Discovering Psychology

The Science of Mind
Miami Dade College PSY 2012

CUSTOM EDITION

Cacioppo | Freberg

CENGAGE
Learning·

Australia • Brazil • Japan • Korea • Mexico • Singapore • Spain • United Kingdom • United States

Discovering Psychology: The Science of Mind: Miami Dade College PSY 2012, Custom Edition

Discovering Psychology: The Science of Mind, Second Edition
John T. Cacioppo, Laura A. Freberg

© 2016, 2013 Cengage Learning. All rights reserved.

For product information and technology assistance, contact us at
Cengage Learning Customer & Sales Support, 1-800-354-9706

For permission to use material from this text or product,
submit all requests online at **cengage.com/permissions**
Further permissions questions can be emailed to
permissionrequest@cengage.com

This book contains select works from existing Cengage Learning resources and was produced by Cengage Learning Custom Solutions for collegiate use. As such, those adopting and/or contributing to this work are responsible for editorial content accuracy, continuity and completeness.

Compilation © 2015 Cengage Learning

ISBN: 978-1-305-76825-3

WCN: 01-100-101

Cengage Learning
20 Channel Center Street
Boston, MA 02210
USA

Cengage Learning is a leading provider of customized learning solutions with office locations around the globe, including Singapore, the United Kingdom, Australia, Mexico, Brazil, and Japan. Locate your local office at:
www.international.cengage.com/region.

Cengage Learning products are represented in Canada by Nelson Education, Ltd.

For your lifelong learning solutions, visit **www.cengage.com/custom.**

Visit our corporate website at **www.cengage.com.**

Brief Contents

From:
Discovering Psychology: The Science of Mind
Cacioppo | Freberg

Concepts

From:
Cengage Advantage Books, Psychology
Bernstein | Penner | Clarke-Stewart | Roy

Brief Contents

Contents

1 The Science of Mind
The Discipline of Psychology

2 The Measure of Mind
Methods of Psychology

Argosy Publishing, Inc.

3 The Evolving Mind
Nature and Nurture Intertwined

Argosy Publishing, Inc.

4 The Biological Mind
The Physical Basis of Behavior

Argosy Publishing, Inc.

5 The Perceiving Mind
Sensation and Perception

Argosy Publishing, Inc.

6 The Aware Mind
Elements of Consciousness

Argosy Publishing, Inc.

7 The Feeling Mind
Motivation and Emotion

Argosy Publishing, Inc.

8 The Adaptive Mind
Learning

Argosy Publishing, Inc.

9 The Knowing Mind
Memory

Argosy Publishing, Inc.

10 The Thinking Mind
Thinking, Language, and Intelligence

Argosy Publishing, Inc.

11 The Developing Mind
Life Span Development

Argosy Publishing, Inc.

12 The Individual Mind
Personality and the Self

Argosy Publishing, Inc.

13 The Connected Mind
Social Psychology

Argosy Publishing, Inc.

14 The Troubled Mind
Psychological Disorders

15 Healing the Troubled Mind
Therapy

Argosy Publishing, Inc.

16 The Healthy Mind
Stress and Coping, Health Psychology, and Positive Psychology

Argosy Publishing, Inc.

Preface

With *Discovering Psychology: The Science of Mind,* we sought to produce a textbook that reflects psychological science in the 21st century and psychology's rightful place as a hub science—a discipline whose work provides foundational material for many other scientific fields. Psychological science is also inherently interdisciplinary. In a scientific community increasingly dominated by interdisciplinary teams, we would like students to see psychology not as an isolated area of study but as one that integrates a range of knowledge into a true science of mind. These goals and our implementation of them resonated with both instructors and students using our first edition, and we have carried this mission forward into our second edition.

The science of psychology developed in the 20th century as a collection of loosely organized, independent subspecialties. Now in our second decade of the 21st century, the discipline is moving rapidly toward maturity as an integrative, multidisciplinary science. Not only are psychologists forming rich collaborations with scholars in other fields, from medicine to business to education to law, but we are returning to original conceptions of psychology put forward by thinkers such as William James, who sought a complete understanding of the human mind and was not content to view psychology from narrow, isolated perspectives. We share a mutual excitement about this evolution of psychological science and a mutual impatience with the slow pace at which existing introductory psychology textbooks—most of which were first written in the 20th century—have adjusted to this sea change.

For many years, the introductory psychology course has served primarily as a jumping-off point for advanced courses in the field, and the textbooks prepared to support the course have reflected this goal. Each chapter in these conventional textbooks provided a capsule of stand-alone information designed to acquaint the student with the terminology and hypotheses of a single psychological perspective. Human behavior is influenced by factors across multiple perspectives, however. We see our introductory textbook as providing a unique opportunity to discuss *all* of psychology in one place and at one time. This approach allows us to reflect on the intersections among various perspectives as they inform the whole of our understanding of the human mind. Given that most students in our introductory classes will only take this one course in the field, we have a responsibility to provide a comprehensive structure that will support their lifelong learning and understanding of human behavior.

We see the introductory course as providing a unique opportunity to discuss all of psychology in one place and at one time.

Our goal is to engage our students in the fascinating, integrated discipline of psychological science as it exists in the 21st century, and we view the second edition of *Discovering Psychology: The Science of Mind* as another plank in the bridge toward this goal. The structure of the bridge is a traditional chapter organization. The piers on which the bridge rests are the foundational theories of the discipline developed in the late 19th, 20th, and early 21st centuries. The steel beams of which the bridge is composed consist of the theories and research painstakingly developed throughout the 20th and 21st centuries, and the rivets, trusses, and tie rods that hold the bridge together are integrative themes that have been reinvented in the past decade or so. Finally, the smooth roadbed that transports students across the bridge is a clear, inviting, warm, and lively writing style and visual narrative.

As active instructors in the introductory psychology classroom, we recognize the balance busy faculty members must find between their preparation for class and their many other duties. Our intent is to make the transition to a 21st-century textbook as seamless and effortless as possible for faculty and students alike. Our discussions of complex and emerging issues, such as epigenetics, include sufficient information and explanation to provide a sense of mastery. Clear writing, frequent examples, visual narratives, and engaging pedagogy energize students and provide the support needed for success. After completing the course, students will be able to appreciate the distinction between how laypeople and how psychologists think about human behavior.

As citizens of the 21st century, community leaders, and influencers, college graduates will need a firm foundation in the understanding of human behavior and critical thinking to confront successfully the myriad issues of privacy, genetic manipulation, free will, human dignity, health, and well-being that will face them in the future. This second edition of *Discovering Psychology: The Science of Mind* is designed to provide that foundation.

Our Integrative and Functionalist Approach

Early writings about psychology were integrated and inclusive. Diverse elements of behavior were combined into the whole. William James (1890) cautions us about the risks of missing the big picture by breaking the phenomenon of mind into little pieces. Mental life for James was not an entity that can be "chopped up in bits" (p. 239). Despite the long-lived popularity of his dominant psychology textbook, James did not prevail. Psychology soon split into camps of scholars who viewed behavior and mental life through their own single, narrow perspectives, rarely speaking with those who held different views and producing curricula and textbooks that emphasized the parts rather than the whole. There are good reasons for specialization in science, but introductory psychology provides an opportunity to put these pieces back together. Doing so shows students how much our notions have changed regarding how the mind and behavior work and how much this understanding can improve their lives.

As psychological science became increasingly siloed in the 20th century, its origins in the late 19th century as a unified whole were forgotten. In 20th-century introductory psychology textbooks, the writings and experiments of Wilhelm Wundt, Edward Titchener, and James are described as the discipline's prehensile tail, long ago lost and interesting only from a historical perspective. The organization of the study of mind into separate, disconnected chapters not only transformed the topics of psychology into islands without bridges but actually built barriers to students' understanding of the connectedness among them. A memory cannot be fully understood from one isolated point of view; only when the social, cognitive, biological and evolutionary, developmental, clinical, and individual differences perspectives are combined can it be thoroughly grasped. James (1890, Vol. 1) warns us that when mental phenomena are "superficially considered, their variety and complexity is such as to leave a chaotic impression on the observer" (p. 1). This confusion, unfortunately, is the legacy for many of our students exposed only to outdated textbooks in psychology.

Breaking from the approach of other textbooks, we reflect throughout our text on the integrative influences of the founders in our functionalist approach to the material. We seek not only to describe behavior but also to answer questions about why a particular behavior occurs. Behavior through this lens is neither random nor unexplainable and shifts into focus when we consider its goals and functions. For example, people do not just experience feelings of loneliness; instead, loneliness acts as a warning signal to remind us of the importance of social connectedness.

Integration in this textbook extends in two directions, both within psychology and between psychology and other disciplines. We hope to highlight for students the many connections within the discipline of psychology, as well as its connections with other disciplines.

Our book is subtitled *The Science of Mind*, and unlike other contemporary texts with their occasional references to *mind*, the word appears in each of the chapter titles, highlighting the scientific study of the nature and behavior of the theoretical construct of the mind. Throughout the book, we emphasize the relationship between rigorous scientific methods and observations, as well as the implications of these observations for competing theories about the structure and operations of the human mind.

Implementing the Goals of Integration

Many introductory psychology textbooks are marketed as "integrated," but saying you are integrated and actually implementing integration are two different things. We have spent a great amount of time and effort discussing ways to provide a truly integrated presentation of the science of mind.

Integration in this textbook extends in two directions, both within psychology and between psychology and other disciplines. We hope to highlight for students the many connections within the discipline of psychology, as well as its connections with other disciplines. Many introductory psychology textbooks share our goal of providing integration, but we would like to make our methods of achieving this goal explicit.

1. Within the body of each chapter, we make frequent connections to material in other chapters, forming bridges that connect subtopics. In the electronic version of the textbook, these connections will be hyperlinked for the convenience of the reader. For example, in a discussion of the causes of anxiety disorders in our chapter on psychological disorders (Chapter 14), we say:

    > A reasonable place to start looking for correlates of anxiety in brain structure and function is the fear circuit involving the amygdala, which we discussed in Chapters 4 and 7. The amygdala is particularly rich in receptors for GABA, a neurotransmitter that inhibits brain activity. As discussed in Chapter 6, drugs such as alcohol and the benzodiazepine tranquilizers (e.g., Valium) have their main anxiety-reducing effects at these GABA receptors.

2. We use frequent examples from other parts of the discipline to illustrate principles within a chapter. For example, when we discuss latent inhibition in our chapter on learning (Chapter 8), we illustrate that principle by linking to clinical research about latent inhibition, creativity, and schizophrenia and to social psychology research on prejudice.

3. We specifically identify and explore six integrative perspectives that weave the standard topics more closely together: **social psychology, cognition, biology and evolution, development, individual differences and personality,** and **clinical psychology.** In keeping with the standard organization of introductory psychology textbooks, the fundamentals of these perspectives are covered in distinct chapters, but the threads of each perspective are woven into all chapters. These perspectives are explained in greater detail in the following section.

4. Each chapter includes six features, which are described in more detail in a later section: **Chapter Opener, Psychology as a Hub Science, Experiencing Psychology, Thinking Scientifically, Connecting to Research,** and **Perspectives on Interpersonal Relationships.** These features are designed to promote active learning and to increase student interest. Three of these in particular (Chapter Opener, Perspectives on Interpersonal Relationships and Psychology as a Hub Science) also contribute to our integrative approach. In the chapter openers, we show how multiple psychological perspectives address a phenomenon by zooming in to see the biological approach and then zooming out again to gain insight from the developmental, cognitive, individual difference, social, and clinical perspectives. Each Perspectives on Interpersonal Relationships feature shows how a particular perspective views questions about successful relationships, so by the end of the textbook, the student can see how integrating 16 approaches to a single issue enriches our understanding of a psychological phenomenon. The Psychology as a Hub Science features address the larger integration picture of where psychology stands in the context of the scientific community.

Integrative Features in Detail

Extensive literature supports the idea that an engaged and cognitively active student is more likely to master content. Although students are accustomed to textbooks, their approaches to learning have been affected by technologies that transfer information at an ever-increasing pace, with a strong emphasis on rapidly presented visual images. Consequently, it becomes all too easy to go through the motions of reading a text without really thinking about what they have read. We have incorporated six features designed to model good textbook-reading practices in students while maintaining a high level of interest and understanding.

Chapter Opener To introduce and engage interest in upcoming chapter material, many textbooks use a vignette or case study, accompanied by either a fine art piece or a photo that is not discussed further. We begin each chapter with a combination of two images—one gives the big picture, and the other gives the microview of the same topic. The chapter opener guides the student through the significance of the images. We use the terms *zoom in* and *zoom out* to emphasize the need to understand the underpinnings of a psychological phenomenon without losing the impact of its larger context. For example, in the biological psychology chapter (Chapter 4), the opening images show a woman watching two friends (zoom out) and a beautiful image of a white blood cell exiting bone marrow (zoom in). Does the woman feel like part of a group of friends or does she feel left out? Depending on how she perceives her social situation, biological cascades are set in motion that prepare her immune system for fighting either the viruses found in close social contact or the bacteria that might be more of a risk when a person is solitary. The reader is drawn into the reciprocal relationships that exist between biology and behavior.

> The integrative Hub feature broadens the discussion of a psychological topic to include ways in which it is engaged in cooperative science with other disciplines, from medicine to the social sciences.

Psychology as a Hub Science In our first edition, this Hub feature was located in its own box, but we feel so strongly about its importance and so concerned about students skipping boxes that we have given this material a new home within the narrative of the chapter. This integrative feature broadens the discussion of a psychological topic to include ways in which psychology engages in cooperative science with other disciplines, from medicine to the social sciences. It is accompanied by a graphic adapted from a citation analysis by Boyack, Klavans, and Börner (2005) that shows psychology citations as nodes with connections to other related disciplines. Tailored to each of the 16 features, this graphic highlights the connections between psychology and the relevant disciplines of psychiatry, nursing, public health, emergency medicine, pharmacology, computer science, law, education, management, and the other social sciences. Given these connections, psychology has a central role to play in our efforts to deal with economic collapses, the spread of pandemics, energy conservation, the spread of terrorism, rising health care costs, and our crumbling educational system. For example, cardiovascular disease is surely a medical condition, but contemporary scientists recognize that a full understanding of this killer requires consideration of psychological domains, including stress appraisal, reactivity to stressors, individual resilience, and a person's social context. Seeing the impact of psychology on many disciplines makes the introductory course relevant for students of all majors, as well as rekindling some "psych pride" in those of us in the field.

Experiencing Psychology This interactive feature provides ways for students to connect the course material to their own lives and interests. Some hands-on examples are the Epworth Sleepiness Scale in the consciousness chapter (Chapter 6), Coren's handedness scale in the biological psychology chapter (Chapter 4), the BFI-10 personality test in the chapter on personality and the self (Chapter 12), and Anderson and Dill's video game violence and aggression instruments in the research methods chapter (Chapter 2). In other cases, this feature provides longer-term opportunities for students to apply their learning, such as working to reduce the frequency of a bad habit (Chapter 8).

Thinking Scientifically This interactive feature models critical thinking skills for students by providing them with opportunities to critique the progress of science. For example, in the chapter on research methods (Chapter 2), students are guided through five steps of critical thinking while evaluating data about the effects of Facebook use on well-being as reported in the popular press. In the chapter on psychological treatments (Chapter 15), students are asked to evaluate the use of mobile technologies to help children with autism spectrum disorder.

Connecting to Research To emphasize psychology as a science, this feature explores either a classic or a contemporary study relevant to the chapter's material and comments on its significance to the field. Sections on the question, methods, results, and conclusions provide a guided introduction for the student to the essentials of the peer-reviewed literature. From Wundt's classic studies of reaction time, to the discovery of mirror neurons, to distinctions between romantic love and lust in the brain, students are given insight into what psychological scientists do.

Perspectives on Interpersonal Relationships In keeping with the integrative mission of this textbook, the goal of this feature is to demonstrate how the information in a particular chapter can be applied to a single topic—building and maintaining important relationships. This issue is personally meaningful to college students, especially first-year students, and it applies across the board—regardless of gender, race, age, ethnicity, sociocultural background, sexual orientation, or level of academic preparation. The feature has two main purposes: (1) to engage and maintain student interest throughout the text and (2) to stitch together into an integrative, thematic quilt the patchwork of traditional introductory psychology topic areas.

Integrative Perspectives in Detail

The separate perspectives taken by psychologists are reviewed for students in the context of the historical discussion in Chapter 1. In each subsequent chapter, we pay especially close attention to the contributions of each of the following perspectives to the topic at hand.

Social English writer and poet John Donne was correct in stating that "no man is an island." The cultural differences that are increasingly apparent as we become a more global world are a testament to how strongly social structures and processes affect the operation of factors from other perspectives. We are a social species, and much of our behavior can be understood in terms of how it maintains our social relatedness with one another. The consequences of failing to maintain connectedness are severe. For example, chronic feelings of social isolation are associated with poor mental and physical health and premature mortality, and longitudinal studies in humans and experimental studies in animals indicate that perceived isolation contributes to these outcomes. In short, feeling left out can be toxic.

Cognitive The human is above all else a thinking organism, and the way we process information affects our behavior. Whether we are considering the development of behavior, learned behavior, or the aberrations of behavior that accompany psychological disorders, an understanding of how we think provides considerable insight. For example, we understand that an effective way to improve depressed people's moods is to help them restructure the way they process information. Instead of students' thinking that flunking an exam means they are not good enough to attend college, we can encourage them to think that although flunking an exam isn't fun, it's not the end of the world and they can make some changes that will lead to better performance next time.

Biological and Evolutionary We believe that all introductory psychology students, even those who will never take another psychology course, will gain a better understanding of contemporary psychology in the context of the relationships between biological processes and behavior. For example, when we discuss attraction and close relationships, we mention data showing that viewing a photograph of somebody we love, as opposed to somebody we like, activates the brain's reward circuits and decreases activity in areas associated with social judgment. Love not only is somewhat socially blind but really does feel good. Throughout the textbook, we stress the role of evolutionary pressures in shaping both the structures and the functions of the mind. We devote a complete chapter to providing students with a foundation for understanding the interactions between genes and environment, including a basic primer on epigenetics. The importance of gene–environment interactions is woven throughout our discussion of development, but it is also highlighted in other contexts, including discussions of children's responses to being bullied.

Developmental The structures and processes of behavior, as well as behavior itself, change over time. Knowing that most children achieve a theory of mind by the age of 4 years not only is relevant to our understanding of children and their behavior but also informs discussions of the development of language and social skills and the deficits found in individuals with autism spectrum disorder. The importance of the developmental perspective does not end in childhood either. January 1, 2011, marked the date at which the oldest of the baby boomers turn 65. From that date, about 10,000 people will turn 65 every day for the next 19 years. As a result of these demographic changes, the percentage of the U.S. population whose social role is retiree is projected to increase dramatically in the coming decades. Understanding developmental changes across the life span is therefore increasingly important.

Individual Differences and Personality Behavioral systems are particularly prone to variation, and we illustrate how such variation can be regarded as a source of important data in its own right. In addition to exploring individual differences within the context of personality, we integrate this facet with other perspectives. For example, we discuss how individual differences in responses to stress are best understood by considering epigenetics, learning, and social factors.

Clinical We can understand behavior by observing what works, but it is also highly useful to see what happens when things go wrong. Just as the neuroscientist learns about normal brain function by observing changes following the damage caused by a stroke, we can learn much about behavior by observing how it changes because of a psychological disorder. For example, we consider the effects of schizophrenia on classical conditioning in the chapter on learning (Chapter 8).

Delivering Complex Content to Contemporary Learners

We were delighted to see that our first edition was embraced by faculty working with students representing a wide range of preparation, from the community colleges to the elite, private universities, as well as by international faculty teaching students with first languages other than English. Our teaching philosophy rejects the common construct of textbook "level." Instead, we believe that all students can master complex content if it is presented in the right way.

Student-Friendly Writing and Pedagogy

Our goal in writing this textbook is to provide students with the best science possible, which means that we do not avoid complex topics or dumb down the material. To make psychological science accessible to a wide range of students, we rely on a student-friendly writing style with supportive pedagogy. We break chapters into meaningful chunks, and we use thumbnail images of chapter photos and figures in our summary tables as a mnemonic device students can use to recall where they read about a topic. Margin definitions and carefully selected key terms help the students focus their learning.

One of our reviewers had this to say about the first chapter of our textbook, which can be one of the most difficult to write: "I am impressed with the History of Psychology chapter in Cacioppo/Freberg. The figures, timeline, interesting AND relevant pictures, and examples throughout the text are fantastic and engaging. It is one of the best history/intro chapters I've read." This reviewer also noticed another one of our goals—to use all photos and figures as teachable moments, not just repetitions of the narrative or pretty placeholders.

Implementation of Guidelines for "Inclusive Psychology"

Today's college and university students represent a wide range of diverse demographic variables, and these variables should be reflected thoughtfully in the textbooks they read. On behalf of the American Psychological Association, Trimble, Stevenson, and Worell (2003) provided considerable guidance to textbook authors and publishers regarding opportunities for including diversity content in an introductory psychology textbook. They focus on the following types of diversity: age, culture, race/ethnicity, gender, disability, language, and sexual orientation. We have used their paper as a blueprint for incorporating the dimension of diversity in our textbook.

We adamantly concur with Trimble et al. (2003) when they state that "Culture, race/ethnicity, gender, disability, sexual orientation, language, and age can be integrated into the main text of every textbook chapter. Highlighting these issues only in special sections or boxes fosters the continued marginalization of members of nondominant groups" (p. 2). Instead of separating diversity from the text into "boxes," we incorporate diversity issues seamlessly throughout the narrative and in illustrations and examples. For example, while we note that Roland Fryer was the youngest African-American professor to obtain tenure at Harvard University, we do so in the context of how his childhood and youth shaped his approaches to educational incentives within a discussion of motivation.

Trimble et al. (2003) provide extensive, detailed suggestions for specific content, such as inclusion of stereotype threat and gender and cultural issues in eating disorders, that we have found useful. For interested faculty and students, we have a comprehensive, separate document with chapter and page references indicating how we have implemented these recommendations. Please feel free to email lfreberg@calpoly.edu to obtain a copy.

In addition, great care has been taken to adhere to American Psychological Association standards on language. Illustrations feature individuals of diverse races, ethnicities, ages, abilities, and gender. Illustrations, when possible, show people in a positive light (e.g., no sad older adults feeding pigeons) and avoid traditional depictions (e.g., male therapist helping female client). Large numbers of illustrations feature cross-cultural examples. Cross-cultural research is featured whenever possible, such as global studies of subjective well-being.

MindTap

MindTap for *Discovering Psychology: The Science of Mind* creates a unique learning path that fosters increased comprehension and efficiency. It engages students and empowers them to produce their best work—consistently. In MindTap, course material is seamlessly integrated with videos, activities, apps, and more.

For students:

- MindTap delivers real-world relevance with activities and assignments designed to help students build critical thinking and analytical skills that can be applied to other courses and to their professional lives.
- MindTap serves as a single destination for all course materials so that students can stay organized and efficient and have the necessary tools to master the content.
- MindTap shows students where they stand at all times—both individually and compared to the highest performers in the class. This information helps to motivate and empower performance.

In MindTap, instructors can do the following:

- **Control the content.** Instructors select what students see and when they see it.
- **Create a unique learning path.** In MindTap, the *Discovering Psychology: The Science of Mind* text is enhanced with multimedia and activities to encourage and motivate learning and retention, moving students up the learning taxonomy. Materials can be used as is or modified to match an instructor's syllabus.
- **Integrate their own content.** Instructors can modify the MindTap Reader using their own documents or pulling from sources like RSS feeds, YouTube videos, websites, Google Docs, and more.
- **Follow student progress.** Powerful analytics and reports provide a snapshot of class progress, time students spend logging into the course, and completion to help instructors assess level of engagement and identify problem areas.

Changes in the Second Edition

Progress in psychological science continues to move forward at a blistering pace, and this second edition has been updated to include many new photos and figures and several hundred new references that reflect the advances in the field since the last edition went to press. One of the biggest content changes was the integration of the fifth edition of the *Diagnostic and Statistical Manual of Mental Disorders (DSM-5)*, which we were only able to preview based on online information when our first edition went to press. In this second edition, all terminology changes and the ordering and categorizing of our discussion of psychological disorders have been modified to be consistent with the *DSM-5*.

We have responded to feedback from our adopters and our own experiences using the textbook in our classrooms to make a few structural changes. The Hub and Interpersonal Relationships features are now more tightly woven into the narrative. We did not want the students to skip these important integrative features, and we wished to avoid interruptions in the flow of the chapter's ideas. We simplified the learning objectives for each chapter while maintaining our commitment to Benjamin Bloom's taxonomy. As mentioned previously, the electronic version of the textbook will provide hyperlinks to relevant sections in other chapters to enhance integration. This experience will make the textbook consistent with the way today's students are accustomed to searching for information.

A sample of the content updates and revisions to each chapter include the following:

Chapter 1 The Science of Mind: The Discipline of Psychology

- Updated information about careers in psychology and related fields
- Included a description of the first official psychology experiment by Wilhelm Wundt
- Added an Experiencing Psychology activity that allows the reader to replicate reaction time experiments in the tradition of Hermann von Helmholtz and Wundt
- Streamlined discussions of psychology's roots in philosophy and the natural sciences

Chapter 2 The Measure of Mind: Methods of Psychology

- Expanded discussions of populations and sampling, commercial online survey services, operationalization of variables, measurement, generalization, and the importance of using multiple methods
- Updated with brief descriptions of "new" statistics, including estimation and confidence intervals
- Refreshed Thinking Scientifically feature using a study on the effects of Facebook participation on well-being

Chapter 3 The Evolving Mind: Nature and Nurture Intertwined

- Expanded and updated discussion of epigenetics
- Expanded discussion of origins of social behavior
- Updated with discussions of the use of genetic profiles by online dating services and controversies surrounding the cycle shift hypothesis

Chapter 4 The Biological Mind: The Physical Basis of Behavior

- Reordered topics to move from the macro level of structures to the micro level of the neuron

- Expanded discussion of the contributions of Santiago Ramón y Cajal
- Updated findings regarding the role of the anterior cingulate cortex in emotional pain
- Updated findings regarding the white matter damage experienced by Phineas Gage
- Added section on the enteric nervous system
- Updated Interpersonal Relationships feature with discussion of new research on lust, love, and the insula

Chapter 5   The Perceiving Mind: Sensation and Perception

- Clarified the processing of the visual field by each hemisphere
- Added illustration demonstrating the McGurk effect
- Updated with research demonstrating the ability to sense carbohydrates in the mouth

Chapter 6   The Aware Mind: Elements of Consciousness

- Updated with discussion of the default mode network and its relationship to unfocused and autobiographical thought, daydreaming, and dreaming during sleep
- Updated to include gamma band waves during waking
- Expanded discussion of lucid dreaming
- Adjusted discussion of sleep–wake disorders to reflect changes in the *DSM-5*
- Expanded and updated discussions of addiction, meditation, and mindfulness

Chapter 7   The Feeling Mind: Motivation and Emotion

- Added discussion of binge-eating disorder category introduced in the *DSM-5*
- Updated and expanded discussion of achievement motivation
- Added discussion of approach and avoidance to section on motivational priorities
- Added discussion of emotions as discrete or continuous
- Updated information about the role of the anterior cingulate cortex in emotion
- Expanded discussion of appraisal theories of emotion
- Refreshed Experiencing Psychology feature with an excellence motivation instrument

Chapter 8   The Adaptive Mind: Learning

- Refreshed Hub feature with discussion of the use of taste aversion to save the endangered Mexican wolf
- Updated discussion of mirror neuron systems

Chapter 9   The Knowing Mind: Memory

- Revised discussion of encoding
- Updated sections on brain correlates of stages of memory
- Added discussions of hyperthymesia and reconsolidation
- Updated discussion of the effects of emotion on memory
- Updated sections on biochemistry and memory and sleep and memory
- Refreshed Thinking Scientifically feature with discussion of our ability to erase traumatic memories
- Refreshed Connecting to Research feature with discussion of caffeine's effects on memory

Chapter 10   The Thinking Mind: Thinking, Language, and Intelligence

- Expanded section on problem solving to include well-defined and ill-defined problems

- Expanded discussion of the importance of understanding probability to problem solving
- Updated discussion of the brain correlates of decision making
- Expanded discussion of the importance of gesture to language
- Updated discussion of the benefits of multilingualism
- Updated discussion of IQ testing and motivational factors leading to success in mathematics
- Refreshed Hub feature with discussion of how beliefs about intelligence influence educational strategies and outcomes
- Updated section on intellectual disability to reflect changes made in the *DSM-5*

Chapter 11 The Developing Mind: Life Span Development

- Updated debate about the endpoint of adolescence
- Expanded discussion of peer influences in adolescence
- Refreshed Thinking Scientifically feature with discussion of whether millennials are more narcissistic than previous generations
- Refreshed Experiencing Psychology feature with parenting type instrument

Chapter 12 The Individual Mind: Personality and the Self

- Updated section on brain correlates of personality to include behavioral approach, fight–flight–freeze system, and behavioral inhibition systems
- Expanded discussion of self-report and personality inventories
- Updated discussion of the depletion effect in self-regulation
- Incorporated discussion of the default mode network in thinking about the self
- Refreshed Thinking Scientifically feature by reviewing criticisms of the reliability and validity of the Myers–Briggs Type Indicator

Chapter 13 The Connected Mind: Social Psychology

- Provided additional clarification about the distinction between the correspondence bias and the fundamental attribution error
- Updated discussion of Milgram experiments with more detail from Jerry Burger's replications
- Updated discussion of groupthink
- Updated discussion of aggression
- Refreshed Interpersonal Relationships feature with discussion of marriages that begin online
- Refreshed Thinking Scientifically feature with discussion of the effects of stereotype threat on people working in groups

Chapter 14 The Troubled Mind: Psychological Disorders

- Reordered chapter outline to reflect ordering and groupings of disorders in the *DSM-5*
- Updated all terminology, groupings, and diagnostic criteria to reflect changes made in the *DSM-5*
- Updated information about causal factors and biological correlates, especially for autism spectrum disorder and bipolar disorder
- Updated information about genetic similarities found in schizophrenia, bipolar disorder, and autism spectrum disorder and the implications of these types of results for the organization of the *DSM-5*
- Updated information about the causes of posttraumatic stress disorder

Chapter 15   Healing the Troubled Mind: Therapy

- Reordered chapter outline to reflect ordering in the *DSM-5*
- Updated information about applied behavior analysis particularly in the treatment of autism spectrum disorder
- Refreshed Experiencing Psychology feature with a progressive relaxation exercise
- Refreshed Connecting to Research feature with discussion of the use of mindfulness to prevent relapse in patients with major depressive disorder
- Refreshed Thinking Scientifically feature with discussion of the use of mobile technologies to aid children with autism spectrum disorder

Chapter 16   The Healthy Mind: Stress and Coping, Health Psychology, and Positive Psychology

- Added section on socioeconomic status and disparities in stress and health, including the potential impact of the Affordable Care Act
- Expanded managing stress section to include mindfulness and meditation
- Updated statistics related to alcohol use, tobacco use, and diet
- Refreshed Interpersonal Relationships feature with discussion of gratitude for a partner's investment in the relationship
- Refreshed Connecting to Research feature with discussion of the effects of early childhood stress on the immune system
- Refreshed Thinking Scientifically feature with discussion of the effects of being a parent on happiness

Acknowledgments

We thank William James for bringing so many disparate threads of scholarship together to form the backbone of what continues to be the study of psychology.

Cengage Learning Team

We are grateful to our Cengage Learning team. Jon-David Hague shared our vision for this textbook from the outset and went many extra miles to make it a reality. Clay Austin, Michelle Newhart, Jennifer Wahi (Art), Jasmin Tokatlian, Kyra Kane, Michelle Clark, Cassie Carey, Carly Bergey, and Brittani Morgan gave us their full support through each step of the process. We also thank Michelle Shiota of Arizona State University and instructional designer Jan Johnson.

Manuscript Reviewers

The current edition builds on contributions from reviewers from the first edition. We would also like to acknowledge our colleagues who reviewed early drafts of the first edition manuscript. Their suggestions helped to make this a better book.

First Edition Full Manuscript Reviewers

John Allen, *University of Arizona*
Ted Barker, *Northwest Florida State College*
Mark Basham, *Regis University*
Kyle Baumbauer, *Texas A&M University*
Kathy Becker-Blease, *Oregon State University*
Rachel Blaser, *University of San Diego*
Christina M. Brown, *Saint Louis University*
Eric Bruns, *Campbellsville University*
Kathryn Caldwell, *Ithaca College*

Aimee A. Callender, *Auburn University*
David Campbell, *Humboldt State University*
Brian D. Carpenter, *Washington University, St. Louis*
Lawrence Cohen, *University of Delaware*
Brian Cowley, *Park University*
Verne Cox, *University of Texas, Arlington*
Natalie Dautovich, *University of Alabama*
Robert DuBois, *Waukesha County Technical College*
Kimberly Duff, *Cerritos College*
Darlene Earley, *Southern Union State Community College*
Kathy Erickson, *Pima Community College*
Carlos Escoto, *Eastern Connecticut State University*
Kendall Eskine, *Loyola University New Orleans*
Melanie Evans, *Eastern Connecticut State University*
Stephen L. Forssell, *George Washington University*
Debra Lynn Frame, *University of Cincinnati*
Andrea Friedrich, *University of Kentucky*
Perry Fuchs, *University of Texas, Arlington*
Philip Gable, *University of Alabama*
Bridgett Galvin, *Framingham State College*
Deborah Garfin, *Georgia State University*
Bryan Gibson, *Central Michigan University*
Allen Gorman, *Angelo State University*
Ruth Grahn, *Connecticut College*
Ruth M. Grant, *Sacred Heart University*
Anthony Greene, *University of Wisconsin, Milwaukee*
Christina Grimes, *Duke University*
Scott Gustafson, *University of Mississippi*
Erin E. Hardin, *Texas Tech University*
Robert J. Hines, *University of Arkansas, Little Rock*
Linda Jackson, *Michigan State University*
Irene P. Kan, *Villanova University*
Craig Kinsley, *University of Richmond*
Megan L. Knowles, *Franklin and Marshall College*
Jordan Labouff, *Baylor University*
Carrie Lane, *Florida State University*
Jennifer Lee, *Cabrillo College*
Fabio Leite, *Ohio State University, Lima*
Robin Lightner, *University of Cincinnati*
Christine Lofgren, *University of California, Irvine*
Nicolette Lopez, *University of Texas, Arlington*
David Malcolm, *Fordham University*
Michael Mangan, *University of New Hampshire*
Abigail Marsh, *Georgetown University*
Anna Medina, *Gonzaga University*
Sean P. Meegan, *University of Utah*
Antoinette Miller, *Clayton State University*
Robin K. Morgan, *Indiana University Southeast*
Hajime Otani, *Central Michigan University*
Marion Perlmutter, *University of Michigan, Ann Arbor*
Gabriel Radvansky, *University of Notre Dame*
Cynthia Reidi, *Morrisville State College*
Ann E. Renken, *University of Southern California*
Heather J. Rice, *Washington University, St. Louis*
Michael Roberts, *DePauw University*
Catherine Sanderson, *Amherst College*
Patrick Saxe, *State University of New York, New Paltz*

Luis Schettino, *Lafayette College*
David Schroeder, *University of Arkansas*
Dennis Shaffer, *Ohio State University, Mansfield*
Donald Sharpe, *University of Regina*
Mikle Don South, *Brigham Young University*
Brian Thomas, *Baldwin-Wallace College*
Lisa Thomassen, *Indiana University, Bloomington*
Anre Venter, *University of Notre Dame*
Craig Vickio, *Bowling Green State University*
Mark Walter, *Salisbury University*
Shannon Welch, *University of Idaho*
John Wright, *Washington State University*
Erin Young, *Texas A&M University*

First Edition Focus Group Reviewers

Judith Addelston, *Valencia College, East*
Anthony Ahrens, *American University*
Roxanna Andersen, *Palm Beach State College, Boca Raton*
Stacy Anderson, *Florida Gulf Coast University*
Richard Bernstein, *Broward College, South*
Kathleen Bey, *Palm Beach State College, Lake Worth*
Sara Broaders, *Northwestern University*
John Timothy Cannon, *University of Scranton*
John Connor, *Daytona State College*
David Seth Crystal, *Georgetown University*
Jennifer Engler, *York College of Pennsylvania*
Gregory Harris, *Polk State College*
Jeffrey Henriques, *University of Wisconsin, Madison*
Jennifer Johnson, *Bloomsberg University*
Todd Joseph, *Hillsborough Community College, Dale Mabry*
Irene Kan, *Villanova University*
Kevin Keating, *Broward College, North*
Cheri Kittrell, *State College of Florida, Manatee-Sarasota*
Debra Laino, *Philadelphia University*
Natalie Lawrence, *James Madison University*
Daniel McConnell, *University of Central Florida*
Ronald Morrison, *Daytona State College*
Kevin O'Neil, *Florida Gulf Coast University*
Gwendolyn Parsons-Spurrier, *Hillsborough Community College, Ybor City*
Lois Pasapane, *Palm Beach State College, Lake Worth*
Ronnie Rothschild, *Broward College, Central*
Sharleen Sakai, *Michigan State University*
Alex Sharpe, *Santa Fe College*
Caroline Shelton-Toney, *Polk State College*
William Suits, *Seminole State College of Florida*
Cyril Svoboda, *University of Maryland University College*
Clarissa Thompson, *University of Oklahoma*
Terry Trepper, *Purdue University, Calumet*
Katherine Urquhart, *Lake Sumter Community College*
Lona Whitmarsh, *Fairleigh Dickinson University*
We thank our colleagues for their diligent and thoughtful readings of our textbook.

Manuscript Reviewers (First Edition)

John Allen, *University of Arizona*
Ted Barker, *Northwest Florida State College*
Mark Basham, *Regis University*
Kyle Baumbauer, *Texas A&M University*

Kathy Becker-Blease, *Oregon State University*
Rachel Blaser, *University of San Diego*
Christina M. Brown, *Saint Louis University*
Eric Bruns, *Campbellsville University*
Kathryn Caldwell, *Ithaca College*
Aimee A. Callender, *Auburn University*
David Campbell, *Humboldt State University*
Brian D. Carpenter, *Washington University, St. Louis*
Lawrence Cohen, *University of Delaware*
Brian Cowley, *Park University*
Verne Cox, *University of Texas, Arlington*
Natalie Dautovich, *University of Alabama*
Robert DuBois, *Waukesha County Technical College*
Kimberly Duff, *Cerritos College*
Darlene Earley, *Southern Union State Community College*
Kathy Erickson, *Pima Community College*
Carlos Escoto, *Eastern Connecticut State University*
Kendall Eskine, *Loyola University, New Orleans*
Melanie Evans, *Eastern Connecticut State University*
Debra Lynn Frame, *University of Cincinnati*
Andrea Friedrich, *University of Kentucky*
Stephen L. Forssell, *George Washington University*
Perry Fuchs, *University of Texas, Arlington*
Philip Gable, *University of Alabama*
Bridgett Galvin, *Framingham State College*
Deborah Garfin, *Georgia State University*
Bryan Gibson, *Central Michigan University*
Allen Gorman, *Angelo State University*
Ruth Grahn, *Connecticut College*
Ruth M. Grant, *Sacred Heart University*
Anthony Greene, *University of Wisconsin, Milwaukee*
Christina Grimes, *Duke University*
Scott Gustafson, *University of Mississippi*
Erin E. Hardin, *Texas Tech University*
Robert J. Hines, *University of Arkansas, Little Rock*
Linda Jackson, *Michigan State University*
Irene P. Kan, *Villanova University*
Craig Kinsley, *University of Richmond*
Megan L. Knowles, *Franklin and Marshall College*
Jordan Labouff, *Baylor University*
Carrie Lane, *Florida State University*
Jennifer Lee, *Cabrillo College*
Fabio Leite, *Ohio State University, Lima*
Robin Lightner, *University of Cincinnati*
Christine Lofgren, *University of California, Irvine*
Nicolette Lopez, *University of Texas, Arlington*
David Malcolm, *Fordham University*
Michael Mangan, *University of New Hampshire*
Abigail Marsh, *Georgetown University*
Anna Medina, *Gonzaga University*
Sean P. Meegan, *University of Utah*
Antoinette Miller, *Clayton State University*
Robin K. Morgan, *Indiana University, Southeast*
Hajime Otani, *Central Michigan University*
Marion Perlmutter, *University of Michigan, Ann Arbor*
Gabriel Radvansky, *University of Notre Dame*
Cynthia Reidi, *Morrisville State College*

Ann E. Renken, *University of Southern California*
Heather J. Rice, *Washington University, St. Louis*
Michael Roberts, *DePauw University*
Catherine Sanderson, *Amherst College*
Patrick Saxe, *State University of New York, New Paltz*
Luis Schettino, *Lafayette College*
David Schroeder, *University of Arkansas*
Dennis Shaffer, *Ohio State University, Mansfield*
Donald Sharpe, *University of Regina*
Mikle Don South, *Brigham Young University*
Brian Thomas, *Baldwin-Wallace College*
Lisa Thomassen, *Indiana University, Bloomington*
Anre Venter, *University of Notre Dame*
Craig Vickio, *Bowling Green State University*
Mark Walter, *Salisbury University*
Shannon Welch, *University of Idaho*
John Wright, *Washington State University*
Erin Young, *Texas A&M University*

Manuscript Reviewers (Second Edition)
Kristen T. Begosh, *University of Delaware*
Melissa A. Berry, *University of Dayton*
Kathleen Bey, *University of Delaware*
Amy Biegel, *Huntington University*
William O. Boggan, *College of Charleston*
Lauren Brewer, *College of Idaho*
Kyle Evan Conlon, *Boise State University*
Sarah D'Elia, *George Mason University and Northern Virginia Community College*
Matthew Draper, *Utah Valley University*
Patrick Drumm, *Ohio University, Lancaster*
Megan Dunbar, *California State University San Marcos and Palomar College*
Dawn Eaton, *San Jacinto College-South*
Bryan D. Fantie, *American University*
Philip Gable, *University of Alabama*
Jeanette Gassaway, *Ohio University*
Alexis S. Green, *Hanover College*
Carrie E. Hall, *Miami University*
Kelly Huffman, *University of California, Riverside*
Michelle (MiKi) Kitchen, *University of South Carolina*
Jamison D. Law, *Utah Valley University*
Angela M. Legg, *Pace University, Pleasantville*
Carrie A. Lloyd, *Huntington University*
Robin K. Morgan, *Indiana University, Southeast*
Michelle Niculescu, *Lebanon Valley College*
David J. Rademacher, *Carthage College*
Charlotte Nolan-Reyes, *Cabrillo College*
Marylou Robins, *San Jacinto College-South*
Dario Rodriguez, *University of Dayton*
Cindy Sledge, *San Jacinto College-South*
Lara Tedrow, *Tidewater Community College*
Alexa Tullet, *University of Alabama*
Lindsey West, *Georgia Regents University*
Eliah White, *University of Cincinnati, Blue Ash College*

Focus Group Reviewers
Judith Addelston, *Valencia College, East*
Anthony Ahrens, *American University*

Roxanna Andersen, *Palm Beach State College, Boca Raton*
Stacy Anderson, *Florida Gulf Coast University*
Richard Bernstein, *Broward College,* South
Kathleen Bey, *Palm Beach State College, Lake Worth*
Sara Broaders, *Northwestern University*
John Timothy Cannon, *University of Scranton*
John Connor, *Daytona State College*
David Seth Crystal, *Georgetown University*
Jennifer Engler, *York College of Pennsylvania*
Gregory Harris, *Polk State College*
Jeffrey Henriques, *University of Wisconsin, Madison*
Jennifer Johnson, *Bloomsburg University*
Todd Joseph, *Hillsborough Community College, Dale Mabry*
Irene Kan, *Villanova University*
Kevin Keating, *Broward College, North*
Cheri Kittrell, *State College of Florida, Manatee-Sarasota*
Debra Laino, *Philadelphia University*
Natalie Lawrence, *James Madison University*
Daniel McConnell, *University of Central Florida*
Ronald Morrison, *Daytona State College*
Kevin O'Neil, *Florida Gulf Coast University*
Gwendolyn Parsons-Spurrier, *Hillsborough Community College, Ybor City*
Lois Pasapane, *Palm Beach State College, Lake Worth*
Ronnie Rothschild, *Broward College, Central*
Sharleen Sakai, *Michigan State University*
Alex Sharpe, *Santa Fe College*
Caroline Shelton-Toney, *Polk State College*
William Suits, *Seminole State College of Florida*
Cyril Svoboda, *University of Maryland University College*
Clarissa Thompson, *University of Oklahoma*
Terry Trepper, *Purdue University, Calumet*
Katherine Urquhart, *Lake Sumter Community College*
Lona Whitmarsh, *Fairleigh Dickinson University*

We also thank Suzanne Corkin for reading and commenting on sections describing the amnesic patient H.M. (Henry Molaison).

Finally, we could not have done this without the patience and support of our families: Stephanie, Christina, and Anthony (JTC) and Roger, Kristin, Karen, and Karla (LF).

1 The Science of Mind
The Discipline of Psychology

STUDYING THE SCIENCE OF PSYCHOLOGY CAN lead you to see yourself and other people in completely new ways. Hundreds of years ago, people believed that the world was flat and the sun and stars circled the earth. Careful scientific research slowly dispelled these inaccurate notions. Nonetheless, we hold tightly to many equally false common-sense beliefs about the human mind and behavior. We all "know" that

opposites attract, but we also "know" that birds of a feather flock together, so why do we need psychology to tell us what we already know? The problem is that both statements cannot be true at the same time, so the real state of affairs is neither obvious nor simple. Just as careful science was required to understand our planet's place in the universe, the same scientific techniques are providing us with a more accurate, complete view of the human mind.

Let's begin with a seemingly simple and familiar example: our ability to taste. We know a lot about taste—what we like or dislike, the different qualities of taste, and so on. You might even be aware that some types of taste seem stronger than others. Most of us can taste sweetness in a solution made of 1 part sugar and 200 parts water; this ability shows an impressive sensitivity to taste. As remarkable as this sensitivity appears to be, however, people can detect 1 part bitter substance (like quinine or chemicals in broccoli) in 2 million parts water. This contrast in taste sensitivity between sweet and bitter does not reflect the actual difference between sweet and bitter substances—that is, bitter tastes are not 10,000 times stronger than sweet tastes—but rather how we experience them. Why would we have such a vast difference in sensitivity between these types of tastes?

Our observations of taste do not help us out much in answering this question, but psychology can. As it turns out, our greater sensitivity to bitter tastes is highly adaptive: Most poisons or toxins taste bitter, and if you want to stay alive, it is more important to avoid swallowing poison than to enjoy something sweet. Being far more sensitive to tastes that are bitter is a trait that has served our species well, because it helps us avoid eating things that could potentially kill us. Psychology helps us understand why we do the things we do by providing a context for understanding behavior.

◀ Taste buds contained in the papillae of the tongue are far more responsive to bitter tastes than to sweet tastes.

To gain that understanding, psychology has to act like the zoom feature in Google Earth. In some parts of this textbook, we will zoom in on human behaviors, like looking at the highly magnified image of the papillae on the tongue (pictured on page 2), which allow us to taste, and trace the messages about taste sent from the tongue to the brain. At

Introspection is the personal observation of our own thoughts, feelings, and behaviors. Because we are not perfect observers of the operations of our own minds, psychologists developed other methods that provide scientific insight into mind. In this functional magnetic resonance imaging (fMRI) scan, areas of the brain that were more active when participants were hungry than when they were full are highlighted. Through technology, researchers can better understand how the brain regulates hunger.

From D. Fuhrer, S. Zysset, & M. Stumvoll, "Brain Activity in Hunger and Satiety: An Exploratory Visually Stimulated fMRI Study," in *Obesity* (*2008*) *16*: 945–950. © Nature Publishing Group.

other times, we'll zoom out to take in the larger picture and better understand why the boy on the previous page is giving his bitter-tasting broccoli a skeptical look.

Psychologists approach the study of mind using in-depth perspectives, which we will describe in this chapter. For example, we can look at the little boy's reaction to his broccoli from a developmental perspective, which tells us that taste sensitivity decreases over the life span. Or, using the social perspective, we can think about social influences like culture on food preferences. Cottage cheese, enjoyed by many Americans, is viewed with disgust in some other parts of the world. Fruit bat pie, a delicacy in Palau, might not be a popular item for a campus dining facility in the United States.

Although single perspectives can tell us a lot about a phenomenon like our sensitivity to bitter tastes, no one perspective can give us a complete answer. The best view comes from putting multiple perspectives together. You can learn a lot about your house from Google Earth by zooming in, but when you see how your home fits into the larger scene of city, state, country, and planet, that viewpoint adds something special to your understanding.

We'll start by learning more about psychology's main perspectives, along with a little background about their origins. At that point, we'll be in a better position to understand how these perspectives come together to give us the big picture.

Learning Objectives

1. Explain the subject matter that psychologists study.

2. Analyze the contributions of philosophy and the natural sciences to modern psychology.

3. Describe how early movements in psychology are significant for modern psychology.

4. Compare and contrast the major perspectives of modern psychology.

5. Demonstrate how the major perspectives can be integrated to address a single psychological problem.

6. Explain why psychology's role as a "hub science" allows psychologists to pursue a range of career paths.

What Is Psychology?

The study of the **mind** is as fascinating as it is complex. Psychological scientists view the mind as a way of talking about the activities of the brain, including thought, emotion, and behavior. A quick look at this textbook's table of contents will show you the variety of approaches to *mind* that you will encounter, such as the thinking mind (cognitive psychology) and the troubled mind (abnormal psychology).

The word **psychology** is a combination of two Greek words: *psyche* (or *psuche*), or "soul," and *logos*, meaning "the study of." For the ancient Greeks, a soul was close to our modern view of a spirit or mind. *Logos* is the source of all our "ologies," such as biology and anthropology. Literally translated, therefore, *psychology* means "the study of mind." Contemporary definitions of psychology refine this basic meaning. Most psychologists today define their field as "the scientific study of behavior and mental processes"—that is, the scientific study of mind.

The phrase "behavior and mental processes" has undergone several changes over the history of psychology. *Behavior* refers to any action that we can observe. As we will see in our chapter on research methods, observation has been an important tool for psychologists from the early days of the discipline. Our definition does not specify whose behavior is to be examined. Although the bulk of psychology focuses on human behavior, animal behavior has been an essential part of the discipline, both for understanding animals better and for comparing and contrasting animal and human behavior.

The study of *mental processes* has been highly dependent on the methods available to psychologists. Early efforts to study mental processes were generally unsatisfactory, because they relied on the use of **introspection**, or the personal observation of your own thoughts, feelings, and behaviors. Because it is difficult for others to confirm your introspections, this subjective approach does not lend itself well to the scientific method. If you say that you are

mind The brain and its activities, including thought, emotion, and behavior.
psychology The scientific study of behavior and mental processes.
introspection Personal observation of your own thoughts, feelings, and behavior.

Psychology as a Hub Science
Why Is Psychology a Hub Science?

Psychology is all about people, and few occupations do not require an understanding of people and their behavior. An architect cannot design a functional space without considering how people respond to crowding. An attorney cannot cross-examine a witness without an understanding of memory, motivation, emotion, and stress. A teacher cannot encourage students to reach their potential without an understanding of child development and learning. The study of psychology, then, provides you with better insight into and understanding of many occupations and fields of study.

You probably have seen applications that allow you to map your friendship networks on social media, with shorter links indicating greater connectivity and with larger bubbles indicating more overlapping friendships with another person. Kevin Boyack and his colleagues generated a similar map of the sciences (see ● Figure 1.1) but used reference lists in journal articles instead of friendship networks (Boyack, Klavans, & Börner, 2005). The resulting analysis shows that psychology is one of the seven major hub sciences, with strong connections to the medical sciences, the social sciences, and education. In our upcoming chapters, we will highlight these connections with examples that are relevant to each particular chapter. ●

FIGURE 1.1

Psychology as a Hub Science. This map of science was generated by comparing citations from more than 1 million papers published in more than 7,000 journals since 2000. Psychology appears among the seven major areas of science, indicated in the map by large font. The other six major areas are social sciences, mathematics, physics, chemistry, earth sciences, and medicine.
Source: Adapted from "Mapping the Backbone of Science," by K. W. Boyack et al., 2005, *Scientometrics, 64*(3), 351-374. With kind permission from Springer Science+Business Media.

feeling hungry, how can anyone else know whether your observation is accurate? In addition, your mind and behavior are governed by a host of structures, factors and processes, most of which are not available through introspection. Innovations in the methods and mathematics used to investigate brain activity and behavior have allowed psychologists to revisit the question of mental processes with greater objectivity and success.

What Are Psychology's Roots?

The empiricists had a profound influence on the foundations of American political thought—all of us are created equal. For generations, Europe had been ruled by people who were born into positions of power instead of earning the privilege of leading through hard work and education. If knowledge is not innate or inborn, any of us can learn enough to grow up to be President.

philosophy The discipline that systematically examines basic concepts, including the source of knowledge.
natural science Sciences that study the physical and biological events that occur in nature.

Psychology is a relatively young discipline, dating back only to the 1870s. However, topics that interest modern psychologists go back farther in the history of human thought. People living as long ago as 6000 to 5000 BCE in Assyria described their dreams (Restak, 1988). Among these accounts are descriptions of being chased, which are still among the most common dreams experienced by people (Nielsen et al., 2003). See ● Figure 1.2 for common dream themes that many people experience.

The psychology family tree includes two major roots: **philosophy** and the **natural sciences**. Psychologists answer questions traditionally posed by philosophers by borrowing the methods of the natural sciences. We examine scientific methods in detail in Chapter 2.

Philosophers and psychologists share an interest in questions regarding the nature of the self, the effects of early experience, the existence of free will, and the origin of knowledge. Both disciplines consider the relative balance of biological factors (nature) and environmental factors (nurture) in the resulting human behavior. Both attempt to determine the relationships

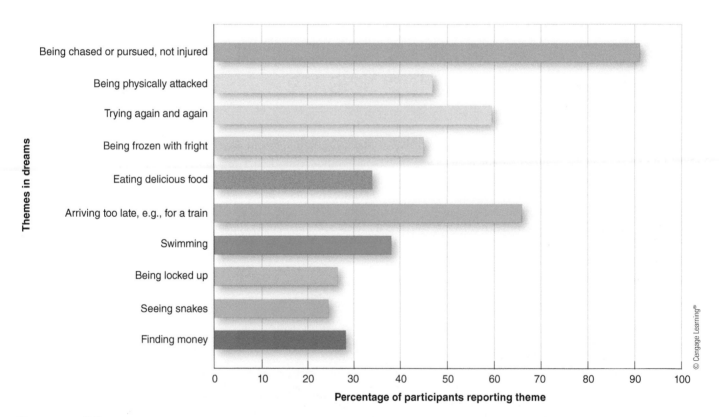

© Cengage Learning®

FIGURE 1.2

Many People Report Dreams With the Same Themes. Although we don't understand why we dream about certain things, many people report similar themes in their dreams.

Source: Adapted from "Typical Dreams of Canadian University Students," by T. A. Nielsen et al., 2003, *Dreaming, 13,* 211–235.

Desperate conditions in Romanian orphanages in the 1970s left many children without the experiences they needed for optimum cognitive or social development.

FIGURE 1.3

Microscopes Changed the World of Science. This light microscope was used by Anton von Leeuwenhoek to discover red blood cells in 1676. Microscopes opened a new world to scientists interested in living things.
A = Screw for adjusting the height of the object being examined
B = Metal plate serving as the body
C = Skewer to impale the object and rotate it
D = Lens, which was spherical

Aristotle (384–322 BCE) believed that we gain knowledge through our senses.

John Locke (1632–1704) and other empiricist philosophers believed that the mind was a "blank slate" at birth and that knowledge was gained through experience.

between self-interest and community welfare, between body and mind, and between humans and other species with which we share the planet. Although we typically consider questions of the unconscious mind and abnormal behavior to be the realm of the psychologist, philosophers investigated these issues thousands of years before the first psychologist was born.

One of the most significant questions shared by philosophy and psychology asks whether the mind is inborn or is formed through experience. Some philosophers, including René Descartes (1596–1650), argued that ideas and emotions were innate or inborn. More commonly, philosophers beginning with Aristotle (384–322 BCE) believed that all knowledge is gained through sensory experience. Beginning in the 17th century, this idea flourished in the British philosophical school of *empiricism*. The empiricists viewed the mind as a "blank slate" at birth that was filled with ideas gained by observing the world.

This philosophical debate about the source of knowledge is echoed in psychology when researchers consider the relative contributions of inborn or innate factors (nature) and of experience (nurture) to particular behaviors. Contemporary psychologists no longer view the question of nature and nurture as needing an either–or response. Instead, we see the mind as a result of complex interactions between inborn characteristics and everyday experiences. For example, we might have a genetic predisposition for intelligent behavior, but intelligence depends on experience too. During the 1970s, children in Romanian orphanages experienced extremely deprived social conditions because of a lack of funding for their care. The children had few opportunities to interact with other people or with the environment. The children who were adopted from these orphanages at young ages were able to recover, but the children who endured years of deprivation experienced permanent cognitive deficits (Ames, 1997). In Chapters 3 (Nature and Nurture) and Chapter 11 (Development), we will revisit these debates in depth.

Running along a parallel track to the early philosophers, ancient physicians were laying the foundation of our biological knowledge of the brain and nervous system, discussed in greater detail in Chapter 4. During this pursuit, physicians helped develop the scientific methods that would become central to contemporary psychology and previewed the application of the knowledge they gained to the improvement of individual well-being.

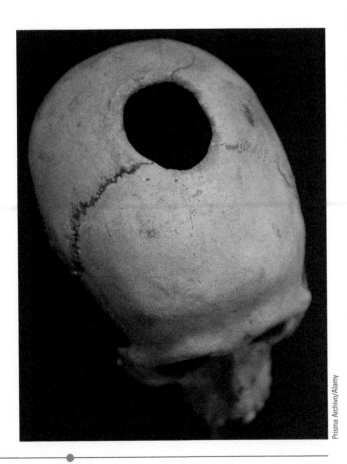

Ancient people might have attempted to cure headaches, seizures, or psychological disorders by drilling holes in the skull. Bone growth around the hole indicates that some patients survived the procedure.

The work of Hermann von Helmholtz (1821–1894) on reaction time helped establish the mind as something that could be studied scientifically.

bilwissedition Ltd. & Co. KG/Alamy

Although some confusion occurred along the way, such as Aristotle's belief that the mind was located in the heart, ancient people had a rudimentary understanding that the head and later the brain were important for mental life. As many as 7,000 years ago, healers using a technique known as trepanation drilled holes in a person's skull to cure some unspecified conditions, possibly headache or hallucination. Subsequent growth of the skull bones indicates that some patients survived this procedure. The early Egyptians correctly understood that paralysis of a part of the body resulted from brain damage and that such damage was permanent (Breasted, 1930).

For centuries, the whole of medicine remained a primitive business. Beginning in the 17th and 18th centuries, scientists armed with new technologies, including the light microscope (see ● Figure 1.3), began to make a series of important discoveries about the human body and mind. For example, they demonstrated that a single sensory nerve carried one type of information instead of multiple types. You might have already duplicated this research yourself while rubbing your sleepy eyes—you see a flash of light. The nerves serving the retina of the eye do not know how to process information about touch or pressure. When stimulated, they are capable of only one type of message—light. These types of discoveries about the physical aspects of mind convinced scientists that the mind could be studied scientifically.

The work of Hermann von Helmholtz (1821–1894) on the speed of nerve signaling provided further evidence that the mind had a physical basis. Von Helmholtz asked his participants to push a button when they felt a touch. When a thigh was touched, participants reacted faster than when a toe was touched. Because the toe is farther from the brain than the thigh, signals from the toe required more time to reach the brain. Von Helmholtz used these differences in reaction time to show that voluntary behavior did not occur instantaneously as previously thought. Helmholtz's demonstration that behavior is not instantaneous—rather, it requires time for the system to process physical signals—contributed to a more scientific, less mystical view of the nervous system.

Philosophers began to incorporate physiological and psychological concepts into their work, and natural scientists began to explore the questions asked by philosophers. The gradual merger of these approaches resulted in a series of experiments that looked increasingly like contemporary psychology. Scientists began to ask questions about the relationships between physical stimulation and its resulting sensations. For example, Gustav Fechner (1801–1889) was able to identify the softest sound a person could hear by randomly presenting sounds of different intensities to which a participant would respond "yes" or "no." When the "yes" responses reached 50%, Fechner concluded that the sound was within the range that the human ear could detect (see Chapter 5). The stage was set for a modern science of psychology.

Summary 1.1 Highlights in the Philosophical and Scientific Roots of Psychology

	Person or group	Things to remember
	Ancient Greek philosophers	Provided natural, not supernatural, explanations for their observations.
	British empiricists	Knowledge is the result of experience.
	Ancient physicians	The brain is the source of mind.
	17th- and 18th-century natural scientists	Discoveries about sensation and movement showed that the mind was physical.
	Hermann von Helmholtz	Studies of reaction time reinforced the idea of the mind as physical.

How Did the Science of Psychology Begin?

As psychology developed from the gradual merger of philosophical questions and scientific reasoning, the young discipline struggled to determine which questions and methods were best suited to its goals. Lively debates arose among psychologists who helped to shape the field.

Wilhelm Wundt and Structuralism

The credit for being the first psychologist goes to **Wilhelm Wundt** (1832–1920), a former research assistant to von Helmholtz, who conducted the first documented psychological experiment in his laboratory at the University of Leipzig in 1879. This landmark experiment was a

Wilhelm Wundt (1832–1920), seated in this photo, is considered the first experimental psychologist.

Connecting to Research

The First Official Psychology Experiment

WE HAVE GIVEN CREDIT to Wundt for conducting the first experiments in psychology. What did those crucial first experiments look like?

Wundt's experiments reflected both his interests in consciousness and his training as a medical doctor. Wundt was aware of methods that were used by researchers in physiology, such as the reaction-time measures pioneered by F. C. Donders in the Netherlands, and he sought to apply these methods to measure psychological processes such as attention and decision making (Danzinger & Ballantyne, 1997).

The Questions: Is it possible to "time" mental processes? Are simple reaction times different from reaction times involving choices?

METHODS

Wundt's methods involved two sets of apparatus: one that would deliver a stimulus precisely to a participant and a second that would measure and record the participant's

responses. His imposing-looking brass instruments used to carry out these tasks were displayed to an admiring public at the 1893 Chicago world's fair.

The first experiments carried out by Wundt involved the presentation of stimuli, such as the sound of a ball dropped onto a platform, and measurements of reaction time, as indicated by the participant pressing a telegraph key. In addition to these simple reaction-time experiments, Wundt asked participants to make decisions: When you see this light, press the button on the left, but if you see that light, press the button on the right.

RESULTS

Wundt viewed reaction time as "mental chronometry" (Hergenhahn & Henley, 2013, p. 255). In other words, he believed that reaction time provided a measure of the amount of mental processing required to carry out a task. As his tasks became more complex, reaction time increased accordingly.

CONCLUSIONS

As mentioned earlier in this chapter, Wundt's mentor, von Helmholtz, had performed a number of experiments similar to those performed by Wundt. Von Helmholtz touched the participant on the thigh and toe and discovered that the participant pushed a button faster in response to the thigh touch. What makes von Helmholtz's demonstration a physiological experiment and Wundt's a psychology experiment?

Part of the answer is the interpretation each scientist made of his results. For von Helmholtz, differences in reaction time in these two instances represented the effects of the speed of conduction of neural signaling. Because the toe is farther from the brain than the thigh is, messages take more time to reach the brain from the toe. Wundt's simple reaction-time experiments were not that different, but his experiments on choice were more clearly psychological. As decisions became more complex, reaction time increased. ●

Bettmann/CORBIS

Max Wertheimer (1880–1943) was one of the founders of Gestalt psychology.

simple test of reaction time: How quickly after hearing a ball drop onto a platform could a person respond by striking a telegraph key?

Wundt saw mental experience as a hierarchy. The mind constructs an overall perception (the food I'm eating tastes good) out of building blocks made up of separate sensations, such as taste and vision, and emotional responses. One of Wundt's students, Edward Titchener (1867–1923), expanded on Wundt's views to establish a theory of **structuralism**, in which the mind could be broken down into the smallest elements of mental experience. Titchener's approach to psychology paralleled the general trends in the physical sciences of his day, such as efforts in chemistry to break molecules into elements and attempts by physicists to describe matter at the level of the atom.

Gestalt Psychology

The structuralists' effort to break behavior down into its essential elements was rejected by a group of early 20th-century German psychologists, including Kurt Koffka, Max Wertheimer, and Wolfgang Köhler, who founded **Gestalt psychology**. *Gestalt,* although lacking a clear translation into English, means "form" or "whole." The Gestalt psychologists believed that breaking a "whole" perception into its building blocks, as advocated by the structuralists, would result in the loss of some important psychological information. For example, look at the middle image in ● Figure 1.4. It is the same in both the top and the bottom rows, yet in the context of the first row, most people interpret the image as the letter B. In the context of the bottom row, however, the image looks like the number 13. The structuralists would have a difficult time explaining why the same visual building blocks could lead to such different conclusions.

structuralism An approach in which the mind is broken into the smallest elements of mental experience.
Gestalt psychology An approach that saw experience as different from the sum of its elements.

William James and Functionalism

While the structuralists and Gestalt psychologists continued their debate, a new type of psychology emerged, partly in response to the publication of Charles Darwin's *The Origin of Spe-*

 Experiencing **Psychology**

Testing Reaction Time

YOU HAVE READ about a number of reaction-time experiments in this chapter, including those conducted by von Helmholtz and Wundt. It is possible to conduct similar experiments without the brass equipment used by these early researchers.

This exercise, developed by Dr. Erik Chudler of the University of Washington, is designed to measure your reaction time to a visual stimulus. All you need is a partner and a simple footlong ruler. Hold the ruler vertically, with the highest numbers at the top, and ask your partner to place a hand at the bottom of the ruler without touching it. Tell your partner that you will drop the ruler sometime in the next 5 seconds and to grab the ruler as quickly as possible and hold it. Note the number at the top of the person's hand after the ruler is caught, and use this

2 in. (~5 cm)	0.10 seconds or s (100 ms)
4 in. (~10 cm)	0.14 s (140 ms)
6 in. (~15 cm)	0.17 s (170 ms)
8 in. (~20 cm)	0.20 s (200 ms)
10 in. (~25.5 cm)	0.23 s (230 ms)
12 in. (~30.5 cm)	0.25 s (250 ms)
17 in. (~43 cm)	0.30 s (300 ms)
24 in. (~61 cm)	0.35 s (350 ms)
31 in. (~79 cm)	0.40 s (400 ms)
39 in. (~99 cm)	0.45 s (450 ms)
48 in. (~123 cm)	0.50 s (500 ms)
69 in. (~175 cm)	0.60 s (600 ms)

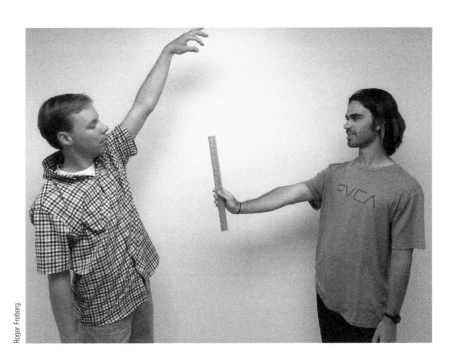

© Cengage Learning®

FIGURE 1.4

Gestalt Psychologists Challenged Structuralism. Participants usually see the middle figure as a B when instructed to look at the first row but see a 13 when instructed to read the second row. The structuralists, who believed that experiences could be reduced to small building blocks, would have difficulty explaining these results. In contrast, Gestalt psychologists, who emphasized the role of context or the "whole" in perception, would have no difficulties.

cies in 1859 and *The Descent of Man* in 1871. **Functionalism** viewed behavior as purposeful, because it led to survival. Instead of restricting themselves to exploring the structure of mind, functionalists were more interested in why behavior and mental processes worked in a particular way.

Functionalism's chief proponent was **William James** (1842–1910), whose textbook, *Principles of Psychology* (1890), dominated the field of psychology for 50 years. There are few topics in psychology that James did not address in his book, and many of his ideas sound modern. For example, James coined the term *stream of consciousness* to describe the flow of ideas people experience while awake. Throughout his discussions of mental processes and behavior,

Mary Evans Picture Library/The Image Works

William James (1842–1910) proposed functionalism, an approach to mind that viewed behavior as purposeful.

functionalism An approach that saw behavior as purposeful and contributing to survival.

chart to convert your results to reaction time.

Test your participant five times, and average the responses. Wundt eventually discarded reaction time as a measure because he became so frustrated with the variability he observed among participants and across tasks (Hergenhahn & Henley, 2013), but you can have some fun exploring these same sources of variability. Are you faster than your friends? Try testing people who are older than you. Are they faster or slower? Do your participants improve with practice? What happens to your reaction time if you dim the lights? ●

Roger Freberg

Measuring the spot where a person catches a falling ruler gives you a rough estimate of that individual's reaction time to a visual stimulus.

James emphasized the role of evolution. For the functionalist, the value of an activity depended on its consequences. Behaviors that enhance survival are repeated, and those that are either irrelevant or damaging to survival are abandoned. If we dream, it must be because dreaming improves our chances of survival. If we enjoy ice cream, it must be because eating sweet, high-fat foods enhances survival—at least it did for our ancestors, for whom famine was a more likely problem than obesity.

It is difficult to overestimate the impact of James on psychology. Although he didn't establish a particular "school" or train large numbers of students, as did Wundt and other early psychologists, James's ideas have become so dominant in psychology that we no longer refer to any separate "functionalist" approach. Structuralism came and went, but all contemporary psychologists are generally functionalists at heart. As described by psychology historians, "As a systematic point of view, functionalism was an overwhelming success, but largely because of this success it is no longer a distinct school of psychology. It was absorbed into the mainstream psychology. No happier fate could await any psychological point of view" (Chaplin & Krawiec, 1979, p. 53).

James, like the Gestalt psychologists, rejected the notion that we can study the mind by breaking it into elements or building blocks, because this division would result in a loss of understanding. As psychology entered the 20th century, this big-picture approach eventually broke up into a variety of separate perspectives as psychologists attempted to gain understanding by limiting their research to particular aspects of mind and behavior.

Mary Whiton Calkins (1863–1930) was a student of James at Harvard University, although she could not officially register because of her gender. She studied memory and the self and served as president of the American Psychological Association in 1905.

Clinical Roots: Freud and the Humanistic Psychologists

When a case of capital punishment occurs, we often read about the prisoner's terrible childhood from one side and the need to protect society from further misdeeds by this person from the other side. Where would the Freudians and humanistic psychologists line up in this debate?

With the exception of occasional bursts of insight from the ancient Egyptians and Greeks, the most common view of psychological disorders over the course of history has been the supernatural approach. According to this view, psychological disorders resulted from the actions of evil spirits or other external, magical forces. Although improvements in science and medicine led to more natural than supernatural explanations of psychological disorders, effective treatments were not rapidly forthcoming. Patients in the 17th and 18th centuries were often subjected to bizarre treatments, including being spun around in a chair. As recently as the 1940s, patients with schizophrenia were subjected to frequent experimentation. They were exposed to questionable techniques such as insulin shock therapy, in which insulin injections led to comas, and were restrained in lukewarm baths. We discuss schizophrenia and its treatment in more detail in Chapters 14 and 15.

Between the 17th and the 19th centuries, supernatural explanations for psychological disorders began to give way to two scientific approaches: a medical model and a psychological model. The medical model of psychological disorder emphasized physical causes of abnormal behavior and medical treatments, such as medication. The psychological model suggested that abnormal behavior can result from life experiences, leading to fear, anxiety, and other counterproductive emotional responses. Psychological treatments take many forms, from offering support to applying cognitive and behavioral methods to help people think and problem solve in new ways. As we will see in Chapters 14 and 15, contemporary psychologists typically combine these approaches to understand disorders and develop effective treatments. For example, we know that feeling depressed has both physical components (changes in the activity of chemical messengers in the brain) and experiential components (exposure to stressful situations). Treatment for depression often combines medication with efforts to change the way a person thinks about situations.

The work of Sigmund Freud (1856–1939) on consciousness, sexuality, abnormal behavior, and psychotherapy played a dominant role in psychology during the first half of the 20th century.

Sigmund Freud **Sigmund Freud** (1856–1939) built a bridge from his medical training as a physician to his belief in the impact of life experiences on behavior. His *psychodynamic* theory and its applications to the treatment of psychological disorders dominated much of psychological thinking for the first half of the 20th century. Freud managed to combine and communicate ideas about the existence of the unconscious mind, the development of sexuality, dream analysis, and psychological roots of abnormal behavior in such a way that his theories influenced not just psychology but also culture. He nearly single-handedly founded the study of personality in psychology, and we will explore his theories more fully in Chapter 13. He developed the techniques of psychoanalysis for treating mental disorders, which we discuss in Chapter 15. He popularized the use of psychological principles for explaining everyday behavior, and his theories are as likely to be discussed in an English literature course as in a psychology course.

Our enthusiasm for Freud is tempered by a number of valid concerns. As you read about Freud throughout the remainder of this textbook, keep in mind that his methods were not scientific. His theories are based primarily on his introspections, along with those of his patients, who as primarily upper-class Viennese housewives were not typical of the human population. Freud's theories do not lend themselves to experimentation, an essential requirement for any scientific theory, as we discuss further in Chapter 2. For example, how could you design an experiment to demonstrate that dreaming about water indicates you have unconscious concerns about sex? Finally, although psychoanalysis is still used as a therapy technique, it is rarely conducted in the strict Freudian manner. Other techniques, discussed in Chapter 15, exceed psychoanalysis in effectiveness and popularity among therapists.

Humanistic Psychology By the 1960s, American psychology was primarily characterized by behaviorism (discussed in a later section) on one side and Freud's theories on the other. Structuralism had fallen into disfavor, and functionalism and Gestalt psychology were no longer distinct schools of thought. Just as other aspects of American culture began to feature rebelliousness against current ways of thinking, some psychologists began to push against the restrictions of psychoanalysis. Many of these disenchanted psychologists had been trained in psychoanalysis but were not seeing the results they desired. This dissatisfaction with prevailing views led these psychologists to propose new ways of thinking about the human mind through an approach known as **humanistic psychology**.

Humanistic psychologists rejected the idea that people are innately uncivilized and must be taught to be good. Freud, James, and the behaviorists all believed that human behavior was on a continuum with animal behavior, which led to their assumption that humans naturally shared the aggressive impulses of animals. For Freud in particular, society had a civilizing function on the otherwise selfish and aggressive human. In contrast, the humanistic psychologists extended the philosophy of Jean-Jacques Rousseau and other 18th-century Romantic philosophers into a belief that people are innately good, are motivated to improve themselves, and only behave badly when corrupted by society.

Instead of focusing on what went wrong in people's lives, humanistic psychologist **Abraham Maslow** (1908–1970) asked interesting questions about what made a person "good." Maslow introduced a major theory of motivation, which we describe in more detail in Chapter 7. According to Maslow, the pinnacle of motivation is the goal of *self-actualization*. The 1990s U.S. Army slogan, "Be all you can be," captures much of the flavor of self-actualization. We will see Maslow's emphasis on what is good about people, as opposed to Freud's focus on what goes wrong with people, reemerge in the form of contemporary positive psychology.

Humanistic therapists rebelled against Freudian approaches to treatment. One humanistic therapist, **Carl Rogers** (1902–1987), developed a new approach to therapy, *client-centered therapy*. In this type of therapy, the people receiving treatment are called clients rather than patients, reflecting their equal standing with the therapist and their active role in the therapy process. Humanistic approaches to therapy have also influenced communication, group process, parenting, and politics. The emphasis on active listening and the use of "I hear what you're saying" reflections have become nearly cliché in courses of leadership training and interpersonal communication. Advice to parents to provide "unconditional" love to their children is a direct application of humanistic beliefs, which we discuss in more detail in Chapter 11. Finally, humanistic psychology continues to flavor our political and social domains. When issues such as capital punishment arise, the humanistic contention that there are no bad people, just bad societies, typically appears as part of the debate.

Ann Kaplan/CORBIS

Abraham Maslow (1908–1970) contributed a theory of motivation and ideas about exceptional people to the growing humanistic psychology movement.

Jerry Cooke/Getty Images

Until about 60 years ago, no effective treatments for psychological disorders existed. The application of scientific principles to treatment has finally led to real help.

humanistic psychology An approach to psychology that saw people as inherently good and motivated to learn and improve.

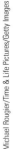

Humanistic therapists, like Carl Rogers (1902–1987), often rebelled against Freudian approaches to therapy. For example, Rogers (in the white shirt leading a group therapy session) referred to people as clients rather than patients, the term Freud used.

In 1920, Francis Cecil Sumner (1895–1954) became the first African American to receive a doctorate in psychology for his work on psychoanalysis. Sumner's later work focused on religion and racism.

behaviorism An approach to psychology that features the study and careful measurement of observable behaviors.

The Behaviorists and the Cognitive Revolution

Beginning at the dawn of the 20th century, the mental processes in our definition of psychology took a backseat to observable behavior for the better part of the next 50 years, because psychologists following the approach of **behaviorism** concentrated on observable, measurable behaviors. As part of their effort to measure behavior carefully, many behaviorists restricted their research to studies using animals. Armed with Darwin's evidence linking humans to animals, the behaviorists comfortably drew parallels between their observations of animals and their assumptions about human behavior. In particular, behaviorists were fascinated by learning, which we define as any persistent change in behavior due to experience. We will examine the behaviorists' contributions to this area in depth in Chapter 8.

Ivan Petrovich Pavlov (1849–1936) had a particularly significant impact on the course of behaviorism and psychology. While studying digestion in dogs, he realized that the dogs' salivation in response to the arrival of the handler or to being harnessed for an experiment indicated that the dogs had associated, or linked, these signals with the arrival of food. The dogs' ability to use this learned association to anticipate important future events was a remarkable advantage in terms of survival. This type of learning is now called classical or Pavlovian conditioning, which we will discuss in detail in Chapter 8.

Psychology textbooks would spend little time on Pavlov if his research applied only to salivating dogs. Although classical conditioning occurs in rather primitive organisms, including fruit flies, snails, and slugs, it also occurs quite frequently in humans. Many of our emotional responses associated with environmental cues are the result of this type of learning. If you feel especially anxious prior to taking an exam, you can thank classical conditioning. If you are repulsed by the idea of eating a food that you once consumed just before becoming ill, this is again a likely result of classical conditioning. A war veteran who experiences distress while filling a pickup truck with diesel fuel (a common battlefield smell) is also likely to be experiencing the results of classical conditioning.

John B. Watson (1878–1958) began experimenting with learning in rats and independently came to many of the same conclusions as Pavlov. Watson also echoed the blank-slate approach of the British empiricist philosophers in his emphasis on the role of experience in forming human behavior. In a famous speech given in 1926, Watson made the following claim:

Give me a dozen healthy infants, well-formed, and my own specified world to bring them up in and I'll guarantee to take any one at random and train him to become any type of specialist I might select—a doctor, lawyer, artist, merchant-chief, and yes, even into beggarman and thief, regardless of his talents, penchants, tendencies, abilities, vocations and race of his ancestors. (Watson, 1925, p. 10)

The Freudians and humanistic psychologists had conflicting views on human nature, with the Freudians believing that we are naturally selfish and aggressive and the humanistic psychologists believing we are naturally good. These philosophical differences continue to color our discussions of topics: Is a criminal a "bad" person who was never properly socialized or a "good" person who was corrupted?

Later in Watson's career, he applied his understanding of behavior to the budding American advertising industry. By 1930, Watson was earning $70,000 per year as an advertising executive, an astronomical salary for the time and quite different from the $3,000 per year he earned as a professor. After discovering that blindfolded participants couldn't tell the difference between brands of cigarettes, Watson concluded that to be successful, a product must be associated with an appealing image. The advertising industry was never the same, and today's advertisers continue to apply Watson's principles.

Watson's legacy in psychology was enormous. He restricted psychology to the study of observable behavior. As we will see in Chapter 2 and throughout this text, even psychologists who are interested in internal events, like the visual recognition of an object, seek related observable behaviors, such as brain images or reaction time.

Like Pavlov, Watson approached psychology with a focus on the relationships between environmental cues and behavior. Other behaviorists were more interested in the effects of consequences on behavior, an idea that was derived from basic functionalism. **Edward Thorndike** (1874–1949) proposed a law of effect, which suggested that behaviors followed by pleas-

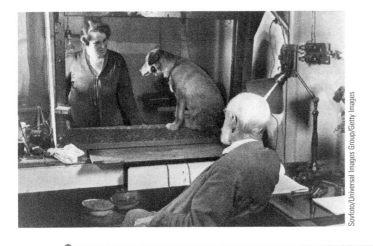

While studying digestion, Ivan Petrovich Pavlov (1849–1936) realized that his dogs could learn that certain signals meant food was on the way.

Classical conditioning helps us understand the links we make between environmental cues and our emotions. If a soldier associated the smell of diesel fuel with traumatic experiences, smelling diesel fuel at a gas station back home could trigger distress.

ant or helpful outcomes would be more likely to occur in the future, whereas behaviors followed by unpleasant or harmful outcomes would be less likely to occur. Thorndike based his law on observations of cats' behavior in a puzzle box he had constructed (see ● Figure 1.5). To escape the box, a cat was required to complete a sequence of behaviors. Through trial-and-error learning, the cat would escape faster and faster on successive trials. In other words, the cat repeated effective behaviors and abandoned ineffective ones.

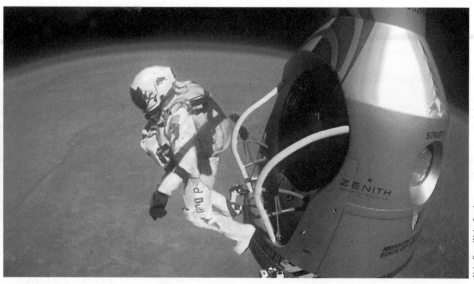

John B. Watson (above left, 1878-1958) was a strong believer in the blank-slate approach of the earlier empiricist philosophers. After working as a psychology professor, he applied his knowledge of human behavior to advertising with great success. Watson believed that a product would sell better if it were paired with an appealing image. The maker of energy drink Red Bull applied Watson's ideas when pairing its brand with daredevil skydiver Felix Baumgartner's record-setting jump from 24 miles above the earth's surface (above right).

FIGURE 1.5

Thorndike's Law of Effect Emerged From Observations of Cats. If you own a cat, you probably know that cats don't like to be enclosed in boxes. Edward Thorndike (1874–1949) studied the escape strategies of a cat to build his law of effect.

© 2016 Cengage Learning®

Like Thorndike, **B. F. Skinner** (1904–1990) was interested in the effects of consequences on how frequently behaviors were performed. Skinner shared Watson's belief that psychology did not benefit from consideration of consciousness or internal mental states. Skinner believed that inner, private states such as thinking and feeling existed, but he viewed them as behaviors that followed the same rules as public behaviors, like driving a car (Jensen & Burgess, 1997). He not only reduced his study of behavior to the actions of rats and pigeons in adapted cages that came to be known as Skinner boxes, but he also was comfortable generalizing from the behavior of rats and pigeons to complex human behaviors. Despite its strong focus on a limited set of animals and situations, Skinner's behaviorism has provided a wealth of beneficial applications. Smokers attempting to quit, doctors and nurses engaging in self-paced continuing education courses, and children receiving treatment for autism spectrum disorder are all likely to be benefiting from Skinner's efforts.

By the 1950s, the behaviorists' disinterest in mental states and activity was challenged by scientists from diverse fields, including linguistics and computer science, leading to a cognitive revolution. Cognition covers the private and internal mental processes the behaviorists avoided studying—information processing, thinking, reasoning, and problem solving. **Ulric Neisser** (1928–2012) gave the new field its name in his 1967 book, *Cognitive Psychology*.

Breakthroughs in computer technology allowed these new cognitive psychologists to use mathematical and computer models to illuminate the mental processes leading to observable behaviors. Alan Newell (1927–1992) and Herbert Simon (1916–2001) wrote groundbreaking artificial intelligence programs using human information processing as their model. The hardware of the computer was viewed as a metaphor for the brain, and its software

B. F. Skinner (1904–1990) was interested in the effects of reward and punishment on future behavior.

Nina Leen/Time Life Pictures/Getty Images

Ulric Neisser (1928–2012) contributed the term *cognition* to the emerging field that studied information processing, thinking, reasoning, and problem solving.

mirrored the brain's activity. By the 1980s, most university psychology departments were offering courses in cognition. By the 1990s, collaborations between cognitive and biological psychologists led to the new field of cognitive neuroscience, which seeks to identify brain structures and functions involved in processing information. In Chapter 10, we will explore the contributions of cognitive psychologists in more detail.

To illustrate how the behaviorist and cognitive approaches differ, we can look at how each explains language learning by children. Behaviorists like Skinner believed that children acquired language in response to feedback, such as parental approval or being understood. In contrast, linguist Noam Chomsky proposed that humans are born with innate mechanisms for learning language, which is the type of specialized internal mental processing Skinner rejected. As we will see in Chapters 10 and 11, the cognitive approach to language learning dominates our current understanding.

In contemporary departments of psychology, behaviorist approaches are represented by professors and researchers specializing in learning, who continue to explore the nuances of the effects of experience on behavior. Many of the big questions tackled by behaviorists are now examined through the lens of the cognitive or biological perspectives. Behavioral approaches make important contributions to real-world problems, including how best to pay employees and how to treat psychological disorders and addiction.

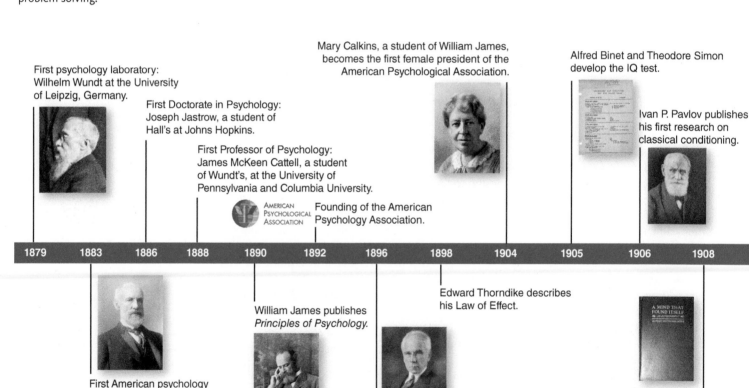

FIGURE 1.6

Milestones in the History of Psychology.

Computers were named after the job title of the women who did most computation tasks before the machines were invented and who continued to operate them. Although these early computers were less powerful than your cell phone (not to mention more expensive), their operation gave psychologists new ideas about how the mind might process information.

John B. Watson publishes *Psychology as the Behaviorist Views It.*

First African-American Doctorate in Psychology: Francis Cecil Sumner, a student of G. Stanley Hall's, at Clark University.

B.F. Skinner's *The Behavior of Organisms* contributes to the dominance of behaviorism.

The Boulder Conference establishes the scientist-practioner model of clinical psychology.

Gordon Allport, a social psychologist, publishes *The Nature of Prejudice.* Wilder Penfield publishes the results of his observations of patients undergoing surgery for epilepsy.

George Miller's "The Magical Number Seven, Plus or Minus Two" stimulates work in Cognitive Psychology.

1913 1920 1921 1928 1929 1938 1942 1949 1954 1956 1959 1976

The first Gestalt journal is published in Germany.

Jean Piaget publishes *Judgment and Reasoning in the Child.*

Hans Berger invents the electroencephalogram (EEG), still used today to study brain activity.

Carl Rogers introduces Humanistic approaches to therapy.

Noam Chomsky's criticism of Skinner's *Verbal Behavior* also contributes to the cognitive revolution.

Richard Dawkins's *The Selfish Gene* popularizes Evolutionary Psychology.

Ferdinand Hamburger Archives, Sheridan Libraries, Johns Hopkins University; Archives of the History of American Psychology, The Center for the History of Psychology, The University of Akron; Farrell Grehan/Historical/Corbis; VEM/Science Source; Nina Leen/Time Life Pictures/Getty Images; Michael Rougier/Time & Life Pictures/Getty Images; Jon Roemer LLC; The magical number seven, plus or minus two: some limits on our capacity for processing information. Miller, George A. *Psychological Review, Vol 63*(2), Mar 1956, 81-97. doi: 10.1037/h0043158; Dennis Van Tine/Retna Ltd./Corbis

Summary 1.2 Pioneering Approaches to Psychology

	Foundation of psychology	Things to remember
Wilhelm Wundt (1832–1920)	Structuralism	Behavior can be broken down into its components.
Max Wertheimer (1880–1943)	Gestalt psychology	Breaking behavior into components loses meaning.
William James (1842–1910)	Functionalism	Behavior is purposeful and contributes to survival.
Sigmund Freud (1856–1939)	Psychodynamic theory	Ideas about the unconscious mind, the role of experience in abnormal behavior, and new approaches to therapy laid a foundation for later study in personality and therapy.
Abraham Maslow (1908–1970)	Humanistic psychology	People are naturally good and are motivated to improve.
Ivan Petrovich Pavlov (1849–1936)	Behaviorism	Experience is the primary source of behavior.
Ulric Neisser (1928–2012)	Cognitive revolution	Private mental processing can be studied scientifically.

What Are Psychological Perspectives?

Like James, the Freudians and behaviorists tried to answer the "big questions" of psychology with a single approach. However, it is difficult to build a big theory (which we discuss in Chapter 2) without a large body of experimental data, and psychology was still a young science. To fill this gap, psychological scientists, like scientists in other fields, began to pursue an understanding by specializing in more specific points of view, or perspectives. By focusing on one part of the discipline, as opposed to trying to answer everything at once, psychologists began to gain an in-depth understanding of at least one aspect of mind.

By the second half of the 20th century, most psychologists were examining psychological phenomena from one of a handful of perspectives. The use of different perspectives does not imply disagreement or conflict. In most cases, the use of each perspective depended on specialized expertise and methods, so different fields of psychology became characterized by their distinct theoretical perspective and methods. For example, understanding how a child learns a new vocabulary word would be investigated using different theories and methods by the biological, developmental, cognitive, social, or behavioral psychologist.

Reflecting the traditional divisions of the field, it is common for psychologists to refer to themselves as social psychologists, developmental psychologists, and so on, indicating their area of specialization and interest. Departments of psychology at universities often continue this organization, and students applying to graduate school in psychology might apply to one particular area of expertise, like choosing an undergraduate major. To illustrate the distinctions among some of the main perspectives, we will consider how each might approach the question of human memory, discussed in detail in Chapter 9.

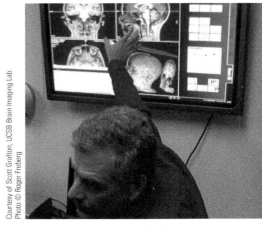

Courtesy of Scott Grafton, UCSB Brain Imaging Lab. Photo © Roger Freberg

Biological psychologists explore the relationships among mind, behavior, and their underlying biological processes. They often use technology such as functional magnetic resonance imaging (fMRI), such as Scott Grafton of the University of California, Santa Barbara, is doing to point out the features of the brain of one of your authors.

Six Perspectives of Psychology

Biological psychology, also called behavioral neuroscience, focuses on the relationships between mind and behavior and their underlying biological processes, including genetics, biochemistry, anatomy, and physiology. In other words, biological psychologists are interested in the physical mechanisms associated with behavior. As we will see in Chapter 4, technological advances beginning in the 1970s, especially new methods for observing brain activity, initiated an explosion of knowledge about the connections between brain and behavior. Using these new technologies, biological psychologists have approached the question of storage and retrieval of memories in many ways, ranging from observing changes in communication between nerve cells in slugs to investigating the effects of stress hormones on the ability to form memories. The focus of this perspective is on the mechanisms used to store and retrieve memories, such as changes in the structure of nerve cells or in the biochemical environment of the nervous system.

A special part of the biological perspective, **evolutionary psychology**, attempts to answer the question of how our physical structure and behavior have been shaped by their contributions to our species' survival. This perspective should sound familiar—it is a modern extension of James's functionalism, which we discussed previously. Earlier, we also saw evolutionary psychology at work in the shaping of our sensitivity to bitter tastes. The basic principle of evolutionary psychology is that our current behavior exists in its present form because it provided some advantage in survival and reproduction to our ancestors. An evolutionary psychologist might be interested in our good memory for faces, and particularly for faces of people who have cheated us in the past (Barclay & Lalumière, 2006). In the world of the hunter–gatherer, being cheated out of a fair share of the hunt was likely to lead to starvation for a family, and people who could not keep track of the cheaters were unlikely to survive and reproduce.

biological psychology The psychological perspective that focuses on the relationships between mind and behavior, as well as their underlying biological processes, including genetics, biochemistry, anatomy, and physiology; also known as behavioral neuroscience.
evolutionary psychology The psychological perspective that investigates how physical structure and behavior have been shaped by their contributions to survival and reproduction.

Evolutionary psychologists are interested in how our modern behaviors were shaped by our species' history.

Cognitive psychology focuses on the process of thinking, or the processing of information. Because our ability to remember plays an integral part in the processing of information, a cognitive psychologist is likely to have a lot to say about the storage and retrieval of memories. A cognitive psychologist might ask why processing seems different when we are trying to remember names and dates while taking a history test compared to remembering how to ride a bicycle. What processes lead to the frustrating experience of having something on the "tip of your tongue," in which you remember the first letter or a part of the word you're trying to retrieve but not the whole thing? What strategies can we use to make our memories more efficient? We address these and similar issues in Chapters 9 and 10.

Social psychology describes the effects of the social environment, including **culture**, on the behavior of individuals. Social psychologists recognize that we construct our own realities and that the social environment influences our thoughts, feelings, and behavior. Early psychologists were limited in their understanding of mind by their exclusive focus on their own sociocultural contexts. More recently, social psychologists have emphasized the need to explore the influences of sociocultural context and biology on our behavior. Returning to our memory example, the social psychologist might ask how being in the presence of others influences the storage and retrieval of data. When we sit comfortably in our own homes, the answers to *Jeopardy* questions come relatively easily. In front of millions of viewers, however, we might be lucky to remember our own names.

Developmental psychology explores the normal changes in behavior that occur across the life span. Using the developmental perspective, a psychologist might look at how memory functions in people of different ages. Without further practice, 3-month-old babies can retain for about a month the memory that kicking moves a mobile suspended above their crib (Rovee-Collier, 1997). However, most adults have difficulty recalling events that occurred before the age of 3 or 4 years. Teens and young adults are able to remember names faster than are older adults (Bashore, Ridderinkhof, & van der Molen, 1997). We explore these and other age-related changes in memory in Chapter 11.

The **clinical psychology** perspective seeks to explain, define, and treat psychological disorders. More recently, clinical and counseling psychologists have expanded their perspective to include the promotion of general well-being, which we describe in Chapter 16. Many types of psychological disorders affect memory. Freud believed that traumatizing experiences were

cognitive psychology The psychological perspective that investigates information processing, thinking, reasoning, and problem solving.

social psychology The psychological perspective that examines the effects of the social environment on the behavior of individuals.

culture The practices, values, and goals shared by groups of people.

developmental psychology The psychological perspective that examines the normal changes in behavior that occur across the life span.

clinical psychology The psychological perspective that seeks to explain, define, and treat abnormal behaviors.

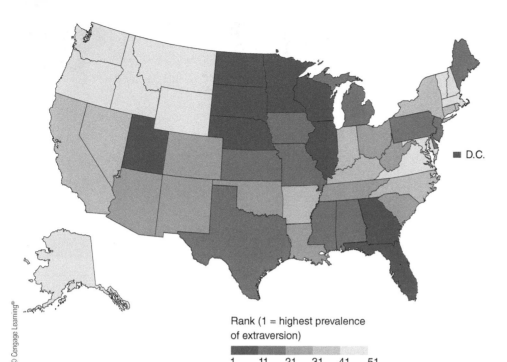

Rank (1 = highest prevalence
of extraversion)

1   11   21   31   41   51

FIGURE 1.7

Individual Differences: The Geography of Personality. Where in the United States do you think the most outgoing, extroverted people live? Would you believe that North Dakota has a higher percentage of extroverts than California or New York? Why would this be the case? Perhaps the need to develop tight social networks to survive the harsh climate in this part of the United States favored extroverts. Introverts, who tend to be more cautious, might choose to live in less challenging environments.

Cognitive psychologists investigate the ways the human mind processes information. This cognitive psychologist is studying the use of mirrored images to help individuals overcome phantom pain due to the loss of a limb. Seeing images of what appears to be a healthy limb in place of the missing limb changes the way the mind thinks about the missing limb, leading to a reduction in perceived pain.

more difficult to remember, a process he labeled *repression* (which will be discussed later in Chapters 9 and 14). In other cases, war veterans and others who have experienced trauma might be troubled by memories that are too good, producing intrusive flashback memories of disturbing events.

Finally, although much of psychology explores how the average person thinks, feels, or acts, some people are not average. Psychologists interested in all varieties of behavior, not just the most typical types, pursue an **individual differences** perspective (see ● Figure 1.7). Recognizing individual differences is especially important to psychologists interested in variations in **personality**. Using our example of memory, we can see how individual differences in "need for cognition" can predict memory for verbal material (Cacioppo, Petty, Feinstein, & Jarvis, 1996). People who have a high need for cognition enjoy mental challenges, like solving difficult puzzles. As we'll see in Chapter 13, individuals who are high in need for cognition also remember more of the messages to which they are exposed and respond differently to persuasive messages.

A New Connectivity: Integrating Psychology's Six Perspectives

Entering the 21st century and armed with in-depth research results compiled in the various perspectives, psychologists are returning to the more comprehensive view of the mind envisioned more than 100 years ago by James. Their questions and methods are more likely to blur the lines of the perspectives outlined earlier, often with remarkable results.

individual differences An approach to psychology that investigates variations in behavior from one person to the next.
personality An individual's characteristic way of thinking, feeling, and behaving.

Social psychologists explore the effects of the social environment on our individual behavior. In this example, the man in the middle is deciding whether to conform with the other two men in a simple judgment of line length.

Although the 20th-century perspective approach to psychology generated detailed understanding of aspects of behavior and mental processes, it has become apparent that single perspectives are insufficient for fully describing and explaining psychological phenomena. For example, if we want to understand the phenomenon of illicit drug use, many perspectives can contribute to our understanding, but no one specialty offers a complete explana-

 # Thinking Scientifically

Can the Use of a Single Perspective Be Misleading?

WE HAVE ARGUED that restricting our thinking about an aspect of mind to the information provided by one perspective can result in an incomplete picture, but can this single-perspective approach actually lead us in the wrong direction?

The answer to that question is a resounding "yes." Consider the following example. You are a biological psychologist interested in the effects of amphetamines on aggression. You know that amphetamines make individual rhesus monkeys quite a bit more aggressive than usual (Haber & Barchas, 1983). (We are unlikely to do this study with humans because of ethical concerns discussed in Chapter 2.) But you also know that rhesus monkeys are social animals, so it makes little

sense to study them in isolation. To your surprise, you find that amphetamines produce no effects on the aggressiveness of a colony of rhesus monkeys (Dawe, Davis, Lapworth, & McKetin, 2009).

Your single biological psychology perspective can help explain why the individual monkeys are more aggressive under the influence of amphetamines, but it provides little help in explaining why you don't see the same results when you study the monkeys in a group. However, when you add the insights of social psychology to those of biological psychology, a clearer picture emerges. The social world of the rhesus monkey consists of a strong hierarchy, or pecking order, with each male monkey

knowing his position relative to all others in the colony. Higher ranking monkeys engage in dominance behaviors, including vocalizations and threats, to remind the lower ranking monkeys about who is the boss. Lower ranking monkeys avoid aggression and other signs of dominance by engaging in submissive behaviors designed to prevent aggression, such as imitation (Adams, 1982).

When you take a monkey's rank in the social hierarchy into account (adding the social perspective to the biological one), a clear picture of the results emerges. Amphetamines have different results on aggression that depend on the social status of the animal. Amphetamines increase dominance behavior by dominant monkeys and

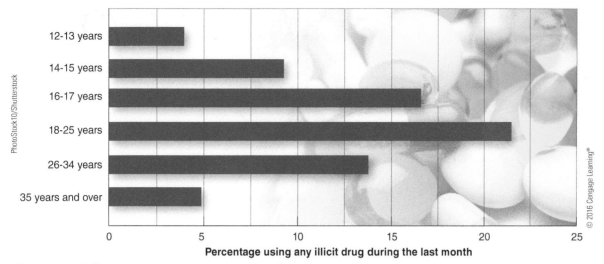

Percentage using any illicit drug during the last month

FIGURE 1.8

Using Multiple Perspectives Can Help Us Better Understand Complex Phenomena Like Drug Abuse. What accounts for the different patterns of drug use at each stage of life? Single perspectives can only give us parts of the answer. Combining perspectives can give us the big picture.

tion. Biological psychologists approach drug use by tracing pathways in the brain correlated with cravings, developmental and social psychologists consider the family and peer influences, and so on. In each case, we learn something about drug use, but understanding the whole phenomenon requires us to zoom out for a more comprehensive perspective (see ● Figure 1.8).

increase submissive behavior by submissive monkeys. If you added up all effects of amphetamines for the group, the increases and decreases would cancel each other out, making it look like amphetamines had no effects. By adding the social perspective to the question, the discrepancy between the individual and the group results can be explained easily. This example illustrates how restricting ourselves to one perspective might cloud our understanding. ●

Studying individual rhesus monkeys will provide useful information, but for these social animals, incorporating a social perspective helps us understand them more fully.

FIGURE 1.9

Contemporary Psychology Integrates Six Perspectives.
Viewing the mind by zooming in and using specialized perspectives has led to significant increases in our understanding, but 21st-century psychology is characterized by efforts to zoom out and integrate multiple, cross-cutting perspectives.

Scientific research methods

© 2016 Cengage Learning®

We don't have a crystal ball that will allow us to foresee psychology's future. However, we strongly believe that this future will be one of combining and integrating new and existing perspectives. Many of these new ways of looking at the mind will take advantage of the revolution in techniques for studying the brain that began in the 1970s and continues. Already, today's cognitive neuroscientists investigate the brain as an information-processing system and search for the biological basis of topics such as attention, decision making, and memory. Social neuroscientists investigate the biological factors that vary with people's feelings and experiences of social inclusion, rejection, or loneliness. Behavioral neuroscientists pick up previous lines of research on learning, memory, motivation, and sleep and search for connections between these processes and our biology. Clinical and counseling psychologists are likely to consider biological processes in their theories about the causes of psychological disorders. By merging the six perspectives of mind, we stand a better chance of tackling the remarkable problem of understanding the human mind (see ● Figure 1.9).

Thierry Berrod, Mona Lisa Production/Science Source

Developmental psychologists look at the behavior that is typical for people of certain ages, from infancy to old age.

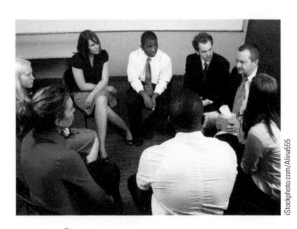

iStockphoto.com/Alina555

Clinical psychologists seek to understand and treat psychological disorders.

What Does It Mean to Be a Psychologist?

In 2010–2011, more than 100,000 students in the United States received a bachelor's degree in psychology (U.S. National Center for Education Statistics, 2012). This amounts to approximately 6% of the 1.7 million bachelor's degrees awarded that year. What are these students likely to be doing in the workforce?

Psychology is unlike some other disciplines in which people with a bachelor's degree can refer to themselves as a practicing member of the relevant profession, such as a chemist or biologist. Calling oneself a psychologist is restricted to holders of graduate, usually doctorate, degrees. This does not mean that students who completed a bachelor's degree in psychology cannot be employed in relevant fields. Some students with undergraduate degrees in psychology prefer employment in fields that are directly related to psychology, such as working in research facilities or rehabilitation centers for drug abuse or brain damage. Others are quite successful in a variety of people-oriented jobs, such as those found in management, sales, service, public affairs, education, human resources, probation, and journalism. This diversity of career pathways reflects the hub nature of psychology to other fields, as described earlier in this chapter.

Forensic psychologists attempt to understand the criminal mind and to develop effective treatments for criminal behavior.

Graduates with a master's degree in psychology, usually requiring 1 to 2 years of additional study past the bachelor's degree, can teach at the community college (2-year) level and obtain licensing as therapists in most states, as we discuss further in Chapter 15. Many psychologists with a master's degree are employed in health, industry, and education (American Psychological Association [APA], 2009). School psychologists typically work on elementary, middle school, or high school campuses. These psychologists participate in academic and career counseling, as well as the identification and remediation of problems that interfere with student success.

Many people working in psychology have earned doctoral degrees, which usually take 2 to 5 years of study beyond the master's level. As shown in ● Figure 1.10, about 32% of new doctoral-level psychologists do what your professor and the authors of this textbook do: teach and conduct research at colleges and universities. About 37% of new doctoral-level psychologists work as therapists, either in private practice or in hospitals and clinics. Smaller numbers of new doctoral-level psychologists find employment in business and government settings, elementary and secondary schools, and other related fields.

Psychologists entering doctoral programs traditionally identify with one of the major perspectives we discussed earlier, such as social, cognitive, or biological. Choosing a graduate perspective is similar to choosing an undergraduate major. Although all psychology graduate students might take core courses in research methods and statistics, they typically pursue

Sports psychologist Vietta Wilson uses biofeedback to help Canadian biathlete Graham Mater maximize his performance.

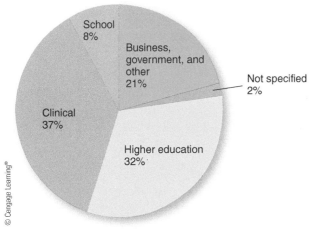

School 8%

Business, government, and other 21%

Not specified 2%

Clinical 37%

Higher education 32%

FIGURE 1.10

Where Psychologists Work. Within 1 year of graduation, individuals earning a doctoral degree between 2008 and 2009 found work in a variety of settings. Most were employed in clinical and higher education settings, but opportunities for psychologists also exist in schools, businesses, government, and other settings in which an understanding of human behavior is helpful. *Source:* Data from "2009 Doctorate Employment Survey," by D. Michalski, J. Kohout, M. Wicherski, and B. Hart, 2011, retrieved from http://www.apa.org/workforce/publications/09-doc-empl/index.aspx.

coursework and research in their particular area of specialization. However, training of psychologists in the 21st century is beginning to reflect the connections occurring in the field. Increasingly, students are being trained in combined specialties (e.g., cognitive neuroscience) as psychology becomes an increasingly integrated field of study.

The most rigid distinction occurs between graduate students who plan to specialize in clinical or counseling psychology and those who do not. The clinical or counseling track includes extensive internships and supervised training prior to government-regulated licensure that usually add at least 1 year to students' graduate studies. Do not assume that your psychology professors are all therapists; it is most likely they are not. It is important to distinguish between therapists with doctoral degrees in psychology and psychiatrists, who are medical doctors. The biggest difference between the two professions is that psychiatrists can prescribe medication but psychologists usually cannot. In New Mexico and Louisiana, however, specially trained psychologists can legally prescribe medications, and this trend might spread to other states. In Chapter 15, we will provide more detail about the types of therapists who treat adjustment problems and psychological disorders.

Interpersonal Relationships
How Can We Use Relationships to Illustrate Psychological Perspectives?

We gave quite a lot of thought to how we might help you, the students reading our book, to see psychology more as an interconnected discipline than as a collection of separate perspectives. The introductory psychology course provides a unique opportunity to see all perspectives at one time, in contrast to upper division courses that typically focus on one specialty area at a time (biological, developmental, social, cognitive, clinical, and so on). At the beginning of each chapter, we will take a question relevant to the chapter, such as "Why are we sensitive to bitter tastes?" and explore it using multiple perspectives. At the end of each chapter, we'll mirror this process by taking a single problem and seeing how the material in the chapter can be applied.

This feature of the textbook will have more of a perspective flavor than the beginnings of each chapter, but by the end of the textbook, you will have seen how each of the major perspectives in psychological science contributes to the whole picture. Because it is most helpful to know something about the perspectives before you see how they can be applied, we save this feature for the end of each chapter. Ideally, seeing the chapter material in action will make it more memorable for you.

The single problem we have chosen to consider this way is one that we know to be on the minds of many of our students: their relationships with others. We are a social species, and the quality of our relationships has a huge impact on our physical and psychological well-being (Cacioppo & Hawkley, 2009). We will see how each of the major perspectives views the question of relationship quality and how the perspectives work together to give us the best understanding possible of this important aspect of life. ●

OlegD/Shutterstock.com

Summary 1.3 Six Psychological Perspectives

	Perspective	Things to remember
	Biological and evolutionary psychology	Investigates the connections among mind, behavior, and biological processes, and asks how our evolutionary past continues to shape our behavior
	Cognitive psychology	Investigates mental processes including thinking, problem solving, and information processing
	Social psychology	Asks how our behavior is affected by the presence of others
	Developmental psychology	Investigates the normal changes in behavior that occur across the life span
	Clinical psychology	Explains, defines, and treats psychological disorders and promotes general well-being
	Individual perspective and personality	Recognizes that behavior varies around averages and that individual differences often interact with environments

Credits: Top Row: Courtesy of Scott Grafton, UCSB Brain Imaging Lab. Photo, Roger Freberg; Publiphoto/Science Source. Second Row: Pascal Goetgheluck/Science Source; Third Row: Joel Gordon 2001. Fourth Row: Thierry Berrod, Mona Lisa Production/Science Source.

Summary 1.3 (continued) What Do Psychologists Do?

Typical academic degree	Possible areas of employment
Bachelor's degree	Rehabilitation, research assistance, management, sales, service, public affairs, education, human resources, probation, journalism
Master's degree	Community college teaching, marriage and family counseling, health, education
Doctor of philosophy (PhD)	University teaching and research, therapy, business, government, education
Medical doctor (MD)*	Psychiatry

*Medical doctors who practice psychiatry are not psychologists, as implied by the title of the table, but we think it's important for you to know how they relate to psychologists.

KEY TERMS The Language of Psychological Science

Be sure you can define these terms and use them correctly.

behaviorism, p. 16
biological psychology, p. 23
clinical psychology, p. 24
cognitive psychology, p. 24
culture, p. 24
developmental psychology, p. 24
evolutionary psychology, p. 23

functionalism, p. 13
Gestalt psychology, p. 12
humanistic psychology, p. 15
individual differences, p. 25
introspection, p. 5
mind, p. 5

natural sciences, p. 6
personality, p. 26
philosophy, p. 6
psychology, p. 5
social psychology, p. 24
structuralism, p. 12

2 The Measure of Mind
Methods of Psychology

AMONG THE MANY CELEBRITIES WHO STUTTER is action actor Samuel Jackson. At a gala for the American Institute for Stuttering, Jackson shared one of his strategies for avoiding stuttering—uttering a particular swear word under his breath.

Stuttering involves disruptions in normal speech production, such as repeating the starting letter of a word (b-b-b-bird), holding a vowel sound for a long time (ah ah ah), or having difficulty initiating speech. About 5% of the population experience stuttering (Månsson, 2000), with males 2 to 5 times more likely to stutter than females (Craig & Tran, 2005).

Stuttering has been described since the days of the ancient Greeks and occurs across all cultures and ethnicities. Many interesting myths exist regarding its causes and remedies (Kuster, 2005). South African traditions suggest that stuttering results from leaving a baby out in the rain or tickling a baby too much. A Chinese folk remedy for stuttering was to hit the person in the face when the weather was cloudy. In Iceland, people believed that a pregnant woman who drank from a cracked cup was likely to produce a child who stuttered.

Many of us might ask, "How could anybody believe these things?" But how do we know these are merely myths and not facts? How can we be so sure? Instead of dismissing these efforts to explain and predict, think about what might have happened to lead people to these particular conclusions. What is missing from these conclusions is a system for reaching logical, objective results. Science provides us with this system.

What does science have to say about stuttering? Based on the careful evaluation of stuttering using the methods outlined in this chapter, scientists have concluded that there are multiple causes for stuttering (Kang et al., 2010). Many cases seem to have a basis in genetics, which we discuss in the next chapter. Scientists have used brain imaging technologies to zoom in on brain structures and functions that appear to differ between stutterers and fluent speakers, with stutterers showing more activation of the right hemisphere during speech (Gordon, 2002). As we mentioned in our previous chapter, some of the most thorough explanations combine multiple psychological perspectives (Ward, 2006). A complete explanation of stuttering zooms back out to combine a predisposition for the problem resulting from genetics and biology with developmental, emotional, and social factors, like feeling embarrassed or anxious about speaking in front of peers.

◀ Scientific methods, including brain imaging, have allowed researchers to pinpoint structural and functional differences between the brains of fluent speakers and those of people who stutter.

iStockphoto.com/EdStock

Argosy Publishing, Inc.

Although there is no "cure" for stuttering, carefully tested scientific explanations combining input from various perspectives are leading to more effective treatments. In this chapter, you will learn how science provides a system that allows us to construct increasingly realistic models of the world around us.

Learning Objectives

1. Differentiate scientific reasoning from common sense.

2. Explain the use of case studies, naturalistic observations, and surveys to describe behavior.

3. Describe the key features, strengths, and limitations of correlational and experimental methods.

4. Define reliability and validity.

5. Differentiate between descriptive and inferential statistics.

6. Analyze the ethical guidelines for using human and animal participants in research.

What Is Science?

Science is a special way of learning about the world through systematic observation and experimentation. These children are learning about the science of mind during the Dana Foundation's Brain Awareness Week.

science A method for learning about reality through systematic observation and experimentation.
objectivity The practice of basing conclusions on facts without influence of personal emotion and bias.

Throughout human history, we have been motivated to understand, predict, and control the world around us. To meet these goals, we need methods for gaining knowledge.

We often take contemporary scientific knowledge for granted, but our ancestors did not enjoy the benefits of science while trying to explain their world. Early in history, people attempted to understand natural phenomena by applying human characteristics to nature (Cornford, 1957). Skies could look angry or a lake could be calm. Other explanations involved spirits, which were found in humans and all other objects. Earthquakes and illness were viewed as the actions of spirits, and people attempted to influence these spirits through magical rituals.

People often form strong beliefs about their world based on faith, which literally means "trust." Faith is belief that does not depend on logical proof or evidence. We might accept friends' excuses for being late based on our faith in their honesty, without knowing for certain whether our friends are telling the truth. Science, in contrast to faith, requires proof and evidence. Our word **science** comes from the Latin *scientia*, which means "knowledge." *Science* doesn't refer to just any type of knowledge but rather to a special way of learning about reality through systematic observation and experimentation. The methods we describe in this chapter are designed to supply that evidence.

The Scientific Mindset

Not all observations are scientific. How does science differ from everyday observations, like the belief that "opposites attract"? As you will learn in Chapter 13, "opposites" do not, in fact, find each other very attractive.

First, science relies on **objectivity**, rather than subjectivity. Objectivity means that conclusions are based on facts, without influence from personal emotions or biases. In contrast, subjectivity means that conclusions reflect personal points of view. In a study by Allport and Postman (1945), research participants described what they had heard about photos from memory. Some participants switched the race of a man threatening another person from

White (which was the objective fact in the photo) to Black (possibly to fit a biased subjective worldview).

Scientists strive to be objective, but any observation by a human is, by definition, subjective. Recognizing when we are being subjective can be difficult, so scientists cannot rely on their introspections to maintain objectivity. Most of us have had the experience of witnessing an accident in the presence of other people. It can be astonishing to hear the different accounts of what happened. Didn't we all see the same thing? We like to believe our view of the events is the accurate one. As we discuss in Chapters 9 and 10, objective facts can be altered easily when processed subjectively by individuals. The scientific methods described in this chapter promote objectivity and help prevent biased, subjective observations from distorting a scientist's work.

The second important difference between science and everyday observations is the use of systematic as opposed to hit-or-miss observation. By "hit or miss" we mean making conclusions based only on whatever is happening around us. If we want to make conclusions about the human mind, we cannot restrict our observations to our immediate circle of acquaintances, friends, and loved ones. Our observations of the people we see frequently are probably quite good. It's just that the people we know represent a small slice of the greater population. We might be surprised to learn that our favorite candidate lost an election, because "everyone we know" voted for that candidate.

Based on observations of their surroundings, college students often believe that drinking alcohol, and even binge drinking (five drinks on one occasion for men, four drinks for women), is a nearly universal behavior for anyone over the age of 18 or so. We can see why a college student might believe this after making hit-or-miss observations. Among 18- to 22-year-olds enrolled in college, 40% reported binge drinking in the previous 30 days (White & Hingson, 2014). In contrast, the overall prevalence of binge drinking among U.S. adults was 17.1%, and the rate among all young adults between 18 and 24 years was 28.2% (see ● Figure 2.1), well below the frequency observed among those in college (Centers for Disease Control [CDC], 2012b). Possibly even more surprising to college students, 48% of the adult population either drink infrequently or do not drink alcohol (Centers for Disease Control [CDC], 2012a).

Finally, science relies on observable, repeatable evidence, whereas everyday observation often ignores evidence, especially when it runs counter to strongly held beliefs. Many people are convinced that women talk more than men. We're not certain where that idea originated, but it does not appear to be true. One group of researchers recorded students' talking throughout the day and concluded that "the widespread and highly publicized stereotype about female talkativeness is unfounded" (Mehl, Vazire, Ramírez-Esparza, Slatcher, &

Science has provided us with explanations for many natural phenomena, like tornadoes, that were probably quite frightening for our ancestors.

Science strives to be objective, making judgments that are free from personal emotion or bias. In contrast, people's subjectivity emerged in a classic experiment by Allport and Postman (1945). Some participants remembered hearing that this picture illustrated a Black man threatening another person rather than the objective fact—a White person is doing the threatening.

Corepics VOF/Shutterstock

We have all had the experience of witnessing an event with other people only to discover that everyone seems to have a different memory of what happened.

Pennebaker, 2007, p. 82). Other studies make the argument that in most circumstances, men actually talk more than women (James & Drakich, 1993; Leaper & Ayres, 2007).

Scientific knowledge is both stable and changing. It is a work in progress, not a finished product. The fact that we may learn something new tomorrow should not convince you that today's knowledge is flawed. Most change occurs slowly on the cutting edges of science, not quickly or at the main core of its knowledge base. Unlike with many other fields, we expect science to improve over time. An important feature of scientific literacy is to learn to be comfortable with the idea that scientific knowledge is always open to improvement and will never be considered certain (American Association for the Advancement of Science, 2009).

The Importance of Critical Thinking

Critical thinking, or the ability to think clearly, rationally, and independently, is one of the foundations of scientific reasoning. The skilled critical thinker can follow logical arguments, identify mistakes in reasoning, prioritize ideas according to their importance, and apply logic to personal attitudes, beliefs, and values.

Critical thinking is not built in; rather, it is a skill people need to learn. You can begin by using five critical thinking questions to evaluate new information you come across in your everyday life, starting with what you read in this textbook (Bernstein, 2011):

- What am I being asked to believe or accept?
- What evidence supports this position?
- Are there other ways this evidence could be interpreted?
- What other evidence would I need to evaluate these alternatives?
- What are the most reasonable conclusions?

It is also helpful to recognize the signs that you are not thinking critically (Excerpt taken from Lau & Chan, 2009):

- Instead of figuring out the answer to a problem myself, I prefer to be given the answer.
- I prefer to use "gut feelings" about decisions instead of using reason to choose a solution.
- I do not review my mistakes or change my mind if evidence contradicts my original position.
- I resent criticism of my ideas.
- I am unwilling to consider alternative explanations.

critical thinking The ability to think clearly, rationally, and independently.

FIGURE 2.1

Scientific Observations Are Systematic, Not Hit or Miss.
Science provides ways to make systematic observations. Judgments we make based on the people we know might not apply to larger groups of people. College students often overestimate the prevalence of binge drinking because of their on-campus observations. Binge drinking is more common among college students (40%) than it is among 18- to 24-year-olds in general (28.2%). Among all adults, 48% either drink infrequently or do not drink. *Source:* CDC, 2012.

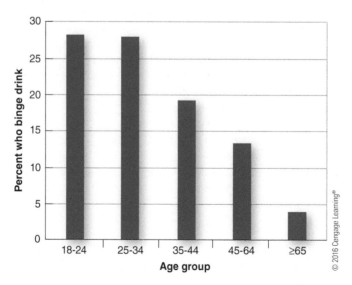
© 2016 Cengage Learning®

Critical thinking not only is essential to good science but also provides the underpinning of a free society. Our ability to think clearly, rationally, and independently gives us the confidence to question the actions of people in authority instead of engaging in blind obedience. We hope you will continue to practice good critical thinking skills long after you complete this textbook.

Scientific research results do not support the common stereotype that women talk more than men.

The Scientific Enterprise

Learning scientific facts is not the same as understanding how science works. Science, including psychological science, is more than a collection of facts—it is a process.

Scientific Theories Science seeks to develop **theories**, which are sets of facts and relationships between facts that can be used to explain and predict phenomena (Cacioppo, Semin, & Berntson, 2004). In other words, scientists construct the best possible models of reality based on the facts known to date. Unfortunately, the English language can be the source of considerable confusion regarding the nature of scientific theories. In addition to its use in science, the word *theory* can be used in nonscientific ways to describe a guess, such as "I have a theory about why my professor seems unusually cheerful this morning," or a hypothetical situation, as in "that's the theory, but it may not work in practice." Confusion over the multiple meanings of the word *theory* have led people mistakenly to view truly scientific theories, like the theory of evolution, as nothing more than casual guesses or hunches rather than the thoroughly investigated and massively supported principles that they are.

The best scientific theories not only explain and organize known facts but also generate new predictions (see ● Figure 2.3). The word *prediction* comes from the Latin words for "saying before." A scientific prediction is more than a guess or hunch. It is usually stated in a rigorous, mathematical form that allows the scientist to say that under a certain set of circumstances, a certain set of outcomes are likely to occur (if A, then B). In some cases, a theory's predictions can be surprising. For example, you might believe that it's impossible to be happy and sad at the same time. However, one model of emotion, discussed in Chapter 7, predicted that it is quite possible to feel happy and sad at the same time (Cacioppo, Berntson, Norris, & Gollan, 2011). This prediction was confirmed by research showing that first-year college students reported feeling either happy or sad, but not both, on a normal day of school but experiencing both emotions simultaneously on the day they moved out of campus housing to go home for the summer.

Before attempting to generate your own scientific questions, it pays to become familiar with relevant theories and previous discoveries. As Sir Isaac Newton noted, scholars stand on the shoulders of giants (Turnbull, 1959, p. 416)—we build on the work of those who came before us. New lines of research can also originate in observation. Scientists are observers not just in the laboratory but also in everyday life. Scientific progress often takes a giant leap forward when a gifted observer recognizes a deeper meaningfulness in an everyday occurrence, such as when Newton observed a falling apple and considered its implications for a law of gravity. As we discovered in Chapter 1, Ivan Petrovich Pavlov realized that when his dogs learned to salivate to signals predicting the arrival of food, something more significant than slobbering dogs was happening. The learning he observed explains why we get butterflies in our stomach before a performance and avoid foods that we think made us ill.

Generating Good Hypotheses Once you understand the theoretical foundations of your area of interest, you are ready to generate a **hypothesis**. A hypothesis is a type of inference, or an educated guess, based on prior evidence and logical possibilities.

Scientists can never "prove" that a hypothesis is true because some future experiment, possibly using new technology not currently available, might show the hypothesis to be false. All they can do is show when a hypothesis is false. A false hypothesis must always be modified or discarded.

Evaluating Hypotheses Once you have a hypothesis, you are ready to collect the data necessary to evaluate it. The existing scientific literature in your area of interest provides con-

theory A set of facts and relationships between facts that can explain and predict related phenomena.
hypothesis A proposed explanation for a situation, usually taking the form "if A happens, then B will be the result."

FIGURE 2.3

How to Develop and Test a Theory.
Theory building begins with generating hypotheses that are then systematically tested. Hypotheses that are not rejected contribute to the theory and help generate new hypotheses.

Theoretical hypothesis (e.g., a causal mechanism or a mathematical relation)

Systematic observation (experimental or nonexperimental)

Confirmation

Testable prediction

© 2016 Cengage Learning®

siderable guidance regarding your choice of materials, types of data to collect, and methods for interpreting your data.

To explore the many techniques available to psychologists, we will use an ongoing question about whether playing violent video games increases physical aggression. We could benefit from many other studies that specify features of violent video games, measures of physical aggression, and statistical procedures for evaluating this type of question. Scientists do not have to reinvent the wheel. Results will be given greater consideration if the researchers use methods that are well established and familiar in their area of research. Once data have been collected, theories allow scientists to evaluate the importance and implications of their observations.

Science is a vastly collaborative enterprise. Not only do we stand on the shoulders of giants because we benefit from the work that has been done previously, but we depend on many others in the scientific community to help us improve our work and avoid mistakes. Normally this evaluation is done by submitting research to conferences or for publication. During this process, research undergoes **peer review**, in which it is scrutinized by other scientists who are experts in the same area. Only if other experts conclude that new research is important, accurate, and explained thoroughly will it be added to the existing body of scientific knowledge. To demonstrate the importance of this peer review, contrast this process to what happens

peer review The process of having other experts examine research prior to its publication.

Thinking Scientifically

Using the Five Steps of Critical Thinking to Evaluate Survey Data

LET'S SEE HOW we might apply the five steps of critical thinking to examine the results of a recent research study about the social media platform Facebook. Kross et al. (2013) reported that frequent users of Facebook experienced reduced well-being. Their results were widely publicized in the popular press. The *Economist* featured the study in an article with the headline "Facebook Is Bad for You: Get a Life!" An article in the *Guardian* carried the headline "Facebook Causes Depression, New Study Says." What did Kross et al. (2013) find? How are their findings related to these headlines?

1. *What am I being asked to believe or accept?* I'm being asked to believe that there is a direct link between the amount of time people spend on Facebook and their ratings of personal well-being.

2. *What evidence supports this position?* Kross et al. (2013) recruited 82 college students, who were texted 5 times per day between 10 a.m. and midnight at random intervals. Each time, the participants received five questions: (a) How do you feel right now? (b) How worried are you right now? (c) How lonely do you feel right now? (d) How much have you used Facebook since the last time we asked? (e) How much have you interacted with other people "directly" since the last time we asked? Responses were collected on sliding scales of 100 points, such as not a lot (0) to a lot (100) for use of Facebook.

Results showed that the best predictor of mood was the mood reported on the prior occasion. However, the results also showed that people's reported amount of Facebook use predicted their reported mood. As Facebook use increased, participants reported more negative mood (see ● Figure 2.2).

3. *Are there other ways this evidence could be interpreted?* The researchers were careful to evaluate an alternate hypothesis: Could people use Facebook more when they are in a nega-

Dick Blume/Syracuse Newspapers/The Image Works

Joe Raedle/Hulton Archive/Getty Images

A contemporary theory of emotion correctly predicted the circumstances for when we might experience mixed emotions of happiness and sadness. Graduation from college is an important accomplishment, but we might feel sad about leaving our friends.

The methods of psychological science can help us evaluate questions like what effects, if any, playing violent video games has on physical aggression.

when a person simply decides to transmit a tweet or launch a personal website. The author is solely responsible for the content, and there are no checks on the accuracy of that content.

During peer review, research that fits with existing knowledge is typically accepted more rapidly than work that is less consistent with previous reports. Unconventional findings often undergo **replication**, which means that other scientists independently attempt to reproduce the results of the study in question (Klein et al., 2014). If the data are replicated, they will be accepted quickly. If other scientists are unable to replicate the data, their extra effort will have prevented inaccurate results from cluttering the scientific literature. Although this process might slow the publication of some innovative research, the result—more accuracy—is worth the effort.

replication Repeating an experiment and producing the same results.

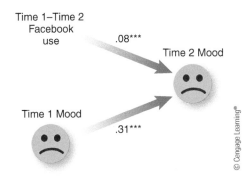

© Cengage Learning®

FIGURE 2.2

What Do These Data Mean? Kross et al. (2013) reported that both Facebook use between two responses to experimenter text messages (Time 1, or T_1, and Time 2, or T_2) and reported mood at Time 1 predicted participants' mood at Time 2. The results were highly significant ($p < .0001$).
Source: Kross et al., 2013.

tive mood? Their analysis did not support this conclusion. People were not more or less likely to turn to Facebook when they were in a positive or negative mood.

4. *What other evidence would I need to evaluate these alternatives?* It is always useful to compare the results of a single study to the existing literature. The literature on the effects of social media on well-being is mixed. Another study using a similar group of participants and methodology did not find evidence of a relationship between the use of social networking sites like Facebook and depressed mood (Jelenchick, Eickhoff, & Moreno, 2013). Yet another study reported that Facebook use was associated with lower rates of depression

and anxiety (Grieve, Indian, Witteveen, Anne Tolan, & Marrington, 2013).

5. *What are the most reasonable conclusions?* A single study with 82 college students is a start but by no means an end to our understanding of the relationship between Facebook use and mood. The authors admit that although their results are statistically significant (this concept is discussed later in the chapter), the size of the effects they observed are quite small. Along with the mixed results from other studies, these factors suggest that more research is necessary and that the strongly stated headlines in the popular press are premature. ●

Summary 2.1 Steps to Critical Thinking

Questions for detecting good critical thinking	Questions for detecting poor critical thinking (all answers should be no)
What am I being asked to believe or accept?	Am I accepting another person's conclusion without working out the problem myself?
What evidence supports this position?	Am I using "gut feelings" instead of reason?
Are there other ways this evidence could be interpreted?	Am I forgetting to review my conclusions to check for mistakes?
What other evidence would I need to evaluate these alternatives?	Am I oversensitive to criticism about my conclusions?
What are the most reasonable conclusions?	Am I unwilling to consider alternative explanations?

How Do Psychologists Conduct Research?

Psychological scientists use a variety of research methods, including descriptive, correlational, and experimental methods, depending on the type of question being asked. Descriptive methods, including surveys, case studies, and observations, provide a good starting place for a new research question. Correlational methods help psychologists see how two variables of interest, like the number of hours spent playing video games and level of physical aggression, relate to each other. Psychologists use experiments to test their hypotheses and to determine the causes of behavior.

In the next sections, we will describe the common research methods used in psychological science and then compare how they might be used to approach a particular question—whether exposure to video game violence increases aggression. Each method—descriptive, correlational, and experimental—provides a different view of the phenomenon in question, and each has a particular profile of strengths and weaknesses. Each requires different types of statistical analyses, which are described in more depth later in the chapter. Many psychological studies combine several of these methods. When similar outcomes are observed using multiple methods, we have even more confidence in our results.

Descriptive Methods

Descriptive methods include case studies, naturalistic observations, and surveys. As we have seen, personal observations and common-sense ideas are especially vulnerable to bias, but descriptive methods allow a researcher to make careful, systematic, real-world observations. Descriptive methods can illuminate associations between variables and establish prevalence rates. Armed with these scientific observations, the researcher will be in a strong position to generate hypotheses.

The Case Study   A **case study** provides an in-depth analysis of the behavior of one person or a small number of people. Many fields, including medicine, law, and business, use the case

descriptive method Research methods designed for making careful, systematic observations.
case study An in-depth analysis of the behavior of one person or a small number of people.

study method. Psychologists often use case studies when large numbers of participants are not available or when a particular participant possesses unique characteristics, as in the case described in this section. Interviews, background records, observation, personality tests, cognitive tests, and brain imaging provide information necessary to evaluate the case. Case studies not only are a useful source of hypotheses but also can be used to test hypotheses. If you did a case study on a planet outside our solar system and discovered life there, you would disprove a hypothesis that no life exists outside our solar system.

One of the most productive case studies in psychology chronicled more than 50 years of examinations of Henry Molaison (1926–2008), known in the scientific literature as "the amnesiac patient H.M." In 1953, Molaison underwent brain surgery to control his frequent, severe seizures. Although the surgery may have saved his life, Molaison was left with profound memory deficits, which we describe in Chapter 9. Through painstaking testing and evaluation of Molaison, psychologists learned a great deal about the brain structures and processes that support the formation of memories (Corkin, 2002). Even after his death, Molaison continues to contribute to our knowledge. Researchers from the Massachusetts Institute of Technology, the Massachusetts General Hospital, and the University of California, San Diego, are analyzing Molaison's brain.

How could you use the case study method to learn about exposure to video game violence and aggression? You could conduct a case study of Michael Carneal, who was sentenced to life in prison after he began shooting students at his high school, killing three students and seriously wounding five others. Carneal had never shot a real gun before, but he was fond of playing first-person shooter games like *Doom.* To conduct your case study, you gather background facts about Carneal's case, possibly by interviewing others associated with the case, viewing legal and medical documents, and observing media accounts. You interview Carneal and possibly administer established personality and clinical tests like those we discuss in Chapters 12 and 15.

What are the advantages of using the case study method to learn about the effects of playing violent video games on aggression? Mass shooters are thankfully quite rare, and the case study method is well suited to learning about unusual situations. A case study can contribute to science by testing hypotheses. If a hypothesis made a strong prediction that all mass shooters play violent video games, finding and documenting a case of a mass shooter who did not play violent video games would require rejection of the hypothesis. Based on the detailed data you obtain from Carneal's case, you will be better prepared to generate and test additional hypotheses.

Naturalistic Observation If you are interested in learning about larger groups of people than are possible with the case study method, you might pursue **naturalistic observation**, or in-depth study of a phenomenon in its natural setting. Compared to the case study method, we are looking at a larger group of people, which will strengthen our ability to apply our results to the general population. We also have the advantage of observing individuals in their natural, everyday circumstances.

A classic example of the method of naturalistic observation is the careful, long-term study of chimpanzees conducted in their habitat by Jane Goodall. In the summer of 1960, then-26-year-old Goodall began her painstaking observations of chimpanzees living in Gombe National Park in Tanzania. Among her discoveries was that chimpanzees were not vegetarians, as previously assumed:

One of the most famous case studies in psychology is that of Henry Molaison (left), who was known in the literature as "the amnesic patient H.M.," until his death in 2008. For more than 50 years, Molaison allowed psychologists to evaluate his memory deficits resulting from brain surgery. After his death, scientists like Jacopo Annese (below) of the University of California, San Diego, began a careful examination of Molaison's brain.

Photograph of Henry Molaison. Copyright © Suzanne Corkin, used by permission of the Wylie Agency LLC.

s44/ZUMA Press/Newscom

naturalistic observation An in-depth study of a phenomenon in its natural setting.

Corbis

I saw that one of them was holding a pink-looking object from which he was from time to time pulling pieces with his teeth. There was a female and a youngster and they were both reaching out toward the male, their hands actually touching his mouth. Presently the female picked up a piece of the pink thing and put it to her mouth: it was at this moment that I realized the chimps were eating meat. (Goodall, 1971, p. 34)

As a result of Goodall's years spent following the chimpanzees, scientists have a rich, accurate knowledge of the animals' behavior in the field.

Impressed by Goodall's results, you plan to pursue further knowledge about violent video games and aggression by attending local area network (LAN) parties, where attendees bring their computers to a gathering place to play multiplayer, networked video games. You hope that by observing people playing violent video games and watching their subsequent behavior for signs of aggression, you might reach some conclusions about the relationships between video game violence and aggression. As in Goodall's case, this approach has the advantages of providing insight into natural, real-world behaviors with large numbers of participants.

Michael Carneal is now serving a life sentence in prison after he shot and killed fellow students at his high school in 1997, when he was 14.

Some naturalistic observations are conducted when people know they are being observed, while in other cases, people are unaware of being observed. Both situations raise challenges. If we know we are being observed, we might act differently. Your LAN party participants know that aggression is not viewed positively in our culture, so they might act less aggressively when they know they're being watched. Watching people who do not know they're being watched raises ethical issues, which we explore later in this chapter. How would you feel if you discovered you had been an unwitting participant in a study?

The use of naturalistic observation illustrates the importance of choosing a method that is well suited to the research goals. Like the case study method, naturalistic observation can be helpful for developing hypotheses, but other methods must be used to test them. Most hypotheses in psychology look at the relationships between two or more concepts, like the exposure to violent video games and aggression in our example. Testing a hypothesis would allow you to say whether a relationship between exposure to violent video games and aggression exists, how strong the relationship is, what direction it is, and so on. It might appear to you that the people you observe are more aggressive following their LAN parties, but you have no way to demonstrate your point. People engage in lots of behaviors during LAN parties. Perhaps eating pizza or staying up all night at LAN parties enhances aggressive tendencies. With only your naturalistic observations to go on, you can't say for sure.

BRUCE COLEMAN INC./Alamy

Jane Goodall used naturalistic observation to illuminate the world of the chimpanzee.

The Survey **Surveys** or questionnaires allow us to ask large numbers of people questions about attitudes and behavior. Surveys provide a great deal of useful information quickly at relatively little expense. Commercial online survey services make conducting surveys easier than in the past.

One of the primary requirements for a good survey is the use of an appropriate **sample**, or subset of a population being studied. The **population** consists of the entire group from which a sample is taken. Good results require large samples that are typical, or representative, of the population we wish to describe. Major pollsters, like the Pew Research Center and Gallup, take great pains to recruit survey participants who mirror the characteristics of the public across factors such as gender, age, education, occupation, income, and geographical location.

Surveys use self-report, so results can be influenced by people's natural tendency to want to appear socially appropriate (Corbett, 1991). As we will discover in Chapter 13, people have strong tendencies to conform to the expectations of others. In some surveys, this factor is not

survey A descriptive method in which participants are asked the same questions.
sample A subset of a population being studied.
population The entire group from which a sample is taken.

a problem. If you ask people whether they prefer lattes or mochas, you will probably get a fairly honest answer. However, when people believe that their true attitudes and behaviors will not be viewed favorably by others, they are likely to lie, even when their answers are confidential and anonymous.

Let's see how scientists have used the survey method to explore video game violence. One survey involved 1,254 middle school students attending public schools in South Carolina and Pennsylvania (Olson, 2010). Although the sample did not include children from other geographic locations or children who are homeschooled or attending private schools, it appeared to be relatively representative of this age group. Children were asked to respond to 17 motives for playing video games on a 4-point scale, from strongly agree to strongly disagree. Like all surveys, this one depended on self-report, which raises the possibility that children would give "the right answer" instead of responding honestly.

What did this scientific survey discover about violent video games? As shown in ● Figure 2.4, a surprising outcome of the survey was the more than 20% of boys who reported a violent video game "helps me relax" and "helps me get my anger out." You will have the opportunity to take a survey on video games and aggression after you read the next section.

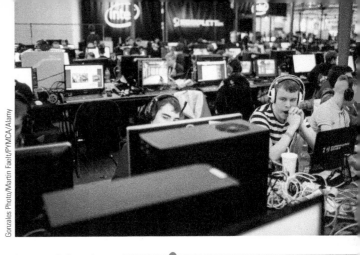

To pursue the question of the effects of violent video games on aggression, you could do a naturalistic observation at a LAN party.

Correlational Methods

Correlations measure the direction and strength of the relationship between two **variables**, or factors that have values that can vary, like a person's height and weight. Correlations allow psychologists to explore whether hours of sleep are related to student grade point averages (GPAs; Trockel, Barnes, & Egget, 2000) or whether the age of parents is related to the rate of autism spectrum disorder among their children (Reichenberg, Gross, Kolevzon, &

People taking surveys might be more interested in pleasing others or appearing "normal" than in answering honestly.

correlation A measure of the direction and strength of the relationship between two variables.
variable A factor that has a range of values.

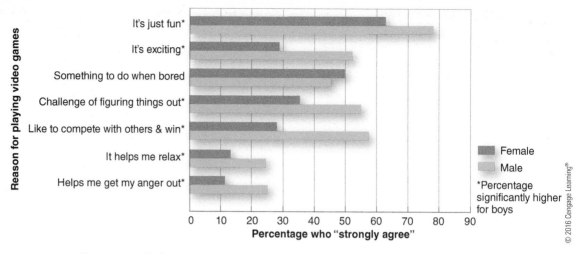

© 2016 Cengage Learning®

FIGURE 2.4

Results From a Real Survey on Video Game Use. Cheryl Olson (2010) asked middle school students why they liked to play violent video games. More than 20% of the boys agreed that a game "helps me relax" and "helps me get my anger out." *Source:* Adapted from "Children's Motivations for Video Game Play in the Context of Normal Development," by C. K. Olson, 2010, *Review of General Psychology, 14*(2), pp. 180–187. doi:10.1037/a0018984.

Susser, 2011). If you're curious about the results of these studies, the first showed that sleep and GPA were not related, and the second showed that age of parents is related to the rate of autism spectrum among their children.

We begin our analysis of correlations by measuring our variables. A **measure** answers the simple question of "how much" of a variable we have observed. After we obtain measures of each variable, we compare the values of one variable to those of the other and conduct a statistical analysis of the results. Three possible outcomes from the comparison between our two variables can occur: positive, negative, or zero correlations. In a positive correlation, high levels of one variable are associated with high levels of the other variable. Height and weight usually show this type of relationship. In most cases, people who are taller weigh more than people who are shorter. Two variables can also show a negative correlation, in which high values of one variable are associated with low values of another. For example, high levels of alcohol consumption among college students are usually associated with low GPAs. The third possible outcome is a zero correlation, in which the two variables do not have any systematic relationship with each other. When variables have a zero correlation, knowing the value of one variable does not tell us anything about the value of the other variable (see ● Figure 2.5). For example, emergency room and law enforcement personnel are often convinced that they are busier with emergencies and crime on nights with a full moon. In contrast, numerous scientific studies of lunar cycles show zero correlations with emergency room admissions, traffic accidents, or other types of trauma (Stomp, ten Duis, & Nijsten, 2011).

Correlational research results are frequently misunderstood. Correlations permit us to discuss the relationships between two variables but tell us nothing about whether one variable causes changes in the other. Let us say that we discover a positive correlation between violent video games and aggression: Youth who play the most hours of violent video games have the most reports of physical aggression at school. However, we still cannot say that playing violent video games causes physical aggression at school. This conclusion may seem reasonable, and it may be true, so why must we abandon it? First, the two variables in a correlation can influence each other simultaneously. Although it may be true that playing violent video games leads to physical aggression at school, youth who experience physical aggression at school may be more attracted to violent video games as an outlet for their frustration. Second, we might be observing a situation in which a **third variable** is respon-

measure A method for describing a variable's quantity.

third variable A variable that is responsible for a correlation observed between two other variables of interest.

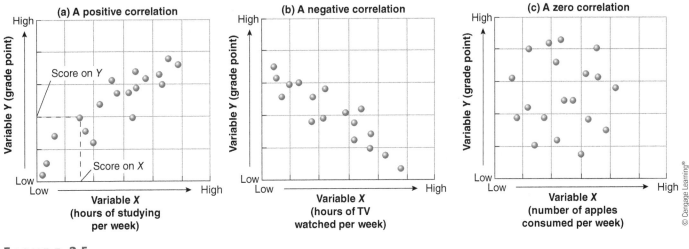

(a) A positive correlation

Variable Y (grade point)
High / Low

Score on Y

Score on X

Variable X
(hours of studying
per week)
Low / High

(b) A negative correlation

Variable Y (grade point)
High / Low

Variable X
(hours of TV
watched per week)
Low / High

(c) A zero correlation

Variable Y (grade point)
High / Low

Variable X
(number of apples
consumed per week)
Low / High

© Cengage Learning®

FIGURE 2.5

Correlations Describe the Direction and Strength of Relationships Between Two Variables.
(a) In positive correlations, high levels of one variable are associated with high levels of the other variable. (b) In negative correlations, high values of one variable are associated with low levels of the other variable. (c) In zero correlations, the two variables do not have any relationship with each other.

sible for the correlation we see between our two variables of interest. Consider the observation that many school shootings have been perpetrated by people who had been bullied relentlessly by others. Perhaps the experience of having been bullied (the third variable in this case) predisposes both a choice of violent recreation and a tendency to engage in aggressive behavior at school (see ● Figure 2.6).

If we cannot make conclusions about causality using correlations, why would we use correlations? In a number of circumstances, correlations are more appropriate than other research methods. For example, it would be unethical to ask pregnant women to consume different amounts of alcohol to assess the effects of prenatal alcohol on their infants. Instead, we can ask pregnant women to identify their alcohol intake in diaries, which can then be correlated with various measures of infant functioning. Although this method will not allow us to conclude that drinking during pregnancy causes damage to the fetus, we can correctly identify the strength and direction (positive, negative, or zero) of any relationship between drinks consumed and infants' outcome measures (see ● Figure 2.7). Using this approach, researchers have shown that heavy maternal alcohol consumption is correlated with abnormal amounts of thickening of the outer layer of the brain (the cortex, discussed in Chapter 4; Sowell et al., 2008).

When you're reading or listening to the news, watch for the use of words like "link," "association," or "relationship" used to describe two variables, such as a headline that states "lack of sleep linked to depression" or "drinking red wine associated with lower rates of heart disease." These key words usually mean that the data are correlational, but are often mistaken for causal. Now you know how you should and should not interpret these reports.

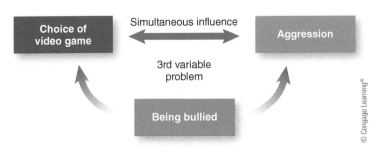

Choice of video game ← Simultaneous influence → Aggression

3rd variable problem

Being bullied

© Cengage Learning®

FIGURE 2.6

Third Variables and Correlations. Third variables can be responsible for the correlation we observe in two other variables. In our example of video game violence and aggression, being bullied could be a third variable that predicts both a choice of violent games and a tendency to be aggressive at school. The possibility of third variables is one reason we must be careful when we reach conclusions based on correlational data.

FIGURE 2.7

Correlations Can Help Us Learn About Situations in Which Experiments Would Be Unethical. Even though we cannot make conclusions about causes based on correlations, we can obtain useful information. It would be unethical to assign pregnant women to drinking and nondrinking groups, but the negative correlation we see between drinks consumed by pregnant women and measures of infant mental development can tell us that drinking during pregnancy is not a good idea. The more alcohol the women consumed, the lower their children scored on tests of infant mental development. *Source:* Adapted from "The Effects of Prenatal Alcohol Exposure on Infant Mental Development: A Meta-analytical Review," by M. Testa, B. M. Quigley, & R. D. Eiden, 2003, *Alcohol and Alcoholism, 38*(4), pp. 295–304. doi:10.1093/alcalc/agg087.

Experimental Methods

The scientist's most powerful tool for drawing conclusions about research questions is the formal **experiment**. Unlike cases in which descriptive methods are used, the researcher conducting an experiment has a great deal of control over the situation. Unlike correlational methods, the use of the formal experiment allows us to talk about cause (see ● Figure 2.8).

A researcher begins designing an experiment with a hypothesis, which can be viewed as a highly educated guess based on systematic observations, a review of previous research, or a scientific theory. An experimental hypothesis takes this form: "If I do this, that will happen." To test the hypothesis, the researcher manipulates or modifies the value of one or more variables and observes changes in the values of others. The variable controlled and manipulated by an experimenter ("If I do this") is known as the **independent variable**. We need some way to evaluate the effects of this manipulation. We use a **dependent variable**, defined as a measure used to assess the effects of the manipulation of the independent variable, to tell us "that will happen" as a result of the independent variable. Like the independent variable, our choice of dependent variable is based on our original hypothesis.

After determining our independent and dependent variables, we still have quite a bit of work to do. In most experiments, we want to know how simply going through the procedures of being in an experiment influences our dependent variable. Perhaps the hassle of going to a laboratory and filling out paperwork changes our behavior. To evaluate these irrelevant effects and establish a baseline of behavior under the experimental conditions, we assign some of our participants to a **control group**. In many experiments, the control group will experience all experimental procedures with the exception of exposure to the independent variable. When a new treatment is being tested, the control group might experience the standard treatment for

experiment A research method that tests hypotheses and allows researchers to make conclusions about causality.
independent variable An experimental variable controlled and manipulated by the experimenter; the "if A happens" part of a hypothesis.
dependent variable A measure that demonstrates the effects of an independent variable; the "result" part of a hypothesis.
control group A group that experiences all experimental procedures with the exception of exposure to the independent variable.

FIGURE 2.8

How to Design an Experiment. A good experimental design features random assignment of participants to groups, appropriate control groups, control of situational variables, and carefully selected independent and dependent variables.

a condition. The experience of the control group should be as similar as possible to that of the **experimental groups**, who experience different values of the independent variable.

We want to ensure that our dependent variables reflect the outcomes of our independent variables, instead of individual differences among the participants' personalities, abilities, motivations, and similar factors. To prevent these individual differences from masking or distorting the effects of our independent variable, we randomly assign participants to experimental or control groups. **Random assignment** means that each participant has an equal chance of being assigned to any group in an experiment. With random assignment, differences we see between the behavior of one group and that of another are unlikely to be the result of the individual differences among the participants, which tend to cancel each other out.

Individual differences among participants are an example of **confounding variables**, or variables that are irrelevant to the hypothesis being tested that can alter or distort our conclusions. For example, a researcher might want to test the effects of aerobic exercise on blood pressure. If some participants competed in triathlons without the researcher's knowledge, their athletic experience would confound the interpretation of the results. Random assignment to groups typically controls for confounds because of these types of individual differences, but other sources of confounds exist. Situational confounds, such as time of day or noise levels in a laboratory, could also affect the interpretation of an experiment. Scientists attempt to run their experiments under the most constant circumstances possible to rule out situational confounding variables.

Let's return to our question about violent video games and aggression and see how one real experiment addressed the issue. The researchers tested a hypothesis stating that playing video games varying in violent content (the independent variable) would influence subsequent levels of aggression (the dependent variable; Anderson & Dill, 2000). The experimental group played a violent game *(Wolfenstein 3D)*, while the control group played a nonviolent game *(Myst)*. Participants were randomly assigned to groups. You can imagine how the results

Researchers attempt to reduce the impact of confounding variables on their results. In a test of the effects of aerobic exercise on blood pressure, situational confounding variables, such as (1) traffic outside the building, (2) a noisy treadmill, and (3) a neighbor breathing heavily, can be controlled by holding the environment as constant as possible for all participants. Individual differences, such as (4) an early morning after little sleep or (5) superior fitness, can be controlled by randomly assigning participants to groups.

experimental group A group of participants that is exposed to the independent variable.
random assignment The procedure in which each participant has an equal chance of being assigned to any group in an experiment.
confounding variable Variables that are irrelevant to the hypothesis being tested but can alter a researcher's conclusions.

Experiencing Psychology

Taking a Video Game and Aggression Survey

IN ADDITION TO using experimental methods to study our question about video games and aggression, Anderson and Dill (2000) compared responses on a standard physical aggression questionnaire (Buss & Perry, 1992) and on a video game questionnaire they devised. After you complete your questionnaires, we will tell you how the college students participating in the Anderson and Dill study responded.

As you complete your questionnaires, consider the limitations we raised earlier about the survey method. Physical aggression is a sensitive topic, and we suspect that Anderson and Dill's survey participants might have been tempted to answer in socially appropriate ways that may not have been completely truthful. See whether you find yourself wanting to do the same.

The Video Game Questionnaire (Anderson & Dill, 2000) asked students to rate their five most frequently played games. In the interests of time and space, we are asking you to rate only your most frequently played game. Before reading further, complete the two surveys.

Let's add up some scores. To score the Physical Aggression Questionnaire (Buss & Perry, 1992), reverse Question 7 ("I can think of no good reason. . . .") by subtracting your score from 8. Now add your scores for all nine items. You do not get a single score for the Video Game Questionnaire (Anderson & Dill, 2000), but it is helpful to add your scores for Items a–d to get a measure of long-term exposure to video games.

The main point of this activity is to get an idea of what it was like to be one of Anderson and Dill's survey participants. You cannot make conclusions about the relationship between video games and physical aggression based on your single scores, but you can compare your results to those reported by Anderson and Dill and by Buss and Perry.

On the Physical Aggression Questionnaire, Buss and Perry (1992) reported that the average score for men was 24.3 and the average score for women was 17.9 out of a possible high of 45. If you're curious, the sex difference in physical aggression was statistically significant, a concept we discuss later

---

Physical Aggression Questionnaire (Buss and Perry, 1992)

Please rate each of the following items in terms of how characteristic they are of you. Use the following scale for answering these items:

1	2	3	4	5
Extremely uncharacteristic of me				**Extremely characteristic of me**

1. Once in a while I can't control the urge to strike another person.

2. Given enough provocation, I may hit another person.

3. If somebody hits me, I hit back.

4. I get into fights a little more than the average person.

5. If I have to resort to violence to protect my rights, I will.

6. There are people who pushed me so far that we came to blows.

7. I can think of no good reason for ever hitting a person.

8. I have threatened people I know.

9. I have become so mad that I have broken things.

Sources: Buss, A. H., & Perry, M. (1992); also adapted from Anderson, C. A., & Dill, K. E. (2000).

---

might be distorted if the experimental group consisted of football players and the control group consisted of members of the chess club. Following their game playing, participants had an opportunity to choose the intensity and duration for a blast of noise to punish a remotely located loser (who didn't exist) in a competitive reaction time activity, and their choices served as the dependent variable. We're assuming that laboratory conditions were held constant to avoid situational confounds. For example, we know that people feel more aggressive in hot temperatures (Carlsmith & Anderson, 1979). What would happen to our experiment if the air conditioner in the laboratory broke while some participants played violent video games but was fixed right before the next participants played nonviolent games? Results of this carefully in this chapter. This concept means that we believe the sex difference observed by Buss and Perry represents a real difference, not just a chance occurrence.

Comparing your data to those of Anderson and Dill is a bit difficult, because these researchers combined the Buss and Perry questionnaire with another measure of aggression in their analysis of their results.

However, they found that this combined physical aggression score was positively correlated with long-term exposure to video game violence (a combination of Items a–d for exposure and Items e–f for violence) and with amount of recent play time (Item a).

Now that you understand correlations, you know what you can and cannot say about these results. Based on the results of the An-

derson and Dill correlations, we still do not know whether (a) having an aggressive personality leads to spending more time playing violent video games, (b) playing violent video games leads to more physical aggression, (c) both of these relationships are true, or (d) some third variable, such as experience of being bullied, contributes to both physical aggression and choice of violent video games. ●

Video Game Questionnaire (Anderson and Dill, 2000)

For the following items, rate your most played game:

a. In recent months, how often have you played this game?

1	2	3	4	5	6	7
Rarely			Occasionally			Often

b. During 11th & 12th grades, how often did you play this game?

1	2	3	4	5	6	7
Rarely			Occasionally			Often

c. During 9th & 10th grades, how often did you play this game?

1	2	3	4	5	6	7
Rarely			Occasionally			Often

d. During 7th & 8th grades, how often did you play this game?

1	2	3	4	5	6	7
Rarely			Occasionally			Often

e. How violent is the content of this game?

1	2	3	4	5	6	7
Little or no violent content						Extremely violent content

f. How bloody/gory are the graphics of this game?

1	2	3	4	5	6	7
Little or no blood & gore						Extremely bloody & gory

g. Which of the following categories best describe this game? Check all that apply.

__ Education   __ Sports   __ Fantasy   __ Fighting with hands/feet   __ Fighting with weapons   __ Skill

---

controlled experiment confirmed the researchers' hypothesis: Playing the violent game led to the stated intent to administer longer noise blasts to another person (see ● Figure 2.9).

As powerful as it is, the experimental method, like the other methods discussed previously, has some limitations. Experiments can be somewhat artificial. Participants know that they are in a research study, and they may vary their behavior as a result. However, making a laboratory experiment more realistic can raise ethical challenges. In a study conducted in 1962, before current ethical guidelines for research had been adopted, military personnel were led to believe that their lives were in danger so that experimenters could "realistically" assess the effects of panic on performance (Berkun, Bialek, Kern, & Yagi, 1962). Although the re-

FIGURE 2.9

Experimental Method in Action. Anderson and Dill (2000) randomly assigned participants to groups playing violent and nonviolent video games. After playing, each participant was asked to choose the strength and duration of a blast of noise to be administered to another person. Keeping conditions in the laboratory as constant as possible would help to reduce the impact of situational variables.

operationalization Defining variables in practical terms.
meta-analysis A statistical analysis of many previous experiments on a single topic.

To conduct an experiment, we must carefully operationalize, or define our variables in practical terms. One way to operationalize physical aggression is to measure how often a preschooler has a physical fight with others.

sponses of these participants were probably quite representative of real life, few of us would want to be put in their position. This type of research could not be conducted under today's ethical standards, as explained later in this chapter.

Artificiality is also a problem in the Anderson and Dill (2000) video game study. Our real-world question relates to the likelihood that playing violent video games may elicit real physical violence in real situations. Is a person's willingness to inflict a loud sound on another person in a professor's laboratory truly representative of the type of violence involved in mass shootings like the Carneal case? It may or may not be; we need additional research to find out.

Another issue with the experimental method arises from differences in the choices of independent and dependent variables. Independent (controlled) and dependent (measured) variables have to be defined and implemented in some concrete fashion. The process of translating abstract independent and dependent variables into measurable forms is called **operationalization**. The first step in operationalization is to identify the concept to be measured clearly, such as the violence in a video game. Next, the quantitative measures of the concept must be determined. What measures do you need to tell a violent video game from a nonviolent one? You might develop a rating scale based on the number of times violent images, such as depictions of physical injury or blood, are presented in a particular game. Finally, a method for obtaining this measure must be developed. The Entertainment Software Rating Board (ESRB) uses a panel of trained raters to evaluate a DVD of representative game play submitted by a manufacturer of a new game to establish an appropriate age group rating (ESRB, 2014).

There are many ways we can operationalize variables in practical terms. Anderson and Dill (2000) operationalized aggression in terms of how lengthy a sound blast a person was willing to inflict on another person. One of the odder dependent variables used in video game aggression research is the hot sauce paradigm, in which the participants' recipes for hot sauce to be administered to another participant are used to measure aggression (Lieberman, Solomon, Greenberg, & McGregor, 1999). Other researchers might choose different ways to operationalize aggression, such as frequency of physical fights among preschoolers. As a result, even though there is a large body of work regarding the impact of violent video games on aggression, the variables used are so different that few direct comparisons can be made among the many studies.

Meta-analyses The point of this discussion is not to convince you that scientists don't know what they're talking about but rather to impress upon you the importance of reviewing research results using your best critical thinking skills. In seeking to understand something as complicated as the science of mind, it is unlikely that any single study could provide complete information about a phenomenon. Instead, progress in our understanding results from the work of many scientists using diverse methods to answer the same question. Conducting a **meta-analysis**, or a statistical analysis of many previous experiments on the same topic, often provides a clearer picture than do single experiments observed in isolation. As shown in ● Figure 2.10, a meta-analysis of about 300 studies, using diverse

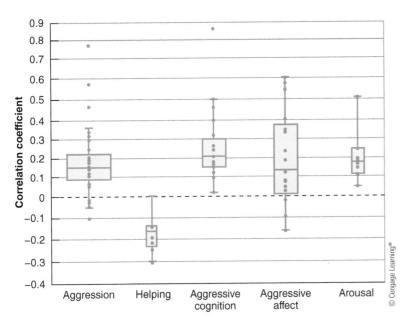

FIGURE 2.10

Insights From Meta-analyses. Combining the findings of more than 300 studies representing more than 50,000 participants, Anderson and Bushman (2002) argued that a positive relationship exists between exposure to video game violence and aggression, aggressive cognitions, aggressive affect or mood, and arousal. Video game violence was negatively correlated with helping behaviors. This type of graph is known as a boxplot. The width of each box corresponds to the number of studies of each type. Of the results, 25% fall below the bottom of the box and another 25% are above the top of each box. The line in the middle of a box shows the median, which we define later in this chapter as the point where half of the data are above and half are below the line. *Source:* Adapted from "Effects of Violent Video Games on Aggressive Behavior, Aggressive Cognition, Aggressive Affect, Physiological Arousal, and Prosocial Behavior," by C. A. Anderson & B. J. Bushman, 2001, *Psychological Science, 12*(5), pp. 353–359.

methods and more than 54,000 participants, demonstrated a positive relationship between video game violence and aggression (Anderson & Bushman, 2001). The observed effects, however, are somewhat small. A correlation coefficient between $-.35$ and $.35$ is considered weak, even if it is statistically significant (Taylor, 1990).

The Importance of Multiple Perspectives As we will see in so many examples in this textbook, even the best research designs might mislead us if they fail to take multiple perspectives into account. Most of the research we have discussed so far regarding video games and aggression has involved single participants playing alone. What happens when we "zoom out" using the social perspective to look at the effects of video games on groups of people playing together? Playing video games cooperatively is associated with less subsequent aggressive behavior, regardless of whether the game played was violent or not (Jerabeck & Ferguson, 2013).

The research discussed through the remainder of this textbook has been subjected to considerable skeptical review by the researchers' peers. Most has stood the dual tests of peer review and replication by others. Converging evidence from descriptive, correlational, and experimental research provides us with confidence in our conclusions. Psychology, like any science, has followed its share of wrong turns and dead ends, but most knowledge presented here has been carefully crafted to present the most accurate view possible of behavior and mental processes.

Psychology as a Hub Science
Testing the Effects of Food Additives on Children's Hyperactivity

The methods described previously can be used by psychologists to provide guidance across many disciplines. For example, how many times have you heard a parent complain about a child's out-of-control behavior and blame it on too much sugar? How would a scientist know whether sugar or any other food ingredient affected children's behavior? Scientific discoveries in this area could benefit the fields of nutrition, health, medicine, and child development.

Psychologists have employed the objective, scientific methods needed to provide guidance to both parents and the food industry on this type of topic. So how can scientists objectively test the idea that kids may become out of control after eating too much sugar? What

Double-blind, placebo-controlled studies have provided insight into the relationship between common food additives in fruit drinks and hyperactivity in children.

tools can a scientist use? The gold standard for demonstrating the objective effects of any substance, whether a food additive, medication, or recreational drug, is the **double-blind procedure**. This procedure requires a **placebo**, an inactive substance that cannot be distinguished from a real, active substance.

The first "blind" aspect of this procedure is the inability of participants to know whether they have taken a real substance or a placebo. This feature controls for effects of the participants' expectations. When we drink coffee, for example, we expect to feel more alert, or when we take an aspirin, we expect our headache to disappear; therefore, we may "feel" better long before the substance has had time to produce effects. Not letting subjects know whether they received the real substance or the placebo helps offset these misleading effects.

The second "blind" is achieved when the researchers do not know whether a participant has been given a real substance or placebo until the experiment is over. This aspect ensures that the researchers' expectations do not tilt or bias their observations. If scientists expect participants to act more alert after drinking coffee, this bias could be reflected in their observations and conclusions.

Returning to our question of food additives, what do double-blind, placebo-controlled studies have to say about their effects on child behavior? In one careful study, young children were given drinks that either had no additives (placebo) or a combination of colorings and preservatives used frequently in packaged foods (McCann et al., 2007). Because it was a double-blind study, the children did not know which drink they had received, and the researchers responsible for observing the children did not know which drink had been served to each child. The outcome of this study showed that general measures of hyperactivity, or unusually large amounts of movement, were higher in the groups that had consumed the additives than in the group that had consumed the placebo. This finding has implications for attention deficit hyperactivity disorder, which we discuss in Chapter 14. The ability of these common food additives to make normal children more hyperactive is cause for concern and worthy of further study (see ● Figure 2.11). ●

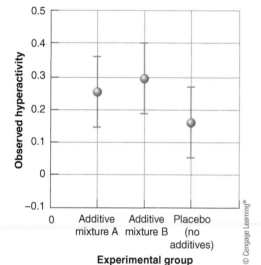

FIGURE 2.11

Hyperactivity and Food Additives. The results obtained by McCann et al. (2007) showed that hyperactivity was higher in children who consumed one of the drinks containing common food additives (left and middle bars) than in children who consumed the placebo drink containing no additives (right bar).

double-blind procedure A research design that controls for placebo effects in which neither the participant nor the experimenter observing the participant knows whether the participant was given an active substance or treatment or a placebo.

placebo An inactive substance or treatment that cannot be distinguished from a real, active substance or treatment.

cross-sectional study An experimental design for assessing age-related changes in which data are obtained simultaneously from people of differing ages.

How Do We Study the Effects of Time?

Modifications of the methods discussed previously might be necessary for answering specific questions. Psychological scientists frequently ask questions about normal behaviors related to age. As we will see in Chapter 11, aggression in preschoolers means something different from aggression in a 16-year-old. Considering the impact of video game violence on aggression within the context of age-related change adds a new and useful dimension to our hypothesis, but it requires additional attention to the research methods to be used.

Psychologists have three specific techniques for assessing the normal behaviors associated with age: cross-sectional, longitudinal, and mixed longitudinal designs. To do a **cross-**

sectional study, we might gather groups of people of varying ages and assess both their exposure to violent video games and their levels of physical aggression. We might be able to plot a developmental course for age-related differences in both video game exposure and aggressive behavior. However, the cross-sectional method introduces what we refer to as cohort effects, or the generational effects of having been born at a particular point in history. Being 20 years old in 1955 was different from being 20 years old in 1985 or in 2015 because of a variety of cultural influences. Today's 10-year-olds, who do not know of a time without the Internet, might respond differently to violent video games than today's 40-year-olds for reasons that have nothing to do with age. Any such cohort effects could mask or distort our cross-sectional results.

A method that lessens this dilemma is the **longitudinal study**, in which a group of individuals is observed for a long period (see ● Figure 2.12). One of the longest running longitudinal studies is the Fels Longitudinal Study, housed in the Wright State University School of Medicine. This study began in 1929 to observe the effects of the Great Depression on children, and it now has enrolled great-grandchildren of the original participants. To use the longitudinal method to answer our question, we could start with a group of infants and carefully plot their exposure to violent video games and their levels of physical aggression into adulthood. The longitudinal approach has few logical drawbacks but is expensive and time consuming. Participants drop out of the study because of moves or lack of incentive. Researchers then must worry about whether those who remain in the study still comprise a representative sample.

The third approach, the **mixed longitudinal design**, combines the cross-sectional and longitudinal methods. Participants from a range of ages are observed for a limited time, usually about 5 years. This approach is faster and less expensive than the longitudinal method and avoids some of the cohort effects of the pure cross-sectional method.

Cross-sectional studies usually show that intelligence scores decrease with age. These results are most likely a cohort effect. Performance on IQ tests has risen approximately 3 points per decade over the past 100 years for reasons that are not fully understood (Flynn, 1984).

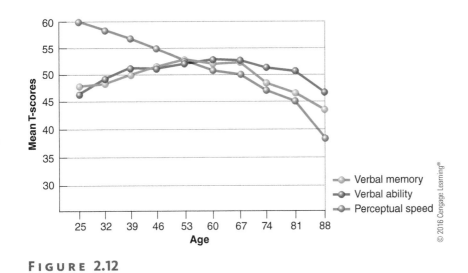

FIGURE 2.12

Special Designs Let Us See Behaviors Associated With Age. Longitudinal designs control for the cohort effects that are often seen in cross-sectional designs. This longitudinal study shows that verbal ability and verbal memory are fairly stable over the lifetime but that perceptual speed gradually worsens with age. *Source:* Adapted from *Intellectual development in adulthood: The Seattle Longitudinal Study* p. 271, K. W. Schaie, 1996, Cambridge, United Kingdom: Cambridge University Press.

© 2016 Cengage Learning®

longitudinal study An experimental design for assessing age-related changes in which data are obtained from the same individuals at intervals over a long period.
mixed longitudinal design A method for assessing age-related changes that combines the cross-sectional and longitudinal approaches by observing a cross-section of participants over a shorter period than is used typically in longitudinal studies.

Summary 2.2 Principles of Research Methods

Research method	Strengths	Weaknesses
Descriptive methods		
Case study	Can explore new and unusual phenomena; can falsify a hypothesis	Has limited generalization
Naturalistic observation	Provides insight into natural, real-world behaviors	Participants act differently when watched; has ethical issues
Survey	Provides large amounts of data quickly and inexpensively	Requires a large representative sample; people wish to appear socially appropriate and may lie
Correlations	Allow us to predict behavior; stimulate development of hypotheses; address some difficult ethical situations	Cannot be used to discuss causality
Experiments	Allow control of situations, strong hypothesis testing, and judgments of causality	Raises artificiality and ethical concerns; is time consuming
Assessing the effects of time		
Cross-sectional study	Is quick and relatively inexpensive	Is subject to cohort effects
Longitudinal study	Reduces the impact of cohort effects	Is expensive and time consuming; people drop out
Mixed longitudinal study	Is less expensive and time consuming than longitudinal, with some control of cohort effects	Is still relatively expensive and time consuming; dropout problem remains

How Do We Draw Conclusions From Data?

Asking the right questions and collecting good information are only the beginning of good science. Once we have collected our results, or data, we need to figure out what those data mean for our hypotheses and theories. The interpretation of data is not an arbitrary act—scientists follow specific rules when drawing their conclusions.

The Importance of Valid and Reliable Measures

Data are only as good as the measures we use to obtain them. How would we know whether a measure is good or bad? Two standards that any measure must meet are reliability and validity.

Reliability refers to the consistency of a measure. There are several meanings of reliability in science, including test–retest, inter-rater, intermethod, and internal consistency. For example, test–retest reliability of the Scholastic Aptitude Test (SAT) is quite good, as you might have noticed if you took the test more than once. If you were ill for the first test, or you invested in a preparation course before taking it the second time, your score might change; otherwise, your scores are likely to be about the same. Good measures also show high inter-rater reliability, or consistency in the interpretation of a measure across different observers. You can imagine how distressing it would be if, for example, one lab identified you as having a fatal disease on the basis of a blood test and another did not. Intermethod reliability describes the positive correlation of several approaches to measure a feature in an individual. Returning to the SAT example, it is likely that your SAT and high school grades are positively correlated, which supports the reliability of these measures. Finally, internal consistency results from measures within a single test that positively correlate with one another. Earlier in this chapter, you had the opportunity to complete a survey. Often, students taking tests like this for the first time complain that they are "answering the same question over and over again." In a sense, this is true, because most tests include a number of items related to the same concept to see whether the participant answers them in similar ways, which allows the researcher to assess the test's internal consistency.

Validity means that a measure leads to valid conclusions, or measures the concept it is designed to measure. For example, your bathroom scale is supposed to measure how much you weigh. The data obtained from your bathroom scale can lead you to a valid conclusion (this is how much I weigh) or an invalid conclusion (oh wow, I'm much lighter than the doctor's scale said I am).

How would we determine whether a measure leads to valid conclusions? One approach is to see whether a measure correlates with other existing, established measures of the same concept. Many universities use the SAT to help select the best candidates for admission. This test is supposed to measure a student's aptitude for success in college, but some universities have abandoned it in favor of other measures. We could ask which of the following measures—the SAT, SAT Subject Tests, or high school GPA—shows the highest positive correlation with first-year college grades. The results of this comparison indicate that the SAT Subject Tests show the highest positive correlation with first-year college grades compared to both the SAT and the high school GPA (Geiser & Studley, 2001). Thus, we can conclude that the SAT Subject Tests are the most valid of the three measures for predicting first-year college grades.

Reliability and validity are not the same. You can obtain a consistent result (reliability) that lacks meaning (validity), but a measure cannot be valid without also being reliable. For example, if you weigh 200 pounds and your bathroom scale consistently reports that you weigh 150 pounds, whether you're looking at the number or your roommate reads it for you, the scale has reliability but not validity. If you get a wildly different number each time you step on the scale, you have neither reliability nor validity. The measure is not consistent (no reliability) and fails to measure the construct—weight in this case—that it is designed to measure (no validity).

A valid measure actually measures what it is supposed to measure. In this case, your bathroom scale is supposed to tell you how much you weigh.

reliability The consistency of a measure, including test–retest, inter-rater, intermethod, and internal consistency.
validity A quality of a measure that leads to valid conclusions (i.e., the measure measures the concept it was designed to measure).

Descriptive Statistics

Just as we might explore a new research topic using the descriptive research methods outlined earlier, we can use descriptive statistics to explore the characteristics of the data we obtain from our research. **Descriptive statistics** help us organize individual bits of data into meaningful patterns and summaries. For example, research investigating the ability of the SAT, SAT Subject Tests, and high school grades to predict grades in colleges and universities across the country would be overwhelming in the absence of some way of summarizing the individual data points for tens of thousands of students in meaningful ways. Descriptive data tell us only about the sample we have studied. To determine whether the results from our sample apply to larger populations requires additional methods, described in a subsequent section.

We might approach this mass of data first by asking how the scores and grades are distributed. We could arrange SAT scores from high to low and note how many students obtained each score. The result of our work would be a frequency distribution. We often illustrate frequency distributions with a bar chart, or histogram, like the one shown in ● Figure 2.13.

Central Tendency Frequency distributions are a useful starting place, but we might also be interested in identifying the "average" score on our measures, or the central tendency of our data set. There are three types of measures for central tendency: the mean, median, and mode for each group of scores. The **mean** is the numerical average of a set of scores, computed by adding all scores together and dividing by the number of scores. For all students taking the SAT in 2009, the mean on the critical reading section was 501, the mean on the mathematics section was 515, and the mean on the writing portion was 493.

descriptive statistics Statistical methods that organize data into meaningful patterns and summaries, such as finding the average value.
mean The numerical average of a set of scores.

FIGURE 2.13

Frequency Distributions.
Descriptive statistics, such as these frequency distributions of SAT mathematics scores, allow us to see meaningful patterns and summaries in large sets of data. *Source:* Adapted from "2009 College-Bound Seniors: Total Group Profile Report," by The College Board, 2009, retrieved from http://professionals.collegeboard.com/profdownload/cbs-2009-national-TOTAL-GROUP.pdf.

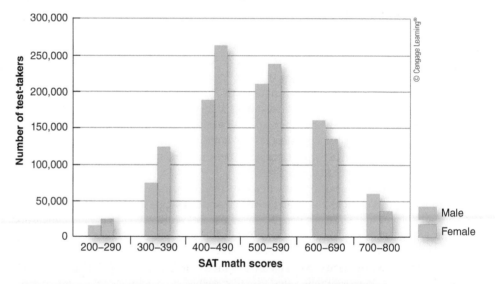

Many colleges and universities use the SAT or other standardized tests to predict success in college courses. Evaluating the resulting data is easier if we use descriptive statistics to summarize the performances of the thousands of individual students who take the tests.

The **median** represents a halfway mark in the data set, with half of the scores above and half below it. The median is far less affected by extreme scores, or outliers, than the mean. In our SAT data, the median scores—500 for critical reading, 510 for mathematics, and 490 for writing—are quite close to the means. Why, then, would you ever need to consider a median? In some sets of results, you might find some extreme scores that could affect the mean. For example, if you asked employees at a small business to report their current annual salaries, you might get the following results: $40,000, $45,000, $47,000, $52,000, and $350,000 (we're assuming this is the boss). The mean in this example would be $106,800, but that figure doesn't provide a good summary of these numbers. The median, $47,000 in this case, is more representative of your overall results. Look at ● Figure 2.14 for another example.

The **mode** refers to the score that occurs most frequently, and it is easy to determine by looking at a histogram. We do not have exact numbers for modal scores on the SAT example, but the most frequent range of scores is between 400 and 490 for all three tests (critical reading, mathematics, and writing). The usefulness of the mode depends on the research question you are asking. In the case of the SAT, the mode provides little interesting information, so let's return to our drinking data mentioned earlier in the chapter. It might surprise you to learn that although the modal pattern of drinking among U.S. adults overall is "current regular," among Asian adults living in the United States, the modal pattern is "lifetime abstainer" (Centers for Disease Control [CDC], 2012b).

The mode is also an advantage over a mean or median when there is more than one mode in a set of data. For example, the mean age of onset for the eating disorder anorexia nervosa, which we discuss in Chapter 7, is 17 years of age, but the distribution is bimodal, which means it has two sub-

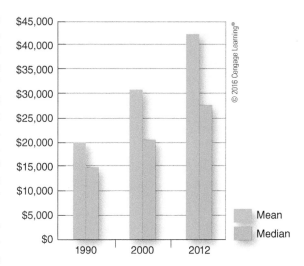

FIGURE 2.14

What New Information Can We Learn From a Median? In many cases, like the SAT data, means and medians are similar. In other cases, such as annual income, these two measures of central tendency provide different pictures. This figure shows mean and median annual incomes in the United States. The ratio of the median to the mean has decreased from 72% in 1990 to 68% in 2000 to 65% in 2012. This suggests that the poorer citizens' income has not increased as fast as the wealthier citizens' income. *Source:* http://www.ssa.gov/oact/cola/central.html

FIGURE 2.15

What New Information Can We Learn From a Mode? The average age of onset for the eating disorder anorexia nervosa is 17 years, but this measure masks the important fact that age of onset shows two modes—one at 14 years and a second at 18 years. For public health officials wishing to target vulnerable groups for preventive education, the modes provide better information than the mean. *Source:* Adapted from "Unique Features Associated With Age of Onset of Anorexia Nervosa," by K. A. Halmi, R. C. Casper, E. D. Eckert, S. C. Goldberg, & J. M. Davis, 1979, *Psychiatry Research, 1*(2), pp. 209–215.

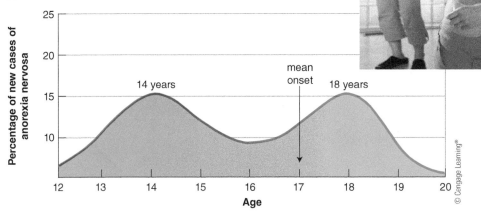

median The halfway mark in a set of data, with half of the scores above and half below.
mode The most frequently occurring score in a set of data.

stantial modes. One peak occurs around the age of 14, when many teens struggle with their changing shapes, and another occurs around the age of 18, when many teens leave home and make food choices without the watchful eyes of their parents (Halmi, Casper, Eckert, Goldberg, & Davis, 1979). An intervention program designed to coincide with the most likely ages of onset would probably be more effective than one timed to coincide with the mean age of onset (see ● Figure 2.15).

Variance In addition to being curious about central tendency, we might want to know how clustered our scores are. The traditional way to look at the variance of scores is to use a measure known as the **standard deviation**. This measure tells us how tightly clustered a group of scores is around the mean. A smaller standard deviation suggests that most scores might be found near the mean, whereas a larger standard deviation means that the scores are spread out from the mean. Returning to our salary example, we had five salaries with a mean of $106,800. To obtain the standard deviation, which is easy to do with a calculator, you subtract each salary from 106,800, square each difference (to eliminate minus signs), add the squares, divide the total by 5 (the number of salaries), and take the square root of the result. In this case, we end up with a standard deviation of 136,021, which means that the average difference between a salary and the mean of the salaries is 136,021. If we discard the extreme salary ($350,000) and find the standard deviation of the remaining four salaries, it turns out to be smaller: 4,966.56. These results suggest that the distribution of the first four salaries is tightly clustered, whereas the distribution of all five salaries is more spread out.

The Normal Curve Many measures of interest to psychologists, such as scores on intelligence tests, which we discuss in Chapter 10, appear to form a **normal distribution**, illustrated in ● Figure 2.16. The ideal normal curve in this illustration has several important features. One, it is symmetrical. Equal numbers of scores should occur above and below the mean. Second, its shape indicates that most scores occur near the mean, which is where our measure of variability plays a role. In the standard normal curve, shown in (a), 68% of the population falls within one standard deviation of the mean, 95% falls within two standard deviations, and 99% of the population falls within three standard deviations. Instruments for assessing intelligence, discussed in Chapter 10, frequently convert raw scores earned by many participants to fit a normal distribution with a mean of 100 and a standard deviation of 15. As a result, we

FIGURE 2.16

The Normal Curve. Many measures of interest to psychologists take the approximate form of a normal distribution. This figure compares a standard normal curve, shown in (a), to the distribution of scores on a standardized test of intelligence, the Wechsler Adult Intelligence Scale, shown in (b).

standard deviation A measure of how tightly clustered a group of scores is around the mean.
normal distribution A symmetrical probability function.

would expect 68% of test takers to receive an IQ score between 85 and 115. Another 95% would most likely score between 70 and 130, leaving only 2.5% to score above 130 and another 2.5% to score below 70.

Descriptive Statistics With Two Variables In our discussion so far, we have been describing single variables, such as number of drinks consumed, salaries, and SAT scores. In psychological research, we often want to describe the relationships among multiple variables.

We can illustrate the relationship between two variables in a scatter plot, like the one shown in ● Figure 2.17. Each dot represents the intersection between scores on two variables of interest. For example, we can compare the distributions of math SAT scores as a function of GPA. From our scatter plot, it looks like math SAT scores and GPAs are systematically related to each other. As one increases, the other does as well, which you should recognize from our earlier discussion as a positive correlation.

Although our scatter plot gives us a sense that GPAs and math SAT scores have a systematic relationship, we can compute that relationship exactly using a correlation coefficient. Correlation coefficients can range from −1.00 to +1.00. A correlation of −1.00 and a correlation of +1.00 are equally strong but differ in the direction of the effect. A zero correlation indicates the two variables have no systematic relationship. The closer a correlation coefficient is to +1.00 or to −1.00, the stronger is the relationship between the two variables. When the score is +1.00 or −1.00, the correlation is perfect—all data points follow the pattern. A value between 0 and 1 indicates a correlation direction, but the relationship is not perfect—not every data point conforms to the pattern. Earlier in this chapter, we referred to height and weight as a common example of a positive correlation: As height increases, weight typically increases as well. Our previous example of a negative correlation is the amount of alcohol consumed and a student's GPA: As alcohol consumption increases, the GPA decreases.

© Cengage Learning®

FIGURE 2.17

A Scatter Plot. A scatter plot allows us to visualize the relationship between two variables, such as the math SAT score and the high school GPA for one small sample of college students. This relationship should look familiar to you—it is an example of a positive correlation. *Source:* Adapted from "The Pearson Correlation Coefficient," by F. Young, 2011, retrieved from http://forrest.psych. unc.edu/research/vista-frames/help/ lecturenotes/lecture11/pearson.html.

Inferential Statistics

Although we can learn a great deal from descriptive statistics, most research described in this textbook features the use of **inferential statistics**, so called because they permit us to draw inferences or conclusions from data. Descriptive statistics allow us to talk about our sample data but do not allow us to extend our results to larger groups. To reach conclusions about how our observations of a sample might fit the bigger picture of groups of people, we use inferential statistics.

Although inferential statistics can be powerful, we must be continually cautious about making **generalizations** from our results to larger populations. To generalize means to extend your conclusions to people outside your research sample. Psychology over the years has been justifiably criticized as being the "psychology of the college sophomore." This criticism arises because researchers are usually college professors and the students in their courses are a convenient source of willing participants, especially when extra credit is available. Today's psychological scientists recognize that college students do not comprise a representative sample of people, and they go to great lengths to recruit samples of participants that are more diverse in age, race, ethnicity, socioeconomic background, and other demographic variables. Having a diverse sample supports more generalization than using a sample of college students.

To illustrate the use of inferential statistics, let's consider the 2009 SAT mathematics test. Men scored an average of 534 and women scored an average of 499 on this test. Does this mean that men perform better than women on this test? Or do men and women perform similarly, and this group is just an unusual sample of test takers? The default position stating that there is no real difference between two measures (math scores produced by men and women in this example) is known as the **null hypothesis**. Recall that we cannot "prove" a

inferential statistics Statistical methods that allow experimenters to extend conclusions from samples to larger populations.
generalize To extend conclusions to larger populations outside your research sample.
null hypothesis A hypothesis stating the default position that there is no real difference between two measures.

hypothesis to be correct, but we can demonstrate that a hypothesis is false (see ● Figure 2.19). Rejecting the null hypothesis suggests that alternative hypotheses (there might be a relationship between gender and math scores) should be explored and tested.

How do we know when a hypothesis should be rejected? Like most sciences, psychology has accepted odds of 5 of 100 that an observed result is due to chance as an acceptable standard for **statistical significance**. We can assess the likelihood of observing a result due to chance by repeating a study, like throwing dice multiple times. We could give the mathematics portion of the SAT to 100 randomly selected samples of male and female college-bound students. If men and women score about the same or women score higher than men in 5 or more of these 100 samples, we would reject our hypothesis as false.

This type of careful analysis of the SAT data has confirmed that the differences on the mathematics portion of the test between male and female test takers is statistically significant (Halpern et al., 2007). Does this result mean that we should consider this difference when deciding on a major or career? Probably not. Keep in mind that the goal of the SAT is to predict college grades. If you compare the SAT scores of men and women receiving the same letter grade in a mathematics course at the same university, the women have scored 33 points less on the math SAT than the men (Wainer & Steinberg, 1992). This is about the same differ-

statistical significance A standard for deciding whether an observed result is because of chance.

Connecting to Research

Do You Believe in ESP?

ESP STANDS FOR EXTRASENSORY PERCEPTION, with *extra* in this case meaning "outside" the boundaries of the normal information we obtain from our various senses, such as vision, hearing, and touch. The study of ESP is part of a larger field of parapsychology, or the study of psychic phenomena lying outside the typical boundaries of the field of psychology described in our first chapter. Among the abilities grouped as ESP are telepathy (the ability to communicate with other minds without using the usual methods of speaking or writing), clairvoyance (the ability to perceive objects that do not affect the known senses), precognition (knowledge of future events), and premonition (emotional anticipation of future events). In 2005, Gallup pollsters found that 41% of Americans said they believed in ESP, with 25% not sure and 32% not believing (Gallup Poll News Service, 2005). Of the scientists who are members of the National Academy of Sciences, 96% said they did not believe in ESP (McConnell & Clark, 1991).

A recent study of ESP (Bem, 2011) generated considerable discussion in the scientific community about everything from the statistics we use to the effects of investiga-

tor bias. Evaluating this study provides a good opportunity to practice your critical thinking skills and to apply what you have learned about validity and reliability.

The Question: Nine experiments involving more than 1,000 participants tested different types of precognition and premonition. We will focus our attention on the first experiment, which tested the following hypothesis: Participants should be able to anticipate the position (right side or left side of a computer screen) of an erotic photograph (see ● Figure 2.18). Is the following study of this hypothesis valid and reliable?

METHODS

One hundred undergraduates (50 men and 50 women) participated. Stimuli, both erotic and nonerotic photographs,

were selected from a standard set known as the International Affective Picture System. On each trial, participants saw two curtains on a computer screen and were asked to predict which curtain hid a picture. The sequencing of the erotic and nonerotic pictures and the left–right positions was determined by a random number generator after the partici-

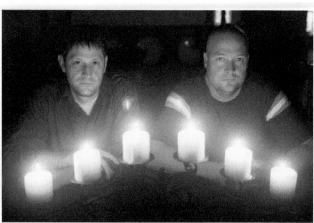

Syfy Channel/Courtesy Everett Collection

Popular television shows like *Ghost Hunters* might contribute to the large number of Americans who report a belief in ESP (41%). In contrast, 96% of the members of the National Academy of Sciences say they do not believe in ESP.

ence that we observed between the mean scores of men and women on the SAT math test. It appears that for some unknown reason, the SAT might be underestimating women's ability to achieve in college mathematics courses.

Although psychology, and most other sciences, has relied heavily on testing the significance of the null hypothesis using the 5 times out of 100 ($p < .05$) odds as a criterion, this approach has its share of weaknesses. Testing and rejecting a null hypothesis tend to encourage us to view variables, like exposure to violent video games, as producing discrete either–or outcomes (aggression or no aggression) when that is unlikely to be the case in reality. An alternative approach is the use of estimation, which includes a report of the 95% confidence interval in addition to the mean (Cumming, 2012). Applying estimation to the video game question might look like this. You could report that the average score on a measure of aggression was 37 ± 2 following exposure to a violent game and 32 ± 2 following exposure to a nonviolent game. This means that 95% of participants are likely to score between 35 and 39 following exposure to an aggressive game, while 95% of participants are likely to score between 30 and 34 following exposure to a nonviolent game. The additional information provided by the confidence interval helps us evaluate the magnitude of the difference better than a simple reporting of the statistical significance of the difference.

Illustration: © Cengage Learning®, photo: © Anson0618/Shutterstock

pant made a selection. This timing was designed to test the precognition of future events (the participants selected a side of the screen before the random number generator selected a location for the picture).

Here is where Bem's methods get a bit murky. The first 40 participants saw 12 erotic pictures, 12 negative pictures (unpleasant images), and 12 neutral pictures. Then, for reasons not well explained in the paper, the method was changed for the remaining 60 participants. These participants saw 18 erotic and 18 nonerotic photos, 8 of which were described as romantic but not erotic (couple at a wedding, etc.). It is quite unusual for researchers to change their methods in the middle of an experiment and more troubling when there doesn't seem to be a good reason to do so.

RESULTS

If we have two choices, we have a 50% chance of guessing correctly on each trial. Bem reported that the future position of the erotic images was chosen correctly on 53.1% of the trials, and the future position of the nonerotic images was chosen correctly on 49.8% of the trials. Bem reported that his results were statistically significant, or were unlikely to happen because of chance.

CONCLUSIONS

Bem concluded that the choices made by his participants were better than chance, supporting his hypothesis that precognition could be demonstrated.

What do others think of Bem's results? James Alcock, writing for the *Skeptical Inquirer*, concluded that "just about everything that could be done wrong in an experiment occurred here" (2011, p. 31). Among Alcock's concerns were Bem's changing of his method midway through the experiment

and his questionable use of statistical analyses.

As we discussed earlier, replication provides an important check on possible researcher bias, and failure to replicate indicates serious flaws in an experiment. So far, the three known replications of Bem's experiments have failed to produce significant results. Despite the flaws, however, Bem's experiments have contributed to science by stimulating a lively discussion of scientific and statistical methods. ●

FIGURE 2.18

Evidence of ESP?
Participants in Bem's (2011) study were supposed to predict behind which of two curtains a picture would appear.

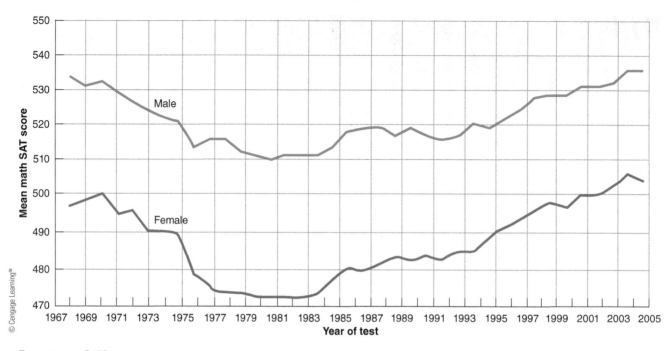

FIGURE 2.19

Are Male and Female Scores on the Math SAT Different? Inferential statistics allow us to decide whether the observed differences between the performance of males and that of females on the math SAT represents a real gender difference or chance. *Source:* Adapted from The College Board (2009).

How Can We Conduct Ethical Research?

Many populations that are interesting to psychologists are unable to sign informed consent forms legally and require additional ethical protection. In the case of research with infants, parents are required to sign informed consent forms on their child's behalf.

We mentioned earlier that deceiving participants into thinking they were truly in danger raised ethical questions. On what basis do researchers decide what they can and cannot do to their research participants?

Although most studies published in psychological journals involve the use of human participants, psychology also has a rich heritage of animal research. Consequently, separate guidelines have been developed for each type of subject. Researchers working in universities and other agencies receiving federal funding must receive the approval of institutional review boards (IRBs) for human participant research and institutional animal care and use committees (IACUCs) before conducting research. The IRBs and IACUCs are guided by federal regulations and research ethics endorsed by professional societies such as the American Psychological Association (APA), the Association for Psychological Science (APS), and the Society for Neuroscience (SfN). IRBs and IACUCs must include at least one member of the community outside the university or agency, avoiding the possibility that inappropriate research might be conducted in secret. These procedures do not apply to institutions that do not have federal funding, such as private genetics research corporations or consumer product corporations (cosmetics, etc.), although efforts are being made to bring these organizations into compliance with federal standards.

As you review the ethical guidelines for both human and animal research participants, keep in mind that the guidelines look simpler when you read about their provisions than when you try to implement them in the context of real research. This is why the final approval decision lies with a committee as opposed to single individuals.

The Tuskegee syphilis experiment, conducted by the U.S. Public Health Service from 1932 to 1972, involved 400 African American men who had contracted syphilis. Failure to treat or inform these participants about their health led to new regulations to prevent such unethical research from being repeated.

Department of Health, Education, and Welfare. Public Health Service. Health Services and Mental Health Administration. Center for Disease Control. Venereal Disease Branch (1970 - 1973)/National Archives

Human Participants

At the core of ethical standards for human research is the idea that participation is voluntary. No participant should be coerced into participating. Although psychologists are well aware that people who volunteer to participate in research are probably quite different in important ways from those who don't volunteer, we have chosen to give research ethics a higher priority than our ability to generalize research results.

To ensure that a participant is a willing volunteer, researchers must make provisions for reasonable incentives. Incentives, such as pay or extra credit for participation, must not be so extreme that they become the primary motivation for prospective volunteers. To decide whether to volunteer for research, a person must have some knowledge of what the research will entail. Researchers must provide prospective participants with an **informed consent** form, which provides details about the purpose of the study and what types of procedures will occur.

In psychological research, we have the added burden of occasionally dealing with participants who are limited in their abilities to provide informed consent because of the conditions that make them interesting to study. Developmental psychologists have an obvious interest in children, but a person cannot sign a legal informed consent form until age 18. Can you obtain informed consent from a patient with schizophrenia, who suffers from hallucinations and irrational, delusional beliefs? Or from a person in the later stages of Alzheimer's disease, whose memory and reasoning have deteriorated because of the condition? In these cases, legal permission must be obtained from a qualified guardian. The university IRBs play an essential role in evaluating these ethical dilemmas case by case.

Research should also be conducted in a manner that does no irreversible harm to participants. In some cases, to avoid participants' desire to appear normal and their tendency to try to outguess the research, researchers might say they are investigating one factor when they are interested in another. Most cases of deception are quite mild, such as when participants are told that a study is about memory when it is actually a study of some social behavior. When researchers must deceive their participants, extra care must be taken to debrief participants and answer all their questions following the experiment.

Research using human participants should be rigorously private and confidential. Privacy refers to the participants' control over the sharing of their personal information with others, and methods for ensuring privacy are usually stated in the informed consent paperwork. For example, some studies involve the use of medical records, which participants' agree to share

© Wellesley College/MCT/Newscom

While examining the papers of Dr. John Cutler, who led the Tuskegee syphilis study, Wellesley College historian Susan Reverby discovered that during the 1940s, U.S. and Guatemalan health officials had deliberately exposed prisoners, soldiers, and mental patients to syphilis and gonorrhea to test the effectiveness of penicillin.

informed consent Permission obtained from a research participant after risks and benefits of an experimental procedure have been thoroughly explained.

with the researchers for the purpose of the experiment. Confidentiality refers to the participants' right to have their data revealed to others only with their permission. Confidentiality is usually maintained by such practices as substituting codes for names and storing data in locked cabinets. Collecting data anonymously, so that even the researchers do not know the identity of participants, is the surest way to protect privacy and confidentiality.

Science learns from its past ethical lapses. One of the most egregious examples of unethical research was the Tuskegee syphilis experiment, which lasted from 1932 until 1972. Researchers from the U.S. Public Health Service recruited about 400 impoverished African American men who had contracted syphilis to study the progression of the disease. None of the men were told they had syphilis, and none were treated, even though penicillin became the standard treatment for syphilis in 1947. Many current federal regulations related to research ethics were developed in response to this experiment.

Animal Subjects

The topic of using animals in research is guaranteed to stimulate lively, and possibly heated, discussion. Some people are adamantly opposed to any animal research, whereas others accept the concept of using animals as long as certain conditions are met. About 7% to 8% of published research in psychology journals involves the use of animals as subjects (APA, 2005a). Ninety percent of the animals used are rodents and birds, with 5% or fewer studies involving monkeys and other primates. According to the APA, the use of dogs and cats in psychological research is rare.

Research using animals must demonstrate a clear purpose, such as benefiting the health of humans or other animals. In addition to serving a clear purpose, animal research requires excellent housing, food, and veterinary care. The most controversial ethical standards relate to minimizing the pain and suffering experienced by animal research subjects. The APA provides guidelines for the use of pain, surgery, stress, and deprivation with animal subjects, as well as the termination of an animal's life. The standards approximate the community standards we would expect from local humane societies tasked with euthanizing animals that are not adopted.

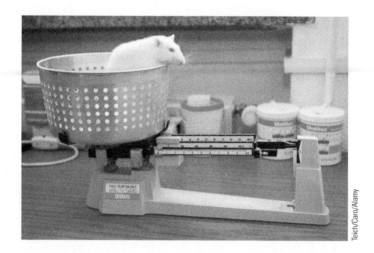

Ethical guidelines for animal research require setting a clear purpose for the experiment, providing excellent care for the animals, and minimizing pain and suffering.

Interpersonal Relationships
The Methodological Perspective
Can We Differentiate "Like" from "Love?"

At the end of Chapter 1, we noted that each chapter would feature a discussion of how the chapter's material could be used to talk about relationships. For this chapter on research methods, we ask whether psychological research methods can be used to differentiate between liking and loving another person.

Using the methods described in this chapter, you can probably think of many ways to approach this question. You could observe friends and compare their behavior to that of romantic partners. You could conduct a survey, asking people to rate certain characteristics of people they love versus those of people they like. Perhaps you could correlate physiological arousal measures, like pupil diameter or heart rate, with ratings of how much a participant likes or loves another person. Conducting an actual experiment might be a bit tricky, though, in terms of both methods and ethics. How could people be randomly assigned to love and like groups?

A fun example of research on relationships was contributed by Bartels and Zeki (2000). These researchers chose to use correlational methods in the form of brain imaging, which we discuss further in our chapter on biological psychology. Brain imaging studies are typically correlational, because we assume that brain activity in particular areas has a relationship with some ongoing behavior. It is important to recall that we cannot make conclusions about causality based on correlational data.

Bartels and Zeki's participants were instructed to supply photographs of people they like and people they love. The photographs were then presented to the participants while their brain activity was observed using functional magnetic resonance imaging (see Chapter 4). Several differences in brain activity occurred when the participants viewed a lover as opposed to a friend. Not too surprisingly, areas of the brain associated with reward became more active when viewing lovers than when viewing friends. Areas of the brain associated with social judgment, negative emotions, and assessing the intentions and emotions of other people were less active when viewing lovers than when viewing friends. Love, according to these results, appears to be a combination of reward and less social judgment (see ● Figure 2.20).

The results of this scientific research might help us understand some of our everyday experiences with relationships. We feel rewarded in the presence of a loved one, and we have to admit that we may miss a flaw or two in someone we love. Friends and family members, whose social judgment has not been silenced, do not miss these flaws and often try in vain to alert us to them. ●

When you view a person you love rather than like:

■ These areas increase their activity.   ■ These areas decrease their activity.

© Cengage Learning®

FIGURE 2.20

Imaging Love. When people view a photo of a person they say they "love," brain imaging shows increased activation in reward areas of the brain and decreased activation in areas involved with social judgment.

Summary 2.3 Principles of Ethical Research

Human participants	Animal subjects
No coercion	Necessity
Informed consent	Excellent food, housing, and veterinary care
No harm	Minimal pain and suffering
Confidentiality and privacy	

Credits: Left: Department of Health, Education, and Welfare. Public Health Service. Health Services and Mental Health Administration. Center for Disease Control. Venereal Disease Branch (1970–1973)/National Archives. Right: Teich/Caro/Alamy

KEY TERMS The Language of Psychological Science

Be sure you can define these terms and use them correctly.

case study, p. 42
confounding variable, p. 49
control group, p. 48
correlation, p. 45
critical thinking, p. 38
cross-sectional study, p. 54
dependent variable, p. 48
descriptive method, p. 42
descriptive statistics, p. 58
double-blind procedure, p. 54
experiment, p. 48
experimental group, p. 49
generalize, p. 61
hypothesis, p. 39
independent variable, p. 48

inferential statistics, p. 61
informed consent, p. 65
longitudinal study, p. 55
mean, p. 58
measure, p. 46
median, p. 59
meta-analysis, p. 52
mixed longitudinal design, p. 55
mode, p. 59
naturalistic observation, p. 43
normal distribution, p. 60
null hypothesis, p. 61
objectivity, p. 36
operationalization, p. 52
peer review, p. 40

placebo, p. 54
population, p. 44
random assignment, p. 49
reliability, p. 57
replication, p. 41
sample, p. 44
science, p. 36
standard deviation, p. 60
statistical significance, p. 62
survey, p. 44
theory, p. 39
third variable, p. 46
validity, p. 57
variable, p. 45

3 The Evolving Mind

Nature and Nurture Intertwined

WE ALL KNOW THAT IDENTICAL TWINS, LIKE THE little girls appearing in the inset photo, are, well, identical. Or are they?

For a long time, scientists were puzzled not by the similarities between identical twins but by their differences. If two people share the same deoxyribonucleic acid (DNA), as identical twins do, why does one get cancer while the other stays healthy? Why does one become obese while the other remains fit?

When science began to unravel some mysteries about genes and how they work, answers to these questions emerged. You have the same DNA in each cell of your body, yet some cells develop into heart cells, others into brain cells, and so on. How does the same set of DNA know how to make these different types of cells? Genes can be turned on and off. The genes that are not turned off are free to produce the proteins needed to build a particular kind of cell, whether that is a skin cell or a liver cell.

Genes do not just turn on and off as they build a body during development. Your ongoing interactions with the environment can also turn genes on or off. What you eat, whether you smoke or drink, your stress levels, and other environmental factors can influence how your DNA works. Our understanding of these ongoing interactions between genes and the environment is the reason psychologists no longer argue about the separate contributions of nature and nurture. In this chapter, we will explore these interactions in more detail.

Let's zoom in to see what's happening when the environment interacts with DNA. You can see a strand of DNA in the large chapter opener image. In mice, a gene called Agouti produces yellow fur and obesity when it is turned on but brown fur and normal weight when it is turned off (Dolinoy, Huang, & Jirtle, 2007). Certain environmental factors can influence whether the gene is turned on or off. For example, if pregnant mother mice ate food containing bisphenol A (BPA), a chemical found in food and beverage containers, baby bottles, dental sealants, and food cans, their babies were more likely to have yellow fur and be obese than were babies of mice that were not fed BPA. The BPA seems to have turned on the Agouti gene.

How does studying the fur color of mice help us understand the differences between identical human twins? The young twins on this page have a great deal in common, but as they get older, they are more likely to eat different foods and have different experiences. These environmental influences can change the way their genes are turned

◀ Environmental factors such as stress, diet, smoking, and exercise, can influence whether a gene is turned on or off.

71

Courtesy Randy L. Jirtle, Ph.D.

on or off, just as the BPA affected the Agouti gene in the mice. These changes accumulate over time, so identical twins become less similar as they age.

In this chapter, we will explore how nature and nurture interact with each other to build the mind across the life span and how the interactions between nature and nurture have been shaping the human mind over millennia.

When pregnant mice are fed a diet containing BPA, found in plastics and other consumer products, their offspring are more likely to have yellow fur and to be obese.

Learning Objectives

1. Analyze the role of genes as the building blocks of human nature.

2. Assess the importance of heritability estimates, twin studies, adoption studies, and epigenetic analyses in the field of behavioral genetics.

3. Analyze the roles played by mutation, natural selection, migration, and genetic drift as mechanisms of evolution.

4. Discuss how the human brain might represent an adaptation for coping with complex social behavior.

5. Explain the mechanisms by which intrasexual and intersexual selection might influence the evolution of human behavior.

6. Explain the cultural mechanisms by which nature and nurture can interact to influence human behavior.

These identical twins probably do not look as similar as they did as small children. The twin on the left is a non-smoker, while her sister on the right smoked for 29 years.

AP Images/Rex Features/American Society of Plastic

Why Do We Say Nature and Nurture Are Intertwined?

Along with an understanding of the structures and processes of the brain, which we cover in Chapter 4, knowing how our biological history shapes our behavior is an important part of understanding the mind. In Chapter 1, we explained how contemporary psychologists view the contributions of **nature**, our heredity or innate predispositions, and **nurture**, the results of our experience with the environment, to be closely intertwined as opposed to somehow competing with each other for control over structure and behavior.

Scholars have not always thought about nature and nurture the way we do today. Instead of viewing the actions of nature and nurture as inseparable, earlier scholars talked in terms of nature versus nurture and debated the relative contributions of nature or nurture to a particular type of behavior. Credit for describing the contrast between heredity and environment as "nature versus nurture" usually goes to scholar Francis Galton (1869), who was Charles Darwin's cousin. Galton believed that intelligence was largely the result of inheritance, a topic we tackle in Chapter 10. Over the next 150 years or so, many thinkers engaged in a highly spirited debate on this question. As we will see in Chapter 10, contemporary psychologists view intelligence as another example of an outcome shaped by both genetic inheritance and environment.

We can say with some certainty that the either–or approach to human behavior has produced some of the most contentious discussions in the history of psychology. Our motive for arguing in favor of the intertwined approach to nature and nurture is intended not to sidestep difficult questions but rather to support good science. By zooming out to integrate a number of perspectives, both biological and experiential, we reach a more accurate understanding of these questions.

Ridley (2003) summarizes the need for an integrated nature–nurture approach as follows:

> Genes are not puppet masters or blueprints. Nor are they just the carriers of heredity. They are active during life; they switch each other on and off; they respond to the environment. They may direct the construction of the body and brain in the womb, but then they set about dismantling and rebuilding what they have made almost at once—in response to experience. They are both cause and consequence of our actions. (p. 6)

Francis Galton was the first to use the phrase "nature versus nurture."

What Are the Building Blocks of Behavior?

Before we explore the interactions between nature and nurture that contribute to psychological phenomena, like a person's reactions to being bullied, let's look at the genetic mechanisms that help shape the mind.

Every nucleus in the approximately 37 trillion cells of your body, with the exception of your red blood cells and sperm or eggs, contains two complete copies of the human genome, a set of instructions for building a human. Your personal set of instructions is known as a **genotype**, which interacts with the environment to produce observable characteristics known as a **phenotype**. Your genotype might include a gene for blond hair and another for brown, while your phenotypical, or observable, hair color is light brown.

One half of your genotype was provided by your mother's egg, and the other was provided by your father's sperm. Each parent contributes a set of 23 chromosomes, which in turn are composed of many molecules of DNA. Smaller segments of DNA located in particular places on a chromosome are known as **genes**. Each gene contains instructions for making a particular type of protein. **Gene expression** occurs when these genetic instructions are converted into a feature of a living cell. Each cell contains the instructions for an entire human organism, but only a subset of instructions is expressed at any given time and location. Gene expression in a nerve cell is different from gene expression in a muscle cell or a skin cell.

nature The contributions of heredity to our physical structure and behaviors.

nurture The contributions of environmental factors and experience to our physical structure and behaviors.

genotype An individual's profile of alleles.

phenotype Observable characteristics.

gene Small segment of DNA located in a particular place on a chromosome.

gene expression The process in which genetic instructions are converted into a feature of a living cell.

Some genes have a large number of alleles. Of the more than 500 alleles for the *BRCA1* (Breast Cancer 1) gene, a small number are associated with a higher risk for breast and other cancers. Actress Angelina Jolie, who possesses the high-risk alleles, chose to undergo a preventive mastectomy to reduce her chances of developing breast cancer.

allele One of several versions of a gene, as in having an A, B, or O blood type allele.

homozygous Having two of the same alleles for a gene.

heterozygous Having two different alleles for a gene.

recessive A feature of an allele that only produces a phenotype in the homozygous condition.

dominant A feature of an allele that determines a phenotype in either the homozygous or the heterozygous condition.

Twenty-three pairs of chromosomes make up the human genome.

Different versions of a gene, or **alleles**, can give rise to different phenotypical traits. Many alleles can occur for a given gene, but an individual receives only two, one from each parent. For example, alleles for blood type include A, B, and O, but typically, nobody can have all three. Combinations of your two alleles make your blood Type A (AA or AO), Type B (BB or BO), Type AB (AB), or Type O (OO). See ● Figure 3.1, which illustrates possible blood type combinations.

If both parents contribute the same type of allele, such as a gene for curly hair, the child would be considered **homozygous** for that gene (*homos* means "same" in Greek). If the parents contribute different alleles, such as a gene for curly hair from one parent and a gene for straight hair from the other, the child is **heterozygous** for that gene (*hetero* means "different" in Greek). **Recessive** alleles only determine a phenotype when an individual is homozygous for a particular gene, whereas **dominant** alleles determine a phenotype in either the homozygous or the heterozygous condition. Because alleles for straight hair are recessive and alleles for curly hair are dominant, the only way an individual can have straight hair is if that person receives two copies of the straight hair allele, one from each parent. An individual receiving one straight hair allele and one curly hair allele will have curly hair (see ● Figure 3.2).

Whether you have straight or curly hair is a simple example of how dominant and recessive genes interact, but in many human characteristics, one allele does not entirely dominate another. In the research on bullying we discuss on page 77, we note that individuals could have SS, SL, or LL genotypes for the serotonin transporter gene. Neither the S nor the L allele dominates the other. As you can see in ● Figure 3.3, The SL group had levels of emotional disturbance that fell between the extremes of the SS and the LL groups (Sugden et al., 2010). If either the S or the L alleles were dominant, the SL group would behave like that dominant group instead.

Genetic Variation

If you have siblings, you are aware that having the same biological parents does not guarantee similar appearance, personality, and behavior.

The development of an egg or sperm cell is like shuffling a deck of cards. In both cases, a large number of possible outcomes may occur. When a parent's cell divides to make an egg or sperm cell, each resulting cell contains 23 chromosomes, one chromosome from each of the parent's original 23 chromosome pairs. As a result, a single human can produce eggs or sperm with 2^{23} (8,388,608) combinations of chromosomes. Add this variability to the different possibilities provided by the other parent, and it may seem surprising that we resemble our relatives as much as we do.

	Father's allele		
Mother's allele	A	B	O
A	AA (Type A blood)	AB (Type AB blood)	AO (Type A blood)
B	AB (Type AB blood)	BB (Type B blood)	BO (Type B blood)
O	AO (Type A blood)	BO (Type B blood)	OO (Type O blood)

FIGURE 3.1

Genotypes and Phenotypes of Blood Type. The three possible blood type alleles—A, B, and O—can be combined to produce Type A, Type B, Type O, or Type AB blood.

Relatedness

Despite this potential variability, we remain similar to our genetic relatives. We will revisit this important point later in the chapter when we discuss the evolution of social behavior. **Relatedness** is defined as the probability that two people share copies of the same allele from a common ancestor. If we go back in history far enough, we all share common ancestors. Relatedness, however, is usually computed within a limited number of generations.

The chance that you share an allele with one of your parents is one half, as is the chance that you share an allele with a sibling. You have a one quarter likelihood of sharing an allele with an aunt or uncle (see ● Figure 3.5). These types of calculations led geneticist J. B. S. Haldane to allegedly proclaim, "I would lay down my life for two brothers or eight cousins!" (Connelly & Martlew, 1999). Haldane was computing the likelihood that his genes would be passed down to future generations. As we discuss later in the chapter, evolutionary psychologists suggest that sacrificing yourself for others is more likely when the others are genetically related relatives.

Sex Chromosomes

Of the 23 pairs of human chromosomes from each parent, 22 pairs are perfectly matched. In other words, a gene appearing on one of a pair of chromosomes, perhaps a gene for hair color or blood type, has a corresponding gene on its partner. The remaining pair, the X and Y sex chromosomes, does not carry the same genes. Females carry two copies of the X chromosome, whereas males carry one X and one Y chromosome. Most of the genes located on the Y chromosome are

FIGURE 3.2

Effects of Dominant and Recessive Genes. Curly hair (C) is dominant, whereas straight hair (c) is recessive. The only way a child can have straight hair is to inherit two of the recessive straight hair alleles from parents. In this example, both parents are heterozygous (Cc) with curly hair.

Huntstock.com/Shutterstock.com

© Cengage Learning®

	Father's allele	
Mother's allele	Curly (C)	Straight (c)
Curly (C)	CC (homozygous curly)	Cc (heterozygous curly)
Straight (c)	Cc (heterozygous curly)	cc (homozygous straight)

relatedness The probability that two people share the same allele from a common ancestor.

FIGURE 3.3

Some Alleles Do Not Show Dominance. Neither the S nor the L allele of the serotonin transporter gene dominates the other. Among children who have been bullied frequently, those with the SL genotype (shown in green) experience a level of emotional problems midway between the levels of those with the SS and LL genotypes. If either the S or the L allele was dominant, we would expect the SL group to behave the same way as the homozygous dominant group. *Source:* Adapted from "Serotonin Transporter Gene Moderates the Development of Emotional Problems Among Children Following Bullying Victimization," by K. Sugden, L. Arseneault, H. Harrington, T. E. Moffitt, B. Williams, & A. Caspi, 2010, *Journal of the American Academy of Child and Adolescent Psychiatry, 49*(8), pp. 830–840. doi:10.1016/j.jaac.2010.01.024.

■ SS (short/short)
■ SL (short/long)
■ LL (long/long)

Serotonin transporter gene genotype
(y-axis) Mean emotional problems score

 Connecting to **Research**

Genes, Bullying, and Emotional Problems

EARLIER IN THIS CHAPTER, you learned about how a mother mouse's diet could influence the fur color and weight of her offspring. We are not mice, so it is fair to ask whether this same type of interaction between genes and experience can happen in humans. The answer to that question is "yes."

Researchers have known for a long time that early victims of bullies often develop serious emotional problems later in childhood or adolescence. We also know that having a particular genetic profile involving serotonin, one of the chemical messengers we discuss in Chapter 4, can lead to emotional problems but, again, not in all cases. How can we integrate these findings to learn why some children seem at higher risk than others for developing emotional problems after being victimized by bullies? A good answer to this question would allow psychologists to target the right groups of children for treatment. Sugden et al. (2010) tackled this question by studying bullying and a particular type of serotonin gene in 2,232 children.

The Question: Does a particular type of genotype, or individual genetic profile, interact with the experience of bullying to produce a higher risk for emotional problems?

METHODS

More than 2,000 children enrolled in the British Environmental Risk (E-Risk) study participated in this analysis. The research-

Abby Hardy, 13, front and Ellie Seaman, 14, back, attach valentines to hundreds of lockers Thursday, Feb. 13, 2014, as part of an anti-bullying campaign at Upton Middle School in St. Joseph, Mich.

ers evaluated the children's exposure to bullying during interviews at home when they were 12 years old. Emotional problems were assessed using standard instruments, one to be filled out by parents and the other by teachers. Parents and teachers filled out these instruments twice, once when the child was 5 years old and a second time when the child was 12 years old. Genetic samples were obtained by swabbing the inside of the children's mouths, which is also a standard procedure.

RESULTS

The serotonin gene studied in this research, the serotonin transporter gene, has a long (L) version and a short (S) version, which means that individuals can have one of three genotypes: SS, SL, and LL. These genotypes did not predict emotional problems by themselves, but a history of being victimized by bullies did predict emotional problems.

One of the strengths of this study was its use of a longitudinal design, which we discussed in our chapter on research methods. As you can see in ● Figure 3.4, never or involved with male fertility. The X chromosome contains genes not duplicated on the Y chromosome that influence a variety of characteristics.

The allele responsible for hemophilia, or the failure of blood to clot, is found on the X chromosome. This allele is recessive, leading to different outcomes based on the sex of the child receiving the alleles. Generally, if a female receives a healthy allele on the X chromosome from one parent and a disease-causing allele on the X chromosome from her other parent, she will be a carrier for the condition but will not experience it. In contrast, a male receiving a disease-causing allele on the X chromosome from his mother will have the condition. Because there is no equivalent allele on the Y chromosome to offset the disease-causing recessive allele, it will be expressed. As a result, conditions such as hemophilia are more frequent among males and are called sex-linked characteristics (see • Figure 3.6). Queen Victoria of Great Britain (1819–1901), through two of her five daughters (Princess Alice and Princess Beatrice), passed the mutation for hemophilia to various royal houses across the continent. Victoria's son Prince Leopold, Duke of Albany, suffered from the disease. Therefore, hemophilia was once popularly called "the royal disease." We can trace hemophilia in Queen Victoria's family, as illustrated in • Figure 3.7.

Epigenetics

Having identical genotypes, as is the case with identical twins, does not guarantee identical phenotypes, or observed characteristics. As we explained in the example of the Agouti gene and the fur color and weight of baby mice, different phenotypes can

MARCOCCHI GIULIO/SIPA/Newscom

Given that each parent can pass along more than 8 million combinations of chromosomes, it might be surprising that family resemblance can be so strong, as it is in actors and brothers Liam (left) and Chris (right) Hemsworth.

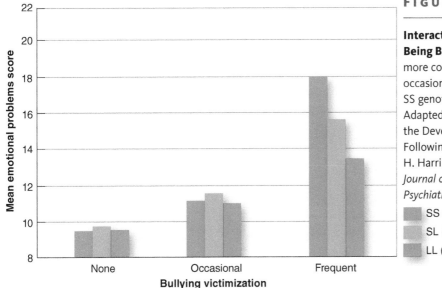

FIGURE 3.4

Interactions Between Genotype and the Experience of Being Bullied. Childhood emotional problems become more common when a child experiences frequent, but not occasional, bullying, especially when the child has the SS genotype for the serotonin transporter gene. *Source:* Adapted from "Serotonin Transporter Gene Moderates the Development of Emotional Problems Among Children Following Bullying Victimization," by K. Sugden, L. Arseneault, H. Harrington, T. E. Moffitt, B. Williams, & A. Caspi, 2010, *Journal of the American Academy of Child and Adolescent Psychiatry, 49*(8), pp. 830–840. doi:10.1016/j.jaac.2010.01.024.

■ SS (short/short)
■ SL (short/long)
■ LL (long/long)

occasionally being bullied is not associated with an increase in emotional problems from age 5 to 12, but being bullied frequently is associated with an increase in emotional problems, especially for children with the SS genotype. Without this longitudinal design, we might not be able to say whether the behavioral problems among the bullied 12-year-olds were related to genotype or to other possibilities, such as

stress at home or a greater likelihood of being victimized because of existing emotional problems.

CONCLUSIONS

The results show that being victimized by bullies leads to emotional problems but that children with the SS genotype who are bullied frequently are more likely than children with either the SL or the LL genotype

to experience increased emotional problems at age 12.

These results shed light onto the question of why some bullied children appear to be more negatively affected by the experience than others. The results also allow psychologists to target specific children for treatment before the emotional problems at age 12 develop into later problems with mental health. ●

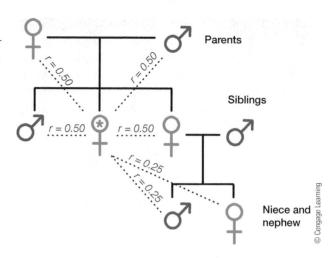

© Cengage Learning

FIGURE 3.5

Relatedness. Relatedness refers to the probability that two people share a particular allele from a common ancestor. The chance that you share an allele with one of your parents or a brother or sister is 0.50, or one half. The chance that you share an allele with a niece or nephew is 0.25, or one quarter.

X chromosome

Biophoto Associates/Science Source

Y chromosome

Biophoto Associates/ Science Source

result from the same genotype because of interactions between the organism and its environment. When factors other than the genotype produce changes in a phenotype, we say that an **epigenetic** change has occurred. *Epi* is Greek for "over" or "above," so *epigenetics* refers to the reversible development of traits by factors that determine how the genes perform. The field of epigenetics explores these gene–environment interactions.

Epigenetic change influences gene expression, the process by which DNA forms proteins that contribute to features of living cells. The process of epigenetic change begins with a chemical signal that originates either within the organism or from the external environment. Internal signals could come from chemicals released by neighboring cells or from hormones circulating in the blood. Environmental signals might come from the food you eat or the nicotine in cigarette smoke that you inhale as you pass a smoker. Cells "listen" for signals, using receptors on their outer membranes. Information from the signals is transferred to the nucleus of the cell, where it can interact with proteins that regulate gene expression. These regulatory

 Experiencing **Psychology**

Reading a DNA Fingerprint

DNA BELONGING TO different individuals can be compared using autoradiographs. An autoradiograph is formed by labeling DNA fragments with a radioactive marker and then exposing the DNA to x-ray film.

In this case, we are looking at a simple paternity test (Public Broadcasting Service, 1998). Four DNA samples have been taken from three people: a mother, her child, and the possible father of the child. The two letters for each segment represent the individual's genotype. For example, in the first autoradiograph, the mother is an AD, the child is an AC, and the possible father is a BC.

Use the autoradiographs to complete Table 3.1.

To evaluate the likelihood of the possible father's paternity, identify which letters the child inherited from the mother and which from the father. The child will receive one allele from each parent, so the child's combinations of alleles must be possible based on the mother's and father's genotypes. For example, if the child had AD in the first column instead of AC, this man would not be the father, because he has neither the A nor the C allele to contribute. Overall, is it possible for this man to have fathered this child?

From A Science Odyssey (http://www.pbs.org/wgbh/aso/resources/guide/earthhappenact3.html) Copyright 1998 WGBH Educational Foundation.

"Epigenetic differences arise during the lifetime of monozygotic twins," by Mario Fraga et al., 2005, in Proceedings of the National Academy of Sciences 2005 Jul 102(30) 10407–8. Fig. 3. © 2005 National Academy of Sciences, U.S.A.

Fraga et al. (2005) studied 160 identical twin pairs between the ages of 3 and 74. The two chromosomes on the left belong to a pair of 3-year-old twins, and those on the right belong to a pair of 50-year-old twins. Areas of red indicate differences between the two chromosomes in each pair related to differences in gene expression. As twins age, their gene expression becomes more different, as indicated by the greater amount of red in the chromosomes from the older twins. Twins who had spent the most time apart showed the greatest epigenetic differences.

proteins produce epigenetic tags, which serve as a cell's memory of the signals it has received and which stimulate changes in gene expression. Epigenetic tags can be added or removed, providing a means for the cells to adapt to ongoing change.

Two processes that can produce lasting but reversible changes in gene expression are histone modification and DNA methylation (see ● Figure 3.8). Histones are protein structures around which your DNA is wound. If the DNA in a single cell were not wound up in this fashion, it would be over 6 feet long (Annunziato, 2008). When either the core or the tail of a histone interacts with regulatory proteins, the expression of nearby segments of DNA can become more or less likely. DNA methylation occurs when a methyl group (one carbon atom bonded to three hydrogen atoms) is added to the DNA molecule. This has the result of turning genes off. You can think about DNA methylation as being similar to stapling some pages in a book together. Because of the staples, you can't read the pages.

A human being has about 100 trillion meters of DNA. To put this in perspective, this means our DNA could go to the Suan and back more than 300 times.

epigenetics The study of gene–environment interactions in the production of phenotypes.

TABLE

3.1 Autoradiograph Results

	1 (A, B, C, D)	2 (E, F, G)	3 (H, I, J, K)	4 (L, M, N, O)
Mother		GG		
Child	AC			MO
Possible father			HK	

© Cengage Learning®

SOLUTION

Keep in mind that genetic tests never prove a relationship: They can only disprove one. In our chapter on research methods, we made this same point about all hypotheses. Based on the evidence in this case, we cannot prove the hypothesis that this man is the child's biological parent. All we can do is show that he is not the father. If the child had an AD genotype instead of an AC genotype in the first box, as mentioned earlier, this man could not possibly be the father, because he could not supply either the A or the D allele. Such an exclusion result is considered absolute evidence of nonpaternity. In contrast, the results of this test suggest that it is very likely that this man is the biological parent of the child. ●

FIGURE 3.6

Hemophilia Is a Sex-Linked Trait. If a daughter inherits her mother's X chromosome containing the allele for hemophilia (X_H), she will be a carrier but will not have the disease. If a son inherits this X_H chromosome, he will have the disease. Unlike his sister, he does not have a healthy X chromosome to offset the disease allele.

Although many studies in epigenetics examine physical features like fur color, we assume that more complex features of interest to psychologists are also subject to epigenetic influences. In one dramatic example, rats that were licked frequently during infancy by their mothers (the rat equivalent of getting a hug from mom) were calmer than rats licked infrequently when faced with stress later in life (Champagne, Francis, Mar, & Meaney, 2003). By licking their pups, these mothers had influenced the expression of genes that determined responses to a stress hormone. The nurture provided by the mother had lifelong impact on the offspring's ability to cope with stress. Children exposed to child abuse have been found to have similar long-lasting changes in the expression of genes related to stress hormones (Neigh, Gillespie, & Nemeroff, 2009), as well as a number of genes associated with later medical problems and psychological disorders (Yang et al., 2013). Happily, these changes appear to be reversible in children who experience consistent and responsive caregiving by foster parents (Fisher, Van Ryzin, & Gunnar, 2011).

The concept that epigenetic changes could be maintained across generations, allowing the experience of parents and grandparents to affect subsequent generations, remains controversial. In one intriguing report, however, father mice seemed to be able to pass along to their offspring a learned sensitivity to an odor that had been paired with electric shock (Dias &

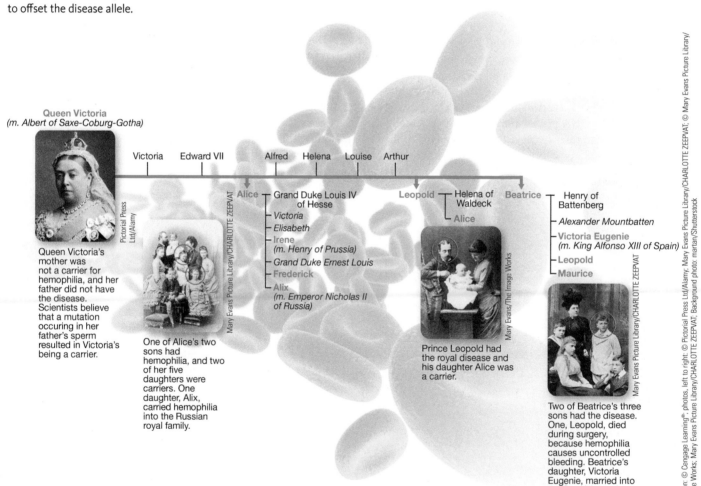

FIGURE 3.7

Hemophilia and European Royalty. Queen Victoria of Great Britain (1819–1901) had nine children. One son (Prince Leopold, Duke of Albany) had hemophilia, and two daughters (Princess Alice and Princess Beatrice) were carriers for the condition. As a result of their marriages to other European royalty, the three children spread the hemophilia gene to the royal families of Germany, Russia, and Spain. Therefore, hemophilia was once popularly called "the royal disease."

FIGURE 3.8

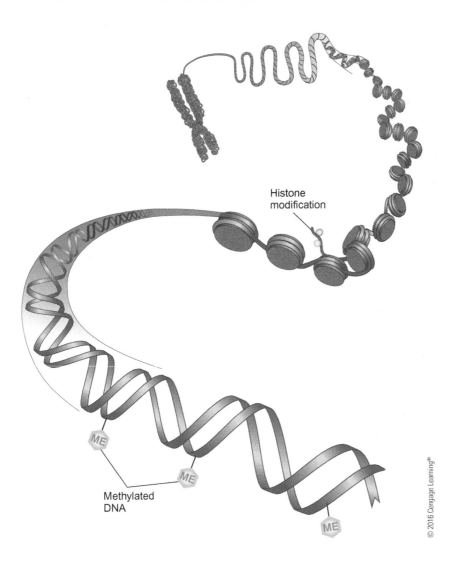

Histone
modification

Methylated
DNA

ME

ME

ME

© 2016 Cengage Learning®

Mechanisms of Epigenetic Change.
Two processes for producing
epigenetic change are histone
modification and DNA methylation.
Histone modification occurs when
certain chemicals interact with the tail
or core of a histone. DNA methylation
occurs when a methyl group (one
carbon atom bonded to three
hydrogen atoms) attaches to the DNA
molecule. These modifications affect
the likelihood that particular genes
will be expressed or silenced.

Ressler, 2013). This is an example of classical conditioning, which we discuss in more detail in Chapter 8. In DNA taken from the sperm of both the father and the son mice, the gene that produces the receptor for the odor showed changes in methylation.

Although the application of epigenetics to psychology is quite recent, it is likely that interest in this approach will continue to grow. Epigenetic change provides a process by which the human mind responds to the interplay between nature and nurture.

What Is the Field of Behavioral Genetics?

The field of **behavioral genetics** attempts to identify and understand the links between genetics and behavior. These links can help explain individual differences among humans, as well as the differences we see between our species and others.

Although we can say that all humans share 100% of their genes, we do not share 100% of our alleles, or variations in each gene, giving each of us a unique version of the genome. In other words, we all share genes that produce eye color of some sort, but our different combinations of alleles result in a variety of shades. There are at least 3 million DNA variations in the human genome, enough for us to differ from one another in nearly every gene (Plomin & Spinath, 2004).

behavioral genetics The scientific field that attempts to identify and understand links between genetics and behavior.

Our species shares genes for eye color, but combinations of alleles produce many possible shades.

Our species also shares quite a few genes with chimpanzees, mice, fruit flies, yeast, and a weed known as thale cress (see ● Figure 3.9). Behavioral geneticists are less interested in genes we share with other species than in those that make us different from them. For example, research points to differences between humans and chimpanzees in a single gene, the *FoxP2* gene, that appears to have had a significant effect on distinctly human behaviors, including spoken language (Konopka et al., 2009).

A common misunderstanding of behavioral genetics is the belief that we can identify a gene for a particular behavior. For instance, the headline of an article written for the popular website WebMD trumpets "Researchers Identify Alcoholism Gene" (Davis, 2004). It is important to remember that genes encode for proteins, not behaviors. Genes build proteins that are used to construct brains, and brains may or may not initiate the behavior of drinking alcohol. Rather than viewing a gene as causing a complex behavior, it is more useful and accurate to view genes as contributing to the development and functioning of the nervous system, which in turn generates observable behavior.

Occasionally, it appears that single genes or a small number of genes have a disproportionately significant effect on a behavior. However, most behavioral differences occur because of interactions among the small effects of large numbers of genes. As we will discuss in Chapter 14, schizophrenia has a clear genetic basis, but more than 70 genes have been implicated in the development of the disorder (Mirnics, Middleton, Marquez, Lewis, & Levitt, 2000). Fortunately, methods for analyzing the simultaneous influence of whole sets of genes, as opposed to analyzing one gene at a time, are advancing rapidly. Researchers using these new techniques have identified multiple genes involved with reading disability (Gayan et al., 2005). No one gene can account for reading difficulties, but small differences in clusters of genes can.

Comparisons of twins are often used in behavioral genetics to evaluate relative contributions of genetics and environment. The differences between identical twins, who share identical DNA, and fraternal twins, whose DNA shows the same approximately 50% of overlap found in any two siblings, are particularly useful, because both types of twins share similar environments. The Minnesota Study of Twins Reared Apart (Bouchard, 1994; Bouchard, Lykken, McGue, Segal, & Tellegen, 1990) not only compares identical to fraternal twins but

FIGURE 3.9

Genes Shared With Other Species. Humans share quite a few genes with other species, such as the 18% of genes we share with a weed known as thale cress. However, geneticists are most interested in the genes that differ from those of other species, like the *FoxP2* gene, which appears to be responsible for spoken language. Mutations of this gene cause severe speech and language disorders.

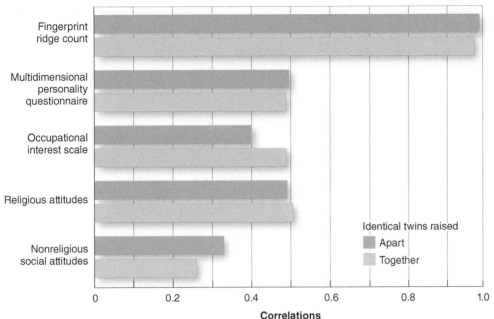

FIGURE 3.10

Twins Raised Together or Apart Show Comparable Levels of Similarity Across Several Traits.
Comparisons of identical twins raised together or in separate adoptive families show that some traits are more similar in twin pairs (fingerprint ridge count) than others (nonreligious social attitudes). However, regardless of the degree of similarity for a trait, living apart or together seems to have had relatively little impact on the degree of similarity within twin pairs. In other words, twins raised apart are just about as similar on each trait as twins raised together. *Source:* Adapted from "Sources of Human Psychological Differences: The Minnesota Study of Twins Reared Apart," by T. Bouchard Jr., D. T. Lykken, M. McGue, N. L. Segal, & A. Tellegen, 1990, *Science, 250,* pp. 223–228.

includes pairs of identical twins and fraternal twins adopted at birth and raised in separate homes (see ● Figure 3.10).

Twin studies are also useful in establishing **concordance rates**, which are statistical probabilities that a trait observed in one person will be seen in another. Concordance rates are especially useful to psychologists interested in psychological disorders, because they provide estimates of the genetic influence on developing a condition. For example, concordance rates for autism spectrum disorder (see Chapter 14) are high in identical twins (95.2%) relative to fraternal twins (4.3%; Nordenbæk, Jørgensen, Kyvik, & Bilenberg, 2014). Because both types of twins share a uterine environment and are exposed to similar parenting, this discrepancy makes a strong argument for the importance of genetic influences on autism spectrum disorder.

Behavioral geneticists often speak in terms of the **heritability** of a particular trait, or the statistical likelihood that variations observed across individuals in a population are because of genetics. Heritability is usually presented as a ratio of the amount of variation observed in a population because of genetics relative to the total amount of variation due to both genetic and environmental influences. If genes play no part in producing phenotypical differences among individuals, heritability is zero. For example, genes are responsible for human hearts, but there is no individual variation in the population in terms of the presence of a heart—we each have one. Consequently, the heritability of having a heart is 0.0. If genes are totally responsible for all phenotypical differences among individuals, heritability is 1.0. All variation in the population in terms of having or not having a fatal neurological condition known as Huntington's disease is entirely because of genetics. If you inherit a Huntington's gene from one parent, you will develop the condition, so the heritability of Huntington's is 1.0. Heritability of most human traits is typically found between these extremes, in the range of 0.30 to 0.60.

Heritability is a concept that is frequently misunderstood. Heritability always refers to populations, not to individuals. Saying that a trait such as shyness is 40% heritable does not say that 40% of one individual's shyness is produced by genes and the other 60% by the environment. Instead, a 0.40 heritability ratio suggests that the variations in shyness we see across the population (some people are shy and some people are not) are the result of both genetic and environmental factors (see ● Figure 3.11).

Heritability cannot be assessed without taking the environment into account, which is another source of potential confusion. If the environment is held constant (everybody is treated the same way), the heritability of a trait will look high. For example, if you plant seeds in trays with identical nutrients, water, and sunlight, the height of the resulting plants will

concordance rates The statistical probability that a trait in one person will be shared by another; usually discussed in relation to identical and fraternal twins.
heritability The statistical likelihood that variations observed in a population are because of genetics.

Heritability of Some Human Conditions. Heritability rates tell us how much of the variability seen in a population can be because of genetics. According to these data, we can say that genes have a greater influence on autism spectrum disorder than on reading disabilities. *Source:* Adapted from "Toward Behavioral Genomics," by P. McGuffin, B. Riley, & R. Plomin, 2001, *Science, 291*(5507), pp. 1232–1249. doi:10.1126/science.1057264.

largely come from their genetic differences. In variable environments, heritability is lower. If you plant seeds in trays receiving different amounts of nutrients, water, and sunlight, the height of the resulting plants will appear to be less influenced by genetics. If you studied the heritability of human intelligence in participants living in extremely wealthy circumstances, genetic influences would be exaggerated, just as they are when you hold the nutrients, water, and sunlight constant for your plants. Researchers assessing heritability of human traits attempt to do so within a "typical" range of environments.

Because of these concerns about the influence of environment on heritability, some researchers question the use of the type of adoption studies mentioned previously for assessing the relative influences of genetics and environment on development. These studies compare adopted children to their biological and adoptive parents in an effort to assess the relative impact of heritability. Like our plants with constant amounts of nutrients, water, and sunlight, adoptive families share many common features as a result of the screening process they go through before adopting. Consequently, adoptive parents rarely represent as much diversity as the group of biological parents whose children they adopt. If all adoptive families provide a consistent environment, this factor would inflate the apparent heritability of characteristics examined in the adopted children.

The environments provided by adoptive parents are more similar to one another than to the environments provided by biological parents. This environmental similarity can exaggerate genetic influences, a result that must be taken into account when investigating heritability using adopted children.

Psychology as a Hub Science
The Need to Understand Risk Taking

A better understanding of risk taking provides important insights for many fields, including public health, law enforcement, economics, and education.

Risk taking is an example of a behavior that demonstrates an interaction between genetic and environmental factors. Risk-taking behavior can lead to a number of outcomes that affect society negatively, including risky financial investments, unprotected sex, accidents, violence, substance abuse, gambling, and victimization.

Researchers have reported that risk taking is significantly heritable (Anokhin, Golosheykin, Grant, & Heath, 2009). However, not only does risk taking vary across the life span (adolescents are notoriously riskier than adults) and between genders (males take more risks than females), but factors such as whether you are a parent, whether you expect to be a parent, your birth order (lastborns are more risky), and how long you expect to live can influence risk-taking behavior (Wang, Kruger, & Wilke, 2009). To give you an idea about how complex risk taking can be, consider the following: In 12-year-olds, heritability in both males and females is modest but significant (28% for males and 17% for females), but at the age of 14, heritability rises to 55% in males and becomes nonsignificant for females (Anokhin et al., 2009). Again, when we're discussing heritability, we're describing the role of genetics in the variations we see across a population. So in 14-year-old males, genetics account for 55% of the variations (high to low) we see in risk taking.

Risk taking is not the type of behavior that lends itself to simple explanations. The genetic perspective featured in this chapter provides considerable insight, but if professionals in the fields of public health and education want to understand the effects of risk taking on rates of unprotected sex or alcohol abuse, for example, a comprehensive exploration of underlying developmental, cognitive, social, and clinical factors will be needed. ●

Risk taking is a complex behavior that demonstrates interactions between genetics and the environment that change over the life span. Psychologists can contribute to public health, medicine, law, and education by providing more insight into this type of behavior.

Kristin Saling

Summary 3.1 Major Concepts in Genetics

Concept	Definition	Example
Genotype	An individual's genetic makeup	A person might have a gene for straight hair and a gene for curly hair.
Phenotype	An individual's observable trait	A person has green eyes.
Gene	A sequence of DNA in a specific location on a chromosome that contains the instructions for making a protein	The serotonin transporter gene is located on chromosome 17.
Gene expression	Information from a gene is used to produce a protein	Maternal diet in mice can affect the expression of the Agouti gene.
Allele	One of two or more possible variations of a gene	A small number of *BRCA1* alleles are associated with cancer risk.
Homozygous	Having two of the same alleles	A person has the SS or the LL form of the serotonin transporter gene.
Heterozygous	Having two different alleles	A person has the SL form of the serotonin transporter gene.
Dominant	An allele that is expressed regardless of whether it is homozygous or heterozygous	The allele for curly hair is dominant.
Recessive	An allele that is expressed only when it is homozygous	The allele for straight hair is recessive.

Credits: Top Row. ISM/Phototake. Second Row. Richard A. Sturm, IMB, University of Queensland. Third Row: Epigenetic differences arise during the lifetime of monozygotic twins, by Mario Fraga et al., in *Proceedings of the National Academy of Sciences* 2005 Jul 102 (30) 10407-8, Fig. 3. 2005 National Academy of Sciences, U.S.A. Fourth Row: Courtesy Randy L. Jirtle, Ph.D. Fifth Row: Featureflash/Shutterstock.com. Sixth Row: © Cengage Learning® Bottom Row. Huntstock.com/Shutterstock.com.

How Does Evolution Occur?

The human genome is the product of millions of years of **evolution**, defined by biologists as descent with modification from a common ancestor. The study of evolution allows us to trace the family tree of living things.

In his book *The Origin of Species,* Charles Darwin proposed that species evolve or change from one form to the next in an orderly manner (Darwin, 1859). Darwin was well aware of the procedures used by farmers to develop animals and plants with desirable traits by mating particular individuals. A farmer's goal to raise the strongest oxen for pulling a plow might be accomplished by breeding the strongest available oxen to each other. In these cases, the farmer is making the determination of which individuals have the opportunity to produce offspring. Darwin suggested that instead of a farmer choosing which animals would breed and pass their genes along, the pressures of survival and reproduction in the wild would make the choice, a process he named **natural selection**. Organisms that survive long enough to reproduce would pass their traits to the next generation. Organisms that did not reproduce would not have the opportunity to pass their traits to future generations. As geneticists often remind us, we have no infertile ancestors.

In the more than 150 years since *The Origin of Species* was first published, our understanding of genetics and the fossil record has expanded exponentially, lending substantial further support for Darwin's views. Surprisingly, Darwin was able to derive his theory without the benefit of a basic understanding of genetics. He was unable to account for the variations he observed in a particular trait. That understanding was provided by Gregor Mendel (1822–1884), who discovered ways to outline and predict the inheritance of particular traits, like the color of flowers, in his research on pea plants (Mendel, 1865). Mendel, in turn, was working without our modern understanding of genes and chromosomes. Combining current understanding of genetics with the natural selection processes proposed by Darwin provides scientists with powerful hypotheses about the progression of species over time.

Charles Darwin's theory of evolution described how species change in an orderly manner.

Mechanisms of Evolution

In addition to the process of natural selection described by Darwin, evolution can result from mutation, migration, and genetic drift.

Mutations are errors that occur when DNA is replicated. The average human baby is born with about 130 new mutations, but most have no effect (Zimmer, 2009). Mutant alleles that provide some advantage often spread through the population, but most mutant alleles that result in a disadvantage disappear from future generations. **Migration** occurs when organisms move from one geographical location to the next. Moving to a new location can affect the

Darwin understood that breeders could influence the traits of offspring by mating particular individuals. He believed that natural selection operated according to the same principles. The pressures of survival and reproduction in the wild would take the role of the breeder—determining which traits are passed to the next generation.

evolution Descent with modification from a common ancestor.
natural selection The process by which survival and reproduction pressures act to change the frequency of alleles in subsequent generations.
mutation Errors that occur when DNA is replicated.
migration Movement to a new location.

akg-images

survival of individuals and the frequency of certain alleles in the population. Phenotypical traits that are advantageous in one environment might be less so in another. **Genetic drift** produces change from one generation to the next through chance or accident. Type B blood is virtually absent in contemporary populations of Native Americans, most likely due to chance (Halverson & Bolnick, 2008). The handful of ancestors crossing the Bering Strait 10,000 years ago appears to have included no individuals with the Type B allele. If the blood type alleles of the ancestors had been more representative of the entire human population, more of their descendants would have Type B blood.

We can demonstrate the effects of evolutionary processes—mutation, migration, genetic drift, and natural selection—on the history of one allele: the recessive allele for blond hair. The original appearance of the allele for blond hair was probably the result of a random mutation that occurred in northern Europe some 10,000 years ago (Frost, 2006). Migration, or rather the lack of it, might account for the relatively restricted area in northern Europe populated by blonds until fairly recent times. Geographical barriers of mountain and ocean contained the allele for centuries. Genetic drift, or changes in the genome because of chance or accident, undoubtedly reduced the global frequency of the blond allele between 1300 and 1700, as waves of bubonic plague decimated the European population, which at that time contained nearly everyone carrying the blond allele. If by chance every person carrying the blond allele had died from the plague before reproducing, the allele would have disappeared from the human genome (see ● Figure 3.12).

Has natural selection influenced the blond gene? Some anthropologists and biologists believe it has. When a person has a choice of mates of equal value, he or she will select the one that stands out from the crowd (Frost, 2006). Individuals with blond hair, which was different and rare, might have enjoyed more reproductive success than those with more common, darker hair colors. In Germany, with its high percentage of blonds, the trait of blondness is viewed differently than in other countries where blonds are relatively rare. German men report that they would marry a blond because she is likely to be a good homemaker but that they find women with dark hair more sexually attractive. Where blonds are rarer, these attitudes are usually reversed. This finding supports the idea that rare things tend to be viewed as valuable (in this case, attractive; Bem, 2001).

Any consideration of evolution must include the question of what natural selection selects. Natural selection favors the organism with the highest degree of **fitness**, defined as the ability of one genotype to reproduce relative to other genotypes. The concept of fitness includes survival to adulthood, ability to find a mate, and reproduction. Fitness is not some static characteristic, such as being strongest or fastest. Instead, fitness describes the interaction between characteristics and the environment in which they exist. A genotype that succeeds during the Ice Age may be at a significant disadvantage during periods of global warming. Animals in cold climates tend to have short legs and stocky bodies, which help retain heat, whereas animals in warm climates have long legs and slim bodies, which release heat. Again, we see the need to consider nature within the context of nurture.

Gregor Mendel (1822–1884) made important discoveries about inheritance at about the same time that Darwin was working on his theory of evolution, but neither scientist knew about genes and chromosomes. Modern geneticists combine this knowledge to form powerful hypotheses about the nature of living things.

genetic drift Change in a population's genes from one generation to the next because of chance or accident.
fitness The ability of one genotype to reproduce more successfully relative to other genotypes.

20TH CENTURY FOX / Album/Newscom

Marilyn Monroe and Jane Russell starred in the 1953 film *Gentlemen Prefer Blondes*. In some parts of the world, that appears to be true.

FIGURE 3.12

Spread of the Blond Allele. After the first appearance of the blond hair allele about 10,000 years ago as a result of a chance mutation, its frequency might have been affected by migration, genetic drift, and natural selection.

Over 80%　　　　　　　　　　Under 1%

70% 60% 50% 40% 30% 20% 10%

Percentage of light hair in Europe

© Cengage Learning®

Adaptation

Adaptation can refer to either the process or the result of change because of natural selection. In other words, a species can respond to an environmental change by adapting, and features of the new phenotype may be called adaptations. Adaptations can take many forms. Adaptations can be behaviors, such as jumping higher to better avoid a predator, or anatomical features, such as eyes that can see color. Adaptations do not necessarily produce perfection. Any adaptation that is good enough to contribute to the fitness of an organism will carry forward into future generations.

A classic example of rapid adaptation is the case of the English peppered moth *(Biston betularia)*. Before the Industrial Revolution, most peppered moths found in England were light gray, which allowed them to hide against the similar colors of tree bark. Darker moths occasionally appeared beginning around 1848, but because they were less capable of hiding from predators, they made up only about 1% of the population. With increasing industrialization, tree bark became frequently coated in soot. The once-camouflaged light gray moths became an easy target for predators against the darker background of the sooty trees. The darker moths rapidly became the norm, reaching frequencies of about 98%. As pollution came under better control, tree bark returned to its original light gray, and the lighter moths again became the norm. The peppered moth population successfully adapted to changing environmental circumstances, with color playing the role of an adaptation. The moths did not "decide" to change color. Natural selection, in the form of greater rates of reproductive success on the part of moths with a particular color, changed the frequencies of color alleles within the population.

Adaptations often appear to be compromises between costs and benefits. Adult human males have about 10 times as much testosterone as adult human females. Testosterone

adaptation A change because of natural selection.

Fitness varies across environments. Characteristics like long ears and long legs work in hot, desert climates, but short ears and legs conserve heat in colder climates.

The dark and light coloring of the peppered moth population in Great Britain changed in response to pollution from soot that collected on trees and changed again when pollution controls reduced the soot.

conveys a reproductive advantage, because men with higher testosterone report having more sex partners and earlier age at intercourse (Lassek & Gaulin, 2009). On the negative side, however, high testosterone levels might be responsible for lower immune system functioning, making the high testosterone males more vulnerable to disease (Muehlenbein & Bribiescas, 2005).

Adaptation is only one source of evolutionary change. Random events, such as the collision of meteors with the earth and resulting climate changes, are believed to have destroyed some types of life and provided broad opportunities for others. We are also limited in our ability to use adaptation to predict the future. The study of evolution is similar to the study of history. Although we gain insight into wars by studying the causes of World War II, we cannot use our knowledge to predict future wars with precision. We can be fairly certain that antibiotic-resistant bacteria, climate change, pollution, and reproductive technologies are probably changing the face of the human population as this text goes to press, but where all these changes will lead us remains unknown.

Evolution of the Human Brain

Our interest as psychologists is in the mind, and the mind and the behavior it produces originate in the structures and processes of the brain and nervous system. Nervous systems are fairly recent innovations that separate animals from plants (see Figure 3.13). We can place the origin of the earth at 4.5 billion years ago and the first single-celled life forms 1 billion years later, but the first neural nets appeared only 700 million years ago. In these primitive animals, the nerves in the abdomen were as likely to be important to behavior as the ones in the head. True brains residing in heads did not appear until animals formed skeletons, around 500 million years ago. The first decidedly human brain made its appearance only 7 million years ago, a small blip in the timeline of evolution (Calvin, 2004). The current model of the human brain has only been available for the last 100,000 to 200,000 years.

Anthropologists use the term *hominin* to describe species that walked on two feet, had large brains, and are assumed to be related to modern humans. Over the 7 million years of hominin evolution, brains grew rapidly, suggesting that improved intelligence was quickly translated into substantial advantages in survival. Early tool-using hominins, the australo-

Males with high testosterone report more chances to reproduce, but testosterone might also lower the response of the immune system. Extremely high levels of testosterone, because of the use of performance enhancing drugs, might be contributing to the early deaths of some professional wrestlers, like Curt Hennig (1958-2003).

pithecines, had brains that were about the same size as those of modern chimpanzees, or about 400 cm³. *Homo erectus,* a hominin living about 1.5 million years ago, had a brain of about 700 cm³, and the brains of modern humans, or *Homo sapiens,* are about 1,400 cm³.

Hominins were not the only creatures who evolved large brains and considerable intelligence. The other primates, elephants, and whales are not lacking in these areas. Although the challenges of finding food, avoiding predators, and navigating through territories require considerable intelligence, these ecological challenges are no match for the complexity of social life faced by the hominins. The major factor distinguishing human intelligence from intelligence of other species is the richness and complexity of the social behavior supported by the human brain. Managing the abilities to distinguish friend and foe; imitate the behavior of others; use language to communicate; recognize and anticipate the emotions, thoughts, and behavior of others; maintain relationships; and cooperate required the evolution of a special brain (Cacioppo, Berntson, et al., 2002; Hrdy, 2005; Roth & Dicke, 2005). Comparisons of the challenges faced by different species support a stronger role for social complexity than for ecological complexity in building bigger brains (Cacioppo & Decety, 2011a; Dunbar & Schultz, 2007).

18 hours ago — 3 hours 45 minutes ago — 2 hours 40 minutes ago — 2.5 minutes ago — 3 seconds ago

single-cell organism — jellyfish (first nervous systems) — lamprey (first brains) — first hominins — homo sapiens

Sebastian Kaulitzki/Shutterstock.com
pan demin/Shutterstock.com
Blickwinkel/Alamy
imageBROKER/Alamy
Natural History Museum, London/The Natural History Museum/Alamy

FIGURE 3.13

Timeline of Brain Evolution. If the 4.5 billion-year history of the earth were expressed as a 24-hour day:
- The first single-celled organisms would have emerged 18 hours ago.
- The first nervous systems would have emerged about 3 hours and 45 minutes ago.
- The first true brain would have emerged about 2 hours and 40 minutes ago.
- The first hominin brain would have emerged less than 2.5 minutes ago.
- The current version of the human brain would have emerged less than 3 seconds ago.

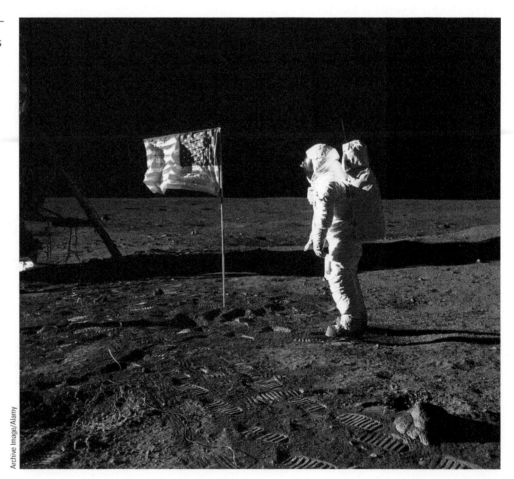

The Contemporary Human Brain

You surf the Internet, complete your calculus homework, and read this textbook with a brain that is essentially the same size as that of your early *Homo sapiens* ancestors.

Although we can understand the advantages to survival of big, intelligent brains, we do not know why advances such as agriculture, literacy, and urbanization have not been accompanied by additional increases in brain size. It is possible that we have reached equilibrium between our needs for intelligence and the costs of a big brain. Brains are expensive to run in terms of nutrients. Although the brain comprises only about 2% of the body's weight, it requires about 15% of the body's resources when at rest. In addition, brain size may be limited by the dimensions of the birth canal. Further change may not occur unless we experience a drop in the costs of big brains, a change in nutrients, or additional pressures for greater intelligence.

Although brain size has changed little during *Homo sapiens*'s time on the earth, the evolution of the human brain has not ended and average intelligence has not remained the same. Modern genetic techniques allow researchers to date changes in a particular gene. Genes involved with brain development appear to have changed as recently as 6,000 years ago (Evans et al., 2004, 2005). As we discuss in Chapter 10, IQ test scores have increased dramatically worldwide over the last 100 years (Flynn, 1999). If brain size has not changed for 100,000 years, let alone during the last 100 years, how can we account for the observed increase in intellectual performance? It is likely that environmental factors, including nutrition and education, might explain the improvement.

Early hominins, like the one on the left, had brains that were about the same size as those of chimpanzees. However, brain size quickly doubled by the time our species, the modern *Homo sapiens*, shown on the right, appeared sometime between 100,000 and 200,000 years ago. (From left to right: *australopithecus*, *Homo erectus*, and *Homo sapiens*.)

It is somewhat surprising that humans figured out how to go to the moon and back with brains that were the same size as those of *Homo sapiens* living 100,000 years ago.

Summary 3.2 Principles of Evolution

Concept	Definition	Example
Natural selection	A trait's frequency in a population is determined by the survival and reproductive success of the organisms with the trait	Faster rabbits are more likely to survive and reproduce than slow rabbits, leading to more fast rabbits in subsequent generations.
Mutation	Genetic changes that occur spontaneously or because of external factors like radiation	A mutation about 10,000 years ago led to the appearance of blond hair.
Migration	Populations move from one area to another	Moving from a cold to a warm climate might change the natural selection of traits in a species.
Genetic drift	Chance events influence the frequency of alleles	Huntington's disease is more common than usual among the Afrikaner population of South Africa, because a carrier of the disease was among the small number of Dutch immigrants who survived to reproduce.
Fitness	The ability of one genotype to reproduce relative to other genotypes in a particular environment	The recessive sickle-cell trait has low fitness in general because it can produce disease, but because the trait protects the individual from malaria, it has higher fitness in populations living where malaria is common.
Adaptation	Evolutionary changes whereby a population becomes better suited to its environment	The moth population changed from primarily light to dark colors when the trees they inhabited became darker because of pollution.

How Does Evolution Influence Behavior?

We mentioned in an earlier section that behavior can be adaptive. If an animal that is good at hiding in the bushes is more successful than others of its species in escaping predators, it is likely that the ability to hide will spread through subsequent generations of the population.

Behavior like hiding, however, is unlike the other adaptations we have discussed so far, such as the color of a moth or blond hair. Color is a physical characteristic, and it is a fairly simple matter to identify the genes associated with these phenotypes. Behavior as a phenotype is considerably more complex. Behavior is not an anatomical structure like a wing or an eye. Can we assume that behavior is shaped by the same evolutionary forces that affect physical traits? Darwin thought so. In *The Descent of Man and Selection in Relation to Sex,* Darwin writes:

> The difference in mind between man and the higher animals, great as it is, certainly is one of degree and not of kind. We have seen that the senses and intuitions, the various emotions and faculties, such as love, memory, attention, curiosity, imitation, reason, etc., of which man boasts, may be found in an incipient, or even sometimes in a well-developed condition in lower animals. (1871, p. 126)

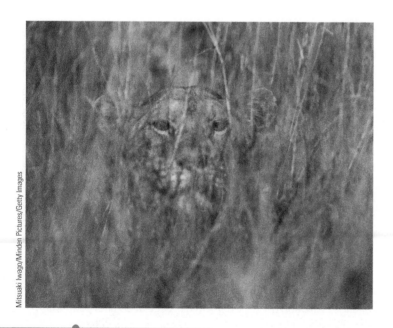

Mitsuaki Iwago/Minden Pictures/Getty Images

Physical features, like the coloring of an animal that allows it to hide, are well-understood types of adaptations. Evolutionary psychologists attempt to explain how behaviors can be adaptive too.

The Evolutionary Psychology Perspective

Among the psychological specialties we discussed in Chapter 1, biological and evolutionary psychology is the most relevant to our current discussion of the evolution of behavior. This approach to mind assumes that our current behavior exists in its present form because it provided some advantage in survival and reproduction to our ancestors (Cosmides & Tooby, 1997).

The biological and evolutionary psychology approach not only owes an obvious debt to Darwin but also is a direct descendant of the functionalism supported by William James. As the term *functionalism* implies, behavior is seen as promoting survival, as opposed to being random and pointless. The goal of evolutionary psychology is to explain how the patterns of behavior we share with other humans have been shaped by evolution.

Origins of Social Behavior

Reconstructing the evolution of the nervous system is difficult, and tracing the origins of individual behavior is even more challenging, but identifying the roots of social behavior might be the most difficult task. Occasionally, physical evidence has allowed scientists to determine whether dinosaur parents stayed around to look after their young, but such accounts leave much detail unexplored and unexplained.

Individuals belonging to social species congregate in a number of ways, from pairs to families to whole societies. Belonging to a social group provides the benefits of mutual protection and assistance. Predatory fish are most likely to hunt in the perimeter of a school of fish because it's easier to isolate prey there than in the middle of the school (Ioannou, Guttal, & Couzin, 2012). For much of human history, the greatest danger to one human has been other humans, and being on the social perimeter is risky for our species as well. Being social carries costs as well as benefits. Social animals face injury in competition for food and mates and are

Predator fish typically hunt on the perimeter of a fish ball, where it is easier to isolate and capture prey. Humans who are on the social perimeter may also be at risk from predation, but usually from their own kind.

exposed to contagious illnesses (Alexander, 1974), but the benefits of being social have clearly outweighed the costs for many species.

The assembly of social groups requires certain types of behaviors, which in turn involve nervous system structures and hormones that contribute to survival and reproductive success. We will see how these factors might have shaped the unique social lives of early humans.

Humans as a Social Species Despite our admiration of the rugged individualist, one of the outstanding features of humans is our rich and essential social nature, which we explore in more detail in Chapter 13. To understand the evolution of social behavior, we need to explore its advantages for survival and reproduction.

In typical environments, individual animals are likely to come into contact with others, leading to a variety of possible interactions and outcomes. In each case shown in Table 3.2, individuals either benefit or do not benefit from the interaction, ultimately affecting their survival and reproductive success. Both parties benefit equally if they cooperate. For example, two hunters can work together to bring down an animal that neither could successfully hunt alone. Sharing the resulting meat with the families of both hunters would contribute to their survival and reproductive success. Much social behavior probably

Although no cultures today exist exactly like the hunters–gatherers of the past, the Ache of Paraguay are often used as a model of how that life might have been. Here, the Ache cooperate with one another to fish. Social behaviors like cooperation might have allowed humans, who are not particularly strong individuals, to survive.

TABLE 3.2	Outcomes of Social Interactions	
	And the second organism:	
The first organism:	**Wins**	**Loses**
Wins	Cooperation	Selfishness
Loses	Altruism	Spite

© Cengage Learning®

Gherasim Rares/Shutterstock.com

Altruism, or the sacrifice of yourself for others, is more common among related individuals, but it also occurs when we are in close social contact with others. Honeybees sting to defend their hive, but in doing so, they end their own lives.

originated in these types of situations, in which the benefits of cooperation for an individual's survival and reproduction outweighed the disadvantages of cooperating.

Cooperation, however, is not the only way two individuals can interact. In selfish interactions, one person could steal food from another, allowing the thief's family to survive while the victim's family starves to death. In spiteful interactions, both participants lose. In some divorce proceedings, the partners are so determined to keep each other from maintaining resources that everything goes to the attorneys. In these cases, the reproductive success of both would be in danger. Finally, in **altruism**, one individual's self-sacrifice is designed to benefit another individual.

Altruism is widespread in the animal kingdom. Most of us have experienced a honeybee sting, which is suicidal behavior on the part of the bee in an effort to protect its hive (Wilson, 1975). Altruism can extend to entire social organizations, regardless of the degree of relatedness (Chicago Social Brain Network, 2011). Among emperor penguins (*Aptenodytes forsteri*), survival of the chicks in the hostile Antarctic cold depends not only on an individual parent but on the larger huddle formed by other parents.

As we will discuss in greater detail in Chapter 13, altruism is one of the most challenging social behaviors to explain in evolutionary terms. Darwin himself was puzzled by the apparent sacrifice of some individuals that led to the survival of the group. If altruism results in the destruction of the individual with altruistic genes, why doesn't this behavior disappear? To explain this phenomenon, we return to the concept of relatedness presented earlier in the chapter. Sacrificing your life to save a close blood relative might increase the likelihood that your alleles would be passed along to subsequent generations. Self-sacrifice in this case does not need to be a conscious decision. Any behavior that results in a greater frequency of the relevant genes in subsequent generations will become more common.

At this point, you are probably thinking that you often behave altruistically with people who are not related to you. You might have stayed to comfort a friend who just experienced a death in the family, even though you flunked your midterm the next day as a result. How can we explain these behaviors, which are known as **reciprocal altruism** (Trivers & Burt, 1999)? In cases of reciprocal altruism, it is customary to help another individual when you can reasonably expect the other individual to return the favor at some future date. Reciprocal altruism is likely to flourish when individuals are in regular contact with one another. Reciprocal altruism also requires the ability to recognize and remember cheaters.

For a gene to survive in subsequent generations, not only the individual carrying the gene but that individual's offspring must survive to reproduce. Because of our long period of dependency in childhood, along with our rather puny fighting equipment in the form of teeth or claws, we humans are especially in need of our social structures for survival. To the extent that genes build structures consistent with social tendencies, they are more likely to survive into future generations.

Sexual Selection

Sexual selection was Darwin's term for the development of traits that help an individual compete for mates (Darwin, 1871). To what extent is human behavior influenced by sexual selection?

Parental Investment Sexual selection is influenced by the different investments in parenting made by males and females (Emlen & Oring, 1977). In many species, including our own, the female bears most costs of reproduction, from the carrying of the developing organism until birth to the nurturance of the young until adulthood. As a result, human females face sharper limitations than human males on the number of children they can produce in a lifetime. If the goal is to pass your genes to subsequent generations and you are only going to produce one or two children, each child had better be as healthy and well nurtured as possible. The average number of children per woman worldwide dropped dramatically between 1950 and 2005 (United Nations, 2009). Between 1950 and 1955, the number of children per woman was 3.45 in the United States, 5.91 in India, and 6.11 in China. Between 2000 and 2005, those

altruism Behavior on behalf of another that fails to benefit or harms the individual performing it.
reciprocal altruism Help you provide for another person when you expect the person to return the favor in the future.
sexual selection The development of traits that help an individual compete for mates.

numbers dropped to 2.04, 3.11, and 1.77, respectively (see ● Figure 3.14).

Because males have a lower investment of time and resources in reproduction compared to females, it might seem that the best reproductive strategy for males would be promiscuity, but this is not usually the case. In species such as our own, with lengthy and complex development leading to adulthood, a male who abandons his offspring puts their survival at risk (Gibson, 2008). Even if a man fathers many children, his genes are less likely to make it into the next generation if most or all perish from lack of care or protection.

The mother can maximize her children's chances of survival by choosing a father who will not only pass along healthy genes but also participate in the raising of children. Women have the ability to make accurate predictions of a man's interest in children simply by looking at a photograph of his face (Roney, Hanson, Durante, & Maestripieri, 2006). Men with facial features correlated with high testosterone (strong brow ridge, square chin—a Patrick Dempsey look) are viewed as less likely to participate in childrearing than are men with facial features correlated with lower testosterone (a Justin Bieber look). These results suggest that women would be able to determine a man's potential as a father before reproductive investment occurs.

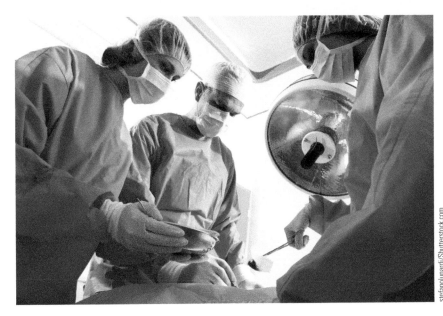

Cooperation allows humans to carry out complex behaviors that would be impossible for a single individual to perform successfully.

Traits Possibly Influenced by Sexual Selection Earlier in this chapter, we discussed how blond hair might have provided a reproductive advantage, because its relative novelty made it an attractive feature. What other types of human traits appear to fit Darwin's ideas about sexual selection?

Survival of emperor penguin chicks in the hostile cold of the Antarctic depends not just on the individual parent but also on the larger huddle formed by the other parents.

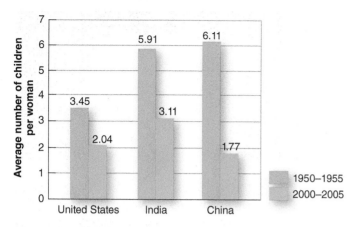

FIGURE 3.14

The Human Birthrate Is Dropping Rapidly. The average number of children per woman worldwide dropped dramatically between 1950 and 2005. *Source:* Adapted from "World Population Prospects: The 2008 Revision," by United Nations, June 2009, Retrieved from http://data.un.org/Data.aspx?d=PopDiv&f=variableID%3A54.

Sexual selection might occur in two ways. In intrasexual selection (*intra* means "within"), members of one sex compete with one another for access to the other sex. In some species, such as deer, males engage in fights that determine which males are able to mate and which are not. Features like large antlers that assist in winning a fight could become sexually selected. In intersexual selection (*inter* means "between"), characteristics of one sex that attract the other might become sexually selected. The male peacock's luxurious and costly tail appears to have developed for the sole purpose of attracting mates.

Evolutionary psychologists have argued that a number of human traits might have been subjected to sexual selection, including humor and vocabulary. According to this argument, human males use humor (Cherkas, Hochberg, MacGregor, Snieder, & Spector, 2000) and their vocabularies (Rosenberg & Tunney, 2008) to impress females with their intelligence because of intersexual selection. In romantic situations, males use more uncommon, fancy words than they do in other situations. We can also tell you about one behavior that does not successfully attract females—taking unnecessary risks (Wilke, Hutchinson, Todd, & Kruger, 2006). However, risky activities might have indirect positive outcomes for males. Dominant, successful males are likely to attract more females, and dominance among males is often decided on the basis of intrasexual competition in risky endeavors.

Culture

Not only are human societies directly influenced by our biological history, but they also bear the stamp of the inventions of the biological brain in the form of culture (see Chapter 1). Cultures provide practices, values, and goals that can be shared by groups of people. Human cultures arise from knowledge that is transmitted socially. Languages, morality, arts, laws, and customs make up a diverse and vibrant part of human social interactions.

Experiences shaped by culture, like other types of experience, interact with survival and reproductive pressures. How might cultural differences have affected our ancestors' survival? We can gain insight into our species' cultural history by observing contemporary preagricultural societies, such as the Waorani and Yanomamö of the Amazonian Basin. These groups are remarkably warlike. Fights between villages account for 30% of the deaths among Yanomamö males (Chagnon, 1988) and 54% of deaths among Waorani males (Beckerman et al., 2009). These observations suggest that aggression was probably an important part of our ancient past, but we cannot assume this behavior is strictly biological. Instead, cultural traditions in the two groups have led to different patterns of interactions between aggression and reproductive success. Aggressive Yanomamö men produce more children than less aggressive Yanomamö, but less aggressive Waorani men have more surviving offspring than aggressive Waorani (Beckerman et al., 2009). A simple cultural distinction—the Yanomamö practice of standing down for a period of time between raids, which is not a practice shared by the Waorani—appears to account for the differences observed in the impact of aggression on reproductive success.

Our social minds were shaped by the cultures of hunter–gatherer groups until the development of agriculture approximately 10,000 years ago. With improved control of the food supply, less geographical mobility, and larger communities, humans entered a new era of social interaction. Although we believe that many features found in modern human behavior, such as reciprocal altruism, originated in the hunter–gatherer society, further social adjustments were required as groups became larger and more complex.

Genghis Khan may have been the most prolific human male in history. His distinctive Y chromosome has been identified in 16 million living men, or 0.5% of the world's current total (Zerjal et al., 2003).

Women show the ability to predict a man's score on the Infant Interest Questionnaire, which might indicate how involved a father he would be, by detecting the influence of testosterone on his facial features. The face at the top indicates higher testosterone, while the one at the bottom indicates lower testosterone.

Agriculture, with its emphasis on land ownership, might have been the origin of patriarchal systems, in which men maintain control of resources, and inheritances follow the male line. Unlike hunter–gatherer societies, which are relatively egalitarian as far as the rights of men and women go, agricultural societies tilted the control of food and important resources in favor of men. Early industrialization merely built upon agricultural systems and, if possible, accentuated the power differential between males and females. Contemporary trends are again moving in a more egalitarian direction, with women in industrialized countries enjoying considerable financial independence and reproductive choice. These changes will no doubt have further effects on our social environment.

As societies became larger, humans took advantage of their large brains to devise new cultural systems to maintain group cohesion. Emerging societies shared many of the same types of internal conflict, so we typically find similar moral, religious, and legal systems across diverse cultures that attempt to control marriage, "character" issues such as honesty, and the transfer of precious resources.

With all the flaws of our groups, whether we're looking at families, communities, or nations, we retain a strong need to belong. As we will see on many occasions in this textbook, humans do not thrive in isolation. Our dependence on kinship, friendship, and group membership, honed over the course of 100,000 years or more of social living, continues to influence our behavior today.

The Waorani (left) and Yanomamö (right) of the Amazon basin share high rates of aggression yet experience different reproductive outcomes. Reproductive success is higher among the most aggressive Yanomamö and the least aggressive Waorani. This outcome is probably the result of the Yanomamö practice, not shared by the Waorani, of standing down between raids. This gives aggressive Yanomamö men chances to rest, heal, and reproduce that are not available to aggressive Waorani men.

Humans have developed a strong need to belong and often adopt traditions that enhance a sense of group membership.

Chuck Liddy/Raleigh News & Observer/MCT/Getty Images

Thinking Scientifically

Do Women Prefer Different Male Characteristics at Different Times in Their Menstrual Cycles?

THIS CHAPTER EMPHASIZES how the human mind has been shaped by its history. Because of the critical role our social behavior played in our species' survival over thousands of years, it should come as no surprise that the evolutionary perspective has so much to say about important human relationships. However, in its functionality, this evolutionary approach to choosing partners is rarely romantic.

As rational beings, we like to think that we choose our partners on the basis of compatibility, shared values, and common interests. While this may be true, evolutionary perspective suggests that women also prefer male features that reflect genetic quality. Because of the interest of evolutionary psychologists in reproductive success, most studies involve heterosexual at-

traction. The study of homosexual and bisexual attraction is relatively sparse and in need of additional emphasis.

Not only do women show preferences for certain male features, but some psychologists believe that preferences are most obvious when women are most fertile (Gildersleeve et al., 2013). This is known as the cycle shift hypothesis. According to this approach, on high-fertility days close to ovulation, women show a more pronounced preference for more masculine (high testosterone-related) facial features, variations in scent that are correlated with a male's degree of physical symmetry (also believed to be a sign of genetic health), and other characteristics associated with genetic health in males (see ● Figure 3.15).

In case you are thinking "I don't do that" or "the women I know wouldn't do that,"

keep in mind that evolutionary psychologists are careful to state that they do not know how ancient these tendencies are and whether they remain "fitness enhancing" in contemporary humans (Gildersleeve et al., 2013). Other psychologists are not so sure that a cycle shift effect occurs at all. Harris (2013) argued that the effects of cycle shifts on preference for masculine faces failed to replicate. A meta-analysis by Wood, Kressel, Joshi, and Louie (2014) also failed to support the cycle shift hypothesis. Instead, these researchers found that women, regardless of fertility status, showed a steady preference for masculine, dominant, symmetrical and healthy men.

These types of debate form an essential part of science, and further research should help clarify the issues. ●

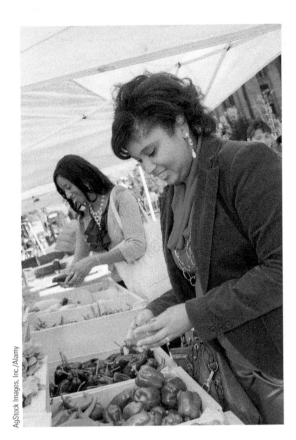

The development of agriculture 10,000 years ago changed the shape of human cultures.

AgStock Images, Inc./Alamy

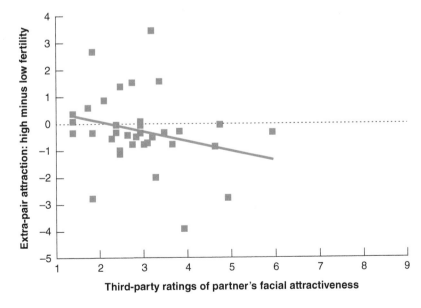

FIGURE 3.15

Evidence for the Cycle Shift Hypothesis. Consistent with the cycle shift hypothesis are findings that when the attractiveness of the face of a woman's partner is rated by others as low (closer to 1 on this scale), she is more likely to report attraction to men other than her partner (4 means far more than usual, while −4 is far less than usual) at periods of high as opposed to low fertility. Attraction to other men did not differ between high- and low-fertility periods in women with attractive partners (ratings closer to 9 on this scale). These results suggest that facial attractiveness, a sign of genetic health, may be more important to women when they are most fertile. *Source:* Adapted from Larson, Pillsworth, & Haselton (2012).

Interpersonal Relationships
The Evolutionary Perspective
Can We Use Odor to Select a Mate, Even Online?

A cluster of genes known as the major histocompatibility complex (MHC) appears to be subject to sexual selection (Wedekind & Füri, 1997). As described in this chapter, this type of sexual selection operates on traits in one sex that influence the choices by the other. A child with a heterozygous set of MHC genes is better prepared to battle infections than is a child with MHC genes that are similar to one another. As a result, our children are more likely to survive if we select a mate that has a different set of MHC genes than we do.

There is some evidence that too much MHC similarity affects not just our children but also our relationships. Garver-Apgar et al. (2006) reported that among romantic couples, increases in the number of MHC alleles shared by a couple reduced the woman's sexual responsivity to her partner and increased her number of extrapair sexual partners and her attraction to men other than her partner.

In a world before genetic testing, it appears that we were able to select partners with compatible MHC profiles on the basis of odor. Different configurations of the MHC genes produce distinctive body odors. When participants were asked to rate the pleasantness of the odors of T-shirts that had been worn by other people, they preferred smells associated with MHC genotypes that were different from their own (Wedekind & Füri, 1997).

Not only do we have relatively inexpensive genetic testing today, but we also have online dating and matchmaking. A company by the name of Instant Chemistry combines the two. In their For Matchmakers webpage (2014), the company explains how a dating service can "significantly increase the number of successful matches." A genetic test kit is sent to the matchmaker's clients, allowing MHC profiles to be added to the factors considered for recommending contact.

It is too soon to tell whether such endeavors will be successful in improving the relationships of modern people. The concept of being influenced by odors associated with a genetic profile, however, reminds us that not all of the attraction we experience toward others operates on the conscious level. ●

Participants in a study preferred the smell of T-shirts worn by people who have MHC genotypes different from their own. Historically, these smell preferences might have helped people select partners with whom they are most likely to have healthy children.

Boris Ryaposov/Shutterstock

Summary 3.3 Evolutionary Influences on Behavior

Concept	Definition	Example
Cooperation	Working together to benefit all parties involved	Hunters work together to kill an animal that an individual could not kill alone.
Altruism	Sacrificing your personal interests to benefit another	A young mother threw herself over her infant during a parking lot shootout. She died, but the infant survived.
Reciprocal altruism	Sacrificing when you expect the recipient might do the same for you at some future time	You share food with a hungry person thinking that someone might share with you later.
Sexual selection	The evolutionary pressure on traits that help individuals find mates	A woman may choose a man whose facial appearance is correlated with being a good father.

Credits: Top Row. stefanolunardi/Shutterstock.com. Second Row. Gherasim Rares/Shutterstock.com. Third Row: Stefan Christmann/Corbis. Bottom Row: Detail from F. Moore et al. Figure 1, "Composite male faces constructed to differ in levels of T and C, from the article "Evidence for the stress-linked immunocompetence handicap hypothesis in human male faces," Proc. R. Soc. B, March 7, 2011, by permission of the Royal Society.

KEY TERMS The Language of Psychological Science

Be sure you can define these terms and use them correctly.

adaptation, p. 89
allele, p. 74
altruism, p. 96
behavioral genetics, p. 81
concordance rates, p. 83
dominant, p. 74
epigenetics, p. 78
evolution, p. 87
fitness, p. 88

gene expression, p. 73
gene, p. 73
genetic drift, p. 88
genotype, p. 73
heritability, p. 83
heterozygous, p. 74
homozygous, p. 74
migration, p. 87
mutation, p. 87

natural selection, p. 87
nature, p. 73
nurture, p. 73
phenotype, p. 73
recessive, p. 74
reciprocal altruism, p. 96
relatedness, p. 75
sexual selection, p. 96

4 The Biological Mind
The Physical Basis of Behavior

THROUGHOUT HISTORY, HUMAN SURVIVAL HAS been threatened by the various bacteria and viruses that try to make us their home. The bacteria-driven Black Death decimated Europe between 1346 and 1400, killing an estimated 30% to 60% of the population (Austin Alchon, 2003). Smallpox, measles, and influenza carried by Europeans to the Western Hemisphere killed as many as 90% of native populations (Public Broadcasting Service, 2005). The "Spanish flu" of 1918, which is related to contemporary bird flu strains, killed between 50 million and 100 million people worldwide in about a year (Patterson & Pyle, 1991).

Although you might think surviving a pandemic is more a question of biology and medicine, behavior and mental processes have a considerable amount of influence on our abilities to fight bacteria and viruses (Cacioppo & Berntson, 2011). Again, zooming out to the human social environment and then zooming back in to a smaller scale gives us a complete and interesting picture.

A. Inden/Cusp/Corbis

Humans, who lack impressive teeth or claws, formed groups to enhance the odds of their survival. Anyone who was socially excluded from these groups experienced a more hostile environment. Social exclusion not only separated a person from the help of others in life-threatening situations, perhaps in fending off a predator, but worse, could lead to outright conflict with others, including combat. Under such hostile circumstances, socially excluded people faced a greater risk from bacterial infections than from viruses. Bacteria enter the body through cuts and scratches, whereas viruses are transmitted through body fluids (e.g., sneezing), so you are most likely to be exposed to them when you are in close contact with other people.

With that background in mind, look at the group of people in the image above. Do you think the woman on the left is feeling included or excluded? Surprisingly, whether we typically feel socially isolated or socially connected can have serious implications for our health (Cole, Hawkley, Arevalo, & Cacioppo, 2011). If this woman normally feels isolated and often left to fend for herself, she will, like her excluded ancestors, face a greater threat from bacteria than from viruses. Her brain will respond to her feelings of isolation by generating hormonal signals that will tell her immune system (shown in the larger image to the left) to gear up to protect her against bacteria.

◀ Perceived social isolation or connectedness can produce changes in the cells of our immune system.

Argosy Publishing, Inc.

In contrast, if she usually feels socially connected to others, her brain will initiate a cascade of hormonal signals that tell her immune cells to prepare to protect her against viruses. This is just one example of how the mind's perceptions of the social

105

Courtesy of Dr. Skirmantas Janusonis/University of California, Santa Barbara; photo by Roger Freberg

Human brains like this one, carefully held by one of your authors, weigh about 3 pounds and contain approximately 100 billion neurons. That's about the same number as the stars in our galaxy, the Milky Way.

Not only does biology influence behavior, but behavior (thinking about winning in this case) affects biology. Players and even fans of a winning team experience a temporary increase in testosterone, while players and fans of a losing team experience a temporary decrease in testosterone.

AP Images/Matt Slocum

environment—whether it is friendly or not, for instance—can affect biological processes that are important to health and survival.

In Chapter 3, we learned how the challenges of surviving and reproducing in particular physical and social environments could shape a species' biology and behavior. In turn, the resulting biological structures and processes of the mind exert profound influences on our physical and social environments. In this chapter, we will provide a foundation for understanding the biological bases of behavior and mental processes by exploring the structures of the nervous system and the ways that they function.

Learning Objectives

1. Describe the relevance of brain structures and processes for understanding mind and behavior.

2. Differentiate the major branches of the nervous system, explaining the core biological function of each branch.

3. Associate key structures in, and regions of, the brain and peripheral nervous system with important aspects of physical and psychological functioning.

4. Explain the process by which hormones influence psychological experience and behavior.

5. Explain the process by which neurons communicate with one another, allowing the nervous system to integrate complex information.

6. Differentiate the roles played by major neurotransmitters in supporting physical functioning and psychological experience.

What Is Biological Psychology?

Many of us find the concept that our "minds" are somehow a result of the activity of nerve cells a bit unsettling. How could our feelings, thoughts, and memories be caused by a bunch of cells? Shouldn't there be more to who we are than something so physical? Such ideas led thinkers like Renaissance philosopher René Descartes to propose a philosophy of dualism, which suggests that our mind is somehow different and separate from our physical being. If you are more comfortable with thinking about mind this way, go ahead, as long as you recognize that the field of biological psychology, and the neurosciences in general, embraces the competing philosophy of monism. According to the monistic approach, the mind is what the brain does.

Biological psychology, also known as behavioral neuroscience, is a rich, interdisciplinary field of study that combines the methods and theories of psychology with those of biology, physiology, biochemistry, the neurosciences, and related fields. While investigating a particular behavior, the biological psychologist focuses on links between observed behavior and genetic factors, biochemical factors, and the activity level and structural characteristics of the nervous system. These links do not travel in one direction only, such as from biological factors to behavior, but are more accurately viewed as reciprocal. For example, we know that if you administer extra testosterone to human males, raising their testosterone so that it is above a normal level, they are likely to behave more aggressively (Pope, Kouri, & Hudson, 2000). In this case, biology (raising testosterone levels) is influencing behavior (aggression). However, we also know that watching his favorite sports team lose lowers a man's testosterone level (Bernhardt, Dabbs, Fielden, & Lutter, 1998). Here, we see the influence of behavior (supporting a particular team and watching the team lose) on biology (testosterone level).

Early Attempts to Understand Biological Psychology

Advances in the methods we use to observe the structure and function of the nervous system have driven the history of biological psychology. The discovery of contemporary methods, such as the recording and imaging of brain activity, opened new areas of inquiry to biological psychologists. Before these methods were available, however, most of our knowledge of the nervous system resulted from clinical observations of injured or mentally ill individuals or from autopsy, the examination of bodies after death. When used with other contemporary methods, clinical observation and autopsy are quite accurate, but early thinkers lacking contemporary methods often struggled in their attempts to understand the physical basis of mind. They understood many things correctly while making some notable errors. Aristotle (384-322 BCE), who was accurate on many issues, mistakenly believed that the heart, not the brain, was the source of mental activity.

An interesting historical mistake was phrenology. Toward the end of the 18th century, phrenologists proposed that the pattern of bumps on an individual's skull correlated with that person's personality traits and abilities (Simpson, 2005). The brain supposedly worked like a muscle, getting larger through use, which led frequently used areas of the brain to grow so much that the skull above these areas would bulge. Phrenologists "read" a person's character by locating the bumps on a person's head and identifying the personality traits below each bump according to a map. None of these ideas were close to being accurate. Although the phrenologists were wrong about the significance of bumps on the skull and the effects of activity on the structure of the brain, they did reach one correct conclusion: Their notion that some behavioral functions are localized to certain areas of the brain is one we share today.

Contemporary Approaches in Biological Psychology

More modern perspectives of the nervous system emerged from the work of scientists like Nobel Prize–winning anatomist Santiago Ramón y Cajal (1852–1934) and neurologist John Hughlings Jackson (1835–1911). Ramón y Cajal's work helped us understand the microscopic level of the nervous system, while Jackson's conclusions illuminate the relationships among the larger structures of the brain.

Surprisingly, it took scientists a long time to accept the idea that the nervous system was made up of separate cells just like other tissues in the body. Even in the late 19th century, scientists like Camillo Golgi still argued that the nervous system was a single continuous network. Ironically, Ramón y Cajal used a microscopic stain invented by Golgi to prove him wrong. Using Golgi's stain, Ramón y Cajal was able to demonstrate conclusively that the nervous system was made up of separate cells, an idea that became known as the neuron doctrine. Both men shared the 1906 Nobel Prize in Physiology or Medicine.

Based on observations of his patients with seizure disorders, Jackson proposed that the nervous system is organized as a hierarchy, with progressively more complicated behaviors being managed by more recently evolved and complex structures (Jackson, 1884). We can see Jackson's hierarchy at work when we observe people drinking alcohol. Alcohol specifically decreases the activity of parts of the brain involved with judgment and decision making. When a person has had too much to drink, the more complex social controls (e.g., knowing how close you should stand to a stranger) normally provided by higher level areas of the brain are diminished. Without the influence of these controls, people start doing things that they would not do while sober. This change in behavior reflects the now-unrestrained influence of the more primitive parts of the brain involved with behaviors such as aggression and sexuality. You might, for example, pick a fight with someone when you normally think fighting is wrong.

Autopsy has been used since 3000 BCE, and it remains a useful source of information, especially in forensics. Dr. Bill Bass, a forensic anthropologist, studies donated bodies as they decompose at the "Body Farm" at the University of Tennessee, Knoxville. The knowledge gained from these investigations makes it possible to determine time of death at crime scenes.

Phrenologists believed that "reading" the bumps on a person's head, using a bust like this as a reference, could tell them about a person's character.

The aggression and sexuality were there all along, but the normal activity of the higher levels of the nervous system usually restricted their expression to more appropriate circumstances (Siever, 2008).

The 20th century saw a burst of knowledge about the nervous system, culminating in the 1990s being designated by the U.S. Congress as the decade of the brain. Our understanding of the correlations between brain and behavior leaped forward with continuing improvements in research methods, including many of those found in Table 4.1. In particular, methods that allow scientists to observe the activity of the living brain, including positron emission tomography (PET) and functional magnetic resonance imaging (fMRI), began to answer questions that were impossible to study previously. For example, we can differentiate between musicians who are improvising jazz, who show activity in parts of the brain normally associated with language, and musicians playing memorized pieces, who do not show activity in these areas (Donnay, Rankin, Lopez-Gonzalez, Jiradejvong, & Limb, 2014). In another application of imaging technologies, researchers found that people engaging in risky activities do so because the parts of the brain normally associated with self-control are relatively inactive at the time (Helfinstein et al., 2014).

Moving into the 21st century, the ranks of neuroscientists continue to grow, from 500 members of the Society for Neuroscience in 1969 to more than 40,000 members today (Society for Neuroscience, 2014). We can look forward to continued innovations in both technology and our knowledge about the biological basis of mind.

 Thinking **Scientifically**

When Does Reductionism Work? When Does It Fail?

REDUCTIONISM IN SCIENCE is defined as the explanation of complex things as sums of simpler things. Taking a rather extreme reductionist approach, science fiction often features scenes in which an android reminds a human that they're not so different after all—the brain is just a computer made up of chemicals, nothing more, nothing less.

In some ways, all modern science is reductionist. Scientists assume that whether you are studying particle physics or human behavior, a single set of fundamental laws explains much of what we observe. We do not need new sets of rules for the features of table salt (sodium chloride) in each context in which it appears. Regardless of whether the chemical is participating in neural signaling, flavoring our food, contributing to high blood pressure, or making us

float more easily when we swim in the ocean, the fundamental principle is the same: Salt is salt.

The scientific search for fundamental principles has been fruitful, but it does have limitations. Although we can learn a lot by breaking apart complex things to study simple things, in Chapter 1 we saw some risks to this approach in the debates between structuralists and Gestalt psychologists. Fish swim in schools, geese and ducks fly in a V formation, ants and bees swarm, cattle form herds, and humans form societies. We could never understand these complex phenomena by studying the behavior of an individual member of the group. Nobel laureate physicist P. W. Anderson reminded scientists that large collections of simple things do not always behave in the same way that simple things

behave in isolation. He wrote that "at each stage (of complexity) entirely new laws, concepts, and generalizations are necessary, requiring inspiration and creativity to just as great a degree as in the previous one. Psychology is not applied biology, nor is biology applied chemistry" (Anderson, 1972, p. 393).

This chapter on the biological foundations of behavior and mental processes relies extensively on reductionist thinking. As you work through the chapter, however, it is important to keep Anderson's cautions in mind. Some aspects of behavior will continue to be governed by rules that explain the actions of simple things, while others will require the introduction of rules better suited to more complex combinations and interactions of simple things. ●

How Is the Nervous System Organized?

To examine the relationships between nervous system and behavior, we will first zoom out to examine the larger view of the structures making up the nervous system, and then we'll zoom in later in the chapter to look at the microscopic world of the nerve cells, or neurons. Talking about the connections between structures of the nervous system and behavior requires a quick word of caution. As mentioned in Chapter 3, saying that we have a "gene for" a behavior is overly simplistic and inaccurate. Saying we have a "center for" a behavior in the brain is equally misleading. Although we can identify structures that participate in certain behaviors, the biology of mind involves intricate and overlapping patterns of activity involving networks made up of many richly connected structures.

The nervous system can be divided into two major components: the central and the peripheral nervous systems (see ● Figure 4.1). The **central nervous system (CNS)** consists of the brain and the **spinal cord**, which extends from the brain down the back of the body. Although we often see the brain and spinal cord referred to as separate structures, they form one continuous unit of tissue. Nerves branch outward from the CNS to all areas of the body—the lungs, heart, and other organs; the eyes and ears; and the arms, legs, fingers, and toes. As soon as a nerve branches outward from the CNS, it is considered part of the **peripheral nervous system (PNS)**. Another way to know you have left the CNS for the PNS is to look for the protection of bone. Nerves of the CNS are encased in bone, but those of the PNS are not.

central nervous system (CNS) The brain and spinal cord.
spinal cord A long cylinder of neural tissue extending from the medulla of the brain down to the middle of the back; part of the central nervous system.
peripheral nervous system (PNS) The nerves exiting the central nervous system that carry sensory and motor information to and from the rest of the body.

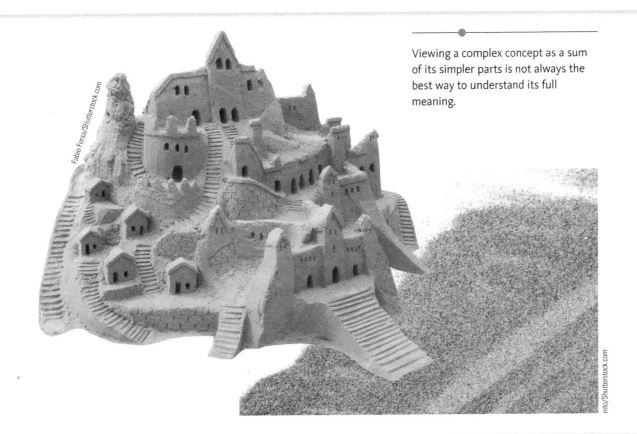

Fabio Fersa/Shutterstock.com

nito/Shutterstock.com

Viewing a complex concept as a sum of its simpler parts is not always the best way to understand its full meaning.

TABLE
4.1   Research Methods in Biological Psychology

Research method	Description	What questions can we answer?
Skin conductance response (formerly galvanic skin response)	Measurement of electricity passed between two surface electrodes placed on the skin of the hand or finger	What is a person's state of arousal?
Electroencephalogram (EEG)	Measurement of the brain's electrical activity using electrodes placed on the scalp	What is a person's state of arousal?
Event-related potential (ERP)	Measurement formed by averaging EEG responses to a stimulus, such as a light or tone	Did the person perceive the stimulus?
Single cell recording	Measurement of a single neuron's activity obtained through a surgically implanted electrode	What types of stimulation make this neuron respond?
Magnetoencephalography	Recording of the tiny amounts of magnetic output of the brain	What parts of the brain react to this stimulus?
Positron emission tomography (PET)	Measurement that uses the accumulation of radioactively tagged glucose or oxygen to identify activity levels in parts of the brain	What parts of the brain are active during a particular task?
Functional magnetic resonance imaging (fMRI)	Identification of active parts of the brain using magnetism to track the flow of oxygen	What parts of the brain are active during a particular task?
Electrical stimulation	Application of small amounts of electricity through a surgically implanted electrode	What behaviors occur if we stimulate this part of the brain?
Transcranial magnetic stimulation	Application of magnetic fields to the brain through an instrument held near the scalp	What behavioral changes occur when magnetism is applied to the brain?
Lesions	Naturally occurring or deliberate damage to the brain	What behavioral changes are correlated with brain damage?

© Cengage Learning®

What Are the Structures and Functions of the Central Nervous System?

The brain and spinal cord are among the best protected parts of your body, which is not surprising given their importance for your survival. Surrounding the brain and spinal cord are the heavy bones of the skull and spinal vertebrae. Under these bones, membranes known as meninges provide further protection. Infections of these membranes result in potentially life-threatening cases of meningitis, for which you were likely vaccinated before beginning your college studies.

The brain and spinal cord are further protected by a clear, plasmalike fluid known as cerebrospinal fluid (CSF). CSF seeps out of the lining of hollow spaces in the brain known as the ventricles (see ● Figure 4.2). Near the base of the skull, openings enable CSF to flow from the ventricles into a space within the meninges, allowing the fluid to flow around the outer surfaces of the brain and spinal cord. Without the cushioning provided by the CSF, a blow to the head would cause considerable damage to the brain. In addition, the CSF "floats" the brain within the skull, preventing false signals that might result from the weight of some neurons pressing down on others.

FIGURE 4.1

THE NERVOUS SYSTEM

Central nervous system (CNS)
— Brain
— Spinal cord

Peripheral nervous system (PNS)

Somatic nervous system

Autonomic nervous system

Sympathetic nervous system

Parasympathetic nervous system

© Argosy Publishing, Inc.

The Organization of the Nervous System. The nervous system has two major divisions: the central nervous system (CNS), containing the brain and spinal cord, and the peripheral nervous system (PNS), containing all nerves that exit the brain and spinal cord. The CNS is protected by bone, but the PNS is not.

To diagnose some medical conditions, it is helpful to obtain a sample of CSF. This is done through a spinal tap, in which a physician removes some of the CSF circulating through the meninges surrounding the spinal cord. CSF is constantly produced, so blockages in its circulation cause the fluid to build up. The result is hydrocephalus, which means "water on the brain."

The Spinal Cord, Brainstem, and Cerebellum

The spinal cord extends from the lowest part of the brain down into the middle of your back (see ● Figure 4.3). If you feel the back of your skull where it curves to meet your spine, your fingers will be just below the junction of the spinal cord and the lowest structure of the brain. Although the spinal cord is only 2% of the weight of the CNS, its functions are vital, as evidenced by the challenges faced by people with spinal damage. The spinal cord serves as a major conduit for information flowing to and from the brain along large bundles of nerve fibers, carrying sensory information from the body and delivering commands. Thirty-one pairs of spinal nerves exit the spinal cord to serve the body. These nerves exit and enter the spinal cord between segments of the bony vertebrae in your spine.

A number of important reflexes are initiated by the spinal cord without the assistance from the brain. One type of spinal reflex makes you pull your body away from any source of pain. It doesn't take long for your hand to fly up when you've touched something hot on the

Jeff Morgan 16/Alamy

stove. When tapping your knee with a hammer during a routine physical, your doctor is checking another type of spinal reflex, the knee-jerk reflex (see ● Figure 4.4). This reflex is interesting to your doctor, because certain medical conditions, such as diabetes, affect the strength of the reflex. Still other spinal reflexes help us stand and walk.

Spinal reflexes give us an opportunity to look at the functions of three types of nerve cells, or neurons. Sensory neurons carry information from the external environment or from the body back to the CNS. In the knee-jerk reflex, sensory neurons tell the spinal cord that a muscle has been stretched by the tap of the hammer. Motor neurons carry commands from the CNS back to the muscles and glands of the body. In response to information about the stretched muscle, the spinal cord sends a message through motor neurons back to your leg, telling the muscle to contract to counteract the stretch. You know what happens next—your foot kicks as the muscles contract. Neurons that have neither sensory nor motor functions are called interneurons. *Inter* in this case means "between," because many interneurons form bridges between sensory and motor neurons. The knee-jerk reflex forms a simple arc between a sensory neuron and a motor neuron and does not require interneurons. However, interneurons play important roles in other reflexes and throughout the nervous system.

Moving up from the spinal cord brings us to the brainstem. Early in prenatal development, the emerging brain forms three bulges. The most forward of these bulges develops into the two large cerebral hemispheres, which we discuss in a later section. The remaining two bulges form the **brainstem**. If you examine ● Figure 4.5, you can see that the brainstem looks like the stem of a flower, supporting the larger blossom of the cerebral hemispheres. Directly branching from the brainstem are the cranial nerves, which perform the same functions for the head and neck areas that the spinal nerves manage for the remainder of the body. We will discuss the cranial nerves in more depth in a later section on the PNS.

The spinal cord merges with our first brainstem structure, the **medulla**. Like the spinal cord, the medulla contains large bundles of nerve fibers traveling to and from higher levels of the brain. Because the medulla manages many essential functions, such as heart rate and

Some cases of potentially fatal meningitis, or infection of the membranes covering the brain, can be prevented by vaccinations.

brainstem The part of the brain containing the midbrain, pons, and medulla.
medulla The brainstem structure that lies just above the spinal cord.

FIGURE 4.2

The Ventricles of the Brain. The ventricles of the brain are filled with circulating cerebrospinal fluid (CSF), which floats and cushions the brain.

Lateral ventricles

Third ventricle

Fourth ventricle

© Argosy Publishing, Inc.

French neurologists were shocked when they saw brain images taken of a middle-age man who sought treatment for some minor weakness in one leg. His lateral ventricles (LV) take up most of the volume in his skull, and the brain appears as a thin layer on the outside. The patient reported that he had been treated for hydrocephalus from infancy until the age of 14. The patient was a married father of two who worked as a civil servant with a low but still normal IQ of 75.

The Lancet, Volume 370, Issue 9583, Page 262, 21 July 2007

blood pressure, damage to this structure usually results in quick death.

Just above the medulla is the **pons**, which contains structures involved with the management of sleep, arousal, and facial expressions. *Pons* means "bridge" in Latin. The pons not only serves as a bridge between higher and lower portions of the brain but also connects the **cerebellum** to the rest of the brain. Essential for maintaining balance and motor coordination, the cerebellum is one of the first structures in the brain to be affected by alcohol. As a result, alcohol consumption impairs balance (walking a straight line) and motor coordination (touching your finger to the tip of your nose

pons A part of the brainstem located between the medulla and the midbrain.
cerebellum A structure attached to the brainstem that participates in skilled movement and, in humans, complex cognitive processing.

FIGURE 4.3

The Spinal Cord and the Spinal Nerves. Thirty-one pairs of spinal nerves exit between the bones of the vertebrae to bring sensory information back to the central nervous system and to carry motor commands to muscles.

Gray matter (cell bodies)
White matter (nerve fiber pathways)
Spinal nerve
Vertebra

with your eyes closed). Most sobriety tests are the same tests a neurologist would use to assess the function of the cerebellum.

Surprisingly, the cerebellum contains more nerve cells than the rest of the brain combined. Not only does the cerebellum contain huge numbers of neurons, but it is also richly connected with the rest of the CNS. Because of the cerebellum's position on the brainstem, which is relatively ancient in terms of evolution compared to the cerebral hemispheres, neuroscientists initially underestimated its importance to human behavior. They believed that the cerebellum's activities were restricted to managing the timing and strength of movements. While we still do not know exactly what the cerebellum does, today's neuroscientists believe that it has a broader role in making mental and motor skills more automatic. Damage to the human cerebellum produces subtle deficits in language, cognition, and perception. In autism spectrum disorder, a condition that affects language, sensory, and social behaviors, abnormalities in the cerebellum are common (Courchesne, 1997).

Opiate painkillers like morphine and OxyContin produce some of their analgesic effects by interacting with opioid receptors in the periaqueductal gray.

midbrain The part of the brainstem that lies between the pons and the cerebral hemispheres.

The **midbrain** sits above the pons and contains a number of structures involved in sensory reflexes, movement, and pain. For example, the periaqueductal gray of the midbrain plays

Connecting to Research

The Discovery of Mirror Neurons

IN THE EARLY 1990s, Giacomo Rizzolatti and a team of Italian scientists were busy studying the brain correlates of movement when they noticed something odd (Di Pellegrino, Fadiga, Fogassi, Gallese, & Rizzolatti, 1992). They had observed that certain neurons in a part of a monkey's brain became especially active when the monkey performed certain actions, like reaching for a piece of banana or a peanut. When an experimenter picked up a piece of food to place it within the monkey's reach, some of the same neurons began to fire. Suspecting something important was behind these observations, the researchers began to study these "mirror neurons" more carefully.

The Question: Can we identify neurons that respond to a particular action, regardless of who performs the action?

METHODS

A monkey (*Macaca nemestrina*) served as the research subject. The technique used in this experiment was single cell recording (see Table 4.1), in which surgically inserted microelectrodes allowed the activity of individual cells to be measured. A total of 184 neurons were tested by observing their activity during the monkey's movements and during movements performed by an experimenter. The experiments were videotaped. The experimenters also recorded the muscle movements in the monkey's hand and arm.

RESULTS

Of the observed neurons, 39 appeared to be most active when either the experimenter or the monkey performed the same action. The cells' responses were specific. For example, a cell that became active when the experimenter grasped a piece of food would also become active when the monkey grasped the food but not when the monkey put food in its mouth. A cell that activated when the experimenter put food in his mouth also activated when the monkey put food in its mouth but not when the monkey grasped the food.

CONCLUSIONS

The scientists believed they had discovered neurons that provided a mechanism for understanding the actions of others. These cells are now called mirror neurons (Caggiano et al., 2011). Although the existence of mirror neurons in humans is still controversial, this discovery stimulated new hypotheses regarding imitation, autism spectrum disorder, and empathy. ●

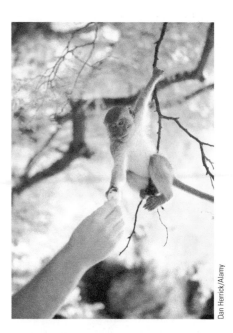

Dan Herrick/Alamy

When a monkey reaches for a banana or sees someone else reach for the fruit, some of the same neurons in the brain become active. Rizzolatti and his colleagues named these mirror neurons.

an important role in the body's management of pain because it contains receptors for endorphins, our natural opioids, which we discuss further later in this chapter. When endorphins are present in the periaqueductal gray, they reduce the perception of pain by decreasing the strength of pain messages traveling up the spinal cord to higher levels of the brain.

Running the length of the brainstem's core from the upper medulla into the midbrain is the **reticular formation**, which participates in the control of mood, arousal, and sleep, as discussed further in Chapter 6. The neurons in these areas are the major sources of two important chemical messengers in the brain, serotonin and norepinephrine. As a result of the actions of the reticular formation, we are able to respond differently to the world as a function of our state of arousal. The same sound that grabs your attention in a quiet library will be ignored while you are sound asleep.

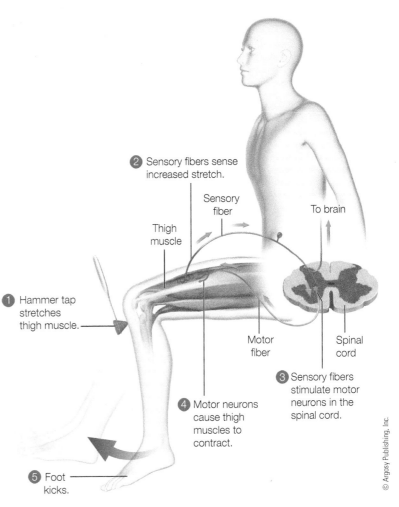

FIGURE 4.4

Checking Spinal Reflexes. When your physician taps on your knee, your thigh muscle stretches. Information about the stretch is carried to the spinal cord by a sensory nerve. The spinal cord sends a command to the muscle to contract to counteract the stretch, and your foot kicks out. The spinal cord manages this reflex alone. No higher level of processing in the nervous system is necessary for this reflex to occur.

FIGURE 4.5

Structures of the Brainstem. The brainstem contains structures responsible for reflexive behaviors, heart rate and breathing, arousal and sleep, preliminary sensory analysis, and balance and movement.

reticular formation A collection of structures located along the midline of the brainstem that participate in mood, arousal, and sleep.

Subcortical Structures

Embedded within the vast tracts of nerve fibers or white matter that make up the bulk of the cerebral hemispheres are a number of subcortical structures that participate in self-awareness, learning, emotion, movement, communication, the inhibition of impulses, and the regulation of body states. We call them *subcortical* because they lie *sub*, which means "below," the cerebral cortex, which comprises the wrinkled outermost covering of the cerebral hemispheres.

Early anatomists collected some of these subcortical structures into a limbic system (*limbic* means "border," and these structures form a gentle curve below the cerebral cortex), but this term is losing popularity with contemporary anatomists. You might also have heard the limbic system called "your emotional brain." As you will see in the next few sections, subcortical structures, including some formerly listed in the limbic system, participate in our emotional life, but they perform many other functions as well. We usually discuss these structures in the singular, as in *thalamus* or *hippocampus*, but they actually are paired sets of structures, one on either side of the brain.

Most sobriety tests assess the function of the cerebellum, which helps us maintain balance and muscle coordination.

This image is taken from a man who is blind because of damage caused by a stroke to his visual areas, indicated by the red and green arrows. The orange area indicates activation of his amygdala when he is shown a photo of an angry face. This man couldn't tell you whether he is looking at a tree, a building, or a face, let alone a happy or angry one, but his amygdala knows and reacts appropriately.

From A. J. Pegna, et al., "Discriminating Emotional Faces Without Primary Visual Cortices Involves the Right Amygdala," in Nat Neurosci, Jan. 2005, 8(1): 24–25. © 2005 Nature Publishing Group

The Thalamus Almost at the center of the brain lies the **thalamus**. The thalamus is often called the "gateway to the cortex," because input from most of our sensory systems (vision, hearing, touch, and taste) travels first to the thalamus, which then forwards the information to the cerebral cortex. The cortex, in turn, forms large numbers of connections with the thalamus. In addition to its role in sensation, the thalamus is involved with memory and states of consciousness. Lesions in the thalamus are associated with profound memory loss (Cipolotti et al., 2008). As you will learn in Chapter 6, during our deepest stages of sleep, the thalamus coordinates the activity of cortical neurons, "tuning out" the outside world and making it difficult to awaken. Disturbances in the circuits linking the thalamus and the cortex accompany some) seizures.

The Basal Ganglia The **basal ganglia** are several large structures involved with voluntary movement that curve around to cup the thalamus (see ● Figure 4.6). The basal ganglia receive substantial input from all areas of the cerebral cortex and from motor structures located in the brainstem. In turn, the basal ganglia send information to the cortex.

Degeneration of the basal ganglia occurs in Parkinson's disease, a condition that makes the initiation of voluntary movement extremely difficult. Involvement of the basal ganglia is also suspected in a number of psychological disorders that we will encounter in Chapter 14, including obsessive-compulsive disorder (OCD) and attention deficit hyperactivity disorder (ADHD). These disorders are characterized by inadequate control of voluntary movement. In the case of OCD, patients may endlessly repeat a behavior, such as hand washing, while in ADHD, voluntary movements can be unusually frequent, rapid, and impulsive. Children with the hyperactivity type of attention deficit disorder are often described as "driven by a motor."

The Hypothalamus The **hypothalamus** is a collection of structures involved with motivation and homeostasis (see Chapter 7), or the regulation of body functions such as temperature, thirst, hunger, biological rhythms, and sexual activities (see ● Figure 4.7). The hypothalamus is often described as contributing to the "4F" behaviors: feeding, fleeing, fighting, and, well, sex (fornication). The hypothalamus carries out its motivational and homeostatic tasks by directing the autonomic nervous system and the endocrine system and its hormones, which we discuss in detail later in this chapter.

The Hippocampus The **hippocampus**, named for its shape after the Greek word for seahorse, is essential to the formation of long-term memories, which we discuss in more detail in

thalamus A subcortical structure involved with the processing of sensory information, states of arousal, and learning and memory.
basal ganglia A collection of subcortical structures that participate in the control of movement.
hypothalamus A subcortical structure that participates in the regulation of thirst, temperature, hunger, sexual behavior, and aggression.
hippocampus A subcortical structure that participates in memory.
cingulate cortex A subcortical structure above the corpus callosum. Its anterior (forward) segment participates in decision making and emotion, and its posterior (rear) segment participates in memory and visual processing.
amygdala A subcortical structure located in the temporal lobe believed to participate in emotional processing.

FIGURE 4.6

The Thalamus and the Basal Ganglia. Near the center of the brain, the thalamus receives input from most of our sensory systems and relays the information to the cerebral cortex. Curving around the thalamus are the basal ganglia, which form an important part of our voluntary movement systems.

Chapter 9. Memories are not stored permanently in the hippocampus, but it is likely that the hippocampus is involved in the storage and retrieval of memories located elsewhere in the brain. Damage to the hippocampus results in profound impairments in the ability to form new memories, but intelligence, personality, and most memories of events that occurred before hippocampal damage remain intact.

The Cingulate Cortex The **cingulate cortex** forms a fold of tissue on the inner surface of each cerebral hemisphere. The forward two thirds of this structure, known as the anterior cingulate cortex (ACC), participate, along with the hypothalamus, in the control of the autonomic nervous system, which we discuss later in this chapter. The ACC also plays significant roles in decision making, emotion, anticipation of reward, and empathy. The rear third, or posterior cingulate cortex (PCC), participates in memory and visual processing.

The Amygdala The **amygdala** gets its name from the Greek word for "almond" because of its shape. One amygdala is deeply embedded in the temporal lobe, the wing of cortex that curves around the side of the brain, in each hemisphere. The amygdala appears to have a role in identifying, remembering, and responding to fear and aggression. Research studies have found that the amygdala becomes more active when people are looking at pictures of fearful facial expressions. The more intense the expression of fear, the more activation is observed in the amygdala (Vuilleumier, Armony, Driver, & Dolan, 2001). Monkeys with damaged amygdalae approached unfamiliar monkeys boldly and fearlessly, which is uncharacteristic of these animals (Emery et al., 2001). They also failed to show their species' typical fear of rubber snakes and unfamiliar humans (Mason, Capitanio, Machado, Mendoza, & Amaral, 2006).

Several behavioral deficits have been identified in a patient, known as Patient S.M., who experienced a rare medical condition that damaged the amygdala in both her right and her left hemisphere (Adolphs, Tranel, & Damasio, 1998) (see ● Figure 4.8). Although the patient can identify facial expressions of happiness, sadness, and disgust in photographs, she has a specific difficulty identifying expressions of fear. When researchers exposed Patient S.M. to snakes, spiders, and scary movies, she showed no signs of fear (Feinstein, Adolphs, Damasio, & Tranel,

FIGURE 4.7

Other Important Subcortical Structures. Subcortical structures located under the cerebral cortex participate in attention, decision making, learning, memory, and emotion.

FIGURE 4.8

SM's preferred distance

Control participant's average preferred distance

0.34 m

0.64 m

© 2016 Cengage Learning®

Results of Damage to the Amygdala. In addition to her difficulties in responding to fear stimuli, Patient S.M. shows other behavioral deficits related to her damaged amygdalae. Personal space, although variable across cultures, is consistent within cultures. Healthy control participants in the United States stand about 0.64 meter (about 2 feet, or arm's length) away from people they don't know. In contrast, Patient S.M. prefers to stand nearly twice as close to others, or 0.34 meter (about 1 foot). Standing closer to strangers than is normal for your culture is likely to send inappropriate social messages of either threat or intimacy. *Source:* Kennedy, D. P., Gläscher, J., Tyszka, J. M., & Adolphs, R. (2009). Personal space regulation by the human amygdala. *Nature Neuroscience, 12,* 1226-1227. doi: 10.1038/nn.2381

2011). Although Patient S.M. shows no signs of antisocial behavior, other research indicates that people who harm others without feeling guilt are also impaired in their abilities to perceive fear in facial expressions or voices (Blair et al., 2002; Marsh & Blair, 2008). The condition affecting Patient S.M. does not usually begin until after the age of 10, so having functional amygdalae in childhood might have helped Patient S.M. learn to act in prosocial ways.

The Nucleus Accumbens The **nucleus accumbens** is an important part of the brain's reward and pleasure circuitry. Whether you are eating, having sex, using addictive drugs, gambling, or simply enjoying a beautiful sunset, this circuit comes into play (Comings & Blum, 2000). The circuit originates in cell bodies located in the midbrain that form connections with many subcortical structures and with the nucleus accumbens in particular.

The activity of the nucleus accumbens is related to a person's sense of social inclusion. When people who have strong connections to friends and family view a happy social scene, their nucleus accumbens becomes active. In contrast, when people with weaker social connections view the same happy scenes, their nucleus accumbens shows less activity than those of the socially connected people (Cacioppo, Norris, Decety, Monteleone, & Nusbaum, 2009).

nucleus accumbens A subcortical structure that participates in reward and addiction.

corpus callosum A wide band of nerve fibers connecting the right and left cerebral hemispheres.

cerebral cortex The thin layer of neurons covering the outer surface of the cerebral hemispheres.

frontal lobe The most forward of the four lobes of the cerebral cortex; location of the primary motor cortex and areas responsible for some of the most complex cognitive processes.

parietal lobe The lobe of the cerebral cortex that lies at the top of the head between the frontal and the occipital lobes; location of the primary somatosensory cortex.

occipital lobe The lobe of the cerebral cortex located at the back of the brain; location of the primary visual cortex.

temporal lobe The lobe of the cerebral cortex that curves around the side of each hemisphere; location of the primary auditory cortex.

The Cerebral Cortex

Above the brainstem, we find the two large cerebral hemispheres, which are connected by a large bundle of nerve fibers known as the **corpus callosum**. The thin layer of cells covering the outer surface of the cerebral hemispheres is the **cerebral cortex** (see ● Figure 4.9). The *cortex*, which means "bark" in Latin, covers the cerebral hemispheres like the bark of a tree. Most of the remaining bulk of the hemispheres is made up of white matter, or nerve fiber pathways, that connects the cortex with other parts of the nervous system. The average 20-year-old human brain has around 100,000 miles (162,500 kilometers) of white matter (Marner, Nyengaard, Tang, & Pakkenberg, 2003). The subcortical structures discussed earlier are distributed within this white matter.

If stretched out flat, the human cerebral cortex would cover an area of about 2.5 square feet (about 0.23 square meters). To fit within the confines of the skull, the cortex is convoluted, or wrinkled. The degree of cortical convolution positively correlates with the general intellectual capacities of a species. For instance, human brains are more convoluted than sheep brains, which in turn are more convoluted than rat brains (see ● Figure 4.10).

Each hemisphere of the cerebral cortex may be divided into four lobes, named after the bones of the skull that cover them (see ● Figure 4.11). Toward the front of the brain, we find the **frontal lobe**, and directly behind the frontal lobe lies the **parietal lobe**. At the back of the brain is the **occipital lobe**. Curving around the side of each hemisphere, we find the

From Heiner L The Human Brain and Spinal Cord: Functional Neuroanatomy and Dissection Guide, second ed., Springer, 1995 (after Brodmann)

FIGURE 4.9

The Cerebral Cortex. The cerebral cortex (*cortex* means "bark") is a thin layer of cells on the outer surface of the brain. The close-up shows different views of the cortex, including the distribution of complete single cells, cell bodies, and myelin, the insulating material that covers most nerve fibers.

temporal lobe. Because we have two hemispheres, it follows that we have pairs of each type of lobe, usually denoted right or left (e.g., right frontal lobe and left frontal lobe).

Localization of Functions in the Cerebral Cortex As we mentioned earlier in this chapter, the phrenologists were wrong in assuming that behavioral characteristics were reflected in bumps of the skull, but they were correct in suggesting that some functions were localized in particular parts of the brain.

The functions performed by different areas of the cerebral cortex within the lobes fall into three categories: sensory, motor, and association. The sensory cortex processes incoming information from the sensory systems, such as vision

Diffusion tensor imaging highlights the rich arrays formed by the white matter in the brain.

Simon Fraser/Science Source

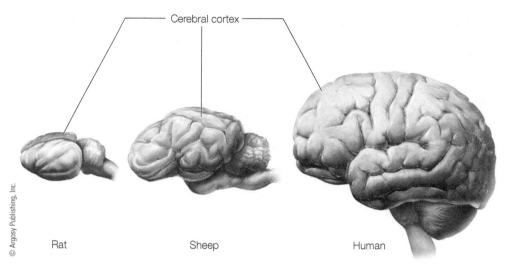

FIGURE 4.10

Degree of the Convolution of the Cortex Predicts Intellect. As species' behavior becomes more complex, we see a corresponding increase in the degree of convolution (wrinkling) of the cerebral cortex. This wrinkling of the brain permits more brain tissue to fit within the skull. As a result, cortical size has increased more quickly over the course of evolution than skull size—an important adaptation given that large skulls are difficult to get through the birth canal.

© Argosy Publishing, Inc.

Cerebral cortex

Rat   Sheep   Human

or hearing, which we describe in Chapter 5. The primary visual cortex is located in the occipital lobe, and the primary auditory cortex is located in the temporal lobe. The primary somatosensory cortex (*soma* refers to "body") is located in the parietal lobe and processes information about touch, pain, body position, and skin temperature. The primary motor cortex is located in the rearmost portion of the frontal lobe and provides the highest level of voluntary control over movement. Areas of the cortex that do not have specific sensory or motor functions are known as association cortex. *Association* means "connection" in this case, and association cortex helps us form bridges between sensation and action, language, and abstract thought. Association areas are distributed throughout the cortex.

The Frontal Lobe In addition to being the home of the primary motor cortex, the frontal lobe has a number of important, sophisticated cognitive functions. Adjacent to the primary motor cortex is Broca's area, named after Paul Broca, who helped identify its functions in the 1860s. Broca's area participates in the production of speech. Consequently, damage to Broca's area caused by a stroke or tumor produces considerable difficulty in speaking, although comprehension of speech remains good. The most forward portion of each frontal lobe, known as

FIGURE 4.11

Lobes of the Cerebral Cortex. The cerebral cortex is traditionally divided into four lobes: frontal, parietal, occipital, and temporal.

Primary motor cortex

Primary somatosensory cortex

Frontal lobe

Prefrontal cortex

Broca's area

Orbitofrontal cortex

Primary auditory cortex

Parietal lobe

Wernicke's area

Occipital lobe

Primary visual cortex

Temporal lobe

© Argosy Publishing, Inc.

the **prefrontal cortex** (*pre* means "before"), is involved with the planning of behavior, attention, and judgment. Abnormalities of frontal lobe activity may account for characteristics of some psychological disorders, including schizophrenia and ADHD, which we will discuss in detail in Chapter 14.

The role of the frontal lobes in the planning of behavior is illustrated by a bizarre condition known as alien hand syndrome, which occurs when connections between the prefrontal cortex and the lower areas of the brain that are involved in movement are damaged (Kikkert, Ribbers, & Koudstaal, 2006). This condition has no effect on sensory feedback from the limb, such as touch and position. However, patients with this condition do not seem to have control over their affected limbs and often remain unaware of the limbs' activities until they are pointed out by another person. For instance, a hand might undo a button or remove clothing without the patient's awareness of the activity. Patients do not recognize the rogue limb as their own and may use the other hand to wrestle with it in an attempt to control it forcibly or punish it for its activities.

The importance of the frontal lobes is also illustrated by the results of a terrible accident that befell a young railroad worker named Phineas Gage in 1848. While Gage was preparing to blast through some granite, a freak accident sent an iron tamping rod through his head like a bullet before it landed about 30 feet (about 9 meters) away. The rod entered his head under his left cheekbone, passed behind his left eye, and exited out the middle of his forehead. Remarkably, Gage survived but he was not the same person as before his accident. Although outwardly normal in his intelligence, speech, and movement, Gage became prone to angry outbursts and unreliability, which made it difficult for him to find and keep employment. As his doctor noted, "His contractors, who regarded him as the most efficient and capable foreman in their employ previous to his injury, considered the change in his mind so marked that they could not give him his place again" (Fleischman, 2002, p. 20).

Gage suffered his accident when modern imaging technologies were nowhere to be seen on the scientific horizon. Today, we know more about why Gage behaved the way he did as a result of his accident. Scientists initially recreated the pathway that Gage's tamping rod must have traveled (Damasio, Grabowski, Frank, Galaburda, & Damasio, 1994). More recent analyses show that the rod did more damage to the fiber pathways in Gage's brain than to the cells of his cerebral cortex (Van Horn et al., 2012). The rod disrupted 11% of the connections in Gage's brain, compared to 4% of the cells in his cortex.

The rod missed areas involved in speech, voluntary movement, and the senses of touch, body position, and pain. Thus, Gage had no difficulty speaking or performing complex movements, like driving a stagecoach, following his accident. Modern patients with damage in this area exhibit many of the same social deficits that Gage demonstrated (Damasio & Anderson, 1993; Damasio, Tranel, & Damasio, 1991; Eslinger & Damasio, 1985). They are impulsive, emotionally unstable, unpredictable, and unable to make reasonable decisions.

Knowing the outcome of the Gage case, you might be astonished to learn that physicians in the 1940s and 1950s deliberately damaged the frontal lobes of nearly 50,000 American patients in a procedure known as a frontal lobotomy. The intent of the procedure was to reduce fear and anxiety in patients with serious psychological disorders, which it accomplished in many cases but at great expense to the patient. As you might suspect from reading about Gage, many patients who underwent the procedure were unable to work or live normal lives because of their impulsive, antisocial behavior.

The **orbitofrontal cortex**, a part of the prefrontal cortex located just behind the bony orbits protecting the eyes, plays an important role in our emotional lives (see ● Figure 4.12). People with damage to the orbitofrontal cortex demonstrate dramatic deficits in their social behavior and experience of emotion, despite retaining their intelligence, language skills, and abilities to pay attention, learn, and remember (Bechara, Damasio, & Damasio, 2000; Damasio, 1994; Damasio & Anderson, 1993).

Patient E.V.R. experienced orbitofrontal damage during surgery for a tumor (Eslinger & Damasio, 1985). Before his surgery, E.V.R. was considered a role model and a respected

Image Shop/Cardinal/Corbis

Early scientists discovered that nerves carry only one type of information. When you take a blow to the back of the head, where your primary visual cortex is found, your occipital lobe does not know how to say, "ouch." Instead, it responds to the blow as if you saw a flash of light (not necessarily the tweeting birds or stars indicated in cartoons).

prefrontal cortex The most forward part of the frontal lobe of the cerebral cortex.
orbitofrontal cortex A part of the prefrontal cortex located right behind the eyes that participates in impulse control.

Patrick Landmann/Science Source

member of his community. Following his surgery, E.V.R. lost his job, went bankrupt, and divorced his wife to marry a prostitute, whom he divorced 2 years later. Although he had no difficulties talking about moral dilemmas, he experienced enormous problems when trying to make everyday decisions, such as buying toothpaste or choosing a restaurant.

Researchers are making other connections between abnormalities in the orbitofrontal cortex and antisocial behavior. In a sample of 21 individuals diagnosed with antisocial personality disorder, a condition characterized by disregard for others that we discuss in Chapter 14, the volume of the prefrontal cortex, which includes the orbitofrontal cortex, was about 11% less than in control participants who did not have the condition (Raine, Lencz, Bihrle, LaCasse, & Colletti, 2000). Individuals with antisocial personality disorder or orbitofrontal damage not only fail to anticipate the emotional consequences of situations but also are unable to delay gratification. They typically choose immediate rewards over long-term benefits, like stealing something now despite knowing the long-term benefits of staying out of jail.

Phineas Gage suffered a terrible injury to his frontal lobes. Modern imaging techniques allowed scientists to re-create the pathway of Gage's tamping iron through his brain. Remarkably, Gage survived, although his friends described him as a "changed man".

The Occipital Lobe The occipital lobe, located at the back of the brain, is home to the primary visual cortex. The primary visual cortex begins the process of interpreting input from the eyes by responding to basic information about an image, such as its borders, shading, color, and movement. This amount of processing, by itself, does not allow you to read this page or recognize your professor in the library. Two important pathways link the occipital lobe with the rest of the brain. A pathway connecting the occipital lobe with the temporal lobe allows you to recognize objects you see. A second pathway connects the occipital lobe with the parietal lobe and allows you to process the movement of objects. We discuss these processes further in the next sections.

The Temporal Lobe The temporal lobe has a number of areas that are specialized for particular functions. The temporal lobe is home to the primary auditory cortex, which allows us to process incoming sounds. As mentioned earlier, the temporal lobe processes some higher visual system tasks, including the recognition of objects and the faces of familiar people. Patients with damage to the temporal lobe are often unable to recognize their loved ones by sight. They have to wait until the person speaks. We discuss this processing of vision and hearing by the temporal lobe in more detail in Chapter 5.

We saw earlier how damage to Broca's area in the frontal lobe produced difficulty in speaking. Damage to another language area located in the temporal lobe, Wernicke's area, produces different results (see Figure 4.11). As we discuss in Chapter 10, patients with damage to their Wernicke's area speak fluently but make no sense. They cannot comprehend speech, but they seem blissfully unaware of their deficits.

© Argosy Publishing, Inc.

Orbitofrontal cortex

FIGURE 4.12

The Orbitofrontal Cortex. People with damage to their orbitofrontal cortex have difficulty controlling impulses and anticipating the negative outcomes of poor decisions. This part of the brain is one of the last areas to mature.

The Parietal Lobe The parietal lobe is home to the primary somatosensory cortex, which helps us localize touch, pain, skin temperature, and body position. Damage to the parietal lobe can produce the odd symptoms of neglect syndrome. Patients with this condition have difficulty perceiving part of their body or part of the visual field (see ● Figure 4.13).

The parietal lobe processes input about taste and, like the temporal lobe, engages in some complex processing of vision. Whereas the temporal lobe participates in visual recognition, the parietal lobe tells us how quickly something is moving toward us. This can be an essential bit of information when deciding whether it is safe to make a left turn in front of oncoming traffic. We discuss these functions of the parietal lobe in depth in Chapter 5.

FIGURE 4.13

Damage to the Parietal Lobe Causes Neglect. Patients with certain types of brain damage in the parietal lobe experience "hemispatial neglect," or the inability to pay attention to stimuli located in space on the opposite side relative to their damage. They seem unaware that there is anything wrong with their perceptions. The patient whose drawings are featured in this figure experienced damage to the right hemisphere, resulting in neglect for anything to the left in space. Neglect does not affect vision alone, but can also affect the sense of body location. One patient was unable to recognize his own leg and suspected the hospital staff of putting a cadaver leg into his bed.

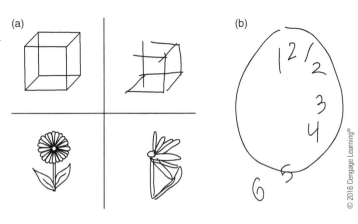

© 2016 Cengage Learning®

One patient with neglect syndrome could not recognize his own leg and believed the hospital staff was playing a horrible trick on him by placing a cadaver leg in his bed. Fortunately, the patient's condition improved over time.

Psychology as a Hub Science
Law, Responsibility, and the Brain

In 1843, Daniel M'Naghten was planning to assassinate British Prime Minister Sir Robert Peel but shot his secretary, Edward Drummond, instead. M'Naghten was acquitted "by reason of insanity" and spent the remainder of his life in hospitals for the insane rather than prison. M'Naghten's legacy in English and American law is the insanity defense, which means that a person can be judged as not responsible for a criminal act if he or she has a mental condition that prevents understanding of the act and/or the wrongfulness of the act (Mobbs, Lau, Jones, & Frith, 2007).

As our understanding of correlations between brain and behavior improves, psychology is likely to have a great deal to say to the criminal justice system regarding a person's capacity for responsible behavior.

These issues came close to the home of one of the authors, the sleepy little town of San Luis Obispo, California (population of about 45,000). In 2005, a 13-year-old boy used a skateboard to bludgeon 87-year-old Jerry O'Malley to death. The boy told police, "I knew it was wrong; I just did it." Joseph Wu, director of the Brain Imaging Center at the University of California, Irvine, told the court that the young murderer had "abnormally reduced activity in parts of his brain that govern a person's judgment" (Sneed, 2006, p. B1).

If somebody has evidence of abnormalities in parts of the brain "that govern a person's judgment," does the insanity defense apply? Is this a situation that calls for medical and psychological treatment or incarceration? We do not have answers for these questions today, but further understanding of the brain's structure and function in both law-abiding people and criminals will contribute to the legal system's ability to handle such cases fairly.

If you're curious about the young murderer's outcome, the court rejected suggestions that he needed treatment instead of incarceration. He was sentenced to a state juvenile corrections facility from which he will be automatically freed in 2017 (Parrilla, 2006). ●

Jessica Ridgeway, 10 years old, was murdered near her home in Colorado by a 17-year-old community college student Austin Sigg. Perpetrators of crime at Sigg's age are usually treated differently than adults by the criminal justice system. How old do people need to be before they are responsible for their actions?

Splash News/Newscom

FIGURE 4.14

The Split-Brain Operation. To save patients from life-threatening seizures, physicians cut the corpus callosum, a large band of nerve fibers connecting the right and left hemispheres.

Fibers to cortex

Corpus callosum

Skull

Location of incision

© Argosy Publishing, Inc.

Right Brain and Left Brain A special type of localization of function in the cerebral cortex is known as lateralization, or the localization of a function in either the right or the left cerebral hemisphere. A basic type of lateralization occurs in the somatosensory and voluntary motor systems in the brain. Movement and sensation on the right side of the body are processed by the left hemisphere, and movement and sensation on the left side of the body by the right hemisphere. If you observe a person who is paralyzed on the right side of the body, you can be fairly certain that this paralysis is a result of motor cortex damage in the left hemisphere. In a similar manner, the visual cortex of the left hemisphere processes all data from the right half of the visual field, while the right hemisphere processes all data from the left half of the visual field. In other words, when you look straight ahead, holding your eyes and head still, everything to the right or left of center is processed by the opposite hemisphere.

Much of our knowledge of lateralization of the human brain resulted from the careful analysis of a surgical procedure known as a split-brain operation (see ● Figure 4.14). To treat rare cases of life-threatening seizures, surgeons in the 1960s cut the patients' corpus callosum and other pathways connecting the right and left cerebral hemispheres (Bogen, Schultz, & Vogel, 1988). The procedure not only succeeded in reducing or eliminating seizures, but it also produced no changes in personality, intelligence, or speech. Only when patients were studied in the laboratory were the consequences of their surgery evident.

In one typical experiment, illustrated in ● Figure 4.15, participants were instructed to fixate on a dot at the center of a screen (Gazzaniga, 1967). The word *he* appeared to the left of the dot, while the word *art* appeared to the right. As mentioned earlier, this positioning means that the word *he* is processed by the right hemisphere and the word *art* is processed by the left. Because the corpus callosum and other connections between the two hemispheres were cut in the split-brain procedure, one hemisphere would not know what the other had seen. When asked to indicate the word seen, the participants said "art," because that is the word seen by their verbal left hemisphere. When shown a card with the two words printed on it and instructed to point with the left hand rather than verbalizing the word that was seen, participants pointed to *he*. As mentioned earlier in this section, the right hemisphere provides motor control for the left side of the body, so the left hand was pointing out the word "seen" by the right hemisphere.

Subsequent research indicated that language, for most people, is lateralized to the left hemisphere, although a minority of individuals process language either in the right hemisphere or in both hemispheres (Rasmussen & Milner, 1977). The lateralization of language is correlated, although not completely, with a person's handedness. As shown in a later section, nearly all right-handed people lateralize language to the left hemisphere, as do about 70% of people who are left-handed. The remaining individuals process language either in the right hemisphere or in both hemispheres.

Language is not the only cognitive process to show evidence of lateralization. Other suspected lateralized processes include mathematical computation and logical reasoning (left hemisphere) and some music functions, spatial information, intuition, and the visual arts (right hemisphere). Emotional behavior also appears to be lateralized. In most people, activity of the left hemisphere is correlated with positive emotions, whereas activity in the right hemisphere is correlated with negative emotions, providing the cortex with a rough distinction between approaching positive things (left hemisphere activity) and avoiding negative things

FIGURE 4.15

The Hemispheres Have Different Capacities for Language Functions. When asked verbally what word was seen, participants answered "art," which was seen by the verbal left hemisphere. When asked to point with the left hand (which is controlled by the right hemisphere) to the word that was seen, the participants pointed to *HE*, which is the word seen by the right hemisphere.

(right hemisphere activity; Davidson & Irwin, 1999). Anesthetizing the left hemisphere results in temporary feelings of depression, while anesthetizing the right hemisphere produces happiness (Lee et al., 2004).

Right–Left Brain Myths A word of caution is in order here. As noted by Roger Sperry, who won the 1981 Nobel Prize for his investigations of lateralization in the human brain, "The left–right dichotomy in cognitive mode is an idea with which it is very easy to run wild" (Sperry, 1982, p. 1225). Most of us have not undergone a split-brain procedure. Our intact corpus callosum and other connections between the two cerebral hemispheres allow information to pass rapidly from one hemisphere to the other. Suggestions that you can improve your artistic or athletic talent or reduce inattention by "learning to access your right brain" have gained considerable attention in the popular press, but they do not hold up to scrutiny in the laboratory. One of the most popular myths about lateralization is the idea that individual differences in artistic talent or logical thinking correlate with a person's dominant hemisphere. Hemisphere dominance, as measured by the relative size of the hemispheres and the localization of language and handedness, does not predict occupational choice or artistic talent (Springer & Deutsch, 1998).

The Function of Lateralization What are the advantages of lateralization? Most species of animals show a preference for one "hand" or the other, such as when a cat reaches for its prey (Cole, 1955; Holder, 1999).

Lateralization might provide organisms with the ability to multitask (Rogers, 2000). Chicks raised in the dark fail to lateralize visually guided responses normally and are at a

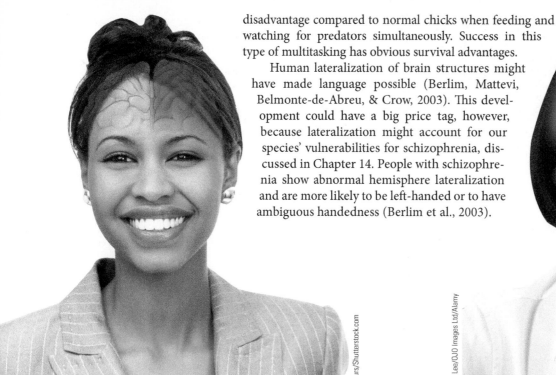

disadvantage compared to normal chicks when feeding and watching for predators simultaneously. Success in this type of multitasking has obvious survival advantages.

Human lateralization of brain structures might have made language possible (Berlim, Mattevi, Belmonte-de-Abreu, & Crow, 2003). This development could have a big price tag, however, because lateralization might account for our species' vulnerabilities for schizophrenia, discussed in Chapter 14. People with schizophrenia show abnormal hemisphere lateralization and are more likely to be left-handed or to have ambiguous handedness (Berlim et al., 2003).

Yuri Arcurs/Shutterstock.com

Anthony Lee/OJO Images Ltd/Alamy

Experiencing Psychology

Handedness

LATERALIZATION OF LANGUAGE is correlated with handedness. Milner (1974) used the Wada test to determine hemisphere dominance for language and then correlated these results with people's handedness. In the Wada test, usually administered before brain surgery, anesthesia is applied to one hemisphere at a time. Once anesthetized in this manner, the subject is asked to speak. When the anesthesia wears off, the other hemisphere is anesthetized, and the subject's language ability is checked again. When the hemisphere used to process language is anesthetized, the subject is unable to speak or understand language, but that person does fine when the other hemisphere is anesthetized. Mixed dominance refers to people who show relatively little lateralization for language and use both hemispheres approximately equally for this function. These people would have trouble with language when either hemisphere is anesthetized. Milner's results are summarized in Table 4.2.

Handedness represents a continuum, with some people being nearly ambidextrous and others having strong preferences for using one hand or the other. Although most of us would have no trouble answering a question asking whether we are right- or left-handed, researchers like Milner must apply systems for determining a person's handedness. One of the frequently used instruments follows.

Simply read each of the questions in Table 4.3. Decide which hand you use for each activity, and then circle the answer that describes you the best. If you are unsure of any answer, try to act out the action.

To find your score, count the number of circled "right" answers and subtract the number of circled "left" answers. Ignore "either" answers. Ambidextrous people will score around 0, very right-handed people will score near +12, and very left-handed people will score near −12.

Although this test can't tell you which hemisphere you use for language (and it's unlikely you'd like to spend your afternoon taking the Wada test), your odds of using your left hemisphere for language if you're very right-handed are quite high. ●

TABLE 4.2 Relationships Between Handedness and Language Localization

Handedness	Language left	Language right	Mixed dominance
Right-handed (90%)	96%	4%	0%
Left-handed (10%)	70%	15%	15%

© Cengage Learning®

Humans are not the only animals to have a preferred hand. However, other primates, like this chimpanzee using a stone to open nuts, are equally likely to be right- or left-handed. In contrast, more than 90% of humans are right-handed.

Martin Harvey/Alamy

TABLE
4.3 The Lateral Preference Inventory

1. With which hand do you draw?	Left	Right	Either
2. Which hand would you use to throw a ball to hit a target?	Left	Right	Either
3. In which hand would you use an eraser on paper?	Left	Right	Either
4. Which hand removes the top card when you are dealing from a deck?	Left	Right	Either
5. With which hand do you normally write?	Left	Right	Either
6. In which hand do you use your racquet for tennis, squash, etc.?	Left	Right	Either
7. With which hand do you use your toothbrush?	Left	Right	Either
8. Which hand holds a knife when you are cutting things?	Left	Right	Either
9. Which hand holds the hammer when you are driving a nail?	Left	Right	Either
10. In which hand would you hold a match to strike it?	Left	Right	Either
11. Which hand holds the thread when you are threading a needle?	Left	Right	Either
12. In which hand would you use a fly swatter?			

Source: Adapted from "The Lateral Preference Inventory for Measurement of Handedness, Footedness, Eyedness, and Earedness: Norms for Young Adults," by S. Coren, 1993, *Bulletin of the Psychonomic Society, 31*(1), pp. 1–3.

Although efforts to connect brain lateralization, which is highly correlated with handedness, with occupational choice or artistic talent have not been successful, being in the left-handed minority might provide advantages in sports and in combat. Right-handed pitchers, like Tim Lincecum, are often challenged by left-handed hitters like Adrian Gonzalez.

Summary 4.1 Structures of the Central Nervous System

	Structure	What to remember
	Spinal cord	• Continuous with brainstem • Large white matter pathways • Reflexes
	Brainstem and cerebellum	• Large white matter pathways, arousal, reflexes, and body functions (heart rate, etc.) • Midbrain • Pons • Cerebellum • Medulla • Reticular formation
	Subcortical structures	• Embedded in the white matter of the cerebral hemispheres • Thalamus • Basal ganglia • Hypothalamus • Hippocampus • Cingulate cortex • Amygdala • Nucleus accumbens
	Cerebral cortex	• Thin layer of gray matter enveloping the hemispheres • Divided into four lobes • Areas with sensory, motor, or association functions • Some localized and lateralized functions

The Peripheral Nervous System (PNS) and the Endocrine System

The brain and spinal cord (the CNS) are spectacular processing units, but without input or ability to implement commands, they would be no different from your computer's central processing unit (CPU) without its mouse, keyboard, monitor, printer, and Internet connection. The lights may be on, but not much is going to happen.

In this section, we will explore the structures of the PNS that provide these essential input and output functions in the body. The PNS can be separated into two divisions: the somatic nervous system and the autonomic nervous system. The somatic nervous system includes the peripheral portions of the sensory and voluntary movement systems. The autonomic nervous system is responsible for the actions of many glands and organs. Additional output is provided by the endocrine system, through which the CNS can communicate with the body by releasing chemical messengers into the bloodstream. These systems coordinate their efforts to produce consistent patterns of movement, hormone release, and arousal.

The Somatic Nervous System

The **somatic nervous system** is the part of the PNS that transmits commands for voluntary movement from the CNS to the muscles and brings sensory input back to the CNS for further processing. These functions are carried out by the 31 pairs of spinal nerves serving the torso and limbs and the 12 pairs of cranial nerves serving the head, neck, and some internal organs (see ● Figure 4.16).

FIGURE 4.16

The Cranial Nerves. Twelve pairs of cranial nerves carry sensory and motor information from the brain to the head, neck, and some internal organs.

III. Oculomotor
IV. Trochlear
VI. Abducens
Eye movements

V. Trigeminal
Touch
Pain
Jaw muscles

II. Optic
Vision

I. Olfactory
Smell

VII. Facial
Face muscles
Taste

XII. Hypoglossal
Tongue movements

VIII. Auditory
Hearing
Balance

XI. Spinal accesory
Neck muscles

X. Vagus
Internal organs
(parasympathetic)

IX. Glossopharyngeal
Taste
Muscles of throat and larynx

© Argosy Publishing, Inc.

somatic nervous system The part of the peripheral nervous system that brings sensory information to the central nervous system and transmits commands to the muscles.

Biofeedback training helps people gain conscious control over some autonomic processes that normally run in the background. People who suffer from migraine headaches can be trained to reduce blood flow to the brain.

Kurt Jones

Stress activates the sympathetic nervous system, preparing the body for fight or flight or, in this case, fast paddling.

The Autonomic Nervous System

The function of the **autonomic nervous system** is the control of tissues other than the skeletal muscle (Langley, 1921)—in other words, our glands and organs. The term *autonomic* has the same root as the word *autonomy*, or independence. You might think of this system as the cruise control of the body, because it ensures that your heart keeps beating and your lungs continue to inhale and exhale without your conscious direction. The autonomic nervous system contains three subdivisions: the sympathetic, the parasympathetic, and the enteric.

The sympathetic and parasympathetic divisions are active under different circumstances. The **sympathetic nervous system** prepares the body for situations requiring the expenditure of energy, while the **parasympathetic nervous system** directs the storage of energy. You have probably experienced sympathetic arousal, perhaps because of a close call on the highway. In the aroused state produced by the sympathetic nervous system, our hearts race, we breathe rapidly, our faces become pale, and our palms sweat. All these activities are designed to provide the muscles with the nutrients they need for a fight-or-flight reaction. The sympathetic nervous system is important to our understanding of stress, described further in Chapter 16. In contrast, the parasympathetic nervous system controls the glands and organs at times of relative calm. Instead of using up energy like the sympathetic nervous system does, the parasympathetic nervous system allows you to store nutrients, repair your body, and return the activities of internal organs to baseline levels.

The responses of the internal organs to environmental stimuli reflect a sophisticated combination of inputs from both the sympathetic and the parasympathetic nervous systems (Berntson, Cacioppo, & Quigley, 1991). These systems usually have antagonistic effects on the organs they serve and are designed to alternate their activities (see ● Figure 4.17). We cannot be simultaneously relaxed and aroused. The sympathetic nervous system dilates the pupils of the eye, whereas the parasympathetic nervous system constricts the pupils. The heart responds to sympathetic commands by beating faster but responds to parasympathetic commands by slowing down. The two divisions do manage, however, to cooperate during sexual activity.

The **enteric nervous system**, shown in ● Figure 4.18, consists of nerve cells embedded in the lining of the gastrointestinal system. This system is often called a "second brain," because it contains as many nerve cells as are found in the spinal cord. The enteric nervous system communicates with the endocrine system, described later, that releases a number of chemicals essential to digestion. Some functions of the enteric nervous system result in conscious perceptions, such as gastrointestinal pain, hunger, and satiety (fullness), while others operate below the threshold of conscious awareness. The latter give rise to our references to having a "gut feeling." The enteric nervous system is the source of 95% of the body's serotonin, a neurochemical discussed later in this chapter. Individuals with autism spectrum disorder (see Chapter 14) show higher than normal levels of serotonin in their blood (Janusonis, 2008) and often experience gastric distress (Kazek et al., 2013).

The Endocrine System

The nervous system communicates by passing messages along nerves. In contrast, the **endocrine system** is made up of a number of glands that release chemical messengers known as hormones into the blood (see ● Figure 4.19). These chemicals are often identical to the ones used by one nerve cell to communicate with another, but their action affects more distant cells and can affect many parts of the body in a coordinated fashion. Ultimately, the endocrine

autonomic nervous system The division of the peripheral nervous system that directs the activity of glands, organs, and smooth muscles.
sympathetic nervous system The division of the autonomic nervous system that coordinates arousal.
parasympathetic nervous system The part of the autonomic nervous system associated with rest, repair, and energy storage.
enteric nervous system A division of the autonomic nervous system consisting of nerve cells embedded in the lining of the gastrointestinal system.
endocrine system A system responsible for the release of hormones into the bloodstream.

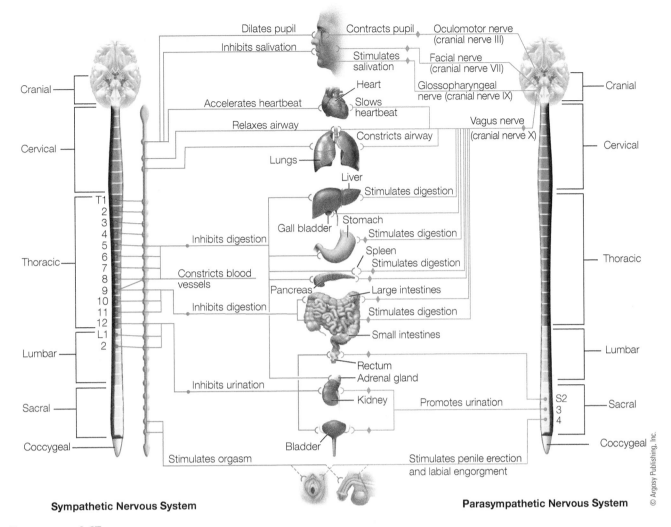

Sympathetic Nervous System

Parasympathetic Nervous System

© Argosy Publishing, Inc.

FIGURE 4.17

The Autonomic Nervous System. The sympathetic nervous system (left) usually has the opposite effect on an organ compared with the parasympathetic nervous system (right). For example, sympathetic input tells the heart to beat faster, while parasympathetic input tells the heart to slow down. However, both systems cooperate during sex.

FIGURE 4.18

The Enteric Nervous System. The enteric nervous system is often called a "second brain." It has about the same number of neurons as the spinal cord, or about as many found in the entire brain of an adult cat.

© 2016 Cengage Learning®

THE PERIPHERAL NERVOUS SYSTEM (PNS) AND THE ENDOCRINE SYSTEM   **131**

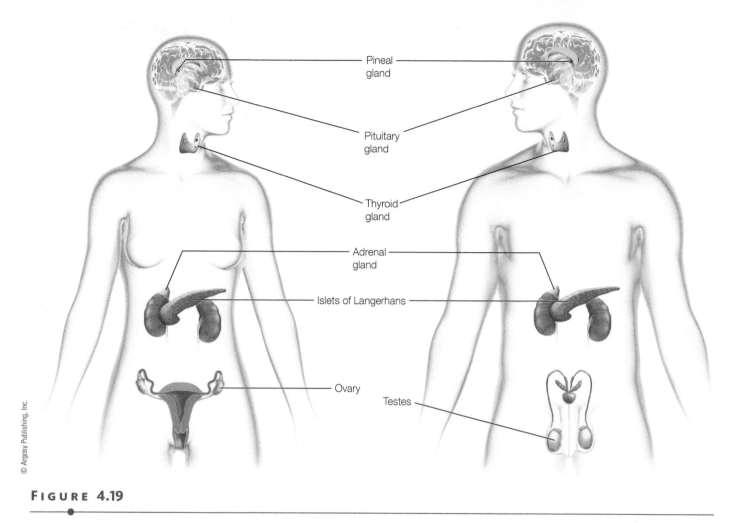

FIGURE 4.19

Glands of the Endocrine System. The endocrine system communicates with other body tissues by releasing hormones from glands into the bloodstream.

system responds to input from the nervous system and from the hypothalamus in particular. The endocrine system is especially involved with arousal, metabolism, growth, and sex. Among the important glands of the endocrine system are the pineal gland, the pituitary gland, the thyroid gland, the adrenal glands, the islets of Langerhans, and the ovaries in females and testes in males.

Human growth hormone, released normally by the pituitary gland, has become a popular but illegal performance-enhancing substance among elite athletes like baseball's Mark McGwire.

The pineal gland, and its release of the chemical messenger melatonin, is important in the maintenance of our sleep–wake cycles, which we discuss in Chapter 6. Although not an officially approved and tested medication, melatonin is used by some travelers in an effort to offset the unpleasant effects of jet lag. Melatonin is normally released in the early evening, and it breaks down in the presence of light. Our ancestors had no problems with this, but our modern exposure to artificial light can have negative implications for our health. For example, higher rates of cancer among people working night shifts in hospitals have been attributed to the breakdown of melatonin by light (Dopfel, Schulmeister, & Schernhammer, 2007).

The pituitary gland, located just above the roof of your mouth, is often called the body's master gland, because many of the hormones it releases activate the body's other glands.

The pituitary in turn is regulated by the hypothalamus, which lies directly above it. The pituitary hormones form two groups. One group, including oxytocin and vasopressin, is released directly from the pituitary. The second group consists of several hormones that influence the release of hormones by other glands. Oxytocin and vasopressin participate in a number of important physical functions, such as breastfeeding and maintenance of fluid levels, respectively. However, these hormones are also implicated in cooperation and trust, memory for social information, recognition of emotions, and resilience during stress (Meyer-Lindenberg, Domes, Kirsch, & Heinrichs, 2011).

Pituitary hormones direct the release of growth hormone, which stimulates growth and regeneration, making it a popular performance-enhancing substance used illegally by some elite athletes. Other pituitary hormones control the production and release of sex hormones by the ovaries and testes, initiating puberty and maintaining fertility. In response to pituitary hormones, the thyroid gland—located just below your larynx, or voice box, in your throat—raises or lowers your rate of metabolism, or the chemical processes your body needs to sustain life. Low levels of thyroid can mimic the symptoms of depression, described further in Chapter 14. At times of stress, pituitary hormones activate the adrenal glands, located just above the kidneys in the lower back. In response, the adrenal glands release other hormones, including cortisol, that travel throughout the body and brain to provide a general wake-up message.

The islets of Langerhans, located in the pancreas, produce a number of hormones essential to digestion, including insulin.

Oxytocin released by the pituitary gland is correlated with human bonding between parent and child and between romantic partners.

R. Gino Santa Maria/Shutterstock.com

Summary 4.2 Peripheral Nervous and Endocrine Systems

	Structure	What to remember
	Somatic nervous system	• Sensation and movement • 12 pairs of cranial nerves • 31 pairs of spinal nerves
	Autonomic nervous system	• Sympathetic nervous system: arousal and fight or flight • Parasympathetic nervous system: rest and repair • Enteric nervous system: control of the gastrointestinal system
	Endocrine system	• Metabolism, arousal, growth, sex • Glands • Hormones

Credits: Top Row. © Argosy Publishing, Inc. Second Row. © Argosy Publishing, Inc. Bottom Row: © Argosy Publishing, Inc.

How Do Neurons Communicate?

Although it sounds like a script from a science fiction film, researchers are capable of growing neurons, like these from the retina of the eye, on silicon chips. The chip is able to electrically stimulate the growing neurons. Future uses of this type of technology might include brainlike computer networks and better prostheses for people who have lost a limb.

We now zoom in to explore the microscopic building blocks of the nervous system, which are the nerve cells, or **neurons**. Human brains have about 100 billion neurons. To put this number into perspective, consider the following: If each neuron represented a second, ticking off the neurons in your body alone would take more than 3,170 years. With each neuron forming an average of several thousand connections with other neurons, the connections in the human brain number in the hundreds of trillions. In addition to these large numbers of neurons, the nervous system contains many supporting cells, known as glia.

Once you are familiar with the structure of neurons and glia, we will explore the ways neurons communicate with one another. Neural communication is a two-step process. The first step takes place within a single neuron and involves the generation of an electrical signal. The second step takes place between two neurons and involves the release of a chemical messenger from one neuron that affects the activity of the second.

Neurons and Glia

Neurons share many characteristics with other cells found in the body. Like other cells, a neuron has a large central mass, or **cell body**, and within the cell body, it has a nucleus (see ● Figure 4.20). Most housekeeping tasks of the cell, such as the translation of genetic codes into the manufacture of proteins, take place in the cell body. Like other cells, neurons feature an outer membrane, which surrounds the neuron and forms a barrier between the fluid outside the cell (the extracellular fluid) and the fluid inside the cell (the intracellular fluid). The neural membrane is composed of fatty materials that do not dissolve in water, so even though it is only two molecules thick, it is able to hold apart the water-based fluids on either side. Pores within the membrane act as channels that allow chemicals to move into or out of the cell.

Unlike many other types of body cells, neurons have two types of branches that extend from the cell body to allow the neuron to perform its information-processing and communication functions. The branches known as **axons** are responsible for carrying information to other neurons, while the branches known as **dendrites** receive input from other neurons. Although neurons may have many dendrites, each neuron typically has only one axon.

Many axons communicate with immediately adjacent cells and are therefore only small fractions of a millimeter in length, but other axons are quite a bit longer. When you stub your big toe on a rock, the neurons that process this information have cell bodies in your lower back and axons that extend all the way down to your sore toe, a distance of around 3 feet (about 9 meters), depending on your height. At its farthest point from the cell body, an axon bulges to form a terminal. If you look inside an axon terminal with an electron microscope, you can see round, hollow spheres, known as synaptic vesicles, which contain molecules of chemical messengers.

We have been using the term white matter to describe pathways formed by nerve fibers, or axons. You have probably heard the term *gray matter* as well. Now that you understand the structure of neurons, these terms will make more sense. Live neural tissue looks rather pink. When we prepare neural tissue for study using microscopes, the chemicals used to preserve the tissue are absorbed by cell bodies. This gives cell bodies a pink–gray coloring. In contrast, these chemicals are repelled by the insulating material covering most axons, because the insulation has a fatty composition that doesn't mix well with the watery preservatives (we discuss the nature of this insulation shortly). As a result, axons look white, like the fat in a steak. When we examine images of the brain, areas that look gray have a high density of cell bodies, whereas areas that look white consist of large bundles of axons.

If neurons are the stars of the nervous system team, glia are the trainers, coaches, and scorekeepers. They make it possible for neurons to do their job effectively. Some glia (from the

neuron A cell of the nervous system that is specialized for sending and receiving neural messages.
cell body The large, central mass of a neuron, containing the nucleus.
axon The branch of a neuron that is usually responsible for transmitting information to other neurons.
dendrite A branch from the neural cell body that usually receives input from other neurons.

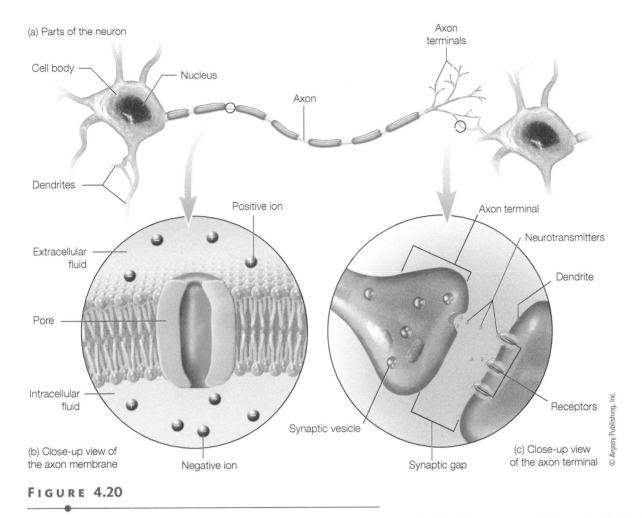

(a) Parts of the neuron

Cell body

Nucleus

Axon terminals

Axon

Dendrites

Positive ion

Axon terminal

Neurotransmitters

Extracellular fluid

Dendrite

Pore

Intracellular fluid

Receptors

(b) Close-up view of the axon membrane

Negative ion

Synaptic vesicle

Synaptic gap

(c) Close-up view of the axon terminal

© Argosy Publishing, Inc.

FIGURE 4.20

The Neuron. Neurons share many features with other living cells but are specialized for the processing of information. **(a) Parts of the neuron.** Like other types of animal cells, the neuron features a nucleus in its cell body and a fatty membrane that separates the intracellular and extracellular fluids. Unlike most other cells, the neuron has specialized branches, the axon and the dendrites, that pass information to and receive information from other cells. **(b) A close-up view of the axon membrane.** A thin oily membrane separates the intracellular fluid inside the neuron from the extracellular fluid outside the neuron. Pores spanning the membrane act as channels that allow ions to move into and out of the neuron. **(c) A close-up view of the axon terminal.** Within the axon terminal are synaptic vesicles, which contain chemical messengers called neurotransmitters that transmit signals between neurons. Later in the chapter, we'll see how these neurotransmitters communicate with receptors on the dendrites of other neurons.

Greek word for "glue") provide a structural matrix for neurons, ensuring that the neurons stay in place (see ● Figure 4.21). Other glia are mobile, allowing them to move to a location where neurons have been damaged to clean up debris. Glia form tight connections with the blood vessels serving the nervous system. This forms a blood–brain barrier that prevents many toxins circulating in the blood from exiting into brain tissue where neurons could be harmed. Psychoactive drugs, by definition, are substances capable of penetrating the blood–brain barrier with ease. We discuss psychoactive drugs and the ways in which they act on the nervous system in Chapter 6.

In vertebrates like us, glia wrap around some axons like sausages on strings at a delicatessen, forming an important layer of insulation called **myelin**. Myelin makes neural signaling fast and energy efficient. We will discuss how myelin accomplishes this in a later section on neural signaling. Not all axons in the human nervous system are myelinated. When you hurt yourself, the fast, sharp "ouch" message is carried to the brain by myelinated axons, but the dull, achy message that lasts a lot longer is carried by unmyelinated axons.

One type of glia forms the myelin in the brain and spinal cord, and a second type forms the myelin in the remainder of the nervous system (see ● Figure 4.22). These two types of glia behave quite differently from each other when they are damaged. Glia in the brain and spinal

myelin The insulating material covering some axons.

FIGURE 4.21

The Blood–Brain Barrier. Glia form tight connections with the blood vessels in the nervous system, preventing many toxins from entering the brain. Glia also help hold neurons in place and form the myelin on some axons.

Blood vessel

Neuron

Glia

© Argosy Publishing, Inc.

cord form scar tissue, inhibiting repair to the damaged nerves. Because of this feature, we consider damage in the central nervous system to be permanent. Considerable research is under way to figure out how to repair such damage, including work using stem cells to grow bridges across the damaged areas. In contrast, damaged glia in the peripheral nervous system do not form scar tissue and instead help the damaged axons regrow. As a result, nerve damage in these areas can heal. If this were not so, operations to reattach limbs would be doomed to failure. Nowadays, not only are digits and even limbs that were lost in accidents routinely reattached to their rightful owners, but a number of patients whose own hands or faces were damaged beyond repair have undergone successful transplants from cadavers (Clarke & Butler, 2009; Dubernard, Owen, Lanzetta, & Hakim, 2001).

As we explore further in Chapter 11, myelin growth in the human nervous system begins before birth, but it is not completed until early adulthood, possibly as late as the age of 25. The last area of the nervous system to be myelinated is the prefrontal cortex, which is involved with judgment and morality (Hayak et al., 2001). Until myelin in this area is mature, these neurons do not work as efficiently, which is one of the possible reasons teenagers and adults sometimes make different decisions (Baird et al., 1999). You may recall some experiences from your early teens that appear shocking and overly risky to your adult brain. Worse yet, as you move through your 20s, you might find yourself agreeing more frequently with your parents.

Frontal lobes

Reprinted with permission from the *American Journal of Roentgenology.*

The image on the left shows myelin (in white) in the brain of a 2-year-old child. The image on the right shows the greater amount of myelin in the brain of an 18-year-old. Myelination of the human brain is not complete until people are in their early to mid-20s. The last areas to be myelinated are the frontal lobes, which are involved in self-regulation, decision making, and judgment.

Neural Signaling

Now that we have a working knowledge of the structure of neurons, we are ready to talk about how they function. A neuron is a sophisticated communication and information-processing system that receives input, evaluates it, and decides whether to transmit information to neurons downstream. Its actions are similar to

FIGURE 4.22

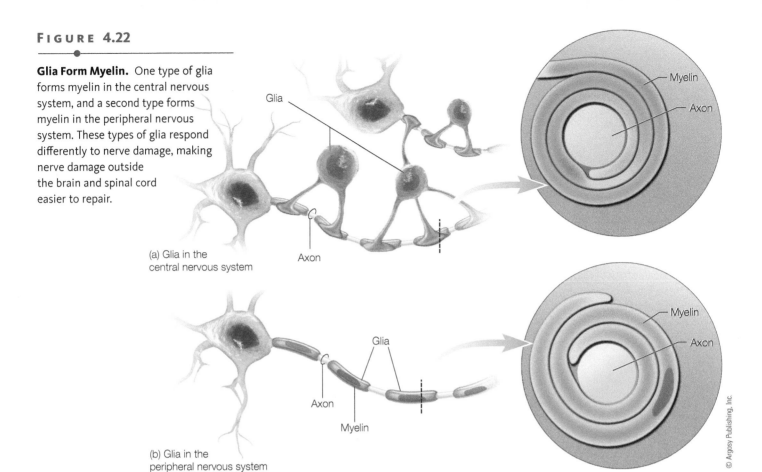

Glia Form Myelin. One type of glia forms myelin in the central nervous system, and a second type forms myelin in the peripheral nervous system. These types of glia respond differently to nerve damage, making nerve damage outside the brain and spinal cord easier to repair.

Glia

Axon

(a) Glia in the central nervous system

Myelin

Axon

Glia

Axon

Myelin

(b) Glia in the peripheral nervous system

Myelin

Axon

© Argosy Publishing, Inc.

your own when you receive a juicy bit of gossip from a friend and then decide whether to tell somebody else.

As we mentioned earlier, neural communication is a two-step process. In the first step, which takes place in the signaling neuron's axon, the neuron generates an electrical signal known as an **action potential**. This signal travels the length of the axon from its junction with the cell body to its terminal. In the second step, which takes place between two neurons, the arrival of an action potential at the axon terminal of the first neuron signals the release of chemical messengers, which float across the extracellular fluid separating the two neurons. These chemicals influence the likelihood that the second neuron will respond with its own action potential, sending the message along.

Electrical Signaling The production of action potentials can be demonstrated using axons dissected from a squid and placed in a tub of seawater, which has a chemical composition similar to the fluid surrounding our body cells (Hodgkin & Huxley, 1952). Of all the possible sources of axons on the earth, why choose squid? Certain axons from a squid can be as much as 1 millimeter in diameter, large enough to see with the naked eye. The squid axon is also large enough that you can insert a recording electrode into its interior without disrupting its function. The readings from inside the axon can then be compared with readings from a recording electrode placed in the seawater.

When a neuron is not processing information, we say that it is at rest. When a cell is at rest, the difference between the readings from the interior of the axon and the external fluid is known as the **resting potential**. Our

Alba Lucia Cardona of Colombia lost both hands in an accident 30 years ago and recently had two cadaver hands surgically attached. This type of operation would be useless unless the nerves in her arms could communicate with her new hands.

action potential The electrical signal arising in a neuron's axon.
resting potential The measure of the electrical charge across a neural membrane when the neuron is not processing information.

Kai Forsterling/epa/Corbis

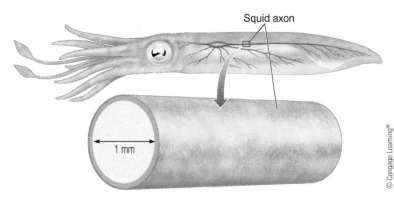

Squid axon

1 mm

© Cengage Learning®

Some squid axons are large enough to be seen with the naked eye and remain active in a bath of seawater for hours. These features make studying neural activity in a squid axon relatively simple.

The blood–brain barrier might offer too much protection to the brain in some cases. Many chemotherapy agents used to treat cancer in other parts of the body cannot penetrate the blood–brain barrier, which complicates the treatment of tumors in the brain.

recording will show that the interior of the neuron is negatively charged relative to its exterior, due to the different chemical composition of the intracellular and extracellular fluids.

Let's assume that our resting neuron now begins to receive chemical messages from another neuron, a process we discuss in more detail shortly. Neurons can respond to incoming chemical signals by becoming either depolarized or hyperpolarized. The word *polarized* means "far apart," such as when political factions disagree. Being depolarized means we have moved closer together, and being hyperpolarized means we have moved even farther apart than before. In the case of neurons, depolarization means that the difference between the electrical charges of the extracellular and the intracellular recordings is decreasing. Hyperpolarization means that the difference is increasing.

When a neuron is depolarized by sufficient input, it reaches a threshold for producing an action potential. A threshold is the point at which an effect, the action potential in this case, is initiated. Once this threshold is reached, the generation of an action potential is inevitable. Approaching the threshold for initiating an action potential is similar to pulling the trigger of a gun. As you squeeze the trigger, nothing happens until you reach a critical point. Once that critical point is reached, the gun fires, and there is nothing you can do to stop it.

Reaching threshold initiates a sequence of events that reliably produces an action potential (see ● Figure 4.23). These events involve the opening and closing of pores, or channels, in the neural membrane, which in turn allow certain chemicals to move into and out of the cell. These chemicals are in the form of ions, or electrically charged particles dissolved in water. When threshold is reached, channels open, allowing one type of ion, sodium, to rush into the neuron. Because sodium ions carry a positive electrical charge, we can see their movement reflected in a steep rise in our recording of the difference between the internal and the external electrodes. At the peak of the action potential, our recording has reversed itself from the resting state. Now the interior of the cell is more positively charged than the outside.

Near the peak of the action potential, channels open that allow another type of ion, positively charged potassium, to move across the membrane. Potassium begins to leave the cell. As the interior loses these positively charged potassium ions, our recording heads in the negative direction again. Following the production of the action potential, the neuron requires a timeout, or refractory period, during which it returns to its resting state. During this refractory period, the cell is unable or unlikely to respond to further input by producing another action potential.

The size and shape of action potentials are always the same, whether we're recording them in a squid or in a human. You won't see recordings of short, fat action potentials or tall, skinny ones. Either an action potential occurs or the cell remains at rest—there is no middle ground. Because of this consistency, we say that action potentials are all or none.

Action potentials do not affect the entire axon all at once. The process we just described takes place first in a small segment of the axon where the axon connects to the cell body. The next step is propagation, or the duplication of the electrical signal down the length of the axon to the axon terminal, where it initiates the release of chemical messengers.

We mentioned earlier that myelinated neurons enjoyed some advantages in efficiency and speed, and we are now ready to discuss why that is the case. Propagation takes place differently in myelinated and unmyelinated axons. In an unmyelinated axon, action potentials occur step by step, from one small section of the axon to the next, adjacent section, down the entire length of the axon. In contrast, action potentials in myelinated axons are formed only at the sections of the axon membrane between adjacent segments of myelin, known as nodes of Ranvier. In other words, propagation in myelinated axons can "skip" the sections covered by myelin. You might think about propagation in unmyelinated versus myelinated axons as being similar to shuffling your feet versus taking long strides. Which covers the most ground faster and more efficiently?

Propagation in unmyelinated axons works well, as evidenced by the wealth of invertebrate life on the earth, from the snails in your garden to the giant squid of the oceans. These animals

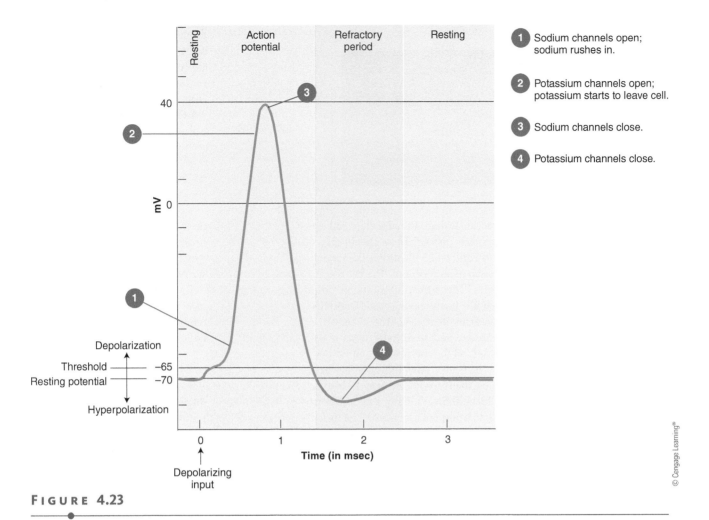

FIGURE 4.23

The Action Potential. Once threshold is reached, an action potential is triggered. The movement of sodium and potassium ions across the axon membrane is reflected in the rise and fall of our recording, respectively. A refractory period follows each action potential, and triggering another action potential during this time is more difficult.

survive with no myelin, but their neural communication is not fast or energy efficient compared to ours. Forming action potentials at each section down the length of the axon is time consuming, like taking the local bus that stops at every block. In addition, cleaning up after all these action potentials uses a lot of energy (Swaminathan, Burrows, & McMurray, 1982). The more action potentials it takes to move a signal down the length of the axon, the more energy is expended returning the cell to its resting state.

Propagation in myelinated axons is fast and efficient (see ● Figure 4.24). After an initial action potential is generated near the cell body, the current flows beneath a segment of myelin until it reaches a node of Ranvier, where another action potential occurs. Like the express bus, the action potentials skip the myelinated sections of the

Sushi made from puffer fish, known as *fugu,* is a delicacy, but when prepared poorly, it can result in sickness or death. Chefs who prepare *fugu* undergo extensive training and licensing in Japan. The puffer fish toxin blocks the movement of sodium into cells, making electrical signaling impossible. As a result, diners who eat poorly prepared *fugu* can become paralyzed and suffocate to death.

Nodes of Ranvier

The Science Picture Company/Alamy

A node of Ranvier, located between two adjacent segments of myelin, is rich in sodium channels, which makes the formation of action potentials at the node possible.

synapse A point of communication between two neurons.
neurotransmitter A chemical messenger that communicates across a synapse.
receptor A special channel in the membrane of a neuron that interacts with neurotransmitters released by other neurons.
reuptake A process in which molecules of neurotransmitter in the synaptic gap are returned to the axon terminal from which they were released.

axon, reaching their destination, the axon terminal, about 20 times faster than if the axon were unmyelinated. By covering the same distance with fewer action potentials, the myelinated axon uses less energy returning to the resting potential than an unmyelinated axon would need.

Once the action potential reaches the axon terminal, the neural communication system switches from an electrical signaling system to a chemical signaling one.

Chemical Signaling The point of communication between two neurons is known as a **synapse**. At the synapse, neurons do not touch one another physically. Instead, they are separated by tiny gaps filled with extracellular fluid. Because electrical signals are unable to jump this gap, neurons send chemical messengers instead. These chemical messengers are called **neurotransmitters** (see Table 4.4).

● Figure 4.25 illustrates the sequence of events triggered by the arrival of an action potential at an axon terminal. The neurotransmitters in the axon terminal are contained in synaptic vesicles. The arrival of an action potential releases the vesicles from their protein anchors, much like boats leaving a dock, and the vesicles migrate rapidly to the cell membrane. Because the vesicles are made of the same thin, oily material as the membrane, they easily fuse with the membrane and spill their contents into the synaptic gap. Following release, the vesicles are pinched off the membrane and refilled.

The neurotransmitters released across the synaptic gap come into contact with special channels on the receiving neuron, known as receptors. **Receptors** work with the neurotransmitters like locks and keys. Only a neurotransmitter with the right shape (the key) can attach itself, or bind, to a particular receptor (the lock). Neurotransmitters do not stay bound to receptors long. Once they pop out of the receptor binding site, neurotransmitter molecules drift away from the gap, are broken down by enzymes, or return to the axon terminal from which they were released in a process called reuptake. In **reuptake**, special channels in the axon terminal membrane allow the neurotransmitters to move back into the releasing neuron, where they are repackaged for later use. Many important drugs, including the antidepressant drug fluoxetine (Prozac), interfere with or inhibit this reuptake process.

The interaction between neurotransmitters and their receptors can have one of two effects on the receiving neuron: excitation or inhibition. When a neurotransmitter has an excitatory

FIGURE 4.24

Propagation of the Action Potential. Action potentials move down the length of the myelinated axon more quickly than they move down an unmyelinated axon.

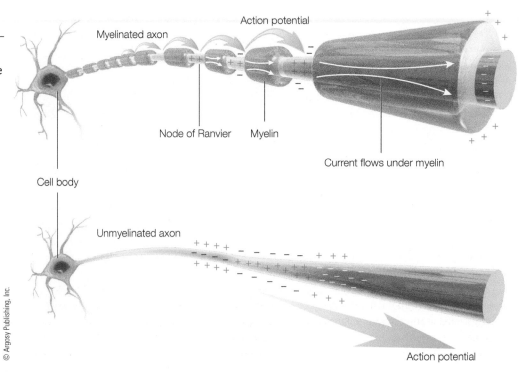

Action potential

Myelinated axon

Node of Ranvier   Myelin

Current flows under myelin

Cell body

Unmyelinated axon

Action potential

© Argosy Publishing, Inc.

140   Chapter 4 | THE BIOLOGICAL MIND: THE PHYSICAL BASIS OF BEHAVIOR effect, it slightly depolarizes the receiving neuron, increasing the likelihood that the neuron will reach threshold and initiate an action potential. Recall that depolarization reduces the difference between the electrical environments inside and outside the neuron. When a neurotransmitter has an inhibitory effect, it slightly hyperpolarizes the receiving neuron, moving the cell farther from threshold and reducing the likelihood that it will initiate an action potential. Recall that hyperpolarization increases the difference between the electrical environments inside and outside the neuron.

Excitatory messages seem logical. One neuron is telling another to "pass the message along." Inhibitory messages, however, seem somewhat strange at first glance. Why would our nervous systems need a message that says, "Don't pass the message along"? Tetanus, for which you probably have been vaccinated, provides a dramatic example of what can happen when inhibition doesn't work properly. The toxin produced by the bacteria responsible for tetanus selectively damages inhibitory neurons in the parts of the nervous system that control muscle contraction. Normally, excitatory inputs that contract muscles coordinate their activity with inhibitory inputs that tell muscles to relax, allowing the steady hands we

Eye of Science/Science Source

Two axons (in purple) are forming synapses, or junctions where communication will occur, with a neuron's cell body (in yellow).

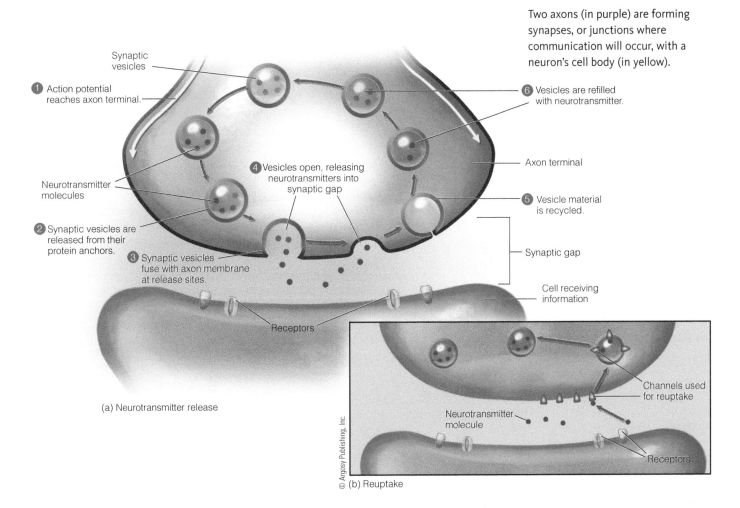

① Action potential reaches axon terminal.

Synaptic vesicles

Neurotransmitter molecules

② Synaptic vesicles are released from their protein anchors.

③ Synaptic vesicles fuse with axon membrane at release sites.

④ Vesicles open, releasing neurotransmitters into synaptic gap

Receptors

⑥ Vesicles are refilled with neurotransmitter.

Axon terminal

⑤ Vesicle material is recycled.

Synaptic gap

Cell receiving information

(a) Neurotransmitter release

© Argosy Publishing, Inc.

Neurotransmitter molecule

Channels used for reuptake

Receptors

© (b) Reuptake

FIGURE 4.25

Chemical Signaling. Because most neurons are separated from one another by extracellular fluid, the action potential cannot jump from one neuron to the next. To cross the gap between neurons, chemical signals are used instead. **(a) Neurotransmitter release.** The arrival of an action potential at the axon terminal triggers a sequence of events that results in the release of neurotransmitter molecules, which float across the synaptic gap to interact with receptors on the receiving neuron. **(b) Reuptake.** After interacting with receptors, neurotransmitter molecules are often recaptured by the neuron that released them to be recycled and used again later.

TABLE 4.4 Important Neurotransmitters

Neurotransmitter	Behaviors influenced by the neurotransmitter
Acetylcholine (ACh)	• Movement • Memory • Autonomic nervous system function
Epinephrine (Adrenalin)	• Arousal
Norepinephrine (Noradrenalin)	• Arousal • Vigilance
Dopamine	• Movement • Planning • Reward
Serotonin	• Mood • Appetite • Sleep
Glutamate	• Excitation of brain activity
GABA	• Inhibition of brain activity
Endorphins	• Pain

© Cengage Learning®

The "SSRI" label for some antidepressant medications, including Prozac, stands for selective serotonin reuptake inhibitor. People who are depressed often have lower than normal serotonin activity at the synapse. If you inhibit reuptake of serotonin, then more molecules remain in the synaptic gap longer, where they can continue to interact with receptors. Serotonin activity increases, relieving depression, because we get more "bang for the buck" each time serotonin is released.

need to put in a contact lens, for example. Without the input of the inhibitory neurons, the system is left with excitation only, and the result is the extreme muscle contraction that gives tetanus its other name—lockjaw (see ● Figure 4.26).

Synapses usually occur in many locations on the dendrites or cell body of the receiving neuron, and the depolarizing or hyperpolarizing current that results from neurotransmitter activity at these synapses drifts to the junction of the cell body and axon. If there is sufficient depolarization to reach threshold at this junction, the neuron generates an action potential. If not, it remains at rest. The neuron's "decision" to generate an action potential or not is called summation; the neuron is adding up all incoming messages and making a decision based on that information. The neuron's task is not unlike the situation we face when we ask friends and family for advice. We will receive some excitatory advice (Go for it!), along with some inhibitory advice (Don't even think about it!). Our job, like the neuron's, is to sum our input and make a decision. Unlike us, however, the neuron cannot disregard the advice it receives.

Types of Neurotransmitters

Researchers have identified more than 50 chemicals that serve as neurotransmitters. Table 4.4 lists some neurotransmitters that are particularly interesting to psychologists, and we will highlight a few of these in this section. In Chapter 6, we explore examples of psychoactive drugs, both therapeutic and recreational, that interact with the normal biochemistry of the nervous system.

Acetylcholine (ACh) is a neurotransmitter found in a number of systems important to behavior. ACh is found at the neuromuscular junction, the synapse at which the nervous system commands muscles. Interference with the action of ACh at the muscles can result in paralysis and death, making drugs that act on ACh popular for use as pesticides and as bioweapons. ACh also serves as a key neurotransmitter in the autonomic nervous system, discussed previously, which carries commands from the brain to the glands and organs. ACh is also intimately involved in the brain circuits related to learning and

FIGURE 4.26

Tetanus Blocks Motor Inhibition. The severe muscle contraction that gives tetanus its nickname of lockjaw results from the toxin's blocking the release of inhibitory neurotransmitters in the motor systems of the brain and spinal cord. (a) Normally, inhibitory input balances contraction to maintain smooth movements. (b) Without the counterbalance of inhibition, too much muscle contraction occurs.

memory. These brain circuits are among the first to deteriorate in Alzheimer's disease. Not surprisingly, memory deficits are among the earliest symptoms of Alzheimer's disease to appear. Among the many drugs that act on ACh systems is the nicotine found in tobacco.

Norepinephrine is released in the brain and leads to arousal and vigilance. Consistent with this role in arousal, norepinephrine is also released by the sympathetic nervous system. As we observed previously, the sympathetic nervous system prepares us to react to emergencies by providing the resources needed for extra activity, like the extra oxygen that is needed to run or throw a punch. Abnormalities in norepinephrine activity have been implicated in a number of psychological conditions that feature disturbances in arousal and vigilance, including bipolar disorder and posttraumatic stress disorder (PTSD), discussed in Chapter 14.

Dopamine is involved with systems that govern movement, planning, and reward. Parkinson's disease, which makes normal movement difficult, results when dopamine-releasing neurons in the brain's movement circuits begin to die. In addition, dopamine participates in the brain's reward and pleasure circuits by becoming active whenever we engage in behaviors that promote survival and successful reproduction, such as eating a great meal or having sex. Most drugs that produce addiction, including cocaine and methamphetamine, stimulate increased activity in dopamine circuits. In Chapter 14, we will see how disruptions to dopamine circuits have been implicated in schizophrenia and ADHD.

Serotonin is involved with systems regulating sleep, appetite, and mood. Consequently, these three behaviors are tightly linked. As we will see in Chapter 14, people who experience depressed mood also show abnormalities in appetite and sleep. Sleep deprivation can result in changes in mood and appetite, even leading to significant overeating (Spiegel, Tasali, Penev, & Van Cauter, 2004).

Endorphins (short for endogenous morphine, or morphine produced by the body) modify our natural response to pain. In evolutionary terms, it makes a great deal of sense to have a system that will reduce your chances of being disabled by pain during an emergency. All too frequently, however, we underestimate the extent of our injuries until we wake up the next morning feeling sore. "Runner's high," in which people who regularly engage in endurance sports experience a sense of well-being and reduced sensation of pain, is probably because of the release of endorphins initiated by high levels of activity. Opioid drugs such as morphine, heroin, and OxyContin produce their pain-relieving effects by mimicking the action of endorphins at the synapse. In other words, the opioid drugs are so similar in chemical structure to our natural endorphins that the receptors cannot tell them apart and treat the opioids as if they were natural endorphins.

Botox, which is used to treat muscle spasms or reduce wrinkles, is made from an inactive form of the toxin responsible for botulism, which is produced by bacteria that spoil food. Botox interacts with ACh by preventing its release from the axon terminal. Without the activity of ACh telling a muscle to contract, the muscle remains paralyzed.

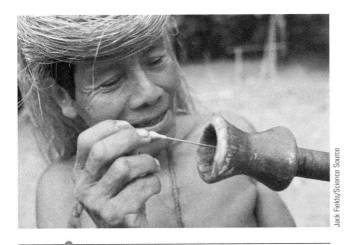

A Yagua hunter in Peru loads a dart tipped with curare into the mouthpiece of his blowgun. Curare is derived from native plants and causes paralysis by blocking receptors for acetylcholine (ACh) at synapses between the nervous system and the muscle fibers.

This image highlights areas of the human brain that are rich in receptors for endorphins, our natural opioid. The red areas have the most endorphin receptors, followed by the yellow areas. Opioid drugs, such as heroin or morphine, affect our behavior by interacting with these receptors.

Interpersonal Relationships
The Biological Perspective
Is There a Difference Between Love and Lust?

For many people, love and lust seem close together. Using the biological perspective, however, these two states can look related yet still quite distinct.

On a neurochemical level, sexual desire or lust is driven primarily by levels of testosterone for both men and women (Welling et al., 2007), while the bonding we associate with romantic love is largely associated with oxytocin (Diamond, 2004). This suggests that at least on a hormonal level, it is possible to differentiate the two states.

Further understanding of the relationship between lust and love comes from brain imaging research. Of particular interest is the insula, an area of cortex lining the lateral sulcus, which separates the temporal lobes from the frontal and parietal lobes. Pulling the temporal lobe away from the rest of the brain reveals the insula within the sulcus. As shown in ● Figure 4.27, researchers found that activation of the posterior part of the insula, or the part toward the back of the brain, is more closely associated with the pleasant sensations that we think of as lust (Cacioppo, Bianchi-Demicheli, Frum, Pfaus, & Lewis, 2012). In contrast, these same researchers found that activation of the anterior, or forward, part of the insula is more associated with romantic feelings of love. They conclude that "love grows out of and is a more abstract representation of the pleasant sensorimotor experiences that characterize desire" (Cacioppo et al., 2012, p. 1048).

Additional support for the role of the anterior insula in love comes from a unique case study (Cacioppo et al., 2013). The male patient who was the subject of the case study had experienced damage to his anterior insula. The researchers presented the patient with a task that required him to indicate whether a series of attractive individuals could be the object of his lust or his love. Compared to healthy control participants that matched the patient for age, gender, and ethnicity, the patient showed a selective deficit in his decisions about love yet performed normally on decisions about lust. The patient was similar to the controls in the number of people he categorized as objects of love or lust, and his response time to objects of lust appeared normal. However, his response time for categorizing objects of love was slower than that of the healthy controls.

Should we conclude that the anterior insula is a "love center" of the brain? It would be better to conclude, as Cacioppo et al. (2013) do, that the anterior insula participates in a larger network that helps us figure out internal states, which includes feelings of romantic love. ●

© 2016 Cengage Learning®

FIGURE 4.27

Brain Areas Associated With Sexual Desire and Romantic Love. Areas shown in blue are uniquely active during sexual desire, while areas shown in red are uniquely active during romantic love. One of the areas where activity reliably varies between the states of sexual desire and romantic love is the insula. Activity in the posterior insula (toward the back of the brain) is associated with sexual desire, while activity in the anterior insula (toward the front of the brain) is associated with romantic love.

Summary 4.3 Neural Communication

	Structure	What to remember
	Neuron	• Cell body: contains the nucleus and carries out most house-keeping functions • Axon: used to send information • Dendrite: used to receive information
	Glia	• Hold neurons in place • Clean up debris • Form myelin • Blood–brain barrier
	Action potentials	• Propagated down the axon to the terminal • Resting potential: no incoming signals • Action potential: occurs when cell reaches threshold • Refractory period: follows action potential
	Synapse	• Point of communication between two neurons
	Neurotransmitters	• Released when an action potential arrives at a terminal • Interact with receptors in the receiving neuron's membrane • Deactivated if they remain in the synaptic gap • ACh • Norepinephrine • Dopamine • Serotonin • Endorphins

Credits: Top Row. MPI Biochemistry/Volker Steger/Science Source. Second Row. © Argosy Publishing, Inc. Third Row: © Argosy Publishing, Inc. Fourth Row: Eye of Science/Science Source. Bottom Row: Jack Fields/Science Source.

KEY TERMS The Language of Psychological Science

Be sure you can define these terms and use them correctly.

5 The Perceiving Mind

Sensation and Perception

WE LIKE TO THINK WE UNDERSTAND REALITY. After all, we can see, hear, touch, smell, and taste it. We don't live in some science fiction universe where things are not how they appear. Or do we?

The human eye can see many different colors, but what does it mean to "see" a color? Is color something that is a fixed quality of an object? Is the sky really blue, and is an apple really red? Or does the human mind construct these colors from the light reflected from these objects into the eye? Stop for a moment to look at the *Discovering Psychology* image to the left. In the upper part of the image, the area with many stripes, do the words *Discovering* and *Psychology* look the same? Do the words *Cacioppo* and *Freberg* look the same? If you're like most people, your answer to these questions will be "no." But in the lower part, you can see the words without the stripes in their actual colors. You might think we're being tricky and changing the colors in the upper image, but honestly, we wouldn't do that to you. What makes the words look different in the upper image is the colors surrounding them. The light reflecting from the words into your eye hasn't changed, but the way your mind interprets the information changes because of the words' context. Something happens between the time we zoom in to study the function of the rods and cones of the eye, shown in the larger image to the left, and when we zoom out again to learn how the brain processes vision. Incidentally, this image is an example of the Munker illusion, named after its discoverer (Munker, 1970).

What can we learn from phenomena like the Munker illusion? First, we believe there is an objective reality out there that follows the laws of physics. At the same time, our experience of that reality is personal. For example, some people have a type of red–green color deficiency. As you will learn in this chapter, *colorblindness* is not an accurate term. Individuals with color deficiencies see color, just differently from the way the rest of us see it. Would having a color deficiency change the way a person sees the Munker illusion? See for yourself. We can reconstruct how the images would look to a person with one type of red-green color deficiency (see • Figure 5.1). The illusion still works to a point, because the colors of *Discovering* and *Psychology* in the striped image look different, and they're not. Is the "reality" seen by a person with a color deficiency different from your reality? We're going to argue that it is not reality that changes but rather the way the brain views that reality.

◀ The rods and cones in the retina begin the process of interpreting the light energy that enters the eye.

147

© Cengage Learning®

FIGURE 5.1

The Munker Illusion and Color Deficiency. Color is constructed by the human mind from light waves that reach the retina, so the experience of color can be intensely personal. Here, we see the same images as shown on the previous page, but this time they are shown as they would appear to a person with a common form of red–green color deficiency.

As you'll see in this chapter, we carefully construct models of reality from the information we obtain through our senses. We like to think that we are aware of the world around us, and it is somewhat unsettling to realize that the world might be quite different from the representations of reality formed by the human mind. You will learn how the models built by the human mind have promoted our survival over many generations. Our models of reality are quite different from those built by the minds of other animals, whose survival often depends on obtaining different types of information from the environment around them.

Learning Objectives

1. Explain basic concepts of sensation and perception, including transduction of stimuli into neural signals, distinctions between bottom-up and top-down perceptual processing, thresholds, and measurement.

2. Analyze the process by which the physical structures of the eye transduce light waves into neural signals producing the sense of vision.

3. Explain the processes responsible for color vision, object recognition, and depth perception.

4. Analyze the process by which physical structures of the ear transduce sound waves into neural signals, producing perception of pitch, loudness, and spatial location in hearing.

5. Summarize the mechanisms by which the somatosensory and chemical sense systems produce perception of body position, touch, skin temperature, pain, smell, and taste.

6. Analyze the causes of various individual differences in perception (including development and culture) in terms of biology, experience, and their interaction.

How Does Sensation Lead to Perception?

sensation The process of detecting environmental stimuli or stimuli arising from the body.

Our bodies are bombarded with information, whether we are asleep or awake. This information can take many forms, from the electromagnetic energy of the sun to vibrations in the air to molecules dissolved in the saliva on our tongue. The process of **sensation** brings information to the brain that arises in the reality outside our bodies, like a beautiful sunset, or originates from within, like an upset stomach.

Sensory systems have developed through natural selection, described in Chapter 3, to provide information that enhances survival within a particular niche. We sense a uniquely human reality, and one that is not necessarily shared by other animals. Your dog begins howling seconds before you hear the siren from an approaching ambulance, because the dog's hearing is better than yours for these high-pitched sounds. Horses seem to bolt at the slightest provocation, but they may be reacting to the vibration of an approaching car or animal that they sense through their front hoofs, a source of information that is not available to the rider. Some animals sense light energy outside the human visible spectrum. Insects can see ultraviolet light, and some snakes can use infrared energy to detect their prey.

Differences in sensation do occur from person to person, such as the need to wear corrective glasses or not, but they are relatively subtle. However, once we move from the process of sensation to that of **perception**, or the interpretation of sensory input, individual differences become more evident. For example, friends voting for different presidential candidates will come to different conclusions about who won a debate. Everyone watching the exchange probably sensed similar information from the environment, but each person's perceptions are likely to be unique.

Some types of snakes (vipers, boas, and pythons) can sense prey using infrared energy.

Sensory Information Travels to the Brain

Sensation begins with the interaction between a physical stimulus and our biological sensory systems. A stimulus is anything that can elicit a reaction from our sensory systems. For example, we react to light energy that falls within our visual range, as we will see later in this chapter, but we cannot see other types of light energy that fall outside that range, such as the microwaves that cook our dinner or the ultraviolet waves that can harm our skin (see ● Figure 5.2).

Before you can use information from your senses, it must be translated into a form the nervous system can understand. This process of translation from stimulus to neural signal is

We have all had the experience of watching events with others (sensation) and then being shocked by the different interpretations we hear of what just happened (perception).

perception The process of interpreting sensory information.

FIGURE 5.2

All Species Experience an Adaptive Reality. Humans see only a small part of the electromagnetic energy emitted from the sun. Some animals see even less. Dogs apparently do fine seeing blues, yellows, and grays, whereas humans have evolved to see a more colorful world. The dog's view of the world is simulated in the photo on the right.

Leah Warkentin/AGE Fotostock

Wavelength in meters

| 10⁻¹⁵ | 10⁻¹⁴ | 10⁻¹³ | 10⁻¹² | 10⁻¹¹ | 10⁻¹⁰ | 10⁻⁹ | 10⁻⁸ | 10⁻⁷ | 10⁻⁶ | 10⁻⁵ | 10⁻⁴ | 10⁻³ | 10⁻² | 10⁻¹ | 10¹ | 10² | 10³ |

Cosmic rays | Gamma rays | X-rays | Ultraviolet | Visible | Infrared | Microwaves | Radar | TV FM AM Radio waves | Short waves

VISIBLE RANGE

Human's view

400   450   500   550   600   650   700   750

Wavelength in nanometers

Dog's view

known as **transduction**. You might think of sensory transduction as similar to the processing of information by your computer. Modern computers transduce a variety of inputs, including voice, keyboard, mouse clicks, and touch, into a programming language for further processing.

The Brain Constructs Perceptions From Sensory Information

Once information from the sensory systems has been transduced into neural signals and sent to the brain, the process of perception, or the interpretation of the sensory information, can begin. Perception allows us to organize, recognize, and use the information provided by the senses.

An important gateway to perception is the process of attention, defined as a narrow focus of consciousness. As we discuss in Chapters 6, 9, and 10, attention often determines which features of the environment influence our subsequent thoughts and behaviors. What types of

transduction The translation of incoming sensory information into neural signals.

stimuli are likely to grab our attention? Unfamiliar, changing, or high-intensity stimuli often affect our survival and seem to have a high priority for our attention. Unfamiliar stimuli in our ancestors' environment might have meant a new source of danger (an unknown predator) or a new source of food (an unfamiliar fruit) that warranted additional investigation. Our sensory systems are particularly sensitive to change in the environment. Notice how you pay attention to the sound of your heating system cycling on or off but pay little attention to the noise it makes while running. This reduced response to an unchanging stimulus is known as **sensory adaptation**. High-intensity stimuli, such as bright lights and loud noises, invariably draw our attention because the situations that produce these stimuli, such as a nearby explosion, can have obvious consequences for our safety.

We rarely have the luxury of paying attention to any single stimulus. In most cases, we experience divided attention, in which we attempt to process multiple sources of sensory information. Many of us try to walk to class without getting run over by a car while texting. These divided attention abilities are limited. We simply cannot process all the information converging simultaneously on our sensory systems. To prioritize input, we use selective attention, or the ability to focus on a subset of available information and exclude the rest.

We refer to the brain's use of incoming signals to construct perceptions as **bottom-up processing**. For example, we construct our visual reality from information about light that is sent from the eye to the brain. However, the brain also imposes a structure on the incoming information, a type of processing known as top-down. In **top-down processing**, we use the knowledge we have gained from prior experience with stimuli to perceive them. For example, a skilled reader has no trouble reading the following sentences, even though the words are jumbled:

All you hvae to do to mkae a snetnece raedalbe is to mkae srue taht the fisrt and lsat letrtes of ecah wrod saty the smae. Wtih prcatice, tihs porcses becoems mcuh fsater and esaeir.

How can we explain our ability to read these sentences? First, we require bottom-up processing to bring the sensations of the letter shapes to our brain. From there, however, we use knowledge and experience to recognize individual words. Many students have learned the hard way that term papers must be proofread carefully. As in our example, if the brain expects to see a particular word, you are likely to see that word, even if it is misspelled, a mistake that is unlikely to be made by the literal, bottom-up processing of a computer spell-checker.

Can we predict when the mind will use bottom-up or top-down processing? There are no hard and fast rules. Obviously, we always use bottom-up processing, or the information would not be perceived. It is possible that bottom-up processing alone allows us to respond appropriately to simple stimuli, like indicating whether you saw a flash of light. As stimuli become more complicated, like reading a sentence or recognizing a friend in a crowd, we are more likely to engage in top-down processing in addition to processing from the bottom up.

AP Images/Google

Divided attention abilities are limited, and the advent of wearable technologies like Google Glass might push the boundaries of those limitations.

If you think about the most memorable advertisements you have seen lately on television or online, it is likely that they share the features of attention-getting stimuli: novelty (we don't see talking geckos every day), change (rapid movement, use of changing colors, and the dreaded pop-up), and intensity (the sound is often louder than the program you're watching).

sensory adaptation The tendency to pay less attention to a nonchanging source of stimulation.
bottom-up processing Perception based on building simple input into more complex perceptions.
top-down processing A perceptual process in which memory and other cognitive processes are required for interpreting incoming sensory information.

skyhawk x/Shutterstock

Selective attention, or our focus on a subset of input, prioritizes incoming information. However, we can sometimes be so focused that we miss important information. An astonishing 20 out of 24 expert radiologists completely missed the image of a gorilla superimposed on scans of lungs while scanning for signs of cancer. Source is Drew, T., Võ, M. L.-H., & Wolfe, J. M. (2013). The invisible gorilla strikes again: Sustained inattentional blindness in expert observers. Psychological Science, 24(9), 1848-1853. doi: 10.1177/0956797613479386

FIGURE 5.3

Connecting the Physical World and the Mind.

"Golden" rectangles, named for their proportions rather than color, appear in art and architecture dating back to ancient Greece, but why are they attractive? Gustav Fechner (1801–1887) made many attempts to link physical realities with human psychological responses. He asked people to choose which rectangles are most pleasing or least pleasing. His results indicated that the most pleasing rectangle was fourth from the right. This rectangle is the closest to having golden proportions (1:1.618). Its sides have a ratio of 13:21.

Most pleasing
- - - Least pleasing

The Golden Rectangle

psychophysics The study of relationships between the physical qualities of stimuli and the subjective responses they produce.

absolute threshold The smallest amount of stimulus that can be detected.

difference threshold The smallest detectable difference between two stimuli.

Measuring Perception Gustav Fechner (1801–1887) developed methods, which he called **psychophysics**, for studying the relationship between stimuli (the physics part) and perception of those stimuli (the psyche or mind part) (see ● Figure 5.3). Fechner's careful methods not only contributed to the establishment of psychology as a true science but are still used in research today.

The methods of psychophysics allow us to establish the limits of awareness, or thresholds, for each of our sensory systems. The smallest possible stimulus that can be detected at least 50% of the time is known as the **absolute threshold**. Under ideal circumstances, our senses are surprisingly sensitive (see ● Figure 5.4). For example, you can see the equivalent of a candle flame 30 miles (about 48 kilometers) away on a moonless night. We can also establish a **difference threshold**, or the smallest difference between two stimuli that can be detected at least 50% of the time. The amount of difference that can be detected depends on the size of the stimuli being compared. As stimuli get larger, differences must also become larger to be detected by an observer. For example, it is easier to detect the difference between a 5-pound weight and a 10-pound weight (2.3 to 4.5 kilograms) than between a 400-pound weight and a 405-pound weight (181.4 to 183.7 kilograms), even though the absolute difference in weight is the same in both cases.

FIGURE 5.4

Absolute Sensory Thresholds. An absolute threshold is the smallest amount of sensation that can be processed by our sensory systems under ideal conditions. Moving from left to right in this image, we see that the absolute threshold for touch is the equivalent of feeling the wing of a fly fall on your cheek from a distance of 0.4 inch (about 1 centimeter), the absolute threshold for olfaction is a drop of perfume in the air filling a six-room apartment, the absolute threshold for sweetness is the equivalent of 1 teaspoon (about 5 grams) of sugar in 2 gallons (about 7.5 liters) of water (the absolute threshold for bitter tastes is even more sensitive), the absolute threshold for hearing is the equivalent of the sound of a mosquito 10 feet (about 3 meters) away, and the absolute threshold for vision is seeing a candle flame 30 miles (about 48 kilometers) away on a dark, clear night.

The wing of a fly falling on you from a distance of .4 inch (about one centimeter)

A drop of perfume diffused into the entire volume of air in a six-room apartment

Illustration: © Cengage Learning®; photos, left to right: © Gladskikh Tatiana/Shutterstock.com, © Kuttelvaserova Stuchelova/Shutterstock.com, © Christopher Elwell/Shutterstock.com, © AlexRoz/Shutterstock.com

Signal Detection Many perceptions involve some uncertainty. Perhaps you're driving rather fast, and you think a distant car behind you might be a police officer. Do you slow down right away? Or do you wait until the car is close enough that you know for sure it's a police officer? How do your expectations affect your decision to drive fast? Maybe you are convinced that as long as you're following another car, you won't get a ticket. How do your personal feelings about making mistakes affect your decision? Would the cost of a ticket ruin your budget?

This type of decision making can have serious implications, such as in the case of decisions made by radiologists after examining the results of mammograms for signs of cancer. Is there reason for concern or not? This situation is different from the thresholds described earlier, because it adds the cognitive process of decision making to the process of sensation. In other words, **signal detection** is a two-step process involving (a) the actual intensity of the stimulus, which influences the observer's belief that the stimulus did occur, and (b) the individual observer's criteria for deciding whether the stimulus occurred.

Experiments on signal detection provide insight into this type of decision making. In these experiments, trials with a single, faint stimulus and trials with no stimulus are presented randomly. The participant states whether a stimulus was present on each trial. The possible outcomes of this experiment are shown in Table 5.1. In the case of driving fast on the highway, we can use such experiments to help us understand why two people might respond differently, even if they were sensing the same information. If you are more concerned about correctly identifying patrol cars (maximizing hits), you might use more lenient standards for identifying patrol cars and slow down frequently (false alarms), but you would get few tickets. In contrast, another person might use stricter criteria for identifying a patrol car than you use. That driver would have fewer false alarms but would run the risk of missing real patrol cars (maximizing misses), which is likely to be expensive.

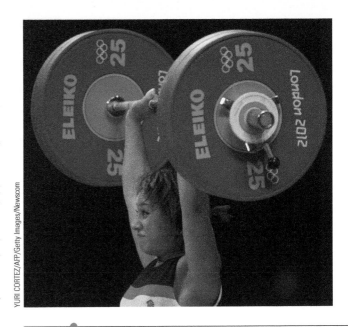

YURI CORTEZ/AFP/Getty Images/Newscom

According to Fechner's work on the difference threshold, British Olympian Zoe Smith would be more likely to notice the difference between 2- and 4-pound (between 1 to 2 kilograms) weights than the difference between her new record of 121 kilograms (266.76 pounds) in the clean and jerk event and the former record of 120 kilograms (264.56 pounds).

Another example of signal detection is a jury's decision about whether a person is guilty. Based on frequently uncertain and conflicting evidence, jurors must weigh their concerns about convicting an innocent person (false alarm) or letting a real criminal go (miss).

signal detection The analysis of sensory and decision-making processes in the detection of faint, uncertain stimuli.

A teaspoon of sugar (about 5 grams) in two gallons (about 7.5 liters) of water

The sound made by a mosquito flying three meters (about 10 feet) away

A candle flame seen at 30 miles (about 48 kilometers) on a clear night

Does this mammogram indicate the woman has cancer or not? Many decisions we make are based on ambiguous stimuli. Signal detection theory helps us understand how an individual doctor balances the risks of missing a cancer and those of alarming a healthy patient.

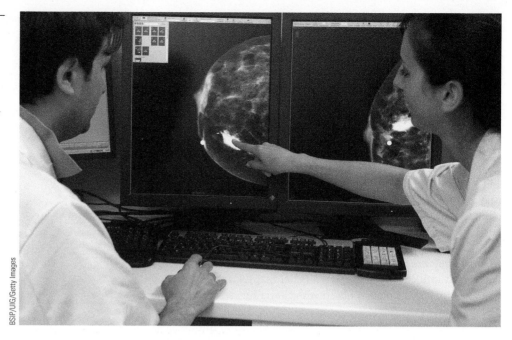

BSIP/UIG/Getty Images

TABLE

5.1 Possible Outcomes in Signal Detection

Participant response	Stimulus present	Stimulus absent
Yes	Hit	False alarm
No	Miss	Correct rejection

© Cengage Learning®

Summary 5.1 Assessing Perception

Concept	Definition	Example
Absolute threshold	The smallest amount of stimulation that is detectable	Seeing light from a candle flame 30 miles away on a dark night
Difference threshold	The smallest difference between two stimuli that can be detected	Being able to detect the difference between two different weights
Signal detection	Correctly identifying when a faint stimulus is or is not present	A radiologist correctly detecting cancer from a mammogram

Credits: Top Row. Karen H. Ilagan/Shutterstock. Second Row. YURI CORTEZ/AFP/Getty Images/Newscom. Bottom Row: BSIP/UIG/Getty Images.

How Do We See?

Vision, the processing of light reflected from objects, is one of the most important sensory systems in humans. Approximately 50% of our cerebral cortex processes visual information, in comparison to only 3% for hearing and 11% for touch and pain (Kandel & Wurtz, 2000; Sereno & Tootell, 2005). We will begin our exploration of vision with a description of the visual stimulus, and then we will follow the processing of that stimulus by the mind into a meaningful perception.

The Visual Stimulus

Visible light, or the energy within the electromagnetic spectrum to which our visual systems respond, is a type of radiation emitted by the sun, other stars, and artificial sources such as a lightbulb. As shown in ● Figure 5.5, light energy moves in waves, like the waves in the ocean. Wavelength, or the distance between successive peaks of waves, is decoded by our visual system as color or shades of gray. The height, or amplitude, of the waves is translated by the visual system into brightness. Large-amplitude waves appear bright, and low-amplitude waves appear dim.

The human visual world involves only a small part of this light spectrum (review Figure 5.2). Gamma rays, x-rays, ultraviolet rays, infrared rays, microwaves, and radio waves lie outside the capacities of the human eye.

The Biology of Vision

Human vision begins with the eye. The eye is roughly sphere shaped and about the size of a ping-pong ball. Its hard outer covering helps the fluid-filled eyeball retain its shape. Toward the front of the eye, the outer covering becomes clear and forms the **cornea**. The cornea begins the process of bending light to form an image on the back of the eye. Traveling light next enters the **pupil**, which is actually an opening formed by the muscles of the **iris** (see ● Figure 5.6). The iris, which means "rainbow" in Greek, adjusts the opening of the pupil in response to the amount of light present in the environment and to signals from the autonomic nervous system, described in Chapter 4. Arousal is associated with dilated pupils, while relaxation is associated with more constricted pupils.

Directly behind the pupil and iris is the main optical instrument of the eye, the **lens**. Muscles attached to the lens can change its shape, allowing us to adjust our focus to see near or distant objects. This adjustment is known as accommodation. Behind the lens is the main chamber of the eye, and located on the rear surface of this chamber is the **retina**, a thin but complex network of neurons specialized for the processing of light.

Located in the deepest layer of the retina are specialized receptors, the rods and cones, that transduce the light information. However, before light reaches these receptors, it must pass through numerous blood vessels and neural layers. We normally do not see the blood vessels and neural layers because of sensory adaptation. As we mentioned previously in this chapter, adaptation occurs when sensory systems tune out stimuli that never change. Because the blood vessels and neural layers are always in the same place, we see them only under unusual circumstances, such as during certain ophthalmology (eye) tests.

vision The sense that allows us to process reflected light.
cornea The clear surface at the front of the eye that begins the process of directing light to the retina.
pupil An opening formed by the iris.
iris The brightly colored circular muscle surrounding the pupil of the eye.
lens The clear structure behind the pupil that bends light toward the retina.
retina Layers of visual processing cells in the back of the eye.

© 2016 Cengage Learning®

FIGURE 5.5

Light Travels in Waves. The distance between two peaks in a light wave (wavelength) is decoded by the visual system as color and the height, or amplitude, of the wave as brightness.

FIGURE 5.6

The Human Eye. Light entering the eye travels through the cornea, pupil, and lens before reaching the retina. Among the landmarks on the retina are the fovea, which is specialized for seeing fine detail, and the optic disk, where blood vessels enter the eye and the optic nerve exits the eye.

Illustration: Argosy Publishing, Inc.; photo: © James P. Gilman, C. R. A./Phototake

We can identify several landmarks on the surface of the retina. The blood vessels serving the eye and axons that leave the retina to form the optic nerve exit in a place known as the optic disk. Because there are no rods and cones in the optic disk, each eye has a blind spot. Normally, we are unaware of our blind spots because perception fills in the missing detail. However, if you follow the directions in ● Figure 5.7, you should be able to experience yours. Toward the middle of the retina is the **fovea**, which is specialized for seeing fine detail. When we stare directly at an object, the image of that object is projected onto the fovea. The fovea is responsible for central vision, as opposed to peripheral vision, which is the ability to see objects off to the side while looking straight ahead.

The image projected on the retina is upside down and reversed relative to the actual orientation of the object being viewed (see ● Figure 5.8). You can duplicate this process by looking at yourself in both sides of a shiny spoon. In the convex, or outwardly curving side, you see your image normally. In the concave, or inwardly curving side, you see your image as your retina sees it. Fortunately, the visual system has no difficulty decoding this image and providing us with realistic perceptions of the actual orientations of objects.

Rods and Cones **Rods** and **cones** are named after their shapes. The human eye contains about 90 million rods and between 4 million and 5 million cones.

Rods and cones are responsible for different aspects of vision. The rods are more sensitive to light than the cones, and they excel at seeing in dim light. As we observed previously, under ideal circumstances, the absolute threshold for human vision is the equivalent of a single candle flame from a distance of 30 miles (about 48 kilometers; Hecht, Shlaer, & Pirenne, 1942). Rods become more common as we move from the fovea to the periphery of the retina, so your peripheral vision does a better job of viewing dim light than your central vision does (see ●

fovea An area of the retina that is specialized for highly detailed vision.
rod A photoreceptor specialized to detect dim light.
cone A photoreceptor in the retina that processes color and fine detail.

FIGURE 5.7

Now You See It—Now You Don't. There are no photoreceptors in the optic disk, producing a blind spot in each eye. We do not see our blind spots because our brain fills in the hole. You can demonstrate your blind spot by holding your textbook at arm's length, closing one eye, focusing your other eye on the dot, and moving the book toward you until the stack of money disappears.

Figure 5.9). Before the development of night goggles, soldiers patrolling in the dark were trained to look to the side of a suspected enemy position rather than directly at their target.

This extraordinary sensitivity of rods has costs. Rods do not provide information about color, nor do they provide clear, sharp images. Under starlight, normal human vision is 20/200 rather than the normal daylight 20/20. In other words, an object seen at night from a distance of 20 feet would have the same clarity as an object seen in bright sunlight from a distance of 200 feet. Cones function best under bright light and provide the ability to see both sharp images and color.

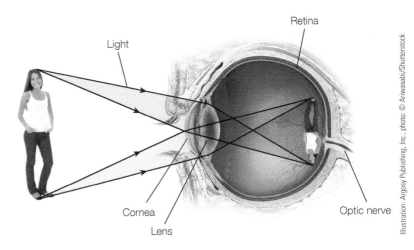

Illustration: Argosy Publishing, Inc.; photo: © Ariwasabi/Shutterstock

FIGURE 5.8

What the Retina "Sees." The image projected on the retina is upside down and reversed, but the brain is able to interpret the image to perceive the correct orientation of an object.

Visual Pathways The rods and cones are the only true receptors of the visual system. When they absorb light, they trigger responses in four additional layers of neurons within the retina. Axons from the final layer of cells, the ganglion cells, leave the back of the eye to form the **optic nerve**. The optic nerves cross the midline at the optic chiasm (named after its X shape, or the Greek letter *chi*). At the optic chiasm, the axons closest to the nose cross over to the other hemisphere, while the axons to the outside proceed to the same hemisphere. This partial crossing means that if you focus straight ahead, everything to the left of center in the visual field is processed by the right hemisphere, while everything to the right of center is processed by the left hemisphere. This organization provides us with significant advantages when sensing depth, which we discuss later in the chapter.

optic nerve The nerve exiting the retina of the eye.

Argosy Publishing, Inc.

FIGURE 5.9

Distribution of Rods and Cones Across the Retina. In humans, cones, indicated by red, blue and green dots, become less frequent as you move from the fovea to the periphery of the retina. The colors of the dots representing cones indicate the colors to which each shows a maximum response (see Figure 5.12). Rods (light brown dots) and cones are named according to their shapes.

FIGURE 5.10

Visual Pathways. Visual information from the retina travels to the thalamus and then to the primary visual cortex in the occipital lobe.

Primary visual cortex (occipital lobe)

Midbrain

Thalamus

Optic chiasm

Retina

Optic tract

Optic nerve

Visual field of right eye

Visual field of left eye

Argosy Publishing, Inc.

Beyond the optic chiasm, the visual pathways are known as **optic tracts** (see ● Figure 5.10). About 90% of the axons in the optic tracts synapse in the thalamus. The thalamus sends information about vision to the amygdala and to the primary visual cortex in the occipital lobe. The amygdala uses visual information to make quick emotional judgments, especially about potentially harmful stimuli. The remaining optic tract fibers connect with the hypothalamus, where their input provides information about light needed to regulate sleep–wake cycles, discussed in Chapter 6, or with the superior colliculi of the midbrain, which manage a number of visually guided reflexes, such as changing the size of the pupil in response to light conditions.

optic tracts Nerve pathways traveling from the optic chiasm to the thalamus, hypothalamus, and midbrain.

The primary visual cortex begins, but by no means finishes, the processing of visual input. The primary visual cortex responds to object shape, location, movement, and color (Hubel & Livingstone, 1987; Hubel & Wiesel, 1959; Livingstone & Hubel, 1984). Two major pathways radiating from the occipital cortex into the adjacent temporal and parietal lobes continue the analysis of visual input. The parietal pathway helps us process movement in the visual environment. The temporal pathway responds to shape and color and contributes to our ability to recognize objects and faces.

Visual Perception and Cognition

To actually see something requires the brain to interpret the information gathered by the eyes. How do you know your sweater is red or green based on the information sent from the retina to the brain? How do you recognize your grandmother at your front door?

Color Vision   Most of us think about colors in terms of the paints and crayons we used in elementary school. Any kindergartner can tell you that mixtures of red and yellow make orange, red and blue make purple, and yellow and blue make green. Mixing them all together produces a lovely muddy brown. Colored lights, however, work somewhat differently (see ● Figure 5.11). The primary colors of light are red, green, and blue, and mixing them together produces white light, like sunlight. If you have ever adjusted the color on your computer monitor or television, you know that these devices also use red, green, and blue as primary colors. Observations supporting the existence of three primary colors of light gave rise to a **trichromatic theory** of color vision.

Trichromatic theory is consistent with the existence of three types of cones in the retina that respond best to short (blue), medium (green), or long (red) wavelengths. Our ultimate experience of color comes not from the response of one type of cone but from comparisons among the responses of all three types of cones (see ● Figure 5.12).

Very rarely, individuals have either one type of cone or none. To these people, the world appears to be black, white, and gray. People with two types of cones are often called colorblind, but as we observed at the beginning of the chapter, this term is not accurate. With two cone types that respond differently to the same light, distinctions between colors can be made. Individuals with two types of cones see color, but they match color samples differently than the rest of us.

Trichromatic theory does a good job of explaining color deficiency, but it is less successful in accounting for other color vision phenomena, like color afterimages. For example, if you stare at the yellow, green, and black flag in ● Figure 5.13 and then focus on the dot within the

FIGURE 5.11

Mixing Colored Lights. The primary colors of paint might be red, yellow, and blue, but in the world of light, the primary colors are red, green, and blue.

trichromatic theory A theory of color vision based on the existence of different types of cones for the detection of short, medium, and long wavelengths.

FIGURE 5.12

Responses by Cones to Colored Light. Our perception of color results from a comparison of the responses of the red, green, and blue cones to light. A 550-nanometer light is perceived as yellow and produces a strong response in green cones, a moderate response in red cones, and little response in blue cones.

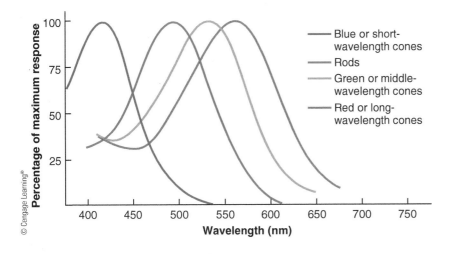

Blue or short-wavelength cones
Rods
Green or middle-wavelength cones
Red or long-wavelength cones

FIGURE 5.13

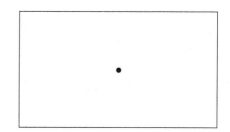

Afterimages Demonstrate Opponent Process Theory. If you stare at the dot in the center of the yellow, green, and black flag for a minute and then shift your gaze to the dot in the white space on the right, you should see the flag in its traditional red, white, and blue.

Monty Roberts, known as the Horse Whisperer, attributes his abilities to observe horse behavior to his complete lack of color vision. This condition is quite rare, occurring in only 1 person out of every 30,000.

opponent process theory A theory of color vision that suggests we have a red–green color channel and a blue–yellow color channel in which activation of one color in each pair inhibits the other color.

white rectangle to the right, you will see an afterimage of the flag in its more traditional colors of red, white, and blue.

An **opponent process theory** of color vision does a better job than the trichromatic theory in explaining these color afterimages. This theory proposes the existence of opposing color channels: a red–green channel and a blue–yellow channel. In other words, we cannot see a color like reddish green or bluish yellow because the two colors share the same channel. Opponent process theory gets support from our understanding of the anatomy of the visual system. Groups of cells that process yellow and blue or red and green are located together (see ● Figure 5.14). Stimulation of one color group in each pair, such as red from the red–green pair, reduces activity in the cells in the other group, or green in this case. You can't see reddish green because stimulating the red cells inhibits activity in the green and stimulating the green cells inhibits activity in the red.

Returning to our green, yellow, and black flag, how can we use opponent process theory to explain our experience of the red, white, and blue afterimage? By staring at the flag, you are producing fatigue in some of your visual neurons. Recall that activity in one color group in a channel reduces activity in the other. At the same time, reducing activity in one color group, as we do when we fatigue green by looking at the flag, increases activity in the other group, which in this case is red. So fatiguing green, black, and yellow causes a rebound effect in each color channel, and your afterimage looks red, white, and blue. (Black and white also share a channel.) If you stare at an image of a real red, white, and blue flag and then look at a white piece of paper, your afterimage looks green, black, and yellow.

Which of these two theories of color vision, trichromatic theory or opponent process theory, is correct? The trichromatic theory provides a helpful framework for the functioning of the three types of cones in the retina. However, as we move from the retina to higher levels of visual analysis in the thalamus and cerebral cortex, the opponent process theory seems to fit observed phenomena neatly. Both theories help us understand color vision but at different levels of the visual system.

FIGURE 5.14

Color Channels in the Retina. Recordings from cells in the monkey visual system support the existence of the red–green and yellow–blue channels predicted by opponent process theory. Groups of cells that process yellow and blue or red and green are located together in doughnut shapes in the retina. Although the red–green channel features both red-center and green-center versions, the yellow–blue channel has only one version featuring a blue center.

Psychology as a Hub Science
Color and Accessible Web Design

Now that you have an understanding of the perception of color, we can consider one of the practical problems associated with individual differences in color vision. Between 7% and 10% of males and about 0.4% of females have a form of red–green color deficiency (see ● Figure 5.15). The reason that males are more affected than females is that the genes for the pigments used by red and green cones are located on the X chromosome, making red–green color deficiency a sex-linked condition (see Chapter 3). Smaller numbers of people lack blue cones (0.0011%) or cones altogether (0.00001%). Given the rather common occurrence of color deficiency, making visual materials accessible to people with all types of color vision is a serious concern.

Color can be an effective tool for designing exciting and engaging websites, but many graphic web designers (who typically have excellent vision) fail to consider how the site might look to a person with a color deficiency. One clue for designing an accessible site can be found in other systems based on color, like traffic lights. Although most of us rely on the color information from the red, yellow, or green lights, the lights also vary in location. In other words, color should never be the only basis for extracting meaning. A second major concern is contrast, which we discuss in the next section. The strong contrast between black letters on the white pages makes text easy to read for most people. Colored text against a colored background might add interest but runs the risk of being harder to read, especially when reds and greens are used. As shown in ● Figure 5.16, various resources exist online that show how a web page looks to a person with color deficiency, which helps designers maximize accessibility. ●

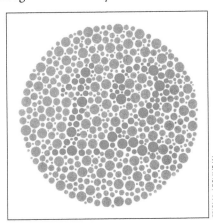

FIGURE 5.15

Detecting Color Deficiency. The Ishihara Color Test, designed by Shinobu Ishihara in 1917, is a standard method for detecting color deficiency. The test is printed on special paper, so the recreated image here would not be considered a valid basis for diagnosing color deficiency.

PRISMA ARCHIVO/Alamy

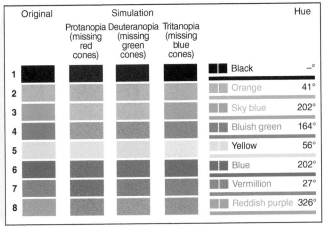

© 2016 Cengage Learning®

FIGURE 5.16

Making Websites Accessible. Web designers have found colors that work for people with typical color vision and people who have color deficiency. This set of colors shows how different shades would be seen by people with typical vision and by people with three of the most common forms of color deficiency. Even though these colors are seen differently by the three groups, nobody mistakes one shade for another.

(a)   (b)

FIGURE 5.17

Can You Figure Out What These Images Are? (a) This might look like a splattering of black dots on a white page until you learn that it represents a Dalmatian dog. (b) Top-down processing ensures that once you know this is a photo of a cow, you can pick out its features easily.

(a) From Richard L. Gregory, "The Medawar Lecture 2001 Knowledge for vision: Vision for knowledge," Phil. Trans. R. Soc. B 2005 360, 1231–1251, by permission of the Royal Society. (b) From American Journal of Psychology. Copyright © 1951 by the Board of Trustees of the University of Illinois. Used with permission of the University of Illinois Press. K. M. Dallenbach, "A puzzle-picture with a new principle of concealment," 64:3 (July 1951): pp. 431-433.

Recognizing Objects

We asked earlier how your brain uses incoming visual signals to recognize your grandmother standing at the front door. A bottom-up approach to this question assumes that as information moves from the retina to higher levels of visual processing, more complicated responses are built from simpler input. In this hierarchical model, the result would be a hypothetical "grandmother cell," or a single cell that could combine all previous input and processing to tell you that your grandmother is at the door.

Although the hierarchical model is attractive in many ways, it does not fit perfectly with what we know about the visual system. First, we would need a large number of single neurons to respond to all the objects and events that we can recognize visually. In addition, the hierarchical model is unable to account for top-down processing, as when our expectations influence what we see. ● Figure 5.17a may appear to be a random pattern of black dots on a white background. Figure 5.17b may not appear to be a recognizable object at all. The sensations produced by these stimuli lead to no meaningful perceptions. However, once we tell you that the first image is a Dalmatian dog and the second image is a cow, you can instantly pick out their shapes. Now that you know what the images are, you will probably never see them again the way you did initially. Recognizing these objects requires knowledge and memory of what Dalmatians and cows look like. It is unlikely that a single cortical cell acting as a Dalmatian or cow detector could incorporate such complex inputs from memory.

 Connecting to **Research**

Can We Identify a Jennifer Aniston Cell?

THE IDEA OF A hierarchical model received some interesting support from an experiment in which the activity of single neurons in patients being prepared for neurosurgery was recorded while they viewed faces, landmark buildings, objects, and printed words (Quain Quiroga, Reddy, Kreiman, Koch, & Fried, 2005).

The Question: Is it possible to identify neurons that preferentially respond to particular faces compared to other faces or stimuli?

METHODS

Eight patients undergoing presurgical testing had recording electrodes implanted in parts of the brain that might be affected by their scheduled surgeries. While the participants were lying in bed, images were projected onto a laptop in front of them, and they were supposed to press the "Y" or "N" key to indicate whether the image was a human face. This process ensured that they were paying attention to the images. Images included famous and unfamous faces, animals, landmarks, and objects. Activity in

individual cells was correlated with the image viewed.

RESULTS

The participants did show activity in single cells that correlated with the images they viewed. One participant had a single cell that became significantly more active when he viewed the actress Halle Berry, whether she appeared in photographs, in drawings, or dressed as Catwoman. The cell activated even when the image consisted of the letters spelling out her name. Another partici-

If we don't use single cells to recognize objects, how else can we accomplish this task? One suggestion is that the visual system may perform a mathematical analysis of the visual field (De Valois & De Valois, 1980). While the hierarchical model implies a reality built out of individual bars and edges, the mathematical approach suggests that we analyze patterns of lines. The simplest patterns of lines are gratings, as shown in ● Figure 5.19. Gratings can vary along two dimensions: frequency and contrast. High-frequency gratings have many bars in a given distance and provide fine detail, while low-frequency gratings have relatively few bars. High-contrast gratings have large differences in intensity between adjacent bars, like black next to white. The print you are reading in is an example of high contrast, because the black letters are quite different from the white background. Low-contrast gratings have subtler differences in intensity between bars, such as dark gray next to black.

Observing responses to gratings can give us a window into the visual capacities of other species. At a certain point of contrast and frequency, gratings look plain gray. Animals can be trained to make a distinction between gratings and gray circles. For example, if a bird is rewarded with food for pecking at a disk with a grating but not for pecking a uniform gray disk, any performance that is better than 50-50, or chance, indicates that the bird can see the difference between the grating and the gray. We can graph the range of gratings that are visible to the observer as a function of their contrast and frequency. ● Figure 5.20 illustrates the visible ranges for human adults and cats. Compared to human adults, cats see less detail. However, cats see large (low-frequency), low-contrast objects better than humans. Large, low-contrast shadows on the wall may get kitty's attention but not yours. You will think kitty is chasing ghosts again.

Gestalt Psychology As we observed in Chapter 1, a group of German researchers known as the Gestalt psychologists tackled visual perception with a number of ingenious observations. The word *Gestalt* is derived from the German word for "shape." These psychologists objected to efforts by Wilhelm Wundt and the structuralists to reduce human experience to its building blocks, or elements. Instead, the Gestalt psychologists argued that some experiences lose information and value when divided into parts. The main thesis of the Gestalt psychologists, as stated by Kurt Koffka, maintains, "It is more correct to say that the whole is something else than the sum of its parts" (Koffka, 1935, p. 176).

pant had a "Jennifer Aniston cell" that activated when he viewed her photograph, but the cell remained quiet when the photograph included Aniston's ex-husband, Brad Pitt (see ● Figure 5.18).

CONCLUSIONS

The results of this study support the hierarchical model of perception. However, as the Gestalt psychologists pointed out, there is more to a whole perception than the sum of its parts (activity of single cells). ●

F I G U R E **5.18**

A Jennifer Aniston Cell. Recordings show that a single cell became active whenever a photo or drawing of actress Jennifer Aniston was presented to the patient, unless the actress was pictured along with her now ex-husband Brad Pitt.

From R. Quian Quiroga, L. Reddy, G. Kreiman, C. Koch, & I. Fried, Invariant visual representation by single neurons in the human brain, Nature 435, 1102–1107 (23 June 2005), doi:10.1038/nature03687

Helga Esteb/Shutterstock

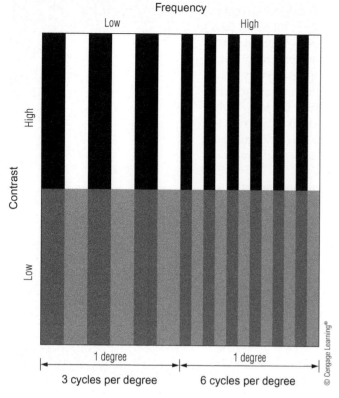

Frequency

Low   High

1 degree | 1 degree

3 cycles per degree | 6 cycles per degree

© Cengage Learning®

FIGURE 5.19

Features of Gratings. An alternative to the hierarchical model suggests that the visual system analyzes the visual environment as a collection of patterns, like these gratings. Gratings vary in frequency (number of bars in a given distance) and contrast (the difference in light intensity from one bar to the next).

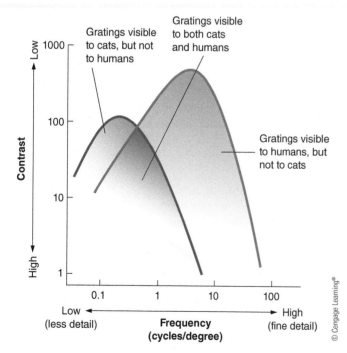

Gratings visible to cats, but not to humans

Gratings visible to both cats and humans

Gratings visible to humans, but not to cats

Low
(less detail) **Frequency (cycles/degree)** High
(fine detail)

© Cengage Learning®

According to the Gestalt psychologists, we are born with a number of built-in tendencies to organize incoming sensory information in certain ways. This natural ability to organize simplifies the problem of recognizing objects (Biederman, 1987). The first organizing principle suggests that we analyze visual input by dividing a scene into figure and ground. In other words, we identify the main object in the scene (the figure), which stands out from the background. We frequently assume that the figure stands in front of most of the ground, and it seems to have more substance and shape. It is possible to construct ambiguous images, like the one created by the vase on the next page in which the parts of the image seem to switch roles as figure or ground. Although you can switch back and forth between the faces and the vase, efforts to see both at once are likely to be frustrating.

A second Gestalt principle is proximity (see ● Figure 5.21). Objects that are close together tend to be grouped together. The dots that make up our Dalmatian in Figure 5.17a are close together, suggesting they belong to the same object. The principle of similarity states that similar stimuli are grouped together. On a close examination of the dog image, the dots that make up the dog are similar to one another and slightly different (more rounded perhaps) than the dots making up the remainder of the image.

The principle of continuity suggests that we assume that points that form smooth lines when connected probably belong together (see ● Figure 5.22). In our dog picture, continuity helps us see the border of the curb or sidewalk and the ring of shadow around the base of the tree. Continuity is perhaps a little less useful in identifying the dog, although we can pick out the lines forming the legs.

Closure occurs when people see a complete, unbroken image even when there are gaps in the lines forming the image (see ● Figure 5.23). We use this approach in viewing the dog in Figure 5.17a when we "fill in the blanks" formed by the white parts of its body.

Finally, the Gestalt psychologists believed in the principle of simplicity, which suggests that we will use the simplest solution to a perceptual problem. This principle may help explain the fun in pictures like that of our Dalmatian dog. It is simpler to assume that this is a random splash of black dots on white background. Finding a hidden picture within the dots is not the simplest solution, which may account for some of our surprise.

Recognizing Depth An image projected onto the retina is two dimensional, as flat as the sheet of paper on which these words appear. Somehow, the brain manages to construct a three-dimensional (3D) image from these data. Adelbert Ames constructed a room that was named in his honor, the Ames Room, which illustrated vulnerabilities in our **depth perception** (Ittleson, 1952). When viewed directly from the front, the room appears to be a rectangle. People within the room, shown in ● Figure 5.24, seem to be larger

FIGURE 5.20

What Do Cats See? Using gratings, we get a window into the visual world of the cat. By comparing gratings to a uniform gray disk, we can learn when a grating with a certain contrast and frequency simply looks gray to humans or cats. We can see better detail than kitty, but she sees large shadows that we don't even notice.

The Gestalt psychologists believed we naturally see the difference between objects and their background, but this figure is designed to make us switch back and forth from vase to background faces. This vase was designed to commemorate an anniversary of Queen Elizabeth II of England (face on the right) and her husband, Prince Philip (face on the left).

or smaller than normal. This distortion of perceived size results from the room's ability to confuse our judgment of distance.

To construct a 3D image, we use both **monocular cues** (one eye) and **binocular cues** (two eyes). Many monocular cues are found in paintings, because the artists attempt to provide an illusion of depth in their two-dimensional pieces. The use of linear perspective, or the apparent convergence of parallel lines at the horizon, by Italian artists during the 15th century provided a realism unknown in earlier works. Linear perspective revolutionized the video game and movie industries, beginning humbly with Sega's *Zaxxon* in 1982 and advancing to the ever more realistic environments of *Halo,* Pixar's animated films, and the 2009 film *Avatar.* Other monocular cues include texture gradients and shading. We can see more texture in objects that are close to us, while the texture of distant objects is relatively blurry. Shading and the use of highlights can be used to suggest curved surfaces.

SSPL/Science Museum/Art Resource, NY

depth perception The ability to use the two-dimensional image projected on the retina to perceive three dimensions.
monocular cue A depth cue that requires the use of only one eye.
binocular cue A depth cue that requires the use of both eyes.

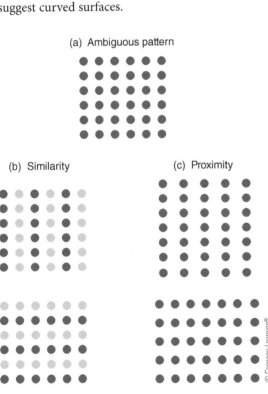

(a) Ambiguous pattern

(b) Similarity   (c) Proximity

© Cengage Learning®

F I G U R E 5.21

The Gestalt Principles of Proximity and Similarity. The set of dots in (a) do not appear to have any particular relationship with one another, but when we color rows in (b), we suddenly see the dots in columns or rows. Moving two columns or rows slightly closer to each other in (c) makes us see the array differently too.

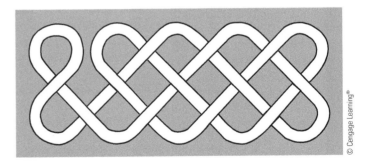

© Cengage Learning®

F I G U R E 5.22

The Gestalt Principle of Continuity. The Gestalt principle of continuity says that we perceive points forming a smooth line as belonging to the same object. If you follow this knot, you can see that it is formed by two objects, but our initial perception is of a single form.

FIGURE 5.23

The Gestalt Principle of Closure.
Because of the principle of closure, we "fill in the blanks" to see a single object, the World Wildlife Fund logo, although it is made up of several objects.

Among the most powerful monocular depth cues is occlusion, or the blocking of images of distant objects by closer objects. We also use relative size to judge the distance of objects, although this method requires you to be familiar with the real size of an object. We know how big people are. When the retinal image of a person is small, we infer that the person is farther from us than when the retinal image of a person is larger.

Several illusions result from our use of monocular cues to judge depth. Relative size helps to explain the moon illusion. You may have noticed that the moon appears to be larger when it is just above the hills on the horizon than when it is straight overhead. The moon maintains a steady orbit 239,000 miles (385,000 km) above the earth. How can we account for the discrepancy in its apparent size? When viewed overhead, the moon is seen without intervening objects, such as trees and hills, that might provide cues about its size and distance. However, when viewed near the horizon, we see the moon against a backdrop of familiar objects whose sizes we know well. We expect trees and hills to be smaller at the horizon than when they are close to us, and if we group the moon with those objects, we adjust its apparent size as well. The next time you are viewing the full moon as it rises over the hills, form a peephole with your hand, and you will see the moon in its normal small size. Although some researchers argue that atmospheric differences between the two viewpoints may contribute to the illusion, viewing the moon through your hand should demonstrate that most of the effect arises from your use of other objects to judge distance.

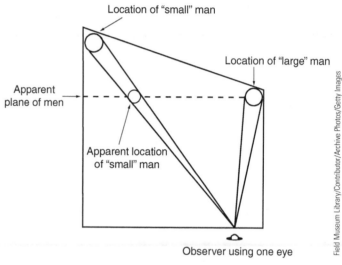

Location of "small" man

Location of "large" man

Apparent plane of men

Apparent location of "small" man

Observer using one eye

FIGURE 5.24

The Ames Room Tricks Our Depth Perception. Many distance cues, such as the apparently rectangular windows, conspire to make these two people look different. The person on the right is much closer to us than the person on the left. The diagram shows the actual layout of the Ames Room.

retinal disparity The difference between the images projected onto each eye.

The Müller–Lyer illusion, shown in ● Figure 5.25, would not cause us problems except that we perceive the images as having corners. Even though the main lines project images of equal length on the retina, we tend to see the line with outward-pointing arrowheads as being farther from our position. The Ponzo illusion, shown in ● Figure 5.26, confounds size and distance judgments in a similar fashion. The parallel lines signal depth, leading us to believe that the upper horizontal line is farther away than the lower line. If both lines project the same image on the retina, the more distant line must be longer.

So far, we have discussed monocular cues that involve a person and a scene that is not moving. The introduction of motion can heighten the impression of depth. As you ride in a car, focus your gaze at a distant point. The objects you pass will appear to be moving in the opposite direction of your car, with closer objects appearing to move faster than distant objects. Next, focus on a point about midway between you and the horizon. Now, the closer objects will continue to move in the opposite direction, but more distant objects appear to be traveling with you. This motion parallax has also been used with great effectiveness to enhance the 3D feeling in video games.

One of our most effective depth cues is **retinal disparity**. Because this cue requires the use of both eyes, we refer to retinal disparity as a binocular cue. Predator species, including ourselves, usually have eyes placed in the front of the head facing forward. As a result of this configuration, the visual scenes observed by the two eyes are different, as shown in ● Figure

F I G U R E   5.25

The Müller–Lyer Illusion. You might find it hard to believe that the two red vertical lines are actually the same length.

5.27. The differences between the images projected onto each eye are called disparities. These disparities do not tell us how far away an object is. Instead, they provide information about the relative distance between two objects in the visual field. As the distance between the objects increases, disparity increases. To illustrate the sensitivity of this system, you can identify an object as being 1 millimeter (about .04 inch) closer than another at a distance of 1 meter (about 3.3 feet) from your body, or a difference of 0.1% (Blake & Sekuler, 2006).

Why would this binocular depth system be an advantage to predators? Most prey species do an excellent job of hiding, often aided by an appearance that blends into the nearby environment. However, retinal disparity allows us to spot tiny variations in the depths of objects in the visual field. This might make an animal stand out against its background,

Video games, like *Minecraft,* incorporate many monocular cues to provide an experience of depth. The standard-sized blocks used to build structures in the game are separated by lines, which when placed in a row provide linear perspective. Texture gradients, shading, and relative size (players understand the size of the blocks well) also contribute to perceived depth.

The two lenses of 3D cameras are separated by about 2 inches (about 50 millimeters), mimicking the distance between two human eyes that makes retinal disparity possible.

FIGURE 5.26

The Ponzo Illusion. We perceive depth because of linear perspective, which in turn make us see the upper horizontal bar as more distant than the lower bar. Even though they are the same length, the bar perceived as more distant looks longer.

even though it is well camouflaged. Retinal disparity has been used to identify camouflaged military equipment and counterfeit currency. Retinal disparity is imitated by cameras used to film 3D movies, which have two lenses separated by about the same distance as our two eyes.

Developmental and Individual Differences in Vision

Although we can't ask human infants what they can or can't see, we can take advantage of their longer gazing at patterns than at uniform stimuli, like a patch of a single color. This allows us to construct graphs of the contrasts and frequencies to which children respond, similar to those we saw previously for cats. Based on these analyses, we know that human infants can see everything human adults can see, but with less detail. To see well, the infant also needs more contrast than the adult. These findings help explain children's preferences for large, high-contrast objects.

The photographs shown on the next page provide insight into the visual world of the infant. Frequencies that cannot be seen by the infant have been removed from each photograph. Other research shows that infants as young as 4 months not only show binocular disparity, as discussed earlier, but also show normal adult responses to color (Bornstein, Kessen, & Weiskopf, 1976). Other depth cues discussed previously develop quite early too. Infants as young as 2 months understand occlusion (Johnson & Aslin, 1995), and the use of the relative size of objects to judge depth appears between the ages of 5 and 7 months (Granrud, Haake, & Yonas, 1985). Infants' abilities to perceive faces also develop quite rapidly, because 2-day-old newborns spend more time gazing at their mothers' faces than at a stranger's face (Bushnell, 2001).

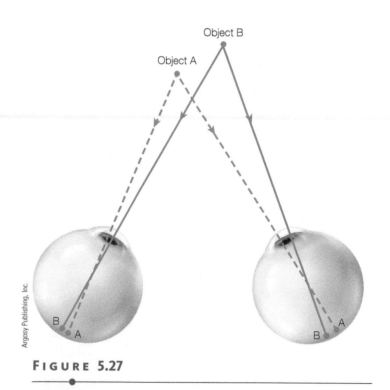

FIGURE 5.27

Retinal Disparity. The right and left eyes see slightly overlapping versions of the visual scene in front of us. We can use the retinal disparity, or discrepancy between the locations of two objects on the two retinas, as a sensitive depth cue.

| 1 month | 2 months | 3 months | adult |

Felix Mizioznikov/Shutterstock.com

We can filter out the frequencies and contrast that a baby cannot see to simulate what the world looks like to an infant.

Predictable changes occur in other aspects of human vision as we grow older. Accommodation of the lens, which allows us to change focus from near to far objects, becomes slower beginning in middle adulthood. Older adults also respond more slowly to changes in brightness, such as leaving a dark theater into the sunlight. The muscles of the iris begin to lose their elasticity, so pupils remain smaller, further reducing vision by limiting the amount of light that enters the eye. The lens of the eye begins to yellow, which protects the eye from ultraviolet radiation but affects the perception of color.

At any age, individual differences shape what people see. In addition to the color deficiencies discussed previously, people differ in their abilities to see near and far objects. Those who deviate from the average often wear corrective lenses or undergo laser surgery to reshape the cornea. The most common visual problems result from eyeball length, with elongated eyeballs interfering with a person's vision for distant objects (nearsightedness) and shortened eyeballs interfering with vision for close-up objects (farsightedness), as in reading. Vision is also affected by astigmatism, which means that the surface of the cornea is uneven. You can test yourself for astigmatism by looking at ● Figure 5.28.

© Cengage Learning®

F I G U R E 5.28

Astigmatism. If you have astigmatism, which results from an uneven surface of your corneas, some spokes of this figure will appear darker than others.

© Hannah Faye Chua

FIGURE 5.29

Cultural Differences in Viewing Scenes. When viewing this photo of a tiger, American participants spent more time viewing the tiger than the background, whereas Asian participants spent approximately equal amounts of time viewing the tiger and the background. This image shows tracings of eye movements from one representative American participant (left) and one representative Asian participant (right).

 Thinking Scientifically

The Roger Shepard Parallelogram Illusion: "Turning the Tables"

ANYONE CAN TELL, simply by looking, whether two tabletops are the same shape, right? For instance, most people would agree that the shapes and sizes of the two tabletops depicted in ● Figure 5.30 are different. One tabletop appears to be rectangular, the other more square. As much as our perceptions may tell us otherwise, these tabletops are identical. (To verify this, trace one of the tabletops and then rotate it to place it above the other. You will be able to prove that these tables have identical tops.) It is not our eyes (sensory receptors) that deceive us; it is our brains.

Roger Shepard combined a profound scientific curiosity with a love of mischief.

Shepard developed a number of creative visual illusions, including "Turning the Tables," which he illustrated himself (Shepard, 1990). The visual illusion produced in this illustration results from our use of a visual system designed to cope with the three dimensions of the physical world on stimuli that have only two dimensions.

In Roger Shepard's words:

The drawings . . . achieve their effects by means of various visual tricks. But to call them tricks is not to imply that they are without psychological significance. The tricks work by taking advantage of fundamental perceptual principles that have been shaped by natural selection in a three-dimensional

world. Our ability to make pictures, which emerged only recently on an evolutionary time scale, enables us to present the eyes with visual patterns that systematically depart from the patterns that we and our ancestors experienced in nature. In considering the ways pictures can trick the eye, we can gain insight into the nature and ultimate source of the principles of visual perception. (Shepard, 1990, p. 121)

More generally, examples like this underscore the importance of relying on scientific investigation and evidence to unveil how sensation and perception work. ●

Sociocultural Influences on Visual Perception

Earlier in the chapter, we explored a number of illusions of depth. There is some evidence that experience plays a role in whether these stimuli provoke an illusion. When tested in 1905, residents of Papua, New Guinea, and the Todas of southern India were less likely than Western participants to see the Müller–Lyer illusion (Rivers, 1905). Similar results were found among participants in Africa and the Philippines (Segall, Campbell, & Herskovits, 1966). The Western experience with a carpentered world of right angles, rectangles, and straight lines might account for these cultural differences.

In addition, the idea that a figure–ground organization is a built-in aspect of the human condition has been challenged (Chua, Boland, & Nisbett, 2005). Eye movements of American and Chinese college students were recorded as they scanned photographs. As shown in ● Figure 5.29, the American students were more likely to focus quickly on the figure, whereas the Chinese students gave approximately equal viewing time to the figure and to its context, or ground. Subsequently, the American students did a better job of identifying which objects they had seen previously, even when the object was shown against a new background. The researchers suggested that some differences they observed stem from cultural differences in the importance of context. According to this view, the American emphasis on individualism makes context less important than it might be for the Chinese students, for whom context provides important cues for proper social functioning. Further cross-cultural research would be helpful in determining the universality of perceptual principles.

© Cengage Learning®

FIGURE 5.30

Are These Tables the Same or Different? You will probably want to use a ruler to prove to yourself that the lines marked "a" are the same and that the lines marked "b" are the same.

Summary 5.2 Important Features of the Visual System

Feature	Significance
Cornea	Bends light toward the retina
Pupil	Forms an opening in the iris
Lens	Focuses light onto the retina
Retina	Contains rods, cones, and other visual neurons in its layer of cells
Fovea (area of the retina)	Processes detailed vision
Thalamus	Acts as the target for most axons forming the optic tracts
Primary visual cortex (area in the occipital lobe)	Receives visual input from the thalamus and performs initial analysis of input

Credits: Top Row. Argosy Publishing, Inc. Second Row. Argosy Publishing, Inc. Third Row. Argosy Publishing, Inc. Fourth Row. Argosy Publishing, Inc. Fifth Row. Argosy Publishing, Inc. Sixth Row. Argosy Publishing, Inc. Bottom Row: Argosy Publishing, Inc.

How Do We Hear?

We have spent a considerable amount of time and space on the sense of vision, which might be considered a dominant source of information for humans. However, when Helen Keller, who was both blind and deaf, was asked which disability affected her the most, she replied that blindness separated her from things while deafness separated her from people. **Audition**, our sense of hearing, not only allows us to identify objects in the distance but also plays an especially important role in our ability to communicate with others through language.

The Auditory Stimulus

Sound begins with the movement of an object, setting off waves of vibration in the form of miniature collisions between adjacent molecules in air, liquid, or solids. Because sound waves require this jostling of molecules, sound cannot occur in the vacuum of space, which contains no matter. Those explosions we enjoy in *Star Wars* films are great entertainment but not good science.

Earlier in this chapter, we described light energy as waves with different amplitudes and frequencies. Sound waves may be described using the same dimensions. However, in the case of sound, the height or amplitude of the wave is encoded as loudness or intensity and the frequency of the wave is encoded as pitch. High-amplitude waves are perceived as loud, and low-amplitude waves are perceived as soft. High-frequency waves (many cycles per unit of time) are perceived as high pitched, whereas low-frequency sounds are low pitched. In sound, amplitude is usually measured in units called decibels (dB), and frequency is measured in cycles per second, or hertz (Hz; see ● Figure 5.31).

As we observed in the case of the light spectrum, parts of the auditory spectrum are outside the range of human hearing. Ultrasound stimuli occur at frequencies above the range of human hearing, beginning around 20,000 Hz (see ● Figure 5.32). Ultrasound can be used to clean jewelry or your teeth or to produce noninvasive medical images. Infrasound refers to frequencies below the range of human hearing, or less than 20 Hz. Many animals, including elephants and marine mammals, use infrasound for communication. Infrasound is particularly effective in water, because it allows sound to travel long distances.

In addition to dizziness and nausea, being exposed to infrasound makes people report feelings of chills down the spine, fear, and revulsion, even though they cannot consciously detect the sound. Some scientists believe that infrasound produced in certain places leads people to conclude the places are haunted.

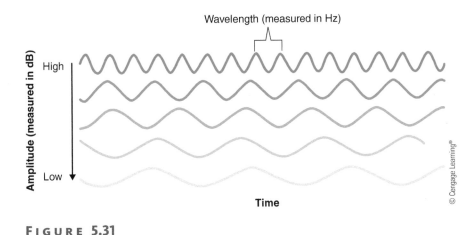

FIGURE 5.31

Features of Sound. Like the light energy we see, sound waves are characterized by frequency and amplitude. We perceive frequency as the pitch of the sound (high or low), measured in hertz (Hz), and we perceive amplitude as the loudness of the sound, measured in decibels (dB).

audition The sense of hearing.

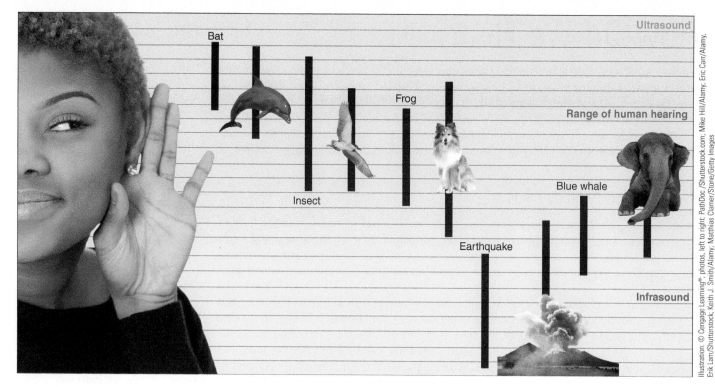

FIGURE 5.32

Range of Hearing. Ultrasounds are above the range of human hearing, and infrasounds are below the range of human hearing.

The Biology of Audition

Human audition begins with an ear located on either side of the head. The components that make up the ear are usually divided into three parts: the outer ear, the middle ear, and the inner ear (see ● Figure 5.33).

The outer ear consists of the structures that are visible outside the body. The pinna, the outer visible structure of the ear, collects and focuses sounds, like a funnel. In addition, the pinna helps us localize sounds as being above or below the head. Sounds collected by the pinna are channeled through the auditory canal, which ends at the tympanic membrane, or eardrum, at the boundary between the outer and the middle ear. The boundary between the middle and the inner ear is formed by another membrane, the oval window. The gap between these two membranes is bridged by a series of tiny bones. The purpose of these bones is to transfer sound energy from the air of the outer and middle ear to the fluid found in the inner ear. Sound waves are weakened as they move from air to water. When you try to talk to friends underwater, the result is rather garbled. Without the adjustments provided by these small bones, we would lose a large amount of sound energy as the sound waves moved from air to liquid within the ear.

The fetus has no bubble of air in the middle ear, having never been exposed to air. Because fluids do a better job than air of transmitting sound waves, there is good evidence that the fetus can hear outside sounds, such as mother's voice, quite well during the final trimester of pregnancy.

The inner ear contains two sets of fluid-filled cavities embedded in the bone of the skull. One set is part of the vestibular system, which we will discuss later in this chapter. The other set is the **cochlea**, from the Greek word for "snail." When rolled up like a snail shell, the human cochlea is about the size of a pea. It contains specialized receptor cells that respond to vibrations transmitted to the inner ear.

The cochlea is a complex structure, which is better understood if we pretend to unroll it (see ● Figure 5.34). The cochlea may be divided into three parallel chambers divided from one another by membranes. Two of these chambers, the vestibular canal and the tympanic canal, are connected at the apex of the cochlea, or the point farthest from the oval window. Vibrations transmitted by the bones of the middle ear to the oval window produce waves in the fluid of the vestibular canal that travel around the apex and back through the tympanic canal. Lying be-

cochlea The structure in the inner ear that contains auditory receptors.

tween the vestibular and the tympanic canals is the cochlear duct. The cochlear duct is separated from the tympanic canal by the **basilar membrane**. Resting on top of the basilar membrane is the **organ of Corti**, which contains many rows of hair cells that transduce sound energy into neural signals. Each human ear has about 15,500 of these hair cells.

As waves travel through the cochlea, the basilar membrane responds with its own wavelike motion, similar to the crack of a whip. The movement of the basilar membrane causes the hair cells of the organ of Corti to move back and forth within the fluid of the cochlear duct. Bending the hair cells stimulates the release of neurotransmitters onto the cells of the **auditory nerve**. The basilar membrane needs to move very little before the hair cells are stimulated. If the hairlike structures extending from the top of the hair cells were the size of the Eiffel Tower in Paris, the movement required to produce a neural response would be the equivalent of 1 centimeter (about 0.4 inch or about 10 mm; Hudspeth, 1983).

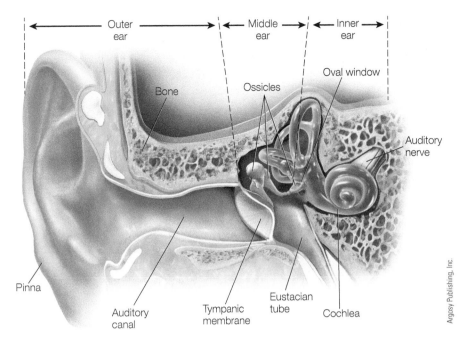

FIGURE 5.33

Parts of the Ear. The human ear is divided into the outer, middle, and inner ear.

Auditory Pathways As we mentioned earlier, hair cells stimulate axons forming the auditory nerve. One branch of each auditory nerve cell makes contact with the hair cells, while the other branch proceeds to the medulla of the brainstem. From the medulla, sound information is sent to the midbrain, which manages reflexive responses to sound, such as turning toward the source of a loud noise. In addition, the midbrain participates in sound localization, or the identification of a source of sound.

The midbrain passes information to the thalamus, which in turn sends sound information to the primary auditory cortex, located in the temporal lobe. The primary auditory cortex conducts the first basic analysis of the wavelengths and amplitudes of incoming information (see ● Figure 5.35). Surrounding the primary auditory cortex are areas of secondary auditory cortex that respond to complex types of stimuli, like clicks, noise, and sounds with particular patterns.

basilar membrane Membrane in the cochlea on which the organ of Corti is located.
organ of Corti A structure located on the basilar membrane that contains auditory receptors.
auditory nerve Nerve carrying sound information from the cochlea to the brain.

Cochlear structure unrolled for clarity

FIGURE 5.34

Perception of Pitch. Sound waves produce peak responses on the basilar membrane according to their frequencies. Like the strings on a musical instrument, high tones produce the greatest response at the narrow, stiff base of the basilar membrane, while low tones produce the greatest response at the wide, floppy part of the basilar membrane near the apex. Sound waves travel through the cochlea from the oval window, around the apex, and back to the round window. The waves cause movement of tiny hair cells in the cochlear duct, which we perceive as sound.

HOW DO WE HEAR?   **175**

The movement of tiny hair cells in the inner ear produces neural signals that travel to the brain.

Auditory Perception and Cognition

Now that we have an understanding of the structures and pathways used to process the sensations that lead to the perception of sound, we turn our attention to the brain's interpretation and organization of these sounds in terms of pitch, loudness, and spatial localization.

Pitch Perception Perception of pitch begins with the basilar membrane of the inner ear (see ● Figure 5.34). Place theory suggests that the frequency of a sound is correlated with the part of the basilar membrane showing a peak response. The base of the basilar membrane, closest to the oval window, is narrow and stiff. In contrast, at its farthest point near the apex, the basilar membrane is wide and flexible. If you are familiar with a stringed instrument like a guitar, you know that high tones are produced by striking the taut, small strings and low tones are produced by striking the floppy, wide strings. The same principle holds for the basilar membrane. High-frequency tones produce the maximum movement of the basilar membrane near the base, while low-frequency tones produce maximum movement near the apex. The hair cells riding above these areas of peak movement show a maximum response. Place theory works well for sounds above 4,000 Hz (which is about the frequency produced by striking the highest key on a piano, C8). Below frequencies of 4,000 Hz, the response of the basilar membrane does not allow precise localization. In these cases, we appear to use another principle described as temporal theory, in which the pattern of neural firing "matches" the frequency of a sound.

Perceiving Loudness Humans can perceive sounds that vary in intensity by a factor of more than 10 billion, from the softest sound we can detect up to the sound made by a jet engine at takeoff (which causes pain and structural damage to the ear). Table 5.2 identifies the intensity levels of many common stimuli, measured in the logarithmic decibel scale. Our perception of loudness does not change at the same rate as actual intensity. When the intensity of a sound stimulus is 10 times greater than before, we perceive it as being only twice as loud (Stevens, 1960).

The frequency of a sound interacts with our perception of its loudness. Humans are maximally sensitive to sounds that normally fall within the range of human speech, or between 80 and 10,000 Hz (see ● Figure 5.36). Sounds falling outside the range of speech must have higher intensity before we hear them as well. One feature that distinguishes an expensive sound system from a cheaper model is its ability to boost these frequencies that fall outside our most sensitive range.

Localization of Sound The pinna helps us localize sounds in the vertical plane, or in space above or below the head. Our primary method for localizing sound in the horizontal plane (in front, behind, and to the side) is to compare the arrival time of sound at each ear. As illustrated in ● Figure 5.37, the differences in arrival times are quite small, between 0 milliseconds for sounds that are directly in front of or behind us to 0.6 millisecond for sounds coming from a source perpendicular to the head on either side. Because arrival times for sounds coming from directly in front of or behind us are identical, it is difficult to distinguish these sources without further information. In addition to arrival times, we judge the differences in intensity of sounds reaching each ear. Because the head blocks some sound waves, a

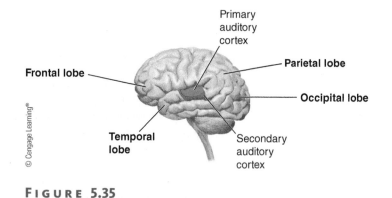

FIGURE 5.35

Auditory Cortex. The auditory cortex is located in the temporal lobe. The primary auditory cortex processes basic features of sound while the surrounding secondary auditory cortex processes more complex sounds, like clicks and general noise.

sound "shadow" is cast on the ear farthest from the source of sound. As a result, a weaker signal is received by this ear.

Just as our visual systems can be fooled by certain types of input, our ability to localize sounds is influenced by the interactions between human vision and audition. Even before the invention of surround sound, which provides a number of effective sound localization cues, moviegoers perceived sound as originating from the actors' lips even though the speakers producing the sound are typically above and to the sides of the screen. Our willingness to believe that the sound is coming from the actors' lips probably results from our everyday experiences of watching people speak. In more abstract laboratory conditions, people are more likely to report that a sound moving left to right is going in the opposite direction if they see an object going right to left at the same time. Our experience has taught us that objects and the sounds they make usually travel together (Soto-Faraco, Kingstone, & Spence, 2006).

Auditory Groupings In our previous discussion of visual perception, we reviewed the grouping principles developed by Gestalt psychologists. Similar types of groupings occur in audition. Sounds from one location are grouped together, because we assume they have the same source, whereas sounds identified as coming from different locations are assumed to have different sources. Sounds that start and stop at the same time are perceived as having the same source, while sounds with different starting and stopping

TABLE 5.2	Loudness of Common Sounds	
Source of sound	**Intensity (measured in decibels, or dB)**
Threshold of hearing	0 dB
Rustling leaves	10 dB
Whisper	20 dB
Normal conversation	60 dB
Busy street traffic	70 dB
Vacuum cleaner	80 dB
Water at the foot of Niagara Falls	90 dB
iPod with standard earbuds	100 dB
Front rows of a rock concert	110 dB
Propeller plane at takeoff	120 dB
Threshold of pain/machine gun fire	130 dB
Military jet takeoff	140 dB
Instant perforation of the eardrum	160 dB

© Cengage Learning®

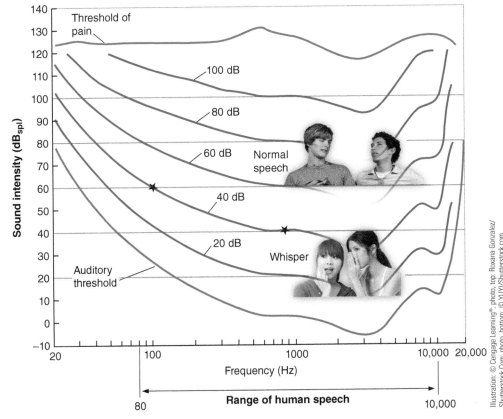

FIGURE 5.36

Human Sensitivity to Sound. These functions plot the results of allowing participants to adjust the intensity of different tones until they sound equally loud. Each curve represents the intensity (dB) at which tones of each frequency match the perceived loudness of a model 1000 Hz tone. The stars indicate that a 100 Hz tone at 60 dB sounds about as loud as a 1000 Hz tone at 40 dB, because they fall on the same line. Low frequencies are usually perceived as quieter than high frequencies at the same level of intensity. We are especially sensitive to frequencies found in speech.

FIGURE 5.37

Where Is That Sound Coming From?
We localize sound to the left and right by comparing the differences between the arrival times of the sounds to our two ears.

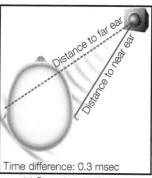

(a) Sound perpendicular to head

Distance to near ear

Distance to far ear

Time difference: 0.6 msec

Time difference: 0.0 msec

(b) Sound directly in front of or behind head

Distance to far ear

Distance to near ear

Time difference: 0.3 msec

(c) Sound at 45 degrees from head

times usually arise from separate sources, like two voices having a conversation or two instruments in a band or ensemble. Grouping plays an especially significant role in the perception of music and speech. In these cases, we see evidence of top-down processing as well, because our expectations for the next note or word influence our perceptions (Pearce, Ruiz, Kapasi, Wiggins, & Bhattacharya, 2010). The similar processing of music and language has led researchers to argue in favor of including more music in school to assist children with language learning (Strait, Kraus, Parbery-Clark, & Ashley, 2010).

Developmental and Individual Differences in Audition

Because of the importance of audition to language learning, it should not be surprising that hearing begins before birth and develops rapidly in human infants. The human fetus is capable of hearing sounds, especially mother's voice. Newborns as young as 2 days show evidence of recognizing their mother's voice (DeCasper & Fifer, 1980) and respond preferentially to their native language (Moon, Cooper, & Fifer, 1993). Infants younger than 3 months show strong startle reactions to noise. By the age of 6 months, infants turn their heads in the direction of a loud or interesting sound. It is likely that their thresholds for sounds are nearly at adult levels by this age (Olsho, Koch, Halpin, & Carter, 1987). By the age of 1 year, children should reliably turn around when their name is called.

The McGurk effect is an auditory illusion that occurs when we combine vision and hearing. In this demonstration, people reported hearing "fa" when viewing the face on the left and "ba" when viewing the face on the right. If they closed their eyes, all they heard was "ba." In some sound combinations, people perceive a third, illusory syllable that is neither heard nor seen.

Perception

Da-da

Sound from monitor

Ba-ba

Lips ga-ga

An important developmental change in audition is the hearing loss that often accompanies aging. Hearing loss tends to occur first at higher frequencies. After the age of 30, most people cannot hear sounds above 15,000 Hz. After the age of 50, most people cannot hear above 12,000 Hz, and people older than 70 years have difficulty with sounds above 6,000 Hz. Because speech normally ranges up to 8,000 to 10,000 Hz, many seniors begin to have difficulty understanding the speech of others, particularly female voices with their higher frequency range.

Among individual differences in hearing is having perfect pitch, which means that you can name a musical tone that you hear. The brains of individuals with perfect pitch appear to be structurally different from those of people who do not have this ability. Areas of the left hemisphere appear to be larger in musicians with perfect pitch (Schlaug, Jäncke, Huang, & Steinmetz, 1995). At the same time, extensive early musical training can shape the structure of the brain (Schlaug et al., 2009).

Sociocultural Influences on Auditory Perception

Human culture and social life often provide a framework for the interpretation of stimuli. A dramatic example of this type of influence is our reaction to sine wave speech. To produce this stimulus, scientists artificially alter recordings of speech to resemble regular, repeating sine waves, as shown in ● Figure 5.38 (Davis, 2007). When people hear these artificial sounds without further instructions, they describe them as tweeting birds or other nonlanguage stimuli. However, if people are told the sounds represent speech, they suddenly "hear" language elements (Remez, Rubin, Pisoni, & Carell, 1981).

Sine wave speech shows us how culture in the form of experience with language can shape perception, but in other instances, perception can shape culture. For many people with hearing loss, and for their families and friends, being deaf means something other than having a disability. Instead, deafness is viewed as a culture, complete with its own set of attitudes, language, and norms. American Sign Language (ASL) is viewed as being quite distinct from signed English and is difficult for signing people in Great Britain and Australia to understand (Mindess, 2006).

Natural utterance ("jazz and swing fans like fast music")

Sine-wave replica of natural utterance

Remez R. E. (1998). Sine-wave speech. Scholarpedia, 3, 2394

FIGURE 5.38

Expectations Influence the Interpretation of Sine Waves. Sine waves are regular and repetitive waveforms, like the ones we included earlier to show how the height and frequency of light and sound waves are interpreted by the mind. Researchers can record speech sounds and transform the recordings into artificial sine waves, like those in this image. If the sounds are played without information about their source, most people interpret the sounds as tweeting birds. However, if people are told that the recordings are language, they report "hearing" language, another example of top-down cognitive influences on perception.

How Do We Feel Body Position, Touch, Temperature, and Pain?

Somatosensation (*soma* comes from the Greek word for "body") provides us with information about the position and movement of our bodies, along with touch, skin temperature, and pain. Although these senses may not seem as glamorous as vision and hearing, we are severely disabled by their loss. You might think it would be a blessing to be born without a sense of pain, but people who have impaired pain reception often die prematurely because of their inability to respond to injury. Although unpleasant, pain tells us to stop and assess our circumstances, which may have promoted the survival of our ancestors.

Somatosensory Stimuli

Unlike the visual and auditory stimuli we have discussed so far in this chapter, somatosensory stimuli arise from within the body or make contact with its surface. As a result, these stimuli provide an organism little time to react. We can deal with a predator seen or heard from a distance using strategies different from those we use for one that is touching us. Nonetheless, the somatosenses provide essential feedback needed for movement, speech, and safety.

The Biology of the Somatosenses

The transition from walking on four legs to walking on two placed selective pressure on the evolution of primate vision and, to some extent, audition. By standing up on two legs, primates distanced themselves from many sources of information, like smell. If you don't believe us, try getting down on your hands and knees and smelling your carpet. This transition did not place the same evolutionary pressure on the human somatosenses, which work about the same way in us as they do in other animals.

Peter Mumford/Alamy

The vestibular system helps us maintain a steady view of the world, even when riding the most extreme roller coaster.

somatosensation The body senses, including body position, touch, skin temperature, and pain.
vestibular system The system in the inner ear that provides information about body position and movement.

Body Position To begin our exploration of the somatosensory systems, we return to the inner ear. Adjacent to the structures responsible for encoding sound, we find the sensory structures of the **vestibular system**, which provide us with information about body position and movement. The proximity of these structures to the middle ear, which can become congested because of a head cold, is often responsible for those rather unpleasant feelings of dizziness that accompany an illness. The receptors of the vestibular system provide information about the position of the head relative to the ground, linear acceleration, and rotational movements of the head. We sense linear acceleration when our rate of movement changes, such as when our car pulls away from a stop sign or when our airplane takes off.

Like the cochlea, the vestibular receptors contain sensitive hair cells that are bent back and forth within their surrounding fluid when the head moves. When extensive movement stops suddenly, perhaps at the end of an amusement park ride, these fluids may reverse course. You may have the odd sensation that your head is now moving in the opposite direction, even though you are sitting or standing still. The movement of these hair cells results in the production of signals in the auditory nerve, the same nerve that carries information about sound. These axons form connections in the medulla and in the cerebellum. You may recall from Chapter 4 that the cerebellum participates in balance and motor coordination, functions that depend on feedback about movement. In turn, the medulla receives input from the visual system, the cerebellum, and other somatosenses. This arrangement provides an opportunity to coordinate input from the vestibular system with other relevant information. The medulla forms connections directly with the spinal cord, allowing us to adjust our posture to keep our balance. Vestibular information travels from the medulla to the thalamus, the primary somatosensory cortex of the parietal lobe, and then the primary motor cortex in the frontal lobe. This pathway allows vestibular information to guide voluntary movement.

In humans particularly, information from the vestibular system is tightly integrated with visual processing. As we move, it is essential that we maintain a stable view of our surroundings. To accomplish this task, rotation of the head results in a reflexive movement of the eyes in the opposite direction. This action should allow you to maintain a steady view of the world, even on the most extreme roller coaster.

Touch Touch provides a wealth of information about the objects around us. By simply exploring an object with touch, we are able to determine features such as size, shape, texture, and consistency. These judgments confirm and expand the information we obtain about objects through visual exploration. Touch is not only a means of exploring the environment. Particularly in humans, touch plays a significant role in social communication. Infants who are touched regularly sleep better, remain more alert while awake, and reach cognitive milestones at earlier ages (Ackerman, 1990). We hug our friends and loved ones to provide comfort, pat others on the back for a job well done, and shake hands to greet a colleague or conclude a deal. The contributions of the sense of touch to human sexuality are obvious.

Our sense of touch begins with skin, the largest and heaviest organ in the human body. Embedded within the skin are several types of specialized neurons that produce action potentials whenever they are physically bent or stretched. Different types of receptors respond to certain features of a touch stimulus, such as pressure, vibration, or stretch (see ● Figure 5.39). In addition to their locations in the skin, receptors may be found in blood vessels, joints, and internal organs. Unpleasant sensations from a headache or a too-full stomach or bladder originate from some of these receptors. Some receptor fibers wrap around hair follicles and respond whenever a hair is pulled or bent. Others, as we will see later in this section, participate in our senses of pain and skin temperature.

Information about touch travels from the skin to the spinal cord. Once inside the spinal cord, touch pathways proceed to the thalamus, along with input from the cranial nerves originating in the touch receptors in the skin of the face, the mouth, and the tongue. The thalamus transmits touch information to the primary somatosensory cortex, located in the parietal lobe.

A map of the body's representation in the primary somatosensory cortex, or a sensory *homunculus* ("little man"), is shown in the statue to the right. This odd figure demonstrates how areas of the body are represented on the basis of their sensitivity rather than their size. Different species show different patterns of cortical organization for touch. Humans need sensitive feedback from the lips and hands to speak and make skilled hand movements for tool use and other tasks. Rats devote a great deal of cortical real estate to whiskers, whereas lips have a high priority in squirrels and rabbits.

A notable area that is missing from the homunculus is the brain, which has neither touch receptors nor pain receptors. We can only assume that for much of evolutionary history, intrusion into the brain was likely to be fatal. Consequently, there would be no advantage to "feeling" your brain. Because of the lack of somatosensation in the brain, neurosurgeons are able to work with an alert patient using local anesthesia for the skull and tissues overlying the brain. The surgery produces no sensations of pressure or pain.

The representation of touch in the primary sensory cortex is "plastic," which means that it changes in response to increases or decreases in input from a body part. Many individuals who lose a body part experience a phenomenon known as *phantom limb*, a term first used by

FIGURE 5.39

Touch Receptors. Different receptors in the skin help us sense pressure, vibration, stretch, or pain.

Touch receptors

Argosy Publishing, Inc.

The Natural History Museum/The Image Works

The sensory homunculus illustrates the amount of representation each part of the body has in the sensory cortex. The human homunculus emphasizes the hands and face.

The representation of body parts in the primary sensory cortex changes in response to the amount of input from a body part. Children who study stringed instruments show more space in the sensory cortex devoted to fingers.

Ashlyn Blocker was born with a rare condition preventing her from feeling pain. Without complaint, she went several days with a broken ankle after falling off her bicycle.

gate theory The theory that suggests that input from touch fibers competes with input from pain receptors, possibly preventing pain messages from reaching the brain.

a Civil War physician to describe his patients' experience of "pain" from a missing limb. Phantom sensations can result from the reorganization of the somatosensory cortex following the loss of a body part (Borsook et al., 1998). In one case study, touching different parts of a patient's face produced "feeling" from the patient's missing hand (Ramachandran & Rogers-Ramachandran, 2000). When his cheek was touched, he reported feeling his missing thumb, along with the expected cheek, while touching his lip elicited feeling from the missing index finger, along with the normal lip sensations. In an even more bizarre example, a patient was embarrassed to report that he experienced a sensation of orgasm in his missing foot.

Increased input also changes the organization of the somatosensory cortex. When monkeys were trained to use specific fingers to discriminate among surface textures to obtain food rewards, the areas of the cortex responding to the trained fingertips expanded (Merzenich & Jenkins, 1993). A similar reorganization occurs when blind individuals learn to read Braille (Pascual-Leone & Torres, 1993) or when people train extensively on stringed musical instruments (Elbert, Pantev, Weinbruch, Rockstroh, & Taub, 1995). Using your thumbs for text messaging will probably result in adaptations in cortical representation not seen in older generations (Wilton, 2002).

Pain Given the anguish experienced by patients with chronic pain, it is often tempting to think that not having a sense of pain would be wonderful. However, as mentioned earlier, we need pain to remind us to stop when we are injured, to assess the situation before proceeding, and to allow the body time to heal.

Free nerve endings that respond to pain are triggered by a number of stimuli associated with tissue damage. Some pain receptors respond to mechanical damage, such as that caused by a sharp object, while others respond to temperature or chemicals. Among the chemicals that stimulate pain receptors is capsaicin, an ingredient found in hot peppers (Caterina et al., 1997). Information about pain is carried centrally to the brain by two types of fibers. Fast, myelinated axons are responsible for that sharp "ouch" sensation that often accompanies an injury. Slower, unmyelinated axons are responsible for dull, aching sensations.

Pain fibers from the body form synapses with cells in the spinal cord, which in turn sends pain messages to the thalamus. This information takes a relatively direct route, with only one synapse in the spinal cord separating the periphery of the body and the thalamus in the forebrain. This arrangement ensures that pain messages are received by the brain with great speed. From the thalamus, pain information is sent to the anterior cingulate cortex, which manages the emotional qualities of pain, and to the somatosensory cortex in the parietal lobe.

Pain messages traveling to the brain may be modified by competing incoming sensory signals. Many of us spontaneously rub our elbow after bumping it painfully. A model known as a **gate theory** of pain accounts for this phenomenon (Melzack & Wall, 1965). According to this model, input from touch fibers (reacting to rubbing your elbow) competes with input from pain receptors for activation of cells in the spinal cord (see ● Figure 5.40). Activation of the touch fibers effectively dilutes the amount of pain information reaching the brain.

The perception of pain is affected by the descending influence of higher brain centers. Many forebrain structures form connections with the periaqueductal gray of the midbrain. As we observed in Chapter 4, this area is rich in receptors for our natural opioids, the endorphins. It is likely that the periaqueductal gray is a major target for opioid painkillers, such as morphine. Electrical stimulation of the periaqueductal gray produces a significant reduction in the experience of pain.

Stress provides an example of a higher order cognitive state that influences pain. Survival often depends on the ability to keep moving even in cases of extreme pain. When levels of arousal are high, people can be seriously injured without being aware of the problem. Another example of cognitive influence on pain perception is the phenomenon of placebo effects. A placebo effect occurs when people experience pain reduction even though they have been

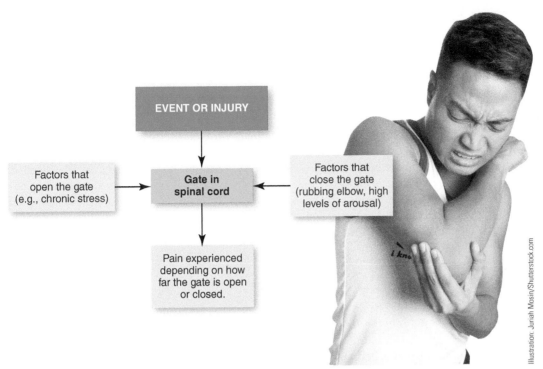

FIGURE 5.40

The Gate Theory of Pain.
According to the gate theory, incoming pain messages can be influenced by factors like chronic stress (opening the gate wider and producing a greater sensation of pain) or rubbing an injured body part (closing the gate and reducing the sensation of pain).

EVENT OR INJURY

Factors that open the gate (e.g., chronic stress)

Gate in spinal cord

Factors that close the gate (rubbing elbow, high levels of arousal)

Pain experienced depending on how far the gate is open or closed.

Illustration: Juriah Mosin/Shutterstock.com

exposed to an ineffective substance or treatment, such as a sugar pill instead of an aspirin tablet. Apparently, people's belief that they are being treated for pain may be sufficient to initiate a real decrease in pain sensation.

Sociocultural Influences on the Somatosenses

No other sensory modality is as dramatically affected by culture, context, and experience as our sense of pain. The connection between culture and experience of pain is vividly illustrated by the hook-swinging ritual practiced in India (Melzack & Wall, 1983). This ritual, designed to promote the health of children and crops, involves hanging a male volunteer from steel hooks embedded into the skin and muscles of his back. Instead of suffering excruciating pain, as Westerners might expect, the volunteers appear to be in a state of exaltation.

Women who have participated in prepared childbirth classes generally report less pain than women who are uninformed regarding the birth process. Although athletes and nonathletes share similar pain thresholds, these groups are quite different in their tolerance of pain (Scott & Gijsbers, 1981). Compared to nonathletes, athletes in contact sports such as boxing, rugby, and football appear to tolerate higher levels of pain before identifying a stimulus as painful. Patients who are allowed to self-administer morphine for pain require less medication than patients who receive injections from hospital staff (Bennett et al., 1982). The sense of control may reduce anxiety and the need for pain medication. In treating patients with chronic pain, the psychological aspects of pain management should not be overlooked in favor of a strictly pharmacological approach.

In one of the most dramatic examples of how stress can interfere with the perception of pain, Guy Gertsch unknowingly ran the final 19 miles (about 30 km) of the 1982 Boston Marathon on a broken leg (Gertsch finished the race with a highly respectable time of 2 hours and 47 minutes).

Louise Batalla Duran/Alamy

Culture, context, and experience can shape our perception of pain. During a festival dedicated to penance and atonement, Tamil Hindus walk through the streets carrying devices called *kavadis* that hold hooks that are pierced through the skin. Without this cultural context, it is likely that most people would find this experience excruciatingly painful.

How Do We Process Smells and Tastes?

The famous philosopher Immanuel Kant (1798/1978) considered **olfaction**, or our sense of smell, to be the "most dispensable" sense (p. 46). Other species rely more heavily on olfaction and **gustation**, or the sense of taste, than humans do. Nonetheless, our chemical senses provide warning of danger, such as smelling smoke from a fire or tasting spoiled food. The chemical senses also contribute a richness to our emotional and social experiences. The smell of perfume or the taste of chocolate may be accompanied by strong emotional reactions. Contrary to Kant's view, people who have lost their sense of smell because of head injury often experience profound depression (Zuscho, 1982). Sharing a meal has a strong effect on bonding for humans and other primates (Brosnan, 2010; Wobber, Wrangham, & Hare, 2010).

Chemical Stimuli

Our chemical senses begin with molecules suspended in the air in the case of olfaction and dissolved in saliva in the case of gustation. Olfaction provides more information from a distance, like vision and audition, whereas gustation, like the somatosenses, involves information from contact with the body.

The Biology of the Chemical Senses

Like the somatosenses, the chemical senses are quite ancient in terms of evolution and have undergone little change over time. However, our sense of smell has been influenced by walking on two feet instead of four. Most olfactory stimuli are relatively heavy and tend to fall to the ground. Consider how your dog puts its nose to the ground when tracking something interesting.

Olfaction Air containing olfactory stimuli is taken in through the nostrils and circulated within the nasal cavities connected to the nostrils, where it interacts with olfactory receptors (see ● Figure 5.41). The receptors are located in a thin layer of cells within the nasal cavity. Unlike most neurons, the olfactory receptors regularly die and are replaced by new receptor cells in cycles lasting 4 to 6 weeks. Cells at the base of the receptors are responsible for producing the mucus surrounding the receptors. One branch of each receptor interacts with molecules dissolved in the mucus. The other branch carries information back to the central nervous system as part of the **olfactory nerve**. The olfactory nerve fibers synapse in one of the two **olfactory bulbs**, located just below the mass of the frontal lobes.

Unlike most other sensory input to the brain, olfactory pathways do not make direct connections with the thalamus before the information reaches the cerebral cortex. Instead, fibers from the olfactory bulbs proceed to the olfactory cortex, located in the lower portions of the frontal lobe, and to the amygdala. Because of the role these areas of the brain play in emotion, which we described in Chapter 4, these pathways may account for the significant emotional reactions we experience (disgust or pleasure) in response to odor.

Taste The most likely original purpose of our sense of gustation, or taste, was to protect us from eating poisonous or spoiled food and to attract us to foods that boost our chances of survival. Although we seem biased toward detecting negative stimuli (Cacioppo & Gardner, 1999), our attraction to certain tastes also reflects our historical past. Because most of our ancestors were constantly facing the threat of famine, we generally find fatty and sugary foods to be especially tasty. Unfortunately, given the current availability of safe and palatable foods, our sense of taste may drive us to eat more than we need.

Most of us are familiar with four major categories of taste: sweet, sour, salty, and bitter. A fifth type of taste has been proposed, known by the Japanese term *umami*, which, roughly

olfaction The sense of smell.
gustation The sense of taste.
olfactory nerve A nerve carrying olfactory information from the olfactory receptors to the olfactory bulbs.
olfactory bulb One of two structures below the frontal lobes of the brain that receive input from the olfactory receptors in the nose.

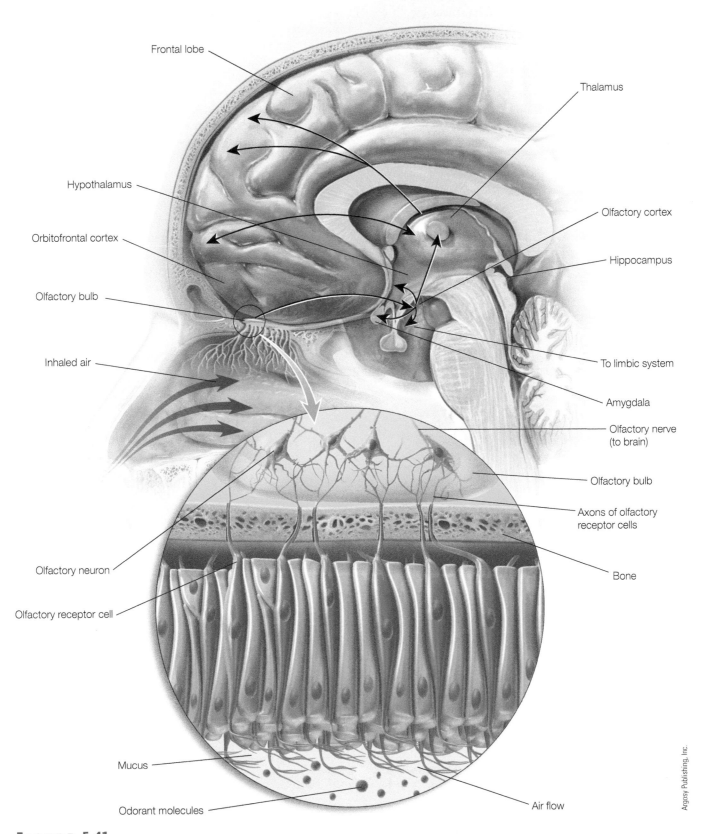

Labels (clockwise from top):
- Frontal lobe
- Thalamus
- Hypothalamus
- Olfactory cortex
- Orbitofrontal cortex
- Hippocampus
- Olfactory bulb
- Inhaled air
- To limbic system
- Amygdala
- Olfactory nerve (to brain)
- Olfactory bulb
- Axons of olfactory receptor cells
- Bone
- Olfactory neuron
- Olfactory receptor cell
- Air flow
- Mucus
- Odorant molecules

Argosy Publishing, Inc.

FIGURE 5.41

Olfactory Receptors. Receptors in the nose interact with airborne chemicals to begin the sensing of odor.

translated, means "savory" or "meaty" (Chaudhari, Landlin, & Roper, 2000). In addition, the tongue and mouth contain receptors for carbohydrates (Turner, Byblow, Stinear, & Gant, 2014) and capsaicin, an active ingredient in hot peppers. Mice lacking capsaicin receptors happily consumed water containing capsaicin at levels that were rejected by normal mice (Caterina et al., 2000).

Taste receptors are located on the tongue and in other parts of the mouth (see ● Figure 5.42). Contrary to a popular myth (usually accompanied by an equally mythological map of "taste centers" on the tongue), receptors sensitive to all types of taste are equally distributed across the tongue. You are probably aware of the bumpy texture of your tongue, which results from the presence of **papillae**. Most papillae contain somewhere between 1 and 100 **taste buds**. Each taste bud contains between 50 and 150 receptor cells, which extend tiny hairlike cilia into the saliva that interact with dissolved taste stimuli and transduce the resulting information into neural signals. Like olfactory receptors, taste buds have a limited life before they are replaced. You may have noticed that if you burn your tongue by drinking hot liquid, your taste is affected for a day or two. However, when the taste buds are replaced, taste should be back to normal.

Information about taste travels from the mouth and tongue to the medulla. The medulla in turn communicates with the thalamus, which sends taste information to the somatosensory cortex of the parietal lobe and to the orbitofrontal cortex, where the emotional pleasantness or unpleasantness of particular stimuli is processed. As we will see in Chapters 7 and 8, taste information interacts with motivation and learning.

papillae Small bumps on the tongue that contain taste buds.
taste bud A structure found in papillae that contains taste receptor cells.

 # Experiencing Psychology

Are You a Supertaster?

ABOUT 25% OF the population are supertasters, or people who are extrasensitive to taste; 25% are nontasters, or people who are relatively insensitive to taste; and the remaining 50% fall between these two extremes. You can use the following exercises to determine your taste category.

1. How Does Mint Taste to You?

Place a mint Life Saver on your tongue and allow it to dissolve (no chewing please). Rate the following qualities of the Life Saver on a scale of 1 to 5, with 1 being "very intense" and 5 being "not intense":

Sweetness	1	2	3	4	5
Smell	1	2	3	4	5
Coolness	1	2	3	4	5
"Rush"	1	2	3	4	5

How to interpret your results: Mint tasters fall into four groups:

Group 1:   Mint is mild, no rush
Group 2:   Mint is moderate, no rush
Group 3:   Mint is moderate, rush
Group 4:   Mint is intense, rush

Table 5.3 shows further characteristics of these taste groups.

2. Count Your Papillae

You need a gummed reinforcer (sticky white ring for notebooks), a swab, blue food coloring, and a mirror.

TABLE 5.3   Interpreting Your Supertaster Results

Mildly sensitive tasters (Group 1)	Moderately sensitive tasters (Groups 2 and 3)	Supertasters (Group 4)
Weak to undetectable sensation from mint	Moderate to strong sensation from mint	Very strong sensation from mint
Flavor of food is not that important	Flavor of food is important	Flavor of food is important
Many foods liked, few foods disliked, and not passionate about food	Many foods liked, few foods disliked, and often passionate about food	Great variation in the number of foods liked and often passionate about food

© Cengage Learning®

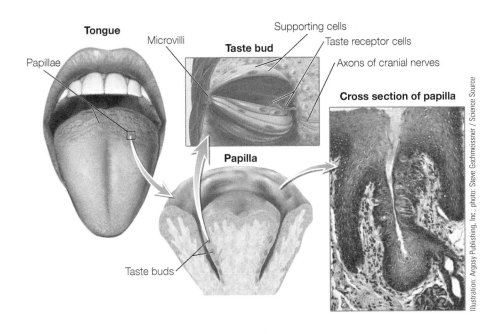

Tongue

Papillae

Microvilli

Taste bud

Supporting cells

Taste receptor cells

Axons of cranial nerves

Cross section of papilla

Papilla

Taste buds

Illustration: Argosy Publishing, Inc.; photo: Steve Gschmeissner / Science Source

FIGURE 5.42

Taste Receptors. Taste buds are located in the bumps, or papillae, located on the tongue.

Place one reinforcer on the front of your tongue just to the side of midline. Use a swab to apply blue food coloring to the part of your tongue that shows through the center of the reinforcer. The blue food coloring should make your papillae (bumps) more obvious. Count the number of papillae you see in the ring.

How to interpret your results: More than 25 papillae within the reinforcer ring means you're a supertaster. The number of papillae of mildly or moderately sensitive tasters will be less than 25, but these two groups cannot be distinguished based on this factor.

3. Other Eating Habits

Rate the tastes of the following foods and drinks using a 1-to-5 scale, with 1 being "dislike strongly" and 5 being "like a great deal":

Broccoli	1	2	3	4	5
Grapefruit	1	2	3	4	5
Coffee (black)	1	2	3	4	5
Dark chocolate	1	2	3	4	5

As a child, were you ever described by a parent, teacher, or other adult as a "picky eater"? (circle one)

YES
NO

Can you easily tell the difference between the fat content of milk (for example, between whole and 2% milk or between 1% and 2% milk)? (circle one)

YES
NO

How to interpret your results: Supertasters tend to dislike bitter foods; they have a lot of low numbers. Supertasters also tend to be picky eaters as children and to be better at detecting differences in fats in foods. ●

Placing blue food coloring on the tongue makes the papillae easier to see. Supertasters have many more papillae, and thus more taste buds, than other people.

Paul Burns/Blend Images/Alamy

Roger Freberg

Perception and Cognition in the Chemical Senses

In both olfaction and gustation, we see three interesting perceptual themes: (a) We can easily identify a number of complex stimuli combining many types of molecules, such as the aroma of coffee; (b) we can detect small differences among similar smells and tastes; and (c) our experience often shapes our perception of an olfactory or gustatory stimulus (Goldstein, 2010). Humans can distinguish among at least 1 trillion odors (Bushdid, Magnasco, Vosshall, & Keller, 2014). An example of the impact of experience on olfaction is the effect of labeling an odor on people's rating of its pleasantness. If participants smell an onion stimulus labeled "pizza," they not too surprisingly rate the odor as more pleasant than if the identical stimulus is labeled "body odor" (Herz, 2003).

The chemical senses interact to provide the perception of flavor. You have probably noticed that food doesn't taste good when your sense of smell is decreased by a bad cold. If you close your eyes and hold your nose, you are unable to distinguish between a slice of apple and a slice of raw potato. Again, the orbitofrontal cortex plays an important role in the perception of flavor, because the pathways serving olfaction and gustation converge in this part of the brain (Rolls, 2000).

Developmental and Individual Differences in the Chemical Senses

Young children are notorious for putting things in their mouths that adults would quickly reject on the basis of taste, including poisonous substances like drain cleaner. However, this propensity does not mean that children lack a sense of taste. Using facial expressions, researchers have demonstrated that newborns differentiate among sweet, bitter, and sour tastes but seem relatively oblivious to salty tastes (Rosenstein & Oster, 1988). As we get older, the overall number of taste buds decreases, reducing the intensity of many tastes and providing a possible explanation for why some strong flavors, such as that of broccoli, are enjoyed more by adults than by children. As we age, our sensitivity to smell also decreases (Cain & Gent, 1991). Because olfaction and taste interact to form the flavor of foods, decreased sensitivity in both senses might affect overall appetite as we age.

Like the other sensory modalities discussed in this chapter, the chemical senses vary from person to person. Females are generally more sensitive to smell than are males (Dorries, 1992; Koelega & Koster, 1974; Ship & Weiffenbach, 1993). The average person has approximately 6,000 taste buds, but this number may vary widely. As we observed previously, supertasters have unusually high numbers of papillae and therefore have more taste buds too (Bartoshuk, 2000).

Disturbances in the chemical senses are correlated with a number of psychological disorders. Olfaction and the experience of post-traumatic stress disorder (PTSD; see Chapter 14) appear to interact in combat veterans. PTSD is often characterized by intrusive, disturbing flashbacks in which the patient essentially relives the traumatic experience. Given the close association between olfaction and memory, researchers hypothesized that some PTSD flashbacks could be initiated by relevant smells. When compared to combat veterans who did not have PTSD, combat veterans with the disorder experienced marked anxiety when exposed to the smell of diesel, accompanied by changes in the activity of the amygdala (Vermetten, Schmahl, Southwick, & Bremner, 2007).

Sociocultural Influences on the Chemical Senses

The sense of smell might seem to play a secondary role to vision and audition in humans, but people have manipulated scent for religious, medicinal, and personal purposes since ancient times. We can speculate that once people learned to control fire, a recognition that some burning things smelled better than others could not have been far behind, possibly leading to the use of incense in religious rituals. Use of natural materials for medicine and self-adornment provides the historical roots for large, contemporary industries that manufacture scent for a host of consumer products, including perfume, air fresheners, "new car smell" products, and detergents.

Although olfaction often seems to run in the background of our other cognitive processes, it is not immune to the effects of culture and experience. Americans spend millions on products that remove or mask body odor, whereas other cultures do not find such odors offensive. One study compared the categorization of odors by French, American, and Vietnamese participants (Chrea et al., 2004). Although the participants sorted odors similarly into broad categories of floral, sweet, bad, and natural, they differed along subtler dimensions. The French and American participants quickly sorted odors into fruit or flower categories, but this separation had little relevance to the Vietnamese participants. How cultural experience contributes to such results remains a mystery.

Experience clearly plays a role in developing an individual's taste preferences. The effects of experience on taste begin in the prenatal environment. Infants whose mothers consumed carrot juice during pregnancy showed stronger preferences for carrot flavor (Mennella & Beauchamp, 1996; Mennella, Jagnow, & Beauchamp, 2001). In terms of survival, this result makes perfect sense. Infants are born with a predisposition to like the safe foods available in their environment. Because the food supply historically has varied widely from place to place, delicacies like fruit bat pie are appreciated in Palau but not necessarily in the United States.

© Kristin Saling

Different cultures can prefer different foods. It is unlikely that you will find fruit bat pie, a delicacy in Palau, in many American restaurants.

Interpersonal Relationships

Sensation and Perception Perspectives

Can Relationships Buffer the Experience of Pain?

We mentioned earlier that of the senses we discussed in this chapter, pain was particularly influenced by cognition and context. Can being in a close relationship affect the way you feel pain?

The answer appears to be "yes." Physical contact with a loved one can affect how the brain processes pain. Women who were expecting an electric shock showed reduced activity in parts of the brain associated with the emotional and arousing aspects of pain when they held their husbands' hands. They even experienced reduced activity, albeit to a lesser degree, when they held the hand of a male they didn't know (Coan, Schaefer, & Davidson, 2006). In addition, the amount of reduction of activity in these pain areas of the brain was correlated with the quality of the marriage—happily married women experienced greater decreases in activity associated with pain than less happily married women.

Perhaps this buffering effect is why you may reach for your partner when frightened during a scary movie. Knowing that such intimacy could literally reduce the pain in a loved one might compel you to make that extra effort to go to the doctor with your partner or make the extra visit to a friend in the hospital. Our understanding of pain in connection with our interpersonal relationships can help us in tangible ways to create and maintain stronger, healthier relationships. ●

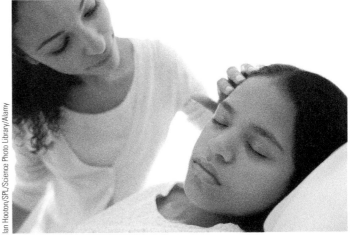
Ian Hooton/SPL/Science Photo Library/Alamy

Research shows that physical contact with loved ones reduces the sensation of pain.

Summary 5.3 Important Structures in Audition

Structure	Function
Pinna	Collects sound and identifies its location as coming from above or below the head
Tympanic membrane	Begins the process of transduction of sound waves to neural signals when movement occurs
Cochlea	Contains auditory receptors
Thalamus	Receives auditory input from the brainstem and connects to the primary auditory cortex
Primary auditory cortex (area in the temporal lobe)	Receives and performs an initial analysis of auditory input from the thalamus

KEY TERMS The Language of Psychological Science

Be sure you can define these terms and use them correctly.

absolute threshold, p. 152
audition, p. 173
auditory nerve, p. 175
basilar membrane, p. 175
binocular cue, p. 165
bottom-up processing, p. 151
cochlea, p. 174
cone, p. 156
cornea, p. 155
depth perception, p. 164
difference threshold, p. 152
fovea, p. 156
gate theory, p. 182
gustation, p. 184

iris, p. 155
lens, p. 155
monocular cue, p. 165
olfaction, p. 184
olfactory bulb, p. 184
olfactory nerve, p. 184
opponent process theory, p. 160
optic nerve, p. 157
optic tracts, p. 158
organ of Corti, p. 175
papillae, p. 186
perception, p. 149
psychophysics, p. 152
pupil, p. 155

retina, p. 155
retinal disparity, p. 166
rod, p. 156
sensation, p. 148
sensory adaptation, p. 151
signal detection, p. 153
somatosensation, p. 180
taste bud, p. 186
top-down processing, p. 151
transduction, p. 150
trichromatic theory, p. 159
vestibular system, p. 180
vision, p. 155

6 The Aware Mind

Elements of Consciousness

WHAT DOES IT MEAN TO HAVE "FREE WILL"? THIS MIGHT sound more like a philosophy question than a psychology question, but advances in biological and cognitive psychology have allowed psychologists to tackle it.

Usually, we think of free will as the ability to consciously control our actions and decisions. In the children's game of "rock, paper, scissors," we feel like we are making a conscious decision to choose one of the three options. But how would such a decision be made? What types of processes in the brain correspond to choosing scissors over the other two possibilities?

Research into voluntary movements, like forming your hand into scissors, has shown that the brain makes a commitment to a choice as much as 10 seconds before we become aware of the decision (Soon, Brass, Heinze, & Haynes, 2008). Other research shows that the brain can be manipulated to make an unusual choice without disrupting the individual's sense of free will. Right-handed people normally use their right hand 60% of the time or more when forced to choose to use one hand over the other, but when researchers exposed right-handed subjects' right hemispheres to transcranial magnetic stimulation (TMS), illustrated in the large image on the previous page, they chose to use their left hand 80% of the time (Ammon & Gandevia, 1990). Despite making the uncharacteristic choice to use "the wrong hand," the participants in this experiment reported feeling in control of their hand movements. If the brain has already committed to a movement, what purpose does a conscious sense of having decided to move serve?

Insight into this question emerged from the study of split-brain patients described in Chapter 4. These patients have undergone surgery that severs the connections between their right and their left hemispheres, making it possible to expose one hemisphere at a time to a stimulus. For example, you can show the relatively nonverbal right hemisphere the word *stand,* and the patient usually stands up. However, because of the limitations of the right hemisphere in processing language, the patient is consciously unaware of having read the word. When asked why they stood up, patients responded by saying they felt the need to stretch. In other words, the mind is building a theory about the behavior that was just performed (Gazzaniga, 2011). This type of observation leads to a view of consciousness as an interpreter, making sense out of our actions and the world within and around us. This view helps us understand the observed delay between the brain's commitment to an action and

LeventeGyori/Shutterstock.com

◄ Do we have free will? Transcranial magnetic stimulation switched the hand chosen to carry out a task from right to left, but participants insisted that switching hands was their own idea.

Argosy Publishing, Inc.

193

our conscious awareness of that decision—the interpreter needs time to analyze the situation.

In this chapter, we will explore many situations that affect the performance of the interpreter, from the variations found in stages of sleep and waking to the alterations produced by psychoactive drugs and damage to the brain. This journey will require us to zoom in to observe underlying processes in the brain and then zoom out again to understand the influences of the social context on the phenomenon of conscious awareness.

Maximilian Weinzierl/Alamy

Social context plays a role in sleep, even for the fruit fly. Fruit flies living with other fruit flies rather than alone need more sleep, suggesting that one of the functions of sleep is to process learning about social experiences. The larger the group of flies, the longer each fly needed to sleep. From Ganguly-Fitzgerald, I., Donlea, J., & Shaw, P. J. (2006). Waking experience affects sleep need in *Drosophila*. *Science, 313*(5794), 1775-1781. doi: 10.1126/science.1130408

Learning Objectives

1. Analyze the different meanings of consciousness.

2. Describe the effects of different stages of waking and sleep on consciousness, electroencephalogram (EEG) patterns, autonomic nervous system function, and muscle activity.

3. Compare and contrast several sleep-wake disorders in terms of their symptoms and the type of sleep disturbed.

4. Explain disorders of consciousness in terms of damage or dysfunction of the brain.

5. Differentiate the neurochemical mechanisms and effects on consciousness of major types of psychoactive drugs.

6. Describe the use of hypnosis, meditation, and other nondrug methods for altering consciousness.

What Does It Mean to Be Conscious?

Our English word *conscious* is derived from the Latin *conscientia*, which means "to know." **Consciousness** refers to knowing or being aware of ongoing experiences occurring both internally and in the world around us. We understand that to be unconscious, perhaps because of a blow to the head, means that we are unaware of what is happening within and around us. However, the term *consciousness* has multiple meanings. Consciousness can refer to a state of awareness (alert versus drowsy, for example) or the current content of awareness (while reading this page, you hear your neighbor's music). A special type of consciousness, **self-awareness**, occurs when we focus on ourselves as individuals.

Consciousness has been a favorite topic among psychologists for many years. William James (1890) coined the term "stream of consciousness" to capture the moving, seemingly unbroken flow of conscious awareness. Sigmund Freud used the term *consciousness* to refer to aspects of the mind that could be retrieved voluntarily, in contrast to the unconscious parts of the mind that remain hidden to voluntary searches for information. Contemporary cognitive psychologists debate why some information becomes conscious while other information does not (Baars, 1988).

consciousness A state of awareness.
self-awareness The special understanding of the self as distinct from other stimuli.

The Evolution of Consciousness

Most of us would agree that bacteria do not possess consciousness but people do. This implies that consciousness emerged at some point in the course of evolution. The exact location of that point remains highly debatable. James maintained that "consciousness grows the more complex and intense the higher we rise in the animal kingdom. That of a man must exceed that of an oyster" (1890, p. 141). If consciousness evolved as suggested by James, what advantages might account for this development?

The question of the emergence of consciousness in animals is complicated by the multiple meanings of *consciousness* described previously. Most animals show variations in states of awareness. Even the humble fruit fly takes periods of rest, which are believed to be the fruit fly equivalent of sleep (Shaw, Cirelli, Greenspan, & Giulio Tononi, 2000). Consciousness defined as an awareness of ongoing sensations is probably less common in the animal kingdom. Many animals would survive quite well by simply responding automatically to the world around them ("food" or "predator") without necessarily thinking "I smell food" or "I see a predator." The self-awareness aspect of consciousness—as exemplified in "I" statements—might be the rarest of all among living things, as we will see later.

Consciousness as Variations in Alertness Varying states of awareness might allow animals to repair their bodies and conserve energy. Food requirements would be higher if we stayed awake for 24 hours (as you may have noticed while studying for final exams). Another possible benefit of varying states of awareness is maximizing safety. Most animals are specialized for activity in either the light or the dark. Sleeping during the cycle for which an animal is poorly equipped for activity might contribute to its survival. However, being inactive is not a safe thing to do unless you have a safe place to hide (Allison & Cicchetti, 1976). Horses and rabbits are both frequently preyed upon, but horses sleep in the open while rabbits sleep in burrows. Consequently, wild horses sleep as little as 1 or 2 hours per day, while wild rabbits sleep at least 8 hours.

ARCO/W Dolder

Sleeping habits of different species reflect how likely they are to be preyed upon by other animals and whether they have shelter. The lion has few predators and is likely to fall asleep wherever it is convenient.

Consciousness as an Awareness of Ongoing Sensations One possible advantage of being consciously aware of ongoing sensations is the ability to choose responses rather than to respond instinctively (Gazzaniga, 2011). If suddenly faced with a predator, any animal could respond automatically using reflex and instinct, which we discuss in Chapter 8. Horses are notorious for running whenever the slightest stimulus bothers them. It is unlikely that the horse in these cases is thinking, "I hear a mountain lion—I should run." Conscious awareness of sensations provides more options. If a conscious animal hears a sound in the distance that might indicate the presence of a predator, it could choose to continue on, flee, or pause while obtaining further information. This flexibility would be likely to increase the animal's chances of survival.

Consciousness as Self-Awareness The self-awareness aspect of consciousness could heighten an animal's drive to survive. Recognition and understanding of being alive is correlated with heightened meaningfulness of self-preservation.

Developmental psychologists have provided a technique for demonstrating self-awareness that can be used with many species. Recognizing one's self in the mirror is believed to be a major developmental milestone in achieving self-awareness. In the so-called rouge test, a dot of rouge or other odorless dye is placed on a child's forehead, and the child is allowed to look in a mirror (Lewis & Brooks-Gunn, 1979). Before the age of about 18 months, children do not seem to indicate that they understand the image in the mirror is their own. At about that age, they rub at the spot of rouge or turn their bodies to get a better look, thus demonstrating self-awareness.

Chimpanzees "pass" the rouge test by demonstrating behavior similar to that of 18-month-old children (Gallup, 1970). In addition to chimpanzees, orangutans, gorillas raised by humans, bottle-nosed dolphins, Asian elephants, and even parrots have demonstrated self-awareness in this type of experiment (Gallup & Suarez, 1986; Patterson, 1984; Patterson &

Babies 18 months and older are able to recognize themselves in a mirror, which psychologists believe indicates a sense of self-awareness. Happy the elephant, a resident of the Bronx Zoo, repeatedly used her trunk to touch a mark that researchers placed above her eye, suggesting that she too can recognize her image in the mirror.

Cohn, 1994; Plotnik, de Waal, & Reiss, 2006; Povinelli, 1993). Dogs, wild-raised gorillas, and most monkeys do not pass the test.

Other researchers restrict the possibility of self-aware consciousness to species that exhibit complex social behavior. Of what use would self-awareness be if one did not frequently interact with others of the same kind? Social animals must be able to recognize other individuals and respond to them accordingly. Dolphins appear to have special whistles that they seem to use for particular individuals, like names (Janik, Sayigh, & Wells, 2006). Some social animals, including chimpanzees and elephants, show an awareness of death and appear to grieve at the loss of family members. Elephants in particular have been known to remain in the area of a relative's bones for lengthy periods (McComb, Baker, & Moss, 2006).

Organisms like the army ant stretch our definitions of what it means to be conscious. Individual army ants *(Eciton)* are not impressive, but colonies of army ants show signs of collective intelligence and sophisticated problem solving, such as using their bodies to build nests of up to 700,000 individuals (Franks, 1989). Computer programs based on ant problem solving provide superior results compared with many more conventional approaches (Chen, Wu, & Chen, 2012).

Psychology as a Hub Science
Can Machines Become Conscious?

Extending the question of what creatures are conscious a step further, we can ask whether it is possible to construct an artificial consciousness. From the Terminator to *Her*'s Samantha, Hollywood loves to tell the story of the machine that develops consciousness. How would we judge whether a machine has achieved consciousness? In 1950, Alan Turing devised a test of a machine's ability to think. According to the Turing Test, if a human had a conversation with two other beings, one human and one machine, without being able to distinguish between them, then the machine would have passed the test. The 2014 Eugene Goostman program, which impersonated a 13-year-old from the Ukraine, managed to convince 10 out of 30 judges that "he" was human. The ability to meet Turing's criteria may be within reach.

Daniel Dennett (1991) argues that it might be more interesting to set aside the question of consciousness and simply build the most human robot possible. Such an effort is under way

Saya the robot was originally programmed to serve as a receptionist, but she taught a science and technology class to 10-year-olds in Tokyo in 2009. She is capable of producing six basic emotions: happiness, surprise, fear, disgust, anger, and sadness. Nobody is arguing that she is conscious, but she is remarkably human for a machine.

at the Massachusetts Institute of Technology, where a robot named Cog has been developed (Humanoid Robotics Group, n.d.). Cog may not have legs yet, but it can see and play in a human way with a slinky toy. Among the plans for Cog are language abilities, hearing, and touch. Saya, a Japanese robot 15 years in the making, has graduated from receptionist duties to the elementary school classroom, where she calls roll, communicates assignments, and even scolds children for misbehavior. Cog and Saya might not meet our criteria for self-awareness and consciousness, but their behavior is becoming increasingly human. ●

Searching for Consciousness in the Brain

Is it possible to find consciousness in the brain? Consciousness, the mind, and the brain are like a set of nested Russian dolls. The brain, the outside doll, houses the mind but has other functions as well, such as maintaining breathing and body temperature. The mind, the middle doll, houses consciousness, the innermost doll, but also manages unconscious functions such as long-term memory, discussed in Chapter 9.

In this chapter, we will examine a number of natural, artificial, and pathological circumstances that correlate with variations in consciousness. As a result of these investigations, we can begin to view consciousness as requiring complex interactions between areas of the cerebral cortex and the thalamus, discussed in detail in Chapter 4. In particular, lesions of the thalamus result in the type of profound unconsciousness typically associated with brain death (Bogen, 1995). We discuss the concept of brain death more fully in a later section of this chapter.

Certain structures in the brain, such as the thalamus, might be necessary, but not sufficient, for consciousness. For example, observing that your television screen no longer produces a picture after you remove a component does not necessarily imply that the sole source of the picture is that particular component; it's likely that other components need to be attached simultaneously and contribute to the creation of the visual image. Likewise, additional brain structures, such as the reticular formation of the brainstem, play an active role in raising or lowering the thresholds of conscious awareness (see ● Figure 6.1). Because of these variations,

FIGURE 6.1

Brain Structures Associated With Consciousness. Among the brain structures that are believed to participate in consciousness are the cerebral cortex, thalamus, and reticular formation, as well as the complex pathways connecting these parts of the brain. These structures make consciousness possible, which we know because damage to these circuits results in unconsciousness, but they do not determine the content of consciousness.

FIGURE 6.2

The Default Mode Network (DMN) of the Brain. Activity of the DMN corresponds to mind wandering, thinking about the self, and preparing for conscious thought. *Source:* Adapted from "The Brain's Dark Energy," by M. E. Raichle, 2010, *Scientific American, 314;*(5803) pp. 44–49.

you are far more likely to hear and respond to a sound while awake than while deeply asleep. Structures such as the thalamus and reticular formation have been described as "enabling" consciousness, but they do not produce its content (Crick & Koch, 2003).

Instead of looking for consciousness as resulting from the activity of particular structures, it is more useful to consider consciousness as resulting from activity changes in brain networks. Neuroscientists initially believed that when your thought is unfocused during a state known as *mind wandering,* the brain would be quiet, but that as you focus on a specific task, the brain would "light up." This does not seem to be the case. The brain uses only about 5% more energy when people are focused compared to when they are unfocused (Raichle & Snyder, 2011). These observations have led to the identification of a default mode network (DMN), which maintains a high level of unconscious, background activity as it helps prepare the brain for conscious thought (see ● Figure 6.2). Activity in the DMN actually decreases a bit when the person engages in a conscious task. One group of researchers was able to predict participants' mistakes in a computer test by watching the activity of the DMN (Eichele et al., 2008). As much as 30 seconds before a mistake occurred, the DMN would take over and activity in areas involved with focused attention decreased.

Despite average people spending about 50% of their waking hours in the relatively unfocused mind wandering state managed by the DMN, activity in this network is correlated with feelings of relative unhappiness (Brewer et al., 2011). DMN activity is also correlated with thoughts about the self, which we discuss further in Chapter 12. It is unclear how, or even if, these two correlates of DMN activity interact.

Summary 6.1 Definitions of Consciousness

Aspect of consciousness	Definition	Examples
State of awareness	The level of conscious awareness of internal states or surroundings, which can be high or low and realistic or distorted	• Asleep or awake • Perceiving realistically or hallucinating • Hypnotized or not • Meditating or not
Content of awareness	The ongoing catalog of internal and external stimuli that are the focus of current attention	• Hearing a neighbor's music • Thinking that you're hungry and it's time to eat • Considering the implications of a news report
Self-awareness	The special understanding of the self as distinct from other stimuli	• Knowing that you are looking at your-self in the mirror • Knowing that you are sleeping and dreaming

Credits: Top Row. ARCO/W Dolder. Second Row. Argosy Publishing Inc. Bottom Row: Ghislain & Marie David de Lossy/Getty Images.

What Happens to Consciousness During Waking and Sleep?

Our first meaning of consciousness involves variations in an animal's state of awareness. Awareness changes dramatically across cycles of **sleep** and **waking**. These cycles follow **circadian rhythms**, or daily rhythms. The term *circadian* comes from the Latin words for "about a day."

Circadian rhythms are only one example of a number of important biorhythms. Animals have birth seasons and migration patterns. Human females experience menstrual cycles. Within a single day, we also see regular fluctuations in arousal, with peaks occurring every 90 to 120 minutes.

Circadian Rhythms

Circadian rhythms respond to a combination of internal and external factors. Internal **biological clocks**, controlled by the hypothalamus, provide an approximate schedule for various physical processes, including sleep and waking, body temperature, and hunger. These internal biological clocks interact with external stimuli, known as *zeitgebers* (*zeit* means "time" and *geber* means "to give" in German; hence, these stimuli are "time givers").

Light is one of the most important zeitgebers for humans. Exposure to the rising sun each day helps to reset the internal biological clocks to the correct "time." In the absence of light, our internal clocks run a few minutes longer than a 24-hour cycle. We become like a wristwatch that is running too slowly. Over time, the distortion adds up, and behavior is only occasionally synchronized with "normal" cycles of day and night. Totally blind people and sailors on submarines experience longer than normal circadian cycles because of their lack of exposure to natural light (Kelly et al., 1999; Skene, Lockley, & Arendt, 1999).

sleep A normal state of consciousness characterized by reduced awareness of external stimuli.
waking A normal state of consciousness characterized by alertness and awareness of external stimuli.
circadian rhythm A daily biological rhythm.
biological clock An internal mechanism that provides an approximate schedule for various physical processes.

| Wake time | Time before leaving for work 1 hour 35 minutes | Commute 23 minutes | Workday 9 hours 28 minutes | Commute 23 minutes | Time before bed 6 hours 6 minutes | Time in bed 6 hours 55 minutes |

5:00 a.m. 5:35 a.m.   7:45 a.m.   8:09 a.m.   5:04 p.m.   5:27 p.m.   10:53 p.m.   5:35 a.m.

FIGURE 6.3

A Day in the Life of a Typical American Worker. Americans are believed to be somewhat sleep deprived because the average adult spends only 6 hours and 55 minutes in bed, which includes time needed to initiate sleep. Although people try to make up for lost sleep on weekends by sleeping longer, this solution is not very effective. *Source:* Data from "2008 Sleep in America Poll," by National Sleep Foundation, 2008, retrieved from http://www.sleepfoundation.org/sites/default/files/2008%20POLL%20SOF.PDF.

Illustration: © Cengage Learning®; photos, left to right: Hurst Photo/Shutterstock.com; Martin Novak/Shutterstock.com; StockLite/Shutterstock.com; Martin Novak/Shutterstock.com; iStockphoto.com/hocus-focus; funkypoodle/iStock

Eating patterns are also significant zeitgebers, as many midnight snackers know. Mice normally sleep during the day and feed at night. However, when mice are fed only during the day, they quickly adapt to the new feeding schedule and begin sleeping at night and exploring more during the day (Mieda, Williams, Richardson, Tanaka, & Yanagisawa, 2006).

Modern Living and Circadian Rhythms It is likely that our human ancestors remained awake during daylight and slept throughout the dark of night, and they lacked the technology needed to travel rapidly across time zones. Technology, particularly the invention of artificial light, has shaped our contemporary sleep–wake patterns into something quite different (see ● Figure 6.3). For example, that course you need for graduation might only be offered at 7 a.m., or you might work until midnight to juggle your work and class schedules. Businesspeople might travel across eight or nine time zones to make an important sales presentation on another continent. These distortions in our natural circadian rhythms can result in problems.

Some occupations, such as hospital and public safety jobs, involve work around the clock, which in turn is correlated with physical and psychological problems. Between 40% and 80% of workers on graveyard shifts (11:00 p.m. to 7:30 a.m.) experience shift maladaptation syndrome, characterized by health, personality, mood, and interpersonal problems (Wagner, 1996). Accident rates in the industrial swing shift (3:00 p.m. to 11:30 p.m.) are higher than in the traditional day shift, and the graveyard shift (11:00 p.m. to 7:30 a.m.) is the most dangerous work period (Hänecke, Tiedemann, Nachreiner, & Grzech-Sukalo, 1998). Not only do shift workers experience more accidents, but they also make more errors. Hospital workers are more likely to make significant errors during evening shifts than during day shifts (Narumi et al., 1999).

Our modern ability to cross time zones leads to the experience of jet lag, which produces fatigue, irritability, and sleepiness. The travel is not to blame, because north–south travel of equal distance does not produce the symptoms of jet lag (Herxheimer & Waterhouse, 2003). Chronic jet lag has even more serious consequences. Flight attendants with 4 or more years of experience in which time zones were crossed at least once a week had reduced reaction times and made 9% more mistakes on memory tasks than local crews (Cho, Ennaceur, Cole, & Suh, 2000).

As you probably already know from personal experience, some of these challenges to our circadian rhythms are easier to manage than others. It is easier to adjust to time changes when we set the clock to a later point than to an earlier point. For example, let's compare the experiences of two people, one traveling from Los Angeles to New York City (setting the clock forward) and the other traveling from New York City to Los Angeles (setting the clock back). Let's assume both travelers usually go to bed at 10:00 p.m. and get up at 6:00 a.m. To stay on the same sleep schedule, the LA–NYC traveler must now go to sleep at 7:00 p.m. and wake up at 3:00 a.m., which is difficult, whereas the NYC–LA traveler must stay up until 1:00 a.m. but can sleep until 9:00 a.m., which is easier because it adheres more closely to the normal sleeping arrangement of going to bed in darkness and waking up in daylight (see ● Figure 6.4).

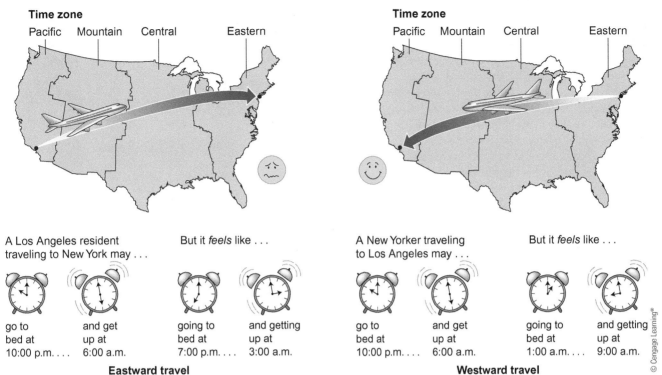

Eastward travel

A Los Angeles resident traveling to New York may . . .

go to bed at 10:00 p.m. . . . and get up at 6:00 a.m.

But it *feels* like . . .

going to bed at 7:00 p.m. . . . and getting up at 3:00 a.m.

Westward travel

A New Yorker traveling to Los Angeles may . . .

go to bed at 10:00 p.m. . . . and get up at 6:00 a.m.

But it *feels* like . . .

going to bed at 1:00 a.m. . . . and getting up at 9:00 a.m.

© Cengage Learning®

FIGURE 6.4

Daylight saving time offers another opportunity to observe our responses to abrupt changes in our daily schedules (see ● Figure 6.5). This energy-saving relic from World War I requires the setting of clocks forward 1 hour in the spring and back 1 hour in the fall. Even though the shift occurs on a Sunday, behavior the subsequent Monday is impaired. When Canadian traffic accident data were correlated with the two annual daylight saving shifts, the shift back in the fall resulted in a 7% decrease in traffic accidents on the following Monday compared to other fall Mondays. In the spring setting of the clock forward, a comparable 7% increase in traffic accidents occurred (Coren, 1996b).

When less light is available for setting the body's internal clocks, approximately 4% to 6% of the population experience **major depressive disorder with seasonal pattern** (Jepson, Ernst, & Kelly, 1999; American Psychiatric Association [APA], 2013). This condition was formerly known as seasonal affective disorder (SAD). During the winter months at higher latitudes, the reduction in daylight hours may interfere with the setting of circadian rhythms. This disruption may lead to symptoms of depression, discussed in more detail in Chapter 14, that lift once the days become longer again. Rates of seasonal depression vary from 1.4% in Florida to 9.7% in New Hampshire (Jepson et al., 1999). Seasonal depression is typically treated by exposure to bright lights with or without antidepressant medications. The lights used in this therapy are stronger than what is normally experienced indoors but not as strong as the light at the beach on an August afternoon.

The invention of artificial lighting has changed our historical sleep–wake cycles by making it easy to be awake at night. Artificial lighting affects sleep by breaking down melatonin, a hormone released in the evening that regulates sleep cycles. Changes in melatonin release have been implicated in a long list of human diseases, including cancer and heart disease, which are more common among people who work night shifts (Navara & Nelson, 2007).

Individual Variations in Circadian Rhythms

You might believe that the day should start around 2:00 p.m., whereas your roommate pops out of bed smiling at an alarming 6:30 in the morning. What accounts for these individual differences in sleep patterns?

Some individual differences become evident in infancy and remain consistent over the life span. "Morning" people have been called larks, and "night" people have been called owls (Åkerstedt & Fröberg, 1976). Many people fall somewhere between these two extremes and

Jet Lag Is Worse When Traveling East. Traveling eastward is more disruptive to circadian rhythms than traveling westward. The Los Angeles resident visiting New York feels like he or she is going to bed 3 hours earlier than usual (7:00 p.m. Los Angeles time) and waking up in the middle of the night (3:00 a.m. Los Angeles time). The New Yorker traveling to Los Angeles has to stay up a little later (1:00 a.m. New York time) but then can sleep later to compensate (9:00 a.m. New York time). Most people find the latter scenario easier.

major depressive disorder with seasonal pattern A mood disorder in which depression occurs regularly at the same time each year, usually during the winter months; formerly known as seasonal affective disorder (SAD).

FIGURE 6.5

Daylight Saving Time Affects the Number of Heart Attacks. Fifteen years of data show that rates of heart attack (a) increase significantly in the days following the spring shift in daylight saving time and (b) decrease following the fall shift. The incidence ratio is computed by comparing the number of heart attacks on the specified day following the shift to the mean number of heart attacks for the same day 2 weeks before and 2 weeks after the shift. The likely reason for the increase is sleep deprivation; it increases sympathetic nervous system activation and inflammation, which can be dangerous to people with existing health problems. *Source:* Adapted from Janszky and Ljung (2008).

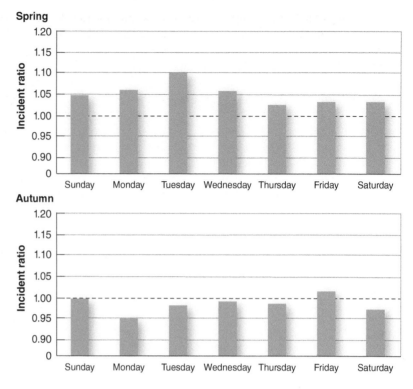

are at their best in the middle of the day. Research on the genetic basis of circadian rhythms suggests that the different patterns may result from different versions of the genes responsible for the activity of our internal clocks (Katzenberg, Young, Finn, Lin, & Mignot, 1998).

Other differences appear to be more age related. Nearly everyone acts like an owl during adolescence and young adulthood (Carskadon, Wolfson, Acebo, Tzischinsky, & Seifer, 1998). In their mid- to late 20s, many temporary owls revert to their previous lark or medium state. The exact cause for such a shift during and after adolescence and young adulthood is unclear, but researchers suspect that the shift correlates with a burst of brain development that is initiated at puberty. Some researchers view the return to a previous sleep pattern in young adulthood as a reliable indicator that the brain is fully mature (Roenneberg et al., 2005).

Waking

Varying states of awareness can be described using electroencephalogram (EEG) recordings, which provide a general measure of overall brain activity. During waking, we alternate among three patterns of activity indicated by

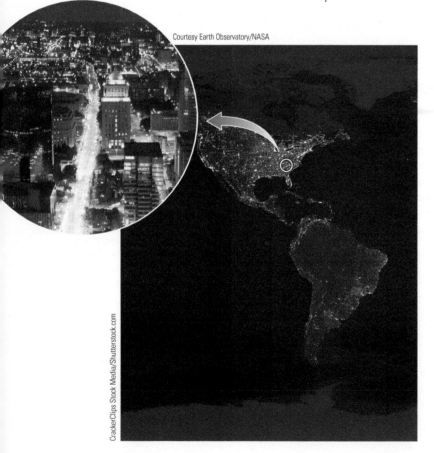

Courtesy Earth Observatory/NASA

CrackerClips Stock Media/Shutterstock.com

Modern artificial light breaks down the hormone melatonin, which is released only at night. Disruptions caused by the effects of light on melatonin might be responsible for higher rates of disease, and cancer in particular, among employees who work at night in hospitals.

the recording of **beta waves, alpha waves,** and **gamma waves** in the EEG (see ● Figure 6.6). During beta activity, a person is actively thinking and alert. Beta activity is characterized by rapid (15–30 cycles per second), irregular, low-amplitude waves that indicate the cerebral cortex is processing large amounts of diverse data. A person showing alpha activity is awake but relaxed. Alpha waves are slightly slower, larger, and more regular than beta waves, with a frequency of 9 to 12 cycles per second. Improvements in EEG technology provided the means to record waking waveforms that are faster than 30 cycles per second, known as **gamma waves** (Miller, 2007). Gamma waves accompany the processing of sensory input, particularly visual stimuli.

Daydreaming, or mind wandering, "refers to spontaneous, subjective experiences in a no-task, no-stimulus, no-response situation" (Vaitl et al., 2005, p. 100). Daydreaming is correlated with activity in the DMN, as described earlier in the chapter. Although the DMN is usually investigated using brain imaging technologies, EEG studies show that activity in the DMN is most closely correlated with alpha waves (Knyazev, Slobodskoj-Plusnan, Bocharov, & Pylkova, 2011). The purpose of the ability to daydream is unclear. We might daydream simply because we evolved the ability to divide our attention, as described in Chapter 5 (Mason et al., 2007). However, during activation of the DMN, we often think about our past experiences and plan our future (Kahn, 2013). This contradicts the commonly held view that daydreaming is a "waste of time."

Stockbyte/Photos.com

Regardless of whether they were larks or owls as children, most teens act like owls by naturally staying up late and sleeping in. Usually by the mid-20s, young adults go back to whichever sleeping pattern they showed before puberty, a change that may mark the final maturity of the brain.

Sleep

We spend one third of our lives sleeping. Despite all that experience, few of us know what is going on during sleep. We know from painful experience that skipping sleep makes us feel terrible, but again, our introspection into our personal experience does not provide many answers. By carefully recording and observing the experience of volunteers sleeping in laboratories, psychologists have been able to unravel many mysteries of sleep.

Stages of Sleep On the basis of observations of sleeping volunteers, we divide sleep into two types: **rapid eye movement (REM) sleep,** and **non–rapid eye movement (N-REM) sleep.** These types of sleep are differentiated by EEG recordings, muscle tone, autonomic activity, and mental activity (see ● Figure 6.7).

N-REM sleep is divided into four stages. Stage 1 usually occurs when we first go to sleep. Our examination of the participant's EEG shows patterns that are difficult to distinguish from those of the drowsy, waking volunteer. Some **theta waves** (4–7 cycles per second), which are larger and slower than alpha waves, are now observed. At this stage, people may not be aware that they are sleeping. Frequently, we awaken a friend or family member who has fallen asleep in front of the television by turning off the program only to have the sleeping person deny being asleep.

After 10 to 15 minutes, Stage 1 of N-REM sleep gives way to Stage 2. Now there is no doubt that the person is asleep. Further reductions in heart rate and muscle tension occur, and the EEG begins to show special waveforms called K complexes and sleep spindles that occur only in sleep. These particular types of activity might reflect the brain's efforts to keep us asleep while continuing to monitor the external environment. We usually sleep through familiar stimuli, such as the hum of an air conditioner, while waking in

Awake Alpha waves　　　　　　Beta waves

© Cengage Learning®

FIGURE 6.6

The EEG During Waking. EEG recordings during waking alternate between alpha waves and beta waves. Alpha waves are associated with a relaxed, possibly drowsy state, whereas beta waves are associated with alertness. *Source:* Adapted from *Why We Sleep: The Functions of Sleep in Humans and Other Mammals,* by J. Horne, 1988, New York, NY: Oxford University Press.

beta wave A waveform of 15 to 30 cycles per second recorded by electroencephalogram that usually indicates alert waking.
alpha wave A waveform of 9 to 12 cycles per second recorded by electroencephalogram that usually indicates relaxed waking.
gamma wave A waveform of more than 30 cycles per second recorded by electroencephalogram that indicates attention to sensory input.
rapid eye movement (REM) sleep The component of sleep characterized by waveforms resembling

waking, as measured by electroencephalogram, accompanied by rapid motion of the eyes, muscular paralysis, and sympathetic nervous system activation.
non–rapid eye movement (N-REM) sleep The components of sleep characterized by theta and delta wave activity, as recorded by electroencephalogram, and deep physical relaxation.
theta wave A waveform of 4 to 7 cycles per second recorded by electroencephalogram that is characteristic of lighter stages of non–rapid eye movement sleep.

FIGURE 6.7

The EEG During Sleep. Sleep is divided into two components: rapid eye movement (REM) sleep and non-REM (N-REM) sleep. The EEG during REM sleep is similar to wakefulness. Stages 1 and 2 of N-REM sleep feature theta waves. Special waveforms known as sleep spindles and K complexes, which might represent the brain's attempts to tune out environmental stimuli, appear in Stage 2. Stages 3 and 4 of N-REM sleep feature delta waves and represent the deepest stages of sleep. *Source:* Adapted from *Why We Sleep: The Functions of Sleep in Humans and Other Mammals,* by J. Horne, 1988, New York, NY: Oxford University Press.

response to unexpected stimuli, such as the sound of a door opening.

After about 15 minutes in Stage 2, we enter Stage 3 and then Stage 4 N-REM sleep. Both of these stages show **delta wave** activity, which is the largest, slowest (1–4 cycles per second) EEG waveform we will observe. Stages 3 and 4 differ primarily in the amount of delta activity that occurs, with Stage 4 having the most. We are deeply asleep in these stages. Awakening from Stage 4 is difficult, and considerable disorientation may occur before a person becomes fully awake. You may have received a telephone call about an hour after you first go to sleep, when you are likely to be experiencing Stage 4 N-REM sleep. If you hear the telephone, it may take several seconds to locate the phone and wake up enough to have a decent conversation.

The first episode of REM sleep occurs between 90 and 120 minutes after the onset of sleep. This stage is often called paradoxical sleep, reflecting a combination of brain activity resembling waking with the external appearance of deep sleep. During REM sleep, the EEG shows activity similar to waking activity. The eyes make the periodic movements back and forth that give this stage its name. The sympathetic nervous system becomes very active. Heart rate, blood pressure, and breathing become rapid or irregular. Males experience erections, while females experience increased blood flow in the vicinity of the vagina (Hirshkowitz & Moore, 1996). If awakened during this stage, most people report vivid, storylike dreams, which we discuss in more detail in a later section.

Major postural muscles are inactive during REM sleep, effectively paralyzing the sleeper, although smaller muscles in the fingers and toes might twitch. You might have experienced dreams in which something terrible was coming but you couldn't move. Your dream probably reflects recognition on the part of the brain that you are paralyzed. This paralysis provides a protective mechanism that prevents you from acting out your dreams. In cases of REM sleep disorder, paralysis fails and people injure

Experiencing Psychology

The Epworth Sleepiness Scale

COLLEGE STUDENTS OFTEN neglect sleep time to study, work, and socialize. Sixty percent of students reported staying awake for an entire night at least once since coming to college (Thacher, 2008). Poor sleep habits lead to daytime sleepiness, which can affect how much you learn in your classes, how well you work, and your safety when

driving and operating other machinery. How much sleepiness is too much?

Try using the Epworth Sleepiness Scale to see how sleepy you tend to be (Johns, 1991). In contrast to just feeling tired, how likely are you to doze off or fall asleep in the situations in the list? (Even if you have not done some of these things recently, try

to work out how they would have affected you.) Use the scale to choose the most appropriate number for each situation. A score greater than 10 indicates excessive daytime sleepiness. If you scored at this level or above, it's time for some lifestyle changes. ●

themselves or their sleeping partners. When one patient dreamed of playing football, he knocked everything off his dresser, hit his head against the wall, and banged his knee on the dresser (Schenck, Bundlie, Ettinger, & Mahowald, 1986).

Because the body is paralyzed during REM sleep, sleepwalking does not happen in this stage. Instead, sleepwalking occurs when a person is in Stage 3 or 4 of N-REM sleep. Sleep talking, however, usually occurs at the lighter Stages 1 and 2 of N-REM sleep. The talker may be sufficiently aware of the environment to politely wait for a turn to speak. These phenomena become progressively less common with age.

The cycling between REM sleep and N-REM sleep in humans follows a characteristic pattern over a period of 8 hours of sleep (see ● Figure 6.8). The first half of a night's sleep is characterized by longer periods of N-REM sleep and brief periods of REM sleep. Stages 3 and 4 of N-REM sleep are especially dominant during these first 4 hours. The second half of the night's sleep switches to a different pattern. REM sleep is now dominant, and N-REM sleep remains in the lighter stages. Stages 3 and 4 may be infrequent or absent during the last 4 hours of sleep. We usually spend the last half hour or so of the night's sleep in REM sleep and often wake up with the awareness that we have been dreaming.

The Benefits of Sleep   Although we still have many unanswered questions about why we spend one third of our lives sleeping, we know that lack of sleep can have many negative effects. Excess sleepiness on the part of decision makers has contributed to many disasters, including the Three Mile Island nuclear meltdown, the *Challenger* space shuttle explosion, and the grounding of the oil tanker *Exxon Valdez* (Coren, 1996a). In 2014, a commuter train at Chicago's O'Hare airport controlled by an operator who admitted to "dozing off" ran off the tracks and climbed an escalator. Staying awake for 17 to 19 straight hours produces worse reaction time than being legally drunk (Williamson & Feyer, 2000).

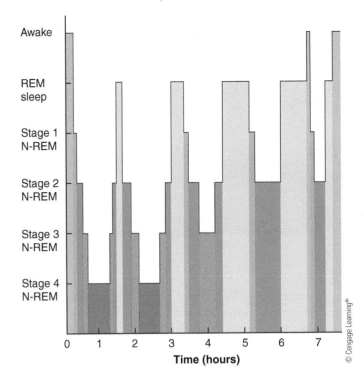

FIGURE 6.8

Nightly Sleep Patterns.   Sleep shows a typical progression over the night. The first 4 hours are dominated by N-REM sleep, and most Stage 3 and 4 N-REM sleep occurs at this time. The second 4 hours feature large amounts of REM sleep. *Source:* Adapted from *A Primer on Sleep and Dreaming*, by R. D. Cartwright, 1978, Reading, MA: Addison-Wesley.

delta wave   A waveform of 1 to 4 cycles per second recorded by electroencephalogram that usually indicates deep non–rapid eye movement sleep.

Situation	Chance of dozing
Sitting and reading	
Watching television	
Sitting inactive in a public place (e.g., a theater)	
Riding as a car passenger for an hour without a break	
Lying down to rest in the afternoon	
Sitting and talking to someone	
Sitting quietly after lunch without alcohol	
In a car, while stopping for a few minutes in traffic	
TOTAL SCORE	

0 = Would never doze
1 = Slight chance of dozing
2 = Moderate chance of dozing
3 = High chance of dozing

Jonathan Ernst/Reuters/Landov

AP Images/Bruce Weaver

Human error, and sleep deprivation in particular, frequently contributes to major accidents and disasters. The 1979 nuclear meltdown at Three Mile Island changed the power industry in the United States. The 1986 explosion of the space shuttle *Challenger* rattled confidence in the U.S. space program. The 1989 oil spill caused by the running aground of the tanker *Exxon Valdez* energized concerns about environmental protection. More recently, the operator of a commuter train that ran off the tracks up an escalator at Chicago O'Hare International Airport admitted to "dozing off."

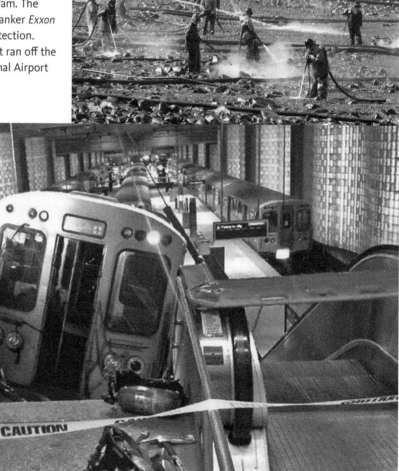

Bob Hallinen/Anchorage Daily News/MCT/Landov

AP Images/Kenneth Webster/ NBC Chicago

FIGURE 6.9

Human Growth Hormone Release.
Human growth hormone stimulates growth and repair. Most human growth hormone release occurs during the first 4 hours of sleep each night, primarily during Stages 3 and 4 of N-REM sleep. The drop in time spent in Stages 3 and 4 among older adults might contribute to reduced abilities to heal compared to those of younger adults. *Source:* Adapted from *Wide Awake at 3:00 a.m. by Choice or by Chance?* by R. M. Coleman, 1986, New York, NY: W. H. Freeman.

Sleep, and in particular Stages 3 and 4 of N-REM sleep, plays an important role in repairing the body. Sleep deprivation slows the healing of injuries (Murphy et al., 2007), reduces the activity of the immune system (Zager, Andersen, Ruiz, Antunes, & Tufik, 2007) and results in the production of fewer new neurons in adult brains (Guzman-Marin et al., 2003). Nearly all human growth hormone, which plays important roles in repairing the body, is released during Stages 3 and 4 of N-REM sleep but rarely during other stages of sleep and waking (Savine & Sönksen, 2000) (see ● Figure 6.9). Another line of evidence supporting the restorative hypothesis of sleep is the behavior of people following intense physical activity. Runners competing in ultramarathons (races that are twice the length of a normal marathon) experience greater amounts of N-REM sleep the night after their performance.

It is possible to selectively deprive volunteers in a sleep laboratory of Stage 3 and 4 N-REM sleep. After a night of such deprivation, volunteers typically complain of muscle and joint pain (Moldofsky & Scarisbrick, 1976). Because time spent in N-REM sleep decreases about 30 minutes per decade after the age of 50 (Van Cauter, Leproult, & Plat, 2000), it is possible that reduced N-REM sleep is the source of some of the muscle and joint aches and pains experienced by older adults.

Sleep plays a significant role in memory. Staying up all night results in poor memory performance, and two subsequent nights of normal sleep do not make up for the initial sleep deprivation effects (Stickgold & Walker, 2007). Sleep may serve as a special state for consolidating memories, in contrast to the acquisition and initial processing of new memories that occurs during waking (Rasch & Born, 2013). During N-REM sleep, memories are reactivated and transformed into versions that can be stored in long-term memory (see Chapter 9). REM sleep stabilizes the newly transformed memories. Students who wish to retain the material they've studied would be well advised to get a good night's sleep.

The Special Benefits of REM Sleep Birds and mammals are the only creatures to show clear evidence of REM sleep, suggesting that this sleep stage is a fairly recent development in the course of evolution. When volunteers are specifically deprived of REM sleep, they show many of the same symptoms as people who experience an overall lack of sleep, including irritability and difficulty concentrating. In addition, REM sleep–deprived individuals show a phenomenon known as REM rebound (Dement, 1960). When allowed to sleep normally, they spend an unusually large amount of their sleep time in REM sleep. You may have experienced REM rebound during a nap following a night with little sleep. You might be aware of having dreamed vividly during the nap, and you're unlikely to feel rested. These attempts to make up for lost REM sleep suggest that REM sleep has a necessary function in the adult brain.

One clue to a possible function of REM sleep is the association of REM sleep with the activity of the immature brain. The proportion of sleep spent in REM sleep is a function of a species' relative maturity at birth (Siegel, 2001). The human infant, born at an immature stage of brain development relative to other primate species, spends about half of its sleep time in REM sleep (see ● Figure 6.10), compared to the 20% of sleep time spent in REM sleep by adolescents and adults (McCarley, 2007). Premature infants spend up to 80% of their sleep time in REM sleep. REM sleep may provide at least part of the stimulation necessary to correctly "wire" the immature brain (Marks, Shaffery, Oksenberg, Speciale, & Roffwarg, 1995).

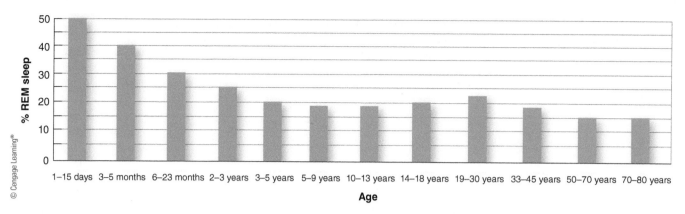

FIGURE 6.10

REM Sleep Over the Life Span. Infants and young children spend greater percentages of their sleep time in REM sleep than do adolescents and adults, suggesting that brain activity during REM sleep might help wire the developing brain. *Source:* Adapted from "Ontogenetic Development of the Human Sleep–Dream Cycle," by H. P. Roffwarg, J. N. Muzic, and W. C. Dement, 1966, *Science, 152,* pp. 604–619.

REM sleep and mood are tightly interwoven, providing us with a further clue regarding the possible functions of REM sleep. As we will see in Chapter 14, individuals with depression experience disruptions in their normal sleep patterns. Without treatment, they enter REM sleep earlier in the night than typical participants do, and they spend a greater proportion of their sleeping time in REM sleep. One of the possible mechanisms by which antidepressant medications regulate mood is their suppression of REM sleep. Individuals with bipolar disorder, which is characterized by moods that swing from euphoria to depression, also experience sleep abnormalities. Patients show an abnormally low need for sleep. The euphoric manic phase of the disorder can be initiated in some patients by sleep deprivation. Consequently, individuals with a diagnosis of bipolar disorder should take great care to obtain appropriate amounts of sleep.

 Connecting to **Research**

Loneliness Affects Sleep

MOST OF US ARE aware that mood and stress can have negative impacts on our sleep, but it might surprise you that loneliness can be a problem for good sleep quality too. Understanding the impact of loneliness on sleep helps explain some of the negative health outcomes associated with feeling socially disconnected. For example, loneliness in older adults predicted lower rates of survival 6 years later in the United States (Luo et al., 2012) and in China (Luo & Waite, 2014). You might think that loneliness affects people by making them less likely to follow good health habits, like taking their medication and exercising, but research didn't support this hypothesis. Instead, researchers suspected that loneliness led to poor health in part by disrupting sleep, which plays an important role in healing the body (Cacioppo, Hawkley, et al., 2002; Kurina et al., 2010).

The Question: Is sleep quality affected by loneliness?

METHODS

Sixty-four undergraduates at Ohio State University participated in the study. Their levels of perceived loneliness were assessed using the Revised UCLA (University of California, Los Angeles; UCLA-R) Loneliness Scale (Russell, Peplau, & Cutrona, 1980). Their sleep quality was measured using a sleep monitor called Nightcap while they spent the night in the campus's Clinical Research Center. Sleep quality measures included sleep onset, sleep duration, number of awakenings, and wake time after onset. The participants' sleep quality was assessed 2 weeks later at home over five consecutive nights.

RESULTS

The participants were divided into high-, medium-, and low-loneliness groups on the

basis of their scores on the UCLA-R Loneliness Scale. Sleep quality did vary significantly among these groups, with the high-loneliness group experiencing the lowest sleep quality and the low-loneliness group experiencing the best sleep quality. The medium-loneliness group had sleep quality scores between these two extremes. In particular, the loneliest participants were more likely to experience restless sleep, as indicated by their spending more time awake during the night after they had fallen asleep once.

CONCLUSIONS

The results of this study indicated that lonely people experienced poor quality of sleep. However, there are several ways these results could be explained, as we outlined in Chapter 2. First, it is possible that the experience of loneliness causes poor sleep quality. Second, poor sleep quality could interfere with a person's ability to

These correlations between REM sleep and mood may represent a common underlying biochemical mechanism. Brainstem neurons that release serotonin and norepinephrine are especially quiet during REM sleep, although they are active during waking and somewhat active during N-REM sleep (Gottesman, 2002). These same neurotransmitters have also been implicated in the regulation of mood states, which helps explain links between REM sleep and mood.

Dreams

From the earliest times in our history, people have searched for the significance and meaning of their dreams. In ancient Egypt, many people believed that dreams predicted the future. In his classic book *The Interpretation of Dreams,* Freud (1900/1953) argued that the unconscious mind expressed itself symbolically through our dreams. These are interesting ideas, but what does science have to say about **dreaming**? The use of EEG technology to track a volunteer's sleep patterns allowed researchers to awaken volunteers and assess a dream experience scientifically for the first time (Aserinsky & Kleitman, 1953; Dement & Kleitman, 1957).

An activation–synthesis theory of dreaming suggests that the content of dreams simply reflects ongoing neural activity. For example, dreams of being unable to move in a dangerous situation might accurately mirror the muscle paralysis present during the REM state (Hobson & McCarley, 1977). Common dreams of flying or falling may be caused by the unusual activation of the vestibular system during REM sleep (Hunt, 1989). In Chapter 5, we discussed the vestibular system's role in helping us maintain balance. Dreams with sexual content are consistent with the physical sexual arousal that occurs during REM sleep. Combining results of brain imaging experiments and cognitive psychology leads to yet another view of dreams. Dreaming behavior correlates with activity in circuits that overlap substantially with the DMN (Fox, Nijeboer, Solomonova, Domhoff, & Christoff, 2013). According to this view, daydreaming and dreaming during sleep are on a continuum. Simultaneous changes in brainstem

dreaming A mental state that usually occurs during sleep that features visual imagery.

function well socially, leading to loneliness. Third, loneliness and sleep quality could influence each other reciprocally. Finally, some third variable or set of variables could lead to both disruptions of feeling socially connected and sleep quality. If you think that a likely candidate for one of these third variables is depression, the researchers controlled for this by assessing depression before the study and excluding potential participants who appeared to be depressed.

These results indicate that the relationships between loneliness and health are more complicated than a simple connection between loneliness and the likelihood that an individual would follow good health practices. ●

Jessica Bell

activity result in lower sensitivity to outside stimuli, and reduced overall frontal lobe activity might lead to even less self-awareness and logical thought than occurs during daydreaming. Once the dream state is initiated, the brain draws on memories of general knowledge and personal experience to produce a story line (Foulkes, 1999).

Although we have characterized dreaming as lacking self-awareness, this is not true of all dreams. In **lucid dreaming**, dreamers become aware that they are dreaming and may use this awareness to control or direct the content of the dream. This improved insight during REM sleep is associated with increased activity in the dorsolateral prefrontal cortex, an area of the brain believed to participate in higher order executive functions, including people's sense of control and voluntary behavior (Dresler et al., 2013). In a sense, lucid dreaming appears to occur when frontal areas of the brain inexplicably "wake up" during a dream (Mota-Rolim & Araujo, 2013).

The activation–synthesis theory of dream content suggests that the content of dreams represents the mind's efforts to make sense out of real physical sensations. During REM sleep, the vestibular system of the inner ear is quite active. Because the vestibular system normally informs us about the position and movement of the head, vestibular activity during REM sleep might lead to the commonly experienced dreams of flying or falling.

Sleep Disorders

Observing what goes wrong in sleep provides additional insights into the natural variations of consciousness we experience.

Nightmares and Sleep Terrors When the content of a REM dream is especially upsetting, we refer to the experience as a nightmare. If lucid dreamers become stuck in a nightmare, they may have the option of "changing channels" and exiting that line of content. Some researchers report that training in lucid dreaming may serve as an effective treatment for recurring, upsetting nightmares (Mota-Rolim & Araujo, 2013; Zadra & Pihl, 1997).

Nightmares are often mistaken for **sleep terrors**, but they are different phenomena. Nightmares are dreams that occur during REM sleep, while sleep terrors occur during N-REM sleep, particularly during the first 3 hours of sleep. In sleep terrors, the usually smooth transition from Stage 4 N-REM sleep upward into REM sleep goes awry. The sleeper becomes acutely distressed despite remaining deeply asleep. If awakened, the person shows the disorientation and confusion typically demonstrated when a sleeper is disturbed during deep N-REM sleep. There is usually no memory of the sleep terror the next day. Twin studies suggest that there is a genetic predisposition to sleep terrors (Taheri & Mignot, 2002).

Insomnia After nightmares, the most common sleep problem is **insomnia**, in which a person has difficulty initiating or maintaining sleep. Clearly, there are substantial individual differences in the healthy amount and patterning of sleep. Although most people seem to need about 7 to 9 hours of sleep per night to function effectively, wider healthy variations exist. In one case of "healthy insomnia," an elderly woman slept only 1 hour per night without apparent detrimental effects (Meddis, Pearson, & Langford, 1973).

Insomnia occurs in one of two forms. In cases of onset insomnia, a person lies in bed for what seems to be a long period but is unable to go to sleep. Stress and anxiety are frequent causes of this type of insomnia. Maintenance insomnia occurs when sleep is frequently interrupted or early waking occurs. These cases typically result from stress, substance use, or psychological disorders. Insomnia medications, such as zolpidem (Ambien), have minor effects on sleep, producing sleep 15 minutes faster and lengthening it for about 30 minutes, which might not offset significant side effects, including dependence on the medication, driving or walking while asleep, memory loss, and loss of coordination (Buscemi et al., 2007).

lucid dreaming A conscious awareness of dreaming accompanied by the ability to control the content of the dream.
sleep terror A sleep disorder occurring in non–rapid eye movement sleep in which the sleeper wakes suddenly in great distress but without experiencing the imagery of a nightmare.
insomnia A sleep disorder characterized by an inability to either initiate or maintain normal sleep.
narcolepsy A sleep disorder characterized by the intrusion of rapid eye movement phenomena into waking.

Narcolepsy and Cataplexy Probably the most dramatic sleep disorder is **narcolepsy**. Narcolepsy consists of "sleep attacks," in which REM sleep occurs during wakefulness (Dahl, Holttum, & Trubnick, 1994). In addition to sleep attacks, other aspects of REM sleep may intrude into the wakefulness of patients with narcolepsy. Cataplexy occurs when the muscle paralysis normally associated with REM sleep occurs during wakefulness without loss of consciousness. Many patients with narcolepsy also experience sleep paralysis, or muscle paralysis that either precedes actual sleep or lingers once the person has awakened. Although upsetting, this paralysis is easy to resolve. Simply touching the person is enough to end the paralysis.

Cells in the hypothalamus that normally secrete neurochemicals known as orexins are missing or damaged in the brains of patients with narcolepsy (Thannickal et al., 2000). Although researchers have been able to selectively breed for narcolepsy in dogs (Foutz, Mitler, Cavalli-Sforza, & Dement, 1978), the contribution of genetics to human narcolepsy is more complex. Narcolepsy results from a combination of genetic vulnerability and autoimmune processes that attack the cells in the brain that produce orexins (Taheri & Mignot, 2002).

Breathing-related Sleep Disorders
We take it for granted that automatic functions like breathing continue uninterrupted during sleep, but this is not the case in the breathing-related sleep disorder called **sleep apnea**. In a person with sleep apnea, breathing can stop for a minute or two, and the sleeper awakens abruptly gasping for air. Not only does this lack of air disrupt the sleep quality of the person with sleep apnea, but it can increase the risk for heart disease (Kendzerska, Gershon, Hawker, Leung, & Tomlinson, 2014). Because most cases of sleep apnea occur in people who are obese and who snore (obstructive sleep apnea hypopnea), losing weight and surgical correction of airway blockages are common treatments. Other cases occur when brainstem neurons responsible for maintaining breathing during sleep malfunction (central sleep apnea). In these cases, the use of a machine that regulates airflow during sleep is an inconvenient but effective solution.

Sudden Infant Death Syndrome (SIDS)
Sudden infant death syndrome (SIDS), occurs when a healthy infant simply dies while asleep. Between 1992 and 2003, rates of SIDS in the United States were cut in half when the American Academy of Pediatrics (AAP) began telling parents to put their infants to sleep on their backs instead of on their stomachs (National Institute of Child Health and Human Development, 2003). As we will see in Chapter 11, young infants cannot turn over easily for the first few months of life, making suffocation on blankets and stuffed animals a greater risk.

Despite these improvements, SIDS remains the most common cause of death in the first six months of life in industrialized nations, even as the cause of these cases remains elusive (Krous, 2014). Although some cases might include biological vulnerabilities in serotonin function (Paterson et al., 2006), most affected infants have additional risk factors, such as exposure to tobacco smoke (Ostfeld, Esposito, Perl, & Hegyi, 2010).

Courtesy A. R. Braun, National Institute of Deafness, NIH, Bethesda

Brain imaging can be used to compare activity during waking with activity during sleep. In this image, areas that are blue or purple are less active during REM sleep than during waking, and areas that are red or yellow are more active during REM sleep than during waking. The bizarre content of dreams occurring during REM sleep might be the result of the lower activity in the frontal lobes (purple) at the top of the image. The visual vividness of dreams might be accounted for by the higher amount of activity in the visual areas of the occipital lobes toward the bottom of the image (yellow and red).

Findings that new narcolepsy cases resulted from either infection with or vaccination for the H1N1 flu virus support the idea that narcolepsy is linked to activity in the immune system. American vaccines provoking weaker immune responses were less likely to result in narcolepsy than stronger European vaccines and the disease itself (Dauvilliers, Montplaisir, Cochen, Sesautels, Einen, Lin, et al., 2010).

sleep apnea A sleep disorder in which the person stops breathing while asleep.
sudden infant death syndrome (SIDS) A sleep disorder in which an otherwise healthy infant dies while asleep.

Bettmann/Corbis

Despite her suspected narcolepsy, Harriet Tubman (1820–1913) helped hundreds of slaves escape through the Underground Railroad during the Civil War era. Tubman appears on the left in this photo with some of the former slaves whom she helped. Unfortunately, narcoleptic attacks are often brought on by stress. Tubman had a number of close escapes when she experienced sleep attacks while being pursued by Confederate troops and irate slave owners.

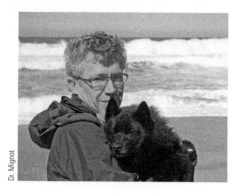

Sleep researcher Emmanuel Mignot is holding Bear, one of his dogs with narcolepsy. Research on dogs like Bear showed that narcolepsy is a genetic disorder involving abnormalities in neurotransmitters known as orexins.

The number of deaths from SIDS dropped dramatically when the American Academy of Pediatrics began telling parents in 2003 to put their babies to sleep on their backs instead of on their stomachs. SIDS still occurs, however, so sleeping position is only one of many risk factors, including exposure to cigarette smoke in the home.

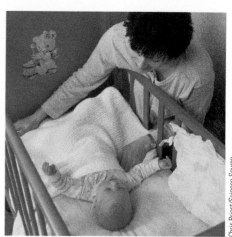

restless legs syndrome (RLS) A disorder characterized by the involuntary movement of an extremity, usually one leg.

Restless Legs Syndrome (RLS) **Restless legs syndrome (RLS)**, occurs when one of a person's limbs, usually a leg, experiences a tingling feeling and moves at regular intervals. RLS appears to be quite common, with 15% of a large sample of adults in the United States reporting these symptoms (National Sleep Foundation, 2009). RLS results from a gene variant that is active only during early prenatal development in the basal ganglia, a part of the brain involved with voluntary movement (Spieler et al., 2014) (see Chapter 4). Of special interest to psychologists is the high frequency of RLS among children and adults with attention deficit hyperactivity disorder (ADHD) and the potential genetic links between these two conditions (Schimmelmann et al., 2009). As we will see in Chapter 14, ADHD is characterized by differences in dopamine functioning, a characteristic shared by restless leg syndrome (Taheri & Mignot, 2002).

Summary 6.2 Features of Wakefulness and Sleep

Stage of waking or sleep		Brain activity recorded by EEG	Observations
Waking Awake ~ Alpha waves Beta waves		Alpha, beta, gamma	• Alternating periods of alertness and relaxation • Logical thought • Voluntary movement • Responsive to stimuli
N-REM sleep Stage 1 N-REM ~ Theta waves	Stage 1	Some theta	• Logical thought • Reduced heart rate and muscle tension • Some responsiveness to stimuli
Stage 2 N-REM ~ Sleep spindle—K-complex	Stage 2	Larger amounts of theta	• Less responsiveness to stimuli • Further reductions in heart rate and muscle tension
Stage 3 N-REM ~ Delta waves	Stage 3	Some delta	• Further reductions in heart rate and muscle tension
Stage 4 N-REM ~ Delta waves	Stage 4	Larger amounts of delta	• Profound reductions in heart rate and muscle tension • Very low responsiveness to stimuli
REM sleep REM sleep ~ Beta waves		Similar to waking	• Rapid motion of the eyes • Muscle paralysis • Irregular autonomic activity • Vivid dreams

© Cengage Learning®

How Is Consciousness Affected by Brain Damage?

If consciousness is a function of the brain, we should be able to identify aspects of consciousness that change reliably when the brain is damaged.

Specific Areas of Brain Damage and Consciousness

In this section, we will explore lessons about consciousness that have emerged from the clinical study of patients with damage to specific parts of the nervous system.

The effects of brain damage on face recognition provide an opportunity to consider how the brain integrates sensory information, memory, and emotion to form a conscious experience. Prosopagnosia is a condition that affects a person's ability to recognize faces (Bauer, 1984). In one case, a patient was unable to identify familiar faces. However, the patient was still able to show differing autonomic responses to familiar versus unfamiliar faces. Separate pathways process the features of faces, emotional responses to faces, and recognition of faces.

In a situation that is reminiscent of many horror film and science fiction classics, patients with Capgras syndrome are convinced that imposters have taken the place of familiar people. In certain tragic instances, patients with Capgras even try to harm the "imposters." This condition appears to be a type of problem opposite that of prosopagnosia. Here, the ability to recognize faces remains intact, but the sense of emotion and familiarity is distorted. The damage associated with Capgras syndrome is not thoroughly understood, but it is assumed to involve connections between visual areas of the brain and the amygdala (Ramachandran, 1998).

These clinical cases demonstrate the varied aspects of consciousness that contribute to our overall awareness of ourselves and the world around us. When we observe the precise loss of a conscious capacity, such as recognizing your friend's face, leaving all other aspects of your awareness intact, we gain an appreciation for the richness of brain activity that must underlie what we call consciousness.

Prosopagnosia results from damage to a part of the temporal lobes on the bottom of the brain known as the fusiform face area (FFA). In this scan using functional magnetic resonance imaging (fMRI), the FFA activity indicates that the person is looking at the image of a face as opposed to a landscape or building. From Timothy J. Andrews, et al.; Internal and External Features of the Face Are Represented Holistically in Face-Selective Regions of Visual Cortex, *The Journal of Neuroscience*, 2010, 30(9): 3544–3552, doi:10.1523/JNEUROSCI.4863 -09.2010.

Coma, Vegetative State, Brain Death, and Near-Death

Consciousness is clearly altered not only by damage in particular areas of the brain but by the severity of damage as well.

Coma Our word *coma* comes from the Greek *koma,* which means "deep sleep." **Coma** produces a profound state of unconsciousness. In a state of coma, a person does not have sleep–wake cycles, cannot be awakened, does not respond to pain or light, and is incapable of voluntary behavior. Coma occurs whenever both cerebral hemispheres or the reticular formation are damaged (Liversedge & Hirsch, 2010). A stroke affecting a single hemisphere typically does not lead to coma. Comas last anywhere from a few days to several weeks. After a period of 2 to 4 weeks, most patients recover, move into a vegetative state (described later in this section), or die. Among those who recover, improvement is usually slow and gradual.

EEG recordings of comatose patients vary depending on the problem that initially led to coma. Following resuscitation from cardiac arrest, many patients show a pattern of alpha rhythms, especially in the frontal lobes, or the so-called alpha coma (Chatrian, 1990). These alpha patterns do not change when the patient is exposed to various types of stimulation. Other patterns feature a low level of overall activity occasionally interrupted by spikes. None of these patterns are found in the typical, healthy EEG described previously in our section on sleep and waking (see ● Figure 6.11).

Vegetative State (VS) Coma can be distinguished from other similar conditions, such as **vegetative state (VS)** and brain death. VS often follows a period of coma. VS is characterized by waking without consciousness. In contrast to the patient with coma, patients with VS look

coma An abnormal state of deep unconsciousness.
vegetative state (VS) An abnormal state following brain injury featuring wakefulness without consciousness.

Normal EEG

Comatose EEG

© Cengage Learning®

FIGURE 6.11

Normal Versus Comatose EEGs.
Even though the patient with the normal EEG recording is drowsy, which should produce a dominant pattern of alpha waves, the normal recording is quite different from the more uniform alpha activity recorded from a patient in a coma.

near-death experience An altered state of consciousness reported by people who were close to death because of cardiac or other medical problems that features out-of-body experiences, light-at-the-end-of-a-tunnel perceptions, and a state of calmness.

rather normal. Their eyes open periodically, and they grind their teeth, scream, smile, or cry. Some are responsive to pain. Despite data from imaging studies, whether there is conscious awareness in VS remains debatable (Celesia, 2013; see ● Figure 6.12).

Brain Death With the advent of technologies that can artificially maintain certain bodily functions, including respiration and blood circulation, we have been placed in the odd position of requiring a new definition of death. Brain death is now defined as a complete and irreversible lack of measurable brain activity, as evidenced by two flatline EEG recordings taken 24 hours apart or lack of blood circulation to the brain (see ● Figure 6.13). In brain death, the patient shows no responses to external stimuli, including pain, and no reflexes related to the cranial nerves described in Chapter 4.

Near-Death Experiences Because of improvements in technology that literally bring people "back to life," more than 8 million Americans have reported a **near-death experience** (Mauro, 1992). Patients who recover following a cardiac arrest or some other life-threatening condition often report similar experiences. These experiences typically feature an out-of-body experience, in which people feel they are viewing their body from a floating position above it. In addition, many people report a "light at the end of the tunnel" visual experience, which may include images of deceased friends and relatives or deities. These visual sensations are accompanied by a peaceful, calm emotional state and followed by a reluctant return to the body.

 Thinking **Scientifically**

Can Patients in Vegetative States (VS) Communicate?

IT IS HARD to imagine a more traumatic experience than to be conscious but trapped in an unresponsive body. This outcome does occur in rare cases of locked in syndrome (LIS), in which damage to the brainstem results in the loss of movement of all voluntary muscles except the eye muscles (Gosseries et al., 2014). LIS patients are fully aware, but can only communicate using eyelid movements. Some scientists working with patients with VS fear that these patients might also be more aware than their bodies' responses indicate. This fear has led to a search for ways to communicate with these patients.

Following a traffic accident more than 20 years ago, Rom Houben has been in a

VS. Doctors attempted to communicate with Houben by asking him to type with his right index finger, which was not paralyzed. Messages from Houben immediately gained worldwide attention. Unfortunately, follow-up research showed that Houben's speech therapist, who was supposed to be providing support for his hand, was responsible for the messages. This "facilitated communication" has often produced similar false results. However, the doctors continue to look for a way to reach Houben, whose brain appears to be acting only slightly differently than normal in imaging studies (Schnakers et al., 2009).

Using fMRI, other scientists have identified VS patients whose brains showed reliable and distinct patterns of activity when asked to imagine playing tennis or walking around their homes (Monti et al., 2010). Using "tennis" for "yes" and "home" for "no," the patients were able to correctly answer a series of questions, such as "Do you have brothers?" or "Is your father's name Thomas?" Despite the accuracy of these responses, the patients show no outward signs of consciousness, nor do they show normal behavioral reactions to stimuli.

VS patients with these higher levels of awareness might differ from less responsive patients in the amount and type of cortical activity their brains show during fMRI (Gosseries et al., 2014). Most VS patients demonstrate low levels of cortical activation re-

A Healthy Controls

B Patient 54

FIGURE 6.12

Is Consciousness Possible in VS Patients? Using functional magnetic resonance imaging (fMRI), a small number of patients in a vegetative state (VS) showed brain activation to specific tasks that closely resembled the activation of healthy control participants. The yellow–red areas were active when thinking about movement, and the bluish areas were active when thinking about a spatial task. This research emphasizes the need to develop new ways of assessing the cognitive correlates of brain injuries so that patients can receive the best care possible. From Martin M. Monti et al. (2010). Willful modulation of brain activity in disorders of consciousness. *New England Journal of Medicine, 362*(7), 579-589, doi: 10.1056/ NEJMoa0905370

A

B **C**

FIGURE 6.13

Determining Brain Death. Brain death is often determined by a study of blood circulation. In these images, blood can be seen flowing into the neck, scalp, and face (particularly the nose, which leads to the phrase "hot nose sign"). However, no blood flow is seen in the brain itself, which remains dark. A careful determination of brain death is required because of the common practice of organ donation following death. Reprinted by permission of the Society of Nuclear Medicine from: MacDonald A. and Burrell S. Infrequently Performed Studies in Nuclear Medicine: Part 2. *J Nucl Med Technol.* 2009; *37*(1): 1-13. Figure 5

stricted to the primary sensory areas. More "aware" patients with VS, like the patients evaluated by Monti et al. (2010), show higher levels of cortical activity in areas of the brain involved with executive function as well as in the sensory areas. Scientists used an "own-name" paradigm to evaluate patient cognition and awareness in which patient responses to hearing their own names were evaluated using fMRI. VS patients who showed higher cortical responses in addition to primary auditory cortex responses to hearing their own names were more likely to show later improvements in functioning (Gosseries et al., 2014). ●

REUTERS/Romain Eyckens/Corbis

After 20 years in an apparent vegetative state (VS), Rom Houben was able to type with his nonparalyzed finger with the assistance of his speech therapist. Unfortunately, further studies suggested that the therapist was typing, not Houben. However, the appearance of relatively normal patterns of activity in Houben's brain, as seen in imaging studies, has led physicians to seek other ways to communicate with him.

FIGURE 6.14

Pathways for the Spread of Partial and Generalized Seizures. (a) Partial seizures originate in a focal area and spread to cortical and subcortical structures. (b) Generalized seizures do not originate in a focal area. Once they begin, generalized seizures spread through the brain symmetrically via connections between the thalamus and the cortex.

Primary seizure focus

Corpus callosum

Thalamus

Argosy Publishing, Inc.

(a) Partial seizure

(b) Generalized seizure

The similarities among documented cases of near-death experiences lead us to assume that the dying–revival experience produces consistent responses in the human brain (Negovsky & Gurvitch, 2004). In animal models of cardiac arrest, a surge of brain activity occurs near death, suggesting a state of heightened consciousness (Borjigin et al., 2013). Strong out-of-body sensations and other near-death phenomena occur in volunteers using ketamine (Jansen, 1996). A damaged brain may release its own chemicals, similar to ketamine, in an effort to minimize cell loss.

Seizures

Seizures are uncontrolled electrical disturbances in the brain that are often correlated with changes in consciousness, providing further evidence that cortical activity is correlated with consciousness. People with recurring seizures are diagnosed with epilepsy. Seizures frequently occur as a result of brain injury or infection but can also appear without an obvious cause. Disturbances in the activity of the inhibitory neurotransmitter GABA might account for many seizures. Drugs that inhibit GABA reliably produce seizures, while drugs that enhance GABA activity, like barbiturates, prevent or control seizures.

Most seizures are classified as either partial seizures or generalized seizures. Partial seizures originate in a particular part of the brain, known as the focal area, and are often accompanied by an aura, or a premonition that a seizure is about to occur. Generalized seizures do not arise from a focal area. Instead, these seizures are characterized by the abnormal activation of circuits connecting the cortex and thalamus. Generalized seizures are typically not accompanied by an aura (see ● Figure 6.14).

Partial seizures originating in the temporal lobe often produce distortions of consciousness, leading to the experience of *déjà vu* (French for "already seen"), a feeling that one is reliving the past, or *jamais vu* (French for "never seen"), a sense that one's familiar circumstances are suddenly foreign or strange. Consciousness is lost in generalized seizures. The two major categories of generalized seizure are tonic–clonic and absence seizures. Tonic–clonic seizures begin with a loss of consciousness, cessation of breathing, and intense muscular contraction. This phase usually gives way to violent, rhythmic contractions that may result in broken bones or other physical injuries. These phases are followed by a period of coma, lasting about 5 minutes. In an absence seizure, the person loses consciousness and awareness of surroundings, and motor movements are limited to blinking, head turns, and eye movements.

seizure An abnormal level of brain activation with a sudden onset.

How Do People Intentionally Alter Their States of Consciousness?

Humans have intentionally altered consciousness in religious, recreational, and healing contexts. Methods may vary dramatically, but we will see that some common themes of these efforts emerge. Individuals who deliberately alter their state of consciousness may be seeking insight, positive emotion (bliss or ecstasy), or a sense of unity or "oneness." The universality of such efforts, which often underlie religious behavior, strongly suggests that these states confer some advantages, although what those advantages may be remains unknown.

General Features of Psychoactive Drugs

Historically, humans have gone to great lengths to obtain **psychoactive drugs**, or substances that alter consciousness. Humans may be unique among animals in their willingness to voluntarily seek alterations in consciousness through the deliberate use of psychoactive substances. Most psychoactive substances are quite poisonous (livestock eating tobacco leaves in the field will die) and usually have the bitter taste associated with most poisons. On the rare occasions when nonhuman animals consume psychoactive substances (cats and catnip or elephants and alcohol), we have no way of knowing whether this consumption is motivated by a desire to alter consciousness.

Before we explore some of the drugs most frequently used to alter consciousness, we will outline several general principles related to the use of drugs, including tolerance, withdrawal, and addiction.

Tolerance and Withdrawal **Tolerance** occurs when a person must take larger quantities of a drug to produce the desired effects. The nervous system is always working to maintain homeostasis, a steady internal balance or equilibrium. When a person takes a drug repeatedly, the nervous system attempts to compensate for the drug's effects. These compensations are both biological and learned (via mechanisms described in more detail in Chapter 8).

When some habitually used drugs are no longer available, the user might experience **withdrawal**, a set of behaviors that are the opposite of those produced by the drug. Withdrawing from alcohol, which inhibits the nervous system, produces a rebound effect characterized by so much excess brain activity that life-threatening seizures often occur. Withdrawing from stimulants like caffeine can make the user sluggish and lethargic. Although many abused drugs produce significant withdrawal, others do not. Heroin and nicotine produce powerful withdrawal effects, but cocaine usually does not (Coffey, Dansky, Carrigan, & Brady, 2000).

Addiction **Addiction** is traditionally viewed as a compulsive physical or psychological dependence on a substance or activity that continues in spite of negative consequences. Although tolerance and withdrawal are two hallmark symptoms of physical dependence on a drug, not all addictive drugs display these features. For example, cocaine is quite addictive despite its lack of withdrawal symptoms. The defining features of an addiction are the compulsive repetition of drug use or an activity and the inability to abstain from the addictive behavior despite serious negative consequences. Addiction overwhelms normal control of behavior, distorts typical systems of reward, and interferes with the recognition of problems.

In addiction, people make choices on the basis of short-term outcomes (getting high) instead of on the basis of long-term outcomes (family, finances, job, and staying out of jail). This disruption in normal, logical decision making can occur because of distortions in one or more of three related neural systems: an impulsive system involving dopamine pathways connecting the midbrain and the basal ganglia, a reflective system in the frontal lobes that weighs the pros and cons of a decision and controls impulses, and a craving system involving the

AP Images/Per Johansson

Most animals avoid psychoactive substances, but this Swedish moose managed to get stuck in a tree after eating fermented apples that had fallen on the ground. We have no way of knowing whether the moose was motivated by a desire to experience an altered state of consciousness or it simply liked the taste of the fruit.

psychoactive drug Any drug with the capability of altering a person's state of consciousness.
tolerance The need to administer greater quantities of a drug to achieve the same subjective effect.
withdrawal Physical responses to the removal of some habitually administered drugs.
addiction A compulsive physical or psychological dependence on a substance or activity that continues in spite of negative consequences.

FIGURE 6.15

Addiction Involves Multiple Brain Networks. Addiction is correlated with activity in a number of brain circuits. (a) An impulsive, reward-seeking system that uses the neurochemical dopamine connects the midbrain (ventral tegmental area and substantia nigra) with the basal ganglia, including the nucleus accumbens. A reflective system involving the frontal lobes controls impulses and makes decisions. (b) A craving system involves the insula.

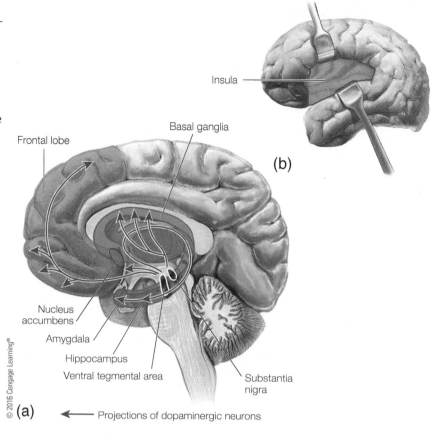

Insula

Basal ganglia

(b)

Frontal lobe

Nucleus accumbens

Amygdala

Hippocampus

Ventral tegmental area

Substantia nigra

© 2016 Cengage Learning®

(a)

◄─── Projections of dopaminergic neurons

Zalmai/Edit/Getty Images

insula (Noël, Brevers, & Bechara, 2013) (see ● Figure 6.15). Activity in the insula is correlated with participants' ratings of the urge for their drug of choice, and strokes that damage the insula eliminate the urge to use some addictive drugs (Verdejo-Garcia, Clark, & Dunn, 2012). Excess activity in the impulsive system, inadequate activity in the reflective system, and increased desire appear to set the stage for maintaining compulsive addictive behaviors.

Understanding human drug use requires us to zoom out to incorporate multiple perspectives. In addition to biological and social factors, we might ask about the possible adaptations provided by altering human consciousness or why younger people seem more vulnerable to addiction than older adults. Individual differences predict which people are more likely than others to become addicted. Through exploring the different examples of drugs historically used by humans with this more integrated perspective, we gain insight into why the human mind seeks altered states of consciousness in the face of substantial restrictions, consequences, and disapproval.

Should we be concerned about military veterans returning from service in Afghanistan with opium addictions? If the experiences of returning Vietnam veterans are repeated, the answer will be "no." Even though heroin was readily available in Vietnam and large numbers of soldiers used heroin while serving, nearly all quit using upon their return to the United States. These observations remind us that addiction is a complex phenomenon with multiple causes.

Commonly Used Psychoactive Drugs

Marijuana Cannabis, from the *Cannabis sativa* plant, has a long human history. It was included in the pharmacy written by Chinese Emperor Shen Neng nearly 5,000 years ago. Marijuana, the smoked form of cannabis, remains the most commonly used federally illegal substance in the United States today. The behavioral effects of cannabis are often so subtle that people may report no changes in response to its use. Most individuals experience some excitation, vivid imagery, and mild euphoria. Others respond with depression and social withdrawal. At somewhat higher doses, cannabis produces hallucinations, leading to its formal classification as a **hallucinogen**.

Cannabis contains more than 50 psychoactive compounds, known as cannabinoids. The most important of these is tetrahydrocannabinol (THC). THC produces some of its behavioral effects by interacting with receptors for endogenous cannabinoids, natural substances that are similar to THC in chemical composition. One type of receptor is located in parts of the brain involved with pain, appetite, learning, reasoning, and movement (see ● Figure 6.16). Another type is found elsewhere in the body, particularly in structures associated with the immune system. THC has the ability to stimulate dopamine activity, which in turn is usually associated with a potential for dependency (Merritt, Martin, Walters, Lichtman, & Damaj, 2008). In addition, genetic vulnerability for schizophrenia interacts with heavy and chronic use of marijuana among teens and young adults to increase their risk of developing psychotic symptoms (Fergusson, Horwood, & Ridder, 2005; Henquet, Di Forti, Morrison, Kuepper, & Murray, 2008; Hill, 2014).

LSD In 1938, researcher Albert Hoffman reported some unusual sensations after working with lysergic acid diethylamide (LSD). Hoffman deliberately ingested some of the chemical and reported vivid, colorful visual hallucinations.

LSD is chemically similar to serotonin, and it interacts with serotonin receptors (Gonzalez-Maeso et al., 2007, 2008). LSD's ability to produce hallucination remains poorly understood. One of the interesting cognitive outcomes of LSD use is the experience of flashbacks, intrusive and involuntary hallucinations, even after the drug has been discontinued (Halpern & Pope, 2003). Further research is necessary to identify the mechanisms for this experience.

Caffeine Caffeine is a **stimulant** found in a range of sources, including coffee, tea, cola and energy drinks, and many over-the-counter pain relievers (see ● Figure 6.17). Caffeine interferes with the inhibition normally produced by adenosine in the brain. If you keep an inhibitory substance like adenosine from doing its job, the result is increased excitation and alertness.

Caffeine produces a withdrawal syndrome characterized by headaches and fatigue. Some people experience problems with heart rhythms related to caffeine use. Caffeine crosses the placenta easily and also enters breast milk, leading to reduced rates of growth and other complications in the fetus and breastfed infant of a mother using the drug (Bakker et al., 2010). On the positive side, caffeine use is correlated with a lower risk of Parkinson's disease, which causes difficulty moving (Ross & Petrovitch, 2001), as well as Alzheimer's disease and other forms of dementia (Eskelinen & Kivipelto, 2010). Because these are correlations, we don't know whether the apparent protection against these conditions is because of some specific action of caffeine in the brain or is simply the result of the characteristics of people who enjoy large amounts of caffeine.

Nicotine After caffeine, the most commonly used stimulant in the United States is nicotine, usually in the form of smoked or chewed tobacco (see ● Figure 6.18). Nicotine mimics

FIGURE 6.16

Locations of Cannabinoid Receptors in the Brain. Cannabinoids, such as THC, interact with receptors located in a number of parts of the brain. In particular, cannabinoid receptors are numerous in the hippocampus and the prefrontal cortex.

Basal ganglia (movement)

Prefontal cortex (reasoning)

Hypothalamus (appetite)

Hippocampus (memory)

Medulla (nausea)

Cerebellum (movement)

Spinal cord (pain)

© 2016 Cengage Learning®

Laguna Design/Science Photo Library/Corbis

Lysergic acid, a metabolite of LSD (left) is similar in chemical structure to naturally occurring serotonin. Although the exact mechanism responsible for producing hallucinations is poorly understood, we do know that lysergic acid interacts with serotonin receptors.

hallucinogen A drug that stimulates the experience of false perceptions.
stimulant Any drug that increases the activity of the nervous system.

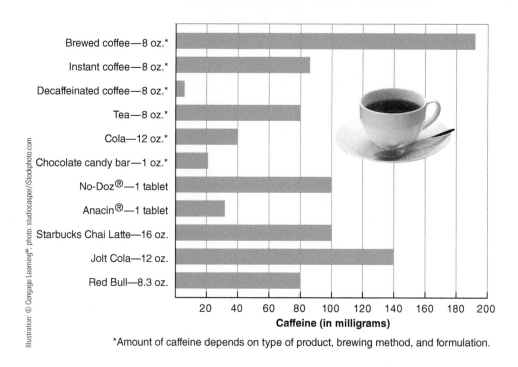

FIGURE 6.17

Sources of Caffeine. Although most people think immediately of coffee when they hear the word *caffeine*, caffeine can be found in many beverages, foods, and over-the-counter medications. *Source:* Adapted from *Living Well: Health in Your Hands* (2nd ed.), by C. O. Byer and L. W. Shainberg, 1995, New York, NY: HarperCollins. The Starbucks Jolt and Red Bull data are from Somogyi, L. P. (2010). Caffeine intake by the U.S. Population. Retrieved from http://www.fda.gov/downloads/AboutFDA/CentersOffices/OfficeofFoods/CFSAN/CFSANFOIAElectronicReadingRoom/UCM333191.pdf

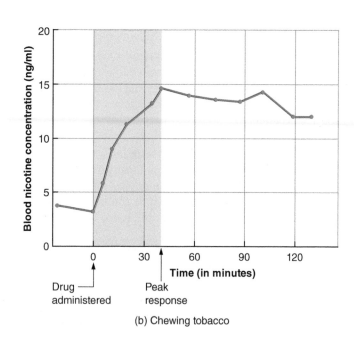

FIGURE 6.18

Concentration of a Drug in the Blood Supply Depend on the Method of Administration. Drug effects depend on the concentration of the drug in the blood supply, and some methods of administration produce effective concentrations faster than others. In the case of nicotine, smoking a cigarette (a) produces a faster increase in blood nicotine concentration than produced by chewing an equivalent dose of tobacco (b). However, chewing tobacco produces higher sustained concentrations of nicotine than smoking does. *Source:* Adapted from "The Nicotine Fix," by W. Bennett, 1983, *Rhode Island Medical Journal, 66*, pp. 455–458.

(a)

Areas of Greatest Loss
— Emotion, Reward (Limbic system)
— Memory (Hippocampus)

0%   3%   5%
Loss   Loss   Loss

Average difference in brain tissue volume of
methamphetamine users, as compared with
non-users.

(b)

Courtesy of the Minnesota Department of Corrections

FIGURE 6.19

**Methamphetamine
Produces Serious Health
Consequences.**
(a) Methamphetamine
users are likely to
experience psychotic
symptoms, probably
because of substantial loss
of brain volume in areas
related to memory,
emotion, and reward.
(b) Methamphetamine also
stimulates clenching and
grinding of teeth, leading
to a pattern of dental
decay known as "meth
mouth."

the action of the neurotransmitter acetylcholine, increasing heart rate and blood pressure, reducing fatigue, and improving cognitive performance while at the same time producing muscular relaxation. Normally, our bodies feel somewhat tense when we are mentally alert, so nicotine's combination of relaxation with alertness is unique.

Despite repeated warnings of the dangers of using nicotine, it continues to be a widely used substance (see Chapter 16). Nicotine use typically begins in adolescence, and adolescents become more rapidly dependent on the substance than do adults (Dani & Harris, 2005). People with psychological disorders, schizophrenia and depression in particular, are very likely to use nicotine (Dani & Harris, 2005). Again, because these are correlations, we do not know whether nicotine has any causal role in the development of psychological disorders or whether people vulnerable to disorders are simply more likely to enjoy the effects of nicotine.

Cocaine and Amphetamines The behavioral effects of cocaine and amphetamines are quite similar. At moderate doses, cocaine and amphetamines produce alertness, elevated mood, confidence, and a sense of well-being. At higher doses, these drugs can produce symptoms that are quite similar to schizophrenia (see Chapter 14). Users experience hallucinations, such as a feeling of bugs running on the skin, and delusional fears that others are trying to harm them. Some users experience repetitive motor behaviors, such as chewing movements or grinding the teeth. Methamphetamine, the current commonly abused form of amphetamines, is particularly likely to lead to symptoms of psychosis (McKetin, McLaren, Lubman, & Hides, 2006; see ● Figure 6.19).

HOW DO PEOPLE INTENTIONALLY ALTER THEIR STATES OF CONSCIOUSNESS? **221**

Although they produce similar types of behavior, cocaine and amphetamines act somewhat differently at the synapse. Cocaine is a dopamine reuptake inhibitor, while amphetamines and their cousin methamphetamine both stimulate dopamine and norepinephrine release while also inhibiting their reuptake. Because of their direct actions on the dopamine reward systems in the brain, these drugs are among the most addictive available substances.

Methylphenidate (Ritalin) As we will see in Chapter 15, many children diagnosed with ADHD are treated with stimulant medications. The two most common choices are methylphenidate or a combination of amphetamine salts (Adderall). Both of these drugs boost the activity of dopamine and norepinephrine, which in turn increases users' ability to stay alert and concentrate. At clinical doses, these drugs do not seem to produce dependence, although they affect sleep and appetite. It is a common misconception that only people diagnosed with ADHD respond to these drugs with increased concentration. Everybody reacts to these drugs in similar ways (Agay, Yechiam, Carmel, & Levkovitz, 2010), which has led to an increase in their nonprescribed use by college students and others wishing to get a competitive edge in intellectual work.

MDMA (Ecstasy) 3,4-Methylenedioxymethamphetamine (MDMA, or Ecstasy) is a relative of amphetamines and the hallucinogen mescaline that increases heart rate, blood pressure, and body temperature. MDMA increases sociability by stimulating the activity of serotonin and oxytocin (Thompson, Callaghan, Hunt, Cornish, & McGregor, 2007). Side effects can include dehydration, exhaustion, hypothermia (low core body temperature), convulsions, and death (Pilgrim, Gerostamoulos, & Drummer, 2011).

Use of MDMA is controversial, with some scientists expressing concern about its apparent detrimental effects on neurons that release serotonin (Biezonski & Meyer, 2011; Capela et al., 2007). Some therapists, however, argue that MDMA might be beneficial to individuals with post-traumatic stress disorder (PTSD). Strong research evidence for such benefits is lacking (Parrott, 2007), but a study using 20 participants with PTSD who had not responded to conventional treatments showed some promise (Mithoefer, Wagner, Mithoefer, Jerome, & Doblin, 2011).

Alcohol Alcohol is one of the earliest psychoactive drugs used by humans, dating back into our prehistory. In addition to seeking the relaxation produced by alcohol, early humans might have turned to fermented beverages as a safety precaution against contaminated water supplies, because alcohol has natural antiseptic qualities.

At low doses, alcohol dilates blood vessels, giving people a warm, flushed feeling. It reduces anxiety, which makes relatively shy people more outgoing at a party. At higher doses, alcohol's inhibition of the higher levels of the brain leads to aggression, risky behaviors, and poor motor coordination. At very high doses, alcohol can produce coma and death, either from suppression of breathing or aspiration of vomit.

Alcohol produces its main behavioral effects by boosting the effects of GABA, the main inhibitory neurochemical in the brain. By boosting an inhibitor, alcohol depresses the activity of the brain, particularly that of the cerebral cortex. Alcohol also stimulates the reward pathways using dopamine, which probably accounts for its addictive potential. Further discussion on the detrimental effects of alcohol on the developing fetus will be discussed in Chapter 11. Alcohol's impact on health in general is discussed in Chapter 16.

Before World War I, many commercial products contained cocaine. Freud originally believed that cocaine was an effective antidepressant. The ability of cocaine to produce rapid addiction eventually changed people's minds about the safety of the drug.

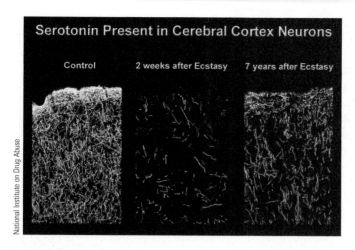

Serotonin Present in Cerebral Cortex Neurons

Control   2 weeks after Ecstasy   7 years after Ecstasy

MDMA (Ecstasy) appears to have long-term detrimental effects on neurons that release serotonin, associated with mood, appetite, and sleep.

Opioids Natural or synthetic substances that interact with endorphin receptors are known as opioids. Opioids that are derived from the opium poppy are known as opiates. The opium poppy is the source of several psychoactive opiates, including morphine and codeine. Heroin can be synthesized through further processing of morphine. These substances are effective because they imitate the action of endorphins (short for endogenous morphine).

Opioids have legitimate medical purposes, including pain control, cough suppression, and control of diarrhea. At low doses typical in medical practice, opioids produce a sense of euphoria, pain relief, reduced anxiety, muscle relaxation, and sleep. The higher doses characteristic of opioids abuse affect consciousness by producing a tremendous euphoria, or rush. With even higher doses, opioids exert a strong depression on breathing, occasionally leading to death.

Among the current frequently abused forms of opioids is the relatively new painkiller oxycodone hydrochloride (OxyContin), reportedly used by more than 8% of recent 12th graders (Johnston, O'Malley, Bachman, & Schulenberg, 2011). In 2010, the U.S. Food and Drug Administration (FDA) approved a new formulation of OxyContin designed to reduce rates of abuse (FDA, 2010). Unfortunately, efforts to reduce OxyContin abuse usually result in compensatory increases in heroin use (Cicero, Ellis, & Surratt, 2012). Abuse of painkillers in general continues to be a serious concern in public health.

Scott A. Schneider/Getty Images Sport/Getty Images

The National Hockey League's Derek Boogaard was found dead in his apartment just before he would have celebrated his 29th birthday. An autopsy indicated that Boogaard died of a combination of alcohol and oxycodone (OxyContin).

Nondrug Methods for Altering Consciousness

Hypnosis is "a state of consciousness involving focused attention and reduced peripheral awareness characterized by an enhanced capacity for response to suggestion" (The Society of Psychological Hypnosis, Division 30 of the APA, n.d., para. 2)."

Misunderstandings about what hypnosis can and cannot do are common. Early research suggested that hypnotized people were more likely to comply with requests to do dangerous things, such as pick up a poisonous snake or throw a beaker of what they believed to be acid into an experimenter's face (Rowland, 1939; Young, 1952). However, later experiments showed

hypnosis An altered state of consciousness characterized by relaxation and increased suggestibility.

© Cengage Learning®

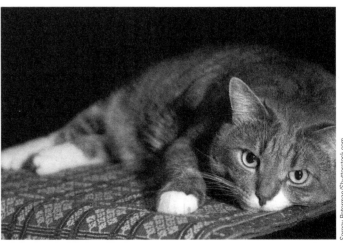

Sergey Peterman/Shutterstock.com

Frustrated licensed psychotherapist Steve Eichel demonstrated the lack of regulation of hypnotherapists by acquiring a number of impressive-looking credentials for Zoe D. Katze, who happens to be Eichel's cat. Zoe's name is a wordplay on the German *die Katze*, which literally means "the cat."

(a)

Red
Yellow
Blue
Green
Green
Yellow
Blue

(b)

Blue
Green
Yellow
Red
Green
Blue
Red

F I G U R E 6.20

Hypnosis and the Stroop Test.
Under normal circumstances, results of the Stroop Test show that participants identify ink colors faster when (a) the color of the letters matches the word being read (the word *red* appears in a red font) than when (b) it doesn't match (the word *red* appears in a yellow or green font). Highly suggestible hypnotized participants who were told that they were reading nonsense words instead of real words did not show this typical difference. Their reaction time for naming the ink color was the same whether it matched the color name or not.

meditation A voluntary alteration of consciousness characterized by positive emotion and absence of thought.

that equal compliance could be obtained with participants who were not hypnotized (Orne & Evans, 1965). In these situations, the participants' strong belief that the experimenters would be unwilling to harm them overrode any measurable influence of hypnosis. Contrary to popular belief (and a number of television crime shows), hypnosis does not sharpen memory and is instead likely to make it worse (Kihlstrom, 1997; Kihlstrom & Barnhardt, 1993; Kihlstrom & Eich, 1994). Hypnosis does have legitimate uses in therapy, however, especially in cases of habit change (quitting smoking, etc.) and pain relief.

One study that illustrates both the power and the limitations of hypnosis used a task known as the Stroop Test (Raz, Kirsch, Pollard, & Nitkin-Kaner, 2006; Stroop, 1935). In this test, participants are simply asked to respond to the color of the letters they are shown (see ● Figure 6.20). When the ink color and the word are congruent (e.g., the word *red* appears in red ink), reaction time is significantly faster (100–200 milliseconds faster) than when the ink color and the word are incongruent (e.g., the word *red* appears in green ink). Nearly everyone who can read shows a robust Stroop effect, and extensive training does not make the effect go away. This effect is typically explained in terms of a well-practiced skill (reading) taking precedence over a less practiced skill (naming the colors of letters). When instructed to ignore the practiced skill, attention is compromised and reaction time becomes slower.

Using a posthypnotic suggestion, Raz, et al. (2006) told their participants to respond to a cue by viewing the stimuli as gibberish instead of real words. Participants were assessed for their individual differences in suggestibility, or the ease with which someone can be hypnotized. Participants who were rated as having low suggestibility performed in a typical manner on the Stroop Test. In contrast, participants rated as having high suggestibility demonstrated little difference between the amount of time needed to identify the ink colors in the congruent and the incongruent conditions. The ability of posthypnotic suggestion to minimize the Stroop effect is remarkable, because other efforts to modulate the effect have all failed. Clearly, hypnotic suggestion has the ability to reorganize cognitive processes, at least in highly suggestible individuals.

Meditation **Meditation** techniques vary widely and may occur in either religious or nonreligious contexts. When experienced practitioners are asked to describe the subjective experience produced by meditation, they describe a conscious state without thought, accompanied by a blissful emotional state (Travis, 2001). A variation on meditation known as mindfulness meditation has been used more frequently over recent years to treat a variety of psychological disorders and substance abuse (Hölzel et al., 2011). Mindfulness refers to "nonjudgmental awareness of experiences in the present moment" (Hölzel et al., 2011, p. 537). Meditation incorporating mindfulness also appears to produce benefits in immune function, blood pressure, stress hormone levels, and cognitive functioning.

EEG recordings during meditation feature increased proportions of alpha waves, which we described earlier as being characteristic of an awake but relaxed state. In participants who had meditated more than 3 years, increased theta activity, normally found in lighter stages of sleep, was observed over the frontal lobes of the brain (Aftanas & Golocheikine, 2001). Theta activity in the prefrontal areas of the brain has been correlated with positive emotions (Aftanas, Varlamov, Pavlov, Makhnev, & Reva, 2001).

Imaging studies using functional magnetic resonance imaging (fMRI), suggest that meditation represents a voluntary regulation of attention and autonomic functions (Lazar et al., 2000). Brain imaging studies have discovered that experienced meditators showed less activity in the brain's DMN, which was described earlier in this chapter (Brewer et al., 2011). As we noted previously, activity in the DMN is usually correlated not only with mind wandering and thinking about the self but also with unhappiness. Relative inhibition of the activity of the DMN through meditation might be responsible for the feelings of bliss associated with this practice (see ● Figure 6.21).

Meditation appears to result in physical changes in the brain. Meditation has been correlated with increased cortical thickness (Lazar et al., 2005) and increased gray matter in the brainstem (Vestergaard-Poulsen et al., 2009). The increased cortical thickness was more noticeable in older participants, suggesting that meditation might offset typical age-related thinning of the cortex.

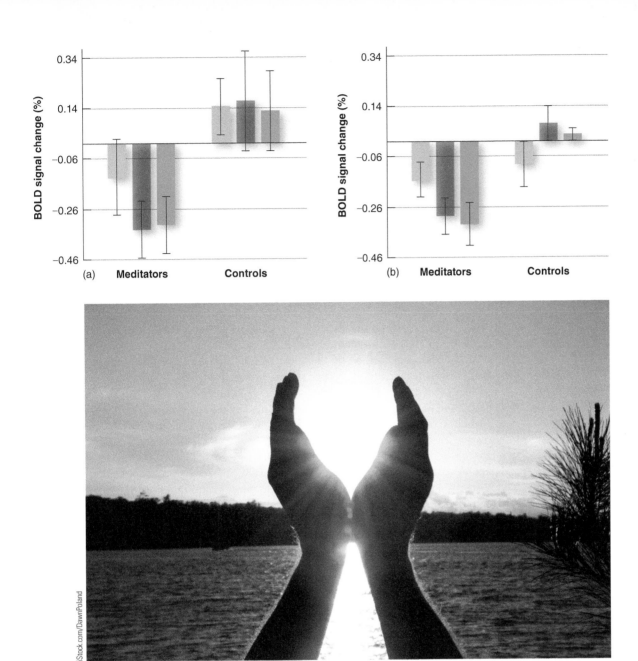

FIGURE 6.21

Meditation Is Correlated With Decreased Activation of the Brain's default mode network (DMN). Meditation is associated with a decrease in activation in the prefrontal cortex and posterior cingulate gyrus, which are important parts of the DMN, of experienced meditators compared to control participants who were introduced to the meditation methods right before being scanned. The amount of decrease in signal strength is shown (a) in the prefrontal cortex and (b) in the posterior cingulate cortex. The colored bars represent three methods of mindfulness meditation: choiceless awareness is shown in green, loving kindness is shown in red, and concentration is shown in blue.

Sufis belong to a mystic Muslim sect that uses spinning as a means of inducing a state of meditation. Spinning can last an hour or more, after which the Sufi typically falls to the ground and experiences a sense of oneness with the earth.

Other Methods for Altering Consciousness A variety of environmental conditions have significant effects on consciousness, including exposure to high altitudes during mountain climbing, underwater conditions in scuba diving, starvation, sleep deprivation, sensory deprivation, twirling, and rhythm-induced trance. These conditions may lead to hallucination and other consistent changes in cognition and emotion.

Several of these environmental factors characterize vision quests, which typically take place within religious contexts. In the traditional Native American vision quest, preparation typically involved 3 to 4 days of starvation and sleep loss. The individual would travel to an isolated location where no shelter could be built. The seeker would then be instructed to concentrate and watch for the appearance of a "guardian." This combination of events reliably led seekers to experience the following phenomena: a distorted sense of time, a sensation of "oneness," the appearance of light, the emotion of ecstasy or bliss, and a sense of improved insight (Steiger, 2000).

We have all observed young children experiment with their bodies by spinning. Although we do not know the precise reason for such spinning behavior, other than that it is fun, spinning probably represents the child's efforts to alter sensory and cognitive states. Spinning is also used as a meditation-inducing method by the Sufis, a mystic Muslim sect. Sufis may whirl for an hour or more before falling to the ground, where they seek a feeling of oneness with the earth.

It is likely that dancing has been a part of human cultures for thousands of years, both for recreational and for religious purposes. Accompanied by the equally ancient practice of drumming, dance is capable of initiating trancelike states in the participants (Vaitl et al., 2013). A trance state typically refers to an induced state of consciousness in which a person is less responsive to external stimuli (Tassi & Muzet, 2001). The altered states induced by drumming and dancing include distortion of time, vivid imagery, and strong positive emotions (ecstasy, bliss; Vaitl et al., 2013). Participants listening to rhythmic drumming showed more theta wave activity in their EEGs, normally associated with light N-REM sleep, than did participants listening to unstructured beat sequences (Maxfield, 1990).

Modern youth are fond of combining dance and psychoactive drugs to alter consciousness, particularly in the context of raves, which are large parties featuring electronic music, darkness, and the use of hallucinogens or MDMA. The raves feature some themes common to the contexts we have described previously. Unity, or oneness, and positive emotion are again primary goals reported by the participants.

Interpersonal Relationships
The Consciousness Perspective
How Does Imitation Influence Liking?

We engage in a variety of unconscious behaviors, and not just when we're asleep. Among the unconscious behaviors that have been identified by psychologists is one that is particularly relevant to relationships—the effect of mimicry on liking and feeling close to others (Lakin, Chartrand, & Arkin, 2008). A substantial body of research supports the idea that we unconsciously copy the behavior of others and that when we do copy another person's behavior, that person likes us better without necessarily knowing why.

Under what circumstances are we most likely to copy the behavior of other people? One possible answer is that we mimic others to avoid or repair social exclusion. Jessica Lakin and her colleagues (2008) made their participants feel socially excluded (temporarily) and then observed that these excluded participants were more likely to mimic another person than were participants who had not been socially excluded. This process extends to group membership as well. Participants excluded by an in-group were subsequently more likely to mimic an in-group member than an out-group member. These results suggest that mimicry developed as an automatic behavior that we could use to respond to threats to our social connectivity, which as we have stated many times previously, could have been a matter of life or death to our hunter–gatherer ancestors.

Because this mimicry is quite automatic and unconscious, we are usually not aware that we are behaving this way. Knowing now that this is an adaptive behavior, look more closely at how you behave when encountering situations in which you feel excluded. It could be a social situation, such as at a party or an organizational event, where you are trying to mingle or initiate a dialogue with others. Or perhaps you observe mimicry when you are around someone you like romantically. Do you feign interest in things you wouldn't necessarily be interested in otherwise? Are you more apt to align yourself with the personality of the person you find interesting? Do you see this kind of behavior in friends or family? ●

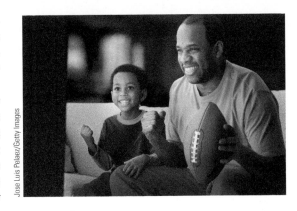

Jose Luis Pelaez/Getty Images

We often imitate the behavior of others without being consciously aware that we're doing so. Imitation seems to enhance liking and social inclusion.

Summary 6.3 Commonly Used Psychoactive Drugs and Their Methods of Action

Drug class	Acts on
LSD	Serotonin
Marijuana	Endogenous cannabinoids
Caffeine	Adenosine
Nicotine	Acetylcholine
Cocaine, amphetamines, and methamphetamine	Dopamine
Methylphenidate	Dopamine
MDMA (Ecstasy)	Serotonin, Oxytocin
Alcohol	GABA, dopamine
Opioids	Endogenous endorphins

Credits: Top Row. Laguna Design/Science Photo Library/Corbis. Second Row. © 2016 Cengage Learning®. Third Row. studiocasper/iStockphoto.com. Fourth Row. © Cengage Learning®. Fifth Row. Courtesy of the Minnesota Department of Corrections. Sixth Row. National Institute on Drug Abuse. Bottom Row. Scott A. Schneider/Getty Images Sport/Getty Images.

KEY TERMS The Language of Psychological Science

Be sure you can define these terms and use them correctly.

addiction, p. 217
alpha wave, p. 203
beta wave, p. 203
biological clock, p. 199
circadian rhythm, p. 199
coma, p. 213
consciousness, p. 194
delta wave, p. 204
dreaming, p. 209
gamma wave, p. 203
hallucinogen, p. 219
hypnosis, p. 223
insomnia, p. 210

lucid dreaming, p. 210
major depressive disorder with seasonal
    pattern, p. 201
meditation, p. 224
narcolepsy, p. 210
near-death experience, p. 214
non–rapid eye movement (N-REM)
    sleep, p. 203
psychoactive drug, p. 217
rapid eye movement (REM)
    sleep, p. 203
restless legs syndrome (RLS), p. 212
seizure, p. 216

self-awareness, p. 194
sleep, p. 199
sleep apnea, p. 211
sleep terror, p. 210
stimulant, p. 219
sudden infant death syndrome (SIDS),
    p. 211
theta wave, p. 203
tolerance, p. 217
vegetative state (VS), p. 213
waking, p. 199
withdrawal, p. 217

7 The Feeling Mind

Motivation and Emotion

MOTIVATION AND EMOTION, THE TOPICS OF THIS CHAPTER, involve neural circuits that often operate below the level of our conscious awareness. We can zoom in to look at these neural circuits, like these sympathetic axons (in blue in the large image on the previous page) forming connections with the gut. We have all had the feeling of butterflies in our stomach when we are excited, and neural pathways like these are responsible for such feelings.

Zooming out, we can examine motivation and emotion in the larger context of the individual using the example of elite athletes at the Olympic Games. The 2012 London Games featured 10,568 athletes who represented the best in their respective sports, a tiny fraction of the millions of people who compete in athletics worldwide. To stand out among these elites takes even more extreme motivation, not to mention talent and hard work. Many athletes competing at this level have focused on their sport to the exclusion of most other activities since they were in elementary school. Yet of the more than 10,000 participants, only 962 (or 9%) went home with a medal.

Given the odds of obtaining a medal, you would think that any athlete winning one would be ecstatic, but that is not always the case. As you can see in the photograph above of Olympic swimmers on the medal stand, the athletes are showing a range of emotions. Look for a moment at the way the three athletes are holding their flower bouquets. The gold and bronze medalists are holding their bouquets straight up, but the silver medalist is close to dropping his bouquet. His entire demeanor says dejection and disappointment.

Why would a silver medalist be disappointed with such an exceptional achievement? To answer this question, we must zoom out even farther from the individual to consider the social context. Psychologists have found that the reactions of these swimmers are quite typical (McGraw, Mellers, & Tetlock, 2005; Medvec, Madey, & Gilovich, 1995). Apparently, silver medalists are more likely to compare themselves to gold medalists, which leads to disappointment, while bronze medalists are comparing themselves to the fourth-place finishers who do not get a medal, which leads to joy.

In this chapter, we will explore the mechanisms responsible for our motivations and emotions, beginning with the underlying physical mechanisms and zooming out to look at individual and, ultimately, social influences on these behaviors.

◀ Axons from the sympathetic nervous system form connections in the gut, contributing to those butterflies we feel at times of excitement.

Michael Steele/Allsport/Getty Images

Argosy Publishing, Inc.

Alan Williams/Axiom/Aurora Photos

Learning Objectives

1. Define and differentiate between emotion and motivation.

2. Analyze the physiological and environmental factors that influence hunger and sexual behavior.

3. Describe motivations of affiliation and achievement in light of systems explaining the prioritization of motives.

4. Explain the biological, social, and cognitive correlates of emotional expression and assessment.

5. Compare and contrast the major theories of emotion.

Emotions are spontaneous, automatic responses to our ongoing perceptions and thoughts.

Steve Cole/Photodisc/Getty Images

If we are thirsty following a tough workout, we are motivated to seek a drink of water. It is unlikely that a thirsty person would be motivated to find a hamburger instead.

emotion A combination of arousal, physical sensations, and subjective feelings that occurs spontaneously in response to environmental stimuli.
motivation A process that arouses, maintains, and guides behavior toward a goal.

How Are Motivation and Emotion Related?

Motivation and emotion are tightly related processes that share the experience of subjective feelings and engage similar processes and structures in the brain. Efforts to differentiate between motivation and emotion can be somewhat frustrating, given their overlapping characteristics and similar definitions.

An **emotion** is defined as a brief combination of physical sensations, such as a rapid heartbeat, and conscious, subjective feelings, like feeling afraid, that prepares an individual for action. Emotions are usually spontaneous, automatic responses to our ongoing perceptions and thoughts. We often communicate our emotions to others through behaviors such as facial expression, body language, gestures, and tone of voice.

Emotions can be distinguished from moods. A mood is a more general state than an emotion. You can be in a good mood while feeling a variety of specific emotions, such as happiness, pride, or relief. A mood generally lasts longer than a single emotion. For example, when we discuss psychological disorders in Chapter 14, we will see that criteria for depression specify that depressed mood should characterize at least half a day every day for 2 weeks (American Psychiatric Association [APA], 2013). Because emotions are responses to the ongoing and ever-changing flow of environmental information, it is unlikely that any single emotion would last this long.

Motivation is defined as a process that arouses, maintains, and guides behavior toward a goal. For example, we are motivated to seek a drink of water in response to thirst. The process of motivation is accompanied by distinct emotional states. Thirst is generally quite unpleasant, and taking a drink of water can produce positive emotions like relief and happiness.

Motivation and emotion share the ability to arouse an organism and stimulate behavior, but motivation does so more directly and precisely than emotions do. People who feel motivated by thirst are likely to do one thing: seek something to drink. In contrast, experiencing the emotion of sadness stimulates behavior, but that behavior may take many forms. Some people respond to sadness by crying in a room by themselves, while others seek the company of friends.

Laura Freberg

What Does It Mean to Be Motivated?

Animals, including humans, have limited time and resources, and a state of arousal is expensive in terms of the energy it requires. Motivational systems allow an animal to be aroused only when necessary, such as when it needs food, and then reduce arousal following the solution of a problem, such as after a meal. Preventing the waste of precious energy resources provides a significant survival advantage. Motivation also provides the benefit of helping an animal prepare to meet future needs. Most animals are motivated to explore their environments, because familiarity with an environment allows them to act more effectively when a need arises.

Many animals are motivated to explore their surroundings even when they have no immediate needs, because being familiar with your neighborhood saves time when a need does arise, whether that is food, water, shelter from a storm, or a gas station. Many people enjoy using technology that helps us deal with unfamiliar places, like Google Glass.

We can think of motivation as a process that maintains **homeostasis**, a term introduced by psychologist Walter Cannon to describe a steady internal balance or equilibrium (Cannon, 1932). To achieve homeostasis, organisms actively defend certain values known as set points. Under normal circumstances, we carefully regulate such variables as core body temperature, fluid levels, and body weight around **set points**. Deviations from these set points stimulate behavior by the organism that is designed to reestablish the original values. You might think about this process as analogous to your home's temperature control. A set point of air temperature is established using your thermostat. If your home's temperature drops below that set point, the furnace is activated until the set point is again established. If your home's temperature rises above the set point, the air-conditioning system is activated until the set point is regained. Similarly, if your core body temperature drops below 98.6 °F (37 °C), your body initiates a number of processes designed to increase its temperature, such as producing heat by the muscle contractions we know as shivering. If your core body temperature rises above its set point, cooling mechanisms are activated. You sweat, and the evaporating moisture cools your skin. Blood is diverted to the outer parts of the body, leading to a flushed appearance.

homeostasis A steady internal balance, or equilibrium.
set point A value that is defended to maintain homeostasis.
drive A state of tension and arousal triggered by cues important for survival.
drive reduction The state of relief and reward produced by removing the tension and arousal of the drive state.

Motivation begins with a stimulus, from either the internal or the external environment of the organism, that serves as a cue for motivated behavior. Stimuli that are important to survival, such as the presence of a predator or a deficit in body fluids, generate arousal and tension, a state frequently called **drive** (Hull, 1943). Being in a drive state propels the organism into some sort of action related to the stimulus, whether that means running from the predator to safety or pulling a bottle of water from a backpack to quench thirst. If actions are successful in regaining equilibrium, we experience **drive reduction**, accompanied by a rewarding feeling of relief.

Drive theories of motivation are often described as push theories, because drive is seen as pushing an organism toward a goal. However, not all psychologists agree that motivation requires the push of drive. Instead, they suggest that rewards, or **incentives**, have the capacity to pull an organism in a particular direction. According to this view, animals are viewed as naturally inclined to act on their environment rather than wait passively for a need to arise (Deci & Ryan, 2000). In incentive theories, no reference to unpleasant internal drive states is required to explain motivated behavior.

Incentives or rewards may be intrinsic or extrinsic. **Intrinsic rewards** arise internally, such as feelings of accomplishment when a goal is met. **Extrinsic rewards** come from outside sources, such as money for completing work or praise from a supervisor. These different types of reward can interact in complex ways (see ● Figure 7.1). In some cases, certain extrinsic rewards can have negative effects on intrinsic motivation. For example, if a child who enjoys reading suddenly gets paid for each book completed, the child's enjoyment of reading might decrease because the motivation shifts from intrinsic (the love of reading) to extrinsic (the love of reward money; DeCharms, 1968).

Sonia Moskowitz-Globe Photos, Inc./Newscom

FIGURE 7.1

Economist Roland Fryer Asks Whether Incentives Work. Harvard University economist Roland Fryer overcame a tough childhood in Daytona, Florida, to become the youngest tenured African American professor in the history of the university. Drawing on his personal experiences, Fryer experimented with different incentives for a variety of school-related behaviors. His results suggest that the relationships among intrinsic rewards, extrinsic rewards, and behavior can be quite complex. Although previous research has shown that extrinsic rewards can undermine intrinsic motivation, it is important to remember that this result occurs only when behavior is intrinsically motivated in the first place. If children do not intrinsically enjoy reading, Fryer suggests paying them to read might work. Unfortunately, Fryer has been the target of death threats for suggesting this simple solution to illiteracy.

Location	DALLAS	CHICAGO	WASHINGTON	NEW YORK CITY
What students were paid for	Reading	Grades	Various†	Test scores
Grade level participating	Second-graders	Ninth-graders	Sixth-, seventh-, and eighth-graders	Fourth- and seventh-graders
How much	$2 per book	$50 for A's $35 for B's $20 for C's	Up to $100 every two weeks	$25 (fourth-graders) to $50 (seventh-graders) per test
Average student earned	$13.81	$695.61	$532.85	$139.43 (fourth-graders) $231.55 (seventh-graders)
Study size*	1,780 from 22 schools	4,396 from 20 schools	3,495 from 17 schools	8,320 from 63 schools
Results	**Very Positive** Paying children to read dramatically boosted reading-comprehension scores.	**Mixed** Children cut fewer classes and got slightly better grades. Standardized test scores did not change.	**Positive** Rewarding five different actions, including attendance and behavior, seemed to improve reading skills.	**No Effect** Paying children for higher test scores did not lead to more learning or better grades — or any measureable changes.

© Cengage Learning®

*Not including control groups

† A combination of metrics that varied from school to school but always included attendance and behavior

Humans consume a range of diets, from the nearly all-meat diet of the traditional Inuit cultures to the vegan diet.

Psychologists have studied a range of motives, from the mostly physical motives of temperature control and thirst to the more cognitive and social motives to affiliate with others and achieve. We will explore this range by discussing some specific motives in detail, including hunger, sexuality, affiliation, and achievement. After discussing these examples, we will examine the ways humans set priorities when faced with competing motives.

Hunger and Eating

Hunger is a complex motive. In comparison to the regulation of body temperature through processes like sweating or shivering, the reduction of hunger through eating is more heavily influenced by emotion, learning, and culture. Humans take in a remarkable variety of nutrients. The traditional diet of the Inuit people living in Arctic regions contains little plant material, whereas vegans strictly adhere to a diet that contains no animal material.

The Sensation of Hunger We respond to combinations of external and internal cues that make us feel hungry. External cues for hunger may include time of day, the sights and smells of favorite foods, admonitions that we should "clean our plates," or the social settings in which food is presented. These external cues may encourage us to eat when our bodies do not need nutrients or to eat more food than we require. Individuals who are very responsive to external cues might find maintaining a healthy weight to be somewhat challenging.

Internal cues for hunger are generated when our bodies are genuinely short on nutrients. "Short on nutrients" applies to the maintenance of current, not necessarily ideal, weight. A morbidly obese person is likely to feel as hungry as a thin person when sufficient nutrients are not available to maintain the status quo.

Cannon provided an early hypothesis about hunger cues. He believed that stomach contractions were an important component in the detection of hunger. Cannon persuaded his colleague A. L. Washburn to swallow a balloon attached to an air pump (Cannon & Washburn, 1912). The balloon allowed Washburn's stomach contractions to be monitored. Although Washburn's feelings of hunger (as expressed by his pushing a telegraph key, because he couldn't talk with a tube down his throat) correlated with his stomach contractions, these signals do not tell the whole story. People who have had their stomachs surgically removed

FIGURE 7.2

Walter Cannon. Walter Cannon (1871-1945) and his assistant, A. L. Washburn, performed one of the earliest experiments on the relationship between stomach contractions and feelings of hunger. The large waves at the top were Cannon's recordings of Washburn's stomach contractions, and the smaller waves at the bottom represent Washburn's key taps indicating hunger. Although these two events are correlated, there is more to hunger than a growling stomach.

glucose A type of sugar that plays an important role in hunger levels.

still experience a sense of hunger in the general region where the stomach used to be. Most of us start eating long before our stomachs begin to growl, indicating that additional types of signaling must be at work (see ● Figure 7.2).

A likely candidate for an important hunger cue is a low level of circulating sugars, particularly **glucose**. Glucose concentrations in the blood are highest just following a meal. As glucose levels drop over time, a person begins to feel hungry again. Glucose levels are intimately connected with levels of the hormone insulin. Insulin, released by the pancreas, moves circulating glucose from the blood into cells awaiting nutrients. Typically, glucose and insulin levels are positively correlated. Right after a meal, both are high. Glucose levels rise as glucose is extracted from the food that has been consumed, and insulin is high because its release is triggered by the anticipation and consumption of food. As time goes by without more food, glucose moves from the blood into other tissues, and insulin is no longer released, leading to lower levels of both substances in the blood. These lower levels of glucose and insulin should signal the need for more food (see ● Figure 7.3).

This is an overly simplistic conclusion, however. You may know people with diabetes mellitus who must check the glucose levels in their blood several times per day, because high levels of circulating glucose can harm many organs. High glucose levels occur in untreated diabetes because of either a lack of insulin production (type 1 diabetes) or the body's resistance to insulin (type 2 diabetes). Without sufficient insulin activity, circulating glucose is unable to move out of the blood into the cells that need nutrients. If hunger results from low levels of circulating glucose, we would expect people with untreated diabetes to not feel very hungry, but this is not the case. Most people with diabetes who have high blood sugar report feeling hungry all the time. This makes sense when you consider that their cells are starving because of their inability to obtain glucose from the blood. It is more accurate to say that the amount of glucose that is available to cells is an indicator of hunger (Mayer, 1955). Hunger results whenever cells are unable to obtain the glucose they require.

Hunger also occurs in response to low levels of stored fats (Kennedy, 1953). If you maintain a healthy weight, you are carrying sufficient body fat to survive 5 to 6 weeks of total

FIGURE 7.3

Insulin Release Is Reduced in Type 2 Diabetes.
Following a meal (time 0), a healthy person experiences a large spike in insulin levels. In contrast, a person with type 2 diabetes has a slower and less dramatic release of insulin. The person with diabetes will not be able to move glucose out of the blood into cells requiring nutrients. The appetite-suppressing action of insulin will be less effective, and the person with diabetes will remain hungry. Source: Pfeifer, M. A., Halter, J. B., Beard, J. C., Judzewitsch, R., & Porte, D. (1982). Insulin responses to nonglucose stimuli in non-insulin-dependent diabetes mellitus during a tolbutamide infusion. *Diabetes, 31*(2), 154-159. doi: 10.2337/diab.31.2.154

starvation. The heavier the person, the longer that individual can survive without food. One person survived a total fast of 382 days, during which time his weight dropped from 455.4 pounds (207 kilograms) to 179.5 pounds (81.6 kilograms) (Stewart & Fleming, 1973).

The body monitors fat stores by assessing levels of the hormone **leptin**. Leptin, from the Greek word *leptos,* or "thin," is produced and secreted by fat cells (Zhang et al., 1994). Because fat stores and leptin levels are positively correlated, leptin levels provide a measure for the amount of fat that has been stored. Leptin appears to be an important key to feeding behavior. As shown in ● Figure 7.4, leptin levels and their associated fat stores initiate a cascade of events that influence eating behavior. When fat stores and leptin levels are low, brain areas that include the lateral hypothalamus (LH) initiate feeding. When the LH is lesioned, rats fail to eat and die of starvation unless force-fed (Anand & Brobeck, 1951). Stimulation of the LH typically initiates immediate eating.

Low fat stores and leptin levels also activate the parasympathetic division of the autonomic nervous system, enhancing the body's ability to digest and store nutrients. Metabolism, or the chemical reactions required by life, slows down, allowing nutrients to be stored rather than used up right away.

Activation of the parasympathetic nervous system, initiation of feeding behavior, and reduction in metabolic rate allow the animal to find, eat, and store nutrients. As fat stores return to normal, leptin levels increase, and the feeding cycle tapers off. Unfortunately for the person trying to lose weight, the leptin system does a good job of defending a set point. As the dieter successfully decreases body fat levels, the associated low levels of leptin initiate a feeding cycle. The dieter feels constantly hungry, making the maintenance of weight loss often more difficult than the initial loss.

Feeding is stimulated by two additional hormones: ghrelin, which is released by the pancreas and the lining of the stomach (Inui et al., 2004), and orexins, produced in the LH (de Lecea et al., 1998; Sakurai et al., 1998). Ghrelin appears to contribute to the rewarding aspects of feeding, while the orexins also participate in sleep (see Chapter 6), suggesting that they might link feeding, activity levels, and sleep.

The Sensation of Satiety

We reach the point of **satiety**, or fullness, long before the nutrients we have eaten can make their way to waiting cells.

Just as stomach contractions serve as signals for hunger, an obvious sign of satiety is a feeling of stomach fullness. In extreme cases of obesity, some people choose to have a portion of the stomach stapled or banded to produce this feeling of fullness after less food has been eaten.

In the brain, the ventromedial hypothalamus (VMH) participates in sensing satiety. As shown in ● Figure 7.5, lesions of the VMH produce a syndrome of large weight gains (Hoebel & Teitelbaum, 1966). Although the VMH plays a significant role in satiety, it is overly simplistic to assume that it works alone and directly. Among the many indirect effects of VMH lesions are boosts in insulin production, which in turn produce low blood glucose levels and hunger.

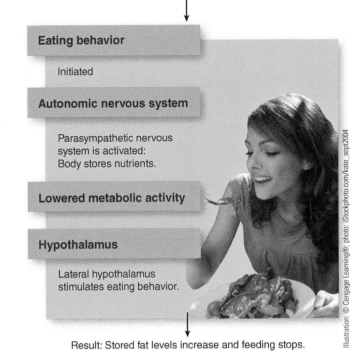

When fat stores are low, leptin levels are low, and ghrelin and orexins are active:

Eating behavior

Initiated

Autonomic nervous system

Parasympathetic nervous system is activated: Body stores nutrients.

Lowered metabolic activity

Hypothalamus

Lateral hypothalamus stimulates eating behavior.

Result: Stored fat levels increase and feeding stops.

FIGURE 7.4

Mechanisms of Hunger.

People of normal weight carry enough fat to survive 5 to 6 weeks of total starvation, although this is obviously not a good thing to do for one's health. Baba Ramdev, a yoga guru, was hospitalized after losing 12 pounds by the seventh day of a hunger strike against corruption. It is likely that Ramdev was already quite thin at the beginning of his fast.

leptin A hormone secreted by fat cells that helps the body maintain an appropriate level of stored fat.
satiety A sense of feeling full and not requiring further food.

FIGURE 7.5

Lesions of the Ventromedial Hypothalamus (VMH) Lead to Obesity. Following lesioning of the VMH, rats nearly tripled their normal weight, suggesting that the VMH plays a significant role in satiety. However, satiety is too complex to be explained as the function of a single part of the brain. *Source:* Adapted from "Ventromedial Hypothalamic Hyperphagia in the Hypophysectomized Weanling Rat," by R. G. Kurtz, P. Rozin, and P. Teitelbaum, 1972, *Journal of Comparative and Physiological Psychology, 80*(1), 19–25.

Other participants in satiety include the gut hormone cholecystokinin (CCK), released by the digestive system in response to the arrival of food, especially fatty foods. CCK not only acts in the digestive tract but also serves as a chemical messenger in the brain. CCK limits meals by activating pathways that connect the hindbrain to the digestive system (Blevins et al., 2009). Drugs that inhibit CCK's action in the brain increase eating behavior, further supporting the hypothesis that CCK normally acts to inhibit further eating (Cooper & Dourish, 1990).

Earlier we observed the cascade of events initiated by low levels of stored fat and leptin that led to feeding and the storage of nutrients. What happens when fat and leptin levels rise again? With increased storage of fat, leptin levels rise. Again, the assessment of circulating leptin levels by the brain initiates a sequence of events, this time directed at inhibiting feeding (see ● Figure 7.6). The sympathetic division of the autonomic nervous system is activated, leading to the expenditure of energy, metabolic rate increases, and inhibition of feeding. As time without food progresses, fat and leptin levels drop and the feeding sequence is reinitiated.

Because of leptin's role in satiety, scientists initially believed it might be helpful as a dieting aid. Mice genetically engineered to lack genes that produce leptin are enormously obese. Injections of leptin allow them to lose weight (Halaas et al., 1995). Unfortunately, people do not respond like mice; obese humans have very high circulating leptin levels but appear to become resistant to the satiety messages this state should produce (Friedman & Halaas, 1998). Adding further leptin is unlikely to lead to weight loss.

Keep in mind that our ancestors rarely had to worry about having too much food. Those who lived and reproduced exhibited characteristics best suited for surviving famine. As we will see in the next sections, the same motivational mechanisms that evolved to prevent starvation among hunter–gatherers might not work well in a society featuring cultural influences on body image and an ample and calorie-rich food supply. Through an examination of the interactions between social and cultural factors with hunger motivation, we gain a better understanding of hunger's mechanisms.

Obesity What do we mean by obesity? Expert opinions regarding ideal weight and the likely impact of obesity on health vary widely, with opinions ranging from doomsday predictions to complaints that the problem has been overstated.

A well-respected approach to body weight is the **body mass index (BMI)**, shown in ● Figure 7.7. The BMI is a simple height-to-weight ratio computed by dividing weight in kilograms by the square of height in meters. We have converted Figure 7.7 to inches and pounds for convenience. A BMI score between 18.5 and 24.9 is considered healthy. A BMI score between 25 and 30 is considered overweight, and a BMI score above 30 is considered obese. This system works well for most people, but it does not account for those who have unusually heavy

body mass index (BMI) A height-to-weight ratio used to identify healthy weight, underweight, overweight, and obesity.

skeletons or musculature. Many elite athletes would score in the overweight or even obese range, despite being quite fit.

Using a BMI score of 30 or above as a criterion, rates of obesity in the United States tripled from 12% of the adult population in 1991 to 37% in 2012 (Flegal, Carroll, Ogden, & Curtin, 2010; Ogden, Carroll, Kit, & Flegal, 2014; see ● Figure 7.8). Obesity rose in all age groups. How can we account for this rapid increase in obesity over the last two decades? It is unlikely that current obesity levels are the result of a single cause. Genetic predispositions, lifestyle issues, and social comparisons all make significant contributions to obesity.

Genes can influence factors such as set point and rate of metabolism, and twin studies indicate that some people are more likely than others to become obese (Livshits, Kato, Wilson, & Spector, 2007). Although genes are unlikely to have changed dramatically over a few decades, complex interactions between genes and environmental factors, like the bisphenol A in plastic products discussed in Chapter 3, could affect current rates of obesity (Dolinoy, Huang, & Jirtle, 2007). Genes might also interact with the bacteria populations in the gut, which differ considerably between obese and lean humans (Million et al., 2013). Manipulations of bacteria through antibiotics and probiotics have been used to promote weight gain in livestock for decades.

A cultural contribution to obesity is our contemporary, sedentary lifestyle, with many people spending hours sitting in front of televisions or computers. Humans use energy efficiently. At rest, we use only 12 kilocalories (kcal; usually described simply as calories) per pound per day. This means that the average 150-pound couch potato needs only about 1,800 calories of food per day. Even the most demanding activities require a remarkably small investment in resources. Cyclists competing in the challenging Tour de France use an average of 5,900 calories per day (Armstrong & Jenkins, 2000). A single entree at a typical chain restaurant, such as Chili's or The Cheesecake Factory (not counting beverages, appetizers, or dessert), can contain as much as 2,500 calories, the total daily requirement for a person who weighs 208 pounds and has a typical level of activity.

When fat stores are high and leptin levels are high:

Eating behavior

Stops

Autonomic nervous system

Sympathetic nervous system is activated: Body expends nutrients.

Higher metabolic activity

Hypothalamus

Ventromedial hypothalamus supresses eating behavior.

Result: Stored fat levels decrease and feeding stops.

Illustration: © Cengage Learning®. photo: Christopher Nash/Alamy

FIGURE 7.6

Mechanisms of Satiety.

FIGURE 7.7

Body Mass Index (BMI).

Height (inches)	80	90	100	110	120	130	140	150	160	170	180	190	200	210	220	230	240	250
80	9	10	11	12	13	14	15	17	18	19	20	21	22	23	24	25	26	28
78	9	10	12	13	14	15	16	17	19	20	21	22	23	24	25	27	28	29
76	10	11	12	13	15	16	17	18	20	21	22	23	24	26	27	28	29	30
74	10	12	12	14	15	17	18	19	21	22	23	24	26	27	28	30	31	32
72	11	12	14	15	16	18	19	20	22	23	24	26	27	28	30	31	33	34
70	12	13	14	16	17	19	20	22	23	24	26	27	29	30	32	33	35	36
68	12	14	15	17	18	20	21	23	24	26	27	29	30	32	34	35	37	38
66	13	15	16	18	19	21	23	24	26	27	29	31	32	34	36	37	39	40
64	14	15	17	19	21	22	24	26	28	29	31	33	34	36	38	40	41	43
62	15	17	18	20	22	24	26	27	29	31	33	35	37	38	40	42	44	46
60	16	17	20	22	23	25	27	25	31	33	35	37	39	41	43	45	47	49
58	17	19	21	23	25	27	29	31	34	36	38	40	42	44	46	48	50	52
56	18	21	22	25	27	29	31	34	36	38	40	43	45	47	49	52	54	56
54	19	22	24	27	29	31	34	36	39	41	43	46	48	51	53	56	58	60
52	21	23	26	29	31	34	36	39	40	44	47	49	52	55	57	60	62	65
50	23	25	28	31	34	37	39	42	45	48	51	53	56	59	62	65	68	70
48	24	28	31	34	37	40	42	46	49	52	55	58	61	64	67	70	73	76

Weight (pounds)

© Cengage Learning®

☐ BMI under 18.5: Underweight
☐ BMI between 18.5–24: Healthy weight
☐ BMI between 25–29: Overweight
☐ BMI between 30–39: Obese
☐ BMI over 40: Severely/morbidly obese

FIGURE 7.8

Obesity Trends* Among U.S. Adults
1990, 2000, 2010
(*BMI ≥30, or about 30 lbs. overweight for 5'4" person)

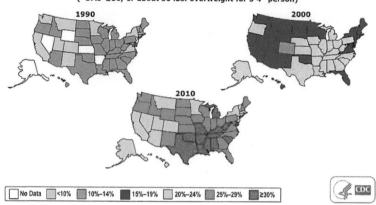

| No Data | <10% | 10%–14% | 15%–19% | 20%–24% | 25%–29% | ≥30% |

U.S. Obesity Rates Have Risen Dramatically. In 1990, no state reported that more than 15% of its population was obese, and the overall national rate of obesity was 12%. By 2012, the overall national rate of obesity rose to 37%, more than triple the rate in 1990. *Source:* Behavioral Risk Factor Surveillance System, CDC.

Our natural preference for sweet, fatty foods is also contributing to our growing size. To avoid starvation, our ancestors developed strong preferences for calorie-rich foods containing sugars and fats. When food supplies are limited, these preferences ensured that humans would spend the greatest amounts of time and energy seeking these rich sources of calories. Unfortunately, we retain these preferences today and continue to gravitate to sugary, fatty foods when they are available, like our frequenting of popular restaurant food chains with the 2,500-calorie meals or our late-night snacking on pizzas and chips.

Zooming out from individual factors to the larger social context, we see that social factors also contribute to obesity. We apparently "keep track" of how we are doing by comparing our size to that of those in our social circles. Having an obese spouse raises your risk of obesity by 37%, and having obese friends raises your risk by 57% (Christakis & Fowler, 2007).

The path to a healthy weight can be difficult. Unfortunately, weight loss for our ancestors usually meant they were one step closer to death by starvation, and we are well prepared to prevent that occurrence. Once a person is obese, a new set point is established and subsequently staunchly defended. Even the surgical removal of fat, or liposuction, does not result in permanent weight loss, because the fat removed by the process is eventually replaced (Dark, Forger, Stern, & Zucker, 1984; U.S. Food and Drug Administration, 2002).

Beginning in the 1800s, in an effort to prevent starvation, initiatives leading to increased cheap sources of high-calorie foods were adopted worldwide. Currently, global agriculture produces 2,600 calories per person per day, which is expected to rise to 3,000 calories per person per day by 2030 (Caballero, 2007). With such a plentiful food supply, we can see why obesity is becoming a global problem even as starvation remains a serious concern in many parts of the world.

Calorie-reducing diets work, but dietary changes cannot be viewed as something to do until a goal weight is reached. If the dieter returns to previous eating habits, the lost weight is quickly regained. Successful diets should be viewed as lifestyle changes that are sustainable for an individual. For example, removing one sugared soft drink per day should result in about a 10-pound weight loss over the next year. It is essential for the dieter to avoid triggering mechanisms designed to prevent starvation, like lowering metabolic rates. By keeping activity levels up and restricting weight loss to a pound or two per week at most, it is possible to slide weight loss under the radar of our vigilant weight maintenance systems.

The average adult weighing 150 pounds needs only 1,800 calories per day. When a single dessert item like cheesecake provides about 70% of that daily requirement, it becomes easy to see how people eating out frequently could become overweight or obese. It is also likely that before eating the cheesecake, a diner might have had an appetizer, salad, entrée, and beverage. This doesn't include meals and snacks consumed at other times throughout the day.

Efforts to use chemicals to control weight have been discouraging. Most medications used to reduce weight do so by suppressing appetite.

During the 1950s and 1960s, it was not uncommon for American doctors to prescribe amphetamines for weight loss. Although amphetamines suppress appetite, their psychoactive and addictive properties make this approach less than desirable. Approved chemical approaches for treating obesity include orlistat (Xenical), which reduces the absorption of fats by the digestive tract, and lorcaserin (Belviq), which is a serotonin agonist (O'Neil et al., 2012). Unfortunately, taking these drugs produces modest weight loss of 5 to 10 pounds per year, which might not be enough to offset diarrhea and other side effects in the minds of dieters (Rucker, Padwal, Li, Curioni, & Lau, 2007).

Some individuals who become discouraged with diets and medication have begun to turn instead to surgical interventions, including stomach stapling and gastric bypass procedures, which literally reduce the amount of nutrients that can be consumed or processed. While the resulting weight loss can be dramatic (the average gastric bypass patient loses 90 pounds within 3 months of surgery; Maggard et al., 2005), these procedures represent major surgery, often result in complications, and should be considered carefully.

Although it is feasible that current research into brain mechanisms for hunger and satiety may eventually lead to better treatments for obesity, lifestyle changes leading to healthier eating and exercise habits remain the most reliable approach.

Drew D. Saur

Contrary to popular opinion, many people lose weight by dieting and are successful in maintaining their weight loss for years. The National Weight Control Registry tracks more than 5,000 case studies of successful maintainers, including Drew Saur. Saur lost more than 150 pounds and has maintained his loss since 2005. He began by counting the calories he was consuming and was astonished to find that he was eating about 5,000 calories per day, not surprising given his starting weight of 325 pounds. By gradually reducing calories and waiting to eat until he felt hungry, Saur lost about 2 to 3 pounds per week. He began walking, and when his weight loss permitted more activity, he switched to running. Successful dieters and maintainers like Saur do not view dieting as something drastic to do before a wedding or class reunion but as a gradual lifestyle change that is livable.

Anorexia Nervosa, Bulimia Nervosa, and Binge-Eating Disorder Coexisting with our ongoing obesity epidemic are eating disorders characterized by unusual patterns of eating and distortions of a person's body image. Normally, we have a fairly accurate view of what we look like. People with distorted body image can be convinced that they are obese when they are in danger of starvation.

Traditionally, eating disorders have been viewed as a problem for women and less typical for men. However, contemporary research suggests that increasing numbers of men are experiencing eating disorders (Hudson, Hiripi, Pope, & Kessler, 2007) and body dissatisfaction (Pope, Katz, & Hudson, 1993). As many as 25% of individuals with eating disorders in the United States today are male. Rates of eating disorder are about 6 times higher among homosexual and bisexual men compared to heterosexual men, although sexual orientation does not seem to be associated with additional risks for eating disorder among women (Feldman & Meyer, 2007).

Anorexia nervosa is characterized by the maintenance of unusually low body weight, an intense fear of gaining weight, and a distorted view of the body as obese (APA, 2013). *Anorexia* literally means "loss of appetite." People with anorexia can show two patterns of behavior (APA, 2013). In the restricting type, people simply eat little food. In the bingeing–purging type, people combine restricted eating most of the time with behaviors associated with bulimia nervosa, which we discuss later.

Anorexia nervosa is dramatic but rare, affecting about 0.4% of females and perhaps 0.04% of males (APA, 2013). Anorexia nervosa is one of the few psychological disorders that can kill, with up to 5% of people with the disorder dying per decade from causes related to the condition, which includes an elevated risk for suicide (APA, 2013). Other symptoms include interruption of normal menstruation in females, very dry and yellow skin, fine downy hair (lanugo) on the face and other parts of the body, increased sensitivity to cold, and cardiovascular and gastrointestinal problems.

Bulimia nervosa is characterized by cycles of binge eating, in which unusually large amounts of food are consumed, and purging through the use of vomiting or laxatives. Bingeing is often followed by feelings of depression, disgust, and a sense of lost control. Bulimia is more common than anorexia, affecting 1.5% of women and between 0.15% and 0.5% of men (APA, 2013; Hudson et al., 2007).

anorexia nervosa An eating disorder characterized by the maintenance of unusually low body weight and a distorted body image.

bulimia nervosa An eating disorder characterized by bingeing, purging, and having feelings of depression, disgust, and lost control.

We have defined healthy weight as a BMI score between 18.5 and 24.9, yet the typical runway model held up as a cultural standard for beauty has an average BMI score of only 16.5. In response to a number of deaths of ultrathin models, some European countries now require models to maintain a minimum BMI score of 18.5. The United States has not followed suit, and American designers have complained that this standard would require a 6-foot-tall model to "balloon" to 136 pounds. In contrast, a 6-foot-tall model with a BMI score of 16.5 would weigh a scant 121 pounds. It is not surprising that young women exposed to these standards of beauty occasionally develop distorted images of their own bodies.

Binge-eating disorder is similar to bulimia nervosa in regards to eating abnormally large amounts of food at one sitting and feeling that eating is out of control, but it does not include compensatory behaviors such as induced vomiting or the use of laxatives (APA, 2013). People with binge-eating disorder eat rapidly, eat until they are uncomfortably full, eat when they are not hungry, and often eat alone because of embarrassment about the quantities they consume. Compared to other eating disorders, differences between males and females with binge-eating disorder are smaller. Approximately 1.6% of adult females and 0.8% of adult males are estimated to meet the criteria for this disorder (APA, 2013).

Environmental factors, especially cultural attitudes toward beauty, can play a significant role in the development of eating disorders. Anne Becker and her colleagues were observing eating patterns in the Fiji Islands when American television became available in 1995 (Becker, Burwell, Herzog, Hamburg, & Gilman, 2002). Prior to this time, Becker reported that dieting was unknown in this culture, which valued a "robust, well-muscled body" for both men and women. The Fijian language has a term for "going thin" that is used to express concern about someone who may be losing weight because of health problems. In the United States, people may say, "Have you lost weight? You look great!" In Fiji, a person is more likely to say, "Are you OK? You look like you're going thin."

These cultural norms underwent nearly overnight change with the introduction of American television, with its frequent images of glamorous, ultrathin actresses. Suddenly, 74% of the adolescent girls in Becker et al.'s study reported themselves as being "too big or too fat." Teens began to report dieting with the same frequency as their American counterparts, a radical shift from the researchers' observations since 1988. Because Becker et al.'s data are correlational, we cannot conclude that watching television produced disordered eating in Fiji. However, the results are suggestive of strong cultural influences on patterns of disordered eating.

Evidence from twin studies has been mixed, with some authors reporting heritability of 48% to 88% for eating disorders and others finding no evidence of genetic influences (Hinney & Volckmar, 2013). People might have a genetic vulnerability to disordered eating but not toward a specific type of disorder (Bulik et al., 2010). It is likely that general personality characteristics that increase a person's risk for eating disorders may be heritable, not the disorders themselves (Hsu, Chesler, & Santhouse, 1990).

binge-eating disorder An eating disorder characterized by eating abnormally large amounts of food at one sitting and feeling that eating is out of control, without compensatory behaviors such as induced vomiting or the use of laxatives.

 Thinking **Scientifically**

The Impact of Pro-Ana Websites

FREEDOM OF SPEECH is a cherished right, especially in the United States, and we decide to restrict access to data reluctantly, as in the case of movie and video game rating systems. Despite these strong values, many health professionals cringe when viewing so-called pro-ana sites online. Some of

these communities are designed to help people with eating disorders, but many are unabashedly in favor of promoting thinness at any cost.

One example, worldsbestdietingtips.com, is written by a self-described former

model. The site features links for "fasting help and answers," "purging tips," and "pro-ana tips," along with "thinspiration" photos of painfully thin celebrities, actresses, and models. The site is typically first to show up on a Google search for pro-ana sites and reports thousands of hits per day.

Once an eating disorder is established, biological factors contribute to maintaining abnormal patterns of eating. Even after people with anorexia nervosa regain normal weight, some still show evidence of elevated levels of hormones that typically raise metabolism and inhibit feeding (Stanley et al., 2003). The binge–purge cycling of bulimia involves processes similar to those of addiction (Avena, Rada, & Hoebel, 2008). When food-deprived rats are given access to sugar water, they tend to binge by consuming larger than normal amounts. Subsequently, if the bingeing rats are given naloxone, a chemical that blocks the action of opioid drugs (discussed in Chapter 6), they respond as if they had been addicted to opioids. For both bingeing and addicted rats, naloxone produces anxiety, agitation, and chattering teeth. People who fast and then binge on sweets may set up a similar addictive process that is difficult to stop.

Effective treatments exist for anorexia nervosa, bulimia nervosa, and binge-eating disorder. Treating anorexia nervosa can be challenging, because the therapist is frequently facing a person who is terrified of gaining weight. The first priority is keeping the person alive, and this effort typically involves hospitalization and careful monitoring of food intake. Cognitive behavioral therapy may be used to address distortions of body image (see Chapter 15), but no known medications are effective in treating anorexia (Berkman et al., 2006). About 50% of people with anorexia make a full recovery, but nearly 20% fail to respond. Treating bulimia and binge-eating disorder is somewhat more encouraging. Antidepressant medications, particularly selective serotonin reuptake inhibitors (SSRIs), are usually quite effective, especially when combined with cognitive behavioral treatment (Johnson, Tsoh, & Vanrado, 1996; Kass, Kolko, & Wilfley, 2013).

Sexual Motivation

Although sexual behavior is essential for the survival of a species, unlike eating, it is not essential to the survival of an individual organism. However, individuals' sexual behavior appears to be maintained by processes similar to the life-sustaining motivations we have already discussed. The evolutionary psychology perspective, discussed in Chapter 3, maintains that the goal of a species' sexual behavior is to produce offspring who will in turn reproduce. According to this approach, males and females experience different pressures that shape their reproductive behaviors.

Historically, cross-cultural data comparing the importance of different characteristics in a mate also showed gender differences (Buss, 1989). Both men and women from 37 cultures worldwide agreed that kindness, emotional stability, dependability, and a pleasant disposition were valuable characteristics in a mate. However, women were more influenced by the financial prospects of their potential mates, whereas men were more influenced by physical attractiveness. More recent data from the United States, illustrated in ● Figure 7.9, showed that male college students place more value on a prospective mate's earning power in 2008 than they did in 1985 but that college women's attitudes about the importance of a mate's being a "good financial prospect" were unchanged (Boxer, Noonan, & Whelan, 2013).

Michael DeFreitas/Photoshot

Before the introduction of American television programming to the islands of Fiji in 1995, the cultural ideal for both men and women was a "robust, well-muscled body," as evidenced by this traditional dancer. Dieting and eating disorders were unknown. A short time after American television was available, however, Fijian rates of dieting and eating disorders grew to match American rates and ideal beauties became slimmer.

What do we know about the influence of these sites? Teens already diagnosed with eating disorders visit pro-ana sites regularly, and few of their parents were aware of either the existence of these sites or their teens' use of the site (Wilson, Peebles, Hardy, & Litt, 2006). Individuals with eating disorders who frequent pro-ana sites show more disturbed body image and eating habits than people who view medical information sites about their disorders (Harper, Sperry, & Thompson, 2008).

Further research would be helpful in finding out how the use of these sites influences the recovery of people with eating disorders. In the meantime, raising awareness among parents, peers, and health advisers of the existence and content of these sites might increase our ability to help those who have eating disorders. ●

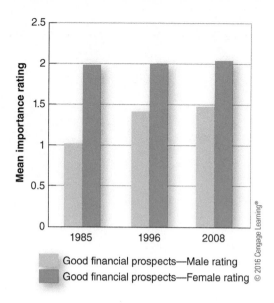

FIGURE 7.9

Preferences in Mate Characteristics Change Over Time. Between 1985 and 2008, female ratings of the importance of a mate being a good financial prospect didn't change. Male ratings of the same trait increased between 1985 and 1996 but did not change further between 1996 and 2008. The rating scale was as follows: 0 = irrelevant or unimportant, 1 = desirable, 2 = important, and 3 = essential. *Source:* Adapted from "Measuring Mate Preferences: A Replication and Extension," by C. F. Boxer, M. C. Noonan, and, C. B. Whelan, 2013, *Journal of Family Issues* 6, 229-249. doi:10.1177/0192513x13490404.

testosterone A male hormone.

FIGURE 7.10

Women Close to Ovulation Judge Male Sexual Orientation More Accurately. Women asked to judge the sexual orientation of men based on a brief presentation of a photograph of a man's face were most accurate at their approximate time of ovulation within their menstrual cycles (approximately day 14). This study suggests that even though women are receptive to sex throughout the menstrual cycle, interest in sex is likely to be highest at a time of increased fertility. *Source:* Adapted from "Mating Interest Improves Women's Accuracy in Judging Male Sexual Orientation," by N. O. Rule, K. S. Rosen, M. L. Slepian, and N. Ambady, 2011, *Psychological Science, 22*(7), 881–886, doi:10.1177/0956797611412394.

Sexuality is an extremely complex aspect of human behavior. In this chapter, we will focus on the more physical aspects of sexual motivation. In Chapter 11, we will explore sexuality across the life span, and in Chapter 13, we will discuss phenomena related to attraction and maintaining relationships.

Hormones and Sexual Motivation The females of most mammalian species undergo estrus, a period of hours or days during which the female is receptive, or willing to have sex. In these species, hormone levels and sexual behavior are tightly linked. In humans and Old World primates, menstrual cycles replace periods of estrus. The sexual behavior of these nonestrus species is quite different (Rushton et al., 2001).

Human females show receptivity throughout the menstrual cycle. Some women report feeling slightly more interest in sex around the time of ovulation, a situation that has obvious advantages for the reproduction of the species, because this is when sexual behavior is most likely to lead to pregnancy (Slob, Bax, Hop, Rowland, & van der Werff ten Bosch, 1996). As shown in ● Figure 7.10, women who are near ovulation make more accurate assessments of the sexual orientation of men but show no comparable change in their ability to identify the sexual orientation of other women (Rule, Rosen, Slepian, & Ambady, 2011). Accuracy improved even more when the experimenters manipulated the women to think romantic thoughts, reminding us that while the physical aspects of sexual motivation can be significant, they always interact with social and cognitive influences.

Around ovulation, women provide subtle cues about their fertility. Participants in one study could accurately identify women who were near ovulation based on how "attractively" they were dressed (Haselton, Mortezaie, Pillsworth, Bleske-Rechek, & Frederick, 2006). Ovulating women showed more attention to detail regarding dress, hair, and makeup. Women also speak in higher, more feminine tones when they are ovulating than at other times of the menstrual cycle, especially in social situations (Bryant & Haselton, 2009).

Because women's behavior around ovulation reflects the activity of hormones responsible for the menstrual cycle, it is surprising that these hormones appear to have little influence on sexual interest. Menopause produces substantial changes in a woman's female hormone levels but has little impact on her sexual interest and activity (Galyer, Conaglen, Hare, & Conaglen, 1999). If anything, women often respond to this change in fertility with greater interest in sexual activity because of the relief of no longer worrying about unplanned pregnancy.

If levels of female hormones do not correlate with a woman's level of sexual interest, are there other biological factors that do? Perhaps surprisingly, female sexual interest and activity are correlated with levels of **testosterone**. Women typically produce about one tenth the amount of testosterone that males produce. Medical conditions that reduce a woman's testosterone production often lead to sexual dysfunction. When these women are treated with low doses of testosterone provided through a skin patch, they report having sex more frequently and enjoying it more (Shifren et al., 2000).

Testosterone is also correlated with sexual interest in males. However, as long as a man's testosterone falls within a normal range, it does not provide a strong predictor of an individual's sexual frequency (Gray et al., 2005; Mazur & Booth, 1998). Below normal levels of testosterone, as in castration, are usually accompanied by very low sexual desire and activity.

Because most oral contraceptives prevent ovulation, women using this form of birth control do not show the characteristic changes in dress and voice observed in ovulating women.

Male testosterone levels fluctuate over the course of a day and are influenced not only by a man's biology but also by a number of environmental factors, notably competition. Male collegiate athletes experience increases in testosterone in anticipation of competition. Following a competition, testosterone continues to rise among the winners and temporarily decreases among the losers (Booth, Shelley, Mazur, Tharp, & Kittok, 1989). Simply observing a competition may influence testosterone levels. Men cheering for the successful Brazilian soccer team at the 1994 World Cup experienced increased testosterone levels, whereas men supporting the losing Italian team experienced a decrease (Bernhardt, Dabbs, Fielden, & Lutter, 1998). These fluctuations are more dramatic when taking the location of the venue into account. Losing at home produces a more dramatic decrease in testosterone than losing a game as the visiting team. This response to losing a competition at home may represent a remnant of our ancestors' need to defend their territory. We can assume that losing a battle is catastrophic in any circumstance, but losing near your family and home makes them especially vulnerable to destruction.

Humans show wide variations in sexual satisfaction (see ● Figure 7.11). Cross-cultural studies show that subjective sexual satisfaction depends on a number of factors, including relative equality between men and women, mental and physical health, and the importance of sexual behavior for an individual (Laumann et al., 2006). The stability of relationships, which also affects sexual satisfaction in a positive way, is related to hormone levels. Men in stable, long-term relationships have lower testosterone levels than single men or men who are within a few years of divorce (Mazur & Michalek, 1998). Men's testosterone levels also drop significantly after the birth of a child (Gettler, McDade, Feranil, & Kuzawa, 2011). These correlations do not allow us to make judgments about causality, as we explained in Chapter 2. It is possible that the competition for mates and pressure for reproduction that single men experience produces an increase in testosterone. Conversely, it is also possible that men with higher testosterone levels are not as successful at maintaining stable relationships. Evidence supporting this second hypothesis was provided by a long-term study in which partnering and unpartnering did not affect men's testosterone levels (van Anders & Watson, 2006). In other words, if a man's

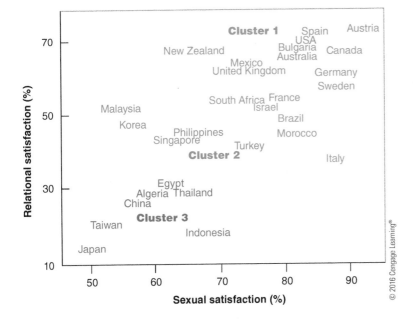

FIGURE 7.11

A Cross-Cultural Comparison of Relational and Sexual Satisfaction. A survey of nearly 30,000 people in 29 countries showed wide variations in sexual satisfaction. In most countries, there was a strong correlation between relational satisfaction (defined as a combination of physical pleasure with a partner and emotional satisfaction with a partner) and sexual satisfaction. Gender differences in satisfaction with sexual function were the smallest in Cluster 1 countries. *Source:* Adapted from "A Cross-National Study of Subjective Sexual Well-Being Among Older Women and Men: Findings From the Global Study of Sexual Attitudes and Behaviors," by E. O. Laumann, A. Paik, D. B. Glasser, J.-H. Kang, T. Wang, B. Levinson, et al., 2006, *Archives of Sexual Behavior, 35*(2), 145–161.

testosterone was fluctuating as a result of competition, as suggested in the first hypothesis, this study should have provided evidence for changes in testosterone as a function of relationship status, but none were observed. For both men and women, individuals with the lowest testosterone levels were more likely to be in monogamous, committed relationships. Single individuals had higher levels of testosterone, and individuals with multiple, committed relationships (such as married men with long-term mistresses) had the highest testosterone levels (van Anders, Hamilton, & Watson, 2007).

An important feature of human social behavior across our evolutionary history has been the importance of forming families to provide supportive, reproductive, and nurturant advantages. Although the resulting cultural values have often linked sexual desire and romantic love, these two functions represent distinct biological and emotional states. Romantic love involves the establishment of long-term relationships, whereas sexual desire promotes mating and reproduction. Romantic love and sexual desire are on a continuum, with the pleasant sensorimotor experiences associated with sexual desire leading to the more cognitive feelings of romantic love (Cacioppo, Bianchi-Demicheli, Frum, Pfaus, & Lewis, 2012).

We have seen how sexual desire or interest is correlated with testosterone for both men and women, but romantic love is associated with two other hormones, oxytocin and vasopressin (see ● Figure 7.12). In humans, both hormones are active in the brain, but vasopressin is expressed more by males and oxytocin is expressed more by females (Ishunina & Swaab, 1999; van Londen et al., 1997). In both sexes, oxytocin enhances bonding. Women release oxytocin during breastfeeding and even respond to a brief hug from their partners with a spike in oxytocin release

FIGURE 7.12

Oxytocin, Vasopressin, and Two Species of Voles. The discovery of the importance of oxytocin and vasopressin to bonding originated in the study of two types of rodents: the prairie vole and the montane vole. Although similar in many ways, the two types of vole differed in both their bonding to a partner and their parenting behaviors. Prairie voles are monogamous for life, but montane voles are not. Prairie voles share parenting duties, but montane voles do not. Differences between the two types of vole in oxytocin and vasopressin were closely associated with the behavioral differences, with the prairie voles showing higher levels of both hormones than the montane voles. In one type of study, voles are allowed to mate, and then they are placed in a test box. On either side of the male, who can move freely, are two females—a stranger and the partner—who are tethered in their boxes and can't move. The chart shows how much time the average male prairie vole and montane vole spend with the partner, with the stranger, or alone. As you can see, the prairie voles prefer to be with their partners, but the montane voles prefer to be alone. *Source:* Cacioppo, S., Bianchi-Demicheli, F., Frum, C., Pfaus, J.G., & Lewis, J.W. (2012). The common neural bases between sexual desire and love: A multi level kernel density fMRI analysis. *Journal of Sexual Medicine, 9*(4), 1048–1054.

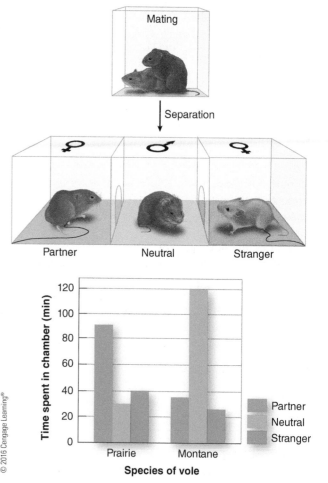

(Light, Grewen, & Amico, 2005). Oxytocin is released at orgasm in both sexes. However, because of the greater overall expression of oxytocin in the brains of females, along with the 10 times higher testosterone levels in men, it appears that women are more likely than men to equate sexual desire with feelings of romantic love (Diamond, 2004). We do not mean to imply that men do not bond, but high testosterone levels are likely to make sexual activity highly salient for young men, with or without the bonding associated with oxytocin release.

In light of these sex differences, it is not surprising to learn that college women report a preference for interacting with men sexually through traditional, planned dates with an expectation for further contact, while college men report a preference for interacting sexually with women through "no strings attached" hookups (Bradshaw, Kahn, & Saville, 2010). Complicating contemporary relationships still further is the ability of oxytocin release to be classically conditioned, a process we describe in Chapter 8. With each successive sexual encounter with a person, that individual becomes a stronger learned signal for oxytocin release, which in turn facilitates bonding (Witt, Carter, Lederhendler, & Kirkpatrick, 1997). Women intending to hook up might find themselves bonding with their partners instead. Counselors in university health centers are well aware that women often seek counseling following a hookup but men typically do not (Grossman, 2007).

Sexual Orientation Individual differences in human sexuality are substantial and normal. One of the ways individuals vary is in their **sexual orientation**, which refers to a stable pattern of attraction to members of a particular sex. Orientation is not synonymous with behavior. Many people engage in same-sex behavior and fantasy while maintaining a strong heterosexual orientation. In the Sambia tribal culture of New Guinea, all adolescent males are expected to engage in same-sex behavior before marrying women (Stoller & Herdt, 1985). The adult sexual orientation of these men remained overwhelmingly heterosexual.

It is difficult to determine the number of individuals who are homosexual (Savin-Williams, 2006). Among adults in the United States, 1.5% of women and 1.8% of men identify themselves as homosexual, and 0.4% of men and 0.9% of women describe themselves as bisexual (Ward, Dahlhamer, Galinsky, & Joestl, 2014).

Genetics appears to influence sexual orientation, although the exact mechanisms are not well understood and are likely to be quite complex. Like most human behaviors, sexual orientation is likely to be the result of an interaction between genetic factors and other aspects of the individual's experience, which can include prenatal factors. To assess the genetic contribution to sexual orientation, researchers have compared rates of homosexuality in twins. If one identical male twin is homosexual, his twin has about a 50% chance of also being homosexual (Kirk, Bailey, & Martin, 2000).

Among the other possible biological variables affecting sexual orientation are levels of prenatal, but not adult, sex hormones. Women with a condition known as congenital adrenal hyperplasia (CAH) experienced high prenatal levels of male hormones. Consequently, they are often born with masculinized external genitalia, are more likely to describe themselves as "tomboys," and are more likely to engage in lesbian or bisexual behavior (Meyer-Bahlburg, Dolezal, Baker, & New, 2008). However, most women with CAH are heterosexual, just as most lesbian and bisexual women do not have a history of CAH or similar conditions.

An interesting clue to the origin of sexual orientation arises from the observation that birth order influences the odds that a man is homosexual. Men who have older brothers are more likely to be gay than men who have no siblings, younger siblings only, or older sisters (Blanchard, 1997). Theoretically, carrying a male fetus could provoke a mother's immune response, which would become stronger with each successive male fetus she carries. Her immune response could influence the development of her fetus by altering significant hormonal processes. Additional research is needed to identify the ways an immune system response of the mother could change the structure of her fetus's developing brain (James, 2006).

Gilbert Herdt/Anthro-Photo

A homosexual orientation is carefully defined as a stable pattern of attraction to people of the same gender. Homosexual behavior can occur with or without a homosexual orientation. Among the Sambian people of New Guinea, young males are separated from their mothers and expected to engage in homosexual behavior with older males. The Sambian people believe that obtaining semen in this manner transforms them into powerful warriors (Herdt, 1987). After marriage, the now-adult man is no longer expected to engage in homosexual behavior.

sexual orientation A stable pattern of attraction to members of a particular sex.

FIGURE 7.13

Some Brain Differences May Correlate With Sexual Orientation. Simon LeVay reported that an area of the hypothalamus known as INAH-3 differs between heterosexual and homosexual men. If you compare the samples in (b) and (c), you can see that INAH-3, indicated by the four dark arrows, appears to be larger in the heterosexual male sample than in the homosexual male sample. The impact of this size difference on adult sexual behavior or sexual orientation remains unknown, however, because these are correlational data. *Source:* Adapted from "A Difference in Hypothalamic Structure Between Heterosexual and Homosexual Men," by S. LeVay, 1991, *Science, 253,* 1034–1037.

© Argosy Publishing, Inc.

(a) Location of INAH-3

(b) Heterosexual man

(c) Homosexual man

Several structures in the brain are known to be different in males and females and also seem to differ between homosexual and heterosexual males. Among these is a small cluster of neurons located in the hypothalamus known as the interstitial nucleus of the anterior hypothalamus (INAH; see ● Figure 7.13). There are four separate nuclei in INAH. Two of these, INAH-2 and INAH-3, are notably larger in males than in females (Allen, Hines, Shryne, & Gorski, 1989). The exact function of these nuclei in humans is unknown, although animal research suggests that they participate in sexual behavior. Building on this research about differences between the brains of men and those of women, Simon LeVay asked whether INAH-3 might be different in heterosexual and homosexual males. After examining the brains of more than 40 individuals, LeVay (1991) concluded that INAH-3 in homosexual men was about 2 to 3 times smaller than in heterosexual men, or about the same size as typically found in women.

LeVay was quite cautious in his interpretation of his results. The homosexual individuals in his sample had all died from AIDS. Otherwise, there would be little reason to note sexual orientation on a person's medical records. Although it is unlikely that AIDS would produce this type of change in the brain, LeVay could not rule out that possibility based on his data. LeVay also raised the possibility that engaging in homosexual behavior might influence INAH-3, even in the adult, although he gave little credence to that possibility. Nonetheless, LeVay's research had a profound effect on the way psychologists and the public looked at sexual orientation. Before the 1990s, the medical and psychological research literatures used the term *sexual preference* instead of today's *sexual orientation.*

Because of the difficulties arising from this type of research in humans, others have investigated the correlations between brain structure and sexual behavior in animals. Among domestic sheep, 6% to 8% of rams (males) mate exclusively with other males. The sheep equivalent of INAH-3 is about the same size in ewes (females) as in the rams that mated with other rams. This structure is larger in rams that mated with ewes (Roselli, Larkin, Resko, Stellflug, & Stormshak, 2004).

Cognitive and Social Motives

So far, our discussion has focused on motivational behavior that is central to maintaining life. In addition, humans experience a range of complex cognitive and social motives. A lengthy list of these types of complex motives published in 1938 included achievement, affiliation, autonomy, nurturance, dominance, play, and order (Murray, 1938). More recent work focuses on needs for competence and relatedness (Deci & Ryan, 2000). Although some psychologists retain strong distinctions between biological and psychological motives, the dividing line is surely blurred. When an individual's need for affiliation is not met, the consequences of the resulting loneliness include biological factors, such as increased rates of illness and death (Cacioppo, Cacioppo, Capitanio, & Cole, 2015).

The Motivation to Affiliate Humans are a social species. Our need to belong might not seem to be in the same category to you as our need for nutrients and sexual behavior, but the results of many studies show that affiliation works similarly to the other motivations we have discussed so far (Baumeister & Leary, 1995). When people are asked to identify which pleasures are most important to their happiness, the overwhelming majority rate love, intimacy, and social **affiliation** above wealth, fame, and even physical health (Cacioppo & Patrick, 2008).

Not only do people value affiliation, but a perceived lack of connection with others can have devastating effects. Solitary confinement is viewed as one of the worst punishments humans inflict on one another. The effects of social isolation can be as detrimental to good health as high blood pressure, lack of exercise, obesity, or smoking (House, Landis, & Umberson, 1988). Not all behaviors associated with feeling isolated or rejected are self-destructive. In some cases, feeling isolated can result in outwardly hostile behavior (see ● Figure 7.14). Students told in an experiment that a personality test had shown that they were "the type likely to end up alone later in life" showed less empathy and more aggression toward other students than did students told that they would enjoy "rewarding relation-

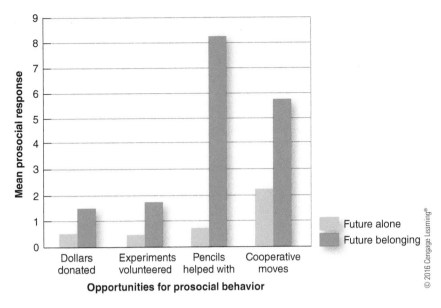

FIGURE 7.14

Effects of Social Exclusion on Helping Behaviors. People who were told that a personality test indicated they were likely to spend their future alone, without significant relationships, were far less helpful across different types of tasks than participants who were told that they were likely to have a future featuring acceptance and belongingness. *Source:* Adapted from "If You Can't Join Them, Beat Them: Effects of Social Exclusion on Aggressive Behavior," by J. M. Twenge, R. F. Baumeister, D. M. Tice, and T. S. Stucke, 2007, *Journal of Personality and Social Psychology, 81,* 1058–1069.

ships throughout life" (Twenge, Baumeister, Tice, & Stucke, 2001). It is probably not an accident that most individuals responsible for mass shootings are described as outcasts or loners.

The experience of loneliness appears to serve as an aversive signal that, like hunger, thirst, and pain, evolved to warn humans that they are facing a threat to their survival and that their social connections are in need of repair (Cacioppo & Patrick, 2008). Social connections are especially important to the survival of humans. Compared to other species, humans require the greatest amount of parenting to survive to adulthood and reproduce. In addition, as we discuss in Chapter 13, humans are not well equipped to survive in isolation. Our ancestors formed hunter–gatherer groups because the cooperative sharing of responsibilities enhanced the survival of all group members.

Individuals differ in the amount of social connection they desire. Early work on affiliation by Henry Murray (1938) and David McClelland (1985) viewed the need for others as similar to a personality trait, as we discuss further in Chapter 12. Some people are relatively happy working in a cubicle for hours on end, while this lack of social contact would be intolerable for others. Still others might feel lonely even when surrounded by large numbers of caring friends and family members. We appear to have a set point for social activity that operates similarly to the set points we mentioned in our discussion of hunger. When we sense a gap between our actual social connectivity and what we desire, we experience the unpleasant state of loneliness, which in turn motivates us to seek more social experiences. Twin studies show that this set point, like the others we have discussed, is influenced by our genetics (Boomsma, Willemsen, Dolan, Hawkley, & Cacioppo, 2005). Knowing one identical twin's need for affiliation helps predict the other twin's need.

Individual predispositions interact with people's situations to predict desire for affiliation. We frequently join others to share good events, whether that means a birthday, a wedding, a promotion, or simply the end of another round of final exams. We have all enjoyed the camaraderie of staying in the stands long after our team has won an important game, celebrating with nearby fans and exchanging high fives.

affiliation Being associated with other people.

People affiliate not only to share happy occasions, like the introduction of a royal baby, but also to reduce stress in sad times, such as when family members of victims of the September 11, 2001 terrorist attacks gathered to throw flowers in the memorial pools at Ground Zero.

Affiliation is not just for good times, however. People often find that the company of others helps to reduce stress. In a classic series of experiments, Stanley Schachter (1959) showed that people expecting to be given a painful electric shock were more likely to seek the company of other study participants than to wait for their shock alone. Not all stressful situations are equally likely to produce affiliation, however. In one study, participants were told that they would be performing embarrassing behaviors, such as sucking on large pacifiers (Sarnoff & Zimbardo, 1961). These participants made different choices than the participants expecting shock in the previous study: They preferred to be alone.

Exactly what does the company of other people contribute to reducing stress? It appears that we appreciate the company of others when we expect them to reduce our stress. In many cases, other people can reduce our stress by providing information. Hospital patients awaiting dangerous surgeries preferred roommates who had already been through the procedure to those who had not yet had surgery (Kulik, Mahler, & Moore, 1996).

Achievement Motivation **Achievement motivation**, or the desire to excel or outperform others, has been a topic of interest to psychologists beginning with William James (1890). Using measures of individual achievement motivation, people who are high in achievement motivation have been shown to seek and typically succeed in competitive, entrepreneurial occupations (McClelland, 1985). The role of individual achievement motivation in predicting performance has been of great interest in the fields of education, management, and athletics.

Many psychologists have recognized that individual differences in achievement motivation seem similar to personality traits, which we discuss in Chapter 12 (Elliot & Murayama, 2008). A trait is a stable characteristic that shows relatively little variation over time. However, traits also typically interact with situations. An introverted person might seem more introverted at a big party than when out to dinner with one friend. According to this more complex view, a person's trait achievement motivation interacts with the opportunities present in the environment (Hart & Albarracin, 2009). For example, achieving excellence might be viewed as an alternative to having fun or enjoying leisure time. High-achieving people do not dislike fun but are prepared to avoid or postpone some fun to meet their achievement goals. Low-achieving people may be perfectly capable of success but, for a variety of reasons, have simply prioritized fun alternatives and inhibited the achievement alternatives. Fear of failure is another factor that possibly keeps competent people from attempting a task (Elliot & Murayama, 2008).

achievement motivation A desire to excel or outperform others.

A person's trait level of achievement motivation interacts with the opportunities to achieve available in the environment.

A number of practical implications emerge from the study of achievement motivation. Many teachers, managers, and coaches emphasize competition, such as sales contests, as a way to promote achievement. While this competitive approach works well for people who are high in trait achievement motivation, it might not work so well for those who are lower on this scale (Hart & Albarracin, 2009). For lower achievers, messages that emphasize the fun and relaxing aspects of a task might be more likely to elicit the best outcomes.

Motivational Priorities

We have discussed a number of different motivations, from hunger to sex to affiliation to achievement. If faced simultaneously with a number of drives and demands, how do we decide which motivations to follow first?

Approach and Avoidance As we observed in the case of achievement motivation, situations often present us with multiple, overlapping opportunities and goals (Elliot, 1999). Approach and avoidance differ in valence or natural attractiveness, with approach involving positive and desirable outcomes and avoidance involving negative and undesirable outcomes. A

 Experiencing **Psychology**

Excellence Motivation

THIS SHORT QUESTIONNAIRE (Cassidy & Lynn, 1989; revised by Hart & Albarracin, 2009) will give you an idea of where you are in terms of trait achievement motivation, sometimes called chronic achievement motivation. For each item, select a number on a scale of 1 (not at all like me) to 5 (extremely like me).

_____ 1. I hate to see bad workmanship.
_____ 2. Part of the satisfaction in doing something comes from seeing how good the finished product looks.

_____ 3. It is no use playing a game when you are playing with someone as good as yourself.
_____ 4. I get a sense of satisfaction out of being able to say I have done a very good job on a project.
_____ 5. I find satisfaction in working as well as I can.
_____ 6. I find satisfaction in exceeding my previous performance even if I don't outperform others.
_____ 7. There is satisfaction in a job well done.

Add up all of your scores. Scores can range from a low of 7 to a high of 35. The authors do not provide "cut points" for high or low scores. If you're curious about where you stand relative to others, you might suggest that your classmates share their scores. Keep in mind that college students are not a representative sample of the adult public, particularly in regards to achievement motivation. ●

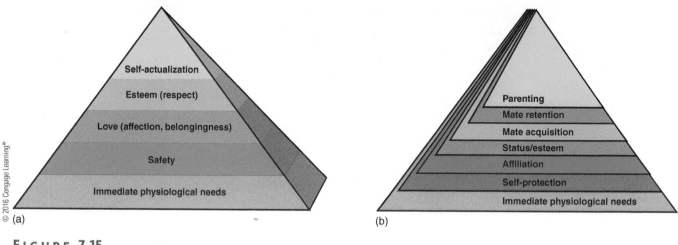

(a)   (b)

FIGURE 7.15

Classic and Contemporary Hierarchies of Needs. Maslow's classic pyramid depicting his hierarchy of needs is shown in (a). Kenrick et al. (2010) have proposed an updated version of the pyramid (b) that incorporates developmental and evolutionary perspectives. *Source:* Adapted from "Renovating the Pyramid of Needs: Contemporary Extensions Built Upon Ancient Foundations," by D. T. Kenrick, V. Griskevicius, S. L. Neuberg, and M. Schaller, 2010, *Perspectives on Psychological Science, 5*(3), 292–314, doi:10.1177/1745691610369469.

Miller (1944) shocked rats while they were eating a food reward they had earned by running down a maze alley, setting up a conflict between approach and avoidance toward the food box. Subsequently, the rat would run down the alley but stop without entering the food box. Miller could adjust where the rats stopped (a point of equilibrium between approach and avoidance) by changing either the rats' hunger levels or the intensity of the shock.

self-actualization A state of having fulfilled your potential.

particular situation might stimulate us to engage in a behavior to approach an outcome, avoid one, or possibly do both simultaneously. When you think about your motivation for studying this textbook right now, you might think you are working to get a good grade in the course (approach), avoid getting a poor grade (avoidance), or do some combination of the two. In any case, you are motivated to study.

This example is only one of several forms conflicts among motives can take. In the example mentioned previously of the student facing a choice between doing well in school and enjoying fun and leisure time, the conflict occurs between two positive choices, or approach–approach. The individual must decide which goal has priority. In still other cases, choices occur between two unpleasant alternatives (avoidance–avoidance). If you don't stay late at work, your boss will think you're a lazy employee, but if you do stay late at work, your significant other will be angry. In most real-world situations, choices typically have multiple, overlapping approach–avoidance aspects, making the prioritization of goals essential.

Motivational Theories An early effort to provide a model for how motivations could be prioritized was contributed by Abraham Maslow in 1943. Maslow viewed motivation as a hierarchy of needs, in which lower levels must be satisfied before the individual has the time and energy to pursue higher level needs. As shown in ● Figure 7.15, Maslow's model is typically illustrated as a pyramid.

At the lowest level of the pyramid, we find physiological needs, including food, water, and shelter. These basic needs must be met daily; otherwise, life will be threatened. Consequently, if meeting these needs is a challenge for a person, Maslow predicted that the person is unlikely to care about needs appearing at higher levels of the hierarchy. In a classic study of caloric restriction, young healthy men were given approximately 1,500 calories per day for 6 months, which resulted in a loss of about 25% of their normal body weight (Keys, Brozek, Henschel, Mickelsen, & Taylor, 1950). Not only did the men become obsessed with food, but their interest in sex declined dramatically.

Once physiological needs are generally met, Maslow suggests that we turn our attention to safety and then to belongingness, represented by the love and affection of others. For Maslow, these three lower categories are essential to human life. Unfortunately, we don't need to look too far in the daily news to read about large numbers of the world's population who do not attain these basic needs.

Freed from the challenges of meeting basic needs, we begin to seek esteem, or the respect we receive from other members of the community. At the pinnacle of human striving, however, is the goal of **self-actualization**, according to Maslow. People seeking self-actualization desire to fully meet their potential, as suggested by the U.S. Army slogan "Be all you can be." Cultures differ dramatically in their emphasis on self-actualization, with individualistic nations like the United States embracing this value more than collectivist nations in Southeast Asia, where harmony and belongingness are highly valued (Hofstede, 1984).

Maslow's classic theory received a recent modification that retained the overall hierarchical organization but added three new perspectives: the evolutionary functions of motives, the development of motives over the life span, and the cognitive priorities assigned to motives in response to environmental stimuli (Kenrick, Griskevicius, Neuberg, & Schaller, 2010). This modified pyramid, illustrated in Figure 7.15, replaces self-actualization with mate acquisition, mate retention, and parenting. The authors of the revision noted that self-actualization was interesting but that they could not find an evolutionary explanation for why we would seek to reach this level. Many of the activities described by Maslow as helping people to reach self-actualization, such as art and poetry, might be better explained as efforts to gain status, which in turn would attract mates.

Schoolteachers often face students who come to school hungry or sick because of poverty or neglect. According to Maslow, it is difficult for teachers to interest these children, whose basic needs are unmet, in learning about long division and other subjects.

AP Images

Abraham Maslow did not believe that everyone achieves self-actualization. Among the select few he believed had reached this pinnacle of motivation were Abraham Lincoln and Mahatma Gandhi—as well as U.S. First Lady Eleanor Roosevelt, shown in this photograph with Madame Chiang Kai-shek. Maslow's self-actualized people shared common attributes, including independence and a good sense of humor. Who would you add to this list of self-actualized people?

Summary 7.1 Important Concepts in Motivation

Term	Meaning	Example
Motivation	A process that arouses, maintains, and guides behavior to a goal	Being thirsty leads you to seek a drinking fountain and get a drink of water.
Homeostasis	A steady internal balance or equilibrium	We are motivated to maintain a constant internal temperature. If we feel cold, we shiver and put on more clothing.
Set point	A value actively defended to maintain homeostasis	It is hard to lose weight because we actively defend our previous weight by slowing our metabolism when fewer calories are consumed.
Drive	A state of arousal or tension resulting from stimuli that are important to survival	Being hungry is unpleasant.
Drive reduction	The feelings of relief and reward following a return to equilibrium	Quenching your thirst on a hot day is rewarding.
Incentives	Rewards that motivate behavior without the experience of any unpleasant drive state	You enjoy throwing a great surprise party for a friend's birthday.

Why Are We Emotional?

Whether we're experiencing happiness or sadness, anger or disgust, an emotion combines a physical sensation, such as a rapid heartbeat, and a conscious, subjective feeling, like fear or sadness. Psychologists have asked questions about how these two aspects, the physical sensations and subjective feelings, might relate to one another.

Psychologists have also debated whether emotions should be viewed as discrete stand-alone states or whether it would be more useful to view them as existing on a continuum. The discrete approach views emotional states like happy, sad, or angry as being like primary colors of red, yellow, or blue, while the continuous view sees emotions like a rainbow, with particular emotions being located closer to some than others and even blending together (Russell, 1980; see ● Figure 7.16). Like many of the either–or discussions that we encounter in psychology, a compromise might be the best strategy. If we think instead of emotions as being stars, we can imagine a constellation containing clusters of positive emotions like happiness and pride and another constellation containing clusters of negative emotions like anger and sadness.

Emotional behavior is not unique to humans. Charles Darwin (1872) made a careful study of the facial expressions produced by humans and other primates. He concluded that all primates form facial expressions using the same muscles, which in turn led him to state that emotional facial expression must have evolved. Although we are frequently cautioned about anthropomorphism, or the attributing of human qualities to other animals, it is easy to identify with the anger of a mother bear defending her cubs or the fear of a gazelle trying to outrun a cheetah.

The evolution of a behavior implies that it makes survival more likely. The survival benefits of motivation are rather obvious, but what about those of emotion? A major advantage provided by emotion is the ability to produce arousal. The word *emotion* is derived from the

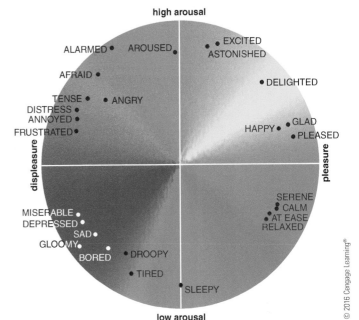

© 2016 Cengage Learning®

FIGURE 7.16

Continuous Versus Discrete Views of Emotion. Russell (1980) suggested that emotions could be viewed along dimensions of pleasant/unpleasant and high arousal to low arousal instead of as isolated states. This approach to emotion suggests that some emotions are closer together than others.

British Library/Robana/Hulton Fine Art Collection/Getty Images

Sergey Lavrentev/123rf

Darwin discovered that humans and other primates use the same facial muscles to produce emotional expressions, leading him to hypothesize that emotions evolved. Can you figure out what emotion is being expressed by both the chimpanzee and the man? Try imitating the expression and think about how you feel. Still no luck? The emotion being expressed is disappointment.

FIGURE 7.17

The Effects of Arousal on Performance. The Yerkes–Dodson law predicts that the complexity of a task interacts with an organism's arousal level to determine the quality of performance. For simple tasks, like running to escape a predator, greater arousal leads to a relatively steady improvement in performance. For difficult tasks, like completing an exam, moderate amounts of arousal lead to the best performance, and high arousal can lead to weaker performance. Adapted from Yerkes, R. M., & Dodson, J. D. (1908). The relation of strength of stimulus to rapidity of habit-formation. *Journal of Comparative Neurology and Psychology*, *18*(5), 459-482.

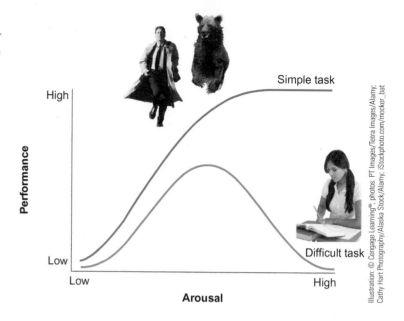

Latin word meaning "to move." The arousal produced by an emotion stimulates action, which might be life saving. According to the classic **Yerkes–Dodson law**, the ideal amount of arousal interacts with the complexity of a task (Yerkes & Dodson, 1908). For simple tasks, such as outrunning a predator, greater arousal leads to greater performance. For more complex tasks, like taking a difficult exam, arousal levels that are too high can begin to interfere with performance (see ● Figure 7.17). We have all had the experience of "choking," or performing badly because of too much arousal. In addition to providing general arousal, each emotion, like the motivations we discussed previously, is associated with a positive or negative quality or valence, which "moves" us in the direction of either approach or avoidance (Davidson & Irwin, 1999). The negative emotion of disgust tells us to avoid rotting food, and positive feelings of happiness cement our social bonds.

In addition to producing beneficial arousal, emotions enhance survival by providing an important means of communication. Nonverbal forms of communication such as facial expression, calls, and body language were used to provide information to others long before humans began using spoken words (see ● Figure 7.18). If one person assumes a body posture indicating fear, the emotion ripples through a crowd to its edges in a short amount of time (de Gelder, Snyder, Greve, Gerard, & Hadjikhani, 2004). Human infants communicate a range of needs to their parents before developing the ability to speak. You have no difficulty interpreting the facial expressions, body language, and gestures of a driver behind you who doesn't approve of your lane-change technique.

Long before infants learn to speak, they are able to communicate with adults by using facial expressions.

Yerkes–Dodson law A description of the relationships among task complexity, arousal, and performance.

An additional and welcome benefit of having emotions is our ability to enjoy the arts. Evidence for a coordinated development of language and emotional communication remains in our contemporary brain, which uses the same pathways for language and for the perception and appreciation of music (Schön et al., 2010). Without the capacity to feel, we would find it difficult to appreciate a Picasso or the moving strains of "Yesterday" by the Beatles. We wouldn't enjoy a good cry at the end of *Pride and Prejudice* or be glued to the edge of our seats while watching *Gravity*. The universal nature of human responses to many poems, pieces of music, and other artistic accomplishments points to shared underlying mechanisms, shaped through our evolutionary past. Shared enjoyment of the arts contributes greatly to social bonding in human societies. When we dance together, sing together, or watch plays and other visual displays of art, shared emotional responses contribute to feelings of community and closeness.

© Cengage Learning®

FIGURE 7.18

Body Language. One of the advantages of emotions is the ability to communicate nonverbally. Even with these simple stick figures, it is easy to interpret how each character feels.

We can identify further advantages of emotion by studying people whose emotional lives have been affected by brain damage. In Chapter 4, we reviewed the case of Phineas Gage, whose frontal lobe damage changed him from a responsible, well-liked member of the community to an impulsive, indecisive, and emotionally volatile individual who had difficulty keeping a job. More recently, Antonio Damasio (1994) described the case of a young man named Eliot, who had frontal lobe surgery to remove a tumor. Like Gage, Eliot maintained his intelligence and other skills after his surgery, with the notable exception of his ability to establish priorities. Damasio hypothesized that emotions provide a bridge to past experiences that can be used to set priorities like approach and avoidance. In the absence of normal feedback from the body that can be used to identify emotional states ("my heart is beating fast, so I must be scared"), Eliot can no longer use these past experiences to guide his current decisions.

The Biology of Emotion

In Chapter 4, we identified a number of nervous system structures that participate in our emotional lives. Emotional responses combine bottom-up processing, in which information from lower parts of the nervous system sends "alerts" to the cerebral cortex, with top-down processing, in which cortical executive functions such as attention and appraisal or judgment of a situation modify the activity of the lower structures.

The autonomic nervous system, which controls many activities of our glands and organs, participates in the general arousal associated with emotional states. In particular, activity of the sympathetic division of the autonomic nervous system is correlated with our fight-or-flight response to perceived danger. The autonomic nervous system is under the immediate control of the hypothalamus, a structure that also plays an important role in most motivated behavior.

The mind's priority for processing negative events has been described in earlier chapters. For example, in Chapters 1 and 5, we discussed how we are far more sensitive to bitter tastes, because these are often associated with poisons, than we are to sweet tastes, which are rarely life threatening.

Researchers have asked whether specific patterns of autonomic activity occur during particular emotional states. In an analysis of a large number of studies conducted over the last 50 years, autonomic measures did not reliably predict particular emotional states, such as happiness or sadness (Cacioppo, Berntson, Larsen, Poehlmann, & Ito, 2000). However, the analysis indicated that the autonomic responses associated with negative emotions generally appear to be stronger than those associated with positive emotions. Fear, with its rapid heartbeat and sweaty palms, provokes a more dramatic set of physical reactions than feelings of happiness.

In addition to the hypothalamus, several other subcortical structures, described in Chapter 4, participate in the regulation of emotion. Among these, the amygdala, the cingulate cortex, and the insula appear to play particularly important roles in our emotional lives. Other areas that play major roles in emotion include the basal ganglia and the cerebral cortex.

The Amygdala and the Insula

The amygdala and the **insula**, regions located within the fold at the junction of the frontal and temporal lobes, aid in the identification of emotional stimuli and the initiation of arousal in response to the perception of these stimuli.

insula Regions of cortex located at the junction of the frontal and temporal lobes.

One of the first clues to the importance of the amygdala to emotion resulted from an experiment conducted in 1939 in which researchers removed both temporal lobes, which include the amygdalae, from rhesus monkeys (Klüver & Bucy, 1939). After recovery, the normally hard-to-handle adult rhesus monkeys became tamer, and their emotions were less intense. They allowed themselves to be picked up and stroked and appeared to be relatively oblivious to stimuli that normally elicit intense fear, such as snakes. They made fewer fear-related grimaces and vocalizations.

Subsequent research has refined our understanding of the role of the amygdala. This structure acts to evaluate environmental stimuli for potential danger and coordinate appropriate responses (Schumann, Bauman, Machado, & Amaral, 2006). The activity of the amygdala changes when study participants look at faces expressing happiness or fear (Williams et al., 2006). As fearful expressions become more intense, activity in the amygdala increases as well. If the amygdala is damaged, animals typically respond inappropriately to danger. Rats with damaged amygdalae fail to learn to fear a tone or other stimulus that reliably predicts the onset of electric shock (LeDoux, Cicchetti, Xagoraris, & Romanski, 1990). Rhesus monkeys with lesioned amygdalae show less fear of rubber snakes and less restraint around unfamiliar monkeys, a potentially dangerous way of behaving in a species that enforces strict social hierarchies (Emery et al., 2001; Mason, Capitanio, Machado, Mendoza, & Amaral, 2006).

Insight into the role of the amygdala in humans has been provided by case studies in which disease has damaged this structure (see ● Figure 7.19). Patient S.M. experienced damage to both amygdalae because of a rare disease (Adolphs, Tranel, Damasio, & Damasio, 1994). Although S.M. can recognize the emotions of happiness, sadness, and disgust portrayed in photographs, she has selective difficulty identifying fear correctly (Adolphs, Tranel, Damasio, & Damasio, 1994, 1995). As shown in Figure 7.19, Patient S.M. has particular difficulty using information from the eye region of the face in judging emotion, although when she was instructed to pay attention to eyes, her performance improved (Adolphs et al., 2005; Adolphs, 2007). Individuals with autism spectrum disorder, discussed in Chapter 14, share Patient S.M.'s reluctance to make eye contact and difficulty identifying other people's emotions, especially fear. One of the most consistent biological correlates of autism spectrum disorder is abnormal development of the amygdala (Amaral, Schumann, & Nordahl, 2008). These findings suggest that the amygdala participates in both the active exploration of the social environment and the interpretation of the results of that exploration (Adolphs, 2007).

When the amygdala perceives danger, it initiates a hormonal cascade involving the pituitary gland and the adrenal glands that produces an increased release of neurochemicals in the brain, leading to an increase in overall arousal. We will discuss this process in greater detail in Chapter 16.

The amygdala is part of a tightly connected circuit that includes the frontal lobes of the cortex, the cingulate cortex (discussed in the next section), and the insula (see ● Figure 7.20). This circuit plays an important role in the identification and classification of emotional stimuli. The role of the insula in emotion was illustrated by an experiment in which people with damage to the insula were asked to rate pictures on a scale from very pleasant to very unpleasant and to indicate how arousing each picture was (Berntson et al., 2011). These participants showed an overall decrease both in their ratings of positivity or negativity and in their arousal ratings when compared to control participants. In contrast, people with damage to their amygdalae did not show deficits in assessing positivity and negativity. However, the people with damage to their amygdalae indicated less arousal in response to unpleasant pictures. These results suggest that the amygdala plays an important role in initiating arousal, particularly to

FIGURE 7.19

Amygdala Damage and the Perception of Emotion. People with amygdala damage, like Patient S.M., do not always use information about people's eyes to judge their emotions. Eyetracking shows (a) how a healthy control participant scans an emotional image and (b) how a person with amygdala damage might scan the same face. (c) For all emotions studied, Patient S.M. showed fewer eye fixations than normal controls (NC). *Source:* Adolphs, R., Gosselin, F., Buchanan, T.W., Tranel, D., Schyns, P., & Damasio, A.R. (2005). A mechanism for impaired fear recognition after amygdala damage. *Nature, 433,* 68-72.

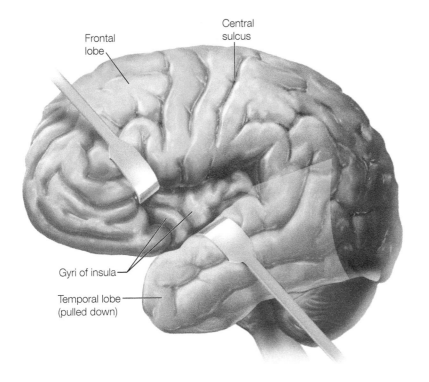

Frontal lobe

Central sulcus

Gyri of insula

Temporal lobe (pulled down)

© Argosy Publishing, Inc.

FIGURE 7.20

The Insula.

negative stimuli, while the insula more broadly helps us make the important distinction between positive and negative stimuli.

The Cingulate Cortex and the Basal Ganglia The cingulate cortex, shown in ● Figure 7.21, serves as a major gateway between the amygdala and other subcortical structures and the frontal areas of the cortex. The cingulate cortex is the target of a number of pathways communicating information about physical pain. The emotional quality of physical pain probably results from its processing at this level of the brain.

Cingulate cortex

Frontal lobe

Basal ganglia

Hypothalamus

Amygdala

Hippocampus

© Argosy Publishing, Inc.

FIGURE 7.21

The Cingulate Cortex and Basal Ganglia. The cingulate cortex forms circuits with the frontal cortex, the amygdala, and other subcortical structures involved with emotional processing. The basal ganglia are part of the brain's voluntary movement systems and help coordinate movement in response to assessments of emotion. The basal ganglia show particularly strong activation that correlates with the emotion of disgust.

The anterior cingulate cortex, along with the dorsomedial prefrontal cortex, participates in the more conscious appraisal of threat compared to the less conscious signals arising from the amygdala (Kalisch & Gerlicher, 2014). As we will see in Chapter 14, some individuals are unusually anxious. Worrying and catastrophizing (focusing on the worst possible outcomes) by anxious people involves exaggerated appraisals of threat. Unusually high levels of activation in the anterior cingulate cortex have been observed during episodes of catastrophizing and worry.

As we discussed in Chapter 4, the basal ganglia are large, subcortical structures that participate in the generation of voluntary movement. These structures coordinate movements in response to emotional stimuli. In particular, the basal ganglia show considerable activity in response to facial expressions of disgust (Phan, Wager, Taylor, & Liberzon, 2002). This finding is consistent with clinical observations of people with diseases that damage the basal ganglia, such as Huntington's disease. These people have particular difficulty recognizing facial expressions of disgust, although their recognition of other major emotional facial expressions appears intact (Hennenlotter et al., 2004). Strokes that damage the basal ganglia result in an overall reduction in the experience of emotional intensity (Paradiso, Ostedgaard, Vaidya, Ponto, & Robinson, 2013).

We often dislike our own photographs even when other people seem to think they look fine. Part of the problem is that we rarely see ourselves the way others do—we usually see ourselves in a mirror, which reverses our emotional expressions. Because our facial expressions are not symmetrical, because of the stronger role of the right hemisphere in emotion, that crooked smile looks wrong when we see it on the opposite side of our face.

The Cerebral Cortex and Emotion As we observed in Chapter 4, damage to the frontal lobes produces changes in emotional behavior. People often experience a reduction in fear and anxiety, which may contribute to their engagement in impulsive, risky behaviors. In these cases, the impaired ability to anticipate negative outcomes of behavior might prove disastrous.

The two cerebral hemispheres participate differently in the processing of emotion. Activity in the left hemisphere is correlated with the experience of positive emotions, while activity in the right hemisphere is correlated with negative emotions (Davidson & Irwin, 1999). As we observed previously in our discussion of the autonomic nervous system, our minds give higher priority to the negative in assessing an emotional stimulus. The right hemisphere usually processes emotion faster and more accurately than the left hemisphere (Bryden, 1982).

We can quickly demonstrate the role of the right hemisphere in the detection of negative emotion. As discussed in Chapters 4 and 5, the right and left hemispheres process different parts of the visual field. If you stare straight ahead at a focal point, all visual information to the right of the focal point will be processed by your left hemisphere, and all information to the left will be processed by your right hemisphere. Take a moment to look at the faces in ● Figure 7.22 and determine quickly whether they look happy or sad. Most people see the top image as happy and the bottom image as sad, although the pictures are just mirror images of each other. The expression on the left side of each face, processed by the right hemisphere, usually determines your judgment.

We do not appear to have "happy centers" or "sad centers" in the cerebral cortex. Instead, the experience of different emotions produces different patterns of cortical activation. When people are asked to recall a specific event from their past associated with the emotions of anger, sadness, fear, and happiness, brain imaging scans identify distinct patterns of activity for each emotion (Damasio et al., 2000). However, the same brain regions usually participate in more than one of these states.

FIGURE 7.22

The Right Hemisphere and the Assessment of Emotional Expression. These faces are mirror images of each other, but most people perceive them as expressing different emotions. Because the left half of the visual field is processed by the more emotional right hemisphere, the expression on the left side of the face is more likely to influence your judgment. Thus, the face on top will look happy, whereas the face on the bottom will look sad. For left-handed and ambidextrous people, these results might vary.

Expressing Emotion

Humans express emotion with their entire bodies. People who are feeling threatened or scared generally cross their arms and hunch forward. Angry, aggressive people typically lean forward, perhaps rising onto the balls of their feet, and raise their shoulders to appear larger and more intimidating. However, humans rely heavily on the face for expressing emotion.

The smiles, frowns, and other facial expressions we make are influenced by the way the brain controls the tiny muscles of our faces. These muscles receive input from the motor areas of the cerebral cortex, which control voluntary movement, as well as from subcortical areas,

© Cengage Learning®

This man has a tumor in his right primary motor cortex that prevents him from voluntarily smiling on the left side of his face when asked to do so, as shown in the photo on the left. In contrast, he is able to smile spontaneously and naturally in response to a genuine, involuntary emotion, as shown in the photo on the right. These observations support the hypothesis that voluntary and spontaneous emotional expressions are managed by different areas of the brain. *Source:* From Armin F. Haerer, *DeJong's The Neurologic Examination*, Fifth Edition, 1992 J. B. Lippincott Company. Fig. 13-4. http://lww.com

including the basal ganglia. The cortical input allows us to voluntarily "smile" for the camera. The subcortical input is responsible for more spontaneous expressions of emotion, such as laughing at a funny joke. It is possible to lose one type of input without affecting the other. The young man shown in the photo above has a tumor that affects his right motor cortex. When asked to smile voluntarily, his smile appears quite crooked because of the importance of the cortex in voluntary expression. When he smiles spontaneously to a joke, his smile appears more natural, because his subcortical areas can still react normally. People with Parkinson's disease, which damages the subcortical emotional pathways, show the opposite pattern. They may be unable to smile spontaneously in response to a joke, but they can smile voluntarily when asked to do so.

Do we learn how to express emotions, or are these behaviors built in? Darwin (1872) believed that human emotional expression had been shaped through evolution. If he is correct, we would expect humans in all parts of the world to share common means of expression. Some major emotional expressions appear to be universal across cultures (Keltner & Ekman, 2000). These "primary colors" of emotional expression include anger, sadness, happiness, fear, disgust, surprise, contempt, and embarrassment. Most people, regardless of the culture in which they live, have little difficulty correctly identifying these major emotional expressions.

Further support for a view of emotional expression as being innate comes from the predictable developmental course shown by young children. Infants' social smiles (as opposed to smiles resulting from gas, etc.) emerge near the same age (around 3 months), regardless of whether an infant can see faces or is born blind (Freedman, 1964). Monozygotic (identical) twins are more similar than dizygotic (fraternal) twins in the ages at which they first show fear of strangers. As shown in ● Figure 7.23, children raised in diverse cultures (African bush, urban Guatemala, rural Guatemala, and Israeli kibbutz) showed similar age-related distress at being separated from their mothers (Kagan, Kearsley, & Zelazo, 1978).

Developmental timelines for emotional behavior are also characteristic of nonhuman primate species. Rhesus monkeys raised in isolation performed typical fear responses when shown pictures of other monkeys engaging in threatening behaviors. The isolated monkeys demonstrated these fear responses at the same stage in development as monkeys raised in normal social conditions (Sackett, 1966).

These photos represent the possibly universal expressions of happiness, anger, surprise, disgust, sadness, and fear.

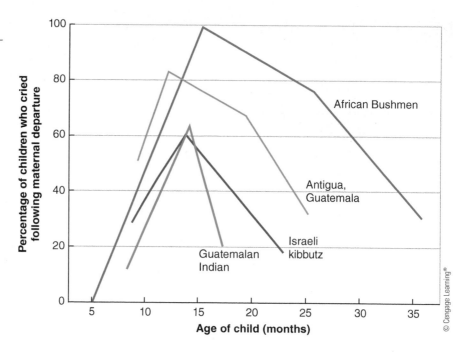

FIGURE 7.23

Infants' Separation Protests Occur at the Same Point in Development. Children in diverse cultures show the strongest emotional reactions to separation from their mothers around the same stage in development, suggesting that this emotional behavior has a biological origin.

Percentage of children who cried following maternal departure (y-axis)

Age of child (months) (x-axis)

African Bushmen

Antigua, Guatemala

Israeli kibbutz

Guatemalan Indian

© Cengage Learning®

Blind athlete

Sighted athlete

David Matsumoto carefully compared thousands of photographs from the 2004 Olympic and Paralympic Games and found that all competitors, sighted or blind, displayed the same expressions in response to winning or losing. These results suggest that, as Darwin suggested, some emotional expressions are innate to the human species.

display rule A cultural norm that specifies when, where, and how a person should express an emotion.

Other researchers point to the universality of words for different emotional states as evidence of emotion's common biological source. Words for emotions have been evaluated in a sample of 60 of the world's languages (Hupka, Lenton, & Hutchison, 1999). The findings indicate a similar approach to major emotions across many cultures. The exceptions, however, are also intriguing. The Japanese term *ijirashi* refers to a feeling that occurs when we see another person overcoming an obstacle. No equivalent term exists in English.

Although biology plays a significant role in emotional expression, there is no question that an individual's environment also has the ability to influence emotional behavior. We can learn to withhold or inhibit expressions of emotion. For example, medical personnel undergo training that affects their expression of disgust. Most patients would not appreciate a physician or nurse who said "oh, gross" during an examination. Military personnel learn to maintain their composure when a superior is yelling at them face to face, a skill that may be important when a soldier is captured by enemy forces.

Many cultures have **display rules**, or norms that specify when, where, and how a person should express emotion (see ● Figure 7.24). The reactions of Japanese and American university students were recorded as they watched emotional movies either alone or with a group of students they did not know (Ekman, Friesen, & Ellsworth, 1972). The Japanese students showed more emotion when alone than when in the group of strangers. In contrast, the American students were about as emotional in either case. If anything, Americans tend to show more emotion when in a group than when alone. Americans made more intense expressions of disgust in response to an odor when in a group than when they were alone (Jäncke & Kaufmann, 1994).

Display rules also differ for males and females. In the United States, a young boy who skins his knee at school is not supposed to cry. If he does cry, the response is typically one of disapproval rather than sympathy. A little girl in the same situation is likely to elicit consider-

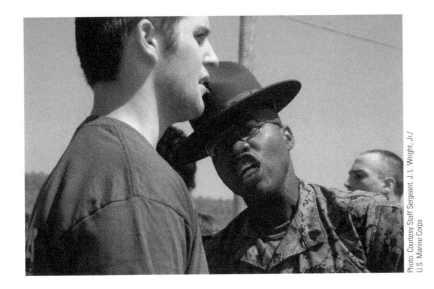

Photo: Courtesy Staff Sergeant. J. L. Wright. Jr./
U.S. Marine Corps

Despite the strong evolutionary and biological heritage
we have for spontaneous emotional expression, we can
learn to control our emotional expressions to fit a
situation. This Marine recruit is expected to remain
calm while his drill instructor applies a "correction."
This skill is believed to help military personnel maintain
composure in highly emotional situations.

Average suppression of emotional score

© 2016 Cengage Learning®

FIGURE 7.24

Cultures Vary in Suppression of Emotional Expression. Although cultures worldwide
are fairly similar in their emotional expressiveness, variations occur. Switzerland, with a
suppression score of 3.05, shows emotion most freely of all these countries, and Hong
Kong, with a suppression score of 4.72, shows the least emotion. *Source:* Adapted from
"Culture, Emotion Regulation, and Adjustment," by D. Matsumoto, S. H. Yoo, S. Nakagawa,
et al., 2008, *Journal of Personality and Social Psychology, 94*(6), 925–937.

able sympathy by crying. This example shows that significant differences in emotional expressiveness can result from socialization, and we should not be too quick to assume that observations of differences in adults are the result of biological processes.

In addition to biological and cultural influences on emotional expression, we can observe
significant individual differences. When young children are exposed to strong, novel stimuli,
such as the odor of alcohol on a swab, some react strongly to the stimuli while others appear
to ignore them. Still others show a moderate response to the stimuli (Kagan, 1997). As we will
see in Chapters 11 and 14, children who are highly responsive often develop into cautious,
anxious adults. In contrast, children who are relatively oblivious to stimulation may develop
into bold, fearless risk takers. If their insensitivity extends to social signals produced by others,
this lack of sensitivity to stimuli may lead to antisocial behavior. Psychopaths incarcerated for
murder show significantly reduced reactions to slides of pleasant, neutral, and unpleasant situations when compared to typical control participants (Herpertz et al., 2001).

Psychologist Jerome
Kagan described
individual differences
in emotionality
based on children's
responsiveness to the
environment, ranging
from the cautious
child to the bold.

Suzanne Tucker/Shutterstock.com

Liudmila P. Sundikova/Shutterstock.com

Although fake and genuine smiles look similar, we usually do a good job of distinguishing between them. Which of these smiles do you think is real? Which is fake?"

Interpreting Emotion

Human adults are quite accurate in their ability to read emotions. When research participants watched only 10 seconds of a videotaped interaction between a teacher and an off-camera student, they were able to judge whether the teacher liked the student with considerable accuracy (Babad, Bernieri, & Rosenthal, 1991). We might think we do a good job of hiding our feelings, but the subtleties of emotional expression often give us away. At the same time, our ability to distinguish between genuine and fake expressions, while good, is far from perfect (Ekman, Davidson, & Friesen, 1990; Frank & Ekman, 1993).

Individual differences in the ability to perceive the emotions of ourselves and others do occur. Twin studies demonstrate that individual differences in the ability to read emotional expression are heavily influenced by genetics (Anokhin, Golosheykin, & Heath, 2010). These differences form one of the key aspects of emotional intelligence (Mayer & Salovey, 1997). Emotional intelligence refers to our abilities to perceive, use, understand, and manage emotions. Individual differences in emotional intelligence predict the success of both work and personal relationships.

In addition to providing display rules, cultures influence interpretations of emotional expressions. Japanese and American study participants were asked to correctly identify emotional expressions with varying levels of intensity (Matsumoto et al., 2002). Individuals from both cultures identified the emotion being expressed with considerable accuracy, even at low levels of intensity. However, intensity was interpreted quite differently by the Japanese and the Americans. When emotional expression occurred at low intensities, Japanese participants assumed that people were feeling more than they were willing to express. In contrast, when emotional expression was highly intense, the American participants assumed that people were exaggerating their feelings.

A person's ability to read others' emotional expressions can be reduced by certain psychological disorders (see Chapter 14). Individuals with schizophrenia have normal abilities to process facial features but perform worse than typical controls on tasks requiring them to distinguish among facial expressions (Kohler et al., 2003; Schneider et al., 2006). People diagnosed with autism spectrum disorder and those with antisocial personality disorder have specific difficulties recognizing expressions of fear (Marsh & Blair, 2008).

Psychology as a Hub Science
Lie Detection and the Law

Even though we view emotional expression as a major means of communication, our abilities to read emotions are not perfect. Our legal system relies on finding the truth. Unfortunately, current polygraph methods are not admissible in court because of their poor record of accuracy (Kleinmuntz & Szucko, 1984). New technologies such as functional magnetic resonance imaging (fMRI) eventually might improve our ability to detect honesty, but further study is needed before they are used in court (see ● Figure 7.25). Until better technologies are available, what do psychologists know about lying that can help the legal system identify truthfulness and deception?

Lying is a difficult thing to do, especially in high-stakes situations in which levels of arousal are high. As a result of arousal, people betray their lying in predictable ways (Ekman, 1996). The liar may stumble verbally, adding "um" and "uh" while seeking to assemble a plausible lie. Inappropriate smiling and nervous laughter might reflect the person's high arousal. A person who is lying tends to stiffen the upper body, nodding the head less frequently and using fewer hand gestures than normal. In contrast to the reduced mobility of the upper body, the feet may start swinging. Many people also view an unwillingness to make eye contact as indicative of dishonesty. However, in many cultures, making eye contact is considered impolite, and failure to make eye contact should not be misinterpreted as dishonesty.

An excellent signal that someone is lying is the use of "scripted" stories, which are lacking in detail. People telling the truth add 20% to 30% more detail to a story compared to liars (Colwell, Hiscock-Anisman, Memon, Rachel, & Colwell, 2007). Another reliable way to identify lying is to ask people to tell their story backward in time (Fisher & Geiselman, 2010). A person telling the truth can simply move from one event to the next, but constructing a false story backward quickly overwhelms a person's memory for details. ●

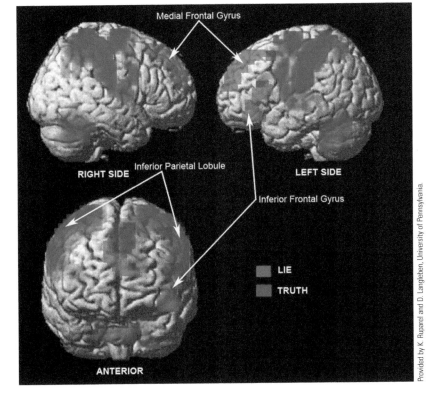

Medial Frontal Gyrus

RIGHT SIDE   Inferior Parietal Lobule   LEFT SIDE

Inferior Frontal Gyrus

■ LIE

■ TRUTH

ANTERIOR

Provided by K. Ruparel and D. Langleben, University of Pennsylvania.

FIGURE 7.25

Will fMRI Be Used to Detect Lies? During a standardized task known as the modified Guilty Knowledge Test which is used to assess deception, participants' brains showed significantly different activation when lying compared to when they told the truth. Red areas represent brain regions that are more active when the participant is lying, and blue areas represent brain regions that are more active when the participant is telling the truth. So far, laboratory studies have used small numbers of law-abiding participants rather than real criminals and concrete tasks like reporting which playing card is being held (e.g., ace of spades). It is unknown whether this technology will advance to the point where results will be admitted in a court of law.

(a) Perceived stimulus → Specific physical responses → Subjective feeling

(b) Perceived stimulus → Physical responses / Subjective feeling

(c) Perceived stimulus → General arousal → Assessment of surroundings → Subjective feeling

FIGURE 7.26

Three Classic Theories of Emotion.
Each of these theories of emotion—
(a) the James–Lange theory, (b) the
Cannon–Bard theory, and (c) the
Schachter–Singer two-factor theory—
attempts to explain how physical
responses and subjective feelings
occur when we experience an
emotion.

© 2016 Cengage Learning®

James–Lange theory A theory of
emotion that proposes that physical
sensations lead to subjective feelings.
catharsis A theory of emotion that
views emotion as a reservoir that fills
up and spills over; it predicts that expressing an emotion will reduce
arousal.

Theories of Emotion

Several major theories of emotion attempt to describe the relationship between physical sensations and subjective feelings
during the experience of an emotion. In other words, what are
the connections between those butterflies in your stomach and
the knowledge that you're feeling afraid? These theories of emotion are similar in many ways to efforts to explain perception in
Chapter 5. Some attempt to work from the bottom up (from
physical sensation to cognitive appraisal), while others work
from the top down (from appraisal to physical sensation).

The James–Lange Theory of Emotion Working independently, William James and Danish physiologist Carl Lange
developed similar descriptions of the relationship between
physical sensations and subjective feelings in emotion (James,
1890; Lange, 1885/1912). Consequently, our first theory, the
James–Lange theory, bears the names of both men (see ●
Figure 7.26).

James believed that emotions could arise from several sources, including the recall from
memory of events that were emotional. However, his greatest interest was in emotions "that
have a distinct bodily expression" (James, 1884, p. 189). At the core of the James–Lange theory
is the idea that this class of emotions is the result of a sequence of events. Once the individual
perceives a stimulus, such as a grizzly bear, that person experiences a physiological response.
This physiological response is subsequently interpreted by the individual, giving rise to a conscious awareness of a subjective feeling. The James–Lange theory depends on the assumption
that physical states related to each type of feeling (sadness and happiness, for instance) are
highly distinct from one another. The theory also assumes that we are capable of correctly associating and labeling these distinct physical states as separate feelings. As James wrote, "We
feel sorry because we cry, angry because we strike, afraid because we tremble" (1890, p. 1006).

James's statement may seem counterintuitive to you at first glance. Shouldn't a good cry
make us feel less sad, not more? Many people also believe that holding anger inside instead of
expressing it somehow makes feelings of anger build up and become worse. These "commonsense" notions support the concept of **catharsis**. According to this approach, emotions are
viewed as filling an emotional reservoir. When the reservoir fills up, there is a possibility that
the emotion will spill over in a less controlled manner. For example, we talk about a "buildup
of hostility or anger" that somehow overflows, producing a more extreme response than is
warranted by the situation. Catharsis theorists recommend that we avoid this buildup by regularly expressing our emotions. In other words, it might be better to express some anger regularly than to repress your anger and "explode."

Catharsis and the implications of the James–Lange theory are contradictory. One suggests
that expressing an emotion reduces that feeling, while the other argues that expressing an
emotion leads to the subjective feeling. Which is correct? If we are feeling sad, does having a
good cry make us feel better or more aware of our sadness?

One clue to our dilemma comes from an experiment in which participants were directed
to make specific movements of the face (Levenson, Ekman, & Friesen, 1990). For example,
they might be instructed to raise their eyebrows and form their mouth into the shape of an O.
They were not informed that they were to make any particular facial expression, nor were they
allowed to view their face in a mirror. They did, however, report "feeling" the emotion they
had portrayed; you might have experienced a feeling of surprise if you followed the same directions. This result is consistent with the notion that expressing an emotion leads to the
subjective feeling, rather than reducing it in ways predicted by catharsis theories. This experiment also supports the James–Lange approach by suggesting that feedback from the body
helps us consciously determine the state of our emotions.

One of the more dramatic examples challenging catharsis theory is the Maori *haka*. Traditional Maori warriors of New Zealand prepared for battle by performing ritual grimaces,
vocalizations, and battle moves. In similar ways, athletes frequently engage in pregame rituals

or "psyching up." A contemporary rugby team, the New Zealand All Blacks, uses the traditional *haka* of the players' homeland to prepare for games. Not only do these performances contribute to the physical and emotional preparation for participation in a rather violent sport, but they no doubt intimidate the opposing team as well.

One implication of the James–Lange theory is that we might be able to influence our subjective feelings by changing our physical sensations. By appearing to be happy, we might begin to feel happier. Another practical outcome of this approach is the impact of modeling facial expression in the development of empathy. The early back-and-forth imitations of facial expressions by adults and infants may contribute to the capacity to read others' emotions. The use of imitation to assess the emotions of others continues into adulthood. When students are asked to determine the emotions expressed in the photos on page 261 during a classroom presentation, it is not uncommon to see some individuals spontaneously copy the facial expression in question to identify it correctly.

There is some evidence that suggests we may not be as good at reading our physical states as the James–Lange theory requires us to be. One experiment that challenged our ability to distinguish correctly among the physical states of different emotions was carried out in Capilano Canyon, located in British Columbia (Dutton & Aron, 1974). Capilano Canyon may be crossed at one of two locations. The first crossing involves a 450-foot-long bridge with low handrails, suspended about 230 feet above rocks and rapids. Farther upstream, the canyon may be crossed on a solid wooden bridge that is less frightening. In the study, an attractive female experimenter approached single men crossing one of the two bridges. After completing a short interview, the experimenter gave each man her telephone number, in case he had further questions about the experiment. Not only did the men on the frightening bridge include more sexual content in their interviews, but they were about 4 times as likely to telephone the female researcher later.

The results of this study suggest that its participants were not very good at discriminating the physical sensations associated with fear and sexual arousal. We can assume that the attractiveness of the female would be constant, suggesting that the setting in which she was seen largely accounted for the differences in sexual content in interviews and the likelihood of seeking further contact with her. One might speculate that similar mistakes underlie the popularity of horror films and amusement parks with impossibly high roller coasters as dating activities. Scare your date to death, and he or she may interpret feelings of fear as love. These results suggest that in some circumstances, we might not be as good at interpreting our physical sensations as predicted by the James–Lange theory.

The Cannon–Bard Theory of Emotion

Walter Cannon disagreed with the James–Lange theory and proposed his own theory, which was later modified by Philip Bard (Bard, 1934; Cannon, 1927). The product of these two men's work is known as the **Cannon–Bard theory**. The James–Lange theory proposes a sequence of events, from physical sensations to

Consistent with the James–Lange theory of emotion, the physical expression of an emotion might lead to subjective feelings. Traditional Maori warriors prepared for battle by performing a *haka*. The New Zealand All Blacks rugby team also uses the *haka* before a game. The James–Lange theory would predict that these men would feel more aggressive after performing the *haka*.

Cannon–Bard theory A theory of emotion featuring the simultaneous and independent occurrence of physical sensations and subjective feelings during an emotional experience.

subjective feeling, but the Cannon–Bard theory proposes that both factors occur simultaneously and independently.

How are these theories different? Let's assume that you are innocently reading your textbook in your room when a bear walks in the door. According to the James–Lange theory, the sight of the bear would immediately set off physical sensations that you would then cognitively interpret as fear. According to the Cannon–Bard theory, the sight of the bear would immediately and simultaneously trigger a subjective feeling of fear ("whoa, there's a bear in my room") and physical sensations (probably the autonomic nervous system's fight-or-flight response in this example). Unlike the James–Lange theory, the Cannon–Bard theory does not assume that the experience of a subjective feeling depends on physical sensations.

The Cannon–Bard theory fares somewhat better in explaining the Capilano Canyon results. Cannon and Bard would be comfortable with the notion that fear and sexual arousal would produce similar physical sensations and that study participants may simply have erred in their cognitive assessment of the situation. Instead of saying, "I'm really scared because I'm on this bridge," the participants would say, "I think this interviewer is very attractive." According to this model, a person's cognitive assessments of an emotional situation work independently of any physical sensations that might occur.

Connecting to Research

Botox and the Ability to Read the Emotions of Others

BOTOX, A DEACTIVATED FORM of the same toxin that causes botulism poisoning from spoiled food, helps people with neurological disorders of movement, but it is more commonly used for cosmetic purposes. Botox reduces wrinkling by paralyzing the small muscles that are used in facial expressions. The ability of Botox to prevent facial movement provides an interesting test for the James–Lange theory. Without feedback from our facial expressions, can we identify our own emotions? Without the ability to imitate the facial expressions of others, can we still identify how they're feeling? These questions were scientifically investigated by Neal and Chartrand (2011).

The Question: How would increasing and decreasing the ability to move facial muscles affect participants' judgments of the emotions of others?

METHODS

In a first experiment, 31 female participants were recruited from cosmetic surgery clinics. Although 16 participants had been treated with Botox, and the other 15 had been treated with a dermal filler material, which does not restrict the movement of facial muscles. Participants viewed photographs of eyes and the surrounding area and were asked to choose which of four emotional adjectives (happy, sad, and so on) best fit the expression they saw (see ● Figure 7.27). In a second experiment, a gel that forced participants to put more effort into their facial movements was placed on the faces of half of a group of 95 participants and on the arms of the other half as a control. Participants completed the same test of identification of emotion as before, along with two control tests: identifying emotion in voices, which is unlikely to be affected by facial expression, and a set of arithmetic questions.

RESULTS

In Experiment 1, the Botox group performed significantly more poorly on the identification of emotions task than the control group that had received the dermal filler instead of Botox. In Experiment 2, participants with the gel placed on the face that made them work harder to copy facial expressions performed better than those with the gel on their arms.

Actress Rachel Weisz, star of *The Mummy* and *The Bourne Legacy*, is not a fan of Botox. She told an interviewer, "Acting is all about expression; why would you want to iron out a frown?"

The Schachter–Singer Two-Factor Theory Stanley Schachter and Jerome Singer proposed a two-factor theory of emotion. Schachter and Singer (1962) believed that each emotional experience begins with an appraisal of our physical sensations. Because these reactions can be similar among emotional states (fear and sexual arousal on the Capilano Canyon bridge), they suggested that interpreting these states requires another step. Emotional arousal signals us to make a conscious, cognitive appraisal of our circumstances, which then allows us to identify the emotion we're experiencing. Physical sensations may lead to several interpretations, based on the way an individual assesses a situation.

Returning to our example of the bear entering your room, we can see how the **Schachter–Singer two-factor theory** differs from the James–Lange and Cannon–Bard approaches. For Schachter and Singer, the sight of the bear would initiate a general state of arousal. To identify the source of your arousal, you would assess your situation, attribute your arousal to the presence of a bear in your room, and identify your feelings as fear (with considerable accuracy, we would assume).

Schachter and Singer (1962) directly tested this approach by injecting volunteers with epinephrine (adrenalin), which causes a high level of arousal. The participants had been told that they were getting an injection of a vitamin and that their vision would be tested as soon as another volunteer arrived to participate in the experiment. The second volunteer was actually an actor employed by the researchers. In half of the trials, the actor behaved in a happy,

Schachter–Singer two-factor theory A theory of emotion in which general arousal leads to assessment, which in turn leads to subjective feelings.

CONCLUSIONS

Both experiments support the idea that feedback from facial expressions of emotion influences the ability to identify emotional states in other people. The participants in the first experiment who used Botox had less facial mobility than the participants who had used the dermal filler. The lack of facial mobility caused by Botox appears to have interfered with the participants' ability to accurately assess another person's emotional state as indicated by a facial expression. In the second experiment, making the muscles work harder to imitate a facial expression by applying a restrictive gel actually improved the participants' ability to identify the facial expressions of others. These results are quite consistent with the James–Lange theory's emphasis on feedback from the body as important to the subjective identification of emotion, not just in ourselves but also in other people. These results suggest that an important side effect of Botox might be a reduction in social competence and empathy because of an inability to read the emotions of other people correctly. ●

FIGURE 7.27

Botox Reduces the Ability to Identify Facial Expressions in Others. Following treatment for wrinkles with either Botox or an injected dermal filler (Restylane), study participants were asked to identify the emotional expression of faces presented on a computer screen. The dermal filler group was significantly better than the Botox group at correctly identifying the emotions. This result suggests that by reducing the ability to imitate another person's facial expressions, Botox limits a person's perception of the emotions of other people. *Source:* Adapted from "Embodied Emotion Perception: Amplifying and Dampening Facial Feedback Modulates Emotion Perception Accuracy," by D. T. Neal and T. L. Chartrand, 2011, *Social Psychological and Personality Science, 2*(6), 673–678, doi:10.1177/1948550611406138.

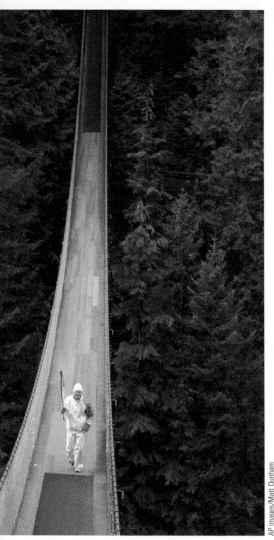

AP Images/Matt Dunham

silly manner; in the other half, he acted angry and stomped out of the room. The results supported a role for cognitive appraisal of the environment in the identification of emotion. Participants who were exposed to the happy actor rated themselves as feeling happy, while participants exposed to the angry actor felt more negative. Importantly, when the participants were accurately informed that they were getting a drug that produced arousal instead of a vitamin, the behavior of the actor did not influence their assessment of the situation. Instead, they attributed their feelings to the drug.

A later attempt to replicate Schachter and Singer's study did not succeed (Marshall & Zimbardo, 1979). As we discussed in Chapter 2, a failure to replicate a study casts serious doubts on the results. Nonetheless, Schachter and Singer's theory has provided considerable insight into how we identify our subjective feelings. Schachter and Singer account easily for the Capilano Canyon bridge study. Once aroused by being on the scary bridge, the male subjects assessed their circumstances and attributed their feelings to sexual attraction. Additional support is provided by research that demonstrates that arousal produced by one emotion can transfer to and intensify a second emotion. People who have just exercised (producing physiological arousal) are more likely to become angry or sexually aroused when exposed to relevant stimuli (Reisenzein, 1983).

Contemporary Approaches Each of these classic theories offers important insights into our experience of emotion, yet none definitively resolves our original question regarding the relationship between physical sensations and subjective feelings. The same patterns of physical activity may occur during a variety of emotions, and a single emotion may be associated with a variety of physical states. That mistakes can and do happen is certain. Nonetheless, we seem to manage quite well at interpreting our emotions in most situations.

A more contemporary model reconciles the debate regarding the impact of physical sensations on subjective feelings (Cacioppo, Berntson, & Klein, 1992). The **somatovisceral afference model of emotion (SAME)** begins with a recognition that physical responses to a stimulus can range from quite specific to quite general. For example, the physical sensations associated with disgust can be more precise than the physical sensations associated with pride.

The initial degree of specificity of the physical response leads to different cognitive processing. A highly specific physical response leads to unambiguous recognition of a subjective feeling. This is the situation that appeared most interesting to James. A bear walks in, you react physically, and you know you're scared. At the other extreme, instead of specific physical responses, a situation might produce general arousal, which requires significant cognitive processing and evaluation. For example, a valedictorian giving a graduation speech might not understand her arousal until she sees her parents and other members of the audience clapping and realizes the emotion she is feeling is pride. This scenario is closest to that proposed by Schachter and Singer (1962).

SAME provides middle ground between the James–Lange and the Schachter and Singer theories. If a physical response is only partially specific, an ambiguous message is sent forward that is clarified by the presence of additional cues or information (see ● Figure 7.28). The model correctly predicts that emotional responses range from immediate to delayed, based on the amount of cognitive processing that is required. Emotions that are associated with a precise set of physical responses, like fear, occur quickly, but emotions that are associated with more general arousal, like pride, occur relatively slowly.

Contemporary cognitive approaches to emotion place little emphasis on the physical correlates that are featured so prominently in the classic theories. Instead, these approaches emphasize the role of **appraisals**, or the detection and assessment of stimuli with relevance for well-being, in eliciting emotion (Moors, Ellsworth, Scherer, & Frijda, 2013). For example, Ellsworth (1994) expresses some frustration with the approach taken by James when she says, "Bears do not automatically cause us to run or tremble." Instead, the interpretation of the stimulus, the bear in this case, forms the critical starting point for the emotional cascade. Appraisal theory further assumes that interpretation is a continuous process rather than a single

John Stibbard, son of the owner of the Capilano Suspension Bridge, poses on the bridge with the Olympic torch after completing his leg of the torch run in preparation for the 2010 Winter Olympics in Vancouver, Canada.

somatovisceral afference model of emotion (SAME) A model of emotion in which a range of physical sensations from precise to general requires varying degrees of cognitive processing prior to subjective feelings.
appraisal The detection and assessment of stimuli that are relevant to personal well-being.

decision about a stimulus (Ellsworth, 1991; Moors et al., 2013). For example, attention may be aroused by some change in the environment. A recognizable emotion has not yet occurred, and if the appraisal of the stimulus determines it to be of no significance, arousal returns to baseline. However, if the stimulus is found to have positive or negative value to the individual making the appraisal (a source of food or a predator, for instance), feelings and physiological responses change yet again.

An emphasis on appraisal as a starting point for emotion may help us account for the vast range of emotional reactions that individuals might have to the same event (Moors et al., 2013). One person may view material wealth as essential to happiness, whereas another may view successful relationships with others as a primary goal. These different cognitive patterns should produce different emotional responses to the same event. A letter to an advice columnist described a situation in which a man's wife had wrecked his expensive antique automobile in a serious accident ("Dear Abby," 2006). Our first person, who values money, is likely to respond with dismay at the loss of the expensive car. Our second person, who values relationships, is likely to be happy that his beloved wife survived the accident in one piece.

Appraisal theory, then, brings us full circle in regards to the content of this chapter. Our motivations and goals provide the context in which we appraise the significance of a situation or event for our personal well-being. Depending on how we assign value to the event, we will react with the cognitions, physical responses, actions, and feelings that characterize emotions.

Ian Paterson/Alamy

FIGURE 7.28

The Somatovisceral Afference Model of Emotion (SAME). This ambiguous image (you should find yourself alternating between seeing a young woman and seeing an old woman) can serve as a model for how the mind processes a range of emotional situations, from simple to complex. If we look at a simple image, we need little cognitive assessment to respond appropriately. As images become more complex, we require increasing amounts of cognitive assessment before we respond. Processing the simple emotion of fear is similar to processing an unambiguous image. Processing more complex, ambiguous emotions, like pride, requires more cognitive assessment, just like viewing this ambiguous image does.

Asier Romero/Shutterstock.com

Monkey Business Images/Shutterstock

According to appraisal theory, a person who values wealth and a person who values family might experience different emotions in response to the same event.

Interpersonal Relationships

The Emotional Perspective

What Is the Impact of Positive and Negative Interactions on Relationships?

The idea that good relationships are characterized by positive emotional interactions and that bad relationships feature many negative emotions sounds obvious. However, it is unrealistic to think that happy couples never experience conflict. They do, but the way they fight can have a big influence on the likelihood that they will stay together.

Psychologist John Gottman uses a combination of heart rate, facial expression, and analysis of the way people talk about their relationships to each other and to others to predict whether a relationship will last (Gottman, 2011). He is correct more than 90% of the time. One of Gottman's key observations is the ratio of positive to negative comments in a couple's discussion of a problem. Happy couples make 5 times more positive comments about each other and their relationship during these discussions (e.g., we laugh a lot versus we never have fun).

In several places in this textbook, we have emphasized how the human mind is skewed toward the negative, like noticing bitter tastes over sweet. This slant suggests that it is all too easy to focus on your partner's negative qualities, which will lead to negative emotions and conflict. If we put our relationships on evolutionary cruise control, the ratio of positive to negative comments might drop to a point where the relationship is in danger. Maintaining a positive outlook on your partner requires attention and work.

Try observing how people you know talk about their significant others (or watch your own behavior, if you're brave enough). Are you achieving Gottman's 5:1 ratio of positive to negative comments? ●

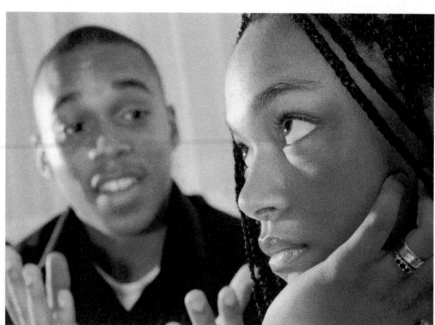

Research by John Gottman shows that happy couples do experience negative emotions with each other. However, for every negative incident, they tend to experience 5 times as many positive emotional interactions.

Summary 7.2 Theories of Emotion

Name of theory		Major features
James–Lange theory		Specific physical sensations lead to an identification of the subjective feeling.
Cannon–Bard theory		Physical sensations and subjective feelings occur simultaneously and independently.
Schachter–Singer two-factor theory		General arousal, not specific physical states, leads to an appraisal of our surroundings, which allows us to identify our subjective feelings.
SAME		Different emotional states produce physical responses ranging from specific to ambiguous. Ambiguous responses require more appraisal than specific responses before a subjective feeling is identified.
Appraisal theory		Emotions begin with the detection and assessment of stimuli that are relevant to personal well-being.

Credits: Top Row. © 2016 Cengage Learning®. Second Row. © 2016 Cengage Learning®. Third Row. © 2016 Cengage Learning®. Fourth Row. Ian Paterson/Alamy. Bottom Row. Asier Romero/Shutterstock.com; Monkey Business Images/Shutterstock.com.

KEY TERMS The Language of Psychological Science

Be sure you can define these terms and use them correctly.

achievement motivation, p. 250
affiliation, p. 249
anorexia nervosa, p. 241
appraisal, p. 270
binge-eating disorder, p. 242
body mass index (BMI), p. 238
bulimia nervosa, p. 241
Cannon–Bard theory, p. 267
catharsis, p. 266
display rule, p. 262
drive, p. 233

drive reduction, p. 233
emotion, p. 232
extrinsic reward, p. 234
glucose, p. 236
homeostasis, p. 233
incentive, p. 234
insula, p. 257
intrinsic reward, p. 234
James–Lange theory, p. 266
leptin, p. 274
motivation, p. 232

satiety, p. 237
Schachter–Singer two-factor theory, p. 269
self-actualization, p. 253
set point, p. 233
sexual orientation, p. 247
somatovisceral afference model of emotion (SAME), p. 270
testosterone, p. 244
Yerkes–Dodson law, p. 256

8 The Adaptive Mind

Learning

ALTHOUGH YOU MAY NOT HAVE HAD AN opportunity to learn to surf, we're assuming that in your role as a student you are familiar with the process of learning. Knowing how to learn, however, is different from understanding how and why learning occurs. What is going on in the minds of the people in the small photo as they learn to do something new?

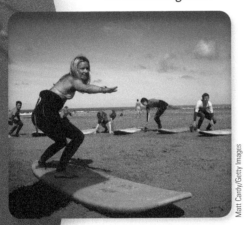

Matt Cardy/Getty Images

A behavior like learning to surf is complicated, so scientists interested in learning often begin their examinations using animals that are simpler than humans, observing as they learn to do behaviors simpler than surfing. Scientists have zoomed in to observe changes that happen in single neurons, like the image on the left, found in simple animals like the *Aplysia californica* sea slug. The sea slug is capable of learning to anticipate an electric shock that happens every time it is touched, and it demonstrates this knowledge by protectively withdrawing its body in response to touch before the shock is administered. Because the slug has such a simple nervous system compared to ours, scientists have been able to identify which neurons are involved in this learning and to describe the changes in a neuron's functioning that make new behaviors—like withdrawing prior to shock—possible.

Is it possible that human learning has anything in common with learning in slugs? The answer to this question is "yes and no." Zooming out, we will see that some types of learning are common across animals with vastly different evolutionary histories and complexities, like humans and sea slugs. In other cases, we see interactions between nature and nurture. Experience, or nurture, frequently interacts with the nature of the organism exposed to the experience. You can talk to your kitten and to an infant, but only the infant will respond to this experience by learning to understand what you're saying and how to reply. Each species brings unique and innate building blocks of learning, accumulated over many generations, to any given situation.

Zooming out still farther, we will see how learning in groups can often be different from learning as an individual. Even the lowly sea slug learns differently when alone than when in a group of fellow slugs. Slugs in isolation seem to have a terrible time learning to stop trying to eat food that is too tough to swallow (Schwarz & Susswein, 1992), but they learn this task easily when in the presence of other slugs (Susswein, Schwarz, & Feldman, 1986). Apparently, the slugs can communicate with one another using pheromones, and the presence or absence of these chemicals has a powerful effect on

◀ Learning something new produces structural changes in neurons.

Argosy Publishing, Inc.

their ability to learn (Schwarz, Blumberg, & Susswein, 1998). The people on the previous page who are learning to surf in a group might have had a different experience if they were taking individual lessons.

Animals respond to the environment with reflexes, instinctive behaviors, and learned behaviors. Animals, like this "ferocious" kitten, use a reflex, piloerection, to make themselves look bigger. The evolutionary purpose of this behavior is to appear so menacing that they can avoid conflict.

Jane Burton/Dorling Kindersley/Getty Images

Learning Objectives

1. Compare and contrast reflexes, instincts, and learned behaviors.

2. Identify the components of a classical conditioning experiment and discuss major phenomena and applications related to classical conditioning.

3. Describe the major components of operant conditioning, and distinguish operant conditioning from classical conditioning.

4. Analyze the processes that result in observational learning.

5. Discuss the interactions between learned processes and animals' preparation to learn in species-specific ways.

6. Apply learning principles and terminology to everyday situations and problems.

How Do Animals Use Reflexes, Instincts, and Learning to Respond to Their Environments?

Animals, including ourselves, behave in response to their environments. Behavior can take the form of either externally observable actions or internal processes, such as emotions, thoughts, and physiological responses. These behaviors fall into three broad categories: reflexes, instincts, and learned behaviors. Each type of behavior has its role in helping us survive but differs dramatically in its ability to adapt to a changing world.

Reflexes are inevitable, involuntary responses to stimuli. In casual conversations, we sometimes attribute a baseball player's high batting average or our ability to step on the brake in time to avoid an automobile accident to great reflexes, but in fact, these examples involve learned behaviors that have become fast and automatic as a result of lots of practice. Nobody is born knowing how to hit baseballs or use the brakes of a car, so these behaviors do not meet our definition of a reflex.

Goose bumps are what is left of piloerection in humans. These signals of arousal are remnants of a time when we had enough hair to make this an easily noticeable response.

In humans, most reflexes are controlled by nervous system circuits located in the spinal cord and brainstem, described in Chapter 4. Your physician checks one of these reflexes by tapping your knee with a hammer. The tap stretches your leg muscles, and the stretch is sensed by neurons in the spinal cord. Motor neurons in the spinal cord tell your thigh muscle to contract to compensate for the stretching, and your foot kicks out. No experience with knee-tapping is necessary to produce this behavior, nor can you voluntarily prevent it. By the time your brain realizes your knee was tapped, you have already reacted. Other reflexes pull our bodies away from painful stimuli, such as when we step on a tack or piece of glass or touch a hot stove, turn our heads in the direction of loud sounds, and help us stand upright and walk.

Reflexes produce fast, reliable responses that promote your welfare. If you've ever touched a hot stovetop and found yourself pulling your hand back seemingly before you even knew what you had done, you know at least one benefit of reflexes. Reflexes have the disadvantages of being inflexible. For example, we respond to stress or cold by forming goose bumps, or bumps on the skin. This reflex appears to be left over from when our species had more body hair. Goose bumps raise each strand of hair, which in times of stress makes an individual look larger, scaring off predators or competitors, and, in response to cold, traps more insulating air near the skin. As humans lost most of their body hair over time, the advantages of this reflex decreased, but we still retain the behavior.

Instincts, also called fixed action patterns, are inborn patterns of behavior elicited by environmental stimuli. Once they begin, instinctive behaviors run to completion. Instincts share reflexes' reliability and lack of dependence on experience, but the resulting behaviors are more complex, requiring many more neurons than the number involved in a reflexive kick of your foot. Instinctive behaviors occur in the mating and parenting behaviors of many species (Tinbergen, 1951). For example, a mother dog instinctively licks clean her first litter of pups immediately after birth. An example of a human instinct is contagious yawning, or yawning in response to seeing others yawn (Provine, 1986). Although yawning has multiple functions, including cooling the brain (Gallup & Eldakar, 2012), contagious yawning might be related to empathy, helping to synchronize the arousal state of whole groups. Children with autism spectrum disorder, a psychological disorder in which empathy is distinctly impaired, fail to show contagious yawning (Senju et al., 2007).

Although some scientists disagree, contagious yawning might represent an instinct for a number of species, including our own. Puppies over the age of 7 months were susceptible to contagious yawning in response to seeing humans yawn.

Psychologists define learning as a relatively permanent change in behavior (or the capacity for behavior) due to experience. The core of this definition is the phrase "change in behavior." After learning, we can do something new that we couldn't do before, providing us with enormous advantages in surviving a changing world. Not all changes in behavior are because of learning, however. Our behavior changes as we mature from infancy through adulthood, as we will see in Chapter 11. Behavior can be changed by brain damage or by having a psychological disorder. So our definition of learning limits the changes we consider to be learned to those that result from experience. The other qualification in our definition,

reflex An inevitable, involuntary response to stimuli.
instinct An inborn pattern of behavior elicited by environmental stimuli; also known as a fixed action pattern.
learning A relatively permanent change in behavior or the capacity for behavior due to experience.

"relatively permanent," prevents the labeling of brief or unstable changes—such as when we experience different moods or suffer from an illness—as learning. How permanent learning is will be discussed in Chapter 9.

Twentieth-century psychology was dominated by the beliefs that, compared to other animals, humans have relatively few reflexes and instincts and that most human behavior results from learning. William James argued that humans have more instincts than other animals, although we are usually unaware of them (James, 1887). According to James, our behavior simply appears more complex and thoughtful because we often face the need to choose among competing instincts. Animals with fewer instincts experience fewer conflicts, so their behavior appears to be more automatic and less thoughtful.

James's approach to instinct and learning is echoed in the writings of contemporary evolutionary psychologists, who argue for an innate learning instinct that prepares humans to learn certain things in particular ways based on our evolutionary history (Cosmides & Tooby, 1997). Cognitive psychologists also revive the flavor of James by suggesting that learned behavior resulting from experience can look automatic and instinctive (Bargh & Chartrand, 1999). For example, prejudice toward a group of people requires learning, but prejudiced behavior often occurs without much conscious awareness, as we explore further in Chapter 13. People who consciously believe that they are without prejudice toward members of a minority group nonetheless sit farther from an individual from that group than from members of the majority (Dovidio & Gaertner, 2005).

The interactions between instinct and learning also provide an explanation for another observation: experience has different effects at different times in an organism's life span, as we discuss further in Chapter 11. We do not attempt to teach philosophy to 2-year-old children because they are not yet capable of learning this material. Imprinting, the tendency of young animals to bond with and follow an adult, depends on timing. Birds that see a human immediately upon hatching follow that person everywhere, but birds that first see a human after having been hooded for their first few days out of the shell attempt to flee in terror (James, 1887).

Mark Bridger/Shutterstock.com

Elena Rooraid/PhotoEdit

Imprinting, in which a young organism bonds with adults, provides an example of how experience has different effects at different times in the life span. These baby swans are following their parents because the parents were the first things they saw when they hatched. After a delay of a day or two, exposure to the parents would not lead to following. If the baby swans saw a human experimenter instead of their parents upon hatching, they would follow the human instead.

Organisms usually show imprinting by the time they are mobile, which for swans means the first day of life but for human children means closer to 1 year. Because these children have imprinted on their primary caregivers instead of their preschool teacher, the teacher needs a bit of technological help to encourage his charges to follow him on a walk.

What Are the Three Main Types of Learning?

Learning is traditionally divided into three categories: associative, nonassociative, and observational. More than one type of learning can operate simultaneously in the same situation.

Associative learning occurs when we form associations, or connections, among stimuli, behaviors, or both. Associative learning helps us to predict the future based on past experience. In other words, if A happens, then B is likely to follow. The ability to anticipate the future provides enormous survival advantages, because through it animals gain time to prepare. Psychologists who study learning describe two types of associative learning: classical conditioning and operant conditioning. In **classical conditioning**, we form associations between pairs of stimuli that occur sequentially in time. If a child sees a bee for the first time and then gets stung, the child forms a connection between seeing bees and the pain of being stung. The next time a bee flies by, the child is likely to feel quite frightened. In **operant conditioning**, we form associations between behaviors and their consequences. If you study hard, you will get good grades. We will discuss each of these forms of associative learning in more detail in later sections.

Nonassociative learning involves changes in the magnitude of responses to a single stimulus rather than the formation of connections between stimuli. Two important types of nonassociative learning are habituation and sensitization. **Habituation** reduces our reactions to repeated experiences that have already been evaluated and found to be unchanging and harmless. For example, you might sleep better the second night than the first in the same hotel, because you have adjusted to the unfamiliar noises in that environment. Sometimes, we habituate to things that we should, ideally, still be noticing. A major concern about exposing children to violent media is the possibility that their emotional responses to violent images will habituate, leading to higher tolerance for violent behavior (Gunter, 1994).

In contrast to habituation, **sensitization** increases our reactions to a range of stimuli following exposure to one strong stimulus. Following an earthquake, people often experience exaggerated responses to movement, light, or noise. If you are awakened by a loud crash, even if you figure out it's just your roommate coming home late at

treasure dragon/Shutterstock.com

It is likely that the first time this dog's owner attempted to dress it up the dog was a bit upset. After repeated experiences of being dressed up, however, the dog probably has habituated, which means that it has learned that no harm results from the process. Now it remains calm.

Vitalij Lang/Shutterstock.com

Following an earthquake, this little boy is likely to be extra jumpy for a while in response to other stimuli, like loud noises, because of sensitization.

associative learning The formation of associations or connections among stimuli and behaviors.

classical conditioning A type of learning in which associations are formed between two stimuli that occur sequentially in time.

operant conditioning A type of learning in which associations are formed between behaviors and their outcomes.

nonassociative learning Learning that involves changes in the magnitude of responses to a stimulus.

habituation A simple form of learning in which reactions to repeated stimuli that are unchanging and harmless decrease.

sensitization An increased reaction to many stimuli following exposure to one strong stimulus.

Many universities offer special programs for students who are the first in their extended families to attend college in recognition of the need to level the playing field with students who enter college having already learned a great deal about college life from observing their college-educated family members.

observational learning Learning that occurs when one organism watches the actions of another organism; also known as social learning or modeling.

Watching others is an efficient way to learn new skills, like dancing. Imagine for a moment how difficult it would be to write a description of how this dance should be performed. Watching others is also a useful way to learn what is harmful to do.

night, it might be harder to get back to sleep because of your suddenly increased state of arousal. Every little sound now seems magnified.

Why would we show habituation to some stimuli and sensitization to others? In general, habituation occurs in response to milder stimuli, whereas sensitization occurs in response to stronger stimuli. Habituation ensures that we do not waste precious resources monitoring low-priority stimuli. Sensitization is particularly useful in dangerous situations. After detecting one harmful stimulus, raising our overall level of responsiveness should improve reaction time should other dangers arise.

Observational learning, also known as social learning or modeling, occurs when one organism learns by watching the actions of another organism. If your knowledge of table manners does not extend to the many forks, knives, and spoons at a fancy dinner, you might want to watch what others do before diving into your food. Observational learning provides the advantage of transmitting information across generations within families and cultures.

Ariel Skelley/Blend Images/Alamy

Summary 8.1 Types of Learning

Associative learning	Classical conditioning • Signal → Important event • Snakes → Snake bite Operant conditioning • Behavior → Consequences • Practice → Successfully riding a wave
Nonassociative learning	Habituation • Responses to repeated, unchanging, irrelevant stimuli • Reduced response to neighbor's loud television every evening Sensitization • Responses to many stimuli • "Jumpiness" in response to many stimuli following an earthquake
Observational learning	Watch → Imitate • Copy new dance moves from your favorite music video Watch → Avoid imitating • Watch friend get sick from alcohol—don't drink as much

Credits: Top Row. Matt Cardy/Getty Images News/Getty Images. Second Row. Vitalij Lang/Shutterstock.com. Bottom Row: Ariel Skelley/Blend Images/Alamy.

What Is Classical Conditioning?

As we discussed in Chapter 1, Ivan Petrovich Pavlov (1849–1936) is so tightly connected to the study of classical conditioning that the phenomenon is frequently called Pavlovian conditioning. Pavlov switched his interests from the study of digestion to the study of learning after noticing that his dogs had learned to anticipate the arrival of food. Instead of salivating when presented with food, Pavlov's dogs began to salivate as soon as the lab assistant retrieved them from the kennel or strapped them into their experimental harnesses in the laboratory. Most people would probably not have noticed the differences in the dogs' behavior. Pavlov not only noticed but realized the full significance of his observations: the dogs had formed an association between the stimuli preceding the food and the arrival of the food. In other words, the dogs had learned that certain stimuli served as signals for the eventual appearance of food (see ● Figure 8.1).

If you are like most people reading about classical conditioning for the first time, you are probably wondering why we spend so much time and effort discussing salivating dogs. If classical conditioning were that limited in its scope, it probably wouldn't warrant more than a small footnote in the history of psychology. Instead, classical conditioning explains many of our learned emotional responses to our environment. It forms the basis for many practical applications, from prepared childbirth methods to the treatment of drug addiction and unrealistic fears.

Classical Conditioning Terminology

In describing the process of classical conditioning, Pavlov distinguished between conditioned and unconditioned stimuli and responses. *Conditioned* refers to something that must be learned, while *unconditioned* refers to factors that are reflexive or that occur without learning.

FIGURE 8.1

Classical Conditioning Terminology. (1) and (2) Before conditioning, food (unconditioned stimulus, or UCS) reliably produces salivation (unconditioned response, or UCR) and the sound of the metronome produces no reliable responding. (3) During conditioning, the sound of the metronome is followed by the food (UCS), which again produces salivation (UCR). (4) After conditioning, the sound of the metronome (conditioned stimulus, or CS) by itself is sufficient to produce salivation (conditioned response, or CR). Learning has occurred.

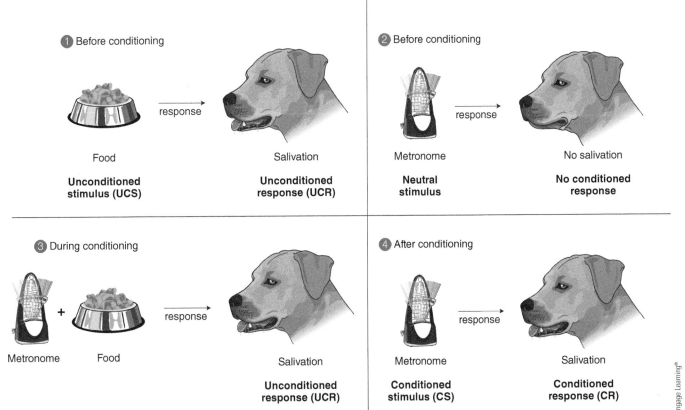

① Before conditioning

Food
Unconditioned stimulus (UCS)

response

Salivation
Unconditioned response (UCR)

② Before conditioning

Metronome
Neutral stimulus

response

No salivation
No conditioned response

③ During conditioning

Metronome + Food

response

Salivation
Unconditioned response (UCR)

④ After conditioning

Metronome
Conditioned stimulus (CS)

response

Salivation
Conditioned response (CR)

© Cengage Learning®

Therefore, a **conditioned stimulus (CS)** refers to an environmental event whose significance is learned, while an **unconditioned stimulus (UCS)** has innate, built-in meaning to the organism. In a typical experiment by Pavlov, dogs heard the sound of a ticking metronome just before food appeared through a small door. Dogs do not have an innate response to the sound of ticking metronomes, but they generally are born knowing what to do with food. By turning on the metronome before delivering food, Pavlov established the ticking sound as the CS, while the food was the UCS. A UCS may be pleasant, like food, but it may also be unpleasant, like an electric shock. The important features of a UCS are its innate biological significance and its reliable ability to elicit a response without prior exposure. Just as dogs don't require training to salivate in response to meat powder, few of us need experience with electric shock before we respond with fear and other negative emotions.

Conditioned responses (CRs) are learned reactions, while **unconditioned responses (UCRs)** don't need to be learned; they appear without prior experience with a stimulus. Salivating when food is put in your mouth is a UCR, because we do this reflexively without prior experience, but salivating to ticking metronomes only occurs as a result of experience. Our definition of learning requires behavior to change, so the appearance of a CR tells us learning has occurred. Once learning has taken place, the organism now responds to CSs that reliably predict the arrival of the UCS. This ability to anticipate future stimuli provides significant advantages to an organism in the struggle for survival.

As we'll see in this section, understanding classical conditioning illuminates a range of behaviors you might have seen in yourself or others, from the avoidance of foods that you associate with feeling sick, to the butterflies you feel in your stomach before a big performance, to the development of social prejudices.

Classical Conditioning Phenomena

Pavlov and those following in his footsteps have extended the usefulness of classical conditioning by exploring its features and development in more detail.

Acquisition **Acquisition** refers to the development of a CR. Pavlov argued that acquisition requires contiguity, or proximity in time between the CS and the UCS. If the CS occurs long before the UCS, the organism may not view the two stimuli as related. A CS that occurs simultaneously with a UCS or, worse yet, following a UCS is not a useful signal. A dinner bell sounded after food has been served is not helpful (see ● Figure 8.2).

Acquisition also requires contingency, or a correlation between the CS and the UCS. Learning about a reliable signal is easier than learning about a signal that only occurs some-

conditioned stimulus (CS) An environmental event whose significance is learned through classical conditioning.
unconditioned stimulus (UCS) A stimulus that elicits a response without prior experience.
conditioned response (CR) A response learned through classical conditioning.
unconditioned response (UCR) A response to an unconditioned stimulus that requires no previous experience.
acquisition The development of a learned response.

FIGURE 8.2

Acquisition of Conditioned Responses (CRs). With each pairing of the conditioned stimulus and unconditioned stimulus, CRs become more likely.

Contiguity + Contingency = Better Learning

Contiguity + Less Contingency = Reduced Learning

© Cengage Learning®

FIGURE 8.3

Contingency Predicts Conditioning. Imagine the experience of the two dogs in this experiment. Food (unconditioned stimulus) always follows hearing the bell (conditioned stimulus) for both dogs, which demonstrates contiguity. However, the first dog only receives food after the bell, while the food is not always signaled by the bell for the second dog. The dog in the first line would learn the association between bell and food faster than the dog in the second line, because the first dog's bell is a more reliable signal for food (contingency).

times. To demonstrate the contingency factor, Robert Rescorla (1968) exposed rats to sound followed by a mild electric shock, which quickly produced fear of the sound. For some rats, a shock was administered only after a sound, while for other rats, shocks were administered following the sound on some occasions and without sound on others. All the rats had the same number of contiguous sound–shock pairings. They differed in the correlation between sound and shock. Learning was faster for rats experiencing signaled shocks 100% of the time. As the percentage of signaled shocks decreased, learning about the signal slowed. If your migraine headaches are always preceded by exposure to bright light, you are more likely to fear bright lights in the future than if your headaches follow exposure to bright lights only once in a while (see ● Figure 8.3).

Extinction and Spontaneous Recovery CRs disappear, or undergo **extinction**, if the association between the CS and the UCS is broken. When Pavlov continued to expose his dogs to the ticking of the metronome without providing food, the dogs eventually stopped salivating in response to the sound of the metronome.

Pavlov believed that extinction is not the same thing as forgetting but is actually new learning that overrides old learning. As evidence for this belief, Pavlov pointed to the occurrence of **spontaneous recovery**, or the reappearance of CRs following periods of rest between sessions of extinction training. Even if a dog has stopped salivating to the sound of the metronome by the end of an extinction session, conditioned salivation reappears at the beginning of the next session. In other words, the CR decreases during a session of extinction training not because the dog is forgetting the relationship between ticking and food but because the dog is now learning that ticking no longer predicts food, and it may take several sessions for this new learning to replace the old (see ● Figure 8.4).

Without the ability to extinguish CRs, adjusting to further changes in the environment would be difficult, if not impossible. We would not be able to learn to enjoy dogs again after being bitten by one. An addict whose associations between needles and the effects of using heroin never extinguished would have an even harder time overcoming addiction.

Inhibition So far, we have been discussing examples of excitatory classical conditioning, in which the organism learns that a CS predicts the occurrence of a UCS. Pavlov was also quite interested in the classical conditioning of **inhibition**, in which a CS predicts the nonoccurrence of a UCS (Pavlov, 1927). To demonstrate inhibition, we can begin by establishing excitatory conditioning by pairing a signal—a light—with shock. After some experience with this pairing, a rat learns to fear the light. Now we continue to present light–shock pairings, but we add other training trials that include the inhibitory CS—a sound—by presenting the light and sound together followed by no shock. Even though the light is present, the rat learns that it is not going to be shocked in the presence of the sound, and it shows no fear.

For a vulnerable animal in the wild, it is important to know not only that a predator at a water hole is in hunting mode (the sight of the prowling predator is an excitatory CS signaling

extinction The reduction of a learned response. In classical conditioning, extinction occurs when the unconditioned stimulus no longer follows the conditioned stimulus. In operant conditioning, extinction occurs when the consequence no longer follows the learned behavior.
spontaneous recovery During extinction training, the reappearance of conditioned responses after periods of rest.
inhibition A feature of classical conditioning in which a conditioned stimulus predicts the nonoccurrence of an unconditioned stimulus.

FIGURE 8.4

Extinction and Spontaneous Recovery. Addiction often involves the association of conditioned stimuli (CSs), such as the syringe, with the unconditioned stimulus (UCS) of a drug. Recovering addicts can be exposed to extinction—viewing the syringe (CS) without receiving the drug (UCS). This process reduces conditioned responses (CRs) that might be contributing to cravings for the drug. However, extinction typically requires multiple sessions. When the recovering addict returns for the next extinction training session after a period of rest, that person is likely to show CRs again. Eventually, with enough training, extinction is complete and no further spontaneous recovery is observed.

fear) but also that a predator relaxing after a recent kill is unlikely to kill again soon (the sight of a predator calmly drinking water is an inhibitory CS that tells the animal that the predator is unlikely to attack soon and that it is safe). For drug addicts, establishing inhibitory CSs associated with the lack of an expected drug effect might provide a more powerful method for rehabilitation (Kearns, Weiss, Schindler, & Panlilio, 2005). If an addict learns that drugs are never available in the presence of a certain signal, turning the signal on whenever the addict's resolve is weak might help prevent a relapse.

Generalization and Discrimination Once a CR is successfully acquired, organisms often show a tendency to respond to stimuli that are similar to the CS. For example, the child who learned to be afraid of bees after being stung might also begin to fear wasps and yellow jackets, a process that Pavlov called **generalization**.

Generalization has obvious survival value. If our ancestors had one bad experience with a lion, it would make sense to avoid all lions, as well as other animals with lionlike characteristics. If you felt sick after eating chocolate bacon at the county fair, it probably would be a good idea to avoid other weird chocolate-covered foods, at least for a while. Unfortunately, our tendency to generalize can have negative outcomes. For example, a soldier traumatized in combat might react with unnecessary fear to sounds that are similar to gunfire on the battlefield, such as the backfiring of a car back at home.

Counteracting our tendency to generalize is another learning process known as **discrimination**, which allows us to make fine distinctions between the implications of stimuli. In the laboratory, if you present food following a high tone but never following a low tone, a dog initially learns to salivate following both tones because of generalization. As learning progresses, the dog eventually learns

Inhibition learning helps organisms behave adaptively when they've learned that something important will not occur. These zebras may have learned that when lions act a certain way, they are already full and unlikely to hunt again. These inhibitory signals tell the zebras that they can drink in safety, at least for a little while.

to discriminate, or differentiate, between the abilities of the two stimuli to predict food. As a result, salivation to the high tone continues, but salivation to the low tone stops (see ● Figure 8.5). If generalization had led the soldier to react with fear to the sound of a backfiring car, further experience with the sound would help distinguish it from real gunfire in combat. Because the sound of a backfiring car is not followed by any fear-producing UCSs, it eventually loses its ability to elicit fear.

generalization The tendency to respond to stimuli that are similar to an original conditioned stimulus.
discrimination A learned ability to distinguish between stimuli.

Higher Order Conditioning We have seen how CRs spread to similar stimuli through generalization. In addition, CRs can occur in response to stimuli that predict the CS, a process known as higher order conditioning.

Higher order conditioning allows us to make even more distant predictions about the occurrence of significant events. A person who was bitten by a dog might show fear the next time the dog is seen, because the sight of the dog (CS) is now associated with the pain of the bite (UCS). Subsequently, the sight of the dog (CS) might begin to act more like a UCS, producing fear in response to other stimuli (seeing the dog's yard or doghouse or hearing the dog bark) that might signal the appearance of the dog.

Latent Inhibition In most of the research we have reviewed so far, the stimuli used as CSs are unfamiliar. Pavlov's dogs had probably never heard a metronome before participating in his experiments. What happens when you are already familiar with a CS? The answer is that you will take a longer amount of time learning to respond to it. It takes more time to learn about a familiar CS than about an unfamiliar CS, a phenomenon known as **latent inhibition** (Lubow & Moore, 1959). The phenomenon is *latent* in the sense that its effects are not seen right away (when the stimuli are first presented) but emerge later when the rate of learning is examined. The *inhibition* part of the term refers to the relatively poor learning that occurs in response to familiar stimuli.

If you have eaten lots of pizzas over time (familiar CS) but get sick after eating one, you are unlikely to associate the pizza with feeling ill. It is more likely that you would need to be sick many times after eating pizza before you learned to connect eating pizza with being ill. In contrast, if you get sick the first time you eat chocolate-covered ants (unfamiliar CS), assuming these are not already your favorite treat, you'll associate eating ants with feeling ill quickly.

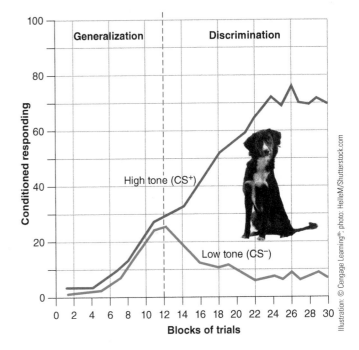

FIGURE 8.5

Generalization and Discrimination.
The dog is receiving food after the high tone but receives nothing after the low tone. Early in training, the dog salivates after both tones because of generalization. Further along in training, the dog learns to discriminate between the abilities of the two tones to signal food and salivates only after the high tone.

Higher order conditioning occurs when stimuli associated with a conditioned stimulus (CS) gain the ability to elicit conditioned responses on their own. If a child has learned to fear dogs (CS) because of a previous bite (unconditioned stimulus), anything that signals "dog" might now produce fear too, including the sight of a doghouse, a dog's feeding bowl, or a chew toy.

higher order conditioning Learning in which stimuli associated with a conditioned stimulus also elicit conditioned responses.
latent inhibition The slower learning that occurs when a conditioned stimulus (CS) is already familiar compared to when the CS is unfamiliar.

Steph and John Cacioppo

Because of latent inhibition, classical conditioning proceeds more slowly when a new conditioned stimulus is familiar than when it is unfamiliar. If you got sick after eating a familiar food (perhaps pizza), you are less likely to associate your illness with the food than if you got sick after eating an unfamiliar food, like this scorpion lollipop one of your textbook authors is about to try.

Cognitive and Biological Influences on Classical Conditioning

Early behaviorists concentrated their study of learning on external behaviors that they could observe directly. As new technologies became available, such as brain imaging methods and more powerful computers used to model thinking and reasoning, psychologists interested in learning began to explore internal processes, leading to revolutionary advances in our understanding of cognition and biology.

Early behaviorists also limited most of their studies to simple animals rather than humans. This restriction resulted from strong beliefs that behavior followed the same rules in all organisms, which meant that it was safe to apply experimental results from studies using rats to the behavior of humans and that having more control over your experimental subjects (food, housing, etc.) led to better science. Although the latter may be true, psychologists discovered that treating the learning animal as some kind of interchangeable black box was overly simplistic. Some learning processes have clearly been conserved over the course of evolution, allowing us to make conclusions relevant to humans about the changes at a synapse that accompany classical conditioning in the *Aplysia californica* sea slug (Carew & Kandel, 1973). In other cases, species bring their unique biology into the learning situation, as we will see in a later section on taste aversion learning. Psychologists have learned to be cautious about generalizing their conclusions across species.

The Element of Surprise In our earlier discussion of the acquisition of classical CRs, we talked about the contributions of contiguity (closeness in time) and contingency (the correlation between the CS and the UCS). It should be easy to learn about a signal that both precedes and is predictive of an important event. The bell on your microwave both precedes and predicts the availability of food, and we would not be surprised if your mouth starts watering a bit whenever you hear it.

What happens, however, if you already possess one good signal but add another one that also precedes and predicts a UCS? Based on past experience, you have learned that if your computer monitor suddenly goes dark (CS), something terrible (UCS) has happened to your computer. Whenever you see a dark screen, you feel extremely stressed (CR). Let's assume that the next time a dark screen appears, the computer also emits a funny sound. Even though the sound both precedes and predicts a hard drive crash, it's unlikely that you will learn much about the sound and its relationship with hard drive crashes. We don't bother to learn much about new signals that provide no additional information, even if they meet our requirements for contiguity and contingency (Kamin, 1968, 1969).

How can we account for this failure to learn under circumstances that should produce strong learning? Rescorla and Wagner (1972) proposed a model of classical conditioning in which learning occurs as a function of how surprising the association between the CS and the UCS appears. Early in training, more learning takes place because the relationship between the CS and the UCS is relatively unexpected. Later in training, less learning takes place with each exposure to the now-familiar relationship between the CS and the UCS (see ● Figure 8.6).

We can't imagine early behaviorists using terms like *expect, surprise,* and *predict,* because these represent internal states they believed were impossible to investigate scientifically. But today, it seems reasonable to discuss some aspects of learning using this vocabulary.

Taste Aversion We have already used some examples of classical conditioning involving food that you dislike because you got sick after eating it. These classically conditioned taste aversions result when the sight, smell, or flavor of the food (CS) has been paired in the past with illness (UCS). Taste aversion, or dislike of the food, is the resulting CR.

Taste aversion isn't just another interesting example of classical conditioning. Its demonstration led to a substantial rethinking not only of classical conditioning but of behaviorism in general. Pavlov believed that stimuli that met the CS or UCS criteria could be successfully paired to produce classical conditioning. He made no provisions in his theory for special interactions between particular types of stimuli. Researcher John Garcia, who had a background not only in psychology but also in biology, did not believe that stimuli were so interchangeable. In what became known as a classic taste aversion study, Garcia and Robert Koelling

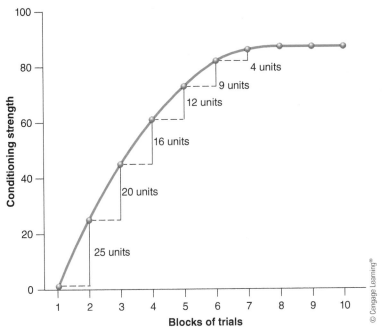

FIGURE 8.6

The Rescorla–Wagner Model. According to the Rescorla–Wagner model, the rate of learning about a conditioned stimulus (CS) depends on how new or surprising the association between the CS and the unconditioned stimulus (UCS) appears to be. Early in training, learning proceeds rapidly (25 units per block or set of trials) because the association is new and surprising. Later in training, gains in conditioning strength (measured by how often a conditioned response occurs) level off, because the association between the CS and the UCS is now familiar and no longer surprising (4 units per block of trials).

(1966) demonstrated that the types of stimuli used as CSs and UCSs matter and that some combinations are learned faster than others. Garcia and Koelling presented groups of rats with either saccharin-flavored water ("tasty water") or plain water. When the rats consumed the plain water, their drinking triggered a light and a clicking sound, which the researchers called "bright-noisy water." After drinking either tasty or bright-noisy water, half the rats were given an injection of lithium chloride, which produces strong sensations of nausea, and the other half received an electric shock (see Table 8.1).

TABLE 8.1	Experimental Design Used by Garcia and Koelling (1966)	
	Conditioned stimulus	
Unconditioned stimulus	**Bright-noisy water**	**Tasty water**
Lithium chloride	Weak learning	Strong learning
Shock	Strong learning	Weak learning

© Cengage Learning®

This type of experiment should look familiar to you by now as an example of classical conditioning. Tasty water or bright-noisy water served as CSs, while shock or lithium chloride served as UCSs. Garcia and Koelling subsequently presented tasty and bright-noisy water to see whether either would be avoided, with avoidance serving as an indication of the CR of disgust with or dislike of the water. Rats immediately learned associations between tasty water and subsequent illness but had difficulty learning to use the bright-noisy water as a signal for illness. Conversely, bright-noisy water, but not tasty water, became an effective signal for shock. After all, if you feel sick, you are more likely to decide that your illness was a result of eating mystery leftovers for breakfast rather than the flickering of the fluorescent lights in your classroom. However, if you receive an electric shock, you might be more suspicious of the flickering lights than of your breakfast.

This experiment had far-ranging implications. Not only did these findings challenge Pavlov's views of the relative interchangeability of stimuli, but they prompted a renewed interest in the biological predispositions of organisms, or their preparedness to learn certain things. Although rats readily formed associations between taste and illness but not between visual stimuli and illness, birds easily formed associations between visual stimuli and illness but not between taste and illness. Rats see poorly, so they usually depend on taste and smell for identifying food. Birds have excellent vision and typically identify food sources using visual cues, such as the markings of particular species of butterfly.

The willingness of behaviorists to treat organisms as interchangeable black boxes with irrelevant internal features was severely challenged by this work, paving the way to an abandonment of the rigid behaviorism that had dominated psychology for most of the 20th century. Many learning theorists closed down their rat and pigeon labs and turned their attention to emerging cognitive, biological, and evolutionary approaches.

Applying Classical Conditioning

Although strict behaviorism no longer dominates research in psychology as it did for the first half of the 20th century, it still provides powerful explanations of human behavior and effective therapeutic tools for producing change. The pervasiveness of classical conditioning in everyday life is quite remarkable. When your palms get sweaty and you feel butterflies in your stomach before a big exam, awaken just before your alarm clock goes off, or feel more awake just because you smell coffee brewing, you can blame your responses on classical conditioning. If you are a clinician working with a traumatized combat veteran who is frightened by the smell of diesel fuel or a coach working with an athlete to overcome "choking" in big games, classical conditioning gives you some answers you need to produce positive change.

Overcoming Fear In 1920, John B. Watson and Rosalie Raynor conducted an experiment with a 9-month-old infant named Albert. By today's standards, this experiment hardly appears well designed or ethical, but the results of the experiment led to research that shed a great deal of light onto human fear. While Albert played with a tame, white laboratory rat (CS), Watson and Raynor made a loud noise (UCS) by hitting a steel bar with a hammer. Albert was quite frightened by this noise (UCR). A week later, Albert was again offered the rat, but this time he was afraid (CR). His fear generalized to other white, furry objects, including a rabbit, a dog, a fur coat, and a Santa Claus mask. Watson and Raynor had successfully demonstrated that fears could result from classical conditioning.

Although Albert left Watson and Raynor's laboratory without treatment for his fear, one of Watson's students, Mary Cover Jones, demonstrated how classical conditioning procedures could be used to reduce learned fears. Her experiment featured a 3-year-old named Peter, who had a serious phobia, or intense, unrealistic fear, of rabbits (Jones, 1924). Could classical conditioning provide a way to reduce Peter's fears? One possible approach would be to use extinction. As we mentioned previously, CRs extinguish if the CS is presented alone, without the UCS. Treating phobias by exposing people to fear-producing stimuli in a manner that is safe until they no longer respond (i.e., extinction) is known as flooding. Although flooding works, it is often traumatic. Being exposed to a stimulus you find frightening until you are no longer afraid is not fun. Imagine forcing a person afraid of heights to bungee jump until the fear of heights is gone.

Instead of using extinction or flooding, Jones treated Peter with counterconditioning, or the substitution of one CR for another, opposite response. Jones associated food, a new UCS, with the presence of a rabbit (CS). Eventually, Peter was able to stroke the rabbit while eating. While not particularly hygienic, this achievement represented a big improvement in Peter's life.

Counterconditioning has many useful applications. **Aversion therapy** can be used to replace inappropriate positive reactions to a stimulus with negative reactions. For example, a compound containing silver interacts with nicotine to make a tobacco cigarette taste terri-

John Garcia and Robert Koelling's work on taste aversion explains why the viceroy butterfly (on the bottom) has evolved to mimic the coloring of the monarch butterfly (on the top). Monarchs taste terrible to birds, so by looking similar to the bad-tasting butterfly, the viceroy might escape being eaten too. The sight of food is important to birds but not as important to rats, which don't see well. The natural capacities of a species prepare it to learn some things better than others.

Psychologists have long been curious about what happened to Albert after he left Watson and Raynor's laboratory. One hypothesis suggests that Albert was Douglas Merritte, the child of one of the foster mothers living at the Harriet Lane home in 1920. Merritte died at age 6 of hydrocephalus. Another strong candidate is William Albert Barger, whose name and physical health appear to some to be a better match for the baby shown in Watson's films of his experiment. Barger died in 2007, at the age of 87. If Barger is indeed the famous Albert, we hope that his strong dislike of animals as an adult was not a remnant of Watson's experiment.

Understanding classical conditioning provides insight into many situations where our emotional responses seem to be triggered by the environment, as in the case of performance anxiety.

aversion therapy An application of counterconditioning in which a conditioned stimulus (CS) formerly paired with a pleasurable unconditioned stimulus (UCS) is instead paired with an unpleasant UCS.

ble. Substituting a negative outcome for a positive outcome of smoking helps some smokers quit more easily (Rose, Behm, Murugesan, & McClernon, 2010).

A variation of counterconditioning used to treat fear is known as **systematic desensitization** (Wolpe, 1958). Associations between a phobic stimulus and fear are replaced by associations between the phobic stimulus and relaxation. The person undergoing treatment is first trained to achieve a state of physical and mental relaxation, usually by tensing and relaxing muscle groups from head to toe. If you would like to try this progressive relaxation technique yourself, we outline the procedure in Chapter 15. Once relaxation is achieved, the fear stimulus is gradually introduced, either in physical form or through guided imagery in which the person is asked to imagine the stimulus. If relaxation falters at any point, the person retreats to an earlier stage of exposure to the fear stimulus until he or she can relax again.

Addiction In addition to the influences on addiction discussed in Chapter 6, classical conditioning can contribute to dependence on a drug or behavior. Stimuli associated with drug use often become CSs for the effects of a drug. For example, peak caffeine levels occur about 45 minutes after drinking a cup of coffee (Liguori, Hughes, & Grass, 1997), yet most coffee drinkers report feeling more awake as soon as they take that first sip in the morning or even smell the coffee brewing.

John B. Watson and Rosalie Raynor observe Little Albert's generalization to a bunny mask worn by Watson. The mask is similar to the original conditioned stimulus in their experiment—a white laboratory rat—which stimulated Albert's conditioned fear.

While still a graduate student, Mary Cover Jones used classical conditioning principles to reduce a small child's fear of rabbits. As a result, she is often called the Mother of Behavior Therapy.

systematic desensitization A type of counterconditioning in which people relax while being exposed to stimuli that elicit fear.

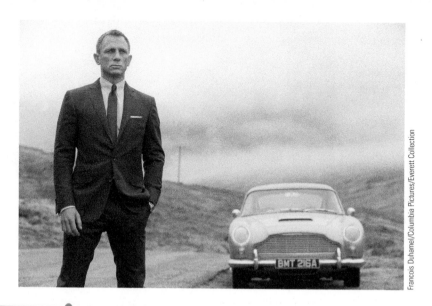

Product placement in movies is expensive, but marketers hope that audiences will form associations between their products and the positive brand of a character. If James Bond drives an Aston Martin, maybe you can be attractive and invincible if you drive one too.

One of the challenges faced by people recovering from addiction to substances is that environmental cues (CSs) associated with the effects of substance use (UCSs) continue to elicit craving (CR) for the drug of choice. Most treatments for substance abuse involve simply abstaining from a drug as opposed to extinction or counterconditioning. There is nothing about avoiding the use of a drug that substantially weakens the previously formed associations surrounding its use. Consequently, being exposed to established CSs, including the people with whom one did the drugs previously or the context in which one used the drugs, often leads to a former addict's relapse (Chaudhri, Sahuque, & Janak, 2008). The sight, smell, or taste of a recovering alcoholic's favorite drink or even a visit to a favorite bar is often enough to undermine the person's abstinence from drinking. Reducing these associations can help the addict continue to abstain.

Attitudes and Prejudice   Classical conditioning contributes to the formation and change of attitudes (Cacioppo & Berntson, 2001). After all, advertisers have been using classical conditioning for years to influence consumer attitudes about products. By forming associations between the products and other stimuli we value, like celebrities, advertisers hope that our opinions of their product will improve.

Prejudice, which is discussed further in Chapter 13, is a negative attitude about a group of people. Like other attitudes, prejudice is influenced by classical conditioning, although it has many other roots as well. In particular, latent inhibition can contribute to the development of negative attitudes (Cacioppo, Marshall-Goodell, Tassinary, & Petty, 1992). Consider the following. Because of latent inhibition, if children grow up with little exposure to people outside their own race, people of their own race are more familiar, and learning to associate their race with other attributes should be slow. In contrast, the children have had less preexposure to people of other races. Latent inhibition would predict that children exposed to news reports about crime would form stronger associations between people of unfamiliar races and crime than between people of their own race and crime.

Creativity and Schizophrenia   By reducing the amount of learning that occurs in response to familiar stimuli, latent inhibition helps us focus our energy on novelty and change in our environments.

Less latent inhibition is seen in creative people and in people diagnosed with schizophrenia than is seen in general (Baruch, Hemsley, & Gray, 1988a, 1988b; Lubow, Ingberg-Sachs, Salstein-Orda, & Gewirtz, 1992). This difference means that creative people and people with schizophrenia form new associations with familiar stimuli faster than most people do. They make connections under circumstances in which most of us would not. Reduced latent inhibition might account for the creative person's ability to see familiar things in new ways, which is a positive outcome, but it also might lead to the tendency of a person with schizophrenia to make odd, inappropriate connections among ideas. In Chapter 14, we refer to this tendency as a "loosening of associations." For example, a person with schizophrenia might suggest that a painting has a headache. This is not the type of association between stimuli that most people would make.

Psychology as a Hub Science
Classical Conditioning Informs Wildlife Conservation

While reading about Ivan Petrovich Pavlov's experiments with salivating dogs, it might be difficult to grasp the full significance of Pavlov's results, but there were some good reasons his laboratory continued to receive considerable resources during difficult times of war and revolution (Gantt, 1928).

As you have seen in this chapter, the possible applications of classical conditioning range widely, from treating addiction to treating phobias to understanding prejudice and schizophrenia. One of the less typical applications was the result of work by John Garcia and one of his graduate students, Carl Gustavson (Gustavson, Kelly, Sweeney, & Garcia, 1976). Gustavson was a child of the rural West, and he had grown up watching the ongoing battles among sheep ranchers, coyotes, and wolves. He asked whether the taste aversion work pioneered by Garcia might provide a useful solution.

With encouragement from Garcia, Gustavson set up an outdoor training facility with six coyotes and two wolves. The coyotes were fed rabbit meat laced with lithium chloride (LiCl), while the wolves were fed sheep meat with LiCl. Gustavson even experimented with a caged cougar that refused to eat deer meat after a single meal of venison laced with LiCl. Some of the researchers' observations of the captive animals were especially dramatic. When a lamb was tethered in the wolves' pen, the wolves approached in a normal threatening manner. The lamb froze, which is also species-typical behavior in this situation. Then, something interesting happened. The wolves sniffed at the lamb and then retreated, showing signs of defensive puppy play (crouching with ears and tail down). In response to these submissive displays, the lamb began to charge the wolves and even chased them around the pen.

Would these observations transfer to the real outdoors? The researchers distributed sheep-flavored bait and sheep carcasses laced with LiCl across a 3,000-acre sheep ranch in Washington state. A comparison of the ranch's loss records demonstrated a 30% to 60% reduction in sheep killed by coyotes following the treatment. A larger-scale test of 10 herds over a 3-year period in Saskatchewan demonstrated a reduction in predator control costs between 86% and 90% per year.

Where does the practice stand today? Unfortunately, when wildlife experts attempted to apply taste aversion to predator control, they made numerous procedural mistakes. They viewed the LiCl as a repellant, as opposed to an unconditioned stimulus. Bait was overdosed with LiCl, which ensured that the predator would link salty tastes with illness instead of the taste of the prey with illness, leading to the discarding of the procedure as ineffective. Contemporary coyote management techniques include propane cannons, horns, sirens, radios, and strobe lights (and we are left wondering what these stimuli do to the sheep), but aversion conditioning is still described by wildlife experts as "speculative" (Wilbanks, 2014).

Gustavson's technique has recently made a comeback in an effort to save the endangered Mexican wolf. When released in the wild, the wolves, like Gustavson's coyotes, naturally run into conflict with ranchers and farmers. Professors Lowell Nicolaus and Dan Moriarty's initial results using conditioned taste aversion with captive gray wolves convinced U.S. government wildlife agencies to prepare to replicate the study with captive Mexican wolves (Tribe, n.d.). If successful, this test could have wide-ranging implications for maintaining endangered predators throughout the world. ●

Use of conditioned taste aversion to provide a nonlethal method of predator control is being explored in efforts to save the endangered Mexican wolf, shown here. Dan Moriarty and his colleague Lowell Nicolaus laced meat with the fungicide thiabendazole. Although the fungicide makes the wolves ill, it causes no permanent damage. If the program is successful in the wild, it could reshape the way endangered predators are managed worldwide.

Summary 8.2 Classical Conditioning Phenomena

Classical conditioning phenomenon	Description	Example
Acquisition	Gradual development of conditioned responses (CRs)	A dog salivates on a higher percentage of trials as training progresses.
Extinction	Reduction of CRs when a conditioned stimuli (CS) is presented without being followed by an unconditioned stimuli (UCS)	If the metronome is no longer followed by food, the dog stops salivating to the metronome.
Spontaneous recovery	Reappearance of CRs following periods of rest between extinction training sessions	The dog shows no salivation at the end of the day's extinction training, but after a night of rest in the kennel, the dog salivates at the beginning of the next extinction session.
Inhibition	CS predicting the nonoccurrence of the UCS	As long as a gauge is "in the green," your equipment will not explode. You do not feel fear.
Generalization	Responding to stimuli that resemble the CS	Albert's fear of white rats generalized to a Santa Claus beard.
Discrimination	Responding to the CS but not to similar stimuli that have not been paired with the UCS	A combat veteran learns to distinguish between the sound of gunfire and the backfire from a car.
Higher order conditioning	CRs to stimuli that predict the occurrence of a CS	A child who has been bitten by a dog begins to fear the street where the dog lives.
Latent inhibition	Acquisition occurring more slowly to a familiar CS than to an unfamiliar CS	An American forms a taste aversion faster to fruit bat pie than to hamburgers.

What Is Operant Conditioning?

In our discussion of behaviorism in Chapter 1, we introduced you to Edward Thorndike and his law of effect. To recap, Thorndike had observed the learning that took place when a cat tried to escape one of his "puzzle boxes." According to Thorndike, the cats learned to escape by repeating actions that produced desirable outcomes and by eliminating behaviors that produced what he called "annoying" outcomes, or outcomes featuring either no useful effects or negative effects (1913, p. 50). Consequently, the law of effect states that a behavior will be "stamped into" an organism's repertoire depending on the consequences of the behavior (Thorndike, 1913, p. 129).

The association between a behavior and its consequences is called operant or instrumental conditioning. In this type of learning, organisms operate on their environment, and their behavior is often instrumental in producing an outcome. B. F. Skinner extended Thorndike's findings using an apparatus that bears his name—the Skinner box, a modified cage containing levers or buttons that can be pressed or pecked by animals (see ● Figure 8.7).

Operant conditioning differs from classical conditioning along several dimensions. By definition, classical conditioning is based on an association between two stimuli, whereas operant conditioning occurs when a behavior is associated with its consequences. Classical conditioning generally works best with relatively involuntary behaviors, such as fear or salivation, whereas operant conditioning involves voluntary behaviors, like walking to class or waving to a friend.

Types of Consequences

As we all know from experience, some types of consequences increase behaviors and some types decrease behaviors. Skinner divided consequences into four classes: positive reinforcement, negative reinforcement, positive punishment, and negative punishment. Both types of reinforce-

Speaker
Signal lights
Lever
Food from dispenser
Food pellet
Electric grid

© Cengage Learning®
From shock generator

FIGURE 8.7

The Skinner Box. A specially adapted cage called a Skinner box, after behaviorist B. F. Skinner, allows researchers to investigate the results of reinforcement and punishment on the likelihood that the rat will press the bar.

TABLE 8.2	Types of Consequences	
	Add stimulus to environment	**Remove stimulus from environment**
Increase behavior	Positive reinforcement	Negative reinforcement
Decrease behavior	Positive punishment	Negative punishment

© Cengage Learning®

ment increase their associated behaviors, whereas both types of punishment decrease associated behaviors (see Table 8.2).

We all have unique sets of effective reinforcers and punishers. You might think that getting an A in a course is reinforcing, making all those extra hours spent studying worthwhile, but top grades may be less meaningful to the student sitting next to you who came to college for the social life. A parent might spank a child, believing that spanking is an effective form of punishment, only to find that the child's unwanted behavior is becoming more rather than less frequent. For some children, the reward of getting the parent's attention overrides the discomfort of the spanking part of the interaction. In other words, the identity of a reinforcer or punisher is defined by its effects on behavior, not by some intrinsic quality of the consequence. The only accurate way to determine the impact of a consequence is to check your results. If you think you're reinforcing or punishing a behavior but the frequency of the behavior is not changing in the direction you expect, try something else.

Positive Reinforcement By definition, a positive reinforcement increases the frequency of its associated behavior by providing a desired outcome. Again, each person has a menu of effective reinforcements. In a common application of operant conditioning, children with autism spectrum disorder are taught language, with candy serving as the positive reinforcement. Benjamin Lahey tells of his experience trying to teach a child with autism spectrum disorder to say the syllable "ba" to obtain an M&M candy (Lahey, 1995). After 4 hours without progress, Lahey turned to the child's mother in frustration, asking her what she thought might be the problem. The mother calmly replied that her son didn't like M&Ms. Lahey switched to the child's preferred treat, chopped carrots, and the child quickly began emitting "ba's." Chopped carrot is probably not the first reinforcer you would try with a 4-year-old boy, but in this case, it made all the difference.

 # Thinking Scientifically

Why Do People Deliberately Injure Themselves?

EDWARD THORNDIKE'S LAW of effect stipulates that behaviors followed by positive consequences are more likely to be repeated in the future and that behaviors followed by negative consequences are less likely to be repeated. Why then, do large numbers of people, particularly in adolescence, engage in self-injury, or deliberate physical damage without suicidal intent (Klonsky & Muehlenkamp, 2007)? In one study, an astonishing 46% of 9th and 10th graders reported a self-injury in the previous year (Lloyd-Richardson, Perrine, Dierker, & Kelley, 2007).

As we learn in this chapter, reward and punishment are in the eye of the beholder. The first challenge we face in our analysis of self-injury is the assumption that pain is always a negative consequence. For most of us, it is. However, adolescents who engage in self-injury report feelings of relief or calm, despite the obvious pain they inflict on themselves. Such feelings probably reinforce further bouts of self-injury. Self-injury often occurs in response to feelings of anger, anxiety, and frustration, and as we will see, alleviation of these negative feelings might also reward the injurious behavior (Klonsky, 2007; Klonsky & Muehlenkamp,

2007). Finally, injury is associated with the release of endorphins, our bodies' natural opiates. The positive feelings associated with endorphin release also might reinforce the behavior.

Self-injury frequently occurs in people diagnosed with psychological disorders, such as depression, anxiety disorders, eating disorders, or substance abuse, which we discuss further in Chapters 7 and 14. Others engaging in the behavior have a history of sexual abuse. Observations that captive animals in zoos and laboratories are often prone to self-injury might provide additional insight into the causes of this behav-

If everyone has a different set of effective reinforcers, how do we know which to use? A simple technique for predicting what a particular animal or person will find reinforcing is the Premack principle, which states that whatever behavior an organism spends the most time and energy doing is likely to be an important behavior to that organism (Premack, 1965). It is possible, therefore, to rank people's free-time activities according to their priorities. If Lahey had been able to observe his young client's eating habits before starting training, it is unlikely that he would have made the mistake of offering M&Ms as reinforcers. The opportunity to engage in a higher priority activity is always capable of rewarding a lower priority activity. Your grandmother may never have heard of Premack, but she knows that telling you to eat your broccoli to get an ice cream generally works.

Both Thorndike and Skinner agreed that positive reinforcement is a powerful tool for managing behavior. In our later discussion of punishment, we will argue that the effects of positive reinforcement are more powerful than the effects of punishment. Unfortunately, in Western culture, we tend to provide relatively little positive reinforcement. We are more likely to hear about our mistakes from our boss than to hear about all the things we've done correctly. Much of our time and effort go into controlling unwanted behaviors with punishment. It is possible that we feel entitled to good treatment from others and therefore feel we should not have to provide any reward for reasonably expected behaviors. The problem with this approach is that extinction occurs in operant, as well as in classical, conditioning. A behavior that is no longer reinforced drops in frequency. By ignoring other people's desirable behaviors instead of reinforcing them, perhaps with a simple thank you, we risk reducing their frequency.

Some reinforcers, known as primary reinforcers, are effective because of

Carolyn Jenkins/Alamy

The Premack principle can help you maintain good time management. If you prefer socializing to studying, use the opportunity to socialize as a reward for meeting your evening's study goals.

According to the Premack principle, a preferred activity can be used to reinforce a less preferred activity. Most children prefer candy over carrots, so rewarding a child with candy for eating carrots often increases carrot consumption. One little boy with autism spectrum disorder, however, preferred carrots to M&Ms, and his training proceeded more smoothly when carrot rewards were substituted for candy rewards.

M. Itani/Alamy

ior (Jones & Barraclough, 1978).Treatment usually consists of therapy for any underlying psychological disorders, along with avoidance, in which the person is encouraged to engage in behaviors that are incompatible with self-harm. To assist these individuals further, we need to be able to see reward and punishment from their perspective, not just our own. ●

If the consequences of a behavior influence how likely a person is to repeat the behavior in the future, how can we explain the prevalence of self-injury? Why don't the painful consequences of the behavior make people stop? In situations like this, operant conditioning tells us that we need to look for possible reinforcers for the behavior that override the painful outcomes. In the case of self-injury, people report feeling calm and relief. To treat such behaviors effectively, psychologists need to understand what advantages they provide from the perspective of the person doing the behavior.

Rusig/Alamy

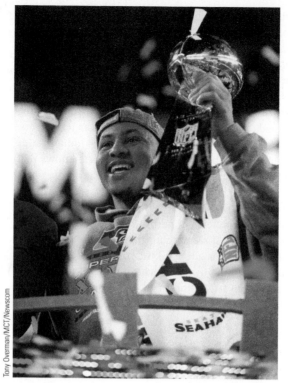

Super Bowl Most Valuable Player Malcolm Smith of the Seattle Seahawks "loves" the Lombardi Trophy not for its intrinsic value (you can't eat it, etc.) but because trophies have become conditioned reinforcers.

Tony Overman/MCT/Newscom

Many superstitious behaviors, like wearing your "lucky socks," can be learned through operant conditioning. Operant conditioning does not require a behavior to cause a positive outcome to be strengthened. All that is required is that a behavior be followed by a positive outcome. Unless you suddenly have a string of bad performances while wearing the lucky socks, you are unlikely to have an opportunity to unlearn your superstition.

their natural roles in survival, such as food. Others must be learned. We are not born valuing money, grades, or gold medals. These are examples of **conditioned reinforcers**, also called secondary reinforcers, that gain their value and ability to influence behavior from being associated with other things we value. Here, we see an intersection between classical and operant conditioning. If you always say "good dog" before you provide your pet with a treat, saying "good dog" becomes a CS for food (the UCS) that can now be used to reinforce compliance with commands to come, sit, or heel (operant behaviors). Classical conditioning establishes the value of "good dog," and operant conditioning describes the use of "good dog" to reinforce the dog's voluntary behavior.

Humans are capable of generating long chains of conditioned reinforcers extending far into the future. We might ask you why you are studying this textbook right now, at this moment. A psychologist might answer that you are studying now because studying will be reinforced by a good grade at the end of the term, which in turn will be reinforced by a diploma at the end of your college education, which in turn will be reinforced by a good job after graduation, which in turn will be reinforced by a good salary, which will allow you to live in a nice house, drive a nice car, wear nice clothes, eat good food, and provide the same for your family in the coming years.

Negative Reinforcement **Negative reinforcement**, which sounds contradictory, involves the removal of unpleasant consequences from a situation to increase the frequency of an associated behavior. Negative reinforcement increases the frequency of behaviors that allow an organism to avoid, turn off, or postpone an unpleasant consequence; these are sometimes called escape and avoidance behaviors. Let's look at a laboratory example of negative reinforcement before tackling real-world examples. If a hungry rat in a Skinner box learns that pressing a bar produces food, a positive consequence, we would expect the frequency of bar pressing to increase. This would be an instance of positive reinforcement. However, if pressing the bar turns off or delays the administration of an electric shock, we would still expect the frequency of bar pressing to increase. This would be an instance of negative reinforcement.

Be careful to avoid confusing negative reinforcement with punishment, which we cover in the next section. By definition, a punishment decreases the behaviors it follows, whereas both positive and negative reinforcers increase the frequency of the behaviors they follow. Returning to our Skinner box example, the rat's bar pressing increases following both positive reinforcement (food) and negative reinforcement (turning off a shock). If we shocked the rat every time it pressed the bar (punishment), it would stop pressing the bar quickly.

Many everyday behaviors are maintained by negative reinforcement. We buckle up in our cars to turn off annoying beeps or bells, open umbrellas to avoid getting wet, scratch an insect bite to relieve the itch, take an aspirin to escape a headache, apply sunscreen to avoid a sunburn or skin cancer, and apologize to avoid further misunderstandings with a friend.

In many real-world cases, positive and negative reinforcement act on behavior simultaneously in a similar fashion as the conflicts between approach and avoidance we observed

conditioned reinforcer A reinforcer that gains value from being associated with other things that are valued; also known as a secondary reinforcer.
negative reinforcement A method for increasing behaviors that allow an organism to escape or avoid an unpleasant consequence.

Greg McWilliams/Icon SMI 408/Newscom

in Chapter 7. A heroin addict uses the drug to obtain a state of euphoria (positive reinforcer) but also to eliminate the unpleasant symptoms of withdrawal (negative reinforcer). You might study hard to achieve high grades (positive reinforcers) while also being motivated by the need to avoid low grades (negative reinforcers).

Punishment   A **punishment** is any consequence that reduces the frequency of an associated behavior. **Positive punishment** refers to applying an aversive consequence that reduces the frequency of or eliminates a behavior. As we observed previously, we can demonstrate that a rat will quickly stop pressing a bar if each press results in an electric shock. **Negative punishment** involves the removal of something desirable. In the Skinner box, we can change the rules for a rat that has learned previously to press a bar for food. Now, food is made available unless the rat presses the bar. Under these conditions, the rat will also quickly stop pressing the bar.

Thorndike and Skinner were in agreement about the relative weakness of punishment as a means of controlling behavior. Part of the weakness of punishment effects arises from the difficulties of applying punishment effectively in real contexts. Three conditions must be met for punishment to have observable effects on behavior: significance, immediacy, and consistency (Schwartz, 1984).

As we observed with reinforcement, consequences have to matter to the person or animal receiving them (i.e., significance). If we use a punisher that is too mild for a particular individual, there is little incentive for that person to change behavior. College campuses usually charge a fairly significant amount of money for parking illegally. However, there will typically be some students for whom that particular punishment is not sufficient to ensure that they will park legally. How high would a parking fee have to be to gain complete compliance on the part of the university community? What if you risked the death penalty for parking illegally? We can be fairly certain that most people would leave their cars at home rather than risk that particular consequence. The point is that punishment can work if a sufficiently severe consequence is selected, but using the amount of force needed to produce results is rarely considered practical and ethical. Free societies have long-standing social prohibitions against cruel and unusual punishments, and these conventions are incompatible with using the force that may be needed to change the behavior of some individuals.

Immediate punishment is more effective than delayed punishment (i.e., immediacy). For the rat in the Skinner box, delays of just 10 seconds can reduce the effectiveness of electric shock as a punisher. Humans are more capable than rats at bridging long intervals. Nonetheless, the same principle holds true. Delayed punishment is less effective than immediate punishment. We should not be too surprised that the months or years that are required to try and convict a serious criminal may greatly reduce the impact of imprisonment on that person's subsequent behavior.

Our final requirement for effective punishment is its uniform application (i.e., consistency). College students are a prosocial, law-abiding group as a whole, yet many confess to determining their highway speed based on the presence or absence of a police car in their rearview mirrors. The experience of exceeding the speed limit without consequence weakens the ability of the possibility of tickets and fines to influence behavior. However, at intersections known to be controlled by cameras, compliance is generally quite high. If you are certain that running a red light will result in an expensive ticket, it would be foolish to test the system.

Skinner recommended extinction as an alternative to punishment (Skinner, 1953). In our discussion of classical conditioning, we used the term extinction to refer to the disappearance of CRs that occurs when the CS no longer signals the arrival of a UCS. Extinction in operant conditioning has a similar meaning. Learned behaviors stop when they are no longer followed by a reinforcing consequence. Attention is a powerful reinforcer for humans, and ignoring negative behavior should extinguish it. Parents and teachers cannot look the other way when

Putting up an umbrella to avoid getting wet from the rain is an example of a negatively reinforced behavior.

punishment A consequence that eliminates or reduces the frequency of a behavior.
positive punishment A consequence that eliminates or reduces the frequency of a behavior by applying an aversive stimulus.
negative punishment A method for reducing behavior by removing something desirable whenever the target behavior occurs.

WHAT IS OPERANT CONDITIONING?   **297**

The likelihood of getting a ticket influences drivers' behavior. At an intersection with cameras, drivers are unlikely to run a red light, but at other intersections, behavior might be determined by whether a police officer is nearby.

one child is being physically aggressive toward another, but in many other instances, Skinner's approach is quite successful in reducing the frequency of unwanted behaviors (Brown & Elliot, 1965). Although ignoring a child's tantrums can be embarrassing for many parents, this can be an effective strategy for reducing their frequency.

Schedules of Reinforcement

Reinforcing a behavior every time it occurs is known as continuous reinforcement. Although it is highly desirable to use continuous reinforcement when a new behavior is being learned, it is inconvenient to do so forever. Dog owners want their dogs to walk with a loose leash, but once this skill is learned, the owners don't want to carry big bags of dog treats for reinforcement whenever they walk their dogs. Once we deviate from continuous reinforcement, however, the manner in which we do so may have a dramatic impact on the target behavior. To obtain the results we want, it is helpful to understand what happens when we use **partial reinforcement**, or the reinforcement of the desired behavior on some occasions but not others.

Psychologists have identified many ways to apply partial reinforcement, but we will concentrate on two variations: ratio schedules and interval schedules. In a ratio schedule of partial reinforcement, reinforcement depends on the number of times a behavior occurs. In an interval schedule of partial reinforcement, reinforcement depends on the passage of a certain amount of time. Either type of schedule, ratio or interval, can be fixed or variable. In fixed schedules, the requirements for reinforcement never vary. In variable schedules, the requirements for reinforcement are allowed to fluctuate from trial to trial, averaging a certain amount over the course of a learning session.

Concerns about the effects of piecework on worker well-being contributed to the Fair Labor Standards Act of 1938, which included a provision for a minimum hourly wage.

Fixed Ratio Schedules A **fixed ratio (FR) schedule** requires that a behavior occur a set number of times for each reinforcer. Continuous reinforcement, discussed earlier, is equivalent to a FR of 1. If we now raise our requirement to two behaviors per reinforcer, we have a FR schedule of 2, and so on. Using the Skinner box, we can investigate the influence of FR schedules on the rate at which a rat will press a bar for food. To do so, we track cumulative responses as a function of time. FR schedules produce a characteristic pattern of responding. In general, responses are fairly steady, with a significant pause following each reward. As the amount of work for each reward is increased, responding becomes slower (see ● Figure 8.8).

In early industrial settings, workers were often paid "by the piece," a real-world example of the use of an FR schedule. In other words, a worker would be paid every time that worker produced a fixed number of products or parts on an assembly line. Most workers find this system less than ideal. If equipment malfunctions, the worker cannot earn money. Lunch breaks would also then be viewed as loss of income rather than a helpful time of rest. Some examples of piecework remain today, including the work of most physicians, who get paid by the procedure, and building contractors, who get paid for constructing a fixed number of homes in a new development.

Variable Ratio Schedules As in FR schedules, **variable ratio (VR) schedules** also involve counting the number of times a behavior occurs. However, this time the required number of behaviors is allowed to fluctuate around some average amount.

In the Skinner box, we might set our VR schedule to 10 for a 1-hour session. This means that over the course of the session, the rat must press an average of 10 times for each food pellet. However, this schedule may mean that only 1 press delivers food on one trial but 30 presses are required on the next trial. The rat is unable to predict when reinforcement is likely to occur, leading to a high, steady rate of responding in our cumulative record. We do not see the characteristic pausing observed following reinforcement in the FR schedule, because the rat cannot predict when the next reward will occur.

partial reinforcement The reinforcement of a desired behavior on some occasions but not others.
fixed ratio (FR) schedule A schedule of reinforcement in which reinforcement occurs following a set number of behaviors.
variable ratio (VR) schedule A schedule of reinforcement in which reinforcement occurs following some variable number of behaviors.

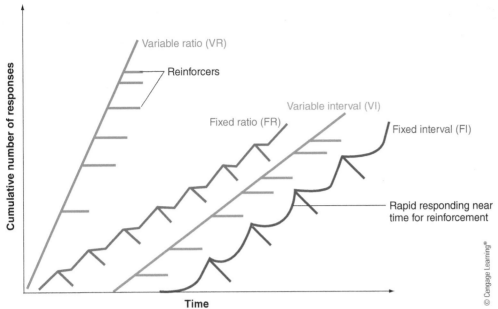

FIGURE 8.8

Schedules of Reinforcement.
The schedule used to deliver reinforcement has a big impact on resulting behavior. In general, the variable schedules produce higher rates of responding than do their fixed counterparts. The fixed interval schedule produces a characteristic pattern of low rates of responding at the beginning of the interval and accelerated responding as the end of the interval approaches.

One of the most dramatic real-world examples of the VR schedule is the programming of slot machines in casinos. Slot machines are human versions of Skinner boxes that use VR schedules. The casino sets the machine to pay off after some average number of plays, but the player doesn't know whether a payoff will occur after one coin or thousands are inserted. You don't have to observe the behavior of people playing slot machines long to see a demonstration of the high, steady responding that characterizes the VR schedule. The programming of slot machines can be sophisticated. Slot machines that are located in places where people are unlikely to return (airports and bus stations) pay off less frequently than those in places where people are more likely to play regularly.

Fixed Interval Schedules Unlike the ratio schedules, reinforcement in interval schedules depends on the passage of time rather than the number of responses produced. In a **fixed interval (FI) schedule**, the time that must pass before reinforcement becomes available following a single response is set at a certain amount. In the Skinner box, a rat's first bar press starts a timer. Responses that occur before the timer counts down are not reinforced. As soon as the timer counts down to zero, the rat's next bar press is reinforced, and the timer starts counting down again. In the FI schedule, the interval is the same from trial to trial. Animals and people have a good general sense of the passage of time, leading to a characteristic pattern of responding in FI situations. Reinforcement is followed by a long pause. As the end of the interval is anticipated, responding increases sharply. A graph of the number of bills passed by the U.S. Congress as a function of time looks similar to the rat's performance on an FI schedule in the Skinner box (Weisberg & Waldrop, 1972). Few bills are passed at the beginning of a session, but many are passed at the end (see ● Figure 8.9).

Variable Interval Schedules As you may have already guessed, the **variable interval (VI) schedule** is characterized by an interval that is allowed to fluctuate around some average amount over the course of a session. This time, our bar-pressing rat experiences intervals that range around some average amount, say, 2 minutes. On one trial, the rat may obtain reinforcement after only 30 seconds, whereas the next trial may involve an interval of 5 minutes. Over the session, the average of all intervals is 2 minutes. As in the VR situation, we see a high, steady rate of responding.

Workers in the garment industry are often paid "by the piece," or with a set amount of money for each finished garment. This compensation system is an example of a fixed ratio schedule. Because workers cannot make money when their equipment breaks down and they tend to view lunch and other breaks as costing them money, this schedule is not considered to be fair to workers.

fixed interval (FI) schedule A schedule of reinforcement in which the first response following a specified interval is reinforced.

variable interval (VI) schedule A schedule of reinforcement in which the first response following a varying period is reinforced.

Most casinos feature a large number of slot machines, which are essentially Skinner boxes for people. The slot machine is programmed on a variable ratio (VR) schedule, which means that the player cannot predict how many plays it will take to win. In response, players exhibit the same high, steady rate of responding that we observe in rats working on VR schedules in the laboratory.

Tetra Images/Photoshot

You are probably quite familiar with VI schedules in the form of pop quizzes administered by your professors. Your professor might tell you that there will be five quizzes given during the term, but the timing of the quizzes remains a surprise. You might have the first two only 1 day apart, followed by a 2-week interval before the next quiz. Your best strategy, like the rat in the Skinner box on a VI schedule, is to emit a high, steady rate of behavior.

Partial Reinforcement Effect in Extinction   Many parents have regretted the day that they unintentionally put an unwanted behavior on a partial reinforcement schedule by uttering the words, "OK, just this once." Perhaps a parent is strongly opposed to buying candy for a child at the supermarket checkout counter (where, because of John Watson and his applications of psychology to advertising, candy is displayed conveniently at child-eye height). Then comes a fateful day when the parent is late coming home from work, the child is hungry because dinner is delayed, and unintentionally, the parent gives in "just this once," putting begging for candy on a variable schedule. Subsequently, when the parent returns to the previous refusal to buy candy, a high, steady rate of begging behavior occurs before it extinguishes.

In the laboratory once more, we compare the behavior of two rats in Skinner boxes. One is working on a continuous, or FR 1, schedule of reinforcement. The other is working on a partial schedule of reinforcement, perhaps a VR 3 schedule. After several sessions of training, we stop reinforcement for both rats. It may surprise you that the rat working on the continuous schedule will stop pressing long before the rat accustomed to the VR 3 schedule. In other words, extinction occurs more rapidly following continuous reinforcement than following partial schedules. This outcome is known as the **partial reinforcement effect in extinction**.

FIGURE 8.9

Congress and Fixed Interval (FI) Behavior. As the end of a congressional session approaches, the U.S. Congress begins to pass more bills in patterns that look similar to the behavior of rats on FI schedules in Skinner boxes.

partial reinforcement effect in extinction   The more rapid extinction observed following continuous reinforcement compared to that following partial reinforcement.

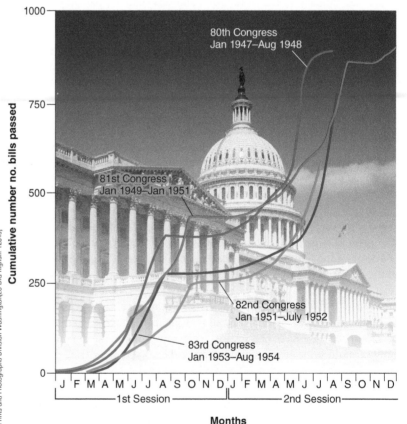

Illustration: © 2016 Cengage Learning®. photo: Library of Congress Prints and Photographs Division Washington[LC-DIG-highsm-12649]

The partial reinforcement effect probably occurs because of one of two factors or a combination of both. First, the transition from continuous reinforcement to extinction is more obvious than the transition from a partial schedule to extinction. If you are accustomed to being paid for a babysitting job every time you work, you will definitely notice any of your employer's failures to pay. In contrast, if your neighbor typically pays you about once a month for raking his yard, you might not notice right away that he hasn't paid you for a while. Second, partial schedules teach organisms to persist in the face of nonreinforcement. In a sense, partial schedules teach us to work through periods in which reinforcement does not occur. Consequently, we might view extinction as just another case where continuing to perform might eventually produce reinforcement. When positive behavior is occurring, such as working on your senior thesis regularly despite a much-delayed grade, persistence is an enormous advantage. However, as shown in our earlier example of begging for candy, placing an undesirable behavior on partial reinforcement makes it more difficult to eventually extinguish.

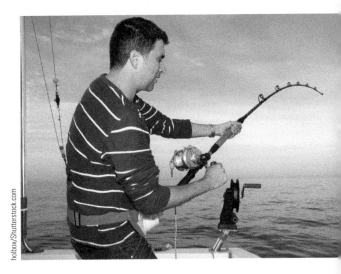

Comparing Schedules What happens if you are exposed to two or more schedules of reinforcement at the same time? This scenario is realistic, because we face these types of choices every day. Which is a more rewarding use of my time: studying for my midterm or making some extra money by working overtime? In making these types of choices, animals and people follow the matching law, which states that the relative frequency of responding to one alternative will match the relative reinforcement for responses on that alternative (Herrnstein & Heyman, 1979). The law powerfully accounts for the effects on behavior of frequency, magnitude, and delays in reward.

Fishing works according to a variable interval (VI) schedule of reinforcement. Fish (the reinforcers) are caught after periods of waiting for fish to bite that vary in length. As in laboratory demonstrations of the VI schedule, fishing usually produces a steady rate of responding.

Time spent playing online video games provides an interesting example of the effects of simultaneous schedules of reinforcement. The millions of users of massively multiplayer online role-playing games, such as *Everquest* and *Star Wars Galaxies,* spend an average of 22 hours per week on their games (Yee, 2006). What compels these people to make such a lopsided choice between online interactions and real-life social experience? One clue to this choice is that substantial numbers of players report that "the most rewarding or satisfying experience" they had over the last 7 or 30 days took place while gaming. We would assume that if the frequency and magnitude of rewards available in gaming were higher than those in real-life socializing, people would choose to spend their time accordingly.

method of successive approximations A method for increasing the frequency of behaviors that never or rarely occur; also known as shaping.

Children are not born with terrific table manners, and parents would have to wait a long time to see perfect table manners that they can reinforce. Instead, we can use the method of successive approximations, or shaping, to gently move behaviors in the desired direction.

The Method of Successive Approximations (Shaping)

So far, our discussion of operant conditioning has centered on increasing or decreasing the frequency of a particular behavior. What happens if you want to increase the frequency of a behavior that rarely or never occurs? Most parents would like to teach their children to use good table manners, but you could wait a long time for the opportunity to reward young children for using the correct utensil to eat their food.

Fortunately, we have a method for increasing the frequency of behaviors that never or rarely occur. Using the **method of successive approximations**, or shaping, we begin by reinforcing spontaneous behaviors that are somewhat similar to the target behavior we want to train. As training continues, we use gradually more stringent requirements for reinforcement until the exact behavior we want occurs. You can think of shaping as a funnel. Using the table manners example, parents start out with generous criteria for reinforcement ("thank you for picking up the spoon") and gradually narrow the criteria ("thank you for putting the spoon in the food") until they are reinforcing only the target behavior ("thank you for using the spoon to eat your applesauce"). One of the most positive features about the shaping process is that behavior doesn't have to be perfect to produce reinforcement.

The rats in Skinner boxes that have been described in this chapter do not spontaneously start pressing levers. We have to teach them to do so.

We begin by making sure the hungry rat understands that food is available in the Skinner box. Using a remote control, we activate the food dispenser a few times. Quickly, the rat forms a classically conditioned association between the sound of the food dispenser (CS) and the arrival of food (UCS) in the cup. However, if we continue to feed the rat in this manner, it is unlikely that it will ever learn to press the bar. There is no reason for it to do so, because it already is obtaining the food it needs. So, we narrow our criteria for obtaining food from simply existing in the box to standing in the corner of the box that contains the bar. If we press our remote control every time the rat is in the correct corner, it will begin to stay there most of the time. Now we want the rat to rear on its back feet so that it is likely to hit the bar with its front feet on the way down. If we begin to reinforce the rat less frequently for staying in the corner, it will begin to explore. Eventually, the rat is likely to hit the bar with its front feet while exploring, pressing the bar. Now it will begin to press the bar on its own. In the hands of an experienced trainer, this process takes about half an hour.

Shaping involves a delicate tightrope walk between too much and too little reinforcement. If we reinforce too generously, learning stops, because there is no incentive for change. If your music teacher always tells you that your performances are perfect, you will stop trying to improve them. However, if we don't reinforce frequently enough, the learner becomes discouraged. Reinforcement provides important feedback to the learner, so insufficient reinforcement may slow or stop the learning process.

Teaching a complex behavior requires chaining, or the breaking down of the complex behavior into manageable steps. Chaining can be done in a forward direction, such as teaching the letters of the alphabet from A to Z, or in a backward direction, such as teaching the last step in a sequence, then the next to the last, and so on. Chaining can be useful when teaching new skills, such as working independently on academic projects, to children with special needs (Pelios, MacDuff, & Axelrod, 2003). Backward chaining is used by most trainers of animals used in entertainment. For example, dogs have been taught to perform complex dances like the Macarena (Burch & Bailey, 1999). The trainer uses a verbal, gestural, or clicker cue while shaping the last step in the dance. When the dog performs this last step reliably, the trainer adds the next-to-last step and so on until the entire complex sequence is mastered.

Cognitive, Biological, and Social Influences on Operant Conditioning

Even the most radical behaviorists, including Skinner, did not deny the existence of cognitive, social, or biological influences on learning (Jensen & Burgess, 1997). Instead, behaviorists believed that internal processes followed the same rules as externally observable behavior. As Skinner (1953) wrote, "We need not suppose that events which take place within an organism's skin have special properties. . . . A private event may be distinguished by its limited accessibility but not, so far as we know, by any special nature or structure" (p. 257). However, as we saw in the case of classical conditioning, the results of some operant conditioning experiments stimulated greater interest in the cognitive, social, and biological processes involved in learning.

Cognitive Influences on Operant Conditioning One of the important principles of operant conditioning is that consequences are required for learning to occur. Edward Tolman (1948) challenged this notion by allowing his rats to explore mazes without food reinforcement. Subsequently, when food was placed in the goal boxes of the mazes, the previously unreinforced rats performed as well as the rats that had been reinforced all along. Tolman referred to the rats' ability to learn in the absence of reinforcement as **latent learning**. He argued that the rats had learned while just exploring but that they did not demonstrate their learning until motivated by the food reward to do so. We usually judge whether learning has occurred by observing outward behavior. Tolman's rats remind us that there is a difference between what has been learned and what is performed. Students are all too familiar with the experience of performing poorly on exams despite having learned a great deal about the material.

In addition to challenging the role of reinforcement in learning, Tolman disputed traditional behaviorist explanations of the nature of the learning that occurred in mazes. Tolman

latent learning Learning that occurs in the absence of reinforcement.

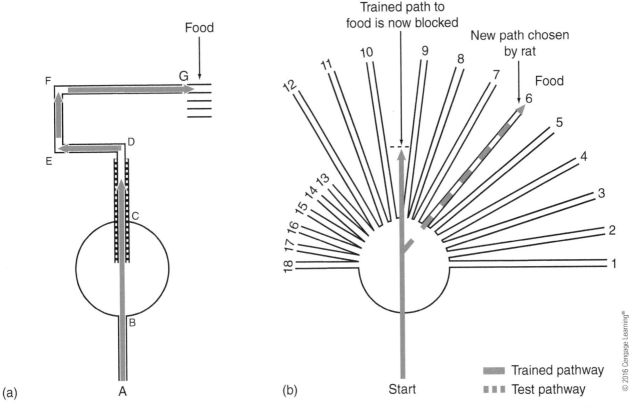

(a)   A

(b)   Start

Trained path to food is now blocked

New path chosen by rat

Food

■■ Trained pathway
■ ■ ■ Test pathway

© 2016 Cengage Learning®

FIGURE 8.10

Tolman's Maze. Edward Tolman did not believe that rats wandering around a maze learned "turn left for food" in the way that early behaviorists believed they did. Instead, Tolman believed the rats were learning a more cognitive map of where they could find food. Tolman provided evidence for his approach by blocking a learned pathway to food. If the behaviorists were right, the rats should choose the path most similar to the trained one. However, the rats did not do that. They showed evidence of having formed cognitive maps and were willing to turn in a different direction if that path led to food.

believed that instead of learning a simple operant "turn right for food" association, rats learned "this is where I can find food" (Tolman, 1948, 1959). After training rats to follow a path in a maze to find food, Tolman blocked the path but allowed the rats to choose from a number of additional paths. If the rats had learned a simple turn left–get food response, they should have chosen the paths that were most similar to the training path. Instead, they showed evidence of choosing paths that required them to turn in a different direction compared to their previously trained path but that led them directly to the goal (Tolman, Richie, & Kalish, 1946; see ● Figure 8.10).

To account for his results, Tolman suggested that the rats had formed cognitive maps, or mental representations of the mazes. Map formation was viewed as a unique, nonassociative learning process that didn't follow the previously established rules of associative learning (O'Keefe & Nadel, 1978). For example, in contrast to the gradual acquisition of learning that usually occurs in classical and operant conditioning, cognitive maps are instantly updated when new information becomes available.

Chimpanzees show considerable abilities in forming cognitive maps (Menzel, 1978). After being carried around a circuitous route in their 1-acre compound as nine vegetables and nine fruits were placed in 18 locations, chimpanzees were released in the center of the compound. They not only navigated to each food location using the shortest pathways, but, given their preference for fruit over vegetables, they visited the spots containing fruit first. They showed no indication that they were attempting to retrace the pathway over which they were carried as the food was put in place.

Biological Influences on Operant Conditioning Just as the work of Garcia and Koelling highlighted the need to consider biological limitations on classical conditioning, biological boundaries in operant conditioning were described by Keller and Marion Breland, two of Skinner's former students. In their 1961 article titled "The Misbehavior of Organisms" (a wordplay on Skinner's classic book, *The Behavior of Organisms*), the Brelands outlined some challenges they encountered while using operant conditioning to train animals for entertainment.

In one instance, the researchers described how they sought to train a pig to pick up large wooden coins and deposit the coins in a large wooden "piggy bank." Initially, all went well. The

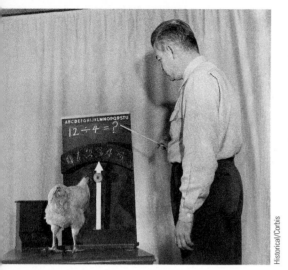

Keller Breland observes the performance of one of the star pupils of the I.Q. Zoo attraction he developed with his wife Marian. Unfortunately, the Brelands discovered that the animals' instinctive behaviors often interfered with their training. The Brelands referred to this phenomenon as instinctive drift.

pig would quickly learn to deposit four or five coins (an example of a FR schedule) for each food reward. Eventually, however, the pig began to work slower and slower to the point where it couldn't obtain enough food for the day. Instead of taking the coins to the piggy bank, the pig would repeatedly toss them in the air and sniff around to find them. Raccoons trained with the coins ultimately tried to wash them instead of depositing them in the bank. The animals' natural approach to food, the rooting by the pigs and the washing by the raccoons, began to interfere with their handling of the coins. You may already have suspected that the coins had become the object of some higher order classical conditioning because of their relationship with food. The Brelands concluded "that these animals are trapped by strong instinctive behaviors, and clearly we have here a demonstration of the prepotency of such behavior patterns over those which have been conditioned. We have termed this phenomenon 'instinctive drift'" (Breland & Breland, 1961, p. 683).

Social Influences on Operant Conditioning   So far in our discussion of classical and operant conditioning, we have focused on the individual in isolation. Learning can take place when people or animals are alone, but it often occurs in the presence of others, especially in a species as social as ours. As we will see in a later section, people are particularly likely to learn by observing others. What do we know about the impact of others on our operant learning?

The presence of others may not just promote learning; it may be necessary for learning. Human infants learn more about language when they are listening to another person face to face than when they are watching a person speak on television (Kuhl, 2007; Meltzoff, Kuhl, Movellan, & Sejnowski, 2009). Although operant conditioning alone cannot account for language learning, as we discuss in Chapters 10 and 11, these results emphasize the importance of social interaction in producing the arousal, focus, and motivation that contribute to effective learning.

As we mentioned previously in our discussion of cognitive maps, learning and the performance of learned behavior are not always identical. Our performance of learned behaviors varies depending on an interaction between the presence of others and the complexity of the learned task. For simple tasks, like pedaling a bicycle or reeling in a fishing line, the presence of others makes us perform faster, a phenomenon known as social facilitation (Triplett, 1898) (see Chapter 13). In complex tasks, such as taking a difficult college entrance exam, the presence of others can make our performance slower and poorer. Again, this effect is not restricted to complex organisms like ourselves; the same results can be observed in the lowly cockroach (Zajonc, 1965). In a straight maze leading to food, cockroaches with an audience of other cockroaches ran quickly. In a more complex maze involving several turns, the cockroaches responded to an audience by running more slowly.

Experienced whale trainer Dawn Brancheau was killed by one of her favorite killer whales during a 2010 show at Sea World in Orlando, Florida. Animal experts believed that the whale had simply reverted to normal whale behavior, similar to the instinctive drift observed by Keller and Marian Breland.

Applying Operant Conditioning

Important applications of operant conditioning may be found in contemporary approaches to psychotherapy, education, advertising, politics, and many other domains.

Possibly one of the oddest applications of operant conditioning was Skinner's secret World War II defense project code-named Project Pigeon. Lagging well behind the Nazis in the area of guided missile technology, the United States invested $25,000 (worth about $400,000 in today's dollars) in Skinner's "organic homing device" (Capshew, 1993). Skinner, who had considerable experience training pigeons to peck at visual stimuli in his laboratory, now trained them to peck at a projected image of a missile's target. Riding in a chamber within the missile, the pigeon's pecks would be translated into updated commands for correcting the path of the bomb. Unfortunately for Skinner (but fortunately for his pigeons), Project Pigeon elicited laughter from military officers instead of approval (Skinner, 1960). Although never implemented, Project Pigeon stimulated Skinner and his intellectual descendents to look outside the laboratory for useful extensions of their work on learning.

B.F. Skinner's Project Pigeon was one of the more bizarre applications of operant conditioning research. Pigeons enclosed in this capsule were trained to peck at projected images of bomb targets. Although Skinner's device was superior to other World War II missile guidance systems, it was never implemented.

Token Economies A widely used application of operant learning is the **token economy**. Money, in the form of coins, bills, bitcoins, or bank statements, is fairly useless. You can't eat it, wear it, or shelter in it. Nonetheless, people value it because it takes on secondary reinforcing qualities due to its history of association with other things that have intrinsic value. The use of money to buy things of personal value is an example of a token economy. You earn money for doing certain things, and then you have the opportunity to trade the money you earned for items of value to you. This system meets the best practices criteria we described for positive reinforcement. Each person can obtain reinforcement that has unique personal value. One friend may spend discretionary money on going out to dinner, while another invests in the stock market. Both find money reinforcing for doing work.

An informed approach to compensating employees should include consideration of learning principles. "Menu" approaches to employee benefits provide an excellent example of this application. Historically, employers offered a set program of health, retirement, and other benefits to their entire workforce regardless of individual needs. We would expect this approach to be minimally reinforcing, because it does not match reinforcers to worker priorities. Catering a benefits package to individual needs is more sensible. A young worker in good health might be more motivated by a benefits package that includes childcare, while a more mature worker may worry about long-term care in the event of a disability. By allowing workers to select their benefits from a menu, everybody can find something worth earning.

All of us respond positively to token economies, but they are especially useful in educational and institutional settings. Teachers provide frequent rewards in the form of checks, stars, or tickets that can be exchanged later for popcorn parties or a night without homework. The key to an effective token economy is to offer ultimate rewards that are truly valuable to the people you wish to motivate. If students don't care about popcorn parties, offering these will have little effect. Token economies are equally useful in prison settings and in institutions serving people with an intellectual disability or mental illness.

Token economies can be effective ways of managing behavior. Tokens, including money, can be traded for a valued reinforcement of the worker's choice. This woman's purchase might motivate her work, but another worker might use the same paycheck to buy a motorcycle or go on vacation.

token economy An application of operant conditioning in which tokens that can be exchanged for other reinforcers are used to increase the frequency of desirable behaviors.

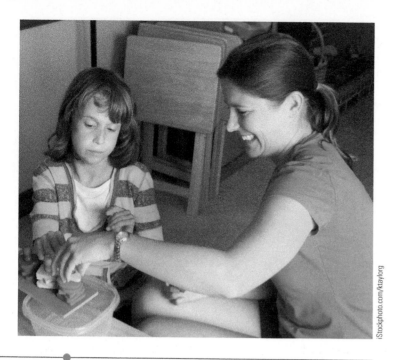

An important application of operant conditioning principles is their use in behavior therapies for conditions like autism spectrum disorder. Operant conditioning can be used to increase the frequency of language use and socially appropriate behaviors, like eye contact.

Behavior Therapies As we will see in Chapter 15, learning theories have also been applied successfully to the clinical setting in the form of behavior therapies, also called applied behavior analysis. After all, our formal definition of learning states that it involves a change in behavior, and changing behavior is precisely what therapists usually seek to do. In addition to the extinction and counterconditioning applications of classical conditioning, behavior therapies use operant conditioning concepts such as extinction, reward, and on rare occasions, punishment.

Coupled with cognitive methods designed to address the way people think about their circumstances, these methods comprise the most popular and effective means for treating many types of disorder, from substance abuse to depression. One of the most dramatic applications of behavior therapy is the treatment for autism spectrum disorder pioneered by O. Ivar Lovaas (Lovaas, 1996; Lovaas et al., 1966). Autism spectrum disorder is characterized by language and social deficits. Although behavior therapy doesn't cure autism spectrum disorder, behavioral interventions, like the use of chaining described previously, typically improve an individual's level of functioning.

 # Experiencing Psychology

How Do I Break a Bad Habit?

WE ALL HAVE behaviors that could use some improvement. Maybe we eat poorly, drink too much, smoke, or lash out angrily at others. An understanding of the processes of learning provides us with powerful tools for changing behavior. Let's as-

sume that your eating habits, like those of many students, do not meet the "my mom would approve" standard. Yet you are learning in your psychology course that good health habits are essential tools for managing stress (see Chapter 16). How do you bring about the necessary changes?

Before doing anything to produce change, you need to understand your current behavior. Many people have a poor understanding of what they actually eat during a day, so you could start by keeping a diary. What foods and how much of them do you eat? What else is going on when you eat well or poorly? What possible reinforcers or punishers are influencing your eating

patterns? For the sake of example, let's say that you observe a tendency to eat high-calorie snacks late at night while studying, even when you are not hungry. Your goal, then, is to eliminate these late-night snacks. Your baseline shows that your snacking is a social behavior. You only consume these extra foods when studying with a group. The social camaraderie and good taste of the food serve as powerful reinforcers for the behavior.

Now that you have a better understanding of your problem behavior, you are in a good position to construct a plan. Some people might say that you should depend on willpower to avoid late-night snacks by just saying that you won't have any. Unfor-

Summary 8.3 Schedules of Reinforcement

Schedule	Features	In the lab	Everyday example
Fixed ratio	Reinforcement occurs after a set number of responses.	A rat presses 3 times for each food pellet.	A garment worker is paid for finishing 10 shirts.
Variable ratio	Reinforcement occurs after a variable number of responses, which average a set number for a session.	A rat is fed on average after 3 responses, but the number of responses required for obtaining food varies between 1 and 15.	People play slot machines and win, sometimes on the first play and other times after thousands of plays, on a schedule determined by the casino.
Fixed interval	Each response begins an interval during which no reinforcement is available. The first response after the interval is reinforced.	A rat's first press after each 1-min interval has timed out is reinforced.	Students study more hours right before finals than at the beginning of the term (although unlike in the rat's case, this behavior contributes to reinforcement).
Variable interval	Each response begins an interval of varying length, with the average length for the session set by the experimenter.	A rat's first press after an interval is reinforced. The interval averages 1 min over the session, but reinforcement could be obtained after intervals ranging between 10 sec and 3 min.	A fisherman trails his line behind the boat, and at various intervals of time, a fish is caught.

tunately, many people have limited quantities of willpower, and using some up temporarily reduces their supply for use on subsequent decisions (Gailliot et al., 2007). Given that the average person makes a stunning 200 to 250 food-related decisions per day, many requiring willpower, anything you can do to lessen the load should be helpful (Wansink & Sobal, 2007). Consequently, engineering your environment to reduce the need to make choices and to use some of your limited supply of willpower would be helpful. This goal could be accomplished by scheduling group study sessions for earlier times in the day, ensuring that you no longer keep high-calorie snacks in your room, substituting healthy food items for high-calorie snacks, or using evening socialization time to engage in activities that do not provide much opportunity for snacking, such as sports.

The next step is to agree on appropriate consequences for your behavior. Again, it is essential that we design consequences that are meaningful to individuals. As we have argued in this chapter, positive reinforcement has many advantages over punishment. You might try placing the money you're saving on junk food in a designated jar to buy a special (nonfood) treat at the end of a successful week or allow yourself an extra study break each night you meet your goals. If you are convinced that the only way you will change is through punishment, you could take an alternate approach. Although some people have successfully stopped smoking through the use of positive punishment, including electric shock (Law & Tang, 1995), this sounds quite unpleasant. Instead, a negative punishment such as losing Facebook privileges for the day following a failure to meet one's goals might work.

As you implement your program, track your progress and make any modifications that seem necessary. In addition to the improvement of your target behavior, a beneficial side effect of applying learning methods to your behavior is the knowledge that given the right tools, you can be in control of your behavior. ●

What Is Observational Learning?

The ability to learn by watching others, known as observational learning, provides considerable advantages, especially in a social species like our own. Learning occurs without personally experiencing negative consequences. This ability to learn from observing others greatly expands our learning capacity, especially when we then generalize from these concrete examples (watching successful students) to produce effective rules (good time management is important to being a successful student). Observational learning can also have a dark side, as we will see in our later discussion of the pioneering work by Albert Bandura (1965) on the modeling of aggression by children.

Not only do we learn by observing others, but it appears that observational learning can override other influences on behavior, possibly because we are such a social species. Parents learn, often the hard way, that children are more likely to pattern behavior after what they observe their parents doing than after what they hear their parents say.

Various behaviors, both positive and negative, appear to be influenced by observation, including aggression, achievement motivation, language development, phobias, cognitive development, moral judgment, and suicidal behavior. People benefit greatly from exposure to positive role models, especially those with whom they can identify. We worry about the relatively small number of women in university math and science faculties not only because of the possibility of discrimination but also because seeing women in these positions might inspire young girls to follow in their footsteps. However, the use of steroids by sports heroes might lead to role modeling of a different sort by young people.

It is easy to find examples of observational learning in our daily lives. New college students identify successful, more experienced students in their classes and copy their behavior. Stumped by your new computer software, not to mention the manual that came with it, you watch as a tech-savvy friend shows you how to make it work. Young athletes pore over films of superstars to perfect their technique. Popular cooking shows on television teach you to prepare a special meal. Cross-generational cycles of domestic violence persist as children continue the patterns of aggressive behavior they observe in their parents and grandparents. Our task in this section is to identify the circumstances in which this type of learning occurs and the variables that affect its outcomes.

Babies learned more Chinese when listening to a person face to face than while watching the same person speak on a television monitor. *Source:* From Patricia K. Kuhl, Brain Mechanisms in Early Language Acquisition, *Neuron 67,* September 9, 2010, (c) Elsevier Inc.

© Elsevier Inc.

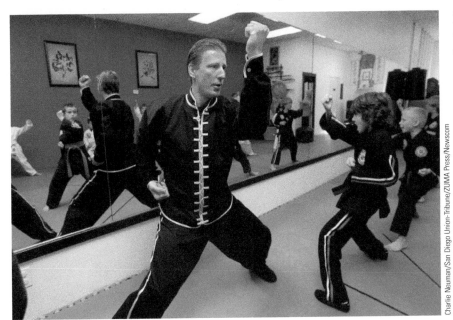

Observational learning can provide a quick and easy way to learn without having to go through individual trial and error.

Charlie Neuman/San Diego Union-Tribune/ZUMA Press/Newscom

Albert Bandura and Aggression

Bandura's work on the observational learning of aggression provides one of the strongest arguments against exposing children to violent media (Bandura, 1965). Bandura was interested in **imitation**, which is defined as the copying of behavior that is unlikely to occur naturally and spontaneously (Thorpe, 1963).

In a series of classic studies of the imitation of aggression in children, Bandura observed children's interactions with a toy known as a Bobo doll. This is an inflatable toy clown with sand in the bottom, allowing it to rock back and forth when pushed. Bandura showed three groups of 3- to 5-year-olds a film in which an adult model physically and verbally assaulted an unfortunate Bobo doll. The adult yelled, "Pow, right in the nose!" when punching the doll in the face, "Sockeroo, stay down!" when hitting the doll with a mallet, "Fly away" when kicking the doll around the room, and "Bang!" when throwing a ball at the doll. The first group of children saw the adult being rewarded for aggression with candy and soda. A second group of children saw the adult being verbally reprimanded, spanked, and threatened. The third group did not see any positive or negative consequences for the adult's actions. Subsequently, when the children who had viewed the film were allowed an opportunity to play with a Bobo doll, they displayed a significant amount of aggression. In all cases, boys were more likely to behave aggressively than girls. The group that witnessed the reprimand of the adult model showed slightly less aggression.

Bandura identified four necessary cognitive processes in the modeling of others' behavior: attention, retention, reproduction, and motivation. Models that get our *attention* are more likely to elicit imitation. A person must *retain* a memory of what the model did. We must be able to *reproduce* the behavior. Many of us enjoy watching elite athletes perform, but no matter how long and often we watch Serena Williams or LeBron James, few of us have the talent to duplicate their movements. If you happen to play tennis or basketball, however, you can learn to improve your game if you carefully observe these superstars. Finally, a person must have a *motivation* for imitating the behavior. Either past or anticipated reinforcement encourages us to model another person's behavior. In vicarious reinforcement, witnessing somebody else getting reinforced for a behavior raises the likelihood that we will imitate the behavior. At the same time, witnessing the other person getting punished for the behavior should reduce the likelihood that you will copy it.

imitation Copying behavior that is unlikely to occur naturally and spontaneously.

Albert Bandura/Stanford University

After watching an adult model assault the Bobo doll, young children copied the adult's movements and verbalizations.

Imitation

Imitation is not limited to the copying of aggression. It occurs frequently in the animal world, which suggests that this behavior provides some adaptive advantages. When rats have observed another rat pressing a bar for food, it takes them less time to learn to press the bar themselves (Del Russo, 1971). Laboratory-raised monkeys quickly learn to fear snakes when exposed to a wild monkey that reacts to snakes with fear (Mineka & Cook, 1988). Imitation of gestures occurs in a number of species in addition to our own, including chimpanzees (Custance, Whiten, & Bard, 1995), dolphins (Harley, Xitco, Roitblat, & Herman, 1998), octopuses (Fiorito & Scotto, 1992), and parrots (Moore, 1992).

As we mentioned in Chapter 7, imitation of facial expressions might serve as a building block on the road to achieving empathy (Iacoboni & Dapretto, 2006; Iacoboni & Mazziotta,

Connecting to Research

Why Do Children Overimitate?

WE HAVE SEEN THAT imitation occurs in many species and might have special advantages for human children. To quickly absorb the benefits of culture, children can watch adults use objects and tools and then replicate those actions. This tendency is so strong that children across many cultural settings have been shown to overimitate. In other words, they copy movements performed by adults that are not required to carry out a task successfully (Nielsen & Tomaselli, 2010).

The Question: Why would children overimitate adults: Do they trust adults so much that they copy everything adults do, or are they overimitating to build stronger relationships and be better liked by adults? (The second explanation is consistent with research suggesting that we like people who imitate us, discussed previously in Chapter 6; see Lakin, Chartrand, & Arkin, 2008.)

METHODS

Thirty-six children between 4 and 5 years old participated in the study. They observed two adults open a box to obtain a toy. One adult would open the box using only the movements that were necessary, while the other adult would open the box after performing some irrelevant actions, such as tapping the right side of the box three times or swiping the top of the lid. After the demonstration, one adult would leave the room, and the other adult would tell the child, "Now it's your turn."

Pier Francesco Ferrari, University of Parma, from PLoS Biology, Sept. 2006, Vol. 4, Issue 9

Imitation forms the basis of much observational learning. A remaining question is whether imitation involves mirror neurons that activate whether you perform a behavior or see someone else perform the behavior. *Source:* "Neonatal Imitation in Rhesus Macaques," by P. F. Ferrari, E. Visalberghi, A. Paukner, L. Fogassi, A. Ruggiero, et al., 2006, *PLoS Biology*, 4(9), e302. doi:10.1371/journal. pbio.0040302.

2007). Individuals with autism spectrum disorder do not participate in the back-and-forth imitation of gestures and facial expressions typically found in infants (Dapretto et al., 2006). Later in life, these individuals usually experience severe deficits in empathy and social skills (Williams, 2008).

Mirror Neurons

Imitation in monkeys and humans involves special neurons known as mirror neurons, which we discussed in Chapter 4. Mirror neurons in monkeys show similar patterns of activity when the individual performs an action or watches another individual perform the same action (Rizzolatti, Fadiga, Gallese, & Fogassi, 1996; cf. Caspers, Zilles, Laird, & Eickhoff, 2010). In monkeys, mirror neurons were observed through surgically implanted electrodes, as we described in our Connecting to Research feature in Chapter 4. Identification of mirror neurons in humans has been complicated by ethical concerns. We can't surgically implant electrodes in people except in rare clinical cases in which patients are undergoing surgical treatment for epileptic seizures. These investigations have revealed the existence of neurons with mirrorlike properties in humans (Keysers & Gazzola, 2010; Mukamel, Ekstrom, Kaplan, Iacoboni, & Fried, 2010).

What purposes might be served by mirror neurons? Although debatable (Kosonogov, 2012), one suggestion is that mirror neurons contribute to our ability to predict the actions of

RESULTS

All the children were able to open the box. If the adult who remained with the child was the one who opened the box with only necessary movements, the child was unlikely to demonstrate unnecessary movements. If the adult who remained was the one who had performed the unnecessary movements, however, the child was likely to overimitate and reproduce the unnecessary movements.

CONCLUSIONS

The results of this study support the social affiliation explanation of overimitation. Children only showed overimitation when the adult remaining with them in the room was the one who had performed the unnecessary actions. The researchers suggest that imitation in humans is not just about learning new skills efficiently—imitation promotes shared experience with other people and builds rapport.

Overimitation has been recently observed in chimpanzees (Price, Lambeth, Schapiro, & Whiten, 2009). Chimpanzees that watched videos of another chimpanzee assembling a tool out of two parts to reach a food reward were more likely than chimpanzees that did not see the video to assemble the tool themselves, even when the tool was unnecessary for obtaining food. We need more research to identify whether the same motives for overimitation observed in children apply to the chimpanzees. ●

others, allowing us to understand intentions (Fogassi et al., 2005). Again, the ability to predict future circumstances would contribute significantly to the survival of an organism. Mirror neurons might also form the basis of empathy. Individuals who appear to be high in empathy show stronger activation than other people in identified mirror systems in the human brain (Gazzola, Aziz-Zadeh, & Keysers, 2006; Jabbi, Swart, & Keysers, 2007).

Children use gestures, like pointing at a cookie jar to indicate "I want a cookie," long before they learn to use words to convey the same meaning. It is likely that preverbal hominins also used gestures to communicate. Mirror neurons might have played a role in the development of language, both for our species and for individual learners (Ramachandran, 2006). Consistent with this argument, mirror neurons in monkeys are located in a part of the brain that is quite similar to the human Broca's area of the frontal lobe (Petrides, Cadoret, & Mackey, 2005). As we discussed in Chapter 4, activation in Broca's area is correlated with the production of speech.

Because individuals with autism spectrum disorder do not show typical imitative behaviors in childhood (see Chapter 14), a natural extension would be to look for possible correlates in the mirror neuron systems. Some researchers have presented evidence that mirror neuron function is disturbed in individuals with autism spectrum disorder, especially when they are engaged in emotional or social tasks (Perkins, Stokes, McGillivray, & Bittar, 2010). Others argue that a "broken mirror" explanation for the social deficits observed in individuals with autism spectrum disorder is overly simplistic and that further research is necessary before making strong conclusions about mirror neuron function in this population (Fan, Decety, Yang, Liu, & Cheng, 2010).

Cultural Transmission of Learning

An individual's learning may serve that person well throughout a lifetime, but the invention of culture provides opportunities to pass the benefits of experience along for many generations. A society is a group of people living together. Culture, in contrast, consists of all the socially transmitted information used by the group of people, including ideas, concepts, and skills. Observational learning in particular provides a powerful tool for transmitting this information over time.

Richard Dawkins (1976) envisioned a way to break culture down into observable parts. He referred to the basic unit of cultural transmission as a meme. Memes, he said, are transmitted by observational learning from one person to another and can take the form of ideas, symbols, or practices. Melodies, religious beliefs, catchphrases, and the technology for building arches are examples of memes. Dawkins viewed memes as the cultural equivalents of genes—they replicate from one person to the next, and they respond to selection pressure. Memes that provide an advantage, such as knowledge of the use of fire, are likely to continue. Those that do not confer much advantage, such as some fads, are likely to die out quickly. Still others, such as pagers, are abandoned when more effective replacements (cell phones) emerge.

Among the most social of memes are Internet memes, which are "inside jokes" passed to others using technologies such as social networking sites and e-mail. Special websites that chronicle Internet memes allow viewers to provide updates of their favorite memes, which contributes to their popularity.

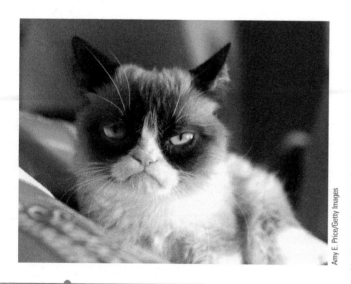

Amy E. Price/Getty Images

Richard Dawkins defined a meme as the basic unit of cultural transmission passed to others by observational learning. If the Grumpy Cat Internet meme does not continue to provide advantages, it is likely to be replaced by something new.

Interpersonal Relationships

The Learning Perspective

Can We Influence the Way Others Behave Toward Us?

Knowledge of the way people learn can improve your social life and possibly even your love life. Operant conditioning can help you decrease unwanted behaviors and increase desired behaviors toward you by people with whom you interact. Your behavior influences the way others behave toward you. If you regularly find that you are treated poorly in relationships, understanding the learning perspective provides powerful tools for change.

In this chapter, we have recommended an emphasis on regularly noticing and rewarding desired behaviors. It is easy to fall into the trap of feeling entitled to good behavior from the people who are close to us, which can lead to these behaviors being taken for granted and ignored. Without positive reinforcement, these good behaviors might be extinguished. It takes little time and energy to thank people for the nice things they do for us, and this simple courtesy can increase the frequency of positive interactions in the future.

When the inevitable undesirable behaviors occur, many people turn to punishment. Skinner believed that part of the love affair we have with punishment is because of the reinforcing properties of punishment to the punisher. Skinner (1971) stated, "We 'instinctively' attack anyone whose behavior displeases us—perhaps not in physical assault, but with criticism, disapproval, blame, or ridicule" (p. 190). Punishing a partner for bad behavior might make you feel better, but this comes at a significant cost. These punishing behaviors are not endearing, and frequent use of them is likely to end relationships.

If punishment is out, what then do we recommend you do when you experience negative behavior from a partner? If possible, try to ignore negative behaviors, putting them on extinction. Unfortunately, some people would rather have negative attention from you than no attention and prefer punishment from you to being ignored. This is particularly likely to be the case if you have forgotten to reinforce positive behaviors. If you combine positive reinforcement of good behavior and extinction of negative behavior, you should notice quite an improvement. Some behaviors like aggression cannot be ignored and require either a complete end to the relationship or professional counseling.

Thoughtfully observing the way you treat other people and their reactions to your behavior, using the learning principles described in this chapter, should provide you with the understanding you need to improve your relationships. ●

Ignoring annoying behavior can be difficult, but you don't want to reinforce it with attention.

Summary 8.4 Features Promoting Observational Learning and Imitation

Feature	Description	Example
Attention	We are more likely to model the behavior of people who get our attention.	Children wear the jerseys of the best players in the sport.
Memory	We must retain a memory of the behavior to be imitated.	A student re-creates from memory a math proof demonstrated earlier that day by a professor.
Reproduction	We must have the ability to reproduce the behavior.	An athlete works on her technique after watching films of an elite athlete in her sport.
Motivation	Past or anticipated reinforcement for the behavior motivates us to perform it.	One student received extra credit for participating in an experiment, so his friends also signed up to participate.

Credits: Top Row. Pier Francesco Ferrari, University of Parma, from PLoS Biology, Sept. 2006, Vol, 4, Issue 9. Second Row. Photos of infants exposed to Mandarin via live interactions or via TV or audio-only, Fig 1 (A) from Patricia K. Kuhl, "Is speech learning 'gated' by the social brain?" *Developmental Science* 10:1 (2007), pp 110-120. Third Row. Charlie Neuman/San Diego Union-Tribune/ZUMA Press/Newscom. Bottom Row: Albert Bandura/Stanford University.

KEY TERMS The Language of Psychological Science

Be sure you can define these terms and use them correctly.

acquisition, p. 282
associative learning, p. 279
aversion therapy, p. 288
classical conditioning, p. 279
conditioned reinforcer, p. 296
conditioned response (CR), p. 282
conditioned stimulus (CS), p. 282
discrimination, p. 284
extinction, p. 283
fixed interval (FI) schedule, p. 299
fixed ratio (FR) schedule, p. 298
generalization, p. 284
habituation, p. 279
higher order conditioning,
      p. 285

imitation, p. 309
inhibition, p. 283
instinct, p. 277
latent inhibition, p. 285
latent learning, p. 302
learning, p. 277
method of successive approximations,
      p. 301
negative punishment, p. 297
negative reinforcement, p. 296
nonassociative learning, p. 279
observational learning, p. 280
operant conditioning, p. 279
partial reinforcement effect in
      extinction, p. 300

partial reinforcement, p. 298
positive punishment, p. 297
punishment, p. 297
reflex, p. 277
sensitization, p. 279
spontaneous recovery, p. 283
systematic desensitization, p. 289
token economy, p. 305
unconditioned response (UCR),
      p. 282
unconditioned stimulus (UCS),
      p. 282
variable interval (VI) schedule,
      p. 299
variable ratio (VR) schedule, p. 298

9 The Knowing Mind
Memory

IN CHAPTER 2, we introduced you to one of the most famous case studies in psychology—the case of Henry Molaison (1926–2008), who is known in the scientific literature as "the amnesic patient H.M." To reduce Molaison's severe seizures, possibly resulting from a minor head injury caused by a childhood accident, his neurosurgeons carried out an experimental procedure that would be considered radical today but was even more so in 1953. As shown in the large image to the left, they removed most of Molaison's hippocampus in both hemispheres, along with some of the surrounding neural tissue. As a result, Molaison's memory functions declined dramatically, although his personality and intellect remained intact.

Photograph of Henry Molaison.

Photos of H.M. by Suzanne Corkin. Copyright © 2013 by Suzanne Corkin, used by permission of The Wylie Agency LLC.

Zooming in to consider the results of this type of surgery, we can ask what scientists learned from their study of Molaison. Brenda Milner, followed by her student Suzanne Corkin, studied Molaison for more than four decades. His case produced a string of surprises, which we discuss in more detail later in this chapter. For example, certain structures in the brain are important for memory, but more so for some types of memories than for others. Some tasks we can perform automatically; that is, we can remember how to do something without remembering that we know how to do it.

Zooming out to Molaison the individual, shown in the smaller photo above, we can see that his story is more extensive than the study of his brain. According to people who knew him, he was a nice man who loved animals, watching trains, and doing crossword puzzles. Even though Molaison was the subject of decades of study, many questions about him remain. Why did he seem less affected by pain than other people? Why was he accurately able to rate the intensity of an odor but unable to tell the difference between a rose and something rotten? Although his ability to learn new facts following his surgery was remarkably impaired, why did he know scattered facts from the following decade? Which of these observations shows the effects of his surgery? Of his accident? Of his seizures?

Zooming out still farther, we ask ourselves how our social interactions would be affected by being unable to remember new people we have met. Molaison remembered people, like his surgeon, whom he had met before his surgery, but he never learned to recognize Milner, Corkin, or other scientists who met him later, even though he saw them regularly for decades. He retained a genuine concern for other people and took great pride in his

◄ The hippocampus plays an important role in memory. In the case of Henry Molaison (above), discussed in this chapter, surgical removal of a large part of the hippocampus reduced his seizures but left him with serious memory deficits.

Argosy Publishing, Inc.

case helping science, but it is hard to imagine that his life was not somewhat lonely and socially isolated.

We often think of memory as something we need to succeed on exams, but in this chapter, you will learn that memory means much more to our human experience. Our memories allow us to form new connections with people, places, and things; to experience a new acquaintance, over time, becoming an old friend; and to experience the continuity of time rather than repeatedly living life as a single, isolated moment.

The careful slicing of Henry Molaison's preserved brain took more than 53 straight hours and was broadcast live on the Internet.

Learning Objectives

1. Define encoding, storage, and retrieval of memory.

2. Differentiate among sensory memory, working memory, and long-term memory, as well as the subtypes of long-term memory.

3. Explain the models describing the organization of long-term memories.

4. Summarize the variables influencing retrieval from short- and long-term memory.

5. Describe forgetting, decay, interference, motivated forgetting, and confabulation.

6. Summarize the biological correlates of memory.

What Are the Advantages of Memory?

Memory is defined as the ability to retain knowledge. The problems encountered by Molaison provide us with a glimpse of how our lives would be altered without certain memory abilities, but can we make more general conclusions about how memory helps animals adapt and survive?

Memory and the Continuum of Information Processing

Take a minute and write down the five most important things you need to remember today. How would your life be affected if you couldn't remember these things?

Memory does not exist in isolation. Instead, cognitive psychologists see memory as part of a continuum of **information processing** that begins with attention, sensation, perception, and learning, which we explored in previous chapters, and progresses to the use of stored information in thinking, problem solving, language, and intelligent behavior, which we discuss in Chapter 10 (see ● Figure 9.1). Information flows in both directions along this continuum, leading to the bottom-up and top-down processing we observed in Chapter 5. Memories of the characteristics of Dalmatian dogs, for example, are gained by learning about Dalmatians through experience with them. These memories helped you identify the photograph of one in Chapter 5 and should help you interact with one appropriately (thinking and problem solving).

Memory can be divided into three steps: encoding, storage, and retrieval. **Encoding** refers to the process of acquiring information and transferring it into memory. In Chapter 5, we described how the sensory systems translate or transduce electromagnetic energy, sound

memory The ability to retain knowledge.
information processing A continuum including attention, sensation, perception, learning, memory, and cognition.
encoding The transformation of information from one form to another.

waves, pressure, and chemical stimulation into action potentials that can be processed by the nervous system. These transduced signals can then be encoded in different forms in memory, such as visual codes, acoustic or sound codes, or semantic or meaningful codes. For example, if you meet your friend on the way to class, you might encode her appearance visually, the sound of her voice acoustically, and how much you value her friendship semantically.

Encoded information needs to be retained, or stored. As we will see later in this chapter, **storage** of memories in the brain can last anywhere from fractions of a second (sensory memory) to several seconds (short-term and working memory) to indefinitely (long-term memory). Storage in the mind differs from storage of information in your computer in one important respect. Computers store encoded information in reliable and unvarying ways, like putting socks in a drawer or papers in a file. What you retrieve is essentially identical to what was stored. In contrast, human memory does not generate such exact records. Instead, bits of information are stored that are later reconstructed into usable memories. Although this process typically results in a useful memory, errors and distortions can occur. We will explore these variations in later sections of this chapter.

The culmination of the memory process is the **retrieval** of stored information. As you have no doubt experienced, storing information is no guarantee that you can find the information again when you need it. Later in this chapter, we will discuss the many ways that memory retrieval can fail in detail. Two of the most common causes of retrieval failure are interference and stress. For example, we seem to know all the answers when watching *Who Wants to Be a Millionaire* in the safety of our homes, but when put on the spot, we might be lucky to remember our names. Fortunately, understanding the strengths and weaknesses of the brain's memory functions may be one of the more practical topics for students that we cover in psychology. Once you understand what can go wrong, you will have an easier time ensuring that your study habits maximize your performance in school.

Memory Provides an Adaptive Advantage

Evolutionary psychologists view memory as "a component of a neural machine designed to use information acquired in the past to coordinate an organism's behavior in the present" (Klein, Cosmides, & Tooby, 2002, p. 308). The evolution of memory allowed animals to use information from the past to respond quickly to immediate challenges, a monumental advance in the ability to survive. Instead of reacting to each predator or source of food as a new experience, an animal with the ability to remember past encounters with similar situations would save precious reaction time.

As we discussed in Chapter 3, useful adaptations often come with a price, like the unwieldy antlers of the male deer that require energy to build yet help the deer fight successfully for mates. The development of a memory system is no exception to this rule. Forming memories requires energy. For memory systems to flourish within the animal kingdom, the survival advantages needed to outweigh the energy costs. Given the 81 years or so of human life expectancy, it would be difficult to demonstrate the energy costs of memory in people, but we can observe the costs in a simpler organism, the fruit fly *(Drosophila)*, which has a life expectancy of only 10 to 18 days. Fruit flies are capable of learning classically conditioned associations between odors and electric shock (see Chapter 8). After experiencing pairings of odor and shock, the flies fly away from the odor 24 hours later (Mery & Kawecki, 2005). However, to form memories about odor and shock, the flies must use more energy than they use for activities that do not require memory. When deprived of food and water, the flies that remembered how to avoid shock died about 4 hours faster than flies that did not form memories. Nearly all animals have the capability of forming memories despite the high energy costs, which is a testament to memory's benefits to survival.

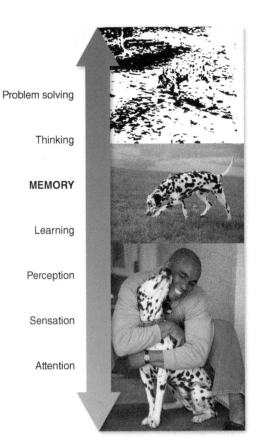

FIGURE 9.1

The Information Processing Continuum. Memory is located on a continuum of information processing that flows both from the bottom up and from the top down. We use our memories of Dalmatian dogs to recognize one in an ambiguous photograph and interact with a new one we happen to meet.

Illustration: © Cengage Learning®; photos, top to bottom: From Richard L. Gregory, "The Medawar Lecture 2001 Knowledge for vision: Vision for knowledge," Phil. Trans. R. Soc. B 2005 360, 1231–1251, by permission of the Royal Society.; AnetaPics/Shutterstock.com; Steve Smith/The Image Bank/Getty Images

Labels on figure, top to bottom: Problem solving / Thinking / **MEMORY** / Learning / Perception / Sensation / Attention

storage The retention of information.
retrieval The recovery of stored information.

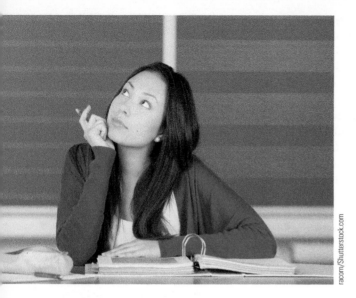

How Are Memories Processed?

Psychologists have proposed a number of models to try to describe how memory works. One of the most influential models of memory was proposed by Atkinson and Shiffrin (1968, 1971). According to this classic model, information flows through a series of separate stages of memory (see ● Figure 9.2). Contemporary cognitive psychologists have continued to modify this original model while retaining the basic ideas that memories can be stored for different lengths of time and that control processes influence the system.

To illustrate the flow of information in this model, let's consider what happens when you use your memory to complete a specific task—remembering a phone number provided to you by a new acquaintance.

Sensory Memory

While settling into your seat before class, you are having a nice conversation with one of your classmates about getting together to study for an upcoming exam. Your classmate gives you her cell phone number so that you can arrange a good time to meet. This incoming information, the auditory signals of your classmate's voice in this case, is processed in a first stage of the Atkinson–Shiffrin model, the **sensory memory**. This stage holds enormous amounts of sensory data, possibly all information that affects the sensory receptors. However, the data remain for brief periods, usually a second or less, that only last as long as the neural activity produced by a sensation continues. The information held in sensory memory has been compared to a rapidly fading "echo" of the real input. You can demonstrate the duration and "fade" of sensory memory information by rapidly flapping your hand back and forth in front of your eyes. When you do this, you can "see" where your fingers were at a previous point in time.

Encoding failure is one of the most common memory problems faced by students. If we don't encode information because we're daydreaming during a lecture, there will be no memory of the information to retrieve later.

Both brains and computers feature the ability to store memories, with one critical difference: The computer stores exact copies of data, but the brain does not. Instead, the brain stores bits of data that are reconstructed later for use. This photo shows the high-security computer memory storage at the Swedish Bahnhof, a facility located 100 feet underground in a concrete bunker. The facility manages servers for many secretive organizations, including WikiLeaks.

sensory memory The first stage of the Atkinson–Shiffrin model that holds large amounts of incoming data for brief amounts of time.
short-term memory (STM) The second stage of the Atkinson–Shiffrin model that holds a small amount of information for a limited time.

Sensory input is translated, or transduced, into several types of codes or representations. A representation of a memory refers to a mental model of a bit of information that exists even when the information is no longer available. Visual codes are used for the temporary storage of information about visual images (Baddeley, Eysenck, & Anderson, 2009). Haptic codes are used to process touch and other body senses. Acoustic codes represent sounds and words. Psychologists believe that input from different sensory systems remains separate in sensory memory, and although these different sensory streams are processed fairly similarly, there are some differences. Acoustic codes, also known as echoic memories, last somewhat longer than visual codes, also known as iconic memories, possibly to meet our needs to hear entire words and phrases before we can begin to understand spoken language.

George Sperling demonstrated the duration of iconic memories by testing recall for matrices of 12 to 16 letters that were presented for as few as 15 milliseconds. Participants were usually able to identify four or five letters. However, the process of verbally instructing participants to do this task takes time, during which the sensory memory for the matrix fades rapidly. If different tones were used to signal a row of the matrix to be recalled instead of verbally asking for a response, participants demonstrated recall for as many as 12 of the original 16 items (Averbach & Sperling, 1961; Sperling, 1960). If the tone was sounded less than a quarter of a second after the presentation of the matrix, participants could usually recall all four letters in a row. After a quarter of a second delay or more, recall fell to one letter (see ● Figure 9.3).

Why do we have a sensory memory? Only a small subset of this incoming data is processed by the next stage. It is likely that we need to collect incoming data until they make enough sense to process further. The first number in your classmate's phone number might be simple (2), but it still contains two speech sounds ("t" and "oo") that must be combined to make sense.

Encoding and storing memories do not guarantee that they can be retrieved when you need them. Stress can make retrieving even the simplest of memories surprisingly difficult.

Short-Term Memory

A tiny amount of information in the sensory memory moves to the next stage of the Atkinson–Shiffrin model, **short-term memory (STM)**, for further processing. If you focus on your new friend's phone number, the information moves from sensory memory to short-term memory. Consider all the other information that might be processed by your sensory memory at the same time. Perhaps you are aware that the professor's first PowerPoint slide has appeared on the screen, that the heater in the classroom cycled on, or that your stomach growled because you didn't have time for breakfast. None of these bits of information are processed in short-term memory unless you pay attention to them. If you are distracted by one of these, it is likely that you will need to ask your friend to repeat her number.

Even though processing memory requires energy, the benefits to survival far outweigh the costs. Without memory, this squirrel would be unable to retrieve the acorns stored weeks ago.

FIGURE 9.2

The Atkinson–Shiffrin Model of Memory. According to this classic model of memory, information flows through a series of stages. If memory is not transferred to the next stage, it is permanently lost. *Source:* Adapted from "The Control of Short-Term Memory," by R. C. Atkinson and R. M. Shiffrin, 1971, *Scientific American, 225*, pp. 82–90.

Short-term memory, like the sensory memory that precedes it, appears to have remarkable limitations in duration. Without additional processing, information in short-term memory usually lasts 30 seconds at most (Ellis & Hunt, 1983). In a classic experiment, participants were shown stimuli consisting of three consonants, such as RBP (Peterson & Peterson, 1959). After seeing one of these triplets, participants counted backward by threes for periods of 0 to 18 seconds to prevent further processing of the consonant triplet. As shown in ● Figure 9.4, accuracy dropped rapidly. It is likely that the Petersons' task actually overestimates the length of time material may be stored in short-term memory. The study's participants were aware in advance that they would be tested on the items, and despite the distraction of counting backward, they may have been able to engage in deliberate efforts to retain the triplets in memory.

You are probably thinking right now that you know what to do to prevent this loss of information. If you repeat the information over and over, a process known as **rehearsal**, information stays in short-term memory indefinitely as long as you are not asked to think about anything else. While you are getting ready to program your classmate's number into your phone, you can rehearse the number in your short-term memory. However, if your attention is diverted from rehearsing the number when the professor calls on you, the phone number will be gone. The incoming information of the professor's question seems to push the previous data out of the system. Data in short-term memory are easily displaced by new, incoming bits of data. If rehearsing the information has been insufficient for moving it into the next stage, long-term memory, the data will be lost.

In addition to limitations of duration, short-term memory is characterized by severe limitations in capacity. George Miller argued that we can process somewhere between five and nine items or "bits" (digits, letters, words, etc.) in short-term memory simultaneously, or in his words, "the magical number 7 plus or minus 2" (Miller, 1956). More recently, other psychologists have set the limit as about four items (Cowan, 2000). Memory capacities vary from individual to individual, and memory tasks appear prominently in standardized tests of intelligence, discussed in Chapter 10. People who enjoy larger than average short-term memory capacity excel at a number of cognitive tasks, including reading (Baddeley, Logie, Nimmo-Smith, & Brereton, 1985).

Our ability to "see" what we have written with a sparkler results from the remaining traces in our sensory memories. The actual light is long gone.

Because our short-term memory holds limited amounts of information for only a short time, smartphone apps that keep track of things we need to remember to do are popular.

rehearsal Repetition of information.

André Babiak/AGE Fotostock

FIGURE 9.3

Sperling's Demonstration of the Duration of Sensory Memory. George Sperling presented a matrix of letters to study participants for as few as 15 milliseconds. When asked to recall the whole matrix (a), most participants could remember about four or five letters. However, when tones instead of verbal commands were used to signal which row to remember (b), participants were able to recall whole rows at a time, which implies they could remember more than four or five items. Sperling concluded that they could "see" the entire matrix in sensory memory briefly, which allowed them to respond correctly. *Source:* Adapted from "The Information Available in Brief Visual Presentations," by G. Sperling, 1960, *Psychological Monographs*, 74 (whole no. 11), 1-29.

FIGURE 9.4

The Duration of Short-Term Memory. In a classic study by Peterson and Peterson (1959), participants were given triplets of letters, like XPJ or BTP, to recall. Their ability to remember the letters decreased as the time between presentation and recall increased. These results led the Petersons to propose that short-term memory might last up to 18 seconds, but more contemporary scientists using different methods think that it lasts as little as 2 seconds. *Source:* Data from "Short-Term Retention of Individual Verbal Items," by L. R. Peterson and M. J. Peterson, 1959, *Journal of Experimental Psychology, 58,* pp. 193–198.

It is easier to remember FBI, IRS, CIA, and EPA in chunks than to remember FBIIRSCIAEPA.

You might be wondering how short-term memory could be useful, given these limitations. However, the limitations of duration and capacity make short-term memory an ideal solution for the tasks we ask it to complete. The brief duration of short-term memories ensures that room is freed regularly for incoming information. Most tasks for which we use short-term memory require us to search its contents to find the right information. If short-term memory were capable of holding dozens of pieces of information instead of nine or fewer, this search process would be lengthy and difficult. It is also convenient to have a mechanism that allows you to use information and then discard it. You may not wish to devote precious room in your memory banks to the telephone number of a plumber you need only once or twice. Short-term memory allows us to use information without overburdening our storage capacities.

Nonetheless, it is often desirable to expand our capacity for information in short-term memory. The best way to accomplish this is to redefine what a "bit" of data is by **chunking**, or grouping, similar or meaningful information together (Miller, 1956). If your friend says the last four digits of her phone number are "one," "five," "seven," and "nine," she could reduce these four bits to two by saying "fifteen seventy-nine." Trying to remember the following sequence of letters—FBIIRSCIAEPA—appears to be an insurmountable task. After all, remembering 12 letters lies well outside the capacity of short-term memory. The task is greatly simplified by chunking the letters into meaningful batches of common abbreviations—FBI IRS CIA EPA. Now you have only 4 meaningful bits to remember rather than 12, which is safely within the capacities of short-term memory. Failure to use chunking as a strategy occurs frequently in people with verbal learning disabilities (Koeda, Seki, Uchiyama, & Sadato, 2011). In the absence of chunking, each item to be remembered is processed as a single, unrelated bit of information, which rapidly overwhelms the capacity of short-term memory.

chunking The process of grouping similar or meaningful information together.

Working Memory The classic description of short-term memory viewed this stage as a place to store information for immediate use. As investigations into memory advanced, researchers proposed an adaptation of this model called **working memory**, shown in ● Figure 9.5 (Baddeley & Hitch, 1974). Short-term memory and working memory differed in two ways. First, short-term memory involves the passive storage of information, while working memory involves an active manipulation of information. Second, short-term memory was viewed as managing a single process at a time, whereas working memory was more complex, allowing multiple processes to occur simultaneously.

The idea that working memory could manage more than one process at a time resulted from observations that people could manage two short-term memory tasks at the same time (Baddeley & Hitch, 1974). For example, study participants could read a list of numbers followed by reading a paragraph. This task should quickly overwhelm the limited capacity of short-term memory, because reading the paragraph should displace the earlier list of numbers. However, this outcome was not what the researchers observed. Participants had no difficulty remembering the numbers, suggesting that the numbers were stored separately from the words in the paragraph.

After further exploration of the types of information that could be maintained separately in short-term memory, four components were proposed (Baddeley et al., 2009): a phonological loop, a visuospatial sketch pad, a central executive, and an episodic buffer.

The phonological loop is the working memory component responsible for verbal and auditory information. As you repeat your friend's phone number while reaching for your phone, you are using your phonological loop. The visuospatial sketch pad holds visual and spatial information. When you describe the route from your friend's dorm to your favorite coffee shop, where you plan to hold your study session, you use your visuospatial sketch pad to help you describe the way. The central executive manages the work of the other components by directing attention to particular tasks (Baddeley, 1996). Divided attention, which we discussed in Chapter 5, requires the skills of the central executive. While discussing the route to the coffee shop with your friend (phonological loop), you visualize the route (visuospatial

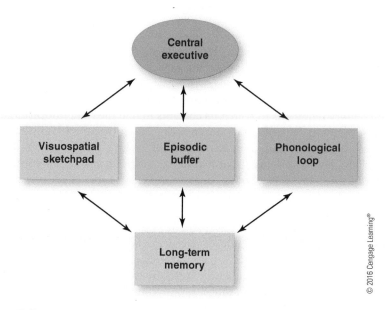

© 2016 Cengage Learning®

FIGURE 9.5

Working Memory. Alan Baddeley's model of working memory differs from short-term memory in two important ways: (1) information in working memory can be actively manipulated, whereas short-term memory passively stores memory, and (2) working memory can manage multiple types of information simultaneously, whereas short-term memory cannot. *Source:* Baddeley, A. D., & Hitch, G. J. (1974). Working memory. In G. Bower (Ed.), *The psychology of learning and motivation* (Vol. *8*, pp. 47–89). New York: Academic Press.

working memory An extension of the concept of short-term memory that includes the active manipulation of multiple types of information simultaneously.

sketch pad), and your central executive parcels out the right amount of attention to allow you to do both tasks well.

The episodic buffer provides a mechanism for combining information stored in long-term memory, which we discuss in the next section, with the active processing taking place in working memory. This component helps explain why chunking the string of letters earlier (FBI IRS CIA EPA) is easier than remembering the letters as individual bits of information—FBIIRSCIAEPA. Without information from long-term memory about what FBI and the other abbreviations mean, making these chunks would not provide any advantage.

Scientists have made progress in their search for brain activity that correlates with working memory, although they continue to debate how the executive processes of working memory are organized (Nee et al., 2013). Studies of people with brain damage suggest that several executive functions are managed by different parts of the frontal lobes but that a single central executive probably does not exist (Stuss, 2011). Working memory does not occur in a separate, isolated part of the brain. Instead, the phonological loop and visuospatial sketch pad use the same posterior parts of the brain that are used in verbal and visual perception (Bledowski, Kaiser, & Rahm, 2010). Top-down influences originating in the prefrontal and parietal cortex provide the attention necessary to maintain stimulus information in working memory (Nee et al., 2013).

Andre Jenny/Alamy

Long-Term Memory

The final stage of memory processing according to the Atkinson–Shiffrin model is **long-term memory**. Unlike sensory, short-term, and working memory, long-term memory seems to have few limitations in either capacity or duration. We do not appear to run out of room in long-term memory for new data, and information can last a lifetime. The oldest person alive can still recall significant childhood memories and learn new things. Although old memories may become more difficult to retrieve, this process is different from losing them simply because of the passage of time.

Moving Information Into Long-Term Memory In most cases, information moves from short-term or working memory to long-term memory through rehearsal. You might find that after you see your new friend's number several times as you text her, you have somehow memorized it without trying to do so. Rehearsal can be divided into maintenance rehearsal, which means simple repetition of the material, and elaborative rehearsal, which involves linking the new material to things you already know.

Of the two types of rehearsal, elaborative rehearsal is a more effective way to move information into more permanent storage. The benefits of elaborative rehearsal can be explained using the **levels of processing theory** (Craik & Lockhart, 1972). When we look at written

Chase and Simon (1973) presented images of chess pieces on chessboards for only 5 seconds to chess masters and people who didn't play chess. When the images were from real games, the chess masters recalled the placement of the pieces better than the nonplayers, because they were able to use their knowledge of chess to chunk the images of the pieces' locations in short-term memory. When the pieces were placed randomly on the boards, however, the chess masters were unable to use chunking and performed no better than the nonplayers.

long-term memory The final stage of the Atkinson–Shiffrin model that is the location of permanent memories.
levels of processing theory The depth (shallow to deep) of processing applied to information that predicts its ease of retrieval.

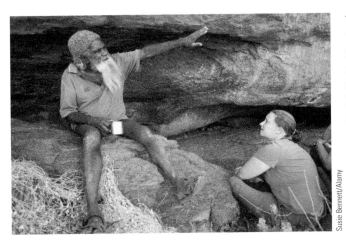
Susie Bennett/Alamy

The accumulated knowledge of a long life, like this Australian aborigine tribal elder's familiarity with his harsh surroundings, probably meant the difference between life and death for many of our ancestors. There is no evidence that old people are unable to add new information to their long-term memories or necessarily lose information they have known a long time.

Our ATMs usually deliver our cash in $20 bills, but handling these regularly does not mean that we remember exactly what they look like. Which president is pictured on the bill? Whose signature as Secretary of the Treasury appears on the bill? Are the fonts used for all the 20s the same or different? Most people can't answer these questions from memory.

Pakhnyushcha/Shutterstock.com

words we want to remember, we can attend to many levels of detail: the visual appearance of the word (font, all caps, number of letters, etc.), the sound of the word, the meaning of the word, and the personal relevance of the word. These characteristics may be placed along a continuum of depth of processing from shallow to deep, with the encoding of the appearance of a word requiring less processing and effort than the encoding of the sound of a word, which in turn requires less processing and effort than the encoding of the meaning or personal relevance of a word, and so on. According to the levels of processing theory, words encoded according to meaning would be easier to remember than words encoded according to their visual appearance, because encoding meaningfulness produces a deeper level of attention and processing (Craik & Tulving, 1975).

In one study designed to test the levels of processing theory, participants recalled more words when their instructions elicited the encoding of word meanings than when they were instructed to determine more surface features of each word, such as whether it appeared in capital letters (see ● Figure 9.6; Craik & Tulving, 1975). In another study, deeper levels of processing were accompanied by more subvocal speech (reminiscent of "talking to yourself"), indicated by measurements of tiny activities in the muscles of speech (Cacioppo & Petty, 1981). However, the levels of processing theory is not very specific about the meaning of deep or shallow processing. How would we apply this approach to evaluate participants' recall for music, touch, or visual images? Further work on this theory needs to identify what determines depth of processing during encoding.

FIGURE 9.6

Levels of Processing Theory. Craik and Tulving (1975) tested the levels of processing theory by investigating their study participants' recognition of words they had seen only briefly (about one fifth of a second) following one of three types of questions. The three types of questions focused the participants' attention on aspects of the word they were about to see. The questions pointed to surface features (Is the word in capital letters?), acoustic features (Does the word rhyme with another word?), or semantic features (Does the word make sense in this sentence?). Theoretically, deciding whether a word is in capital letters takes less processing than deciding whether it rhymes with another word, which in turn takes less processing than thinking about its meaning to answer the sentence question. The results supported the levels of processing theory. Recognition of words preceded by a semantic question was better than recognition of words preceded by a rhyme question, which were recognized better than words preceded by a font question. *Source:* Adapted from "Depth of Processing and the Retention of Words in Episodic Memory," F. I. M. Craik and E. Tulving, 1975, *Journal of Experimental Psychology: General, 104*(3), pp. 268–294. doi:10.1037/0096-3445.104.3.268.

© 2016 Cengage Learning®

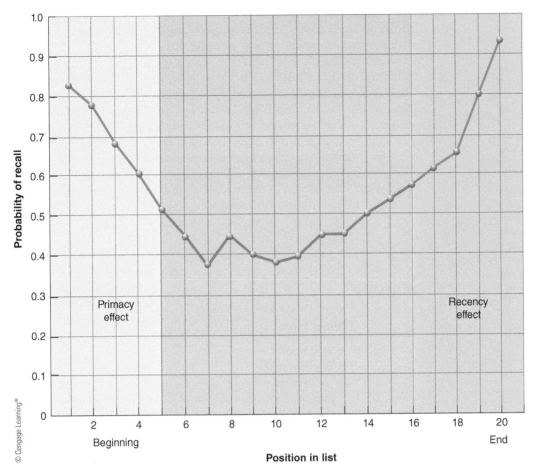

FIGURE 9.7

The Serial Position Effect.
When people are given a list of words to remember and told they can recall the items in any order, the likelihood that a word on the list will be remembered depends on its position in the list. The primacy effect refers to the superior recall for the first words on the list, and the recency effect refers to the superior recall for the last words on the list. The primacy effect probably occurs because people have had more time to place these items in long-term memory. The recency effect probably occurs because these last words still remain in working memory at the time of retrieval. A delay in retrieval erases the recency effect but not the primacy effect.

© Cengage Learning®

Differences Between Working and Long-Term Memory In addition to not sharing the limitations of duration and capacity found with working memory, long-term memory appears to be unique in other ways.

Differences between working and long-term memories can be seen in classic experiments demonstrating the serial position effect. This phenomenon can be observed when people are asked to learn a list of words and recall them in any order they choose. As shown in ● Figure 9.7, recall of items takes on a U-shaped appearance when retrieval is plotted as a function of an item's position in a list during presentation (Murdoch, 1962).

The superior recall for the first items on a list is known as the primacy effect, which is believed to result from the storage of these items in long-term memory. Using a typical list of 20 words, people would have the most rehearsal time for the first word, a bit less for the second, and so on through the list. Because rehearsal can move information from working to long-term memory, the earlier words, with their greater share of rehearsal, would be more likely to be stored in long-term memory than the later words on the list, which probably were not rehearsed much.

The superior recall for the last words on the list is known as the recency effect, which probably occurs because these items remain in working memory at

According to research on primacy, recency, and website menus, we would predict that more people would click on the first and last news articles listed on the Association for Psychological Science's webpage. Which articles are least likely to get attention?

WHAT ARE THE ADVANTAGES OF MEMORY? **327**

the time of recall. The recency effect, but not the primacy effect, disappears if recall is delayed by 30 seconds (Glanzer & Cunitz, 1966). After 30 seconds, items in long-term memory are still available for recall, but items in working memory are long gone.

One of the strongest arguments in favor of the separation of working and long-term memory is the occurrence of clinical cases in which one capacity is damaged while the other remains intact. Henry Molaison (the amnesic patient H.M.), whom we discussed at the beginning of this chapter, was able to remember a small amount of information for a few seconds but experienced enormous difficulties when trying to store new information in his long-term memory. In another case study, a patient with brain damage appeared to have the opposite problem. Patient K.F. had normal long-term memory, as indicated by his ability to form new memories. However, his working memory was seriously impaired (Shallice & Warrington, 1970). When asked to recall a list of digits (a typical working memory task), he could remember only one or two digits at a time, a big deviation from the typical ability to recall five to nine digits.

Summary 9.1 Types of Memory

Type of memory	Major features
Sensory memory	• Large capacity • Brief duration • Separate channels for different sensory types (acoustic, visual, etc.)
Short-term memory or working memory	• Limited capacity (5–9 bits) • Limited duration (30 sec maximum) • Expansion of capacity through chunking • Expansion of duration through rehearsal • Central executive, visuospatial scratchpad, episodic buffer, phonological loop
Long-term memory	• Very large capacity • Very long duration

What Are the Different Types of Long-Term Memory?

declarative memory A consciously retrieved memory that is easy to verbalize, including semantic, episodic, and autobiographical information; also known as explicit memory.

nondeclarative memory An unconsciously and effortlessly retrieved memory that is difficult to verbalize, such as a memory for classical conditioning, procedural learning, and priming; also known as implicit memory.

Long-term memory can be divided into several categories (see ● Figure 9.8). These categories not only help us describe memory more precisely but also represent the activities of different parts of the brain.

Long-term memory can be divided into declarative, or conscious, memories and nondeclarative, or unconscious, memories. **Declarative memories** are easy to "declare," or discuss verbally. Declarative memories are also called explicit memories because they are typically accessed in a conscious, direct, and effortful manner. In contrast to declarative memories, **nondeclarative memories** are difficult to discuss. For example, classical conditioning, which

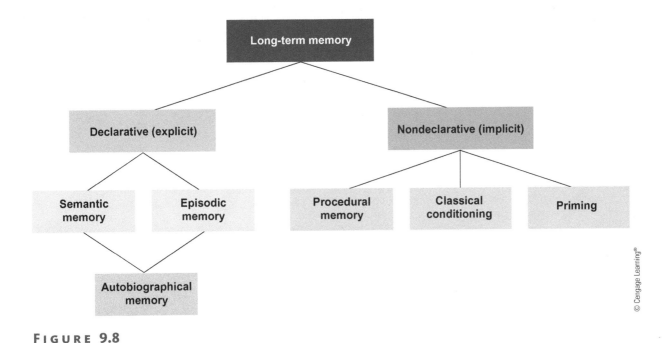

FIGURE 9.8

Types of Long-Term Memory. Long-term memory can be divided into several categories, beginning with a distinction between declarative (also known as explicit, or conscious memories) and nondeclarative (also known as implicit, or unconscious memories). Declarative memories are further divided into semantic and episodic memories, which are combined when we use autobiographical memories. Examples of nondeclarative memories are procedural memories, classical conditioning, and priming.

we examined in Chapter 8, produces nondeclarative memories. We might find it difficult to explain to another person why we get nervous right before an exam or dislike a food we ate once before becoming ill. Nondeclarative memories are also called implicit memories because they affect our behavior in subconscious, indirect, and effortless ways. We are aware of their outcomes ("I don't want to eat that food"), but we are usually unaware of the information processing that led to that outcome.

Declarative Memories

Declarative memories are further divided into semantic and episodic memories (Tulving, 1972, 1985, 1995). **Semantic memory** contains your store of general knowledge in the form of word meanings and facts. Using your semantic memory, you can answer questions such as "Which NFL team won last year's Super Bowl?" or "What is a churro?" **Episodic memory** is a more personal account of past experiences.

We can distinguish between semantic and episodic memories along four dimensions: the type of information processed, the organization of the information in memory, the source of the information, and the focus of the memory (Williams, Conway, & Cohen, 2008). Semantic memories contain general knowledge about the world, whereas episodic memories include more specific information about events, objects, and people. Semantic memory, as we will see later in this chapter, is organized according to categories. For example, we have a category for birds that contains our semantic knowledge of birds. Episodic memory, in contrast, is organized as a timeline. To answer a question from episodic memory, we often use time as a cue: "When I was in the eighth grade, my family took a vacation at the beach." Semantic knowledge originates from others, like your professors, or from repeated experience: "The ocean is colder in California than in Florida, because every time I've gone to the beach in either location, this is what I have observed." An episodic memory can result from a single, personal experience. Finally, the two types of memories serve different purposes. Semantic memory provides us with an objective understanding of our world, whereas episodic memory provides a reference point for our subjective experience of the self.

semantic memory A general knowledge memory.
episodic memory A memory for personal experience.

You might have semantic memories that tell you about the characteristics of Labrador retrievers and episodic memories about the day you chose your first puppy. Your autobiographical memories combine these two elements to give you an account of your life. A semantic element of your autobiographical memory might be that your dog's parents were champions. The episodic elements of your autobiographical memory for the event might include memories of your puppy's warmth and the happy way you felt that day.

Despite the differences just outlined, semantic and episodic memories often overlap. You could form an episodic memory of where you were when you stored a specific semantic memory. A colleague was introduced to a student's parents as follows: "Mom, Dad, this is Professor Jones. He's the one I told you about who taught us that rats can't barf." Not only did the student retain a semantic memory about rat behavior (which incidentally is true and is relevant to understanding the classical conditioning of taste aversion in rats), but the student correctly retained an episodic memory of when and where the fact was learned.

We can see that semantic and episodic memories usually interact dynamically to provide a complete picture of the past. Our semantic knowledge of the relative temperatures of the Pacific and Atlantic Oceans depends on the personal experiences of either hearing the fact in a geology classroom or vacationing on both coasts of the United States. At the same time, we use our semantic knowledge to interpret our episodic memories. Without semantic knowledge of the meanings of the words ocean, temperature, Atlantic, and Pacific, we would be unable to organize our experience into a coherent conclusion—the ocean is colder in California than in Florida.

This type of blending of semantic and episodic memories characterizes **autobiographical memories** (Williams et al., 2008). Autobiographical memories can contain factual, semantic aspects of personal experience without episodic aspects. You might know you were born in Pasadena, California, but you would not have any memory of being born. However, your autobiographical memories of Pasadena might also include episodic memories of attending the Rose Parade on New Year's Day as a child, complete with images of the sights, sounds, and emotions of that experience.

Some people have a condition known as hyperthymesia, or superior memory of autobiographical events (Ally, Hussey, & Donahue, 2013). Patient H.K. showed nearly perfect recollection of dates chosen at random from the time he was 11 years old. His recall was corroborated by entries in his grandmother's diary, interviews with family members, his medical records, and historical facts about his hometown. Compared to control participants, patient H.K. showed richer connections between his amygdala and hippocampus. Activity in the amygdala provides autobiographical memory with emotion and self-relevance. Enhanced amygdala activity might make autobiographical memories especially strong (Ally et al., 2013).

Nondeclarative Memories

Earlier, we defined nondeclarative memories as unconscious or implicit memories. In other words, nondeclarative memories influence our behavior without our conscious awareness of having used a memory. You might have had the experience of just being able to do something, like using roller blades for the first time in many years, without really know-

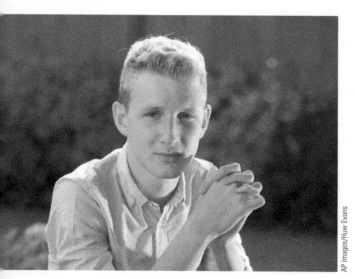

Aurelien Hayman can recall detail from random dates in his past. When asked in 2012, Aurelien accurately recalled that October 1, 2006 was a cloudy day, he listened to "When You Were Young" by the Killers, asked a girl out and was turned down, wore a blue T-shirt, and experienced a power outage at his home. This rare type of memory, known as hyperthymesia, has been the subject of only 20 published case studies.

ing how you are doing it (Tulving, 1985). We also identify nondeclarative memories as those difficult to describe in words (Smith & Grossman, 2008).

Cognitive psychologists have studied three types of nondeclarative memories in detail: classical conditioning, which we discussed in Chapter 8, procedural memories, and priming. **Procedural memories** are also called skill memories because they contain information about how to carry out a skilled movement, like driving a car. **Priming** occurs when exposure to a stimulus changes a response to a subsequent stimulus. For example, people who listened to rude words were more likely to interrupt a researcher than those who listened to polite words (Bargh, Chen, & Burrows, 1996). Hearing the rude words had primed these individuals to respond rudely to the investigator.

Procedural Memories Procedural memories, which are memories for how to carry out motor skills and procedures, are especially difficult to describe in words. Consider the differences between showing somebody how to use scissors (procedural memory) and writing an essay about how to use scissors (semantic and episodic memory). Which would be faster and easier? Explaining in words how to use scissors, particularly when helping a person who had never seen a pair of scissors, would be quite a challenge. In contrast, few of us experience difficulties demonstrating procedures (Squire, 1987).

One great advantage of procedural memories is their ability to automate our performance. When a novice driver first learns to operate a car with a manual transmission, a great deal of conscious effort must go into the correct sequence of procedures—clutch, gas, shift. Once the skill is well learned, it is doubtful that the driver is aware of this sequence; the person "just drives." When procedures become automatic, we are free to direct our limited capacities for divided attention to other aspects of the task. A musician who has mastered the procedure of playing a difficult piece can direct attention to the finer points of expression. Unfortunately, if a procedure is learned incorrectly, like a bad golf swing, considerable effort must be expended to think about fixing the swing, which slows performance. The golfer must put in sufficient practice time to make the new, correct swing automatic.

Priming Priming, or the change in our response to a stimulus because of preexposure to related stimuli, explains many everyday effects of familiarity. We may believe strongly that our behavior is unaffected by exposure to advertising. However, people rate advertisements they have seen previously, even if they can't consciously remember seeing them, more positively than those that they have not seen previously (Perfect & Askew, 1994). We agree that the unconscious way our attitudes can be manipulated is a bit unsettling.

Priming is often studied using a technique called the lexical decision task (see ● Figure 9.9). In this task, a participant views two rapidly presented stimuli and must decide whether the stimuli are both real words (such as *fork-roof*) or not (such as *mork-loof*). Reaction time, in the form of hitting one key for real words and another for nonwords, is the dependent variable. When the two stimuli are related words (e.g., *doctor–nurse*), reaction time is faster than when the stimuli are unrelated words (e.g., *butter–nurse*; Meyer & Schvanevelt, 1971).

Age fotostock/SuperStock

It might have been years since this grandfather last put on a pair of ice skates, but to help his granddaughter learn to skate, he's willing to get back out on the ice. He might be a little wobbly at first, but procedural memories for skilled movement are persistent. He'll quickly be skating as if he'd done it every day.

The distinction between nondeclarative procedural memories and declarative memories is one reason it is so challenging to be a computer help desk technician who must talk people through a repair procedure over the telephone. It would be easier to demonstrate how to fix the computer, which is why some software companies prefer to have the technician take over the computer remotely and apply the needed fixes as opposed to verbalizing procedures for the caller to undertake. It also explains why few star athletes go on to be good coaches. Performing a task is not the same as talking about it.

autobiographical memory Semantic or episodic memories that reference the self.
procedural memory A nondeclarative or implicit memory for how to carry out skilled movement.
priming A change in a response to a stimulus as a result of exposure to a previous stimulus.

Long-Term Memories and the Brain

Through the careful observation of people with brain damage, along with brain imaging studies in healthy participants, scientists have discovered correlations between activity in parts of the brain and specific components of long-term memory. These discoveries support the distinctions made by cognitive psychologists between declarative and nondeclarative memories based on observations of behavior.

Declarative Memories and the Hippocampus In Chapter 4, we described the important role played by the hippocampus in memory. The hippocampus clearly participates in the consolidation of information into long-term memory.

Now that we are familiar with some distinctions between declarative and nondeclarative memories, we can examine the case study of Henry Molaison (the amnesic patient H.M.) in more detail. In follow-up observations of Molaison, Brenda Milner discovered that not all of his memories were equally affected by the surgery that damaged his hippocampus (Milner, 1966, 2005). Molaison retained most of his memory for events leading up to his surgery, but his ability to form new memories was profoundly reduced. The inability to form new memories is known as anterograde amnesia. Much to Milner's surprise, Molaison learned a new procedural task, mirror tracing, as well as typical control participants did. In one of these tasks, Molaison was asked to draw the shape of a star while looking at a sample star and his hand in a mirror. After 3 days, Molaison mastered the task. However, if asked, he would deny ever having performed the task. His procedural memories were intact, but his declarative memories for the details of the task were nonexistent (see ● Figure 9.10).

Declarative Memories and the Cerebral Cortex Semantic, episodic, and autobiographical memories involve the participation of the cerebral cortex.

Semantic memories appear to be widely distributed across the cerebral cortex (see ● Figure 9.11). Using brain imaging, researchers can observe which parts of the cerebral cortex are active when a person is thinking about particular memories. Naming animals is associated with activity in the occipital lobes, suggesting that visualizing an animal's appearance might be helpful in this task (Martin, Wiggs, Ungerleider, & Haxby, 1996). Naming tools activates

Procedural memories quickly become automatic. When you learn to drive, you must attend to each step, but after learning the process, you "just drive."

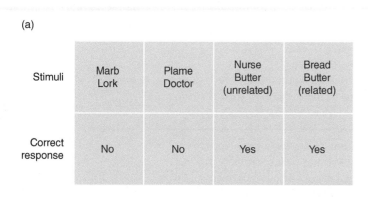

(a)

Stimuli	Marb Lork	Plame Doctor	Nurse Butter (unrelated)	Bread Butter (related)
Correct response	No	No	Yes	Yes

(b)

FIGURE 9.9

Priming. Priming can be investigated within the lexical decision task, in which participants are asked to judge whether two words appearing together are both real words or not (a). Nonreal words are made by switching one letter from a real word, like *plame* from *flame* or *lork* from *fork*. Pairs of real words are either related to each other by meaning or not. The participants' reaction time in this task (b) demonstrates that participants respond faster to related word pairs *(bread–butter)* than to unrelated word pairs *(nurse–butter)*. These results support the idea that we organize items in long-term memory based on their meaning. *Source:* Meyer, D. E., & Schvanevelt, R. W. (1971). Facilitation in recognizing pairs of words: Evidence of a dependence between retrieval operations. *Journal of Experimental Psychology, 90,* 227-234.

(a) Mirror-tracing task

(b) Performance of Henry Molaison

© 2016 Cengage Learning®

FIGURE 9.10

Separating Declarative and Nondeclarative Memories. The mirror-tracing task requires a participant to trace a five-pointed star, which is mounted on a wooden board that blocks the participant's view of the star and his or her hand. The participant must view the star and his or her hand in a mirror. This task is especially challenging because the mirror reverses the image, so if you want the pencil to trace around the star away from your body, you have to move your pencil toward your body instead. Brenda Milner was surprised to observe that Henry Molaison learned the mirror-tracing task at a normal rate, even though he didn't remember the details of the task. This outcome suggested to Milner that nondeclarative, procedural memories like the mirror-tracing task were not managed by the brain the same way as declarative memories. *Source:* Milner, B. (1965). Memory disturbance after bilateral hippocampal lesions. In P. M. Milner & S. E. Glickman (Eds), *Cognitive processes and the brain* (pp. 97-111). Princeton, NJ: Van Nostrand.

(a) Naming animals, but not tools

(b) Naming tools, but not animals

© Argosy Publishing, Inc.

FIGURE 9.11

Semantic Memories Are Widely Distributed in the Brain. Different patterns of activity in the cerebral cortex are correlated with various types of semantic memories. Naming animals (a) is associated with activity in the visual cortex of the occipital lobe, suggesting that we think about what an animal looks like to name it. Naming tools (b) activates areas associated with hand movements, suggesting that we think about how we would use a hammer or saw to name one.

areas of the frontal and parietal lobes normally associated with movements and action words. To name a hammer, for example, we might consider the hand movements associated with using hammers and words such as *pound* or *hit*.

Episodic memories are affected by damage to the prefrontal cortex. Damage in this area can produce a condition known as source amnesia. People with source amnesia maintain their semantic knowledge but do not recall how they acquired it. A man who experienced damage to his prefrontal cortex as the result of a traffic accident retained his semantic and procedural knowledge of the game of chess, but he could not remember how old he was when he learned or who taught him to play the game (Tulving, 1989). Autobiographical memories are perhaps the most widely distributed of all types of memory in the cerebral cortex (Svoboda, McKinnon, & Levine, 2006). Because these memories capture perceptual, factual, and emotional details of past experience, we find activation not only in the prefrontal areas associated with episodic memories but also in the relevant areas of cerebral cortex associated with perception and movement.

Procedural Memories and the Basal Ganglia Procedural memories are correlated with activation of the basal ganglia, forebrain structures that are part of the brain's motor systems (see Chapter 4). People with Huntington's disease and with Parkinson's disease, both of which produce degeneration in the basal ganglia, typically experience great difficulty with learning new procedures (Knowlton et al., 1996; Krebs, Hogan, Hening, Adamovich, & Poizner, 2001). In contrast, their declarative memories remain relatively intact. Recall that Henry Molaison experienced the opposite outcome. His procedural memory abilities were intact, but his declarative memory abilities were severely impaired.

Summary 9.2 Types of Long-Term Memory

Type of memory	Declarative or nondeclarative?	Major features	Correlated brain structures
Semantic memory	Declarative	• General knowledge • Organized by category	Sensory and motor cortex
Episodic memory	Declarative	• Personal history • Organized chronologically	Prefrontal cortex
Autobiographical memory	Declarative	• Combines semantic and episodic memories • References self	Combination of prefrontal, sensory, and motor cortex
Procedural memory	Nondeclarative	• Difficult to verbalize • Easy to demonstrate • Automated skills	Basal ganglia

How Is Long-Term Memory Organized?

Little research exists regarding the organization of nondeclarative memories in long-term memory, but significant efforts have been made to understand the organization of declarative memories. Within the category of declarative memories, far more is known about semantic than about episodic organization. However, both types of memory appear to follow some of the same basic principles. Memories that share characteristics appear to be more closely linked than memories that show little overlap among their various features.

Connectionist Theories

More formal explanations have evolved to account for this tendency to group memories that share overlapping features. These explanations fall under the heading of connectionism, or the view of the mind as an interconnected network made up of simpler units. These models are "connectionist" because they suggest that thinking about one concept automatically leads to thinking about related concepts and their properties.

A **spreading activation model** (Collins & Loftus, 1975) recognizes that people form their own organizations in memory based on their personal experiences (see ● Figure 9.12). For example, if you ask people to report the first words that come to mind when they see the word *red*, you are likely to get many different sets of answers.

The spreading activation model also suggests that concepts differ in the strength of their connections. For example, even though avocados and oranges are both examples of the concept "fruit," it is likely that most people have a closer link in their memories between "orange" and "fruit" than between "avocado" and "fruit." If asked whether an avocado or an orange is a fruit, reaction time to the second statement would be faster.

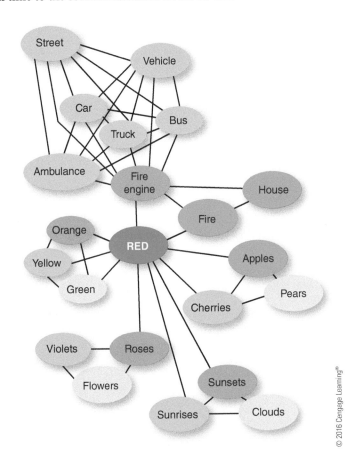

© 2016 Cengage Learning®

FIGURE 9.12

Spreading Activation. According to the spreading activation theory, thinking about *red* will activate nearby concepts (*orange, green,* and *fire*) faster than more distant concepts (*sunsets* and *roses*). This network suggests that a person would answer the question "Is a bus a vehicle?" faster than the question "Is an ambulance a vehicle?" *Source:* Adapted from "A Spreading Activation Theory of Semantic Processing," by A. M. Collins and E. Loftus, 1975, *Psychological Review, 82,* pp. 407–428.

spreading activation model A connectionist theory proposing that people organize general knowledge based on their individual experiences.

HOW IS LONG-TERM MEMORY ORGANIZED? **335**

The spreading activation model does an excellent job of accounting for the results of the lexical decision experiments demonstrating priming that we described earlier. Using the spreading activation model, we could assume that seeing the first word activates a concept. This activation would spread to connected concepts and properties. For closely related concepts like "doctor" and "nurse," activating the "doctor" concept would lead to activation of the "nurse" concept even before the person sees the word *nurse,* allowing a quick decision to be made as soon as the word appears. In contrast, with unrelated words like *butter* and *nurse,* the "nurse" concept would not be activated until the word appears, resulting in a relatively slower decision.

Inferences: Using Schemas

As early as 1932, psychologist Frederic Bartlett observed that memory does not work like a video recording of events (1932/1967). Bartlett read long, involved stories to his study participants and then asked them to recall the stories 20 hours later. Not too surprisingly, the recalled stories were shorter and had less detail than the original story. Somewhat more surprisingly, participants added features to the recalled stories that had not appeared in the original. These additions were not random. In most cases, the details added by participants fit the theme or meaning of the story.

Bartlett concluded that memory storage does not occur in a vacuum. When we encounter new information, we attempt to fit the new information into an existing **schema**, or set of expectations about objects and situations. Details that are consistent with our schemas are more likely to be retained, whereas inconsistent details are more likely to be left out. Details may be added in memory if they make a story more consistent and coherent. For example, you are more likely to recall having seen books in a photograph of a professor's office than in a photograph of a farmer working in the fields. Even if no books appeared in the professor's office, you might recall seeing some, because most professors have offices filled with books. In Chapter 11, we will explore the development of schemas and the formation of concepts during childhood.

We are more likely to remember details that are consistent with our schemas than those that are not. We will remember books in the professor's office and brushes and canvases in the artist's studio.

schema A set of expectations about objects and situations.

Experiencing Psychology

Schemas and False Memories

FREDERIC BARTLETT OBSERVED that using schemas to frame our memories can lead us to add details that improve a memory's consistency and coherence. In other words, we can "remember" things that did not occur because they fit our schemas. We can demonstrate this "fill in the blank" tendency in memory by asking you to memorize some word lists.

1. Read through both lists of words in order, and try to remember as many words as you can.

List 1   sheets, pillow, mattress, blanket, comfortable, room, dream, lay, chair, rest, tired, night, dark, time

List 2   door, tree, eye, song, pillow, juice, orange, radio, rain, car, sleep, cat, dream, eat

2. Without looking back at the list, write down as many words as possible from List 1 in any order.

ANALYSIS

Check your list of recalled words for any that did not appear in List 1. *Pillow* and *dream* appear in both lists, but *sleep* appears in List 2 only. Many people insert *sleep* into their List 1 responses (a false memory) because so many of the words on List 1 fit the sleep schema. It is unlikely that you will insert words into your recalled list that are not related to the schema of sleep. See whether you can construct some lists on your own that produce other false memories. We return to the issue of false memories and retrieval later in this chapter. ●

Schemas appear to be important in the process of memory storage, as demonstrated by a clever experiment in which participants were asked to read the following passage:

> The procedure is actually quite simple. First you arrange things into different groups depending on their makeup. Of course, one pile may be sufficient depending on how much there is to do. If you have to go somewhere else due to lack of facilities that is the next step, otherwise you are pretty well set. It is important not to overdo any particular endeavor. That is, it is better to do too few things at once than too many. In the short run this may not seem important, but complications from doing too many can easily arise. A mistake can be expensive as well. The manipulation of the appropriate mechanisms should be self-explanatory, and we need not dwell on it here. At first the whole procedure will seem complicated. Soon, however, it will become just another facet of life. It is difficult to foresee any end to the necessity for this task in the immediate future, but then one never can tell. (Bransford & Johnson, 1972, p. 722)

Alexander Image/Shutterstock

At this point, you are probably scratching your head in confusion. Reading this passage is bad enough, and remembering much of it later seems impossible. However, what if we tell you that the passage is about doing your laundry? With the laundry schema in mind, try re-reading the passage. It is likely to make a lot more sense than when you read it the first time, and you will remember more of what you read.

The self is one of the most important schemas we have for organizing our thinking. If you can think about how the material you study is reflected in your experience, it will be easier to remember.

How Do We Retrieve Memories?

Storing information does us little good unless we can locate and retrieve the information when we need it. Without a system of retrieval, our stored memories would be no more useful to us than a library in which books were placed on shelves at random. You might get lucky sometimes and find what you are looking for, but in most cases, the search would take so long that the information would no longer be needed.

Retrieval From Short-Term Memory

Imagine that you were told to remember the following letters for a subsequent test:

c a f h k

During the test, you are shown a series of letters one at a time. If the letter you are shown matches one on your list, you pull the "yes" lever as quickly as possible. If the letter is not on your list, you pull the "no" lever. This is the type of procedure used by Saul Sternberg (1966, 1967, 1969) to investigate recall from short-term memory.

Because of the small number of items that we can hold in short-term memory, it is tempting to assume that we can bring them all up simultaneously to perform Sternberg's task correctly. However, this probably is not the way memory works. Sternberg varied the length of the lists of letters from one to five and found that reaction time on his task increased a consistent 38 milliseconds for each additional item added to the list. In other words, if you were asked to say whether "h" was on your list, you would first consider "c," then "a," then "f," and so on until you reached the target letter. Sternberg's results suggest that we search through short-term memory one item at a time rather than retrieving its contents all at once.

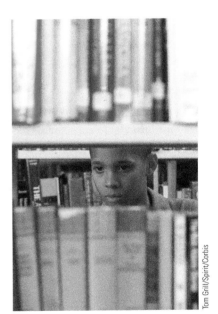

Tom Grill/Spirit/Corbis

Retrieval From Long-Term Memory

The popularity of games like *Trivial Pursuit,* crossword puzzles, and television game shows highlights an interesting aspect of memory retrieval. It feels good when you can remember something. At the same time, most students are all too familiar with the intense feelings of

Retrieval systems help us find the information we need, whether we are searching online, looking for a book, or trying to remember something important. Organized information is always easier to find than disorganized information.

frustration that accompany the inability to retrieve information. You know the answer, but it isn't coming to mind.

The Role of Cues

Students are quite familiar with the impact of cues on the ability to retrieve information. A **cue** is any stimulus that helps you access target information. Most students find recognition tasks, such as true–false or matching exam items, relatively easy. These tasks provide complete cues (the correct information is right on the page in front of you). All you need to do is make a judgment about how well the presented information matches what is stored in memory. Compared to recognition tasks, recall tasks, such as essay exams, require an additional step. Information must be retrieved from memory and then recognized as correct, a process known as generate-recognize (Guynn et al., 2014). Recall tasks provide far fewer cues than recognition tasks and are typically more difficult as a result.

In addition to the amount of information provided, what makes a stimulus an effective cue for recalling a particular bit of information? The most effective cues are those we generate ourselves, a finding that provides a practical application in student life. In one experiment, one group of students wrote down 3 words of their choosing for every 1 of 600 words they were expected to learn while another group studied the same 600 words accompanied by 3 words for each term selected by another person (Mäntylä & Nilsson, 1988). Although recall in the second group was an excellent 55%, the students who selected their own retrieval cues remembered a remarkable 90% of the words. In a later section on improving your memory, we will emphasize the benefits of incorporating your experience when forming new memories. If you are able to put concepts to be learned in your own words and associate them with personal experiences, it is likely that they will be easier to remember.

Why are cues helpful? Cues might work because of a process known as **encoding specificity** (Flexser & Tulving, 1978; Tulving, 1983; Tulving, & Thomson, 1973). Each time you form a long-term memory, bits of information are encoded along with other important bits that were present at the same time. As a result, each memory is processed in a unique and specific way, because this exact combination of bits is unlikely to occur again. Any stimulus that was present and noticed during this encoding process could serve as a cue for retrieving the target memory.

Among the bits of information that get encoded along with target memories are features of the surrounding environment, leading to context-dependent memory. You are probably familiar with advice about studying in a well-lit, quiet, professional environment to perform your best on exams. Duplicating your testing situation when you study should provide the greatest number of retrieval cues. When study participants were asked to learn lists of words in one of two distinctive rooms while either standing or sitting, recall was best when participants were tested in the same room and position as when they learned the information (Greenspoon & Ranyard, 1957). As shown in ● Figure 9.13, scuba divers who learned words either on land or underwater retrieved the most words when their encoding and testing circumstances were the same (Godden & Baddeley, 1975). Although these effects are small, it is still a good idea to study in a quiet classroomlike environment, which may help explain why studying in the library has remained popular through the years.

Mood and other internal states can serve as encoding cues. In one creative study, people with bipolar disorder (described in Chapter 14), whose moods can swing from mania to depression, learned words in one state (mania or depression) and tried to retrieve them in either the same state (mania–mania or depression–depression) or the opposite one (mania–depression or depression–mania; Weingartner, Miller, & Murphy, 1977). The participants were most successful when learning and retrieving occurred in the same state, whether that was mania or depression.

Tip of the Tongue

Retrieval is not an all-or-none phenomenon. Instead, retrieval proceeds step by step, with each new step bringing you closer to the target. This gradual retrieval is best

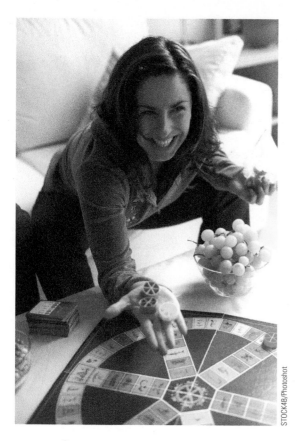

The popularity of memory games, like *Trivial Pursuit*, probably results from the rewarding feeling we get when we retrieve a sought-after memory.

It may be tempting to blame context-dependent memory for the experience of alcohol-related blackouts, but these are more likely to result from alcohol's active interference with the formation of long-term memories (Lisman, 1974). There is no evidence that getting drunk again will make it easier to recall what happened the last time a person got drunk.

cue A stimulus that aids retrieval.
encoding specificity A process in which memories incorporate unique combinations of information when encoded.

FIGURE 9.13

Our Surroundings Are Encoded in Context-Dependent Memories. Features of our environment get encoded along with target memories. Study participants learning lists of words either on land or while underwater recalled more words when tested in the same context compared to when they were tested in the opposite context. This diver might find it more difficult to retrieve information about types of fish if tested on dry land instead of underwater. *Source:* Adapted from "Context-Dependent Memory in Two Natural Environments: On Land and Under Water," D. R. Godden and A. D. Baddeley, 1975, *British Journal of Psychology, 66,* pp. 325–331.

illustrated by the tip-of-the-tongue (TOT) phenomenon. TOT is probably a familiar experience for you. You are trying to remember a word or name, and you might retrieve another word that either starts with the same letter or has the same meaning. You know that the retrieved word is not the one you're looking for, but you're close.

In a classic series of experiments, more than 200 TOT experiences were induced in research participants by presenting definitions of relatively rare English words (Brown & McNeill, 1966). For example, participants were asked to supply a word for "a navigational instrument used in measuring angular distances, especially the altitude of the sun, moon and the stars at sea" (Brown & McNeill, 1966, p. 333). You may be picturing the object right now, or thinking about a movie of an old salt using this instrument—it starts with an *s*—but most of you will have difficulty retrieving the word *sextant.*

Participants in these studies showed considerable evidence of partial recall during their TOT experiences. They were able to identify words that they recognized instantly, unlike words they did not know. Many were able to identify the first letter and the number of syllables in the target word. Incorrect words that were retrieved frequently sounded like the target, although their meanings were usually quite different. In some cases, retrieving the incorrect word appeared to block the retrieval of the correct item, but in other cases, the incorrect word was an additional cue.

Reconstruction During Retrieval What is happening when we retrieve a bit of stored information?

When retrieved, information to be used flows from long-term memory back into working memory. The mind is building a memory out of the stored bits. The mind accomplishes this **reconstruction** by blending retrieved information with new content present in working memory (Bartlett, 1932/1967). When you retrieve the target information, you are reconstructing something sensible to fit the occasion, as opposed to simply reproducing some memory trace. If the memories are rather fresh, such as when you are describing an automobile accident to a police officer, this process might produce updates in the original memory that will then be reconsolidated into long-term memory. Changes you make in the original memory will be stored as the new "truth." However, if you are recalling a memory from a more remote time, less updating is likely to occur (Gräff et al., 2014).

As storytellers begin, they discover that certain aspects of the story provoke more of a reaction from the audience. These aspects are emphasized and perhaps exaggerated for even greater effect, and the new, more exciting story replaces the original version in long-term memory. Fish become larger, vacations become more exciting, and heroes become more heroic. When participants in a study were asked to repeat a complicated story on several occasions, they had a tendency to simplify the story, highlight some aspects more than others, and

Drugs, including the caffeine in coffee, can produce strong context-dependent effects on memory. If you study while drinking coffee, taking a test without coffee is likely to make retrieval more difficult.

reconstruction Rebuilding a memory out of stored elements.

Tip-of-the-tongue experiences were elicited in volunteers by describing rare words in English. One of the items was the name of the weird-looking instrument this naval cadet is learning to use. Study participants were often able to retrieve the first letter of the word (s) and the number of syllables (two) without necessarily retrieving the whole word (*sextant*), which demonstrates retrieval is not all or none.

adjust the story to fit their worldviews (Bartlett, 1932/1967). Such alterations probably form the basis of mythology. In the retelling of the adventures of Odysseus or King Arthur, accounts of the original true events are lost or hopelessly distorted.

Most of us would like to believe that our memories, especially for important life events, are relatively accurate. Elizabeth Loftus set out to evaluate the reliability of eyewitness testimony in courtroom settings and discovered that memories are rather flexible. In one experiment, participants watched a video of an automobile accident and answered a number of questions about what they had seen (Loftus & Palmer, 1974). One group heard the question "How fast was the white sports car going while traveling along the country road?" while the other group heard the same question with a slight addition—"How fast was the white sports car going *when it passed the barn* while traveling along the country road?" There was no barn in the video, but when participants were asked 1 week later whether they had seen a barn, 20% of those who had heard the barn question answered "yes" while fewer than 5% of the other participants did so. One must assume that skilled attorneys are quite aware of this feature of memory and could use such leading questions to the advantage of their clients (see ● Figure 9.14).

If you began this psychology course believing, like many people do, that memory works like a video of life, it might surprise you to learn that this is not the case. It may be quite unsettling to realize that memories are open to change and revision and that those distinct and confident childhood memories we cherish may be somewhat inaccurate or even flat out wrong. However, it also doesn't make sense to think that we would evolve a system of memory that was usually wrong. Instead, fuzzy trace theory suggests that we use precious resources to form different types of memories based on our needs, ranging from verbatim, or exact, accounts to gist, which means we retain the general idea of events (Reyna, 2008). We use gist when a relatively vague level of information is sufficient, because this is a more efficient use of resources. We use the more energy-intensive verbatim memories for situations that require detailed, accurate recall, such as remembering the periodic table of the elements in your chemistry class. This system works well for us most of the time, but later in this chapter, we will see how relying on gist instead of retrieving verbatim information can lead to false memories (see ● Figure 9.15).

A checkpoint for the accuracy of our memories results from source monitoring (Johnson, Hashtroudi, & Lindsay, 1993). Under normal circumstances, we do a good job of dis-

FIGURE 9.14

Memory Reconstruction. After study participants viewed a short video of an automobile accident, Loftus and Palmer (1974) asked one group, "About how fast were the cars going when they *hit* each other?" while a second group was asked, "About how fast were the cars going when they *smashed* each other?" One week later, both groups were asked if they recalled seeing glass on the road after the accident. There was no glass on the road in the video, so the correct answer was "no." Hearing the word *smashed* instead of *hit* increased the likelihood that a participant would "remember" glass on the road and answer "yes." *Source:* Adapted from "Reconstruction of Automobile Destruction: An Example of the Interaction Between Language and Memory," by E. F. Loftus and J. C. Palmer, 1974, *Journal of Verbal Learning and Verbal Behavior, 13,* pp. 585–589.

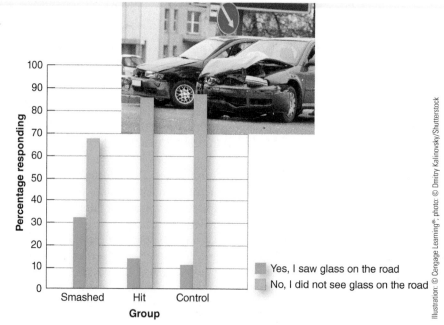

Yes, I saw glass on the road
No, I did not see glass on the road

FIGURE 9.15

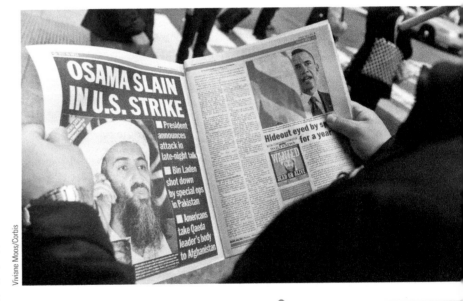

The Use of Gist Increases With Age. Older children, with their improved language skills, use gist more effectively than younger children (Odegard, Cooper, Lampinen, Reyna, & Brainerd, 2009). When children attended birthday parties with a theme (e.g., Harry Potter or SpongeBob SquarePants), older children appeared to be able to use the theme of the party to provide gist, leading to their successful recall of more theme-related events, such as having magic potions at Hermione's party. Younger children, however, could not remember theme-related events better than generic birthday party events like blowing out candles on a cake, suggesting that forming a theme gist was not helpful. *Source:* Adapted from "Children's Eyewitness Memory for Multiple Real-Life Events," by T. N. Odegard, C. M. Cooper, J. M. Lampinen, V. F. Reyna, and C. J. Brainerd, 2009, *Child Development, 80*(6), pp. 1877–1890, doi:10.1111/j.1467-8624.2009.01373.x.

tinguishing between external and internal sources of information, as in "I said that" or "I thought about saying that." Again, this system works well for us most of the time, but it can produce false memories when we attribute a memory to the wrong source. For example, you might think you told your roommate you would be coming in late, but you may have only mentally reminded yourself to do so. You have mistaken an internal source of information ("I thought that") with an external source ("That happened").

Retrieval of Emotional Events

Take a moment and write down the most important five events in your life last year. Do these events have anything in common with one another? We're willing to guess that each of the events on your list is associated with strong emotions. From an evolutionary perspective, this makes good sense. In Chapter 7, we argued that emotions provide quick guidance for approach-or-avoidance decisions. Many of our emotional experiences, while not life threatening, have significance for us, and forming strong memories of these events will help us respond effectively to similar situations in the future.

Emotions, particularly negative emotions, do not have a simple relationship with memory retrieval. In some cases, we seem to have difficulty remembering negative events, which we discuss in a later section on motivated forgetting. Some individuals report that they can recall few or no details of having been sexually molested as children. In other cases, memories for negative events seem more vivid and intrusive than other types of memories. Most adults in the United States seem to have formed a **flashbulb memory** of the terrorist attacks of September 11, 2001, or an especially vivid memory including details of where they were and what they were doing when they first heard the news. Individuals diagnosed with posttraumatic stress disorder (PTSD) often experience intrusive flashbacks of the events that originally traumatized them. How do we reconcile these differences in retrieval for emotional events?

People often report especially vivid episodic memories about where they were and what they were doing when they first heard news that evoked a strong emotional response, although research evidence suggests that these memories are not always as accurate as we think they are.

flashbulb memory An especially vivid and detailed memory of an emotional event.

HOW DO WE RETRIEVE MEMORIES? **341**

As information moves through the stages described by the Atkinson–Shiffrin model, it remains relatively fragile and subject to modification. Stress and strong negative emotions are accompanied by the release of hormones and by patterns of brain activity that can either enhance or impair memory processing, depending on the timing of the emotional response relative to target learning (Joëls, 2006). If stress and learning happen at the same time, an enhanced memory such as a flashbulb memory might be formed (Diamond, Campbell, Park, Halonen, & Zoladz, 2007). Stress occurring either before or after learning tends to impair memory formation (Joëls, 2006). Impairment of memory following an important life event

Thinking Scientifically

Should We Erase Traumatic Memories?

IN CHAPTER 14, we explore a condition known as posttraumatic stress disorder (PTSD) that results when some people experience a traumatic event. Although trauma of many kinds can induce PTSD, one of the most reliable sources of PTSD is combat exposure. Although about 7% to 8% of Americans will experience PTSD at some point in their lives, between 11% and 20% of U.S. soldiers who served in Iraq or Afghanistan and approximately 30% of soldiers who served in Vietnam meet the diagnostic criteria for the disorder (U.S. Department of Veterans Affairs, 2014).

Among the symptoms of PTSD is the experience of vivid, intrusive flashbacks of the traumatic event. These flashbacks can be triggered by environmental stimuli, such as the odor of diesel fumes, according to the principles of classical conditioning we discussed in Chapter 8. Individuals with PTSD would like to eliminate these distressing responses. The current mode of therapy is exposure therapy, which we also discussed in Chapter 8. But what if we could simply erase the memory?

In our discussion of the Atkinson–Shiffrin model, we noted that memories that are retrieved mingle with ongoing material in short-term or working memory. Subsequently, these memories undergo a process of reconsolidation. If you are thinking about something you just read in the chapter, those memories are more "open" to modification, but memories for the more

distant past are less changeable. What if we could get the brain to treat memories from the distant past more like recent memories?

Long-term memories involve structural changes in neurons and their synapses that result from changes in gene expression, which we discussed in Chapter 3. In mice, the state of a chemical called histone deacetylase 2 (HDAC2) correlates with the "open" period of reconsolidation in which memories are modifiable as opposed to the "closed" period characteristic of more remote memories (Gräff et al., 2014). As shown in Figure 9.16, application of HDAC2 inhibitors essentially returns remote memories to the same modifiable state that characterizes fresh memories. Extinction of fear responses during this artificial reconsolidation state should produce more effective reductions in traumatic fear.

We can't imagine that anyone would wish continued suffering on people with PTSD, but not all therapists are comfortable with the concept of "erasing" traumatic memories. As one psychiatrist wrote, "There is pain in life, and it needs to be dealt with in a human way.... Our suffering, trauma included, is not a brain problem, but a human problem" (Berezin, 2014, para. 3).

Perhaps the key here is to consider what "erasing" means. If we are erasing the entire memory for the traumatic event, that is one thing. If we are simply reducing the emotional response to that event, that could be a different matter. ●

FIGURE 9.16

Epigenetic Effects Can Make Old Memories Modifiable Again. Histone deacetylase 2 (HDAC2) activity in the hippocampus differs between situations in which recent memories and those in which remote memories are recalled. HDAC2 affects histone acetylation (A? in the image), which is associated with greater gene expression (see Chapter 3). (a) During recall of recent memories, HDAC2 is associated with nitric oxide (NO), which dissociates it from the histones, allowing acetylation to occur. This leads to greater expression of genes related to learning and memory-induced structural changes in neurons, like cFos. (b) When remote memories are recalled, the association of HDAC2 with histones prevents the expression of cFos. (c) In the presence of HDAC2 inhibitors, histone acetylation occurs again even during recall of remote memories, which returns the memory systems to a modifiable state. Extinction of fear during this state might lead to long-term reductions in the fear associated with traumatic events.

might protect the fragile memories of that event from interference until they are fully consolidated.

So far, we have been considering isolated events that elicit strong negative emotions and stress. As we will see in Chapter 16, chronic stress produces its own set of challenges. Chronic stress produces a number of important changes in the parts of the brain associated with memory formation. For example, chronic stress produces a loss of volume in the hippocampus that is likely to have profound influences on the formation of new memories (Roozendaal, McEwen, & Chattarji, 2009).

Psychology as a Hub Science
How Reliable Are Eyewitnesses?

Our legal system relies heavily on the testimony of eyewitnesses, especially those who have nothing to gain by telling a lie. Given the flexible nature of human memory as discussed in this chapter, is the trust we place in eyewitness accounts reasonable?

Carefully controlled research by Elizabeth Loftus into the use of eyewitness testimony (Loftus, 1979; Loftus & Palmer, 1974), along with the development of forensic deoxyribonucleic acid (DNA) testing in the 1990s, seriously compromised trust in eyewitness testimony. Out of all cases in which an innocent person has been cleared of a crime because of DNA evidence, about 75% involved mistaken identification of the perpetrator by an eyewitness (Wells, Memon, & Penrod, 2006).

Psychologists have used research on eyewitness behavior to make scientifically based recommendations to law enforcement officials. For example, the manner in which photograph lineups of possible suspects are shown to witnesses affects the likelihood of mistaken identification. In the typical procedure, witnesses view lineup photographs simultaneously, which allows them to compare all the people and choose the person who looks most similar to their memories of the perpetrator. Unfortunately, this procedure makes mistaken identification more likely if the real suspect does not appear in the lineup. The witness simply chooses the person who looks most like the remembered perpetrator. If a sequential procedure is used, in which the witness must respond "yes" or "no" to a picture before moving to the next one, mistaken identifications occur less frequently (Steblay, Dysart, Fulero, & Lindsay, 2001).

Perhaps juries could evaluate eyewitness testimony more accurately if they took the witness's apparent confidence into account. In other words, a person who seems confident about identifying a suspect might be expected to be more accurate than a witness with less confidence. Unfortunately, such an appealing idea has major flaws. Even witnesses who express a 95% confidence in their judgment (expecting to be wrong only 5% of the time) are correct only 70% to 75% of the time (Brewer, Keast, & Rishworth, 2002). In addition, witness confidence can be easily manipulated by feedback that confirms an identification. Simply telling witnesses, "Good, you identified the suspect," retroactively changes the witnesses' recollections of how confident they were about an original identification, how good a view they had of the perpetrator and events, and how much attention they paid to the suspect's face during the crime (Wells & Bradfield, 1998).

Special consideration must be given to cases in which the eyewitness is a child. An understanding of children's memory development is critical for evaluating the child's ability to serve as a witness to a crime. Some data indicate that children's memories for significant events, like a trip to an emergency room, are quite reliable as long as 4 to 5 years later (Peterson & Whalen, 2001). However, young children are accustomed to pleasing adults with their answers and are more suggestible than adolescents and adults. Fortunately, understanding the strengths and limitations of children's memory systems has allowed experts to develop methods for obtaining the most accurate reports possible from child witnesses (Bruck & Ceci, 2009).

Further improvements should accompany the development of new, more reliable measures of recognition, such as brain imaging, reaction time, rapid presentation of faces, and analyses of witness eye movements (Wells et al., 2006). ●

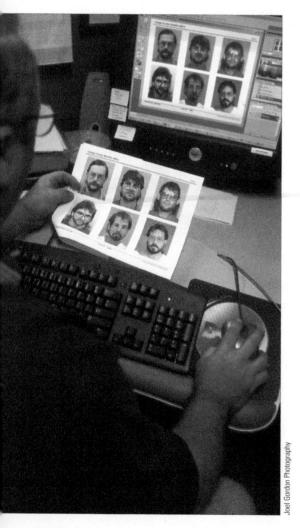

Joel Gordon Photography

The traditional lineup used in the criminal justice system is likely to produce a mistaken identification when the real perpetrator is not included. The witness simply picks the most similar person. Psychologists have shown that giving "yes" or "no" answers to one photo at a time reduces the risk of a mistaken identification.

Why Do We Forget?

Now that we understand the processes involved with the formation, storage, and retrieval of memories, we can turn our attention to the troublesome topic of forgetting. For students, whose job description involves committing large amounts of information to memory, an understanding of the processes leading to forgetting is the source of practical advice for improving memory and avoiding memory failure.

For the purposes of our discussion, we define **forgetting** as a decrease in the ability to remember a previously formed memory. The key here is that to forget a memory, it has to have been formed in the first place. This definition excludes a number of instances that we have discussed previously. For example, many students maintain that they "forgot" information needed for an exam but instead were daydreaming during the lecture covering the material and never learned it. This example is better understood in terms of lack of attention and encoding failure than as an example of forgetting. Using our definition, you can't forget something you never learned. When forgetting is the result of brain injury or disease, we usually refer to the loss of information as amnesia.

Andy Reynolds/The Image Bank/Getty Images

If this woman was never able to forget where she parked all the previous times she used this lot, finding her car today would be extremely difficult.

Understanding forgetting is complicated because we measure memory indirectly by looking at performance. As most students are all too aware, actual memory for a topic can be quite different from performance on an exam. Stress, illness, time pressure, and distractions can temporarily reduce our ability to recall information. When we discuss true forgetting, we are not considering the effects of these temporary difficulties. It would be handy for both students and instructors if some sort of modern imaging technology would allow us to "see" whether introductory psychology had been adequately stored in the brain, but alas, this is not currently possible.

Although forgetting can be frustrating, it also has its adaptive benefits. Forgetting might provide a way to prioritize the things we should remember. For example, we are often asked to change our computer passwords to maintain security. At first, this can lead to annoying competition in memory between the old and the new passwords. Over time, however, the strength of an old password weakens. Functional magnetic resonance imaging (fMRI) studies have shown that prefrontal areas of the brain appear to actively suppress memories that are used less frequently (Kuhl, Dudukovic, Kahn, & Wagner, 2007). By suppressing these lower priority memories, we can avoid confusion and reduce the amount of work we have to do to recall higher priority memories.

Decay

Decay occurs when our ability to retrieve information we do not use fades over time. Imagine taking last term's final exams today. How would you do? It might seem to you that the material you learned last term is gone forever, but just because you can't retrieve something doesn't mean the memories are lost.

A classic method of measuring the retention of material in long-term memory over time is the method of savings. This method compares the rate of learning material the first time to the rate of learning the same material a second time. It might take you 50 practice trials to learn the periodic table of elements for your chemistry class. Perhaps you don't study chemistry again for a year or two. In a subsequent course, you again need to memorize the table. This time, it only takes you 20 trials. The greater speed of learning the table the second time indicates that you retained, or saved, some prior memories of the table. Using this technique, we can demonstrate that people who studied high school Spanish but never used it later in life retained most of their memories for Spanish vocabulary words 50 years later (Bahrick, 1984). Instead of a large amount of forgetting because of the passage of time, we usually see that most of the material we learn is retained nearly indefinitely.

forgetting A decrease in the ability to remember a previously formed memory.

decay A reduction in ability to retrieve rarely used information over time.

Ted Benson/ZUMA Press, Inc./Alamy

People attending their 70th high school reunions might have forgotten the names of some of their classmates whom they hadn't seen in decades.

interference Competition between newer and older information in memory.

Although the idea of decay fits our everyday experience of forgetting quite well, most contemporary psychologists believe that the simple passage of time does not do a good job of predicting memories that are easy or difficult to retrieve (Berman, 2009). It is likely that forgetting occurs because of a combination of factors, which may or may not include decay.

Interference

A significant factor in forgetting is **interference**, or the competition between newer and older information in the memory system. The brain requires a measurable amount of time to consolidate a memory, or to produce a physical representation. In the window of time in which memories are being processed but not yet fully consolidated, they may be subject to distortion, loss, or replacement by interference from other bits of information.

How long is this window? Synaptic consolidation, the physical changes related to memory that occur at the level of the synapse, might take minutes or hours. Memory loss usually occurs when this consolidation is interrupted. Individuals who experience unconsciousness as a result of a head injury rarely remember much about the immediate circumstances leading to the injury. Procedures such as general anesthesia or electroconvulsive therapy (ECT, described in Chapter 15) often produce slight memory deficits spanning a period of hours or possibly a day or two before and after treatment. In contrast, storage of memories in the cerebral cortex might take years, during which time information can be lost or distorted (Dudai, 2004).

Interference can be demonstrated by comparing performance in a list-learning task. The more lists someone must learn, the more difficult it becomes to remember words on the first list (Tulving & Psotka, 1971). In other words, learning new lists of words interfered with memory for the first list.

Does this mean that the first list is somehow erased from memory by the incoming information? To test this hypothesis, researchers gave participants in one experiment a little help in the form of memory cues. The lists all contained categories of items, such as types of buildings (e.g., house, barn, garage, and hut). If the experimenters provided their participants with a cue in the form of the category (types of buildings), the effects of having learned additional lists were quite small. It appears that the words on the first list were maintained in memory but that learning additional lists made them hard to retrieve.

To make matters worse, interference can work in two directions (Underwood, 1957; see ● Figure 9.17). Let's assume your foreign language class is assigned one list of vocabulary words to study each night. You have procrastinated a bit on your homework, and to catch up for a quiz the next day, you now have three lists of vocabulary words to study instead of the usual single list. Our interest will be on how well you can remember the second of the three lists. If we compare your memories for the second list to those of students who studied the first list when it was assigned, we find that your performance is relatively poor. In other words, learning the first list on the same night as the second list produces proactive interference for the second list. Proactive interference refers to reduced memory for target information as a result of earlier learning.

At the same time, we can compare your memories for the second list to the performance of your classmates who studied the third list the night after they studied the second list. Again, your performance is likely to be worse. Reduced memory for target information because of subsequent learning is known as retroactive interference. This type of interference was demonstrated in the multiple lists study we discussed previously (which you may recall unless too much retroactive interference has occurred).

FIGURE 9.17

Proactive and Retroactive Interference. If we measure recall of a target list of words, we find that it is worse both when preceded by learning another list (proactive interference) and when followed by learning another list (retroactive interference).

Learned first	Target learning	Learned last

Proactive interference

Retroactive interference

© Cengage Learning®

Motivated Forgetting

The Internal Revenue Service reports that far more people who owe money fail to sign their tax returns than do those who are due a refund. Assuming that the failure to sign the return is not a conscious act of defiance, how can we account for this lapse in memory? Theories of **motivated forgetting**, or the failure to remember or retrieve unpleasant or threatening information, suggest that the nonsigners are protecting themselves from further unpleasantness by "forgetting" to sign their tax forms.

Memory is a servant to our overarching goals. Retrieval, for better or worse, is often influenced by our motivations, and our motivations can distort the memories we retrieve. While not exactly forgetting in the sense of our earlier definition, motivated distortions of memory can be so extreme that the original information is essentially lost during the process.

Elizabeth Loftus (2003) demonstrated that it was relatively easy to implant a false memory in study participants of having taken a hot air balloon ride during childhood.

In one example of the influence of motivation on recall, study participants were presented with a list of choices, such as between two internships, roommates, or cars for sale, with equal numbers of corresponding positive and negative features (high resale value or some rust in the case of the cars). Subsequently, they remembered the positive features associated with their ultimate choices better than the negative features (Henkel & Mather, 2007). When they were deceived into thinking they had chosen the other option instead (because of a friendly "reminder" from the experimenter), they continued to remember the false choice more positively. In related research, participants conveniently demonstrated less recall for ethical rules after they had been given an opportunity to cheat (Shu, Gino, & Bazerman, 2011). In Chapter 13, we will explore how these types of discrepancies between behavior and attitudes can change the attitudes, not just the memories for them.

Identifying the presence of motivated forgetting can have serious practical implications. Beginning in the 1970s, largely because of greater public recognition that incest was more common than previously believed, many adults began to report having been a victim of sexual abuse during childhood. These cases represented a range of possible motivated forgetting from suppression, in which the individual consciously remembered the incidents but had not reported them to parents or other authorities, to repression, in which the individual reported no conscious memory of the incidents until the memories were suddenly recovered during therapy or while reading a news report of a child molestation case.

A number of psychologists studying memory suspected that not all reports of recovered memories of child abuse were true and that some might represent confabulation, or confusion between imagined and true memories. As we mentioned earlier in this chapter, our source monitoring abilities usually prevent us from mistaking false for true memories, but the system does not perform perfectly. Under the right set of circumstances, it is relatively easy for people to believe strongly in a memory that is simply not true.

We demonstrated in an earlier section on schemas that false recall for verbal stimuli can be produced by presenting words that are associated by meaningfulness (e.g., *bed, rest,* and *awake*). In this case, most study participants formed a false memory for the presentation of the word *sleep* (Deese, 1959). Perhaps you are thinking that memorizing strings of words in a laboratory has little relevance to the experience of traumatized victims of child abuse. Loftus, whom we met earlier in our discussion of memory reconstruction, addressed that concern by demonstrating that more complex false memories were rather easy to implant in study participants. Loftus (2003) described how imagining an event had happened or even reading the testimonials of witnesses could increase a person's confidence that a false event had occurred. Most persuasive is the use of photographs. When a real family photo was superimposed on a hot air balloon, 50% of participants "remembered" taking a ride, including details about how old they had been at the time and that the photo was taken by a particular person.

Until we understand more about the nature of confabulation, a cautious approach to repressed memories is probably the best course of action. We can neither prove nor disprove these memories without additional evidence, so any therapy should be aimed at relieving distressing symptoms without reference to their source (American Psychological Association, 2014).

motivated forgetting Failure to retrieve negative memories.

What Is the Biology of Memory?

In our previous discussions of working and long-term memory, we outlined some brain areas believed to coordinate those processes. In this section, we will zoom in for a closer look to see how the brain in general appears to manage memory at the cellular and biochemical levels.

Memory at the Level of the Synapse

Forming new memories requires changes in the connections neurons make with one another at the synapse, or synaptic consolidation. You might find it strange to think that such a process is going on in your brain as you read this chapter.

Eric Kandel and his colleagues have demonstrated persistent changes in the strength of synapses responsible for several types of learning in the sea slug, including classical conditioning (Antonov, Antonova, Kandel, & Hawkins, 2003; Brunelli, Castellucci, & Kandel, 1976; Carew & Kandel, 1973). In addition to changes in synaptic strength, it appears that learning stimulates a cascade of gene expression, which in turn produces the long-term structural changes in neurons that represent memories. The number of axon terminals increases following sensitization and decreases following habituation (Bailey & Chen, 1983; see Chapter 8). These observations are consistent with the behavior observed in each case—lower levels of responses to stimuli in habituation and higher levels of responses to stimuli in sensitization (see ● Figure 9.18).

One of the major processes responsible for change at the synaptic level during learning is **long-term potentiation (LTP)**, which enhances communication between two neurons. This phenomenon can be demonstrated experimentally by applying a rapid series of electric pulses to one area of the nervous system and observing the increased reactions of cells receiving input from that area (Bliss & Lømo, 1973; see ● Figure 9.19). Results from demonstrations of LTP suggest that the relatively simultaneous activation of a neuron sending information and the neuron receiving this information produces changes that make the synapse more efficient. LTP shares many features with memory, which makes it an attractive candidate for being one of the processes underlying memory phenomena. LTP lasts a long time, possibly indefinitely, which is similar to our thinking about long-term memories. Second, both memories and LTP can be formed after only brief exposure to stimuli.

long-term potentiation (LTP) The enhancement of communication between two neurons resulting from their synchronous activation.

FIGURE 9.18

Learning Changes Neural Structure. Neurons have smaller numbers of axon terminals following habituation but larger numbers following sensitization. *Source:* "Morphological Basis of Long-Term Habituation and Sensitization in *Aplysia*," by C. H. Bailey and M. C. Chen, 1983, *Science, 220*, pp. 91–93.

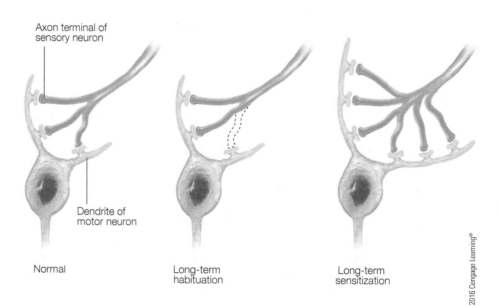

Axon terminal of sensory neuron

Dendrite of motor neuron

Normal

Long-term habituation

Long-term sensitization

© 2016 Cengage Learning®

Biochemistry and Memory

Throughout this chapter, we have emphasized that memory is not a single thing but rather a flexible, multistage process. It should not be surprising, therefore, that we do not have a simple biochemical account for memory.

Acetylcholine (ACh), discussed in Chapter 4, appears to affect memory, especially the encoding of new information (see ● Figure 9.20). Drugs that inhibit systems using ACh as a major neurotransmitter typically interfere with memory formation (Atri et al., 2004). People with Alzheimer's disease, which is characterized by severe memory deficits, typically show degeneration of neural circuits that use ACh. Medications prescribed to reduce the symptoms of Alzheimer's disease typically boost ACh activity (Holzgrabe, Kapkova, Alptuzun, Scheiber, & Kugelmann, 2007). At the same time, high ACh levels might impair memory consolidation and retrieval (Micheau & Marighetto, 2011). Relatively low levels of ACh during sleep might improve the transfer of information from temporary to more permanent storage (Diekelmann & Born, 2010).

Researchers are also interested in the role of the neurotransmitter glutamate in memory formation. One type of glutamate receptor, known as the *N*-methyl-D-aspartate (NMDA) receptor, is a prime candidate for learning-related changes such as those observed in LTP (Qiu & Knopfel, 2007). Not too surprisingly, chemicals that enhance the activity of glutamate receptors have been shown to boost memory formation in rats (Balschuna, Zuschrattera, & Wetzel, 2006). Similar compounds are being tested for possible use in treating Alzheimer's disease.

Baseline   Stimulation   1 week later

© Argosy Publishing, Inc.

FIGURE 9.19

Long-Term Potentiation (LTP). LTP can be demonstrated by applying a series of electrical pulses (center) and observing the increased reactions of cells receiving input (right) compared to their previous baseline (left). LTP shares many features with memory, such as being long-lasting and formed after a brief exposure to stimuli.

Acetylcholine

Illustration: © Cengage Learning®. photo: Daniel Prudek/Shutterstock

FIGURE 9.20

Acetylcholine (ACh), Caffeine, and Memory. Not only do drugs promoting ACh initiate changes in neural structure in honeybees (Weinberger, 2006), but so does caffeine. Bees rewarded with caffeine were 3 times as likely to remember a floral scent as bees rewarded with sucrose (Wright et al., 2013).

How Can We Improve Memory?

Most college students by definition have good memory skills—this is an essential component of academic success, and those who lack these skills generally do not end up in higher education. However, we can always improve, and the observations made by psychologists studying memory provide many practical suggestions.

We have already discussed several lines of research that have practical implications for improved memory. The structure of long-term memory implies that organized material is easier to remember than disorganized material. Elaborative rehearsal, especially when you can connect material to personal experience, anchors new material in your existing memory stores and makes it easier to retrieve. The effects of state, mood, and context on retrieval suggest that studying in circumstances that are most similar to those in which you will retrieve your memories will give you the best outcome.

In addition to these basic suggestions, we would like to offer a few tips that might be especially useful, both during and after your college experience.

Distribute Practice Over Time

Psychology professors will never give up trying to convince students that cramming is a terrible memory strategy. Persistent faith in cramming is surprising, given that we all know that concert pianists and basketball players are better off practicing 1 hour a day each day for a week than practicing 6 hours straight the night before a performance. The mind works in

 Connecting to Research

Does Caffeine Help You to Remember?

CAFFEINE, DISCUSSED IN CHAPTER 6, is a favorite substance among students because of its ability to produce alertness. Previous research has not indicated any benefits of caffeine use for boosting memory functions that could not be attributed to its effects on attention and alertness. As we discovered in this chapter, substances like caffeine often produce context-dependent memories, which further complicates research efforts to observe its results on memory.

A group of researchers at Johns Hopkins University, led by Michael Yassa, looked at the effects of caffeine on memories for photos as much as 24 hours later (Borota et al., 2014). Unlike previous studies, caffeine was administered after the photos were viewed. The group also used a memory test for pattern separation, which indicates a deeper level of processing than simple recognition (Yassa & Stark, 2011).

The Question: Does caffeine administered following learning affect long-term memory for visual images?

METHODS

The researchers used a classic double-blind, placebo-controlled design, discussed further in Chapter 2 (see ● Figure 9.21). A group of 160 students who did not use caffeinated products were divided into placebo and caffeine groups. Five minutes after viewing a series of photographs and making a simple indoor–outdoor discrimination (tree = outdoor, sofa = indoor), participants were given either a placebo pill or a 200-milligram caffeine tablet (approximately the equivalent of one cup of coffee). Participants were unable to correctly determine whether they had received caffeine or the placebo. Saliva samples were taken before administration

of the tablet and 1, 3, and 24 hours later to assess caffeine levels.

The following day, participants viewed photos that were shown the day before, were new photos, or were similar to the photos viewed the day before. The discrimination between familiar and similar is made quite difficult because of the overlapping features of stimuli in these categories (Yassa & Stark, 2011).

RESULTS

The group using caffeine distinguished familiar photos from similar photos better than the placebo group when tested the following day.

CONCLUSIONS

The researchers were able to demonstrate that caffeine administered following learning had a beneficial effect on recall for visual images the next day. Should you rush similar ways whether it learns to play basketball or it learns the periodic table of elements, so the same learning strategies should work in either case.

Nearly all forms of learning show evidence of an advantage of distributed practice (practice spread out over time) as opposed to massed practice (practice condensed to a short period; Russo & Mammarella, 2002). In other words, spacing the input of information to the brain over time produces better memory than cramming. Whether we are discussing the learning of classically conditioned responses by sea slugs or the learning of complex semantic information by college students, the advantage of distributing learning over time is a constant. By giving the brain more time to consolidate each memory, less is likely to be lost to interference.

Take Tests

We usually think about tests as measuring a student's ability to retrieve memories, but test taking is a powerful tool for forming memories too (Roediger & Butler, 2011). Research demonstrates that taking a test produces superior long-term memory when compared with repeated studying of material. In addition, taking tests improved participants' ability to think about learned material with greater flexibility and to apply material to new situations.

We are not advocating that you abandon reviewing your textbook and lecture notes, but we hope you will take advantage of the online testing opportunities that accompany this textbook.

out to your nearest Starbucks to enhance your memories for this chapter? We would not necessarily recommend this. If you enjoy caffeinated beverages and experience no adverse effects, then by all means continue to enjoy them. But you might find some of our recommendations for improving memory in the rest of this section more useful. ●

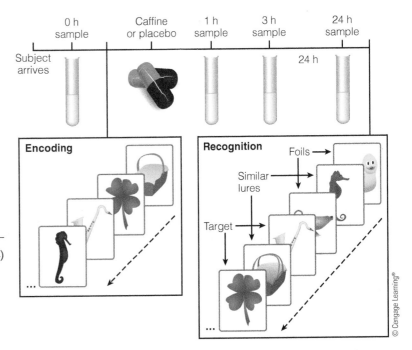

F I G U R E 9.21

Caffeine Enhances Memory Formation. Borota et al. (2014) used a double-blind, placebo-controlled design to test whether caffeine improved retention of visual memories. After providing a saliva sample, participants viewed images. Five minutes after the viewing, they consumed either a caffeine or a placebo tablet. Further saliva samples were taken 1, 3, and 24 hours later. Participants were asked to identify images as targets (seen the day before), foils (not seen the day before), or lures (similar but not identical to items seen the day before). Correct identification of lures as similar has been shown to require hippocampal activity.

Most of us realize that the best way to improve our music or athletic skills is to practice every day (distributed practice). We would think it odd if an athlete or musician crammed practice in the night before a game or performance (massed practice). The same advantage of distributed over massed practice holds for academic work, but unfortunately, that fact does not deter some students from cramming for exams.

Sleep

Initially, many psychologists believed that the positive role of sleep in memory formation resulted from a lack of interference. If you learned something right before going to sleep, no further information would enter the system to cause interference. More sophisticated research, however, has demonstrated that sleep plays an active role in the consolidation of memories. Learning during waking might strengthen new connections, but sleep-related processing might reorganize existing memories to accommodate new information (Stickgold & Walker, 2007).

Most types of memories appear stronger after a period of sleep (Genzel, Kroes, Dresler, & Battaglia, 2014). We can also say with confidence that students who pull all-nighters are not doing their memory systems a favor. In one experiment, staying up all night produced poor memory for a previous task, and two additional nights of adequate sleep did not compensate for the original deprivation (Stickgold, James, & Hobson, 2000).

Putting information you need to remember in your own words is an effective memory strategy. Recitation takes advantage of our tendency to remember things better when they're associated with the self. If they are your words, you will remember them.

Recite

Most students recognize that a certain number of rehearsals of reading and lecture notes are required for success on exams. One of the traps in a dependence on rehearsal is that we can easily mistake the ease with which we cover familiar material for actually knowing the material. Just because you can read something doesn't mean you know it.

A somewhat more efficient method is recitation, or the verbalizing of the material to be learned in your own words. Recitation takes advantage of a general superiority for self-referential information. People who processed words in reference to themselves (e.g., "Does the word 'honest' describe you?") are more likely to remember the word *honest* than are people who processed the definition of the words (e.g., "Does 'honest' mean the same thing as 'trustworthy'?"; Rogers, Kuiper, & Kirker, 1977). This result has obvious relevance for students wishing to improve their memories. If you can think about the information you are trying to learn in self-referential ways ("This example of episodic memories in my textbook reminds me of something that happened to me the other day"), your memory for the information will be enhanced. By putting information in your own words, you make it more relevant to yourself.

Recitation is still used as a classroom technique in small classes, but you can duplicate this process on your own. After you have a reasonable grasp of the material, try talking about it. The most significant benefit of recitation is that you quickly realize what you do not understand when you try to explain the material to someone else. You can think that you understand something, but when you try to explain it, it doesn't come out right. This is a signal that more work on the topic is needed.

Use Mnemonics

The early Greeks devised a number of methods, known as **mnemonics**, for improving memory. Mnemonic devices expand memory capacity by linking the material to be remembered to information that is relatively effortless to retrieve. The first-letter approach takes advantage of chunking. You condense a large amount of information into an acronym. For example, in Chapter 12, we'll use the acronym OCEAN to help remember the five major personality traits: openness, conscientiousness, extraversion, agreeableness, and neuroticism.

One of the classic Greek techniques was the method of *loci,* or places. This technique is particularly handy when you are trying to memorize a list of items in order, such as the planets in our solar system or the cranial nerves. The method takes advantage of the fact that we form excellent representations of visual images in memory. You begin by imagining a familiar place, perhaps your childhood home. As you imagine yourself walking through your home, you visualize each item in a particular location. If you wish to remember your grocery list (although writing the items down is probably easier), you might imagine a carton of eggs on the little table in your entry, a loaf of bread on the sofa, a box of cereal on the television, and so on. To recall your list, all you need to do is to take another imaginary walk through your house, recalling the items you placed as you go. If all goes well, you should remember all your items in the correct order.

This technique may sound like a lot of work, but it can be effective. One of the authors of this textbook had a colleague in graduate school who performed so perfectly on her neuroanatomy exams that her professors accused her of cheating. She related to them how she had been taught the method of loci as a childhood game and had practiced the technique throughout her academic career. After they posed several difficult lists to her, all of which she recalled perfectly, they were convinced of her honesty.

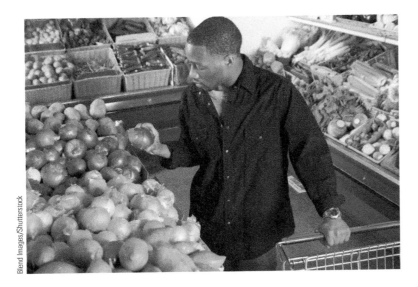

Blend Images/Shutterstock

The ancient Greek mnemonic device, the method of *loci*, takes advantage of our superior memory for visual images of familiar places. Although the method involves consciously imagining things in a particular place, we often use location as a memory aid less consciously. You are probably familiar with the layout of your favorite grocery store and use that mental image to guide your memories for the food you need to purchase. If the store reorganizes its layout between trips, you might forget something.

mnemonics Memory aids that link new information to well-known information.

Interpersonal Relationships
The Memory Perspective
What Is Transactive Memory?

Shared memories are a characteristic of close relationships. You may know people in close relationships who seem to know intuitively what the other is thinking, perhaps even finishing the partner's sentences. According to a theory of transactive memory, couples in long-term relationships also develop a division of labor in regard to memory, in which each partner knows certain things but also knows what information can be retrieved from the partner if needed (Wegner, 1986; Wegner, Giuliano, & Hertel, 1985). For example, one partner might not keep track of where candles are stored in the house but knows that the other partner knows where the candles are and can be called upon to provide that knowledge in the event of an emergency.

How do couples develop systems like this? Three major strategies have been identified (Wegner, Erber, & Raymond, 1991). First, one partner can explicitly agree to take on an area of expertise, such as managing the household finances. Second, as people get to know each other better through self-disclosure, they also learn about each other's relative areas of knowledge and expertise. One partner might have an interest in computer science, while the other thinks that computers work by magic. If something goes wrong with a household computer, the second person will turn to the first. Finally, couples learn about their partner's access to information. If you know that your partner discussed holiday plans with your families, you are likely to assume that your partner knows more about your holiday options than you do.

From an evolutionary standpoint, what are the advantages of working out this division of memory labor? One major advantage of this type of transactive memory is that a couple working well together has access to far more knowledge than either individual could manage separately. We can also assume that the convenience of these systems, in contrast to managing knowledge individually, would contribute to further bonding. Transactive memory is negotiated over long periods between each couple in ways that are unique and not interchangeable with others.

The concept of transactive memory has been extended from intimate couples to larger groups (Peltokorpi, 2008). In the context of larger groups, transactive memory contributes to group cognition, or information processing that differs from individual cognition. Transactive memory is critical to understanding the behavior of teams in organizations (Lee, Bachrach, & Lewis, 2014). As in the case of intimate couples, transactive memory contributes to the group's ability to manage more information than any individual could be expected to do in an efficient manner based on the relevant specialties of the individuals making up the group. Transactive memory contributes to the establishment, maintenance, and adaptation of organizational routines, or ways to solve familiar problems (Miller, Choi, & Pentland, 2014).

Whether transactive memory takes place at the couple or the organizational level, it takes time to develop. People beginning a new relationship can expect some miscommunications and misunderstandings (and overdue bills and lost candles) until their transactive memory system begins to take shape. ●

People in close relationships form transactive memories, or a division of labor for remembering certain things. This woman might remember how to do certain home repair tasks, and her partner might remember others. Together, they have access to far more information than either individual could manage separately.

Bellurget Jean Louis/The Image Bank/Getty Images

Summary 9.3 Types of Forgetting

Type of forgetting	Major feature	Assessment
Decay	Reduced ability to retrieve infrequently used material over time	Savings technique
Interference	Competition between newer and older information in the memory system	Comparison of performance in a list-learning task
Motivated forgetting	Failure to retrieve negative information	Comparison of recall for memories associated with positive or negative emotions

Credits: Top Row. ZUMA Press/Alamy. Second Row. © Cengage Learning®. Bottom Row: © pasphotography/Shutterstock.com.

KEY TERMS The Language of Psychological Science

Be sure you can define these terms and use them correctly.

autobiographical memory, p. 331
chunking, p. 323
cue, p. 338
decay, p. 345
declarative memory, p. 328
encoding, p. 318
encoding specificity, p. 338
episodic memory, p. 329
flashbulb memory, p. 341
forgetting, p. 345
information processing, p. 318

interference, p. 346
levels of processing theory, p. 325
long-term memory, p. 325
long-term potentiation (LTP), p. 348
memory, p. 318
mnemonics, p. 353
motivated forgetting, p. 347
nondeclarative memory, p. 328
priming, p. 331
procedural memory, p. 331
reconstruction, p. 339

rehearsal, p. 322
retrieval, p. 319
schema, p. 336
semantic memory, p. 329
sensory memory, p. 320
short-term memory (STM), p. 320
spreading activation model, p. 335
storage, p. 319
working memory, p. 324

10 The Thinking Mind
Thinking, Language, and Intelligence

DAILY LIFE IS FULL OF DECISIONS—SOME BIG AND SOME SMALL. How does the mind reach a decision?

Psychologists have learned a great deal about the processes involved in reaching a decision and have identified many steps we can take to improve our decision making. Zooming in, we can use imaging technologies to observe how the brain reacts to a number of choices. For example, do you really want to see that movie based on its trailer?

Film producers are using brain imaging when editing movie trailers to elicit the reactions they want from an audience (MindSign, 2010). They have only a few seconds to convince the audience to decide to see their film. Assuming that the ability of a film to elicit emotion drives the decision to see it, filmmakers take out the parts of a trailer that produce a neutral emotional response and splice together the most dramatic parts. Is such a practice scientifically valid? It may be useful in some cases. In Chapter 7, we discussed how emotions can range along a continuum. Some emotions are associated with precise physical responses, as in the case of fear, while others are associated with more ambiguous physical responses, as in the case of pride. It is likely that you could develop a movie trailer that would evoke fear in viewers, but eliciting more complex emotions might be more difficult.

Zooming out to the moviegoers' decision to see a movie, what factors, aside from seeing an emotional trailer, might influence their choice? Individual differences very likely play a key role. One person might enjoy horror films, while another does not. Using the social perspective to zoom out still farther, we can see that people often respond to horror films based on their beliefs about the expectations of others. You might think that males are predisposed to like horror films and females to like "chick flicks," but psychology is rarely that simple. Instead, a person's reaction to horror films is strongly determined by social attitudes and beliefs about how same- and opposite-sex peers would respond to the film (Mundorf, Weaver, & Zillmann, 1989).

In this chapter, we will explore how we use the tools of language and intelligence to think, which in turn guides our behavior. Beginning with the parts of the brain that process information, we will zoom out to the individual differences of personality and experience and farther still to the social and larger cultural contexts that shape the way we think.

IS098U3ZE/Image Source Plus/Alamy

◀ Observing brain activity while a person watches a movie is helping filmmakers produce more effective movie trailers.

Argosy Publishing, Inc.

357

TP/Alamy

TP/Alamy

TP/Alamy

David Bro/ZUMA Press/Corbis

The mind uses symbols, or mental representations, to signify information, just as websites have icons that link to and represent some of your favorite social networks, such as Facebook, Twitter, Instagram, and Yelp.

cognition Internal mental processes including information processing, thinking, reasoning, and problem solving.

Learning Objectives

1. Explain the role of mental representations in thinking, and compare and contrast models of concept formation.

2. Summarize the four steps of problem solving, incorporating existing research on how to approach each step successfully, and apply to a problem.

3. Analyze the building blocks and biological correlates of language.

4. Define general intelligence, and evaluate the evidence for multiple intelligence subtypes.

5. Analyze the interactions between nature and nurture in explaining individual differences in intelligence.

What Do We Think About?

The word **cognition**, as in the term *cognitive psychology*, is derived from the Latin *cogito*, which literally means "to think." Thinking allows us to manipulate information internally to construct models of the world, plan our interactions with that world, and regulate ourselves to meet our goals. Given the extent of these concepts, it should come as no surprise that cognitive psychology covers a broad area of topics. In addition to perception, learning, and memory, which we discussed in previous chapters, cognitive psychology addresses questions of thinking, language, and intelligence.

We think about what we know. In the broadest sense of the word, knowledge is the entire body of information acquired through study, investigation, observation, and experience. To manage this large collection of knowledge, the mind often uses symbols, or mental representations, to signify information. Using mental representations is similar to having an icon on your computer desktop that represents Microsoft Word, and a profile photograph on Facebook that represents your best friend.

The most familiar uses of mental representations are found in language, both written and spoken. Depending on the language you choose, you could represent the animal coming toward you on the sidewalk as a *hund* (German), *chien* (French), *gau* (Chinese), *perro* (Spanish), or *dog* (English). Representations can be visual too. For example, imagine that you snap a photo of the dog using your cell phone or you sketch a picture of the dog. Despite the differences in these two visual representations, the dog to which each refers is the same. We can view the representation of the dog (the sound or appearance of the word used, the patterns of light in your photo or drawing) as a vehicle for carrying information about the content of our knowledge of this dog (it seems to be a friendly, young golden retriever).

Our interest in this chapter is in the ability of minds to form mental representations and manipulate them to make sense of the world. What forms can representations take? What are the relationships between the representations and the content they symbolize?

Thought as Images

Temple Grandin, a college professor with autism spectrum disorder, describes her way of thinking as "thinking in pictures" (Grandin, 2010). Albert Einstein is also widely quoted as relying on mental visualization in the early stages of his thinking and only later putting his ideas into words (Einstein, 1945). To what extent do the rest of us share their ability to think in mental images? By *mental image*, we are referring to a representation of any sensory experience that is stored in memory and can be retrieved for use later. For example, you can call up a visual image of your first car, picture the letters of your name, or silently hum the first bars of "Happy Birthday to You" to yourself quite easily.

People appear to treat mental images much like they would a real object (Kosslyn, 1978, 1980, 1994). We can turn visual mental images around in our minds, zoom in or out, and identify their features (see ● Figure 10.1). If you were to think about a map of the United States (assuming you have a good grasp of geography), it would take you longer to mentally count the major cities between Los Angeles and New York than those between Chicago and New York, just as it would if you were looking at a real map.

Children are particularly likely to use visual images in their thinking. In one study, between 2% and 15% of elementary school children experienced long-lasting and detailed visual images of a complex picture they had seen previously for a short interval (Haber & Haber, 1964). The children described the scene using the present tense, suggesting that they were scanning a mental replica. Except for rare cases like Grandin, few adults can do this. It is possible that language becomes an increasingly important way to organize thinking during childhood and might begin to overwrite or interfere with the ability to directly access visual images.

Regardless of the exact form taken by mental representations, our knowledge would be useless unless we imposed some type of organization on all the bits we know. To supply this organization, we extract special, organizing ideas known as **concepts** from the specific instances and occurrences we experience.

Thought as Concepts

Concept formation is not unique to humans. Nonhuman animals as diverse as pigeons and monkeys demonstrate concept formation (Herrnstein, 1979). In one study, pigeons learned to peck at projected images of water with fish to obtain food rewards but to withhold pecking at images of water without fish (Herrnstein & de Villiers, 1980). Subsequently, a new set of slides was presented. The pigeons successfully distinguished between the fish and the nonfish slides, even though they had not seen these particular images during their prior training. The pigeons appeared to have extracted a "fish" concept from their experience. What does it mean to have a "fish" or any other type of concept? How are we (and pigeons) able to construct a new concept?

Because of the memory processes we discussed in Chapter 9, you already "know" what a dog is. If you were asked to feed your neighbor's dog while your neighbor goes on vacation, it is likely that you could locate the correct animal, provide dog food instead of cat food, and

Kevin Mazur/WireImage/Getty Images

Temple Grandin, a college professor with autism spectrum disorder, is shown here with actress Claire Danes, who portrayed her in a 2010 made-for-television movie. Grandin has described her cognitive experience as "thinking in pictures." It is likely that young children depend on a similar approach to thinking, but learning language provides new dimension to our ability to think.

concept An organizing principle derived from experience.

FIGURE 10.1

Forming Mental Maps. A person familiar with New York City could follow a mental route among these buildings, zoom in or out, and identify important features like landmarks and a favorite place to have coffee.

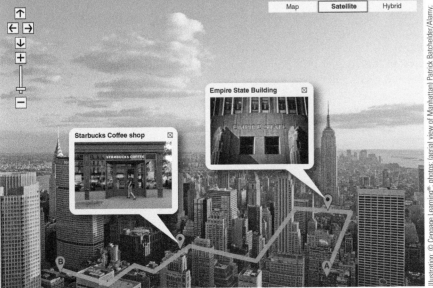

Illustration: © Cengage Learning®, photos: (aerial view of Manhattan) Patrick Batchelder/Alamy, (Empire State Building) Justin Green/Alamy, (Starbucks) Martin Shields/Alamy

Chip East/Reuters/Corbis

London-based artist Stephen Wiltshire, who like Temple Grandin has autism spectrum disorder, has been described as a "human camera." Wiltshire can fly over a major city like New York in a helicopter for about 1 hour and then re-create highly accurate and detailed drawings of the city. His talent is an extreme and unusual form of the use of visual imagery.

Pigeons appear to be able to form concepts, such as "people" and "nonpeople." If their pecking is reinforced with food in the presence of an image containing people but not in the presence of images without people, they will learn to peck only when the people images are present. The experimenters used hundreds of images that showed people but varied in number, distance from the camera, age, ethnicity, and other features, but the pigeons still responded appropriately.

exercise appropriate caution if your neighbor's dog happens to be unfriendly. This activity sounds simple, but what if you found yourself trying to recruit an alien from another planet to help you with your task? What information about dogs would the alien need to know to succeed? Essentially, what you must convey to your alien friend is the concept of "dog" (see Table 10.1).

You might start the discussion with a dictionary definition of *dog*. In the dictionary, however, you find that a dog is "a domesticated carnivorous mammal (*Canis familiaris*) related to the foxes and wolves and raised in a wide variety of breeds." This definition seems rather remote from what we know to be a dog. You don't need to know what dogs eat and who their nearest relatives are to identify one correctly.

Perhaps you could find some common features of dogs that would allow you to distinguish between dogs and nondogs. You could tell your alien friend that dogs are furry animals with four legs that bark and wag their tails. Unfortunately, there is a major logical flaw in this system (Wittgenstein, 1953). No matter how careful your definition, even for the simplest concepts, somebody will be able to think of an exception. Although we can agree that all dogs are animals, this feature alone is insufficient for distinguishing dogs from cats and raccoons. Having fur does not describe Chihuahuas, and basenjis don't bark. A dog that has lost a leg in an accident no longer has four legs. Most dogs we know wag their tails, but there may be an abused dog that keeps its tail perpetually between its legs, as well as dogs that have tails too stubby to wag.

To resolve this dilemma, you can make your definition more flexible. Instead of being rigidly defined by a checklist of features, a concept could describe a group of instances that share overlapping features. This approach is similar to a feature detection model (Smith, Shoben, & Rips, 1974). According to this type of model, people determine the truthfulness of statements like "a canary is a bird" by considering overlapping features (wings, beak, flies, chirps). Using this approach, the alien could compare the features of an animal suspected of being a dog with a checklist of dog features. There are several problems with this approach too. Some categories are quite clear, like triangles, but others do not have precise enough boundaries for the checklist approach to work. People in some cultures would list "taste good" as a feature of dogs, but Americans probably would not. In addition, the feature checklist approach doesn't seem to match personal experience with thinking. When you think about a dog, do you access a mental checklist of dog features?

Science Source

Pigeon in a Skinner box

Top and bottom: Photo courtesy of Will Vaughan

Examples of nonhuman (top) and human (bottom) stimuli for a concept formation experiment.

TABLE 10.1 Approaches to Concept Formation

Approach	Application to dog category	Disadvantages
Dictionary definition	Describe a dog as "a domesticated carnivorous mammal *(Canis familiaris)* related to the foxes and wolves and raised in a wide variety of breeds"	Gives more information than needed to classify a dog correctly
Common features	Describe dogs as furry animals with four legs that bark and wag their tails	Results in too many exceptions (e.g., Chihuahuas are not furry)
Overlapping features	Compare features of a suspected dog with features of the "dog" concept	Lacks precise boundaries for most categories (e.g., "tastes good" might be a category feature for dogs in some cultures but not in others)
Prototype	Average all members of the dog category	Does not provide a good way to think about a category's variability
Exemplar	Use a specific instance of a category a model	Excludes some category members that are too dissimilar to model

© Cengage Learning®

Prototypes and Exemplars An alternate approach to thinking about concepts is to consider some type of "standard" dog, or a **prototype** that represents your entire category (Rosch, 1973, 1983). A prototype results from an averaging of all members of your category, and it may not even resemble a real instance (Posner & Keele, 1970). For example, the prototypical dog has an average size, an average tail, average ears, average coloring, and so on. When thinking about a category, you might also retrieve a specific instance of a concept, or an **exemplar**. This could be the dog you raised during your childhood or a dog featured in your favorite movie.

The processes in which prototypes and exemplars are used are quite similar. Whichever standard you choose, you compare new instances to it to get a sense of "fit." The more similar the new objects are to the standard, the more likely you are to include them in your concept. Both approaches are also able to account for the tendency of people to rate apples as more typical fruits than avocados or robins as more typical birds than penguins (Malt & Smith, 1984). Apples are not only closer to the "average" fruit than avocados are, but they are also more likely to be chosen as an exemplar fruit because of the extensive experience most people have with apples, at least in the United States.

Despite the similarities between the prototype and the exemplar approaches, exemplars have some advantages. Compared to prototypes, exemplars provide a better way of thinking about the variability of a category (Rips & Collins, 1993). Averages, which characterize prototypes, do not provide much information about the range of features that can be found in a category. For example, imagine that you were just introduced to a young man named Christian Cantwell, who tells you that he is an athlete. Judging from Cantwell's imposing physical

prototype A representation of a category formed by averaging all members of the category.
exemplar A specific member of a category used to represent the category.

Although correct, this dictionary definition of a dog might not help you figure out whether an animal standing in front of you is a dog or not.

dog
[dawg, dog]
noun, verb, dogged, dog-ging.

-noun

A domesticated carnivorous mammal *(Canis familiaris)* related to the foxes and wolves and raised in a wide variety of breeds.

Dmitry Kalinovsky/Shutterstock.com

Using common features to identify dogs, such as "has hair" or "has four legs," would exclude these two: a dog with three legs and an American hairless terrier.

appearance (he is 6 feet 5 inches and weighs 300 pounds), he seems more similar to your prototypical NFL football player than what he is—a star track-and-field athlete. In contrast, while your personal exemplar for a track-and-field athlete might be a sprinter or distance runner instead of a shot-putter like Cantwell, the individual instances you know can help you comprehend the variability found within the concept.

Just when you are feeling comfortable about using prototypes and exemplars to solve your alien's dog problem, you run into an additional dilemma. The use of prototypes and exemplars rests on similarity. Similar objects will be included in a concept, and dissimilar objects will be excluded. What if your new friend comes across a lifelike dog robot? In many ways, the robot looks and acts like your prototype and exemplar dogs, yet you know it is not a dog. What if you find an unfortunate dog that has been killed on the highway? It hardly retains much similarity to the prototype and exemplar dogs, yet nobody, except perhaps the alien, would question its identity as a dog. Clearly, you need more than prototypes and exemplars to solve your problem.

Concepts as Theories   It might be useful to view concept formation as a type of theory building. In Chapter 2, we defined theories as "sets of facts and relationships between facts that can be used to explain and predict phenomena." This definition can also apply to a concept. Like theories, concepts can guide our thinking and be continually tested for accuracy against new, incoming information. Also like theories, concepts do not exist in isolation. As we mentioned in Chapter 9, concepts can be viewed as part of a vast, interconnected network of memories.

Thinking about concepts as theories provides insight into the problem of judging category membership, such as deciding whether an avocado is a fruit. Prototypes and exemplars provide a useful starting place for judging category membership. We test our theory that the new item (avocado) fits the category by comparing it to the prototypes (average fruit) and exemplars (apple) of a concept (fruit). We might make the occasional mistake, such as including bats or excluding ostriches in a concept of "bird," but most of the time, we will be successful and fast.

This approach also has the advantage of being consistent with observations of how children acquire new concepts, which we explore in more detail in Chapter 11. A child might start with a prototype or exemplar dog based on the family pet, possibly overapplying the concept to other four-legged animals at the zoo and failing to apply it to dogs of different breeds. With the help of feedback from others ("No, that's a tiger, not a dog" or "Yes, a Chihuahua is a dog"), the concept becomes more refined. Your alien friend is likely to need the same type of feedback from you when attempting to apply the newly learned concept of dog to a variety of animals.

Concepts and Schemas   Our "dog" concept is embedded in a rich, complex set of beliefs and expectations about dogs, animals, nature, and personal experience known as a schema, which we discussed in Chapter 9. This type of schema not only shapes memory storage and retrieval of information relevant to dogs but also allows us to predict new facts about them. If our schema includes "likes to play ball," we know that playing ball with a friend's new dog is likely to be successful.

Under what circumstances do people apply a schema

Apples are more likely than avocados to be a person's exemplar fruit because of the extensive experience we have with apples in the United States.

to new information? Again, comparisons to typical members of a category appear to play a role. People who are told a new fact about a typical instance of a category are more willing to extend the new fact to all members of a category, whereas a new fact about an atypical category member is less likely to be widely applied (Rips, 1975). For example, if you learn about a new fruit disease found in apples (an exemplar fruit for many people), you are more likely to think other fruits are vulnerable than if you learn that the disease targets a less typical member of the fruit category, such as olives or avocados.

Concepts and the Brain Can we find brain activity that correlates with thinking about a particular concept or category of things? In Chapter 9, we described imaging studies that identified different patterns of brain activity when people thought about animals or tools (Martin, Wiggs, Ungerleider, & Haxby, 1996). When asked to name animals, the participants showed activation in the visual cortex, suggesting that they would need to think about what a zebra looks like to name it correctly. Naming tools, in contrast, was accompanied by activation in frontal and parietal lobe areas associated with movement, implying that it is helpful to think about what to do with a screwdriver when attempting to name it correctly.

This specialization in the brain for processing different types of categories is supported by observations of patients with brain damage. A small number of people have been identified who have specific difficulties naming pictures of animals, although they can successfully name other living things (fruits and vegetables) and nonliving things (tools and furniture; Mahon & Caramazza, 2009). Not only do these people have difficulty naming animals, but they also struggle to answer questions about animals, such as "Does a whale have legs?" Similar questions about nonliving things do not cause difficulty.

Although we typically think of amyotrophic lateral sclerosis (ALS, or Lou Gehrig's disease) as a movement disorder, the condition also affects a person's ability to form new concepts. Performance by ALS patients on a concept formation task was correlated with the extent of gray matter loss they had experienced in the left prefrontal and parietal cortices (Libon et al., 2012).

In Chapters 8 and 9, we emphasized the important role played by experience in building up our knowledge. Our discussion so far on concept formation has also stressed experience. However, it appears that this experience interacts with existing structures in the brain that help to organize our incoming information. For example, most patients with specific deficits in processing categories perform differently from control participants in one domain—animals versus nonliving

You might mistakenly put Olympic shot-putter Christian Cantwell in your category of NFL football player because of his appearance, which is closer to the prototypical football player than it is to the prototypical track-and-field athlete. Using exemplars instead of prototypes to guide the use of concepts helps us think about the variability of a category.

Even when a prototype is well understood, like the signs and symptoms of a disease, evidence suggests that exemplars might work better. Physicians diagnosing cancer who had recently seen similar cases (exemplars) made more accurate diagnoses than those who had not (Brooks, 1990; Brooks, Norman, & Allen, 1991).

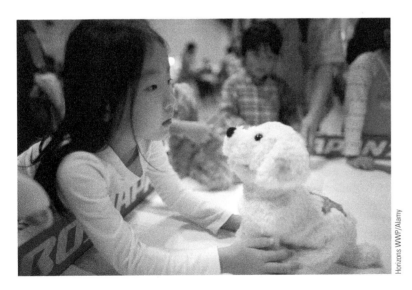

Prototypes and exemplars depend on similarity, which can result in similar items, like this robotic dog, being included in our dog category.

It is unlikely that this toddler has vocabulary words for many of the animals seen for the first time in a zoo. Theories of what kind of animal this is will be shaped with the help of the child's parents.

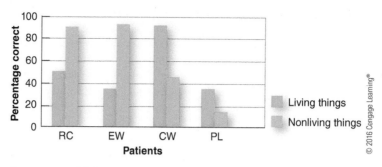

FIGURE 10.2

Some Categories Might Be Hardwired in the Brain. Some individuals with brain damage have difficulty processing certain types of semantic information. The pattern of these deficits varies depending on the location of the damage. For example, patient CW can name living things better than nonliving things, while patient RC names nonliving things better than living things. However, the categories that are affected in this way are relatively few: animals, fruits and vegetables, nonliving things, and members of our own species. This suggests that our brains have been shaped through natural selection to form certain types of categories. *Source:* Adapted from "What Drives the Organization of Object Knowledge in the Brain?" by B. Z. Mahon and A. Caramazza, 2011, *Trends in Cognitive Sciences, 15*(3), pp. 97–103. doi:10.1016/j.tics.2011.01.004.

things (see ● Figure 10.2; Mahon & Caramazza, 2011). This observation might indicate that our brains are predisposed to make this distinction between the two categories. If forming concepts helps to organize appropriate responses, our ancestors' ability to form types of categories quickly might have conferred a significant survival advantage.

How Do We Solve Problems?

One of the primary purposes of thinking is to guide behavior. In particular, thinking helps us deal with the many types of problems we face daily. Whether you are figuring out how to cope with a busy schedule, help a friend who is feeling blue, or complete your calculus homework, a **problem** exists whenever there is a difference between where you are and where you would like to be (Newell & Simon, 1972). For example, when you step on the bathroom scale after days of feasting and indulging around the holidays, the weight shown on the scale might be quite different from the weight you know to be ideal for your health and appearance; you now have a problem. In addition, referring to a situation as a *problem* implies that obstacles exist. Returning to your preholiday weight can be challenging.

Problems can be well defined or ill defined. Well-defined problems have a solution that can be verified as correct or incorrect, like an algebra problem, whereas ill-defined problems have solutions that are evaluated subjectively on the basis of their usefulness (Le, Loll, & Pinkwart, 2013). Our weight-loss problem is well defined, because it is easy to verify whether you lose the newly gained weight or not, but many of the problems we face in everyday life are ill defined. Thinking that you need to improve your appearance would be an example of an ill-defined problem. People might not agree about what makes another person more or less attractive.

Problem solving is defined as the use of information to meet a specific goal (Lovett, 2002). As shown in ● Figure 10.3, problem solving begins with recognizing a problem exists (you now weigh too much) followed by the development and use of strategies that solve it (you go on a diet) and the evaluation of the success of those strategies (you have either lost the holiday weight or not). Ill-defined problems require additional thought about what constitutes an acceptable solution and how the solution should be justified. Reconfiguring an ill-defined problem into a set of well-defined problems can be helpful. If your ill-defined problem is to improve your appearance, you could divide this into well-defined problems like returning to your preholiday weight, eating five servings of fruits and vegetables per day, and running at least 10 miles per week.

problem A situation in which a current state is separated from an ideal state by obstacles.
problem solving The use of information to meet a specific goal.

Effective problem solving puts thinking processes to work in a systematic way. Because good problem-solving skills are so important to psychological well-being, we will examine the process in detail using these four steps (Polya, 1957):

1. Understand the problem.
2. Make a plan.
3. Carry out the plan.
4. Look back.

Given the close relationship between cognitive psychology and computer science, we should not be too surprised to see this problem-solving process as a type of looping computer program. If we reach step 4 and our solution has taken us to where we want to go, we stop. If we reach step 4 and our problem still exists, we return to earlier steps to try another solution or to generate new solutions. This looping of steps, reminiscent of looping statements in computer programs, continues until the problem is resolved, as we might see when we learn by trial and error.

Understand the Problem

Although carefully formulating a problem takes time, this is generally time well spent. All relevant data should be collected, analyzed, and organized. What do we know? What information do we need that is missing? How does all this information fit together?

An important part of this step is to represent or frame the problem in a useful way (Lovett, 2002). What does it mean to represent a problem? Earlier in this chapter, we talked about forming mental representations of experiences that subsequently can be manipulated by the mind. In the case of problem solving, the mental representations we form relate to how we see the problem. For example, you might represent your weight problem as the result of your holiday splurge or as the result of a broken bathroom scale. Your representation of the problem in these two ways clearly leads to separate solutions, and in many cases, your representation will determine how successful you will be at solving the problem.

Psychologists have identified a number of helpful suggestions for making the most useful representations of problems and for avoiding some common mistakes that frequently lead to failure. For example, big, long-term problems are easier to solve if they are approached through components, or intermediate goals. Your primary goal in college is to obtain a degree, but it is useful to consider how you plan to meet intermediate goals such as completing your general education courses, your major courses, and electives.

The representation of a problem can be improved by recognizing personal bias you might have toward particular solutions. In our weight example, your reluctance to cut back on treats might lead you to conclude that the bathroom scale is at fault instead of your behavior. Your amount of self-efficacy, or belief in your abilities to succeed, might also influence the way you conceive a problem (Bandura, 2001). You might believe that your attempts to diet never work, so there is no point in even trying. By recognizing these biases, you can approach your problem with a more open and fair mind.

Another pitfall that interferes with a useful representation of a problem is known as **functional fixedness**, or a person's tendency to think about a concept in its most typical form and no others. For example, in the string problem illustrated in ● Figure 10.4, most people fail to see the potential of the screwdriver as a weight. Instead, they tend to think about the screwdriver in terms of its typical use as a tool to turn screws (Maier, 1931).

Make a Plan

Making a plan to solve your problem requires you to first generate possible solutions and then choose the best one to implement.

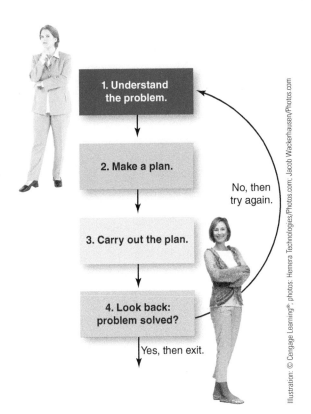

FIGURE 10.3

Problem-Solving Flow Chart.
Effective problem solving can be achieved by following a system proposed by Polya (1957). If you reach step 4 and the problem is solved, you can exit the system. If the problem is not solved, you return to step 1 and try again.

Like ill-defined problems, big complex problems, like world hunger, can be tackled best by breaking the problem into smaller, intermediate problems.

functional fixedness A possible barrier to successful problem solving in which a concept is considered only in its most typical form.

FIGURE 10.4

Functional Fixedness.

Functional fixedness, or our tendency to think about a concept in only one way, can interfere with problem solving. In this classic problem, the person's task is to grab both ropes simultaneously. The only tool available is a screwdriver, which can be tied to one rope and used to make the rope swing within reach. If you only think about the screwdriver one way, as a tool used to turn screws, you cannot solve this problem.

Generating Solutions Generating possible solutions involves some creativity, but most importantly, it requires time. People who spend the most time on a problem typically generate the most diverse solutions. Generating the most solutions raises your chances of finding one that will work.

A number of factors can interfere with finding appropriate solutions. You might be so upset about the numbers on the bathroom scale that you refuse to consider efforts to lose weight. Some people dislike risk so intensely that they fail to consider a full range of alternative solutions. To escape the chaos and ambiguity involved with facing a problem, people can rush to find a solution, overlooking more appropriate courses of action. Judging and discarding solutions too early in the process also leads to failure. Generating impractical solutions requiring resources we don't have is not useful. An expensive stay at a weight reduction spa might work, but it probably doesn't fit a student budget. Understanding that we have these weaknesses in our approach to problem solving should help us avoid them in the future.

Some types of problems lend themselves to precise, step-by-step rules for reaching a particular solution, known as **algorithms**. Algorithms have the advantage of producing an accurate solution reliably. Let's assume you have a three-number combination lock on your bicycle but you have forgotten the combination. You can start with using 001 for the first input, then 002, and so on, until you reach the correct solution for unlocking your bike. Algorithms are efficient when run by a computer, but their cost when used by the human brain can be high. You could be very late to your next class by the time you unlock your bike.

When aggressive children are asked how to solve social problems, such as persuading another child to share a desirable toy, they generate fewer solutions than do more prosocial children. Eventually, most children will generate an aggressive solution (grab the doll and run), but perceiving additional options (trading a piece of candy for the toy or arguing that "sharing is nice") might make it less likely that the prosocial child will use the aggressive solution.

algorithm A precise, step-by-step set of rules that will reliably generate a solution to a problem.

Recipes are examples of algorithms. If you follow the recipe step by step, you should be able to produce the cookies you want every time.

Chocolate chip cookies
Ingredients
1/2 cup unsalted butter
3/4 cup packed dark brown sugar
3/4 cup sugar
2 large eggs
1 teaspoon pure vanilla extract
1 bag semisweet chocolate chips
2 1/4 cups all-purpose flour
3/4 teaspoon baking soda
1 teaspoon fine salt

Because of the time needed to use algorithms, we often substitute rules of thumb, or shortcuts to problem solving, known as **heuristics**. Because heuristics do not go through the exhaustive evaluation of solutions required by algorithms, they are faster. Another advantage of heuristics is that they typically require far less information than algorithms do. However, unlike algorithms, heuristics do not guarantee a solution.

Not only can heuristics fail to find a solution, they can lead us in the wrong direction. Amos Tversky and Daniel Kahneman identified several heuristics that can produce faulty decisions (1973, 1974). The first type, the **availability heuristic**, is used when people predict that events that are easy to think about will be more frequent. For example, dramatic and memorable media reports make people think shark attacks are more common than they are. If we asked which is more common, being killed by a shark or being killed by falling airplane parts, which would you choose (see ● Figure 10.5)? You might be surprised to learn that you have 30 times the risk of being killed by falling airplane parts than by sharks (Plous, 1993). In the aftermath of 9/11, with its vivid media imagery of airplanes crashing, more Americans chose to drive rather than fly. The extra traffic that resulted from fear of flying led to an estimated 9% increase in automobile fatalities, compared to typical rates, in the 3 months following the attacks (University of Michigan Transportation Research Institute, 2004).

As we mentioned earlier in this chapter, people often form prototypes, or average examples, when thinking about a category. These prototypes then represent the category when we are deciding which new examples might also fit the category. Tversky and Kahneman's second type of heuristic, the **representativeness heuristic**, leads people to estimate that stimuli similar to a prototype are more likely to fit the category than are stimuli different from the prototype. To illustrate this heuristic, Tversky and Kahneman asked research participants whether Thomas, who is short, slim, and loves poetry, is more likely to be an Ivy League classics professor or a truck driver. Most people assumed that Thomas would be a classics professor, because his description is closer to that of a prototypical professor than a prototypical truck driver. However, this conclusion is statistically quite unlikely. There are few Ivy League classics professors, and even if most fit Thomas's description, the numbers would still be quite low. In contrast, there are thousands of truck drivers in the United States. Even if a small proportion of them shared Thomas's characteristics, the numbers would be large. Consequently, the odds are that Thomas is a truck driver.

Heuristics are most likely to fail when a correct solution requires a sophisticated understanding of probability (Fenton & Neil, 2012). For example, a classic American television show originating in the 1960s called *Let's Make a Deal* usually ended with a contestant facing three

heuristic A shortcut to problem solving; also known as a rule of thumb.
availability heuristic A rule of thumb in which the frequency of an event's occurrence is predicted by the ease with which the event is brought to mind.
representativeness heuristic A rule of thumb in which stimuli similar to a prototype are believed to be more likely than stimuli that are dissimilar to a prototype.

FIGURE 10.5

The Availability Heuristic. Which is more likely? Being hit by an airplane part or being attacked by a shark? The availability heuristic leads us to believe that events that are easy to think about are more frequent. Because of the frequent media coverage of shark attacks, such as Rodney Fox's close call with a great white in Australia, people think shark attacks are common. You might be surprised to learn that you are 30 times more likely to be killed by falling airplane parts, like this turbine engine that fell from the sky onto a car in Brazil, than by a shark. *Source:* Adapted from *The Psychology of Judgment and Decision Making,* by S. Plous, 1993, New York, NY: McGraw-Hill.

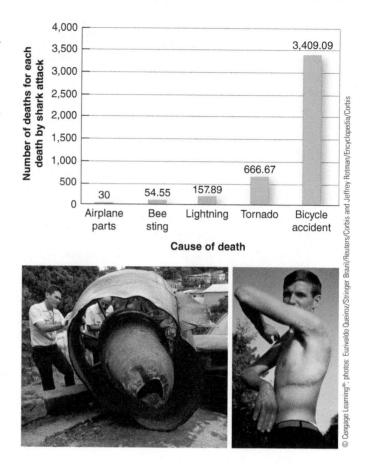

doors ("Behind door number one…") and knowing that a huge prize, like a car, was behind one door and worthless prizes were behind the other two. After the contestant selects a door but before its contents are known, the host reveals that one of the unchosen doors has a worthless prize and asks whether the contestant wishes to switch. Most people erroneously stick with their first door in the mistaken belief that they now have a 50% chance of winning. In fact, their chance of winning with their chosen door remains one third, but they have a two thirds chance of winning if they switch. Here's why. When the contestants first choose, their chance of winning is one third. When the host reveals another door, he has to reveal one of the losing doors no matter what the contestant chose first. If the contestants initially guessed correctly and stay with their original decision, their chance of winning remains one third. However, if the contestants guessed incorrectly when first asked, switching now guarantees a win, making their chance of winning two thirds if they switch. The "trick" here is that all of the options seem equal (there is a one third chance of winning, the host reveals one third of the unknown, and the contestant can switch to the other one third option), yet they are not truly so (Fenton & Neil, 2012).

Although some of these examples make it sound like heuristics lead to bad decisions, it is likely that the ability to use heuristics to make quick, effective, and efficient decisions was a significant adaptive advantage for our ancestors (Haselton et al., 2009). An example of an effective heuristic is the **recognition heuristic** (see ● Figure 10.6), which predicts that people will place a higher value on the more easily recognized alternative (Gigerenzer, 2008). In one study, American college students were asked which of two cities was larger. In making size decisions about German cities, such as Hamburg and Munich, students tended to choose the city they recognized most (Goldstein & Gigerenzer, 2002). They were correct about 73% of the time (Hamburg has about 1.8 million residents compared to Munich's 1.3 million). The recognition heuristic has been shown to beat other, more conventional means of selecting stocks. Companies whose names were recognized by the most people also had stocks that performed better than the overall markets (Reips & Orth, 2006).

recognition heuristic A rule of thumb in which a higher value is placed on the more easily recognized alternative.

affect heuristic A rule of thumb in which we choose between alternatives based on emotional or "gut" reactions to stimuli.

Decide on a Solution Once we have generated a set of solutions, we must decide which one to try first. How is this decision reached?

The **affect heuristic** is particularly relevant to the way people make important choices (Slovic, Finucane, Peters, & MacGregor, 2002). According to this approach, we use our emotional responses to each choice to guide our decisions. Based on our past experience with similar choices, we literally develop a "gut" reaction to our options, pushing us toward alternatives we expect to produce desirable outcomes and away from alternatives we expect to produce undesirable outcomes. Our decision making is also affected by the need to avoid the complex emotion of regret (Connolly & Zeelenberg, 2002). By considering ways to explain and justify the reasons for their decisions in advance, people are able to live more comfortably with the decisions they have made.

An alternate approach to decision making, the utility theory, is also popular in economics. According to this theory, we compute the expected outcomes of our choices and select the best likely one. The expected outcome is computed by multiplying measures of the usefulness of the outcome by its expected probability. For example, to choose an elective course for your next term, you might consider a course that provides positive outcomes, like being interesting and satisfying a graduation requirement. At the same time, you wish to avoid negative outcomes, such as getting a poor grade or spending a lot

The representativeness heuristic makes us believe that stimuli similar to a prototype are more likely than stimuli that are dissimilar. Katrina Hodge, 2009 Miss England, may not fit your prototype of a Lance Corporal and Iraq War veteran. However, there are many more soldiers than beauty queens, so the likelihood that a beautiful woman is a soldier is higher than the likelihood that she is a beauty queen.

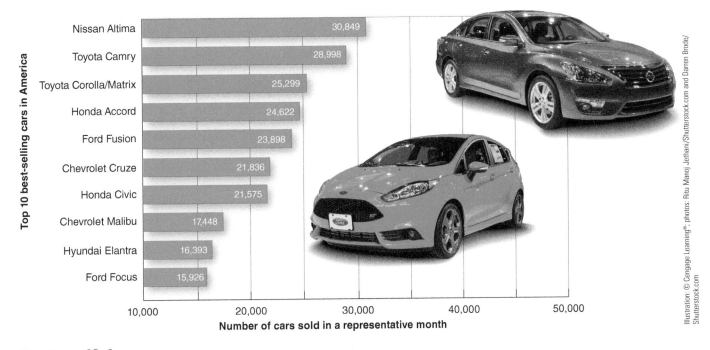

FIGURE 10.6

The Recognition Heuristic. The recognition heuristic predicts that if you think the Nissan Altima (above) looks more familiar than the Ford Focus (below), you will correctly judge the Altima as having better sales in the United States (number 1 seller) than the Focus (number 10 seller).

Even though we might carefully weigh the pros and cons of buying one laptop over another, the affect heuristic suggests that we use our emotional or "gut" responses to make decisions too.

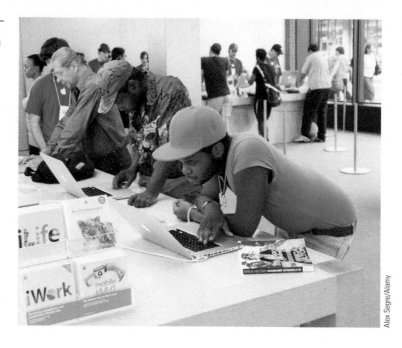

Alex Segre/Alamy

of money on materials. If you weight each outcome according to its probability and add up the results, you will end up with your own mini cost–benefit analysis.

You might find that applying utility theory is a useful exercise when faced with an important decision, like whether to accept a job offer with modest pay in your hometown or one with higher pay in another state. It is clear, however, that we rarely make decisions by solving equations. Even when utility is held constant, people show a preference for one solution or the other based on how the solutions are framed. People rate basketball players who are described as making 75% of their free throws higher than those who are described as missing 25% of the time, even though the math is identical in both cases. Medical treatments that are described as effective 80% of the time are viewed more positively than those that fail 20% of the time.

Tversky and Kahneman (1987) illustrated the importance of framing in decision making using an Asian disease problem. Even though the outcome in both situations is that 400 people will die, 72% of respondents preferred a more secure solution when the problem was framed using the word *saved*. In contrast, when the problem was framed using the word *die*, the secure solution was preferred by only 22% (see ● Figure 10.7). As we mentioned earlier, the way a problem is represented or framed can have a large effect on whether it will be solved. Framing can affect the choice of a solution through its interaction with a person's willingness to select risky solutions. When a problem is framed in terms of losses, as in the *will die* framing of the Asian disease problem, people are more comfortable choosing the risky solution. In contrast, when a problem is framed in terms of gains, as in the *saved* frame of the Asian disease problem, people generally become more cautious. If we have already "saved" 200 people, we don't want to risk saving fewer.

Good decision making is a skill that can be taught (Baron & Brown, 1991), and those who have received formal training in decision making make better real-world choices

FIGURE 10.7

Framing Effects. Amos Tversky and Daniel Kahneman's classic Asian disease problem asks people to choose one of two solutions to the following problem: "If a disease was coming to the U.S., and 600 people were expected to die, what should the president do?" Both solutions resulted in the deaths of the same number of people (400), but one was phrased positively (200 will be saved) and the other was phrased negatively (400 will die). When the question was framed negatively, people were more likely to choose the riskier alternative.

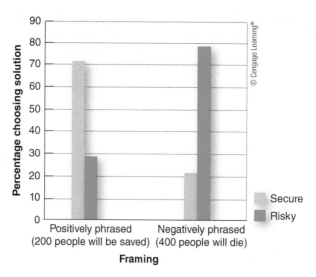

© Cengage Learning®

(Larrick, Nisbett, & Morgan, 1993). Psychologists have identified skills that seem quite powerful in their ability to predict decision-making competence, such as a good understanding of probability (Parker & Fischhoff, 2005). How well do these decision-making skills predict behavior in the real world? When participants' performance on the identified skills was compared with real-life decision making, such as buying new clothes or shoes they never wore, strong correlations were observed between their abilities on the identified skills and the quality of their real-world decision making (Bruine de Bruin, Parker, & Fischhoff, 2007).

Corbis RF/Alamy

Carry Out the Plan

Your belief that you can implement a particular solution will determine whether you decide to pursue that solution or look for another solution. Once you have decided on a solution, it is time to try it out.

At this point, one of the most critical elements in successfully implementing your solution is planning. Solutions that might otherwise succeed can fail when people do not anticipate the time and resources needed for implementation. It is one thing to decide that you need to exercise more to lose your holiday weight, but without further planning, this solution might not work. How much exercise will you need? What activities should you do? When? Where? Is your solution practical? If you are a couch potato, thinking you will implement your exercise solution by training for next month's marathon might not be realistic. If time management is not your strongest skill, you might consider using a Gantt chart, such as the one shown in ● Figure 10.8, to help you set aside the time you need for each part of your solution.

Measures of decision-making skills, such as a person's understanding of probability, are negatively correlated with poor real-world decision making, such as the number of times you buy things you never use.

Look Back

As you implement your solution, you will need to know whether it is bringing you closer to your goal, which usually means that you need some type of measurement of success. In the example of holiday weight gain, the logical way to assess progress is to get back on the scale at regular intervals. At the same time, solutions usually require time to work, and a failure to make immediate progress should not be the basis for discarding a promising solution.

Evaluation is an ongoing process, but it is especially important once a solution has been fully implemented. You might have predicted that 6 months of exercise should return you to your goal weight. At the 6-month point, we return to the original problem. Does it still exist? If not, the problem has been solved, and you can move on to other issues (although keeping up your exercise program is always a good idea). If the problem still exists, you return to the make-a-plan step and try again. Maybe this time you need to combine exercise with counting calories.

People have a reasonably effective commonsense approach to making decisions, but again, careful psychological research can point out where we are vulnerable to poor decision making. If you find yourself unhappy with some outcomes of your previous decisions, following the steps in this section on future occasions might help you find better solutions.

© Cengage Learning®

Week 1 Week 2 Week 3 Week 4 Week 5 Week 6 Week 7

■ Completed
□ Unfinished

FIGURE 10.8

Gantt Charts. Good organization can help you carry out your plan successfully. A Gantt chart is a classic way to break plans into manageable pieces and schedule the time needed for each piece. The chart shows the starting and ending point for each part of the plan.

The Biological Psychology of Decision Making

What processes can we observe in the brain during decision making? As we have seen on previous occasions in this textbook, observing the effects of brain damage on a behavior can illuminate the contributions of particular parts of the brain to that behavior. Damage to the frontal lobes of the brain, as in the case of the unfortunate Phineas Gage described in Chapter 4, reliably produces impulsivity and poor judgment. Patients with this type of damage often begin to gamble obsessively, turn their personal lives upside down, and become unemployable.

 Experiencing Psychology

Are You a Maximizer or a Satisficer?

MANY VARIABLES INFLUENCE an individual's approach to decision making. Classic research suggests that some people are "maximizers," which means that their decision making is aimed at reaching the best outcome. Other people, the "satisficers," are more willing to choose outcomes that are merely acceptable (Simon, 1957). The instrument in Table 10.2 was designed to identify which type of style you use (Schwartz et al., 2002).

Add up all of your answers. Your score can range from a high of 91 to a low of 13. The higher your score, the more likely you are to follow a maximizer strategy. In a sample of nearly 2,000 participants, the average score on this test was 50 (Schwartz

TABLE

10.2 Maximizer/Satisficer Questionnaire

Indicate how much you agree with each of the following by circling the appropriate number:

1. No matter how satisfied I am with my job, it's only right for me to be on the lookout for better opportunities.

1	2	3	4	5	6	7
Completely disagree						Completely agree

2. When I am in the car listening to the radio, I often check other stations to see whether something better is playing, even if I am relatively satisfied with what I'm listening to.

1	2	3	4	5	6	7
Completely disagree						Completely agree

3. When I watch TV, I channel surf, often scanning through the available options even while attempting to watch one program.

1	2	3	4	5	6	7
Completely disagree						Completely agree

4. I treat relationships like clothing: I expect to try a lot on before finding the perfect fit.

1	2	3	4	5	6	7
Completely disagree						Completely agree

5. I often find it difficult to shop for a gift for a friend.

1	2	3	4	5	6	7
Completely disagree						Completely agree

6. Renting videos is difficult. I'm always struggling to pick the best one.

1	2	3	4	5	6	7
Completely disagree						Completely agree

7. When shopping, I have a hard time finding clothing that I love.

1	2	3	4	5	6	7
Completely disagree						Completely agree

Three brain circuits play particularly important roles in decision making (Goschke, 2014). The first circuit assigns value to situations along the lines of pleasure or pain and involves the ventromedial prefrontal cortex, the orbitofrontal cortex, the nucleus accumbens, and the amygdala. The second circuit is an impulse control network that controls unwanted responses and includes the lateral prefrontal cortex and the parietal cortex. The third is an attentional circuit that monitors significant stimuli, and involves the insula, the anterior cingulate cortex, and the amygdala. This circuit also seems to be involved with more complex social decision making, such as deciding whom to trust (Rilling & Sanfey, 2011).

et al., 2002). As we will see in later discussions of personality and happiness, there is no "one size fits all" approach to psychological well-being. We will caution you, however, that people with very high maximizer scores tend to be less happy and more prone to depression (Schwartz et al., 2002).

If your score is very high, we are not suggesting that you lower your standards. However, you might review upcoming decisions with your score in mind to see whether your perfectionist approach is giving you the best overall outcomes. ●

Image Source/Alamy

---

8. I'm a big fan of lists that attempt to rank things (the best movies, the best singers, the best athletes, the best novels, etc.).

1	2	3	4	5	6	7
Completely disagree						Completely agree

9. I find that writing is difficult, even if it's writing a letter to a friend, because it's so hard to word things right. I often do several drafts of even simple things.

1	2	3	4	5	6	7
Completely disagree						Completely agree

10. I never settle for second best.

1	2	3	4	5	6	7
Completely disagree						Completely agree

11. Whenever I'm faced with a choice, I try to imagine what all the other possibilities are, even ones that aren't present at the moment.

1	2	3	4	5	6	7
Completely disagree						Completely agree

12. I often fantasize about living in ways that are quite different from my actual life.

1	2	3	4	5	6	7
Completely disagree						Completely agree

13. No matter what I do, I have the highest standards for myself.

1	2	3	4	5	6	7
Completely disagree						Completely agree

The pleasure and pain circuit, which is impulsive, gradually comes under the control of the impulse control circuit as we mature and are exposed to the social rules of our community (Bechara, 2005). As college students, you are a prime example of this maturity. Spending long hours studying and writing papers produces immediate "pain" but also promises the future pleasure of obtaining an interesting job and making enough money to support yourself and perhaps a family.

Drug addiction provides an interesting example of what happens when these normal decision-making circuits are disrupted. In many ways, drug addicts behave similarly to people who have brain damage in circuits related to decision making. Through their experience with drugs, and possibly because of some biochemical consequences of addictive substances, the impulsive system gains control over the impulse control system. The immediate pleasure promised by the drug experience overwhelms the impact of negative future events such as lost jobs, disrupted family life, and even prison. Addicts begin to experience exaggerated responses to the potential reward of drug cues while becoming less responsive to other types of reward (Bechara, 2005). Hyperactivity in this impulsive reward system seems to progressively weaken impulse control.

As you will see in Chapter 11, the prefrontal cortex is one of the last parts of the brain to mature (development continues into the early 20s), which might account for some of the impulsive, risky decisions made by adolescents (Blakemore & Robbins, 2012). At the same time that their impulse control system is relatively weak, adolescents might be hypersensitive to reward. Developmental changes in brain structure and function also account for the effects of peers on adolescent risk taking. Teens and young adults make about the same number of risky decisions while alone, but teens are more likely than young adults to make risky decisions in the presence of their peers. As shown in ● Figure 10.9, parts of the reward circuit were especially active in adolescents making a risky decision in the presence of peers.

Making simple decisions about what to keep and what to throw away can be difficult for some individuals. Hoarding behavior is correlated with unusually low levels of activity in the anterior cingulate cortex (Saxena et al., 2004).

FIGURE 10.9

Adolescents Make Risky Decisions in the Presence of Peers. (a) The stoplight driving game is a simulation in which participants are told to reach the end of a track as quickly as possible. (b) Adolescents driving alone do not make more risky decisions than young adults or older adults, but they make many more risky decisions in the presence of a peer. (c) The ventral striatum, in orange, is part of the brain's reward pathways. It is also crucial to addiction. (d) This graph shows the amount of change in the ventral striatum for the three age groups in the alone and peer-present conditions.

(a)

(b)

(c)

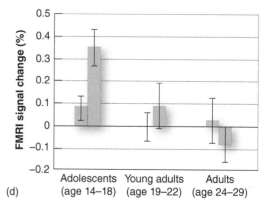

(d)

Summary 10.1 Heuristics

Type of heuristic	Definition	Example
Availability	Events that are easy to think about are more likely.	Despite news and missing child reports that make kidnappings appear to be common, fewer than 100 children per year are abducted by strangers in the United States.
Representativeness	Stimuli that are similar to a prototype are more likely than stimuli that are different from the prototype.	A big, muscular student at Ohio State University is probably a football player (even though fewer than 100 of Ohio State's 60,000-plus students are on the football team).
Recognition	A more recognizable stimulus has a higher value.	Wine labeled as "California wine" is rated higher than the same wine labeled "North Dakota wine."
Affect	We use an emotional response ("gut" feeling) to choose one alternative over another.	Eating dessert instead of staying on your diet is an emotional choice.

Credits: Top Row. Jeffrey Rotman/Encyclopedia/Corbis. Second Row. AP Images/Matt Dunham. Third Row. Ritu Manoj Jethani/Shutterstock.com. Bottom Row: Alex Segre/Alamy.

How Does Language Influence Behavior?

Language has been defined as a system for communicating thoughts and feelings using arbitrary signals, such as voice sounds, gestures, or written symbols. As we discussed previously, language provides us with powerful tools for organizing and manipulating our thinking, problem solving, and decision making. Although thoughts can be represented visually as well as verbally, language extends our thinking abilities to abstract concepts like truth and beauty that would be difficult to visualize. Above all, language connects us with others. Not only can we communicate with people in our immediate vicinity, but language spans time and distance, allowing us to share the thoughts of people living long ago and in distant places. Because of language, the thoughts we record today might reach into the future to influence the thinking of people not yet born.

Language both reflects and shapes thought. Benjamin Lee Whorf's hypothesis of linguistic relativity examines the effect of having a rich vocabulary on a person's ability to think about a topic (Whorf, 1956). According to Whorf, a skier who can name and identify powder, slush, and other variations of snow thinks differently about snow than does a person born and raised in a tropical climate. Whorf's theory predicts that the use of gender-free words such as *server* instead of *waiter* or *waitress* or *flight attendant* instead of *stewardess* would have a real impact

language A system for communicating thoughts and feelings using arbitrary signals.

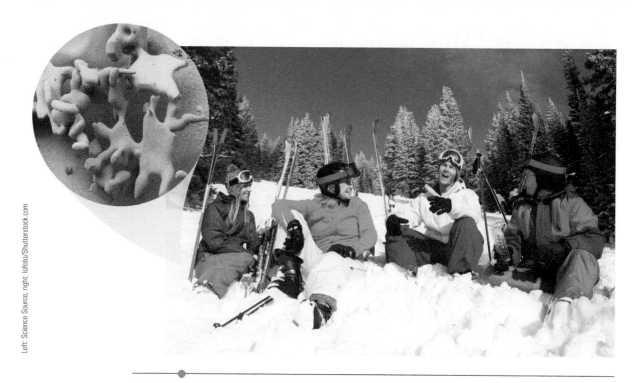

Left: Science Source; right: Iofoto/Shutterstock.com

According to Benjamin Lee Whorf, a skier who knows what *early sintering* means is able to think differently about snow than a person who is unfamiliar with the term. Sintering occurs when snow crystals break down and fuse into larger crystals.

on behavior. Researchers have shown that the use of *he* or *him* as opposed to *she, her,* or *they* in a sentence prompt leads children to produce stories about males (Hyde, 1984).

The Origins of Human Language

To fix the emergence of human languages in time, we can assume that certain complex social behaviors would be difficult to conduct without the ability to speak. Elaborate tool use and cooperation would be easier to accomplish using language. Because our version of the human species, *Homo sapiens,* appeared between 100,000 and 200,000 years ago, most anthropologists are convinced that human language existed at that time, if not earlier. A critical gene mutation in the *FOXP-2* gene occurring around 100,000 years ago possibly marked the start of modern language as we know it (Corballis, 2004). Regardless of timing, the enormous advantages of language to human culture and cooperation would ensure its continuity.

Language is intimately connected to cultural values. For example, the English language contains a large number of words that signify the passage of time. In contrast, the Hopi Native American tribes have only two words relevant to time, loosely translated as "sooner" and "later" (Le Lionnais, 1960). What does this difference tell you about the two cultures?

Much evidence points to Africa as the source of the first human languages. Some anthropologists suggest that it would be difficult for early humans to migrate successfully to other continents without the cooperation provided by language. Taking a different approach, an analysis of more than 500 contemporary languages has demonstrated that the number of speech sounds in a language decreases systematically with the culture's distance from Africa along migration routes (Atkinson, 2011). Many African languages feature more than 100 speech sounds, compared to 45 in English and 13 in Hawaiian (see ● Figure 10.10).

Languages are living entities, under constant pressure to change. A report on endangered languages states that nearly half the world's spoken languages may soon be lost. Following assimilation into larger cultures, speakers might stop using their native languages or fail to transmit them to their children (Malone, 2006). With each language lost goes an opportunity for scientists to understand the unique local knowledge of a culture, along with the historical and cognitive implications of the language.

FIGURE 10.10

Phoneme Diversity Shows the Path of Language. The number of phonemes, or speech sounds, per language decreases with the distance of the culture using the language (indicated by shades of red) along migration routes from the western coast of Africa. Many African languages feature more than 100 speech sounds, compared to 45 in English and 13 in Hawaiian. *Source:* Adapted from "Phonemic Diversity Supports a Serial Founder Effect Model of Language Expansion from Africa," by Q. D. Atkinson, 2011, *Science, 332*(6027), pp. 346–349. © 2011 The American Association for the Advancement of Science

The Basic Building Blocks of Language

Language works like a set of building blocks, beginning with basic speech sounds (phonemes), which are combined into meaningful units (morphemes) and then combined in meaningful strings according to the rules of grammar.

Humans produce more than 500 **phonemes**, or speech sounds, like the *c* in *cat*. The number and types of phonemes are limited only by the physical features of the human vocal apparatus. Not all phonemes appear in all languages. Individual world languages vary from as few as 11 phonemes to more than 140 (Holt, Lotto, & Kluender, 1998). English features about 45 phonemes, which we represent visually using the 26 letters of the alphabet either singly *(s)* or in combination *(sh)*. Most written languages attempt to match visual symbols to phonemes, although many new readers of English struggle with the different pronunciations represented by the same letters, as in the *ough* in *through, rough, trough, slough,* or *thought*.

Phonemes are combined into **morphemes**, which are defined as the smallest components of speech that carry meaning. Most morphemes are words, but word prefixes (as in *pre*school and *sub*urban) and word endings (as in dog*s* and walk*ed*) also qualify as morphemes because they change the meaning of the root word. English contains approximately 100,000 morphemes, which can be used to produce more than a million words. The average high school graduate in the United States knows approximately 80,000 words, but vocabulary continues to increase steadily with years of higher education (Miller & Gildea, 1987).

Morphemes are combined into phrases and sentences according to rules of grammar. For example, different languages have their own rules about the meaningful ordering of nouns and adjectives. In English, you can say "the brown dog" but not "the dog brown," while the reverse is true in Spanish. This type of natural grammar is usually learned early in childhood by interacting with other speakers, in contrast to the formal grammar instruction featured in schools.

Click languages include sounds made by clicking the tongue and might be among the earliest forms of language used by humans.

The Biological Psychology of Language

As we discussed in Chapter 4, language is typically managed by the left hemisphere of the brain. Further insights into the localization of language processing result from investigations of brain damage and efforts to teach language to nonhuman animals.

Lessons From Language Disorders We can learn about the biology of language by surveying problems that arise because of brain damage resulting from head injury or stroke. **Aphasia** is the loss of the ability to speak or understand language. The closely related processes of reading and writing may also be affected by aphasia, but this is not always the case.

phoneme A speech sound.
morpheme The smallest component of speech that carries meaning.
aphasia The loss of the ability to speak or understand language.

HOW DOES LANGUAGE INFLUENCE BEHAVIOR? **377**

Broca's area

Motor control of
mouth and lips

Motor cortex

Primary auditory cortex

Wernicke's area

© Argosy Publishing, Inc.

FIGURE 10.11

**The Major Brain Structures
Participating in Language.**

One of the earliest case studies of aphasia was conducted by Paul Broca in 1861. Broca's subject was a 51-year-old man named Louis Leborgne, who had been institutionalized for more than 20 years (Domanski, 2013). Leborgne came to be called "Tan," because when questioned, "tan" was one of a few syllables he could produce. Leborgne entered the hospital after several months of being unable to speak. He apparently understood much of what was said to him and retained his ability to answer numerical questions by raising an appropriate number of fingers on his left hand (Herrnstein & Boring, 1965). Leborgne died shortly after Broca's examination of him, and Broca performed an autopsy on his patient's brain. Broca found significant damage to the patient's left frontal lobe, possibly because of a Leborgne's long history of epilepsy. The damaged area is now called Broca's area in honor of Broca's discovery (see ● Figure 10.11).

Today, Leborgne would be diagnosed with Broca's aphasia. This condition is characterized by difficulty producing speech. The speech that the patient manages to produce is slow and effortful, but it generally makes sense. In some cases, patients retain the ability to curse, as in one of Broca's other patient's "Sacre nom de Dieu!" ("In the name of God!"), which he uttered in frustration when unable to make himself understood with gestures. A contemporary patient with Broca's aphasia described his condition by saying, "Speech . . . can't say . . . talk, you see" (Gardner, 1976, p. 61).

About 13 years after Broca presented his revolutionary work on Leborgne, Carl Wernicke published his observations on another type of language deficit (Wernicke, 1874). In honor of his contributions, this syndrome is now called Wernicke's aphasia, and the affected area of the brain is known as Wernicke's area. Wernicke's area is located near the primary auditory cortex, located in the temporal lobe.

The symptoms of Wernicke's aphasia could hardly be more different from those of Broca's aphasia. Where Broca's aphasia affects the production of speech, Wernicke's aphasia affects its comprehension. In Broca's aphasia, speech is slow and laborious but generally meaningful. In Wernicke's aphasia, the opposite is true. Speech is rapid and fluent but virtually meaningless. A contemporary patient with Wernicke's aphasia said,

> Oh sure, go ahead, any old think you want. If I could I would. Oh, I'm taking the word the wrong way to say, all of the barbers here whenever they stop you it's going around and around, if you known what I mean, that is typing and tying for repucer, repuceration, well we were trying the best that we could while another time it was with the beds over the same thing. (Gardner, 1976, p. 68)

If you don't pay attention to the meaning, the speech of patients with Wernicke's aphasia sounds rather normal, if slightly fast. Grammar is generally correct. On further examination, we find that meaningfulness is lacking. These patients are locked into a world without social connection, yet they do not seem overly aware of their circumstances or in apparent distress.

It is overly simplistic to assume that the brain has only two main language "centers," Broca's and Wernicke's areas. Instead, contemporary research has identified complex pathways for processing language that connect Broca's and Wernicke's areas to other cortical areas involved in cognition (Dronkers, Pinker, & Damasio, 2000; Friederici, 2011).

Are Nonhuman Animals Capable of Real Language? Later in this chapter, we discuss several approaches to learning language. The evolutionary approach suggests that language results from some innate capacity shaped by natural selection. This view implies that we might be able to find precursors of human language in the behavior of other animals.

Many animals communicate with each other, often in complex ways. All forms of communication, however, do not involve the flexibility and creativity we see in language. We can identify three major patterns of animal communication (Dronkers et al., 2000). Some animals have a fairly inflexible group of calls used for functions such as signaling danger and identifying territories. A second set contains signals that communicate magnitude, as in the case of bee dances that indicate the location of food. Finally, other animals communicate through sequences of behavior, as in the case of birdsong. The extent to which these animal forms of communication may have acted as precursors for human language in an evolutionary sense is speculative at this point.

To search for animal precursors to human language capability, the most logical place to start is with the great apes. Chimpanzees, bonobos, and gorillas have a part of the brain analogous to the human Broca's area. In both humans and apes, this area shows a difference in size between the right and the left hemispheres that might be correlated with language ability (Cantalupo & Hopkins, 2001).

Many researchers have attempted to teach human languages to apes. In one of the earliest experiments in ape language, Winthrop N. Kellogg and his wife "adopted" a baby chimpanzee named Gua in 1931. Gua was raised alongside the Kelloggs' son, Donald. However, because of the limitations of the chimpanzee vocal apparatus, efforts to teach Gua to talk were doomed to failure (Kellogg & Kellogg, 1933). In 1969, Allen and Beatrice Gardner taught sign language to a chimp named Washoe (Gardner & Gardner, 1969). After 4 years of work, Washoe had mastered 132 signs. The Gardners' efforts were followed by Francine Patterson, who trained a gorilla named Koko to use signs (Patterson, 1978). Sue Savage-Rumbaugh and her colleagues have successfully taught a bonobo chimpanzee named Kanzi to associate geometric symbols with words (Savage-Rumbaugh, Shanker, & Taylor, 1998). Even before his training began, Kanzi appeared to have learned 10 symbols simply by observing his mother's training sessions (although his mother never quite mastered the task). Kanzi also seems to be able to understand some human speech. When given 660 verbal requests, such as "Put the collar in the water," Kanzi behaved correctly 72% of the time.

In addition to investigations of language behavior in apes and monkeys, Irene Pepperberg makes a strong case for her African grey parrots (Pepperberg, 2014). While we often use the phrase "to parrot" to indicate mindless mimicry, Pepperberg argues that her parrots demonstrate complex cognitions related to language. Additional debate has also occurred regarding the language abilities of dolphins, whales, dogs, and prairie dogs (Bloom, 2004; Caldwell & Caldwell, 1976; Janik, Sayigh, & Wells, 2006; Lilly, 1967; Slobodchikoff, Perla, & Verdoli, 2009). The ability of animals to demonstrate real language abilities is the subject of ongoing debate. Although children build vocabularies spontaneously, critics point out that ape language must be taught laboriously (Terrace, 1979). Word order does not seem to matter too much to apes, although it has an essential role in human language. Trainers of the apes might be making biased observations. When Washoe signed "waterbird" while observing a swan, the Gardners concluded that she was making a new, creative observation, but Washoe may simply have noticed a "bird" sitting on the "water."

Whether we believe that animals have true language or not, we are left with an enormous respect for both the complexity and the intelligence of animal behavior and the remarkable sophistication of human language.

The soundtracks of horror films, adventure films, dramas, and war films use sound features that characterize animal distress calls to heighten viewer arousal. It is likely that these sounds add to the fear produced by the visual images (Blumstein, Davitian, & Kaye, 2010).

Efforts to teach sign language to chimpanzees have been more successful than efforts to teach them to speak. Here, the human instructor is teaching the chimpanzee to sign "eye."

How Do We Learn Language?

Historically, the topic of language learning has been characterized by the type of splintered, either–or, nature–nurture type of thinking that is rejected by an integrative view of psychology. Several psychological perspectives provide important input into the question of language learning, and no one perspective explains all our observations of the process.

Learning language occurs differently than many types of learning. No specific instruction is needed, as it is for the related skills of reading and writing. A typical child exposed to language will learn language. The type and extent of exposure, however, are important in determining how well an individual child will learn. Social interaction is an essential component of this process, and two-way interaction in the form of conversation produces maximum results. Conversing with children produces greater language competence than simply reading to them (Zimmerman et al., 2009). Even when exposure is one way, such as when a child is listening to a speaker, more language learning occurs when a real person is speaking with the child face to face than when a child is listening to the same speaker on television (Kuhl, 2007; Meltzoff, Kuhl, Movellan, & Sejnowski, 2009). This finding implies that parents using passive television or computer videos to enhance their child's language learning are likely to be disappointed in the outcomes.

Behaviorists, including B. F. Skinner, argued that children learn language through operant conditioning, which we described in Chapter 8 (Skinner, 1970). Using a word correctly is reinforced when it produces a desired outcome. This approach might explain your success in learning key terms for your psychology exams, but there is more to learning language than memorizing vocabulary words and their definitions. The types of mechanisms proposed by the behaviorists simply do not seem to match well with observations of children in the process of learning language. Parents responding to children's sentences are more likely to attend to the meaning of a sentence than to its grammatical structure. When the child says, "We goed to the store today," the parent is likely to respond, "Oh no, that's not right. We went to the store yesterday." The parent is modeling the correct use of the past tense (*went* instead of *goed*) but shows more interest in shaping truthfulness.

Several observations, including the speed and ease with which very young infants can learn complicated language tasks, have led to the assumption by many, including linguists Noam Chomsky (1957) and Steven Pinker (1994), that humans have an inborn capacity for learning language. No human culture on Earth exists without language. Language acquisition follows a common course, regardless of the native language being learned. Whether a child is exposed to English or Cantonese, similar language structures appear around the same point in development. For example, children all over the world go through a stage in which they overapply language rules, as in our previous example of a child saying "goed" instead of "went." Eventually, the child will switch to the correct forms, long before formal instruction. In addition, human brain structure is correlated with language. As we discussed in Chapter 4, most people process language in the left hemisphere of the brain. Damage to these left hemisphere language areas because of stroke or other brain injury produces specific types of language deficits.

It is not necessary to assume, however, that we have a unique "language module" in the brain to account for the development of human language. Many linguists believe that spoken language built on existing structures that allow primates to produce gestures (Corballis, 2009). Simultaneous vocalizations and gestures (pointing and saying "look") could have been followed by a greater reliance on vocalizations, which is the same progression we see in children. Vocalization requires less energy than gesturing, as any sign language interpreter can tell you. It also allows communication to occur at night or when hidden, and it frees the hands for tool use and hand-to-hand combat.

Assuming an inborn capacity for learning language further implies that language has a basis in our genes. Several genetic conditions appear to selectively affect individuals' language learning abilities. For several generations, members of a family known as the KE family have been studied extensively by researchers interested in the genetics of language. Many KE family members have severe difficulties with the production of language accompanied by a mutation in a single gene (Lai, Fisher, Hurst, Vargha-Khadem, & Monaco, 2001). The KE family mutation occurred in the

Irene Pepperberg's African grey parrots have demonstrated sophisticated languagelike behaviors. For example, when shown an object, Alex could correctly state its color, shape, and material. After only six repetitions, he correctly referred to himself as "gray" when asked his color.

Two-way interaction in the form of conversation produces the fastest language learning, reinforcing the social nature of this behavior.

FOXP-2 gene, the same gene suspected of mutating about 100,000 years ago, making human language possible in the first place (see ● Figure 10.12). The *FOXP-2* gene appears to be critical for learning to produce vocalizations (White, 2013).

Another condition affecting language, Williams syndrome, results from a rare genetic mutation and produces a moderate level of intellectual disability. We discuss intellectual disability later in this chapter. In most cases, individuals with intellectual disability experience difficulties with language, but individuals with Williams syndrome are fluent speakers with large vocabularies. Williams syndrome and another genetic disorder, Down syndrome, produce a similar level of intellectual disability, but language use in these two groups is quite different (Bellugi, Wang, & Jernigan, 1994). When asked to name all the animals he knew, a child with Down syndrome replied, "Horsie, dog, ice cream." A child of the same age and with the same IQ score but who has Williams syndrome answered, "Weasel, newt, salamander, ibex, yak."

Although a person's ability to use language is usually consistent with his or her intelligence, we have seen that this is not the case in Williams syndrome. On the other end of the intelligence scale, it is not unusual for a person of normal to high intelligence to have significant difficulties learning language (Tallal, Ross, & Curtiss, 1989). Accomplished people who have been diagnosed with verbal learning disabilities or are suspected of having learning disabilities include such notables as Einstein, Sir Winston Churchill, Leonardo da Vinci, Thomas Edison, and even psychology's own William James.

Variations in Language Processing

Language learning and use can vary widely, and these variations provide us with a richer understanding of how humans can communicate. We examine three variations of particular interest here. Why do some children have such a hard time learning to read? What happens when people learn more than one language? How does American Sign Language (ASL), which uses movement instead of sound, compare with more conventional spoken languages?

Dyslexia Individuals with dyslexia experience difficulties in learning to read despite typical intelligence and exposure to adequate teaching methods (Shaywitz, Morris, & Shaywitz, 2008). The first description of a dyslexic patient, Percy F., was published by W. Pringle Morgan

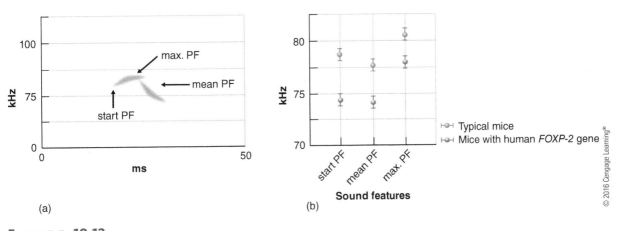

(a)   (b)

FIGURE 10.12

FOXP-2 **and Mice With Lower Voices.** Although it would not be appropriate to call the *FOXP-2* gene "the language gene," evidence suggests that this gene plays an important role in vocalization. When researchers inserted the human version of *FOXP-2* into mice, the mice did not begin speaking of course, but their vocalizations became different from those of typical mice. In (a), an ultrasonic recording of a mouse's squeak shows the starting peak frequency (PF), the maximum PF, and the average or mean PF as a function of time in milliseconds (ms). Ultrasound features frequencies, measured in kilohertz (kHz), that are too high for humans to detect. In (b), you can see that the frequencies emitted by typical mice are higher in all three aspects of vocalization than those emitted by the mice with the human *FOXP-2* gene. *Source:* Adapted from "A Humanized Version of *FOXP-2* Affects Cortico-basal Ganglia Circuits in Mice," by W. Enard, S. Gehre, K. Hammerschmidt, S M. Hölter, T. Blass, M. Somel, et al., 2009, *Cell, 137*(5), pp. 961–971.

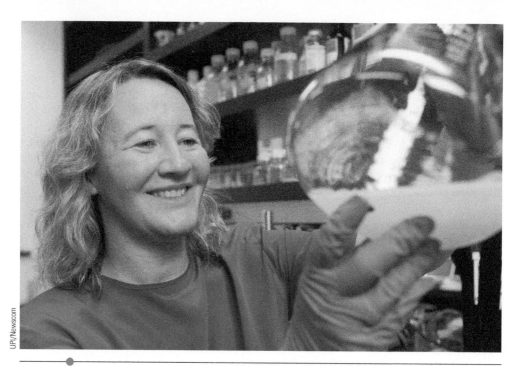

Carol Greider, a Nobel Prize–winning professor of molecular biology and genetics, struggled with dyslexia from elementary school through graduate school. Although the condition was challenging, Greider states, "Perhaps my ability to pull more information out of context and to put together different ideas may have been affected by what I learned to do from dyslexia."

Activity in the right prefrontal cortex during a rhyming task, which requires the ability to discriminate among phonemes, accurately predicted gains in reading skills over the next few years by children with dyslexia. *Source:* From Hoeft et al., "Neural systems predicting long-term outcome in dyslexia," in *Proceedings of the National Academy of Sciences*, January 4, 2011, vol. 108, no. 1, 361-366, Fig. 2.

bilingual Proficient in two languages.

in 1896 (Shaywitz, 1996). Percy F. was described by Morgan as "quick at games, and in no way inferior to others of his age. His great difficulty has been—and is now—his inability to learn to read" (Shaywitz, 1996, p. 98).

Dyslexia is strongly influenced by genetic factors, which in turn result in differences in the symmetry of the cerebral hemispheres (Beaton, 1997; Gilger, Hanebuth, Smith, & Pennington, 1996). People with dyslexia are more likely to be left-handed or ambidextrous than people without dyslexia (Eglinton & Annett, 1994). In addition to these differences in brain structure, people with dyslexia have difficulty distinguishing between similar-sounding phonemes, or basic speech sounds, such as *m* or *n* (Merzenich et al., 1996). Compared to typical readers, their brains show different patterns of activation during rhyming tasks, which are based on the sound of words (Frith & Frith, 1996).

Because reading most languages depends on matching phonemes to the letters that represent them, people with dyslexia show evidence of using a workaround when they read. Brain activity has been recorded while university students with and without dyslexia were reading (Shaywitz et al., 1998). Compared to typical readers, readers with dyslexia showed less activity in a pathway connecting visual cortex in the occipital lobe to Wernicke's area in the temporal lobe. Instead, the readers with dyslexia showed greater activation of Broca's area, which participates in speech production.

Multilingualism More than half the world's population is **bilingual**, or proficient in at least two languages (Chertkow et al., 2010; Kavé, Eyal, Shorek, & Cohen-Mansfield, 2008; see ● Figure 10.13). The 19th-century Italian cardinal Giuseppe Caspar Mezzofanti allegedly spoke 50 languages (Della Rosa et al., 2013). Bilingualism is associated with a number of benefits. Children with several types of bilingualism (Chinese–English, French–English, and Spanish–English) outperformed monolingual English speakers on tests of executive control (Barac & Bialystok, 2012). Older adults who were bilingual seemed to experience a delayed onset of symptoms of Alzheimer's disease compared to monolingual older adults (Bialystok, Craik, & Luk, 2012). Being bilingual possibly contributed to "cognitive reserve," or protection against cognitive decline.

Gauteng
English, Afrikaans,
Zulu, Sepedi

Limpopo
English, Sepedi,
Tsonga, Venda

Mpumalanga
English,
Zulu,
Ndebele,
Swazi

North West
English, Tswana,
Afrikaans

Free State
English, Afrikaans,
Sesotho

KwaZulu-
Natal
English, Zulu

Northern Cape
English, Afrikaans, Tswana

Eastern Cape
English, Xhosa,
Afrikaans

Western Cape
English, Afrikaans,
Xhosa

© Cengage Learning®

FIGURE 10.13

Many People Speak Multiple Languages. Eleven languages are recognized in South Africa, and each province recognizes at least two languages. The most commonly spoken language in homes (23.8%) is Zulu. Many South Africans speak two or more languages.

Are different languages represented in different parts of the brain? Evidence from bilingual people who experience brain damage suggests that the answer to this question is "no." Brain areas involved with multiple languages appear to overlap (Pearce, 2005). The amount of overlap depends on the timing of learning and proficiency in each language. When a person learns two languages early in childhood, the extent of overlap in the brain is greater than when the second language is learned in adulthood (Kim, Relkin, Lee, & Hirsch, 1998). When a person is nearly equally skilled in two languages, more overlap will occur as well (Perani et al., 1998).

Relying on Broca's area while reading, as people with dyslexia do, is like reading out loud to yourself, which slows reading speed. If you have ever read a bedtime story to a child, you are aware of how much slower reading out loud is compared to reading silently.

American Sign Language ASL, used by people with hearing impairments and people who wish to communicate with them, provides further insight into the processing of language. There is no question that ASL constitutes a distinct language, although it uses spatial cues of sight and movement instead of sound (Klima & Bellugi, 1979). ASL provides an interesting contrast between language functions, generally found in the left hemisphere of the brain, and spatial functions, generally managed by the right hemisphere.

Both clinical observation and imaging studies support the notion that the brain manages ASL in the same way it manages other languages, despite its obvious spatial characteristics. Before brain surgery, surgeons first identify which functions are processed by each hemisphere in an individual patient's brain by anesthetizing one hemisphere at a time. When the left hemisphere of an English-speaking patient proficient in ASL was anesthetized, she made errors in both spoken English and ASL signing. Neither anesthetizing the right hemisphere nor performing subsequent surgery on her right hemisphere produced deficits in either language (Damasio, Bellugi, Damasio, Poizner, & Gilder, 1986). Despite the spatial nature of ASL, this case suggests that a language is still a language and the left hemisphere is the likely place for that language to be processed. These clinical observations have been confirmed by imaging studies. The same areas of the brain are activated during language tasks regardless of whether the subject uses spoken English or ASL (Neville et al., 1998).

AP Photo/Tery Gilliam

American Sign Language (ASL) is a distinct language based on sight and movement rather than sound.

Summary 10.2 Aphasia

Type of aphasia	Location of damage	Symptoms
Broca's aphasia Broca's area Broca's aphasia	Broca's area (left frontal lobe in most people)	Slow, effortful speaking combined with good comprehension
Wernicke's aphasia Wernicke's area Wernicke's aphasia	Wernicke's area (left temporal lobe in most people)	Fluent, meaningless speech without comprehension

Credits: Top Row.© Cengage Learning®. Bottom Row: © Cengage Learning®.

Albert Harling/Roger-Viollet/The Image Works

Along with Théodore Simon, Alfred Binet devised a test aimed at identifying schoolchildren with intellectual disability. Binet and Simon's test laid the groundwork for today's intelligence testing.

intelligence The ability to understand complex ideas, adapt effectively to the environment, learn from experience, engage in reasoning, and overcome obstacles.

intelligence quotient (IQ) A measure of individual intelligence relative to a statistically normal curve.

What Is Intelligence?

Intelligence refers to an individual's "ability to understand complex ideas, to adapt effectively to the environment, to learn from experience, to engage in various forms of reasoning, and to overcome obstacles" (Neisser et al., 1996, p. 77).

Assessing Intelligence

The assessment, or testing, of intelligence represents an attempt to assign a number to an individual's abilities, allowing that person to be compared with others.

Formal intelligence testing began in 1904, when Alfred Binet was instructed by the French government to devise an objective means of identifying schoolchildren who needed additional help to succeed. Binet and his colleague, Théodore Simon, assumed that relatively bright children behaved cognitively like older children, while less intelligent children would behave like younger children. They devised items that they believed would indicate children's "mental age" relative to their peers. In this system, children who successfully completed an item at an earlier age than most of their peers would have a higher mental age, while those who were not able to complete an item until they were older would have a lower mental age.

Stanford University professor Lewis Terman adapted Binet's test for use in the United States and named his revised version the Stanford–Binet Intelligence Scales (Terman, 1916). Terman began using the **intelligence quotient (IQ)**, which is computed by dividing children's mental age by their chronological age and, for convenience, multiplying by 100. For example, a bright child with a mental age of 15 and a chronological age of 12 would have an IQ score of 125 ($15/12 = 1.25$; $1.25 \times 100 = 125$).

The most frequently used intelligence tests today include the Stanford–Binet Intelligence Scales and the Wechsler Adult Intelligence Scale (WAIS). These tests no longer use the concept of mental age. Instead, contemporary tests place individual performance on a statistically normal curve, described in Chapter 2. Contemporary tests also incorporate new features designed to more accurately assess people of extremely low or high intellect, the elderly, and individuals with language difficulties.

As we discuss in Chapters 2 and 12, constructing a good test can be difficult. A good test must demonstrate both reliability and validity. In short, the test should provide consistent results that correlate with other measures of the same construct. Although no test is perfect,

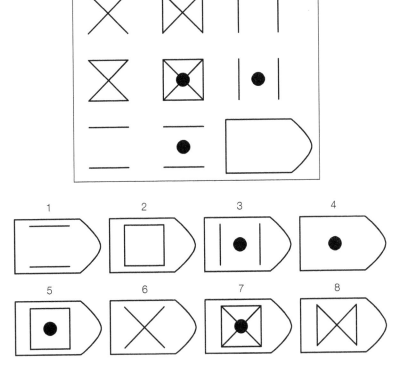

Culture-Free IQ Testing. Matrix reasoning tests are believed to be examples of culture-free and nonverbal intelligence tests. This category of testing is showing the largest increases in performance worldwide, suggesting that our modern experience is making us better at extracting abstract concepts. Which of the items labeled 1 through 8 fits in the lower right corner of the matrix? The correct answer to this item is 4. *Source:* Fox, M. C., & Mitchum, A. L. (2013). A knowledge-based theory of rising scores on "culture free" tests. *Journal of Experimental Psychology: General, 142*(3), 979.

most IQ tests show relatively good reliability and validity (Kaplan & Saccuzzo, 2001). It is important to keep in mind, however, that the intent of IQ tests is to predict school performance as opposed to the complex construct of intelligence described at the beginning of this section. Consequently, it is not surprising to find that correlations between IQ score and performance in mathematics and verbal skills, which are essential for success in contemporary education, are relatively high but correlations between IQ score and performance in art and design are lower (Deary, Strand, Smith, & Fernandes, 2007). Performance on the verbal components of many commonly used IQ tests are influenced by socioeconomic status, which further complicates the interpretations of the scores (Chapman, Fiscella, Duberstein, Kawachi, & Muennig, 2014). Remarkable improvements in scores over the last 60 years on tests that are supposedly culture free suggest that it may be virtually impossible to separate test performance from environmental factors (Fox & Mitchum, 2013; Nisbett et al., 2012; see ● Figure 10.14).

General and Specific Abilities

In discussions of intelligence, some psychologists focus on an individual's overall abilities, while others focus on particular types of abilities.

Using the statistical technique of factor analysis, which he helped develop, Charles Spearman distinguished between a **general intelligence (g)** factor and specific factors that apply to single tasks (Spearman, 1904). For example, Spearman argued that *g* was important for learning Latin but not for distinguishing between two musical tones.

General intelligence can be divided into fluid intelligence and crystallized intelligence (Cattell, 1971). **Fluid intelligence** refers to the ability to think logically without needing previously learned knowledge, like seeing patterns in a visual stimulus, while **crystallized intelligence** requires specific, learned knowledge, like vocabulary or the multiplication tables. A person needs pattern recognition, a type of fluid intelligence, to play chess or Sudoku well, but understanding the rules of the game requires crystallized intelligence. Fluid intelligence peaks in young adulthood and then declines (although it declines slowly in individuals who continue to actively use fluid intelligence), while crystallized intelligence remains more stable through adulthood (see ● Figure 10.15).

general intelligence (*g*) A measure of an individual's overall intelligence as opposed to specific abilities.
fluid intelligence The ability to think logically without the need to use learned knowledge.
crystallized intelligence The ability to think logically using specific learned knowledge.

General intelligence theories do not provide us a way to explain splinter skills, or islands of ability that occur against an overall background of lower functioning. Gloria Lenhoff, who has Williams syndrome and an IQ score of about 55, cannot make change for a dollar or subtract 3 from 5, but she has performed as a lyric soprano with the San Diego Master Chorale and as an accordionist with Aerosmith (Maher, 2001). Leslie Lemke, who is both intellectually disabled and blind, listened one time to Pyotr Ilich Tchaikovsky's Piano Concerto no. 1. Hours later, Lemke sat down at the piano, which he had never studied, and played the entire composition without error (Treffert & Wallace, 2004). Professional musicians are unlikely to be able to duplicate this feat.

The separability of "intelligences" in these exceptional cases suggests that intelligence is a combination of factors rather than a single thing, like the processing speed of your computer. Howard Gardner interprets these and similar findings to mean that we have multiple, independent types of intelligence (Gardner, 1983, 1999). Gardner proposed no less than eight types of intelligence. Robert Sternberg proposed a triarchic theory of intelligence, in which a combination of analytical, creative, and practical abilities allows people to achieve success (Sternberg, 1985; Sternberg & Salter, 1982). He argues that it is possible to be gifted in one aspect without being gifted in others.

Both general and specific approaches to intelligence can be useful. We can assume that people have separate strengths and abilities, like those outlined by Gardner and Sternberg. Among these diverse abilities, purely cognitive abilities, such as verbal, mathematical, spatial, and logical skills, show strong positive correlations with one another, supporting an

FIGURE 10.15

Fluid and Crystallized Intelligence Across the Life Span. Fluid intelligence, like a reaction time measured with a stopwatch, includes abilities that do not require acquired knowledge. Fluid intelligence peaks in young adulthood and then gradually declines over the remaining life span. In contrast, crystallized intelligence, which does require acquired knowledge, remains fairly stable throughout adulthood. Composer John Williams has used his crystallized intelligence of music theory to contribute memorable soundtracks (for films including *Jaws*, *Star Wars*, and the Harry Potter series) in a career spanning more than six decades. *Source:* Adapted from "Transformations in the Couplings Among Intellectual Abilities and Constituent Cognitive Processes Across the Lifespan," by S.-C. Li, U. Lindenberger, B. Hommel, G. Aschersleben, W. Prinz, and P. B. Baltes, 2004, *Psychological Science, 15*(3), 155–163.

Individuals with Williams syndrome provide examples of how general intellect can diverge from other abilities and talents. Gloria Lenhoff (right), has a tested IQ score of 55 but has performed as a lyric soprano and has played her accordion with Aerosmith.

argument for general intelligence, or *g*. At the same time, abilities involving sensory, motor, and personality factors are less likely to show strong correlations, supporting an argument for multiple intelligences in these domains (Visser, Ashton, & Vernon, 2006).

Emotional and Social Intelligence

Traditional views of intelligence focused on education-related skills, but emotional and social skills are important to successful adaptation too. Building on arguments in favor of multiple intelligences, and in recognition that previous work on intelligence seemed to neglect social skills, models of emotional and social intelligence were proposed (Goleman, 2006; Mayer & Salovey, 1993). Social and emotional intelligence allow people to manage emotions and reason about the mental states of others.

Clinical cases involving individuals with brain damage, psychological disorders, and intellectual disability provide evidence for social and emotional abilities that are separate from cognitive abilities. In Chapter 7, we discussed roles for the prefrontal cortex, amygdala, and insula in emotion. Patients with damage to connections between these structures performed very poorly on a standard measure of emotional and social intelligence, even though they have a normal IQ score and show no evidence of other psychological disorders (Bar-On, Tranel, Denburg, & Bechara, 2003). Individuals with autism spectrum disorder often display cognitive abilities that are superior to their social abilities. Individuals with Down syndrome, which produces moderate intellectual disability, display relatively strong social skills (Fidler, Most, Booth-LaForce, & Kelly, 2008).

Even if emotional and social intelligence can be separated from traditional measures of intelligence, these factors can still exert a strong influence on a person's academic and professional outcomes. In comparisons of math and science proficiency in high school seniors in 41 nations, students in the United States came in last (Boe, May, & Boruch, 2002). Motivation for succeeding on these math and science tests accounted for most of the variance among nations. Self-regulation behaviors, such as the ability to delay gratification and persist in solving difficult and possibly boring problems, are emotional skills that clearly predict academic achievement (Nisbett et al., 2012).

Some psychologists view social and emotional intelligence as different from "school-based" intelligence and equally if not more important for success. In a classic study, children were given a single marshmallow with instructions to not eat it when an experimenter left the room. They were told that if they did not eat it, they would receive two marshmallows when the experimenter returned. When the children were tracked down 12 years later, the two thirds who had been able to delay gratification (they didn't eat the marshmallow) were less stressed and more confident than the one third who had not been able to delay gratification (Mischel, Ebbesen, & Raskoff Zeiss, 1972).

Psychology as a Hub Science
How Beliefs About Intelligence Impact Education

According to Carol Dweck (2000), people usually believe one of two theories about their own intelligence. Some people believe in an entity theory that states that people have a certain fixed, unmodifiable amount of intelligence. Others believe in an incremental theory that states that intelligence is something you can improve through learning. This second approach does not deny that learning is easier for some people than for others but simply suggests that everyone can improve through effort.

What are the implications of these theories of intelligence for educators? Students who hold to the fixed, entity theory feel best when they complete easy, low-effort tasks and outperform other students. Challenges in the form of difficult tasks or higher performing peers threaten the self-esteem of the entity theory student. Dweck voices concerns about the lavish praise heaped on today's students, which she believes promotes belief in the entity theory. The result for students is anxiety about looking smart, avoidance of challenges, and an inability to cope with the inevitable educational setbacks.

In contrast to the entity theorists, the incremental theorists like to stretch their skills and put their knowledge to use. They view easy tasks as a waste of time. These students are not as affected by setbacks and worries about looking smart as their entity theorist peers.

Dweck's two types of theories about intelligence parallel cultural differences regarding proficiency in math. In the United States, we tend to hold an entity theory of math ability—you have it or you don't. People feel comfortable admitting that they are "bad at math" and view this as a good reason to stop taking math courses or working to improve. In China, the incremental theory is dominant. Math is simply viewed as a difficult subject for most people that you have to work to master. It probably would not come as a surprise to Dweck that math proficiency is much higher in China than in the West. The children of very poor parents in Shanghai outperformed the children of wealthy British professionals in math (OECD, 2013).

According to Dweck's view, educators who view self-esteem (see Chapter 12) as something you "give" to a student through the application of easy tasks, lavish praise, and avoidance of failure are making a big mistake. Instead, self-esteem could be viewed as something students give themselves. Educators can better promote student self-esteem by teaching students to value learning over the appearance of being smart, promoting the love of challenge and effort, and helping students view mistakes as stepping stones to mastery. ●

In response to research showing that students from the poorest schools in Shanghai outscored the children of doctors and lawyers in the United Kingdom on math tests, the British government flew 60 English-speaking Chinese teachers to London to provide advice about how to improve British math achievement. Chinese teachers recommended teaching to the brightest students in the class, while also ensuring the children with moderate or lower abilities were also served. Chinese teachers and students commonly express a belief that hard work is more important than natural ability in math achievement. Source: http://www.dailymail.co.uk/news/article-2578693/Chinese-teachers-improve-pupils-maths-Sixty-fly-Shanghai-promote-methods-bid-halt-slide-standards.html

Biological Influences on Intelligence

Because the mind is the outcome of the brain, investigations of the brain have been undertaken in search of associations between its structure and activity and an individual's intelligence. For the purposes of this type of research, standardized tests are used as the measure of intelligence.

Brain Structure, Brain Activity, and Intelligence Brain imaging studies demonstrate that standard measures of intelligence positively correlate with overall brain volume (Deary, Penke, & Johnson, 2010; McDaniel, 2000; Pol et al., 2006). More precisely, intelligence measures are positively correlated with the thickness of the cerebral cortex, particularly in the prefrontal cortex and temporal lobes (Deary et al., 2010).

Because intelligence is such a broad concept, it is unlikely that we have "intelligence centers" in the brain. Instead, scientists have suggested that intelligent brains enjoy quick, efficient communication of information from one area to another along axon pathways. This possibility has led to studies investigating white matter health, which also shows positive correlations with measures of intelligence (Achard, Salvador, Whitcher, Suckling, & Bullmore, 2006). Studies of people with brain damage indicate that fluid intelligence, but not crystallized intelligence, is negatively affected by damage to the frontal lobes. These observations are complemented by studies showing high levels of frontal lobe activity during diverse tests believed to demonstrate fluid intelligence (Gray & Thompson, 2004).

Different brain architectures may underlie intelligence in men and women (Haier, Jung, Yeo, Head, & Alkire, 2005). In men, IQ scores were most strongly correlated with the amount of gray matter located in both frontal lobes and the left parietal lobe. In women, IQ scores were highly correlated with the volume of gray matter in the right frontal lobe and Broca's area and with the volume of white matter throughout the brain. According to these researchers, general intelligence was more likely linked to gray matter in men but to white matter in women. These structural differences help to explain why males and females differ in brain size and structure but do not differ significantly in measures of general intelligence (Deary et al., 2010). Apparently, males and females follow different paths to intelligent behavior, which reinforces the complexity of this topic.

Measures of brain activity during tasks requiring intelligence have also demonstrated individual differences. On problems of simple to moderate difficulty, the brains of people with high scores on standard intelligence measures do not have to work as hard as the brains of people with lower scores to solve the same problem (Haier et al., 1992). This research supports the view of intelligence as processing information quickly and efficiently (see ● Figure 10.16). For very difficult problems, however, people with higher intelligence scores increase activity in the prefrontal lobes while people with lower scores show decreased activity in this area (Rypma & Prabhakaran, 2009; Rypma et al., 2006).

Intelligence also seems to be related to the timing of brain development. As children approach puberty, the gray matter of the brain experiences a period of growth that slows down again later in adolescence. Children with average IQ scores showed a peak thickening of cortical gray matter around the age of 8, but children with superior IQ scores experienced a later peak, thickening around age 13 (Shaw et al., 2006).

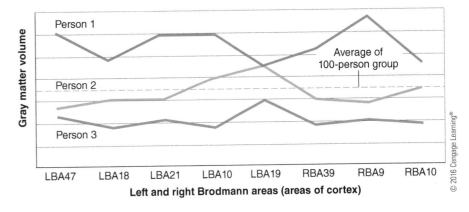

FIGURE 10.16

Correlations Between Brain Structure and IQ Scores Show Multiple Patterns. The relationships between brain structure and IQ scores are complex. The individual depicted with the blue line had the highest IQ score out of 100 participants, and in each area of the brain believed to correlate with IQ results, he showed much higher than average gray matter volume. Person 2 and Person 3 had identical scores on an IQ test, but their patterns of gray matter volume were quite different from each other. Further research might help psychologists better understand the relationships between observed differences in brain structure and intelligence. *Source:* Adapted from "What Does a Smart Brain Look Like?" by R. J. Haier, November/December 2009, *Scientific American Mind*, pp. 26–33.

How Different Are Twins' Brains?

Fraternal Twins (DZ) — Share half their genes

Identical Twins (MZ) — Share all their genes

F — W

A comparison of the amount of gray matter in the brains of identical and fraternal twins showed that the identical twins were more similar to each other than were fraternal twins, as indicated by red and yellow coloring, especially in areas where gray matter volume is correlated with IQ test results. ("F" is for frontal lobe and "W" indicates Wernicke's area.) *Source:* Thompson, P. M., Cannon, T. D., Narr, K. L., van Erp, T., Poutanen, V.-P., Huttunen, M., et al. (2001). Genetic influences on brain structure. *Nature Neuroscience*, 4(12), 1253-1258. doi: 10.1038/nn758

Genetics and Intelligence As we observed in Chapter 3, simple either–or thinking about nature and nurture is rarely correct when considering human behavior, including intelligence. The influences of heredity (nature) interact intimately with experience and other environmental factors (nurture) to produce a result. For example, infants who are breastfed have higher IQ scores than those who are not. However, the experience of being breastfed increases IQ results only in children with one variation of a gene; it has no effect on IQ results in children with another variation of the same gene (Caspi et al., 2007).

To recap the discussion in Chapter 3, heritability estimates how much of the variability in a characteristic observed in a population, such as variations in adult height, is because of genes. If genes play no role in this variation, such as the likelihood that people have tattoos, heritability is 0. When a condition is completely genetic, like Huntington's disease, heritability is 1.0. The heritability of adult intelligence as measured by IQ tests is usually reported to be about .75 (Neisser et al., 1996).When we say that the heritability of intelligence is .75, we are saying that 75% of the variance in intelligence observed in the population can be attributed to genetics, not that 75% of an individual's intelligence is because of that person's genes.

As we observed in an earlier section, both overall brain size and proportion of gray matter are correlated with intelligence, and both are approximately 85% heritable, based on comparisons of identical and fraternal twins (Gray & Thompson, 2004). Although many genes are known to influence brain development, none have been conclusively linked to high IQ test performance. It is likely that a very large number of genes, each having a small impact and interacting with the individual's environment, contribute to the development of the brain.

The fact that a trait demonstrates high heritability does not imply that change or improvement is impossible. A case in point is the highly heritable condition of phenylketonuria (PKU), in which a person cannot properly metabolize a particular amino acid found in many foods. Left unchecked, the condition leads to intellectual disability, discussed in a later sec-

 Connecting to **Research**

What Is Collective Intelligence?

WE HAVE BEEN DISCUSSING the concept of a general intelligence that characterizes an individual, but is it possible for the same sort of measure to describe the abilities of groups of people? Such a measure might be quite useful to organizations using teams.

The Question: Do groups of people have a "collective intelligence" that predicts their performance, and if so, what factors contribute to a group's collective intelligence?

METHODS

Nearly 700 people completed individual intelligence tests and then were randomly assigned to work groups of two to five individuals (Woolley, Chabris, Pentland, Hashmi, & Malone, 2010). Each group was assigned several tasks to complete that varied in the amount of coordinated activity required for success, including solving visual puzzles, brainstorming, making collective moral judgments, and negotiating the allocation of limited resources. Some groups finished their session by playing checkers against a computerized opponent, while others completed an architectural design task. Additional measures were taken of factors believed to be related to group performance, including motivation, satisfaction, group cohesion, social sensitivity, and distribution of speaking turns.

RESULTS

Evidence suggested that a group or collective intelligence did emerge. For each group, performance across the different tasks was highly and positively correlated. Further statistical analyses ruled out the average individual intelligence of the group or the maximum individual intelligence of individuals in the group as significant predictors of group performance, leaving collective intelligence as a single, strong predictor of group performance (see ● Figure 10.17).

What was the basis of this collective intelligence? Surprisingly, typical group features such as motivation, satisfaction, or group cohesion failed to predict group performance. Individual features, such as the individual intelligence of the members, also failed to predict group performance. Instead, the members' scores on the social sensitivity instrument, called the Reading the Mind in the Eyes test, and how evenly tion of this chapter. However, if a person with PKU is given an appropriate diet in which problem foods are avoided, intellectual development proceeds normally. The presence of data showing that IQ results are heritable does not mean we "give up" on anybody's intellectual development.

Worldwide increases in IQ scores of about 3 points per decade over the last 100 years illustrate the potential for change (Dickens & Flynn, 2006, 2001). This increase in IQ scores, known as the Flynn effect, has occurred far too quickly to represent genetic changes. Improvements in nutrition and other health factors probably account for some of the change. Using information from the World Health Organization, researchers have identified strong correlations between a nation's freedom from serious infectious diseases and its citizens' average IQ scores (Eppig, Fincher, & Thornhill, 2010). As nations become wealthier and more capable of battling disease, their citizens' IQ scores increase (see ● Figure 10.18). Surprisingly, the test score gains are most pronounced in supposed culture-free tests like the Raven's Progressive Matrices (Fox & Mitchum, 2013). Participants born after 1990 scored far better on these tests than did participants born in 1940. This change might reflect an improvement in the ability to manage dissimilar items that accompanies living in a modern society.

Psychologists have produced long lists of environmental factors that influence intellectual development, including nutrition and exposure to mentally stimulating activities. Most of these environmental advantages are not cheap. Consequently, it is not surprising to find that socioeconomic status, a measure of family income, education, and other class factors, is positively correlated with IQ score (Turkheimer, Haley, Waldron, D'Onofrio, & Gottesman, 2003). This correlation does not tell us whether more intelligent people enjoy higher socioeconomic status, whether higher socioeconomic status provides means to optimize intelligence, whether some unknown third factor produces both high intelligence and high socioeconomic status, or whether some combination of these factors occurs. Nonetheless, poverty continues to be a significant risk for a low IQ score.

speaking turns were distributed had a large impact on the group's collective intelligence.

CONCLUSIONS

Most students have had significant experience with group projects, and you might have had an opportunity to observe the collective intelligence of your groups. This research shows that bringing together the most intelligent people might not guarantee the best results. Instead, members who are more empathic and do not dominate the conversation might have the greatest success in completing the group work. ●

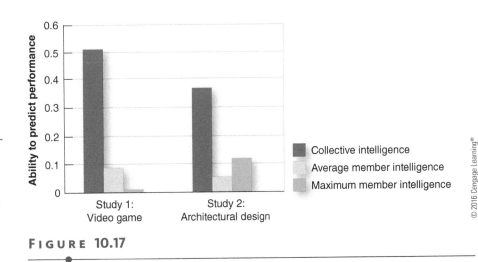

FIGURE 10.17

Collective Intelligence. A group's performance on a variety of tasks, from playing video games to constructing a complex architectural design, was predicted better by the group's collective intelligence than by the average intelligence of the group's members or by the highest IQ score among the group's members. *Source:* Adapted from "Evidence for a Collective Intelligence Factor in the Performance of Human Groups," by A. W. Woolley, C. F. Chabris, A. Pentland, N. Hashmi, and T. W. Malone, 2010, *Science, 330*, pp. 686–688.

FIGURE 10.18

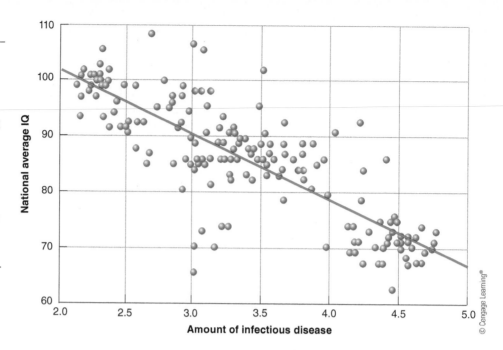

Worldwide, a nation's overall average IQ results have a negative correlation with its rate of infectious disease. This finding raises the possibility that as we improve health, we will also improve IQ scores. *Source:* Adapted from "Parasite Prevalence and the Worldwide Distribution of Cognitive Ability," by C. Eppig, C. L. Fincher, and R. Thornhill, 2010, *Proceedings of the Royal Society of London, Series B: Biological Sciences,* 277(1701), pp. 3801–3808. doi:10.1098/rspb.2010.0973.

FIGURE 10.19

IQ Distribution. IQ test results form an approximately normal distribution, which means that about 68% of the population falls between IQ scores of 85 and 115. Ninety-five percent of the population falls between IQ scores of 70 and 130, with the remaining 5% divided between the two tails.

intellectual disability A condition diagnosed in individuals with IQ scores below 70 and poor adaptive behaviors; also known as mental retardation.

Extremes of Intelligence

Assuming that IQ scores are normally distributed, with an average of 100 and a standard deviation of 15, about 68% of the population should fall within one standard deviation (85–115), and 95% of the population should fall within two standard deviations (70–130). The remaining 5% is divided between the two tails of the distribution, either above 130 or below 70 (see ● Figure 10.19).

Intellectual Disability According to the *Diagnostic and Statistical Manual of Mental Disorders* (*DSM-5*; American Psychiatric Association [APA], 2013; see Chapter 14), **intellectual disability** or intellectual developmental disorder is diagnosed in individuals who show deficits in intellectual functioning beginning early in childhood, accompanied by deficits in independent living skills. Although individually administered standardized IQ tests are often used as a starting point when evaluating an individual who might have an intellectual disability, the clinician's impressions can be used to make the decision too.

Approximately 1% to 3% of the population will score 70 ± 5 or below on a standardized IQ test (Szymanski & King, 1999). In addition to an IQ score between 65 and 75 (APA, 2013), individuals with intellectual disability demonstrate problems with adaptive behaviors, or life skills. These behaviors might include the ability to balance a checkbook, receive correct change from a cashier, read a bus schedule, buy groceries, maintain personal hygiene, and other skills required for independent living.

Intellectual disability is divided into categories of mild, moderate, severe, and profound based on IQ scores and level of adaptive functioning (APA, 2013). Mild intellectual disability is typically accompanied by IQ scores of 55 to 70, or between two and three standard deviations from the mean of 100. With proper intervention, individuals in this group are able to master a sixth-grade curriculum, although it will typically take them until age 18 to do so. Most individuals in this group can live independently, and many work, marry, and have families.

The causal factors for mild intellectual disability provide both good news and bad news. The good news is that mild intellectual disability is typically not the result of genetic or medical problems (Zigler, 1967; Zigler & Hodapp, 1986). As a result, mild intellectual disability is frequently called familial retardation, recognizing that it usually results from preventable, environmental causes. Poverty is an obvious risk factor for this condition, because poor par-

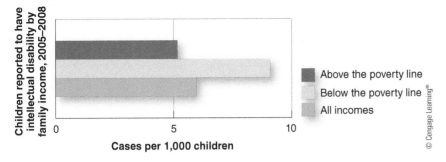

FIGURE 10.20

Poverty Is a Risk Factor for Intellectual Disability. Mild forms of intellectual disability, leading to IQ scores between 55 and 70, are also known as familial retardation because these cases are not due to medical or genetic problems. Poverty is a large risk factor for this level of intellectual disability. A little more than 5 in 1,000 children living above the poverty line have intellectual disability, but this number jumps to 9 in 1,000 among children living below the poverty line.

ents may be unable to obtain the health care, diet, and other environmental benefits needed to produce healthy children (see ● Figure 10.20).

IQ scores between 40 and 55, or between three and four standard deviations from the mean, indicate moderate intellectual disability. Unlike mild cases, moderate intellectual disability typically results from genetic or medical conditions rather than familial factors. Genetic conditions such as Down syndrome are likely to produce disability in this range. The academic attainment of most individuals in this category is limited to the second-grade curriculum, and again, most do not achieve this level until about the age of 18 years. Most of these individuals need some type of assisted living, although the type and extent of needed services vary widely among affected individuals.

Severe intellectual disability is diagnosed in individuals with IQ scores between 25 and 40, or four to five standard deviations below the mean, while profound intellectual disability is diagnosed in individuals with IQ scores below 25. Both severe and profound intellectual disabilities generally result from serious medical conditions and are identified at birth or early in infancy. Individuals with severe intellectual disability can learn a few high-priority words, such as "stop" or "hot." Individuals with profound intellectual disability can learn some basic self-care skills, such as feeding themselves or washing their hands. Depending on the nature of the medical problems, these individuals can require significant assistance and supervision.

Individuals with intellectual disability face a number of common problems. Many children with intellectual disability form insecure attachments with their caregivers, described in detail in Chapter 11 (Clegg & Sheard, 2002). Ideally, children form a secure attachment, characterized by demonstrating a clear preference for a caregiver over strangers, protesting when the caregiver leaves, and indicating a willingness to explore their environment (Ainsworth & Bowlby, 1965).

Depending on the severity of the intellectual disability, language skills are typically affected (Chapman, 1995). Children with intellectual disability have problems expressing themselves clearly, although they may understand a great deal that is said to them. In conjunction with typically poor social skills, these language deficits may result in peer rejection. Consequently, successful intervention programs address language and social skills, in addition to academic and life skill work.

Between 10% and 40% of individuals with intellectual disability experience some type of emotional or behavioral disorder (McGaw, Shaw, & Beckley, 2007). Anxiety, impulsiveness, and mood disorders are the most common disorders seen in this population. When intellectual

Actor Chris Burke, shown here with "Life Goes On" co-star Patti LuPone, has Down syndrome.

These teens, standing with former astronaut and NASA administrator Charles Bolden, are not satisfied by finding the "right answer" to teachers' questions. Instead, they tackled tough problems to compete in the White House Science Fair.

NG Images/Alamy

disability is more severe, individuals may engage in pica, or the eating of nonedibles, or self-injurious behaviors, such as banging the head against the floor or wall.

giftedness An extreme of intelligence defined as having an IQ score of 130 or above.

Giftedness and Genius Just as variations occur on the low side of the IQ distribution, so they do appear on the upper tail. Individuals with intellectual **giftedness**, who make up approximately 1% to 3% of the population, score two or more standard deviations above the

Thinking Scientifically

Can Children's IQ Scores Be Increased With Special Baby Videos?

DESPITE ADVICE FROM the American Academy of Pediatrics telling parents that children under the age of 2 should have zero screen time (television, tablets, phones, or computers), the market for electronic media designed to make babies smarter is booming (Committee on Public Education, 2001). Sporting names like *Baby Einstein, Brainy Baby,* and *Baby Genius,* these materials make their intent clear to consumers. The popularity of these programs indicates that today's parents take the need for nurture seriously.

Surprisingly little scientific research has been done on the use of these products with very young children. Research on the

television show *Sesame Street* showed beneficial effects on outcomes such as vocabulary and school readiness. *Sesame Street* has long-term effects as well, boosting adolescent grades in English, math, and science and overall grade point average (Anderson, Huston, Schmitt, Linebarger, & Wright, 2001; Huston, Anderson, Wright, Linebarger, & Schmitt, 2001). However, the *Sesame Street* studies were conducted with preschoolers, not babies.

One study found that watching baby videos had a detrimental effect on young children's language acquisition. Infants younger than 16 months and exposed to the videos understood from six to eight fewer

words for each hour of exposure compared to nonexposed infants (Frederick, Dimitri, & Andrew, 2007). This finding generated quite a discussion in the nearly $5 billion children's educational media industry.

Earlier in this chapter, we described research demonstrating that young children learn language from a speaker in the room but not from the same speaker being televised. This research suggests that the concerns about language learning and very young children's media use are worth exploring further. In the meantime, we hope that young parents can sit back, relax, play with, and enjoy their children, who grow up all too quickly. ●

mean, or more than 130 on a standardized IQ test. Genius combines unusually high intelligence with creativity and achievement (Renzulli & Delcourt, 1986).

Having a high IQ score provides some significant advantages to individuals in many aspects of life. One of the longest running studies in psychology is a longitudinal examination of gifted children initiated in 1921 (Terman, 1925; Terman & Oden, 1959). The original participants were children who were selected because of their very high IQ scores, averaging 150. The gifted participants not only maintained their high IQ scores but also enjoyed better physical health, emotional stability, occupational attainment, and social satisfaction throughout their adult lives.

High intellect, particularly as measured by an IQ score, does not capture completely what we mean by genius. Despite their successes, the gifted participants in the longitudinal study just cited did not produce "genius" work. Nor do all remarkable thinkers possess particularly high IQ scores. Nobel laureate Richard Feynman was disappointed to learn that his IQ score was "only" 124 (Gleick, 1992).

Like individuals on the lower extreme of IQ scores, children with unusually high IQ scores benefit from educational opportunities tailored to their abilities. Unfortunately, the structure of public education in the United States, with its emphasis on grade levels based on age, rarely provides optimum learning for gifted children. A report by the U.S. Department of Education noted that children with IQ scores of 140 or above typically know at least half of a grade's curriculum before the school year even begins, and those with IQ scores of 170 or above know virtually all of it (U.S. Department of Education Office of Educational Research and Improvement, 1993). Their time in school is subsequently wasted, and the material is so easy that it encourages poor learning habits ill suited to later educational challenges. Ideally, we could begin to offer education targeted to an individual's intellectual strengths and weaknesses.

Vitalinka/Shutterstock

Despite advice from the American Academy of Pediatrics to avoid screen time for children under the age of 2 years, there is a booming market for apps and DVDs advertising their ability to make children smarter.

Interpersonal Relationships
The Cognitive Perspective
How Does Being a Maximizer or a Satisficer Affect Relationships?

Faced with a large array of choices, satisficers will pick one that works, but maximizers will evaluate all the options to find the perfect choice. We're guessing that most of these candies taste good.

Earlier in this chapter, you had an opportunity to take the maximizer–satisficer test (Schwartz et al., 2002). A very high score on this test predicts that you will be quite a perfectionist in your decision making. You might need to evaluate all your choices before you can settle on one, so you are unlikely to be known for making quick decisions. Because maximizers tend to feel more regret when a decision doesn't work out well, they have a tendency to avoid making decisions. Although they may experience better outcomes than satisficers on many occasions, maximizers might still feel worse. Satisficers are more likely to see their glass of life as half full, whereas maximizers are more likely to see their glass as half empty.

What does this distinction mean for interpersonal relationships? Finding a romantic partner and making a long-term commitment to that person involve some important decisions. Romance is consistently ranked among the top regrets in life for most people (Roese & Summerville, 2005). These facts suggest that maximizers might run into some predictable obstacles within the realm of relationships. Either they will let opportunities pass by, because they are still looking for that perfect person, or they will avoid making a commitment for fear of regretting it later. Their perfectionist standards might make it impossible for them to appreciate a partner who is a good match, perhaps because that person does not look like a supermodel or squeezes the toothpaste tube the wrong way.

Does this mean maximizers are doomed in relationships? Not at all. Recognizing that our automatic ways of behaving will not always lead us to our goals can help us identify areas where we need to take conscious, systematic control. Many maximizers blame their partners for a failed romance (the partner just didn't measure up) instead of taking a hard look at their own contributions to the relationship. If you know your maximizing tendencies are leading you in the wrong directions, you can use the steps to effective problem solving outlined earlier in this chapter to supply alternatives that might work better. ●

KEY TERMS The Language of Psychological Science

Be sure you can define these terms and use them correctly.

affect heuristic, p. 368
algorithm, p. 366
aphasia, p. 377
availability heuristic, p. 367
bilingual, p. 382
cognition, p. 358
concept, p. 359
crystallized intelligence, p. 385
exemplar, p. 361

fluid intelligence, p. 385
functional fixedness, p. 365
general intelligence (g), p. 385
giftedness, p. 394
heuristic, p. 367
intellectual disability, p. 392
intelligence quotient (IQ), p. 384
intelligence, p. 384
language, p. 375

morpheme, p. 377
phoneme, p. 377
problem, p. 364
problem solving, p. 364
prototype, p. 361
recognition heuristic, p. 368
representativeness heuristic, p. 367

Summary 10.3 Types of Intelligence

Type of intelligence	Description	Example
General intelligence (g)	A single measure of an individual's intellectual ability that predicts most of that person's intellectual performance	Verbal, mathematical, spatial, and logical skills showing high positive correlations within an individual
Fluid intelligence	A type of general intelligence that allows logical thinking without needing learned knowledge	Recognizing relationships between geometric shapes
Crystallized intelligence	A type of general intelligence that requires learned knowledge	Using your knowledge of the multiplication tables to figure out interest on a new car loan
Multiple intelligences	Single skills that tend to show relatively low correlations with one another and with general intelligence	Strong musical abilities in people with Williams syndrome, which results in a lower than normal IQ score
Emotional and social intelligence	The ability to manage emotions and reason about other people's states of mind	Managing anger appropriately and showing empathy for others
Collective intelligence	A quality of group process independent of individual group members' intelligence that predicts group performance	A team featuring good social sensitivity and conversation sharing that completes a task successfully

Credits: Top Row. © Cengage Learning®. Second Row. iStockphoto.com/acilo. Third Row. Carlo Allegri/LAPA/Getty Images. Fourth Row. DAVE YODER KRT/Newscom. Fifth Row. Bill Aron/PhotoEdit. Bottom Row: © Cengage Learning®.

11 The Developing Mind

Life Span Development

WHAT IS YOUR EARLIEST MEMORY? A BIRTHDAY party? A new puppy? We are guessing that your earliest autobiographical memories, which we discussed in Chapter 9, probably date to when you were between 3 and 5 years old. Why this age period and not another?

iStockphoto.com/Christopher Futcher

Zooming in, we can see that one of the factors driving memory abilities is the development of the brain during childhood. As you will see in this chapter, changes taking place in the hippocampus and frontal lobes somewhere during the third year of life give children a boost in their abilities to form long-term memories, particularly about the sequences of events that make up our autobiographical memories. But there are other parts to this story.

To form an autobiographical memory, children must have a sense of self. As we discussed in Chapter 6, babies as young as 18 months can recognize themselves in a mirror. In this chapter, you will learn about the further development of self-awareness as children gradually separate from their parents and family and move into adult roles in the community.

Zooming out still farther, we find that cultures can influence the formation and timing of autobiographical memories. When White American adults are compared with Chinese adults, the White Americans access more autobiographical memories from earlier ages and provide more episodic details of these memories (Wang, 2008). Wang believes that this difference observed in adults originates earlier in childhood, when White American children show more "emotion knowledge," or an understanding of how situations can lead to emotions, than do Chinese children (see ● Figure 11.1). Emotion knowledge is assessed by asking children such questions as, "What makes people happy?" Cultures can influence emotion knowledge development by focusing on information relevant to the self versus more general aspects of information.

To understand the development of autobiographical memory, psychologists must explore the biological, individual, developmental, social, and cultural contributions to this ability. At the same time, the development of an autobiographical memory capability forms reciprocal influences with these other aspects of the individual's behavior. In this chapter, we will explore many examples of how the normal changes that occur across the life span interact with our behavior and mental processing.

◀ Around the age of 3 years, fiber pathways connecting the frontal lobes with the rest of the brain are developing rapidly, making changes in decision making and memory possible.

Argosy Publishing, Inc.

Learning Objectives

1. Evaluate the evidence for sensory capacities, preferences, and reflexes in newborn infants.

2. Identify major physical, cognitive, and social and emotional differences among the prenatal period, infancy, childhood, adolescence, and adulthood, and give examples of ways in which these three trajectories influence one another.

3. Differentiate Jean Piaget's four stages of cognitive development (sensorimotor, preoperational, concrete operational, and formal operational), and critique Piaget's theory, using research from alternate approaches.

4. Debate the adaptive function of infant attachment, and analyze the roles of temperament, culture, and parenting in driving individual attachment styles.

5. Identify epigenetic processes, critical or sensitive periods, and the impact of experience on biological development.

6. Debate the research evidence for continuity versus discontinuity in the trajectories of physical, cognitive, and social and emotional development.

A major milestone in children's development of a sense of self is the ability to recognize themselves in a mirror by the age of 18 months.

What Does It Mean to Develop?

In Chapter 8, we defined learning as a relatively permanent change in behavior due to experience. In this chapter, we will explore an additional force for changes in behavior—changes that unfold with the passage of time. The study of human development considers changes in behavior that correlate with growth or maturation.

Developmental Themes

As we explore the normal changes that occur at different stages of life, we will concentrate on three interwoven threads: physical development, cognitive development, and social and emotional development. Although we discuss each separately, they are constantly interacting. For example, moving independently by crawling or walking produces a more rapidly changing and interesting environment, which spurs an infant's cognitive growth. At the same time, a mobile infant is likely to elicit different reactions from parents or caretakers than one that is stationary, stimulating further social and emotional development.

In addition to documenting these three types of change over time, the study of development highlights several major questions that stretch across the entire life span. How does nature interact with nurture? Is development gradual and continuous or abrupt and discontinuous? How much of human development is universal across the human species or dependent upon a person's culture?

Nature and Nurture Intertwined Although we will be discussing the genetic heritage of individuals, as well as environmental influences on their development, we will be emphasizing the interactions between nature and nurture that predict developmental outcomes. Signifi-

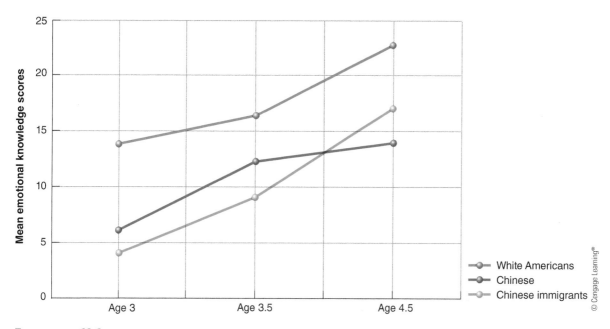

FIGURE 11.1

Cultural Influences on Emotion Knowledge. White American adults recall more childhood autobiographical memories in greater detail than do Chinese adults. These differences may have their roots in earlier cultural influences on emotional knowledge, or an understanding of how a situation can lead to emotions. When asked to describe situations that would make a person happy, sad, fearful, or angry, White American children provided more information than Chinese or Chinese immigrant children. Emotional knowledge increases when a person focuses on information relevant to the self rather than more general information. *Source:* Adapted from "Emotion Knowledge and Autobiographical Memory Across the Preschool Years: A Cross-Cultural Longitudinal Investigation," by Q. Wang, 2008, *Cognition, 108*(1), pp. 117–135.

cant progress has been made in the understanding of how genes and the environment interact. As we discussed in Chapter 3, we now understand that the underlying deoxyribonucleic acid (DNA) that makes up our genes is turned on or off by the surrounding chemical tags (the epigenome) that accumulate through life. Among the external environmental factors that can chemically "tag" our DNA are diet, nurture, and stress.

This epigenetic process is not constant across the life span, just as an individual's physical, cognitive, and social and emotional behaviors change. In prenatal development, most of the chemical tags that influence gene expression come from within the developing organism, with some external influence from the mother's diet and her stress hormones. After birth, internal signals continue to be important in driving physical growth, but the child is now exposed to a wider array of environmental influences, including diet, social interactions, and physical activity. Throughout the remaining life span, epigenetic tags continue to accumulate in response to ongoing experience, which leads to divergence in appearance and health, even among closely related people.

These outcomes mean that epigenetics plays an increasingly dominant role over the life span. Because younger children have had less time for epigenetic interactions between their genes and their experience to take place, they have more in common with one another at any particular age than do older adults, whose decades of experience have caused their epigenetic paths to lead them in many directions. A group of 8-year-olds is more consistent in its physical characteristics and behaviors than a group of 20-year-olds, who still have more in common with one another than any group of 65-year-olds. This contrast between children and adults might have led earlier psychologists to the mistaken belief that development "stopped" at some

Early developmental psychologists described normal age-related changes up through childhood to puberty, but not beyond. Today, we know that the ages represented in these four generations bring their own set of characteristic behaviors.

WHAT DOES IT MEAN TO DEVELOP? **401**

As children develop physically, they are able to move out into the world. Mobile children face new problems that stretch their cognitive abilities and new social and emotional challenges as they learn self-regulation and experience control from their parents.

Jerry Arcieri/Corbis

zygote The term used to describe a developing organism immediately following conception until the embryo stage, or the first 2 weeks following conception in humans.
embryo The term used to describe a developing organism between the zygote and the fetus stages, or between 3 and 8 weeks following conception in humans.
fetus The term used to describe a developing organism between the embryo stage and birth, or between 8 and approximately 40 weeks following conception in humans.

Epigenetic influences accumulate over the life span. Groups of 8-year-olds have more in common than groups of 20-year-olds, who have more in common than groups of older adults. The contrast between the degree of similarity seen in children and that seen in adults might have led early developmental psychologists to the mistaken conclusion that development stops.

point in childhood or adolescence, when all they were seeing was a transition point where internal influences were becoming overshadowed by external ones.

Continuity or Discontinuity Another major question asks whether development proceeds gradually and smoothly over time (continuity) or changes more abruptly from one stage to the next (discontinuity). The gradual approach might be visualized as a rainbow, with one color (stage) gradually merging into the next, with no bold line separating the two. In contrast, the discontinuity approach views development as a staircase to be climbed. The behavior on one step is qualitatively different from that on the step that preceded it, and the change from one step to the other is abrupt (see ● Figure 11.2).

As in the case of nature and nurture, the continuity–discontinuity debate does not have a "right answer." Some features appear to be more continuous in their developmental course, such as the gradual development of infant temperament into later personality. Other features seem to develop more abruptly. Parents are often surprised when their child becomes suddenly more mobile, such as rolling across the bed or walking, although the underlying physical development is probably quite gradual.

Universal or Ecological Development Psychologists taking the universal approach to development look for age-related behaviors that are found across the entire human species, whereas psychologists taking an ecological view ask questions about the impact of culture and environment on development.

Which approach is correct? Both universal and ecological approaches improve our understanding. Although we will see universals of development in this chapter, such as the age at which most children begin walking unassisted, we will also see that children growing up in cultures where early walking is encouraged walk at slightly younger ages than children growing up in cultures where restricting infant movement is the norm. Although a consideration

Radius Images/Alamy

Image Source/Alamy

auremar/Shutterstock

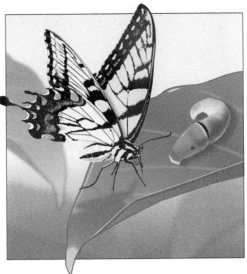

FIGURE 11.2

Continuity Versus Discontinuity in Development. Development can appear as a gradual, continuous process, such as the acorn growing into a mighty oak tree, or as a sudden, discontinuous process, such as the butterfly emerging from a chrysalis.

of human universals is useful, most contemporary psychologists would be unwilling to consider many behaviors outside their context of social relationships and culture.

How Do We Change Prenatally?

Now that we have explored some major themes of development, we are ready to apply them to development beginning with conception, or the merger of the mother's egg with the father's sperm. As we discussed in Chapter 3, this merger combines the genetic material from each parent that will begin to orchestrate development.

The 9 months between conception and birth are full of growth and activity. For the first 2 weeks following conception, the developing organism is known as a **zygote**. During the second week, the zygote typically completes its journey through the mother's fallopian tube to the uterus, where it implants in the lining. During weeks 3 through 8 following conception, we use the term **embryo**, and for the remainder of the pregnancy, we use the term **fetus**.

During the first week following conception, the zygote differentiates into three germ layers—the ectoderm, mesoderm, and endoderm (see ● Figure 11.3). The ectoderm develops into nerve tissue and skin, while the mesoderm gives rise to muscle and bone. The endoderm is the source of much of the body's soft tissue, such as the organs of the digestive tract. By the fourth week following conception, the central nervous system has differentiated into forebrain, midbrain, hindbrain, and spinal cord. During the seventh week, cells that will form the cerebral cortex begin a carefully orchestrated journey from the lining of the neural tube to their ultimate destinations. By the seventh month of pregnancy, most of the brain's cells have been formed (Rakic, 2000).

Other systems, while perhaps not as dramatic as the nervous system, also begin to differentiate and develop during the embryonic stage. The heart, stomach, liver, and other organs are formed during this period, and the initial differentiation between male and female internal sex organs occurs. By 2 months after conception, the fetus is about 1 inch long, weighs about 1 gram (0.04 ounces), and looks decidedly human.

The remainder of the pregnancy involves continued growth and maturation of the systems that are now in place (see ● Figure 11.4). New neurons are born in large numbers and begin the process of forming connections with one another. Myelination of the nervous system begins about 6 months following conception (Rivkin et al., 1995). As you may recall from Chapter 4, myelin allows neurons to communicate faster and more efficiently. During the seventh month of the pregnancy, rapid eye movement (REM) sleep (described in Chapter 6) can be recorded for the first time (Inoue et al., 1986). In children and adults, REM sleep corresponds with vivid dreaming, but we can merely speculate about the quality of the REM

The universal approach sees development as common to all people, whereas the ecological approach emphasizes the influences of environment and culture on development. In the United States, we tend to look at child soldiers, some as young as 10 years old, as being a product of the poverty and lack of opportunity in their environments. However, some universal aspects of being a preteen or young teen, such as an immature sense of morality and greater obedience to adults, might apply equally to very young violent gang members in the United States.

FIGURE 11.3

(a)

Fertilized egg   Zygote   Embryo

Prenatal Development.
(a) For the first 2 weeks after conception, the developing organism is known as a zygote. Cell division continues at a rapid pace as the zygote travels down the mother's fallopian tube, reaching the uterus during its second week. The embryo stage lasts from week 3 through week 8 following conception.
(b) During the zygote stage, cells begin to differentiate into three types: the ectoderm, which is the source of cells making up the nervous system; the mesoderm, which develops into muscle and skeleton; and the endoderm, which will form internal organs.

(b)

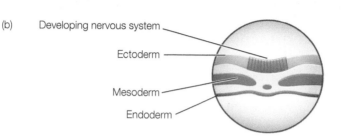

Developing nervous system

Ectoderm

Mesoderm

Endoderm

Illustration: © Argosy Publishing, Inc.; photos, left to right: Eye of Science/Science Source; K H Kjeldsen/Science Source; Dr G Moscoso/Science Source

experience in the fetus. Fetal REM sleep might provide the spontaneous activity necessary for the refinement of connections in the nervous system.

You may be under the impression that the fetus resides in a rather isolated, self-contained environment in the womb, but this is not the case. The fetus's ability to hear noises outside the mother's body is quite good during the last few months of pregnancy (Birnholz & Benacerraf, 1983). Newborn babies show an immediate preference for their mother's voice (DeCasper & Fifer, 1980). When pregnant mothers read the Dr. Seuss classic *The Cat in the Hat* out loud twice a day, their infants later preferred to listen to tapes of their mothers, but not others, reading this story (DeCasper & Spence, 1986). This preference has obvious advantages in the attachment and bonding that occurs between mother and newborn.

We also begin learning food preferences before birth. When pregnant women consumed carrot juice, their infants subsequently chose to eat more cereal prepared with carrot juice than did infants whose mothers did not consume carrot juice during pregnancy. The infants

© Argosy Publishing, Inc.

9	12	16	20	24	28	32	36	40	**weeks**
50	96	140	190	230	270	300	340	380	millimeters

FIGURE 11.4

Fetal Development. During the fetal stage, from 8 to approximately 40 weeks following conception, considerable growth and maturation of organs and tissues prepare the fetus for birth.

exposed prenatally to carrot juice also appeared to enjoy the carrot juice cereal more than infants who were not exposed prenatally (Mennella, Jagnow, & Beauchamp, 2001). Again, this type of learning appears quite adaptive. Children may be born with a familiarity and preference for the safe and available foods in their environment.

Most pregnancies last about 40 weeks, and babies born between 37 and 42 weeks are considered typical, or term, births. Just over 12% of babies born in the United States are born prematurely, or before 37 weeks of pregnancy (Witt et al., 2014) and 2% are born before 32 weeks of pregnancy (Cole et al., 2011). Premature infants are at greater risk than term infants for a number of conditions that can affect lifetime health and development, including disorders of the lungs, vision, and development of the brain (Cole et al., 2011).

Genetic Risks to Development

In most cases, prenatal development proceeds according to plan. As we observed in Chapter 3, genetic abnormalities that have adverse effects are rarely passed along in large numbers.

The more common genetic abnormalities seen in children are those that become more likely when their parents are older. Errors in the development of eggs and sperm are more likely in older parents, particularly in mothers. A woman's eggs are first formed when she is in her own prenatal period. Each of these immature eggs contains a complete set of 46 chromosomes, only half of which (23) are passed along to her child. The child's other 23 chromosomes are contributed by the father through fertilization. The final division of a woman's immature egg into a mature ovum, leaving only 23 chromosomes, does not occur until just before ovulation. Before they make this last crucial division, a 40-year-old woman's eggs have been exposed to 40 years of environmental influences, possibly including harmful factors such as x-rays, which raise the probability that something will go wrong as they divide. In contrast, it takes a little over 2 months for a man to produce a sperm cell, which reduces the chances of the cell's exposure to harmful influences.

Down syndrome, or trisomy 21, results when the child receives three copies of the 21st chromosome instead of the usual two, usually because of faulty cell division during the production of the mature ovum (see ● Figure 11.5). Down syndrome results in intellectual disability (see Chapter 10), a pattern of mild physical abnormalities, and a probable life span of only 40 to 50 years. A woman's chances of giving birth to a child with Down syndrome are only about 1 in 2,000 at age 20 but rise to 1 in 30 at age 45.

Compared to a typical baby born around 40 weeks following conception, who is usually about 20 inches long and weighs about 7 pounds, little Rumaisa Rahman was born only 25 weeks following conception. Rumaisa was about 8 inches long and weighed a little over 1/2 pound. Her twin sister, Hiba, was a little larger, weighing 1 pound, 4 ounces at birth.

Maternal age (years)

FIGURE 11.5

Risk of Down Syndrome and Maternal Age. Many genetic disorders, such as Down syndrome, are more common as the age of the mother increases. Errors in the final cell division forming the mother's egg immediately before ovulation become more likely over time as a woman is exposed to more potentially harmful environmental influences, such as radiation.

Environmental Risks to Development

During pregnancy, the developing fetus is fairly well protected from exposure to a variety of toxins and disease-causing agents by the placenta, an organ attached to the wall of the mother's uterus that provides the fetus with nutrients and oxygen. After all, there are about 7 billion people currently alive, and many have been born under less than ideal conditions. We are a hardy species.

According to one expert in medical ethics, today's technology makes it possible to screen embryos for every known disease-causing mutation in the human genome (Leroi, 2006). What would be the benefits and costs of this practice?

This protection, however, is not perfect. In some cases, substances that are relatively safe for the mother, such as over-the-counter cold remedies and pain medications, have devastating effects on the health and development of her fetus. Any agent that can produce harmful effects in the zygote, embryo, or fetus is known as a **teratogen** (see ● Figure 11.6). Table 11.1 lists some common teratogens and their effects. Commonly used antidepressant medications, discussed in Chapter 15, easily cross the placenta to the fetus. Exposure to these medications has been linked to higher rates of premature birth (Kendall-Tackett & Hale, 2010) and autism spectrum disorder in boys (Harrington, Lee, Crum, Zimmerman, & Hertz-Picciotto, 2014). Because even the safest and most routine substances are capable of acting as teratogens, pregnant women are well advised to consult with health care providers before taking any type of medication.

Recreational drugs consumed by the mother are the most common and preventable sources of adverse effects in the developing fetus. Infants born to women who use tobacco are at risk for premature birth and being underweight, circumstances that are major risk factors for numerous physical and psychological problems later on in the child's life (Centers for Disease Control and Prevention [CDC], 2010b).

There are no known safe levels of alcohol consumption for pregnant women, leading to strongly worded advice to abstain from alcohol. The intricate programming of nervous system

teratogen A chemical agent that can harm the zygote, embryo, or fetus.

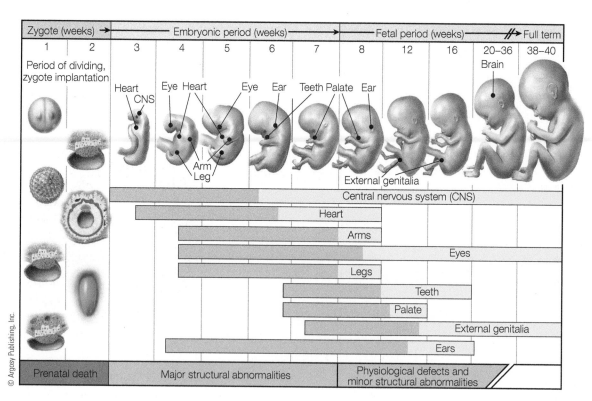

FIGURE 11.6

Risks From Teratogens. The orange bars indicate the overall time during which a system is developing. The yellow bars indicate when particular systems are most vulnerable to disrupted development because of teratogens.

TABLE 11.1 Examples of Some Common Teratogens and Their Effects

Teratogen	Type	Effects on the child
Alcohol	Recreational drug	• Small stature • Facial abnormalities • Hyperactivity • Intellectual disability
Phenytoin (Dilantin)	Prescription medication for epilepsy	• Heart defects • Intellectual disability • Cleft palate • Slow growth
Selective serotonin reuptake inhibitors (Prozac, Zoloft, etc.)	Prescription antidepressants	• Premature birth • Autism spectrum disorder in males
Varicella (chicken pox)	Viral infection	• Scars • Small head size • Blindness • Seizures • Malformed and paralyzed limbs
Aspirin	Over-the-counter pain medication	• Heart defects • Intellectual disability • Slow growth

© Cengage Learning®

development in the fetus appears to be especially vulnerable to interruption by alcohol consumed by the mother during pregnancy (Haycock, 2009). Alcohol consumption by a pregnant woman can result in a condition known as **fetal alcohol syndrome (FAS)**. As shown in ● Figure 11.7, FAS produces a number of physical abnormalities, including growth retardation, skin folds at the corners of the eyes, nose and mouth abnormalities, and small head circumference, as well as cognitive and behavioral problems, including reduced IQ, attention problems, and poor impulse control (Streissguth et al., 1991).

fetal alcohol syndrome (FAS) A condition resulting from alcohol consumption by the mother during pregnancy that produces physical abnormalities and cognitive and behavioral problems in her child.

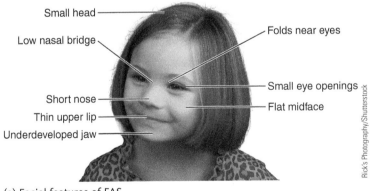

(a) Facial features of FAS

Small head — Low nasal bridge — Short nose — Thin upper lip — Underdeveloped jaw — Folds near eyes — Small eye openings — Flat midface

(b) Brain affected by FAS (left) compared to normal brain (right)

FIGURE 11.7

Fetal Alcohol Syndrome (FAS). No known amount of alcohol consumption is considered safe during pregnancy, yet about 8% of pregnant women in the United States drinks some alcohol and about 1.4% binge drinks (has five or more drinks at one time; CDC, 2012). Drinking during pregnancy can result in FAS, which produces (a) characteristic facial features, (b) reduced brain volume, and attentional and other behavioral problems in children.

Mothers who drink alcohol during pregnancy are often malnourished and have other health problems that indirectly affect their developing fetus (Steinhausen, Willms, & Spohr, 1993). They are more likely to smoke or use other psychoactive drugs, which produce their own sets of problems for the fetus. A mother's use of alcohol, tobacco, marijuana, or cocaine during pregnancy significantly reduces the volume of gray matter of her child's brain, but combinations of two or more of these drugs produce even more dramatic reductions. As we mentioned in Chapter 4, gray matter refers to areas populated by neural cell bodies, and the thickness of cortical gray matter is correlated with measures of intelligence. These are not short-term effects, because children exposed prenatally to multiple drugs show reduced gray matter thickness and head circumference at 10 to 13 years of age (Rivkin et al., 2008).

In addition to following a typically balanced, nutritious diet, pregnant women require particular nutrients to meet the needs of the growing fetus. Folic acid, found in fortified wheat products, green leafy vegetables, citrus, eggs, and chickpeas, reduces the likelihood of spina bifida, in which the early development of the spinal cord is disrupted, leading to movement disorders. Docosahexaenoic acid (DHA), an omega-3 fatty acid found in maternal milk and oily fish, is important for proper development of the fetus's brain and retina of the eye. However, because most oily fishes also contain mercury, which is harmful to brain development, pregnant women should be cautious about choosing a source for this nutrient. Even with a healthy diet, many pregnant women need supplements of vitamin D, calcium, and iron.

A pregnant woman can be exposed to viruses that can trigger conditions that occur immediately or later in the child's life (Cannon, Kendell, Susser, & Jones, 2003). One of the most significant viral risks to the fetus today is the mother's infection with HIV, which can be passed from mother to child during pregnancy, birth, or breast-feeding. Worldwide, mothers transmit HIV to nearly 500,000 babies per year. Fortunately, an infected mother can significantly reduce her offspring's chances of contracting HIV by using medications that slow the reproduction of the virus (Mofenson, 2010). Women with HIV might also be advised to deliver via cesarean section and to avoid breast-feeding to reduce the chances of passing the virus to their children.

What Can Newborns Do?

Human development is characterized by a longer period of dependency than in other primates, including chimpanzees and gorillas. Physical abilities present at birth in other primates, such as independent movement, require about 1 year to develop in human infants (Walker & Shipman, 1996). Human adults house, feed, clothe, protect, and educate their young for the better part of two decades, if not longer. However, even though human newborns are less mature than primate infants of other species, they come into the world with a number of useful capacities.

Newborn babies grasp anything placed in their hand, including a parent's finger.

The Newborn's Reflexes

According to medical definitions, the newborn stage of life begins officially at birth and lasts 28 days. Newborns have a number of reflexive behaviors that begin to operate immediately (see Table 11.2). Babies immediately turn their head to the source of a touch, open their mouth, and search for the mother's nipple. This rooting reflex assists the newborn with the essential process of feeding. If an object is placed in the mouth, babies begin to suck reflexively, which also leads to effective feeding. Other reflexes form the basis for the later development of more sophisticated behaviors. Very young babies reflexively grasp any object placed in the hand, which leads to the later voluntary grasping of objects. If parents hold newborns upright with their feet touching a surface, babies show a stepping reflex, which possibly serves as a basis for later walking (Zelazo, 1998).

11.2 Newborn Reflexes

Reflex name	Action	Possible purpose
Babinski	Stroking the baby's foot causes toes to spread out.	Unknown; disappears as nervous system matures
Blink	Eye closes in response to strong stimuli.	Protects eyes
Moro	If the baby's head falls backward, the arms first spread out and then "hug."	A possible evolutionary remnant allowing primates to cling to an adult
Palmar	Placing an object in the hand produces reflexive grasping.	A possible evolutionary remnant allowing primates to cling to an adult's fur
Rooting	Stroking a baby's cheek results in the baby turning toward the touch and opening the mouth.	Helps the baby nurse
Stepping	Placing the baby's feet on a flat surface initiates stepping.	Possible precursor to walking
Sucking	The baby sucks anything that touches the roof of the mouth.	Helps the baby nurse

© Cengage Learning®

The Newborn's Activity

Newborns spend up to 16 to 18 hours per day sleeping. As we mentioned in Chapter 6, a large proportion of this time is spent in REM sleep, which might participate in the wiring of the newborn's brain.

During times of wakefulness, the baby alternates between periods of alert looking about and periods of physical movement of the arms and legs. Unfortunately for parents, most newborns also spend about 2 to 3 hours per day either crying or being close to tears. As upsetting as this crying may be, it represents the infant's first efforts at communicating with the parents. Babies generally cry for a reason, such as hunger or pain, and most parents are stimulated by the crying to find ways to make their infant more comfortable.

The Newborn's Senses

Newborns have significant, although immature, sensory capacities. Because babies can't talk, researchers have had to be fairly creative in assessing their sensory capacities (see ● Figure 11.8). Measures of heart rate, facial expression, and head movements may correlate with distinctions among stimuli. Researchers also take advantage of habituation, the type of learning in which we reduce responding to repeated stimuli (see Chapter 8). Because of habituation, babies gaze longer at a new stimulus than at one they have seen previously. When babies spend equal time looking at two stimuli, we can assume they cannot tell the difference between them.

Newborns show considerable sensitivity to smells and respond differently to pleasant smells (chocolate or honey) than to unpleasant smells (rotten eggs; Maurer & Maurer, 1988). They are also capable of recognizing their mother by smell, which has obvious survival advantages. Babies even recognize their mother's favorite brand of perfume (Porter, Makin, Davis, & Christensen, 1991). Infants are quite sensitive to taste and can respond differentially to the major taste qualities of sweet, sour, bitter, and salty. They apparently have a sweet tooth and

Illustration: © Cengage Learning®. photo by: Mark Philbrick/Brigham Young University

Facial expression plus voice
Voice alone
Facial expression alone

FIGURE 11.8

Studying Infants Requires Clever Experimental Methods. By studying the amount of time infants look at a new stimulus after habituation, such as the face of a person, Ross Flom and Lorraine Bahrick were able to demonstrate that infants as young as 4 months could correctly perceive emotional expression if they both saw and heard the same expression simultaneously. The ability to perceive emotion using voice alone appeared around the age of 5 months, and the ability to perceive emotion from facial expression alone appeared around 7 months. *Source:* Adapted from "The Development of Infant Discrimination of Affect in Multimodal and Unimodal Stimulation: The Role of Intersensory Redundancy," by R. Flom and L. E. Bahrick, 2007, *Developmental Psychology, 43*(1), pp. 238–252. doi:10.1037/0012-1649.43.1.238.

nurse longer when their breast-feeding mother has consumed sweet-tasting foods (Mennella & Beauchamp, 1996).

The fetus can hear quite well beginning in the seventh month of pregnancy, but improvement in hearing continues after birth. We might tiptoe around a sleeping newborn, but older children and adults have superior hearing for very quiet sounds. The infant's ability to hear is best for sounds found in the range of frequencies that normally occur in human speech. This ability allows infants to learn language.

Infant vision can be tested by measuring the amount of time the child spends viewing a pattern rather than a uniform screen. Using this technique, we can demonstrate that young infants do not see detail at a distance as well as adults do. In addition, infants need more contrast than adults to see well. As we discussed in Chapter 5, contrast refers to differences in intensity between adjacent stimuli. The black letters on this white page are an example of high contrast, whereas dark gray letters on a black background would be an example of low contrast. These features of infant vision probably explain babies' preference for large, high-contrast, colorful objects.

Newborns demonstrate an innate preference for looking at faces (Otsuka, 2014; see ● Figure 11.9). This capacity has obvious advantages in social behavior and language learning. We know that infants who refuse to make eye contact often develop social and language impairments later (Knickmeyer, Baron-Cohen, Raggatt, & Taylor, 2005; Mundy et al., 2007). An early preference for viewing faces is not unique to humans, suggesting that this behavior provides an adaptive advantage. Other primates show similar preferences for faces, which may be related to the importance of social relationships in primate species, including our own (Thierry, 1994).

The emerging picture of the newborn infant is one of immature yet formidable capacities. The remainder of this chapter will explore the unfolding of these capabilities as the individual matures.

FIGURE 11.9

Newborns Show a Preference for Facelike Stimuli. Newborns looked at the stimulus on the left for about 16 seconds longer than the less facelike stimulus on the right. Looking time has been used as one measure of preference for infants. *Source:* Adapted from "Newborns' Preference for Faces: What Is Crucial?" by C. Turati, F. Simion, I. Milani, and C. Umiltà, 2002, *Developmental Psychology, 38*(6), pp. 875–882.

Summary 11.1 Milestones of Prenatal and Newborn Development

Stage	Timing	Highlights
Zygote	1–2 weeks postconception	• Differentiation into germ layers
Embryo	3–8 weeks postconception	• Nervous system and organs form • Sex organs differentiate into males and females
Fetus	Week 9 postconception through remainder of pregnancy	• Growth and maturation of existing organs • REM sleep in seventh month of pregnancy • Good hearing from seventh month of pregnancy
Newborn	First 28 days of life	• Reflexive movement • Large amounts of sleep • Improving sensory capacities • Preference for faces

Credits: Top Row. K. H. Kjeldsen/Science Source. Second Row. Dr G. Moscoso/Science Source. Third Row. © Argosy Publishing, Inc. Bottom Row: Tony Wear/Shutterstock.com.

What Physical Changes Occur in Infancy and Childhood?

Physical development in infancy and childhood features rapid growth, particularly during the first year of life, when children triple their birth weight (see ● Figure 11.10).

4 months (fetal) 5 months (fetal) Newborn 2 years 6 years 12 years 25 years

FIGURE 11.10

Physical Growth Is Rapid in Childhood. Infants grow rapidly, tripling their birth weight during the first year alone. As they grow, their proportions also change significantly. The head takes up approximately one quarter of a newborn's height, versus about one seventh to one eighth of an adult's height. In contrast, the ratio of the trunk to the overall height, about three eighths, remains the same over the life span. *Source:* Adapted from *Human Development: A Life-Span View* (5th ed., p. 93), by R. V. Kail and J. C. Cavanaugh, 2010, Belmont, CA: Wadsworth/Cengage Learning.

Nervous System Development

In the latter months of pregnancy and for the first 18 months of life, the human brain shows rapid growth in gray matter, or collections of neural cell bodies, which we discussed in Chapter 4. Following this burst of brain growth, cells and connections that are not useful are systematically deleted. In other words, we produce more neurons and synapses than we will eventually need and then keep only those that are working well for us (see ● Figure 11.11).

What does it mean to have neurons and synapses that are working well? The nervous system develops according to a "use it or lose it" principle, which emphasizes the important role of experience in wiring the brain. Children who are raised in a stimulating and enriched environment, with many things to explore, are likely to have the best outcomes. Children living in intellectually impoverished circumstances may retain too few connections, which may lead to mild forms of intellectual disability (see Chapter 10).

If a child's rate of growth during the first year of life continued, a 10-year-old would be about the size of a jumbo jet (McCall, 1979).

Myelination, the growth in white matter that begins about 6 months after conception, continues to develop at a fairly regular rate throughout childhood and adolescence (see ● Figure 11.12; Houston, Herting, & Sowell, 2013). An interesting spurt in myelination occurs between the ages of 6 and 13 years in parts of the brain associated with language and spatial relations (Thompson et al., 2000). The rather sudden end of this white matter growth coincides with the end of a sensitive period for language development. Bilingual individuals who learn language after the age of 10 or so process their second languages differently than do native-language speakers (van Hell & Tokowicz, 2010). Unfortunately, most students in the United States begin foreign language study after this age.

Motor Development

As we mentioned earlier, newborn human infants are relatively helpless compared to their chimpanzee and gorilla counterparts. Newborn humans' mobility is handicapped by their proportions. One quarter of their length is made up by newborns' head. In contrast, adults'

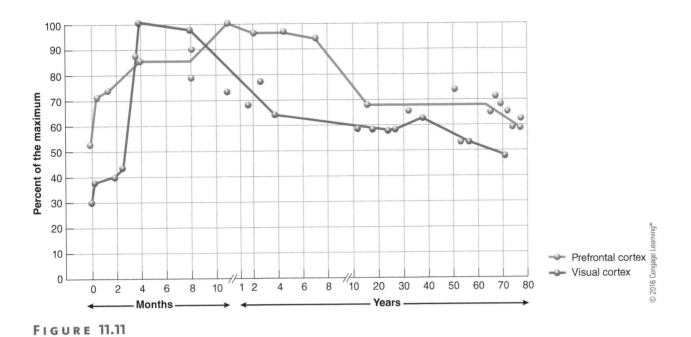

FIGURE 11.11

Synaptic Connections Are Pruned in Response to Experience. During development, we produce more synapses than necessary. Synapses that are not useful are deleted in a process known as synaptic pruning. This process emphasizes the importance of experiencing enriched environments during development. *Source:* Huttenlocher, P. R. (1994). Synaptogenesis, synapse elimination, and neural plasticity in human cerebral cortex. *Threats to optimal development: Integrating biological, psychological, and social risk factors, 27,* 35-54.

heads make up approximately one seventh to one eighth of their height. Motor development, or change in our ability to move and perform physical skills, is largely driven by our human genetic blueprint. Identical twins typically reach motor milestones such as walking with more similar timing than that of fraternal twins or nontwin siblings (Fox, Hershberger, & Bouchard, 1996). Because identical twins share more genes in common compared with fraternal twins, reaching milestones at the same time indicates an important role for genetics in early motor development.

Motor development in childhood proceeds simultaneously in two directions. First, we see development in the head-to-toe direction. Controlling the muscles of the neck and shoulders allows 2-month-old infants to raise their head to look around. This achievement is followed by development of the muscles of the torso around 3 months of age, which are necessary for rolling and sitting. Between 6 and 9 months, babies begin to crawl, although some happily skip this stage. Finally, around the first birthday, the muscles of the legs are developed sufficiently to support the weight of a child when standing or walking. Well into middle childhood, children continue to improve their movement and coordination, demonstrated by the abilities to skip rope, hop on one foot, and combine movements, such as throwing a ball while running (see ● Figure 11.13).

The second direction of motor development begins at the midline, an imaginary line dividing the human body in equal halves, and proceeds outward. Infants can bat at toys suspended above their cribs (3 months) before they are able to grasp objects (5 months). In other words, accurately directing the arms precedes the ability to direct the hands and fingers. Incidentally, infants learn to grasp objects before they learn to release them, a fact parents may wish to consider before wearing long hair or dangling earrings. Well into elementary school,

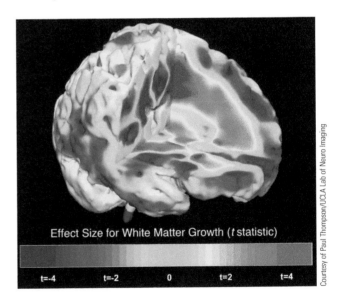

FIGURE 11.12

Myelination Increases During Childhood. Imaging technologies have captured the progress of myelination (white matter growth) in childhood. Red and yellow areas show the largest changes. Myelinated systems are faster and more efficient than unmyelinated systems.

WHAT PHYSICAL CHANGES OCCUR IN INFANCY AND CHILDHOOD? **413**

Parents in most cultures attempt to teach toileting practices when children are about 2 years old. Not coincidentally, the motor systems required to achieve sphincter control are generally myelinated somewhere around 21 months of age (Largo, Molinari, von Siebenthal, & Wolfensberger, 1996).

children are continuing to master control over the fine muscle movements of the hands and fingers required for writing. Perhaps you recall the rather large-lined paper you used in first grade and the challenges of coloring "within the lines." Females enjoy a slight advantage in developing fine motor skills (Hampson, 1990; Hampson & Kimura, 1988; McEwen, 2001). In contrast, boys enter kindergarten with significantly more muscle mass than girls of the same age and often prefer large-scale movements such as running, climbing, and jumping (Wang et al., 1999).

We can predict with some certainty the average age at which each motor milestone will be reached. However, we must be cautious when measuring the progress of one child against the average age. Around these average ages is a range of normal development. Although most children might walk unassisted around their first birthday, some children walk as early as 9 or 10 months of age, while others do not take their first steps alone until about 18 months of age.

Although early motor milestones are driven largely by biology, they respond to experience. It is possible to slow down motor milestones by restricting movement. Some cultures, out of safety concerns, restrict the movement opportunities of young children, which slightly delays motor milestones such as walking alone (Kaplan & Dove, 1987). In other cases, motor milestones may be reached slightly earlier by providing specific practice in sitting, standing, and walking (Super, 1976). These changes in the developmental timeline are usually slight, because myelination of motor nerves usually just precedes the achievement of a new skill. Once the relevant parts of the nervous system are sufficiently mature, new skills develop rapidly with little practice.

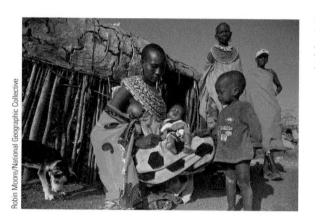

Kenyan parents often encourage early walking in their children. Compared to American children, whose average age of walking unassisted is about 1 year, Kenyan children observed by Super (1976) walked between the ages of 7 and 11 months. In contrast, practices such as swaddling young infants are associated with slightly later attainment of motor milestones.

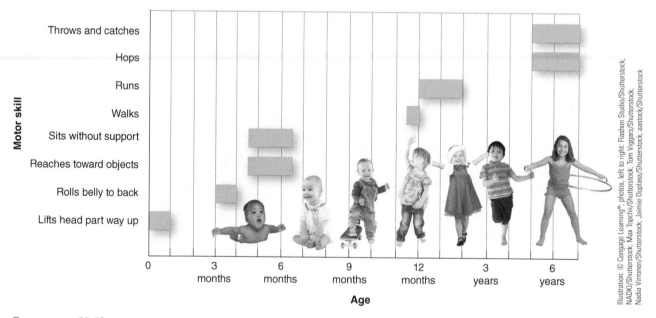

FIGURE 11.13

Motor Milestones. These motor milestones emerge at predictable times over the course of childhood but can range significantly from child to child. The ages in this chart represent the average time at which children reach a milestone.

How Does Cognition Change During Infancy and Childhood?

Interacting with brain development and the child's ability to move and explore the environment are changes in the way children process information and solve problems. Even when children are exposed to the same information as adults, their thinking often leads them to different conclusions. When asked why clouds move across the sky, a 4-year-old might suggest that the clouds are pulled by airplanes, but an adult is unlikely to come to this conclusion. Both child and adult have observed clouds and airplanes moving across the sky, but viewing these occurrences as related is something that only a small child would do. To understand these differences, we need to examine how cognition changes as a function of age and experience.

One of the classic theories about the development of cognition was proposed by Swiss psychologist Jean Piaget (1896–1980). While working with Théodore Simon, who along with Alfred Binet developed some of the first intelligence tests (see Chapter 10), Piaget became more interested in the errors made by the children than in their correct responses. He believed that these errors were representative of growth in the child's ability to reason. Later, Piaget's views were challenged and revised by psychologists who believed that he underestimated the capabilities of children at particular ages. We will explore these contemporary approaches after we look more carefully at Piaget.

A preschool child might believe that airplanes pull clouds across the sky, but an adult is unlikely to come to the same conclusion, even though they are watching the same events.

Jean Piaget's Theory of Cognitive Development

According to Piaget's theory, cognitive abilities develop through regular stages, making Piaget's work a classic example of the discontinuity approach discussed earlier in this chapter. Cognition matures as the child increasingly uses concepts and organizing schemas to think. We discussed concepts and schemas in Chapter 10.

Two types of adjustments can be made to a schema, depending on the nature of discrepancies between the new information and the existing category. Assume that a child has a rather well-developed schema for birds, which includes features such as "has wings," "has feathers," and "can fly." If the child then learns about a new species of bird, such as a hawk, the

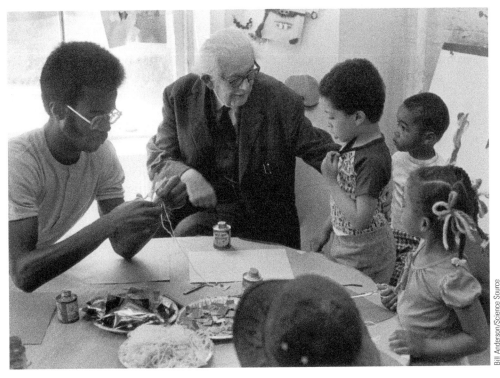

Jean Piaget (1896–1980).

11.3	Jean Piaget's Theory of Cognitive Development	
Stage	**Approximate age**	**Highlights**
Sensorimotor stage	Birth to age 2	• Here and now rather than past and future • Exploration through moving and sensing • Object permanence
Preoperational stage	2–6 years	• Language acquisition • Egocentrism • Illogical reasoning
Concrete operational stage	6–12 years	• Logical reasoning • Mastery of conservation problems • Learning by doing
Formal operational stage	12 years and older	• Abstract reasoning • Idealism • Improved problem solving

© Cengage Learning®

Eric Isselee/Shutterstock.com

If children can learn about robins without making changes to their schema of "bird," assimilation will occur. In contrast, learning about kiwis might require changes in the bird schema, and accommodation will occur.

assimilation The incorporation of new learning into an existing schema, without the need to revise the schema.

accommodation The incorporation of new learning into an existing schema that requires revision of the schema.

sensorimotor stage Jean Piaget's stage of development beginning at birth and ending at the age of 2 years and characterized by active exploration of the environment.

object permanence The ability to form mental representations of objects that are no longer present.

child can assimilate the new information into the existing bird schema: Hawks have wings and feathers and the ability to fly. In **assimilation**, no changes to the existing schema are required to add the new instance. However, let's now assume that the child meets a kiwi, a small, flightless bird from New Zealand. The kiwi doesn't fit neatly into the existing schema, which assumes that all birds can fly. The schema must be adapted to fit the new information, a process Piaget called **accommodation**. Through accommodation, the child now understands that although most birds can fly, some exceptions occur.

In addition to his interest in the development and refinement of schemas, Piaget made many other observations about cognition at different ages. We will now explore the particular characteristics found in each of Piaget's four stages (see Table 11.3).

The Sensorimotor Stage Piaget's first stage, the **sensorimotor stage**, begins at birth and lasts until the child's second birthday. The name of this stage reflects the infant's existence in the here and now. The child at the sensorimotor stage does not think extensively in terms of past and future. Sensations immediately evoke motor responses. As soon as they can crawl, infants work their way (usually quite rapidly) through the environment, exploring new objects by interacting with them physically, particularly by putting them in their mouths. Infants do not seem particularly deterred by features such as taste and are very likely to sample the drain cleaner under the sink unless parents take appropriate precautions to babyproof their home.

One of the major milestones that occur during the sensorimotor stage is the achievement of **object permanence**. Infants under the age of 8 months or so do not seem to be able to form clear memories, or mental representations, for objects once they are removed from the immediate present. Piaget carried a rather beautiful gold pocket watch, which was quite attractive to young children. If Piaget covered the watch with his beret while an infant watched, the infant would not show signs of searching for the now missing watch. Around the age of 8 months or so, infants become more persistent. If he hid the pocket watch, 8-month-olds would look for it. Object permanence coincides with achieving sufficient growth in the prefrontal cortex (Diamond & Goldman-Rakic, 1989).

During the sensorimotor period, the child's language abilities are developing rapidly. By the age of 18 months, children usually have a working vocabulary of 10 to 50 words, and by the age of 2 years, they are beginning to combine words into short but meaningful sentences, such as "Want cookie" or "Go bye-bye." These new ways of thinking symbolically lead the child into the subsequent preoperational stage.

The Preoperational Stage Piaget's **preoperational stage** lasts from approximately age 2 to age 6, or the child's preschool years. While significant advances in cognitive and language abilities occur during this stage, thinking is still relatively immature. The stage gets its name from the notion that children are still incapable of engaging in internal mental operations or manipulations, such as following the transformation of objects from one form to another.

Piaget used a variety of creative tasks to demonstrate the characteristics of the reasoning of the preoperational child. **Conservation** tasks require the child to recognize that changing the form or appearance of an object does not change its quantity. One of the observations that led Piaget to consider cognitive development as occurring in stages is the rather abrupt way in which conservation tasks are often solved. Children who could not solve the problem a few weeks earlier suddenly look at the adult experimenter with pity, as if to say, "This may be the world's stupidest grown-up."

In addition to difficulty with transitions, preoperational children have limited abilities to understand points of view other than their own, a characteristic described by Piaget as **egocentrism**. One kindergarten teacher asked his class where the sun went at night and received an enthusiastic response of "Yuba City" (which is located in northern California) from one of the students. As it turned out, the young student had moved recently from Yuba City to his current home in San Luis Obispo. Because these were the only two places on earth the child knew, if he was in one place and the sun wasn't there, there was only one other logical place for the sun to be. You guessed it—Yuba City.

Preoperational thinking is also limited by beliefs that appearances are real. While older children understand that movies feature real people dressed up and acting like superheroes, the younger child might believe that not only is the superhero real but also that he can really fly.

The Concrete Operational Stage Piaget referred to the stage between the ages of 6 and 12 as the **concrete operational stage**. Rather suddenly, problems of conservation are easily solved, and thinking becomes more logical. The only remaining limitation is an inability to handle abstract concepts, which will not be resolved until the next and final stage.

Piaget used the term *concrete operations* for this stage because he observed that children reasoned best when allowed to engage in hands-on learning. This observation of Piaget's has had an enormous impact on the way early childhood education is conducted in many nations. Endless paper-and-pencil worksheets requiring students to regurgitate math facts have given way to colorful boxes of manipulatives, which allow children to count and sort real things. Children's museums, petting zoos, interactive websites, and other opportunities for experiential learning have become commonplace.

The Formal Operational Stage For Piaget, cognitive development matures in the **formal operational stage**, which begins around the age of 12. The final piece to be added to the child's cognitive skill set is the ability to handle abstract concepts. Abstract concepts usually involve "what if" types of questions and form the heart of scientific inquiry. If you were to ask a group of sixth graders what would happen if everyone on earth became blind tomorrow, they would likely struggle to come up with a reasonable answer. A group of high school students, however, would readily reply that people who were already blind would become instant leaders, because they would have existing skills for coping with blindness.

Accompanying the ability to think abstractly is a big improvement in problem solving. Younger children tend to approach problems by trying things out and seeing what happens, a rather inefficient trial-and-error approach. Teens are more likely to think through several alternatives more systematically. Abstract thinking ability also appears to stimulate a burst of idealism. What if we could solve world hunger? These are the types of questions teens begin to ask, and they are not always content with the more practical and less idealistic responses of older adults.

Preoperational children are unlikely to recognize that pouring liquid from one glass to another of a different size and shape does not change the amount of liquid. They usually believe that the glass that is "higher" holds more. The abruptness with which children master conservation tasks led Jean Piaget to suggest that cognitive development proceeds in stages, but other psychologists believe changes occur more gradually.

The young child's inability to distinguish fantasy from reality has led to a lively debate about managing entertainment materials for children. Is it appropriate to let young children believe that fairy tales are real?

preoperational stage Jean Piaget's stage of development beginning at the age of 2 years and ending at the age of 6 years and characterized by use of symbols, egocentrism, and limits on the ability to reason logically.

conservation The ability to understand that changing the form or appearance of an object does not change its quantity.

egocentrism Limitations on the ability to understand the point of view of other people.

concrete operational stage Jean Piaget's stage of development beginning at the age of 6 years and ending at the age of 12 years and characterized by logical but not abstract reasoning.

formal operational stage Jean Piaget's stage of development beginning at age 12 and extending through adulthood and characterized by mature reasoning capabilities.

One of Jean Piaget's legacies to early childhood education is his emphasis on hands-on learning. Colorful objects, or manipulatives, have replaced endless worksheets used to teach math concepts such as sorting to older generations of students.

Criticisms of Jean Piaget's Theory Piaget's classic theory sets the standard for his time, but more contemporary developmental psychologists argue that some aspects of his view of cognitive development need updating and revising.

Piaget's strong interest in biology led him to look at human development from a species perspective, which in turn reduced his interest in individual differences. Other psychologists point out that individual cognitive development can be quite variable. Some adults fail to achieve the ability to reason abstractly or do so only on some problems and not on others. This variability makes cognitive development look more gradual and continuous than stagelike, as suggested by Piaget.

Piaget did not specify mechanisms responsible for moving from one stage to the next. Today, using brain imaging methods, we can explain some of these changes, such as the correlation between the achievement of object permanence and frontal lobe development. Other transitions, such as the relatively sudden mastery of conservation problems, are not so easily explained.

Many psychologists believe that Piaget underestimated the capabilities of young children. At the same time, he might have overestimated the cognitive abilities of adolescents. As we discussed in Chapter 4, the human brain is not fully mature until a person's early 20s, so we would not expect fully adult cognition in an adolescent. For example, adolescents perceive risk as well as adults do, but unlike adults, adolescents are likely to be enticed by a large reward into selecting a risky alternative (Reyna et al., 2011).

Finally, Piaget has been criticized for viewing developing children in relative isolation from their family, community, and culture. These criticisms have formed the basis for extensions to Piaget's approach, described in the next section.

Alternative Approaches to Cognitive Development

Although Piaget provides a useful starting place for the evaluation of cognitive development, not all researchers agree with his conclusions. In the next sections, we will explore some of these alternatives to Piaget's classic approaches to cognitive development.

A burst of idealism, leading to a desire to make the world a better place, often accompanies the onset of formal operational thinking in adolescence.

Lev Vygotsky An alternative to Piaget's approach was proposed by Soviet psychologist Lev Vygotsky (1896–1934). Piaget and Vygotsky illustrate the theme of universal versus ecological development introduced at the beginning of the chapter. Unlike Piaget, whose interest viewed human development as universal across cultures, Vygotsky (1934/1962) stressed the role of culture and cultural differences in the development of the child. For Vygotsky, cultures teach children not only what to think but also how to think.

Piaget's developing individual learns to understand the world by actively exploring it, like a miniature scientist, whereas Vygotsky's individual gains knowledge of the world by interacting socially and collaboratively with parents, teachers, and other members of the community (see ● Figure 11.14). Language was a particularly impor-

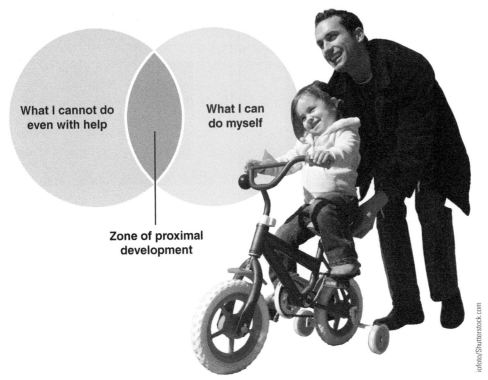

FIGURE 11.14

Zone of Proximal Development.
Unlike Jean Piaget, Lev Vygotsky viewed development as taking place within the social and cultural environments. His zone of proximal development included tasks that the child could learn to do with the assistance of parents, teachers, or other adults or peers. Vygotsky's advice is to provide children with activities that are within reach but neither too easy nor too hard.

What I cannot do even with help

What I can do myself

Zone of proximal development

iofoto/Shutterstock.com

tant aspect of cognitive development for Vygotsky. Children first use language to initiate social contact and opportunities to learn. Later, self-directed talk, such as "I need to finish my game before dinner," aids in problem solving and, in the older child, forms inner speech.

Information Processing An information processing model of cognitive development provides important extensions to Piaget's theory (Kail & Bisanz, 1992).

The overall rate of processing information, analogous to your computer's CPU speed, increases during childhood (Cerella & Hale, 1994). In tasks that require judgment, such as deciding which of two numbers is larger, adults are 3 times faster than 4- and 5-year-olds and twice as fast as 8- and 9-year-olds (Kail & Bisanz, 1992). Surprisingly, by the time children enter elementary school, their performance on tasks requiring focused attention and disregard of distracters reaches adult levels (McKay, Halperin, Schwartz, & Sharma, 1994). In contrast, the ability to sustain attention over time remains limited until the age of 11 years. Around this age, attention span begins to lengthen significantly each year until adulthood.

Children's memory abilities change dramatically following their second year of life (Bauer, Larkina, & Deocampo, 2011; Bauer & Lukowski, 2010). These changes are likely because of maturation of brain structures related to memory. The amygdala and most of the hippocampus are relatively mature at a very early age, around 6 months, but changes in the frontal lobe and hippocampus during the third year of life allow children to form more long-term memories, particularly for sequences of events. Improved memory and a growing sense of self combine to produce some of the first autobiographical memories between the ages of 3 and 5 years (Wang, 2008).

Naïve Theories Piaget suggested that children's abilities to understand objects in their world develop slowly over time. Contemporary developmental psychologists believe that Piaget's assertion was wrong. Instead, very young children seem to understand a great deal about objects and how they work, even before they have had much experience interacting with them (Baillargeon, Li, Gertner, & Wu, 2011). For example, infants as young as 2-1/2 months old looked longer at an impossible situation (a toy mouse that should have been seen moving between two blocks did not appear), as shown in ● Figure 11.15.

Theory of Mind Piaget used the concept of egocentrism to describe the young child's relative lack of awareness of the viewpoints of others. An elaboration of this concept,

HOW DOES COGNITION CHANGE DURING INFANCY AND CHILDHOOD?   **419**

FIGURE 11.15

Children Possess Naïve Theories. Many contemporary psychologists believe that Jean Piaget underestimated the reasoning abilities of young children. Children as young as 2-1/2 months of age looked longer at this impossible situation (the mouse toy, which is moved from left to right behind the blocks, should have been visible as it passed between the two blocks). *Source:* Adapted from Baillargeon, Gertner, and Wu (2011).

FIGURE 11.16

Testing Theory of Mind (TOM). Children who have achieved TOM recognize that their personal knowledge of the whereabouts of Sally's ball is different from Sally's knowledge, and they will predict correctly that she will look in the basket.

This is Sally.   This is Anne.

Sally puts her ball in the basket.

Sally goes away.

Anne moves the ball to her box.

Where will Sally look for her ball?

theory of mind (TOM) The understanding that others have thoughts that are different from one's own.

theory of mind (TOM), has emerged as an important tool in tracking typical and abnormal development. TOM occurs when people understand that others have beliefs, desires, and intentions that are different from their own (Premack & Woodruff, 1978). The classic procedure for demonstrating TOM is the false belief task, often called the "Sally–Anne" task (Wimmer & Perner, 1983). Imagine that one doll, Sally, places her ball in a basket and then leaves the room. Another doll, Anne, enters the room, moves the ball from the basket to a box, and then leaves. If Sally comes back, where will she look for her ball? Children who have developed a TOM understand that their personal knowledge of where the ball is located is different from the knowledge of Sally, who was absent when the ball was moved. They will correctly decide that Sally will look in the basket (see ● Figure 11.16).

Developmental psychologists generally agree that TOM emerges in children around the age of 3 to 4 years, somewhat earlier than the end of Piaget's preoperational period. Although the presence of TOM in even younger children has been hotly debated, finding tasks that are appropriate for testing these age groups is difficult. However, we can identify behaviors in younger children that seem to act as building blocks leading to the achievement of TOM. Joint attention, which includes such behaviors as following another person's gaze with one's own and using pointing to direct another person's attention to something in the environment, emerges in the first year of life (Barresi & Moore, 1996). Others mention the ability of young children to distinguish between living and nonliving objects as another important step in the development of TOM. Finally, young children appear to make distinctions between intentional and unintentional behaviors, because 3-year-olds will imitate the former but not the latter (Williamson, Jaswal, & Meltzoff, 2010).

Regardless of the age at which we decide children have TOM, its existence appears critical to further social development, the topic of our next section. A failure to develop a typical TOM has been linked to the development of autism spectrum disorder, a condition characterized by extreme social difficulties that we discuss in more detail in Chapter 14 (Gopnik, Capps, & Meltzoff, 2000).

How Do Social and Emotional Behaviors Change During Infancy and Childhood?

In contrast to the writings of philosophers such as John Locke and strict behaviorists such as John B. Watson, developmental psychologists believe that children do not begin life as a *tabula rasa,* or "blank slate." Their personal characteristics, many of which are influenced by genetics, immediately predispose them to certain patterns of experience and elicit different reactions from other people. The bold, adventurous, noisy child will seek different activities than the shy, cautious, quiet child, contributing to a different set of experiences in life. Parents, teachers, and peers are likely to respond differently to these two individuals, further shaping their experience, opportunities, and behavior. These interactions among predispositions, the responses the predispositions elicit in others, and resulting experiences converge to produce the adult personality, which we explore in Chapter 12.

Temperament

Children's temperaments reflect their prevailing patterns of mood, activity, and emotional responsiveness. Alexander Thomas and Stella Chess proposed that children showed evidence of different temperaments within the first few months of life (Thomas & Chess, 1977, 1989). The nine separate temperament traits proposed by Thomas and Chess were distilled more recently by Mary Rothbart (2007) and her colleagues into three categories: surgency or extroversion (happy, active, vocal, and social), negative affect or mood (angry, fearful, shy, and frustrated), and effortful control (the ability to pay attention and inhibit behavior). Differences along these initial dimensions predict adult personality. Because these individual differences emerge so early in life, it is likely that they represent genetic differences, a topic we revisit in Chapter 12. In addition, temperaments are predictive of later psychological disorders. Children who are fearful and shy are at greater risk for anxiety disorders and depression, while children who are frequently angry are at greater risk for externalizing disorders, or problems with aggression and self-control (Rothbart, 2007).

Thomas and Chess (1977, 1989) reminded us that children do not develop within a vacuum. While temperament may predispose a child to interact with the environment in certain ways and affect the behavior elicited from caregivers and others, the environment in which children find themselves also has an impact. Thomas and Chess refer to this concept as goodness of fit. Rothbart came to the same conclusion. For example, fearful children with gentle parents develop a stronger internal sense of right and wrong than do fearful children with punitive parents (Rothbart, 2007). Similar interactions between temperament and parenting have also been reported in rhesus monkeys, emphasizing the possible biological and evolutionary contributions to these outcomes (Suomi, 2006). Rhesus infants with a particular genotype were more aggressive, but only if they were raised by their mothers rather than by peers (see ● Figure 11.17).

Temperament interacts not only with the socialization provided by parents but also with the larger-scale socialization provided by culture. In the United States, but not in China, children with higher effortful control showed lower levels of negative affect, such as anger. In

China, but not in the United States, higher effortful control was correlated with less surgency or extroversion (Ahadi, Rothbart, & Ye, 1993).

Attachment

Because of the physical dependency of the human infant on the adult caregiver, maintaining closeness is a high priority. Infants engage in a number of behaviors, such as smiling, cooing, and crying, that are effective in ensuring adult attention.

FIGURE 11.17

Parenting and Temperament Interact. In rhesus monkeys, variations in a gene called monoamine oxidase A (MAOA) are related to aggressive behavior. Monkeys with the low-activity variant are typically more aggressive and attain higher rankings within the monkeys' dominance hierarchy than do monkeys with the high-activity variant of the gene. This relationship is seen when the monkeys are raised normally with their mothers. However, when monkeys are raised in peer groups without contact with their mothers, the relationship is reversed: The monkeys with the high-activity version are more aggressive. This research supports the goodness-of-fit interactions between child temperament and parenting style proposed by Alexander Thomas and Stella Chess and by Mary Rothbart. *Source:* Adapted from "Monoamine Oxidase: A Gene Promoter Variation and Rearing Experience Influences Aggressive Behavior in Rhesus Monkeys," by T. K. Newman, Y. V. Syagailo, C. S. Barr, J. R. Wendland, M. Champoux, M. Graessle, et al., 2005, *Biological Psychiatry, 57*(2), pp. 167–172.

Connecting to Research

The Evolution of Attachment Behavior

THERE IS A BIG DIFFERENCE between a newly hatched goose following its mother because of imprinting and the two-way interactions that promote attachment between human mothers and their newborns, including body contact, mutual gaze, and exaggerated facial expressions. Are these more sophisticated interactions exclusively human? Research evidence suggests that the answer to this question is "no." Rhesus monkeys also show complex mutual behaviors between mothers and their newborns (Ferrari, Paukner, Ionica, & Suomi, 2009).

The Question: Do rhesus monkeys have behaviors that are the equivalent of human mother–infant behaviors that promote bonding?

METHODS

Fourteen mother–infant rhesus monkey pairs were observed while they were living among social groups housed in indoor–outdoor enclosures. Six additional pairs were observed in a more naturalistic setting. For the first 2 months of the infants' lives, the researchers filmed and recorded the frequencies of mutual gaze (infants and mothers making eye contact) and lipsmacking (an important rhesus social behavior).

RESULTS

The rhesus infant–mother pairs engaged in frequent mutual gaze and lipsmacking behaviors. The infants spent more time gazing at their mothers than at other individuals,

and this time increased with the age of the infant. Lipsmacking behavior was also a frequently observed method for mothers and infants to interact with each other. This behavior is never observed among adults, so it is exclusive to interactions with infants.

Mutual gaze and lipsmacking both appear to be sensitive to the age of the infant. By the time the infant is in its second month of life, it is spending considerable time outside the mother's vicinity, much as a human child might do when it attends day care or preschool. As the infant physically separates more frequently from the mother, the frequency of the mutual gaze and lipsmacking behaviors also decreases. The behaviors observed in the enclosed area were

Harry Harlow (1905–1981) studied infant attachment by removing baby rhesus monkeys from their mothers at birth and providing them with a wire mother, such as the one shown here, and a similar mother covered with carpet. Regardless of which "mother" provided food, the infant monkeys spent more time cuddling with the cloth mother than the wire one. Harlow concluded that "contact comfort" provided by the mother was more important to attachment than the food she provided.

Attachment between child and parent is not unique to humans. Harry Harlow (1905–1981) was interested in identifying the behaviors that led to attachment between infants and their mothers, and he investigated attachment in rhesus monkeys (Harlow, 1958). The Freudian theories still popular in Harlow's day suggested that the pleasure obtained through feeding formed the basis of infants' bond with their mothers. Behavioral approaches suggested that the infant was positively reinforced with food for staying near the mother. Harlow was not convinced by either of these arguments and set out to contrast the mother's ability to provide food with her ability to provide comfort, security, and safety.

To observe this distinction between the mother's provision of food and comfort, Harlow removed newborn rhesus monkeys from their biological mothers. The infant monkeys were presented with two surrogate mothers, one made of wire and the other of cloth. Either surrogate could be rigged with a milk bottle, allowing Harlow to investigate all combinations of comfort and feeding. Regardless of which "mother" provided food, infant monkeys spent most of their time clinging to the cloth mother and ran to her immediately when threatened by a novel toy. The wire mothers were visited only if they provided food, and then for only as long as the infant was feeding. Based on his observations, Harlow concluded that the Freudian and behavioral emphasis on feeding was wrong. Instead, the mother's ability to provide contact comfort was critical in forming a strong attachment on the part of her infant.

A key factor in predicting the timing of attachment appears to be mobility. Young birds that are mobile upon hatching need to form immediate attachments to a protective adult. Human infants, who are not particularly mobile until the second half of their first year of life,

attachment Emotional bond linking an infant to a parent or caregiver.

confirmed by observations in the more naturalistic setting.

CONCLUSIONS

Rhesus monkeys show some of the same types of mother–infant interactions, believed to enhance bonding, that have been observed in humans. This finding suggests that behaviors that set the stage for social interactions in humans are not unique to our species but, rather, have their roots in the evolutionary past. ●

Rhesus monkey mothers and infants show many of the same types of behavior that enhance bonding in human mothers and infants, including mutual gaze. *Source:* Reprinted from Ferrari et al. (2009). Reciprocal face-to-face communication between rhesus macaque mothers and their newborn infants. *Current Biology*, 19(20), 1768–1772. Copyright © 2009, with permission from Elsevier.

Secure attachment results from responsive parenting that teaches children that the parent is there for them. Unresponsive parenting teaches children that their needs may or may not be met, so their best strategy is to make regular, frequent, and persistent demands for the parent's attention.

secure attachment A pattern of infant–caregiver bonding in which children explore confidently and return to the parent or caregiver for reassurance.
insecure attachment A pattern of infant–caregiver bonding that can take several forms but is generally characterized as less desirable for the child's outcomes than secure attachment.

have more time to bond with a caregiver. About the same time infants begin to crawl, usually between 6 and 8 months, they also begin to show evidence of having bonded with particular people in the form of separation anxiety (Bowlby, 1969/1982, 1973/1999a, 1973/1999b). Before this stage, infants tolerate being handed around to admiring relatives and babysitters without much protest. Once children demonstrate stranger anxiety, however, they respond to unfamiliar people with crying and distress.

Although stranger anxiety may be a nuisance for parents hiring a new sitter or an insult to visiting relatives, it is an important step forward in infants' social development. The children recognize who does and, more importantly, who does not belong in their social world. Infants who do not make this distinction put themselves at greater risk, because they may venture too far from parents or go off quietly in the company of strangers. As we mentioned in Chapter 7, the timing of separation anxiety appears to be constant across many cultures, which implies that it is an example of a human universal pattern with its roots in biology (Kagan, Kearsley, & Zelazo, 1978).

Several patterns of attachment between infant and caregiver were demonstrated in classic research by Mary Ainsworth and her colleagues (Ainsworth, Blehar, Waters, & Wall, 1978). Young children in a laboratory playroom were observed through a two-way mirror as their mothers or a friendly stranger left or entered the room. Based on the children's reactions to these separations and reunions, their attachment to their mothers was classified as either secure or insecure. Children who demonstrated **secure attachment** played happily and interacted positively with the stranger as long as their mothers were present. However, when their mother left, the children responded by searching for her, crying, and showing other signs of distress. Efforts by a stranger to comfort the children were rejected. When their mother returned, she was greeted warmly, and the children returned to their play.

The remaining children demonstrated different patterns of **insecure attachment**. Two of these, avoidant and anxious–ambivalent attachment, were identified by Ainsworth, and a fourth, disorganized attachment, was identified by other researchers (Main & Solomon, 1986). Children with avoidant attachment did not react to their mother's leaving with distress and allowed themselves to be comforted by the stranger. When the mother returned, the child with an avoidant attachment did not immediately approach her. Children who showed anxious–ambivalent attachment never seemed comfortable, even when their mother was present. Her leaving was greeted with great distress, and the child was alternately clingy and rejecting when she returned. Children with disorganized attachment seemed confused and not well attached. Such children showed contradictory behavior, such as approaching the mother walking backward.

Children's temperament type, discussed previously, interacts with the quality of their attachment to caregivers. Avoidant or anxious–ambivalent attachment is more common in children with high negative affect (Vaughn & Bost, 1999). Because of the challenging aspects of their strong negative emotions, these children might elicit less warm and nurturant behavior on the part of a caregiver. In response to little attention from the caregiver, the infant forms a weaker attachment, and the cycle continues.

Cultural influences on parenting behaviors also influence attachment. Psychologists have compared the frequencies of the attachment types in the United States to frequencies in Japan and Germany (Cole, 1999). The Japanese sample had about the same proportion of securely attached infants as reported by Ainsworth but had higher proportions of anxious–ambivalent attachments and zero cases of avoidant attachment. In Germany, the number of anxious–ambivalent infants was about the same as in the United States, but many more had avoidant attachments. The exact features of each culture's norms responsible for these differences remain to be explored.

What types of parenting behavior might foster secure attachment? When you are in public places, such as parks and malls, take a minute to watch parents interact with their children. Some parents are sensitive and responsive to their children's needs (Cox, Owen, Henderson, & Margand, 1992). The responsive parents are teaching their children that the world is a predictable place in which their parents are there for them when needed. Consequently, these children feel free to explore their environment, knowing that if an emergency arises, they will be able to quickly and reliably obtain assistance from their parents. Small securely attached children have a relatively short radius of exploration, which lengthens gradually as they get older.

Footage from www.davidsonfilms.com

Mary Ainsworth used the "strange situation" to assess the quality of children's attachment to their mothers. While watched through a two-way mirror, the child's mother first leaves and then returns. Using a careful grading scale, researchers rate children as having a secure attachment or one of several variations of insecure attachments.

In contrast, unresponsive or inconsistent parents are teaching their children that the world is an unpredictable place and that the parent may or may not be there for them when needed. In response to such insecure circumstances, children do not venture far from the parent. As suggested by the results of partial reinforcement experiments discussed in Chapter 8, children with unresponsive or inconsistent parents make regular, frequent, and persistent demands for attention, because they know that only a small subset of these demands will be met. It might seem counterintuitive, but ignoring children results in clinginess and constant demands for attention, whereas meeting children's needs promptly and reliably fosters independence.

Although American psychologists view a secure attachment to be ideal, attachment might be better viewed with an ecological approach than with a universal approach. Secure attachment is a good model for relatively safe societies (Belsky, 1999). In a safe society, parents have the time and resources to be attentive to children, and exploration is unlikely to put the children in much danger. In contrast, secure attachments in dangerous societies might be maladaptive. If the environment is dangerous, parents have less opportunity to be responsive to their children, and exploration might put the children in great danger. The message that "The world is an unpredictable place in which we may or may not be able to help you, so stay close" might be more realistic under these circumstances.

Parenting Styles

We rarely face a task as difficult as parenting with so little training or information. We get more guidance about setting up a new computer than about being a good parent. Most parents simply re-create aspects of their own experience, with the more thoughtful parents making a conscious effort to change things that they disliked. If you generally like the way you were parented, chances are that you will feel rather comfortable taking on the parental role. However, if you do not feel that you were treated well by your parents, you might feel somewhat lost when it comes to finding an approach that suits you.

Parenting styles can be divided into four categories. These four parenting styles vary along two dimensions: parental support and behavioral regulation (Baumrind, 1975; Maccoby & Martin, 1983). Parental support takes the form of empathy and recognition of the child's perspective. Behavioral regulation involves supervision of the child's behavior accompanied by consistent discipline and clear expectations (Luyckx et al., 2011).

If we look in the upper left-hand box of Table 11.4, we find the authoritative parenting style, a cross between high parental support and high behavioral regulation. This is the ideal style for parents, as evidenced by the superior outcomes among children raised by parents using this style (Milevsky, Schlechter, Netter, & Keehn, 2007; Simons & Conger, 2007). The authoritative parent is a teacher who disciplines the child with an eye toward making that

HOW DO SOCIAL AND EMOTIONAL BEHAVIORS CHANGE DURING INFANCY AND CHILDHOOD?   **425**

TABLE 11.4 Parenting Styles

	High parental support	Low parental support
High behavioral regulation	Authoritative	Authoritarian
Low behavioral regulation	Indulgent	Uninvolved

© Cengage Learning®

child a productive, prosocial member of the community. Limits are appropriate for the age and stage of the child's development, and consequences are educational, not punitive. For example, a teen who abuses the privilege of using the family car might lose that privilege for a reasonable time. Because of the emphasis on teaching, these parents tend to use little or no physical punishment. They are consistent and firm but also warm and reasonable. They communicate their standards and invite feedback, but there is no question as to who is running the show.

The upper right-hand box contains the cross between low parental support and high behavioral regulation, or the authoritarian parenting style. The high behavioral regulation provided by these parents prepares children for the limits they inevitably meet in the community from other authority figures such as teachers and law enforcement personnel, but this is considered a less-than-ideal approach in most contemporary environments because of lower levels of warmth and support (Luyckx et al., 2011). Authoritarian parents have a greater tendency than authoritative parents to use harsh punishments, including physical punishment. This behavior can prompt some rebelliousness in the child that is not seen as frequently in response to authoritative parents.

Cross-cultural research has found that the impact of authoritarian parenting does not differ between collectivist cultures and individualistic cultures (Sorkhabi, 2005). Authoritarian parenting in China, Egypt, Australia, and the United States is viewed quite similarly by the children exposed to it, and the outcomes for children of authoritarian parents vary little across these cultures. These children tend to have few problems with externalizing (acting out) behaviors, such as drug use. However, compared to children raised in authoritative homes, the children of authoritarian parents have more internalizing symptoms, such as depression (Luyckx et al., 2011).

In the lower left-hand box, we find the indulgent parenting style, produced by crossing high parental support with low behavioral regulation. These parents are warm and loving, but they simply do not want to be the ones who tell their children the dreadful word "no." They are more comfortable letting others, such as teachers, neighbors, and law enforcement, establish rules. Children of indulgent parents are monitored less than children of authoritative and authoritarian parents and show a much higher level of nicotine and alcohol use and antisocial behavior (Luyckx et al., 2011).

The lower right-hand box represents the cross between low parental support and low behavioral regulation, or the uninvolved parenting style. This style generally does not occur unless there is something seriously wrong with the family situation. Illness, marital discord, psychopathology, or substance abuse can prevent parents from carrying out

In her 2011 book *Battle Hymn of the Tiger Mother,* Amy Chua described her initial efforts to raise her daughters in a "strict, Chinese" fashion instead of a Western style emphasizing self-esteem over achievement, followed by adjustments she made in response to her older daughter's rebelliousness at age 13. How do Chua's experiences fit with our discussion of parenting styles?

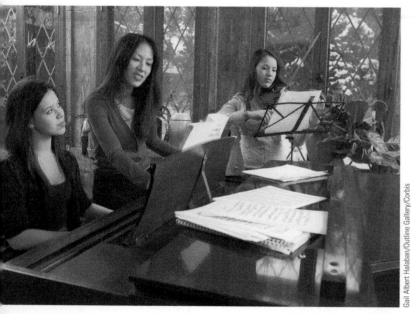

Gail Albert Halaban/Outline Gallery/Corbis

their duties in regard to children. As a result of the incapacity of the parent, the children are basically ignored. In extreme cases, neglect may require the intervention of social services to maintain the health and safety of the child. By the 12th grade, children of uninvolved parents drink and smoke nearly twice as much as children of authoritarian or authoritative parents, and sons of uninvolved parents are at a very high risk of antisocial behavior (Luyckx et al., 2011; see ● Figure 11.18).

Does a parent consistently stay in the same box? The answer to that question is "no." Life circumstances can radically change a parent's style. A competent parent can be thrown off balance by loss of a job, poor health, divorce, or other disruptions. Once the challenging circumstances are resolved, we would expect that parent to get back on track. What if a person's parents each use a different style? Although this does happen occasionally, most couples share a common style of parenting (Milevsky et al., 2007). If the parents do have differing styles, the presence of one authoritative parent can protect the children from the negative outcomes associated with other styles (Milevsky et al., 2007).

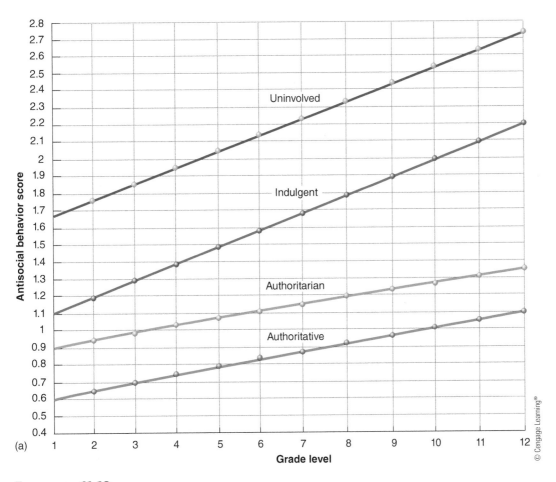

FIGURE 11.18

Parenting Style and Child Outcomes. Authoritative and authoritarian parenting styles are associated with lower rates of antisocial behavior in children than the indulgent or uninvolved parenting styles. However, children with authoritarian parents experience more depression and withdrawal than do children of authoritative parents. *Source:* Adapted from "Parenting and Trajectories of Children's Maladaptive Behaviors: A 12-Year Prospective Community Study," by K. Luyckx, E. A. Tildesley, B. Soenens, J. A. Andrews, S. E. Hampson, M. Peterson, et al., 2011, *Journal of Clinical Child and Adolescent Psychology, 40*(3), pp. 468–478.

Summary 11.2 Highlights of Childhood Development

Aspect of development	Highlights
Physical development	• Height and weight increase rapidly. • Both gray and white matter in the brain increase. • Motor control improves from head to toe and from the midline outward to the periphery of the body.
Cognitive development	• Children demonstrate naïve theories. • Children learn language rapidly. • Assimilation and accommodation of information build better concepts. • Thought becomes more logical and abstract.
Social and emotional development	• Temperament shapes initial responses to the environment. • Children form secure and insecure attachments to caregivers. • Parenting styles interact with temperament.

Credits: Top Row. Robin Moore/National Geographic Collective. Second Row. Lew Merrim/Science Source. Bottom Row: Nina Leen/Getty Images.

What Does It Mean to Be an Adolescent?

Adolescence is an artificial, arbitrary period of development that is a relatively recent phenomenon in human experience. In hunter–gatherer societies, sexual maturity at puberty signaled the young person's entry into adult roles, privileges, and expectations. Our word *puberty* comes from the Latin word for "adult."

Although adolescence is assumed to begin with puberty, we do not have much consensus regarding its endpoint. Legally, an 18-year-old is an adult in the United States. However, we restrict legal alcohol consumption to those over 21, and rental car companies rarely rent cars to young adults under the age of 25. In the United Kingdom, child psychologists are now allowed to work with people up to the age of 25 years. Lifestyle factors associated with adulthood, such as financial independence from parents, separate living arrangements, marriage, and parenthood, are far more descriptive of the end of adolescence than age.

Two factors have resulted in an extended period of adolescence in modern, industrial societies, such that it starts earlier and ends later than in the past. One is the dramatic decrease in the age at which **puberty** occurs. Over the last 100 years, the average age of puberty in the United States has dropped from about age 16 to around age 12 (Frisch, 1983; see ● Figure 11.19). For people living 100 years ago, taking on adult roles around the age of puberty was more realistic than it would be today. A second factor contributing to the length of modern adolescence is the extended period of education and training needed in technological societies. Youth at puberty are simply not prepared to assume adult roles in most modern cultures.

adolescence A period of development beginning at puberty and ending at young adulthood.
puberty A period of physical changes leading to sexual maturity.

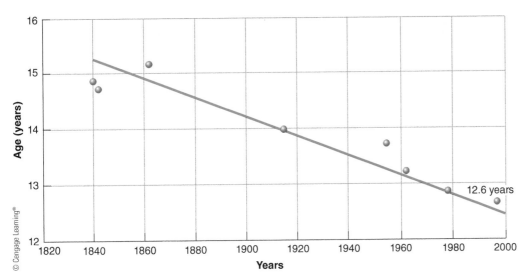

FIGURE 11.19

The Age of Puberty Has Decreased Over the Last 100 Years. Since 1840, the average age of first menstruation, a major indicator of puberty in females, has dropped from nearly 16 years to its current average of 12.6 years.

Physical Changes in Adolescence

Physical changes in adolescence provide individuals with their final preparation for taking on adult roles. Among the most striking physical changes in this period are those related to sexual maturity and brain development.

Sex and the Adolescent The onset of puberty is marked by a cascade of hormone release, culminating in the maturity of reproductive organs and the development of **secondary sex characteristics**. Males experience muscular development, maturity of the external genitalia, growth of facial hair, and enlargement of the larynx, which leads to a deeper voice. Females experience breast growth, maturity of the external genitalia, maturity of the uterus, and changes in fat distribution and quantity. Menarche, or the first menstrual cycle, occurs relatively late in the puberty process for girls. In response to the same hormones, skeletal growth for both boys and girls begins to slow down. Individuals experiencing early puberty stop growing at an earlier age.

The obvious evolutionary purpose of puberty is to prepare an individual for sex, so not too surprisingly, teens respond to the physical changes of puberty with a dramatic increase in sex drive. For the hunter–gatherer, no conflicts occurred, because the assumption of adult roles, including adult sexual relationships, coincided with these feelings. With modern children experiencing puberty as young as 7 or 8 years old, however, we face challenges that are relatively new in our evolutionary history.

Sexual maturation during the teen years parallels further development in gender identity, the assumption of sex-role behaviors, and sexual orientation. As we discussed in Chapter 7, sexual orientation refers to a stable pattern of attraction to people of a certain sex, independent of gender identity, sex-role behavior, and sexual experiences. Gender identity refers to a person's sense of being male or female, and sex-role behavior refers to a pattern of traditionally male or female behavior. Many variations in combinations of these variables occur. People with a homosexual orientation typically demonstrate a gender identity consistent with their biological sex, while showing the same range of variation in sex-role behaviors, from traditionally masculine to traditionally feminine, as people with a heterosexual orientation.

The Adolescent Brain Early developmental psychologists, including Piaget, argued that cognition is rather mature at puberty, which in turn implies that the brain is mature. In some aspects this conclusion is correct. By the teens, areas of the brain that process language, spatial relations, hearing, and other sensory processes appear complete. However, much additional work remains to be done before we can consider the brain to be fully adult. Far from considering the brain complete at puberty, today's psychologists are viewing the early teen years as

The physical growth that accompanies the onset of adolescence does not happen to everyone at the same time. Middle school students show a range of physical maturity.

secondary sex characteristics Physical changes occurring at puberty associated with sexual maturity.

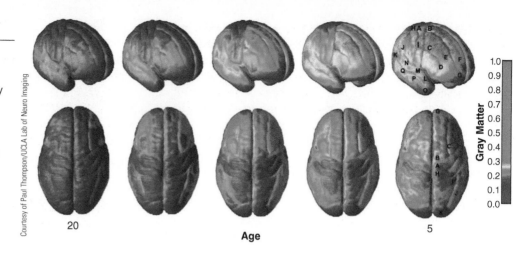

Gray Matter

1.0
0.9
0.8
0.7
0.6
0.5
0.4
0.3
0.2
0.1
0.0

20

Age

5

FIGURE 11.20

Brain Growth in Adolescence. In contrast to early developmental theories such as Jean Piaget's theory that viewed the mind as mature at the outset of adolescence, gray matter growth continues into early adulthood, although the pace slows and the cortex thins in some areas. Areas shown in red and yellow are experiencing the greatest rates of growth.

being a second critical period of brain growth (the first being prenatally up to age 18 months; Kuhn, 2008).

The onset of puberty is accompanied by substantial gray matter growth, which peaks between the ages of 11 and 12 years. Following this burst of growth, the gray matter normally thins somewhat over the remainder of the teen years (see ● Figure 11.20). Abnormalities in this process may be associated with the onset of schizophrenia, described in Chapter 14. Youth with early-onset forms of this disorder show 4 times more loss of gray matter in the frontal lobes than is usually seen in teens of the same age (Rapoport et al., 1999). White matter, or myelin, continues to mature through the teen years and into young adulthood. Myelination of the frontal lobes is greater in adults 23 to 30 years old than in youth between the ages of 12 and 16. Unfortunately, an adolescent's white matter is more susceptible than an adult's to damage, such as that caused by binge drinking (McQueeny et al., 2009).

Structural differences between the brains of teens and those of adults affect their interpretations of the emotions of other people. Functional magnetic resonance imaging (fMRI) has been used to observe brain activity in adolescents and young adults while they react to photographs of facial expressions of emotion (Thomas, De Bellis, Graham, & LaBar, 2007; Yurgelun-Todd, 2007). Adults identified the expressed emotions accurately, but teens frequently misunderstood the emotions being displayed. The amygdala, which provides a quick, subconscious assessment of emotion, showed the same pattern of activity in adults and teens. However, the adults showed more activity in the frontal lobes than the teens did, which might account for the adults' superior judgment of emotional expression.

The earlier maturation of the emotional parts of the brain, such as the amygdala, relative to the logical frontal lobes might account for some "risky" behaviors that characterize the teen years, such as reckless and drunk driving, driving without seatbelts, experimenting with drugs, and having unprotected sex. Risky behavior does not result from the teen's inability to judge what is risky or not. If anything, teens view life as more risky than it is and vastly overestimate their personal risks for becoming crime victims or dying in the near future (Fischhoff, de Bruin, Parker, Millstein, & Halpern-Felsher, 2010). At the same time, teens typically believe that they are somehow immune from the consequences of risky behavior—for example, that drunk driving accidents happen to other people (Reyna & Farley, 2006). The teen brain also responds more vigorously to pleasure than does the adult brain, which means that the immediate pleasurable consequences of a risky behavior can overwhelm the teen's "better judgment" (Galvan, Hare, Voss, Glover, & Casey, 2007).

Cognitive and Moral Development in Adolescence

The continuing maturity of the nervous system, interacting with the expanding physical and social environment of the adolescent, leads to more adult ways of thinking and reasoning.

Adolescent Cognition During adolescence, both working memory and reaction time reach adult levels. Teens' problem-solving abilities continue to improve. While we all use heuristics, or rules of thumb that provide shortcuts to a solution, adolescents begin to think more logically or analytically (Kokis, Macpherson, Toplak, West, & Stanovich, 2002). For example, children often use their personal experience as a heuristic (the teacher didn't catch my friend cheating on the test, so it's safe for me to cheat too) instead of the more logical, statistical reasoning of the teen (my friend might have had a lucky break, but this teacher is extra good at catching cheaters, so my odds of getting caught remain high despite my friend's experience).

Teens are hard at work acquiring data, and as they build up their knowledge bases, their ability to use executive processes such as strategies improves (Peverly, Brobst, & Morris, 2002). As we mentioned in Chapter 9, the more you know about a subject, the easier it becomes to learn new things about it. You acquire skills specific to a subject, such as how to solve statistics problems or prepare for a final covering thousands of pages of reading in your literature course.

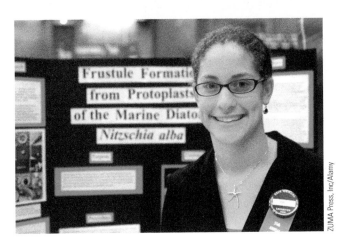

Adolescence is when youths apply their new executive strategies to problems and build their knowledge base for specific subjects. High school senior Ronit Abramson won an Intel International Science and Engineering Fair prize for her science project on marine biology.

Moral Reasoning Our human history and literature are filled with heroes and villains, and we are fascinated by their development. How does one child grow to be Mother Teresa and another to be Adolf Hitler?

Lawrence Kohlberg, a student of Piaget's, attempted to extend Piaget's theory of cognition to explain the development of moral reasoning (Kohlberg, 1981, 1984). To assess changes in moral reasoning, Kohlberg presented children, adolescents, and adults with a number of ethical dilemmas. He was not as interested in the choice participants would make in response to the dilemma as he was in the reasoning participants provided their choice. Consider the following dilemma and imagine the choices you might make:

> In Europe, a woman was near death from a very bad disease, a special kind of cancer. There was one drug that the doctors thought might save her. It was a form of radium that a druggist in the same town had recently discovered. The drug was expensive to make, but the druggist was charging 10 times what the drug cost him to make. He paid $200 for the radium and charged $2,000 for a small dose of the drug. The sick woman's husband, Heinz, went to everyone he knew to borrow the money, but he could get together only about $1,000, which was half of what it cost. He told the druggist that his wife was dying and asked him to sell it cheaper or let him pay later. But the druggist said, "No, I discovered the drug and I'm going to make money from it." Heinz got desperate and broke into the man's store to steal the drug for his wife.

Based on the participants' responses, Kohlberg identified three major stages in moral reasoning, shown in Table 11.5. Children and young adolescents are typically in the **preconventional morality** stage. In this stage, children make moral choices based on their expectations of reward and punishment. Their advice to Heinz might be to steal the drug, because letting your wife die is bad, or to avoid stealing because he might be punished for it. Some individuals never progress beyond this stage, even in adulthood, and believe that stealing or cheating is OK as long as they don't get caught.

Kohlberg believed that during adolescence, most of the population moves to the next stage, **conventional morality**, and stays there throughout adulthood. In this stage, rules are seen as governing moral behavior and are therefore to be followed. Conventionally moral people are also sensitive to public opinion. They want to do the right thing so that others will approve of their behavior. Heinz might be advised to steal the drug or not based on how others would view his behavior. Although conventional morality adds to the stability of a society, it runs the risk of being arbitrary and rigid. In addition, history is full of situations in which local public opinion was supportive of morally abhorrent activities, such as genocide or slavery.

The final step of moral development for Kohlberg was **postconventional morality**. Relatively few people, according to Kohlberg, attain this stage. In conjunction with the abstract reasoning of formal operations, the individual now recognizes that rules are made by humans and can therefore be flawed. Consequently, personal standards are used as reference points. If

preconventional morality Lawrence Kohlberg's stage at which moral choices are made according to expectations of reward or punishment.
conventional morality Lawrence Kohlberg's stage of moral development in which moral choices are made according to law or public opinion.
postconventional morality Lawrence Kohlberg's stage at which moral choices are made according to personal standards and reason.

| 11.5 | Lawrence Kohlberg's Stages of Moral Development |

Stage	Features
Preconventional	Uses probability of rewards and punishments to guide behavior
Conventional	Maintains reputation and follows the law
Postconventional	Follows self-chosen ethical principles

© Cengage Learning®

everybody used postconventional reasoning to select a driving speed on the highway, chaos would ensue. However, the postconventional thinker is likely to evaluate laws and rules critically before complying with them. In the case of Heinz, the legal aspects of theft would be given less attention than the morality of the druggist's request for compensation and Heinz's request for special consideration for his wife.

Kohlberg is not without his critics. Postconventional reasoning has been criticized as characteristic of males in Europe and the United States, rather than representing a universal stage of moral development (Murphy, Gilligan, & Puka, 1994). Children and adults living in the United States give responses to Kohlberg's dilemmas consistent with the culture's emphasis on personal justice and individual rights. Other cultures place a higher priority on interpersonal factors, such as duty and responsibility to others, and these values can lead to different responses to ethical dilemmas (Miller & Bersoff, 1992).

Social and Emotional Development in Adolescence

As the teen prepares to transition to adulthood, questions emerge about what kind of adult to be. The focus of social activity begins to shift from the family to the peer group, which is where most adult interaction will be taking place.

Many teens explore questions of identity by trying on different roles and affiliating with different groups.

Image Source/Alamy

Identity Formation in Adolescence We pick up social development in adolescence by introducing Erik Erikson, a student of Sigmund Freud who outlined stages of social development beginning in infancy, shown in Table 11.6. Erikson made significant contributions to our understanding of **identity**, or a unified, consistent sense of self (Erikson, 1968). For Erikson, social development proceeds in stages, with each stage characterized by a fork in the road between a positive outcome and a less than desirable outcome. Adolescence challenges teens to develop a sense of identity (the positive outcome). If they fail, the result is role confusion (obviously, the less desirable outcome).

Teens begin the process of identity formation by asking such questions as "Who am I?" and "What kind of person do I want to be?" These are profound questions, made possible by the newly developed abstract reasoning skills of the teen. The answers are not immediately apparent. Considerable exploration may be necessary before the teen discovers a direction. Many teens may try on a number of identities, from jock to nerd to goth, before finding one that works.

Because developing an identity may be somewhat unpleasant, teens may be tempted to short-circuit the process. One technique for prematurely adopting an identity is to assume the

identity A consistent, unified sense of self.

TABLE

11.6 Erik Erikson's Psychosocial Stages

Stage	Challenge	Description
Birth to 18 months	Trust versus mistrust	Children view the world as a safe, dependable place.
18 months to 3 years	Autonomy versus shame and doubt	Children begin to explore.
3–6 years	Initiative versus guilt	Children begin to act on the world.
6–12 years	Industry versus inferiority	Children develop self-confidence.
Adolescence	Identity versus role confusion	Teens begin to form an identity by asking "Who am I?" Failure to achieve a stable identity leads to role confusion and problems with subsequent stages.
Young adulthood	Intimacy versus isolation	Young adults with clear identities form stable, intimate relationships, while others experience feelings of loneliness and isolation.
Midlife	Generativity versus stagnation	Midlife adults who find value in their lives, even if they have not met all their earlier goals, experience generativity. They are likely to "put back" energy into family, work, and community.
Late adulthood	Integrity versus despair	Toward the end of life, adults who feel that they have lived fully experience a sense of integrity and calm.

© Cengage Learning®

identity of a group (Erikson, 1968). By affiliating with a particular club, clique, or gang, teens take on a preformed identity and avoid the challenges of finding their individual identities. A second approach is the adoption of readymade identities provided by parents or other mentors. Although parents may have valuable advice regarding choice of college major and career, these are highly individual choices with significant implications. In one tragic instance, a young man was told by his parents from an early age that he should be a physician. He was provided with a doctor's coat and gear as a Halloween costume and was introduced to friends and family members as "our future MD." When the young man began to fail his first-semester premed courses, he attempted suicide to avoid facing his disappointed parents. Fortunately, the attempt was unsuccessful. In subsequent counseling, therapists helped him identify his special talent for helping troubled youth. The young man obtained his teaching credential and has achieved notable success in working with inner-city youth.

The Benefits of Ethnic Identity   For many adolescents, ethnic identity, or how an individual feels about being a member of a particular ethnic or racial group, is a major part of their overall identity (see ● Figure 11.21). As we will see in Chapter 13, having an ethnic identity boosts the overall self-esteem of adolescents and young adults.

An ethnic identity is usually the outcome of an adolescent's exploration of what it means to be a part of the group and a sense of belonging to that group. Many environmental factors contribute to this experience, including family attitudes and the extent of exposure to peers of the same ethnicity (Kiang, Witkow, Baldelomar, & Fuligni, 2010). Ethnic identities differ in centrality, or the degree to which an individual feels pride in and connection with a group (Charmaraman & Grossman, 2010).

A growing number of individuals identify with more than one ethnic or racial group. Psychologists are investigating this multiethnic experience to see what changes might be required in their theories of ethnic identity development (Shih & Sanchez, 2009).

Family and Peer Influences   Running parallel to the search for identity is a tendency on the part of teens to spend more time with peers and less with family. Although this preference

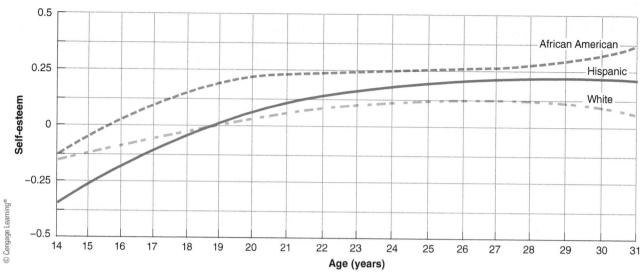

FIGURE 11.21

Ethnic Identity May Lead to Higher Self-Esteem. Identifying with an ethnic group appears to boost the overall self-esteem of African American and Hispanic teens during adolescence and young adulthood. *Source:* Adapted from "Self-Esteem Development From Age 14 to 30 Years: A Longitudinal Study," by R. Y. Erol and U. Orth, 2011, *Journal of Personality and Social Psychology, 101*(3), pp. 607–619. doi:10.1037/ a0024299.

can be upsetting for the parents, especially if the peers are not to their liking, it may be viewed as a natural step in teen development. After all, most significant social relationships in adulthood will be with age peers, rather than individuals who are years older or younger. This affiliation with peers can be taken too far, however, because there is evidence that teens who continue to interact regularly with their parents, such as having regular dinners together, are more likely than teens who don't interact much with parents to avoid pitfalls of substance abuse (see ● Figure 11.22) and promiscuity (Fulkerson et al., 2006). A healthy balance between family and peer influences appears to produce the best outcomes.

The importance of the peer group to adolescents can be demonstrated by their heightened sensitivity to peer exclusion. Compared to adults over the age of 22, adolescents reported significantly worse mood following an experimental procedure designed to instill feelings of social exclusion (Blakemore & Mills, 2014). Teens are also more susceptible than adults to negative peer influence. Compared to young adults and older adults, adolescents made many more risky decisions when in the presence of peer than while alone (Chein, Albert, O'Brien, Uckert, & Steinberg, 2011; Simons-Morton et al., 2014).

In contrast to popular press accounts of the "stormy" teen years, most teens (and their parents) navigate their passage to adulthood with no more than a few bumps and bruises (Steinberg & Levine, 1997). "Generation gaps" may occur, but teens typically do not deviate too far from their parents' values. Research indicates that most teens love their parents, feel

FIGURE 11.22

Family Remains Important in Adolescence. As teens begin to spend more time in the company of peers, balancing that experience with time spent with family is associated with lower risk for substance abuse and other common teen problems. In 2007, 59% of teens reported eating at least five dinners per week with their families. *Source:* http://www .casacolumbia.org/addiction-research/ reports/importance-of-family- dinners-2007

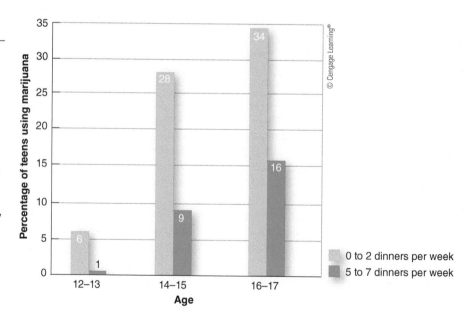

loved by their parents in return, share many of their parents' values, and turn to them regularly for advice. Even "rebellious" teens rarely go in the opposite direction from their parents. Few of the student radicals of the 1960s were the offspring of conservative parents (Troll, Neugarten, & Kraines, 1969). Instead, these young people were slightly more to the left of their already left-leaning parents.

What Is It Like to Be a Young Adult?

As we mentioned previously, defining the exact point when a person becomes an adult is not easy. In developing nations, marriage remains the dominant marker for adulthood, but in industrialized nations, numerous roles are considered, including the completion of education, full-time employment, independent living, marriage, and parenthood. People do not usually assume all these roles simultaneously, leading to a gradual emergence of adulthood over a period of several years.

The timing of many of these milestones has changed over time. In 1970, the average age of a first-time mother in the United States was 21, but this rose to 25 by 2006 (Mathews & Hamilton, 2009). If you reacted to this statistic by thinking, "Oh, that's still too young," it is likely that you are responding to a social clock, or your sense of the "right" time for taking on a role. Compared to their parents' generation, contemporary young adults believe that adult roles should be assumed at later ages and that the social clock is more flexible (Peterson, 1996).

Physical Status

The young adult has reached the pinnacle of physical development. If you are in this age group, you are as tall, strong, and fit as you're ever likely to be. Your brain is mature, and your senses and reaction time are in excellent shape.

Unfortunately, nothing lasts forever. Age-related loss of muscle mass typically begins as early as 25 years of age, and about 3% to 5% of muscle mass is lost in each subsequent decade of life (Nair, 1995). Not too surprisingly, relatively few over-40 football players remain in the NFL. It is not too early for young adults to consider how to best maintain their physical health. Through childhood and adolescence, we have seen that physical development often follows a blueprint that is strongly genetic. In adulthood, however, lifestyle factors begin to play a greater role in a person's outcomes. In a longitudinal study of more than 20,000 adults, following four simple steps added 14 years to life: eating fruits and vegetables, not smoking, drinking alcohol moderately if at all (fewer than two drinks per day for men and fewer than one drink daily for women), and exercising (defined in the study as 1 hour per week; Khaw et al., 2008).

Cognition in Young Adulthood: Postformal Thought

In your college experience, you might have seen a professor become annoyed by a student's inquiry about "the right answer." The search for a single answer, however, is characteristic of formal operations as described by Piaget. At this stage of cognitive development, the teen can follow a logical course of steps to solve a problem (Guignard & Lubart, 2006; Wu & Chiou, 2008). Lack of agreement with the solution is viewed by the formal operational thinker as a sign that the solution is incorrect.

Although many questions we face in college have right answers, such as an element's atomic weight or whether a hypothesis was shown to be incorrect, many more are open to debate. The professor's frustration with your fellow student's interest in only one right answer reflects a difference in adolescent versus adult thinking, or postformal thought. Postformal thought recognizes that the "right answer" is often "it depends" and that many important questions are complex and ambiguous (King & Kitchener, 2002). Adolescents are more likely to think in absolutes and defer to authorities, such as professors (Perry, 1970). Efforts to move

Cultura Creative/Alamy

Becoming a parent is no longer restricted to young adulthood. In 1970, the average age of first-time mothers was 21, and few women became mothers after the age of 35. Today, many women are postponing parenting until midlife.

adolescents toward independent, postformal thought are often described as critical thinking exercises, described in Chapter 2.

Why is it important to embrace postformal ways of thinking? In Chapter 2, we discussed the importance of generating and testing new hypotheses to move science forward. Using formal operations, a student can evaluate a hypothesis and conclude whether it needs to be rejected. However, postformal thinking is an integral part of creativity, in science or in any other field (Guignard & Lubart, 2006). Scientists who are unable to look beyond the "right answers" already existing in their fields are unlikely to make creative contributions that stretch that knowledge.

Relationships in Young Adulthood

As teens enter young adulthood, Erickson suggests that they confront a new challenge: intimacy versus isolation. Frequently, the search for intimacy concludes with marriage and the establishment of a family. Those who fail to find the level of intimacy they seek might experience feelings of loneliness, which in turn can elicit behaviors that are more likely to alienate others instead of promoting intimacy (Cacioppo & Hawkley, 2005). One key to successful intimacy, according to Erikson, is to have established a solid identity in adolescence. If you still don't know who you are, it is unlikely that you will make good judgments about the type of person who will make you happy.

Current trends in the United States include diverse approaches to intimacy and family. In addition to forming traditional families that include two biological parents and their children, large numbers of people are choosing to remain single, live together without being married, be single parents, have children without being married, divorce, and remarry. Along with these changes, public attitudes regarding the question "What is a family?" continue to change. In the United States, 80% of the public consider an unmarried couple with children to be a family (see ● Figure 11.24), although only 43% consider an unmarried couple without children to constitute a family (Pew Research Center, 2010).

Thinking Scientifically

Are Millennials or Gen Yers More Narcissistic Than Previous Generations?

TODAY'S EMERGING ADULTS have been classified as members of the millennial and Gen-Y generation, or those born after 1980. Since the time of Aristotle, it has been almost a tradition to despair over the traits of young people. The millennials have been described alternately as the newest "greatest generation" because of their information-seeking and multitasking abilities but also as "generation whine," whose overprotective parents have raised fragile offspring with no tolerance for adversity (Dannar, 2013). Cohorts like the millennials, and the baby boomers and Gen Xers that preceded them, are shaped by their experience. Social trends have the greatest influence on the young (Twenge, 2013). What effects have the last decades had on emerging adults?

Jean Twenge (2013) argues that despite the technology that connects us around the clock, the U.S. culture is becoming more individualistic and self-oriented. Television shows are more likely to focus on fame, books use more individualistic language than previously, and song lyrics are more narcissistic and antisocial. In response to these cultural trends, Twenge argues that millennials show higher rates of narcissism, or an unrealistically positive, inflated view of the self. Narcissistic personality disorder is quite rare, but scores on scales that measure narcissistic traits are increasing (see ● Figure 11.23).

Increased narcissism has been accompanied by less empathy and more self-oriented behavior, such as increases in elective plastic surgery, cheating in school, and the desire to have authority over others.

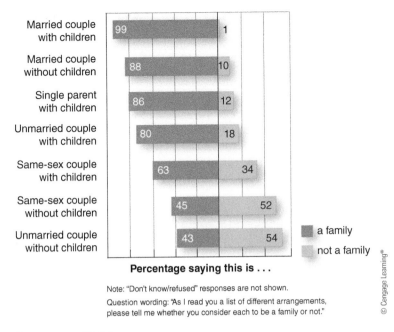

Percentage saying this is . . .

Note: "Don't know/refused" responses are not shown.

Question wording: "As I read you a list of different arrangements, please tell me whether you consider each to be a family or not."

© Cengage Learning®

FIGURE 11.24

What Is a Family? American attitudes about what constitutes a *family,* a term once restricted to two parents living with their biological children, continue to change and expand to recognize diverse approaches to intimacy. *Source:* Adapted from "The Decline of Marriage and Rise of New Families," by Pew Research Center, 2010, from http://www.pewsocialtrends.org/2010/11/18/the-decline-of-marriage-and-rise-of-new-families/.

For those who do choose to have children, the experience of being parents often dominates much of their adult lives. Although most parents are quite happy with their choice to take on this role, many young couples experience a drop in marital satisfaction as they adjust to new responsibilities (Goldscheider & Waite, 1991). After all, it's rather difficult to feel attractive for your partner with peanut butter and jelly in your hair. Marital satisfaction decreases when children are quite young (see ● Figure 11.25) and rebounds when children become more independent. Couples who describe their relationships as successful experience milder impacts from having children.

Narcissism is linked to significant interpersonal problems, including reduced commitment to romantic relationships and increased aggression within those relationships (Keller et al., 2014).

Whether you think Twenge is being fair, is there something we could do to reduce narcissism? Twenge argues that efforts to artificially boost self-esteem (see Chapter 12), such as participation trophies and telling everyone they are "special," should be abandoned. Instead, she advocates emphasis on building empathy and becoming involved in larger social issues. ●

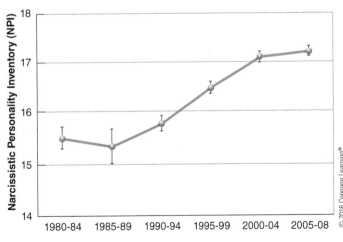

FIGURE 11.23

Millennials and Narcissism. Scores on the Narcissistic Personality Inventory (NPI) have risen since 1990. Twenge, J. M. (2013). The Evidence for Generation Me and Against Generation We. *Emerging Adulthood, 1*(1), 11-16. doi: 10.1177/2167696812466548

© 2016 Cengage Learning®

What Happens During Midlife?

Just as our criteria for leaving adolescence for young adulthood were somewhat vague, we do not have a set of reliable characteristics that signal the transition between young and middle adulthood. Some people view a specific age, such as 40, as a starting point for midlife. Psychologists often point to physical changes, such as graying hair or menopause in women, as signposts for this new transition. Others suggest that a person's growing sense of mortality, possibly boosted by the death of a parent, leads to a feeling of being closer to death than to birth (Jaques, 1965).

As with the urban myths about the "storm" of adolescence, you have probably heard popular accounts assuming that we all have some "midlife crisis" (Levinson, Darrow, Klein, Levinson, & McKee, 1974). For most people, this is simply not true (Rosenberg, Rosenberg, & Farrell, 1999). Middle adulthood is not without its challenges, because many adults find themselves simultaneously caring for children and aging parents, working to meet their career and financial goals, and dealing with physical and possibly marital changes. However, there appears to be no evidence for a large-scale crisis associated with any one age.

 Experiencing Psychology

What Type of Parent Might You Be?

IN TABLE 11.7, select the number that most closely matches your feelings. Your first reaction to each question should be your answer.

The scale you just completed is a subtest of the Adult Adolescent Parenting Inventory 2 (AAPI-2; Bavolek & Keene, 1999). The complete AAPI-2 has four subscales: lack of empathy, value corporal punishment, oppressing power and independence, and role reversal. The preceding subscale measures role reversals, or expectations about the child meeting the parents' needs instead of the parent meeting the child's needs. Higher scores indicate greater expectations that the child has responsibilities for the parents' well-being. Responses to these items vary among ethnic groups; white Americans have the lowest scores, followed by Hispanics, African Americans, Asian Indians, and Asians (Jambunathan, Burts, & Pierce, 2000). None of the groups had positive scores, indicating that all groups generally disagreed with these statements.

As with any pencil-and-paper test you take, the results of this one should not form the basis of life-changing decisions. As you can imagine, this test is subject to large social desirability effects when the results are not confidential, as they are in the real research studies. Most people are going to give the answers they are expected to give. ●

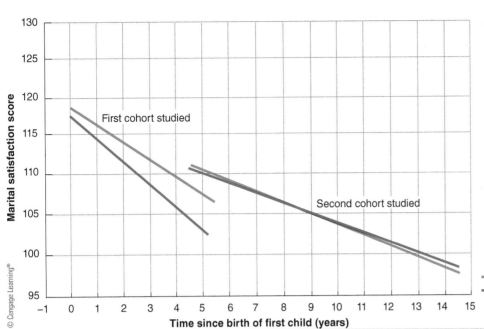

FIGURE 11.25

Marital Satisfaction Drops During Parenting. Couples typically experience a drop in marital satisfaction after the birth of a first child. In this longitudinal study that followed two groups, or cohorts, of participants, marital satisfaction continued to drop up to the first child's 15th birthday. Couples whose marital satisfaction was higher as newlyweds are more likely to weather these challenges than couples whose relationship was rocky from the outset. *Source:* Adapted from "Marital Satisfaction Across the Transition to Parenthood," by E. Lawrence, A. D. Rothman, R. J. Cobb, M. T. Rothman, and T. N. Bradbury, 2008, *Journal of Family Psychology, 22*(1), pp. 41–50. doi:10.1037/0893-3200.22.1.41.

—— Wives
—— Husbands

TABLE 11.7 — Parenting Inventory

Select the number that most closely matches your feelings. Your first reaction to each question should be your answer.

1. Children should offer comfort when their parents are sad.

−2	−1	0	1	2
Strongly disagree				Strongly agree

2. Children need to be potty trained as soon as they are 2 years old.

−2	−1	0	1	2
Strongly disagree				Strongly agree

3. Children should be considerate of their parents' needs.

−2	−1	0	1	2
Strongly disagree				Strongly agree

4. In a father's absence, the son needs to become the man of the house.

−2	−1	0	1	2
Strongly disagree				Strongly agree

5. Older children should be responsible for the care of their younger brothers and sisters.

−2	−1	0	1	2
Strongly disagree				Strongly agree

6. Children should know when their parents are tired.

−2	−1	0	1	2
Strongly disagree				Strongly agree

7. Children should be considerate of their parents' needs.

−2	−1	0	1	2
Strongly disagree				Strongly agree

To evaluate your score, add up your responses to all seven items, giving you possible scores between −14 and +14.

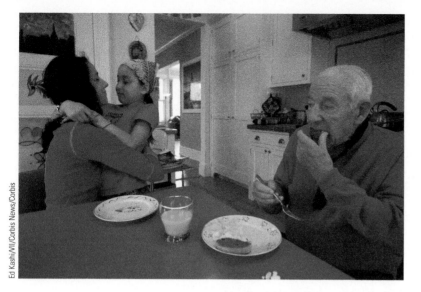

Physical and Cognitive Aspects of Midlife

The major theme of physical and cognitive development in midlife is stability. Assuming that people maintain good health, changes in the physical and cognitive domains tend to be mild and gradual.

The most significant physical change in midlife for women is the end of their ability to reproduce. **Menopause** is the point where menstruation stops. For most women, menopause is complete in their early 50s, but loss of fertility is a gradual process beginning many years earlier. Menstrual cycles may become irregular in a woman's 40s as her sex hormone levels that regulate the cycles begin to drop. During the period of transition between the start of irregular periods and the final disappearance of menstruation, women can experience a number of physical and psychological symptoms. Hot flashes, night sweats, headaches, joint pain, mood swings, and sleep disturbances are common complaints, and the severity of these issues can range from barely noticeable to nearly disabling. Hormone treatments to offset these symptoms are used quite cautiously, because they can also increase a woman's risk of stroke, heart attack, breast cancer, and later dementia (Banks & Canfell, 2009).

Men experience more gradual changes in their reproductive status through the remainder of their lives. Sperm quantity may be reduced, but men in their 80s remain half as fertile as men who are 25. Most men experience little to no decrease in testosterone over the course of the midlife years, although other conditions, such as diabetes, can interfere with the maintenance of an active sex life. For both men and women in midlife, the availability of a partner is more predictive of sexual activity than any health issues (Karraker, DeLamater, & Schwartz, 2011).

With increasing life expectancies on one side and later parenthood on the other, many contemporary midlife adults find themselves "sandwiched," or caring for their aging parents and growing children at the same time.

menopause The complete cessation of a woman's menstrual cycles.

Social Changes in Midlife

In contrast to the relative stability in the physical and cognitive domains during midlife, this period of life is characterized by significant changes in social and work roles. Children grow up and move out. If you are the youngest child in your family, you may have noticed that your parents are beginning to feel somewhat more relaxed. For many parents, the "empty nest" period following

FIGURE 11.26

Responses to the Empty Nest Vary Across Cultures. Although most Americans report positive reactions to their last child leaving home, reactions vary across cultures. Among Canadians of different ethnic groups, being an empty-nest parent has different meanings. Parents from Chinese and Southern European cultures are less likely to report negative responses to their last child leaving home than are parents with a British background. Parents from India experienced the most negative response of all groups studied. *Source:* Adapted from "The Empty Nest Syndrome in Midlife Families," by B. A. Mitchell and L. D. Lovegreen, 2009, *Journal of Family Issues, 30*(12), 1651–1670. doi:10.1177/0192513x09339020.

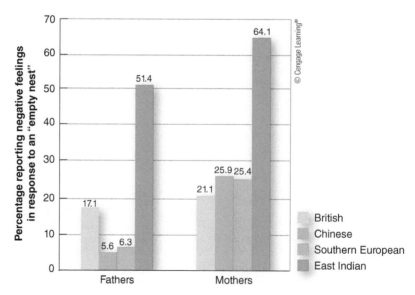

their last child leaving home is accompanied by an improvement in marital satisfaction (Birchler, 1992). Your parents no doubt love you, but they're also relieved to have many of the responsibilities of parenting behind them. However, as ● Figure 11.26 shows, the likelihood that negative emotions will accompany an empty nest varies from culture to culture (Mitchell & Lovegreen, 2009).

Adults in midlife continue to pursue their careers, becoming more expert, or they might initiate a new career that was not previously compatible with the financial and social responsibilities of raising a family. Recent economic and social changes have made midlife work less stable than it has been for previous generations. Today's midlife workers express intent to stay employed longer than previous cohorts (at least until age 65), but some find themselves taking jobs below their levels of skill and experience or withdrawing from employment (Elman, 2011).

During midlife, Erikson suggests that adults experience either generativity or stagnation. Many people, particularly during adolescence, set a number of goals for themselves. You may want to win a Nobel Prize or the Olympics or simply help others have a better life. Whatever your goals, by the time you reach midlife, you will have a rather good idea about whether these goals will be met. In many cases, people find that progress has been made toward their goals, although they perhaps didn't meet them. Wherever an adult finds himself or herself at midlife, the question posed by Erikson is whether value exists. If people feel that their lives have had value, even if they fall short of their goals, they experience generativity. Adults experiencing stagnation, in contrast, have not found much satisfaction in their lives.

What Is Late Adulthood Like?

As we have seen in our discussion of previous stages of development, the starting point of late adulthood is rather vague. You might think of age 65, a common retirement age, as a starting point, but many of today's older adults are living and working longer than ever before and so are conceiving of "old age" differently than in the past. For example, the baby boomers, or individuals born between 1945 and 1964, are more likely than other age groups to choose 72 as the start of old age (Cohn & Taylor, 2010). Current life expectancy at birth in the United States is 78.7 years (Murphy, Xu, & Kochanek, 2013).

Physical Changes in Late Adulthood

Assuming good health, the effects of aging on an adult's physical status are gradual and rather mild. Nonetheless, some physical change is inevitable, and understanding the nature of these changes provides guidance for coping with them.

Reuters/Sport/Corbis

Fauja Singh, born in 1911, competes in marathons worldwide as part of the Sikhs in the City team, a group of four runners whose combined age is more than 330 years. Running marathons isn't necessary to prevent cognitive decline, but people who participate in 20 minutes or more per day of physical activity have the lowest rates of dementia.

The brain reaches maturity around age 25, and few further changes occur until about the age of 45. At that time, the weight of the brain begins to decrease, leading to about a 5% decrease by the age of 80 (Anderton, 1997). However, this decrease is not accompanied by dramatic cognitive and behavioral changes. Results from the Baltimore Longitudinal Study of Aging (n.d.) show that healthy aging is accompanied by mild changes in the speed of learning and problem solving and that most of these observable changes occur very late in life. As with other physical changes, age-related changes in sensory abilities are gradual, and their effects can be offset by the use of technologies, such as eyeglasses and hearing aids.

Cognition in Late Adulthood

Intelligence remains relatively stable during adulthood, as long as general health remains good. Although many people erroneously believe that aging is inevitably accompanied by loss of intellect, only about 6.4% of the population over the age of 60 experiences dementia, such as Alzheimer's disease (Ferri et al., 2005). Cardiovascular disease, including strokes, may have a negative effect on intellect by reducing blood flow to the brain.

Certain types of intelligence change more because of aging than others. As we discussed in Chapter 10, crystallized intelligence, or the use of accumulated knowledge, changes less than fluid intelligence, or a person's basic information processing skills (Horn & Hofer, 1992). Fluid intelligence correlates with speed of processing, whereas crystallized intelligence might be viewed as wisdom, or the ability to draw on past knowledge and experience to solve problems.

Many people maintain high levels of intellectual functioning well into their senior years. Early studies of scientific, scholarly, and artistic accomplishments as a function of age demonstrated a peak in a person's 40s (Dennis, 1966). However, more recent studies show a relatively constant level of professional output. Among professors, research output was far more related to pressure to publish than to a professor's rank or age (Stroebe, 2010).

Psychology as a Hub Science
Entertainment and the Aging Brain

According to the U.S. Centers for Disease Control and Prevention (CDC), the number of Americans over the age of 65 has increased from only 3 million to more than 36 million during the last 100 years (CDC, 2007). Over the next 25 years, this group will balloon to more than 75 million with the addition of the baby boomers. Not only are the overall numbers of older adults growing, but expectations for an improved quality of life have increased. Today's seniors want to remain independent, active, and healthy.

Scientists have identified a number of lifestyle factors, especially physical exercise in midlife and later adulthood, that seem to protect people from developing dementia (Geda et al., 2010). But what about commercial technologies that claim to improve cognitive functioning? A number of high-profile technology firms, including Nintendo and MindWeaver, are marketing "games" designed not just to avoid cognitive decline but to improve mental functioning. Nintendo's Brain Training system even quantifies the improvement in terms of "brain age."

Do these systems work? Nintendo's system is based on "learning therapy," developed by Ryuta Kawashima. Kawashima and his colleagues have pub-

Actress Nicole Kidman serves as a spokesperson for Nintendo's Brain Age training system. While remaining mentally active is good for cognition, scientific research has yet to show a strong impact of the games on the cognition of healthy older adults.

Featureflash/Shutterstock

lished studies that investigate the usefulness of activities such as reading out loud and performing arithmetic for people who already have been diagnosed with dementia (Kawashima et al., 2005; Sekiguchi & Kawashima, 2007). However, the improvements noted on trained tasks may have limited usefulness among healthy adults. A group of 11,430 participants who trained for 6 weeks improved on the specific tasks they completed but did not show improvements on tasks that were not trained, even if the tasks were similar to the trained tasks (Owen et al., 2010).

Further research is necessary to establish the usefulness of these activities for preventing cognitive decline in healthy adults. In the meantime, if you find these games fun, that is probably a good enough reason to play them. ●

Social and Emotional Aspects of Late Adulthood

In later adulthood, Erikson suggests that people experience either integrity or despair. Older people who are happy with their life's experiences generally experience integrity (Sneed, Whitbourne, & Culang, 2006; Vaillant & Koury, 1993). They met their goals for the most part and had a rather fun time doing it. In contrast, people who reach their senior years feeling that life passed them by are likely to experience a sense of despair.

You might hold a common stereotype about older adults being sad and lonely. If so, you will probably be surprised to learn that psychological research has found that depression is higher in young people than in healthy, older adults (see ● Figure 11.27) and that older adults report higher subjective well-being overall than young adults (Carstensen, Isaacowitz, & Charles, 1999). Given the frequent challenges of aging, including physical and cognitive changes, what could possibly account for this increase in emotional well-being? Part of the explanation lies in the way people look at the time they have remaining in life (Carstensen, Fung, & Charles, 2003; Carstensen et al., 2011). When people see a long stretch of time remaining in their lives, they pursue achievement, possibly at the expense of meeting their social and emotional needs. In contrast, when older adults are looking at a shorter period of remaining life, their goals are refocused toward seeking positive emotional experiences.

One thing that doesn't change during our journey through the life span is the need for social connection. Older adults show significant benefits from their friendships, but they have fewer of them than younger adults and are less likely than younger adults to form new ones (Rawlins, 2004). Relationships with siblings can be especially meaningful for older adults (Connidis, 1992).

Grown children and grandchildren play an important part in the social life of many older adults. Unlike other primates, humans live long past their reproductive years, suggesting that grandparents may have historically contributed to the survival of their extended families.

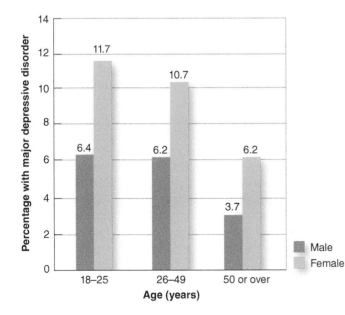

FIGURE 11.27

Depression Rates Decrease Over the Life Span. In contrast to stereotypes about sad, older adults, depression rates are highest in late adolescence and young adulthood and decrease gradually over the life span. *Source:* Adapted from "The Epidemiology of Major Depressive Disorder: Results From the National Comorbidity Survey Replication (NCS-R)," by R. C. Kessler, P. Berglund, O. Demler, R. Jin, D. Koretz, K. R. Merikangas, et al., 2003, *JAMA: Journal of the American Medical Association, 289*(23), pp. 3095–3105.

Relationships continue to play important roles in the social lives of seniors. Marriage is related to continued good health in seniors.

Relationships with grown children and grandchildren also form a significant part of the social life of older adults. Historically, many parents entered the role of grandparent during midlife, but with more young adults postponing parenting, the grandparent role is occurring later as well. Humans are somewhat unusual among primates in their length of life span beyond their productive years, a phenomenon known as the "grandmother effect." A healthy woman might live 40 or 50 years past her age at menopause. It is possible that her contributions to the care of her grandchildren, freeing her children for other tasks, might have provided an adaptive advantage over the course of evolution (Herndon, 2010).

Marriage in late adulthood is typically seen as making an important contribution to continued good health. In married older adults, interacting with the spouse contributes to happiness by buffering the individual from stress (Waldinger & Schulz, 2010). Seniors who have remained married to the same person for decades have seen many changes in their relationships over the years. We observed earlier that parents of young children experience a drop in marital satisfaction, which improves as children leave the home as young adults. Long-term marriage partners show more similarities with each other because of a lifetime spent in each other's company, along with a characteristic lack of attention to past negative events and personality traits (O'Rourke & Cappeliez, 2005). In other words, they believe their relationship has been more positive than it was. These couples also show an interesting pattern of conflict avoidance, which contributes to higher levels of marital satisfaction.

Interpersonal Relationships
The Developmental Perspective
How Do Age and Personality Interact to Predict Marital Satisfaction?

Getting married and being married can mean different things at different stages in life. One of the more interesting age-related changes in marriage is the impact of similar personalities on a couple's marital satisfaction throughout the life span (Shiota & Levenson, 2007). Overall, the saying "Birds of a feather flock together" is quite true. So it is surprising that some similarities in personality are predictive of reduced marital satisfaction and are more so at some life stages than at others. Early in marriage, personality similarities can promote bonding and intimacy. At midlife, however, the focus of the couple often turns to more practical than romantic tasks, such as raising children, advancing careers, and running a household. In this new environment, similarities in the personality trait of conscientiousness are associated with less marital satisfaction (Shiota & Levenson, 2007). The interaction between the highly conscientious person's drive to finish tasks and the midlife tendency to be a bit less flexible in routine suggests that putting two such individuals under the same roof is likely to produce substantial conflict. We might also speculate that two nonconscientious partners might be overwhelmed by the midlife workload, and the stress resulting from constantly playing catch-up on tasks might take a toll on the relationship. Fortunately, as the family workload diminishes later in life, the married couple's focus returns to intimacy, and the negative effects of similar personality recede again. ●

Summary 11.3 Highlights of Adolescent and Adult Development

Aspect of development	Highlights
Physical change	• Adolescents mature sexually and reach adult height and weight. • The brain continues to grow through adolescence and into young adulthood. • Menopause is a major transition for women in midlife. • Among healthy older adults, physical changes are gradual.
Cognition	• Working memory and reaction time reach adult levels during adolescence. • Thinking becomes more logical during adolescence and more independent in young adulthood. • Moral reasoning in adults is usually conventional or postconventional. • Intelligence remains relatively stable in healthy adults.
Social and emotional life	• Adolescents seek to develop identity. • Relationships might lead to marriage and parenting in young adulthood. • Midlife adults may experience changes in family and work domains. • Older adults show significant benefits from social connections.

Credits: Top Row. Universal Images Group Limited/Alamy. Second Row. ZUMA Press, Inc/Alamy. Bottom Row: Image Source/Alamy.

KEY TERMS The Language of Psychological Science

Be sure you can define these terms and use them correctly.

accommodation, p. 416
adolescence, p. 428
assimilation, p. 416
attachment, p. 423
concrete operational stage, p. 417
conservation, p. 417
conventional morality, p. 431
egocentrism, p. 417
embryo, p. 402

fetal alcohol syndrome (FAS), p. 407
fetus, p. 402
formal operational stage, p. 417
identity, p. 432
insecure attachment, p. 424
menopause, p. 439
object permanence, p. 416
postconventional morality, p. 431
preconventional morality, p. 431

preoperational stage, p. 417
puberty, p. 428
secondary sex characteristics, p. 429
secure attachment, p. 424
sensorimotor stage, p. 416
teratogen, p. 406
theory of mind (TOM), p. 420
zygote, p. 402

ALTHOUGH YOU MIGHT BE COMFORTABLE WITH THE IDEA THAT a trait like a moth's color can make it better adapted to one environment over another, how do you feel about your personality as an adaptation? Are there some types of personalities that thrive in some circumstances better than others? Can a culture shape personality? Can the personalities of a group of people shape their culture?

In Chapter 3, we introduced you to an interesting variation in the serotonin transporter gene, which can come in two versions, or alleles: short (S) and long (L). Children with two short alleles (SS) were more likely than children with either a combination of alleles (SL) or two long alleles (LL) to react negatively to the experience of being bullied (Sugden et al., 2010). Zooming out to the map of the world, you can see that these genotypes are not equally distributed worldwide. Lighter and darker yellow areas on the map have very low frequencies of the S allele, and orange and red areas have higher frequencies. South Africa has a relatively small number of people with the S allele (28%) compared to the United States, Australia, and Great Britain (about 40%–45%), which in turn have many fewer than in China (about 80%).

Besides having different distributions of the serotonin transporter gene, what else do you know about these cultures? If you thought about these cultures as differing in their emphasis on individualism versus collectivism, you are correct. Although a number of cultures with lower frequencies of the S allele have more collectivistic cultures than the United States, there is a positive correlation between the percentage of S allele carriers and a culture's rating on a scale from individualistic to collectivistic (Chiao & Blizinsky, 2010). Why would this be the case? Like all correlations, multiple relationships among genetic profiles and culture ratings are possible, and we cannot make conclusions about causes for these relationships. A population with a certain genetic mix might be more likely to form a particular type of culture, a culture might shape the reproductive success of its members, some outside variable could influence both the genetic mix and the form of the culture, or some combination of these factors could influence one another simultaneously (see ● Figure 12.1).

Zooming in to the level of the individual, we find that people carrying the S allele are especially attentive to negative information, like words and pictures that produce negative emotions (Beevers, Gibb, McGeary, & Miller, 2007; Osinsky et al., 2008). This focus on negativity might assist a person in coping well within a collectivistic environment, because

◄ Different versions of the serotonin transporter gene are not equally distributed throughout the world.

Argosy Publishing, Inc.

© Cengage Learning®

it could lead to a heightened sensitivity to another person's anger or fear. Early recognition of impending negative interactions might give people a chance to smooth things over before they escalate. The L allele, however, is associated with reduced responses to psychological and social sources of stress (Nardi et al., 2013), which might enhance coping in the individualistic cultural environment. The person carrying the S allele might be too cautious for the individualistic cultural environment, whereas the person carrying the L allele might act like a bull in a china cabinet in the collectivistic cultural environment (see ● Figure 12.2).

Although the S allele is a risk factor for depression (see Chapter 14), China has a much lower rate of depression than the United States despite the much higher frequency of the S allele in the Chinese population (Chiao & Blizinsky, 2010). The collectivistic cultural environment might buffer an individual with the S allele from the stress that can lead to depression. As you will see in this chapter, individual differences are an important aspect of behavior and mental processing, but they must be viewed within the larger contexts of the social and cultural environment.

Asians have a much higher probability of having the S allele of the serotonin transporter gene than do people living in many other parts of the world.

Learning Objectives

1. Compare and contrast the psychodynamic, humanistic, trait or Big Five, and social–cognitive theories of personality.

2. Debate the validity of self-report inventories versus projective tests as measures of personality.

3. Differentiate and illustrate several distinct aspects of self (self-concept, self-awareness, self-esteem, and self-regulation) in terms of their content, sources, and implications.

4. Analyze evidence for the biological bases of personality and the self.

5. Distinguish between the personal and interpersonal self, and relate these to cultural differences in individualistic versus collectivistic aspects of self-concept.

FIGURE 12.1

The Distribution of the Short (S) Allele as a Function of Culture Type. The percentage of people carrying the S allele varies according to a culture's position on the continuum from individualism to collectivism. Only about 40% of people in highly individualistic cultures such as the United States, Australia, and the United Kingdom carry the S allele, compared to nearly 80% in highly collectivistic cultures such as China, Japan, and Korea. *Source:* Adapted from "Culture–Gene Coevolution of Individualism–Collectivism and the Serotonin Transporter Gene," by J. Y. Chiao and K. D. Blizinsky, 2010, *Proceedings of the Royal Society of London, Series B: Biological Sciences, 277*(1681), pp. 529–537. doi:10.1098/rspb.2009.1650.

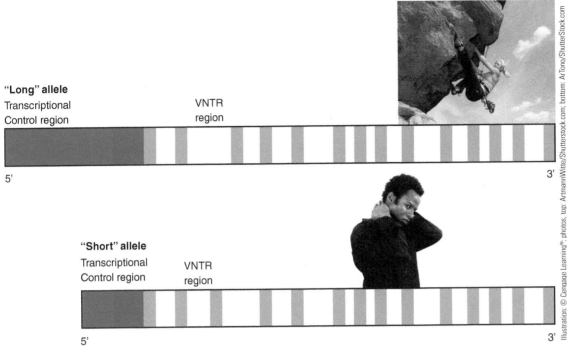

"**Long**" **allele**
Transcriptional
Control region

VNTR
region

5'   3'

"**Short**" **allele**
Transcriptional   VNTR
Control region   region

5'   3'

FIGURE 12.2

The Serotonin Transporter Gene. The serotonin transporter gene comes in two versions, or alleles. People with a copy of the short (S) allele tend to be more anxious and cautious, whereas people with a copy of the long (L) allele are prone to greater risk taking and creativity.

What Is Personality?

Suppose you were given the following feedback about your personality:

> You have a need for other people to like and admire you and yet you tend to be critical of yourself. Although you have some weaknesses, you are generally able to compensate for them. You have considerable unused capacity that you have not turned to your advantage, however. Disciplined and self-controlled on the outside, you tend to be worrisome and insecure on the inside. At times you have serious doubts as to whether you have made the right decision or done the right thing. You prefer a certain amount of change and variety and become dissatisfied when hemmed in by restrictions and limitations. You also pride yourself as an independent thinker and do not accept other's statements without satisfactory proof. But you have found it unwise to be too frank in revealing yourself to others. (Forer, 1949, p. 120)

How well does this description fit your beliefs about your personality? You might be impressed by how this paragraph presents such specific and personalized information about you. Ironically, you probably can relate to this description because it applies to nearly everyone. So the question is: If our personalities are so unique, how can we all be so easily described in a few brief sentences?

The science of personality explores characteristic patterns of thinking, feeling, and behaving. To what extent is a person's personality truly unique, and to what extent is personality based on some general characteristics that describe nearly everyone? That is, how much do our personalities overlap with those of others? How consistent or inconsistent is our behavior across time and across situations? How much of a role does biology or experience play in developing our personalities? Is the basic nature of humans good or bad?

Personality is our characteristic way of thinking, feeling, and behaving. How unique are we? How much do our personalities overlap with the personalities of other people?

Rawpixel/Shutterstock

Personality theories represent far more than simple curiosity about human behavior. These theories are intimately bound to our views of normal and abnormal behavior, which we will discuss in Chapter 14. Many of the psychologists who proposed personality theories also contributed influential ideas to the treatment of psychological disorders.

Historical Approaches to Personality

Our understanding of personality has progressed a great deal over the past century. The study of personality for the first half of the 20th century was dominated by the psychodynamic approaches of Sigmund Freud and his followers, who regarded personality as shaped by early childhood experiences. Behaviorists like B. F. Skinner attempted to apply principles of learning to personality. The humanistic psychologists, including Carl Rogers, actively rebelled against Freud and his psychodynamic approach. While few contemporary psychologists adhere to these historical approaches to personality, these theories stimulated interest in individual differences.

How Do Psychodynamic Theories View Personality?

The term **psychodynamic** was first used in a publication by Ernst von Brücke in 1874 (Hall, 1954). Von Brücke used the term as an extension of the first law of thermodynamics, which states that energy in a closed system can change from one form to another but cannot be created or destroyed. You may not have heard of von Brücke before, but you are likely familiar with one of his students, Freud, who made psychodynamics the foundation of his theory of personality.

As a young physician practicing neurology, Freud became known for his success in treating patients with hysteria, a condition characterized by physical symptoms without medical cause that is known today as somatoform or somatic symptom disorder. Freud sought to incorporate his observations and interactions with his patients into a new, unifying theory of psychology. His treatment approach, which we cover in Chapter 15, was known as **psychoanalysis**.

The Id, Ego, and Superego Personality was viewed by Freud as a closed energy system, in which "psychic" or instinctive energy moves among three compartments: the id, ego, and superego (see ● Figure 12.3). Freud proposed that the **id**, which literally means "it" in Latin, is present at birth and contains the primitive drives that serve as a source of energy for the personality, such as hunger, thirst, and sex. Freud believed that the id operates according to the pleasure principle, in which it seeks immediate gratification and relief. As a child begins to interact with parents and other social influences, the ego and superego begin to control the id. The **ego** is the component of the personality that is readily seen by others, so it acts as the person's "self." Its task is to coordinate the needs of the id with reality. The **superego** develops when a child begins to internalize society's rules for right and wrong, forming what we normally refer to as a conscience. As shown

psychodynamic A theory put forward by Sigmund Freud in which psychic energy moves among the compartments of the personality: id, ego, and superego.
psychoanalysis Sigmund Freud's treatment approach based on his psychodynamic theory.
id The component of Sigmund Freud's personality theory containing primitive drives present at birth.
ego The component of Sigmund Freud's personality theory that is the self that others see.
superego The component of Sigmund Freud's personality theory that internalizes society's rules for right and wrong, or the conscience.

FIGURE 12.3

Superego

Id

Ego

Illustration: © Cengage Learning®. photos, clockwise from top left: Lukaszfus/Shutterstock.com; hartphotography/Shutterstock.com; iko/Shutterstock.com

The Id, Ego, and Superego. Sigmund Freud viewed the mind as a closed system in which energy flows from one compartment to the next. It is the job of the ego, or self, to balance the pleasure-seeking impulses of the id with the morality imposed by the superego. Imbalances can be the source of unhealthy behavior. An overly dominant id can lead to antisocial behavior, and an overactive superego might produce too much guilt.

in Figure 12.4, we are not conscious of the operations of the id, although we might become consciously aware of the operations of the ego and superego.

Freudian Defense Mechanisms Threats to the balance of the id, ego, and superego can result in anxiety, or the sense that danger is around the corner. When the ego is faced with anxiety, it engages in a variety of protective behaviors called **defense mechanisms**. According to Freud, each of these mechanisms helps us channel potentially self-destructive or painful psychic energy into more constructive or manageable behaviors. For example, when we use the defense mechanism of sublimation, we redirect negative energy. An aggressive teen might take up martial arts rather than starting fights at school. Freud noted, though, that each mechanism has its limits; if people continually use defense mechanisms, they risk doing damage to the ego or self as well.

Psychosexual Stages of Development For Freud, the development of the personality is critical to the remainder of his theories and to the therapeutic process of psychoanalysis. When treating patients for various problems, Freud assumed that the origins of the problems could be found in his patients' developmental past, not in their present circumstances. As the word *psychosexual* implies, Freud was interested in how the developing personality would deal with the sexual impulses of the id. Freud proposed five **psychosexual stages** of personality development: oral, anal, phallic, latency, and genital. Personality, according to Freud, is the product of conflict occurring during these psychosexual stages. Personality characteristics emerge as the id, ego, and superego resolve their conflicts and struggle for balance. Should the conflict become so great as to produce a conflict between ego and reality, psychosis (including abnormal behaviors characteristic of schizophrenia and other serious disorders) might occur (Freud, 1938).

Contemporary Assessments of Sigmund Freud's Approach Although there is no question regarding the tremendous influence Freud has had on modern thinking, his legacy today is considered mixed. Freud's approach to development contrasts sharply with the scientific theories of development we explored in Chapter 11. But his work remains important in that it had such a profound influence in psychology and popular culture.

defense mechanism In Sigmund Freud's personality theory, a protective behavior that reduces anxiety.
psychosexual stage A stage in Sigmund Freud's theory of the developing personality.

HISTORICAL APPROACHES TO PERSONALITY   **451**

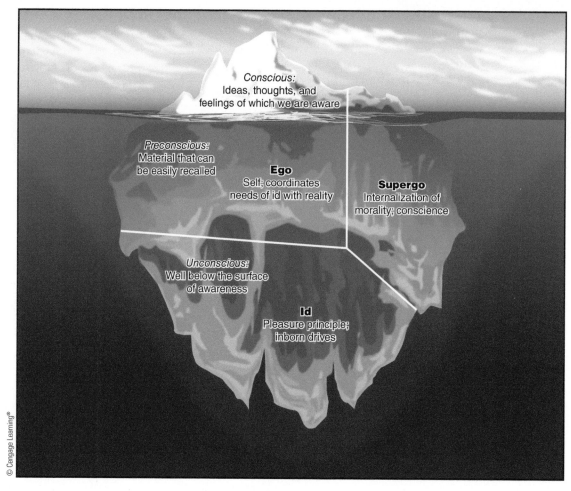

FIGURE 12.4

Sigmund Freud's Levels of Conscious Awareness. According to Freud, we are consciously aware of only a small percentage of the mind's activities. Some information is located in the preconscious mind and can become conscious at any moment. Information in the unconscious mind can affect our behavior without our awareness.

A few Freudian constructs appear to be supported by scientific investigation, even though the theoretical mechanisms he proposed have been refuted. The notion of defense mechanisms, the distinction between conscious and unconscious processes, and the descriptions of some types of adult personalities remain topics of research in psychological science (Kline, 2013). However, contemporary scientists point out that Freud's ideas rarely lend themselves to scientific investigation. Some of his ideas, such as women's penis envy, are viewed today as remarkably sexist (Sprengnether, 1990). Additional criticisms center on the questionable effectiveness of psychoanalysis, which we discuss in more detail in Chapter 15.

The Neo-Freudians No theory as influential as Freud's is likely to be left alone without revision. A number of Freud's followers began to diverge from his approach to construct their own psychodynamic theories. We refer to these as "neo," or "new," Freudians. A common feature of the **neo-Freudian** theories was a substitution of social competence for sexuality and pleasure as the major motivation for human behavior. These theorists brought the psychodynamic approach closer to contemporary views of humans as social animals, a theme we discuss throughout this textbook. Unfortunately, the theories put forward by the neo-Freudians share one of Freud's greatest weaknesses—the proposal of constructs that do not lend themselves to scientific investigation. We will highlight a few of the notable contributions of this group.

neo-Freudian A theorist who attempted to update and modify Sigmund Freud's original theory of personality.

Alfred Adler (1870–1937) contributed the notion of an inferiority complex to psychodynamic thought (Adler, 1956). According to Adler, an inferiority complex, or overwhelming feelings of inferiority, can lead to overcompensation, usually in the form of seeking the appearance of superiority rather than the substance. For example, a person might overcompensate for feelings of inferiority with peers by purchasing a fancy, expensive automobile. Adler was also one of the first psychologists to suggest that siblings, along with parents, could have an influence on development, leading to investigations of the effects of birth order.

Carl Jung (1875–1961), a Swiss psychiatrist, divided the **unconscious mind** into two components. The personal unconscious remained the same as Freud's unconscious mind. Jung added a deeper level, the collective unconscious, composed of our common psychological predispositions as humans passed from generation to generation (Jung, 1928). After observing common themes in cultures around the world during his extensive travels, Jung argued that generations of experience with concepts such as darkness, power, death, and parents would lead to characteristic ways of unconsciously thinking about such topics. Jung's ideas are echoed in today's evolutionary approach to psychology, which views the mind as having adapted over the course of evolution (Walters, 1994).

In addition to his expansion of the concept of the unconscious, Jung deviated from Freud by providing more specific information about differences in individual personality. In particular, Jung's concepts of the personality characteristics of extroversion (outgoing) and introversion (relatively less outgoing) are still very much alive in current discussions of personality. Jung's personality characteristics form the basis for several popular personality tests, such as the Myers–Briggs Type Indicator (MBTI). Unfortunately, as we will see later, the MBTI does not hold up well to analyses of validity and reliability.

Karen Horney (1885–1952; pronounced "horn-eye") was one of the first female psychiatrists. Horney rejected many of Freud's ideas to concentrate on aspects of the culture that contributed to women's feelings of inferiority. Simultaneously, while treating male patients, Horney became convinced that men envied women's ability to become pregnant and be mothers. Her emphasis on the impact of a male-dominated society on women helped set the stage for many subsequent feminist scholars (Horney, 1923–1937/1967, 1950).

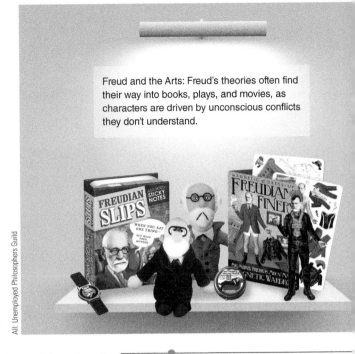

Freud and the Arts: Freud's theories often find their way into books, plays, and movies, as characters are driven by unconscious conflicts they don't understand.

Sigmund Freud has become a mainstay in popular culture.

Classic Behavioral Approaches to Personality

Behaviorist approaches to personality emphasized learning as an important influence on personality development. Because learning is a lifetime process, behaviorists expected to see change and variability in personalities observed over time.

According to Skinner, the principles of operant conditioning, discussed in Chapter 8, would lead to the development of stable "response tendencies" that might appear to others as "traits." For example, if your parents were strict about enforcing rules at home, like finishing chores, you might look like a conscientious person who always finishes assigned tasks on time.

Compared to stable personality traits, Skinner's response tendencies were more flexible and subject to change. If people experienced something new, their ways of responding would change to reflect that new interaction with the environment. If you move away from home to college, and you no longer have your parents to reward or punish you based on your completion of tasks, you may no longer be conscientious about finishing your homework on time.

Alfred Adler suggested that an inferiority complex can lead to overcompensation in the form of seeking the appearance of superiority. "Man heels" that add at least 2 inches of height have become increasingly popular and are worn frequently by Hollywood stars.

unconscious mind The part of mental activity that cannot be voluntarily retrieved.

This Tibetan mandala represents unity formed out of the four elements of earth, wind, water, and fire, a theme that Carl Jung believed was universal in the human collective unconscious.

The Star-Ledger / Aristide Economopoulos / The Image Works

Science Source

Karen Horney (1885–1952) was one of the first female psychiatrists, and although she is considered a neo-Freudian, she rejected many of Sigmund Freud's ideas to concentrate on the sources of women's feelings of inferiority.

How Do Humanistic Psychologists Approach Personality?

Until the 1960s, American psychology was dominated by two perspectives—behaviorism and the psychodynamic approach. At that time, some psychologists began to consider other ways of approaching psychology in general and personality specifically. One alternative approach, initially called third-force psychology (behaviorism and psychodynamic theory were forces one and two), later became known as humanistic psychology.

Humanistic psychology differed from behaviorism and the psychodynamic approach in distinctive ways. Humanistic psychologists were convinced that humans are unique, and they argued that the animal research favored by behaviorists was irrelevant. The humanistic psychologists' belief that human nature is basically good contrasts dramatically with the darker view of human nature put forward by Freud and other psychodynamic theorists. Humanistic psychologists believed that psychodynamic theories placed too much emphasis on abnormal behavior. Instead, they advocated studying exceptional people to see why they succeeded, a tactic continued by contemporary positive psychology approaches, discussed in Chapter 16.

One of the leading humanistic psychologists, Abraham Maslow, was primarily interested in human motivation, and we discussed his contributions to this area in Chapter 7. He did not attempt a full-fledged theory of personality, although he made some interesting conclusions about the characteristics of exceptional people. After reviewing biographies of people like Albert Einstein, Jane Addams, William James, and Abraham Lincoln, Maslow observed that exceptional people had a number of common traits (Maslow, 1950). In addition to expected characteristics, such as creativity, realistic thinking, and concern for others, Maslow's exceptional people had some surprising qualities. They had few friends, well-developed senses of humor, and periodic mystic or peak experiences.

Carl Rogers, another humanistic psychologist, put forward a theory of personality based on his experience as a therapist (Rogers, 1951, 1980). We discuss Rogers's approach to therapy in Chapter 15. Rogers, like Maslow, believed that humans strive toward self-actualization, or maximizing their individual potential. For Rogers, people who follow the path laid out by their feelings will lead productive, healthy lives. They will experience congruence, or similarity, between their real selves and their ideal selves. Congruence is most likely to occur in response to unconditional positive regard, or a nonjudgmental appreciation for a person's true nature. Being treated judgmentally makes people act in ways that are incongruent, or inconsistent, with their ideal selves, which might lead to disordered behaviors (see ● Figure 12.5).

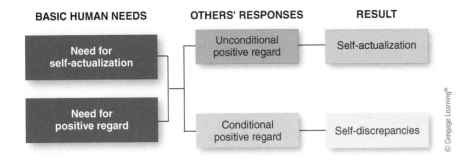

BASIC HUMAN NEEDS — OTHERS' RESPONSES — RESULT

Need for self-actualization

Need for positive regard

Unconditional positive regard → Self-actualization

Conditional positive regard → Self-discrepancies

© Cengage Learning®

FIGURE 12.5

Carl Rogers's Humanistic Theory of Personality. Rogers, like other humanistic psychologists, believed that people were striving for self-actualization, or the ability to maximize their potential. Achieving that goal depended on the response of other people (family, friends, and society) to the self. If people receive unconditional positive regard, or nonjudgmental acceptance, they can reach self-actualization. However, if their acceptance is conditional on whether they please others, the result is "self-discrepancies" that can lead to depression, anxiety, and other negative outcomes. *Source:* Adapted from *Essentials of Psychology* (5th ed.), by D. A. Bernstein, 2011, Belmont, CA: Cengage.

As we observed in the case of psychodynamic theories, it is somewhat difficult to move from the humanistic psychologists' description of personality to our original definition of personality as consisting of stable and consistent patterns of behavior. The humanistic psychologists are more interested in the process by which personality develops than in the actual characteristics that emerge. Like the psychodynamic theories they rejected, the humanistic psychologists are subject to criticisms of being unscientific in their methods (Child, 1973).

How Do Trait Theories Explain Personality?

Following a discussion of psychodynamic, behaviorist, and humanistic approaches to personality, the trait approach seems relatively simple. A **trait** is a stable personality characteristic.

Psychologists were hard at work testing personality traits, using methods described later in this chapter, long before they derived coherent theories to explain their findings. They realized intuitively that traits often clustered together. An outgoing person might also be expected to be brave and cheerful. However, these approaches lacked the precision required by a true theory of personality. Statistical methods of correlation and factor analysis came to the rescue (see ● Figure 12.6). As we discussed in Chapter 2, correlations allow us to see whether two

trait A stable personality characteristic.

FIGURE 12.6

Factor Analysis Identifies Clusters of Personality Traits. The statistical technique of factor analysis allows psychologists to identify factors that positively correlate or cluster together, as well as the strengths of those relationships. Raymond Cattell identified 16 personality factors that formed five clusters (extroversion, anxiety, self-control, independence, and receptivity) that are similar to the factors in the Big Five theory proposed later by McCrae and Costa (1985). The darker lines represent stronger statistical relationships.

Insecurity — O — Q4 Irritability
Anxiety
Perfectionism — Q3
Self-control
Warmth — A
C — Emotional stability
Conformity — G
H — Boldness — L — Skepticism
Independence
Q2 — Self-reliance — F — Impulsivity — E — Dominance — Q1 — Openness to change
Extroversion
Receptivity
N — Privateness — Imagination — M — B — Intelligence
Sensitivity — I

© Cengage Learning®

FIGURE 12.7

The Big Five Theory of Personality.

Big Five theory A trait theory that identifies five main characteristics that account for most individual differences in personality.

openness A Big Five personality trait characterized by an appreciation for fantasy, feelings, actions, ideas, values, and aesthetics.

conscientiousness A Big Five personality trait characterized by competence, order, dutifulness, achievement striving, self-discipline, and deliberation.

variables have some systematic relationship with each other, such as height and weight or speed and strength. Factor analysis allows a researcher to compare large numbers of correlations simultaneously, which makes the technique perfectly suited to the study of clustered personality traits (Spearman, 1904).

Early Trait Theories

One of the earliest efforts to identify personality traits began with the selection of 4,500 words that described observable traits out of a dictionary (Allport & Odbert, 1936). Some of these terms were defined as central traits, or those characteristics that most clearly define and differentiate a person (Allport, 1937). These are the types of terms you might use when trying to describe someone you know: smart, hardworking, and outgoing.

Emerging computer technologies in the 1940s allowed psychologists to refine lists of traits further (Cattell, 1946/1969). Using factor analysis, Allport and Odbert's original list of 4,500 words was reduced to 16 major personality traits. Each trait took the form of a continuum between opposites. For example, the trait of suspiciousness would range from "trusting" at one extreme to "suspicious" at the other. The basic methods and elements for trait theories were now in place.

The Big Five Theory

A common theme found in the work of early trait theorists is that relatively few traits are required to describe and predict an individual's behavior accurately. Based on this work, a **Big Five theory** identified five core traits: openness to experience, conscientiousness, surgency (extroversion), agreeableness, and neuroticism (McCrae & Costa, 1985, 1987; Norman, 1963). To remember the Big Five traits, use the acronym OCEAN. The development of a personality test to measure the five traits has made it possible for many investigators to explore the Big Five theory scientifically (see ● Figure 12.7). The current version of the test is known as the NEO-PI-R Inventory (Costa & McCrae, 2011). You will have an opportunity to take a short version of this test in this chapter.

Each of the Big Five traits consists of a continuum from one extreme to the other. We will discuss the five traits in order of the OCEAN acronym.

Openness to experience involves fantasy, aesthetics (an appreciation for the arts), feelings, actions, ideas, and values. People who score high on openness are curious, unconventional, and imaginative. They are more likely to be interested in exploring aspects of life that are different from their own, whether this means trying new foods, traveling to exotic locations, or studying other religions. People who score low on openness are more likely to be practical, traditional, and conforming. They prefer the familiar over the new, choosing a chain restaurant in a new city rather than experimenting with the local cuisine.

Conscientiousness incorporates competence, order, dutifulness, achievement striving, self-discipline, and deliberation. People scoring high on this trait are reliable, work hard, and complete tasks on time. People scoring low on this trait are unreliable, somewhat lazy, and undependable. It might be frustrating to work on group projects with people who are low in conscientiousness, but under some circumstances, they make valuable contributions. For example, they might help by identifying unnecessary steps in a process, reducing the time pressure felt by a group, or even promoting some forms of "outside the box" thinking and problem solving.

Extroversion is characterized by warmth, gregariousness, assertiveness, activity, excitement seeking, and positive emotion, although extroverts also tend to be a bit insensitive and overbearing. **Introversion** (opposite of extroversion) is characterized by coolness, reserve, passivity, and caution, although introverts also tend to be sensitive and reflective. Extroverts tend to seek social activity and find it invigorating, whereas introverts are more likely to want time to themselves to recharge their batteries.

Agreeableness includes trust, straightforwardness, altruism, compliance, modesty, and tender mindedness. People who score low on this trait tend to be cynical, uncooperative, and rude. Again, we face the challenge of finding advantages for a negative-sounding trait like disagreeableness. At least in employment settings, disagreeable people seem more capable of making tough decisions, whereas their more agreeable colleagues might find it difficult to supervise others (Rust, 1999). In one study, men who scored below the mean on measures of agreeableness earned 18% more than men who were more agreeable (Judge, Livingston, & Hurst, 2012).

Finally, **neuroticism** combines anxiety, angry hostility, depression, self-consciousness, impulsivity, and vulnerability. The opposite trait could be described as emotional stability. Although scoring high on neuroticism sounds quite unpleasant, this trait appears to have survival advantages (Zhang, Chrétien, Meaney, & Gratton, 2005). In threatening and impoverished environments, high neuroticism may be precisely what is required to increase a person's chances of surviving to reproduce. We observed a similar argument in Chapter 11, in which a child's insecure attachment to the parents was shown to have potential benefits for survival in a dangerous environment (Belsky, 1999). Whether considering a personality trait or attachment, the anxious, clinging child is more likely to stay near protection, enhancing survival in dangerous situations.

In the years following the development of the Big Five theory, the traits it outlines have provided a framework for investigating job performance (Barrick & Mount, 1991), parenting style (Prinzie, Stams, Deković, Reijntjes, & Belsky, 2009), psychological disorders and substance abuse (Kotov, Gamez, Schmidt, & Watson, 2010), cognitive decline in older adulthood (Curtis, Windsor, & Soubelet, 2014), happiness (DeNeve & Cooper, 1998), academic performance (Komarraju, Karau, & Schmeck, 2009) and many other specific outcomes. Evidence across diverse cultures, including the United States, Japan, Korea, Germany, Portugal, Israel, and China, suggests that these personality traits represent universal human characteristics (McCrae & Costa, 1997).

People who score high on the trait of openness are curious, unconventional, and imaginative.

Across a range of professional, skilled, and unskilled job descriptions, the conscientiousness variable had the greatest positive correlation with work-related success (Barrick & Mount, 1991). Surprisingly, the same meta-analysis found little relationship between agreeableness and job performance.

Out of the Big Five characteristics, conscientiousness shows the highest positive correlation with work-related success, whether a person is employed in a professional, skilled, or unskilled job.

extroversion One of the Big Five traits characterized by warmth, gregariousness, assertiveness, activity, excitement seeking, and positive emotion; opposite of introversion.
introversion One of the Big Five traits characterized by coolness, reserve, passivity, inactivity, caution, and negative emotion; opposite of extroversion.
agreeableness A Big Five personality trait characterized by trustworthiness, altruism, trust, compliance, modesty, and tender mindedness.
neuroticism A Big Five personality trait characterized by anxiety, angry hostility, depression, self-consciousness, impulsivity, and vulnerability.

Experiencing Psychology

A Short Version of the Big Five Inventory

THE FULL VERSION of one of the tests frequently used to measure Big Five traits, the Big Five Inventory (BFI), contains 44 items. The 10-item version in Table 12.1 has served as a reasonable substitute for the full test for research purposes when time is limited (Rammstedt & John, 2007). If reading about the different Big Five traits has left you wondering about your own personality, this is your chance to get an idea of where you stack up on each of these factors.

To take the test, circle the number that represents your best answer for each item. At the end, we'll tell you how to add up your scores. A self-report test like this is only as good as you make it by answering honestly. Wanting to appear socially desirable by downplaying your negative charac-teristics might make you feel better, but this approach reduces the validity of the test results. At the same time, no paper-and-pencil test is perfect, and if a result does not fit the way you and others honestly view your personality, feel free to disagree with the results. ●

TABLE

12.1 The BFI-10 Personality Test

1. I see myself as someone who is reserved.

1	2	3	4	5
Disagree strongly	Disagree a little	Neither agree nor disagree	Agree a little	Agree strongly

2. I see myself as someone who is generally trusting.

1	2	3	4	5
Disagree strongly	Disagree a little	Neither agree nor disagree	Agree a little	Agree strongly

3. I see myself as someone who tends to be lazy.

1	2	3	4	5
Disagree strongly	Disagree a little	Neither agree nor disagree	Agree a little	Agree strongly

4. I see myself as someone who is relaxed, handles stress well.

1	2	3	4	5
Disagree strongly	Disagree a little	Neither agree nor disagree	Agree a little	Agree strongly

5. I see myself as someone who has few artistic interests.

1	2	3	4	5
Disagree strongly	Disagree a little	Neither agree nor disagree	Agree a little	Agree strongly

6. I see myself as someone who is outgoing, sociable.

1	2	3	4	5
Disagree strongly	Disagree a little	Neither agree nor disagree	Agree a little	Agree strongly

7. I see myself as someone who tends to find fault with others.

1	2	3	4	5
Disagree strongly	Disagree a little	Neither agree nor disagree	Agree a little	Agree strongly

8. I see myself as someone who does a thorough job.

1	2	3	4	5
Disagree strongly	Disagree a little	Neither agree nor disagree	Agree a little	Agree strongly

9. I see myself as someone who gets nervous easily.

1	2	3	4	5
Disagree strongly	Disagree a little	Neither agree nor disagree	Agree a little	Agree strongly

10. I see myself as someone who has an active imagination.

1	2	3	4	5
Disagree strongly	Disagree a little	Neither agree nor disagree	Agree a little	Agree strongly

Here is how you should score your results. To ensure that you don't just pick the same number for each item, half of the questions "reverse" the scale. Follow the directions below carefully so that you obtain a correct score. Scores can range from 1 to 5 on each trait.

Extroversion: Q1R (Reverse) and Q6
  Subtract your answer to Q1 from 6 and add to your answer to Q6. Divide by 2.
  Scores of 1 or 2 are introverted, scores of 4 and 5 are extroverted, and a score of 3 is neutral.

Agreeableness: Q2 and Q7R (Reverse)
  Add your response to Q2 to (6 minus your answer on Q7), and divide the sum by 2.
  Scores of 1 or 2 are disagreeable, scores of 4 and 5 are agreeable, and a score of 3 is neutral.

Conscientiousness: Q3R (Reverse) and Q8
  Add (6 minus your answer on Q3) to Q8, and divide the sum by 2.
  Scores of 1 or 2 are low conscientiousness, scores of 4 and 5 are high conscientiousness, and a score of 3 is neutral.

Neuroticism: Q4R (Reverse) and Q9
  Add (6 minus your answer on Q4) to Q9, and divide the sum by 2.
  Scores of 1 or 2 are low neuroticism, scores of 4 and 5 are high neuroticism, and a score of 3 is neutral.

Openness: Q5R (Reverse) and Q10
  Add (6 minus your answer on Q5) to Q10, and divide the sum by 2.
  Scores of 1 or 2 are low openness, scores of 4 and 5 are high openness, and a score of 3 is neutral.

How Do Situations Affect Personality?

Not all psychologists were convinced by the argument that personality originated in stable traits that produce consistent patterns of behavior across different situations. Research showing that situations could exert a stronger influence on people's behavior than any individual predispositions highlighted limits to the general trait approach. We discuss a number of these situations in Chapter 13. For example, studies of obedience or conformity might be better understood by evaluating the situations people encounter rather than the predispositions or traits they bring to the laboratory (Asch, 1951; Milgram, 1963).

Consistent with their emphasis on experience, learning theorists attempted to capture the effects of circumstances and situations on personality development. Early behavioral learning approaches gave way to social–cognitive learning theories that emphasized the importance of social rewards, such as approval, and internal processes, such as expectations, in shaping personality.

Social–Cognitive Learning Theories of Personality

Midway in the 20th century, some behaviorists began to think in more cognitive terms and believed that learning theories of personality had neglected motivations, emotions, and cognitions. These behaviorists recognized the importance of personality in social contexts, where your behavior is shaped and rewarded by interactions with other people. The resulting **social–cognitive learning theories** are consistent with our observations that single perspectives in psychology do not always capture the whole story.

Locus of Control   One influential social–cognitive learning theory popularized a type of cognitive expectancy known as **locus of control** (Rotter, 1966). If you have an external locus of control (*locus* means "place" in Latin), you expect that most of the things that happen to you occur because of chance, luck, or factors beyond your control. However, if you have an internal locus of control, you believe that most of your outcomes are due to your own efforts.

Due in large part to cultural norms in the United States emphasizing independence, many American psychologists see having an internal locus of control as an advantage. People with an internal locus of control manage stress more effectively, floss their teeth more regularly, are more likely to seek shelter in response to tornado warnings, use their seat belts more consistently while driving, and are more likely to practice effective birth control (Wallston, 2005). However, people with an internal locus of control tend to be less sympathetic with the plight of others, viewing their troubles as due to their choices and behavior as opposed to outside forces they can't control (Lane, 2001).

Reciprocal Determinism and Self-Efficacy   Albert Bandura, whom we met in Chapter 8, attempted to capture a balance between external, environmental factors and internal traits in his theory of **reciprocal determinism** (Bandura, 1990, 1993). Like other social–cognitive learning theorists, Bandura rejected the strict behaviorism of Skinner as applied to personality. He agreed with Skinner that the environment can determine behavior but thought that it does so reciprocally, as people influence the environment through both their internal cognitions and their behavior.

Bandura believed that observation of others' behavior played an important role in the development of personality. Although much of his work centered on aggression, Bandura believed that many other characteristics were learned in this same manner. He was particularly interested in self-efficacy (Bandura, 1990, 1993, 1995). This characteristic refers to your level of confidence in your own abilities to gain reinforcement. If your self-efficacy is high, you have strong expectations that positive outcomes are within reach. If you study hard and get good grades, you expect to obtain a good job in your chosen career. However, if your self-

Is this man helping these women because of his individual personality traits? Or do situational variables do a better job than personality traits at predicting behavior?

social–cognitive learning theory A theory of personality that features cognition and learning, especially from the social environment, as important sources of individual differences in personality.

locus of control A cognitive expectancy featured in social–cognitive learning theories of personality about the source of individual outcomes; an external locus of control sees outcomes as resulting from luck or chance, while an internal locus of control sees outcomes as the result of individual effort.

reciprocal determinism A social–cognitive learning theory of personality that features the mutual influence of the person and that of the situation on each other.

Vibe Images/Shutterstock

efficacy is low, you might doubt your abilities to reach your goals. Self-efficacy can be situation specific. You might be confident in your abilities in science but less so in your abilities in rock climbing. Self-efficacy influences a person's environment and experiences. A confident job candidate is probably more likely to be hired than an applicant who appears insecure.

If–Then Relationships Walter Mischel argued that trait theories could not explain the variation in an individual's behavior across situations (Mischel, 1968). For example, when 51 boys at a summer camp were observed, their extroversion–introversion scores could not predict the extent of their extroverted or introverted behaviors across 21 situations (Newcombe, 1929). Instead of focusing on traits alone, Mischel argued that the stability we expect in a person's behavior arises from that individual's characteristic way of interpreting situations (Mischel, 2004).

To illustrate this process, consider two children who both score high on some measure of aggression. Trait theorists would expect the children to be consistently more aggressive than their low-scoring peers, regardless of circumstances, yet these are precisely the results that Mischel found to be lacking in actual studies (Mischel, 1968). Instead, an individual child's behavior can be predicted by considering "if–then" relationships between situations and behavior (Mischel & Shoda, 1995). One child may be aggressive when approached by peers but respond passively to an adult's efforts to apply discipline, while another might show the opposite pattern. In other words, *if* the child experiences a particular situation (interacting with peers or adults), that child *then* responds with a unique, stable set of behaviors (aggressive or passive). These if–then patterns are characteristic of an individual, leading to the stable characteristics we think of as personality.

People with an internal locus of control believe that most of our outcomes are due to our own efforts, while people with an external locus of control believe that our outcomes are more often due to factors beyond our control. Although people with an internal locus of control experience less stress, they tend to be less sympathetic with the plight of others. The person with an internal locus of control might believe this woman needs to try harder to escape homelessness, while the person with an external locus of control might believe this woman just needs help and better opportunities.

Self-efficacy is the belief that you can handle a challenging situation and obtain future rewards.

What Are the Biological Bases of Personality?

Biological theories of personality attempt to build bridges between observed traits and their underlying biological correlates. Among the biological variables theorists have attempted to connect to personality are temperament, genetic predispositions, and brain structure. When investigating these variables within the context of a specific disorder, like those we discuss in Chapter 14, scientists may refer to them as a *behavioral phenotype* (Skuse, 2000). Constructing a behavioral phenotype allows researchers to compare and contrast underlying genetic profiles associated with the same problem, such as the poor social skills that characterize autism spectrum disorder (van Rijn et al., 2014).

Temperament and Personality

We introduced the concept of **temperament**, or a child's pattern of mood, activity, or emotional responsiveness, in Chapter 11. Contemporary psychologists believe that temperament is biological in origin (Rothbart, 2011) but quickly begins to interact with the social and physical environments. Not only does a bold, fearless child select different activities, but that child is treated differently than a quiet, cautious child by peers, parents, and teachers.

temperament A child's pattern of mood, activity, or emotional responsiveness linked to later personality.

Differences in the temperament dimension of reactivity predict children's responses to novel or challenging stimuli. Children with high reactivity often display high introversion and neuroticism later in life.

Two dimensions of temperament appear particularly important for adult personality: reactivity and self-regulation (Ahadi & Rothbart, 1994; Rothbart, Ahadi, & Evans, 2000; Rothbart & Derryberry, 1981). Reactivity describes differences in people's responses to novel or challenging stimuli. People's responses may vary in terms of both intensity and timing. Some people respond to such stimuli immediately with highly intense anxiety, others respond more slowly, and some barely notice the stimuli. Self-regulation involves the ability to control attention and inhibit responding to perceived stimuli. These dimensions of temperament appear to be related to the Big Five traits. Higher reactivity is characteristic of introversion and neuroticism (Aron et al., 2010), while self-regulation is associated with later conscientiousness (Rothbart, Sheese, Rueda, & Posner, 2011).

Genetics and Personality

The early emergence of temperament in life suggests a possible genetic origin for personality. Most efforts to study the effects of genetics on personality use the twin study method, such as the Minnesota Study of Twins Reared Apart (Bouchard, 1994; Bouchard, Lykken, McGue, Segal, & Tellegen, 1990). In this ongoing research, Thomas Bouchard and his colleagues have studied 59 pairs of identical twins and 47 pairs of fraternal twins who had been raised in separate families, as well as a larger number of twins raised in the same home. The pairs of identical twins were quite similar, regardless of whether they were raised together. Some characteristics showed stronger positive correlations between identical twins, such as their scores on an occupational interest scale. Other characteristics showed relatively weaker positive correlations, such as nonreligious social attitudes. The critical finding was that the identical twins raised apart and together were similar to each other, whether the overall positive correlation for a particular characteristic was strong or weak (see ● Figure 12.8).

The Big Five personality traits show an approximate heritability of .50 in humans (Jang, Livesley, & Vernon, 1996; Loehlin, McCrae, Costa, & John, 1998). As we discussed in Chapter

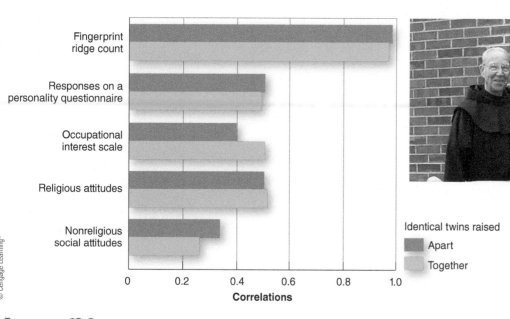

Identical twins raised
■ Apart
■ Together

Adrian and Julian Riester were identical twin friars who died within hours of each other at the age of 92. Their shared experiences of more than 65 years as members of the Franciscan order probably accentuated their genetic similarities.

FIGURE 12.8

Comparisons Between Identical Twins Raised Together or Apart. Some characteristics, such as the number of ridges you have in your fingerprints, are more strongly influenced by genetics than other characteristics, such as your nonreligious social attitudes. Regardless of how much genetic influence a trait might have, identical twins show considerable similarity, whether they grow up in the same household or not.

3, heritability always refers to populations rather than individuals. Saying that a trait such as shyness has a heritability of .40 does not mean that 40% of a person's shyness is produced by genes and the other 60% is produced by the environment. Instead, a .40 heritability ratio suggests that across the human population, the variations we see in shyness from high to low are influenced moderately by both genetics and environmental factors.

If genetics accounts for about half of the variability seen in the population's personality, what is the source of the other half? Environmental influences take the form of shared experiences, which affect all members of a family, and nonshared experiences, which affect an individual. For example, you and your siblings might have the shared experience of attending the same elementary school and always having Thanksgiving dinner with the extended family but the nonshared experiences of studying different musical instruments, having different friends, or playing different sports.

Knowing about the heritability, or variation across the population, for a trait like extroversion does not tell us much about the development of an individual's personality. Our general heritability estimates are similar to knowing the overall average annual temperature in North America. Although this information could be useful for the study of global warming trends, it doesn't tell us much about whether California is likely to have more wildfires or whether the skiing industry in Colorado will have a good year. We know that the population heritability for a factor such as positive emotionality is between .46 and .52, but this fact doesn't tell us much about how heritability interacts with shared and nonshared environments to produce particular outcomes (Krueger, South, Johnson, & Iacono, 2008). For example, depending on teenagers' perceived relationship with their parents, the heritability of positive emotionality can vary widely. The positive emotionality of teens who perceive their relationship with their parents as poor is more strongly predicted by their individual, or nonshared, experiences, whereas the positive emotionality of teens who enjoy strong relationships with their parents is more strongly predicted by genetics (Krueger et al., 2008). These fine-tuned analyses of the interactions of nature and nurture are likely to provide psychologists with more accurate views of the sources of personality (see ● Figure 12.9).

Personality, Brain Structure, and Brain Function

Given the evidence of genetic influence on personality, and the early emergence of temperament in life, it is reasonable to assume that some individual differences in personality are reflected in the structures of the brain. Early efforts to link personality and biology examined the correlations between extroversion and neuroticism traits and the activities of the autonomic nervous system and reticular formation, structures involved with arousal discussed in Chapter 4 (Eysenck, 1967).

Researchers have identified structural correlates in adults for four of the Big Five personality traits: extroversion, agreeableness, neuroticism, and conscientiousness (Canli, 2009; DeYoung et al., 2010). The differences in structure appear to occur in logical places. For ex-

FIGURE 12.9

Genetics and Teen's Relationships With Parents Interact to Predict Positive Emotion. Without taking environment into account, genetics explains between 46% and 52% of the variability we see in positive emotionality. However, we gain a better understanding of positive emotions when we also consider environments, such as teens' relationships with their parents. When teens report a positive relationship with their parents, most of the variation we see in their positive emotionality is genetic, but when their relationship with their parents is poor, their positive emotionality is better predicted by their individual experiences than by their genetics. *Source:* Adapted from "The Heritability of Personality Is Not Always 50%: Gene–Environment Interactions and Correlations Between Personality and Parenting," by R. F. Krueger, S. South, W. Johnson, and W. Iacono, 2008, *Journal of Personality, 76*(6), pp. 1485–1522.

Measures of the Big Five trait of consientiousness are positively correlated with the volume of areas in the prefrontal cortex involved with planning and the voluntary control of behavior. *Source:* From DeYoung, C. G., et al. (2010). Testing predictions from personality neuroscience: brain structure and the big five. *Psychological Science, 21*(6), 820-828. Copyright © 2010 Sage Publications.

© 2010 Sage Publications

ample, people who differ in neuroticism show different volumes of areas of the prefrontal cortex, anterior cingulate cortex, and hippocampus, areas that have been implicated in sensitivity to threat and stress. People with different levels of conscientiousness had different volumes in areas of the prefrontal cortex involved with planning and the voluntary control of behavior (DeYoung et al., 2010). These relationships are correlational, which means that we do not know whether they are responsible for personality, the result of personality, or caused by some unknown additional variables.

An alternate personality model, reinforcement sensitivity theory (RST), attempts to explain individual differences in approach, avoidance, and inhibition of behavior in terms of the activity of three brain networks known as the behavioral approach system (BAS), the fight–flight freeze system (FFFS), and the behavioral inhibition system (BIS; Gray & McNaughton, 2003; Kennis et al., 2013). Variations in the activity of the BAS predict a person's response to reward, or impulsiv-

After noticing that staff at the Seattle Aquarium had been naming their octopuses based on their behavior (from shy Emily Dickinson to destructive Lucretia McEvil), Jennifer Mather tested 44 octopuses systematically for their responses to stimuli, such as being touched with a brush. The octopuses seemed to have unique and stable responses, similar to having a "personality."

Courtesy of Jennifer Mather/University of Lethbridge and Roland Anderson/Seattle Aquarium

ity. The FFFS is active when an organism experiences unlearned punishment or lack of reward, while the BIS is active when an organism senses learned signals for punishment or lack of reward (Gray, 1970, 1987). Individual differences in FFFS activity might correlate with reactivity, described earlier, while BIS activity might be associated with anxiety levels or neuroticism. Using functional magnetic resonance imaging (fMRI; see Chapter 4), researchers have been able to map the networks in which activity successfully predicts individual differences in these three dimensions of behavior (Kennis et al., 2013).

The Evolution of Personality

If we accept the idea that personality characteristics can be influenced by genetic factors leading to individual differences in brain structure and function, an interesting question arises:

How might differences in personality have evolved? Some evolutionary psychologists argue that characteristics such as the Big Five traits are present across a variety of cultures because these are the characteristics that affect survival in our entire social species (Buss, 1996, 1999).

To bolster the evolutionary approach, it would be useful to identify "personality" in other species and observe its development. Ivan Petrovich Pavlov, discussed in Chapter 8, noticed that individual dogs responded differently to frustration: Some responded "cheerfully," others responded with "anger," some went to sleep, and still others appeared to have had a nervous breakdown (Pavlov, 1906). Using a modified human personality questionnaire to evaluate animals, extroversion and neuroticism have been identified in hyenas, octopuses, guppies, rats, pigs, dogs, cats, donkeys, monkeys, gorillas, and chimpanzees (Gosling, Mollaghan, & Van Lange, 2006). Agreeableness, which might form the basis for cooperative behavior, has been observed to vary in nonhuman primates (Adams, 2011). However, the only species identified as showing variations in conscientiousness were humans and chimpanzees (Gosling et al., 2006).

How Can We Assess Personality?

Personality is assessed, or tested, for a variety of reasons, including the refinement of personality theories, the construction of a correct diagnosis of a psychological disorder, or the selection of an ideal employee.

In everyday life, we make assessments of other people's personalities by listening to them and watching their behavior. Observation remains one of the most reliable means of making judgments about other people (Leichtman, 1995). However, observation takes precious time and can be biased, as we will discuss in Chapter 13. In addition to observation, we rely on interviews. When you meet a person for the first time, you ask questions to see "what kind of person" that individual might be. Although a skilled interviewer might be able to obtain reliable information, it is also easy for the person being interviewed to conceal some aspects of personality.

To avoid the pitfalls of observation and interview, many psychologists turn to standardized tests of personality. In Chapter 2, we noted that good tests require validity and reliability. A valid test literally does the job it is advertised to do. For example, if you constructed a test of creativity, people with high scores on your test should demonstrate more creativity than do people with lower scores. A reliable test returns similar results when it is interpreted by different observers or is taken repeatedly.

The results of standardized personality tests are based on self-report, which might introduce several types of errors. Self-reports can be influenced by a person's need to appear socially appropriate (Cyders & Coskunpinar, 2011). An individual who is applying for a job in sales is unlikely to admit to being shy. In Chapter 9, we distinguished between conscious or explicit and unconscious or implicit memories. Self-report measures do a good job of tapping into our explicit information about our personalities but may not capture implicit aspects of personality (Asendorpf, Banse, & Mücke, 2002). Furthermore, answers on a questionnaire may indicate a person's beliefs but have relatively less to say about how a person would behave. Claiming to be honest on a questionnaire says little about whether a cashier will steal money from the cash register or provide free food for groups of friends, as we will explore in Chapter 13.

One solution to these problems with self-report is to observe behavior directly (Asendorpf et al., 2002). Researchers track behavior in the laboratory or in everyday life. Increasingly, analysis of data from cell phones, Google Glass, or social media provides personality psychologists with ecologically valid snapshots of real behavior (see ● Figure 12.10). Alternately, a growing field of personality neuroscience takes another methodological route.

We can learn quite a bit about "what kind of person" we have just met through an interview, but it is also relatively easy for people being interviewed to present an inaccurate view of their personality.

FIGURE 12.10

Social Media and Behavioral Research. Personality psychologists can take advantage of data from social media platforms like Facebook to obtain ecologically valid snapshots of real behavior. Not surprisingly, the Big Five trait of extroversion correlates with the number of friends a person has on Facebook but only for those whose numbers of friends are in the top 50% of users. *Source:* Data from Bachrach et al. (2012).

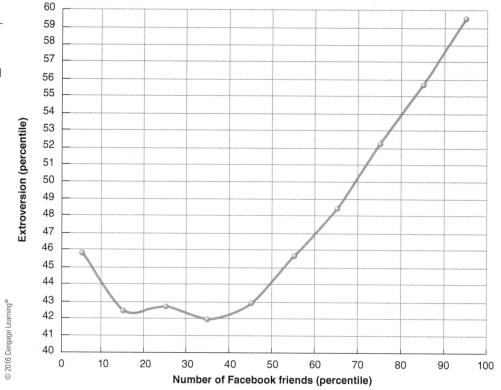

Answers on standardized instruments are correlated with observed differences in brain structure and activity (DeYoung et al., 2010).

Personality Inventories

Personality inventories are objective tests, often using numbered scales or multiple choice, like the short Big Five test that you took earlier in the chapter. These tests have some obvious advantages over more subjective measures, such as interviews or observation. Large numbers of people can be assessed quickly and inexpensively. Many of the tests appear to perform quite well in terms of reliability and validity (McCrae, Kurtz, Yamagata, & Terracciano, 2011).

One of the most frequently used personality inventories is the Minnesota Multiphasic Personality Inventory (MMPI), published in the early 1940s and most recently revised in 2001. This test compares the responses of typical people with those hospitalized for a psychological disorder to a number of true–false items (see ● Figure 12.11; Hathaway & McKinley, 1940, 1943). For example, responses to the statement "I usually feel that life is worthwhile and interesting" might differentiate between people who either are or are not depressed. People with schizophrenia, but not others, are likely to agree with the statement "I seem to hear things that other people can't hear." Although the MMPI was designed to assist with clinical diagnosis, this is only one of its present-day uses. The publisher's website suggests that the test may also be used for college and career counseling recommendations, screening of potential public safety employees, marriage and family counseling, and many other purposes (Pearson Assessments, 2005).

personality inventory An objective test, often using numbered scales or multiple choice, used to assess personality.

The MMPI has been joined by hundreds of additional objective tests featuring personality characteristics, including the NEO-PI-R, which assesses the Big Five traits. Most of these tests use response scales rather than the true–false options of the MMPI. These numbered scales

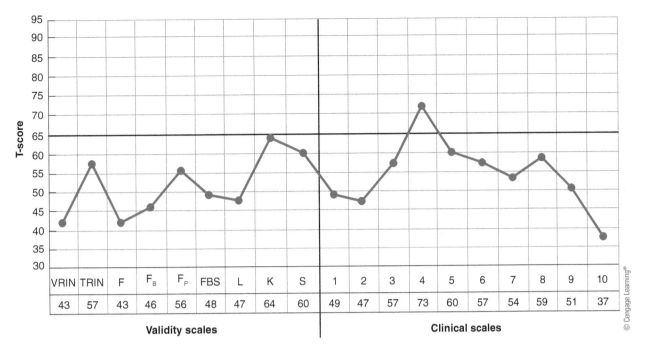

	VRIN	TRIN	F	F$_B$	F$_P$	FBS	L	K	S	1	2	3	4	5	6	7	8	9	10
	43	57	43	46	56	48	47	64	60	49	47	57	73	60	57	54	59	51	37

Validity scales | **Clinical scales**

© Cengage Learning®

FIGURE 12.11

The Minnesota Multiphasic Personality Inventory (MMPI). The MMPI compares a participant's responses along a number of dimensions to people with diagnosed psychological conditions. Scores above 65 are cause for concern. In this case, the individual scored normally with the exception of his score on scale 4, which is the psychopathic deviate scale. This scale measures conflict, struggle, anger, and respect for society's rules. This person might be diagnosed with antisocial personality disorder, which we discuss in Chapter 14.

are often called Likert scales, after one of their earliest proponents, Rensis Likert (Likert, 1932). For example, you might be asked to select the number that best describes you:

Outgoing   7   6   5   4   3   2   1   Withdrawn

Projective Tests

Projective tests are derived directly from projection, one of the Freudian defense mechanisms discussed earlier in this chapter. According to the psychodynamic approach, tests can access the unconscious mind by displaying an ambiguous stimulus, onto which the test participants "project" their personalities as they describe the object.

One of the most famous projective tests is the Rorschach Inkblot Test, which contains 10 different inkblots, some in color and others in black and white (Rorschach, 1921). The job of the participants is to describe what each inkblot looks like to them. These responses are written down by the examiner and scored according to a manual. For example, the examiner might note that a participant talked about a part of the inkblot instead of the entire image. This response would be scored as an indication of the participant's concrete, rather than abstract, way of thinking. Despite serious questions about its reliability and validity (Wood et al., 2010; Wood, Nezworski, & Lilienfeld, 2003), the Rorschach Inkblot Test remains more widely used than the MMPI. Out of a randomly selected group of 1,000 therapist members of the American Psychological Association, 82% reported using the Rorschach at least "occasionally," and 43% use it "frequently" or "always" (Watkins, Campbell, & Nieberding, 1995).

projective test A test of personality based on Freudian theory that provides an ambiguous stimulus onto which test takers "project" their personality.

Swiss psychologist Hermann Rorschach (1884–1922), the son of an artist, was nicknamed "Klecks," or "inkblot," by his high school classmates because of his hobby of making inkblot pictures. After becoming a psychiatrist, he became curious about why people saw the inkblots differently, and he began analyzing their responses. Despite poor validity and reliability, the Rorschach Inkblot Test continues to be used widely.

NetPhotos/Alamy

Thinking Scientifically

Evaluating the Validity and Reliability of Personality Tests

ONE OF THE most widely used personality tests is the Myers–Briggs Type Indicator (MBTI), which is based on the work of one of the neo-Freudians discussed in this chapter, Carl Jung. More than 2 million Americans take the MBTI annually, and most of the top employers in the United States use it for employment purposes (Paul, 2010). After answering a number of forced-choice questions, the MBTI sorts you into 1 of 16 possible personality types combining four dimensions: extroversion–introversion, sensing–intuition, thinking–feeling, and judging–perceiving.

In our discussion of personality testing in general, we noted that validity and reliability were essential features of any good test. How does the MBTI hold up on these criteria? Unfortunately, the answer is not very well (Druckman & Bjork, 1991).

Validity describes how well a test measures what it is supposed to measure. Two approaches to evaluating the validity of the MBTI are using factor analysis, a statistical method described in this chapter that was invented by psychologists interested in personality, and assessing the predictive power of the MBTI (Pittenger, 1993).

Factor analysis allows researchers to explore correlations among items on a personality test like the MBTI. If the MBTI is a valid model, the factor analysis should identify the four clusters, answers to the questions associated with each cluster should be highly correlated with each other, and the questions that fit in a cluster statistically should make sense. In other words, an item stating "I like to be the life of the party" should be found in the extroversion–introversion cluster (Pittenger, 1993). Evidence from the application of factor analysis suggests that the validity of the MBTI is extremely weak.

What about the predictive power of the MBTI? One of the major uses of the test is in career counseling and employment. Unfortunately, there is no evidence that certain MBTI types are more successful than others in an occupation, that certain types are more satisfied with their occupations, or that certain types remain in their occupation longer (Pittenger, 1993).

What about the reliability of the MBTI? In Chapter 2, we discussed a number of meanings for reliability, one of which is test–retest reliability. If your personality as measured by the MBTI is stable, we would expect little variation as you take the test multiple times, but that has not been the case. Instead, even with test–retest intervals as short as 5 weeks, as many as 50% of all test takers will be classified into different types on the second try (Pittenger, 1993).

This leaves us with the real question as to why we continue to use tests that do not meet standard criteria for acceptable levels of validity and reliability. Why is the Rorschach Inkblot Test still admissible to American courts of law? Why do employers invest in the MBTI for their employees?

The Ethics of Personality Testing

Personality tests are widely used by therapists, potential employers, judges, and attorneys (Newitz, 2000). These applications of personality assessment raise important ethical concerns. Who gets to see these data? How are they stored? For what purposes may they be used? Is the examiner trained in the administration and evaluation of tests? In many cases, such as in the use of the MMPI, extremely sensitive and private data may be generated. In other cases, like the Rorschach Inkblot Test, the results are at best controversial. This widely used test has described normal children as having problems approaching psychosis (Garb, Wood, Lilienfeld, & Nezworski, 2005; Hamel, Shaffer, & Erdberg, 2000). Using invalid results to make important real-world decisions could be disastrous.

The American Psychological Association has wrestled with many of these questions, incorporating some conclusions into the organization's code of conduct (American Psychological Association, 2014). Should you be asked to take a personality test, it would be prudent to fully educate yourself regarding the test and make an informed decision about whether to proceed.

Perhaps part of the truth lies in our love of "insight," which drives otherwise reasonable people to consult horoscopes, tarot cards, palm readers, and crystal balls. Upon receiving a description of their MBTI profile, many people have an "aha" moment, but the same could be said of horoscopes. In fairness, however, tests like the MBTI are so well marketed and used by so many reputable institutions that it is natural for the public to feel a level of trust (see ● Figure 12.12).

In Chapter 10, we discussed how decision making depended on a level of understanding of probability theory that might elude even the college graduate, and a similar argument can be made about personality tests. Understanding their strengths and weaknesses requires a sophisticated mastery of statistics that most people simply do not possess. However, what we all can do is use our best critical thinking skills, described in Chapter 2, and at least ask meaningful questions about validity and reliability of the tests we are asked to take rather than passively assuming the tests are what they're advertised to be. ●

Applied to a Target Customer

As a fun example of how this works, let's analyze Carrie—she's an ESFP and the target customer for the Ford Escape compact utility vehicle

ESFP

Personal characteristics	Myers-Briggs preference	Favorite feature
Outgoing and social	Extraversion	Spacious seating for five friends
She lives in the moment and travels to experience life	Sensing	Her powerful EcoBoost engine delivers the fuel efficiency to feed her curiousity
Stays true to her values, beliefs and ideals	Feeling	Intelligent 4WD system helps the vehicle stay grounded
"I know marriage and family is in my future. I crave change!"	Perceiving	Class-exclusive hands-free, foot-activated liftgate is perfect for her evolving lifestyle

Minerva Studio/Shutterstock

FIGURE 12.12

What Not to Do With a Personality Test. Not only is the Myers–Briggs Type Indicator questionable in terms of validity and reliability, but this real-world application of the test to an automobile customer's choice for a "hands-free, foot-activated liftgate" in her car is not in the best scientific tradition.

Summary 12.1 The Big Five Traits

Trait	Description
Openness to experience	Artistic, curious, imaginative, insightful, original, wide interests, unusual thought processes, intellectual interests
Conscientiousness	Efficient, organized, planful, reliable, thorough, dependable, ethical, productive
Extroversion	Active, assertive, energetic, outgoing, talkative, gesturally expressive, gregarious
Agreeableness	Appreciative, forgiving, generous, kind, trusting, noncritical, warm, compassionate, considerate, straightforward
Neuroticism	Anxious, self-pitying, tense, emotionally unstable, impulsive, vulnerable, touchy, prone to worry

What Does It Mean to Have a Self?

One of the most fundamental psychological distinctions we make is the distinction between our self and others. William James argued in favor of "the belief in a distinct principle of self-hood" and believed that such a principle could be studied scientifically (James, 1890, Vol. I, p. 330). Knowing something about the personalities of others makes it easier for us to anticipate what others will feel, think, or do and, therefore, to interact more effectively with them. But what about the patterns of thought, feelings, and actions we see in ourselves? When we think about this personal knowledge, we are thinking about the **self**.

A person's sense of self combines a number of separate factors (Kahn, 2013). Having a self means to have a sense of unity, or of being a single human. The self incorporates a history, or sense of continuity. This aspect of self helps us organize our personal knowledge on a timeline, providing us with a past, present, and future. A sense of embodiment means that the self is embedded in the body (as opposed to the sensation of having an out-of-body experience, discussed in Chapter 6). A self has free will, or the feeling we can do whatever we want to do, and self-location, which means we understand our current location. The self uses a first-person perspective. Finally, the self is embedded in a social network and is influenced by the quality of those relationships.

Scientists have explored a number of questions about the self. What factors influence the development of the self? What are the advantages of a sense of self? Can the sense of self be correlated with brain activity?

Defining the Self

Psychologists approach the study of the self by examining the ABCs: affect, behavior, and cognition. The affective, or emotional, components of the self include our evaluation of the self, or level of self-esteem, which we discuss in greater detail later in this chapter. Behavior and self-concept form reciprocal relationships. We gain self-knowledge by observing our behavior, and our concepts of the type of people we are influence our behavior. Cognitive processes help us organize information and think about the self.

The self does not exist in a vacuum. It both shapes and is shaped by our social environment. Our development of a self sets the stage for our understanding of the behavior of others. Early in infancy, as children begin to recognize themselves as separate beings, they begin to form hypotheses about why others behave in certain ways. This social perception is subject to many of the same strengths and weaknesses that we find in a person's knowledge of the self.

Self-Concept

For the moment, set aside your reading and make a list of 10 things that complete the sentence "I am _____."

If you are like most college students, this description of your **self-concept** includes references to demographic factors, such as age, sex, or student status (first year, psychology major, etc.); personality features (outgoing or shy); relationships with others (friend, lover, daughter, son, sister, brother, etc.); physical attributes (pretty, tall, brown eyed, etc.); and various other roles (athlete, club member, Texan, etc.).

We use **self-schemas** to think about these many aspects of the self (Markus, 1977). As we discussed in Chapters 10 and 11, schemas provide cognitive structures for organizing information. The structure provided by a self-schema influences not only the way you view yourself but also how you view and interact with others.

A major implication of having a self-schema is the suggestion that we may process self-relevant information differently than the same type of information about others. For example, we might think about our own brown hair in different ways than we think about our neighbor's brown hair. In one of the earliest studies on this self-reference effect (SRE), four

f John Cacioppo

f Laura Freberg

Our self-concept captures the way we see ourselves, which we often portray through our choice of social networking profile pictures. Here are your authors' current profile pictures on Facebook. What do your profile pictures say to others about you?

self Patterns of thought, feelings, and actions we perceive in our own minds.
self-concept People's description of their own characteristics.
self-schema A cognitive organization that helps us think about the self and process self-relevant information.

FIGURE 12.13

Using a Self-Schema Improves Recall for Words. Participants in this experiment were asked whether a word was in larger font (structural), rhymed with another word (phonemic), meant the same thing as another word (semantic), or described the participant (self-reference). As you can see from these results, when participants used their self-schemas to consider a word, later recall for the word was better than when the word was considered structurally, phonemically, or semantically. These results suggest that your memory for material you are studying will be improved by thinking about how it relates to your own life. *Source:* Adapted from "Self-Reference and the Encoding of Personal Information," by T. B. Rogers, N. A. Kuiper, and W. S. Kirker, 1977, *Journal of Personality and Social Psychology, 35*(9), pp. 677–688. doi:10.1037/0022-3514.35.9.677.

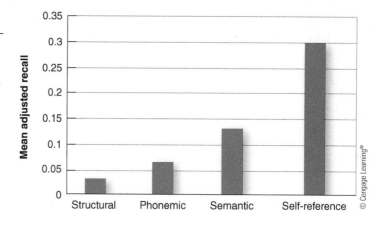

groups of participants were given lists of adjectives to memorize with different instructions (Rogers, Kuiper, & Kirker, 1977). The first group judged the size of letters making up the word, the second group judged whether the word rhymed with another word, the third group judged whether the word had the same meaning as another word, and the last group judged whether the word described them. The fourth group's recall for the words was subsequently superior to recall by the other groups (see ● Figure 12.13). These results implied that the self provided "a superordinate schema" (Rogers et al., 1977, p. 685).

Questions remain, however, as to the true cause of the observed SRE. Is there something special about self-schemas, or is the SRE simply a result of general memory processes, such as depth of processing or elaboration, which we discussed in Chapter 9? For example, memory enhancement also occurred in a group that judged whether words described the study participants' mothers (Bower & Gilligan, 1979). We may remember self-relevant information simply because we know a lot about the subject—ourselves.

Self-Awareness

When answering the questions posed in the previous section, how do you know what to say? To know yourself requires you to make the self an object to be examined. Just as you try to figure out what kind of people your classmates and instructor are, you have the capacity to turn this analysis inward to the self. Self-awareness, or knowledge of your own internal traits, feelings, roles, and memories, is the result of this self-study. In addition, self-awareness allows us to establish boundaries between the self and other people. When we talk about ourselves, look at ourselves in a mirror, watch a video of ourselves, or stand out from the crowd in some way, we become more self-aware than usual. This state of heightened self-awareness is typically quite unpleasant for most people. Many people experience negative mood when they look in a mirror (Fejfar & Hoyle, 2000).

Related to this negative self-awareness is the concept of self-consciousness, our awareness of our own characteristics and the way the self is perceived by others. In many cases, we overestimate how much attention others pay to our behavior, a phenomenon known as the spotlight effect. When student participants wearing an embarrassing T-shirt featuring 1970s pop singer Barry Manilow entered a room full of other students, they expected at least half of their fellow students to notice (Gilovich, Medvec, & Savitsky, 2000). In fact, only 23% of the students paid attention to the T-shirts. The particularly active spotlight effect that often accompanies puberty is responsible for much of the pain of adolescence (Elkind, 1967; Elkind & Bowen, 1979). As a result, teens are typically convinced that every flaw and blemish they possess will be scrutinized by others. How reassuring it would be to understand that other teens are so worried about the imaginary audience's reactions to their own flaws and blemishes that they scarcely have time to notice the flaws of others.

Self-consciousness might be unpleasant, but it makes people behave more ethically. When children were instructed by a sign to "take only one Halloween candy," they were more likely to comply when they could see their image in a mirror (Beaman, Klentz, Diener, & Svanum, 1979). In a similar study, an honor-system coffee bar featured either a poster showing a pair of eyes or a poster showing a bouquet of flowers (Bateson, Nettle, & Roberts, 2006). People were more likely to put money in the box to pay for their coffee when they saw the poster of the eyes (see ● Figure 12.14).

Sources of Self-Knowledge How do we obtain self-knowledge? An obvious source of self-awareness is the process of introspection, or the direct observation of one's own thoughts and feelings. After all, who is in a better position to know what goes on inside our heads than we are? Unfortunately, as we discussed in Chapters 1 and 2, introspection as a scientific method is not considered very reliable.

Perhaps we could bypass mental states and focus instead on our observable behavior. People seem to use their behavior as a clue to their characteristics, just as any other observer does (Bem, 1972). If they see themselves behaving in a kindly and respectful way toward others, maybe they are kindly and respectful people. In support of this approach, people who were gently encouraged to provide flattering descriptions of themselves scored higher on a subsequent test of self-esteem (Jones, Rhodewalt, Berglas, & Skelton, 1981). In other words, if they observe themselves providing a positive self-analysis, it must be true.

The people around us also contribute to our self-knowledge. We use the reactions of other people like a mirror to "see" our own characteristics, developing a looking-glass self. We also incorporate the opinions of significant others about us into our self-concept. If our parents viewed us as brilliant, it is likely that we would view ourselves as brilliant too. Unfortunately, using the reactions of others works better when defining some characteristics than others. If our parents inaccurately view us as brilliant, we soon learn the truth at school. If they unfairly think we're lazy, though, it is more difficult to figure out they're wrong.

An obvious component of self-knowledge arises from autobiographical and episodic memories, described in Chapter 9. Who we are today is intimately linked with the self from the past that we remember. While offering valuable information about "who we are," episodic and autobiographical memories can provide a partial, incomplete, and occasionally inaccurate picture. As one psychologist noted, "The past is remembered as if it were a drama in which the self was the leading player" (Greenwald, 1980, p. 604).

Barry Manilow might have sold millions of records in the 1970s, but students in 2000 thought wearing this shirt would be embarrassing. We tend to overestimate how much attention others pay to us, though, and only 23% of study participants noticed the T-shirt.

Self-Esteem

Not only do we form a self-concept, but we also judge its value. This personal report card is known as **self-esteem**. Self-esteem may be global, based on our overall self-worth, or specific, relating to particular characteristics such as appearance or intelligence. Self-esteem introduces an emotional aspect to our self-concept. Not only do we judge ourselves, but we experience emotional responses to that judgment.

self-esteem A judgment of the value of the self.

FIGURE 12.14

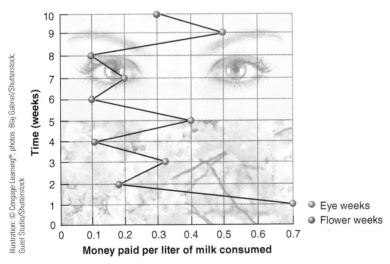

Self-Consciousness and Honesty. The amount of money collected in a college department honor-system coffee bar relative to consumption was measured by tracking milk consumption (this study was conducted in the United Kingdom, where coffee is rarely consumed black). Donations increased when a poster of eyes appeared above the bar and decreased when a poster of flowers appeared above the bar. Self-consciousness, perhaps from feeling "watched" by the photograph of eyes, typically results in more ethical behavior. Whether we are responding similarly to the large numbers of surveillance cameras in our environments remains to be demonstrated through future research. *Source:* Adapted from "Cues of Being Watched Enhance Cooperation in a Real-World Setting," by M. Bateson, D. Nettle, and G. Roberts, 2006, *Biology Letters*, *2*(3), pp. 412–414.

These judgments of the self are not necessarily accurate. Most people experience "positive illusions," which lead them to judge themselves more positively and less negatively than they judge others (Taylor & Brown, 1988). Despite inaccuracies, people who experience positive illusions typically enjoy a heightened sense of well-being.

People with high and low self-esteem respond quite differently to failure. The low self-esteem person tends to overgeneralize from failure (Brown & Mankowski, 1993). In other words, people with low self-esteem who fail one exam might assume that they are going to fail all their classes. This tendency to overgeneralize may explain why people with low self-esteem are more prone to depression (Sowislo & Orth, 2013), discussed further in Chapter 14. In contrast, people with high self-esteem respond to failure in one domain by exaggerating their abilities in other domains (Brown & Smart, 1991). If people with high self-esteem fail an exam, they are more likely to remind others about how great they are in sports, appearance, or dating.

Sources of Self-Esteem Because of the importance of self-esteem to psychological well-being, psychologists have looked at the origins of self-esteem carefully. Many psychologists believe that the process of developing self-esteem begins early in childhood. Long before children have a working model of the self, they are experiencing the emotional consequences of acceptance and rejection (Erikson, 1963; Sroufe, Carlson, & Levy, 2003). As we discussed in Chapter 11, children form a variety of attachments with their primary caregivers (Ainsworth, Blehar, Waters, & Wall, 1978; Bowlby, 1969/1982), which can predict a child's self-esteem at the age of 6 years (Cassidy, 1988). Self-esteem does not appear to change much over the life span (Block & Robins, 1993; Trzesniewski, Donnellan, & Robins, 2003). Early differences in self-esteem seem to be magnified and reinforced over time, because having high or low self-esteem influences both the selection of activities and the reactions of others to the self.

Self-esteem is also influenced by social comparisons, or the judgments we make of our own worth relative to those around us (Festinger, 1954). The impact of social comparisons on self-esteem was demonstrated in an experiment in which researchers placed an advertisement for a research assistant (Morse & Gergen, 1970). Prospective employees found themselves in a waiting room with another candidate, who was actually an actor working for the experimenters. The actor took the role of either Mr. Clean or Mr. Dirty. Participants waiting with Mr. Clean experienced drops in self-esteem, whereas the self-esteem of participants waiting with Mr. Dirty rose.

People with high self-esteem tend to make downward comparisons, in which they compare themselves to those they consider less worthy on a particular dimension. For example, a beautiful woman with high self-esteem is more likely to congratulate herself on how much

Dove, a division of Unilever that produces skin and hair care products, lists its "social mission" as building women's self-esteem. The company reports that only 4% of women worldwide consider themselves beautiful. To combat the influence of upward social comparisons, in which girls and women judge their attractiveness against the impossibly beautiful images of women in the media, Dove produced a video featuring the transformation of a model's real photograph (before on the left) into the Photoshopped product on a billboard (after on the right).

better looking she is than her friends but is unlikely to compare herself with the current crop of Hollywood beauties. In contrast, people with low self-esteem are likely to do the opposite. A beautiful woman with low self-esteem will engage in upward comparisons, chastising herself because she doesn't measure up to the most beautiful women in the world.

Regardless of self-esteem, we all seem to engage in a reassuring type of downward comparison when viewing our own pasts (Wilson & Ross, 2000). Most of us look back in time with a sense that we have improved. Our virtues are greater today than they used to be, and our faults are less.

Gender, Race, and Culture and Self-Esteem Given the influence of social comparisons on self-esteem, we might suspect that belonging to certain social groups would affect an individual's self-esteem. If you are a member of a privileged group in society, for example, shouldn't you have higher self-esteem than that of people who have experienced prejudice and discrimination?

Higher rates of depression among women, discussed further in Chapter 14, might predict that females would have lower self-esteem than males. In a very large meta-analysis representing thousands of participants, males had a very small advantage over females in self-esteem (Kling, Hyde, Showers, & Buswell, 1999). This advantage is larger in adolescence and early adulthood but dissipates with age.

Similar meta-analyses of self-esteem demonstrated differences based on race and ethnicity in the United States (Erol & Orth, 2011; Twenge & Crocker, 2002). As we noted in Chapter 11, beginning in adolescence, Black Americans score higher than White Americans in measures of self-esteem. However, Americans identifying themselves as Asian or Native American scored below White Americans in measures of self-esteem. Hispanic adolescents had lower self-esteem than White teens but reported higher self-esteem at age 30 than White Americans (Erol & Orth, 2011).

Cultural differences among groups might account for some of these results. As we mentioned previously, people in more collectivistic cultures might avoid standing out from the group by giving themselves highly positive ratings (see ● Figure 12.15). Results from tests that tap into implicit attitudes by asking participants to associate themselves with either positive words (*glorious, happy, laughter*) or negative words (*agony, horrible, nasty*) suggest that Asian Americans have about the same level of self-esteem as White Americans but that cultural values of modesty usually override their outward expression of that self-esteem (Greenwald & Farnham, 2000).

Using Self-Enhancement to Protect Self-Esteem The good news is that most of us feel rather positively about ourselves. The bad news is that we are a wee bit unrealistic. People who perform most poorly are the most likely to engage in self-enhancement by inflating their opinions of themselves. College students who performed in the bottom 12% on tests of logic, grammar, and humor guessed that they performed better than 62% of their

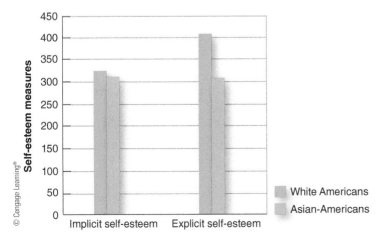

White Americans
Asian-Americans

FIGURE 12.15

Cultural Differences in Explicit and Implicit Measures of Self-Esteem. Apparent cultural differences in self-esteem must be evaluated carefully. Using explicit measures of self-esteem, it appears that White Americans have higher self-esteem than Asian Americans. However, when implicit measures of self-esteem are used, this difference disappears, suggesting that the observed difference is probably because of cultural norms related to modesty. *Source:* Adapted from "Using the Implicit Association Test to Measure Self-Esteem and Self-Concept," by A. G. Greenwald and S. D. Farnham, 2000, *Journal of Personality and Social Psychology, 79,* pp. 1022–1038.

© Sarah Storelli

The bask-in-reflected-glory (BIRG) effect predicts that sales of apparel featuring a winning team are likely to be much higher than those for a losing team. Associating with those we admire can produce self-enhancement.

peers (Kruger & Dunning, 1999). As student performance increased, the amount of inflation decreased.

Some people begin protecting their self-esteem long before a performance takes place. In self-handicapping, people begin to build an excuse in advance, just in case they fail (Berglas & Jones, 1978). People use a number of self-handicapping strategies, including taking drugs, failing to practice or do homework, commenting on poor health or stress, or sandbagging. Sandbagging occurs when you let everyone know how bad you are at something. By lowering expectations of your performance, nobody will notice much when you fail. Although self-handicapping may protect your self-esteem, it does not make you popular with others (Rhodewalt, Sandonmatsu, Tschanz, Feick, & Waller, 1995).

Another protective method for self-enhancement is to associate with others you admire. This approach has been labeled the bask-in-reflected-glory (BIRG) effect (Cialdini et al., 1976). On the Monday following a football game, university students are more likely to wear sweatshirts with their school's name if their team won than if it lost. We are equally quick to distance ourselves from failure. Many an athlete or performer has been surprised at how many "friends" they have during successful times, and how quickly those friends disappear when times are tough.

Self-enhancement may serve to protect self-esteem, but it can have a number of unwanted effects. Primary among these negative side effects is being disliked by others. People who engage in self-enhancement typically make good first impressions, but these impressions do not last (Paulhus, 1998).

The Advantages of Self-Esteem
Having high self-esteem provides a number of benefits both to the individual and to the groups to which the individual with high self-esteem belongs. Among the advantages of high self-esteem to the individual are happiness and persistence (Baumeister, Campbell, Krueger, & Vohs, 2003). These outcomes occur because high self-esteem acts as a buffer. When faced with bad news, people with high self-esteem are more likely to weather the storm than are people with low self-esteem. In addition, high self-esteem enhances social dominance within a peer group (Juvonen, 2005).

Self-esteem contributes to belongingness, or the maintenance of good social relationships (Baumeister & Leary, 1995; Leary, 2004; Leary & Downs, 1995; Leary, Tambor, Terdal, & Downs, 1995). Because social rejection could have such devastating effects on survival in our evolutionary past, self-esteem could have emerged as a way of estimating the likelihood of rejection. Self-esteem drops following the experience of social exclusion (Leary et al., 1995). A drop in self-esteem serves as an early warning signal that rejection by the group is imminent and that behavior designed to regain the favor of the group should be initiated (see ● Figure 12.16).

A terror management theory suggests that self-esteem interacts with a cultural worldview to buffer our fear of death (Greenberg, Pyszczynski, & Solomon, 1986; Pyszczynski, Greenberg, & Solomon, 1991). Cultural worldviews can include shared beliefs that allow us to attain feelings of immortality, whether through producing children, writing books, or believing in an afterlife. By conforming to these cultural worldviews, people enjoy enhanced self-esteem that reduces their anxiety related to death.

Having members with high self-esteem is an advantage to groups in several respects. People with high self-esteem are more likely to speak critically when in groups (LePine & Van Dyne, 1998). Groups that do not have members who are willing to question group decisions might fall prey to poor decision making, discussed further in Chapter 13. People with high self-esteem not only value themselves but also value the groups to which they belong (Aberson, Healy, & Robero, 2000). People with low self-esteem do not show this favoritism. If a group is highly valued by its members, its overall success is likely to be enhanced, which in turn benefits its members.

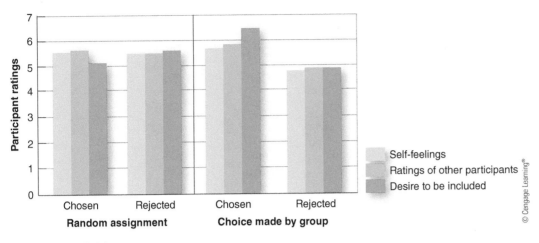

FIGURE 12.16

Self-Esteem as a Signal for Social Rejection. Study participants who believed they had been rejected as group project members by peers experienced reduced self-feelings (self-esteem), rated the other participants more negatively, and expressed a lower desire to be included than participants who either were chosen by the group or believed group membership had been randomly assigned. Believing that you were chosen by the group, however, did not improve self-esteem. These results suggest that feelings of low self-esteem might have developed over the course of human history as a warning signal for social rejection. *Source:* Adapted from "Self-Esteem as an Interpersonal Monitor: The Sociometer Hypothesis," by M. R. Leary, E. S. Tambor, S. K. Terdal, and D. L. Downs, 1995, *Journal of Personality and Social Psychology*, *68*, pp. 518–530.

Terror management theory suggests that self-esteem serves as a protection against our fear of death. When people are reminded of their own mortality, self-esteem can increase. Ironically, these labels proposed by the government for cigarette packages might have the unintended consequences of enhancing, rather than diminishing, favorable attitudes about smoking. Some smokers equate smoking with improving their image, which in turn improves their self-esteem (Hansen, Winzeler, & Topolinski, 2009).

Psychology as a Hub Science

Self-Esteem, Academic Performance, and Juvenile Delinquency

Although many people believe that raising children's self-esteem is a good thing, research suggests that self-esteem is more likely to be the outcome rather than the cause of behavior. Providing feel-good messages that are not based in real achievement can backfire (Forsyth & Kerr, 1999).

The claims made on behalf of self-esteem are often dramatic. The California Task Force on Self-Esteem and Personal and Social Responsibility published a report that declared "many, if not most, of the major problems plaguing society have roots in the low self-esteem of many of the people who make up society" (Mecca, Smelser, & Vasconcellos, 1989, p. 1). Teachers, parents, and therapists express similar beliefs and actively work to increase the self-esteem of others. These approaches mirror a commonsense attitude toward self-esteem. High self-esteem seems more desirable than low self-esteem, and interventions designed to raise self-esteem appear on the surface to be a good thing. How accurate are these views of self-esteem?

Self-esteem and school grades are positively correlated, although the effects are not large (Hansford & Hattie, 1982). The important question, however, is whether high self-esteem is a result or a cause of good grades. As we discussed in Chapter 2, it is not possible to use correlational data to determine causal factors. Consider the example of students who achieve very high grades. Does the students' success reflect the impact of high self-esteem, or does the achievement of high grades make the students feel more positively about themselves? Or like many correlations, is an unidentified third factor such as intelligence or social class responsible for the observed correlation?

Explicit efforts to identify the causal relationships between self-esteem and school performance have failed to support the commonsense hypothesis that high self-esteem produces good performance. A sample of 1,600 young males in the 10th grade was followed for an additional 8 years (Bachman & O'Malley, 1977). No evidence for a causal role for self-esteem in school performance was discovered. Instead, third factors, including socioeconomic status, IQ, and early school performance, appeared to be responsible for the correlation between self-esteem and school performance. Among studies that have reported a causal relationship between self-esteem and school performance, the direction of the relationship is not consistent with the commonsense hypothesis. High self-esteem is more likely to be a result of good grades, not vice versa (Rosenberg, Schooler, & Schoenbach, 1989).

What do these findings mean for efforts like the California Task Force, which sought to raise achievement by improving self-esteem? Unfortunately, interventions intended to boost self-esteem may backfire. When students receiving poor grades on a midterm were sent an e-mail message designed to boost their self-worth, they performed significantly worse on the next exams than did students in control groups (Forsyth & Kerr, 1999). This study provides an important lesson for those who wish to raise self-esteem: Providing indiscriminate feel-good messages that are not anchored in real achievement may result in lower achievement.

If relationships between school achievement and self-esteem are weaker than many believe, what about the relationships between self-esteem and social problems such as aggression? Again, our commonsense hypotheses fail us. We have heard parents, teachers, and legislators lament that many social problems would dissipate if only we could raise self-esteem. Bullies, we were told, were especially likely to suffer from low self-esteem. This commonsense notion was challenged by Roy Baumeister and his colleagues, who discovered that aggressive people were more likely to have positive, and frequently inflated, views of their self-worth (Baumeister et al., 2003; Baumeister, Smart, & Boden, 1996).

Not only are bullies unlikely to suffer from low self-esteem, they are less anxious, less depressed, and less lonely than prosocial youth who do not participate in bullying (Juvonen, 2005). Even more disturbing is the finding that middle school students rate their bullying peers as "the coolest kids in their classes" (Juvonen, 2005, p. 37). Instead of raising the self-esteem of bullies, which might make things worse, school-based programs could try to reduce the reinforcing admiration bullies receive from their peers. ●

Contrary to many stereotypes, bullies typically do not suffer from low self-esteem. They experience less depression, less anxiety, and less loneliness than prosocial youth and are likely to be considered by peers "the coolest kids in their classes" (Juvonen, 2005).

Self-Regulation

To meet the expectations we have for ourselves, we often engage in self-regulation, also known as self-control or willpower. Self-regulation consists of conscious executive efforts to control our thoughts, motives, feelings, and behaviors (Carver & Scheier, 2000). Failures to regulate behavior frequently lead to some of the most perplexing problems facing society, including drug abuse, domestic violence, and binge eating. In addition, deficits in self-regulation characterize a number of psychological disorders we discuss in Chapter 14, including schizophrenia, attention deficit hyperactivity disorder (ADHD), and obsessive-compulsive disorder.

We do not appear to enjoy unlimited supplies of self-regulation (Muraven & Baumeister, 2000). Once we use up our personal supply, we are temporarily more vulnerable to temptation. In an experiment that shouldn't surprise anyone who has been on a diet, female dieting participants watched a documentary in the presence of snacks that were either within reach or across the room (Vohs & Heatherton, 2000). Subsequently, the participants were given the opportunity to "test" as much ice cream as they'd like. The participants who had watched the documentary with snacks right in front of them ate more ice cream than the previously less-tempted participants. The implications of this experiment suggest that dieters and others who wish to change habits would be served well by limiting their exposure to temptation, thus saving their self-regulatory energy reserves.

What is the source of the depletion effect? A major candidate for the limited resource used in self-regulation is glucose (Gailliot & Baumeister, 2007). However, the depletion of willpower effect seems to depend on the study participants' top-down belief that willpower is limited (see ● Figure 12.17). People who already believed that willpower was limited or who were encouraged to hold this belief were the only ones who demonstrated the depletion effect (Job, Dweck, & Walton, 2010; Job, Walton, Bernecker, & Dweck, 2013). People who view willpower as unlimited showed no depletion effects. How do we reconcile these findings with the glucose depletion hypothesis? It appears that we have sufficient quantities of glucose on hand but that our top-down processing determines how much of our available supply we allocate to self-regulation (Beedie & Lane, 2012).

FIGURE 12.17

Top-Down Influences on Willpower. Many studies have duplicated the results demonstrated by the green bars on this graph. Being asked to use willpower before completing a difficult task increases the number of mistakes made. However, the participants represented by the orange bars do not show the willpower depletion effect. They are the participants who believe they have an unlimited supply of willpower. *Source:* "Ego Depletion—Is It All in Your Head? Implicit Theories About Willpower Affect Self-Regulation," by V. Job, C. S. Dweck, and G. M. Walton, 2010, *Psychological Science, 21*(11), pp. 1686–1693.

Self-regulation is made even more difficult because the harder we think about not doing something, the more likely we are to do it (Wegner, 1994). Try, for example, to avoid thinking about a white bear for the next 30 seconds. If you are like most people, your thoughts were suddenly dominated by images of white bears. We can explain this phenomenon as follows. When you try to control your behavior, you simultaneously activate a concern about failing. In an effort to avoid failure, you automatically pay more attention to the item or behavior to be avoided. "What exactly is this white bear thing I should avoid?" Because of this attention, we end up doing what we hoped to avoid doing.

The Brain and the Self

If the mind is the product of the activity of the nervous system, is it possible to locate the self within these patterns of activity? This question suggests that information about the self is processed in unique and special ways by the nervous system (Gillihan & Farah, 2005). As we have seen so far in this chapter, the concept of self can mean many things. Brain correlates have been found for our knowledge of our own bodies—their configuration, appearance, and location—as well as for our memories of personal experiences, our interpersonal connections, and our use of a first-person perspective.

Given the large number of different aspects of the self discussed in this chapter, it should not be surprising that a widely distributed network of brain structures participates in the processing of the self (Cacioppo & Decety, 2011b). Activity in the default mode network (DMN; see Chapter 6) is often associated with thinking about the self (Kahn, 2013). However, during thinking about the self, activity in the DMN is joined by activity in parts of the brain that process external sources of information, such as the awareness of other people and the environment. These observations remind us of our constant use of context when we think about ourselves.

An important aspect of the self is the recognition of our own faces. The right hemisphere appears to play a special role in distinguishing our own faces from those of other people. In one study, one hemisphere of each participant's brain was made inactive using an anesthetic. When study participants then viewed a photograph combining one half of their face with the half-face of a famous person, they recognized themselves when the left hemisphere was anesthetized but reported seeing the famous person when the right hemisphere was anesthetized (Keenan, Nelson, O'Connor, & Pascual-Leone, 2001; see ● Figure 12.18).

In addition to playing an important role in recognizing our own faces, the right hemisphere could be necessary for the construction of our stable traits and attitudes. The location of brain damage because of a type of age-related dementia (right hemisphere only, left hemisphere only, or both hemispheres) can be correlated with observed changes in personal characteristics that usually show little change over time, such as political views and religious beliefs (Miller et al., 2001). Only people with right hemisphere damage alone showed changes in these normally stable characteristics.

Schizophrenia, which we discuss more fully in Chapter 14, often produces distortions in a person's sense of self (Feinberg, 1978). One common symptom is a delusion of control, or the sense that some external agent is either monitoring or influencing a person's behavior. This delusion is highly relevant to our current discussion, because it represents confusion over the behavior produced by the self or by others. For example, people with this symptom might describe their behavior as controlled by others through implants in their brains. A comparison of brain activity during such delusions and after they recede indicated that the delusions of control were correlated with excess activity in the right hemisphere (Spence et al., 1997).

Sometimes when we try to use our self-regulation abilities to not think of something ("Whatever you do, don't think about white bears"), we end up thinking quite a bit about the object we wish to avoid.

▲ Emotional domain: self > nonself
▽ Facial domain: self > nonself
▫ Memory domain: self > nonself
◆ Motor domain: self > nonself
◁ Social domain: self ∩ other
○ Social domain: self > other
✤ Spatial domain: self > nonself
▶ Verbal domain: self > nonself

A widely distributed network of brain structures participates in processing the different aspects of self. Self-referential processing, or the processing of information relevant to ourselves but not others, can occur in our emotional, facial, memory, motor, social, spatial, and verbal domains. *Source:* From Northoff, G., et al. (2006) "Self-referential processing in our brain—A meta-analysis of imaging studies on the self," *NeuroImage 31*(1), 440-457.

(a)

(b)

Illustration: Argosy Publishing, Inc.; photo (Marilyn): Alfred Eisenstaedt/Pix Inc./Time & Life Pictures/Getty Images

FIGURE 12.18

Recognizing Your Own Face. Participants in this experiment viewed blended faces made from one half of their own photograph and one half of a photograph of a famous person. When the participants' left hemispheres (LHs) were anesthetized, leaving the right hemisphere (RH) active, they believed the photo was their own (a). When their right hemispheres were anesthetized, leaving the left hemisphere active, most believed the photo showed the famous person (b). These results suggest that for many people, the right hemisphere plays a role in recognizing our own faces. *Source:* Adapted from "Self-Recognition and the Right Hemisphere," by J. P. Keenan, A. Nelson, M. O'Connor, and A. Pascual-Leone, 2001, *Nature, 409*(6818), pp. 305.

The Social Self

The self we have discussed so far represents the personal self, or the attributes that differentiate an individual's self from all others (Brewer & Gardner, 1996). This self both shapes and is shaped by interactions with others. Just who those others are and how they interact with the self has been the subject of significant psychological inquiry.

The Interpersonal Self William James remarked that an individual has "as many different social selves as there are distinct groups of persons about whose opinion he cares" (James, 1890, Vol. I, p. 294). In other words, in addition to having a personal self, we experience an **interpersonal self**. In current psychological discussions of the self, influences on the interpersonal self fall into two categories—a person's significant others and the social groups to which the person belongs. Significant others include family members, friends, coworkers, and others with whom the self interacts or has interacted. As we interact with significant others, we experience the relational self (Brewer & Gardner, 1996; Chen, Boucher, & Tapias, 2006). The influence of the larger groups to which we belong provides our collective self (Brewer & Gardner, 1996).

The concept of the interpersonal self implies that an individual's self is more flexible and complex than it would be on the basis of a personal self alone. This flexibility is illustrated by the suggestion that we have a relational self when we are with a particular person, such as the "me when I'm with mom" (Chen et al., 2006, p. 153). It is likely that a great deal of overlap occurs among the many interpersonal selves we experience, but recognizing that we may not

interpersonal self The self we are in the presence of other people.

When we interact with significant others, such as family members, we experience the relational self. When we interact with larger groups, such as other fans supporting the same sports team, like these Brazilian soccer fans, we experience the collective self.

 Connecting to **Research**

Effects of Culture on the Self Can Be Modified

OUR DISCUSSION OF CULTURE AND the self has assumed that individualistic and collectivistic values are socially transmitted to people growing up in a culture and that these values in turn result in a stable and relatively unchanging view of the self. However, we can also assume that regardless of culture, all humans share both a need for independence and a need to belong. If this is the case, is it possible to show that a situation can modify a person's emphasis on individualistic and collectivistic values (Gardner, Gabriel, & Lee, 1999)?

The Question: Can cultural influences on the self be modified by a person's situation?

METHODS

Seventy-five White American college students and 82 Chinese students attending the University of Hong Kong participated in this study. Thinking about independence versus interdependence was manipulated by reading a story about a general choosing a warrior to send to the king. The stories differed in the warrior chosen (the best individual for the job versus a member of the family) and in the benefits of the choice (benefits to the general versus benefits to his family). A control group did not hear a story. The effects of the two stories were assessed by asking each study participant to complete a values inventory that measures how obligated a person feels to help others.

RESULTS

Participants hearing the independence version of the warrior story, regardless of culture, produced more individualistic responses to the values survey than collectivistic responses. Participants hearing the interdependence version of the warrior story, again regardless of culture, produced more collectivistic responses to the values survey than individualistic responses. Participants who heard a story that was consistent with their cultural norms (independence for American participants and interdependence for Chinese participants) did not differ in their responses to the values survey from the control groups from their respective cultures.

DISCUSSION

Although we tend to think of culture influencing the self, this experiment demonstrated that views of the self as independent or interdependent can be changed by a person's immediate situation (such as hearing a story that emphasizes one aspect or the other). This result supports the ideas that both the need for independence and the need to belong are human universals and that the relative dominance of one over the other is modifiable through experience and situational variables (see ● Figure 12.19). ●

be consistent across all social situations is important. The differences we experience echo the discussion earlier in the chapter about personality traits and situations.

Cultural Influences on the Self Given the interpersonal dimensions of the self described in the previous section, it should come as no surprise that the concept of the self means different things in different cultures.

One aspect of cultural differences that is particularly relevant to the study of the self is the distinction between individualism and collectivism (see ● Figure 12.20). Individualism is characterized by an emphasis on independence and self-reliance. In contrast, core values of collectivism include interdependence, cooperation, and lack of conflict. As we discussed in the introduction to this chapter, these relative weightings of self and others tend to characterize entire nations. The United States, Australia, Great Britain, Canada, and the Netherlands appear to be the most individualistic, while Venezuela, Colombia, Pakistan, Peru, Taiwan, and China appear to be the most collectivistic (Hofstede, 1980).

Two major differences occur between highly individualistic cultures and more collectivistic cultures (Markus & Kitayama, 1991). The first difference predicts a person's source of satisfaction. People in individualistic cultures feel best about themselves when they experience personal achievement, whereas people in collectivistic cultures feel good about belonging to a

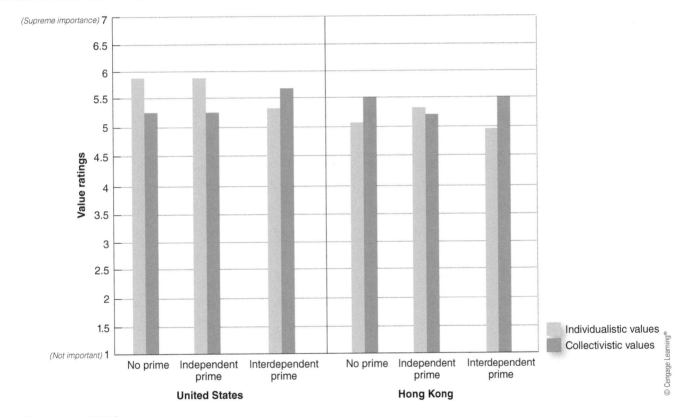

FIGURE 12.19

Individualism and Collectivism Are Modifiable. Listening to a story that emphasized individualistic or collectivistic values elicited congruent responses from study participants, regardless of whether they lived in an individualistic culture (United States) or a collectivistic culture (Hong Kong). These results suggest that both independent and interdependent views of the self are human universals and that the relative dominance of one over the other is modifiable by a person's experience and situation. *Source:* Adapted from "'I' Value Freedom, but 'We' Value Relationships: Self-Construal Priming Mirrors Cultural Differences in Judgment," by W. Gardner, S. Gabriel, and A. Y. Lee, 1999, *Psychological Science, 10*(4), pp. 321–326.

FIGURE 12.20

Individualism and Collectivism.
Geert Hofstede compared cultures on five dimensions relevant to individualism and collectivism. Compared to the Chinese, Americans are less tolerant of unequal distributions of power (PDI), more likely to expect self-reliance (IDV), about equally assertive and competitive rather than modest and caring (MAS), more tolerant of ambiguity and lack of structure (UAI), and far less thrifty and persistent (LTO).

PDI: Less powerful accept and expect that power is distributed unequally.
IDV: Refers to individuals or groups, not the state, and their role in taking care of you.
MAS: Higher numbers indicate more assertive and competitive, rather than modest and caring.
UAI: Tolerance for ambiguity, unstructured situations.
LTO: Thrift, perseverance

© 2016 Cengage Learning®

successful group. For example, a baseball player from an individualistic culture, such as the United States, might take pride in having a terrific batting average, even though his team is losing, whereas the player from a more collectivistic culture, such as Japan, might feel better about being a member of the top team regardless of his personal performance.

The second difference predicts a person's sense of being similar to other group members. In individualistic cultures, people are more likely to see themselves as unique. In collectivistic cultures, conformity and appearing similar to others are more highly valued. White American and Korean study participants were offered the gift of a pen, which they were to choose from a group of three or four pens of the same color and one pen with a unique color. Whereas 74% of the White Americans chose the uniquely colored pen, 76% of the Koreans chose a pen with the more common color (Kim & Markus, 1999).

The individualistic–collectivistic nature of a culture is a moving target across time (Hamamura, 2012), and our characterization of particular social groups requires constant updating. For example, a recent meta-analysis of individualism and collectivism among European Americans, African Americans, Latino Americans, and Asian Americans suggest that although minor differences remain, values related to individualism and collectivism are becoming more similar across these groups (Vargas & Kemmelmeier, 2013).

Interpersonal Relationships
The Personality Perspective
How Does Personality Affect Attraction?

Personality provides a perfect opportunity to revisit the "birds of a feather flock together" theme that we discussed previously in this textbook. Is it true that two people who have similar personalities are attracted to each other?

In Chapter 11, we discussed research that showed that people in long-term relationships who have similar personalities experienced different levels of satisfaction at different stages in their relationships (Shiota & Levenson, 2007). Early in a relationship, similarity was particularly important to promoting bonding and intimacy. But what happens when we take one more step backward in time to look at the effects of similarity when two people first meet each other?

In one study, pairs of heterosexual, opposite-sex college students were left in a waiting room while a researcher ran an "errand" (Cuperman & Ickes, 2009). Without their knowledge, the pairs' interactions were filmed. As predicted by "birds of a feather," pairs of introverts and pairs of extroverts reported having a better conversation and liking their partner more (see ● Figure 12.21). However, similarity in agreeableness was not so important. Leaving two disagreeable people together did not result in a pleasant conversation. Surprisingly, though, having at least one agreeable person produced the same quality of interaction as having two agreeable people. Apparently, agreeable people know how to produce a good interaction whether or not their partner is equally capable.

You might be wondering how personality similarities and differences stack up next to other factors when people first meet, and the answer is not well, at least in the context of a speed-dating session for college students (Luo & Zhang, 2009). Under these circumstances, the overwhelming determinant of attraction for both men and women was physical appearance. No similarity in attitudes and Big Five characteristics was able to significantly predict attraction. This outcome might be one of the reasons we are cautioned to "get to know each other better" before becoming involved in a serious relationship. If similarity plays an important role in long-term satisfaction, even with the bumps and bruises of middle age described by Shiota and Levenson (2007), it appears that we need more time than the speed-dating situation provides to make important relationship decisions. ●

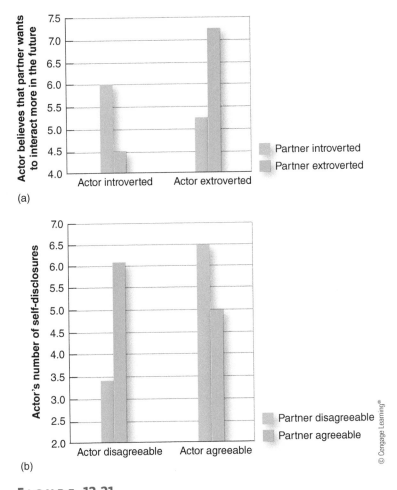

(a)

(b)

FIGURE 12.21

Do Opposites Attract? Introverts conversing with other introverts and extroverts conversing with other extroverts were more likely to believe their partner would want to interact in the future than pairs in which one person was introverted and the other was extroverted. When agreeableness was investigated, one disagreeable person having a conversation with another disagreeable person was not very positive, but as long as one of the partners was agreeable, the conversation went well.
Source: Adapted from "Big Five Predictors of Behavior and Perceptions in Initial Dyadic Interactions: Personality Similarity Helps Extraverts and Introverts, but Hurts 'Disagreeables,'" by R. Cuperman and W. Ickes, 2009, *Journal of Personality and Social Psychology, 97*(4), pp. 667–684. doi:10.1037/a0015741.

Summary 12.2 Some Important *Self* Terms

Trait	Description
Self-concept	Attributes assigned to the self, as in "I am a first-year botany major"
Self-schema	Collection of all self-concept attributes, used to organize thinking about the self
Self-awareness	Knowledge of the self
Self-esteem	Judgments of the self's worth
Self-regulation	Self-control, or conscious efforts to manage the self

Credits: Top Row. Laura Freberg. John Cacioppo. Second Row. © Cengage Learning®. Third Row. Illustration: © Cengage Learning®; photos: Blaj Gabriel/Shutterstock; Guzel Studio/Shutterstock. Fourth Row. Reproduced with kind permission of Unilever PLC and group companies. Reproduced with kind permission of Unilever PLC and group companies. Bottom Row: Iakov Filimonov/Shutterstock.com.

KEY TERMS The Language of Psychological Science

Be sure you can define these terms and use them correctly.

agreeableness, p. 457
Big Five theory, p. 456
conscientiousness, p. 456
defense mechanism, p. 451
ego, p. 450
extroversion, p. 457
id, p. 450
interpersonal self, p. 481
introversion, p. 457
locus of control, p. 460

neo-Freudian, p. 452
neuroticism, p. 457
openness, p. 456
personality inventory, p. 466
projective test, p. 467
psychoanalysis, p. 450
psychodynamic, p. 450
psychosexual stage, p. 451
reciprocal determinism, p. 460
self, p. 471

self-concept, p. 471
self-esteem, p. 473
self-schema, p. 471
social–cognitive learning theory, p. 460
superego, p. 450
temperament, p. 461
trait, p. 455
unconscious mind, p. 453

13 The Connected Mind

Social Psychology

MUCH OF OUR SUCCESS AS A SPECIES CAN BE attributed to our social nature. But as we all know from personal experience, the social world can be challenging; consider, if you can, some truly embarrassing memories you have about social mistakes you've made. Our need to understand our complex social environment was one of the driving forces that shaped the development of our large human brains (Cacioppo & Decety, 2011a).

Among the social environments with the largest minefields is the connection we make with others in intimate, romantic relationships. The two people in the photograph at left appear to find each other attractive, and they are engaged in behaviors—both variable and choreographed—designed to further their relationship. Looking at the developing relationship, psychologists can see a number of processes at work, such as first impressions and the effects of perceived similarities that we discuss in detail in this chapter.

Zooming in, however, we see a different set of processes at work. Although most of us believe that we choose romantic partners on the basis of perceived attractiveness and compatibility, there is some "chemistry" at work here too. Overall, humans share more genes in common with spouses (Domingue, Fletcher, Conley, & Boardman, 2014) and friends (Christakis & Fowler, 2014) than they do with strangers. In some cases, however, being genetically different from your partner is desirable. The highlighted genes in the larger image help determine a person's immune system response. Furthermore, variations of these genes, or alleles, are associated with different detectable body odors (Wedekind & Füri, 1997). As attractive and compatible as these individuals seem to each other, one might reject the other in response to this odor. Our evolutionary history has left us with the ability to detect a genetic compatibility in a partner, as well as more surface compatibilities.

Zooming out from our couple, we see that their romance takes place within a larger social context. What will their families and friends think of their relationship? How do cultural attitudes and biases shape the likelihood of their success? To what extent will they feel comfortable conforming to these cultural expectations or rejecting them? These external factors can help determine the course of their relationship.

◀ Genes on chromosome 6 not only influence a person's immune system but also determine a detectable body odor that affects our choice of a partner.

Maridav/Shutterstock

Argosy Publishing, Inc.

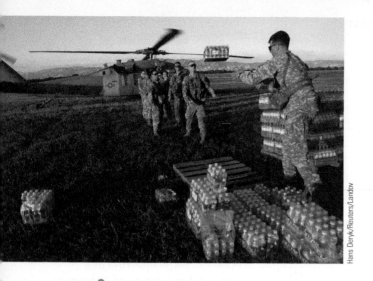

Hans Deryk/Reuters/Landov

Individual humans are not imposing predators, but cooperating in groups makes our species more formidable.

Learning Objectives

1. Discuss person perception, including first impressions, our use of dispositional and situational attributions, and the types of attributional biases that can occur.

2. Define *attitude*, and discuss the origins of attitudes and their susceptibility to change.

3. Differentiate prejudice, stereotyping, and discrimination.

4. Evaluate social influence by distinguishing among conformity, compliance, and obedience.

5. Identify types of group influence, including social facilitation, social loafing, deindividuation, group polarization, and groupthink.

6. Summarize research on the mechanisms of attraction, cooperation and competition, and aggression.

Why Are Humans So Social?

Humans depend on one another. We sit in houses and offices built by contractors and laborers, work on computers designed and built by armies of engineers and technicians, eat food grown and transported by others, wear clothes made by people living halfway around the globe, and look forward to the next text message from a friend.

As far back as the historical record goes, we have evidence that humans lived in groups. What advantages might cooperative living have provided to our early ancestors? As predators or fighters, individual humans have rather modest equipment relative to other species. Our teeth and nails are not particularly frightening, and we are frequently outmatched in speed and strength. It is our human abilities to think and to use tools, to employ and detect deceit, and to communicate, work together, and form alliances that make us such a formidable species.

Early evolutionary pressures favored humans who chose to affiliate, or associate with others, and by doing so, sculpted much of the social behavior we observe today. Social interaction is not just a helpful option but is also a basic human need, which can be more powerful than other basic needs such as hunger, which we addressed in Chapter 7 (Baumeister & Leary, 1995; Cacioppo, Berntson, Sheridan, & McClintock, 2000). A mother's ability to comfort her infant through touch has a greater impact on the infant's attachment to her than her ability to provide food (Harlow & Harlow, 1973). Study participants expecting a painful electric shock prefer the company of strangers to facing their fears alone (Schachter, 1959). We depend on today's mobile technologies that allow us to carry our social networks wherever we go (Taylor, 2002).

We not only need social contact but also react negatively when social support is withdrawn (see ● Figure 13.1). Social isolation shares similar risks of death with high blood pressure, obesity, and a sedentary lifestyle and is positively correlated with risk of suicide (House, Landis, & Umberson, 1988; Trout, 1980). Disruptions of social connections through divorce, bereavement, separation, or ridicule are known to be among the most stressful experiences people may face (Williams, 2007). Perceived isolation, or loneliness, can initiate a cascade of negative interactions that further separate individuals from the social contact they need and want, interfere with the quality of sleep, increase feelings of negative mood and hostility, and lead to a heightened sensitivity to threat and attack (Cacioppo, Cacioppo, Capitanio, & Cole, 2015; Cacioppo, Hawkley, & Thisted, 2010). The isolated person begins to behave in ways that are self-protective but that paradoxically push people away and promote further rejection and isolation. As a result, we are highly motivated to stay in the good graces of our social groups. In the remainder of this chapter, we will see how this need to maintain our social connectivity shapes many types of behavior, from the attitudes we hold about brands of cereal to our responses as members of teams and committees.

Eliciting Feelings of Exclusion.
Psychologists have many ways to make study participants feel socially excluded for short periods so that they can evaluate the effects social exclusion has on everything from brain activity to sharing cookies. Many experiments use this Cyberball game, developed by Kip Williams of Purdue University. The participant, represented by the little hand in the foreground, is initially included in the game of catch with the other two players, who are just part of a computer program. Midway through the game, the other players throw the ball between themselves, excluding the participant, whose little hand is left with nothing to do.

© Cengage Learning®, courtesy of Kip Williams and David Yeager

How Accurate Are First Impressions?

Our success in the social world begins with our ability to perceive the characteristics and intentions of others. What was your immediate reaction to your psychology professor on your first day of class? If you're like most people, you came to some quick conclusions that are likely to last a long time. We form rapid and enduring first impressions of other people.

When we say first impressions are formed "rapidly," we are not talking about months, weeks, days, or hours but, in some cases, less than a minute. In a meta-analysis of research using "thin slices of behavior" (exposure lasting less than 30 seconds), initial impressions did not change much after longer periods of exposure (Ambady & Rosenthal, 1993). Speed-dating provides an interesting environment for observing the accuracy of these thin-slice impressions. Researchers asked men and women to participate in 3-minute social exchanges, followed by their rating each potential partner as date, friend, or no contact (Wilson, Cousins, & Fink, 2006). After only 3 minutes of observation, people accurately predicted their compatibility with a potential partner as measured by a reliable instrument called the compatibility quotient (CQ).

We make quick assessments of others by focusing on a subset of traits and behaviors, rather than trying to sum up an entire person. Halo effects occur when one or a small number of characteristics have a large impact on overall perception. If people see characteristics they value or dislike, they tend to make simple thumbs-up or thumbs-down assessments. One person might be attracted to blue eyes, and another might be turned off by tattoos. In one study, students hearing a professor described as "warm" instead of "cold" were willing to say after a brief encounter that he was a more effective teacher, less ruthless, and more

Speed dating, in which people have a limited time to decide whether they would like further contact with another person, takes advantage of the rapid assessments we make of one another. After only 30 seconds of contact, people make enduring evaluations of other people.

Marmaduke St. John/Alamy

humorous (Widmeyer & Loy, 1988). Although the tendency to make first impressions may be characteristic of all humans, our abilities to shape accurate judgments also interact with culture.

First impressions are not only fast but also persistent. Once we have reached a conclusion about a person, even after a brief social exchange in a speed-dating experiment, we tend to stick with that assessment for a long time, even in the face of contradictory information. Most of us have formed a false first impression of others, either overly positive or overly negative, that breaks down only after extensive further exposure, if at all. Even if we form the occasionally faulty first impression, the fact that we construct first impressions so readily implies that they offer some value to us. In particular, people are likely to use faces to form impressions.

As shown in ● Figure 13.2, Japanese and American participants successfully used their first impressions to predict which political candidates would win an upcoming election, but their predictions were more accurate for candidates from their own culture (Rule et al., 2010).

© Cengage Learning®

Courtesy of the United States Senate

Official White House Photo by Lawrence Jackson

Courtesy of the United States Senate

Junko Kimura/Getty Images

FIGURE 13.2

Judging Winners and Losers Across Cultures. Can you pick which of these candidates won or lost their elections?* Apparently, people can do this quite well, but perform better within their own culture. Based on viewing the photos of candidates' faces, without recognizing the candidate or even knowing the person was running for office, Americans did a good job of predicting the outcome of an election for unfamiliar American candidates for the U.S. Senate but did not do as well when predicting the outcome for Japanese candidates for the *shugi-in* (the Japanese equivalent of the U.S. House of Representatives). Japanese participants predicted the success of Japanese candidates, but most of the American candidates they expected to win ended up losing. *Source:* Adapted from "Polling the Face: Prediction and Consensus Across Cultures," by N. O. Rule, N. Ambady, R. B. Adams Jr., H. Ozono, S. Nakashima, S. Yoshikawa, et al., 2010, *Journal of Personality and Social Psychology, 98*(1), pp. 1–15. doi:10.1037/a0017673.

*The two on the left won; the two on the right lost.

Why Did That Just Happen?

We not only size up other people quickly in terms of their personal characteristics but also ask why they behave the way they do. Being able to predict the behavior of others has significant survival value. Our answers to questions about why others behave in certain ways are **attributions**, or judgments about the causes of other people's behavior.

Behavior can be seen as resulting from some combination of **dispositional attribution** (internal) factors and **situational attribution** (external) factors (Heider, 1958). For example, if your friend just flunked an important exam, you could try to answer the question "Why?" by considering your friend's personal characteristics and circumstances. In considering your friend's disposition, you might recall that she is anxious (being anxious is dispositional), which might have interfered with her performance on a stressful test. In considering your friend's situation, you remember that she just broke up with her romantic partner of several years, which was depressing and distracting for her as she prepared for her test (breaking up is situational).

Thinking that disposition and situation act in an either–or fashion instead of interacting to produce an outcome is not more helpful to our understanding of behavior than using either–or thinking in considering nature and nurture (Funder, 2009; Johnson, 2009). However, as we will see in the next section, the weight placed on dispositional and situational variables as explanations for behavior can vary dramatically from one case to the next. Although our attributions typically guide us in the right direction, we do make errors. We are not able to read minds, so we must make a logical leap from what we observe in a person's behavior to the internal state of mind that produced it. Sometimes that leap takes us in the wrong direction.

The Correspondence Bias and the Fundamental Attribution Error

When you hear about people flunking a test, you are likely to start making conclusions about their disposition ("she is a lazy student" or "he is not very smart"), even though you are aware that the professor giving the test has a reputation for writing brutal exams. This willingness to infer a person's disposition from observed behavior, even when strong situational factors are obvious, is known as the **correspondence bias** (Gilbert & Jones, 1986; Gilbert & Malone, 1995). In other words, we usually expect people's behavior to correspond to their dispositions, even when we know for sure that the situation is having a powerful effect.

Given the importance of making accurate attributions to our survival and social relationships, why would such a bias ever occur? Psychologists are still debating the reasons for this error. One possibility might be the genuine stability of personality traits, discussed in Chapter 12. Although traits interact with situations to produce behavior, people often believe the "you did it because that is the kind of person you are" explanation is accurate. There is some truth to these beliefs, which is why they persist. But at the same time, our discussion of personality showed that situations make important contributions to behavior. You might consider yourself to be a helpful person, but you might ignore someone with a flat tire when you're late for class or work.

Other factors that contribute to the correspondence bias include a lack of awareness of the power of the situation and unrealistic beliefs about how situations should affect people (Gilbert & Malone, 1995). In many everyday instances, we simply do not have enough information about somebody's circumstances to consider situational variables in our attributions. A grumpy, unenthusiastic professor might be having health or personal problems of which students in the classroom are unaware. By default, students believe that the professor is characteristically grumpy and unenthusiastic. In other cases, we seem to misjudge the likelihood that typical people will respond to a situation in a certain way. Later in this chapter, you will learn how a majority of individuals were willing to electrocute another participant simply because they were told to do so by an experimenter. You might think, "I would

Are the famous Walmart Greeters really friendly people? Or are they just doing their jobs? Because of the correspondence bias, we tend to view Walmart Greeters as friendly people, even though we fully understand that their jobs require them to act this way.

attribution A judgment about the cause of a person's behavior.
dispositional attribution A judgment assigning the cause of a person's behavior to personal qualities or characteristics.
situational attribution A judgment assigning the cause of a person's behavior to the environment.
correspondence bias The tendency to view behavior as the result of disposition even when the behavior can be explained by the situation in which it occurs.

never respond to the situation like that," which might lead to your misjudging the power of the situation.

Classic research proposed a global neglect of situational variables in making attributions, a concept labeled the **fundamental attribution error** (FAE; Ross, 1977). According to this view, the correspondence bias occurs because people completely failed to consider situational variables, leading by default to an overestimation of dispositional contributions to the resulting observed behavior. Although this might seem to be the case on some occasions, we have already seen that the correspondence bias can arise from multiple causes. In addition, research evidence for a consistent neglect of observed situational variables is lacking (Gawronski, 2004). For example, in the study mentioned earlier about administering shock, how do you think people view the minority of participants who did not comply? If we globally ignore situational variables as required by the FAE, we should attribute the behavior of these individuals to their strong moral character (disposition), but this is not what usually happens (Gilbert & Malone, 1995). Instead, most people attribute the minority's behavior to simply responding to

fundamental attribution error (FAE) A failure to consider situational variables while making an attribution, leading to an overestimation of dispositional contributions when observing the behavior of others.

 Experiencing Psychology

What Is Your Attributional Style?

WAYS OF ASSIGNING causality are often so stable and characteristic of individuals that they have been called attributional styles, and questionnaires have been devised to identify a person's style (Seligman, Abramson, & Semmel, 1979). Table 13.1 is an adapted, shortened version of the Attributional Style Questionnaire (Peterson et al., 1982).

Instructions: Please try to vividly imagine yourself in the situations that follow. If such a situation happened to you, what would you feel would have caused it? While events may have many causes, we want you to pick only one—the major cause if this event happened to you. Please write this cause in the blank provided after each event. Next, we want you to answer some questions about

the cause and a final question about the situation.

Interpreting your scores: There are 12 situations in the complete questionnaire and we have only provided a quick sample, so you are cautioned to not take your results too seriously.

The first situation is an example of a good situation, and the second situation is

TABLE 13.1 Attributional Style Questionnaire

Situation 1: You become very rich.

1. Write down the *one* major cause. _____

2. Is the cause of your becoming rich due to something about you or to something about other people or circumstances? (circle one number)

1	2	3	4	5	6	7
Totally due to other people or circumstances						Totally due to me

3. In the future, will this cause again be present? (circle one number)

1	2	3	4	5	6	7
Will never again be present						Will always be present

4. Is the cause something that just influences becoming rich or does it also influence other areas of your life? (circle one number)

1	2	3	4	5	6	7
Influences just this particular situations						Influences all situations in my life

the situation "the way people ought to do." Psychologists are continuing to explore the basis of the correspondence bias.

Defensive Attributions

The correspondence bias is not the only flaw in our judgments of behavior. When our personal needs and motives enter the picture, additional errors can occur.

Classic studies suggested that an **actor–observer bias** occurs when we use situational variables to explain our own behavior while continuing to use dispositional variables to explain the behavior of others (Jones & Nisbett, 1972): If my friend and I both flunked a test, I flunked because I was sick, but my friend flunked because he's not a very hard worker. Although this suggestion has some intuitive appeal, a more recent meta-analysis suggested that people judge their own behavior similarly to the behavior of others (Malle, 2006).

actor-observer bias Emphasizing dispositional attributions to explain the behavior of others while emphasizing situational attributions to explain our own behavior.

an example of a bad situation. People often make different attributions in these types of situations, as we discussed in our section on the self-serving bias. Add up your scores on questions 2 to 4 for each situation and divide by 3 to get your composite score. Are these the same or different for the two situations? Higher scores indicate you attribute the situation more to yourself than to your circumstances.

Each question 2 indicates your tendency to form internal attributions (dispositional). Each question 3 indicates the stability of your attributions (these same reasons are usually present), and each question 4 indicates the globality of your attributions (these reasons affect most situations you're in).

Attribution style questionnaires have been used widely to assess people with psy-chological disorders such as depression and potential job applicants. For example, people often view their successes as internal (dispositional) and stable, whereas they view their failures as external (e.g., situational) and unstable. Depressed people, in contrast, view their successes as external and unstable and their failures as the result of internal, stable, and global factors (Seligman et al., 1979). ●

Situation 2: You have been looking for a job unsuccessfully for some time.

1. Write down the *one* major cause. _____

2. Is the cause of your unsuccessful job search due to something about you or to something about other people or circumstances? (circle one number)

1	2	3	4	5	6	7
Totally due to other people or circumstances						Totally due to me

3. In the future when looking for a job, will this cause again be present? (circle one number)

1	2	3	4	5	6	7
Will never again be present						Will always be present

4. Is the cause something that just influences looking for a job or does it also influence other areas of your life? (circle one number)

1	2	3	4	5	6	7
Influences just this particular situation						Influences all situations in my lfie

© Cengage Learning®

Olympic figure skater Rachael Flatt told a newspaper, "I was ultimately responsible for my work, no one else! No excuses! And, that is true in daily training. I am responsible for my own work, no one else." Elite athletes like Flatt rarely indulge in the self-serving bias, in which we attribute our successes to dispositional qualities (I'm a talented athlete) and our failures to situations (the judging wasn't fair or the ice wasn't prepared properly). By avoiding this bias, athletes can learn from their mistakes and continue to improve their performances.

Franck Robichon/EPA/Newscom

self-serving bias Attributing success to dispositional factors while attributing failure to situational factors.

Because of a **self-serving bias**, we view our successes differently than our failures (Miller & Ross, 1975). When we succeed, we are more likely to attribute our success to dispositional variables. For example, if you get an A in this course, you are likely to congratulate yourself on the basis of your brains and hard work. In contrast, if you fail the course, your failure is because of situational factors, such as the professor's asking unfair questions on the final exam. The self-serving bias can make you feel better, but it can also make it harder to learn from experience. Elite athletes, for example, are less likely than less successful athletes to use situational variables to excuse poor performance, such as blaming the weather when they lose a game (Roesch & Amirkhan, 1997). By considering their own contributions to failure, the elite athletes can make the adjustments necessary for future success.

Similar attribution errors occur at the group level (Forsyth & Schlenker, 1977). In a group-serving bias, an organization tends to attribute success to its dispositional characteristics but failures to the situation. If a sports team wins, most members attribute the victory to team disposition, such as talent, good preparation, or sheer will. If a team loses, the members are unlikely to blame the loss on team dispositional factors (Sherman & Kim, 2005). By failing to consider

 Connecting to **Research**

Farming, Collectivism, and Individualism

IT IS ERRONEOUS TO ASSUME that large populations like the people of China are all alike, yet many cross-cultural psychologists have assumed that Chinese culture is uniformly collectivist. Not only is this not the case, but researchers have also suggested some novel contributing factors to explain the variation in social structure that can be observed. For example, differences in the type of crops you raise is probably not the first variable that comes to mind when we consider differences in individualism and collectivism, yet this variable seems to play a role (Talhelm et al., 2014).

The Question: Does the type of crop farmed predict the tendencies of a culture to be collectivist or individualist?

METHODS

More than 1,000 Han Chinese students in six areas of China (see Figure 13.3) com-

pleted measures of cultural thought, implicit individualism, and loyalty/nepotism. None of the measures were self-report, because the researchers expressed concerns that the students would feel the need to answer in socially appropriate ways. For example, the cultural thought task asks you to decide which two items out of a group of three "go together." If we asked you to do this for "train, bus, tracks," what would you choose? People from individualistic cultures tend to make abstract pairings, such as train and bus, which belong to the same category. People from collectivistic cultures tend to make more holistic pairings, such as train and tracks, because they share a functional relationship. The responses of the students were analyzed in terms of their location in the wheat-growing north of China or the rice-growing south. Raising rice requires high levels of cooperation (a married couple cannot grow the rice needed to sup-

port a family by themselves), but growing wheat requires less, so the authors expected more collectivist responses from southern students than from northern students. The authors quoted a 17th-century Chinese farming guide that says, "If one is short of labor, it is best to grow wheat."

RESULTS

The researchers tested their rice explanation against other potential explanations, such as the influence of pathogens or modernization. They found that the rice theory was the only one that consistently fit their cultural data. People from provinces that traditionally farmed rice performed more collectively and holistically, while people from provinces that traditionally farmed wheat performed more individualistically and analytically.

dispositional factors that might be remedied in the future, a group might miss opportunities to correct its course of action.

In addition to the self-serving bias, we frequently engage in other types of defensive reasoning. It is a short step from "your behavior reflects your disposition" to causal judgments about the outcomes of behavior, such as "you get what you deserve." Through the **just-world belief**, people assume that good things happen to good people and bad things happen to bad people (Lerner & Miller, 1978). When you see something bad happen to a good person, you might reduce your anxiety by thinking that the person must have done something to deserve the bad outcome and that you can avoid that outcome by behaving differently. However, this reduction in personal anxiety can come at the expense of the victim, who is being blamed unfairly. Strong just-world beliefs have been positively correlated with negative attitudes toward the poor, people with HIV/AIDS, the elderly, and the unemployed (Sutton & Douglas, 2005).

Marmaduke St. John/Alamy

A just-world belief leads people to expect good things to happen to good people and bad things to happen to bad people. A strong just-world belief might lead people to "blame the victim" thinking, making them less sympathetic to the poor and the sick.

just-world belief The assumption that good things happen to good people and bad things happen to bad people.

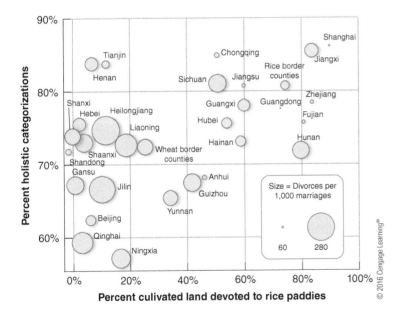

© 2016 Cengage Learning®

DISCUSSION

The participants were unlikely to have ever engaged in farming, but traditional farming practices had shaped their cultural values nonetheless. A history of having had to co-operate to survive might have shaped the local culture for centuries.

These results also remind us that simple answers to psychological problems are usually not good. Rather than thinking of East Asia as a consistent whole, it is more accurate and interesting to investigate the nuances of behavioral differences within cultures. ●

FIGURE 13.3

Collectivism and Individualism Correlate With Regional Farming History. Han Chinese living in areas that have historically farmed rice scored higher on holistic thinking and were less likely to disrupt social organization through divorce than Han Chinese living in areas that have historically farmed wheat. *Source:* Data from "Large-Scale Psychological Differences Within China Explained by Rice Versus Wheat Agriculture," by T. Talhelm, X. Zhang, S. Oishi, C. Shimin, D. Duan, X. Lan, and S. Kitayama, 2014, *Science, 344*(6184), pp. 603–608.

Cultural Influences on Attribution

There are subtle differences in attribution between cultures that value individualism and cultures that value collectivism. Individualistic cultures, including the United States and many other Western nations, stress individual achievement and competition. Collectivistic cultures, including those in many Asian nations, traditionally have valued cooperation as a means of attaining family and work group goals.

Members of collectivistic cultures tend to place more emphasis on situations than on dispositions (Choi, Nisbett, & Norenzayan, 1999; Ho & Fung, 2011). For example, in the United States, murder is viewed as resulting from the disposition of the murderer, whereas in China, murder is often described in terms of the histories of the people involved and the situation in which the murder occurred (Morris & Peng, 1994). As a result, members of individualistic cultures are more likely to demonstrate the correspondence bias in evaluating crime.

These cultural differences in attribution may have their roots in the tendency for people in Eastern cultures to focus on context or situations and relationships, while people in Western cultures are more likely to focus on objects than on situations (Masuda & Nisbett, 2001). As we mentioned earlier, we tend to attribute behavior to the factors we perceive. If being raised in a particular culture leads you to focus on different features of the environment, the attributions that are made vary accordingly (see ● Figure 13.4).

Because of the importance placed on individual achievement in individualistic societies, members of these societies are more likely to use defensive attributions, such as the self-serving bias (Leung, Kim, Zhang, Tam, & Chiu, 2011). Members of more collectivistic cultures show an interesting group-serving bias, in which they attribute more success to the group than it deserves and less of its failures than it deserves (Leung et al., 2011). That is, if you were raised in a collectivistic culture, you would show the same attributional biases about your in-group as an individual raised in an individualistic culture would show about herself or himself.

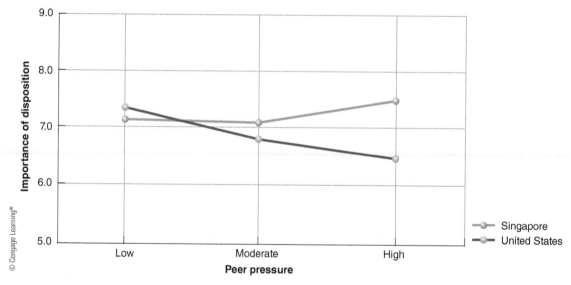

FIGURE 13.4

Situational Attributions and Punishment Across Cultures. In the individualist United States culture, but not in collectivist Singapore, recognition of peer pressure leading to crime (a situational variable) reduces the attribution of the crime to a person's disposition. An American criminal who commits a crime because of peer pressure is not seen to be as bad as a person who acts without such pressure. As a result, extenuating circumstances usually lead to reduced sentences in the United States. Even though collectivist nations like Singapore place a higher emphasis on situational variables when making attributions overall, they do not view peer pressure as a reason to reduce punishment of an individual. If anything, the individual will be blamed for associating with the wrong peer group. *Source:* Adapted from "The Punitiveness Paradox: When Is External Pressure Exculpatory—and When a Signal Just to Spread Blame?" by P. E. Tetlock, W. T. Self, and R. Singh, 2010, *Journal of Experimental Social Psychology, 46*(2), pp. 388–395. doi:10.1016/j.jesp.2009.11.013.

How Are Our Attitudes Influenced by Others?

To survive, all animals must make appropriate approach or avoidance responses to stimuli. The reflexes, fixed action patterns, and unconditioned responses discussed in Chapter 8 provide some guidance in simple situations, such as seeing a predator. To respond to more complex situations, humans form **attitudes**, or favorable or unfavorable evaluations that predispose behavior (Petty & Cacioppo, 1986b).

Attitudes are pervasive. We form positive and negative attitudes about everything from world events to celebrities to brands of peanut butter, and attitudes provide an efficient means of communicating with others. If a friend asks you for a recommendation for a movie, restaurant, or class, a simple attitude statement ("I liked my psychology class!") can serve as a quick and efficient summary for a wide set of beliefs, behavioral experiences, and emotions. Decision making is simpler, faster, and less stressful when attitudes exist to serve as a guide. Attitudes can influence behavior, which is why the advertising industry spends billions of dollars each year in an attempt to shape your attitudes toward various products.

Because we depend on our attitudes to guide our behavior, we want to make sure they are "correct" (Festinger, 1950). Imagine what would happen if you woke up one day to discover that your attitudes about people, objects, and issues were all wrong. Suddenly, your closest friends would dislike you, your major would be a poor match for your interests and abilities, and your entire collection of music would sound dreadful. Occasional mistakes happen, but holding accurate attitudes makes it easier for us to maneuver through the environment successfully.

Attitudes share three basic elements (the ABCs): affect (emotion), behavior, and cognition. For example, how might your attitudes about your college major be affected by hearing a news report about the job market for new college graduates? The affective aspect of an attitude addresses emotional responses to the object. Information about your future job prospects could make you feel quite helpless, frightened, or angry. Behavior reflects the way people respond to the object. After hearing the news, you might schedule an appointment with your adviser to discuss the ways you can pursue the subjects you love and still have a great career. The cognitive aspect of an attitude includes beliefs about the object. In response to the news, you might believe that you have chosen the wrong major.

AFP/Getty Images

If you have any doubt whether people are emotional about their attitudes, just ask some friends whether they prefer an Apple (represented by the late Steve Jobs, left) or a PC (represented by Bill Gates, right). Be prepared to duck for cover.

Attitude Formation

We form many attitudes on the basis of our personal experiences. You like a flavor of ice cream after sampling it, and you dislike the parking situation at your school because you can never find a spot near your classes. In other cases, we absorb attitudes from our contacts with peers, parents and other family members, religious leaders, teachers, and the media.

We often adopt the attitudes of those around us to strengthen our chances of being socially included. As a result, many people prefer to stay on the "winning side" by forming attitudes based on how frequently they hear an opinion expressed by others and in the media (Noelle-Neumann, 1984). Later in this chapter, we explore how fear of social rejection can also lead to conformity and strict adherence to social norms or values.

The learning principles explored in Chapter 8 play important roles in the development of attitudes. Operant conditioning suggests that approval or disapproval shapes a person's attitudes. An opinion expressed in class that is followed by nods and claps will be repeated in the future more than one that is met with horror and disgust. Because of classical conditioning, you are likely to form positive attitudes toward stimuli associated with positive outcomes. If a song is popular at a happy time of your life, it is likely that your subsequent attitude toward the song will be positive too. Observational learning can also be a powerful

attitude Positive or negative evaluations that predispose behavior toward an object, person, or situation.

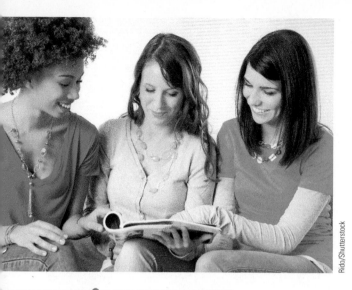

mechanism for learning attitudes. Children who are exposed to particular attitudes in their homes, communities, and media duplicate them, especially if they observe the person expressing the attitude being rewarded.

Can attitudes be influenced by genetics? Identical twins who were adopted by different families at birth, making it unlikely that they were exposed to the same attitudes, still show a surprising amount of similarity among their attitudes as adults (Bouchard, Lykken, McGue, Segal, & Tellegen, 1990). You might have noticed that certain social, political, and religious attitudes seem to follow consistent patterns in the people you know. In other words, a person who holds liberal social and political attitudes is unlikely to hold traditional religious attitudes. Twin studies suggest that this range of attitudes can be explained by a single dimension—traditionalism versus nontraditionalism—which appears to be quite heritable (Ludeke, Johnson, & Bouchard, 2013).

Cognitive Dissonance

Some of our attitudes result from personal experience, but others are quickly absorbed from the world around us, especially through peers and the media.

Cognitive dissonance helps explain why hazing, or requiring an unpleasant initiation to become a member of a group, increases the value of the group (Aronson & Mills, 1959). If you choose to endure so much to join, the group must be something special.

Although our attitudes typically guide us well, attitude change is often desirable. After all, we are sometimes flat out wrong. Addiction, for example, includes attitudes and preferences that are not in the best interests of anybody concerned. The addict by definition cannot easily change these attitudes and preferences, however. Similarly, people who are unable to change their attitudes in the face of new evidence can be quite handicapped. Understanding the circumstances in which attitude change takes place gives us additional insight into the formation of our attitudes and their role in guiding our behavior.

Cognitive dissonance provides a powerful tool for producing attitude change (Festinger, 1957). Cognitive dissonance is an uncomfortable state that occurs when our outward behavior doesn't match our attitudes. For example, you might have been accepted by several colleges and universities, but you can choose to attend only one (the behavior). Thinking about the positive features of the schools you reject causes dissonance (I like these schools but I didn't choose them), which could be resolved either by becoming a "superfan" of your chosen school or by forming negative attitudes toward the schools that you reject. How could you even consider making another choice? Who would want to go to those other schools?

Choosing to smoke despite constant warning messages can produce cognitive dissonance. To reduce dissonance, this smoker may start to think that the warnings are not believable and that smoking isn't that bad for you.

cognitive dissonance The uncomfortable state that occurs when behavior and attitudes do not match and that can be resolved through attitude change.

Cognitive dissonance appears to change attitudes by producing an unpleasant state of arousal, caused by a person's feeling responsible for helping to bring about a negative event (Cooper, 2011). Adolescent participants who evidenced online gaming addictions first rated a new online game and then followed directions to tell peers that the game "really wasn't fun." When asked to rate the game a second time, they gave it more negative rankings than they had before their expressing a negative opinion about it (Wan & Chiou, 2010). In the case of the online gamers, they might believe that their false statements about the game's quality could deprive fellow gamers of the pleasure of playing the game or damage the reputation and income of the company making the game. The resulting negative emotions can be reduced by bringing attitudes more into line with their behavior.

Target sentences — (a)

Neutral sentences — (b)

© Cengage Learning®

Legend:
- Dissonance
- Control

FIGURE 13.5

Cognitive Dissonance and the Anterior Cingulate Cortex (ACC). Study participants undergoing functional magnetic brain imaging (fMRI) were divided into two groups: a dissonance group that was asked to tell the next participant how pleasant the rather unpleasant scanning experience was, and a control group that did not have this experience. Both groups responded to target sentences, such as "I feel calm, peaceful in the scanner," or neutral sentences, which did not involve attitudes toward the scanner experience. (a) The dissonance group responded to the target sentences with more activation in several parts of the brain, including the ACC and the insula (located at the junction of the temporal and frontal lobes), compared to the control group. (b) The groups did not show differences in response to the neutral sentences. (c) The yellow–orange areas are more active during the dissonance situation (dissonant group responding to target sentences) than during the other situations (dissonant group responding to neutral sentences or control group responding to target and neutral sentences). *Source:* Adapted from "Neural Activity Predicts Attitude Change in Cognitive Dissonance," by V. van Veen, M. K. Krug, J. W. Schooler, and C. S. Carter, 2009, *Nature Neuroscience, 12*(11), pp. 1469–1474. doi:10.1038/nn.2413.

Brain imaging studies provide substantial support for cognitive dissonance (see ● Figure 13.5). Many people undergoing functional magnetic brain imaging (fMRI) find being confined in the scanner tube and the loud banging of the magnets to be unpleasant. Still, in one study, participants undergoing fMRI were asked to describe the somewhat unpleasant scanner experience as pleasant (van Veen, Krug, Schooler, & Carter, 2009). Levels of activity in the anterior cingulate cortex (ACC) and insula were higher when a participant made dissonant statements about how pleasant the fMRI experience was compared to neutral statements. Subsequent research has confirmed that the ACC is often engaged during episodes of cognitive conflict, while activity in areas of the insula corresponds to negative arousal (Kitayama, Chua, Tompson, & Han, 2013).

Why Does Persuasion Happen?

Cognitive dissonance can produce attitude change, but not in response to a direct effort by another person. When we change our attitudes in response to information provided by others, **persuasion** occurs. Knowing how to persuade others and understanding the efforts of others to persuade you are important life skills.

The Elaboration Likelihood Model

The **elaboration likelihood model (ELM)** organizes and predicts our responses to persuasive messages by recognizing two major pathways leading to changes in attitudes (Petty & Cacioppo, 1981). The first, known as the central route to persuasion, occurs when a person

persuasion A change in attitudes in response to information provided by another person.
elaboration likelihood model (ELM) A model that predicts responses to persuasive messages by distinguishing between the central and the peripheral routes to persuasion.

FREDERIC J. BROWN/AFP/Getty Images

Experts attending a technology trade show are likely to use the central route to persuasion while evaluating the speaker's message. They will concentrate on the logic of the message and will be relatively unimpressed by peripheral cues, such as the speaker's attractiveness or use of emotion.

Driving down a busy highway requires your full attention, making it unlikely that you will have the resources you need to evaluate persuasive messages using the central route. Instead, the billboards you pass hope to influence you in a few seconds to think better of the product or message they display.

Walter McBride/Corbis

considers persuasive arguments carefully and thoughtfully. The second, known as the peripheral route to persuasion, occurs when a person responds to peripheral cues, which we describe in the following section, without considering the quality of the argument carefully. Importantly, attitudes achieved through the central route are more enduring, more resistant to counterpersuasion, and more predictive of behavior than are attitudes achieved through the peripheral route (Petty & Cacioppo, 1986a).

Why do we need two systems for responding to persuasive messages? Ideally, we would use the central route to consider all messages that we encounter. However, given our limited time, knowledge, and cognitive resources, a thorough evaluation of all the messages we perceive is not practical. Using the peripheral route allows us to use heuristics, or rules of thumb (described in Chapter 10), to react promptly to many situations. If you feel overwhelmed by the large number of candidates on your ballot, you might use the heuristic of voting along party lines or voting like your friends.

Routes to Persuasion

What determines whether we use the central or peripheral route? According to the ELM, a person's motivation influences which route that individual uses to evaluate a particular argument. When students are highly motivated to take time out of their busy schedules to attend a presentation by a guest speaker on campus because they know and care about the topic of the lecture, they are likely to use the central route and evaluate the speaker's points carefully.

People are also likely to use the central route to persuasion when they are well educated about a topic. However, even people who are knowledgeable occasionally take the peripheral rather than the central route. If you know about a topic but do not have the time to think about it or don't care about it, you might find the shortcuts provided by the peripheral route more useful. In addition, because using the central route requires so many cognitive resources, including attention, we are less likely to process persuasive messages this way when we are distracted by other information or activities. As you concentrate on driving down a busy highway, you do not have the cognitive resources to evaluate the messages on billboards carefully.

If a person is using the peripheral route to persuasion, what cues might influence the amount of attitude change that occurs? Peripheral cues usually apply to the persuasive message (e.g., the number of arguments), the manner in which the message is presented (e.g., speed of speech and accent), or the characteristics of the speaker (e.g., credibility or celebrity).

Emotional appeals can influence people using the peripheral route. Both positive and negative emotions can enhance persuasion. Students asked to read persuasive messages about topics such as curing cancer and the state of military forces were more likely to agree with the statement they read while happily snacking on Pepsi and peanuts (Dabbs & Janis, 1965). Efforts to persuade using negative emotions are especially common. We hear daily warnings about the dangers of drinking too much, not using our seatbelts, engaging in risky sex practices, riding a bicycle without a helmet, eating trans fats, and so on (Leventhal & Watts, 1966; Robberson & Rogers, 1988).

Arousing negative emotions, such as fear, can be risky. If people are too frightened by a message, they go into a state of denial. "It's really not that bad," they will say, or "That can't happen here." Denial is most likely to occur if the audience is not given an action step they can use to reduce their anxiety. It is fine to scare smokers to death about the appearance of their lungs, as long as you include a message that tells them where to get help to quit smoking. Having a sense of control over their response will reduce the fear and make the message more persuasive (Ajzen, 1991).

A positive response to the speaker can enhance a message's persuasion. Despite the commonsense warning that "beauty is only skin deep," people have a deep-seated stereotype that what is beautiful is good (Dion, Berscheid, & Walster, 1972). Student evaluations of their professors are heavily influenced by the perceived attractiveness of the professor (Hamermesh & Parker, 2005). People are more likely to be persuaded by people they like and with whom they share some similarity (Cialdini, 2001; Van Knippenberg & Wilke, 1992). Similarities need not be substantial to produce this effect; study participants who shared a first name or birthday with the supposed author of a persuasive essay were more likely to agree with the essay (Silvia, 2005).

A credible speaker is usually more persuasive, especially when listeners are traveling the peripheral route. Credibility in turn is based on the speaker's perceived expertise and trustworthiness. Expertise is often established by a person's history and credentials. We suspect your psychology professors would look different to you if they indicated that their degrees were in other subjects and that they didn't know much about psychology.

Persuasion is also influenced by the medium used to communicate a message, from the face-to-face presentation of the door-to-door salesperson to print media, social media, the Internet, and movies and television. Typically, we find that the closer a medium is to a live interaction with another person, the more effective it is in transmitting a persuasive message. In general, face-to-face contact remains more effective than the use of other media (Bavelas, Hutchinson, Kenwood, & Matheson, 1997). This arrangement is the most natural way for humans to communicate. Face-to-face communication is not only the first medium we learn in childhood, but various technologies allowing communication at a distance developed at much later points in human history.

Finally, the age and intelligence of an audience can influence the effectiveness of a persuasive message. Young children are more likely to respond to persuasive arguments emotionally rather than logically, which might make them more susceptible to attitude change (and advertising) than adults. Intelligent, well-educated audiences are more difficult to persuade in most situations (Rhodes & Wood, 1992).

Again, the influences of cues related to the message, speaker, medium, or audience are greatest when people are using the peripheral route to persuasion. When people are using the central route, their focus remains on the quality of the arguments being presented.

The less a speaker stands to gain by persuading you, the more credibility the speaker appears to have. We understand that athletes and other celebrities are being paid large amounts of money to advertise particular products, so we tend to discount their opinions (Moore, Mowen, & Reardon, 1994). A testimonial by someone who has nothing to gain by speaking in favor of a product or issue is more persuasive. As a result of these findings, bloggers must disclose whether they are being compensated for writing about a brand. Without this information, we might not evaluate their arguments correctly.

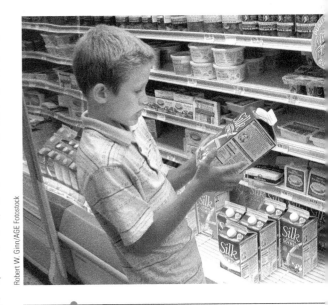

Children are more likely than adults to respond to persuasive messages emotionally rather than logically, making them more susceptible to persuasion. Threatened with lawsuits from public interest groups, several major U.S. food companies agreed to reduce their marketing to children and to make products that appeal to children healthier.

Psychology as a Hub Science
Social Media and Persuasion

The Internet is providing new ways to communicate, from the use of webcams, video, and live chat to Twitter, Facebook, Instagram, and blogs. Many of these new technologies have advantages in providing immediacy and collaboration. To the extent that they duplicate the advantages of face-to-face communication, we would expect them to provide effective means of persuading others.

The Internet not only provides a new medium for communicating persuasive messages but also challenges the status of the credible, expert speaker. Historically, persuasive messages from traditional news outlets such as newspapers, magazines, radio, and television were more of a one-way street. However, in an environment in which everybody with a computer can produce information, receivers of information can be influencers as well by sharing and commenting on messages in blogs and on social networking sites. Initial research in this area suggests that user-generated content in the form of blogs, uploaded videos, comments, and reviews is considered as credible and accurate as formal news reports prepared by professional journalists (Lee, Park, Lee, & Cameron, 2010). In addition, knowing that content is "popular" with other users significantly raises a message's impact (Steyn, Wallstrom, & Pitt, 2010).

Again, we see the power of the social group in shaping our ideas (see ● Figure 13.6). Emerging interactions between new social media and credibility are likely to continue changing the landscape of persuasion. ●

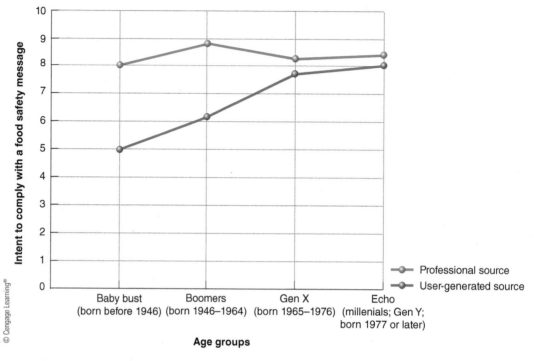

FIGURE 13.6

Responses to User-Generated Messages by Age Group. Social media, with their ability to make users into spokespeople, raise new issues for our understanding of speaker credibility in persuasion. Different age groups have embraced user-generated content, such as blogs, tweets, and articles shared on Facebook, to different degrees. Younger age groups are as likely to say they would comply with a food recall message posted on their Facebook wall by a friend (user-generated message) as they are to an official notice from the Centers for Disease Control and Prevention (professional message), but older age groups are less likely to say they would comply with the user-generated messages. *Source:* Adapted from *Intention to Comply With Food Safety Messages in a Crisis as a Function of Message Source and Message Reliability* (Doctoral dissertation), by K. J. Freberg, 2011, retrieved from http://trace.tennessee.edu/utk_graddiss/970/.

Summary 13.1 Sources of Attribution Error

Type of error	Definition	Example
Correspondence bias	Overestimating the dispositional causes of a person's behavior	My friend flunked her exam because she's not very bright.
Self-serving bias	Attributing personal success to dispositional causes while attributing personal failure to situational causes	I got an A on one test because I'm smart, but I flunked the other test because it was unfair.
Group-serving bias	Attributing group success to dispositional causes while attributing group failures to situational causes	Our team won its first game because we're talented and skilled but lost the second because the referees were biased.
Just-world belief	Assuming that people get what they deserve	That rape victim should have dressed more modestly.

Credits: Top Row: AP Images/The Janesville Gazette/Dan Lassiter. Second Row: Franck Robichon/Epa/Newscom. Bottom Row: Marmaduke St. John/Alamy.

Why Are We Prejudiced?

Among the most damaging perceptions we form about other people are those that are based on their group memberships, which can include factors such as race, gender, age, socioeconomic status, height, weight, disabilities, attractiveness, sexual orientation, and religion.

Psychologists use a group of related terms to discuss the assessment of others based on group membership. **Prejudice**, which literally means "to prejudge," is an attitude (usually negative) about others. Prejudice is supported by cognitions known as **stereotypes**, which are simplified sets of traits that are associated with group membership. A person might believe a stereotype stating that all blondes are dumb, which leads to negative attitudes (prejudice) about blondes. Resulting behavior based on prejudice and stereotyping is considered to be **discrimination**. Hiring practices, housing, educational opportunities, and many other facets of modern living can be conducted in discriminatory ways.

Sources of Prejudice and Stereotyping

Without excusing prejudice and stereotyping and their negative social consequences, it helps to understand that some tendencies to develop prejudice and stereotypes are extensions of the typical ways we process information. In Chapter 10, we observed that humans organize information and experience into schemas made up of categories or concepts, which is generally useful. Our concepts are associated with a variety of characteristics, such as "birds have feathers." We

prejudice A prejudgment, usually negative, of another person on the basis of membership in a group.
stereotype A simplified set of traits associated with membership in a group or category.
discrimination Unfair behavior based on stereotyping and prejudice.

Peter Foley/Landov

People often have negative stereotypes about overweight people as a group. In one online survey, more than 75% of respondents believed that overweight people should either buy a second seat or pay a "fat tax" to travel on airplanes (Siegfried, 2010). Comedian Kevin Smith, ejected from a Southwest Airlines flight for "infringing on a portion of the next seat," tweeted that he "broke no regulation, offered no 'safety risk' (what, was I going to roll over a fellow passenger?)."

frequently have exemplars, or best examples, of each category. If you think of the word *bird,* you are probably more likely to imagine a canary than an ostrich. Finally, we generalize from our known concepts when faced with new information. If we know that birds peck at objects placed before them, we are less likely to stick our fingers near the beak of a new type of bird. In other words, based on our past experience with birds, we are prejudging the behavior of an unfamiliar bird. This process of categorizing information enables us to make rapid decisions about new situations and objects, similar to the rules of thumb, or heuristics, we discussed in Chapter 10.

Effective concepts are inclusive, recognizing a full range of associated characteristics. When our categories are oversimplified, we are left with stereotypes. Although it's true that most birds fly, it is inaccurate to oversimplify the matter by saying, "Birds fly," because ostriches do not. Stereotypes often contain an element of truth but become inaccurate because of the information they exclude. More importantly, stereotypes conflict with our valid desires to be viewed and treated as individuals.

If stereotypes can lead us astray, why are they so pervasive and persistent? People tend to misjudge correlations between groups and their stereotypical behaviors. They might overestimate the percentage of Asian students who excel in math and science or underestimate the number of White athletes who play professional basketball. Attributions, discussed earlier, also contribute to continued stereotyping. If you see an exception to your stereotype, perhaps a female who is running faster than her male friend, you might view her success as the result of situational variables. Perhaps the man is letting her win to be nice. This type of thinking allows us to maintain a "women are weaker" stereotype.

You have probably noticed that people's prejudice toward a group often conflicts with their behaviors toward individual members of that group. Someone might express dramatically prejudiced opinions about a group yet treat members of that group well. Individuals can be viewed as being different or exceptions, allowing people to retain their stereotypes in the face of conflicting observations. Instead of rethinking a stereotype about truck drivers and country music, you view your truck-driving friend who enjoys opera to be one of a kind. Finally, stereotypes are often maintained by people's expectations. In one experiment, students listening to a basketball game were informed that a certain player was either Black or White. After the game, students who believed the athlete was Black expressed their stereotypes by rating the player as being highly athletic, while those who believed the athlete was White gave him praise for his intelligence and hustle (Stone, Perry, & Darley, 1997).

Prejudice, like other types of attitudes, can result from direct experience (I had one boring history professor, so all history professors must be bad) or can be indirectly absorbed from the social world of peers, parents, the community, and the media. Human prejudice based on group membership, however, might have deeper roots in our evolutionary past. Recognizing and reacting to individuals based on group affiliation was probably an important skill for early hunter–gatherers, whose survival often depended on quickly identifying others as potential trading partners or foes. This pressure could have led to a tendency to distinguish between in-groups, or the group to which we belong, and out-groups, or everybody else (see ● Figure 13.7). This categorization is made primarily on the basis of physical appearance, and people still instantly and often unconsciously categorize others on the basis of physically observable features, including age, gender, and race (Fiske, 1998).

This type of categorization was demonstrated by recording brain activity as people viewed photographs of faces and made judgments of either race or gender (Ito & Urland, 2003). Study participants reacted quickly to both race and gender information, even when the information was irrelevant to their task. In other words, a participant who was asked to differentiate between male and female faces still showed evidence of having paid attention to the race of the faces without being asked to do so.

Different emotional responses can accompany these instant categorizations. When study participants viewed faces from their own racial group, activity in the amygdala was lower than when they viewed faces from another racial group (Hart et al., 2000). As we discussed in Chapter 4, activity in the amygdala is correlated with assessments of threat. Either realistic or imaginary threats from an out-group are viewed as a major source of prejudice (Stephan & Stephan, 2000). Furthermore, responses of the amygdala to race are correlated with several implicit measures of prejudice (Phelps et al., 2000). Implicit measures are designed to demonstrate subconscious associations between concepts (literature and math, for example) and attitudes (good and bad, for example; Nosek, 2007). Psychologists continue to debate the extent to which implicit measures predict actual prejudice (Oswald, Mitchell, Blanton, Jaccard, & Tetlock, 2013). White study participants who showed the greatest differences in amygdala activity while viewing Black and White faces were also more likely to associate positive words such as *joy, love,* and *peace* with Whites and negative words such as *cancer, bomb,* and *devil* with Blacks. The amygdala activity in response to viewing Black faces might reflect the fear and other negative assessments made by these participants based on racial stereotypes.

Understanding that biological and evolutionary processes are involved with in-group–out-group differentiation does not make prejudice inevitable or acceptable. By understanding why we develop prejudice, we can better identify ways to reduce it. As we will see later in this section, prejudice can change.

Outcomes of Prejudice

Prejudice, whether subtle or overt, can lead to discriminatory behavior in a number of ways. Not only are African Americans convicted of murder more likely than Whites to be given the death penalty in the United States, but perceptions of "Blackness" are also predictive of a murderer being sentenced to death (Eberhardt, Davies, Purdie-Vaughns, & Johnson, 2006). Researchers presented photographs of African American defendants to participants without telling them that the men depicted had been convicted of murder. The participants ranked the photographs on the basis of stereotypical Black features, such as broad nose, dark skin, and thick lips. The ratings were highly predictive of the men's sentences when the victim was White. Men who appeared more stereotypically African American were more than twice as likely to be given the death sentence as men whose physical appearance was less stereotypical. This difference disappeared, however, when the victim was also African American (see ● Figure 13.8).

Prejudice affects not only the way we view others but also the way we view our own behavior. Raising awareness of a negative stereotype about a group to which we belong has the ability to reduce our performance, a phenomenon known as stereotype threat (Steele, 1997; Steele & Aronson, 1995). Anxiety about confirming a negative stereotype attributed to your group can prevent you from doing your best work.

In a set of studies demonstrating this effect, researchers asked Stanford University undergraduate students to complete difficult items taken from the verbal portion of the Graduate Record Exam (GRE), used as part of the admissions process for some graduate programs (Steele & Aronson, 1995). One group of students, the stereotype threat group, was told that the test accurately assessed their cognitive abilities, a statement that was designed to stimulate thinking about possible racial stereotypes about intelligence. The other group was told that the test was a routine laboratory procedure. Subsequently, the performance of Black and White students on the test was compared. In the stereotype threat condition, the Black students performed more poorly than did the White students with equal verbal abilities, as measured earlier by their entrance scores on the similar SAT. In contrast, in the nonthreatening condition, Blacks and Whites with equal SAT scores performed similarly on the GRE items, which is the result we would expect because of the tests' reliability and validity, discussed in Chapter 2 (see ● Figure 13.9).

Oversimplified categories, such as "girl toys" or "boy toys," can lead to stereotypes.

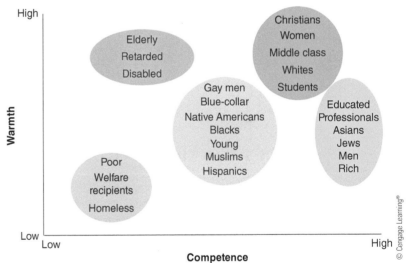

FIGURE 13.7

American Perceptions of Out-Groups. Out-groups often elicit mixed reactions. Some out-groups (rich people) are respected for their perceived competence but disliked for their supposed lack of warmth. Elderly people and the disabled are viewed as low in competence, but they are viewed warmly because of the lack of threat they pose. Groups such as the poor are viewed most harshly as a result of having both low status and representing a threat of exploiting the in-group. *Source:* Adapted from "A Model of (Often Mixed) Stereotype Content: Competence and Warmth Respectively Follow From Perceived Status and Competition," by S. T. Fiske, A. J. C. Cuddy, P. Glick, and J. Xu, 2002, *Journal of Personality and Social Psychology, 82*(6), pp. 878–902. doi:10.1037/0022-3514.82.6.878.

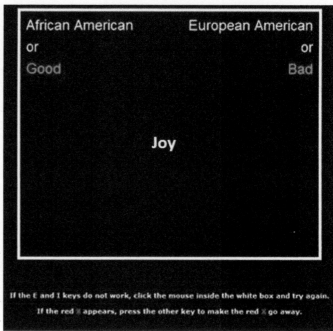

Project Implicit/Dr. Anthony Greenwald

The Implicit Association Test (IAT) measures reaction time to assess people's unconscious attitudes. In this version of the test, either a face (African American or European American) or a word appears at the center of the screen. The participant pushes a specified key on a computer for the face (African American) and then again for the word (*joy* is Good). Later in the test, the combinations at the top of the screen are switched to African American or bad and European American or good. An implicit bias in favor of African Americans would be shown if reaction time in the first condition (African American or Good) is faster than in the second condition (African American or Bad).

 # Thinking Scientifically

Does Working in Groups Affect Stereotype Threat?

AS WE HAVE described in this chapter, stereotype threat refers to the decrease in performance that occurs when people face subtle reminders of stereotypes about their own group's abilities. Most of the stereotype threat research in psychology, which is extensive, has focused on individuals. In keeping with our textbook's theme of looking at behavior from multiple perspectives, we might wonder what would happen if we zoomed out a bit to look at whole groups of people experiencing stereotype threat at the same time.

Fortunately for our discussion, this question has been addressed in an experiment that compared the effects of stereotype threat on individuals working alone or in groups (Aramovich, 2014). Female participants were led to believe that their performance on a set of problems would be used to evaluate the logical abilities of women in general. As shown in ● Figure 13.10, stereotype threat impaired the performance of women working individually but did not affect the work of groups. Groups exposed to stereotype threat performed as well as groups that did not experience stereotype threat. Groups performed better than individuals overall, but the effect was larger when comparing groups and individuals experiencing stereotype threat. The groups even outperformed individual women who were identified as best performers on the problems.

Why do you think that working in a group was able to buffer the women from the detrimental effects of stereotype threat? Aramovich (2014) demonstrated that the perception of the threat was about the same strength for women working individually and in groups, so the results do not reflect a diminished sense of threat in the group members. Stereotype threat is often explained in terms of distraction or increased cognitive load. While you're worrying about the stereotype, you have fewer available resources for thinking about the problem. One advantage of the groups

Less stereotypical
More stereotypical

FIGURE 13.8

Implications of Stereotyping. Study participants' ratings of stereotypical Black features predicted the men's likelihood of being sentenced for murder with the death penalty, but they only did so when the victim was described as White. The men in these photographs have no criminal records but are examples provided by the authors for individuals who were viewed as less stereotypical (left) and more stereotypical (right). *Source:* From Eberhardt, J. L., et al. (2006). Looking deathworthy: Perceived stereotypicality of black defendants predicts capitalsentencing outcomes, *Psychological Science, 17*(5), 383–386. Copyright 2006 Association for Psychological Science. Reprinted by Permission of SAGE Publications.

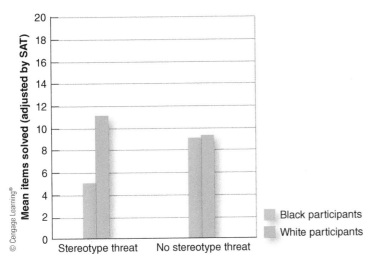

Black participants
White participants

FIGURE 13.9

Stereotype Threat. When Black students at Stanford University were told that a verbal test measured their true abilities (stereotype threat), their subsequent performance was less than when they were told that the test was being used to understand the "psychological factors involved in solving verbal problems" (no stereotype threat). The different instructions did not affect the performance of the White students. *Source:* Adapted from "Stereotype Threat and the Intellectual Test Performance of African Americans," by C. M. Steele and J. Aronson, 1995, *Journal of Personality and Social Psychology, 69*, pp. 797–811.

would be a shared ability to overcome these distractions by catching more errors. Another intriguing possibility is that in a group that shares a threat, the threat might be viewed as a challenge, motivating better performance.

The experience of stereotype threat by entire groups of people working together remains less well explored than the effects of stereotype threat on individuals. What happens when only some members of a group experiencing a threat are from a stigmatized group? Do these results speak to the controversies over female-only educational settings? ●

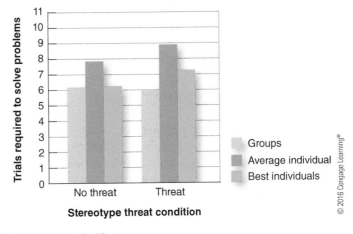

Groups
Average individual
Best individuals

FIGURE 13.10

Groups Are Less Vulnerable to Stereotype Threat. Both average and best-performing individuals performed better (required fewer trials to solve problems) in the no threat condition than in the threat condition. However, groups performed equally in threat and no threat conditions and outperformed even the best individuals in the threat condition.

Reducing Prejudice

Although we would prefer a world in which prejudice never occurred, psychologists at least have gained insight into how prejudice can be reduced.

Increased contact can reduce prejudice (Skerry, 2000). However, not just any contact will have this effect. To be effective in reducing prejudice, contact must occur under certain circumstances. For example, contact between people of equal standing is more effective in reducing prejudice. If people are from different socioeconomic groups, greater contact may increase rather than decrease between-group resentment.

Contact is particularly beneficial in reducing prejudice when groups participate in cooperative activities (see ● Figure 13.11). In a study using two groups of boys at a summer camp, negative feelings between the groups decreased after the boys cooperated to solve false emergencies, such as interruptions to the camp's water supply (Sherif, Harvey, White, Hood, &

FIGURE 13.11

The Reduction of In-Group and Out-Group Bias Through Cooperation. After arbitrarily dividing campers into two groups, the Rattlers and the Eagles, Sherif and his colleagues observed considerable in-group–out-group bias between the groups. During this phase, few of the campers reported having friends from the out-group. To resolve the resulting discord, the researchers set up false emergencies, such as a problem with the camp's water supply, that required the boys to cooperate. After cooperating, many of their previous biases were no longer present, and more boys reported having friends among the out-group. *Source:* Adapted from *The Robbers Cave Experiment: Intergroup Conflict and Cooperation,* by M. Sherif, L. J. Harvey, B. J. White, W. R. Hood, and C. Sherif, 1961, Norman, OK: University of Oklahoma Institute of Intergroup Relations.

◻ Choice of friends from in-group
◻ Choice of friends from out-group

Sherif, 1961). Another classic example of the effectiveness of cooperation in reducing prejudice is the jigsaw classroom, designed to reduce racial tensions in newly desegregated school districts in the 1970s (Aronson, 2011). Children in cooperative groups were assigned a part of the answer that their group needed to learn, leading to interdependence among the group members. Rather than competing for the teacher's approval, the children in the jigsaw task helped their teammates by listening and teaching. Outcome research indicated that students in jigsaw classrooms mastered the material better, liked their group members better, were absent less frequently, and showed evidence of more empathy and higher self-esteem (Aronson, 2011). This type of cooperative contact is used in deliberate efforts to reduce prejudice in about 80% of elementary schools in the United States (Paluck & Green, 2009).

Because so much prejudice originates in categorizing people and then engaging in in-group–out-group thinking, another strategy for reducing prejudice is to expand the definition of the in-group. For example, if a White female and an Asian female concentrate on the similarities they share as women, they should experience fewer feelings of bias toward each other on the basis of race (Deschamps & Doise, 1978). Although this effect is not always seen in the laboratory (Vescio, Judd, & Kwan, 2004), when combined with real-world extended contact, the strategy seems to be promising (Eller, Abrams, Viki, & Imara, 2007). Perhaps if we stop focusing on our group identities, we can consider ourselves members of the human race or residents of the planet. If we cooperate to solve problems of hunger, sickness, poverty, and degradation of the environment, the result could be a reduction in prejudice.

Why Do We Go Along With the Group?

When acceptance by a group is important to us, we are motivated to behave in ways that increase the likelihood of gaining the group's approval and avoiding rejection. Groups typically have rules for behavior, known as **social norms**. Social norms can be explicit, or conscious, like wearing shoes into a restaurant; they can also be implicit, or unconscious, like moving to the back of an elevator and turning to face the doors.

We often conform to social norms without being asked to do so. In contrast, compliance and obedience lead us to fulfill a request from another person. In compliance, the person making the request has no authority over us, but in obedience, the request is coming from an authority figure.

Conformity

Matching your behavior and appearance to the perceived social norms of a group constitutes **conformity**.

In a classic study of conformity by Solomon Asch (1951), participants were asked to match a reference line to one of three comparison lines. As you can see in ● Figure 13.12, the lines are sufficiently different that solving this task was not rocket science. In the conformity condition, one real participant was placed among a group of confederates (fake participants who are employed by the investigator). Before the real participant gave an answer, the confederates provided some wrong answers. Would the real participant tell the truth or conform to the answer given by the confederates? In about one third of the trials, the participants conformed by deliberately choosing a response they knew was wrong. About three quarters of the participants conformed on at least one trial.

Conformity to expectations associated with roles was investigated in the Stanford Prison Study (Haney, Banks, & Zimbardo, 1973). In a short time, young men who had been randomly assigned to prisoner or guard roles quickly adopted behaviors consistent with those roles, leading to such inappropriate behavior that the study was stopped after only 6 days instead of the planned 14 days. The study has been criticized due to the active role taken by researcher Philip Zimbardo, who served as the warden in the study and thus influenced how the guards

social norms Usually unwritten or unspoken rules for behavior in social settings.
conformity Matching behavior and appearance to perceived social norms.

FIGURE 13.12

Conformity. When a lone participant was asked to match the Exhibit 1 line to Line A, B, or C, the person chose the correct line, A. However, when placed in a group of confederates told to pick another line, people became more likely to go along. Conformity reached its peak in groups of three to four people and did not increase as the group became larger. *Source:* Adapted from "Effects of Group Pressure Upon the Modification and Distortion of Judgments" (pp. 177–190), by S. E. Asch, in *Groups, Leadership and Men: Research in Human Relations,* edited by H. Guetzkow, 1951, Oxford, United Kingdom: Carnegie Press.

In 2001, Stephen Reicher and Alexander Haslam re-created aspects of the classic Stanford Prison Study, which was conducted by Philip Zimbardo and his colleagues in the 1970s. Zimbardo argued that the roles of guard or prisoner overwhelmed individuality, but Reicher and Haslam believe that the study's participants were simply responding to Zimbardo's instructions. Scientists do not always agree with one another, and their debates bring us closer to realistic representations of our world.

behaved. A similar prison experiment was conducted for BBC television, and this time, few of the guards acted inappropriately (Reicher & Haslam, 2006). In contrast to Zimbardo's active participation in his own study, the British prison experiment featured little direction from the investigators.). However, the likelihood that we unconsciously fulfill the roles expected of us by others remains an active area of scientific investigation.

Why do people conform? Conformity can be useful in ambiguous situations. If you are uncertain about what to do, such as how to dress at work, observing the behavior of others and conforming to it can be helpful. In a computer simulation comparing the effectiveness of social learning strategies, which includes imitation of others, to nonsocial learning strategies, such as trial and error, the social strategies proved far more successful (Rendell et al., 2010). The availability of others to copy might contribute to the overall success of group over independent living.

Conformity also reduces the risk of rejection by a social group, a situation that would have greatly threatened the survival of our human ancestors. In a study demonstrating the rejection of nonconformists, participants were asked to debate the fate of an imaginary juvenile delinquent named Johnny Rocco (Schachter, 1951). Three members of the group were confederates. One was instructed to agree with the group consistently, another to disagree with the group consistently, and the third to switch positions from disagreeing to agreeing with the group. When the real participants rated how well they liked other members of the group, members who agreed with the majority were all well liked, and the confederate who changed position was liked best. The participants were unanimous in their intense dislike of the confederate who disagreed with the group.

Compliance

Compliance occurs when we simply agree to do something because another person asks us to do it, even if that person has no authority over us. From messages in junk mail that tell us to "Open immediately. Do not discard" and advertising appeals to "Buy now" to medical instructions we receive from our dentist or family physician, we are bombarded with requests for compliance.

Fulfilling requests from authority figures such as teachers or police officers can provide considerable advantages to society. It is more difficult, however, to explain why people would develop the tendency to comply with requests made by strangers who have no authority. It appears that our natural tendency to affiliate leads us to behave in ways that encourage the development of relationships, including being compliant.

Compliance is higher when factors that normally lead to the formation of relationships are present, such as perceived similarity and physical attraction. For example, we are more likely to comply with requests presented by physically attractive people (Lynn & Simons, 2000; McCall, 1997). This behavior provides yet another example of the "beauty is good" stereotype that influences persuasion in general. People are more likely to comply with a request from a person who shares some similarity, even when the similarity represents irrelevant dimensions, such as a shared birthday (Burger, Messian, Patel, del Prado, & Anderson, 2004).

Many seemingly simple yet sophisticated sales techniques exploit our natural tendencies to comply in response to perceiving a social tie with another person (Cialdini & Goldstein, 2004). Once a sense of relationship is established, powerful norms of reciprocation are brought into play. Reciprocation, in which we feel obligated to give something back to people who have given something to us, is one of the most powerful tools of social influence (Gouldner, 1960). The importance of reciprocation to the cohesion of early human groups can probably not be overestimated. If somebody shared food with you, and you reciprocated by sharing yours, a powerful bond would be formed.

Reciprocation has been used to explain compliance in the **door-in-the-face** scenario, in which a large, unreasonable demand is followed by a smaller request, which is the one the requester expects to work (Cialdini et al., 1975). For example, you might be asked to donate a large amount to an organization, followed by a request to "give what you can afford." By lowering the initial demand, the salesperson has made a concession. The rules of reciprocation now suggest that you have an obligation to that person and should respond to this concession with one of your own—you send a donation (see ● Figure 13.13).

In addition to reciprocity, the need to appear consistent may also drive considerable compliance. The **foot-in-the-door** technique, in which a small request is followed up by a larger

FIGURE 13.13

Door in the Face. In a study by Cialdini et al. (1975), participants in the door-in-the-face condition were first asked to volunteer for 2 hours per week for 2 years as a "big brother" or "big sister" at a local juvenile detention center. None agreed. Subsequently, they were asked to spend 2 hours chaperoning a group of delinquents to a local zoo, and 50% agreed. In comparison, only 16.7% of the participants hearing only the zoo request agreed, and 25% of people asked whether they would choose one of the two activities agreed to the zoo request. It is possible that feeling guilty for turning down the first request makes people more likely to agree to a second, smaller request.
Source: Adapted from "Reciprocal Concessions Procedure for Inducing Compliance: The Door-in-the-Face Technique," by R. B. Cialdini, J. Vincent, S. Lewis, J. Catalan, D. Wheeler, and B. L. Darby, 1975, *Journal of Personality and Social Psychology, 31,* pp. 206–215.

compliance Agreement with a request from a person with no perceived authority.
door in the face A persuasive technique in which compliance with a target request is preceded by a large, unreasonable request.
foot in the door A persuasive technique in which compliance with a small request is followed by compliance with a larger request that might otherwise have been rejected.

According to the foot-in-the-door technique, agreeing with a small request, such as clicking the "Like" button on Facebook, makes it more likely that you will agree with larger requests, such as buying products from a company.

request, is especially effective in gaining compliance. "Liking" an organization on Facebook (a small request) can lead to more purchases and brand loyalty (larger requests). Another technique based on the need to appear consistent is the low-balling strategy, in which an initially favorable deal is revised upward once the buyer appears committed (Cialdini, Cacioppo, Bassett, & Miller, 1978). Once you have made a commitment to buy a car, the salesperson leaves to "check" the deal with a supervisor and invariably returns with a few more charges to make the deal "work." The salesperson is counting on you to agree to the higher price, because you have already made a public commitment to buy the car. If you stand up at this point and prepare to leave, it is likely those extra charges will quickly disappear.

Obedience

Obedience is defined as compliance with the request of an authority figure. When you take an exam from a professor or show your driver's license to a police officer, you are being obedient.

In a series of classic experiments, Stanley Milgram demonstrated that when personal ethics come into conflict with demands from an authority, the authority usually wins (Milgram, 1974). Milgram's participants entered his laboratory at Yale University believing that they were to take part in a study of the effects of punishment on learning. The other "participant" present was a confederate, and the situation was rigged so that the real participant would take the role of teacher while the confederate took the role of learner. The punishment for failing to learn pairs of words was an electric shock, to be administered by the teacher to the learner using an intimidating piece of equipment. The learner or confederate received no actual shocks; his verbal responses to shocks were prerecorded.

In most cases, Milgram's experiment began uneventfully. The first challenge to the teacher occurred, however, at 75 volts, at which time the learner's first recorded protest could be heard. When faced with this situation, many of Milgram's participants looked to the experimenter in the room for guidance. The experimenter assured the participant that "the experiment must continue" and "you have no choice." Although most participants showed signs of stress and verbally stated their concerns about the procedure, all of Milgram's original 40 participants went as far as 300 volts, and 26 out of the 40 (65%) fully complied by administering the maximum shock (450 volts). Milgram followed up his original scenario by modifying variables that might have influenced the large number of people willing to obey. No differences in outcome were observed when the experiment was conducted in an off-campus office or with participants of different ages and occupations.

Among the variables that did seem to influence Milgram's results was proximity, both between the teacher and the learner and between the teacher and the experimenter. The proximity between the teacher and the learner ranged from complete separation, in which the two people could neither see nor hear each other, to close, in which the teacher was instructed to physically hold the learner's hand on a shock grid. As proximity between the teacher and the learner increased, rates of obedience dropped to about 30% (see ● Figure 13.14). The implications of this result for modern war technologies are clear. People are more likely to operate a drone that harms a person they can neither see nor hear than they are to harm a person whose pain is apparent. The proximity of the teacher and the experimenter was also quite influential. The experimenter communicated with the teacher while in the room, by telephone, or by tape recording. Obedience dropped dramatically as interaction with the experimenter, who represented authority, became more remote.

Obedience varies across cultures, but no one is immune. Milgram's data suggest that about 65% of the American population, with equal numbers of men and women, would fully comply in his basic experiment (Milgram, 1963). The highest rates of obedience are found in the general public of the Netherlands (92%; Meeus & Raaijmakers, 1995), Austria (80%; Schurz, 1985), and Germany (85%; Mantell, 1971). Australia reports some of the lowest levels of obedience, along with one of the few notable gender differences reported in the obedience literature. Forty percent of Australian male students were fully obedient, but only 16% of Australian female students were fully obedient (Kilham & Mann, 1974).

Milgram's original goal was to illuminate some of the most troubling behavior of modern times, the killing of millions of innocent people in the Holocaust, so it is no surprise that his

obedience Compliance with a request from an authority figure.

FIGURE 13.14

Circumstances Affecting Obedience. After his initial study, in which the teacher could hear but not see the learner, Milgram varied the experimental circumstances to see what variables influenced the amount of obedience his participants displayed. The "teacher, learner together" condition took place with both people in the same room. In the "teacher touches learner" condition, the teacher had to hold the learner's hand down on a shock device. As the teacher and learner came into more contact, obedience dropped, but it remained surprisingly high overall. *Source:* From the film Obedience 1968 by Stanley Milgram, © renewed 1993 by Alexandra Milgram, and distributed by Alexander Street Press. Permission granted by Alexandra Milgram.

results are among the most disturbing in modern psychology. Milgram clearly demonstrated the power of authority to gain compliance. But did he meet his goal of modeling Nazi obedience? He believed so. You may be more comfortable thinking that people who could carry out genocide are different from the students sitting next to you in class. But Milgram's findings show otherwise:

> Ordinary people, simply doing their jobs, and without any particular hostility on their part, can become agents in a terrible destructive process. Moreover, even when the destructive effects of their work become patently clear, and they are asked to carry out actions incompatible with fundamental standards of morality, relatively few people have the resources needed to resist authority. (Milgram, 1974, p. 6)

You might be thinking optimistically that people today are different from Milgram's participants in the 1960s. Between the 1920s and the 1980s, parents in the United States shifted their preferences for their children's outcomes from obedience to autonomy (Alwin, 1988). We can begin to evaluate the impact of this parenting change, because Milgram's experiment has been partially replicated fairly recently by Burger (2009). By "partially replicated" we mean that Burger made procedural changes for the purposes of meeting ethical requirements, such as informing participants that they could leave if they felt uncomfortable. Despite these changes, Burger's results were similar to Milgram's results (82.5% of Milgram's participants obeyed under the same circumstances in which 66.7% of Burger's male participants obeyed). Burger's participants were told explicitly that they could leave at any time, which raises questions about previous explanations of Milgram's results in terms of coercion. Hopefully, now that the major ethical concerns about Milgram's procedures have been resolved, further work in this area can illuminate the exact reasons people choose to stay and continue to administer shocks even when they're free to leave.

No society can exist without obedience. However, history is full of instances in which blindly following orders leads people into highly unethical behavior. Even in more commonplace situations, obedience to authority can overwhelm individual judgment. In one chilling obedience experiment, 22 nurses were telephoned by a doctor they didn't know and instructed to administer a drug not listed on a patient's chart in double its normal dose (Hofling, Brotzman, Dalrymple, Graves, & Pierce, 1966). Astonishingly, 21 of the 22 nurses indicated they would be willing to obey. We could argue that it is desirable for nurses to carry out the directions of physicians, but at what point do we want people to question authority?

AP Images/Jeff Widener

The Power of One

Our discussion of conformity, compliance, and obedience would be incomplete without considering the circumstances in which an individual or small group can influence a larger group. Asch provided a clue to the necessary conditions when he noted that conformity was greatest when a person faced a unanimous group. A single individual's willingness to take an opposing view may encourage others to also resist the pressure to conform to a misguided action, or at least to reconsider their original position.

To successfully influence the majority, a minority voice must display consistency and confidence. In a study designed to determine the factors that enabled a minority to influence a majority, people occasionally agreed with an individual who consistently stated that blue slides were green but never agreed with an individual who judged blue to be green only part of the time (Moscovici, Lage, & Naffrechoux, 1969). Individual voices that are raised confidently, as in the case of Mahatma Gandhi or Martin Luther King Jr., are more likely to influence the majority than are more tentative efforts.

The anonymous Tank Man of the 1989 Tiananmen Square protests in Beijing, China, created a minutes-long standoff by maintaining his position in front of a column of tanks. Single individuals disagreeing with a majority with confidence and consistency can stimulate others to reconsider their positions. We do not know the fate of Tank Man today.

How Do Groups Work Together?

We have explored many instances in which situations seem to have a large impact on people's behavior. Given the sociability of our species, it should not be surprising to learn that one of the most powerful situational influences on our behavior is the presence of other people. How is our behavior different when we are with others compared to when we are alone?

Social Facilitation

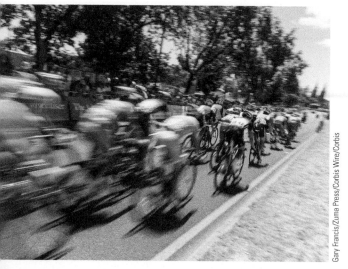

Gary Francis/Zuma Press/Corbis Wire/Corbis

Social facilitation occurs when the presence of other people changes individual performance. In 1898, Norman Triplett reported that cyclists riding in pairs rode faster than cyclists riding alone. Social facilitation is not limited to cycling. Children spinning fishing reels did so faster when in groups than when they were alone.

In contrast to Triplett's observations, we have all seen skilled performers "choke" in front of an important audience. Why does performance improve in front of audiences in some situations and become worse in others? Psychologists noticed that well-practiced skills, like riding a bicycle, improved with an audience but that when people were still learning a new skill, they performed badly (Zajonc, 1965; Zajonc & Sales, 1966). When we're performing a well-practiced skill, most of what we do is correct, but when we are learning something new, most of the things we do are wrong. The presence of the audience appears to enhance whichever patterns of behavior are dominant—the right moves in a well-practiced skill and the wrong moves in a new skill. The moral of this story is to make sure you practice thoroughly before you perform in front of an audience.

The complexity of a task can also interact with the presence of an audience to produce either improved or impaired performance (Bond & Titus, 1983). This result implies that one of the functions of the audience is to increase the performer's level of arousal. The Yerkes–Dodson law, discussed in Chapter 7, states that performance on simple tasks improves steadily with arousal but that performance on complex tasks first improves and then becomes impaired as arousal continues to grow (Yerkes & Dodson, 1908). Improvements in performance are more likely to occur when people are engaged in simple, well-practiced activities, such as

Because of social facilitation, a well-practiced skill like pedaling by these professional cyclists is enhanced by the presence of others.

social facilitation A situation in which the presence of other people changes performance.

riding a bicycle, as opposed to highly complex, novel activities, such as memorizing a difficult list of words.

Social Loafing

While working on group projects, you have probably had opportunities to observe **social loafing**, or the reduced motivation and effort shown by individuals working in a group as opposed to working alone. When engaged in a tug-of-war game at a picnic, members of a team exert less individual effort with each additional person added to their side (Kravitz & Martin, 1986). Individuals cheer less loudly in a large group than they do in a smaller group (Latané, Williams, & Harkins, 1979).

Individual, gender, cultural, and task variables interact to produce social loafing. Women are somewhat less likely to demonstrate social loafing than men, and people from Eastern cultures are less likely to loaf than those from the West (Karau & Williams, 1993). Simple physical tasks, such as screwing and unscrewing nuts and bolts, reliably produce social loafing in most people (Petty, Cacioppo, & Kasmer, 1988). Task complexity interacts with a need for cognition, or the motivation to engage in and enjoy effortful cognitive endeavors (Cacioppo, Petty, & Kao, 1984). People with a low need for cognition showed social loafing during both a physical task and a brainstorming task in which they are asked to generate a list of possible uses for an object (Cacioppo, Petty, Feinstein, & Jarvis, 1996). In contrast, individuals who demonstrate a high need for cognition take pleasure in difficult mental tasks, and although they showed social loafing on the simple physical task, they did not socially loaf during the more intellectually demanding brainstorming task. Individuals appear to be less likely to take the opportunity to socially loaf on tasks that they find intrinsically enjoyable to perform.

Because of social loafing, we would expect the cheering by each of these fans in a nearly empty stadium to be louder than the cheering produced by individual fans in a packed stadium.

Deindividuation

Deindividuation refers to the immersion of the individual within a group, which makes the individual relatively anonymous. Deindividuation can lead normally law-abiding people to commit uncharacteristic atrocities, including riots and lynchings.

Why would people go along with the negative behavior of a surrounding group, especially if they are unlikely to behave this way on their own? One possibility is that anonymous people feel less accountable for their actions. In an experiment using a paradigm similar to Milgram's obedience experiments described earlier, participants dressed in hoods and oversized lab coats administered longer shocks than control participants who were dressed in normal clothing with name tags (Zimbardo, 1969). Other psychologists suggest that you do not necessarily "lose yourself" in a group but that your attention shifts from a personal identity to the identity of the surrounding group (Lea & Spears, 1991). If that surrounding group begins to act in antisocial ways, the personal controls normally present within you might not be enough to resist going along.

If you participate in online discussions, you might notice a difference in the way people relate on platforms such as Facebook compared to the anonymous platforms in some message boards and chat rooms. Deindividuation predicts that anonymous message boards would feature less inhibition, such as less civil discussion, than would platforms where individual identity is obvious.

Group Polarization

Common sense suggests that discussion with others who express different opinions should produce more moderate attitudes for everyone in the group. Surprisingly, this is not always the case. In **group polarization**, a period of discussion pushes group members to take more extreme positions in the direction they were already inclined (Moscovici & Zavalloni, 1969). Group polarization does not reverse the direction of attitudes but, rather, accentuates the attitudes held at the outset (see ● Figure 13.15). If group members began mildly favorable on gun control, their attitudes will be more favorable after discussion, whereas if group members began mildly unfavorable on gun control, their attitudes will be more unfavorable after discussion.

social loafing Reduced motivation and effort shown by individuals working in a group.
deindividuation Immersion of an individual within a group, leading to anonymity.
group polarization The intensifying of an attitude following discussion.

DARREN STAPLES/Reuters/Corbis

Deindividuation, or the loss of personal identity within a crowd, can lead people to do things that they would not do on their own.

Two pressures appear to push individuals to take more extreme positions following a group discussion. First, conformity and desire for affiliation contribute to group polarization. If the majority of a group is leaning in a particular direction, what could be a better way of "fitting in" than agreeing with that majority and maybe even taking its argument one step farther? There is also a tendency for like-minded people to affiliate with one another, which can provide reinforcement for existing opinions, increase people's confidence in those opinions, lead to the discovery of new reasons for those opinions and counterarguments to opposing views, and reduce exposure to conflicting ideas. Second, exposure to discussion on a topic introduces new reasons for holding an attitude. If you are already opposed to gun control and you listen to additional arguments supporting your position, you might end up more opposed than you were originally.

Group polarization is frequently studied in the context of the behaviors of juries. Following deliberations, final sentencing decisions by mock juries are typically more severe or more lenient than the original opinions expressed by individual group members (Bray & Noble, 1978). Group polarization appears to be even more powerful in online discussions, where people are exposed to many more arguments on issues than they might generate on their own (Himelboim, McCreery, & Smith, 2013; Sia, Tan, & Wei, 2002).

Groupthink

As we discovered in our discussion of conformity, the presence of others can influence the process of decision making. In Asch's experiments, individuals appeared to make a choice in favor of group harmony over accuracy. If group members suppress dissenting opinions in the interests of group cohesion, the group may fall into a state of **groupthink**.

This type of flawed decision making might account for a number of unfortunate group decisions throughout history (Janis, 1972). Among the examples most frequently described as results of groupthink are the Bay of Pigs invasion, the Korean and Vietnam Wars, and the Cuban missile crisis (Rose, 2011). These examples are notable because of their disastrous results, but they may not be representative of groupthink outcomes. For example, many terrorist organizations meet the criteria stipulated by Janis (1972) for groupthink, yet they have arguably met a number of their short-term objectives, including the terrorist attacks of 9/11 (Rose, 2011).

groupthink A type of flawed decision making in which a group does not question its decisions critically.

FIGURE 13.15

Group Polarization. We like to think that we can come together and talk out our differences, but that does not always happen. Discussion often moves individuals to take more extreme versions of their original positions. After individually rating French leader Charles de Gaulle and Americans (both of which were rated somewhat positively), groups of four French college students were asked to reach consensus on the ratings and then provide a second set of individual ratings. Following the group discussion leading to consensual ratings, the students' individual ratings were more extreme (more positive in this example) than their first ratings had been.

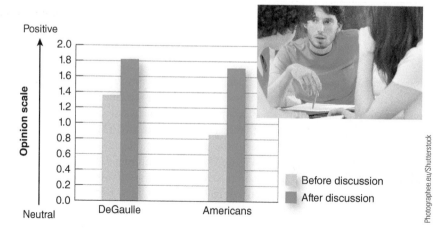

Photographee.eu/Shutterstock

Before discussion
After discussion

Opinion scale

Positive
2.0
1.8
1.6
1.4
1.2
1.0
0.8
0.6
0.4
0.2
0.0
Neutral

DeGaulle   Americans

Groupthink is especially likely in cohesive groups with high morale whose members already share similar attitudes (Baron, 2005). Members of cohesive groups are less likely to consider risks or alternatives associated with their chosen plan of action. In many cases, the group is far from unanimous, but individuals are unwilling to step forward in dissent, just as many of Asch's participants preferred to go along rather than rock the boat. This illusion of a unanimous group further stifles serious consideration of alternatives before making a decision.

Smart, experienced groups of people can make some not-so-smart decisions because of groupthink. In 2001, Yahoo! had the opportunity to buy a company called Google, started by Stanford University graduates Sergey Brin (left) and Larry Page (right). The Yahoo! executives hesitated, and the opportunity passed.

Summary 13.2 Group Processes

Group process	Definition	Example
Social facilitation	Individual performance is influenced by the presence of others.	A jogger runs faster with a buddy than when running alone.
Social loafing	Working in a group decreases individual effort.	A student puts less effort into a group project than into an individual term paper.
Deindividuation	Behavior differs when in a group from when alone and identifiable.	A normally law-abiding citizen loots a store during a riot.
Group polarization	Attitudes become more intense following discussion.	After a late-night debate with like-minded friends, students hold more extreme views about an issue than they did before the discussion.
Groupthink	Flawed group decision making fails to consider dissenting views.	A group of friends decides to engage in a risky behavior that seems dumb in hindsight.

How Well Do We Get Along With Others?

Part of our heritage as a social species involves the need not only to affiliate with a group but also to form important social relationships with individual people. These relationships can be between family members, peers, coworkers, neighbors, or romantic partners. If you think about the people with whom you interact regularly, it is obvious that our relationships with others are not all the same. Learning to get along well with different people, or gaining so-called social skills, is one of the most important tasks we face, and one that can influence important outcomes throughout life. Psychologists have discovered a number of underlying themes that affect this important part of life.

Attraction and Liking

Attraction refers to our attitudes about other people and can vary along a continuum from strong liking to strong disliking. Attraction varies in quality and strength, which in turn help to determine the type of relationship we form with another person. We are attracted to our romantic partners in stronger and more physical ways than we are attracted to our friends and acquaintances. We know what attraction to another person feels like, but it is more difficult to identify the variables that predict our attraction to a particular person.

Before you can be attracted to a person, you need to have some contact with that person. Contact becomes more likely when people work, live, or spend leisure time in proximity to, or near, one another. In an early exploration of this concept, 5,000 marriage licenses in which one or both partners lived in Philadelphia were examined (Bossard, 1932). In about one third of the marriages, the partners had lived five blocks or fewer from each other before marrying. As distance between homes increased, the number of couples decreased. In the contemporary era of online dating, proximity can take forms other than physical closeness.

Proximity is important to relationships because simple contact can increase liking. In contrast to the proverb that states "familiarity breeds contempt," regular exposure to neutral or positive stimuli generally leads to increased liking, a principle known as the **mere exposure effect** (see ● Figure 13.16). In one example of this effect, people who repeatedly viewed nonsense words described as "Turkish" words and Chinese-like symbols reported liking them better than those they were seeing for the first time (Zajonc, 1968). The mere exposure effect applies to people too (Swap, 1977). From an evolutionary point of view, the mere exposure effect might have led people to avoid unfamiliar, and possibly dangerous, stimuli (Young & Claypool, 2010). Unfortunately, having an inclination to make more negative responses to unfamiliar people might also contribute to prejudice.

Musicians recognize the advantages of the mere exposure effect. Hearing a song frequently makes it more likeable. Placement of a song in a television show or movie is virtually guaranteed to boost sales of the artist's work.

mere exposure effect Repeated exposure increases liking.

FIGURE 13.16

Mere Exposure Increases Liking. More frequent exposure to these nonsense "Turkish adjectives" resulted in higher ratings among American college students on their "goodness" of meaning. *Source:* Adapted from "Attitudinal Effects of Mere Exposure," by R. B. Zajonc, 1968, *Journal of Personality and Social Psychology Monograph Supplement, 9,* pp. 1–27.

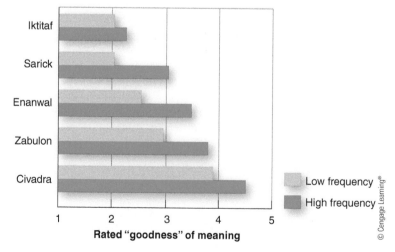

To what extent do similarities and differences influence our friendships and romantic relationships? In one experiment, college students read the results of an attitude survey supposedly filled out by another student (Byrne, 1961). As the attitudes expressed became closer to the students' attitudes, the students reported that the anonymous person was better liked, more intelligent, and better informed about current events. Apparently, assuming we like ourselves, we find it easy to like people with whom we are similar. People tend to choose friends and romantic partners who are similar in race, ethnicity, religion, values, education, and age (Buss, 1985; Kandel, 1978). However, the number of interracial couples in the United States has grown dramatically since 1960 (Joyner & Kao, 2005; Lee, 2010).

Although people may be initially attracted to those with whom they share similar characteristics, being attracted to another person also increases similarity, a process known as attitude alignment. Attitudes of dating partners grow closer together in a gradual process (Davis & Rusbult, 2001). At the same time, partners in stable relationships often overestimate the similarity of their attitudes (Murray, Holmes, Gellavia, Griffin, & Dolderman, 2002).

Physical appearance is a dominant factor in romantic attraction. After completing questionnaires assessing personality and academic achievement, study participants were randomly paired for a "computer dance." Male participants were subsequently asked whether they would ask their partner for a second date. The only significant variable out of all the personality and other data collected that predicted the likelihood of a second date was the woman's physical attractiveness (Walster, Aronson, & Abrahams, 1966).

Cultures frequently have their own definitions of physical beauty, but we appear to have some underlying, biological preferences. Beauty serves as a marker for health and fertility. By choosing a beautiful mate, you may be enhancing your abilities to produce healthy children with a strong chance of survival. Preferences for faces rated as beautiful by adults can be demonstrated in infants as young as 3 months of age (Langlois, Roggman, & Rieser-Danner, 1990). Subjective judgments of beauty are heavily influenced by symmetry, or the degree of similarity between one half of the body or face and the other half. Symmetrical bodies are more likely to be healthy bodies, so they are highly sought in prospective mates (Thornhill & Gangestad, 1994). As further evidence of the importance of symmetry in mate choice, symmetry of faces was more important to heterosexual research participants in opposite-sex judgments of attractiveness than in same-sex judgments of attractiveness (Little, Jones, DeBruine, & Feinberg, 2008).

Most long-term couples share an approximately equal level of attractiveness and may even have similar features or physique, as do Sting and Trudie Styler.

People show strong preferences for symmetrical faces (bottom row) compared to the less symmetrical versions of the same faces (top row). Symmetry may serve as an outward sign of genetic health (Little et al., 2008). *Source:* From Little, A. C., et al. (2008). Symmetry and sexual dimorphism in human faces: interrelated preferences suggest both signal quality. *Behavioral Ecology, 19*(4), 902–908. Copyright © 2008 Oxford University Press.

Liking
Intimacy

Romantic love
Intimacy + Passion

Companionate
Intimacy + Commitment

Consummate Love
Intimacy + Passion + Commitment

Infatuation
Passion

Fatuous (foolish) love
Passion + Commitment

Empty love
Commitment

Illustration: © Cengage Learning®; photo: Yuri Arcurs/Shutterstock.com

FIGURE 13.17

Robert Sternberg's Triangular Model of Love. According to Sternberg, close relationships vary along the dimensions of intimacy, passion, and commitment. Consummate love combines all three.

Most romantic couples share a common level of physical attractiveness, a concept known as the matching hypothesis. Couples who were most similar in terms of physical attractiveness were more likely to be together 9 months later (White, 1980). However, when longer-lasting relationships are examined, female partners tend to be rated as slightly more attractive than their male partners (McNulty, Neff, & Karney, 2008).

Building Relationships

Self-disclosure, or sharing personal information about yourself, follows a regular progression as people become more intimate with one another (Taylor & Altman, 1987). Acquaintances talk about general topics other than themselves. New friends might discuss their personal abilities and attitudes, whereas close friends move on to consider dreams and goals. Intimate friends might share fears and negative past behaviors.

Intimacy is highest when falling in love, but what does love look like under the microscope? Robert Sternberg's triangular model of love distinguishes the building of different types of relationships along dimensions of intimacy, passion, and commitment (Sternberg, 2004). Intimacy refers to the closeness or bonding we experience with another person, passion includes sexual attraction and romance, and commitment describes the intent to maintain the relationship over time. Intimacy without passion or commitment is characteristic of most friendships. Passion by itself characterizes an infatuation or "love at first sight." Commitment alone could describe the situation in which a person remains loyal to a partner whose health makes intimacy and passion no longer possible, as in the case of a partner with dementia (see ● Figure 13.17).

Combinations of intimacy and passion describe romantic love. Without the addition of commitment, this type of love can fade quickly. Intimacy and commitment occur together as companionate love. This love exists without passion in deep friendships, family relationships, and long-term partnerships in which sexuality no longer plays a significant role. A combination of passion and commitment can occur in an impulsive "whirlwind" relationship, in which insufficient time has elapsed for the development of true intimacy. Finally, people who are lucky enough to find all three components in the same relationship experience consummate love.

Maintaining Relationships

What factors keep people together? Some strategies seem particularly important to many types of relationships, including friendships, family relationships, and romantic relationships. People continue to use openness and self-disclosure as relationships mature, along with participation in joint activities, provision of reassurance, and communication (Berscheid, Snyder, & Omoto, 2004; Canary, Stafford, Hause, & Wallace, 1993).

Maintaining a relationship may become easier over time. As couples spend more time together, they build a shared history, which provides them with a stronger basis for understanding each other. Couples who have been together for many years appear to have the ability to communicate a thought or emotion with a single look to each other (Schober & Carstensen, 2010). Long-term relationships can also become boring, however. Couples who continue to engage in novel and exciting activities also have higher relationship satisfaction (Aron, Norman, Aron, McKenna, & Heyman, 2000).

Ending Relationships

As you are no doubt well aware, real life does not typically follow the scripts of fairy tales, in which the lovers ride off into the sunset to live happily ever after. Maintaining relationships takes time and effort, and sometimes people are wrong for one another. A sense of inequity or unfairness in a relationship may cause it to end. Equity in a relationship suggests that costs, such as curtailed freedom and less time to oneself, are offset by benefits, such as companionship and security. In general, more equitable romantic relationships are stable, enjoyable, and sexually intimate.

Most couples experience their share of ups and downs, but the relative number of their positive and negative experiences is related to the likelihood the relationship will survive or end (Gottman, Swanson, & Swanson, 2002). Couples appear to need about five positive interactions to offset one negative interaction. As the ratio of positive to negative interactions slips toward 1:1, the likelihood that the relationship will end increases. Couples with high levels of apparent conflict might still stay together, as long as their conflict is offset by a larger amount of positive times together.

Infidelity often contributes to the ending of a romantic relationship. Data describing how frequently romantic partners cheat on each other are difficult to obtain and show wide variations, as in the 33% to 75% of men and 26% to 70% of women reported to cheat on their partners in one review of the literature (Buss & Schmitt, 1993). Men and women also appear to respond to different aspects of cheating behavior (see ● Figure 13.18). Males become jealous of sexual infidelity, whereas females are more distressed by emotional infidelity (Buss, Larsen, & Westen, 1992). In other words, a woman would be less distressed if her partner had a one-night stand while drunk than if he had an ongoing relationship with a mistress whom he supported financially. In any case, relationship jealousy can have dangerous implications. More than a quarter of homicides in the United States are estimated to involve jealousy (Goldsmith & Zimmerman, 2001).

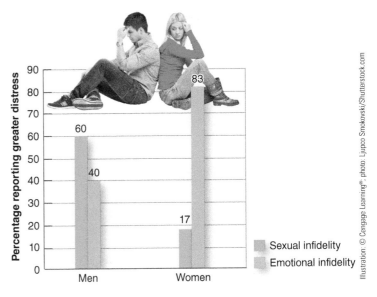

FIGURE 13.18

Gender Differences in Response to Partner Infidelity. When asked which would cause greater distress, your partner cheating on you sexually or becoming deeply emotionally involved with a rival, men reported greater distress from sexual infidelity, whereas women reported greater distress from emotional infidelity. *Source:* Adapted from "Sex Differences in Jealousy: Evolution, Physiology, and Psychology," by D. M. Buss, R. J. Larsen, and D. Westen, 1992, *Psychological Science, 3,* pp. 251–255.

Summary 13.3 Sternberg's Three Types of Love

Type of love	Combines	Excludes
Romantic love	Intimacy + passion	Commitment
Companionate love	Intimacy + commitment.	Passion
Consummate love	Intimacy + commitment + passion	

Why Do We Cooperate in Some Situations and Compete in Others?

Our social interactions with one another can feature cooperation, or working together toward common goals, or competition, where we struggle with one another to obtain limited resources.

Both cooperation and competition have a long history in shaping our behavior. In Chapter 3, we described natural selection as an ongoing race among organisms competing for scarce resources and opportunities to reproduce (Darwin, 1859). The stakes in this race are high. Individuals with characteristics that give them an advantage over others are able to pass their genes along, while losers fail to reproduce or die. At the same time, because humans do not live alone, our survival depends on cooperation.

Competition and Cooperation in Animals

Individual animals frequently compete for food or opportunities to mate. Beginning with observations of "pecking order" among chickens (Schjedlderup-Ebbe, 1922), biologists have cataloged many species that use competition, usually in the form of fighting, to determine the allocation of mating opportunities, food, and other resources both within and between groups.

The advantages of cooperation can be illustrated by a real-life tale of two 1864 shipwrecks in the South Pacific. Members of one crew worked cooperatively with one another as equals, while members of the other maintained their formal command structure. After 1 year, the first crew managed to build a boat and get rescued, while the second was decimated by cold, hunger, and cannibalism (Druett, 2007).

Too much competition among individual members hampers the cohesion of a group, breaking it into factions and possibly resulting in injuries among its members. Consequently, many animals minimize the extent of within-group conflict by displaying clear signals of dominance, or high status. The mandrill, a type of baboon, uses facial expressions and gestures to signify its position in a dominance hierarchy. The coloring of the mandrill's face, rump, and genitalia is also reflective of individual fighting abilities (Setchell & Wickings, 2005).

Do humans have analogous signals of dominance? It appears that the male of the species does (Mazur & Mueller, 1996). Dominant human male faces are handsome and muscular, featuring strong chins, deep-set eyes, and prominent brows. In contrast, "baby-faced" males are rated by observers as being more submissive (McArthur & Berry, 1987). Humans have the advantage of augmenting their natural signals of status by purchasing and displaying expensive automobiles, homes, and jewelry.

Animals minimize the damage caused by competing for dominance by displaying clear signals of submission. The dog on its back is letting the other dog know that its dominance has been recognized.

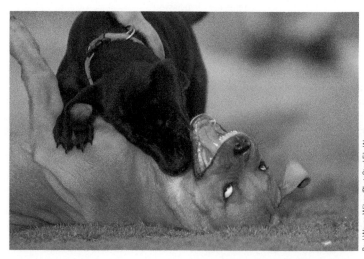

Individual Differences in Cooperation and Competition

Individuals vary in their predisposition to cooperation or competition. In one experiment, groups of participants were given the opportunity to compete (by keeping tokens) or cooperate (by sharing tokens) while they observed the decisions made by their group members (Kurzban & Houser, 2005). Three types of dispositions emerged: 17% of the participants were "cooperators," who gave their tokens freely without paying much attention to the behavior of other group members; 20% were "free riders," who didn't give up any of their tokens; and 63% of the participants were "reciprocators," who cooperated only after seeing others do so. Even though the cooperators were in the minority, their behavior is important to group survival. By contributing selflessly, they encourage the majority of the group to cooperate too.

The Influence of Culture on Competition and Cooperation

Members of successful groups are more likely to survive and reproduce than members of unsuccessful groups. Because it is in our best interest to belong to effective groups, we cooperate with other group members and are quick to conform to their norms and judgments. Cooperation becomes ingrained in the group's culture and is passed along to new members.

Why is cooperation so essential to successful group behavior? Without cooperation, there would be no basis for gathering diverse areas of individual expertise into a meaningful, useful whole. Under the influence of culture, humans have progressed from simple divisions of labor to highly specialized areas of expertise. Individuals might spend their entire academic careers exploring the structure of the frog retina or the surface characteristics of one of Saturn's moons. At the same time, no single person working alone would be able to put humans on the Moon or produce all the special effects expected by contemporary movie audiences. Few fans would pay to see an individual football player demonstrate his skills on an otherwise empty field on Sunday afternoon. Cooperation is the glue that holds productive groups together, from the operating room of a hospital to the baseball stadium.

The importance of group membership to survival is reflected in the remarkable loyalty humans show to their culturally defined groups. Fans of a particular sports team may be every bit as loyal to their group (and as potentially violent toward others) as our early hunter–gatherer ancestors were to their tribe or clan. Unfortunately, the same loyalty and cultural distinctiveness that bind us to our groups may lead us into conflict with other groups, as discussed later in this chapter.

GONZALO FUENTES/Reuters/Corbis

Cooperation is essential to successful group behavior.

Choosing Between Cooperation and Competition

How do people decide when to compete and when to cooperate?

A classic model of competition and cooperation within groups is known as the prisoner's dilemma (Poundstone, 1992). Assume that you and another person have been arrested for a crime but that the police have limited evidence against you. Without being able to communicate with your partner, you are given the choice to confess (defect from your partner) or to remain silent (cooperate with your partner). If you both remain silent, you will each be sentenced to 1 year. If you both confess, you will each receive 10 years. However, if one confesses and the other remains silent, the prisoner who confesses will be set free, and the silent prisoner will receive a 20-year sentence. The dilemma arises because the best individual strategy is to confess or defect from your partner, but if both of you figure this out and subsequently confess, your outcome is worse than if you both remained silent (see ● Figure 13.19). In the prisoner's dilemma, cooperation is moderately rewarded (a 1-year sentence) while defection is punished (10 years). If only one of you confesses, however, the confessor is highly rewarded (freedom) while the other person is severely punished (20 years).

FIGURE 13.19

The Prisoner's Dilemma.

	Prisoner B	
Prisoner A	Prisoner B stays silent.	Prisoner B confesses.
Prisoner A stays silent.	A and B both serve 1 year each.	A serves 20 years. B goes free.
Prisoner A confesses.	A goes free. B serves 20 years.	A and B both serve 10 years each.

For real people, computers, and even animals, the most successful strategy in the prisoner's dilemma situation is the tit-for-tat (TFT) strategy (Axelrod & Hamilton, 1981). Using the TFT strategy, you make cooperation your first move and then repeat your partner's successive moves. The success of the TFT strategy has been attributed to three aspects: It is nice (you begin with cooperation), it is able to retaliate and punish uncooperative behavior (defection by your partner is followed by your own defection), and it is forgiving (you return immediately to cooperation following cooperation on the part of your partner; Brembs, 1996).

The research on individual differences in cooperation discussed earlier found that most human participants were reciprocators, whose behavior is most similar to the TFT strategy (Kurzban & Houser, 2005). The prevalence of this type might reflect its typical success. If most people are reciprocators, how can we explain the existence of the other types? Free riders clearly benefit from their selfish behavior, but what advantages might increase the chances of the cooperators' survival and reproductive success? It is easier to be generous when you are well off, so acting like a cooperator might make people believe you have extensive resources, improving your chances of attracting a mate (Milinski, Semmann, & Jrambeck, 2002). A person's reputation is also a powerful motivator for cooperation. In ongoing prisoner's dilemma games, participants use other people's record of cooperation (or lack thereof) to determine whether to cooperate with them (Milinski et al., 2002). In small hunter–gatherer bands or basketball teams, having a reputation for selfishness is not likely to make you successful.

Culture can shape a person's choice of competition and cooperation. When two people from different countries played the prisoner's dilemma game, less cooperation and more competition occurred than when two people from the same country participated together (Matsumoto & Hwang, 2011). Furthermore, the bigger the difference between the native countries of the participants along the dimension of individualism or collectivism, the less cooperation occurred. This finding reflects the in-group bias we mentioned earlier in the chapter.

Contributing to our cooperative abilities is a deep-seated, possibly biological sense of fair play that is shared with other species in the animal kingdom. Capuchin monkeys will happily trade pebbles for slices of cucumber until they see another monkey receiving a more preferred grape for its pebbles. After seeing the "unfairness" of their situation, they are no longer willing to work for cucumber slices (Brosnan & De Waal, 2003). When people playing a prisoner's dilemma game were observed with fMRI, viewing the faces of cooperators produced activation in brain areas normally linked to reward (Singer, Kiebel, Winston, Dolan, & Frith, 2004). In contrast, when people were treated unfairly, activation occurred in parts of the brain associated with anger, disgust, and pain (Sanfey, Rilling, Aronson, Nystrom, & Cohen, 2003).

Altruism and Helping

We have all read stories about soldiers, firefighters, and others who have risked or even sacrificed their lives to save the lives of others. These instances are examples of altruism, a helping behavior that either fails to reward or actually harms the person who performs it, which we discussed in Chapter 3. Instances of altruism in which the helper is exposed to risk or experiences harm are often described as heroism (Franco, Blau, & Zimbardo, 2011).

If behavior usually leads to improved survival and reproduction, how can we account for altruism? Charles Darwin suggested that "[a] tribe including many members who were always ready to give aid to each other and sacrifice themselves for the common good, would be vic-

Capuchin monkeys refuse to exchange pebbles for a slice of cucumber after seeing another monkey receive a more highly valued grape for its pebble, suggesting that nonhuman primates have a sense of fairness.

torious over most other tribes; and this would be natural selection" (Darwin, 1871, p. 166). Although this suggestion is attractive, it suffers from a major flaw in logic. The system suggested by Darwin would produce free riders who were not altruistic themselves but who would benefit from the altruistic behaviors of the members of their group (Dawkins, 1976). These individuals, because they would undoubtedly live to reproduce, should eventually swamp the group with "selfish" genes.

Several evolutionary mechanisms have been proposed that account for the continuation of cooperative, altruistic behavior (Nowak, 2006). Although altruistic behaviors may have costs for an individual, they may benefit the altruist's genetic relatives. Altruistic genes will survive in the population as long as the cost to an altruist is associated with a large enough benefit to relatives (Hamilton, 1964). Japanese macaque monkeys are more likely to defend close relatives from attack than they are to defend unrelated monkeys (Kurland, 1977). People are more likely to help their relatives than they are to help strangers, such as in helping to raise their children. Altruism is also maintained by expectations that a favor might someday be returned by those you have helped, a process known as reciprocal altruism (Trivers, 1971). Vampire bats often regurgitate blood to share with bats who did not hunt successfully; bats are more likely to share with those who had shared with them recently (Wilkinson, 1984, 1990).

Selfishness might be limited by punishment administered by other group members. Study participants who had the opportunity to punish those who had not cooperated activated reward circuits in the brain, lending credence to the phrase "revenge is sweet" (Fehr & Rockenbach, 2004). Unfortunately, the willingness to pay a big price to carry out revenge against those who seem "unfair" might also lead to irrational acts, such as suicide bombings.

However, other instances of altruism do not fit these models. People adopt unrelated children. Arland Williams, a passenger on an airplane that crashed into the freezing Potomac River in 1982, passed lifelines to other passengers before disappearing beneath the water. These altruistic acts represent psychological altruism, or conscious efforts to help. This type of altruism can be transmitted by a culture through learning (Dawkins, 1976). The role of learning in altruism is supported by observations that the tendency to feel pleasure when helping others is quite low in children and gradually increases into adulthood (Cialdini, Kenrick, & Baumann, 1981).

If cooperation confers so many benefits to individuals and groups, how can we explain the failure of some individuals to provide help when it is desperately needed? In 1964, a young woman named Kitty Genovese was murdered on a New York City street near her home late at night. Sensational news reports at the time stated that 38 of her neighbors watched for more than half an hour while Kitty struggled with her attacker without intervening or calling the police. Although these reports were not confirmed by later court testimony in the case (De May & Gladstone, 2009), the public outrage they stimulated led to a series of experiments into **bystander intervention**. This research demonstrated that an individual's likelihood of helping drops as the number of other observers grows. In a typical experiment investigating this phenomenon, college students filled out a questionnaire as their room filled with smoke (Latané & Darley, 1968). The researchers were interested in how frequently and quickly the students reported the smoke. When the college students were alone, nearly 80% sought help within 6 minutes. When three study participants were tested together, only 40% reported the emergency within 6 minutes.

The designation of *hero* is often given to people who are altruistic to the point of risking their lives to help others. In 2007, Wesley Autrey, shown here with his daughter, selflessly risked his life to save a young man who fell onto New York subway tracks after suffering a seizure.

Sensational, although inaccurate, news accounts of the murder of Kitty Genovese stimulated research in bystander intervention, which asked questions about why people seem to help in some situations but not in others.

bystander intervention The study of situational variables related to helping a stranger, most notably the decreased likelihood of helping as the number of bystanders increases.

The effect of the number of observers on the likelihood of intervention is probably influenced by a sense of individual responsibility. When you are the only person available to help, your responsibility is clear. When a crowd of people is gathered around the scene of an accident, it is easier to assume that others have already called 911 or that a physician or nurse who is better qualified to help will be present. People also fail to act because of fears of appearing foolish as a result of misinterpreting a situation. Emergencies can be ambiguous. What sounds like a case of domestic violence next door might be a loud movie or video game or actors practicing a scene for a play. People who feel anonymous are less likely to help, which is consistent with our previous observations of how anonymity can lead to less socially desirable behavior. Finally, people are more likely to help when it is safe and convenient for them to do so. If you are heading for your car at the end of the day when you notice a classmate with a flat tire, you are likely to lend a hand. However, if you are late for work or a final exam, you may conveniently assume that someone else will take care of the situation as you continue on your way.

Why Are We Aggressive?

Aggression is the conscious intent to harm others, and it can take several forms. Instrumental aggression is the intentional harm, usually physical, done to others to obtain a goal, such as attacking a person to steal a wallet or purse. Relational aggression harms another person's social standing through behaviors such as ignoring, excluding, and gossiping. Other types of aggression include defensive aggression, in which the person may do harm to others in self-defense; passive aggression, in which people who aren't comfortable being openly aggressive get what they want under the guise of still trying to please others; and maternal aggression, a rather common phenomenon in the animal world (and occasionally among humans) in which sickly or unwanted offspring are killed.

Like most of the behaviors we discuss in this textbook, factors leading to human aggression form complex interactions. Efforts to find simple correlations between violence and single variables such as economic growth, population trends, illegal drug trade, availability of guns, and domestic violence versus stranger violence do not tell the whole story. We can capture the flavor of this complexity by examining homicide rates across cultures. The average homicide rate worldwide is about 10 per 100,000 residents per year, or twice the number killed in war (United Nations Office on Drugs and Crime [UNODC], 2014). South Africa has a murder rate of 60 homicides per 100,000 residents, compared to Singapore's rate of 0.2 per 100,000 (UNODC, 2014). Rates in large cities within the United States vary substantially, from Washington, D.C.'s 45 homicides per 100,000 residents to Honolulu's 2 per 100,000 (U.S. Department of Justice, 2006). Across all cultures, women are more likely than men to be killed by intimate partners or family members, but rates again vary. Only 24% of female victims in Australia are killed by someone they don't know, while 66% of female victims in Singapore don't know their murderer (UNODC, 2014).

The Biological Psychology of Aggression

Is a capacity for aggression simply part of being human? Biological explanations of aggression point to several possible sources of human aggression: genetics, biochemistry, and nervous system structure and activity.

Aggression is clearly a disposition that can be selectively bred in animals, as evidenced by the development of the famous fighting bulls of Spain and hyperaggressive laboratory mice (Lagerspetz & Lagerspetz, 1983). Human twin and adoption studies imply that aggressive tendencies in humans are at least partly influenced by genetics (Rushton, Fulker, Neale, Nias, & Eysenck, 1986). As we have seen so frequently in this textbook, genes associated with aggressive behavior interact with nurture or experience. Among children who were abused, those with one version of a gene linked to aggression in animals were likely to behave aggressively, while those with the other form rarely did so, even when the abuse they experienced was severe (Craig, 2007; Fergusson, Boden, Horwood, Miller, & Kennedy, 2011).

aggression The conscious intent to harm another.

Both naturally occurring chemicals and recreational drugs can influence aggression. Among the naturally occurring chemicals implicated in aggression are the androgens, or male hormones such as testosterone (see ● Figure 13.20). Prenatal exposure to high levels of androgens, which can occur naturally or because of medications occasionally given to pregnant women, increases the aggressive play of both male and female preschoolers (Reinisch, Ziemba-Davis, & Sanders, 1991). Adult men with higher levels of prenatal testosterone exposure score higher on standardized questionnaires of aggression (Bailey & Hurd, 2005; Burton, Henninger, Hafetz, & Cofer, 2009). Testosterone levels on the high end of the typical range in teen and adult males are positively correlated with delinquency, drug abuse, and aggression (Dabbs & Morris, 1990). Testosterone levels for both male and female criminals correlate with the violent nature of the crimes for which they were sentenced, as well as the dominance and violence they demonstrate while in prison (Dabbs, Frady, Carr, & Besch, 1987; Dabbs & Hargrove, 1997). Testosterone appears to affect aggressive behavior by increasing the sensitivity of the amygdala to threatening stimuli, such as angry faces (Derntl et al., 2009). When feeling threatened, a person might engage in more aggressive behavior as a preemptive strike.

Serotonin levels are negatively correlated with aggressive behavior. Male vervet monkeys form precise social hierarchies, and higher rank is associated with higher levels of serotonin activity (Raleigh, McGuire, Brammer, Pollack, & Yuwiler, 1991). Monkeys at the bottom of the hierarchy had lower serotonin levels and were much more aggressive than high status monkeys. Serotonin might reduce aggression by enhancing empathy (Siegel & Crockett, 2013) or by promoting activity in frontal lobe areas associated with inhibiting impulsive behaviors (Heinz, Beck, Meyer-Lindenberg, Sterzer, & Heinz, 2011).

Many psychoactive substances affect the likelihood that a person will behave aggressively. For instance, alcohol has been implicated in between 32% and 63% of violent crimes (Giancola, 2013). In addition, many suicides are committed under the influence of alcohol (Sher, 2006). The most likely mode of action for alcohol in stimulating aggression is its general disinhibiting effects on behavior. As we discussed in Chapter 4, alcohol silences higher cortical areas responsible for impulse control, often leading to behavior that is normally actively suppressed, including aggression.

Keeping in mind the complexity of human aggression, we can point to variations in brain structure and function that are correlated with senseless violence. Antisocial, violent behavior is correlated with some types of brain damage, although these findings interact with experience in ways similar to the genetics studies discussed earlier (Davidson, Putnam, & Larson, 2000). The diversity of patterns of brain activity leading to aggression was demonstrated in a study comparing brain activity in murderers who had experienced neglect, poverty, physical abuse, or sexual abuse and murderers who had experienced none of these social deficits (Raine, Stoddard, Bihrle, & Buchsbaum, 1998). The brain activity of the neglected and abused murderers was quite similar to the nonviolent control participants. In contrast, the brain activity of the nonabused murderers was quite different, suggesting that their violent behavior had different roots compared to the murderers with a history of child abuse. The nonabused individuals showed an unusually reduced level of activity in the frontal lobes. Given the essential role of the frontal lobes in higher order judgment and impulse control, this lower level of activity might help account for their inability to control their aggression.

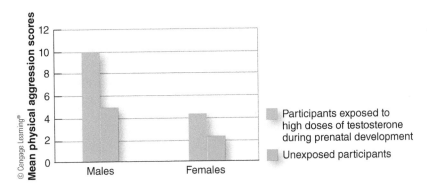

© Cengage Learning®

FIGURE 13.20

Prenatal Exposure to Testosterone and Aggression.
Both male and female preschoolers who had been exposed prenatally to higher than normal levels of testosterone were more physically aggressive than their same-sex siblings who experienced normal levels of prenatal testosterone.

Courtesy of Dr. Adrian Raine, Departments of Criminology, Psychiatry, and Psychology, University of Pennsylvania

These brain images were taken from (a) a person with no history of criminal behavior, (b) a person who was convicted of murder and had a strong history of childhood abuse and neglect, and (c) a person who was convicted of murder but had no history of childhood abuse or neglect. The murderer who had been abused and neglected shows activity that is similar to that of the person without a criminal history. The murderer with no history of abuse or neglect shows little activity in the frontal lobes (toward the top of the image) or in the middle parts of the brain that usually respond to emotional stimuli.

Learning and Aggression

Although it is probably safe to say that our human heritage contains a capacity for aggression, the actual expression of aggression is elicited by environmental factors and modified by experience. As we discussed in Chapter 8, Albert Bandura provided compelling evidence that children who observe aggression are likely to behave aggressively themselves (Bandura, 1973). In Bandura's classic demonstration of social learning, preschoolers who observed an adult attack an inflatable Bobo doll toy mimicked not just the violent actions but also the yells of "sock him in the nose," "knock him down," and "kick him."

Opportunities to observe violence are plentiful. Within the family, children who are disciplined with screaming, slapping, and beating are more likely to be physically aggressive with their peers at school (Patterson, Chamberlain, & Reid, 1982). Even when the parents are violent toward each other, without involving the child directly, the child's level of violent behavior may be affected. In a study of more than 2,000 violent children and teens, recent exposure to violence in the home was a useful predictor for the child's violent behavior outside the home (Singer, Miller, Guo, Slovak, & Frierson, 1998).

Additional opportunities to observe violence are provided by media. By the age of 18, the average American has seen an estimated 200,000 acts of violence on television alone (Strasburger, 2007). Sixty-one percent of television programming includes violence, with only 4% featuring an antiviolence theme (Federman, 1998). Children and youth are exposed to increasingly violent and graphic images and ideas through films, video games, and music lyrics. As we discussed in Chapter 2, however, care must be taken to avoid misinterpretation of the research results showing correlations between media exposure and aggression.

Preventing Aggression

The human species loses a smaller percentage of the population to war today than in the time of our hunter–gatherer ancestors (LeBlanc, 2003), but we still have a long way to go. As in the case of reducing prejudice, redefining the boundaries of the in-group might be contributing to this improvement. Instead of hunter–gatherer clans of 100 or so individuals fighting with their neighboring clans, we have nations of millions that cooperate as units. Increasing economic dependencies among nations further reduces the advantages of between-group violence. Damage to one nation's critical infrastructure, such as its ability to produce or process oil, is likely to have adverse effects for all nations, including the attacker. Despite this progress, we remain plagued not only by continued war deaths but also by homicides, domestic violence, rape, bullying, and other destructive aggressive behaviors. Psychologists continue to search for effective ways to reduce aggression.

There are no simple solutions to the problem of aggression. You might think that we could take advantage of catharsis, or the reduction of an emotion through its expression, but the research results do not support this approach. Catharsis theories of aggression are common but suffer from the same weaknesses shown by catharsis explanations of emotion discussed in Chapter 7. Just as expressing an emotion typically heightens rather than decreasing a feeling, people who engage in aggression experience an increase in aggression. In one typical experiment, participants first were angered by a person who criticized essays they had written (Bushman, 2002). Subsequently, the participants who were given opportunities to hit a punching bag while thinking about the critic administered louder sound blasts to the critic when given the opportunity to retaliate than did participants in control groups. Despite the intuitive appeal of the notion of catharsis, when it comes to aggression, catharsis is generally ineffective.

Another frequent suggestion for reducing aggression that has failed to gain research support is an active teaching approach in which children are rewarded for sensitivity and cooperation. Cross-cultural data show that homicide rates are often high in cultures that feature a loving socialization of children and aversion to interpersonal conflict, such as the Inuit, !Kung Bushmen, and Gebusi of New Zealand, yet very low among cultures where children are explicitly taught to fight, like the Turkana of Kenya (Dyson-Hudson & Dyson-Hudson, 1999, 1995).

Much of the research we have discussed so far focuses on individual variables, whether they are related to a person's genetic makeup or socialization. To truly understand aggression, we need to zoom out to see this behavior within the social context. For example, we know that if groups rarely interact, they are more likely to fight than to cooperate. In contrast, if groups interact regularly and anticipate future interactions, they may still compete, but they tend to do so in more prosocial ways.

The social environment can also determine whether aggressiveness escalates to actual violence. In a study using surveillance footage of public places, researchers observed actual fighting behavior (Levine, Taylor, & Best, 2011). In many cases, one or more third parties (usually friends of the combatants) intervened to stop the fight. In an interesting contrast with the helping behavior observed in the bystander intervention literature discussed previously, third parties are more likely, not less likely, to intervene in a fight when the number of bystanders is larger. Perhaps the implications of the aggression spreading to include the whole group makes stopping the fight a very high priority for members of the group.

Research using surveillance camera footage shows that third parties often intervene in an effort to de-escalate violence (Levine, Taylor, & Best, 2011). Unlike most laboratory studies of bystander intervention, third parties in the filmed incidents were more, not less, likely to intervene as groups of onlookers became larger. Further research should help clarify the exact conditions leading to helping behavior.

Homicides among the Turkana of Kenya are quite rare, even though children are explicitly encouraged to be aggressive to one another, under the watchful eyes of adults. However, the Turkana are exceedingly aggressive toward their neighbors. Over human history, the trait of aggression has probably been valued when turned against other groups but not when it is turned inward.

Interpersonal Relationships
The Social Perspective
What Do We Know About Marriages That Begin Online?

The advent of the Internet is changing our social interactions right in front of our eyes. Classic research reviewed earlier in this chapter showed that Americans typically married someone who lived within a mile of their home (Bossard, 1932). The Internet has changed all of that. Between 2005 and 2012, a surprising number of Americans, one out of three, met their spouses online (Cacioppo, Cacioppo, Gonzaga, Ogburn, & VanderWeele, 2013). Despite the comfort level of younger adults with the Internet, 30- to 39-year-olds were more like to have met their spouse online than were those under 30. Those who met their spouse online were also more educated and had higher income, suggesting that the Internet has provided busy people opportunities to socialize.

Marriages begun online were slightly but significantly less likely to end in divorce or separation than the marriages begun offline. Online marriage partners rated their marriages as more satisfying. Even when factors such as age, education, and income were controlled, because these might account for higher satisfaction by themselves, the online marriages remained more successful.

What other factors might account for the success of the online marriages? People who seek a spouse online might differ from those who don't in important ways. Perhaps they are more motivated to maintain long-term relationships, or they might be more selective in their choices. Self-disclosure differs in the online and offline settings, leading to greater liking for people you meet in the online setting (Cacioppo et al., 2013). Finally, the matching algorithms used by online dating sites might result in people finding more compatible partners than they would through chance meetings in their face-to-face lives.

Further research is necessary to fully understand the impact of online meetings on relationship outcomes, but these initial results indicate that many Americans are using online dating with surprising success. ●

Summary 13.4 Cooperation and Competition

	What is it?	Influential factors
Cooperation	Working together to reach a goal	• Individual differences • Tit-for-tat strategy • Culture • Innate sense of fair play
Competition	A contest for resources	• Availability of resources • Signals for dominance and submission
Altruism	Helping others without personal gain or with personal cost	• Number of potential helpers available • Relatedness to person needing help • Punishment for selfishness • Expectation of future reciprocation • Conscious desire to help • Sense of personal responsibility to help
Aggression	Conscious intent to harm another	• Interactions between genetics and child maltreatment • Use of alcohol and other drugs • Testosterone and serotonin levels • Brain structure and activity • Observational learning

Credits: Top Row. Gonzalo Fuentes/Reuters/Corbis. Second Row. Paul Wayne Wilson/PhotoStockFile/Alamy. Third Row. Lucas Jackson/Reuters/Corbis. Bottom Row: Andrew Aitchison/In Pictures/Corbis News/Corbis.

KEY TERMS The Language of Psychological Science

Be sure you can define these terms and use them correctly.

actor-observer bias, p. 495
aggression, p. 528
attitude, p. 499
attribution, p. 493
bystander intervention, p. 527
cognitive dissonance, p. 500
compliance, p. 513
conformity, p. 511
correspondence bias, p. 493
deindividuation, p. 517

discrimination, p. 505
dispositional attribution, p. 493
door in the face, p. 513
elaboration likelihood model (ELM), p. 501
foot in the door, p. 513
fundamental attribution error, p. 494
group polarization, p. 517
groupthink, p. 518
just-world belief, p. 497

mere exposure effect, p. 520
obedience, p. 514
persuasion, p. 501
prejudice, p. 505
self-serving bias, p. 496
situational attribution, p. 493
social facilitation, p. 516
social loafing, p. 517
social norms, p. 511
stereotype, p. 505

14 The Troubled Mind

Psychological Disorders

OF ALL THE REASONS TO STUDY PSYCHOLOGY, FINDING ways to improve the lives of people with psychological disorders might be one of the most rewarding. This process begins with understanding the features and possible causes of a disorder.

Identifying the causes of psychological disorders requires us to pull together multiple threads leading from the genetic, biological, cognitive, developmental, and social aspects of being human. These causal factors interact with one another in complex ways, so the same disorder might look one way in one individual and quite different in another. We do not know what causes children to develop the symptoms of autism spectrum disorder (ASD), discussed in detail later in this chapter, but we at least know where to start looking.

We have cautioned you on several occasions in this textbook to avoid the idea that we have "genes for" this trait or the next, because the reality is more complex. As we zoom in to analyze the genetic contributions to ASD, you will see that we have zoomed way past the traditional array of 46 human chromosomes featured in Chapter 3. Instead, we are looking at a visual representation of something biologists call an *interactome*, which is a map of all interactions among proteins in a cell. In this particular case, the researchers were attempting to identify the relationships among the 539 proteins that formed interactions with proteins produced by 26 genes already implicated in ASD (Sakai et al., 2011). The resulting map not only confirmed links between ASD and several related conditions but also identified genetic relationships that warranted further study.

What does an interactome mean for the child in the photo on this page? Understanding more about the sources of ASD has not yet, unfortunately, led to improved treatments. As we mention in Chapters 8 and 15, the only effective treatment for ASD today is the use of behavioral therapies. Still, such discoveries have the potential to improve the lives of individuals with ASD down the road or to provide information that will eventually help us prevent further cases.

To fully understand this child's experience requires us to zoom out to consider his overall development. Psychologists point out that we say "a person with autism spectrum disorder" instead of an "autistic person" for good reasons. People are not their disorders, and much is happening in this child's life that has nothing to do with ASD. We could consider the impact of his parents, whose age might have been a risk factor for his ASD, or study their abilities to manage his behavior and help him reach his potential. Zooming

◀ An interactome among genes implicated in autism spectrum disorder with other cellular proteins confirmed links between autism spectrum disorder and several related conditions and identified new genes that warranted further study.

J.R. Bale/Alamy

Argosy Publishing, Inc.

even farther out, we can investigate the effects of ASD on the social connectedness this child experiences as he ventures out into the world.

In this chapter, you will discover a number of types of psychological disorders, each with a unique history and set of characteristics. In Chapter 15, we will explore the treatments and therapies that psychologists have developed to address the challenges to well-being posed by these disorders.

We refer to "people with autism spectrum disorder" instead of "autistic person" because there is so much more to people than their disorders.

Learning Objectives

1. Analyze the general definition of *psychological disorder* and discuss its application in the *Diagnostic and Statistical Manual of Mental Disorders (DSM-5)*.

2. Debate the diagnostic criteria for autism spectrum disorder and attention deficit hyperactivity disorder, considering ways to distinguish symptoms of these disorders from normal childhood behavior.

3. Summarize the symptoms of schizophrenia and their biological and environmental correlates.

4. Discuss the role of bipolar disorder as a bridge between schizophrenia and major depressive disorder.

5. Identify common and differentiating symptoms of the anxiety disorders, obsessive-compulsive disorder, posttraumatic stress disorder, and dissociative and somatic symptom disorders.

6. Assess the psychological mechanisms that may support behavioral symptoms of antisocial and borderline personality disorders.

What Does It Mean to Have a Psychological Disorder?

Mental health experts define a psychological disorder as "a syndrome characterized by clinically significant disturbance in an individual's cognition, emotion regulation, or behavior that reflects a dysfunction in the psychological, biological, or development processes underlying

		NORMAL	MILD
Emotions		Good alertness and positive emotional state.	Feeling sad or down temporarily, but not for long.
Cognitions		"I'm not getting the grades I want this semester, but I'll keep trying to do my best."	"I'm struggling at school this semester. I wish I could study better, or I'll fail."
Behaviors		Going to classes and studying for the next round of tests. Talking to professors.	Going to classes with some trouble studying. Less contact with others.

© Cengage Learning®

mental functioning" (American Psychiatric Association [APA], 2013, p. 20).What does this definition mean?

Many behaviors considered abnormal are quite similar to normal behaviors. We all know what it feels like to be depressed, so how is that different from having a major depressive disorder? This chapter will help you understand the distinctions, but because those distinctions can be subtle, we also caution you against "first-year medical student's disease," or the sense that you have all the disorders you are studying.

The study of psychological disorders is called **abnormal psychology**. It is surprisingly difficult but necessary for psychologists to agree on the differences between typical and abnormal behaviors, because deciding that an individual's behaviors and mental processes are abnormal is the first step toward labeling that person with a psychological disorder and providing treatment (see ● Figure 14.1).

We can start with the literal meaning of the word *abnormal.* In Latin, the prefix *ab* means "away from" and *norma* means "the rule." In other words, abnormal behavior is literally behavior that is not typical, usual, or regular. This meaning implies a statistical definition of abnormality. By this definition, behaviors that most people do are normal, whereas behaviors that characterize a minority of people are abnormal.

This statistical approach has the advantage of being clear (see ● Figure 14.2). For example, intellectual disability is one of the categories in the *Diagnostic and Statistical Manual of Mental Disorders,* a handbook for diagnosis that we discuss in more detail later in the chapter. The diagnosis of intellectual disability relies heavily on statistics. A score of 70 or below on a standard IQ test is the typical cutoff for identifying an individual with intellectual disability (APA, 2013). Even in this relatively clear situation, however, the statistical approach represents merely a starting point. A diagnosis of intellectual disability also requires an individual to demonstrate difficulties with adaptive skills, which include factors such as communication, self-care, safety, and use of community resources.

A purely statistical approach, however, has several major drawbacks. First, it implies a cultural specificity that we would like to avoid. Because most members of one culture may behave in ways different from those of people in another, the purely statistical approach to abnormality might result in different definitions of psychological disorder from one culture to the next. Second, a statistical definition fails to capture the distress that often accompanies a psychological disorder, both for the person experiencing the disorder and for those interacting with that person.

To address these concerns, we might suggest that abnormal behavior deviates from some ideal manner of behaving. This approach succeeds in capturing the general distress most of us experience when observing or experiencing abnormal behavior. Unfortunately, this approach does nothing to avoid cross-cultural differences in defining disordered behavior. Different cultures are often characterized by diverse ideals. In Western nations, hearing voices that others cannot hear is generally considered abnormal. In other cultures, hearing voices may be viewed more positively as a sign of religious giftedness (Al-Issa, 1977; Kurihara, Kato, Sakamoto, Reverger, & Kitamura, 2000). More troublesome is the simple fact that it is difficult, if not impossible, to reach consensus regarding what constitutes ideal behavior. People, including experts in psychology, have deeply divided value judgments regarding sexual conduct, recreational drug use, and a host of other activities.

abnormal psychology The study of psychological disorders.

FIGURE 14.1

A Continuum From Normal to Psychological Disorder.
Psychological disorders can be understood both categorically, which means that each has its own set of distinct characteristics used for diagnosis, and as part of a continuum from normal behavior to severely disordered behavior. The diagnostic criteria we discuss in this chapter guide psychologists in their identification of the types and severity of disorders their patients and clients might have. *Source:* Adapted from *Abnormal Psychology and Life: A Dimensional Approach,* by C. A. Kearney and T. J. Trull, 2012, Belmont, CA: Wadsworth/Cengage Learning.

MODERATE	PSYCHOLOGICAL DISORDER—LESS SEVERE	PSYCHOLOGICAL DISORDER—MORE SEVERE
Feeling sad, but a strong positive experience such as a good grade could lift mood.	Intense sadness most of the day with some trouble concentrating and some loss of appetite.	Extreme sadness all of the time with great trouble concentrating and complete loss of appetite.
"These bad grades really hurt. This may set me back for a while. I'm really worried."	"I'm so worried about these grades that my stomach hurts. I don't know what to do."	"These bad grades just show what a failure I am at everything. There's no hope; I'm not doing anything today."
Skipping a few classes and feeling somewhat unmotivated to study. Avoiding contact with professors and classmates.	Skipping most classes and unable to maintain eye contact with other people. Strong lack of motivation.	Unable to get out of bed, eat, or leave the house. Lack of energy and frequent crying.

MARKA/alberti/Alamy

FIGURE 14.2

Statistical Abnormality. The word *abnormal* literally means "away from the rule." Both intellectually gifted individuals, usually defined as having an IQ over 130, and individuals with intellectual disability, usually defined as having an IQ below 70, are equally "abnormal" in this statistical sense of the word. Academy Award–winning producer Quentin Tarantino (*Pulp Fiction*, *Kill Bill*, and *Django Unchained*) has a reported IQ of 160. Although neither he nor his films are "typical," we are unlikely to refer to Tarantino as "abnormal." Statistics alone do not capture what we mean by abnormal behavior.

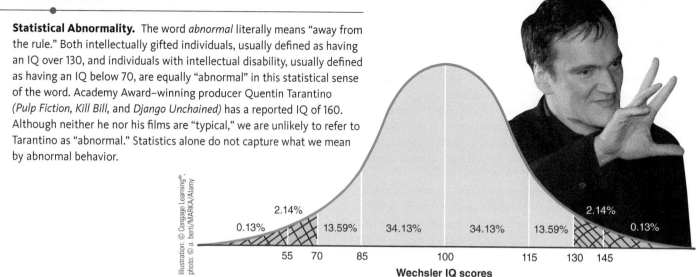

Illustration: © Cengage Learning®. photo: © a. berti/MARKA/Alamy

0.13%   2.14%   13.59%   34.13%   34.13%   13.59%   2.14%   0.13%

55   70   85   100   115   130   145

Wechsler IQ scores

Our tolerance for people engaging in acts that are harmful to themselves is variable. For example, most states in the United States have prohibitions against committing suicide (the irony in prosecuting under such laws appears to have been lost on the legislators).

A simple modification of this "deviation from the ideal" approach can help us to achieve some consensus. Behaviors that cause harm to others are viewed as less than ideal. Unless the person is acting defensively, most of us would agree that such behavior is negative and undesirable. We are also sympathetic to those who have conditions that produce harm to themselves. We can combine the best aspects of each of these approaches to construct a formal definition of abnormal behavior: Abnormal behavior is unusual, distressing, and harmful to self or others.

We don't know how many people have psychological disorders. A person can be diagnosed with **comorbid** disorders, which means more than one disorder occurs at the same time, so simply adding up the rates for each type of disorder is not a solution. Statistics can look different for different time frames. Estimates of the number of people who experience a psychological disorder during the previous year are around 26% (Kessler, Chiu, Demler, & Walters, 2005), but estimates of the number of people experiencing a disorder as least once during their lifetime are as high as 65% (Moffitt, et al., 2010).

Defining abnormal behavior as a deviation from what is considered ideal immediately runs into problems of cultural specificity. Behaviors like hearing voices that others cannot hear might be considered less than ideal in Western cultures but a gift in others. The ability to hear voices was considered an advantage for shamans, like the one represented transforming into his jaguar spirit companion in this Costa Rican piece from 1000–1500 CE.

Peter Horree/Alamy

Although college students have the same rates of psychological disorders as their age peers who are not attending college, as shown in ● Figure 14.3, rates of psychological disorders in young adults are higher than in the general population and appear to be increasing (Hunt & Eisenberg, 2010). Nearly half of the young adults under the age of 24 who were surveyed met criteria for at least one psychological disorder in the previous year, including 18% for a personality disorder, 12% for an anxiety disorder, and 11% for either major depressive disorder or bipolar disorder (Blanco et al., 2008). We discuss each of these categories in more detail in this chapter.

comorbid Two or more disorders in the same individual.

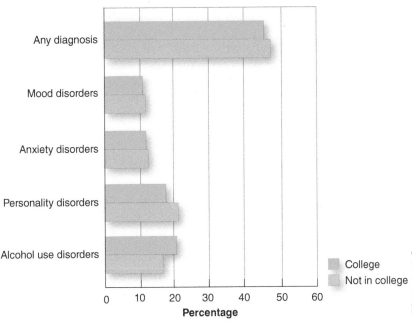

FIGURE 14.3

Rates of Psychological Disorders in College Students. Based on face-to-face interviews, college students and their same-age peers who do not attend college have a high rate (nearly 50%) of meeting the criteria for at least one psychological disorder over the past 12 months. College students and age peers not in college did not differ significantly in their rates of psychological disorder, with the exception of alcohol-use disorders, which were higher among those attending college. *Source:* Adapted from "Mental Health of College Students and Their Non–College-Attending Peers: Results From the National Epidemiologic Study on Alcohol and Related Conditions," by C. Blanco, M. Okuda, C. Wright, D. S. Hasin, B. F. Grant, S.-M. Liu, et al., 2008, *Archives of General Psychiatry, 65*(12), pp. 1429–1437. doi:10.1001/archpsyc.65.12.1429.

How Are Psychological Disorders Diagnosed?

When you visit your physician or student health center complaining of a sore throat, your health care provider notes your symptoms, compares them to known categories of illness, swabs your throat for a sample, and then determines your diagnosis: You have strep throat. Based on that diagnosis, you are given a prescription for an antibiotic. Unlike medical illnesses, however, psychological disorders are diagnosed purely on the basis of observable behaviors. There are no blood tests, scans, or other medical diagnostic procedures that can be used to determine whether a person has a psychological disorder.

To promote consistency in the diagnosis of psychological disorders, mental health professionals typically refer to the **Diagnostic and Statistical Manual of Mental Disorders (DSM)**, first published by the American Psychiatric Association (APA) in 1952. The current, fifth edition is known as *DSM-5* (APA, 2013). A second classification system in wide use is the *International Statistical Classification of Diseases and Related Health Problems,* 10th edition *(ICD-10)*, which was published by the World Health Organization (WHO) in 1992. An updated 11th edition is due to be published in 2015 (WHO, 2011b). Professionals responsible for the

The first official effort in the United States to gather data on psychological disorders was the recording of a single category, "idiocy/insanity," in the 1840 census (APA, 2000).

Diagnostic and Statistical Manual of Mental Disorders (DSM) A system for classification of psychological disorders published by the American Psychiatric Association.

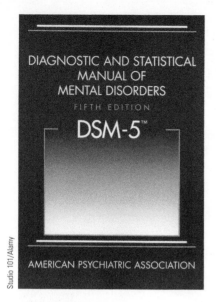

The *Diagnostic and Statistical Manual of Mental Disorders (DSM)* has undergone a number of revisions since its first edition in 1952. Over its history, the *DSM* has become less Freudian and more sensitive to cross-cultural issues. The *DSM* is published by the American Psychiatric Association. *Source:* Reprinted with permission from the *Diagnostic and Statistical Manual of Mental Disorders*, Fifth Edition.

DSM and *ICD* classification systems have coordinated their efforts to reduce the differences between the two systems (APA, 2013).

Although the *DSM* is the standard diagnostic tool used by psychiatrists and psychologists and is required by most health insurance providers in the United States, it is not without its critics. Beginning with *DSM-III* in 1980, some normal behaviors seem to have been categorized as abnormal by the system. Allen Frances, a psychiatrist who chaired the task force in charge of writing the *DSM-IV*, expressed concern that the committee's well-meaning efforts had led to three "false epidemics"—attention deficit disorder, autism, and childhood bipolar disorder—and that the *DSM-5* was even worse (Frances, 2010). For example, the *DSM-5* lists the following as a criterion for attention deficit hyperactivity disorder (ADHD):

> often avoids, dislikes, or is reluctant to engage in tasks that require sustained mental effort (e.g. schoolwork or homework; for older adolescents and adults, preparing reports, completing forms, reviewing lengthy papers). (APA, 2013, p. 59)

It is hard to imagine how this criterion fits the "unusual" aspect of our definition of abnormality. Despite its flaws, the *DSM* remains the most frequently used tool in the United States for the diagnosis of psychological disorders. Our discussion of types of psychological disorders is therefore grounded in the *DSM* system.

What Do the Psychological Perspectives Tell Us About Disorders?

We have seen many examples in this textbook of behaviors that are best understood when viewed from multiple perspectives. The study of psychological disorders provides yet another example of how an integration of multiple perspectives can be useful. This is particularly the case when considering the possible causes for abnormal behaviors.

Philippe Pinel (1745–1826) is often called "the father of modern psychiatry." After observing the more humane treatment of inmates by a former patient turned employee named Jean-Baptiste Pussin at Bicêtre Hospital outside Paris, Pinel followed Pussin's example by removing the patients' iron shackles. Instead of the usual "treatments" of the day—bleeding, purging, and blistering—Pinel made a practice of conversing with the patients regularly.

Philippe Pinel (1745-1826) releasing lunatics from their chains at the Salpetriere asylum in Paris in 1795 (colour litho), Robert-Fleury, Tony (1837-1912) (after) / Bibliotheque des Arts Decoratifs, Paris, France / Archives Charmet / The Bridgeman Art Library
Philippe Pinel (1745-1826) (oil on canvas), Merimee, Anna M. (d.1852) / Musee d'Histoire de la Medecine, Paris, France / Archives Charmet / The Bridgeman Art Library

What might an integrated approach to psychological disorder look like? First, we propose that the various perspectives discussed in this textbook (biological, clinical, developmental, cognitive, individual, and social) all have a great deal to say about disorders, but each has more to say about some disorders than about others. By considering the contributions of factors from multiple perspectives, we should have a greater appreciation of the complex interactions that occur among perspectives.

In addition, an integrated perspective helps us understand the reciprocal relationships among factors leading to psychological disorder. Just as a person who is diagnosed with depression might show low levels of serotonin activity in the brain, being in a leadership position boosts a person's serotonin levels. A simple biological explanation suggesting that chemical imbalances lead to depression or a simple psychological explanation stating that people who feel powerless are more likely to be depressed misses the nuances of these reciprocal relationships. The richer understanding of the causal factors leading to a psychological disorder pays off in the development of more effective treatments. Single-perspective thinking usually leads to single-perspective treatments. If you believe that depression is purely the result of chemical imbalances of the brain, then a simple prescription should do the trick. If you believe that hearing voices others can't hear is the result of childhood communication patterns, you will miss the opportunity to provide medication that can effectively end these troubling symptoms. Inclusive models describing the entire range of causal factors are more likely to result in effective treatments tailored to the needs of individuals.

Which Disorders Emerge in Childhood?

Many disorders might have roots in childhood but are more typically diagnosed in adolescence and adulthood. The *DSM-5* uses the term *neurodevelopmental disorders* to refer to disorders that instead are diagnosed typically in childhood yet often continue throughout the life span (APA, 2013). Two of these neurodevelopmental disorders are examined in this section: autism spectrum disorder (ASD) and attention deficit hyperactivity disorder (ADHD).

Autism Spectrum Disorder

The word *autism* literally means "within oneself." In 1943, psychiatrist Leo Kanner worked with a group of children who shared problems in social communication and interaction and restricted, repetitive patterns of behavior, interests, or activities. Kanner's observations form the basis of our current diagnostic criteria for **autism spectrum disorder** (ASD; APA, 2013), which combines previous categories of autism and Asperger's syndrome. ASD represents a spectrum because the severity of the observed deficits can vary widely from individual to individual. Adjustment can range from relatively normal, allowing independent living, to intellectual disability, requiring living with parents or in institutional settings.

Rates of ASD have been increasing rapidly over the last two decades (see ● Figure 14.4). Approximately 1 child out of every 50 between the ages of 6 and 17 years in the United States has ASD (Blumberg et al., 2013). Rates of ASD in California had already jumped 273% between 1987 and 1998 (Shute, 2000). The rapid increase in rates could be a result of a genuine rise in cases, a relaxation or improved awareness of diagnostic criteria, or some combination of the two (Barbaresi, Katusic, Colligan, Weaver, & Jacobsen, 2005). Males remain far more likely to be diagnosed with ASD than females, possibly by a factor of 4 to 1 (Blumberg et al., 2013; Shute, 2000).

Problems with social relatedness are at the core of this disorder, regardless of the individual's level of intelligence and adjustment. Beginning in infancy, most children with ASD do not make eye contact or take pleasure in reciprocal games like peekaboo. Insight into the thoughts and points of view of others is particularly lacking. As we discussed in Chapter 11, children develop a theory of mind by the time they are 3 to 4 years of age. Many researchers believe that a failure to develop a normal theory of mind is responsible for many of the social

autism spectrum disorder (ASD) A disorder characterized by deficits in social relatedness and communication skills that are often accompanied by repetitive, ritualistic behavior.

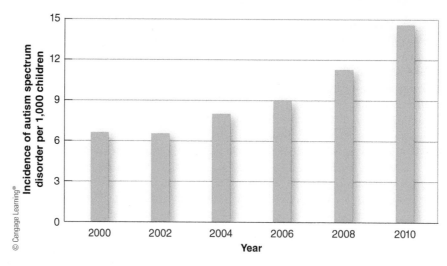

FIGURE 14.4

The Prevalence of Autism Spectrum Disorder Appears to Be Increasing. Rates of autism spectrum disorder continue to increase, but the reasons for this change remain a source of debate in the scientific community. It is possible that the rates are truly increasing, but greater awareness by parents and health care providers, relaxed applications of the diagnostic criteria, and improved availability of services might also be contributing to the observed change. *Source:* Centers for Disease Control and Prevention (CDC, 2014). *Data & statistics.* Retrieved from www.cdc.com/ncbddd/autism/data.html

deficits observed in ASD (Baron-Cohen, 1991; Senju, Southgate, White, & Frith, 2009). Language skills of individuals with ASD can vary widely, from having no language abilities to delayed acquisition of language to normal skills (Ellis Weismer, Lord, & Esler, 2010). Even when language skills are relatively normal, individuals with ASD usually experience difficulty maintaining conversations with others because of their deficits in social skills.

Individuals with ASD often object strenuously to changes in the environment and show a high level of repetitive, routine behavior. Rituals may include repetitive movements, such as rocking, hand flapping, head banging, and twirling. Other individuals may engage in extremely limited preoccupations, such as learning all models of cars ever made by Ford. One possible source of this ritualistic behavior is a general dysfunction in sensory networks. Most individuals with ASD show unusually increased or decreased sensitivity to stimuli (Lane, Young, Baker, & Angley, 2010). They may be relatively insensitive to pain or cold but distressed by normal sound levels (see ● Figure 14.5). Ritualistic behavior may control or override these disparate sensations.

Causes of Autism Spectrum Disorder

Although the causes of ASD remain somewhat mysterious, and probably show variable patterns from case to case, scientists are making progress in their understanding. Family and twin studies provide strong evidence that ASD is influenced by genetics (Frazier et al., 2014). The concordance rate for ASD between identical twins may be 76% to 88% and possibly more (Ronald & Hoekstra, 2011), which means that if one twin has ASD, the other twin has between a 76% and an 88% chance of also having ASD. Very large numbers of genes are probably involved, and research attention is being focused on the expression of these genes during brain development (Sakai et al., 2011). Autopsies of the brains of people with ASD and people with no history of psychological disorder show dramatic differences (Voineagu et al., 2011). In the typical control brains, 174 genes were expressed differently in the frontal lobes compared to the temporal lobes, but in the brains of people with ASD, no gene showed evidence of being expressed differently in the two areas.

Abnormalities in cortical development might lead to unusual minicolumns, vertical arrays of neurons perpendicular to the surface of the cerebral cortex that represent the smallest

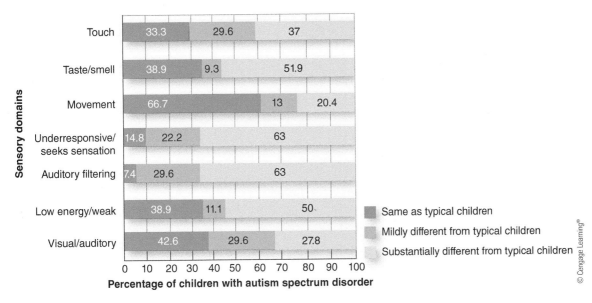

FIGURE 14.5

Sensory Sensitivity Is Different in Autism Spectrum Disorder (ASD). Children with ASD often show differences from healthy children in their sensitivity to environmental stimuli. This graph shows the percentage of children with ASD whose scores on an instrument measuring sensitivity were the same as those of typical children, mildly different from those of typical children (between one and two standard deviations from the mean), and rare compared to those of typical children (more than two standard deviations from the mean). The domains measured included sensitivity to touch (tactile), sensitivity to taste and smell, sensitivity to movement (e.g., fear of falling), underresponsiveness (e.g., touches people), auditory filtering (e.g., fails to respond to name when called), low energy (e.g., tires easily), and visual or auditory (e.g., responds negatively to loud noises or bright lights). *Source:* Adapted from "Sensory Processing Subtypes in Autism: Association With Adaptive Behavior," by A. Lane, R. Young, A. Baker, and M. Angley, 2010, *Journal of Autism and Developmental Disorders, 40*(1), pp. 112–122. doi:10.1007/s10803-009-0840-2.

processing units of the brain. Individuals with ASD have narrower minicolumns containing normal numbers of cells but spaced farther apart than those found in healthy individuals. These structural differences are consistent with a pattern of connectivity that favors detailed focus, which could produce the unusual interests and hobbies of people with ASD, over more global processing, like understanding the social environment (Opris & Casanova, 2014).

Additional structural abnormalities in cases of ASD have been observed in the amygdala, hippocampus, and cerebellum (Barnea-Goraly et al., 2014; Stoodley, 2014). Researchers continue to debate a possible role in ASD for the mirror system, which has been implicated in empathy, imitation, and language (see Chapter 8; Gallese, Rochat, & Berchio, 2013; Hamilton, 2013).

Environmental factors undoubtedly play a part in ASD, and they probably interact with genetic factors during sensitive periods of brain development (Engel & Daniels, 2011). Parental age appears to be one risk factor, with older parents more likely than younger parents to give birth to a child with ASD (Grether, Anderson, Croen, Smith, & Windham, 2009; Shelton, Tancredi, & Hertz-Picciotto, 2010), although the effect is rather small. Exposure to infection and nutritional factors are known risk factors for ASD (Hamlyn, Duhig, McGrath, & Scott, 2013). Use of common antidepressants known as selective serotonin reuptake inhibitors (SSRIs) during pregnancy triples the risk of producing a son with ASD but does not seem to influence risk in daughters (Harrington, Lee, Crum, Zimmerman, & Hertz-Picciotto, 2014).

One of the unfortunate consequences of the uncertainty surrounding the causes of ASD has been the vulnerability of concerned parents seeking answers. In a paper later retracted by the British medical journal *Lancet,* unsubstantiated claims that the routine measles, mumps,

Narrow minicolumns similar to those found in the brains of people with ASD were observed in the brains of three distinguished scientists, none of whom had ASD symptoms, who donated their brains for scientific study. These similarities suggest that the minicolumn structure might account for the extreme focus of interests typical in ASD (Casanova, Switala, Trippe, & Fitzgerald, 2007). Outstanding scientists, like people with autism, have been known to study minute details for long periods.

Minicolumns in the cerebral cortex function like the microprocessors in modern computers by serving as the basic unit that receives input, processes it, and responds. Individuals with autism spectrum disorder (ASD; lower image) have smaller minicolumns than do healthy controls (top image). What does this difference mean for information processing? Smaller minicolumns favor the process of discrimination, described in Chapter 8 as distinguishing among stimuli, while larger minicolumns favor generalization, or applying a response to similar stimuli. Behavioral domains that are difficult for people with ASD, such as language, face recognition, and following another person's gaze, require more generalization than discrimination.

(a) Healthy controls

(b) Individuals with autism

Manuel F. Casanova, M.D., Department of Psychiatry and Behavioral Sciences, University of Louisville

and rubella vaccination caused ASD were published. Similar controversies in the United States about a type of mercury preservative in vaccinations ensued.

The weight of the scientific evidence shows that vaccinations play no part in the development of ASD (Schechter & Grether, 2008; see ● Figure 14.6). Despite the clear data and reassurances from medical experts, worried parents have withheld vaccinations from their children, leading to increasing numbers of cases of life-threatening, preventable diseases that had previously been believed to be under control. For example, in the first half of 2008, measles cases in the United States doubled compared to the rates observed between 2000 and 2007, and all cases involved unvaccinated school children (Centers for Disease Control and Prevention [CDC], 2008).

Attention Deficit Hyperactivity Disorder

Attention deficit hyperactivity disorder (ADHD) is perhaps one of the most contentious categories described in the *DSM-5*. The criteria for the disorder are difficult to distinguish from the behaviors of many typical young children. Because most children diagnosed with ADHD are treated with medication, the stakes for accurately diagnosing the condition are high indeed.

ADHD involves inattention and hyperactivity. Some individuals show both inattention and hyperactivity, but some inattentive people show no hyperactivity (APA, 2013). The core feature of inattention is the inability to maintain sustained attention, or on-task behavior, for an age-appropriate length of time. This problem is evidenced in the diagnostic criteria for inattention, such as difficulties in following instructions, in organizing and completing work, and in avoiding careless mistakes. Children with hyperactivity express a high level of motor activity and find engaging in structured activities, such as waiting in line or sitting quietly in class, challenging. These children are noisy, active, and boisterous, and they often appear to take action without thinking it through. Even as adults, individuals who were diagnosed with ADHD as children have more traffic accidents than do people without the disorder (Barkley & Cox, 2007).

attention deficit hyperactivity disorder (ADHD) A disorder characterized by either unusual inattentiveness, hyperactivity with impulsivity, or both.

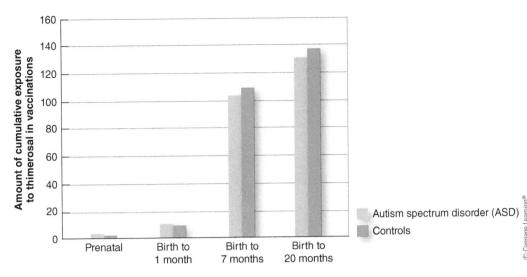

FIGURE 14.6

Cumulative exposure to thimerosal, a mercury-containing preservative that has been used in vaccines, was the same for children diagnosed with autism spectrum disorder (ASD) and healthy controls. Despite clear scientific evidence to the contrary, many people have been influenced by celebrities such as model Jenny McCarthy and have withheld vaccinations from their children. As a result, communities are facing epidemics of clearly avoidable and disabling diseases, such as measles.

Many of these behaviors are seen in children who do not have psychological disorders. Although the *DSM-5* attempts to provide guidelines about making a distinction between normal and abnormal inattentiveness and hyperactivity, fewer than 40% of surveyed pediatricians reported using the *DSM-5* criteria to evaluate cases of ADHD (Wasserman et al., 1999). More than half the children in a large sample who were receiving medication for ADHD did not meet even relaxed diagnostic criteria for the disorder, let alone the carefully constructed criteria spelled out in the *DSM-5* (Angold, Erkanli, Egger, & Costello, 2000).

In 2011, 11% of children between the ages of 4 and 17 years had been diagnosed with ADHD in the United States, representing an increase of 42% over rates of ADHD as recently as 2003 (Visser et al., 2014; see ● Figure 14.7). ADHD is diagnosed at least twice as frequently in males as in females, and females are more likely than males to be diagnosed with inattentiveness without hyperactivity (APA, 2013).

One of the DSM-5 criteria for ADHD is "often fidgets with hands or feet or squirms in seat." If you have visited an elementary school classroom lately, you might have noticed that most children are active. At what point does squirming become a psychological disorder requiring medication?

Causes of Attention Deficit Hyperactivity Disorder

The National Institute of Mental Health (2009, p. 3) concluded that "scientists are not sure what causes ADHD." However, twin and adoption studies support a significant role for genetics in the development of ADHD. Heritability may be 70% or more (Faraone & Mick, 2010). Environmental factors might interact with genetic risk. Known environmental risks for ADHD are lead contamination, low birth weight, and prenatal exposure to tobacco, alcohol, and other drugs (Banerjee, Middleton, & Faraone, 2007).

The frontal lobes may be underactive in cases of ADHD (Barkley, 1997). Because the frontal lobes inhibit unwanted behavior, lower activity in this part of the brain may lead to hyperactivity and impulsivity. The frontal lobes, and the prefrontal areas in particular, appear to mature more slowly in children with ADHD than in healthy controls (Shaw et al., 2007). Peak cortical

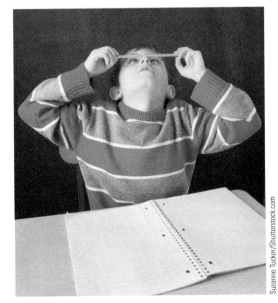

All children can be active and noisy, but most usually learn quickly to restrict those behaviors to the right times and places. Children with attention deficit hyperactivity disorder (ADHD) often struggle to sit quietly in class or wait in line.

FIGURE 14.7

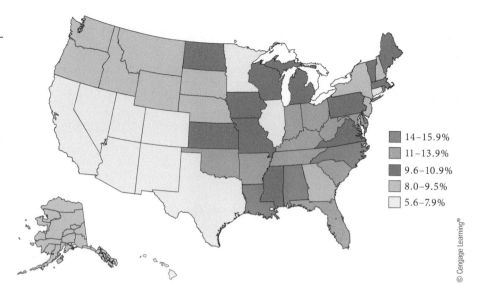

Diagnoses of Attention Deficit Hyperactivity Disorder (ADHD) in the United States. The number of children diagnosed with ADHD in a 2007 report from the Centers for Disease Control and Prevention varies dramatically by region in the United States, from a low of 5.6% to 7.9% in the Southwest to 11% to 15.9% in parts of the Midwest and Southeast. Reasons for these regional discrepancies are not clear, although low socioeconomic status is considered a risk factor for ADHD. The differences might also represent variations in how the diagnostic criteria are applied by local health care providers.

Legend:
- 14–15.9%
- 11–13.9%
- 9.6–10.9%
- 8.0–9.5%
- 5.6–7.9%

© Cengage Learning®

thickness, a measure of brain maturity, occurred in healthy controls around the age of 7.5 years but not until the age of 10.5 years in children with ADHD. Patterns of cortical thinning during adolescence predicted which individuals would continue to experience ADHD symptoms in adulthood and which would "outgrow" their symptoms (Shaw et al., 2013). The caudate nucleus, part of the basal ganglia that we described in Chapter 4, also shows delayed development in ADHD (Krain & Castellanos, 2006). White matter circuits connecting the basal ganglia and the frontal lobes appear to mature differently in people with and without ADHD (Helpern et al., 2011).

The parts of the brain implicated in ADHD, such as the prefrontal cortex and the basal ganglia, feature large amounts of dopamine activity. As we will see in Chapter 15, most of the medications used to treat ADHD, such as methylphenidate (Ritalin), dextroamphetamine (Dexedrine or Dextrostat), or amphetamine salts (Adderall), act by boosting the activity of dopamine, suggesting that dopamine activity might be lower than usual in cases of ADHD (Volkow et al., 2009).

As in ASD, myths about the causes of ADHD are common. Sugar is often blamed for hyperactive behavior, but evidence from carefully controlled studies does not support this belief (Milich & Pelham, 1986; Wolraich, Wilson, & White, 1996). However, as we discussed in Chapter 2, a well-controlled study suggested that combinations of common food additives made normal children demonstrate more hyperactivity (McCann et al., 2007). It is unlikely that "poor parenting" is responsible for these symptoms (Schroeder & Kelley, 2009). Parents can, however, learn new behavioral management techniques that greatly improve their child's behavior.

Among the many differences observed in the brains of children with attention deficit disorder (ADHD) compared to those of healthy controls is the rate of brain maturity, as measured by cortical thickening. These images demonstrate areas of the brain that developed later in children with ADHD than in healthy controls. Peak cortical thickness occurred around the age of 7.5 years in healthy children but was not seen in children with ADHD until an average age of 10.5 years. This finding implies that children with ADHD can be expected to lag behind their age peers in some tasks but will eventually experience improvement. *Source:* From Shaw, P., et al., (2007). Attention-deficit/hyperactivity disorder is characterized by a delay in cortical maturation. Proceedings of the National Academy of Sciences (PNAS), 104(49), 19649-19654. Copyright 2007 National Academy of Sciences. U.S.A.

Legend:
- Greater than 2 years' delay
- 0–2 years' delay

Summary 14.1 Neurodevelopmental Disorders

Disorder	Symptoms	Possible causal factors under investigation
Autism spectrum disorder	• Problems with social relatedness • Problems with communication • Ritualistic behavior	• Genetics • Parental age • Disruptions in brain development • Unknown environmental influences
Attention deficit hyperactivity disorder	• Inattentiveness • Hyperactivity	• Genetics • Brain development/exposure to toxins • Frontal lobe activity • Food additives

What Is Schizophrenia?

Schizophrenia is not the most common type of disorder, affecting approximately 1% of the human population worldwide (Kessler et al., 2007), but it is one of the most dramatic. This condition influences and distorts a range of behaviors, including perception, cognition, movement, and emotion.

Symptoms of Schizophrenia

The *DSM-5* places schizophrenia within a group of disorders called schizophrenia spectrum and other psychotic disorders (APA, 2013). Among the symptoms of schizophrenia are delusions, hallucinations, disorganized speech, and disorders of movement, which together indicate a state of psychosis. Schizophrenia also features negative symptoms (APA, 2013). Negative symptoms are behaviors that are seen in healthy people but not in patients. These symptoms include "diminished emotional expression and avolition" (APA, 2013, p. 88). A person with diminished emotional expression does not show typical outward signs of emotion, such as facial expressions and tone of voice, when an emotional response is expected. Avolition (the *a* means "lack of") refers to a patient's lack of goal-oriented behavior.

Delusions are defined as unrealistic beliefs. These may take a number of forms, including delusions of persecution by others (paranoia) or feelings of unrealistic power or importance (grandiosity).

Hallucinations are false perceptions. Although hallucinations may occur in several sensory modalities, most hallucinations in schizophrenia are auditory (Tien, 1991). Patients often report hearing voices, which can be accusatory or otherwise unpleasant, contributing to the distress associated with the disorder. Auditory hallucinations are not imaginary; they are real sensations correlated with increased activity in the primary auditory cortex of the temporal lobe (Dierks et al., 1999). Simply asking patients to remember or imagine sounds did not produce the type of activity in the auditory cortex seen during an auditory hallucination, indicating that the hallucination experience is different from simple memory or imagination.

A further symptom of schizophrenia involves disorganized patterns of speech. The patient jumps inexplicably from one topic to the next. People with schizophrenia appear to have difficulty inhibiting secondary meanings for some words (Titone, Levy, & Holzman, 2000).

Reuters/Corbis Wire/Corbis

Despite having been diagnosed with schizophrenia, John Nash shared the 1994 Nobel Prize in Economic Sciences. Nash was the subject of the film *The Beautiful Mind*, starring Russell Crowe.

schizophrenia A disorder characterized by hallucinations, delusions, disorganized thought and speech, disorders of movement, restricted affect, and avolition or asociality.
delusion A false, illogical belief.
hallucination A false perception.

For example, the word *jam* can refer to either a fruit spread for toast or an impromptu musical session. Most people would use context (a conversation about food or music) to decide which meaning was appropriate. Patients with schizophrenia might not experience this filtering, leading their thoughts to jump from food to jazz and on to other atypical connections.

This loosening of associations among ideas might occur because of the reduced latent inhibition in patients with schizophrenia, which we discussed in Chapter 8. According to this argument, latent inhibition typically results in fewer associations being made to familiar stimuli. If you have had a lot of experience connecting jam and food, you are unlikely to consider other uses of the word *jam*. The person with schizophrenia, however, would be less inhibited in making connections among ideas, leading to trains of thought that seem bizarre to the rest of us.

Schizophrenia also features "grossly disorganized or abnormal motor behavior" (APA, 2013, p. 88). Some people may be unusually active, while others may barely move throughout an entire day. Unusual behaviors can occur, including grimaces and gestures. The maintenance of awkward or unusual body positions for hours at a time is called catatonia. People experiencing catatonia appear aware of their surroundings, but they don't move. Most of us would find it difficult to sit for a few minutes, let alone hours, without shifting position.

Some people with schizophrenia experience catatonia, which means that they maintain awkward or unusual body positions for hours at a time.

Causes of Schizophrenia

Like many other types of psychological disorders, it is likely that schizophrenia has multiple sources of causality. No one factor is likely to be sufficient to produce the disorder.

Biological Factors in Schizophrenia Significant evidence points to a genetic vulnerability for schizophrenia. People with close family members who have been diagnosed with schizophrenia are more likely to develop the disorder themselves (Gottesman, 1991). If one identical twin is diagnosed with the disorder, the other twin has nearly a 50% lifetime risk of developing the disorder (see ● Figure 14.8). Comparisons of adopted children with their biological and adoptive parents also support a role for genetics (Kety, Rosenthal, Wender, &

Experiencing Psychology

The Remote Associates Test

THE THINKING OF people with schizophrenia shares a feature with the thinking of unusually creative people—more data than usual are viewed as being relevant to a particular problem. The Remote Associates Test (RAT) provides a measure of this type of thinking that correlates with other measures of creativity. Although people diagnosed with schizophrenia tend to do more poorly on the RAT than do people without

disorders, people described as "psychosis-prone" who possess strong coping skills score quite high on this test (Fodor, 1995).

The RAT presents you with sets of three words, and your task is to find a single word that makes sense when paired with the other three words. For example, "star" is the solution for the group of "falling," "actor," and "dust." The list in Table 14.1 is a

small sample of the RAT, which typically contains more than 60 items.

How did you do? If you did well, it is likely that you excel in other creative activities. Do you have to worry now about being diagnosed with schizophrenia? Absolutely not. Schizophrenia and creativity are not the same thing, but analyzing these overlapping characteristics might help us understand schizophrenia better. ●

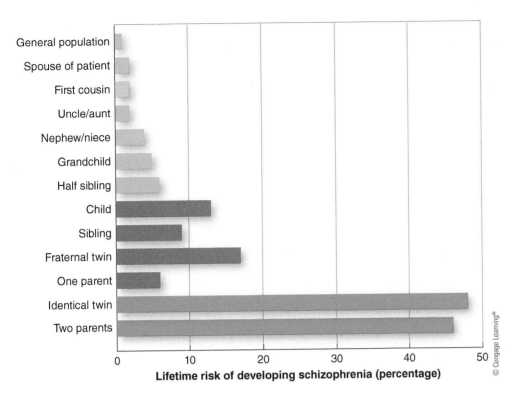

© Cengage Learning®

FIGURE 14.8

Genetics and Schizophrenia. A person's lifetime risk of developing schizophrenia increases when closely related family members have been diagnosed with the disorder, suggesting that genes play a significant role. Having a spouse with schizophrenia doubles the risk (from 1% to 2%), which probably reflects the tendency for people to marry others with whom they share similarities.

Schulsinger, 1968). A large number of genes have been implicated in the development of schizophrenia and overlap with those involved with bipolar disorder (Cross-Disorder Group of the Psychiatric Genomics Consortium, 2013; Owen, Craddock, & Jablensky, 2007). In one case of identical triplets, two of the triplets were diagnosed with schizophrenia and the third was diagnosed with bipolar disorder (McGuffin, Reveley, & Holland, 1982).

A number of structural and biochemical features accompany schizophrenia. One reliable correlate of schizophrenia is the presence of enlarged ventricles (Yotsutsuji et al., 2003). As we discussed in Chapter 4, the ventricles are fluid-filled spaces in the brain that are not responsible for any particular behavior. The ventricles enlarge in response to any condition resulting

TABLE 14.1 Sample Items from the Remote Associates Test

Problem terms	Solution (Write this in now, and then view the answers below.)	Percentage of people who solve the problem
1. Broken Clear Eye		80
2. Cracker Union Rabbit		65
3. Room Blood Salts		60
4. Chocolate Fortune Tin		45
5. Hall Car Swimming		40
6. Note Dive Chair		30
7. Shopping Washer Picture		25
8. Sore Shoulder Sweat		10

© Cengage Learning®

Answers: 1. Glass, 2. Jack, 3. Bath, 4. Cookie, 5. Pool, 6. High, 7. Window, 8. Cold.

Courtesy D. R. Weinberger, NIMH, St. Elizabeth's Hospital

Magnetic resonance images of the brains of a pair of identical twins show the differences in the size of the lateral ventricles (arrows) found in healthy people (left) and in people with schizophrenia (right). The ventricles are fluid-filled spaces and enlarge whenever significant numbers of nearby neurons have died.

in a loss of neural tissue in adjacent areas, so we can assume that schizophrenia is associated with neural degeneration.

Patients with schizophrenia demonstrate differences in brain activity compared with healthy people. For example, patients with schizophrenia often show a lower level of frontal lobe activity than that of healthy controls, both at rest and during effortful cognitive tasks (Berman, Torrey, Daniel, & Weinberger, 1992). The importance of the frontal lobes to higher cognitive processes and attention suggests that this difference would have significant influences on behavior, and lower levels of activity might account for the emotional disturbances and social withdrawal seen in these patients (Andreasen et al., 1992). Pathways in the brain that manage olfaction, or the sense of smell, travel through the frontal lobe. Lower overall frontal lobe activity might account for some difficulties patients with schizophrenia experience with their sense of smell. In addition, distortions in the brain's default mode network (see Chapter 6) predict the severity of patients' psychotic symptoms (Garrity et al., 2007; Pomarol-Clotet et al., 2008).

Schizophrenia might involve abnormal brain development during adolescence. Teens typically experience a burst of cortical gray matter growth at puberty followed by a wave of thinning of the gray matter extending into their early 20s. Healthy teens experience little loss of gray matter, whereas teens diagnosed with schizophrenia experience a loss that has been likened to a forest fire (Thompson et al., 2001).

Abnormalities in dopamine activity might be the major biochemical culprit in schizophrenia. Drugs that boost dopamine activity, such as amphetamine and the Parkinson's disease treatment L-dopa, can produce hallucinations and paranoid delusions (Goetz, Leurgans, Pappert, Raman, & Stemer, 2001). Medications that block dopamine activity are usually quite effective in reducing these same symptoms.

Compiled

151.50

105.00

57.50

10.00

Healthy twin   Twin with schizophrenia

When the brain activity of these identical twins is observed through brain imaging, the frontal lobes (arrows) appear to be more active in the healthy twin (left) than in the twin with schizophrenia (right). Red and yellow areas indicate greater activity, while green and dark areas are relatively inactive.

Daniel R. Weinberger, M.D. E. Fuller Torrey, M.D. (formerly of NIMH) Karen Berman, M.D. NIMH Clinical Brain Disorders Branch Division of Intramural Research Programs, NIMH 1990

However, this dopamine hypothesis of schizophrenia is not perfect. About one fourth of patients with schizophrenia do not respond favorably to drugs that reduce dopamine activity. In particular, the negative symptoms, such as diminished emotional expression, are not improved by these drugs (Goff & Evins, 1998; Kane & Freeman, 1994). In addition, medications that influence neurotransmitters other than dopamine may also be effective (Syvalahti, 1994). Finally, phencyclidine (PCP, or angel dust) produces a syndrome that is quite similar to schizophrenia, although PCP acts on synapses using glutamate, not dopamine, as their neurotransmitter (Mössner et al., 2008). Although it seems certain that dopamine does play a role in schizophrenia, the nature and scope of that role remain unclear.

Environmental Factors in Schizophrenia The nearly 50% concordance rate for schizophrenia in identical twins indicates a role for genetics in the development of the disorder. However, 50% is not 100%, and we need to account for the remaining factors.

Extreme stress seems to play a role in the appearance and severity of schizophrenia among genetically vulnerable people. Schizophrenia appears nearly 5 times more frequently in members of lower than in those of higher socioeconomic groups (Keith, Regier, & Rae, 1991). The stress of living in poverty may trigger schizophrenia in vulnerable individuals. However, others argue that people who are susceptible to schizophrenia "drift" to lower paying jobs. In other words, the disorder reduces the patients' socioeconomic status, accounting for the higher rates of the disorder among the poor. Other stresses might accompany a person's minority status in a community (Boydell et al., 2001). African immigrants living in London neighborhoods with the lowest proportions of African immigrants were twice as likely to be

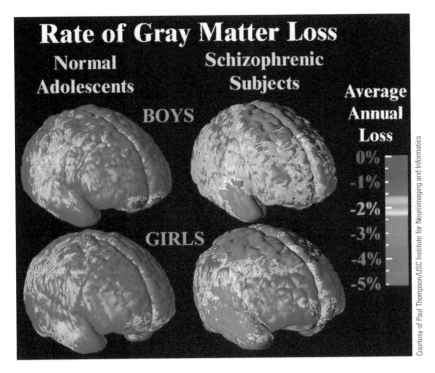

Rate of Gray Matter Loss

Normal Adolescents   **Schizophrenic Subjects**

BOYS

GIRLS

Average Annual Loss

0%
-1%
-2%
-3%
-4%
-5%

Courtesy of Paul Thompson/USC Institute for Neuroimaging and Informatics

Teens typically experience a burst of gray matter growth at puberty followed by a wave of gray matter thinning that extends into the early 20s. Compared with their healthy peers, teens diagnosed with schizophrenia experience much greater gray matter loss. Purple and red areas indicate the greatest amount of loss, followed by yellow and green areas. *Source:* From Thompson, P. M. et. al. (2001). Mapping adolescent brain changes reveals dynamic wave of accelerated gray matter loss in very early-onset schizophrenia. *Proc Natl Acad Sci, 98*(20), 11650-11655.

diagnosed with schizophrenia as African immigrants living in neighborhoods with the highest proportion of minorities (see ● Figure 14.9). The stress of social isolation because of minority status may have contributed to higher rates of schizophrenia.

When we talk about environmental influences, factors such as stress come to mind (see Chapter 16). However, environmental influences also include biological variables such as the prenatal environment, including the pregnant woman's exposure to viral illness. Another environmental variable that might trigger schizophrenia in genetically vulnerable individuals is marijuana use (Ho, Wassink, Ziebell, & Andreasen, 2011; Van Haren, Cahn, Hulshoff Pol, & Kahn, 2012). A 25-year longitudinal study concluded that cannabis use nearly doubled the

© Cengage Learning®

Janine Wiedel Photolibrary/Alamy

FIGURE 14.9

Stress and Schizophrenia. African immigrants living in South London were more likely to be diagnosed with schizophrenia if they lived in a predominantly White neighborhood (lowest and middle thirds of non-White ethnic minority populations) than if they lived in a primarily non-White neighborhood. An explanation based on self-selection (people choosing to live in each type of neighborhood) is unlikely in this case, because nearly all study participants were assigned to public housing units rather than having a choice of where to live. These findings suggest that the stress of minority status might contribute to higher risk for schizophrenia. *Source:* Adapted from "Incidence of Schizophrenia in Ethnic Minorities in London: Ecological Study into Interactions With Environment," by J. Boydell, J. van Os, K. McKenzie, J. Allardyce, R. Goel, R. G. McCreadie, et al., 2001, *British Medical Journal, 323*(7325), pp. 1336–1338.

risk of schizophrenia (Fergusson, Horwood, & Ridder, 2005). As we mentioned in Chapter 11, adolescence is a time of brain growth, and heavy marijuana use during this period produces a reduction in white matter volume in the frontal lobes that might interact with a person's genetic vulnerabilities for schizophrenia (Ho et al., 2011).

What Is Bipolar Disorder?

Bipolar disorder serves as a bridge between psychotic disorders, such as schizophrenia, and depressive disorders in respects of their symptoms, family histories, and genetics (APA, 2013, p. 123). Bipolar disorder features a period of **mania**, which may or may not be followed by a period of depression. The symptoms of depression that can accompany bipolar disorder are identical to those used to diagnose major depressive disorder, which is described in the next section of this chapter.

A manic phase consists of "a distinct period of abnormally and persistently elevated, expansive, or irritable mood, abnormally and persistently increased goal-directed activity or energy" (APA, 2013, p. 124). Patients may demonstrate grandiosity, in which they feel unrealistically special or important. The person's behavior, characterized by little need for sleep, rapid speech, difficulty concentrating, and rapidly shifting ideas, seems to be running at an abnormally high speed. Unlike many other disorders, however, mania increases productive, goal-directed behavior. However, because of the person's tendency to meet the *DSM-5* criterion for "excessive involvement in activities that have a high potential for painful consequences," hospitalization is often necessary for the patient's protection (APA, 2013, p. 124). Many variations occur in the timing and severity of the mania and depression observed in bipolar disorder.

Bipolar disorder affects approximately 2.6% of American adults each year (Kessler et al., 2005). Women are more likely to be diagnosed with bipolar disorder than men by a ratio of approximately 3:2 (CDC, 2011a). The average age of onset for bipolar disorder is 25 years. Children and youth under the age of 18 years with symptoms of bipolar disorder are diagnosed with disruptive mood dysregulation disorder (APA, 2013).

Genetic predispositions play a significant role in bipolar disorder. Concordance rates between identical twins for bipolar disorder are commonly reported to be as high as 70% (Craddock & Sklar, 2013). Adoption studies also support a powerful role for genetics (Taylor, Faraone, & Tsuang, 2002). As mentioned previously, there is considerable overlap between the genes believed to play a role in bipolar disorder and those implicated in schizophrenia. Not surprisingly because of their genetic overlap, bipolar disorder shares some of the same abnormalities in brain structure and function as we observed in schizophrenia (De Peri et al., 2012; Pol et al., 2012).

Among the many possible environmental factors that could interact with genes associated with bipolar disorder is diet. Omega-3 fatty acids, generally found in fish, may provide some protection from bipolar disorder (Noaghiul & Hibbeln, 2003). As shown in ● Figure 14.10, prevalence rates for bipolar disorder are highest in countries where fish is rarely consumed (such as Germany) and lowest in countries where fish is an important diet staple (such as Iceland). However, attempts to improve symptoms in patients with bipolar disorder by administering omega-3 supplements have produced weak results (Murphy et al., 2012; Stahl, Begg, Weisinger, & Sinclair, 2008). The impact of omega-3 fatty acids on a person's vulnerability for bipolar disorder might be more important during prenatal development than later in life.

Many unanswered questions regarding the development of this condition remain. Bipolar disorder may be overrepresented in groups of people with artistic and creative talent (Jamison, 1993, 1995). Based on biographical accounts, the poet William Blake, the composers George Frideric Handel and Gustav Mahler, and visual artists Vincent van Gogh and Michelangelo might have had bipolar disorder. Many noted actors and actresses, including Carrie Fisher *(Star Wars)* and Vivien Leigh *(Gone with the Wind),* have been diagnosed with bipolar disorder. Comparisons between people with bipolar disorder and major depressive disorder and healthy people in creative and noncreative professions support this hypothesis. The patients with bipolar disorder scored similarly on tests of creativity to healthy people in creative oc-

Actors (such as Russell Brand), actresses, poets, painters, and musicians seem to have a disproportionate risk for bipolar disorder compared to people in other occupations. We do not know whether having bipolar disorder allows these creative people to express emotion more effectively in their art or whether the arts are simply more welcoming than the corporate boardroom to those who have psychological disorders.

bipolar disorder A mood disorder characterized by alternating periods of mania and depression.
mania A period of unrealistically elevated mood.

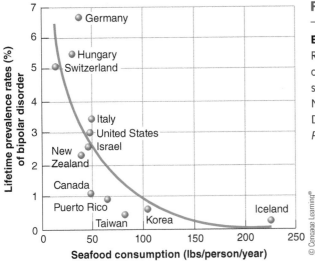

FIGURE 14.10

Bipolar Rates Are Lower in Nations With High Seafood Consumption.
Rates of bipolar disorder are negatively correlated with a nation's consumption of seafood, suggesting that the omega-3 fatty acids contained in seafood might help prevent bipolar disorder. *Source:* Adapted from "Cross-National Comparisons of Seafood Consumption and Rates of Bipolar Disorders," by S. Noaghiul and J. R. Hibbeln, 2003, *American Journal of Psychiatry, 160*(12), pp. 2222–2227. doi:10.1176/appi.ajp.160.12.2222.

cupations and higher than people with major depression and healthy people in noncreative occupations (Santosa et al., 2007). While it is possible that the dramatic mood swings that characterize bipolar disorder might enhance creative activities, it is also possible that the arts provide a more comfortable environment for those who are emotionally volatile. It is hard to imagine a person with bipolar disorder working comfortably within a rigid corporate organization, while artistic organizations frequently embrace people who are different.

What Is Major Depressive Disorder?

Although most of us experience the occasional "blues," these feelings are usually not as severe or chronic as the depressed feelings that characterize major depressive disorder. According to the *DSM-5*, **major depressive disorder** is characterized by depressed mood most of the day, nearly every day, for a period of at least 2 weeks (APA, 2013). Patients with depression complain about feeling sad and empty, and periods of tearfulness are common. The *DSM-5* also notes that depression can produce anhedonia, or loss of pleasure. You are probably already familiar with the term *hedonist*, which refers to a person who is a pleasure seeker. *Anhedonia* refers to a person's disinterest in activities that previously provided pleasure, such as sex, eating, or social activities.

To be diagnosed with major depressive disorder, a person must show at least five symptoms, one of which must be either depressed mood or anhedonia. The remaining symptoms can be divided into physical and cognitive groups. The physical symptoms of major depressive disorder are related to disturbances in autonomic function typically found in the presence of high levels of stress, described in Chapter 16. Appetite and sleep may be disturbed. Some patients experience a loss of appetite, whereas others begin to eat too much. As we observed in Chapter 6, many patients with depression experience frequent wakefulness, whereas others experience oversleeping (more than 9 hours per night). Fatigue or restlessness may occur. Among the cognitive symptoms of depression are difficulty concentrating, feelings of hopelessness and worthlessness, and in some cases, thoughts of suicide (APA, 2013).

Prevalence of Major Depressive Disorder

Major depressive disorder is one of the most frequently diagnosed psychological disorders, affecting approximately 7% of the adult population each year (APA, 2013). Depression decreases with age, and people between the ages of 18 and 29 years have rates that are 3 times as high as those for people over the age of 60 years.

major depressive disorder A disorder characterized by lengthy periods of depressed mood, loss of pleasure in normal activities, disturbances in sleep and appetite, difficulty concentrating, feelings of hopelessness, and possible thoughts of suicide.

Women experience depression more frequently than men do. This discrepancy between rates of depression in men and those in women has been observed to be independent of race, ethnicity, social class, and country of residence (Strickland, 1992; Üstün, Ayuso-Mateos, Chatterji, Mathers, & Murray, 2004; see ● Figure 14.11). It is possible that female hormones participate in mood through some unknown mechanism. Mood disturbances can be associated with hormonal changes in women, including postpartum depression and mood changes accompanying menopause (Rapkin, Mikacich, Moatakef-Imani, & Rasgon, 2002). However, it is also possible that women are more likely than men to admit feeling depressed to others and to seek help with depression. Men may mask or cover their depressed mood by engaging in activities such as drinking alcohol.

The equal rates of depression between Amish men and Amish women in Pennsylvania provide interesting insights into the role of gender in this disorder (Egeland & Hostetter, 1983). Amish men do not drink alcohol, so it is unlikely that masked depression affects their depression rates. Amish women, like men, are expected to work outside the home, making the "sick" role difficult to maintain and possibly keeping their rates of reported depression low. These results support the idea that gender differences in depression may be less biological and are more likely to be due to situational factors such as alcohol use and employment outside the home.

Causes of Major Depressive Disorder

Theories attempting to explain depression range from the learning, social, and cognitive to the strictly biological. It is likely that some combination of these approaches provides the greatest understanding of the sources of depression.

Learning Explanations for Depression According to learning theories, depression occurs when a person experiences a reduction in positive reinforcement or an increase in negative outcomes. The loss of an important relationship can lead to depression, because the loss reduces the amount of positive reinforcement a person experiences.

FIGURE 14.11

Worldwide Gender Differences in Depression. Across many cultures, women are diagnosed with depression more frequently than men. *Source:* Adapted from "Global Burden of Depressive Disorders in the Year 2000," by T. B. Üstün, J. L. Ayuso-Mateos, S. Chatterji, C. Mathers, and C. J. L. Murray, 2004, *British Journal of Psychiatry, 184*(5), pp. 386–392. doi:10.1192/bjp.184.5.386.

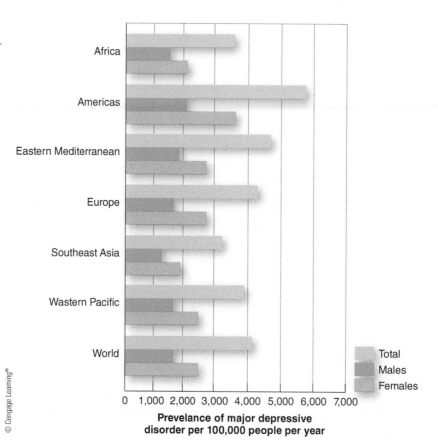

© Cengage Learning®

A variation of the learning approach suggests that depression results from **learned helplessness**, which is an application of operant conditioning. Instead of experiencing consequences that are clearly linked to your previous behavior (I studied hard and earned an A on my test), learned helplessness occurs when consequences of behavior appear to be random or uncontrolled (the amount of studying I do doesn't seem to make a difference in my test grades). If you get low grades whether you study hard or not, you might begin to believe that grades are outcomes that cannot be controlled. You may begin to feel helpless in preparing for your exams, and this belief in your own helplessness can lead to depression.

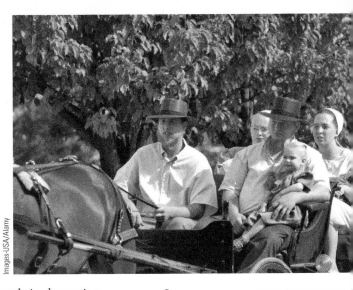

Cognitive Explanations for Depression Cognitive theories frame depression as the result of a combination of negative thoughts about the self, the world, and the future (Beck, 1975). For example, students failing an exam might respond by doubting their academic abilities (self), assuming that they will fail the course (future), and deciding they hate the class (world). The resulting dysfunctional beliefs would result in depression. Beck's view of the development of depression led directly to the use of cognitive therapies for depression, which we discuss in Chapter 15.

Another cognitive process that contributes to the development and maintenance of depressed mood is rumination (Nolen-Hoeksema, 2003). Susan Nolen-Hoeksema describes rumination in depression as "repetitively focusing on the fact that one is depressed; on one's symptoms of depression; and on the causes, meanings, and consequences of symptoms of depression" (Nolen-Hoeksema, 1991, p. 569). Rumination can arise from attempts to gain insight into one's problems, but too much rumination interferes with problem solving (Watkins and Brown, 2002). When rumination is encouraged by asking study participants to focus on their moods, they find it difficult to solve several types of problems (see ● Figure 14.13). When the participants are distracted from this inward focus by thinking about neutral topics (such as "think about the Statue of Liberty"), their problem-solving abilities improve immediately. Typically, rumination is correlated with negative outcomes, including delaying recovery from depression during treatment (Siegle, Sagratti, & Crawford, 1999), predicting depression following the death of a loved one (Nolen-Hoeksema & Girgus, 1994), and increasing a person's likelihood to abuse alcohol (Nolen-Hoeksema, 2003).

Depression might be influenced by the types of attributions a person makes (Abramson, Seligman, & Teasdale, 1978). As we mentioned in Chapter 13, an attribution is a belief about causality. Attributions can vary along several dimensions (internal–external, stable–unstable, or global–specific), and making some types of attributions might predispose a person to depression. The internal–external dimension, which is similar to the locus of control discussed in Chapter 12, represents beliefs that outcomes are because of personal effort or because of luck or chance. The stable–unstable dimension captures beliefs about whether circumstances can change. People make global attributions (I'm stupid) or more specific attributions (I'm not great in algebra, but I'm good at geometry). Overall, people who make internal, stable, and global attributions (what happens to me is my fault, circumstances never change, and I'm always this way) are more prone to depression. People with this attributional style earn lower grades in college, perform more poorly as sales representatives, and experience worse health (Seligman, 1987).

Social Explanations for Depression Depression reflects feeling generally sad, whereas loneliness is a more social process that reflects feeling badly about the state of one's relationships with others. The two states are related, yet they can occur independently. In older adults, loneliness increased depressive symptoms, but depression did not increase loneliness (Cacioppo, Hawkley, & Thisted, 2010). Social and evolutionary theories of depression and loneliness suggest that these states might promote an individual's survival by promoting better relationships with others (Allen & Badcock, 2003; Cacioppo, Cacioppo, & Boomsma, 2014;

In the general population of the United States, women make up about two thirds of all cases of major depressive disorder. In contrast, rates of depression among the Amish are equal for men and women. Psychologists have suggested that because Amish men do not drink alcohol, their depression would not be masked. The workloads of Amish women might keep their rates of reported depression lower than in the general population.

Rates of both depression and rumination drop in middle adulthood. Young adults often find it frustrating when they are trying to ruminate about problems with their parents, only to have their parents immediately shift into problem-solving mode. The young adult might not feel "ready" to fix the problem yet.

learned helplessness A state in which experiencing random or uncontrolled consequences leads to feelings of helplessness and possibly depression.

WHAT IS MAJOR DEPRESSIVE DISORDER? **555**

FIGURE 14.13

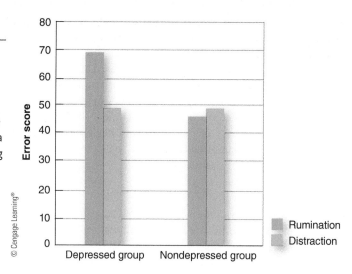

Rumination and Problem Solving. Rumination and distraction were induced in depressed and nondepressed study participants, who then completed a problem-solving task. To induce rumination, participants were instructed to think about "what your feelings mean." To induce distraction, participants were asked to think about "the shape of a large black umbrella." Subsequently, all participants were asked to complete a problem-solving task. More errors occurred in the depressed ruminating group than in the other groups. These results suggest that rumination competes with other cognitive processes, possibly contributing to the problems with concentration experienced by people with depression. *Source:* Adapted from "Rumination and Executive Function in Depression: An Experimental Study," by E. Watkins and R. G. Brown, 2002, *Journal of Neurology, Neurosurgery, and Psychiatry, 72,* pp. 400–402.

Connecting to **Research**

Recognition of Facial Expression by People With Depression

HOW DOES THE WORLD LOOK to a person who is depressed? Does the experience of depression affect a person's attention to negative stimuli? As we mentioned in Chapter 7, positive and negative emotions often serve as guides to approach and avoidance behaviors (Davidson & Irwin, 1999). Because it is usually more important to survival that we avoid predators and other dangers than that we miss approaching something positive, such as a tasty food, we have a bias toward noticing the negative. If we're experiencing ongoing negative mood, does that have an effect on our sensitivities to positive and negative stimuli?

Among the important types of positive and negative stimuli we need to process are facial expressions, because these are our clues to successfully navigating the social environment. Few of us would miss dramatic facial expressions, but the subtle ones require more attention (Gollan, McCloskey, Hoxha, & Coccaro, 2010).

The Question: How do people with depression compare to control partici-

pants in their ability to detect subtle facial expressions of emotion?

METHODS

Eighty-eight study participants, half of whom had been diagnosed with major depressive disorder but were not treated with medication, observed photographs of facial expressions on a computer screen. The photographs depicted four basic emotions: happiness, surprise, sadness, and harsh (a category that combined photos showing disgust, fear, and anger). The photos were morphed to present a range of intensity from mostly neutral to very intense (see ● Figure 14.12). Two hundred photos were presented for only 0.5 second each. The participants pushed one of six keys to identify the emotion being expressed.

RESULTS

The participants with depression were more sensitive to sad faces than the control participants were, especially when the emotion was expressed at a lower intensity. The

groups were equally accurate in identifying the positive emotions (happiness and surprise) and the harsh emotions (fear, anger, and disgust). The severity of the participants' depression was positively correlated with their accuracy in recognizing sad faces but not with their accuracy in recognizing other emotional expressions.

CONCLUSIONS

The participants with depression were not only more sensitive to subtle expressions of sadness than the healthy control participants but also more likely to misidentify other emotional facial expressions as sad. In contrast, they were equally likely as control participants to misidentify happy, surprised, or harsh facial expressions. These findings indicate that people with depression not only are more likely to be attending to more sad stimuli but also might misinterpret neutral stimuli as sad. These tendencies might add to the challenges faced by the person with depression in the social environment. ●

Cacioppo, Hughes, Waite, Hawkley, & Thisted, 2006). Expressions of depression, such as sad facial expressions and crying, can serve as a safe call to others for connection and comforting responses in what the person may feel is a threatening social context. The response of others to these signals may foster the repair of frayed or broken social connections. Even when others do not respond, the symptoms of depression may protect people from additional negative interactions by reducing their social activities.

Biological Explanations for Depression The biological perspective identifies a number of factors contributing to depression. Twin studies suggest that the heritability of major depressive disorder is about 40% (Shi et al., 2011). A number of genes have been implicated in depression, including genes affecting serotonin function (Wurtman, 2005). A large body of research points to a role for serotonin in the regulation of mood. Serotonin's role in brain systems responsible for mood, appetite, and sleep corresponds closely to the symptoms of depression outlined in the *DSM-5*. Most effective medications for the treatment of depression boost the activity of serotonin at the synapse.

Depressed mood is correlated with patterns of activity in the cerebral hemispheres of the brain (see ● Figure 14.14). Depression is correlated with both reduced left frontal lobe activity and increased right frontal lobe activity (Hecht, 2010; Schaffer, Davidson, & Saron, 1983). Because these data are correlational, we cannot make a judgment regarding cause and effect. People who have a tendency to show a particular pattern of brain activity, possibly because of genetic factors, may be more vulnerable to depression. However, it is equally logical to propose that the experience of depression may produce different patterns of brain activity.

0% (neutral)   20%   40%   60%   80%   100% (sadness)

Emil F. Coccaro, M.D. at the University of Chicago

FIGURE 14.12

Heightened Sensitivity to Sad Expressions in Depression. Study participants see one photo for only 0.5 second and must determine which of six emotions (happiness, surprise, sadness, disgust, fear, or anger) is being displayed. Morphed images are made by combining neutral (0%) and high intensity (100%) images. Each emotion is easier to identify as its intensity increases. Participants with depression needed to see the same amount of intensity as healthy control participants before correctly identifying happy, surprised, or "harsh" facial expressions but needed to see less intensity than control participants before correctly identifying sad faces. This heightened sensitivity to the sad moods of others might reinforce the negative feelings of the person with depression. *Source:* Reprinted from *Biological Psychiatry* Volume 62, Issue 2, Pages 168–178, July 15, 2007. Emil F. Coccaroemail, Michael S. McCloskey, Daniel A. Fitzgerald, K. Luan Phan, Amygdala and Orbitofrontal Reactivity to Social Threat in Individuals with Impulsive Aggression, with permission from Elsevier.

Depressed

Control

© Cengage Learning®

FIGURE 14.14

Right Hemisphere Activity and Depression. Imaging studies typically show unusually high levels of activity in the right prefrontal cortex of people with depression, particularly in the area shown in yellow (the dorsolateral prefrontal cortex). In this experiment, the amount of activity observed in this area during an emotional picture judging task was positively correlated with scores on the Beck Depression Inventory, a standard questionnaire used to assess severity of depressive symptoms. In other words, the more severe the person's symptoms of depression, the more extreme was right hemisphere activity displayed. *Source:* From Grimm, S., et al. (2008). Imbalance between Left and Right Dorsolateral Prefrontal Cortex in Major Depression Is Linked to Negative Emotional Judgment: An fMRI Study in Severe Major Depressive Disorder. *Biological Psychiatry,* *63*(4), 369-376. Copyright © 2008 Elsevier

Depression might be part of a larger disturbance in daily, or circadian, rhythms (Soria et al., 2010). Among the genes suspected of being related to depression are those involved with circadian rhythms (see Chapter 6; McClung, 2007). The *DSM-5* criteria for depression include sleeping either less than or more than a normal number of hours per night (7-9 hours; APA, 2013). People who are depressed spend too much time in rapid eye movement (REM) sleep, and most medications that are used to treat depression reduce REM sleep (Rijnbeek, de Visser, Franson, Cohen, & van Gerven, 2003; see ● Figure 14.15).

Thinking Scientifically

What Should We Do When We Think Somebody Might Commit Suicide?

PEOPLE WHO ARE depressed sometimes think about suicide or even make suicide attempts (see ● Figure 14.16). Because of the greater prevalence of major depressive disorder in younger people, younger people are also at greater risk of suicide. Approximately 1,100 college students in the United States die in suicides each year, making suicide the second leading cause of death in this population (Wilcox et al., 2010).

These statistics raise the possibility that as a college student, you may become aware of another person's risk for suicide. According to the American Foundation of Suicide Prevention (AFSP), we can make ourselves aware of risk factors and take action that might save a life (AFSP, 2014). Among these

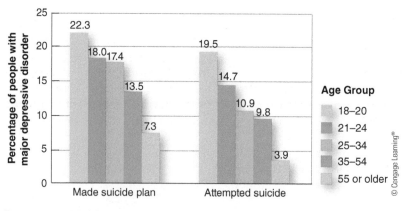

FIGURE 14.16

Depression Carries a High Risk of Suicidal Thinking and Suicide Attempts. Among individuals experiencing at least one depressive episode in the past year, thinking seriously about suicide and making a suicide attempt happened frequently.

Typical person

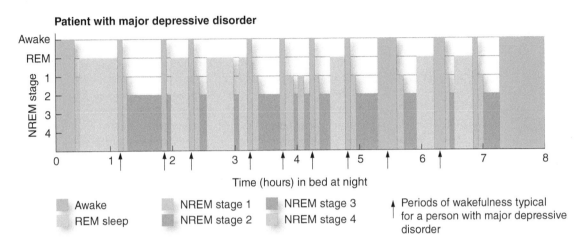

Patient with major depressive disorder

Time (hours) in bed at night

▨ Awake	▨ NREM stage 1	▨ NREM stage 3
▨ REM sleep	▨ NREM stage 2	▨ NREM stage 4

↑ Periods of wakefulness typical for a person with major depressive disorder

FIGURE 14.15

Major Depressive Disorder Disrupts Sleep. These sleep records show the normal progression of non-REM and REM sleep (upper row) and the disrupted sleep of a person with major depressive disorder (bottom row). Note the lack of Stage 3 and 4 non-REM sleep and the frequent waking experienced by the person with depression (see Chapter 6). *Source:* Adapted from Gillin and Borbely (1985).

risk factors are evidence of a psychological disorder (particularly depression), alcohol and other substance use, a history of suicide attempts, being male (males have a 3 to 5 times higher suicide completion rate than females), and impulsivity. More immediately, the occurrence of a traumatic event (job loss or ending of an important relationship) might increase a person's risk.

Approximately 75% of individuals who attempt suicide show prior evidence of their intent (AFSP, 2014). People might say things like "my family would be better off without me" or speak in ways that indicate they are saying good-bye. Purchasing a gun or putting one's affairs in order (giving away prized possessions like a computer) is a sign of risk. Hopelessness, rage, or increased use of drugs and alcohol is also a common response to feeling suicidal (AFSP, 2014).

If you suspect someone of being suicidal, experts advise you to take the situa-tion seriously. Yes, it may be true that some people "cry wolf," but with a life at stake, who wants to take that chance? Be a good listener, and reassure the person that depression can be treated, that he or she is not alone, and that you care. If possible, take your friend to a place where professional help is available, whether that is your campus health center or a local emergency room. Do not leave the person alone, and remove possible means of self-harm (drugs, weapons, etc.). If such steps are not possible, call the National Suicide Prevention Lifeline at 1-800-273-TALK or 911. ●

Understanding that the combination of depression, impulsivity, alcohol or substance use, a history of suicide attempts, and a recent breakup or other traumatic event may increase the risk of suicide can help us offer support to a person who exhibits these characteristics.

Stress and Depression The experience of severe stress, whether arising from the death of a loved one, illness, or frustration of major life goals, frequently occurs immediately before the onset of a depressive episode (Brown & Harris, 1989; Mazure, 1998). The physical and cognitive responses to high levels of stress, such as difficulty sleeping or concentrating, are quite similar to the symptoms of depression. However, most people exposed to such stressors do not respond by becoming depressed, reinforcing the complexity of the development of this disorder. Depression provides an example of a **diathesis–stress model**, which suggests that biological vulnerabilities for a disorder interact with a person's experience with stress (Zubin & Spring, 1977).

Integrating the Perspectives The picture emerging from this discussion of causal factors in depression is complex. It is likely that underlying biological predispositions interact with cognitive patterns and life events to produce the disorder. For example, the serotonin transporter gene, which we have discussed previously in the contexts of personality and responses to bullying, does little by itself to help us predict a person's risk for depression. However, among people experiencing significant stress, those with one or two copies of the short version of the gene were more likely than those with two copies of the long version to develop depression (Caspi et al., 2003).

A biological bridge is formed across the experience of stress, circadian rhythms, and the development of depression by the release of hormones (e.g., cortisol) when the stressor is perceived. Cortisol levels follow circadian patterns, with the greatest cortisol release in the early morning followed by a gradual drop throughout the day and evening. However, cortisol is also released at times of stress and helps prepare the body for fight or flight. Feedback loops involving the hippocampus usually prevent too great a release of cortisol. It is possible that in cases of depression, this feedback loop is not working correctly, and cortisol levels remain high (Stokes, 1995). The body simply cannot maintain high levels of arousal indefinitely, and depression may result.

diathesis–stress model A model that suggests that the experience of stress interacts with an individual's biological predisposition to produce a psychological disorder.

Summary 14.2 Schizophrenia, Bipolar Disorder, and Major Depressive Disorder

Disorder	Symptoms	Possible causal factors under investigation
Schizophrenia	• Delusions • Hallucinations • Disorganized thought and speech • Movement disorders • Restricted affect • Avolition or asociality	• Genetics • Reduced frontal lobe activity • Disruption of brain development • Dopamine and glutamate abnormalities • Stress • Prenatal environment • Marijuana use
Bipolar disorder	• Elevated mood • Grandiosity • Little need for sleep • Rapid speech • Difficulty concentrating • Possible depression	• Genetics • Serotonin disturbances • Diet
Major depressive disorder	• Chronic depressed mood • Lack of pleasure • Sleep disturbances • Appetite disturbances • Difficulty concentrating • Hopelessness • Possible suicidal thoughts	• Loss of positive reinforcement • Learned helplessness • Negative cognitions • Rumination • Attributions • Stress • Genetics • Reduced serotonin activity • Patterns of brain activity • Circadian rhythms

What Is an Anxiety Disorder?

Anxiety disorders take many forms, but all share the core characteristic of unrealistic and counterproductive levels of anxiety. Anxiety has two major components: (1) strong negative emotions and (2) physical tension because of the anticipation of danger (Barlow, 1988). It is the anticipation of danger that separates anxiety from the closely related emotion of fear. When we are afraid, usually something is happening in the present that is producing that feeling, whereas anxiety occurs when we are worried about the future. **Anxiety disorders** represent an exaggeration of what is normally a useful response. Normal levels of anxiety protect us from engaging in risky activities, such as running up debts, driving recklessly, or failing to prepare for work or school, but excessive anxiety can cause a person to withdraw from positive life experiences and interpersonal relationships.

Nearly 30% of all Americans experience one or more anxiety disorders during their lifetime, although not all seek treatment (Kessler et al., 2005). People appear to have genetic vulnerabilities for anxiety disorders in general but not for specific types of anxiety disorders (DiLalla, Kagan, & Reznick, 1994). Families with members who are diagnosed with anxiety disorders are also likely to have members diagnosed with depression, because these types of problems appear to share an underlying genetic basis (Weissman, Warner, Wickramaratne, Moreau, & Olfson, 1997). Anxiety disorders differ across gender and ethnicity for reasons that are not well understood. Women are more likely to be diagnosed with anxiety disorders than are men, and African Americans and Hispanics living in the United States are less likely to be diagnosed with anxiety disorders than are White Americans (Kessler et al., 2005).

Evidence of a predisposition to anxiety appears early in life (Biederman et al., 1990; Schwartz, Snidman, & Kagan, 1999). As we observed in Chapters 11 and 12, children's initial temperament and reactivity can predispose them to anxiety. In one study, young infants showed consistent levels of response to novel stimuli, such as the smell of cotton swabs dipped in alcohol (Kagan, 1997). Twenty percent of the infants in this study were classified as "high reactives" to these stimuli, because of their increased activity and distress when novel stimuli were presented. When the high-reactive children were placed in a novel laboratory environment at the ages of 4 to 5 years, they still showed heightened levels of anxiety compared to their peers.

Unlike most other types of psychological disorders, anxiety disorders do not impair a person's ability to think realistically. In most cases, adults with anxiety disorders recognize that their circumstances do not warrant their extremely anxious responses, but they feel unable to control them. A person looking out the window of a skyscraper is well aware that the likelihood of falling is quite low, but feelings of fear and anxiety persist. Young children with anxiety disorders are usually less aware that their feelings are unrealistic.

Anxiety is the anticipation of danger. Normal levels of anxiety remind us about the risks of engaging in dangerous activities, but disordered anxiety can prevent people from engaging in everyday activities.

Specific Phobias

Specific phobias are fears of objects or situations other than those associated with agoraphobia and social anxiety disorder (see ● Figure 14.17). These fear stimuli may be animals, natural phenomena (water or earthquakes), blood and injury, or situations (flying, heights, bridges, and so on). People do not ordinarily form phobias for harmless objects such as coffee cups and keys (Mineka, Sutton, Craske, Hermans, & Vansteenwegen, 2006).

The evolutionary perspective suggests that phobias might be exaggerations of an otherwise useful sense of caution. The items that become fear stimuli have some realistic potential relationship to harm, such as snakes, spiders, and the sight of blood. As we noted in Chapter 8, the connections formed in phobias can arise from classical conditioning. A stimulus (conditioned stimulus, or CS) becomes associated with a negative experience (unconditioned stimulus, or UCS) that results in fear (unconditioned response, or UCR), giving the CS the ability to elicit fear (conditioned response, or CR). We might be biologically prepared to form connections between certain stimuli and feelings of fear (Seligman, 1971). Learning can also

anxiety disorder A disorder featuring anxiety that is not proportional to a person's circumstances.
specific phobia Fears of objects other than those associated with agoraphobia or social anxiety disorder.

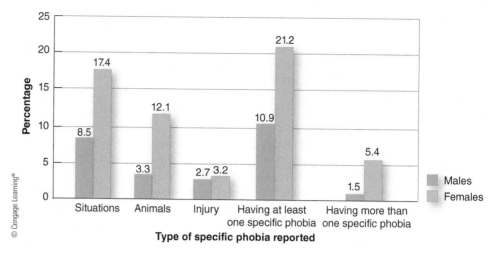

FIGURE 14.17

Prevalence of Different Types of Specific Phobias. In a large random sample of adults, 21.2% of women and 10.9% of men reported having at least one specific phobia, as defined by the *DSM-5*. Gender differences were seen in the prevalence of situational phobias (lightning, enclosed spaces, darkness, flying, and heights) and animal phobias (primarily spiders and snakes). However, no gender differences occurred in injury phobias (injections, dentists, and injuries). More than one type of specific phobia was reported by 5.4% of the women and 1.5% of the men. *Source:* Adapted from "Gender and Age Differences in the Prevalence of Specific Fears and Phobias," by M. Fredrikson, P. Annas, H. Fischer, and G. Wik, 1996, *Behaviour Research and Therapy, 34*(1), pp. 33–39. doi:10.1016/0005-7967(95)00048-3.

People with spider phobias are often convinced that the spider is intent on harming them, when spiders are usually just being spiders.

social anxiety disorder A disorder characterized by an unrealistic fear of being scrutinized and criticized by others.

influence the development of phobias through imitation and observation, such as when a child sees a parent scream when a spider walks across the room.

Cognitions influence specific phobias. Even though a spider in your house or garden is simply minding its own business while doing spider things, people with spider phobias tend to believe that the spider is intending to attack them or move toward them (Riskind, Moore, & Bowley, 1995). People who have height phobias misjudge real physical heights, believing that they are higher up than they really are (Stefanucci & Proffitt, 2009).

Social Anxiety Disorder

Social anxiety disorder is the fear of being scrutinized and criticized by others, particularly during public speaking and when meeting new people. Many of us are a little uneasy in these situations, but for people with social anxiety disorder, the fear and anxiety caused by these situations are out of proportion for the particular situation. In other words, the person with social anxiety disorder feels crippling anxiety while doing things that most people take in stride, like introducing yourself to others at a party. In most cases, social anxiety disorder begins during adolescence. As we discussed in Chapter 11, adolescents often experience a "spotlight effect," or belief that others are scrutinizing them. For an anxious teen, this spotlight effect might be exaggerated, leading to social anxiety disorder.

Cultural variables appear to be particularly significant in the development of social anxiety. Social anxiety is more prevalent in collectivistic cultures, with their emphasis on shame and the opinions of other people, than in individualistic cultures. Asian American college students were more likely than White American students to report negative emotions in social situations (Lee, Okazaki, & Yoo, 2006).

Panic Disorder

The *DSM-5* distinguishes between the experience of a single **panic attack**, characterized by intense fear and autonomic arousal, and the experience of **panic disorder**, which features repeated panic attacks and fear of future attacks (APA, 2013).

Having a panic attack does not mean that you should be diagnosed with panic disorder. It is not unusual for people to experience one or two panic attacks in their lifetime. One quarter to one third of college students report having had at least one panic attack in the previous year (Asmundson & Norton, 1993; Brown & Cash, 1990). However, panic disorder is much less common, affecting 2.7% of the population in any given year (Kessler et al., 2005). Women are more likely to experience panic attacks and panic disorder than are men. More than half of people with panic disorder have also been diagnosed with depression or another type of anxiety disorder (Kearney, Albano, Eisen, Allan, & Barlow, 1997). Panic attacks begin to occur in adolescence and young adulthood (Robins & Regier, 1991).

By all reports, panic attacks are extremely unpleasant. Symptoms typically last about 10 minutes. Feelings of intense fear or discomfort are accompanied by both physical and cognitive symptoms. Strong arousal of the sympathetic nervous system leads to the experience of a pounding heart, sweating, trembling, shortness of breath, chest pain, nausea, and dizziness or faintness. Not too surprisingly, people experiencing such symptoms may believe they are dying or going crazy. For some individuals, panic attacks may be brought on by identifiable stimuli, such as being swept along in a crowd. For others, the attacks seem to come out of nowhere. In either case, many people experiencing repeated attacks may begin to fear leaving their homes, a condition known as agoraphobia, a type of phobia that we will discuss in a later section.

In Japan, some people experience taijin kyofusho, *which is a fear of offending or embarrassing other people with their odor, eye contact, or appearance (Tarumi, Ichimiya, Yamada, Umesue, & Kuroki, 2004). This condition is significantly different from the emphasis on a person's own embarrassment that is typical in social anxiety as experienced in Western cultures.*

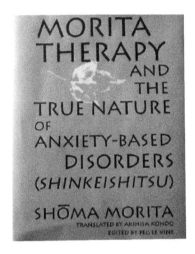

Morita Masatake (1874–1938) founded the Morita Therapy for the treatment of anxiety disorders, including the culture-bound syndrome *taijin kyofusho*, which affects 10% to 20% of the Japanese population. This condition, recognized in the *DSM*, is characterized by fear of offending others, by blushing, or by having an offensive appearance or body odor. Morita recommended treating anxiety by accepting your feelings, knowing your purpose, and doing what needs doing. His therapy continues to be used today. *Source:* Reprinted by permission from "Morita Therapy and the True Nature of Anxiety-Based Disorders" by Shoma Morita, the State University of New York Press 1998, State University of New York. All rights reserved.

Biological Explanations for Panic Disorder A clue to the biological origin of panic attacks is that they can be produced artificially in people with panic disorder, but not in people who do not have panic disorder, by administering an injection of sodium lactate (Papp et al., 1993; Pitts & McClure, 1967). Researchers have suggested that the sodium lactate interacts with orexins, chemical messengers we discussed in Chapters 6 and 7. Orexins, which are released by cells in the hypothalamus, play important roles in wakefulness, vigilance, and appetite. People with panic disorder have larger quantities of orexins than do people without the disorder (Johnson et al., 2010). It is possible that disturbances involving the orexins might lead to panic attacks.

Cognitive Explanations for Panic Disorder Cognitive theories of panic attacks suggest that the interpretation of body symptoms, such as an increased heart rate, could lead to increasing anxiety and, ultimately, to panic (Bakker, Spinhoven, van Balkom, & van Dyck, 2002; Harvey, Watkins, Mansell, & Shafran, 2004). A person might interpret increased heart rate and rapid breathing as a heart attack instead of the result of having walked briskly from a parking lot. Concern about having a heart attack leads to further physiological arousal, which leads to more anxiety, until a full state of panic is reached. Unfortunately for such theories, panic surprisingly does not increase levels of the stress hormone cortisol, which suggests that there is more to a panic attack than just responding to the stress of thinking you are ill (Hollander et al., 1989).

Social Explanations for Panic Disorder Social influences can be seen in the symptoms related by people with panic disorder. Many people worry about appearing weird or crazy to other people, which can lead to increased anxiety and more panic attacks (Hicks et al., 2005). Culture appears to play an important role in how panic attacks are interpreted. Although the underlying physical characteristics remain similar from country to country, interesting variations have been observed. For example, dizziness is an important aspect of panic attacks in China, constipation and shortness of breath are common complaints in Rwanda, and gastrointestinal symptoms signal panic for patients in Thailand (Hinton & Good, 2009). Social factors also influence the development of panic disorder. Panic disorder is more common in

panic attack The experience of intense fear and autonomic arousal in the absence of real threat.
panic disorder A disorder characterized by repeated panic attacks and fear of future attacks.

children who have experienced parental loss or separation and in adults who have recently experienced significant, stressful life events (Klauke, Deckert, Reif, Pauli, & Domschke, 2010).

Integrating the Perspectives A combination of the factors just discussed is likely to provide the best explanation for the development and experience of panic disorder. A panic attack could occur as a result of a chain of events: (1) A person with a biological predisposition to panic, possibly involving the orexin systems of the brain, is (2) exposed to social stressors in the form of parental loss or separation or significant life stressors, (3) interprets physical symptoms of arousal as threatening or embarrassing, and finally (4) has cognitions leading to panic that are modulated by that individual's cultural expectations.

Agoraphobia

Agoraphobia is the fear of open spaces and is named after the ancient Greek *agora,* or "marketplace." As we mentioned previously, agoraphobia is a common outcome of panic disorder. When people become afraid of the embarrassment of having panic attacks in public, they might opt to simply stay at home. Fear can occur in a number of situations, including being outside the home alone, using public transportation, being in open spaces such as parking lots or in shops, or standing in line or in a crowd. Agoraphobia often prevents working or engaging in normal social activities (Kessler et al., 2005).

Generalized Anxiety Disorder

Generalized anxiety disorder (GAD) is diagnosed when a person has experienced excessive anxiety and worry for 6 months that is not correlated with particular objects or situations (APA, 2013). In other words, the person experiences a great deal of worry, but the worry is focused on life in general, not upcoming midterms or spiders. GAD is associated with physical complaints, including headache, stomachache, and muscle tension. GAD is often comorbid, or coexisting, with other anxiety disorders, substance abuse, and depression (APA, 2013).

Biological Explanations for Generalized Anxiety Disorder To explain psychological disorders like GAD, the biological perspective considers underlying genetics, biochemistry, and structure. Like all anxiety disorders, GAD shows evidence of genetic predisposition (Kendler et al., 1995; Molina et al., 2011). A reasonable place to start looking for correlates of anxiety in brain structure and function is the fear circuit involving the amygdala, which we discussed in Chapters 4 and 7. The amygdala is particularly rich in receptors for GABA, a neurotransmitter that inhibits brain activity. As discussed in Chapter 6, drugs such as alcohol and the benzodiazepine tranquilizers (e.g., Valium) have their main anxiety-reducing effects at these GABA receptors. Not too surprisingly, then, people often self-medicate with alcohol and tranquilizers to reduce their anxiety levels, leaving them vulnerable to substance abuse disorders.

The amygdala forms complex connections with the prefrontal areas of the frontal lobe (see ● Figure 14.18). As we observed in our discussion of aggression in Chapter 13, the prefrontal cortex coordinates our decisions based on potential dangers identified by the amygdala. For example, if you see a driver's angry face in your rearview mirror, your amygdala alerts the prefrontal cortex about a potential threat or danger, and your prefrontal cortex uses memories of similar past experiences and reasoning to decide to pull over safely to the slower lane to let the angry driver go by. It is possible that this circuit is not responding typically in cases of GAD.

Cognitive Explanations for Generalized Anxiety Disorder Several cognitive models of GAD have been proposed (Beck, 1985). As we discussed in Chapters 10 and 11, we often organize our thinking about the world into schemas, or systems of belief. If a high-reactive

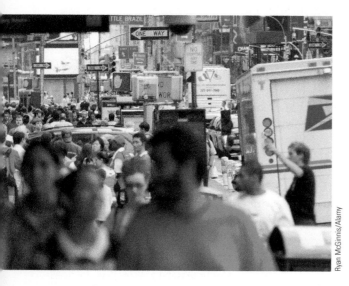

Ryan McGinnis/Alamy

People with agoraphobia or fear of open places often fear being in crowds, like this one in Times Square in New York City.

agoraphobia Unrealistic fear of open spaces, being outside the home alone, or being in a crowd.
generalized anxiety disorder (GAD) A disorder characterized by excessive anxiety and worry that is not correlated with particular objects or situations.

child develops a schema that says "the world is a dangerous place," even safe experiences begin to look dangerous through this filter. A different cognitive approach suggests that worrying can become a coping strategy for anxiety. By examining "what ifs," people might believe that they are coping, but so many situations are capable of triggering the coping response that the result is nearly constant worry (Wells, 2006). Bill Murray's character in the 1991 film *What About Bob?* expresses this type of worry when he asks his psychiatrist, "What if my bladder explodes?"

Social Explanations for Generalized Anxiety Disorder Social perspectives also add to our understanding of GAD. Individuals in lower socioeconomic classes in the United States are about twice as likely to be diagnosed with GAD as people in middle or upper socioeconomic classes (Kessler et al., 2005). Disruptions in social connectivity because of divorce, separation, death of a spouse, or loss of a job are also associated with higher rates of GAD (Wittchen & Hoyer, 2001).

Integrating the Perspectives Pulling these perspectives together into an integrated model, we might predict that GAD is most likely to occur in individuals with a high-reactive temperament, possibly because of their genetic background, who subsequently develop schemas and other cognitive patterns that maintain high levels of worry. When these individuals experience unusual amounts of stress because of socioeconomic factors and disruption of social networks, their risk for developing GAD is likely to be even higher.

Obsessive-Compulsive and Related Disorders

The *DSM-5* groups obsessive-compulsive disorder (OCD), which was formerly an anxiety disorder, with body dysmorphic disorder, hoarding disorder, and other similar problems (APA, 2013).

Obsessive-Compulsive Disorder (OCD)

Individuals with **obsessive-compulsive disorder (OCD)** are haunted by distressing, intrusive thoughts (**obsessions**); the need to engage in repetitive, ritualistic behaviors (**compulsions**); or both. Between 2% and 3% of the U.S. population report experiencing OCD during their lifetime (Ruscio, Stein, Chiu, & Kessler, 2010).

Obsessions are distinct from everyday worries, which usually focus on real-life problems. Common obsessions include concerns about contamination (catching diseases from shaking hands), repeated doubts (wondering whether you have hurt somebody), ordering (needing things arranged in a particular order or configuration), inappropriate impulses (hurting somebody else or shouting obscenities at a funeral), and sexual imagery (APA, 2013).

Compulsions appear to be efforts to ward off the anxiety produced by obsessions or some other feared event. For example, people troubled by obsessions about contamination may engage in compulsive hand washing hundreds of times per day. Other common compulsions include checking (for locked windows or faucets turned off), counting, ordering objects, and requesting or demanding assurances.

Randal Pfizenmaier/Alamy

Thalamus
Prefrontal cortex
Hypothalamus
Amygdala

© Cengage Learning®

FIGURE 14.18

Brain Circuits and Generalized Anxiety Disorder (GAD). People with GAD have higher levels of activity in the cortex, thalamus, amygdala, and hypothalamus (Wittchen & Hoyer, 2001). The prefrontal cortex was especially active when people with GAD saw angry faces, suggesting that this area had to "work harder" to control incoming danger signals from the amygdala (Monk et al., 2008).

Some people with obsessive-compulsive disorder must arrange their possessions in particular ways; otherwise, they will experience overwhelming anxiety.

obsessive-compulsive disorder (OCD) A disorder associated with intrusive obsessions and compulsions.
obsession An intrusive, distressing thought.
compulsion Repetitive, ritualistic behavior associated with high anxiety.

The childhood rhyme "don't step on a crack or you'll break your mother's back" captures the ineffectiveness of obsessive-compulsive thinking.

Biological Explanations for Obsessive-Compulsive Disorder The biological perspective has made important contributions to our understanding of the causes of OCD. Twin studies suggest a strong genetic vulnerability for the disorder, with concordance rates between identical twins of 63% to 87% (Menzies et al., 2008). It is probable that significant interactions between this genetic vulnerability and the environment can occur. Symptoms of OCD may arise following head trauma, the brain inflammation caused by encephalitis, and seizure disorder (Grisham, Anderson, & Sachdev, 2008). Young children who experienced birth complications or streptococcal infections (e.g., strep throat) may be more likely to develop the disorder later in life (Swedo et al., 1997).

Imaging studies provide insight into the patterns of brain activity that accompany obsessions and compulsions (see ● Figure 14.19). Several structures, including the orbitofrontal cortex, prefrontal cortex, the anterior cingulate gyrus, and the caudate nucleus of the basal ganglia, appear to be more active than usual in people with OCD (Saxena, 2003; Szeszko et al., 2004). Individuals with OCD appear to have lower than normal amounts of serotonin activity, and individuals with the lowest levels of serotonin activity experience the most severe obsessions and compulsions (Piacentini & Graae, 1997).

The evolutionary perspective suggests that OCD might have its roots in normal grooming and territoriality behaviors that somehow become overly exaggerated in some cases (Rapoport, 1989). Humans who anticipated threats like disease from dirty hands or threats from the perimeters of their territories probably benefited from proactive strategies like hand washing and checking (Brune, 2006). Disordered behavior similar to OCD does occur elsewhere in the animal kingdom. Dogs may lick and chew their front paws to the point of causing extensive tissue damage, which can be prevented by giving the dogs the same medications used to treat humans with OCD (Seksel & Lindeman, 2001).

Learning Explanations for Obsessive-Compulsive Disorder Learning explanations for OCD focus on the rewarding aspects of compulsions. As we pointed out in our discussion of operant conditioning, any behavior that produces a positive outcome (reducing anxiety associated with an obsession) is likely to be repeated in the future. For example, if hand washing reduced anxiety about germs and disease, hand washing might become progressively more frequent to the point where it would be considered abnormal. The *DSM-5* specifies that engaging in compulsive behavior for more than 1 hour per day is considered abnormal (APA, 2013).

Social Explanations for Obsessive-Compulsive Disorder Culture plays a role in how frequently OCD occurs and what obsessions and compulsions are more likely. Anthropologists have identified interesting parallels between cultural rituals and OCD. For example, many normal cultural rituals involve elements similar to OCD, including washing, special colors, stereotyped actions, and rigid rules (Dulaney & Fiske, 1994). Like the evolutionary perspective, this cultural view suggests that OCD might represent an exaggerated version of normal behaviors.

FIGURE 14.19

Obsessive-Compulsive Disorder (OCD) and the Orbitofrontal Cortex. When compared to healthy controls, people with OCD have greater gray matter density in the areas shown in red. When people with OCD experience symptoms, the areas in yellow become especially active. Areas of the orbitofrontal cortex, shown in orange, are anatomically different from those in healthy controls and are activated during OCD symptoms, suggesting an important role for the orbitofrontal cortex in OCD. *Source:* From Rotge, J.-Y., et al. (2010). Anatomical Alterations and Symptom-Related Functional Activity in Obsessive-Compulsive Disorder Are Correlated in the Lateral Orbitofrontal Cortex. *Biological Psychiatry, 67*(7), e37-e38. Copyright 2010 Elsevier.

Orbitofrontal cortex

Pop entertainer Michael Jackson was described by his mother as "addicted" to plastic surgery. She related that during adolescence, her son became obsessed with his perceived physical flaws. Although Jackson was never formally diagnosed with body dysmorphic disorder, many people with this disorder engage in similar types of behavior.

Body Dysmorphic Disorder

Body dysmorphic disorder is characterized by the unrealistic perception of physical flaws. Many people with this condition undergo numerous cosmetic surgeries. Others continually try to "perfect" their bodies through bodybuilding activities and other strategies.

Body dysmorphic disorder shows a significant influence of heredity (Feusner, Neziroglu, Wilhelm, Mancusi, & Bohon, 2010). In addition, people with this disorder might not be as out of touch with reality as you might think. Their visual perception of subtle facial distortions appears to be much better than normal, so they may be noticing "flaws" that the rest of us cannot see (Reese, McNally, & Wilhelm, 2010).

What Is Posttraumatic Stress Disorder?

Posttraumatic stress disorder (PTSD) is the current term used to describe a condition formerly known as shell shock or battle fatigue. PTSD is unique among disorders listed in the *DSM-5*, because it is the only one with a specified cause: To be diagnosed with PTSD, you must have experienced trauma (APA, 2013). Although combat, especially hand-to-hand combat, is still recognized as one of the most likely experiences leading to PTSD, we now understand that other types of trauma may produce the same results (Insel, 2007). PTSD may follow the experience of automobile accidents, assaults, abuse, and natural disasters.

PTSD symptoms include hypervigilance, avoidance of stimuli associated with the trauma, emotional numbing, and reexperiencing in the form of repetitive, intrusive thoughts, flashbacks, and dreams about the traumatic event (APA, 2013). The last thing a person in this situation wants to do is to "relive" the traumatic event, so these symptoms can be upsetting. Children with PTSD tend to reenact the traumatic event in their play (Cohen, Chazan, Lerner, & Maimon, 2010). In other words, they may play "terrorist attack," "car crash," or "tsunami," possibly in an effort to reduce their fear. This reenactment play can have either positive or negative effects on the child. Children whose play included a reworking of the traumatic event (revenge or a happy ending) were less disturbed than children whose play was repetitive without resolution.

body dysmorphic disorder A disorder characterized by the unrealistic perception of physical flaws

posttraumatic stress disorder (PTSD) A disorder caused by the experience of trauma, which leads to flashbacks, dreams, hypervigilance, and avoidance of stimuli associated with the traumatic event.

Although combat remains the most frequent cause of posttraumatic stress disorder (PTSD), people who experience natural disasters, like the 2011 Japanese earthquake and tsunami, are also at risk for the disorder.

PTSD affects between 3% and 4% of the adult population in the United States every year (Kessler et al., 2007). After large-scale traumatic events, health workers typically expect about 10% of the population to develop PTSD (Kessler, Sonnega, Bromet, Hughes, & Nelson, 1995). For example, more than 12% of lower Manhattan residents developed PTSD following the terrorist attacks of 9/11 (DiGrande et al., 2008). Children appear to be more vulnerable than adults, with 25% developing PTSD following automobile accidents in which they were injured, compared to 15% of their parents (de Vries, 1999). Between 8.5% and 14% of combat soldiers serving in Iraq and Afghanistan experienced severe impairment because of symptoms of PTSD after returning home, and up to 31% experienced some impairment (Thomas et al., 2010).

Biological Explanations for Posttraumatic Stress Disorder

Biological explanations for PTSD focus on the hippocampus, a structure we have discussed previously in the context of the biology of memory formation. Brain imaging studies consistently show that PTSD is correlated with smaller hippocampal volume (Bossini et al., 2008; Bremner et al., 2002). This leaves us with two competing hypotheses: Are people with a naturally smaller hippocampus more vulnerable to PTSD? Or is there something about the experience of trauma that is toxic to the hippocampus? Both hypotheses seem reasonable. As we observed in Chapter 7, stress increases the release of cortisol, which in turn may have toxic effects on the hippocampus (Sapolsky, Krey, & McEwen, 1985). Decreases in hippocampal volume are greater as a function of the amount of time that has elapsed since a traumatic event in Vietnam veterans with PTSD, suggesting that hippocampal damage can continue steadily because of the disorder (Chao, Yaffe, Samuelson, & Neylan, 2014). Comparisons of twins have also identified PTSD-related damage to the anterior cingulate cortex (Kasai et al., 2008).

PTSD is correlated with lower levels of naturally occurring benzodiazepine activity in the frontal cortex (Geuze et al., 2008; see ● Figure 14.20). Extra benzodiazepines can be administered in the form of major tranquilizers, such as Valium, which produce relaxation and lack of anxiety. If naturally occurring benzodiazepine activity was low, anxiety would be the logical result. Lower levels of natural benzodiazepine activity might also explain the unfortunate tendency for people to self-medicate for PTSD with alcohol (Jakupcak et al., 2010). Alcohol reduces anxiety using biological mechanisms similar to those of the benzodiazepines.

FIGURE 14.20

Benzodiazepine Activity Is Reduced in Posttraumatic Stress Disorder (PTSD). Yellow areas show reduced binding of benzodiazepine, which has a tranquilizing effect, in the brains of combat veterans with PTSD compared to those of combat veterans who do not have PTSD. *Source:* From Geuze, E., van Berckel, B. N., Lammertsma, A. A., Boellaard, R., de Kloet, C. S., Vermetten, E., et al. (2008). Reduced GABA$_A$ benzodiazepine receptor binding in veterans with post-traumatic stress disorder. *Molecular Psychiatry, 13*(1), 74-83, 73.

posterior cingulate   prefrontal cortex   superior temporal gyrus   hippocampus   posterior cingulate   thalamus   prefrontal cortex

T-value

Learning Explanations for Posttraumatic Stress Disorder

Learning, and classical conditioning in particular, contributes to the symptoms of PTSD. Individuals with PTSD show conditioned responses to stimuli associated with the traumatic event. Combat veterans with PTSD seem particularly sensitive to smells, such as burning rubber and diesel (Rothbaum, Rizzo, & Difede, 2010). Most people actively avoid any stimuli that remind them of the traumatic event.

Social and Cultural Explanations for Posttraumatic Stress Disorder

Social and cultural factors play significant roles in the development of PTSD. People reporting low social support in the 6 months before 9/11 were twice as likely to be diagnosed with PTSD as people who reported strong social support during this period (Galea et al., 2002). Cultural factors also influence the likelihood of PTSD. Following 9/11, PTSD was more common in New York City residents of some ethnicities than others, affecting 13.4% of Hispanics, 9.3% of Black Americans, 6.5% of White Americans, and 3.2% of Asian Americans (Galea et al., 2002).

What Are Dissociative Disorders?

Dissociative disorders feature disruptions in a person's identity, memory, or consciousness (APA, 2013).

Heisman Trophy winner, NFL star, and mixed martial arts fighter Herschel Walker has spoken about his experience with dissociative identity disorder to encourage military veterans to seek help for psychological disorders.

dissociative disorder A disorder characterized by disruptions in a person's identity, memory, or consciousness.

Dissociative disorders can take several forms. Dissociative amnesia occurs when a person forgets important information about specific events, often following a frightening or traumatic event. In dissociative fugue, people become confused over their identity and often combine this loss of identity with sudden travel and the assumption of a new identity. These situations typically last a few hours or days but not longer periods (Kopelman, 2002).

Depersonalization or derealization disorder occurs when a person experiences strong feelings of unreality about either the self or the surrounding environment (APA, 2013). People might feel as though they are watching their behavior from outside their bodies or that the world is dreamlike. However, they retain their abilities to understand that their feelings are not realistic. In other words, they feel as if they're outside their bodies, but they don't believe this is really happening.

Possibly the most controversial of the dissociative disorders is dissociative identity disorder, which was previously known as multiple personality disorder. According to the *DSM-5*, dissociative identity disorder is characterized by the experience of two distinct "personality states" (APA, 2013).

Dissociative identity disorder experienced a spike in popularity as a diagnosis in the mid-1990s but has since dropped in frequency. Media attention might have contributed to the frequency with which this disorder was diagnosed. Before the popularization of patients named Sybil and Eve in books and films during the 1970s, few cases of dissociative identity disorder had ever been described in the scientific literature. Following this media interest, thousands of cases were diagnosed, primarily in the United States and Canada. Responses to extreme stress frequently include detachment, numbness, or altered memory and cognitions, but this is quite different from the development of additional identities. Well-meaning therapists can misinterpret these stress symptoms as dissociative identity disorder and, worse yet, suggest this possibility to their clients. People diagnosed with dissociative identity disorder, like those with other dissociative disorders, score very high on tests of suggestibility that predict a person's susceptibility to hypnosis and in measures of being likely to fantasize (Giesbrecht, Lynn, Lilienfeld, & Merckelbach, 2010). These findings imply that these people may have difficulty distinguishing between reality and fantasy and might accept a therapist's suggestion without considering it critically.

What Are Somatic Symptom and Related Disorders?

Historically, **somatic symptom disorder** involved physical symptoms that do not have an underlying medical cause (APA, 2013). The *DSM-5* notes that these patients spend excessive amounts of time thinking about the seriousness of their symptoms, which is accompanied by a high level of anxiety. To the patient, the somatic symptoms appear quite serious and often disabling. Among the different symptoms are vague pain complaints, gastrointestinal upset, sexual problems, amnesia, breathing problems, or unexplained sensory or motor problems. People with somatic symptoms usually visit physicians frequently, report high numbers of physical complaints, and are at risk of becoming dependent on pain medications. They can become preoccupied with their health and often insist on unnecessary medical tests and procedures.

somatic symptom disorder A disorder characterized by physical symptoms that do not have an underlying medical cause.

personality disorder A disorder characterized by impairments in identity, in personality traits, and in establishment of empathy or intimacy.

What Are Personality Disorders?

Several types of **personality disorders** are recognized in the *DSM-5* (APA, 2013). A personality disorder is characterized by impairments in identity, in personality traits, and in establishment of empathy or intimacy. Personality disorders cannot be diagnosed in people under the age of 18. To illustrate this category of disorders, we will look at two of the personality disorders in greater detail: antisocial personality disorder (ASPD), which is more common in males, and borderline personality disorder, which is more common in females.

Antisocial Personality Disorder

Antisocial personality disorder (ASPD) is characterized by a "pervasive pattern of disregard for and violation of the rights of others" (APA, 2013, p. 659). Individuals with this disorder have little regard for normal social rules and conventions. Their behavior is frequently risky and irresponsible, and they form shallow, fleeting relationships with others.

ASPD is quite similar to the term *psychopath,* which has not been used by the *DSM* system since its third edition was published in 1980. Criteria for ASPD in *DSM-III* and *DSM-IV* focused on a person's behaviors, especially criminal behaviors, whereas the term *psychopath* implies flaws in the person's consistent traits or character (Hare, 2006). Between 0.2% and 3.3% of the population experiences ASPD within a given year (APA, 2013). Hare (2006) has estimated the number of psychopaths in the United States to be approximately 1%.

Most individuals with ASPD or psychopathy do not engage in outright criminal behavior, and not all criminals have ASPD or psychopathy. Noncriminal individuals with ASPD were easily recruited by placing a newspaper ad calling for "charming, aggressive, carefree people who are impulsively irresponsible but are good at handling people and at looking after number one" (Widom, 1978, p. 72).

Causes of Antisocial Personality Disorder Research on individuals with antisocial parents suggests a genetic contribution to this disorder. Related traits such as fearless dominance, impulsive antisociality, and callousness show substantial heritability rates between .46 and .67

JON ARE BERG_JACOBSEN/AFTENPOSTE/EPA/Newscom

Anders Behring Breivik killed 8 people with a bomb before shooting another 69 people at a nearby youth camp on July 22, 2011. Police told reporters that during a reenactment of the shootings, Breivik "didn't show any remorse." Although we don't know whether Breivik will be diagnosed with antisocial personality disorder, a callous lack of empathy and remorse is typical of people with this diagnosis.

Copyright 2001, with permission from Elsevier

(a)   (b)

The areas marked in blue showed less activity in criminal psychopaths than in noncriminal control participants in a study during the processing of negative emotional words like *rape* or *torture*. These areas are associated with emotional processing and include (a) the cingulate cortex and basal ganglia and (b) the hippocampus and amygdala. The failure of negative emotional stimuli to produce normal levels of arousal might allow the psychopath to engage in harmful behaviors without experiencing normal remorse or empathy. *Source:* Reprinted from Kiehl, K. A., et al. (2001). Limbic abnormalities in affective processing by criminal psychopaths as revealed by functional magnetic resonance imaging. *Biological Psychiatry, 50*(9), 677-684.

antisocial personality disorder (ASPD) A disorder characterized by an unusual lack of remorse, empathy, or regard for normal social rules and conventions.

(Blair, Colledge, Murray, & Mitchell, 2001). Children adopted at birth who have antisocial biological parents are more likely to engage in antisocial behavior (Cadoret & Cain, 1981). When children of biological parents who are not antisocial are adopted by antisocial parents, they are less likely than children with biological parents who are antisocial to engage in antisocial behavior(Mednick & Kandel, 1988). As we have mentioned previously in this textbook, child maltreatment interacts with a genetic predisposition to violent antisocial behavior (Caspi et al., 2003).

A genetic influence on a trait usually implies that the trait provides some advantage, but how can this be the case for a tendency toward antisocial behavior? One suggestion is that fearlessness characterizes both heroes and people with antisocial behavior (Lykken, 1982). Having heroic people in your population might offset the negative impact of having some antisocial people. To test his hypothesis about the similarities between these two groups, Lykken devised an Activity Preference Questionnaire, which asks respondents to choose between a frightening or embarrassing situation and one that is simply unpleasant. For example, would you prefer to wash a car or drive a car 95 miles per hour? People who either engage in antisocial behavior or who have behaved heroically typically choose the risky alternative (driving fast) over a chore (washing car), whereas cautious people typically choose the chore over the risky alternative.

A relative lack of response to emotions, especially those of others, might also contribute to antisocial behavior disorder. While undergoing brain imaging, people with ASPD, unlike the control participants in a study, showed little activation of parts of the brain that are usually active during emotional processing when listening to words such as *torture, rape,* or *cancer* (Hare, 2006; Kiehl et al., 2001). Participants were also shown neutral scenes and rather gruesome images of murder scenes. Again, the people with ASPD showed different patterns of brain activation than did the typical control participants. In particular, the amygdalae of people with ASPD showed relatively little activity. As we discussed in Chapters 4 and 7, the amygdala normally participates in recognition of fear and other negative emotions in others. Other research indicates that children with antisocial tendencies are impaired in their ability to identify expressions of sadness and fear in others, a finding that is consistent with lower activity in the amygdala (Blair et al., 2001).

Antisocial behavior is associated with abnormalities of the orbitofrontal cortex. Orbitofrontal abnormalities occur at higher rates among murderers and those diagnosed with ASPD (Davidson, Putnam, & Larson, 2000). As we observed in Chapter 4, damage to the frontal areas of the cortex often leads to poor judgment and impulsivity. In one representative case, two adults who had been raised in stable, middle-class homes but who had experienced damage to the orbitofrontal cortex in infancy both showed a profound inability to understand the consequences of their negative behavior (Anderson, Bechara, Damasio, Tranel, & Damasio, 1999). They engaged in stealing, lying, and aggressive behavior and were poor parents.

Psychology as a Hub Science
The "Dark Side" of Leadership

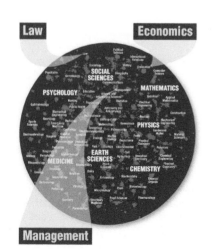

At a 2002 convention of law enforcement officers in Canada, psychologist Robert Hare made a startling suggestion (Hare, 2002). With slides in the background depicting convicted WorldCom Chief Executive Officer Bernard Ebbers and Enron Chief Financial Officer Andrew Fastow, Hare asked his audience why law enforcement personnel are screened for psychopathy but not executives responsible for millions of dollars of people's savings and retirement funds.

When we hear the term *psychopath,* most of us think of characters like Hannibal Lecter of *The Silence of the Lambs.* However, Hare and other psychologists suggest that psychopaths are more likely to be the people next door, your coworkers, and maybe even your friends and relatives. Not only are psychopaths relatively common (around 1% of the population), but their characteristics might also allow them to be disturbingly successful. When profiles of 39 top British executives were compared to those of criminals and psychiatric patients, the executives were found to be more charming, egotistical, manipulative, and lacking in empathy (Board & Fritzon, 2005). Consequently, researchers began to refer to the executives as "successful" psychopaths, whereas the criminals and patients were "unsuccessful" psychopaths. Hare and his colleague Paul Babiak would agree. Using scales they hope to market to corporations wishing to avoid hiring the next Fastow, these researchers have shown that corporate psychopaths score very high on items measuring the callous, selfless, and remorseless use of others (Babiak & Hare, 2006). Unlike criminal psychopaths, however, the corporate psychopaths did not show patterns of instability and social deviance.

Unfortunately, rapid and uncertain change in the business environment may provide fertile ground for corporate psychopaths to rise to the top. In a world of downsizing, an executive like Sunbeam's "Chainsaw" Al Dunlap, who fired half the corporation's workforce, might look like the right person for the job. Dunlap had also been divorced by his first wife for "extreme cruelty," thrown a chair at one of his executives, allegedly altered Sunbeam's financial records to make his performance look better, and demanded additional severance pay when he was fired for cause.

Modern corporations often find it difficult to distinguish between the behavior of the corporate psychopath and the person who is a genuinely visionary leader. Leaders such as Bill Gates and the late Steve Jobs may seem insensitive to others' feelings, according to leadership experts, but they turn their grandiosity toward making their organizations great rather than plundering them for personal gain (Maccoby, 2003). ●

Stephen Chernin/Getty Images

Bernard Madoff built one of the most successful businesses on Wall Street and served as the non-executive chairman of the NASDAQ stock market before being convicted of perpetrating one of the largest financial frauds in U.S. history. Psychologists Paul Babiak and Robert Hare suggest that it might be difficult to distinguish between tough corporate leaders and those with antisocial tendencies.

Borderline Personality Disorder

The term **borderline personality disorder** originated from the idea that the characteristics of this disorder fell on the "border" between anxiety and psychosis.

According to the *DSM-5,* borderline personality disorder is characterized by instability in interpersonal relationships, self-image, and emotion. Individuals with this disorder may engage in "frantic efforts" to avoid abandonment, either real or imagined, and may behave in impulsive, self-destructive ways (see ● Figure 14.21). Suicide and self-mutilating behaviors, which we discussed in Chapter 8, are quite common among people with this disorder. Relationships are often initially intense and idealized, but if the individual perceives any slight rejection, love can turn to anger quickly.

Borderline personality disorder affects about 2% of the population, with women outnumbering men by a factor of three to one (Skodol & Bender, 2003). People with borderline personality disorder appear to be vulnerable to a number of additional disorders, including bipolar disorder, substance abuse, eating disorders, and other personality disorders.

Causes of Borderline Personality Disorder Borderline personality disorder is 5 times more common among close relatives with the disorder than among the general population, suggesting a biological predisposition (APA, 2013). However, as many as 70% of individuals with this diagnosis have histories of abandonment, neglect, and physical, sexual, or both types of abuse (Hunt, 2007). These findings suggest that traumatic experiences interact with a possible genetic predisposition to produce disordered behavior.

borderline personality disorder
A disorder characterized by instability in interpersonal relationships, self-image, and emotion.

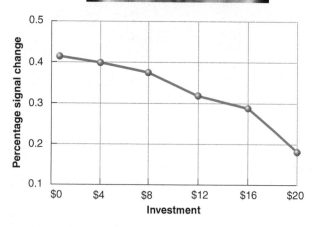

Healthy trustees (n = 38)
(low investment – high investment)

Trustees with borderline personality disorder (n = 55)
(low investment – high investment)

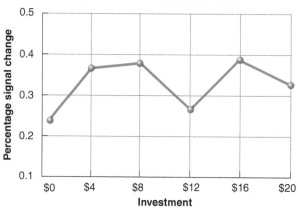

FIGURE 14.21

Abnormal Responses to Trust in Borderline Personality Disorder. Not only do people with borderline personality disorder perform differently than healthy controls in experimental activities measuring trust, but their brain activity during a trust game is also different. In healthy study participants, activity in the anterior insula decreases when an offer is higher or fairer. In the participants with borderline personality disorder, insula activity did not correspond well with the offers they received. This inability to respond to trust normally might explain some difficulties these people experience in building healthy relationships with others. *Source:* From King-Casas, B., et al. (2008). The Rupture and Repair of Cooperation in Borderline Personality Disorder, *Science, 321,* 806-810. Copyright 2008 The American Association for the Advancement of Science.

Interpersonal Relationships
The Clinical Perspective
How Does PTSD Affect Families?

There are hidden costs in war. Soldiers, most of whom are about the same ages as those of you reading this textbook, are permanently changed by their experiences in ways that are often difficult for those of us who have not shared those experiences to understand. They have faced the fear of death and the realities of injury, held dying friends in their arms, and felt guilty that their lives were spared.

Some cope with these challenges better than others. As we stated previously, between 8.5% and 14% of U.S. veterans serving in Iraq and Afghanistan experience severe PTSD, and up to 31% experience some impairment (Thomas et al., 2010). Veterans usually come home to loved ones and families, who are also affected by their soldiers' combat experiences in what has been called secondary traumatization (Galovski & Lyons, 2004). Although not directly threatened, the soldiers' families have had challenges of their own as they cope with their helpless fear of loss. Understanding that bad news comes to the front door in the person of a military chaplain makes each FedEx delivery or visit by a neighbor a heart-pounding experience. The spouses who have learned over the course of a year to run households independently and balance the checkbook might not want to return some of these tasks to their returning partners.

Among the biggest challenges for veterans with PTSD and their families are the results of having symptoms of hyperarousal, emotional numbing, and stimulus avoidance (Monson, Taft, & Fredman, 2009). Although veterans without PTSD have the same rates of intimate aggression as the general population, the risk of intimate aggression is much higher in those with PTSD, and the severity of symptoms predicts the likelihood of aggression. Because of the emotional numbing and avoidance symptoms of PTSD, returning veterans do not engage in much self-disclosure, or discussion of their thoughts, feelings, and experiences. As we discussed in Chapter 13, self-disclosure is an important component of intimacy.

A soldier's existing level of social support is one of the strongest protections against the initial development of PTSD (Brewin, Andrews, & Valentine, 2000). After trauma, a person with PTSD recovers more quickly with strong social support. Unfortunately, with ongoing PTSD, that social support tends to diminish as the symptoms of PTSD take their toll on relationships (Kaniasty & Norris, 2008).

By recognizing the importance of the larger social network to PTSD, psychologists can begin to develop more effective preventions and interventions that take the entire social system into account, not just the individual with PTSD symptoms. ●

AFP/Getty Images

Both soldiers and their families are changed by war, and their reunions, while happy, are not always smooth. Strong social support is a critical variable in the development and course of posttraumatic stress disorder (PTSD) resulting from combat.

Summary 14.3 Anxiety Disorders, Obsessive-Compulsive Disorder (OCD), Body Dysmorphic Disorder, and Posttraumatic Stress Disorder (PTSD)

Disorder	Symptoms	Possible causal factors under investigation
Phobia	• Excessive fear of an object or situation	• Exaggeration of normal caution • Classical conditioning • Cognitions about fear stimulus • Collectivist cultures emphasizing shame
Panic disorder	• Repeated panic attacks accompanied by excessive worry about having panic attacks	• Possible abnormality in orexin function • Cognitions regarding symptoms • Expectations and embarrassment • Cultural influences
Generalized anxiety disorder	• Excessive anxiety for 6 months that is not correlated with objects or situations	• Genetic predisposition • Stress • Fearful schemas • Low socioeconomic status • Disruptions in social connectivity
OCD	• Intrusive, repetitious, and anxiety-producing thoughts and behaviors	• Genetic predisposition • Low serotonin activity • Prefrontal and basal ganglia activity • Extension of grooming and territorial behaviors • Rewarding aspects of compulsions • Extension of cultural rituals
Body dysmorphic disorder	• Unrealistic perception of physical flaws	• Genetic predisposition • Superior perception of facial distortions
PTSD	• Exposure to a traumatic event, following by flashbacks, hypervigilance, and nightmares	• Hippocampus and prefrontal cortex • Benzodiazepine receptors • Classical conditioning • Social support

KEY TERMS The Language of Psychological Science

Be sure you can define these terms and use them correctly.

abnormal psychology, p. 537

agoraphobia, p. 564

antisocial personality disorder (ASPD), p. 571

anxiety disorder, p. 561

attention deficit hyperactivity disorder (ADHD), p. 544

autism spectrum disorder (ASD), p. 541

bipolar disorder, p. 552

body dysmorphic disorder, p. 567

borderline personality disorder, p. 573

comorbid, p. 538

compulsion, p. 565

delusion, p. 547

Diagnostic and Statistical Manual of Mental Disorders (DSM), p. 539

diathesis–stress model, p. 560

dissociative disorder, p. 569

generalized anxiety disorder (GAD), p. 564

hallucination, p. 547

learned helplessness, p. 555

major depressive disorder, p. 553

mania, p. 552

obsession, p. 565

obsessive-compulsive disorder (OCD), p. 565

panic attack, p. 563

panic disorder, p. 563

personality disorder, p. 570

posttraumatic stress disorder (PTSD), p. 567

schizophrenia, p. 547

social anxiety disorder, p. 562

somatic symptom disorder, p. 570

specific phobia, p. 561

15 Healing the Troubled Mind

Therapy

Yuri Arcurs/Shutterstock.com

WE HAVE ALL BEEN TOLD HOW IMPORTANT IT IS to wash our hands to avoid illness, especially during flu season. But people with obsessive-compulsive disorder (OCD) might wash their hands several hundred times each day.

Why do people with OCD behave this way? In Chapter 14, we highlighted some possible causes of OCD, including a genetic vulnerability and the presence of too much activity in several brain structures, including the basal ganglia. In this chapter, we will talk about how psychotherapists can improve the situations of people with OCD and the other disorders we discussed in Chapter 14.

The two most common approaches to treating OCD are cognitive behavioral therapies (CBTs), which we discuss in detail in this chapter, and medications. CBTs have been developed based on the principles of classical and operant conditioning that we discussed in Chapter 8. In the case of OCD, a woman with hand-washing compulsions could be trained to anticipate when she might feel like washing her hands inappropriately. Then, she would engage in some competing activity, perhaps going out to her garden to pull some weeds or pick some flowers. Finally, she would reward herself for resisting the temptation to wash her hands too much.

Is it possible to show differences in brain activity resulting from CBT? The answer is "yes" (Baxter et al., 1992). Zooming in, we can see what happens to a person's brain by using a positron emission tomography (PET) scan following therapy for OCD. A PET scan provides a measure of brain activity. The red and yellow areas are considerably more active than the green, blue, and dark areas. When people with OCD who have been treated with cognitive behavioral methods are compared to people treated with medication, their PET scans show the same decrease in activity in the basal ganglia. Because medication can produce unwanted side effects and are not effective for all people, it is fortunate that alternate therapies are available.

In this chapter, we will be exploring a number of approaches that have been used to improve the situations of people with psychological disorders. Some represent a variety of psychological treatments, like the behavioral approach to OCD discussed

◄ Both medication and behavioral treatments reduce abnormal activity in the basal ganglia that is associated with obsessive-compulsive disorder.

Argosy Publishing, Inc.

here, while others take the form of medication and other biological treatments. The effects of these treatments might have more in common than you think, as in the case of the changes in brain activity that result from the psychological and biological treatments of OCD. Just as we have argued for the advantages of integrating psychological perspectives to understand behavior and mental processes, the field of clinical psychology is recognizing the benefits of applying multiple perspectives to the treatment of psychological disorders.

Learning Objectives

1. Summarize the core principles of evidence-based practice in psychotherapy.

2. Differentiate the training and licensure required for, and the types of care offered by, psychiatrists, clinical psychologists, counselors, hypnotherapists, and life coaches.

3. Analyze the key principles of psychoanalytic, humanistic, behavioral, and cognitive psychotherapy techniques.

4. Explain the biological mechanisms by which medication, electroconvulsive therapy, psychosurgery, deep brain stimulation, and neurofeedback are thought to alleviate symptoms of disorder.

5. Integrate biological and psychotherapeutic approaches to treating neurodevelopmental disorders, schizophrenia, bipolar disorder, major depressive disorder, anxiety disorders, OCD, posttraumatic stress disorder (PTSD), and personality disorders.

How Do Psychologists Provide Therapy?

Chapter 14 explored a diverse range of problems that can contribute to personal and interpersonal distress. Once considered virtually untreatable, many of these disorders respond positively to the treatments available today. Unfortunately, many people with disorders still do not seek help, possibly because of some of the stigma related to having a psychological problem or a lack of awareness that effective help is available (see ● Figure 15.1). Sixty years ago, many people diagnosed with schizophrenia faced a discouraging future of institutionalization and little improvement (see ● Figure 15.2). Today, although about 30% of patients with schizophrenia do not seem to respond to available treatments, the other 70% experience some relief from their troubling symptoms (Bobo & Meltzer, 2010).

Approaches to Treatment

psychotherapy Treatment designed to improve symptoms of psychological disorder through conversation between the therapist and the patient or client.

Psychological treatments, or **psychotherapies**, which generally involve a conversation between the professional providing the therapy and the person seeking help, are often combined with biological treatments, such as the medications described in more detail in later sections of this chapter. For example, a person who is terrified of being part of a crowd might benefit from a combination of psychotherapy and medication for anxiety. As we will see in this chap-

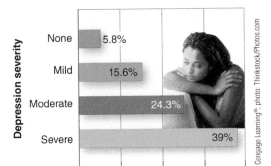

FIGURE 15.1

Many People With Psychological Disorders Do Not Receive Care. As symptoms of depression become more severe, people become more likely to obtain treatment from a psychiatrist or mental health (MH) professional, which would include clinical psychologists. It is difficult to tell whether the remaining individuals receive no care or are seen by their family physicians or other health care providers. *Source:* Adapted from "Depression in the United States Household Population, 2005–2006," by L. A. Pratt and D. J. Brody, NCHS Data Brief No. 7., September 2008, Washington, DC: U.S. Department of Health and Human Services, retrieved from http://www.cdc.gov/nchs/data/databriefs/db07.pdf.

ter, different combinations of methods can be tailored to different types of problems and to the individuals being treated.

Biological Approaches Biological approaches to treatment have their roots in our understanding of the biological factors that contribute to psychological disorders. Along with the overall burst of scientific and medical knowledge beginning in the 18th century, scientists began to learn more about psychological disorders and their causes. This knowledge, in turn, set the stage for the discoveries of more effective biological treatments.

Improved medical knowledge made psychological disorders less mysterious. When untreated, syphilis (a common type of sexually transmitted disease) can produce a characteristic set of abnormal behaviors, including hallucinations, delusions, and changes in mood and personality. As we noted in Chapter 14, these behaviors are characteristic of a number of psychological disorders, including schizophrenia. The discovery that behaviors like hallucinations could have a biological cause (syphilis is caused by a bacterial infection) led to the recognition that abnormal behavior can result from infection or other medical conditions. In these cases, the abnormal behaviors should disappear when the underlying medical condition is treated.

FIGURE 15.2

Recovery in Schizophrenia. Scientists are making progress in identifying which patients with schizophrenia are more responsive to current treatments. A deficit group of patients differed from a nondeficit group primarily in having more emotional disturbances. *Recovery* was defined strictly in this study as no psychiatric hospitalizations, no major symptoms, and at least half-time work or the equivalent level of functioning. In a 20-year study of the patients' outcomes, using a group of patients diagnosed with depression as a comparison group, the nondeficit group made more progress than the deficit group. Identifying which patients respond to existing treatments will help researchers and health care providers develop more effective treatment plans for individuals. *Source:* Adapted from "Periods of Recovery in Deficit Syndrome Schizophrenia: A 20-Year Multi–Follow-Up Longitudinal Study," by G. P. Strauss, M. Harrow, L. S. Grossman, and C. Rosen, 2010, *Schizophrenia Bulletin, 36*(4), pp. 788–799, doi:10.1093/schbul/sbn167.

Australian psychiatrist John Cade searched for alternatives to the electroconvulsive therapy, lobotomies, and psychoanalysis that were commonly used to treat psychological disorders in the 1940s. After observing that lithium salts had a sedating effect on guinea pigs, he tried lithium on himself to test for side effects. He then tried lithium on his patients and noticed that those with bipolar disorder appeared to respond favorably. Lithium is an element, so could not be patented, providing little financial incentive for the pharmaceutical industry. However, lithium was approved for use in the United States in 1970. Lithium salts continue to be used extensively to treat bipolar disorder, although we now understand that this treatment has serious side effects.

The use of one biological approach to treatment, medication, revolutionized the care of people with some psychological disorders. In 1949, an Australian psychiatrist named John Cade discovered that lithium salts could produce remarkable improvements in the behavior of patients with bipolar disorder. Cade's discovery was followed quickly by breakthroughs in the use of medication to treat schizophrenia. Bolstered by these successes with some of the most troubling psychological conditions, the pharmaceutical industry quickly introduced medications for depression and anxiety. These successes not only led to better outcomes for many patients but also strengthened the credibility of using biological approaches to treat abnormal behaviors.

Psychological Approaches Running parallel to the successes of scientists engaged in biological approaches to disorders were significant contributions from those who focused on the psychological and emotional underpinnings of disorders.

During the 19th century, psychologists and psychiatrists were interested in hysteria, a condition that would be diagnosed today as somatic symptom disorder (see Chapter 14). Hysteria did not seem to have any biological basis and did not respond to the medical treatments of the day. Among the first efforts to treat hysteria through nonmedical means was the use of hypnosis by Franz Anton Mesmer (1734–1815), whose name gives us the alternate term for being hypnotized—mesmerized. Mesmer attempted to treat hysteria by inducing a hypnotic state, described further in Chapter 6. In many cases, people with hysteria no longer experienced their symptoms under hypnosis and, following Mesmer's suggestions made during hypnosis, continued to be symptom free even after they left the hypnotic state.

Despite skepticism regarding Mesmer and his techniques, other scientists continued to explore hypnosis, suggestion, and hysteria. When positive outcomes were reported by the noted French neurologist Jean-Martin Charcot (1825–1893), hypnosis and suggestion took on a new legitimacy in the scientific community. Among admirers of Charcot and his work were Josef Breuer (1842–1925) and his more famous colleague Sigmund Freud (1856–1939). As we will see later in this chapter, Freud eventually abandoned his interest in hypnosis in favor of other approaches, which eventually gave rise to psychoanalysis. Instead of hypnotizing people, Freud encouraged them to speak freely about whatever came to mind.

During the 20th century, psychological approaches to treatment reflected the rise of the behavioral and humanistic perspectives, described in Chapters 1, 8, and 12. The behaviorist perspective, unlike the biological and Freudian approaches, focused exclusively on observable behavior and approached the treatment of abnormal behaviors using the principles of classical conditioning, operant conditioning, and observational learning, described in Chapter 8. The cognitive revolution of the second half of the 20th century added a recognition of the role of cognitions in abnormal behavior, leading to the development of CBT. Later in this chapter, we will explore the use of CBT for disorders such as phobias and depression.

The rise of humanistic psychology in the second half of the 20th century also led to new **humanistic therapies**. As we discussed in Chapter 1, the humanists specifically rebelled against psychodynamic thinking and the practice of psychoanalysis. Humanistic therapist Carl Rogers wished to separate his procedures, described in greater detail later in this chapter, from the more traditional Freudian psychotherapies of his time by referring to treatment as

Franz Anton Mesmer (1734–1815), whose name gives us the term *mesmerized*, attempted to use hypnosis to treat people with hysteria, which would now fall under the somatic symptom disorders category. Mesmer's practices inspired Sigmund Freud to use hypnosis, although he eventually abandoned the technique in favor of other approaches.

Mesmer's methods for using hypnosis to treat hysteria were quite theatrical and were denounced as fraudulent by none other than Benjamin Franklin, who was serving as the U.S. ambassador to France at the time.

humanistic therapy A therapy approach patterned after the theories proposed by humanistic psychologists.

counseling rather than psychotherapy or psychoanalysis (Rogers, 1942). Today's field of counseling psychology mirrors the more positive view of human nature held by the humanistic psychologists by focusing on personal strengths and development.

Evidence-Based Practice The beginning of the 21st century has featured greater demands to tie clinical practice to research on the outcomes of treatment. As shown in ● Figure 15.3, evidence-based practice (EBP) combines research evidence, clinical expertise, and individual values to provide the best outcome for a patient (APA Presidential Task Force on Evidence-Based Practice, 2006; Straus, Richardson, Glasziou, & Haynes, 2011). The movement toward EBP began in medicine, but it has since spread throughout the helping professions, including psychology.

EBP combines five steps (Thyer, 2004). The first step is to construct an answerable question, such as "Which treatments produce the best outcomes in cases of PTSD?" Next, clinicians conduct a search of the most current scientific literature related to the question. In other words, doing something "because I've always done it this way in my practice" is no longer an option. Third, clinicians critically evaluate the relevant literature, using the standards for good science that we discussed in Chapter 2. This information is then integrated with data regarding particular cases, including the patients' values and circumstances. Finally, clinicians evaluate their performance based on the patients' outcomes and make necessary adjustments.

If you think these EBP steps sound like the problem-solving system we introduced in Chapter 10, you're right. You might have assumed that your health care provider would take this approach automatically, but historically, many clinicians have been convinced that science can do little to assist them with an individual case and that clinical practice was more art than science. Large numbers of clinicians have traditionally valued their "clinical expertise" over the body of knowledge represented by science (Baker, McFall, & Shoham, 2008). Given the demanding financial realities of health care in the 21st century, however, a logical, scientific evidence–based approach to the delivery of health care services is not just the most effective approach but also the necessary one.

Clinical Assessment Before therapists can provide any type of useful treatment, they need to understand the problems presented by the person to be treated. The choice of assessment methods is guided by the training and experience of the clinician, but it usually includes the methods we described in Chapter 12: interviews, observations, and standardized tests (Groth-Marnat, 2009).

Carl Rogers and the humanistic psychologists rebelled against the practices of psychoanalysis and established new approaches of counseling psychology.

counseling Treatment originally proposed by humanistic therapists that includes a focus on personal strengths and development; it is now used to refer to treatment for adjustment problems as opposed to treatment for severe psychological disorders.

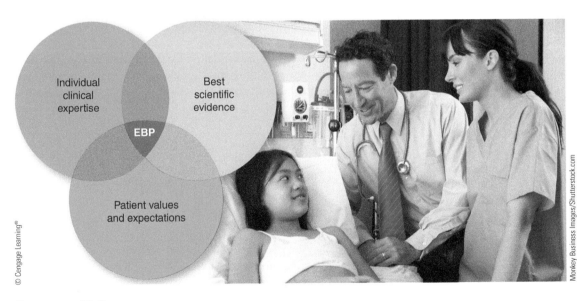

FIGURE 15.3

Evidence-Based Practice (EBP). EBP began in medicine and spread to psychotherapy and other helping professions. EBP combines the personal experience of the clinician, the best scientific evidence, and a consideration of patient values and expectations to tailor scientifically valid treatments to the individual.

The Therapists

A range of professionals, including general medical practitioners, psychiatrists, psychologists, social workers, nurses, and religious leaders, provide counseling and psychotherapy. Licensing of these professionals to provide treatment for psychological disorders is administered by state governments in the United States and provincial governments in Canada. Requirements for licensing can vary widely from state to state and can result in a bewildering array of titles. For example, the simple term *therapist* is not regulated consistently across the United States. We will use the term **psychotherapist** for any of the many types of licensed professionals described in this section who provide psychotherapy.

Psychiatrists first obtain a standard medical doctor (MD) degree and then spend an additional 3 to 4 years specializing in psychiatry. Because of their training and licensure as physicians, psychiatrists are allowed to perform the medical procedures we review later in this chapter, particularly the prescribing of medication. It is difficult to generalize across the entire profession, but psychiatrists are somewhat more likely to look for the causes of disorder in biological factors than in learned or environmental factors and to assume a biological treatment such as medication will be most effective. In addition, the medical model does not see treatment as taking place within a relationship of equals. Instead, expertise is simply transmitted from the doctor to the patient, and little input is expected from the patient. We will see alternatives to this model in the procedures conducted by other types of therapists.

The word *psychologist* is used to describe professionals who have completed advanced degrees in psychology, including those who become psychotherapists. Most psychologists, including the professors teaching your introductory course, earn the traditional academic doctor of philosophy (PhD) degree in psychology, but not all choose career paths as licensed psychotherapists. Clinical psychology is the path taken by psychology graduate students who wish to study, teach, or practice psychotherapy. In addition to completing the academic requirements for a PhD degree, clinical psychology students must spend an additional year providing treatment in a supervised internship.

Beginning in the 1970s, an alternate route to becoming a clinical psychologist arose from suggestions that the practice of psychology could be modeled after dental and medical schools (Norcross & Castle, 2002). The doctor of psychology (PsyD) degree was developed to train students to provide services without undergoing the extensive training in research methods that characterizes the PhD degree.

Both PhD and PsyD programs can earn accreditation by the American Psychological Association (APA). PsyD programs are becoming increasingly popular with students (see ● Figure 15.4). However, the lack of emphasis on research characteristic of the PsyD degree has led to concerns about the ability of these graduates to think scientifically about their choice of methods (Baker et al., 2008). For example, without a solid background in science, objective evaluation of and adherence to the EBP model could be quite difficult. Sixty-five percent of the faculty members in institutions granting the traditional PhD degree teach scientifically supported cognitive behavioral techniques (Norcross & Castle, 2002). In contrast, only about 30% of faculty members in PsyD programs teach cognitive behavioral techniques.

How do clinical psychologists and psychiatrists differ, other than that they earn different degrees? One of the traditional distinctions has been psychiatrists' ability to prescribe medication, but that difference is gradually disappearing. In 2002, New Mexico became the first state to allow select psychologists to prescribe medication, followed by Louisiana in 2004 (Daly, 2006). The requirements for already-licensed clinical psychologists to gain prescription privileges are quite rigorous. Psychologists wishing to prescribe medication in these states must go through an additional 450 classroom hours of neuroscience study, 80 hours of clinical practicum, and 400 physician-supervised hours of care with at least 100 patients.

In addition to treating people with diagnosed psychological disorders, clinical psychologists often provide marriage and family counseling, substance abuse counseling, vocational

Benjamin Rush (1749–1813), "the father of American psychiatry," believed that psychological disorders were caused by the "irritation" of the blood vessels in the brain. He invented the tranquilizer chair for patients and wrote a textbook published in 1812, *Medical Inquiries and Observations Upon Diseases of the Mind,* that was the standard in the field for the next 50 years.

psychotherapist A licensed professional who provides psychotherapy.
psychiatrist A medical doctor who specializes in psychiatry and can use medical procedures, such as the prescribing of medication, to treat psychological disorders.

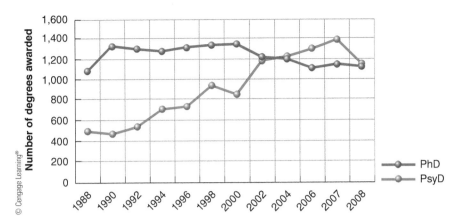

FIGURE 15.4

PsyD Degrees Are Becoming More Common.
While PhD degrees awarded in psychology have
remained fairly constant, the number of PsyD
degrees has grown dramatically since 1988. There
are now approximately equal numbers of clinical
PhD and PsyD degrees awarded each year. *Source:*
Hart and Pate, 2011.

counseling, grief counseling, rehabilitation counseling, and prison counseling. However, these
types of service are also provided by counselors, who typically do not provide services for
psychological disorders such as schizophrenia. In other words, a couple experiencing marital
conflict might seek either a counselor or a clinical psychologist, whereas a person experiencing hallucinations and delusions is more likely to be treated by a clinical psychologist or a
psychiatrist. Counselors hold master's or doctoral degrees in psychology and related fields,
such as education and social work.

Students pursuing undergraduate psychology degrees frequently ask whether they can do
anything in the mental health field without a graduate degree. About one third of undergraduates in psychology obtain jobs that are closely related to the field (see ● Figure 15.5). Students
completing an undergraduate degree in psychology often work in group homes and camps for
troubled youth or in hospital or outpatient settings under supervision. Many others seek work
in "people"-related professions, including human resources, sales, and teaching (see Chapter 1).

In recognition of the historical role of religious leaders in providing counseling to members of their congregations, most states allow religious leaders to provide this service without
further licensure. The master of divinity (MDiv) degree typically includes human development and counseling courses taught within schools of divinity. In a fairly new development,
some universities are offering MDiv degrees that prepare students to be either religious leaders
or licensed counselors in the outside community.

Among the least frequently regulated practitioners are hypnotherapists. Only two states
(Florida and Texas) require that a person using hypnotherapy be a licensed psychotherapist.
Three states (Indiana, New Mexico, and Washington) insist that hypnotherapists register with
the state. As we mentioned in Chapter 6, there are many legitimate uses of hypnosis in therapy,
and there are many legitimate therapists who use the technique. We also recounted the adventures of Zoe D. Katze, who is a hypnotherapist certified by the National Guild of Hypnotists,
the American Board of Hypnotherapy, and the International Medical and Dental Hypnotherapy Association. She is a professional member of the American Association of Professional Hypnotherapists. Zoe also happens to be a cat, owned by a real psychotherapist named
Steve Eichel (Eichel, 2002).

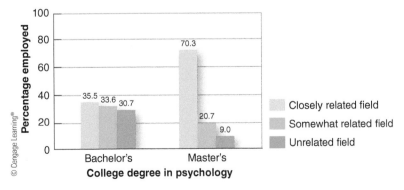

FIGURE 15.5

**Job Opportunities for Workers With Bachelor's or
Master's Degrees in Psychology.** More workers with
master's degrees in psychology are employed in degree-
relevant fields than are workers with bachelor's degrees.
Closely related fields include substance abuse counselor and
applied behavior analysis therapist. Somewhat related fields
include human resources administrator and nonprofit
organization program coordinator. *Source:* Salazar and
Frincke, 2005

HOW DO PSYCHOLOGISTS PROVIDE THERAPY?   **585**

Donald Asher writes and speaks about career hunting, college applications, and resume building, topics often presented by life coaches. Although unlicensed, coaches also do many of the same tasks as psychotherapists and counselors. Licensed psychotherapists have found that referring to themselves as *coaches* rather than *therapists* reduces some of the stigma their clients might feel in using their services.

Another unregulated area in the provision of psychological services is the field of life coaching, which requires no licensing. According to the International Coach Federation (n.d., para. 5), "Professional coaching focuses on setting goals, creating outcomes and managing personal change." Substitute *psychotherapy* for *coaching* in this definition, and few would disagree with the resulting statements. Coaches seem to perform the same duties as psychotherapists and counselors. Some psychotherapists have found that referring to themselves as *coaches* expands their practices, possibly because of the lower stigma of seeing a coach rather than a therapist in the minds of some clients. Few studies have attempted to evaluate the effectiveness of coaching, but those that have done so note that clients are satisfied with the services (Grant, 2003) and experience improved coping and self-regulation (Theeboom, Beersma, & van Vianen, 2014). Life coaching provides the advantage of being more appealing to men, who generally seek more traditional psychotherapy in much smaller numbers than do women (McKelley & Rochlen, 2007).

Although licensure provides significant protection for the public, any consumer of psychological services must thoroughly investigate prospective psychotherapists. Zoe D. Katze may be an extreme example, but we suspect she is not alone. Credentials are not always what they seem. For example, the author of the 1992 best seller *Men Are From Mars, Women Are From Venus,* lists himself as "John Gray, PhD" (MarsVenus.com, 2007). Gray's resume includes 9 years as a monk under the leadership of Beatles' guru Maharishi Mahesh Yogi, a bachelor's and a master's degree in the Science of Creative Intelligence from the Maharishi European Research Institute in Switzerland, and a PhD degree from the now-defunct Columbia Pacific University in California, which was described by the state government as a "diploma mill."

So far, we have focused our discussion on credentialing practices in the United States. Worldwide, an even greater variety of professionals perform psychotherapy and counseling under diverse licensure and oversight practices. The United Kingdom, Australia, and Canada provide systems that are similar to those in the United States for delivering psychotherapy (Priebe, 2006). In these countries, psychotherapy is conducted by a number of professionals, including physicians, psychologists, social workers, nurses, and others in similar professions. In each case, performing psychotherapy requires training beyond that needed to simply obtain the appropriate professional degree. Some European countries are more restrictive. Germany and Russia are particularly strict in their accreditation rules. Because of the prevalence of state-run health systems in Europe, assessments of treatment outcomes are regularly conducted (Priebe, 2006). In the United States, treatment outcomes are a question of interest to academic researchers but are rarely assessed as comprehensively as in many other nations, although that circumstance is likely to change with further government involvement in health care.

Delivering Psychotherapy

Many people imagining a session of psychotherapy think of a stereotypical Freudian scenario. The patient reclines on a couch, while a bearded man sitting in a chair scribbles copious notes. Although some therapy continues to take place using such a setting, many more options are available.

Celebrity psychologists like "Dr. Phil" McGraw are often criticized by the profession for offering overly simple versions of psychological advice to the public.

Variations in Length of Treatment Most psychotherapy occurs in the form of individual therapy, involving face-to-face, hourlong meetings between the therapist and the patient or client (as we will see in a subsequent section, terminology varies among practitioners). In traditional psychoanalysis, such meetings are quite frequent (4 to 5 times per week) and take place over the course of years. In CBT, described in detail in a later section, sessions might occur once per week for about 6 weeks. Given the approximate rates of up to $150 per hour for individual therapy, insurance providers are pressuring psychotherapists to find faster, more efficient ways to provide treatment. Many insurance plans limit psychotherapy sessions to 10 per calendar year.

Brief therapy, advocated by Milton Erickson and others, specifically avoids spending long periods searching for the historical basis of a person's problems. Instead, therapists using this approach focus on "solution-building rather than problem-solving" (Iveson, 2002, p. 149). Consequently, practitioners argue that only three to five sessions are necessary. Many brief therapy interventions involve only one session, and no cases require more than eight.

Alternatives to Individual Therapy In addition to individual sessions, psychotherapy can take place with groups of patients or clients in **group therapy**.

Group therapy does not imply particular types of treatment approaches. Although some treatment approaches seem better suited for group work than others, therapists of all persuasions are known to use groups in their work. The groups formed by the therapist can be homogeneous, in the sense that the group members share a common problem, or heterogeneous, in which the group members have diverse diagnoses. In most cases, groups are limited to between 6 and 12 individuals. People with severe conditions, such as psychotic, suicidal, or antisocial tendencies, are usually excluded from groups until they progress sufficiently to act as good group members.

Although many groups are organized and supervised by a licensed psychotherapist, leaderless self-help groups are also quite popular. Weight Watchers, Alcoholics Anonymous (AA), and other groups modeled after AA have become popular sources of support and self-improvement. These groups often operate with a member–leader who is not a psychotherapist, and they function outside the realm of government licensure and supervision.

In addition to the obvious cost-effectiveness of having a group split the therapist's fee, group therapy offers a number of other advantages (Yalom, 1995). For example, group therapy offers hope to members, who benefit from seeing others who have made more progress with their condition. Group members also benefit from knowing that others share their condition, decreasing their sense of isolation. Although practitioners generally believe that group therapy

Many people thinking about psychotherapy imagine a bearded man scribbling notes next to a client reclining on a couch, but this stereotype is usually far from the truth.

People participating in group therapy benefit from reduced feelings of isolation. Seeing the progress of others with the same condition raises hope and provides opportunities to model successful strategies.

brief therapy Psychotherapy provided in a short time frame, usually between three and five sessions.
group therapy Psychotherapy conducted with a group of people rather than individually.

Family therapy combines individual sessions with sessions that include some combination of family members, like these parents and their young daughter.

family therapy A type of therapy in which family members participate individually and in combination with other family members.

couples therapy A type of family therapy that focuses on intimate relationships.

The benefits of privacy, engaging in therapy from home, frequent 24-7 coverage, video interactions using Skype or similar technologies, and the ability to choose a suitable therapist regardless of location provide significant advantages for some clients. Online delivery of cognitive behavioral therapy has been shown to be as effective as face-to-face delivery (Ruwaard et al., 2011).

is effective, research on group therapy outcomes is difficult to conduct because of the large number of variables that must be considered. The need to control for such factors as different disorders and previous treatment history make this area challenging for researchers.

Family therapy, in which various family members participate in therapy individually and in combination with other family members, is another alternative to the purely individual provision of treatment. **Couples therapy** is a type of family therapy that focuses on intimate relationships. Family therapy is frequently used when a child or teen is experiencing problems, because these problems typically affect and are affected by the behavior of other family members. Family therapists face a number of significant challenges. In some cases, the member who seems to need treatment the most refuses to participate. In others, maintaining the confidentiality of all participants can be difficult. Teens might disclose information that will help the parents do their job better, but sharing this information with the parents could interrupt the trust the therapist has built up with the teen.

Innovative Delivery Systems An emerging delivery system for psychotherapy is online therapy. When "online therapy" is used as a Google search term, more than 416,000 results are returned. The benefits of privacy, engaging in therapy from home, and the ability to choose a suitable therapist regardless of location provide significant advantages for some clients. In its early days, online therapy was conducted through e-mail or chat services. Because the written word conveys less information than a therapist obtains face to face, this method could be viewed as less desirable. However, many online therapists have taken advantage of Skype and other voice and video technologies. Online delivery of CBT has been shown to be as effective as face-to-face CBT (Herbst et al., 2014; Ruwaard, Lange, Schrieken, & Emmelkamp, 2011; Sethi, 2013).

Other technologies have influenced the delivery of psychotherapy. Therapists can buy products such as Wiley's TheraScribe, a computer program that includes more than 2,500 prewritten interventions, goals, objectives, and suggested diagnoses. The program generates reports catering to Medicare and other managed care organizations. The time savings provided by these technologies can be useful in controlling costs, but receiving a prewritten evaluation might seem somewhat impersonal to individuals seeking therapy. If you receive a treatment plan from your campus health center that is nearly identical to a friend's, you might not feel the counselor cared about you.

Contemporary Challenges in Treatment

Providing treatment for psychological disorders has changed dramatically since the days of Freud. Originally, therapy was provided by individual professionals in small private practices.

In the latter part of the 20th century, however, this model became increasingly rare as psychological treatments became more likely to be managed by large organizations, including insurance companies. Many of the concerns about these new models of managed psychological treatment echo complaints from the medical community regarding contemporary medical treatment. Decisions formerly made by the therapist about the types of disorders that warranted treatment and the length, frequency, and type of treatment to be offered are now more likely to be made by insurance company personnel without medical or psychological training (Baker, McFall, & Shoham, 2008).

In addition to the need to adapt to the managed care of psychological disorders, psychotherapy faces many of the same challenges as medicine in providing scientifically valid treatments. Just as we would expect our physician to provide a scientifically supported treatment for cancer, we should expect a psychotherapist to provide equally well-documented treatments for depression. In our earlier section on EBP, we joined most research clinical psychologists and psychiatrists in endorsing the use of science in selecting, implementing, and evaluating psychological treatments. However, as we saw in our discussion of the Rorschach Inkblot Test in Chapter 12, a lack of scientific support does not always prevent an approach from being widely used.

Frustration over the lack of emphasis on science in psychotherapy has led to considerable debate. The APA has the primary responsibility for accrediting programs that train clinical psychologists with either PhD or PsyD degrees. This system has been challenged by a new accreditation body, the Psychological Clinical Science Accreditation System (PCSAS, 2011), which specifically aims to increase the scientific basis of clinical treatment and research literacy among clinical psychologists. The program has accredited 24 programs, with several more under review (PCSAS, 2014). Time will tell whether PCSAS will be able to nudge the clinical psychology community into a greater reliance on research-based methods.

Summary 15.1 **The Psychotherapists**

Title	Degrees	Specialties
Psychiatrist	Medical doctor (MD)	• Treats psychological disorders • Prescribes medication
Clinical psychologist	Doctor of philosophy (PhD) or doctor of psychology (PsyD)	• Treats psychological disorders and problems with adjustment • If specially licensed, prescribes medication
Counselor	PhD, PsyD, doctor of education (EdD), or various master's degrees	• Specializes in problems with adjustment

Credits: Top Row. Stock Montage/Getty Images. Second Row. Frank Pedrick/The Image Works. Bottom Row: Michael Rougier/Time & Life Pictures/Contributor/Getty Images.

Historical Approaches to Psychotherapy

Because Freud is typically credited with being the first person to use "talking therapy" in his efforts to improve his patients' psychological symptoms, we begin our discussion of specific treatment approaches with **psychoanalysis**. A psychotherapist who uses psychoanalysis is typically known as a psychoanalyst. Psychoanalysis has not fared well in scientific studies of its effectiveness, although supporters continue to argue in its favor (Leichsenring, 2005; Lichtenberg, Lachmann, & Fosshage, 2013). The absence of strong evidence for its efficacy has led to a decline in its use. However, psychoanalysis served as an important step to contemporary treatments.

Freud's study featured not only the famous couch but also Persian rugs and a sample of Freud's collection of antiquities.

Freud called his slips "faulty actions." For example, a man texting his partner "I wish you were her" instead of "I wish you were here" would have a great deal of explaining to do. Modern cognitive psychologists are more likely to blame slips on conflicts between grammar sequences than between the unconscious and the conscious minds.

psychoanalysis The treatment approach developed by Freud and practiced by those who believe psychodynamic theories.
insight therapy A therapy that improves symptoms of psychological disorder by building the people's understanding of their situation.
free association The psychoanalytic technique of encouraging a patient to say whatever comes to mind without attempting to censor the content.

Psychoanalysis

Freud's approach to psychotherapy reflected several key themes from his theory of personality (see Chapter 12). In particular, Freud emphasized the importance of conflict among the self (ego), the aggressive energy of the id, and the restrictions supplied by society (superego). Freud's view of the ability of the unconscious mind to affect behavior is also central to his therapeutic approach. Because of Freud's training as a physician, the psychoanalysts take a directive role, which means that they are in charge of the session. Like your physician, the psychoanalyst does not expect contributions from you other than information about your symptoms.

Freud's psychoanalysis is a classic example of an **insight therapy**. Insight therapies assume that people will improve once they understand their problems. For Freud, many psychological disorders arose from problems that resided in the unconscious mind, out of conscious awareness. Although the person might not be consciously aware of these continuing conflicts, the conflicts exert their influence on behavior and through dreams. For example, a patient might arrive at the therapist's office complaining about her inability to enjoy a satisfactory sex life with a beloved spouse. Although many factors could contribute to such problems, the psychoanalyst is likely to suspect the influence of some traumatic experience that is relatively unavailable to the patient's conscious thoughts. Perhaps the patient is the victim of childhood sexual abuse, or she might be experiencing a conflict between the ultrastrict morality she learned from her parents and her current desire to have a fulfilling relationship with her partner. For the psychoanalyst, the "cure" lies in uncovering the unconscious contributions to the patient's problems. Once she understands the source of her problems (the insight), her situation should improve.

How does one go about uncovering unconscious material? Although Freud experimented with the use of hypnosis to access the unconscious mind, he became dissatisfied with the results and abandoned the procedure. Instead, Freud decided to use the technique of **free association**. Free association occurs when a person says whatever comes to mind. As we mature, most of us become aware that we do not literally "speak our mind" out of consideration for our fellow humans. Although small children might tell a person, "You're fat," such comments, although they may be true, are not the type that most adults consider polite. We learn to think before we speak. To engage in free association, this self-censor must be turned off, allowing the patient to verbalize those thoughts that are typically withheld. Without the self-censor, the famous "Freudian slips" might occur and are assumed to reflect unconscious wishes.

Not all psychoanalysts engage in dream analysis, but it is likely that therapists interested in dream analysis are psychoanalysts. For Freud, dreaming represented a censored reflection of unconscious wishes and, therefore, a potential source of useful insight into the unconscious mind. If patients are undergoing dream analysis, they are taught to awaken following a dream to jot some notes that can later be reviewed with the therapist, who will attempt to interpret the dream's symbolic meanings.

In addition to reviewing the content of free association, dreams, and Freudian slips, the analyst looks for signs of transference and resistance. **Transference** occurs when a patient uses an earlier relationship, usually with a parent or other authority figure, as a prototype for a current relationship, such as that between the patient and the therapist. If the patient begins yelling at the therapist, the therapist might infer that the patient reacted similarly to parents and others in authority under similar circumstances in the past. **Resistance** occurs when the patient is getting closer to insight. Freud believed that we have unconscious wishes to maintain infantile fantasies and avoid punishment and that efforts to uncover this material will be resisted by the patient. Resistance, for the psychoanalyst, can be expressed in many forms. When a patient changes the subject, disagrees with the analyst's interpretation, or even misses an appointment because of a flat tire, the analyst might suspect the patient is getting closer to the uncomfortable truth.

In recent years, psychoanalysis has changed in the length and frequency of treatment. Driven by demands from insurance providers, psychoanalysts have developed new, briefer treatments. These briefer approaches tend to be less past oriented as well. In other words, the psychoanalyst might ask a person about recent experiences at work rather than about experiences as a toddler.

Does psychoanalysis work? Some published meta-analyses suggest that psychoanalysis produces better results than no treatment and occasionally produces results comparable to more modern approaches to therapy (Leichsenring & Rabung, 2008; Shedler, 2010). However, these studies have been criticized on the basis of their methods, such as including Rorschach Inkblot results as measures of patient improvement (McKay, 2011).

Humanistic Therapies

As we mentioned in Chapter 12, humanistic approaches developed in direct opposition to the theories and techniques of Freud and his followers. Where Freud believed that humans are inherently selfish and aggressive, the humanistic psychologists believed that humans are inherently good, possessing natural drives to grow and improve. Society for Freud had a beneficial effect on behavior by providing controls on our selfish and aggressive tendencies. For the humanistic psychologists, society can interfere with growth by providing judgmental feedback.

Not too surprisingly, this conflict in theory led to an equal opposition in treatment approaches. As we mentioned previously, the psychoanalyst takes a powerful, directive role reminiscent of an MD. The individual seeking therapy is identified as a patient. As in the medical setting, the therapist identifies the nature of the patient's problems and prescribes a course of action. Other than supplying information, the patient has a relatively passive role in the process. In contrast, the humanistic therapist is nondirective and treats the person seeking therapy, called a client instead of a patient, as more of an equal in the process. Clients are expected to take an active role in helping to identify their problems and a positive course of action.

Primary among the humanistic approaches to treatment is the **person-centered therapy** of Carl Rogers (1942). In place of the psychoanalytic goal of uncovering unconscious sources of problems, person-centered therapy aims to achieve congruence, which we discussed in Chapter 12. For Rogers, discrepancies between the ideal and the real selves, such as when we fail to live up to our ideals, can lead to psychological disorders. Therapy techniques that bring the selves into alignment should effectively treat the disorders.

Among the techniques used to achieve this congruence are empathy, unconditional positive regard, and the reflection and clarification of feelings. Empathic therapists attempt to see the world through the eyes of the client, as opposed to imposing their worldview. Allowing the client to feel understood in this manner contributes to the establishment of a safe, supportive environment where natural growth can occur. Unconditional positive regard, discussed in Chapter 12, also contributes to the safety of the therapeutic setting.

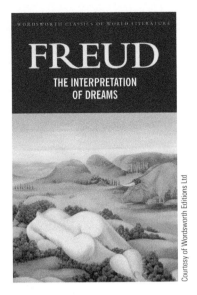

The Interpretation of Dreams by Sigmund Freud was originally published in German in 1900. The 600 copies of the first edition sold slowly, and the publisher did not issue a second edition until 1909. Nonetheless, this book is considered one of Freud's most influential.

transference A psychoanalytic technique in which the therapist uses the responses of the patient to the therapist to understand the patient's approach to authority figures in general.
resistance A psychoanalytic technique in which the patient's reluctance to accept the interpretations of the therapist indicate that the interpretations are correct.
person-centered therapy A humanistic therapy approach developed by Carl Rogers to help clients achieve congruence.

Although we think that dressing and sitting like your client is not necessary to demonstrate empathy, attempting to see situations through the client's eyes is an important part of humanistic therapies.

Reflecting feelings takes practice to avoid sounding silly or reverting to the cliché "I hear what you're saying," but you might give it a try the next time someone confronts you. Reflecting the other person's feelings instead of focusing on your own helps you stay calm, and it's hard to carry on a one-sided argument with a calm person.

According to the humanistic psychologists, people who learn they have value only when their behavior is pleasing to authority figures can benefit from a therapy setting that features unconditional positive regard.

Rogers believed that much human unhappiness resulted from conditional regard, in which children learn they have value only when their behavior is pleasing to an authority figure. The nonjudgmental, unconditional positive regard of the therapy setting is designed to compensate for those earlier, potentially damaging experiences.

Reflection techniques consist of the therapist restating some of the client's comments in a way that conveys understanding. As such, reflection contributes to empathy and the client's sense of being fully understood. For example, a client might state that he felt helpless when his boss reprimanded him for losing an important account. The therapist might simply comment, "You sound like you were very angry and frustrated when your boss yelled at you." Clarification allows the therapist to point out important insights the client might have reached. The therapist might clarify the situation with the boss by pointing out its similarities with the feelings we have as children when we are corrected by an adult.

Even when psychotherapists use therapy techniques other than a person-centered approach, they frequently incorporate some or all of Rogers's communication strategies, such as reflection. These strategies have also become quite popular in programs designed to improve interpersonal communication and group process. For example, it is not uncommon for teens to stomp into the house and declare that they "hate" their parents. The typical response of the parent at that point is to become hurt and angry. The argument escalates as the parent retaliates with a hurtful statement, perhaps "I wish you were never born!" Rogers suggests that such immature battles are easily avoided. Instead of retaliating, the parent might say, "I know it makes you very angry when I restrict your privileges, but we had a deal, you broke it, and that means there will be consequences." Reflecting another's emotions in this way may increase the chances of defusing needless hostility and of coming to a mutual understanding, because people will know more concretely that they are "being heard."

Like psychoanalysis, humanistic approaches to therapy work better in some instances than in others. Rogers referred to his approach as counseling, and his techniques are probably better suited to problems of adjustment than cases of serious disorders, such as schizophrenia. Efforts to assess the outcomes of humanistic therapy scientifically have been rejected by its followers. For example, one group of proponents argued that "natural science methodology should not be privileged over human science methodology" (Bohart, O'Hara, & Leitner, 1998, p. 141). By now, you probably understand that we would reject this suggestion and argue instead that science is science, regardless of the phenomenon being examined.

Contemporary Approaches to Psychotherapy

Although a small minority of psychotherapists continue to use Freudian or humanistic approaches, most contemporary therapists use other methods.

Behavioral Therapies

Freud's psychodynamic theory, humanistic theory, and behaviorism were among the most dominant influences in psychology during the 20th century. We have seen how psychodynamic and humanistic theories were applied to psychotherapy in the form of psychoanalysis and Rogers's person-centered therapy, so it should come as no surprise to find that behaviorism has similar applications. Given our formal definition of learning as "a relatively permanent change in behavior or the capacity for behavior due to experience," it seems logical to use learning as a way to increase the frequency of desirable behaviors and decrease unwanted behaviors in the therapy setting.

Behavior therapies represent applications of classical and operant conditioning to problems of adjustment and psychological disorders. These techniques have proved helpful in both reducing unwanted behaviors and increasing the frequency of desirable behaviors over a range of psychological conditions, including autism spectrum disorder and schizophrenia. The first book to use the term *behavior modification* in its title was Leonard Ullman and Leonard Krasner's *Case Studies in Behavior Modification,* published in 1965. The public initially distrusted behavioral treatment methods, because they were based on animal research and assumed human behavior was relatively simple. The mysticism of the psychoanalysts' unconscious drives and impulses seemed far more romantic. However, when behavior modification produced successful results in cases that were previously considered untreatable, such as in autism spectrum disorder, respect for the approach grew.

Like behaviorism in general, behavior modification, now known as applied behavior analysis (ABA), focuses on what can be observed and makes few assumptions about such unseen factors as an unconscious mind. We can contrast the way Freud and a therapist using ABA might approach Freud's case of Little Hans, a 5-year-old boy who had a phobia of horses (Freud, 1909/1976). For Freud, Hans's phobia resulted from the Oedipus complex issues that were supposedly at their height at his age. Horses, Freud argued, symbolized Hans's father. The boy had noted that he was especially frightened of horses with black bits in their mouths, which Freud suggested represented the father's moustache. Freud concluded that Hans's fear of horses resulted from his unconscious fear of retaliation by the father for sexual fantasies about his mother and would disappear with the resolution of Hans's Oedipus complex.

Now it is the behaviorist's turn. According to classical conditioning theory, phobias can result from conditioned fears. In Hans's day, horses were the most frequently used means of transportation, especially in large cities. Accidents involving horses were frequent and quite serious. Hans related that he was frightened of horses falling, and with good reason, because it is likely that viewing such accidents would be quite traumatic. Horses could become classically conditioned fear stimuli through their association with accidents and the resulting fear. To reduce the fear, Hans could be gradually exposed to horses in a safe environment (desensitization), rewarded for approaching horses (counterconditioning), or allowed to play with a group of children interacting with a horse (peer modeling). It is not necessary to know why Hans fears the horses to successfully apply behavioral treatment.

ABA has been used frequently to reduce unwanted habits. For example, let us suppose that Jennifer would like to stop smoking. The behavior therapist begins by evaluating Jennifer's current behavior by observing the circumstances in which she smokes. Based on these observations, the therapist might note that Jennifer rarely smokes alone. Instead, her smoking is quite social. If she is at a party or with friends who are smoking, she smokes. The therapist also takes notes of reinforcers or punishers that might be influencing the behavior. Perhaps Jennifer's friends praise her when she smokes but her parents get angry when they notice

Bettmann/Corbis

The subject of Freud's famous case study of "Little Hans" was actually named Herbert Graf. Graf grew up to be a successful opera producer at New York's Metropolitan Opera and the Salzburg Festival in Austria. He is shown here directing the great Marion Anderson as she rehearses for her operatic debut in Giuseppe Verdi's *Masked Ball* in 1954.

behavior therapy Applications of classical and operant conditioning principles to the treatment of symptoms of psychological disorder and adjustment problems.

Behavioral treatments for phobias have been improved with the development of virtual reality for exposing clients to fear-producing stimuli. Researchers at the University of Washington have developed SpiderWorld and successfully demonstrated that participants could reduce their fear of real spiders after undergoing three treatment sessions.

Behavior therapies have helped many people change negative habits.

evidence of her smoking. Jennifer's dentist might warn her about the poor state of her oral hygiene.

Based on these observations, the behavior therapist might attempt a number of techniques that will separate Jennifer from high-risk situations for smoking. Jennifer might be encouraged either to gain the support of her friends for her efforts to quit smoking or to spend more time with her nonsmoking friends. Jennifer's parents might be willing to provide some incentives for her to quit smoking. She could set aside the money she normally spends on cigarettes for some special treat. Counterconditioning in the form of asking Jennifer to smoke until she feels sick is an unpleasant but effective strategy (Lichtenstein, Harris, Birchler, Wahl, & Schmahl, 1973).

The effectiveness of behavior therapies is not restricted to changing negative habits such as tobacco use. As we discussed in Chapter 8, token economies, in which reward tokens are later exchanged for preferred rewards, have been shown to increase the frequency of desirable behaviors across a variety of settings, including classrooms, prisons, and institutions (Barkley, 2002; Glynn, 1990).

Cognitive Therapies

As the name implies, cognitive therapies are based on the notion that the way we think about our circumstances is essential to our health and adjustment. According to this view, situations do not cause abnormal behavior, but the way we think about situations might do so.

One of the earliest versions of cognitive therapy was developed beginning in the 1940s by Aaron Beck. According to Beck (1975), people run into psychological trouble when they adopt irrational, self-defeating ways of thinking. For example, it is unrealistic to think that other people will always treat you fairly and kindly or that you must be perfect to be loved. An important aspect of the therapy process occurs when the therapist attempts to change the irrational beliefs of the client. For example, let's assume a therapist is trying to help a group of students who suffer from test anxiety. Each student has an irrational belief that he or she is going to flunk out of school, despite having an adequate grade point average. To help the students realize that this belief is irrational, the therapist might ask each student to provide evidence of the likelihood of flunking out or to identify the worst possible outcome of giving up the belief. Faced with logic, each student begins to substitute a new, rational belief for the old, irrational belief. This substitution of rational for irrational beliefs is termed **cognitive restructuring**.

cognitive restructuring A technique used in cognitive therapies in which new, rational beliefs replace earlier, irrational beliefs held by the client.

A variation of cognitive therapy emerged out of work by Albert Ellis, beginning in the 1950s. Ellis's version of cognitive therapy is known as rational emotive behavioral therapy (REBT; Ellis, 1975). Compared to many other types of psychotherapy, REBT is somewhat confrontational, because the therapist is more openly critical of a client's thinking. Ellis retained the need to produce cognitive restructuring but deemphasized the supportive role of the therapist.

As cognitive therapy expanded further, therapists began to use the term **cognitive behavioral therapy (CBT)**. In addition to promoting cognitive restructuring, therapists wanted to help clients initiate behavioral changes. For example, a person with major depressive disorder, described in Chapter 14, can have irrational beliefs about hopelessness and worthlessness coupled with behavior that is counterproductive to good mood, such as staying at home in bed watching television. Not only can the irrational beliefs be addressed by CBT, but behavioral methods can be used to encourage the client to take a brisk walk and to provide self-rewards for using more positive, rational patterns of thought (see ● Figure 15.6).

CBT has an excellent record of success, particularly in the treatment of major depressive disorder (Roth & Fonagy, 1996; Westbrook & Kirk, 2005). Because CBT typically requires fewer than 16 sessions and can be used for a variety of conditions, it is a favorite among insurance providers.

Biopsychosocial Approaches

Patient characteristics, the type of problems being addressed, and other variables influence the success of any particular treatment. Consequently, many therapists use the **biopsychosocial approach**, which combines elements of therapies designed to address the biological, psychological, and social underpinnings of an individual case. The therapist focuses on what works for an individual client, without adopting a single theoretical orientation (Lazarus, 2005). For example, a therapist might find that relaxation training seems to help one client while role-playing is more effective with another.

CLEM MURRAY/MCT/Landov

Aaron Beck (1921–), shown here addressing a workshop at the Beck Institute, developed one of the earliest types of cognitive therapies. Beck's approach featured cognitive restructuring, in which irrational beliefs, such as "everyone must love me or I can't be happy," are replaced with more rational beliefs, such as "I can be happy because I have some people who love me."

FIGURE 15.6

Cognitive Behavioral Therapy (CBT) Produces Clear, Long-Lasting Improvements in Many Conditions. The use of CBT is best understood in the treatment of major depressive disorder, but CBT can improve many conditions, including insomnia. In this experiment, CBT produced improvements in the amount of time needed to get to sleep (sleep onset latency), the amount of wakeful time after the onset of sleep, and total sleep time. *Source:* Adapted from "Nonpharmacological Interventions for Insomnia: A Meta-Analysis of Treatment Efficacy," by C. M. Morin, J. P. Culbert, and S. M. Schwartz, 1994, *American Journal of Psychiatry, 151*(8), pp. 1172–1180.

cognitive behavioral therapy (CBT) A combination of cognitive restructuring with behavioral treatments that has been shown to be effective in reducing symptoms of many psychological disorders.

biopsychosocial approach An integrated approach to therapy that combines treatments addressing the biological, personal, and social underpinnings of psychological disorders.

What Are Biological Therapies?

The major types of biological treatments for psychological disorders include medication, electroconvulsive therapy (ECT), psychosurgery, deep brain stimulation, and neurofeedback.

Medication

Medication is the most commonly used of the medical therapies. Particularly in the last 60 years, the discovery of medications that effectively treated psychological disorder has dramatically shaped the outcomes of millions of patients. A comprehensive review of psychoactive medications is clearly beyond the scope of this text, but we will discuss the use of medication for some specific disorders later in this chapter.

A patient is shown being prepared for electroconvulsive therapy (ECT) for serious depression. The patient is anesthetized before electricity is applied through electrodes to the head, inducing seizures. ECT is believed to increase responsiveness to dopamine and norepinephrine and to stimulate neural growth.

Electroconvulsive Therapy

Electroconvulsive therapy (ECT) is used in some severe cases of depression that do not respond to other treatments. In ECT, the patient is anesthetized and given a muscle relaxant before the induction of general seizures, which are produced by electricity applied through electrodes on the head. Between 6 and 12 treatments, at a rate of 3 treatments per week, are typically given.

Ladislas Meduna (1896–1964) recommended ECT for patients with schizophrenia after observing that people who had epilepsy had unusually high numbers of glia and people with schizophrenia had low numbers of glia (Kalinowsky, 1986). ECT was first used with patients with schizophrenia in the 1930s, with poor results. However, observations of improved mood in these patients following ECT led to further use with patients diagnosed with major depressive or bipolar disorder. This procedure is used primarily with patients who do not respond to conventional treatments with medication (Medda, Perugi, Zanello, Ciuffa, & Cassano, 2009). Although the exact mode of action of ECT is unknown, most patients experience an increase in responsiveness to dopamine and norepinephrine, along with the desired reduction in subjective feelings of depression.

Although many people have a negative view of ECT, perhaps as a result of reading Ken Kesey's *One Flew Over the Cuckoo's Nest* or viewing the film or play of the same name, ECT is considered as safe as any minor surgery conducted under general anesthesia (American Psychiatric Association [APA], 2001). However, approximately one third of patients experience persistent memory loss following the procedure (Rose, Fleischmann, Wykes, Leese, & Bindman, 2003). This memory loss specifically affects autobiographical memory, discussed in Chapter 9, which can be impaired for at least 6 months following treatment (Sackheim et al., 2007).

Psychosurgery

As we observed in Chapter 1, trepanation, or the drilling of holes in the skull by ancient people, might represent the first effort to use psychosurgery. Although particular functions might be localized to parts of the brain, it is a giant leap of faith from our current understanding of localization and brain networking to the idea that someone can use **psychosurgery** to treat psychological disorders.

Historically, one of the most frequent types of psychosurgery aimed at changing behavior was the frontal lobotomy, which we discussed in Chapter 4. After hearing about the calm that resulted following the procedure in chimpanzees, Egas Moniz encouraged his colleagues to try the procedure on psychotic patients in the 1930s (Valenstein, 1986). Walter Freeman popularized the procedure in the United States, traveling in a vehicle he called his lobotomobile. Be-

electroconvulsive therapy (ECT) A biological treatment in which seizures are induced in an anesthetized patient; it is used primarily in the treatment of mood disorders that have not responded to medication or other treatments.

psychosurgery The attempt to improve symptoms of psychological disorders through the use of brain surgery.

tween 40,000 and 50,000 patients received the procedure between the 1930s and the 1950s, sometimes for vague problems such as depression in housewives or misbehavior in children (Sabatini, 1997). John Fulton, whose research with chimpanzees had formed the basis for Freeman's operation, was horrified. "What are these terrible things I hear about you doing lobotomies in your office with an ice pick?" he asked Freeman. "Why not use a shotgun?" (Kopell, Machado, & Rezai, 2005, p. 192).

As we have emphasized in several contexts in this textbook, the frontal lobes participate in some of the highest order cognitive functions carried out by the human brain. Consequently, the deliberate damage to the frontal lobes and their connections to other parts of the brain involved with the lobotomy procedure has harmful effects on a person's judgment, personality, initiative, social behavior, and sense of self. Despite the outrage among many in the medical community, frontal lobotomies were performed well into the 1960s, until the use of medications for psychological disorders became an established practice (Sabatini, 1997). Radiation and precise lesions are still used today to treat small numbers of people with depression or OCD (Kopell et al., 2005).

Brain Stimulation

Brain stimulation has a number of advantages over psychosurgery. Most importantly, most of the effects are reversible. In contrast, once the brain has been damaged by psychosurgery, there is no going back.

Following observations of mood changes in people undergoing **deep brain stimulation** through surgically implanted electrodes for the relief of Parkinson's disease, physicians attempted to use stimulation to address OCD and depression. Microelectrodes are surgically inserted into specific parts of the brain, and in many cases, the patient controls the application of any current (Mayberg et al., 2005). Fifty percent of patients with severe depression who had not responded to more conventional treatments achieved improvements in mood following stimulation of the nucleus accumbens (Bewernick et al., 2010). In Chapter 4, we indicated that the nucleus accumbens was part of a circuit that processes feelings of reward. Stimulating this area improved patients' mood and led to their engagement in more pleasurable activities.

Deep brain stimulation requires surgery to implant the microelectrodes. Repeated transcranial magnetic stimulation (rTMS) provides an alternative way to stimulate the brain without surgery. When applied through a handheld device touching the scalp, low-frequency magnetic pulses change activity in underlying cortical regions. This technique has been recommended for use in depression (Speer, Wassermann, Benson, Herscovitch, & Post, 2014; see ● Figure 15.7) and some cases of schizophrenia, but it appears to have a negative effect in cases of OCD (Slotema, Blom, Hoek, & Sommer, 2010).

Trepanation has made a bizarre modern comeback in the form of an alternative medicine or elective procedure. People are doing this in their own homes, in a possible variation of the self-injurious behavior we discussed in Chapter 8. They argue that the procedure improves brain circulation and metabolism, but research support for such claims is lacking (Moskalenko et al., 2008).

Walter Freeman (1895–1972) performed more than 3,400 lobotomies at $25 per procedure, despite having no formal training in surgery. Although this procedure is considered barbaric today, Freeman enjoyed the respect of many of his colleagues, serving as cofounder and president of the American Board of Psychiatry and Neurology from 1946 to 1947. He nominated his mentor, Egas Moniz, for the Nobel Prize in Physiology and Medicine, which Moniz won in 1949.

After the successful use of deep brain stimulation for Parkinson's disease, the method was used to treat people with depression. The image on the right shows where an electrode was implanted in this woman's brain.

deep brain stimulation Electrical stimulation applied through surgically implanted electrodes that is used to treat some anxiety and mood disorders.

BSIP SA/Alamy

© Cengage Learning®

FIGURE 15.7

Effects of Repeated Transcranial Magnetic Stimulation (rTMS) on Depression. Compared to participants with depression undergoing a placebo version of rTMS (sham rTMS), participants receiving active rTMS showed significantly reduced scores on the standard Hamilton Depression Rating Scales. Participants showed rather strong placebo effects in the sham condition (note the drop in depression at week 2), which emphasizes the need for placebo-controlled studies in assessing the effectiveness of all types of treatment. *Source:* Adapted from "Efficacy and Safety of Transcranial Magnetic Stimulation in the Acute Treatment of Major Depression: A Multisite Randomized Controlled Trial," J. P. O'Reardon, H. B. Solvason, P. G. Janicak, S. Sampson, K. E. Isenberg, Z. Nahas, et al., 2007, *Biological Psychiatry, 62*(11), pp. 1208–1216, doi:10.1016/j.biopsych.2007.01.018.

Neurofeedback, a type of biofeedback training that focuses on brain activity, can be used to treat attention deficit hyperactivity disorder in children.

Dr. Lise DeLong/cognitive-connections.com

Neurofeedback

As we mentioned in Chapter 4, biofeedback training allows participants to gain some conscious control over some otherwise unattended physical functions. For example, people can be taught to overcome "white coat hypertension," or the classically conditioned spike in blood pressure that occurs when a nurse or doctor (in a lab coat) takes a measurement. By learning to relax instead of becoming tense in this situation, people can reduce their blood pressure, which is not a process we typically try to control.

Neurofeedback is a type of biofeedback that concentrates on the activity of the brain. Recordings of brain activity, usually from electroencephalography (EEG) but increasingly from functional magnetic resonance imaging (fMRI), are usually displayed for the participant, who is trained to keep readings in a desired range. In most cases, people are not consciously aware of what they are doing to comply. So far, however, rigorous double-blind, placebo-controlled studies have not indicated that this approach is effective in the treatment of attention deficit hyperactivity disorder (ADHD), which is the disorder most likely to be treated with neurofeedback (Vollebregt, van Dongen-Boomsma, Slaats-Willemse, & Buitelaar, 2014).

neurofeedback A type of biofeedback used to treat attention deficit hyperactivity disorder and seizures by teaching the client to keep measures of brain activity within a certain range.

Summary 15.2 Approaches to Treating Psychological Disorders

Type of therapy	Theoretical perspective	Defining features
Psychoanalysis	• Psychodynamic theory	• Directive therapy • Free association • Dream analysis • Analysis of resistance • Analysis of transference
Humanistic therapy	• Humanistic theory	• Nondirective therapy • Unconditional positive regard • Reflection • Empathy
Behavior therapy	• Behaviorism	• Application of classical and operant learning principles in behavior modification • Therapy based on observed behavior only
Cognitive therapy	• Cognition	• Cognitive restructuring • Combination of restructuring with behavior modification in cognitive behavioral therapy
Biological treatments	• Biology	• Medication • Electroconvulsive therapy • Psychosurgery • Brain stimulation • Neurofeedback

How Are Specific Disorders Treated?

As we have mentioned previously, approaches to treatment have differing success rates when applied to specific types of disorders. In this section, we will outline the typical approaches to the psychological disorders we discussed in Chapter 14.

Treating Neurodevelopmental Disorders

All therapy approaches discussed previously in this chapter have been applied to the treatment of children and adolescents. However, special care must be given to the use of biological therapies in childhood and adolescence, because of the possible adverse effects of these treatments on the development of the nervous system.

Treating Autism Spectrum Disorder Although autism spectrum disorder (ASD) is accompanied by abnormalities in the neurotransmitters serotonin, GABA, and glutamate, no medications have proved effective in alleviating symptoms (Pardo & Eberhart, 2007). This lack of a beneficial result does not mean that medications are not prescribed in cases of ASD. Two antipsychotic medications have been approved by the U.S. Food and Drug Administration for use in ASD and appear helpful in severe cases involving self-injury (Posey, Stigler, Erickson, & McDougle, 2008). Unfortunately, children treated with antipsychotic drugs experience the same side effects as adults, including weight gain, diabetes, motor dysfunction, and immune system problems. Antidepressants and several other types of drugs are commonly prescribed for children with ASD off-label, which means that the drugs have not been officially approved for this purpose on the basis of research demonstrating effectiveness (see ● Figure 15.8).

The most commonly used psychological treatment for ASD is ABA, which builds on the principles of operant conditioning outlined in Chapter 8 (Smith & Lovaas, 1998). ABA focuses on observable, socially important behavior such as language and should produce lasting

 Thinking Scientifically

Can Mobile Technologies Improve the Behavior of Individuals with Autism Spectrum Disorder?

PARENTS AND TEACHERS of individuals with autism spectrum disorder (ASD) are anxious to find new methods for improving academic, communication, employment, and leisure outcomes. Subjective observations might lead us to think that computers, and better yet, mobile devices like tablets and smartphones, would be perfect for this purpose. But do the results of scientific research demonstrate true benefits?

The answer, happily, appears to be "yes" (Kagohara et al., 2013). A review of 15 studies carefully selected based on the strength

of their methodology demonstrated that mobile technologies have advantages for the person with ASD. The most frequent uses of mobile technology were using the device to access preferred stimuli, such as snacks and toys, that might otherwise be difficult for individuals with language delays. In cases of severe language disability, the devices could generate speech that would allow the individual to request preferred stimuli.

Other uses included videos that teach specific academic skills, such as how to use

the spell-check function of a word processing program. Video modeling of skills can be useful given the reluctance to engage in face-to-face instruction that characterizes this disorder. Using an iPad to improve math skills produced mixed results (O'Malley, Lewis, Donehower, & Stone, 2014). However, the students using the math app were more likely to complete their work with fewer prompts on the part of the teacher.

The overall advantages of using these technologies include people's ability to ad-

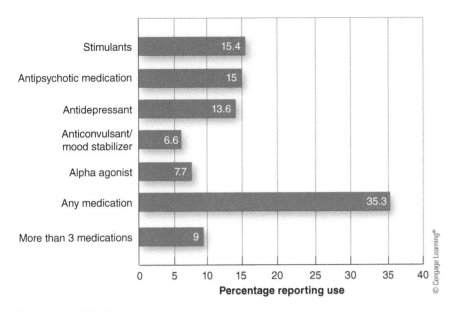

FIGURE 15.8

Medications and Autism Spectrum Disorder (ASD). Although only two medications (antipsychotic medications typically used to treat schizophrenia and bipolar disorder) have been approved by the U.S. Food and Drug Administration for use in autism spectrum disorder (ASD), large-scale studies show that many other medications are routinely prescribed by psychiatrists and neurologists for children with ASD. Alpha agonists are usually prescribed for high blood pressure and have a sedative effect. In this sample, 35.3% of the children had at least one prescription, and 9% had three or more drugs they were taking simultaneously. *Source:* Adapted from "Psychotropic Medication Use Among Children With Autism Spectrum Disorders Enrolled in a National Registry, 2007–2008," by R. Rosenberg, D. Mandell, J. Farmer, J. Law, A. Marvin, and P. Law, 2010, *Journal of Autism and Developmental Disorders, 40*(3), pp. 342–351, doi:10.1007/s10803-009-0878-1.

vance at their own pace with minimal supervision. At the same time, use of the devices should not substitute for face-to-face interaction, because this experience is essential to improvements in behavior in individuals with ASD. However, social skills themselves might be the object of mobile apps. Results of evaluations of apps specifically designed to enhance children's creative, expressive, and collaborative social activities seem encouraging, but use of apps for this purpose is in need of further study (Hourcade, Williams, Miller, Huebner, & Liang, 2013). ●

Research supports the use of tablets and other mobile technologies for improving the skills and behaviors of children with autism spectrum disorder.

improvements that generalize to settings outside the therapy setting (Baer, Wolf, & Risley, 1968). ABA in the treatment of ASD often involves therapy that takes up most of a child's waking hours, which is a large investment for families in terms of time and resources. As shown in ● Figure 15.9, although studies are complicated by the child's initial level of functioning and many other variables, meta-analyses of the outcome of intensive, early-childhood behavioral interventions show a strong positive effect of treatment on language acquisition but more moderate effects on social skills and daily functioning (Virués-Ortega, 2010).

Because of the severity and lifelong nature of ASD, parents of children with this disorder are especially vulnerable to "cures" that have little research support. Dietary interventions have become popular in recent years, but these appear to have few benefits. People with ASD show evidence of excess peptides from gluten (found in wheat) and casein (found in dairy products), but controlled studies do not demonstrate benefits from restricting these foods (Millward, Ferriter, Calver, & Connell-Jones, 2008). Treatments designed to remove heavy metals from the body are also popular but lack research support (Weber & Newmark, 2007). Even worse, at least one child died from this type of treatment because a physician substituted a toxic chemical for the correct one with a similar name (Sinha, Silove, & Williams, 2006). Among the other "treatments" that are advertised to parents are hyperbaric oxygen treatment (typically used to treat the bends in scuba divers), sensory integration treatment, massage, music, special diets, and animal-assisted therapies.

Treating Attention Deficit Hyperactivity Disorder Many children with a diagnosis of ADHD are treated with medication, either alone or in combination with behavior therapy

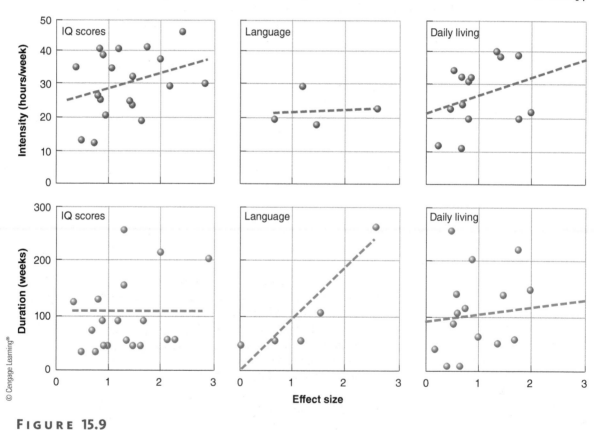

FIGURE 15.9

Outcomes for Early Behavioral Intervention in Autism Spectrum Disorder (ASD). A meta-analysis demonstrated that early behavioral intervention in autism spectrum disorder (ASD) produced measurable improvements in IQ scores, language, and daily living. High-intensity treatment (measured by hours per week) seemed to have the greatest effects on IQ, but duration of treatment seemed to have the biggest impact on language. Most clinical psychologists suggest that an effect size of 1 for a treatment means that the treatment is very effective. *Source:* Adapted from "Applied Behavior Analytic Intervention for Autism in Early Childhood: Meta-Analysis, Meta-Regression and Dose-Response Meta-Analysis of Multiple Outcomes," by J. Virués-Ortega, 2010, *Clinical Psychology Review, 30,* pp. 387–399.

(Conners et al., 2001). The use of medications for attention problems resulted from an accidental discovery. In 1937, Charles Bradley used a stimulant (benzedrine sulfate) to treat a group of children hospitalized for learning and behavior problems. He noted that during the week the children used the drug, half demonstrated "a spectacular improvement in school performance" (p. 584).

The most commonly prescribed drugs for ADHD are the closely related stimulants methylphenidate (Ritalin), dextroamphetamine (Dexedrine or Dextrostat), and a combination of amphetamine salts (Adderall). These drugs increase the activity of dopamine and norepinephrine. Most patients tolerate these medications well, but side effects of weight loss and sleep disturbance can occur. If children take the medications continuously for long periods, growth can also be suppressed. Methylphenidate does produce tolerance, and patients should stop the drug under medical supervision rather than on their own (Ross, Fischhoff, & Davenport, 2002). Although it is chemically quite similar to amphetamine, methylphenidate is not considered an addictive drug given its slower action on the brain (Volkow, Wang, Fowler, & Ding, 2005). Individuals who do not respond well to the stimulant drugs are often treated with nonstimulant drugs that increase norepinephrine activity (Prasad & Steer, 2008).

It might appear odd to treat a disorder that often features hyperactivity, or high levels of impulsive behavior, with a stimulant. Wouldn't it make more sense to try medications that have a calming effect? The rationale for stimulant treatment of ADHD suggests that impulsive hyperactivity occurs if the parts of the brain responsible for planned, thoughtful behavior, such as the basal ganglia and frontal lobes, are not active enough. Raising the activity in these areas theoretically should reduce impulsive behavior. One of the common myths about medications for ADHD, however, is that they are ineffective in people who do not have the disorder. This is not the case, and medications prescribed for ADHD are commonly abused (Arnsten, 2006).

The use of medication for ADHD in the United States is 5 times higher than in any other nation, leading to criticism of the practice (see ● Figure 15.10). However, approximately 75% to 80% of children treated with medication alone experience significant improvements on ratings of social compliance and sustained attention (Barkley, 1995). As a result of studies comparing treatment effectiveness, medication continues to be the primary choice in ADHD (Conners et al., 2001). However, these effects are short term, and research has not demonstrated long-term benefits of stimulant use on later outcomes in adolescence and adulthood (Loe & Feldman, 2007). In other words, children with ADHD treated with medication do not enjoy superior outcomes later in life compared to children with ADHD who do not receive medication.

Although medications are widely prescribed, behavioral methods for treating ADHD can be helpful. In particular, behavioral parent training, which builds the skills of parents of children with ADHD to use operant conditioning methods effectively, and behavioral classroom management, which extends classical conditioning into the school setting, are especially effective (Pelham & Fabiano, 2008). Another behavioral approach featuring peer-focused treatments in recreational settings has also shown promise (Pelham & Fabiano, 2008). Unfortunately, it is often difficult to maintain the consistency needed for successful behavioral interventions without a great deal of cooperation among teachers, parents, and others working with the child. A combination of individually tailored doses of medication and behavioral therapy had the best outcome in a large-sample study of children with ADHD (Hoza, Waschbusch, Pelham, Molina, & Milich, 2000).

Charles Bradley observed the behavior of 30 institutionalized children, who had a variety of problem behaviors, after they were administered a type of amphetamine used at the time for asthma and other breathing problems. Bradley's observations about the children's "spectacular improvement in school performance," as well as their becoming "emotionally subdued," led to the modern treatment of attention deficit hyperactivity disorder with stimulant medication, including other types of amphetamine.

College students are not the only ones using ADHD medications inappropriately. A survey in the prestigious scientific journal Nature found that 65% of the scientists who responded knew a colleague who used methylphenidate or similar drugs without a prescription to improve focus and concentration (Maher, 2008).

Treating Schizophrenia

Before the 1950s, effective treatment for schizophrenia was virtually nonexistent. Patients were often subjected to odd "treatments" that had no basis in any scientific understanding of their condition and that were frankly dangerous in some cases. They were forcibly restrained in lukewarm baths with canvas covers that prevented their escape. Insulin shock therapy, in

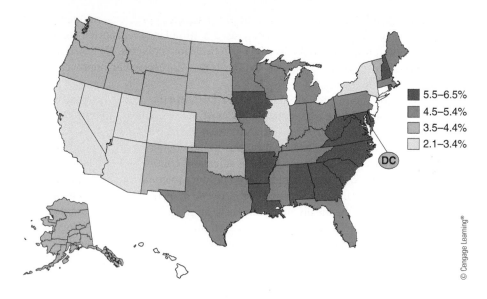

FIGURE 15.10

Use of Medication for Treating Attention Deficit Hyperactivity Disorder (ADHD). This map of medication use for ADHD from the Centers for Disease Control and Prevention shows the same regional variations that we observed in Chapter 14 for the prevalence of ADHD diagnoses. Together, these data suggest that about half of all children diagnosed with ADHD are prescribed medication. The use of medication produces short-term improvements in about 75% to 80% of children with ADHD. However, children with ADHD who are treated with medication are no better off in adolescence or adulthood than children with ADHD who were not treated with medication. *Source:* Adapted from "State-Based Prevalence Data of ADHD Medication Treatment," by Centers for Disease Control and Prevention, 2003, retrieved from http://www.cdc.gov/ncbddd/adhd/medicated.html.

which injections of insulin were used to place patients in daily comas, enjoyed a brief fad status, as did the frontal lobotomy discussed earlier in this chapter.

The discovery of effective medications for schizophrenia was accidental. A French surgeon, Henri Laborit, was impressed by the calming effects of the phenothiazines. He experimented with one of the drugs, chlorpromazine (Thorazine), to reduce stress and shock in his surgical patients. Based on his promising results, Laborit encouraged his psychiatric colleagues to try the drug on their psychotic patients, which they did with dramatic success. A new era of treatment began. Largely as a result of this new type of treatment, institutionalized populations dropped by about 50% in the United States between 1955 and 2000 (see ● Figure 15.11). People responding well to medication could now return to their communities instead of living in institutions.

Initially, nobody understood how the phenothiazines reduced psychosis. One clue came from high doses of the drug producing symptoms that were similar to those of Parkinson's disease, such as muscular tremor. Parkinson's disease was known to result from the degeneration of motor neurons that used dopamine as their primary neurotransmitter. Further research indicated that the phenothiazines acted as dopamine antagonists, blocking dopamine at the receptor site.

The phenothiazines are not without their share of problems. Nearly one quarter of patients with schizophrenia do not respond to these drugs (Kane & Freeman, 1994).The drugs successfully reduce psychotic symptoms, such as hallucinations and delusions, but are often less effective in reducing negative symptoms, such as social withdrawal and emotional disturbance (Carpenter, Conley, Buchanan, Breier, & Tamminga, 1995). The phenothiazines can produce significant side effects because of their ability to block dopamine activity at the syn-

FIGURE 15.11

The Discovery of Effective Medications for Schizophrenia Had Dramatic Effects. The percentage of the U.S. population that was institutionalized in asylums because of mental disorders was cut almost in half in the years following the discovery of antipsychotic medications.

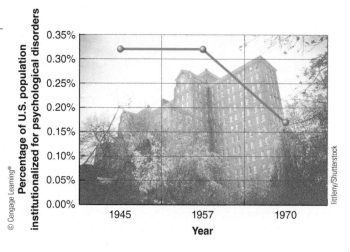

apse. **Tardive dyskinesia**, (*tardive* means "slow" and *dyskinesia* means "difficulty moving") is a syndrome that results from the use of phenothiazines by some patients. The syndrome produces tremors and involuntary movements, especially of the face and tongue. These problems often continue even when medication stops.

To address these deficits of the phenothiazines, often called "typical" antipsychotic medications, new "atypical" antipsychotic medications, such as clozapine (Clozaril), were introduced. Approximately half of all patients with schizophrenia are now using the atypical antipsychotics (Meltzer, Bobo, Lee, Cola, & Jayathilake, 2010). These newer drugs are often more effective than the phenothiazines in treating the negative symptoms of schizophrenia, because they affect a wider range of neurotransmitters, including serotonin. Although risk of tardive dyskinesia seems lower than with the typical antipsychotics (Correll & Schenk, 2008), these drugs have their own set of side effects, including diabetes, weight gain, reductions in white blood cell count, aggravation of existing cancers, and seizure disorders.

Most individuals with schizophrenia are treated with medication, but psychological treatments still have much to offer. The World Health Organization noted that people with schizophrenia in developing countries, such as Nigeria, India, and Colombia, were recovering more frequently than patients in the United States and Europe (Hopper, Harrison, Janca, & Sartorius, 2007). Further research suggested that improved outcomes occur when patients remained in their homes and were given opportunities to do meaningful work. These observations led to the increased use of psychosocial rehabilitation for patients with schizophrenia (Bustillo, Lauriello, Horan, & Keith, 2001). This approach emphasizes providing opportunities to do meaningful work, social skills training, education about schizophrenia and the importance of medication, affordable housing linked to services, and information about symptom management.

Treating Bipolar Disorder

The primary method of treating bipolar disorder is the use of medication. The most commonly prescribed medication is a simple salt, lithium carbonate. Lithium's actions are specific to bipolar disorder. People who do not have bipolar symptoms show no changes in behavior when given lithium. If we can discover what lithium is doing for patients with bipolar disorder, we should have an improved understanding of the disorder; however, lithium's actions remain poorly understood. Lithium has antioxidant effects (Jornada et al., 2011) and appears to both promote the birth of new neurons and prevent further loss of neurons (Quiroz, Machado-Vieira, Zarate, & Manji, 2010). Administration of lithium in patients with bipolar disorder results in increased gray matter relative to patients who are not treated with lithium (see ● Figures 15.12 and 15.13).

Unfortunately, lithium carbonate has a number of unpleasant and potentially dangerous side effects. Toxic levels of lithium produce nausea, vomiting, muscular tremor, coma, and seizures. Because of these risks,

Helene Rogers/Art Directors & TRIP/Alamy

Medications used for schizophrenia often produce a movement disorder known as tardive dyskinesia in patients. This patient is experiencing the intrusive, involuntary movements and tremors that characterize this condition, which is usually permanent. Newer medications for schizophrenia are somewhat less likely to produce tardive dyskinesia but have their own side effects including diabetes, weight gain, reductions in immune system functioning, aggravation of existing cancers, and seizure disorders.

tardive dyskinesia A movement syndrome that results from the use of medications used to treat symptoms of schizophrenia.

Courtesy of Transitions-Mental Health Association

Psychosocial rehabilitation for schizophrenia includes opportunities to do useful work. For more than 20 years, Growing Grounds Farm in San Luis Obispo, California, has provided horticultural therapy and vocational training within the setting of a wholesale "green" nursery business. Socializing with peers, engaging in healthy outdoor physical activity, and earning a paycheck contribute to the clients' personal growth.

HOW ARE SPECIFIC DISORDERS TREATED? **605**

FIGURE 15.12

Effects of Lithium Treatment on Gray Matter Volume. Newly diagnosed participants with bipolar disorder were randomly assigned to groups treated with lithium or valproic acid, which is also used to treat bipolar disorder. Over the next 16 weeks, these groups were compared to healthy controls using no medications. Gray matter volume increased in the group treated with lithium but did not change in the healthy controls or in the group treated with valproic acid. These results support the ability of lithium to increase neural growth, which might also explain its effectiveness in treating bipolar disorder. *Source:* Adapted from "Lithium-Induced Gray Matter Volume Increase as a Neural Correlate of Treatment Response in Bipolar Disorder: A Longitudinal Brain Imaging Study," by I. K. Lyoo, S. R. Dager, J. E. Kim, S. J. Yoon, S. D. Friedman, D. L. Dunner, et al., 2010, *Neuropsychopharmacology, 35*(8), pp. 1743–1750.

patients must have regular blood tests to monitor their lithium levels. The unpleasantness of these side effects also contributes to the poor compliance with their treatment plan that characterizes patients with bipolar disorder. These patients are less likely to follow treatment instructions than any other kind of patient on any other type of medication (Sajatovic, Valenstein, Blow, Ganoczy, & Ignacio, 2007). Fortunately, research into alternatives to lithium carbonate is active, and patients might soon enjoy improved treatment.

Research demonstrating that bipolar disorder is more common in nations in which consumption of seafood is low, discussed in Chapter 14, has led to suggestions that dietary omega-3 fatty acids might provide some protection from bipolar disorder (Noaghiul & Hibbeln, 2003). Lower levels of omega-3 fatty acids have been observed in patients with bipolar disorder (Balanzá-Martínez et al., 2011). The use of omega-3 supplements improves symptoms of depression in these patients, but it does not seem to have much effect on the symptoms of mania (Grosso et al., 2014). While not a substitute for treatment with lithium, the benefits of omega-3 fatty acids are obtained without side effects.

You have probably noticed that our discussion of treating bipolar disorder has not emphasized psychotherapy. Most individuals with bipolar disorder appear to require medication for the alleviation of their symptoms, and psychotherapy alone is not typically considered an option. However, psychotherapy aimed at assisting individuals and their families with coping with bipolar disorder and adhering to treatment is often beneficial. Even in conditions like bipolar disorder that have strong bases in biology, integrating several perspectives when selecting treatment approaches can produce superior outcomes.

FIGURE 15.13

Gain in Gray Matter Density With Lithium Use. These images compared gray matter density between (a) patients with bipolar disorder using lithium treatment and control participants and (b) patients with bipolar disorder who were not using lithium treatment and control participants. As indicated by the colors (blue = little to no difference and red/white = statistically significant difference), the patients taking lithium experienced considerable growth in gray matter density in many areas of the cerebral cortex. *Source:* From Bearden, C. E., et al., (2007). Greater Cortical Gray Matter Density in Lithium-Treated Patients with Bipolar Disorder. *Biol Psychiatry;*62: 7-16.

Treating Major Depressive Disorder

Given the range of suspected causal factors in depression, it should not surprise you that treatment approaches are equally diverse. Treatments range from medical, to cognitive, to behavioral, to simple aerobic exercise, and combinations of these approaches are common.

The most popular method for treating major depressive disorder today is the use of medication. Nearly 170 million prescriptions for **antidepressant medications** were written in the United States in 2005 (Stagnitti, 2008). In the United Kingdom, where health statistics are easier to obtain because of nationalized medicine, annual prescriptions for antidepressants went from less than 10 million in 1991 to nearly 40 million in 2009 (Middleton & Moncrieff, 2011). Far from reducing reported problems, this 400% increase in prescriptions was accompanied by an equal increase in the number of disability claims for related disorders. Keep in mind that antidepressant medications are often prescribed for conditions other than major depressive disorder, such as anxiety disorders. This is still a remarkable number of prescriptions and raises the distinct possibility that, like barbiturates and benzodiazepines before them, antidepressants are being overprescribed (see ● Figure 15.14). In addition, studies have shown that these medications are effective in severe cases of depression, but they do not show benefits compared to placebos in mild to moderate cases of depression (Fournier et al., 2010).

The most widely prescribed antidepressant medications are the selective serotonin reuptake inhibitors (SSRIs), which include popular brands like Prozac and Zoloft. As their name implies, these medications increase serotonin activity at the synapse by interfering with reuptake of the neurotransmitter, a process we discussed in Chapter 4. As a result, more serotonin is available in the synapse (see ● Figure 15.15). The use of SSRIs is based on a belief that depression results from unusually low serotonin activity and that boosting serotonin activity should therefore improve mood.

In addition to inhibiting the reuptake of neurotransmitters at the synapse, antidepressants provide further benefit by increasing the number of neurons in the hippocampus, at least in rats (Nasrallah, Hopkins, & Pixley, 2010). Stress and depression both appear to reduce the

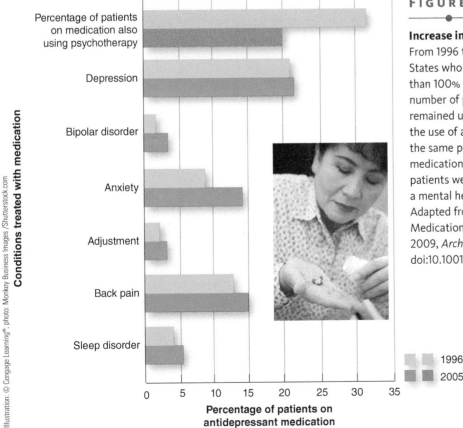

Illustration: © Cengage Learning®, photo: Monkey Business Images /Shutterstock.com

FIGURE 15.14

Increase in Antidepressant Use in the United States.
From 1996 to 2005, the number of people in the United States who used antidepressant medications grew more than 100% from 13.3 million to 27.0 million people. The number of people using antidepressants for depression remained unchanged, so the growth in use resulted from the use of antidepressants for other conditions. During the same period, use of psychotherapy by patients on medication dropped from 31.5% to 19.87%, and more patients were seen by a general health professional than by a mental health professional for their treatment. *Source:* Adapted from "National Patterns in Antidepressant Medication Treatment," by M. Olfson and S. C. Marcus, 2009, *Archives of General Psychiatry, 66*(8), pp. 848–856, doi:10.1001/archgenpsychiatry.2009.81.

antidepressant medication A medication designed to alleviate symptoms of depression but often prescribed for other types of conditions.

FIGURE 15.15

Selective Serotonin Reuptake Inhibitors (SSRIs). SSRIs increase the amount of serotonin in the synaptic gap that is available to interact with serotonin receptors. These drugs achieve this effect by interacting with the serotonin transporters located in the membrane of the neuron releasing the serotonin. This interaction slows the rate of reuptake, or the process by which the neuron retrieves and repackages the molecules of serotonin it has just released.

Seratonin molecule

Seratonin receptor

SSRI

Seratonin transporter

Argosy Publishing, Inc.

number of neurons found in the hippocampus, and the administration of antidepressants may not only halt this loss but also promote the birth of new neurons in this area. Results from experiments with rats showed a 20% to 40% increase in neurons in the hippocampus in response to administration of antidepressant drugs.

These medications have their share of risks and side effects. Increases in thinking about suicide following use of SSRIs, especially among children and youth, have prompted stronger warnings for close supervision by attending physicians (Hall, 2006; Wessely & Kerwin, 2004). Other side effects of SSRIs include nausea, reduction of rapid eye movement (REM) sleep, headache, weight gain, and sexual dysfunction. Between 30% and 60% of patients treated with SSRIs report problems with sexual activity (Gregorian et al., 2002). SSRIs reduce the activity of nitric oxide (NO), the gaseous neurotransmitter that helps maintain erections in men and genital engorgement in women (Yu et al., 2003). In contrast, erectile dysfunction medications, such as Viagra and Cialis, act by boosting NO activity. When patients fail to respond to medication, other biological treatments might be used to treat depression, such as ECT and rTMS (Demitrack, 2007; O'Reardon et al., 2007).

In addition to biological treatment options, a number of psychotherapy alternatives are quite successful in alleviating depression and have the added benefit of producing no adverse side effects. One of the most popular approaches is the use of CBT. As we described previously, this approach combines the restructuring of negative cognitions ("nobody loves me" becomes "not everybody loves me, but some people do") and behavioral techniques aimed at increasing the person's activity levels and social skills (Beck, Rush, Shaw, & Emery, 1979). Between 40% and 60% of people with depression treated with CBT not only experience relief from their symptoms but also appear to be less susceptible to repeated bouts of depression than people who use medication alone (Hollon, Thase, & Markowitz, 2002).

People who are depressed also benefit from adding aerobic exercise to their routine (see ● Figure 15.16). A brisk 30-minute walk or jog only 3 times per week produces the same relief from depression as typical treatment with medication, with none of the side effects (Blumenthal et al., 1999). Not only is exercise an effective treatment for depression, but it might act to prevent depression as well (Ströhle, 2009).

608   Chapter 15 | HEALING THE TROUBLED MIND

FIGURE 15.16

Exercise and Major Depressive Disorder. Participants with major depressive disorder who had not been previously treated were randomly assigned to medication alone, exercise alone, and medication plus exercise groups for a 12-week study period. Because the participants were randomly assigned to groups, there were no statistically significant differences in the severity of their depression before treatment. All three treatment groups experienced improvement in their symptoms, as shown by their reduced scores on the Beck Depression Inventory. Although it appears that the medication group might have improved more than the exercise and combination groups, the differences between these three groups were not statistically significant. Therefore, we can conclude that exercise alone was equally effective in reducing symptoms of depression as medication alone or medication in combination with exercise. *Source:* Adapted from "Effects of Exercise Training on Older Patients With Major Depression," by J. A. Blumenthal, M. A. Babyak, K. A. Moore, W. E. Craighead, S. Herman, P. Khatri, et al., 1999, *Archives of Internal Medicine, 159*(19), pp. 2349–2356.

Connecting to Research

Mindfulness and the Prevention of Relapse in Major Depressive Disorder

ALTHOUGH OUR METHODS FOR TREAT-ING major depressive disorder are typically effective, there is a significant risk of recurrence. Some individuals experience low rates of recurrence when continuing to take antidepressant medications even when their depressive symptoms are gone. However, these medications produce significant side effects, making this approach undesirable for many people. Continuation of CBT after recovery is typically more helpful than continuing to take medication, but many health plans only pay for limited numbers of sessions.

Recurrences of depression might occur because people who have experienced episodes of major depressive disorder tend to think differently than people with no history of depression when a mildly negative mood state occurs (Teasdale et al., 2000). A technique known as mindfulness-based cognitive therapy (MBCT) combines aspects of CBT and mindfulness-based stress reduction. The idea of MBCT is to teach people to

"detach" from depression-related thoughts and feelings by endorsing statements like "thoughts are not facts" and "I am not my thoughts." How well does this approach work to prevent repeated episodes of major depressive disorder?

The Question: Does the addition of MBCT to major depressive disorder treatment as usual produce better outcomes than treatment as usual alone?

METHODS

In a study, 145 patients in recovery from major depressive disorder were randomly assigned to continue with their treatments as usual or to receive additional MBCT training. Their progress at a 1-year follow-up was assessed.

Treatment as usual meant that the patients would seek help as they normally would, perhaps from a family doctor, if they experienced mood difficulties. Participants assigned to receive MBCT training attended

eight weekly 2-hour group training sessions and completed daily homework exercises. Key themes include empowerment, freedom of choice, and awareness of experience in the moment.

RESULTS

Among participants with three or more previous episodes of depression, who made up 77% of the sample, the addition of MBCT reduced recurrence rates by nearly 50% compared to treatment as usual alone.

CONCLUSIONS

This study indicated that MBCT provides a powerful tool for preventing further episodes of depression, a finding that has since been replicated and supported by a significant amount of research (Khoury et al., 2013; Tang & Posner, 2009). Use of MBCT has been extended successfully from the treatment of depression to the treatment of anxiety and stress (Khoury et al., 2013). ●

Treating Anxiety Disorders

Anxiety disorders, including general anxiety disorder, phobias, and panic disorder, are typically treated by using medication, CBT, or a combination of the two (see ● Figure 15.17).

As we discussed in Chapter 14, anxiety is associated with a heightened level of brain activity because of anticipated danger. Consequently, most efforts to medicate anxiety attempt to reduce brain activity, or produce a "tranquilizing" effect.

Because GABA is the major inhibitory neurotransmitter in the brain, a common method for slowing brain activity is to enhance the effects of GABA. As we described in Chapter 6, many substances interact with the GABA receptor to produce stronger inhibition in the brain, including alcohol, barbiturates, and benzodiazepines. Each of these types of substances produces a tranquilizing effect on the brain. Because these drugs have additive effects with one another and work at the same receptor site, taking combinations of these drugs is frequently fatal because of a life-threatening level of brain inhibition.

Knowing that one of the motivations for alcohol use might be to reduce the anxiety resulting from social events and other stressors can be helpful in avoiding problem drinking. If a person feels like she "can't face" a situation without being drunk, it would be more positive to seek professional help than to continue drinking.

Barbiturates, developed in 1903, continue to be quite useful in the treatment of seizures, but their use as a treatment for anxiety is no longer considered desirable. Barbiturates were one of the first of several medications used for psychological treatments to become vastly overprescribed. By the mid-1960s, enough barbiturates were being made to provide every American man, woman, and child with 40 to 50 doses per year (Regan, 2000). The addictive properties of barbiturates, as well as their frequent use in suicides, were definite drawbacks.

The discovery of benzodiazepines after World War II changed the treatment of anxiety dramatically, but like the barbiturates, the benzodiazepines became overused. By the 1970s,

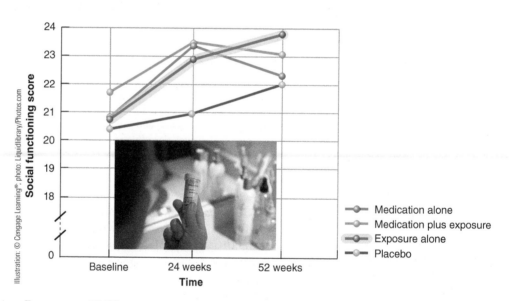

FIGURE 15.17

Comparisons of Treatments in Social Anxiety Disorder. Medication, exposure therapy (in which the individual is gradually introduced to anxiety-producing situations), and combined medication and exposure therapy appear to produce approximately equal improvements in the functioning of people with social anxiety disorder. Scores of social functioning of people randomly assigned to these treatment conditions were significantly better than scores of the placebo group after 24 weeks of treatment. However, when treatment was discontinued after 24 weeks, the functioning of the groups that received medication and medication combined with exposure therapy deteriorated at the 1-year follow-up assessment, whereas the exposure-alone group continued to improve. These results suggest that patients choosing to use medication should continue treatment to maintain gains in functioning. *Source:* Adapted from Haug et al. (2003).

chlordiazepoxide (Librium) and diazepam (Valium) were the most frequently prescribed drugs of their day. Alprazolam (Xanax) remains a widely used benzodiazepine, typically prescribed for panic disorder, general anxiety disorder, and premenstrual syndrome. In some cases, alprazolam seems to be helpful in treating major depressive disorder, but its mechanism for doing so is not understood.

You might think that tranquilizers would be a logical choice of medication for treating anxiety disorders. Although these drugs are used occasionally, the antidepressants we discussed in a previous section are typically more effective. This result might reflect a common underlying cause for both depression and anxiety.

Behavioral and cognitive behavioral techniques are commonly used to treat anxiety disorders and have the advantage over medication of having no side effects. Phobias, for instance, can be treated with exposure therapy, in which the person is gradually exposed to the fear stimulus or to other people interacting harmlessly with the fear stimulus while the person relaxes.

Treating Obsessive-Compulsive Disorder

OCD can be treated with antidepressant medication, CBT, or a combination of both. CBT for OCD involves training the person to anticipate compulsive behavior and then to engage in a competing behavior. As mentioned earlier, a compulsive hand-washer could go outside away from faucets and soap to do some gardening. Meta-analyses show that CBT is a highly effective approach to treating OCD (Olatunji, Davis, Powers, & Smits, 2013).

 # Experiencing Psychology

Progressive Relaxation

AS YOU HAVE seen in this chapter, administering therapies for psychological disorders and problems with adjustment is typically the domain of highly trained professionals. However, there are a few activities people can do safely on their own to reduce stress and change habits. In Chapter 8, we outlined a method you could use to change unwanted habits based on behavioral therapies. In this section, we review a progressive relaxation technique that you can use to reduce stress. These same techniques are often implemented during exposure therapy.

To enhance your ability to relax, it is often beneficial to make an audio recording of the instructions. To begin, put on some loose, comfortable clothing and either lie down on your back or sit in a chair with your head supported. Breathe slowly and deeply. Each muscle group is tensed for 5 seconds (silently count "one–one thousand" at a normal speaking pace) followed by a pause of 20 seconds during which you relax

the muscle group and think of tension "draining" from that part of the body. The procedure can be repeated for more dramatic relaxation. With practice, you should be able to "will" yourself into a relaxed state rather easily. Here is the order of muscle groups to tense and relax:

1. Tense the muscles of your head and face.
2. Tense the muscles of your neck (gently).
3. Tense your elbows and biceps for 5 seconds, and then relax and straighten your arms.
4. Clench your fists tightly.
5. Tense the muscles of your chest.
6. Tense the muscles of your stomach.
7. Tense the muscles of your calves.
8. Tense the muscles of your feet and toes (gently, to avoid cramping).

If you are successful in achieving deep relaxation, someone should be able to pick up your arm or leg and it will be limp and unresisting. ●

Anan Kaewkhammul/Shutterstock.com

Tensing then relaxing each muscle group in the body leads to a deep state of relaxation.

Treating Body Dysmorphic Disorder

CBT is particularly helpful in cases of body dysmorphic disorder (Allen & Woolfolk, 2010). In CBT, cognitive restructuring can help the individual think more realistically about perceived physical flaws. Many individuals with this disorder, however, insist on continued treatment by cosmetic surgeons and resist suggestions that they should obtain psychotherapy.

Treating Posttraumatic Stress Disorder

PTSD is typically treated using exposure therapy with or without SSRI medications (Le, Doctor, Zoellner, & Feeny, 2014). Because many people with PTSD also develop a variety of substance use disorders, additional treatment addressing these disorders is necessary for full recovery (Back et al., 2014).

Psychology as a Hub Science
Using Virtual Reality to Treat Anxiety and Posttraumatic Stress Disorder

Psychiatry **Computer Science**

PSYCHOLOGY

Public Health

You might expect virtual reality (VR), the presentation of realistic stimuli through a device worn on the head, to be more exciting to video gamers than to therapists. However, this new technology is showing remarkable promise for the treatment of phobias and PTSD.

As we discussed in this chapter and in Chapter 8, one of the best ways to address these stress- and fear-related problems is to combine relaxation with a controlled exposure to the fear-producing stimuli. This application of classical conditioning was popularized by Joseph Wolpe in the 1950s (Wolpe, 1958). For example, if a person is afraid of heights, he could imagine progressively more stressful situations (climbing a ladder or visiting the Empire State Building) while remaining relaxed. Eventually, the fear of heights should be reduced.

Imagination is a wonderful capability of the mind, but it has its limitations. This is where VR comes in. Instead of asking a client to imagine a situation, the scenario can be presented in a realistic way through the use of VR technology. As our height-phobic client maneuvers through elevators, construction sites, and other high places, wind, vibration, and sound can be added to make the visual experience even more realistic. In addition to treating phobias, VR is being used to help combat veterans recover from PTSD (Spira et al., 2006). In these cases, odors from diesel fuel and gunpowder can be added to enhance the reality of the virtual experience.

Research comparing the effectiveness of VR therapies, alone or in conjunction with traditional cognitive behavioral therapy (CBT), suggests that VR therapy alone is about as effective as CBT alone in treating phobias but might have an advantage in certain situations, such as fear of flying (Krijn et al., 2007). VR also performed well in comparisons with CBT in cases of PTSD (Baños et al., 2011). In particular, VR therapy appealed to people with PTSD who were unwilling to undergo more traditional treatments. People who grew up playing video games might find the VR approach more effective and comfortable. ●

The U.S. Army is testing "Virtual Iraq," a 360-degree, interactive, computer-generated environment, as a treatment for soldiers with posttraumatic stress disorder (PTSD). Soldiers are able to relate their traumatic experiences to the therapist, who can then program the environment to reproduce weather conditions, terrain, helicopter flyovers, types of attacks, and sound. Soldiers treated with virtual reality are being compared with soldiers treated with other traditional psychotherapy approaches and a control group of soldiers on the waiting list for treatment.

Treating Dissociative Identity Disorder

The treatment of dissociative identity disorder can be quite controversial, as is the diagnosis of this condition, as we explained in Chapter 14.

Some psychotherapists work on the assumption that dissociative identity disorder is a valid diagnostic category that often results from serious trauma, childhood sexual abuse in particular. Treatment is aimed toward integrating the various personalities by first identifying and "working through" the traumatic memories related to the disorder (International Society for the Study of Dissociation, 2005). Hypnosis is commonly used by these therapists to assist in the recovery and resolution of traumatic memories, but this practice is not well advised. Under hypnosis, a suggestible person might be vulnerable to the manufacture of false memories, and individuals identified as having dissociative identity disorder appear to be far more suggestible than the general public (Frischholz, Lipman, Braun, & Sachs, 1992). In one notable case study, a woman sought therapy to cope with a traumatic event involving her daughter. Her psychiatrist employed hypnosis and convinced her that she had experienced horrific abuse as a child and now had more than 120 separate personalities, including one that was a duck, thereby illustrating the influence therapists can have on the "memories" they help recover (Loftus, 1997).

A particularly damaging finding regarding the state of treatment for dissociative identity disorder is the suggestion that individuals labeled with the disorder subsequently show even worse symptoms (Piper & Merskey, 2004). Critics of the dissociative identity disorder classification suggest that psychotherapists should restrict their actions to resolving the stress, anxiety, and depression of the individual without referring to dissociation.

Treating Somatic Symptom Disorders

Both biological and psychological treatments are commonly used to treat somatic symptom disorders, which involve physical symptoms such as pain that have no apparent physical basis.

Among the biological treatments for somatic symptom disorders are medication with antidepressants and increases in physical activity. Psychological treatments usually take the form of CBT (Allen & Woolfolk, 2010). Complicating the treatment of these disorders, most of these patients are seen by their primary physicians, and relatively few are willing to pursue psychotherapy. Between 50% and 80% of patients referred for psychological treatment by their

British painter Kim Noble has been diagnosed with dissociative identity disorder. This disorder is characterized by the experience of two or more "personality states." Noble paints quite differently when she feels she is in one of her personality states compared to the others and believes she has improved her well-being by expressing her perceived personalities through her art.

physicians do not comply, possibly because of their continued belief that they have a real medical condition that has not yet been appropriately diagnosed (Allen & Woolfolk, 2010).

Treating Antisocial Personality Disorder

Finding effective treatments for antisocial personality disorder has a high priority, given the extent of harm individuals in this category inflict on the rest of society. Unfortunately, effective treatments appear elusive.

No known medications specifically reduce antisocial behavior, although many incarcerated individuals are treated with tranquilizing drugs, including antipsychotic and anticonvulsant medications (such as barbiturates), to make their aggressive, violent behavior more manageable. Even if effective medications are eventually discovered, individuals with antisocial personality disorder tend to view themselves as "okay" and not in need of treatment. Compliance with effective treatments is likely to remain a problem.

Psychological treatments for antisocial personality disorder include learning models that emphasize anger control, social skills, and moral reasoning (Goldstein, Glick, & Gibbs, 1998). These models appear to be modestly effective in reducing antisocial behavior in children and youth, but they do not appear to have much benefit for individuals who show evidence of true psychopathy, or lack of guilt and empathy (Hornsveld, Nijman, Hollin, & Kraaimaat, 2008). Individuals with antisocial personality disorder might benefit from training in "character formation" (Salmon, 2004). Addressing the selfishness inherent in people with antisocial personality disorder, therapists can attempt to convince the person that doing the right thing will produce more favorable outcomes (e.g., staying out of prison), even if the person fails to grasp the underlying value of respecting the rights of others. Despite these efforts, many nations consider this condition untreatable and rely on incarceration of criminals with antisocial personality disorder to protect the public.

Treating Borderline Personality Disorder

No medications are currently approved specifically for the treatment of borderline personality disorder, but medications are frequently prescribed. Among the commonly prescribed medications are antidepressants, antipsychotic medications, mood stabilizers (e.g., lithium), anti-anxiety medications (e.g., benzodiazepines), and anticonvulsants. Because of the potential for self-destructive behavior and serious depression in borderline personality disorder, individuals are occasionally hospitalized for a few days for their own safety.

Psychotherapy for borderline personality disorder often takes the form of CBT. In this case, the individual learns to manage stress, emotions, and relationships. In particular, psychotherapists emphasize skills aimed at reducing the individual's potential for suicidal thinking and behavior. A therapy specifically designed for individuals with borderline personality disorder, dialectical behavior therapy (DBT), attempts to address symptoms in the order of their importance: reducing suicidal thoughts, reducing behaviors that interfere with therapy, and finally reducing behaviors that interfere with the quality of life (Linehan, Armstrong, Suarez, Allmon, & Heard, 1991). Outcomes using dialectical behavior therapy for borderline personality disorder appear superior to those produced by more conventional treatments with CBT (Linehan et al., 1991).

Integration of Specific Treatments

Perhaps after reading through the variations in both biological and psychological treatments available for specific types of disorders, you will better appreciate why people who want to be therapists spend such a long time in school perfecting their skills and learning about their options.

Although some disorders seem to defy our available treatment methods, we do not want to leave you with the impression that therapy is somehow ineffective. Quite the contrary is true. Compared to the state of available therapies as recently as 60 years ago, psychologists and psychiatrists have made great strides in their ability to alleviate the distress of many millions of people. As we learn more about the causal factors underlying these disorders, as we surely will by pursuing integrative approaches, our abilities to help will expand. At the same time, we are making significant progress in our understanding about the prevention of many of these disorders, which we hope will make these problems a thing of the past.

The use of dialectical behavior therapy for borderline personality disorder has been simplified by the development of a new smartphone app, which takes the place of keeping diary cards of emotions, events, and problem behaviors. *Source:* Adapted from "A Pilot Study of the DBT Coach: An Interactive Mobile Phone Application for Individuals With Borderline Personality Disorder and Substance Use Disorder," by S. L. Rizvi, L. A. Dimeff, J. Skutch, D. Carroll, and M. M. Linehan, 2011, *Behavior Therapy, 42,* pp. 589–600. Copyright © 2011 Elsevier.

Interpersonal Relationships
The Treatment Perspective
Can Couples Therapy Help in Cases of Infidelity?

We have spent most of our time in this chapter talking about how psychotherapists tackle some of the most challenging psychological disorders, but that is not what they do all the time. The everyday problems faced by psychotherapists in their practices can be challenging too, and the well-being of clients is often at stake.

When a couple is hitting some hard times together, we often hear them advised to seek counseling. Does that work? How often can counselors help people patch up relationships? What do they do to achieve successful outcomes?

One of the biggest problems that drives couples to counseling is infidelity, which we discussed in Chapter 13. The lifetime prevalence of infidelity in married couples in the United States is estimated to be between 20% and 40% (Atkins, Baucom, & Jacobson, 2001). In surveys of psychotherapists who specialize in couples therapy, infidelity is reported to be one of the most damaging situations faced by couples and one of the most difficult for the therapist to treat effectively (Whisman, Dixon, & Johnson, 1997). The therapist's job is further complicated by the impact of the infidelity on the partners' well-being. Many people respond to their partner's infidelity by developing symptoms of depression and anxiety (Gordon, Baucom, & Snyder, 2004).

To assess the outcomes of therapy in cases of infidelity, couples entering therapy with at least one partner indicating concerns about infidelity were compared to couples entering therapy without infidelity concerns (Atkins, Marín, Lo, Klann, & Hahlweg, 2010). The infidelity couples reported greater initial distress and more depression than the other couples. However, by the end of the therapy process, both types of couples had made similar, positive progress. All couples (with or without infidelity), however, still scored rather high on measures of couple distress at the end of their therapy, indicating that despite their progress, their relationships were still at risk (see ● Figure 15.18).

One interesting aspect of this study was the wide use of techniques by the couples therapists, which included behavioral, biopsychosocial, and psychodynamic approaches. This study used a large, community sample, so researchers were unable to assign therapists to particular approaches. It is possible that the use of infidelity-specific counseling, emphasizing trust and forgiveness, might have produced even better outcomes for the couples with infidelity. However, even in this less-targeted counseling approach, the results are encouraging. Couples do seem to benefit from seeking counseling for one of the more difficult problems they may face together. ●

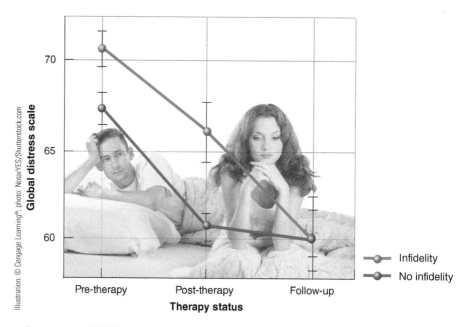

FIGURE 15.18

Response of Couples With and Without Infidelity to Therapy. Couples entering therapy with a history of infidelity showed more initial distress than couples without infidelity, but both types made similar, positive progress after 6 months of treatment. In a follow-up assessment 6 months after the end of treatment, or 1 year since the beginning of the study, both types of couples reported similar, lower levels of distress. *Source:* Adapted from "Outcomes of Couples With Infidelity in a Community-Based Sample of Couple Therapy," by D. C. Atkins, R. A. Marín, T. T. Y. Lo, N. Klann, and K. Hahlweg, 2010, *Journal of Family Psychology, 24*(2), pp. 212–216, doi:10.1037/a0018789.

KEY TERMS The Language of Psychological Science

Be sure you can define these terms and use them correctly.

antidepressant medication, p. 607
behavior therapy, p. 593
biopsychosocial approach, p. 595
brief therapy, p. 587
cognitive behavioral therapy (CBT),
    p. 595
cognitive restructuring, p. 594
counseling, p. 583
couples therapy, p. 588

deep brain stimulation, p. 597
electroconvulsive therapy (ECT), p. 596
family therapy, p. 588
free association, p. 590
group therapy, p. 587
humanistic therapy, p. 582
insight therapy, p. 590
neurofeedback, p. 599
person-centered therapy, p. 591

psychiatrist, p. 584
psychoanalysis, p. 590
psychosurgery, p. 596
psychotherapist, p. 584
psychotherapy, p. 580
resistance, p. 591
tardive dyskinesia, p. 605
transference, p. 591

Summary 15.3 Common Treatments for Psychological Disorders

Disorder	Psychological treatment	Biological treatment
Autism spectrum disorder	• Applied behavior analysis	• Antipsychotic medications for self-injury
Attention deficit hyperactivity disorder	• Behavior therapy	• Stimulant medications
Schizophrenia	• Psychosocial rehabilitation • Evaluation of expressed emotion	• Medication with antipsychotic drugs
Bipolar disorder	• Supportive Cognitive behavioral therapy (CBT)	• Medication with lithium carbonate • Electroconvulsive therapy (ECT) for depression
Major depressive disorder	• CBT	• Medication with antidepressant drugs • ECT • Exercise
Anxiety	• CBT	• Medication with antidepressant or antianxiety drugs
Personality disorders	• Learning models for antisocial personality disorder • Dialectical behavior therapy for borderline personality disorder	• No effective biological treatments, although medications are sometimes prescribed

16 The Healthy Mind

Stress and Coping, Health Psychology, and Positive Psychology

WE HAVE ALL HAD DAYS LIKE THE WOMAN IN THIS PHOTO. Whether it comes in relatively minor forms (losing your keys, getting a traffic ticket, or doing poorly on an exam) or in large forms (death of a loved one or serious illness), stress is a fact of life.

Ghislain & Marie David de Lossy/Cultura Creative (RF)/Alamy

We don't know what kind of stress is producing this woman's reactions, but we know a great deal about what is happening to her physically and psychologically in response to her stress. Zooming in, we look at one of her adrenal glands, shown in the larger image. Your adrenal glands are located on top of your kidneys in your lower back, and they are the source of hormones that are dumped into your bloodstream at times of stress. How does feeling stressed get translated into activity by a gland?

Here is how the system works. First, the woman must identify something as a threat to her. Making that cognitive appraisal, or judgment, of her situation begins a cascade of processes designed to mobilize her to either run (flight) or fight. Messages from her amygdala to her hypothalamus result in the activation of hormones that tell the adrenal glands to release a hormone called cortisol. In Chapter 6, we noted that cortisol levels are naturally high in the morning. In other words, circulating cortisol wakes you up. In response to the cortisol released by the adrenal glands, the body is mobilized for action.

We also have had enough stress in our lives to understand that too much is not a good thing. Again, if we zoom in, we can understand that our bodies are usually protected from too much cortisol by a feedback loop that reduces cortisol release once circulating levels reach a certain point. It is likely that this feedback loop malfunctions in stress-related disorders, such as depression (see Chapter 14).

While still at the microscopic level, we might also see that one person's genetic makeup might predispose that individual to have a more or less dramatic response to perceived stressors. By now, you can probably anticipate that we have to zoom back out again to fully understand this situation. These genetic differences among individuals interact with developmental and social factors, such as the possibility that this woman was maltreated as a child or now enjoys a strong social network of family and friends.

We can't make your stress go away, and it is probably not in your best interests for us to do so. Some stress, such as the stress associated with exercise or even surviving a

◀ The adrenal glands are the source of several important hormones that are released into the bloodstream at times of stress.

Argosy Publishing, Inc.

Patrick Tuohy/Shutterstock

traumatic experience, can have quite beneficial effects on your overall health. Instead, we can acquaint you with research findings on coping and resilience that might help you deal with life's inevitable challenges.

Learning Objectives

1. Define *stress*, identifying key neural and hormonal aspects of Hans Selye's general adaptation syndrome.

2. Distinguish among adaptive elements of the short-term stress response with health problems linked to chronic stress.

3. Compare and contrast strategies for coping with stress, including problem-, emotion-, and relationship-focused strategies.

4. Summarize the psychosocial factors associated with smoking, nutrition, alcohol use, and lack of exercise, and propose a behavioral interventions for these problems.

5. Differentiate the aims and principles of positive psychology from those of other major movements in psychology, as described in Chapter 1.

6. Distinguish among meanings of *happiness* (pleasant, good, and meaningful lives), and analyze the research evidence on what makes people happy.

Professional athletes like Grace Park have learned to cope with stress to perform their best.

What Is Stress?

College students rarely need much introduction to the concept of stress. They are no strangers to the stress that accompanies worrying about assignments and grades, money matters, world affairs, and relationships. **Stress** is an unpleasant emotional state that results from the perception of danger. The source of stress is called a **stressor**.

The key to our definition is the word *perception*. No one set of stressors reliably produces stress in everybody. People's stressors are highly individual and idiosyncratic. The object of one person's phobia may be another person's beloved, although scaly and slithery, pet. Regardless of the stressor responsible for feelings of stress, once people perceive that they are in some kind of danger, a common and predictable set of responses to the stressor is set in motion.

Psychologists have identified positive outcomes of our responses to stress (Selye, 1975). Stress, by its nature, is a powerful adaptive response that mobilizes the body's resources to enhance survival in dangerous situations (Meaney, 2010). Although sometimes unpleasant, stress can motivate us to perform well and makes us healthier in the long run. The exercise we do at the gym is undeniably stressful, but it produces significant benefits down the road. Many of us do some of our best work under time pressure and are not too much the worse for the wear as a result.

However, in other cases, stress can be counterproductive and interfere with our performance and well-being. In extreme cases, as we observed in Chapter 14, a diathesis–stress model predicts that stress can contribute to the development of depression, schizophrenia, posttraumatic stress disorder (PTSD), and other serious conditions. These negative outcomes are more likely when we are unable to cope with or adapt to a stressor. We will be focusing most of our discussion on these negative situations.

stress An unpleasant emotional state that results from the perception of danger.
stressor A stimulus that serves as a source of stress.

The Stress Response

Walter Cannon, whom we met in Chapter 7, demonstrated the ability of a number of stressors to activate the sympathetic division of the autonomic nervous system, described in Chapters 4 and 7 (Cannon, 1929). Cannon reported that extreme cold, lack of oxygen, and emotional experiences all had the capacity to initiate a fight-or-flight response. During such a response, heart rate, blood pressure, and respiration all increase, while nonessential functions, like digesting food, are inhibited. Stored energy is released, and blood is shunted from the surface of the body to the muscles needed for exertion. These physical responses reflect a process that has been finely tuned through evolution to maximize our survival in emergencies.

Hans Selye, in a research career lasting more than 40 years, extended Cannon's findings by studying the effects of stronger, longer lasting stressors. Selye worked primarily with rats, exposing them to a variety of stressors and measuring the amount of time they could subsequently swim before giving up. (They were then rescued.) Cold water, restraint, electric shock, surgery, and having their whiskers cut off were some of Selye's stressors that greatly reduced the amount of time the rats would swim before giving up. Regardless of the nature of the stressor, Selye found that the rats responded with a consistent pattern of behavior, which he labeled the **general adaptation syndrome** (GAS; Selye, 1946).

The GAS occurs in three stages (see ● Figure 16.1). An alarm reaction is initiated when a stressor is first perceived and identified. Selye's **alarm reaction** is essentially the same process as Cannon's fight-or-flight response. All possible resources are deployed to survive the danger, and all nonessential systems are inhibited. It is likely that you have had at least one close call while driving a car, and you can probably remember how that felt. Your heart pounds, you breathe rapidly, your hands may be sweaty, and you feel unusually mentally alert and focused. This is precisely the way your autonomic nervous system is supposed to react in an emergency.

Some sources of danger do not go away as quickly as your close call on the freeway. Many students think, "Oh, if only I survive this term—everything else will be easy," only to find themselves facing the same problems next term, along with some new ones. One of the challenges of modern living that our ancestors did not face is the need to worry about many future events. For the hunter–gatherer, the challenge was usually surviving that day. In contrast, today's college student may be concerned not only with fairly immediate problems, such as paying the rent and passing a midterm, but also more distant problems of future job markets, world events, climate change, and the future of Social Security. If these uncertainties are perceived as threatening or dangerous, they will act as stressors with the ability to initiate GAS.

When stressors are prolonged, Selye suggests we enter a stage of **resistance**. During this stage, we continue to experience ongoing stress, which requires us to adapt and cope as well as possible. Although resistance is not as dramatic as the briefer and more intense alarm reaction, it still takes its toll. Under normal circumstances, we alternate between periods of calm

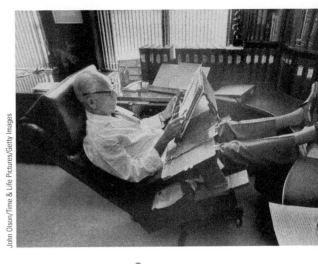

Hans Selye identified a general adaptation syndrome, which is our characteristic set of responses to stressors.

general adaptation syndrome (GAS) Hans Selye's three-stage model for an organism's response to stressors.
alarm reaction The first stage of the general adaptation syndrome, characterized by sympathetic arousal and mental clarity.
resistance The second stage of the general adaptation syndrome, characterized by coping with ongoing stress.

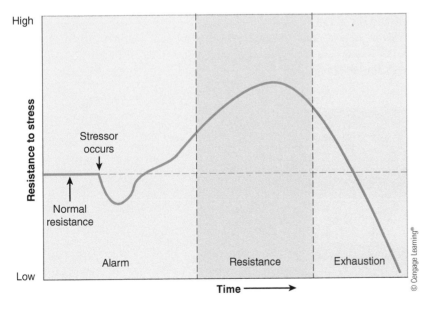

FIGURE 16.1

The General Adaptation Syndrome (GAS) Has Three Stages. Hans Selye's GAS has three stages: alarm, resistance, and exhaustion. During the alarm stage, all resources are mobilized for fight or flight. If stress is prolonged, we enter the resistance stage, where we adapt and cope as well as possible. Finally, resources are depleted when we reach the exhaustion stage.

and periods of relative arousal. You might calmly enjoy your lunch on the lawn between classes but feel aroused while taking a quiz in a later class. During the calm periods, we have an opportunity to store nutrients and rest and repair the body. During periods of arousal, such as during the quiz, we expend energy instead of storing it. In the resistance phase of GAS, we attempt to take care of both arousal and resting functions simultaneously. Neither function operates as smoothly under these circumstances as when it is operating alone. You might get an upset stomach when digesting your lunch is combined with the excitement of giving an oral presentation to your classmates. In contrast to the mental clarity that typically accompanies the brief alarm reaction, judgment during the longer periods of resistance may not be as good.

During extended periods of stress, judgment can suffer. You might have had the experience of looking back at the decisions you made during a stressful time, scratching your head, and asking, "What was I thinking?"

If stressors are severe and last long enough, a person might reach Selye's **exhaustion** stage. Strength and energy drop to very low levels. As we mentioned in Chapter 14, stress is a risk factor for depression, and the exhaustion stage has much in common with the criteria for major depressive disorder. Exhaustion can even lead to death. Forced marches during war produce higher rates of death than the rate that might be expected to occur because of injuries and lack of food. Similar observations of stress, exhaustion, and death have been made among baboons in Kenya (Sapolsky, 2001). Under normal circumstances, lower status baboons avoid higher status baboons whenever possible. Unfortunately, because of fears of losing their crops, the Kenyan villagers caged the local baboons 1 year. While caged, the lower status baboons had no way to escape the higher status animals, and many died as a result. They did not die, as you might have guessed, from battle wounds resulting from fights with the higher status animals. Instead, the baboons died from stress-related medical conditions such as cardiovascular disease.

Sources of Stress

Stressors exist in the eye of the beholder. Stressing over an exam might seem reasonable to many students, but this behavior might look silly to people stressed by war, poverty, and disease, who would probably be thrilled to have the opportunity to attend college.

Cognitive appraisal models help us to predict when a particular stimulus or event is likely to be a stressor for an individual person (Lazarus, 1966). According to this approach, we make appraisals, or rapid initial assessments, of potential stressors to determine whether they are irrelevant or harmless, positive or negative. Because people appraise situations from the vantage point of their own strengths and experiences, we would expect that a single potential stressor might produce different amounts and intensity of stress for different people.

Despite this variability in response to stressors, we can identify several types of events that are likely to produce significant stress in most people (see ● Figure 16.2). Large-scale disasters, such as the terrorist attacks of 9/11, the Haiti earthquake of 2010, the 2011 Japanese earthquake and tsunami, and the 2013 Oklahoma tornadoes typically produce stress in large numbers of people. PTSD in New York following 9/11 was estimated to affect 130,000 people in that city alone. In the 3 to 5 days following the attacks, 90% of Americans reported feeling unusually stressed (Schuster et al., 2002).

exhaustion The third and last stage of the general adaptation syndrome, characterized by depletion of physical and psychological resources.

Older zoos featured cages that often contributed to stress and illness among the animals. Modern zoos go to great lengths to provide more natural, less stressful habitats for their animals in recognition of the stress that often accompanies captivity.

Stress because of disasters can produce long-range and cross-generational effects. Researchers identified women who witnessed the 9/11 attacks in New York while pregnant and who subsequently developed PTSD (Yehuda et al., 2005). One year later, the women and their infants showed indications of long-term, chronic stress. As preschoolers, the children born to the women who were diagnosed with both PTSD and depression following 9/11 showed evidence of higher reactivity to stimuli and more aggressive behavior than did children of terrorism-exposed mothers who did not develop these disorders (Chemtob et al., 2010). The ability of cortisol and other stress hormones to cross the placenta probably accounts for the effects of stress beginning in the prenatal environment (Weinstock, 2005).

As we mentioned in Chapter 14, children are especially susceptible to PTSD. Three weeks after a 2004 tsunami, prevalence of PTSD among children in areas of Sri Lanka ranged between 14% and 39% and could be predicted by variables such as family loss and severity of exposure (Neuner, Schauer, Catani, Ruf, & Elbert, 2006). To put these very high numbers of childhood cases into perspective, we would expect about 10% of the general population to experience PTSD after most large disasters (Kessler, Sonnega, Bromet, Hughes, & Nelson, 1996). Automobile accidents appear to be a major source of PTSD in childhood, with about 25% of children developing the disorder after being injured in an accident (de Vries, Kassam-Adams, Cnaan, Sherman-Slate, Gallagher, & Winston, 1999).

Although disasters are dramatic, they are not the only sources of stress we face. Changes, including some changes for the better, can also trigger stress. In the 1960s, Holmes and Rahe compiled a list of life events they believed might be correlated with stress and then surveyed

This man is obviously stressed. Is somebody being injured? Is he in danger? No—he is witnessing a tense moment during a baseball game. Cognitive appraisal theories of stress suggest that different people are likely to respond to stimuli with varying levels of stress, based on their individual appraisals of a situation.

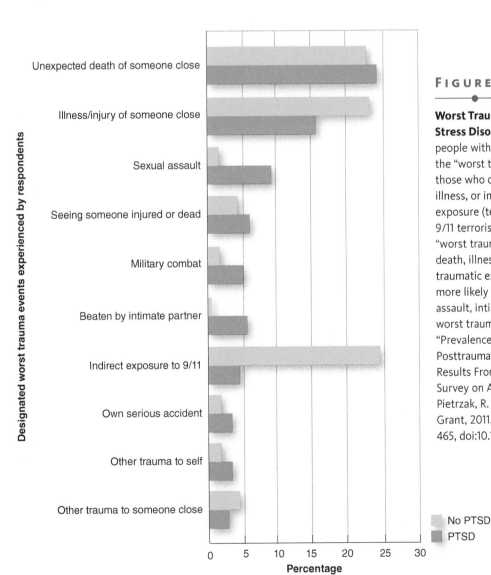

FIGURE 16.2

Worst Traumatic Exposures and Posttraumatic Stress Disorder (PTSD). Approximately 30,000 people with and without PTSD were asked to identify the "worst trauma they had ever experienced." Among those who did not have PTSD, the unexpected death, illness, or injury of someone close and indirect exposure (television and other news reports) to the 9/11 terrorist attacks were the most commonly named "worst traumas." Among those with PTSD, unexpected death, illness, or injury were also commonly noted traumatic experiences, but people with PTSD were more likely than healthy controls to identify sexual assault, intimate partner violence, and combat as their worst traumatic experiences. *Source:* Adapted from "Prevalence and Axis I Comorbidity of Full and Partial Posttraumatic Stress Disorder in the United States: Results From Wave 2 of the National Epidemiologic Survey on Alcohol and Related Conditions," by R. H. Pietrzak, R. B. Goldstein, S. M. Southwick, and B. F. Grant, 2011, *Journal of Anxiety Disorders, 25*(3), pp. 456–465, doi:10.1016/j.janxdis.2010.11.010.

According to Holmes and Rahe (1967), positive life events, such as weddings and holidays, can be equally or even more stressful than some negative events, such as flunking an important assignment.

participants about the amount of adjustment each event required (Holmes & Rahe, 1967). Subsequently, researchers used the Holmes and Rahe scales to predict vulnerability to physical illness and psychological disorder because of different stressors (Derogatis & Coons, 1993; Scully, Tosi, & Banning, 2000). According to the scales, Christmas is more stressful than minor violations of the law. Getting married is more stressful than being fired from your job. Research results from studies using the Holmes and Rahe scales suggest that we should consider spreading out controllable changes over time. In other words, it may not be the best strategy to graduate from college, get married, move to a new city, and start a new job all at the same time.

Not all psychologists are convinced that "good" life events are as stressful as bad ones, nor are they convinced that change per se is a reliable predictor of stress. Critics of the Holmes and Rahe approach argue that most items on their list are quite negative and that these negative items are responsible for more stress (McLean & Link, 1994). It is likely that most of the stress associated with "good" changes occurs when the anticipated event does not live up to the person's expectations. Vacations and holidays may not be inherently stressful, but trying to fulfill unrealistic fantasies about what vacations and holidays should be like is probably stressful indeed.

Relatively insignificant sources of stress, often called hassles, can also contribute to a person's overall level of stress. Waiting in long lines, losing your keys, getting a parking ticket, and oversleeping on the day of an important exam are not life-threatening events. However, if enough of these hassles occur within a short period, people begin to react as if something larger had occurred. The number of hassles people report experiencing predicts psychological symptoms of stress, even when the impact of major life events is factored out (Kanner, Coyne, Schaefer, & Lazarus, 1981). You might hear advice to avoid "sweating the little stuff," because enough little stuff happening at the same time can still affect your well-being.

Social relationships and their disruption can be a significant source of stress for many people. When we feel socially isolated, we feel unsafe, and at this point in our discussion, you probably know what happens whenever we feel unsafe—more stress. Because lonely people see the social environment as threatening, they respond with feelings of hostility, stress, pessimism, anxiety, and low self-esteem (Hawkley & Cacioppo, 2010). Their behavior begins a loop of self-fulfilling prophesies. Thinking that nobody wants to be around them, they begin to act in negative ways that ensure nobody wants to be around them, yet they do not see the reactions of others as related to their own negativity. There are no easy fixes for loneliness, but most people cope more effectively with feelings of loneliness when they consciously attend to the needs of other people rather than focusing on their own situations (Cacioppo & Patrick, 2008).

Feeling socially isolated makes us feel unsafe, which triggers stress responses. Loneliness makes people behave in ways that make them difficult to be around, such as displaying greater pessimism, anxiety, and hostility, beginning a loop of self-fulfilling prophesies and more loneliness.

What Are the Biological Correlates of Stress?

Regardless of the identity of a stressor, once you appraise a stimulus as a danger, you initiate Selye's GAS. The first stage, the alarm stage, is accompanied by a coordinated reaction including physical, cognitive, and behavioral responses to perceived danger. Imagine for a moment that one of your ancient ancestors was out hunting and suddenly found himself face to face with a hungry lion. Physically, the autonomic nervous system prepared your ancestor for fight or flight. The brainstem, described in Chapter 4, initiated the release of the neurotransmitter norepinephrine, which increased vigilance and fear. Cognitively, your ancestor accessed his memory for information about lions, which he hoped would include ideas about how similar situations were handled in the past. Behaviorally, your ancestor carried out his plan for escape. We assume that given your presence today, your ancestor was successful.

Stress and the Amygdala

We can trace the neural pathways that coordinate these responses to potentially dangerous stimuli. Sensory pathways provide information to higher cognitive centers in the cerebral cortex, letting our hunter know that the object in front of him is a lion. Memories of lion behavior, including eating habits, contribute to accurately identifying the lion as a stressor.

Simultaneously, sensory input travels from the thalamus to the amygdala, which plays an important role in the identification of dangerous stimuli, as discussed in Chapters 4 and 7. The amygdala participates in a "fear circuit" that provides a rapid assessment of a stimulus or situation as potentially dangerous (LeDoux, 2000, 2014). If the amygdala is lesioned, animals no longer respond with conditioned fear to previously learned classically conditioned associations between a stimulus (perhaps a tone or light) and an electric shock, an example of classical conditioning discussed in Chapter 8 (see ● Figure 16.3). Animals with lesions in the amygdala are also unable to learn to respond appropriately to unfamiliar dangerous stimuli (Wilensky, Schafe, Kristensen, & LeDoux, 2006).

Because sensory information can reach the amygdala along routes that are separate from the pathways for information going to the cortex, we might find ourselves frightened by stimuli that we don't immediately understand or consciously view as dangerous (Knight, Nguyen, & Bandettini, 2003). As we mentioned in Chapter 4, a man who was blind because of damage to his visual cortex still showed normal response in his amygdala when shown faces expressing fear (Pegna, Khateb, Lazeyras, & Seghier, 2005). You might have found yourself feeling anxious while

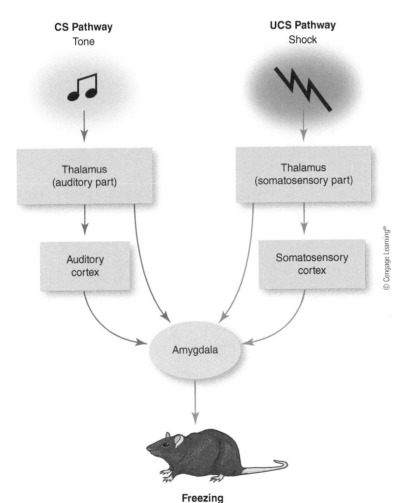

FIGURE 16.3

The Amygdala and Fear. The amygdala participates in a "fear circuit" that provides a rapid response to a potentially dangerous stimulus. After rats learn a classically conditioned association of a tone (a conditioned stimulus, or CS) that signals the arrival of an electric shock (an unconditioned stimulus, or UCS), they freeze whenever they hear the tone. If the amygdala is lesioned, the rat no longer freezes when it hears the tone, and it is unable to learn about new signals for shocks.

© Cengage Learning®

returning to your car after an evening class without knowing why you are reacting this way, but it is probably a good idea to listen to your amygdala until further information becomes available.

Once the amygdala has identified a stimulus as potentially dangerous, it communicates with the hypothalamus. As we mentioned in Chapter 4, the hypothalamus most directly commands the autonomic nervous system, particularly the sympathetic division. This part of the autonomic nervous system is responsible for our fight-or-flight response to danger.

Stress, the Sympathetic Adrenal–Medullary System, and the Hypothalamic–Pituitary–Adrenal Axis

Perceiving a potential source of danger mobilizes the body's resources using two systems—the **sympathetic adrenal–medullary (SAM) system** and the **hypothalamic–pituitary–adrenal (HPA) axis**. The SAM system initiates the release of adrenaline (also known as epinephrine) and norepinephrine into the bloodstream from the adrenal glands located above the kidneys in your lower back. These chemical messengers circulate to many organs and to the brain, producing many of the immediate, short-lived, fight-or-flight responses to stress, such as a pounding heart and rapid breathing (see ● Figure 16.4).

sympathetic adrenal–medullary (SAM) system A circuit that responds to perceived stressors by initiating the release of epinephrine and norepinephrine into the bloodstream.
hypothalamic–pituitary–adrenal (HPA) axis A circuit that responds to perceived stressors by initiating the release of cortisol into the bloodstream.

FIGURE 16.4

Two Systems Respond to a Stressor.
In response to the appraisal of a stimulus as a stressor, two systems mobilize the body's resources. The sympathetic adrenal–medullary (SAM) system responds quickly by initiating the release of epinephrine (adrenaline) and norepinephrine into the bloodstream by the adrenal glands. These chemical messengers initiate many immediate, short-lived responses, such as a pounding heart and rapid breathing. Simultaneously, activation of the hypothalamic–pituitary–adrenal (HPA) axis results in the release of cortisol into the bloodstream by the adrenal glands. Cortisol acts to boost the energy available for dealing with the stress. Cortisol receptors in the hippocampus serve as a feedback loop to keep the system from overreacting. The effects of HPA axis activity are slower to develop and longer lasting than those of the SAM response. HPA axis activity is associated with more of the outcomes of chronic stress, such as suppression of the immune system.

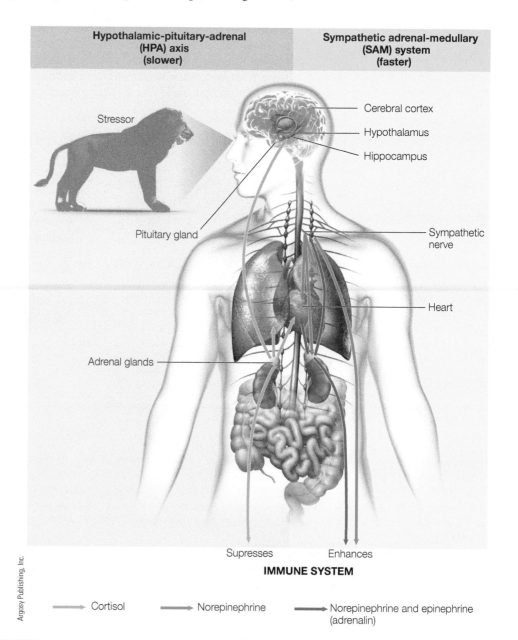

Argosy Publishing, Inc.

Simultaneously, activation of the HPA axis sets an entirely different system in motion. Here's how the circuit works. The hypothalamus (H) communicates with the pituitary gland (P), located just above the roof of your mouth, which in turn tells the adrenal glands (A) to release a hormone known as **cortisol** into the bloodstream. Circulating cortisol boosts the energy available for dealing with a stressor. The HPA axis response to stress can continue longer than the SAM response, which explains many of the outcomes of chronic stress.

One of the possible outcomes of chronic stress is prolonged high levels of circulating cortisol. Long-term exposure to cortisol can produce a number of harmful effects, including the death of neurons. When rats received daily injections of the rat equivalent of cortisol, neural death began to occur in just a few weeks (Stein-Behrens, Mattson, Chang, Yeh, & Sapolsky, 1994). Identical amounts of neural death occurred if the rats were stressed daily instead of receiving the injections, suggesting that the action of cortisol is responsible for most of the neural damage observed to result from stress. Studies in humans who have a medical condition called Cushing's disease that results in unusually high cortisol levels suggest that cortisol abnormalities might contribute to reduced hippocampus volume, memory problems, abnormal sleep patterns, and depression (Langenecker et al., 2012). Not only can high levels of cortisol damage neurons, but these same levels appear to inhibit the neurogenesis, or birth of neurons, that might help to offset the damage (Cowen, 2010).

Normally, activity of the HPA axis is regulated by a feedback loop involving the hippocampus (Stokes, 1995). The hippocampus works like a rev limiter in an automobile engine that prevents the driver from going over a certain speed. The hippocampus contains large numbers of receptors for cortisol and other stress hormones. When the hippocampus detects high levels of these hormones, it signals the hypothalamus, which in turn tells the adrenal glands to reduce the release of cortisol, and arousal dissipates.

The role of the hippocampus as the rev limiter of the HPA axis might be the bridge between extreme stress and depression. As we observed in Chapter 14, many cases of depression are preceded by unusually stressful events. Consistently elevated levels of cortisol because of stress can overwhelm the hippocampus's feedback loop, leading instead to the continuous release of cortisol and constant arousal. Without the regulation of cortisol usually provided by the hippocampus acting as a rev limiter, a person can begin to experience depression (Stokes, 1995). People who are treated with cortisol and similar stress hormones for medical conditions such as rheumatoid arthritis are often troubled by deep depression, reinforcing the role of excess cortisol in depressed mood.

Not only can the hippocampus fail to regulate cortisol release under conditions of extreme stress, but continued stress can damage the hippocampus further. The stressed baboons mentioned earlier in this chapter experienced neural death, particularly in the hippocampus, in addition to their other medical problems (Sapolsky, 2001). People with PTSD, discussed in Chapter 14, also show evidence of having a smaller than average hippocampus (Bossini et al., 2008; Bremner et al., 1995). Having a smaller than average hippocampus appears to be a result of PTSD as opposed to a risk factor for PTSD (Chao, Yaffe, Samuelson, & Neylan, 2014).

Gender Differences in the Stress Response

Although psychologists typically discuss fight or flight as the common response to stressors, an alternate response has been suggested that might be more typical of women's responses to stressors (Taylor, 2006). Noting that from an evolutionary standpoint, a mother with small children is unlikely to find either fight or flight easy to do, Taylor (2006) suggested that women are more likely to **tend and befriend** in response to stressors. Soothing frightened children, hiding, and forming social alliances for further protection might be more effective strategies.

Instead of the traditional hormones associated with fight and flight, a tend-and-befriend response is more closely associated with the release of oxytocin, a hormone related to social bonding that we discussed in Chapters 4 and 7. As we mentioned in Chapter 4, added oxytocin relieves stress in animals but only when the animals are in a social group as opposed to being isolated (Taylor & Master, 2010; Yee et al., 2010).

cortisol A hormone released into the bloodstream from the adrenal glands.
tend and befriend An alternative to fight or flight as a response to stressors that is possibly more characteristic of females.

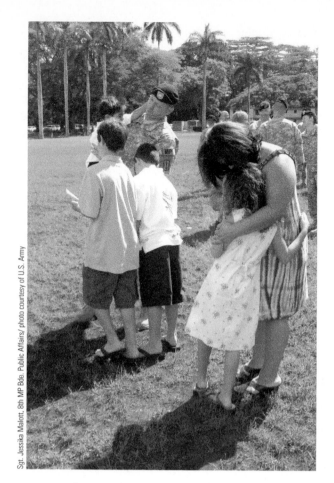

Sgt. Jessika Malott, 8th MP Bde. Public Affairs/ photo courtesy of U.S. Army

As this family faces the stress of the father's overseas deployment, the mother responds with a tend-and-befriend approach by comforting her daughter.

Socioeconomic Status and Stress

Beginning with initial observations that death rates were negatively correlated with increases in occupational grades among British civil servants (Marmot, Rose, Shipley, & Hamilton, 1978; Marmot, Shipley, & Rose, 1984), scientists have become aware that health disparities exist worldwide as a function of wealth. People with lower socioeconomic status (SES) experience worse health. Absolute wealth is not the only factor here. People's subjective estimation of their own status in the community also predicts susceptibility to disease (Cohen et al., 2008).

What processes can explain SES effects on health disparities? The poor are exposed to more noise, more toxins, more carcinogens, more violence, fewer resources, less health care, higher levels of drugs and alcohol abuse, less exercise, more anger, less control, and less trust (Adler, 2013). This long list has something in common—all of these factors are associated with high stress. In essence, this type of stress accelerates the aging process, including the shortening of telomeres, the "caps" found at the end of chromosomes (Needham et al., 2013). Premature aging, of course, is also going to lead to earlier death.

The Epigenetics of Stress

In Chapter 3, we discussed the significant role played by the environment in determining whether and when a particular gene is expressed. We defined epigenetics as the influence on traits by factors that determine how genes perform; the field of epigenetics explores gene–environment interactions. For example, we observed how both rats and human children who were well nurtured by their mothers showed more resilience to stress later in life. The nurture received from the mother had influenced how the genes responsible for producing and reacting to stress hormones behaved during later stressful experiences (Champagne, Francis, Mar, & Meaney, 2003; Neigh, Gillespie, & Nemeroff, 2009).

Genes and life stress also interact to produce depression. As we observed in Chapter 14, depression is often accompanied by dysfunction in systems using the neurotransmitter serotonin. Life stress affects people differently depending on whether they possess a short form or a long form of a gene related to serotonin function. Having the long or short version of the gene interacts with life stress to produce different levels of activity in the amygdala and hippocampus, differences in the pathways connecting the amygdala and hippocampus with other regions of the brain, differences in gray matter, and different levels of rumination, the repetitive rethinking of problems that is particularly characteristic of depressed people (Canli et al., 2006). These gene–stress interactions help explain why some people are more vulnerable to life stress while others seem relatively well protected against stress.

Health disparities, or the differences between the health of wealthy and that of poor individuals, can result from the greater exposure of poor people to stressors.

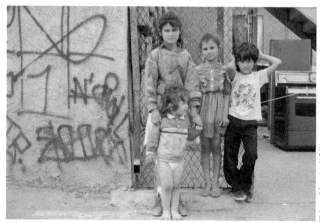

Visions of America, LLC/Alamy

How Does Stress Affect Our Health?

Our stress response was forged by the challenges our hunter–gatherer ancestors were most likely to face. The result is a system that has beneficial effects in the short term but can lead to negative effects when stress becomes chronic (Cacioppo & Berntson, 2011). After all, it would not take your ancestors hours, days, months, or years to figure out what to do to escape a hungry lion. For better or for worse, the outcome would be decided quickly.

In contrast, many of the stressors we face in modern living are not brief, and as a result, we are fairly constantly experiencing Selye's resistance phase, which combines stress and coping. You might be worried about finding a job after you graduate from college, which might be years away. Any long-term, chronic stress has the potential to affect health in negative ways. Not only does responding to stress require large amounts of energy, but while in the resistance stage, you do a less efficient job of storing nutrients and giving your body the rest and repair it needs. Improved understanding of the relationships between stress and health can guide our quest for physical and psychological well-being.

Stress and the Immune System

Very short-term bursts of stress can have a beneficial effect on many biological systems, including the **immune system**, your body's frontline defense against infection and cancer. Participating in a stressful memory task was correlated with an improvement in the response of the immune system, as measured by markers of immune system activity in the saliva of volunteers (Bosch, De Geus, & Kelder, 2001).

However, the immune system does not perform as well in the face of long-term, chronic sources of stress (see ● Figure 16.5). When responding to an emergency, our stress response system prioritizes body functions. Those that are not necessary for handling the immediate emergency are taken offline. Unfortunately for those suffering from chronic, ongoing stress, one of those expendable systems is the immune system (Thornton, Andersen, Crespin, & Carson, 2007). As a result, stress can lead to greater frequency and severity of illnesses, as you may have noticed immediately following final exam periods (Wadee, Kuschke, Kometz, & Berk, 2001).

Numerous studies indicate that people experiencing chronic stress are more vulnerable to infectious diseases, like colds and the flu (Cohen, Tyrrell, & Smith, 1991). White blood cells, or **lymphocytes**, protect us from invading organisms. Unfortunately, stress hormones directly suppress the activity of lymphocytes (Calcagni & Elenkov, 2006). Flare-ups of both oral and genital herpes are most likely to occur when a person is experiencing unusual stress (Cohen & Herbert, 1996). The progression of HIV infection to AIDS is influenced by the person's level of stress (Harper et al., 2006). Stressed students show greater vulnerability to the virus

immune system The body system that defends against infection and cancer.
lymphocyte White blood cells that are products of the immune system.

FIGURE 16.5

Stress Interacts With Anxiety to Predict Immune Response. Students with high anxiety, but not those with low anxiety, experienced a drop in immune function in anticipation of an exam coming up in 2 weeks. Immune system function had returned to normal 2 weeks following the exam. *Source:* Adapted from "Personality Factors, Stress and Immunity," by A. A. Wadee, R. H. Kuschke, S. Kometz, and M. Berk, 2001, *Stress and Health: Journal of the International Society for the Investigation of Stress, 17*(1), pp. 25–40.

Many of the dangers faced by these San hunters in South Africa are likely to arise and resolve quickly. Our responses to stress are better suited for short-term stressors than for many of the ongoing, chronic sources of stress we face in industrialized settings.

responsible for mononucleosis, which normally is kept in check by a robust immune system (Cacioppo & Berntson, 2011). Unfortunately, knowledge of these relationships can place an even greater burden on sick people, who may be led to believe that their illness wouldn't be so bad if they were somehow better at managing stress.

Stress related to our social relationships seems to be especially harmful to our ability to stay healthy. A meta-analysis of almost 300 studies and about 20,000 participants demonstrated that chronic stressors affecting people's social roles (e.g., death of a loved one or divorce) produce the greatest suppression of the immune system (Segerstrom & Miller, 2004). In particular, stressors that are outside a person's sense of control and lead to little hope for improvement have the most damaging effects. Those who are older and already ill are especially susceptible to adverse consequences of stress.

Stress and Heart Disease

Type A personality A competitive, workaholic, and in some cases hostile personality type.
Type B personality A mellow, laid-back personality type.

In the 1970s, Meyer Friedman and Ray Rosenman (1974) stimulated a large quantity of research by suggesting that highly competitive workaholics, whom they called **Type A personalities**, were more susceptible to heart disease than the mellower, laid-back people they called **Type B personalities**.

Connecting to **Research**

Social Challenges Early in Life Affect the Developing Immune System

IN THIS TEXTBOOK, WE HAVE explored a number of examples of interactions between people's genetic makeup and their life experiences that predict psychological and physical health. We have also seen how some early life experiences, such as child maltreatment, seem to have especially pronounced effects on people's outcomes throughout the rest of their life. What is there about experiences early in life that is so important? How does the experience of stress early in life affect health later? To examine these questions, researchers evaluated the effects of early stress on genetic

pathways that shape the immune system (Cole et al., 2012).

The Question: How does adverse early life experience produce effects on later health?

METHODS

In Chapter 11, we reviewed work by Harry Harlow in which infant rhesus monkeys were raised by cloth and wire surrogate "mothers" to investigate questions about attachment. Steven Cole and his colleagues (2012) also exposed infant rhesus monkeys

to surrogate mothers, other peers, or both instead of their real mothers. The researchers then conducted analyses of genetic changes in the infant monkeys' immune systems.

RESULTS

When the monkeys were only 4 months old, the researchers identified changes in the expression of genes in the monkeys' developing immune systems. Genes that were related to inflammation and activation of the immune system were more active in monkeys raised by peers or by peers plus a sur-

Further study, however, showed that simply being competitive had little to do with increased risk of heart disease. Instead, the Type As who did develop heart problems exhibited a pattern of interpersonal hostility. The Type As most at risk for heart disease were frequently suspicious, angry, and resentful of others. It is possible that their own hostile behavior provoked more hostile situations and reactions from others, confirming their worldview and maintaining their negative behavior. In addition, hostile people are not likely to build up networks of friends and loved ones, who are often our best protectors from the untoward effects of stress (Jackson, Kubzansky, Cohen, Jacobs, & Wright, 2007). In middle-age adults, frequent conflict with members of a person's social network raised the risk of death 200% to 300% (Lund, Christensen, Nilsson, Kriegbaum, & Hulvej Rod, 2014).

Stress puts the cardiovascular system at risk by affecting the ability of blood vessels to expand when necessary. People whose arteries are already stiff or clogged because of age, poor fitness, or disease often suffer from high blood pressure and might be especially susceptible to heart attacks following stress. In a heart attack, interruptions of blood flow to the heart trigger death of a part of the cardiac muscle. Flexible blood vessels maintain blood flow and blood pressure and lessen the chances of a heart attack. To test the effects of stress on blood flow, healthy participants were given a standardized mental stress task in which colored buttons were to be pushed as quickly as possible in response to flashing lights of the same color (Spieker et al., 2002). For the following 45 minutes, the ability of the participants' blood vessels to expand was reduced by a factor of 50%. A participant's change in blood pressure in response to a stressful situation was predictive of a later diagnosis with hypertension, or high blood pressure, which can lead to heart attacks or stroke (Spieker et al., 2002).

Research shows that in middle-age adults, frequent conflict with members of a person's social network increased the risk of death by 200% to 300%.

Stress, Mood, Sleep, and Obesity

As we mentioned in Chapters 4 and 14, mood, sleep, and appetite are closely intertwined. A change in one of these behaviors usually results in changes in the others. Long-term, chronic stress can begin a cascade of changes in mood, sleep, and appetite that compromise well-being. Disruptions of sleep because of stress are particularly hazardous to health, because we need sleep to restore our bodies after the challenges of the day. Both sleep quantity and sleep quality are associated with both overall health and cognitive outcomes (Hawkley & Cacioppo, 2010).

Stress frequently serves as a trigger for depressed mood. Self-reports of daily stressors, like having an argument with a friend, were correlated with the participants' mood (Stader &

rogate mother than in monkeys raised by their biological mothers. Genes involved in basic defenses against bacteria and viruses were less active than in the monkeys raised by their biological mothers.

CONCLUSIONS

The researchers believed that sympathetic nervous system responses to the stress of being raised by peers or a surrogate mother and peers changed the basic way genes important to the immune system were expressed. Their results were similar to genetic studies of adults who had experienced adverse childhood events. These changes help to explain why people with early social challenges have a more difficult time responding to diseases caused by bacteria or viruses. ●

Rhesus infants raised by surrogate mothers or peers experienced changes in the expression of genes related to their immune systems. These results help explain the connection between adverse childhood experience and poor adult health outcomes.

Hokanson, 1998). The ability of stress to alter levels of circulating cortisol, discussed earlier in this chapter, might form the basis for this connection between stress and depressed mood. As we observed in Chapter 14, many people diagnosed with depression show signs of abnormal cortisol function (Aihara et al., 2007).

Cortisol is not just released in response to perceived stressors. As we observed in Chapter 6, cortisol also plays a role in maintaining our natural cycles of sleep and waking. Cortisol is released in large quantities early in the morning, contributing to wakefulness. As the day progresses, cortisol levels drop off, reducing wakefulness and setting the stage for sleep. If you experience a big jolt of cortisol because of a stressor late in the evening, getting to sleep is going to be difficult, even when you're tired. Even when you do get to sleep, high levels of cortisol interfere with good sleep quality (Van Cauter, Leproult, & Plat, 2000). Both high levels of stress and depression can produce sleep disturbances, especially the experience of waking frequently throughout the night (Koenigsberg et al., 2004).

Mood and sleep can both affect appetite. Among the criteria for major depressive disorder, discussed in Chapter 14, are changes in appetite. Some people who are depressed lose weight without dieting, while others gain weight. By now, it shouldn't surprise you to learn that stress, along with depression, can also contribute to obesity. In response to stress-related hormones, fat cells behave differently, growing in both size and number (Kuo et al., 2009). Stressed mice gained more weight than mice that were not stressed, even when both were fed the same high-fat, high-sugar diet. In addition to this direct effect of stress on appetite, stress can produce indirect effects on obesity by interfering with sleep. Dieters who enjoyed a full-night's sleep lost the same amount of weight as dieters who slept less, but there was a difference in the kind of weight that was lost (Nedeltcheva, Kilkus, Imperial, Schoeller, & Penev, 2010). Dieters who slept well lost a healthy amount of fat. Sleep-deprived dieters lost only half as much fat as the sleeping dieters, and three quarters of their weight loss consisted of precious bone and muscle tissue instead (see ● Figure 16.6).

Long before vaccinations and antibiotics were available, death rates because of infectious diseases began to drop in the United States. Improved wages and nutrition, coupled with more rest time away from work, allowed people to recuperate from their daily stresses (Cacioppo & Berntson, 2011).

An Integrated View of Stress and Health

We have reviewed a number of studies in this section that demonstrate the adverse effects that chronic, prolonged stress can have on our health. Popular wisdom suggests that people with

FIGURE 16.6

Sleep and Diet Interact. Participants who slept 8.5 hours per night lost about the same amount of weight during a treatment program as participants who slept 5.5 hours per night, but the two groups differed in the amount of body fat and lean body mass that was lost. The group that slept 8.5 hours per night lost more body fat and less lean body mass, which is characteristic of desirable weight loss, than the group that slept 5.5 hours per night. These results remind us that many of our health habits are intimately interconnected and that changing one can have a large effect on others. *Source:* Adapted from "Insufficient Sleep Undermines Dietary Efforts to Reduce Adiposity," by A. V. Nedeltcheva, J. M. Kilkus, J. Imperial, D. A. Schoeller, and P. D. Penev, 2010, *Annals of Internal Medicine, 153,* pp. 435–441.

the highest levels of stress should therefore experience the worst health. However, we have already seen one example, the healthy Type As, in which this was not the case. In another study, 5,000 men reported their stress levels, which were then compared 20 years later to their medical records. Surprisingly, the men who had reported the highest levels of stress had experienced the least amount of heart disease (Macleod, Davey Smith, Heslop, Metcalfe, Carroll, & Hart, 2002). How can we explain these apparently contradictory results?

One approach to reconciling the good health enjoyed by some stressed people with data demonstrating the harmful effects of stress in others is to step back and look at the whole person within her environment over the entire life span. Health can be described as not just the absence of disease but also as the ability to respond to the challenges of being alive (Juster, McEwen, & Lupien, 2010; McEwen & Gianaros, 2011).

Personal factors, including your genes, interact with the parental care you receive, as we discussed previously in this chapter. Other protective factors, such as your social networks and sense of meaning or purpose in life, contribute to your resilience in the face of the negative and cumulative effects of a lifetime of responding to stressors (Cacioppo & Berntson, 2011). These protective factors occur at critical periods, such as the impact of parenting in early childhood, so a complete understanding of protective mechanisms should be examined within the context of life-span development. Once we fully understand these protective processes, psychologists should be in the exciting position of being able to design effective interventions for improving health and well-being (see ● Figure 16.7).

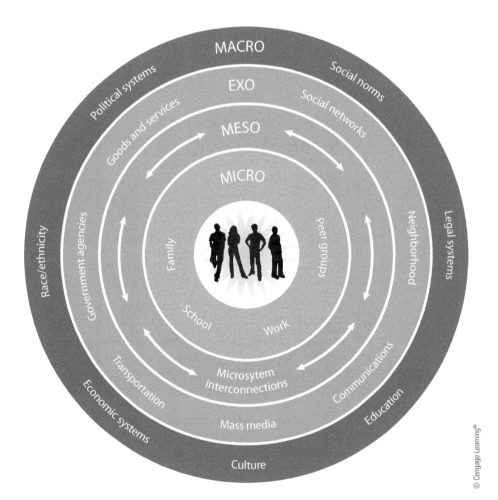

FIGURE 16.7

An Interactive View of Stress and Health. Individuals do not experience stress in a vacuum. Personal factors, like genes and everyday experiences, influence outcomes within an environment consisting of ever larger circles of social connectivity. The relationships between social environment and personal factors are reciprocal. Individual actions influence the social environment, which in turn influences individual factors. *Source:* Adapted from "Allostatic Load Biomarkers of Chronic Stress and Impact on Health and Cognition," by R.-P. Juster, B. S. McEwen, and S. J. Lupien, 2010," *Neuroscience and Biobehavioral Reviews, 35*(1), pp. 2–16, doi:10.1016/j.neubiorev.2009.10.002.

© Cengage Learning®

Psychology as a Hub Science
Belongingness, Stress, Achievement, and Health

We don't need to tell you that being in college can be stressful. For many students, college can mean new environments, new rules and routines, new social interactions, less sleep, not-so-great eating habits, and more sitting than exercising. Can the application of psychological research make the transition into college easier and less stressful?

We can't make many of these stressors go away, but a simple, one-time intervention at the beginning of the first year of college made a large difference in the academic performance and health of a group of students (Walton & Cohen, 2011). Incoming first-year students at Stanford University were randomly assigned to a control group or a social-belonging group. The social-belonging group read what they thought were the results of a survey of older students, who said that they had worried about fitting in during their first year but had grown more confident over time. Participants were asked to write an essay comparing their own first-year experiences with the survey results and then deliver a speech based on their essay to a video camera for use with future students. At no time were the participants aware that they were actually experiencing a "treatment" designed to make them see the social stressors of college life as typical of all students and of short duration.

Over the next 3 years, the participants' grade point averages and health were monitored. The "belongingness" intervention had little impact on the health and grades of European American students, but it had significant and positive effects on African American students. Compared to African American students in the control group, the students who had received the one-time reassurance that their concerns about fitting in were normal and were not permanent had higher grades, fewer visits to the doctor, and higher subjective happiness (see ● Figure 16.8).

While further research is necessary to know how far these results can be generalized to other students, the results emphasize the importance of how you interpret your situation and whether you feel like you belong to your overall performance, health, and well-being. ●

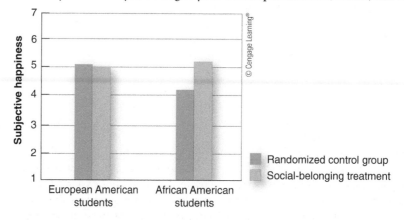

FIGURE 16.8

A Belongingness Intervention Improved the Performance and Health of African American College Students. A one-time treatment aimed at framing the stress of fitting in to the college experience as common to most students and limited in duration significantly improved the grade point averages, happiness ratings, and health of African American students at Stanford University 3 years later. European American students did not experience the same treatment-related differences, with both treated and nontreated European American students experiencing the same health and subjective happiness as the treated African American students. This result suggests that "fitting in" was already framed by European American students in positive ways. *Source:* Adapted from "A Brief Social-Belonging Intervention Improves Academic and Health Outcomes of Minority Students," by G. M. Walton and G. L. Cohen, 2011, *Science, 331*(6023), pp. 1447–1451, doi:10.1126/science.1198364.

How Can We Cope Effectively With Stress?

Stress is inevitable. That simple statement does not imply that there is nothing you can do about stress. Psychologists have identified a number of strategies people can use to effectively reduce the negative impacts of stress on their happiness and health.

One of the most positive aspects of stress is that we adapt to it over time. Take a minute to jot down the things you found most stressful 5 years ago and then make a list of the stressors you face today. Would you trade today's list for the one from 5 years ago? Most people would do so in a heartbeat. Life gets more complicated and often more stressful, but our skills for coping improve at the same time. People tend to report less stress as they get older (Shields, 2004).

Earlier in this chapter, we described the role of cognitive appraisal in identifying a stimulus or event as a stressor. Appraisal plays an important role in coping with identified stressors as well. Once a stressor has been identified, a second set of appraisals occurs that guides our coping responses (Lazarus, 1966). What harm has already occurred? What threats remain? What resources do we need to overcome the challenge?

The stress of middle school, such as attending school dances, is real to students at the time, but as we get older and more experienced, our capacity to manage stress improves. With age, people report feeling less stress, even though stressors tend to become more complicated and numerous at the same time.

Managing Stress

An obvious starting place for keeping your levels of stress low is to ask whether stressors can be eliminated. If you feel stressed about having too much to do and too little time to do it, it might be possible to reduce your workload or practice better time management skills. If money is tight, a visit to your campus's financial aid office might provide you with solutions you had not considered. The worst possible approach is to withdraw and avoid stressors in the vain hope that they will go away. Your latest credit card statement is not going to get better magically if you ignore it. In fact, your emotional response to seeing the statement on your desk every day is likely to get a lot worse over time.

A major variable that predicts our response to stress is the sense of control. Feeling surprised by life or out of control can lead to significant stress. Some of the worst stressors are those that seem to strike randomly, such as being diagnosed with lung cancer when you never smoked (Pietrzak, Goldstein, Southwick, & Grant, 2011). These seemingly random events undercut our sense of control, countering the belief that "If I don't smoke, I am ensuring my lungs will stay healthy."

Even when a stressor takes us by surprise, we can regain a sense of control. Viktor Frankl (1959, p. 161), a Holocaust survivor, developed what he described as "tragic optimism" for coping with unforeseen disasters. Instead of asking why these disasters should happen to us, Frankl recommends that people exert a sense of control by asking, "How can I face this disaster with courage and responsibility?"

Many stressors are out of our control. We can't wish our cancer away or magically ensure that enough money appears in our bank accounts to pay this month's bills. However, we can respond to our stressors in ways that reduce our overall stress. This approach is consistent with the elements of positive psychology, which we review later in this chapter. Even if you are struggling with a life-threatening disease, stress can be reduced by educating yourself as much as possible about your condition and participating fully in decisions about your treatment. Residents of nursing homes who have more control over their choice of daily activities live longer than those who are not given such choices (Rodin, 1986). We observed in Chapter 12 that stressors have less effect on people who experience an internal locus of control, which means that they believe most of their outcomes are because of their personal efforts as opposed to luck, chance, or other external forces.

Because of the inevitability of stress, people cope best when they keep themselves as healthy as possible. If you follow good health habits, stress will still deplete your reserves and inhibit your immune system, but a healthy body can take more abuse than an unhealthy one. Students are more likely to get sick during final exams if they have neglected good eating and sleeping habits all term.

Regular aerobic exercise appears to be especially helpful. In one experiment, people with heart disease were observed as they engaged in exercise as part of their rehabilitation programs. The exercise reduced the overall stress levels of all participants (Milani & Lavie, 2009). Exercise seemed particularly beneficial for the participants who also scored high on psychosocial stress.

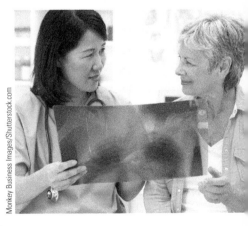

Patients who educate themselves about their conditions and participate fully in treatment decisions experience less stress.

FIGURE 16.9

Exercise Reduces Mortality in Stressed Cardiac Patients. People with cardiovascular disease were assessed for psychosocial stress levels during a rehabilitation program that included exercise. A control group did not have a formal exercise program. Based on their improvement in physical measures following the exercise program, the study participants were divided into low and high exercise change groups. In a follow-up 5 years later, high levels of physical improvement because of exercise did not affect the mortality of the low psychosocial stress group but significantly reduced mortality in the high-stress group. *Source:* Adapted from "Reducing Psychosocial Stress: A Novel Mechanism of Improving Survival From Exercise Training," by R. V. Milani and C. J. Lavie, 2009, *American Journal of Medicine, 122*(10), pp. 931–938, doi:10.1016/j.amjmed.2009.03.028.

Specialist Lawrence Shipman and Sergeant First Class Jonathan Zeke, a combat stress–relief dog, received an award for their work in reducing the stress of soldiers deployed in Iraq. Shipman notes that Zeke acts as an icebreaker, encouraging soldiers to talk to the behavioral health counselors.

None of the high-stress participants who showed the greatest physical benefits from exercise (such as increased oxygen uptake) died in the follow-up period compared to 19% of the high-stress participants who showed relatively low physical benefits from exercise (see ● Figure 16.9). Students would be wise to engage in some level of activity in college to offset the effects of increased stress.

In Chapter 15, we discussed the use of mindfulness in the treatment of anxiety and depression. Mindfulness, or the trained awareness of our current thoughts, emotions, and actions, has also been shown to be an effective method for reducing stress (Tang & Posner, 2009). In Chapter 6, we explored the effects of the altered state of consciousness produced through meditation. Although many people meditate within a religious context, a large meta-analysis indicated that meditation is an effective strategy for reducing psychological stress (Goyal et al., 2014).

One of the most powerful antidotes to the unhealthy effects of stress is social connectedness and support. Social support from friends and family and belief systems that allow a person to make sense out of the world provide powerful buffers against stress (Montpetit, Bergeman, Deboeck, Tiberio, & Boker, 2010). As we have argued on many occasions in this textbook, people with good social relationships and support are far less vulnerable to adverse health and psychological conditions than are people who are lonely and isolated (Cacioppo, Cacioppo, Capitanio, & Cole, 2015; Hostinar, Sullivan, & Gunnar, 2013). In times of distress, people frequently turn to others in an effort to cope. According to a study of responses to the terrorist attacks of 9/11, nearly 100% of the participants reported talking about their thoughts and feelings about the attacks with other people (Schuster et al., 2002). More than 90% reported either praying or engaging in spiritual contemplation appropriate to their faith. More than 60% engaged in relevant public activities. Nearly 40% focused on the needs of others by donating money or blood to relief efforts.

Understanding the importance of social support for coping helps to explain why people living in poor neighborhoods often experience more stress and have higher rates of depression. Living in a neighborhood where few people know one another or help one another with tasks like child care increases the risk of developing major depressive disorder (Russell & Cutrona, 2010). These socially disconnected neighborhoods become more prevalent as the income of residents decreases, making people living below the poverty line especially vulnerable to stress and depression.

Although it is ideal to receive your social support from other people, having a pet can also provide benefits to your health. Stockbrokers with high blood pressure who lived alone were selected to receive a cat or dog from a local shelter (Allen, 2003). When stressed, the pet owners experienced a much lower increase in blood pressure than their petless counterparts. The effect was most obvious among participants who listed few social connections with other people.

Many people find that having religious beliefs helps them cope with stress. People who report having religious beliefs appear to withstand the challenges of unemployment, low income, and widowhood better than people who report no religious beliefs (Diener & Seligman, 2004). Across a number of nations practicing different forms of religion, a higher rate of belief in a god predicts higher ratings of life satisfaction and lower rates of suicide (Helliwell, 2003).

Three Types of Coping

Coping with a stressor can take three forms: problem-focused, emotion-focused, and relationship-focused coping (O'Brien & DeLongis, 1996). In each case, positive and negative versions of each style can be observed.

Problem-focused coping is designed to address the problem. If you just flunked an important exam, positive problem-focused coping strategies might include making an appointment with your professor to discuss your options, hiring a tutor, taking a study skills seminar, or joining a study group formed by your classmates. Negative problem-focused coping can include escape and avoidance. Instead of confronting the problem, a student might stop going to class. Problem-focused coping is more frequently used for work-related stressors (which would include schoolwork) than for interpersonal stressors (like the breakup of an important relationship; Terry, 1994).

Emotion-focused coping helps you deal with the negative emotions associated with a stressor. Flunking an exam might make you feel sad, discouraged, and depressed. Positive coping with these negative emotions might involve sharing your concerns with your friends or family, taking a break from your studies to enjoy a movie or go for a jog, or, when the negative emotions seem overwhelming, visiting your campus's counseling center for advice. Negative emotion-focused coping, such as eating food you do not need or using alcohol to dull your stress, might simply add to your problems and increase your overall levels of stress.

Relationship-focused coping helps you maintain and protect social relationships in response to stress (O'Brien & DeLongis, 1996). This type of coping has both positive and negative aspects. For example, people caring for Alzheimer's patients, which can be stressful, exhibited both positive coping (empathy, support, and compromise) and negative coping (confronting, ignoring, blaming, and withdrawal; Kramer, 1993).

As we have seen so frequently in our discussions of human behavior, the choice of a coping approach results from interactions between people and their situation (Aldwin, 1994). For example, people who score high on the Big Five trait of neuroticism, which we discussed in Chapter 12, tend to experience more distress than people with low neuroticism scores (Bolger & Schilling, 1991). When responding to stressors in the work situation, people high in neuroticism are more likely to engage in negative problem-focused coping, such as escaping the situation (O'Brien & DeLongis, 1996). When dealing with interpersonal stress, however, people with high neuroticism use the negative relationship-focused coping strategy of confrontation. People with high neuroticism also cope differently with stress involving close relationships (significant others, family members, and close friends) than with stress involving distant relationships (coworkers and neighbors). They are more likely to use a positive relationship-focused coping method,

At times of stress, we often engage in three types of coping. (a) Problem-focused coping is usually used to solve problems at work. (b) Emotion-focused coping helps us deal with the negative emotions of stress. The use of strategies like overeating, however, can lead to more problems. (c) Relationship-focused coping helps us maintain and strengthen social networks at times of stress.

problem-focused coping A response to stress designed to address specific problems by finding solutions.
emotion-focused coping A response to stress that targets the negative emotions arising from the situation.
relationship-focused coping A response to stress designed to maintain and protect social relationships.

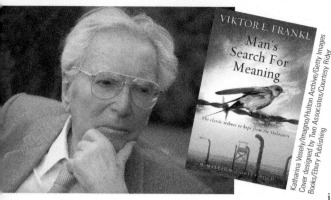

empathy, when dealing with distant relationships than when dealing with close relationships (O'Brien & DeLongis, 1996).

Resilience: Individual Differences in Response to Stress

You might have observed that under the same stressful circumstances, such as an upcoming exam, some students seem calm and others appear to be in a state of panic. What determines these individual differences in coping?

We have already seen how epigenetic interactions between genes and nurturing can influence later responses to stress. In addition, people differ in resilience, or the ability to adapt to life's challenges in positive ways. Resilient people do not ignore feelings of sadness or stress, but like Holocaust survivor Viktor Frankl, they harness their inner strengths to enable them to remain optimistic and get on with the business of life. In contrast, when people lack **resilience**, they feel overwhelmed, helpless, and victimized. They become more vulnerable to the use of negative coping strategies, including alcoholism and drug abuse, to escape their problems. Early research in resilience focused on children's ability to thrive even in conditions of poverty, neglect, and abuse (Masten et al., 1999).

Some psychologists refer to individual differences in the ability to cope with stress as resulting from a personality trait of hardiness (Hystad, Eid, Laberg, Johnsen, & Bartone, 2009; Maddi, 2013). As we mentioned in Chapter 12, a personality trait is likely to be stable and enduring over time. Compared to less hardy people, people with high hardiness experience less threat or disruption in response to the normal stressors of life. Hardiness combines commitment, control, and challenge (Bartone, 2000). People with high commitment see the world as interesting and seek involvement rather than withdrawal. Control refers to individuals' belief in their ability to influence events. Challenge is a state of mind that sees change and new experiences not as negative stressors but as opportunities for learning and personal growth. Among college students, hardiness did not predict grades, but it was negatively correlated with health complaints and stress related to academic work (Hystad et al., 2009; see ● Figure 16.10).

Other protective factors contributing to individual differences in resilience are cognitive skills, social skills, and flexibility in response to new situations (Garmezy, 1991). Individual differences in resilience might also have their roots in emotion. People who are generally more positive in mood tend to build the resources they need, including strong social networks, to sustain them at difficult times (Cohn, Fredrickson, Brown, Mikels, & Conway, 2009).

Austrian psychiatrist Viktor Frankl (1905–1997) was sent to the dreaded Nazi concentration camp Auschwitz, where he lost his pregnant wife, parents, and brother. Frankl used his experiences in developing his theories of *logotherapy*, after the Greek word for "meaning." The ability to find meaning even in the depths of despair by recalling pleasant memories or helping a suicidal inmate helped Frankl survive the stress and horror surrounding him.

People who write "scripts" for how their life "should" happen, such as thinking that everyone should enjoy a set schedule of activities over a holiday, often experience high stress levels when events take an unexpected turn. Maintaining a flexible approach to meeting your life's goals is far less likely to produce stress.

FIGURE 16.10

Hardiness Protects Students From the Health Impacts of Stress.
A personality trait of hardiness, which combines commitment, a sense of control, and the appraisal of stressors as challenges, seems to protect college students from the health consequences of high academic stress. *Source:* Adapted from "Academic Stress and Health: Exploring the Moderating Role of Personality Hardiness," by S. W. Hystad, J. Eid, J. C. Laberg, B. H. Johnsen, and P. T. Bartone, 2009, *Scandinavian Journal of Educational Research, 53*(5), pp. 421–429, doi:10.1080/00313830903180349.

resilience The ability to adapt to life's challenges in positive ways.

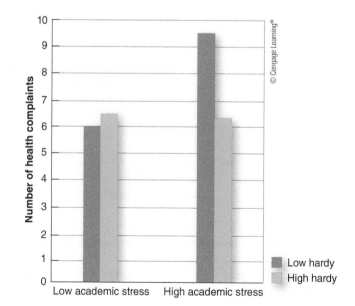

Summary 16.1 Stages in Hans Selye's General Adaptation Syndrome

Stage	What's happening?
Alarm	Mobilization of resources for fight or flight
Resistance	Continued coping with chronic stress
Exhaustion	Systems begin to fail

Credits: Top Row. AP Images. Second Row. Sgt. Jessika Malott, 8th MP Bde. Public Affairs/photo courtesy of U.S. Army. Bottom Row: oliveromg/Shutterstock.com.

What Is the Relationship Between Psychology and Health?

You might be surprised to see a section about **health psychology** in your psychology textbook. Isn't health the exclusive domain of medical personnel rather than of psychologists? It all depends on how you define *health*. For most of its history, the field of medicine viewed health as a lack of disease (Juster et al., 2010). Treatments were designed to make sick people feel better. In more recent years, health has been more commonly defined as the attainment of a positive state of well-being, rather than simply the absence of disease. Medicine today is more likely to use a **biopsychosocial model** of health, in which health is viewed as the sum of biological (such as genetics, infection, and injury), psychological (such as lifestyle, stress, and health beliefs), and social factors (such as culture, family, and social support; McEwen & Gianaros, 2011). In 1948, the World Health Organization (WHO) proposed a definition that reflects this more contemporary model of health: "a state of complete physical, mental and social well-being and not merely the absence of disease or infirmity" (WHO, 2003, para. 1). In addition to making sick people feel better, which is an important function of medicine, this new view of health seeks to improve the well-being of people who are not sick (see ● Figure 16.11).

One reason for this transition from the biomedical model to the biopsychosocial model is the changing face of health and medicine over the last 100 years or so. Because of improved sanitation and vaccination, the threats to health faced today are quite different from those faced by earlier generations. In 1900, the leading causes of death in the United States were pneumonia, influenza, and tuberculosis, but by 2005, the leading causes of death were heart

health psychology A branch of psychology that investigates the relationships between psychological variables and health.
biopsychosocial model A model that sees health as the result of biological, psychological, and social factors.

FIGURE 16.11

A Biopsychosocial Model of Health. Health today is viewed as the product of interactions among individual characteristics, life experiences, cognitions, and behavior. *Source:* Adapted from "Allostatic Load Biomarkers of Chronic Stress and Impact on Health and Cognition," by R.-P. Juster, B. S. McEwen, and S. J. Lupien, 2010," *Neuroscience and Biobehavioral Reviews, 35*(1), pp. 2–16, doi:10.1016/j.neubiorev.2009.10.002.

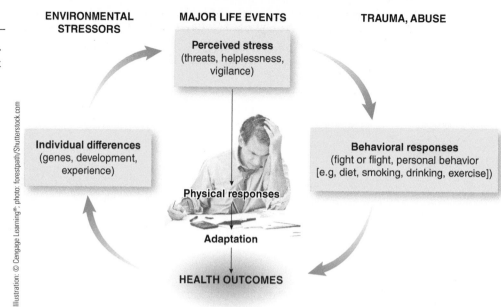

disease, cancer, lung disease, and stroke (see ● Figure 16.12). In other words, we have gone from facing major threats from infectious, short-duration conditions to noninfectious, long-term conditions. In the last few decades, considerable progress was made in the treatment of heart disease, cancer, and stroke. This improvement in turn has resulted in a larger number of Americans who are living long enough to be diagnosed with age-related conditions such as Alzheimer's disease and Parkinson's disease.

The contemporary leading causes of death just listed (heart disease, cancer, lung disease, and stroke) form significant interactions with behavior, because their risk factors include obesity, smoking, lack of exercise, and alcohol consumption. Even when we consider infectious diseases, we see evidence of strong behavioral components, such as the amount of stress you're experiencing (Cohen et al., 1991) or the likelihood you practice prevention by washing your hands during flu season. In addition, lifestyle factors and adherence to treatment plans can be extremely important to achieving and maintaining wellness. Health psychologists are interested in helping people to better prevent and recover from disease and to cope with the stress of chronic health problems and pain.

FIGURE 16.12

Leading Causes of Death in the United States. Over the last 100 years, infectious diseases have been replaced as the major causes of death in the United States by heart disease, cancer, lung disease, and stroke. As medical progress decreases deaths because of these causes, age-related diseases such as Alzheimer's disease have become more common causes of death. *Source:* Adapted from "Sitting Time and Mortality From All Causes, Cardiovascular Disease, and Cancer," by P. T. Katzmarzyk, T. S. Church, C. L. Craig, and C. Bouchard, 2011, *Medicine and Science in Sports and Exercise, 41*(5), pp. 998–1005, doi:10.1249/MSS.0b013e3181930355.

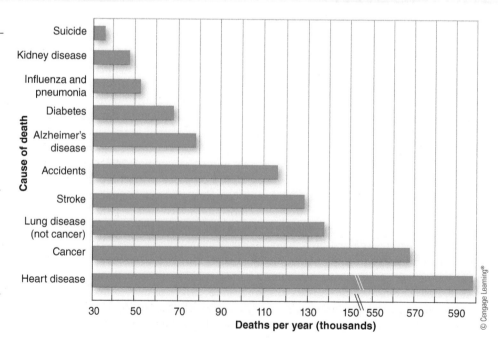

When we discuss the contributions of behavior to health, by no means do we want to "blame the victims" of poor health. People who have never smoked still get lung cancer, and thin, fit people get heart disease. The relationships between lifestyle factors and health are derived from the statistical analyses of large populations, not single individuals. At the same time, understanding that most people who engage in particular behaviors have certain health outcomes can provide us with clues for maintaining the healthiest lifestyles possible.

Behavior and Health

In 2009, *Consumer Reports* conducted a survey of 1,000 Americans to see how many engaged in everyday prevention behaviors (Consumerreports.com, 2009). As shown in Table 16.1, the respondents did rather well in a number of categories (91% read the warnings that come with a prescription drug, and 87% report not drinking beer while using a power tool or mower) but neglected some obvious preventive steps (58% never wear a bike helmet, 24% report being in a car without using a seat belt, and 27% do not use sunscreen when outdoors for an extended period). We do worry about those 13% who are drinking beer while using power tools or mowing the lawn. The point is that many of our choices contribute to the prevention of accidents and disease.

Behaviors that contribute to our major causes of death include smoking, poor nutrition, alcohol use, and lack of exercise (see ● Figure 16.13), which we discuss in more detail in the next sections.

Tobacco Use Cigarette smoking is considered to be the leading preventable cause of death in the United States, with a direct responsibility in one of five deaths each year (Centers for Disease Control and Prevention [CDC], 2014. On average, smokers die 13 to 14 years earlier than nonsmokers. Tobacco use can lead to additional health problems. Nicotine is a well-established gateway drug, capable of producing epigenetic changes that increase the likelihood of addiction to cocaine (Li et al., 2014). Tobacco's effects are not restricted to its users. In the

TABLE 16.1 Americans' Safety Practices

Behavior	Yes	No
Use cotton swabs to clean ears	73%	26%
Let your kids play on trampoline	43%	56%
Eat raw dough when making cookies	39%	61%
Use top step of ladder	31%	69%
Fail to use car's seat belt	24%	75%
Drink beer while using power tool or mower	13%	87%
Have a rubber mat in shower	39%	61%
Have a carbon-monoxide detector in home	51%	48%
Eat burgers only well done	67%	32%
Change batteries in smoke alarm annually	79%	21%
Clean lint trap in dryer after each use	81%	18%
Read warnings on prescription medicines	91%	9%
Wear a bike helmet	42%	58%
Wear sunscreen when outside for an extended time	73%	27%

Source: Adapted from "Risky Business," by Consumerreports.org, 2009, retrieved from http://www.consumerreports.org/cro/magazine-archive/march-2009/money/risk-taking/overview/risk-taking-ov.htm

FIGURE 16.13

Four Simple Habits Make Major Contributions to Health. Following four simple health habits—never smoking, exercising 30 minutes per day, maintaining a nonobese weight, and eating a healthy diet including fruits and vegetables—reduced overall risk of chronic disease by 78%. Unfortunately, only 9.1% of a sample of more than 20,000 adults between 35 and 65 years of age had all four habits. Most people reported following only one to three of the four health habits. *Source:* Adapted from "Healthy Living Is the Best Revenge: Findings From the European Prospective Investigation into Cancer and Nutrition–Potsdam Study," by E. S. Ford, M. M. Bergmann, J. Kroger, A. Schienkiewitz, C. Weikert, and H. Boeing, 2009, *Archives of Internal Medicine, 169*(15), pp. 1355–1362, doi:10.1001/archinternmed.2009.237.

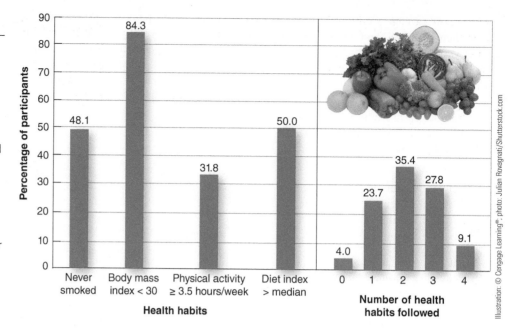

FIGURE 16.14

Geographical Distribution of Smokers in the United States. In the United States, nearly one in five adults is a smoker. In 2012, an estimated 18.1% of adults in the United States were current smokers. Smoking is more common among men, ethnic minorities, people with less education, people living below the poverty line, and people diagnosed with a psychological disorder. *Source:* Adapted from "Vital Signs: Current Cigarette Smoking Among Adults Aged ³18 Years—United States, 2005–2010," by Centers for Disease Control and Prevention, 2011b, *Morbidity and Mortality Weekly Report.* Retrieved from http://www.cdc.gov/mmwr/pdf/wk/mm60e0906.pdf.

United States, exposure to secondhand smoke leads to 3,400 lung cancer deaths, 46,000 heart disease deaths, 430 cases of sudden infant death syndrome (SIDS), 24,500 low-birth-weight babies, 71,900 preterm deliveries, and 200,000 episodes of childhood asthma each year (WHO, 2008).

Despite considerable educational efforts aimed at smoking prevention, 18.1% of American adults smoked as of 2012 (CDC, 2014c). Worldwide, rates of smoking are even higher than those found in the United States and other developed countries. According to the WHO (2008), two thirds of current smokers live in developing countries, with 30% of smokers residing in China and 10% in India. Gender, race, ethnicity, education, mental health, and income are strong determinants of the likelihood of smoking. In the United States, men are more likely to smoke than women (20.5%, as opposed to 15.8%). Multirace individuals reported the highest incidence of smoking (26.1%), followed by American Indians or Alaska Natives (21.8%), non-Hispanic Whites (19.7%), non-Hispanic Blacks (18.1%), Hispanics (12.5%), and Asians (10.7%). Smoking drops with increasing education, from 41.9% of individuals with a general equivalency diploma (GED) certificate to 5.9% of adults with a graduate degree. Poverty plays a strong role in smoking; 27.9.1% of adults living below the poverty line compared to 17.0% living at or above the poverty line report smoking (see ● Figure 16.14).

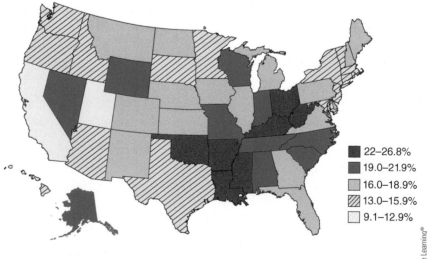

Percentage of persons age 18 years or more who reported smoking at least 100 cigarettes during their lifetime and who, at the time of the survey, reported smoking cigarettes every day or some days.

22–26.8%
19.0–21.9%
16.0–18.9%
13.0–15.9%
9.1–12.9%

Given the carnage produced by tobacco, why do people start smoking and then continue? An understanding of the initiation of tobacco use requires combining many of the perspectives we have discussed in this textbook—in particular, development, biological psychology, learning, and social psychology.

Most tobacco users begin smoking in childhood or early adolescence, long before decision-making abilities are mature. Because of the addictive nature of nicotine, about half of those who experiment with tobacco continue to use it. In addition to its action on synapses where the neurotransmitter acetylcholine is released, as discussed in Chapter 6, nicotine has the ability to stimulate the dopamine reward circuits of the brain and to produce a particularly unpleasant set of withdrawal symptoms. As we discussed in Chapter 11, adolescence is also a time when people try out new roles and learn important skills for getting along with peers, making them frequently susceptible to peer pressure. Teens often overestimate how many other people are using tobacco, so they might begin using it to avoid looking "different" (Institute of Medicine, 1994). Finally, most smokers have friends and parents who also smoke, suggesting a role for social learning (Biglan, Duncan, Ary, & Smolkowski, 1995).

A troubling aspect of the initiation of smoking is the prevalence of tobacco use among people with diagnosed psychological disorders. Of the approximately 20% of American adults diagnosed with any mental disorder (see Chapter 14), 36.1% were current smokers, a much higher rate than that found in the general population (CDC, 2013). Adults diagnosed with mental disorders smoke 31% of all cigarettes consumed by adults in the United States (CDC, 2013). Tobacco use among people with schizophrenia and other severe mental illnesses is about 70% in the United States, more than 3 times as high as the approximately 20% of users in the general population as reported by the CDC (Dixon et al., 2007). In addition, the severity of smoking among these individuals, which includes such factors as how many cigarettes are smoked per day, appears to be much higher among people with psychological disorders than in the general population. In a large-scale study of more than 50,000 adults who did not live in mental institutions, individuals with serious psychological distress, a global measure of psychological disorder, were more likely to smoke currently and heavily and were less likely to quit than individuals without serious psychological distress (Sung, Prochaska, Ong, Shi, & Max, 2011). Although many smokers with psychological disorders report using cigarettes to feel better, most began smoking long before their symptoms emerged and they were diagnosed with a disorder (Sacco, Termine, & Seyal, 2005).

People do quit smoking, although some find it difficult. Again, the social nature of our species plays a role in this process. A person's chances of successfully quitting are reduced by 67% if a spouse smokes, 25% if a sibling smokes, 36% if a friend smokes, and 34% if a coworker smokes (Schroeder, 2008). We are not advocating that a prospective quitter abandon the essential social support needed at a difficult time; rather, we are suggesting that people trying to quit physically separate themselves when friends and family light up. As we noted in Chapter 8, being exposed to conditioned stimuli, such as the smell of tobacco, can initiate a variety of conditioned behaviors that might make refusing a cigarette difficult for the person trying to quit.

Smoking cessation programs can also take advantage of the self-reference effect that we discussed in Chapter 12. The self-reference effect explains the superior recall for information relevant to the self by suggesting that the self serves as an important schema for organizing information. Participants experiencing interventions for smoking that were tailored to their own lives, needs, interests, and obstacles not only were more successful at

One of every three cigarettes lit each day is smoked by a person in China, where it is a conventional courtesy for one businessperson to greet another by offering a cigarette. The 2011 ban on smoking in bars, in restaurants, and on transportation does not apply to offices and factories. The ban was required when China signed the World Health Organization Framework Convention on Tobacco Control five years ago. Public health officials fear that the lack of an awareness program and penalties will encourage the population to ignore the ban.

In the United States, ex-smokers now outnumber smokers (47 million to 46 million; Chapman & MacKenzie, 2010). Smokers use a variety of techniques to quit, including simply stopping all use abruptly (cold turkey), gradually reducing intake, using nicotine patches and gum or other nicotine replacement tools, participating in counseling and support groups, or some combination of these.

quitting smoking but also showed brain activity in parts of the prefrontal cortex believed to participate in thinking about the self (Chua et al., 2011).

The benefits of quitting smoking appear within minutes to hours as the body begins to repair itself. After 5 years of abstention from smoking, risk of stroke is the same for ex-smokers and nonsmokers. After 10 years of abstention, the risk of lung cancer is cut in half. If the smoker quits before the age of 30 years, life expectancy remains the same as for someone who has never smoked (Doll, Peto, Boreham, & Sutherland, 2004). Eliminating all tobacco smoking in the United States would produce a gain of 1.73 years of life expectancy for an 18-year-old (Stewart, Cutler, & Rosen, 2009).

Nutrition Nutrition plays a significant part in overall physical development, including brain development, and is believed to be responsible for many differences in psychological and health outcomes related to SES (Rosales, Reznick, & Zeisel, 2009). People need the right amount and quality of nutrients to support optimum health and brain functioning, and being either underweight or obese is associated with reduced health. Obesity increases the rates of many chronic conditions, including heart disease, stroke, diabetes, arthritis, and breast and colon cancers. As we noted previously, maintaining a BMI below 30 (nonobese) was one of the four protective factors associated with much lower risk of disease. Returning the United States population to normal weight (a body mass index, or BMI, between 18.5 and 24.9) would produce about the same improvement in overall life expectancy as the elimination of smoking (Stewart et al., 2009).

As we mentioned in Chapter 7, not only do we face problems in the form of eating disorders, such as anorexia and bulimia, but the world has also experienced an unprecedented obesity epidemic over the last two decades (see ● Figure 16.15). In the United States, the percentage of obese adults rose from 12% in 1991 to 35% in 2012 (Ogden, Carroll, Kit, & Flegal, 2014). It is likely that multiple factors have contributed to this change, including our sedentary lifestyle, increases in caloric intake, changes in the types of food we eat, changes in sleep patterns, and social factors. WHO (2006) describes low- and middle-income countries as facing a "double burden" of disease, because undernutrition and obesity occur at the same time, often

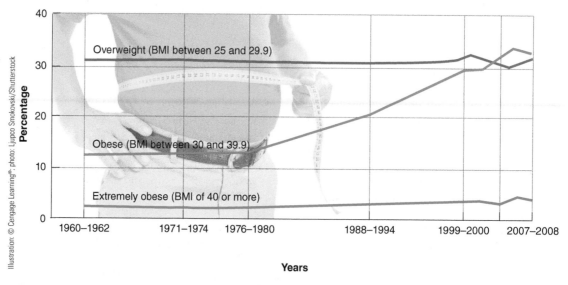

FIGURE 16.15

The Obesity Epidemic. In 1960, fewer than 15% of American adults were obese (body mass index, or BMI, ≥ 30), but today about one third are obese. The number of people who are extremely or morbidly obese (BMI ≥ 40) has also climbed during this period. The reasons for the obesity epidemic are not well understood and are likely to be complex. *Source:* Adapted from "Prevalence of Overweight, Obesity, and Extreme Obesity Among Adults: United States, Trends 1960–1962 Through 2007–2008," by C. L. Ogden and M. D. Carroll, June 2010, *NCHS Health E-Stats.* Atlanta, GA: Centers for Disease Control and Prevention. Retrieved from http://www.cdc.gov/NCHS/data/hestat/obesity_adult_07_08/obesity_adult_07_08.pdf.

in the same households. A combination of inadequate nutrition prenatally and in childhood followed by exposure to high-calorie but nutrient-poor foods sets the stage for a lifetime of poor health, possibly because of epigenetic factors (Haemer, Huang, & Daniels, 2009).

As was the case in smoking, we can also see evidence of social factors that maintain our eating habits and weight. Our recent history of cheap, fatty, and sugary foods is now colliding with increased rates of poverty because of a downward spiraling economy. Nutritionists have raised the alarm that eating healthy foods is becoming more expensive than ever. We seem to use the people around us as a measure of "how we're doing" in terms of our weight. Having an obese spouse increases your risk of obesity by 37%, and having obese friends increases your risk by 57% (Christakis & Fowler, 2007).

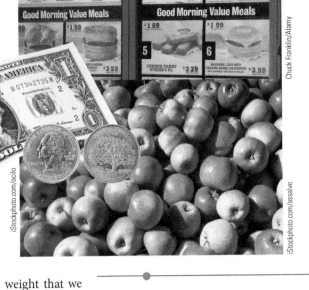

One of the challenges we face today is the high cost of eating a healthy diet. If you have $1.50 in your pocket, you can buy about 1,100 calories at McDonald's (pancakes and sausage breakfast) or 250 calories of fresh apples. We can guess which choice financially struggling parents with hungry children are likely to make.

As we observed in Chapter 7, there are no quick fixes for obesity and poor nutrition. Many of the same challenges face people who want to lose weight that we observed among people attempting to quit smoking. One advantage would-be ex-smokers enjoy, however, is the option of complete abstinence. In contrast, we cannot abstain from eating but instead must choose to eat differently. Research identifying the contagious aspects of smoking and obesity might provide a hopeful note. If people in your social circle begin to eat healthier diets and maintain healthier weights, perhaps it will become easier for you to do so as well. Although losing weight can seem difficult, small changes in behavior can be helpful. People using smaller plates unconsciously ate less (Wansink, 2006).

In addition to addressing concerns about obesity, current research in nutrition focuses on the specific nutrients we need for healthy development and psychological well-being. As we mentioned in Chapter 14, prevalence of bipolar disorder is much lower in countries consuming large amounts of seafood than in countries where seafood consumption is rare (Noaghiul & Hibbeln, 2003). Although much remains to be explored in this area, a further understanding of the consequences of changes in our modern diet should help us achieve a healthier lifestyle.

Alcohol Alcohol is widely used in the United States and in many other countries around the world (see ● Figure 16.16). According to the National Institute on Alcohol Abuse and Alcoholism (2014), 87.6% of American adults consumed alcohol at some point in their lifetime, 71% consumed alcohol in the past year, and 56.3% consumed alcohol in the past month. Nearly one quarter of the adult population engaged in binge drinking (five or more alcoholic beverages on the same occasion) during the past month, and 7% reported heavy drinking (five or more alcoholic beverages on one occasion on each of five or more days in the past month).

The largest threats to health from alcohol use are to the liver, which is responsible for clearing the body of toxins, but alcohol use also contributes to lower life spans because of stroke, high blood pressure, and some cancers (breast, digestive, and liver). In the United States alone, excessive alcohol consumption leads to approximately 88,000 deaths and 2.5 million years of potential life lost annually at an annual cost of $223.5 billion (CDC, 2014a).

Alcohol also poses a risk of abuse and dependence for many people. Psychologists define alcohol abuse as repeated use despite adverse consequences and alcohol dependence as alcohol abuse accompanied by tolerance, withdrawal, and a compulsive urge to drink more (American Psychiatric Association [APA], 2013). As we observed in Chapter 4, *tolerance* is defined as the need to administer greater quantities of a drug to maintain the same subjective effect, and *withdrawal* refers to symptoms that occur when a habitually used drug is no longer used.

As we have seen in so many other domains of human behavior, complex interactions between biological and environmental factors lead to alcohol abuse and dependence. Genes related to the body's ability to break down alcohol in the liver are not evenly distributed across the world's populations. Certain types of genes found primarily in Asians are correlated with lower rates of alcohol dependence (Eng, Luczak, & Wall, 2007). To illustrate the need to consider more than simply genetic predisposition, however, we find that Native Americans have much higher rates of alcohol dependence than those of many other ethnic groups in the United States, despite a high prevalence of the supposedly "protective" genes (Ehlers, 2007).

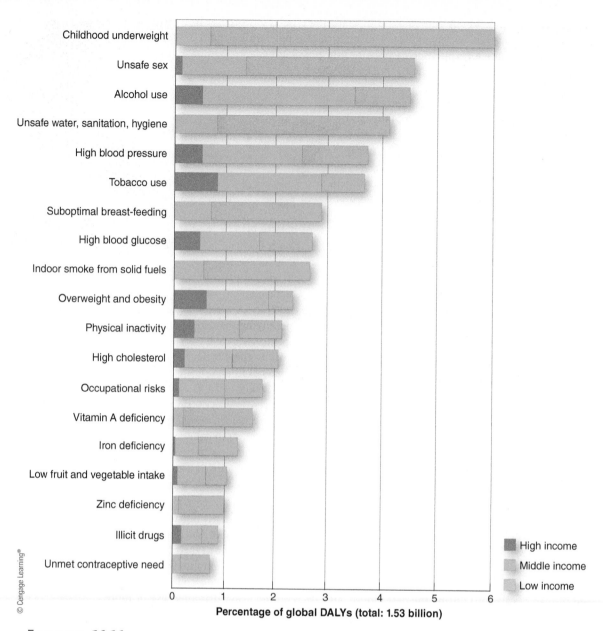

Childhood underweight
Unsafe sex
Alcohol use
Unsafe water, sanitation, hygiene
High blood pressure
Tobacco use
Suboptimal breast-feeding
High blood glucose
Indoor smoke from solid fuels
Overweight and obesity
Physical inactivity
High cholesterol
Occupational risks
Vitamin A deficiency
Iron deficiency
Low fruit and vegetable intake
Zinc deficiency
Illicit drugs
Unmet contraceptive need

High income
Middle income
Low income

0   1   2   3   4   5   6

Percentage of global DALYs (total: 1.53 billion)

© Cengage Learning®

FIGURE 16.16

Alcohol Is the Third-Leading Cause of Worldwide Loss of Disability-Adjusted Life Years (DALYs). The World Health Organization reports that worldwide, alcohol is third behind only childhood starvation and unsafe sex (leading to HIV/AIDS) as a cause of loss of years of "healthy life" because of disability and poor health. *Source:* Adapted from "Alcohol (Fact Sheet)" by World Health Organization, 2011a, retrieved from http://www.who.int/mediacentre/factsheets/fs349/en/index.html.

Many of the same factors that encourage teens to begin smoking also operate to encourage drinking. Most people who go on to abuse alcohol are drinking heavily by late adolescence, and most cases of alcohol dependence are well established by the age of 30 years (Enoch, 2006). This timeline provides insight into when prevention programs are likely to be most effective. Peer pressure, the need to fit in or look cool, overestimates of "everybody's doing it," modeling the behavior of parents and other family members, and the teen's characteristic sense of being immune to harm from risky behaviors can contribute to decisions to begin drinking. Because alcohol reduces anxiety, socially anxious teens are especially at risk for problem drinking. If teens feel more socially competent while drinking, they are likely to continue this practice because of operant conditioning, as described in Chapter 8. Reduced feelings of anxiety are rewarding, so a person is likely to repeat the behavior (alcohol consumption in this case) that is associated with this reward.

Among the environmental influences on problem drinking is the age at which people take their first drink. Individuals exposed to alcohol at earlier ages show a much higher rate of alcohol dependence later in life. Again, we find that age of first drink interacts with a person's genetic predisposition to alcohol dependence (Agrawal et al., 2009). In yet another example of the epigenetic mechanisms we discussed in Chapter 3, early exposure to alcohol might affect the expression of genes related to problem drinking. A similar interaction is found between the maltreatment and neglect of a child and the genetic vulnerability to alcohol dependence. Not all children who are maltreated go on to become dependent on alcohol, although many do (Shin, Edwards, & Heeren, 2009; Shin, Edwards, Heeren, & Amodeo, 2009). The maltreated children who do not develop drinking problems are likely to be protected by combinations of genetic predisposition and the presence of peer and parental support (Enoch, 2006).

People who are exposed to alcohol at younger ages have the highest risk for alcohol abuse.

Treatment for very heavy drinkers often requires medical supervision, because withdrawal from alcohol can produce life-threatening seizures. Recall from Chapter 4 that alcohol boosts the inhibition produced by GABA, leading to alcohol's classification as a central nervous system depressant. Because withdrawal symptoms are usually the opposite of drug effects, withdrawing from a depressant produces excitation, and too much excitation leads to seizures.

One of the remaining controversies in the treatment of alcohol dependence is whether a person can safely return to moderate drinking. Most psychologists do not believe it is possible for recovered problem drinkers to resume alcohol consumption without relapse. In one 60-year longitudinal study of men with problem drinking, few returned to moderate drinking without experiencing a relapse (Vaillant, 2003).

Exercise Exercise was not a question for our hunter–gatherer ancestors, for whom physical work meant the difference between death and survival. In today's sedentary lifestyle, in which many workers spend hours commuting in cars to sit for more hours in front of computers, exercise becomes something we have to consciously remember to do. Children in previous generations would dash from school to play out of doors, but social changes including lack of supervision at home and safety concerns have led to much less spontaneous, outdoor activity. Parents might prefer that their children stay indoors playing video games rather than ride their bicycles in the neighborhood. For many middle-age and older adults, loneliness might lead to less physical activity (Hawkley & Cacioppo, 2010; Hawkley, Thisted, & Cacioppo, 2009).

In contrast to previous generations, who simply "played," it is not uncommon today to find children as young as 3 to 5 years of age involved with adult-organized formal sports. Further research is necessary to determine the long-term impacts of this social trend on adult patterns of play and exercising.

Lack of exercise and sitting are related but different. Today's children and adults in the United States spend an average of 55% of their day sitting while riding in cars, watching television, sitting at work or school, and playing video games or doing other computer work (Matthews et al., 2008). Sitting predicts risk of death independently from a person's level of exercise (see ● Figure 16.17). Although the highest risk of death occurs in obese individuals who spend nearly all their time sitting, the amount of time spent sitting also predicts mortality within a group of active individuals (Katzmarzyk, Church, Craig, & Bouchard, 2009).

Exercise not only benefits our bodies by keeping our muscles and cardiovascular systems in good shape but also benefits our psychological well-being. A brisk 30-minute walk has emerged as an effective way to treat major depressive disorder, as discussed in Chapter 15 (Blumenthal et al., 1999). In addition to improving mood, exercise increases cognitive performance (Hogan, Mata, & Carstensen, 2013). One mechanism for this improvement could be the increased delivery of oxygen to the brain that results from a fit cardiovascular system. Other research suggests that exercise also has the capacity to boost neurogenesis, the production of new neurons, particularly in the hippocampus of the brain (Gibbons et al., 2014). As you learned in Chapter 4, the hippocampus plays important roles in learning and memory.

WHAT IS THE RELATIONSHIP BETWEEN PSYCHOLOGY AND HEALTH? **647**

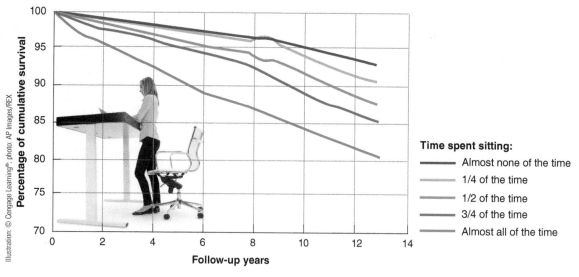

Illustration: © Cengage Learning®. photo: AP Images/REX

FIGURE 16.17

Time Spent Sitting and Mortality. Data showing decreased survival as a function of the amount of your day spent sitting have led to a market for "standing desks." If you find these desks comfortable, by all means use them, but recall that again, the sitting data are correlational, and we cannot conclude that sitting causes death. We are not randomly assigning people to sitting groups. People who sit all day are likely to be obese or have other health problems that contribute to their higher risk of mortality. *Source:* Adapted from "Sitting Time and Mortality From All Causes, Cardiovascular Disease, and Cancer," by P. T. Katzmarzyk, T. S. Church, C. L. Craig, and C. Bouchard, 2009, *Medicine and Science in Sports and Exercise, 41*(5), pp. 998–1005, doi:10.1249/MSS.0b013e3181930355.

We mentioned in an earlier section that stress can be detrimental to the functioning of the immune system. Exercise can be stressful. Not too surprisingly, we find complex relationships between the amount and type of exercise a person experiences and the response of the immune system. Compared to sedentary people, those who engage in regular moderate exercise enjoy a lower rate of infection (Gleeson, 2007). However, too much of a good thing, in the form of continuous, prolonged, and high-intensity exercise, such as competition in marathons and triathlons, can produce a temporary decrease in immune system function for about a day. Elite athletes, because of their constant and intense training schedules, often experience more minor illnesses, such as sniffles and colds, but the long-term benefits of exercise far outweigh these small vulnerabilities.

Culture and Health

Many health-related variables, including poverty, education, access to medical care, nutrition, and substance abuse, vary widely from country to country and within ethnic groups living in the United States. The United States, despite its high standard of living, ranks 36th among countries of the world in terms of life expectancy, suggesting that wealth alone is not sufficient to guarantee good health (United Nations, 2007; see ● Figure 16.18).

In the United States, death rates for all ethnic groups have declined over the last decade, but ethnic differences remain. Risk of death is lowest among Asians and Pacific Islanders and highest among the non-Hispanic Black population (CDC, 2013). Although life expectancy for White and Black Americans differs, the gap continues to narrow. In 2000, life expectancy for Whites was 5.5 years more than life expectancy for Blacks, but this gap was reduced to 3.8 years by 2010. Increases in life expectancy across all ethnic groups result from reductions in the rate of death from leading causes, including heart disease, cancer, chronic respiratory diseases, and stroke.

Before the implementation of the Affordable Care Act, African Americans, Hispanics, and Native Americans were 2 to 3 times more likely to be uninsured (Derksen, 2013). Not only

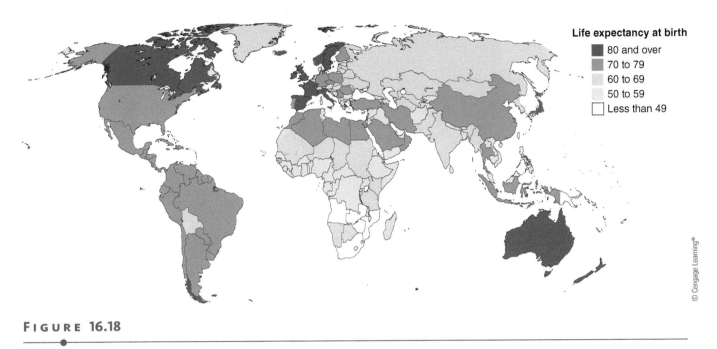

FIGURE 16.18

Culture and Health Interact to Predict Life Expectancy. Many health-related variables, including poverty, education, access to medical care, nutrition, and substance abuse, vary widely from country to country and interact to determine average life expectancy. *Source:* Adapted from World Population Prospects: The 2006 Revision" in United Nations, 2007, retrieved from http://www.un.org/esa/population/publications/wpp2006/WPP2006_Highlights_rev.pdf.

do these discrepancies burden minorities with increased disability, but they contribute to continued poverty and violence affecting society as a whole. A shortage of physicians willing to treat racial and ethnic minorities and non-English-speaking patients contributes to health disparities (Marrast, Zallman, Woolhandler, Bor, & McCormick, 2013).

In addition to ethnic and cultural differences in overall health and health habits, discrepancies occur in mental health. Minorities living in the United States have less access to mental health services, are less likely to receive needed services, receive a poorer quality of care, and are underrepresented in mental health research (Department of Health and Human Services, U.S. Public Health Service, 2007). Among possible variables accounting for increased mental health problems among minorities are poverty, discrimination, and violence. Poverty in particular is an important risk factor for psychological disorders, with people living at the lowest levels of the socioeconomic scale experiencing 2 to 3 times greater rates of psychological disorder (Department of Health and Human Services, U.S. Public Health Service, 2007). The exact prevalence remains unknown, because many people living in poverty do not have access to care. Stress from poverty, discrimination, and violence might contribute to higher rates of stress-related health problems and disorders. Distrust of clinicians who might seem to be disrespectful or whose approach is culturally insensitive might also deter people from obtaining the treatment they need.

Culture contributes to risk for suicide. Between 2005 and 2009, the highest rates of suicide in the United States among individuals aged 10 years or older occurred among American Indians/Alaska Natives (17.48 per 100,000). Whites had higher risk of suicide (15.99 per 100,000) than non-Hispanic Blacks, Hispanics, and Asian or Pacific Islander groups (between 6 and 7 per 100,000; CDC, 2014b). These data suggest the presence of protective mechanisms within some cultures that offset the negative effects of minority status.

An Integrated Understanding of Health Behaviors

If you haven't already noticed during our discussions of stress, sleep, nutrition, smoking, alcohol use, and exercise, all of these variables interact. Stress can lead to poor sleep, additional consumption of calories, more smoking, more drinking, and less exercise. People who eat

Poverty is a significant risk factor for many types of psychopathology.

poorly are unlikely to sleep well or feel like going to the gym. Smoking reduces weight (the choice of the tobacco industry to market a cigarette called "Virginia Slims" to women was no accident) but of course has negative effects on health that far outweigh that advantage. Problem drinkers either cut back on nutritious food or become obese (Breslow & Smothers, 2005). College students engage in "drunkorexia," or the deliberate restriction of calories before planned alcohol consumption for the purpose of avoiding weight gain (Burke, Cremeens, Vail-Smith, & Woolsey, 2010). Most, if not all, of these behaviors are affected by our social context. We eat, drink, and smoke but also exercise more in the company of our fellow humans.

These interactions in health behaviors remind us of the need to zoom out to look at the whole picture of individuals within their social contexts when we attempt to apply interventions leading to better health (see ● Figure 16.19). We have amassed a significant amount of data on why people engage in a particular problem behavior, whether that is smoking, drinking, or overeating, and we are now in a better position to identify the overlapping patterns of epigenesis, stress, child maltreatment, peer pressure, and motivation that underlie these behaviors.

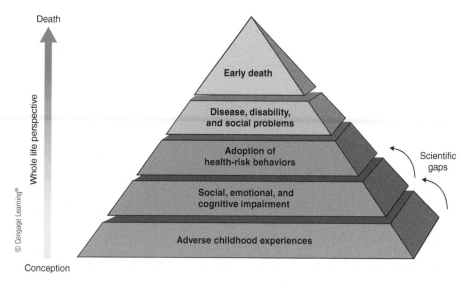

FIGURE 16.19

The Adverse Childhood Experiences (ACE) Study: An Integrated Model of Health. An example of contemporary research that uses an integrated model of health is the ACE Study, being undertaken by researchers affiliated with the Centers for Disease Control and Prevention. The study plans to address identified gaps in our understanding about the relationships between adverse childhood experiences, such as abuse and neglect, and later social, emotional, and cognitive impairments, which in turn could influence the adoption of risky health behaviors. *Source:* Adapted from "Pyramid: Adverse Childhood Experiences (ACE) Study." in Centers for Disease Control and Prevention, 2010a, retrieved from http://www.cdc.gov/ace/pyramid.htm.

Summary 16.2 Four Domains of Health Behavior

Domain	Correlates
Tobacco Use	• Smoking is the leading preventable cause of death in the United States.
Nutrition	• Obesity increases rates of many chronic diseases, including heart disease, stroke, diabetes, arthritis, and some cancers. • Specific nutrients, not just calories, are necessary for optimum functioning.
Alcohol	• Alcohol's main effect on life span is its contribution to accidents, but use is also correlated with liver disease, stroke, high blood pressure, and some cancers.
Exercise	• Exercise improves overall health, mood, and cognition.

Credits: Top Row. Carlos Barria/Reuters/Corbis. Second Row. Chuck Franklin/Alamy; iStockphoto.com/assalve; iStockphoto.com/Arsgera; iStockphoto.com/acilo. Third Row. Diverse Images/Universal Images Group/Getty Images. Bottom Row: Stockbroker/MBI/Alamy.

What Is Positive Psychology?

Although helping people with problems is an important part of psychology, some psychologists have pointed out that there are differences between making people less uncomfortable and helping them live happier, more fulfilling lives. The interventions we explored in Chapter 15 are designed to alleviate psychological pain, but these treatments are not intended to make people who do not have psychological disorders happier. At the same time, we know a great deal about people with psychological problems, whom we described in Chapter 14 as representing a minority of the population. What about most people, who lead relatively untroubled, typical lives? As we observed in Chapter 10, we quite possibly know the least about people with unusual strengths, such as talent and genius. The field of **positive psychology** focuses on these relatively neglected areas of behavior and mental processes by using scientific methods to understand positive human experiences and adjustment. A new set of interventions should emerge from this understanding that will guide individuals, families, and communities in their attempts to maximize their potential (Seligman & Csikszentmihalyi, 2000).

William James foreshadowed positive psychology in his 1902 book *The Varieties of Religious Experience*. In this book, James discussed people who achieve "healthy mindedness" as having an understanding of the "goodness of life" and a soul (a word often used by people in James's era as synonymous with *mind*) with "a sky-blue tint" (James, 1905, pp. 79–80). James

positive psychology An approach to psychology that emphasizes normal behavior and human strengths.

The Varieties of Religious Experience

WILLIAM JAMES

In his book *The Varieties of Religious Experience*, William James foreshadowed the development of positive psychology by considering what makes some people healthy minded and gives others a "sick soul."

goes further to speculate about the origins of healthy mindedness. For the lucky few, healthy mindedness occurs naturally and effortlessly. For others, it must be achieved through effort.

Despite James's efforts, psychology continued its fascination with the abnormal and the unhealthy into the 20th century and did not direct the same energy toward understanding the normal and healthy. Voices of dissent arose from among the humanistic psychologists, including Abraham Maslow, whom we discussed in Chapters 7 and 12. Maslow argued that psychologists could learn more about human behavior by studying outstanding individuals than by studying people with severe problems. As part of Maslow's thinking about self-actualization, the pinnacle of social motivation in his theory, he took detailed notes on people he admired in a "GHB (Good Human Being) notebook" that he kept between 1945 and 1949 (Lowry, 1973). In addition to making observations of living people he admired, Maslow combed through biographies and autobiographies of famous people looking for common features of healthy mindedness.

Running parallel to the humanistic psycholgists' rejection of a negative, sickness model of human behavior were innovations among cognitive and behavioral approaches. As we mentioned in Chapter 15, Albert Ellis and Aaron Beck were achieving excellent results with cognitive restructuring around the same time the humanistic psychologists began reconsidering Freud. Ellis and Beck were able to help their clients with depression see a glass of water as half full as opposed to half empty, improving their mood and optimism in the process.

One of the most significant voices leading to contemporary positive psychology approaches is that of Martin Seligman. We discussed his concept of learned helplessness in Chapter 14. If people's outcomes do not seem connected to their behaviors, the resulting feelings of helplessness and lack of control could result in depression. Based on his investigations of learned helplessness, Seligman proposed that **optimism**, or thinking positively about the future, can be learned, as well as helplessness (Seligman, 1990).

Positive psychology embraces humanistic emphases on human growth and fulfillment, yet applies the scientific reasoning and research characteristic of cognitive and behavioral psychology. Positive psychology has focused on the study of positive emotions, positive traits, and positive institutions.

Positive Emotions

Positive emotions and the experiences that produce them, including happiness, love, gratitude, contentment, and hope, contribute to our well-being. For our social species, it is not an

Martin Seligman (right) and the Dalai Lama (left), spiritual leader of Tibetan Buddhism, discussed the important role of positive emotions at a Mind and Its Potential conference in 2009.

optimism Thinking positively about the future.

accident that many of the situations, such as promotions at work, marriage, and victories, that produce these positive feelings involve other people who are important to us.

What Is Happiness? We all know happiness when we experience it, and most people prefer the state of happiness to the alternatives of unhappiness and depression. Yet happiness often seems fleeting or transient. The primary reason for this elusiveness is that happiness is typically relative (see ● Figure 16.20). We quickly adapt to our current circumstances, and it is only change in those circumstances that provokes feelings of happiness or unhappiness.

Research with identical twins suggests that we have a happiness "set point" that is largely influenced by genetics (Lykken & Tellegen, 1996). Changes in circumstances might raise or lower happiness from the set point, but the effect would be temporary. However, having a genetic predisposition to being happy or to being cranky does not mean that a person's behavior has no influence. Instead, people can do a great deal to improve their happiness. Rather than looking for external things to boost happiness, such as a new car or a new nose, looking within is more effective. Happiness can be improved by thinking carefully about what things interfere with our happiness, such as allowing ourselves to stay mad at a partner following an argument, and working to avoid these situations.

One critical factor in people's happiness is the strength of their interpersonal relationships. When participants are asked, "What is necessary for your happiness?" or "What is it that makes your life meaningful," nearly everybody talks about their close relationships first—family, friends, and romantic partners (Berscheid & Peplau, 1983). This finding is consistent with one of the ongoing themes of this text: social environment plays a central role in human behavior.

Happiness and Marriage Among interpersonal relationships, the institution of marriage is particularly likely to contribute to happiness (see ● Figure 16.21). In a study of more than 42,000 Americans beginning in 1972, 40% of married adults, but only 22% of never-married adults, report that they are "very happy" (Davis, Smith, & Marsden, 2006). Eighteen percent of divorced adults report being "very happy," and remarriage increases happiness only in a minority of cases. In a large-scale study that followed 13,000 adults for 5 years, people who

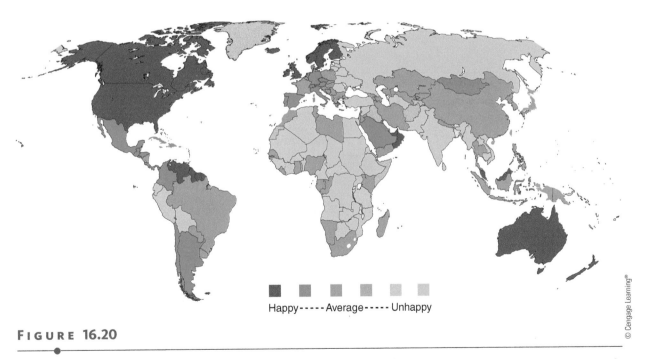

Happy - - - - - Average - - - - - Unhappy

© Cengage Learning®

FIGURE 16.20
●

Global Happiness. In a study of life satisfaction, health, wealth, and education were the three most important predictors of happiness. The five happiest countries were Denmark, Switzerland, Austria, Iceland, and the Bahamas, with the United States ranked 23, China ranked 82, Japan ranked 90, and Russia ranked 167. *Source:* Adapted from "First Ever World Map of Happiness Produced," by PhysOrg.com, July 28 2006, retrieved from http://www.physorg.com/news73321785.html.

FIGURE 16.21

Relationship Status and Happiness. Many studies have pointed to a strong relationship between being married and subjective well-being. *Source:* Adapted from "The Long-Term Consequences of Relationship Formation for Subjective Well-Being," by J. P. M. Soons, A. C. Liefbroer, and M. Kalmijn, 2009, *Journal of Marriage and Family,* 71(5), pp. 1254–1270, doi:10.1111/j.1741-3737.2009.00667.x.

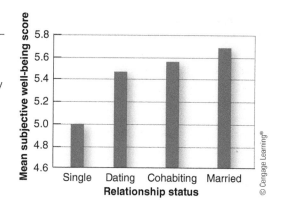

remained married experienced higher well-being than those who separated or divorced (Waite, Luo, & Lewin, 2009). Among the benefits of marriage are reduced infidelity, longer-lasting relationships, and longer life (Waite, & Gallagher, 2001). People who are married and living with their spouse enjoy a significantly lower death rate than those who are unmarried. People who have never married, particularly males, experience an especially high risk for premature death (Kaplan & Kronick, 2006).

Why would marriage make people happy? One possibility is that the relationship between marriage and happiness is a false one because of the likelihood that happy people produce happy marriages instead of the other way around. Careful research that controls for premarital happiness does not support this hypothesis (Horwitz, White, & Howell-White, 1997). Regardless of how happy you are before marrying, on average being married makes people happier. If you're thinking of cases you know in which married couples are miserable, time together seems to help. Among the unhappiest couples, only 12% report being unhappy 5 years later. Seventy percent of the formerly unhappy partners report being "very" or "quite" happy (Horwitz et al., 1997).

What is the source of this marital happiness? Traditionally, psychologists have suggested that marital happiness results from the perceptions one partner has of the other. More sophisticated analyses have shown that the factors associated with marital happiness are more complicated (Luo, Zhang, Watson, & Snider, 2010). While it's true that perceptions of your partner influence how satisfied you are in a relationship ("I'm with a great person"), it is also true that your overall satisfaction with the relationship affects how you see your partner ("I'm happy, so

Thinking Scientifically

Does Parenting Increase Happiness?

IN CHAPTER 7, we noted that an update of Abraham Maslow's hierarchy of needs pyramid featured parenting at the top to represent this role's importance from an evolutionary perspective (Kenrick, Griskevicius, Neuberg, & Schaller, 2010).

Parenting in the 21st century, however, probably shares little similarity with parenting for our hunter–gatherer ancestors. The goal of contemporary marriages has less to do today with financial survival or raising families than it has with meeting partners' emotional needs (Dew & Wilcox, 2011). A major predictor of marital satisfaction is

time spent with a partner, so where does that need fit with the challenges of meeting the demands of a family of young children?

Some research suggests that parenting results in lower marital satisfaction, which increases with the number of children (Twenge, Campbell, & Foster, 2003). This result is most pronounced among younger, higher income mothers of infants. Even in the 21st century, the arrival of the first child has a tendency to "traditionalize" the gender roles of the new parents. Fathers begin to take on more of the income-earning responsibilities and mothers take on more of

the childcare and housework. Her changing roles might make the new mother less happy with her circumstances (Dew & Wilcox, 2011).

Other researchers disagree. In another set of studies, parents evaluated their lives more positively than nonparents, felt better than nonparents from day to day, and found more satisfaction in caring for their children than in other daily activities (Nelson, Kushlev, Dunn, & Lyubomirsky, 2014; Nelson, Kushlev, English, Dunn, & Lyubomirsky, 2013). Parenting contributed to more positive emotions on a daily basis and to the

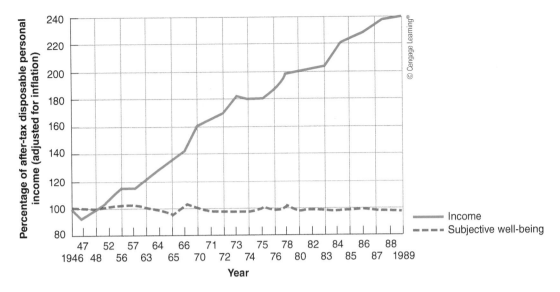

FIGURE 16.22

Wealth and Happiness. When adjusted for inflation, Americans' after-tax disposable income grew dramatically between 1946 and 1989, but measures of subjective well-being remained flat. Increases in income above a certain point where basic needs can be met tend to have mild, if any, long-term impacts on happiness. *Source:* Adapted from "Subjective Well-Being: Three Decades of Progress," by E. Diener, E. M. Suh, R. E. Lucas, and H. L. Smith, 1999, *Psychological Bulletin, 125*(2), Figure 1, doi:10.1037/0033-2909.125.2.276.

I must be with a great person"). Then, what is the source of that satisfaction? A major factor in satisfaction with a relationship is how you see yourself perceived by your partner ("My partner thinks I'm terrific, which makes me happy, and because I'm happy, I must be with a great person").

Happiness and Wealth Another commonsense notion about happiness is that wealth can make you happy. After all, we see frequent images of ecstatic lottery winners and smiling sports superstars who have signed megabuck contracts. At both national and individual levels, being poor does appear to be correlated with being unhappy. However, once basic needs are met, additional money does not guarantee happiness (see ● Figure 16.22). Interviews with the

sense of having a meaningful life, concepts consistent with the approach to happiness held by some positive psychologists.

What might be the source of the discrepancies? One possibility is that parents as a group are highly diverse. Parenting under some circumstances can be more stressful than under others. Young, unpartnered parents not too surprisingly reported less happiness and satisfaction than their nonparent age peers yet still indicated they felt their lives were meaningful (Nelson et al., 2013). ●

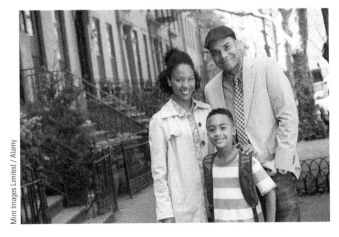

Evolutionary theories view parenting as an important motivation for human behavior, yet contemporary psychologists debate whether parents are truly happier than nonparents.

Lottery winners experience an increase in happiness, but they tend to be cautious about changing their lifestyles. Most continue working and attempt to maintain as normal a life as possible.

100 richest people in the United States indicated that they were only slightly happier than average (Diener, Horwitz, & Emmons, 1985). In addition, how people use their wealth can influence happiness. People who are less materialistic report being happier than people who are materialistic (Tsang, Carpenter, Roberts, Frisch, & Carlisle, 2014).

We return to the idea that happiness occurs because of changing circumstances. Perhaps the 100 richest Americans had simply adapted to their wealthy lifestyles. What about people who suddenly become wealthy? The Camelot Group, which manages the United Kingdom national lottery, reported that winning the lottery did have an impact on happiness (Camelot Group, 2004). Sixty-five percent of winners reported that they were happier following the win because of financial security and increased freedom. Thirty-five percent said that they were about as happy after winning as before. None reported feeling less happy than before the win. Although the winners traded up in terms of lifestyle (most had bought new cars and new homes), 92% of those who were married when they won were still married to the same spouse.

The correlation between happiness and income has been assumed to reflect the effect of money on happiness. However, longitudinal research suggests that happiness may influence income (Cacioppo et al., 2008). As in prior studies, happiness and income in middle-age and older adults were correlated. However, happiness predicted bigger increases in income, whereas higher income did not predict increases in happiness. Additional analyses by these same researchers further indicated that happy people form better relationships and that these better relationships contribute to larger increases in income, perhaps because of improved job performance, better performance reviews and promotions, and better "networking" opportunities that lead in financially productive directions.

Results from the Gallup World Poll, the first representative sample of all people on the planet, showed that financial wealth and social psychological "wealth" predict different types of well-being across many cultures (Diener, Ng, Harter, & Arora, 2010). Social psychological wealth is measured by the respect you received; closeness with family and friends; the opportunities to learn, do what you do best, and choose how to spend your time; and the need to work long hours. A single "happiest nation" measure does not seem supported by the data. Central American and some African nations have greater social psychological wealth than financial wealth, while nations previously in the Soviet bloc experience much higher financial wealth than social psychological wealth. The United States ranks first in financial wealth and 19th in social psychological wealth. Financial wealth predicted global measures of life satisfaction, but social psychological wealth made much stronger predictions of the presence of positive emotions like happiness.

Can We Increase Happiness? Some psychologists have moved past research identifying the causes and correlates of happiness to make recommendations for how to increase individual happiness. Among the steps recommended for improving happiness are practicing time management, exercising regularly, sleeping well, finding interesting work to do, nurturing close relationships, and following a chosen religious faith (Myers, 1993).

Methods for increasing happiness can be tailored to three types of happiness: the pleasant life, the good life, and the meaningful life (Seligman, 2002; Seligman & Csikszentmihalyi, 2000). The pleasant life describes the pleasures we enjoy from moment to moment. Enjoying a great meal or a beautiful sunset enhances our daily experience. The good life occurs when we are maximizing our strengths in our work, hobbies, and other activities, making time subjectively slow down. The meaningful life describes our ability to focus away from the self to serve others or participate in something more permanent and "larger" than ourselves.

In general, people taking tests designed to assess their involvement with these three types of happiness are happiest overall if either their good life or their meaningful life scores are high. If scores on one of these aspects are high, then a high score on the pleasant life can raise overall happiness, like having a cherry on top of an already-delicious ice cream sundae. Unfortunately, those who score highest on the pleasant life, without comparable scores in either the good or the meaningful life category or both, tend to be less happy (Seligman, 2002). Two reasons help explain why isolated pleasant life scores fail to greatly affect overall happiness.

First, these scores tend to be highly heritable, which means that you can't do much to improve your sense of pleasure. Some people seem to respond more intensely than others to pleasurable experiences. Second, these feelings do not last long and habituate quickly. Think about the last time you had a delicious dessert. The first few bites are fantastic, but the last ones are usually less so. A short time later, you might have forgotten how delicious the dessert was.

Even if heritability affects our ability to experience pleasure, positive psychology has some suggestions for enhancing our experiences. How often have you eaten your meals while watching television, reading, or working on your computer? If you try to multitask in this way, it is unlikely that you will derive much pleasure or satisfaction from your food, which can lead to overeating. Learning to "savor" pleasurable experiences by paying more attention to them can make them more memorable and enjoyable (Bryant & Veroff, 2007).

The good life is somewhat easier to modify than the pleasant life. To enhance your happiness from the good life, all you have to do is identify your strengths and find ways to use them in your important work and hobby activities. During activities that contribute to the good life, people experience **flow**, in which they are absorbed in their current activity, usually related to work, problem solving, or creativity (Csikszentmihalyi, 1990, 1996). The word *flow* was chosen to describe this experience on the basis of interviews in which people spontaneously used the metaphor to explain their own experiences. These experiences may qualify as altered states of consciousness and are usually perceived as highly positive. Time appears to stand still for people who are immersed in flow.

People who do not play video games are often astonished by the nearly compulsive attractiveness of the activity for those who do play. However, video games meet many of the criteria for a flow experience (Csikszentmihalyi, 1990). The games have clear goals (reaching the next level or beating a dungeon boss), they provide the opportunity to focus, they encourage a merging of action and awareness (as opposed to self-consciousness), and players generally experience a distortion of subjective time (hours go by quickly). In addition, games provide instant and precise feedback (you succeed or not), a balance between ability and difficulty (gamers reject games that are either too easy or too challenging), and a sense of personal control (you're the one making the moves). Finally, gaming, like other flow activities, is intrinsically reinforcing. Many a parent has diabolically used access to gaming as a reinforcer for other desired behaviors, such as chores or homework. It is likely that video games, at least for some people, tap into a predisposition to find activities that meet these flow criteria to be highly reinforcing.

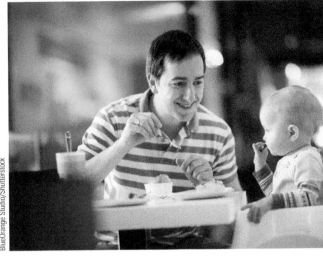
BlueOrange Studio/Shutterstock

Researchers studying happiness identify three types. The pleasant life consists of pleasures, like ice cream, that are enjoyed from moment to moment. The good life features "flow" and a sense that time is standing still. The meaningful life describes the positive emotions obtained by helping others.

We are not suggesting that happiness can be found by spending all your time playing video games; instead, we recommend that you seek this type of flow in the work and hobbies you enjoy.

Positive Traits

In an effort to further understand the sources of well-being, positive psychologists have built upon the trait theories we discussed in Chapter 12. Among the traits that contribute to well-being are hope, resilience, spirituality, and gratitude.

wavebreakmedia/Shutterstock

According to Mihaly Csikszentmihalyi, video games can be compelling because they meet many of the criteria required of a flow-inducing experience, such as clear goals, the opportunity to focus, the merging of action and awareness, and the experience of a distortion of time for the player.

flow A state characterized by complete absorption in a current activity, such as work, problem solving, or creativity.

Hope refers to an expectation that your goals will be met in the future. You are probably hopeful that you will complete your college education and find a good job. The trait of hope is tightly linked to feelings of optimism, or a belief in a positive future. Hope in turn is determined by motivation and planning (Snyder, 1994). Your expectations for a college degree are based on beliefs that you can achieve a degree through hard work and that following your plans will give you the results you desire. Being a hopeful person provides a number of benefits to well-being. Hopeful people withstand more pain and stress, because they believe the future will be better (Snyder et al., 2005). Hopeful people are more capable problem solvers, because they are likely to consider alternate pathways for meeting their goals instead of giving up at the first obstacle. Finally, hopeful people usually enjoy strong social networks, because other people find hope attractive (Snyder, Rand, & Sigmon, 2002). You can test your levels of hope in the following section.

Hopeful people are capable problem solvers who believe that their goals can be met in the future.

We discussed resilience in an earlier section of this chapter. Resilience not only serves as a buffer for stress but can lead to growth following a traumatic experience (Davis & Nolen-Hoeksema, 2009). None of us likes being traumatized, but when we look back on difficult episodes of our lives, we often feel like a traumatic experience led to growth and improved strength. Among the positive changes associated with posttraumatic growth are perceptions of the self as a survivor rather than a victim, increased self-confidence and self-efficacy, and greater appreciation for the fragile nature of life. Many people respond to prior trauma with increased compassion for others, closer bonds with family and friends, and enhanced willing-

 Experiencing Psychology

The Trait Hope Scale

USE THE SCALE in Table 16.2 to respond to the items listed on the next page. Select the number that best describes you in the space provided.

Scores on this test can range from 8 to 64. To obtain your overall hope score, add your responses to items 1, 2, 4, 6, 8, 9, 10, and 12. (The other items are distractors.) The higher your score, the greater hope you have for the future. The average score among college students in 1991 was 25 (Snyder et al., 1991). How does that compare with your score and your classmates' scores? What factors in your life do you think influence your score? ●

16.2 The Trait Hope Scale							
1 Definitely false	2 Mostly false	3 Somewhat false	4 Slightly false	5 Slightly true	6 Somewhat true	7 Mostly true	8 Definitely true

ness to share emotions. Trauma can also lead people to reduce the value they place on material aspects of life, such as money and possessions, while increasing their sense of what is truly meaningful about life.

As we mentioned in a previous section, the experience of a meaningful life enhances well-being and happiness. Although finding meaning simply refers to recognizing things that are bigger than one's personal existence, some people achieve meaningfulness through religious practice (Myers, 1993). Religious beliefs and practice have also been associated with a long list of health benefits, because most major world religions promote healthier lifestyles (Emmons, Barrett, & Schnitker, 2008). Many people find religious prohibitions to be a helpful tool for resisting the temptation to engage in risky, unhealthy behaviors. Although participation in religious or spiritual activities is a behavior, it is strongly predicted by a person's need for deeper meaning, or trait spirituality (Pargament & Krumrei, 2009).

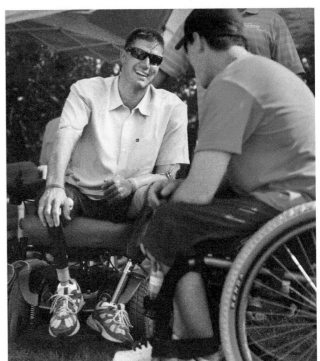

ZUMA Press, Inc/Alamy

Nobody wants to experience trauma, but some survivors report experiencing posttraumatic growth. Mike Atherton lost both legs and his left arm in a boating accident but has returned to performing with the Tampa Bay Water Ski Show Team and reports feeling optimistic about his future.

_____ **1.** I can think of many ways to get out of a jam.

_____ **2.** I energetically pursue my goals.

_____ **3.** I feel tired most of the time.

_____ **4.** There are lots of ways around any problem.

_____ **5.** I am easily downed in an argument.

_____ **6.** I can think of many ways to get the things in life that are important to me.

_____ **7.** I worry about my health.

_____ **8.** Even when others get discouraged, I know I can find a way to solve the problem.

_____ **9.** My past experiences have prepared me well for my future.

_____ **10.** I've been pretty successful in life.

_____ **11.** I usually find myself worrying about something.

_____ **12.** I meet the goals I set for myself.

SERVICE Above Self

Organizations such as Rotary International often reinforce the values of their members, such as "service above self." *Source:* Service Above Self and the Service Above Self logo are trademarks of Rotary International and used herein with permission.

The idea of individual traits related to well-being has been extended to include shared social values and experiences, resulting in values or virtues. A value can be defined as "an enduring belief that a specific mode of conduct or end state of existence is personally or socially preferable to an opposite or converse mode of conduct or end state of existence" (Rokeach, 1968, p. 5). The voluntary nature of values is stressed by many psychologists, including Gordon Allport, who defines a value as "a belief upon which a man acts by preference" (1961, p. 454). One effort to identify values combined those listed by major world religions and such organizations as the Boy Scouts, Rotary International, and Alcoholics Anonymous with data from major personality tests (Franken, 2002). The resulting values are social, cheerful, peaceful, tolerant, kind, generous, trusting, assertive, self-control, self-confidence, communication, leading, and autonomous. Additional lists have added some interesting items, such as awe and forgiving (Peterson & Seligman, 2004).

One interesting difference between the positive psychologist's discussion of values and the personality psychologist's discussion of traits is the judgmental approach to values. In discussing personality traits, we don't want to think of traits as necessarily good or bad. A variety of personalities, such as the introverted computer programmer and the extroverted salesperson, helps meet the needs of societies. In contrast, the values discussed by positive psychologists are good, and to be without them is not so good. This deviation from being nonjudgmental represents a significant departure by the positive psychologists from the humanistic psychologists, who argue strongly against any type of outward judgments of others.

Do values matter in everyday life? As we saw in Chapter 13, attitudes and behavior may or may not correlate. However, possessing certain values seems to correlate with a number of positive outcomes. Participants' self-ratings on the 13 values mentioned earlier are positively correlated with measures of self-esteem (Franken, 2002). In addition, explosiveness, or a propensity to violence, was negatively correlated with a person's values ratings. As ratings on the values increased, a person's potential for violent behavior decreased. People with high values scores were the least likely to experience alcohol or tobacco addictions or to experience anxiety and depression.

Positive Institutions

Positive psychologists study the roles of institutions such as workplaces, schools, and families in promoting well-being in the community. What characteristics should we strive for in our institutions to raise the likelihood that members of the community will lead satisfying lives? Positive institutions share several features (Peterson, 2006). They share a purpose in the form of institutional goals. Their rules and consequences are fair. They feature a reciprocal caring by the institution for its members and by the members for the institution. A positive institution provides safety for its members and treats them with respect.

One of your goals in completing a college education is probably related to the type of work you'll be able to do as a result. Your future working conditions will have significant influence on your overall well-being. Positive psychologists have identified three ways people feel about their work (Wrzesniewski, McCauley, Rozin, & Schwartz, 1997). Some people just have jobs. A job is viewed as a way of supporting your family, and workers with jobs emphasize this role without asking more of their work life. A career not only pays the bills but also fulfills workers' needs for status and achievement. Finally, a calling satisfies both personal and cooperative goals. The worker pays the bills while gaining both personal achievement and a sense of contributing to the community. When workers view their employment as a calling, they are less concerned with work conditions, salary, benefits, and status. Positive workplaces facilitate the workers' abilities to meet their personal work-related goals.

Schools from kindergarten through college are particularly important to the health and future of a community. In a manner similar to psychology's emphasis on disorders, most of the research in education has focused on what goes wrong in schools rather than on what schools are doing well. Positive schools promote growth and produce a sense of satisfaction in students. Although this area is sparsely studied, student satisfaction with schools predicts a

Google captured the coveted number one spot in the 2014 *Fortune* list of the top employers. The company encourages the "meaningful life" by donating $50 for every 5 hours of volunteer work completed by an employee. Google's practice of making every employee a stockholder is an example of a positive institution's reciprocal caring.

number of positive outcomes, including higher grades and fewer problem behaviors, even as early as kindergarten (Ladd, Buhs, & Seid, 2000).

Significant challenges face today's families, and identifying what works could provide guidance for many. Family-centered positive psychology (FCPP) focuses on the characteristics of positive families (Sheridan & Burt, 2009). Consistent with the general approach of positive psychology, FCPP identifies the strengths of families rather than emphasizing their failures and weaknesses.

Positive Psychology and the Future

Positive psychology is not without its critics. Among the weaknesses seen in positive psychology are its unintended negative effects on people who face medical and psychological challenges (Held, 2004). Although research indicates that optimism and health are linked, this finding might give sick people the unfortunate impression that all they have to do to cure their illness is to maintain a positive attitude. A second criticism is related to the integration theme we have featured in this textbook. Positive strengths are valuable, but they are best studied within the entire context of individuals interacting in environments. Positive and negative emotions can coexist, and we cannot fully understand one type of experience without considering the other (Cacioppo, Berntson, Norris, & Gollan, 2011).

It is unlikely that psychology will ever abandon its goal of helping troubled people feel better, but positive psychology's emphasis on what goes right is also illuminating. We do not know at this time whether the label of *positive psychology* will drop out of favor like Wilhelm Wundt's structuralism or enjoy the fate of William James's functionalism by becoming so integrated into mainstream psychology that a label is no longer necessary. By applying the same evidence-based criteria we described for evaluating interventions for "negative" behaviors to interventions based on positive psychology, we will figure out the role positive psychology should play in our continued search for understanding the human mind.

Interpersonal Relationships
The Health Psychology Perspective
How Do Investment and Experiences of Gratitude Affect Relationships?

We have studied relationships from the vantage points of 15 psychological perspectives so far in this textbook, and we end the journey with an analysis of the role of a positive emotion—gratitude—on relationship building.

Psychologists traditionally have focused on how an individual invests in relationships and report that individuals' perceptions of how much they have already invested (time, energy, and other resources) influences how committed they feel. However, researchers know relatively little about how our perceptions of our partner's investment in the relationship influence our commitment.

When a partner invests in a relationship, the typical response is the experience of the positive emotion of gratitude. Gratitude includes the feelings of thankfulness and appreciation felt for the partner, which in turn affects perceptions of who the partner is as a person (Joel, Gordon, Impett,

It's often the little things that people do for their partner that result in gratitude and a stronger commitment to the relationship.

Matthias Tunger/Corbis

MacDonald, & Keltner, 2013). When people experience gratitude for a partner, it stimulates further commitment. The amount of commitment an individual experiences is linked to the perceived investment in the relationship on the part of the partner.

What types of investment promote stronger gratitude, and through those feelings, greater commitment? You might guess that financial investments would be important, but research has shown that intangible investments, like emotional involvement, have a greater impact on commitment (Goodfriend & Agnew, 2008). This is reminiscent of the finding discussed earlier that it is not wealth that makes us happy but rather our social connectivity. •

Summary 16.3 Types of Happiness

Source of happiness	How to get it	Examples
The pleasant life	Savor your experience without trying to multitask.	Turn off the TV when you're trying to enjoy a meal.
The good life	Find ways to incorporate your key strengths into your activities.	Choose an occupation that you truly enjoy, not just one that pays the bills.
The meaningful life SERVICE Above Self	Focus on something bigger than yourself.	Volunteer for a cause that's important to you.

Credits: Top Row. BlueOrange Studio/Shutterstock. Second Row. wavebreakmedia/Shutterstock. Bottom Row: Rotary International.

KEY TERMS The Language of Psychological Science

Be sure you can define these terms and use them correctly.

alarm reaction, p. 621
biopsychosocial model, p. 639
cortisol, p. 627
emotion-focused coping, p. 637
exhaustion, p. 622
flow, p. 657
general adaptation syndrome (GAS), p. 621
health psychology, p. 639

hypothalamic–pituitary–adrenal (HPA) axis, p. 626
immune system, p. 629
lymphocyte, p. 629
optimism, p. 652
positive psychology, p. 651
problem-focused coping, p. 637
relationship-focused coping, p. 637
resilience, p. 638

resistance, p. 621
stress, p. 620
stressor, p. 620
sympathetic adrenal–medullary (SAM) system, p. 626
tend and befriend, p. 627
Type A personality, p. 630
Type B personality, p. 630

References

Aberson, C. L., Healy, M., & Robero, V. (2000). Ingroup bias and self-esteem: A meta-analysis. *Personality and Social Psychology Review, 4*, 157–173. doi: 10.1207/S15327957PSPR0402_04

Abramson, L. Y., Seligman, M. E. P., & Teasdale, J. D. (1978). Learned helplessness in humans: Critique and reformulation. *Journal of Abnormal Psychology, 87*, 49–74. doi: 10.1037/0021-843X.87.1.49

Achard, S., Salvador, R., Whitcher, B., Suckling, J., & Bullmore, E. (2006). A resilient, low-frequency, small-world human brain functional network with highly connected association cortical hubs. *Journal of Neuroscience, 26*(1), 63–72. doi: 10.1523/JNEUROSCI.3874-05.2006

Ackerman, D. (1990). *A natural history of the senses.* New York, NY: Vintage Books.

Adams, D. B. (1982). A statistical analysis of the social behavior of the male stumptail macaque *(Macaca arctoides). American Journal of Primatology, 2*, 249–273. doi: 10.1002/ajp.1350020303

Adams, M. J. (2011). Evolutionary genetics of personality in nonhuman primates. In M. Inoue-Murayama, S. Kawamura, & A. Weiss (Eds.), *From genes to animal behavior* (pp. 137–164). Tokyo: Springer Japan.

Adler, N. E. (2013). Health disparities: Taking on the challenge. *Perspectives on Psychological Science, 8*(6), 679–681. doi: 10.1177/1745691613506909

Adolphs, R. (2007). Looking at other people: Mechanisms for social perception revealed in subjects with focal amygdala damage. *Novartis Foundation Symposium, 278*, 146–159.

Adolphs, R., Gosselin, F., Buchanan, T. W., Tranel, D., Schyns, P., & Damasio, A. R. (2005). A mechanism for impaired fear recognition after amygdala damage. *Nature, 433*, 68–72. doi: 10.1038/nature03086

Adolphs, R., Tranel, D., & Damasio, A. R. (1998). The human amygdala in social judgment. *Nature, 393*, 470–474. doi: 10.1038/30982

Adolphs, R., Tranel, D., Damasio, H., & Damasio, A. (1994). Impaired recognition of emotion in facial expressions following bilateral damage to the human amygdala. *Nature, 372*, 669–672. doi: 10.1038/372669a0

Adolphs, R., Tranel, D., Damasio, H., & Damasio, A. (1995). Fear and the human amygdala. *Journal of Neuroscience, 15*, 5879–5891.

Aftanas, L. I., & Golocheikine, S. A. (2001). Human anterior and frontal midline theta and lower alpha reflect emotionally positive state and internalized attention: High-resolution EEG investigations of meditation. *Neuroscience Letters, 310*, 57–60. doi: 10.1016/S0304-3940(01)02094-8

Aftanas, L. I., Varlamov, A. A., Pavlov, S. V., Makhnev, V. P., & Reva, N. V. (2001). Affective picture processing: Event-related synchronisation within individually defined human theta band is modulated by valence dimension. *Neuroscience Letters, 303*, 115–118. doi: 10.1016/S0304-3940(01)01703-7

Agay, N., Yechiam, E., Carmel, Z., & Levkovitz, Y. (2010). Non-specific effects of methylphenidate (Ritalin) on cognitive ability and decision-making of ADHD and healthy adults. *Psychopharmacology, 210*(4), 511–519. doi: 10.1007/s00213-010-1853-4

Aggarwal, P., & O'Brien, C. L. (2008). Social loafing on group projects: Structural antecedents and effect on student satisfaction. *Journal of Marketing Education, 30*(3), 255–264. doi: 10.1177/0273475308322283

Agrawal, A., Sartor, C. E., Lynskey, M. T., Grant, J. D., Pergadia, M. L., Grucza, R., et al. (2009). Evidence for an interaction between age at first drink and genetic influences on DSM-IV alcohol dependence symptoms. *Alcoholism: Clinical and Experimental Research, 33*(12), 2047–2056. doi: 10.1111/j.1530-0277.2009.01044.x

Ahadi, S. A., & Rothbart, M. K. (1994). Temperament, development, and the Big Five. In G. Kohnstamm, C. Halverson, & R. P. Martin (Eds.), *The developing structure of temperament and personality from infancy to adulthood* (pp. 189–207). Hillsdale, NJ: Erlbaum.

Ahadi, S. A., Rothbart, M. K., & Ye, R. (1993). Children's temperament in the U.S. and China: Similarities and differences. *European Journal of Personality, 7*(5), 359–377. doi: 10.1002/per.2410070506

Aihara, M., Ida, I., Yuuki, N., Oshima, A., Kumano, H., Takahashi, K., et al. (2007). HPA axis dysfunction in unmedicated major depressive disorder and its normalization by pharmacotherapy correlates with alteration of neural activity in prefrontal cortex and limbic/paralimbic regions. *Psychiatry Research, 155*(3), 245–256. doi: 10.1016/j.pscychresns.2006.11.002

Ainsworth, M., & Bowlby, J. (1965). *Child care and the growth of love.* London, United Kingdom: Penguin Books.

Ainsworth, M. D. S., Blehar, M. C., Waters, E., & Wall, S. (1978). *Patterns of attachment: A psychological study of the strange situation.* Hillsdale, NJ: Erlbaum.

Ajzen, I. (1991). The theory of planned behavior. *Organizational Behavior and Human Decision Processes, 50*(2), 179–211. doi: 10.1016/0749-5978(91)90020-t

Åkerstedt, T., & Fröberg, J. E. (1976). Interindividual differences in circadian pattern of catecholamine excretion, body temperature, performance, and subjective arousal. *Biological Psychology, 4*, 277–292. doi: 10.1016/0301-0511(76)90019-3

Alcock, J. (2011). Back from the future: Parapsychology and the Bem affair. *Skeptical Inquirer, 35*(2), 31.

Aldwin, C. (1994). *Stress, coping, and development: An integrative perspective.* New York, NY: Guilford Press.

Alexander, R. D. (1974). The evolution of social behavior. *Annual Review of Ecology and Systematics, 5*, 325–383.

Allen, K. (2003). Are pets a healthy pleasure? The influence of pets on blood pressure. *Current Directions in Psychological Science, 12*, 236–239. doi: 10.1046/j.0963-7214.2003.01269.x

Allen, L. A., & Woolfolk, R. L. (2010). Cognitive behavioral therapy for somatoform disorders. *Psychiatric Clinics of North America, 33*(3), 579–593. doi: 10.1016/j.psc.2010.04.014

Allen, L. S., Hines, M., Shryne, J. E., & Gorski, R. A. (1989). Two sexually dimorphic cell groups in the human brain. *Journal of Neuroscience, 9*, 497–506.

Allison, T., & Cicchetti, D. (1976). Sleep in mammals: Ecological and constitutional correlates. *Science, 194*, 732–734. doi: 10.1126/science.982039

Allport, G. W. (1937). *Personality: A psychological interpretation.* New York, NY: Henry Holt.

Allport, G. W., & Odbert, H. S. (1936). Trait names: A psycho-lexical study. *Psychological Monographs, 47*, 171.

Allport, G. W., & Postman, L. J. (1945). The basic psychology of rumor. *Transactions of the New York Academy of Sciences, 8*, 61–81.

Ally, B. A., Hussey, E. P., & Donahue, M. J. (2013). A case of hyperthymesia: Rethinking the role of the amygdala in autobiographical memory. *Neurocase, 19*(2), 166–181. doi: 10.1080/13554794.2011.654225

Alwin, D. F. (1988). From obedience to autonomy: Changes in traits desired in children, 1924–1978. *Public Opinion Quarterly, 52*(1), 33–52. doi: 10.1086/269081

Amaral, D. G., Schumann, C. M., & Nordahl, C. W. (2008). Neuroanatomy of autism. *Trends in Neurosciences, 31*(3), 137–145. doi: 10.1016/j.tins.2007.12.005

Ambady, N., & Rosenthal, R. (1993). Half a minute: Predicting teacher evaluations from thin slices of nonverbal behavior and physical attractiveness. *Journal of Personality and Social Psychology, 64*, 431–441. doi: 10.1037/0022-3514.64.3.431

American Association for the Advancement of Science. (2009). Benchmarks online. Retrieved from http://www.project2061.org/publications/bsl/online/index.php?chapter=1

American Foundation for Suicide Prevention. (2014). Risk factors and warning signs. Retrieved from http://www.afsp.org/understanding-suicide/risk-factors-and-warning-signs

American Psychiatric Association. (2000). *Diagnostic and Statistical Manual of Mental Disorders—Text Revised*. Washington, DC: Author.

American Psychiatric Association. (2001). *The practice of ECT: Recommendations for treatment, training, and privileging*. Washington, DC: American Psychiatric Press.

American Psychiatric Association. (2013). *Diagnostic and statistical manual of mental disorders* (5th ed.). Washington, DC: Author.

American Psychological Association. (2005a). Guidelines for ethical conduct in the care and use of animals. Retrieved from http://www.apa.org/science/anguide.html

American Psychological Association. (2005b). What is hypnosis? Retrieved from http://www.csj.org/infoserv_articles/apa_what_is_hypnosis.htm

American Psychological Association. (2014). Ethical principles of psychologists and Code of Conduct: Including 2010 amendments. Standard 9: Assessment. Retrieved from http://www.apa.org/ehtics/code/index.aspx?item=12

American Psychological Association. (2009). Careers in psychology. Retrieved from http://www.apa.org/topics/psychologycareer.html

American Psychological Association. (2014). Questions and answers about memories of child abuse. Retrieved from http://www.apa.org/topics/trauma/memories.aspx?item=2

American Psychological Association Presidential Task Force on Evidence-Based Practice. (2006). Evidence-based practice in psychology. *The American Psychologist, 61*(4), 271. doi: 10.1037/0003-066X.61.4.271

Ames, E. (1997). *The development of Romanian orphanage children adopted to Canada*. Barnaby, British Columbia, Canada: Simon Fraser University.

Ammon, K., & Gandevia, S. C. (1990). Transcranial magnetic stimulation can influence the selection of motor programmes. *Journal of Neurology, Neurosurgery, and Psychiatry, 53*(8), 705–707. doi: 10.1136/jnnp.53.8.705

Anand, B., & Brobeck, J. R. (1951). Hypothalamic control of food intake in rats and cats. *Yale Journal of Biology and Medicine, 24*, 123–140.

Anderson, C. A., & Bushman, B. J. (2001). Effects of violent video games on aggressive behavior, aggressive cognition, aggressive affect, physiological arousal, and prosocial behavior. *Psychological Science, 12*(5), 353–359. doi: 10.1111/1467-9280.00366

Anderson, C. A., & Bushman, B. J. (2002). The effects of media violence on society. *Science, 295*, 2377–2378. doi: 10.1126/science.1070765

Anderson, C. A., & Dill, K. E. (2000). Video games and aggressive thoughts, feelings, and behavior in the laboratory and in life. *Journal of Personality and Social Psychology, 78*, 772–790. doi: 10.1037/0022-3514.78.4.772

Anderson, D. R., Huston, A. C., Schmitt, K. L., Linebarger, D. L., & Wright, J. C. (2001). Early childhood television viewing and adolescent behavior: The recontact study. *Monographs for the Society for Research in Child Development, 66*, 1–147.

Anderson, P. W. (1972). More is different. *Science, 177*(4047), 393–396. doi: 10.1126/science.177.4047.393

Anderson, S. W., Bechara, A., Damasio, H., Tranel, D., & Damasio, A. R. (1999). Impairment of social and moral behavior related to early damage in human prefrontal cortex. *Nature Neuroscience, 2*(11), 1032–1037. doi: 10.1038/14833

Anderton, B. H. (1997). Changes in the ageing brain in health and disease. *Philosophical Transactions of the Royal Society, B: Biological Sciences, 352*(1363), 1781–1792. doi: 10.1098/rstb.1997.0162

Andreasen, N. C., Rezai, K., Alliger, R., Swayze, V. W., Flaum, M., Kirchner, P., et al. (1992). Hypofrontality in neuroleptic-naïve patients and in patients with chronic schizophrenia: Assessment with xenon 133 single-photon emission computed tomography and the Tower of London. *Archives of General Psychiatry, 49*(12), 943. doi: 10.1001/archpsyc.1992.01820120031006

Andrews, T. J., Davies-Thompson, J., Kingstone, A., & Young, A. W. (2010). Internal and external features of the face are represented holistically in face-selective regions of visual cortex. *Journal of Neuroscience, 30*(9), 3544–3552. doi: 10.1523/JNEUROSCI.4863-09.2010

Angold, A., Erkanli, A., Egger, H. L., & Costello, E. J. (2000). Stimulant treatment for children: A community perspective. *Journal of the American Academy of Child and Adolescent Psychiatry, 39*, 975–984. doi: 10.1097/00004583-200008000-00009

Annunziato, A. (2008). DNA packaging: Nucleosomes and chromatin. *Nature Education, 1*(1), 26.

Anokhin, A. P., Golosheykin, S., Grant, J., & Heath, A. C. (2009). Heritability of risk-taking in adolescence: A longitudinal twin study. *Twin Research and Human Genetics, 12*(4), 366–371. doi: 10.1375/twin.12.4.366

Anokhin, A. P., Golosheykin, S., & Heath, A. C. (2010). Heritability of individual differences in cortical processing of facial affect. *Behavior Genetics, 40*(2), 178–185. doi: 10.1007/s10519-010-9337-1

Antonov, I., Antonova, I., Kandel, E. R., & Hawkins, R. D. (2003). Activity-dependent presynaptic facilitation and hebbian LTP are both required and interact during classical conditioning in *Aplysia. Neuron, 37*, 135–147. doi: 10.1016/S0896-6273(02)01129-7

Ansbacher, H. L. & Ansbacher, R. R. (1956). *The individual psychology of Alfred Adler*. In New York, NY: Harper Torchbooks.

Aramovich, N. P. (2014). The effect of stereotype threat on group versus individual performance. *Small Group Research, 45*(2), 176–197. doi: 10.1177/1046496414523508

Armstrong, L., & Jenkins, S. (2000). *It's not about the bike: My journey back to life*. New York, NY: Penguin Putnam.

Arnsten, A. F. (2006). Stimulants: Therapeutic actions in ADHD. *Neuropsychopharmacology, 31*(11), 2376–2383. doi: 10.1038/sj.npp.1301164

Aron, A., Ketay, S., Hedden, T., Aron, E. N., Markus, H. R., & Gabrieli, J. D. E. (2010). Temperament trait of sensory processing sensitivity moderates cultural differences in neural response. *Social Cognitive and Affective Neuroscience, 5*(2–3), 219–226. doi: 10.1093/scan/nsq028

Aron, A., Norman, C. C., Aron, E. N., McKenna, C., & Heyman, R. E. (2000). Couples' shared participation in novel and arousing activities and experienced relationship quality. *Journal of Personality and Social Psychology, 78*(2), 273–284. doi: 10.1037//0022-3514.78.2.273

Aronson, E. (2011). Jigsaw basics. Retrieved from http://www.jigsaw.org/pdf/basics.pdf

Aronson, E., & Mills, J. (1959). The effect of severity of initiation on liking for a group. *Journal of Abnormal and Social Psychology, 58*, 177–181. doi: 10.1037/h0047195

Asch, S. E. (1951). Effects of group pressure upon the modification and distortion of judgments. In H. Guetzkow (Ed.), *Groups, leadership and men: Research in human relations* (pp. 177–190). Oxford, United Kingdom: Carnegie Press.

Asendorpf, J. B., Banse, R., & Mücke, D. (2002). Double dissociation between implicit and explicit personality self-concept: The case of shy behavior. *Journal of Personality and Social Psychology, 83*(2), 380–393. doi: 10.1037//0022-3514.83.2.380

Aserinsky, E., & Kleitman, N. (1953). Regularly occurring periods of eye motility and concomitant phenomena during sleep. *Science, 118*, 273–274. doi: 10.1126/science.118.3062.273

Asmundson, G. J. G., & Norton, G. R. (1993). Anxiety sensitivity and its relationship to spontaneous and cued panic attacks in college students. *Behavior Research and Therapy, 31*, 199–201. doi: 10.1016/0005-7967(93)90072-3

Atkins, D. C., Baucom, D. H., & Jacobson, N. S. (2001). Understanding infidelity: Correlates in a national random sample. *Journal of Family Psychology, 15*, 735–749. doi: 10.1037/0893-3200.15.4.735

Atkins, D. C., Marín, R. A., Lo, T. T. Y., Klann, N., & Hahlweg, K. (2010). Outcomes of couples with infidelity in a community-based sample of couple therapy. *Journal of Family Psychology, 24*(2), 212–216. doi: 10.1037/a0018789

Atkinson, Q. D. (2011). Phonemic diversity supports a serial founder effect model of language expansion from Africa. *Science, 332*(6027), 346–349. doi: 10.1126/science.1199295

Atkinson, R. C., & Shiffrin, R. M. (1968). Human memory: A proposed system and its control processes. In K. W. Spence & J. T. Spence (Eds.), *The psychology of learning and motivation: Vol. 2. Advances in research and theory* (pp. 89–195). New York, NY: Academic Press.

Atkinson, R. C., & Shiffrin, R. M. (1971). The control of short-term memory. *Scientific American, 225*, 82–90.

Atri, A., Sherman, S., Norman, K. A., Kirchhoff, B. A., Nicolas, M. M., Grecius, M. D., et al. (2004). Blockade of central cholinergic receptors impairs new learning and increases proactive interference in a word paired–associate memory task. *Behavioral Neuroscience, 118*, 223–236. doi: 10.1037/0735-7044.118.1.223

Austin Alchon, S. (2003). *A pest in the land: New world epidemics in a global perspective.* Albuquerque, NM: University of New Mexico Press.

Avena, N. M., Rada, P., & Hoebel, B. G. (2008). Evidence for sugar addiction: Behavioral and neurochemical effects of intermittent, excessive sugar intake. *Neuroscience & Biobehavioral Reviews, 32*(1), 20-39. Doi: 10.1016/j.neubiorev.2007.04.019

Averbach, E., & Sperling, G. (1961). Short term storage of information in vision. In C. Cherry (Ed.), *Information theory* (pp. 196–211). London, United Kingdom: Butterworth.

Axelrod, R., & Hamilton, W. D. (1981). The evolution of cooperation. *Science, 211*(4489), 1390–1396. doi: 10.1126/science.7466396

Baars, B. J. (1988). *A cognitive theory of consciousness.* Cambridge, United Kingdom: Cambridge University Press.

Babad, E., Bernieri, F., & Rosenthal, R. (1991). Students as judges of teachers' verbal and nonverbal behavior. *American Educational Research Journal, 28*, 211–234. doi: 10.3102/00028312028001211

Babiak, P., & Hare, R. D. (2006). *Snakes in suits.* New York, NY: Regan.

Bachman, J. G., & O'Malley, P. M. (1977). Self-esteem in young men: A longitudinal analysis of the impact of educational and occupational attainment. *Journal of Personality and Social Psychology, 35*, 365–380.

Bachrach, Y., Kosinski, M., Graepel, T., Kohli, P., & Stillwell, D. (2012). *Personality and patterns of Facebook usage. Proceedings of the 4th Annual ACM Web Science Conference,* 24-32. doi: 10.1145/2380718.2380722

Back, S. E., Killeen, T. K., Teer, A. P., Hartwell, E. E., Federline, A., Beylotte, F., et al. (2014). Substance use disorders and PTSD: An exploratory study of treatment preferences among military veterans. *Addictive Behaviors, 39*(2), 369–373. doi: 10.1016/j.addbeh.2013.09.017

Baddeley, A., Eysenck, M. W., & Anderson, M. C. (2009). *Memory.* London, United Kingdom: Psychology Press.

Baddeley, A. D. (1996). Exploring the central executive. *Quarterly Journal of Experimental Psychology, 49A*, 5–28. doi: 10.1080/713755608

Baddeley, A. D., & Hitch, G. J. (1974). Working memory. In G. Bower (Ed.), *The psychology of learning and motivation* (Vol. 8, pp. 47–89). New York, NY: Academic Press.

Baddeley, A. D., Logie, R. H., Nimmo-Smith, I., & Brereton, J. (1985). Components of fluent reading. *Journal of Memory and Language, 24*, 119–131. doi: 10.1016/0749-596X(85)90019-1

Baer, D. M., Wolf, M. M., & Risley, T. R. (1968). Some current dimensions of applied behavior analysis. *Journal of Applied Behavior Analysis, 1*(1), 91–97. doi: 10.1901/jaba.1968.1-91

Bahrick, H. P. (1984). Semantic memory content in permastore: Fifty years of memory for Spanish learned in school. *Journal of Experimental Psychology: General, 113*, 1-29. doi: 10.1037/0096-3445.113.1.1

Bailey, A. A., & Hurd, P. L. (2005). Finger length ratio (2D:4D) correlates with physical aggression in men but not in women. *Biological Psychology, 68*, 215–222. doi: 10.1016/j.biopsycho.2004.05.001

Bailey, C. H., & Chen, M. C. (1983). Morphological basis of long-term habituation and sensitization in *Aplysia. Science, 220*, 91–93. doi: 10.1126/science.6828885

Baillargeon, R., Li, J., Gertner, Y., & Wu, D. (2011). How do infants reason about physical events? In U. Goswami (Ed.), *The Wiley-Blackwell handbook of childhood cognitive development* (2nd ed., pp. 11–48). Walden, MA: Wiley–Blackwell.

Baird, A. A., Gruber, S. A., Fein, D. A., Maas, L. C., Steingard, R. J., Renshaw, P. F., et al. (1999). Functional magnetic resonance imaging of facial affect recognition in children and adolescents. *Journal of the American Academy of Child and Adolescent Psychiatry, 38*(2), 195–199. doi: 10.1097/00004583-199902000-00019

Baker, T. B., McFall, R. M., & Shoham, V. (2008). Current status and future prospects of clinical psychology: Toward a scientifically principled approach to mental and behavioral health care. *Psychological Science in the Public Interest, 9*(2), 67–103. doi: 10.1111/j.1539-6053.2009.01036.x

Bakker, A., Spinhoven, P., van Balkom, A. J. L. M., & van Dyck, R. (2002). Relevance of assessment of cognitions during panic attacks in the treatment of panic disorder. *Psychotherapy and Psychosomatics, 71*(3), 158–161. doi: 10.1159/000056283

Bakker, R., Steegers, E. A., Obradov, A., Raat, H., Hofman, A., & Jaddoe, V. W. (2010). Maternal caffeine intake from coffee and tea, fetal growth, and the risks of adverse birth outcomes: The Generation R Study. *American Journal of Clinical Nutrition, 91*(6), 1691–1698. doi: 10.3945/ajcn.2009.28792

Balanzá-Martínez, V., Fries, G. R., Colpo, G. D., Silveira, P. P., Portella, A. K., Tabarés-Seisdedos, R., et al. (2011). Therapeutic use of omega-3 fatty acids in bipolar disorder. *Expert Review of Neurotherapeutics, 11*(7), 1029–1047. doi: 10.1586/ern.11.42

Balschuna, D., Zuschrattera, W., & Wetzel, W. (2006). Allosteric enhancement of metabotropic glutamate receptor 5 function promotes spatial memory. *Neuroscience, 142*, 691–702. doi: 10.1016/j.neuroscience.2006.06.043

Baltimore Longitudinal Study of Aging. (n.d.). About BLSA. Retrieved from http://www.blsa.nih.gov/

Bandura, A. (1965). Influence of models' reinforcement contingencies on the acquisition of imitative responses. *Journal of Personality and Social Psychology, 1*, 589–595. doi: 10.1037/h0022070

Bandura, A. (1973). *Aggression: A social learning analysis.* Oxford, United Kingdom: Prentice-Hall.

Bandura, A. (1990). Perceived self-efficacy in the exercise of personal agency. *Journal of Applied Sport Psychology, 2*, 128–163. doi: 10.1080/10413209008406426

Bandura, A. (1993). Perceived self-efficacy in cognitive development and functioning. *Educational Psychologist, 28*, 117–148. doi: 10.1207/s15326985ep2802_3

Bandura, A. (1995). Exercise of personal and collective efficacy in changing societies. In A. Bandura (Ed.), *Self-efficacy in changing societies* (pp. 1–45). New York, NY: Cambridge University Press.

Banerjee, T. D., Middleton, F., & Faraone, S. V. (2007). Environmental risk factors for attention-deficit hyperactivity disorder. *Acta Paediatrica, 96*(9), 1269–1274. doi: 10.1111/j.1651-2227.2007.00430.x

Banks, E., & Canfell, K. (2009). Invited commentary: Hormone therapy risks and benefits—The Women's Health Initiative findings and the postmenopausal estrogen timing hypothesis. *American Journal of Epidemiology, 170*(1), 24–28. doi: 10.1093/aje/kwp113

Baños, R. M., Guillen, V., Quero, S., García-Palacios, A., Alcaniz, M., & Botella, C. (2011). A virtual reality system for the treatment of stress-related disorders: A preliminary analysis of efficacy compared to a standard cognitive behavioral program. *International Journal of Human-Computer Studies, 69*(9), 602–613. doi: 10.1016/j.ijhcs.2011.06.002

Barac, R., & Bialystok, E. (2012). Bilingual effects on cognitive and linguistic development: Role of language, cultural background, and education. *Child Development, 83*(2), 413–422. doi: 10.1111/j.1467-8624.2011.01707.x

Barbaresi, W. J., Katusic, S. K., Colligan, R. C., Weaver, A. L., & Jacobsen, S. J. (2005). The incidence of autism in Olmsted County, Minnesota, 1976–1997: Results from a population-based study. *Archives of Pediatric and Adolescent Medicine, 159*, 37–44. doi: 10.1001/archpedi.159.1.37

Barclay, P., & Lalumière, M. L. (2006). Do people differentially remember cheaters? *Human Nature, 17*(1), 98–113. doi: 10.1007/s12110-006-1022-y

Bard, P. (1934). Emotion: I. The neurohumoral basis of emotional reactions. In C. Murchison (Ed.), *Handbook of general experimental psychology* (pp. 264–311). Worcester, MA: Clark University Press.

Bargh, J. A., & Chartrand, T. L. (1999). The unbearable automaticity of being. *American Psychologist, 54*(7), 462–479. doi: 10.1037/0003-066X.54.7.462

Bargh, J. A., Chen, M., & Burrows, L. (1996). Automaticity of social behavior: Direct efforts of trait construct and stereotype activation on action. *Journal of Personality and Social Psychology, 71*(2), 230–244. doi: 10.1037/0022-3514.71.2.230

Barkley, R. A. (1995). *Taking charge of ADHD: The complete, authoritative guide for parents.* New York, NY: Guilford Press.

Barkley, R. A. (1997). *ADHD and the nature of self-control.* New York, NY: Guilford Press.

Barkley, R. A. (2002). Psychosocial treatments for attention-deficit/hyperactivity disorder in children. *Journal of Clinical Psychiatry, 63*(Suppl. 12), 36–43.

Barkley, R. A., & Cox, D. (2007). A review of driving risks and impairments associated with attention-deficit/hyperactivity disorder and the effects of stimulant medication on driving performance. *Journal of Safety Research, 38*(1), 113–128. doi: 10.1016/j.jsr.2006.09.004

Barlow, D. (1988). *Anxiety and its disorders: The nature and treatment of anxiety and panic.* New York, NY: Guilford Press.

Barnea-Goraly, N., Frazier, T. W., Piacenza, L., Minshew, N. J., Keshavan, M. S., Reiss, A. L., et al. (2014). A preliminary longitudinal volumetric MRI study of amygdala and hippocampal volumes in autism. *Progress in Neuro-Psychopharmacology and Biological Psychiatry, 48*, 124–128. doi: 10.1016/j.pnpbp.2013.09.010

Baron, J., & Brown, R. V. (1991). *Teaching decision making to adolescents.* Hillsdale, NJ: Erlbaum.

Baron, R. S. (2005). So right it's wrong: Groupthink and the ubiquitous nature of polarized group decision making. In M. P. Zanna (Ed.), *Advances in experimental social psychology* (Vol. 37, pp. 219–253). San Diego, CA: Elsevier Academic Press.

Bar-On, R., Tranel, D., Denburg, N. L., & Bechara, A. (2003). Exploring the neurological substrate of emotional and social intelligence. *Brain, 126*, 1790–1800. doi: 10.1093/brain/awg177

Baron-Cohen, S. (1991). The development of a theory of mind in autism: Deviance and delay? *Psychiatric Clinics of North America, 14*, 33–51.

Barresi, J., & Moore, C. (1996). Intentional relations and social understanding. *Behavioral and Brain Sciences, 19*, 107–122. doi: http://dx.doi.org/10.1017/S0140525X00041790

Barrick, M. R., & Mount, M. K. (1991). The Big Five personality dimensions and job performance: A meta-analysis. *Personnel Psychology, 44*, 1–26. doi: 10.1111/j.1744-6570.1991.tb00688.x

Bartels, A., & Zeki, S. (2000). The neural basis of romantic love. *NeuroReport, 11*(17), 3829–3834. doi: 10.1097/00001756-200011270-00046

Bartlett, F. C. (1967). *Remembering: A study in experimental and social psychology.* Cambridge, United Kingdom: Cambridge University Press. (Original work published 1932)

Bartone, P. T. (2000). Hardiness as a resiliency factor for United States forces in the Gulf War. In J. M. Violanti, D. Paton, & C. Dunning (Eds.), *Posttraumatic stress intervention: Challenges, issues, and perspectives* (pp. 115–133). Springfield, IL: Charles C. Thomas.

Bartoshuk, L. M. (2000). Comparing sensory experiences across individuals: Recent psychophysical advances illuminate genetic variation in taste perception. *Chemical Senses, 25*, 447–460. doi: 10.1093/chemse/25.4.447

Baruch, I., Hemsley, D. R., & Gray, J. A. (1988a). Differential performance of acute and chronic schizophrenics in a latent inhibition task. *Journal of Nervous and Mental Disease, 176*, 598–606.

Baruch, I., Hemsley, D. R., & Gray, J. A. (1988b). Latent inhibition and "psychotic proneness" in normal subjects. *Personality and Individual Differences, 9*, 777–783. doi: 10.1016/0191-8869(88)90067-0

Bashore, T. R., Ridderinkhof, K. R., & van der Molen, M. W. (1997). The decline of cognitive processing speed in old age. *Current Directions in Psychological Science, 6*, 163–169. doi: 10.1111/1467-8721.ep10772944

Basu, A., Alzaid, A., Dinneen, S., Caumo, A., Cobelli, C., & Rizza, R. A. (1996). Effects of a change in the pattern of insulin delivery on carbohydrate tolerance in diabetic and nondiabetic humans in the presence of differing degrees of insulin resistance. *Journal of Clinical Investigation, 97*(10), 2351–2361. doi: 10.1172/JCI118678

Bateson, M., Nettle, D., & Roberts, G. (2006). Cues of being watched enhance cooperation in a real-world setting. *Biology Letters, 2*(3), 412–414. doi: 10.1098/rsbl.2006.0509

Bauer, P. J., Larkina, M., & Deocampo, J. (2011). Early memory development. In U. Goswami (Ed.), *The Wiley–Blackwell handbook of childhood cognitive development* (2nd ed., pp. 153–179). Walden, MA: Wiley–Blackwell.

Bauer, P. J., & Lukowski, A. F. (2010). The memory is in the details: Relations between memory for the specific features of events and long-term recall during infancy. *Journal of Experimental Child Psychology, 107*(1), 1–14. doi: 10.1016/j.jecp.2010.04.004

Bauer, R. M. (1984). Autonomic recognition of names and faces in prosopagnosia: A neuropsychological application of the Guilty Knowledge Test. *Neuropsychologia, 22*, 457–469. doi: 10.1016/0028-3932(84)90040-X

Baumeister, R. F., Campbell, J. D., Krueger, J. I., & Vohs, K. D. (2003). Does high self-esteem cause better performance, interpersonal success, happiness, or healthier lifestyles? *Psychological Science in the Public Interest, 4*(1), 1–44. doi: 10.1111/1529-1006.01431

Baumeister, R. F., & Leary, M. R. (1995). The need to belong: Desire for interpersonal attachments as a fundamental human motivation. *Psychological Bulletin, 117*(3), 497–529. doi: 10.1037/0033-2909.117.3.497

Baumeister, R. F., Smart, L., & Boden, J. M. (1996). Relation of threatened egotism to violence and aggression: The dark side of high self-esteem. *Psychological Review, 103*(1), 5–33. doi: 10.1037/0033-295X.103.1.5

Baumrind, D. (1975). *Early socialization and the discipline controversy.* Morristown, NJ: General Learning Press.

Bavelas, J. B., Hutchinson, S., Kenwood, C., & Matheson, D. H. (1997). Using face-to-face dialogue as a standard for other communication systems. *Canadian Journal of Communication, 22*, 5–24.

Bavolek, S. J., & Keene, R. G. (1999). *Adult–Adolescent Parenting Inventory (AAPI-2) administration and development handbook.* Asheville, NC: Family Development Resources.

Baxter, L. R., Jr., Schwartz, J. M., Bergman, K. S., Szuba, M. P., Guze, B. H., Mazziotta, J. C., et al. (1992). Caudate glucose metabolic rate changes with both drug and behavior therapy for obsessive-compulsive disorder. *Archives of General Psychiatry, 49*(9), 681–689. doi: 10.1001/archpsyc.1992.01820090009002

Beaman, A. L., Klentz, B., Diener, E., & Svanum, S. (1979). Self-awareness and transgression in children: Two field studies. *Journal of Personality and Social Psychology, 37,* 1835–1846. doi: 10.1037/0022-3514.37.10.1835

Bearden, C. E., Thompson, P. M., Dalwani, M., Hayashi, K. M., Lee, A. D., Nicoletti, M., et al. (2007). Greater cortical gray matter density in lithium-treated patients with bipolar disorder. *Biological Psychiatry, 62,* 7–16. doi: 10.1016/j.biopsych.2006.10.027

Beaton, A. A. (1997). The relation of planum temporale asymmetry and morphology of the corpus callosum to handedness, gender, and dyslexia: A review of the evidence. *Brain and Language, 60,* 252–322. doi: 10.1006/brln.1997.1825

Bechara, A. (2005). Decision making, impulse control and loss of willpower to resist drugs: A neurocognitive perspective. *Nature Neuroscience, 8*(11), 1458–1463. doi: 10.1038/nn1584

Bechara, A., Damasio, H., & Damasio, A. R. (2000). Emotion, decision-making, and the orbitofrontal cortex. *Cerebral Cortex, 10,* 295–307. doi: 10.1093/cercor/10.3.295

Beck, A. T. (1975). *Cognitive therapy and the emotional disorders.* Madison, CT: International Universities Press.

Beck, A. T. (1985). Cognitive therapy, behavior therapy, psychoanalysis, and pharmacotherapy: A cognitive continuum. In M. Mahoney & A. Freeman (Eds.), *Cognition and psychotherapy* (pp. 197–220). New York, NY: Plenum Press.

Beck, A. T., Rush, A., Shaw, B., & Emery, G. (1979). *Cognitive therapy of depression.* New York, NY: Guilford Press.

Becker, A. E., Burwell, R. A., Herzog, D. B., Hamburg, P., & Gilman, S. E. (2002). Eating behaviours and attitudes following prolonged exposure to television among ethnic Fijian adolescent girls. *British Journal of Psychiatry, 180,* 509–514. doi: 10.1192/bjp.180.6.509

Beckerman, S., Erickson, P. I., Yost, J., Regalado, J., Jaramillo, L., Sparks, C., et al. (2009). Life histories, blood revenge, and reproductive success among the Waorani of Ecuador. *Proceedings of the National Academy of Sciences, 106*(20), 8134–8139. doi: 10.1073/pnas.0901431106

Beedie, C. J., & Lane, A. M. (2012). The role of glucose in self-control another look at the evidence and an alternative conceptualization. *Personality and Social Psychology Review, 16*(2), 143–153. doi: 10.1177/1088868311419817

Beevers, C. G., Gibb, B. E., McGeary, J. E., & Miller, I. W. (2007). Serotonin transporter genetic variation and biased attention for emotional word stimuli among psychiatric inpatients. *Journal of Abnormal Psychology, 116*(1), 208–212. doi: 10.1037/0021-843x.116.1.208

Bellugi, U., Wang, P. P., & Jernigan, T. L. (1994). Williams syndrome: An unusual neuropsychological profile. In S. H. Broman & J. Grafman (Eds.), *Atypical cognitive deficits in developmental disorders: Implications for brain function* (pp. 23–56). Hillsdale, NJ: Erlbaum.

Belsky, J. (1999). Modern evolutionary theory and patterns of attachment. In J. Cassidy & P. R. Shaver (Eds.), *Handbook of attachment: Theory, research and clinical applications* (pp. 141–161). New York, NY: Guilford Press.

Bem, D. J. (1972). Self-perception theory. In L. Berkowitz (Ed.), *Advances in experimental social psychology* (Vol. 6, pp. 1–62). New York, NY: Academic Press.

Bem, D. J. (2001). Exotic becomes erotic: Integrating biological and experiential antecedents of sexual orientation. In A. R. D'Augelli & C. J. Patterson (Eds.), *Lesbian, gay, and bisexual identities and youth: Psychological perspectives* (pp. 52–68). New York, NY: Oxford University Press.

Bem, D. J. (2011). Feeling the future: Experimental evidence for anomalous retroactive influences on cognition and affect. *Journal of Personality and Social Psychology, 100*(3), 407–425. doi: 10.1037/a0021524

Bennett, W. (1983). The nicotine fix. *Rhode Island Medical Journal, 66*(11), 455–458.

Berezin, R. (2014). A new drug to erase traumatic memory is not a good thing. Retrieved from http://www.psychologytoday.com/blog/the-theater-the-brain/201401/new-drug-erase-traumatic-memory-is-not-good-thing

Berglas, S., & Jones, E. E. (1978). Drug choice as a self-handicapping strategy in response to noncontingent success. *Journal of Personality and Social Psychology, 36*(4), 405–417. doi: 10.1037/0022-3514.36.4.405

Berkman, N. D., Bulik, C. M., Brownley, K. A., Lohr, K. N., Sedway, J. A., Rooks, A., et al. (2006). Management of eating disorders. *Evidence Report/Technology Assessment, 135,* 1–166.

Berkun, M. M., Bialek, H. M., Kern, R. P., & Yagi, K. (1962). Experimental studies of psychological stress in man. *Psychological Monographs, 76*(15), 1-39. doi: 10.1037/h0093835

Berlim, M. T., Mattevi, B. S., Belmonte-de-Abreu, P., & Crow, T. J. (2003). The etiology of schizophrenia and the origin of language: Overview of a theory.

Comprehensive Psychiatry, 44(1), 7–14. doi: 10.1053/comp.2003.50003

Berman, K. F., Torrey, E. F., Daniel, D. G., & Weinberger, D. R. (1992). Regional cerebral blood flow in monozygotic twins discordant and concordant for schizophrenia. *Archives of General Psychiatry, 49,* 927–934. doi: 10.1001/archpsyc.1992.01820120015004

Berman, M. G. (2009). In search of decay in verbal short term memory. *Journal of Experimental Psychology: Learning, Memory, and Cognition, 35*(2), 317–333. doi: 10.1037/a0014873

Bernhardt, P. C., Dabbs, J. M., Jr., Fielden, J. A., & Lutter, C. D. (1998). Testosterone changes during vicarious experiences of winning and losing among fans at sporting events. *Physiology and Behavior, 65,* 59–62. doi: 10.1016/S0031-9384(98)00147-4

Bernstein, D. A. (2011). *Essentials of psychology* (5th ed.). Belmont, CA: Cengage.

Berntson, G. G., Cacioppo, J. T., & Quigley, K. S. (1991). Autonomic determinism: The modes of autonomic control, the doctrine of autonomic space, and the laws of autonomic constraint. *Psychological Review, 98,* 459–487. doi: 10.1037/0033-295X.98.4.459

Berntson, G. G., Norman, G. J., Bechara, A., Bruss, J., Tranel, D., & Cacioppo, J. T. (2011). The insula and evaluative process. *Psychological Science, 22*(1), 80–86. doi: 10.1177/0956797610391097

Berscheid, E., & Peplau, L. A. (1983). The emerging science of relationships. In H. H. Kelley, E. Berscheid, A. Christensen, J. H. Harvey, T. L. Huston, G. Levinger, E. McClintock, L. A. Peplau & D. R. Peterson (Eds.), *Close relationships* (pp. 1–19). New York, NY: Freeman.

Berscheid, E., Snyder, M., & Omoto, A. M. (2004). Measuring closeness: The Relationship Closeness Inventory (RCI) revisited. In D. J. Mashek & A. P. Aron (Eds.), *Handbook of closeness and intimacy* (pp. 81–101). Mahwah, NJ: Erlbaum.

Bewernick, B. H., Hurlemann, R., Matusch, A., Kayser, S., Grubert, C., Hadrysiewicz, B., et al. (2010). Nucleus accumbens deep brain stimulation decreases ratings of depression and anxiety in treatment-resistant depression. *Biological Psychiatry, 67*(2), 110–116. doi: 10.1016/j.biopsych.2009.09.013

Bialystok, E., Craik, F. I., & Luk, G. (2012). Bilingualism: Consequences for mind and brain. *Trends in Cognitive Sciences, 16*(4), 240–250. doi: 10.1016/j.tics.2012.03.001

Biederman, I. (1987). Recognition-by-components: A theory of human image understanding. *Psychological Review, 94,* 115–147. doi: 10.1037/0033-295X.94.2.115

Biederman, J., Rosenbaum, J. F., Hirshfeld, D. R., Faraone, S. V., Bolduc, E. A., Gersten, M., et al. (1990). Psychiatric correlates of behavioral inhibition in young children of parents with and without psychiatric disorders. *Archives of General Psychiatry, 47*(1),

21–26. doi: 10.1001/arch-psyc.1990.01810130023004

Biezonski, D. K., & Meyer, J. S. (2011). The nature of 3,4-methylenedioxymethamphetamine (MDMA)–induced serotonergic dysfunction: Evidence for and against the neurodegeneration hypothesis. *Current Neuropharmacology, 9*(1), 84–90. doi: 10.2174/157015911795017146

Biglan, A., Duncan, T. E., Ary, D. V., & Smolkowski, K. (1995). Peer and parental influences on adolescent tobacco use. *Journal of Behavioral Medicine, 18*(4), 315–330. doi: 10.1007/bf01857657

Birchler, G. R. (1992). Marriage. In V. B. V. Hassett & M. Hersen (Eds.), *Handbook of social development: A lifespan perspective.* New York, NY: Plenum Press.

Birnholz, J. C., & Benacerraf, B. R. (1983). The development of human fetal hearing. *Science, 222*(4623), 516–518. doi: 10.1126/science.6623091

Blair, R. J., Colledge, E., Murray, L., & Mitchell, D. G. (2001). A selective impairment in the processing of sad and fearful expressions in children with psychopathic tendencies. *Journal of Abnormal Child Psychology, 29*, 491–498. doi: 10.1023/A:1012225108281

Blair, R. J. R., Mitchell, D. G. V., Richell, R. A., Kelly, S., Leonard, A., Newman, C., et al. (2002). Turning a deaf ear to fear: Impaired recognition of vocal affect in psychopathic individuals. *Journal of Abnormal Psychology, 111*(4), 682–686. doi: 10.1037/0021-843X.111.4.682

Blakemore, S.-J., & Mills, K. L. (2014). Is adolescence a sensitive period for sociocultural processing? *Annual Review of Psychology, 65*, 187–207. doi: 10.1146/annurev-psych-010213-115202

Blakemore, S.-J., & Robbins, T. W. (2012). Decision-making in the adolescent brain. *Nature Neuroscience, 15*(9), 1184–1191. doi: 10.1038/nn.3177

Blanchard, R. (1997). Birth order and sibling sex ratio in homosexual versus heterosexual males and females. *Annual Review of Sex Research, 8*, 27–67. doi: 10.1080/10532528.1997.10559918

Blanco, C., Okuda, M., Wright, C., Hasin, D. S., Grant, B. F., Liu, S.-M., et al. (2008). Mental health of college students and their non-college-attending peers: Results from the National Epidemiologic Study on Alcohol and Related Conditions. *Archives of General Psychiatry, 65*(12), 1429–1437. doi: 10.1001/archpsyc.65.12.1429

Bledowski, C., Kaiser, J., & Rahm, B. (2010). Basic operations in working memory: Contributions from functional imaging studies. *Behavioural Brain Research, 214*(2), 172–179. doi: 10.1016/j.bbr.2010.05.041

Blevins, J. E., Morton, G. J., Williams, D. L., Caldwell, D. W., Bastian, L. S., Wisse, B. E., et al. (2009). Forebrain melanocortin signaling enhances the hindbrain satiety

response to CCK-8. *American Journal of Physiology—Regulatory, Integrative and Comparative Physiology, 296*(3), R476–R484. doi: 10.1152/ajpregu.90544.2008

Bliss, T. V. P., & Lømo, T. (1973). Long-lasting potentiation of synaptic transmission in the dentate gyrus of the anesthetized rabbit following stimulation of the perforant path. *Journal of Physiology, 232*, 331–356. doi: 10.1016/0006-8993(88)91499-0

Block, J., & Robins, R. W. (1993). A longitudinal study of consistency and change in self-esteem from early adolescence to early adulthood. *Child Development, 64*(3), 909–923. doi: 10.1111/j.1467-8624.1993.tb02951.x

Bloom, P. (2004). Can a dog learn a word? *Science, 304*, 1605–1606. doi: 10.1126/science.1099899

Blumberg, S. J., Bramlett, M. D., Kogan, M. D., Schieve, L. A., Jones, J. R., & Lu, M. C. (2013). Changes in prevalence of parent-reported autism spectrum disorder in school-aged U.S. children: 2007 to 2011–2012. *National Health Statistics Reports, 65*, 1–11.

Blumenthal, J. A., Babyak, M. A., Moore, K. A., Craighead, W. E., Herman, S., Khatri, P., et al. (1999). Effects of exercise training on older patients with major depression. *Archives of Internal Medicine, 159*(19), 2349–2356. doi: 10.1001/archinte.159.19.2349

Blumstein, D. T., Davitian, R., & Kaye, P. D. (2010). Do film soundtracks contain nonlinear analogues to influence emotion? *Biology Letters, 6*, 751–754. doi: 10.1098/rsbl.2010.0333

Board, B. J., & Fritzon, K. (2005). Disordered personalities at work. *Psychology, Crime, and Law, 11*(1), 17–32. doi: 10.1080/10683160310001634304

Bobo, W. V., & Meltzer, H. Y. (2010). Duration of untreated psychosis and premorbid functioning: Relationship with treatment response and treatment-resistant schizophrenia. In H. Elkis, & H. Y. Meltzer (Eds.), *Therapy-resistant schizophrenia* (Vol. 26, pp. 74-86). Basel, Switzerland: Karger. doi: 10.1159/000319810.

Boe, E. E., May, H., & Boruch, R. F. (2002). *Student task persistence in the Third International Mathematics and Science Study: A major source of achievement differences at the national, classroom, and student levels.* (Center for Research and Evaluation in Social Policy, University of Pennsylvania, Philadelphia), Research Report 2002-TIMSS1.

Bogen, J. E. (1995). On the neurophysiology of consciousness: Part II. Constraining the semantic problem. *Consciousness and Cognition, 4*, 137–158. doi: 10.1006/ccog.1995.1020

Bogen, J. E., Schultz, D. H., & Vogel, P. J. (1988). Completeness of callosotomy shown by magnetic resonance imaging in the long term. *Archives of Neurology, 45*,

1203–1205. doi: 10.1001/archneur.1988.00520350041013

Bohart, A., O'Hara, M., & Leitner, L. (1998). Empirically violated treatments: Disenfranchisement of humanistic and other psychotherapies. *Psychotherapy Research, 8*(2), 141–157. doi: 10.1080/10503309812331332277

Bolger, N., & Schilling, E. A. (1991). Personality and the problems of everyday life: The role of neuroticism in exposure and reactivity to daily stressors. *Journal of Personality, 59*, 355–386. doi: 10.1111/j.1467-6494.1991.tb00253.x

Bond, C. F., & Titus, L. J. (1983). Social facilitation: A meta-analysis of 241 studies. *Psychological Bulletin, 94*, 265–292. doi: 10.1037/0033-2909.94.2.265

Boomsma, D. I., Willemsen, G., Dolan, C. B., Hawkley, L. C., & Cacioppo, J. T. (2005). Genetic and environmental contributions to loneliness in adults: The Netherlands Twin Register Study. *Behavior Genetics, 35*, 745–752. doi: 10.1007/s10519-005-6040-8

Booth, A., Shelley, G., Mazur, A., Tharp, G., & Kittok, R. (1989). Testosterone, and winning and losing in human competition. *Hormones and Behavior, 23*, 556–571. doi: 10.1016/0018-506X(89)90042-1

Borjigin, J., Lee, U., Liu, T., Pal, D., Huff, S., Klarr, D., et al. (2013). Surge of neurophysiological coherence and connectivity in the dying brain. *Proceedings of the National Academy of Sciences, 110*(35), 14432–14437. doi: 10.1073/pnas.1308285110

Bornstein, M. H., Kessen, W., & Weiskopf, S. (1976). Color vision and hue categorization in young human infants. *Journal of Experimental Psychology: Human Perception and Performance, 2*, 115–119. doi: 10.1037/0096-1523.2.1.115

Borota, D., Murray, E., Keceli, G., Chang, A., Watabe, J. M., Ly, M., et al. (2014). Post-study caffeine administration enhances memory consolidation in humans. *Nature Neuroscience, 17*(2), 201–203. doi: 10.1038/nn.3623

Borsook, D., Becerra, L., Fishman, S., Edwards, A., Jennings, C. L., Stojanovic, M., et al. (1998). Acute plasticity in the human somatosensory cortex following amputation. *NeuroReport, 9*, 1013–1017. doi: 10.1097/00001756-199804200-00011

Bosch, J. A., De Geus, E. J. C., & Kelder, A. (2001). Differential effects of active versus passive coping on secretory immunity. *Psychophysiology, 38*, 836–846. doi: Differential effects of active versus passive coping on secretory immunity.

Bossard, J. H. S. (1932). Residential propinquity in marriage selection. *American Journal of Sociology, 38*, 219–224. doi: 10.1086/216031

Bossini, L., Tavanti, M., Calossi, S., Lombardelli, A., Polizzotto, N. R., Galli, R., et al. (2008). Magnetic resonance imaging volumes of the hippocampus in drug-naïve patients with post-traumatic stress disorder without comorbidity conditions. *Journal of Psychiatric Research, 42*(9), 752–762. doi: 10.1016/j.jpsychires.2007.08.004

Bouchard, T., Jr. (1994). Genes, environment, and personality. *Science, 264,* 1700–1701. doi: 10.1126/science.8209250

Bouchard, T., Jr., Lykken, D. T., McGue, M., Segal, N. L., & Tellegen, A. (1990). Sources of human psychological differences: The Minnesota Study of Twins Reared Apart. *Science, 250,* 223–228. doi: 10.1126/science.2218526

Bower, G. H., & Gilligan, S. G. (1979). Remembering information related to one's self. *Journal of Research in Personality, 13*(4), 420–432. doi: 10.1016/0092-6566(79)90005-9

Bowlby, J. (1982). *Attachment and loss. Vol. 1: Attachment.* New York, NY: Basic Books. (Original work published 1969)

Bowlby, J. (1999a). *Attachment and loss. Vol. 2: Separation, anxiety and anger.* New York, NY: Basic Books. (Original work published 1973)

Bowlby, J. (1999b). *Attachment and loss. Vol. 3: Loss; Sadness and depression.* New York, NY: Basic Books. (Original work published 1973)

Bowmaker, J. K., & Dartnall, H. J. (1980). Visual pigments of rods and cones in a human retina. *Journal of Physiology, 298*(1), 501–511.

Boxer, C. F., Noonan, M. C., & Whelan, C. B. (2013). Measuring mate preferences: A replication and extension. *Journal of Family Issues.* doi: 10.1177/0192513x13490404

Boyack, K. W., Klavans, R., & Börner, K. (2005). Mapping the backbone of science. *Scientometrics, 64*(3), 351–374. doi: 10.1007/s11192-005-0255-6

Boydell, J., van Os, J., McKenzie, K., Allardyce, J., Goel, R., McCreadie, R. G., et al. (2001). Incidence of schizophrenia in ethnic minorities in London: Ecological study into interactions with environment. *British Medical Journal, 323*(7325), 1336–1338. doi: http://dx.doi.org/10.1136/bmj.323.7325.1336

Boyle, C. A., Boulet, S., Schieve, L. A., Cohen, R. A., Blumberg, S. J., Yeargin-Allsopp, M., et al.. (2011). Trends in the prevalence of developmental disabilities in U.S. children, 1997–2008. *Pediatrics, 127*(6), 1034–1042. doi: 10.1542/peds.2010-2989

Bradley, C. (1937). The behavior of children receiving Benzedrine. *American Journal of Psychiatry, 94,* 577–585.

Bradshaw, C., Kahn, A. S., & Saville, B. K. (2010). To hook up or date: Which gender benefits? *Sex Roles, 62*(9–10), 661–669. doi: 10.1007/s11199-010-9765-7

Bransford, J. D., & Johnson, M. K. (1972). Contextual prerequisites for understanding: Some investigations of comprehension and recall. *Journal of Verbal Learning and Verbal Behavior, 11,* 717–726. doi: 10.1016/S0022-5371(72)80006-9

Bray, R. M., & Noble, A. M. (1978). Authoritarianism and decisions of mock juries: Evidence of jury bias and group polarization. *Journal of Personality and Social Psychology, 36,* 1424–1430. doi: 10.1037/0022-3514.36.12.1424

Breasted, J. H. (1930). *Edwin Smith papyrus.* Chicago, IL: University of Chicago Press.

Breland, K., & Breland, M. (1961). The misbehavior of organisms. *American Psychologist, 16,* 681–684. doi: 10.1037/h0040090

Brembs, B. (1996). Chaos, cheating and cooperation: Potential solutions to the prisoner's dilemma. *Oikos, 76,* 14–24.

Bremner, J. D., Randall, P., Scott, T. M., Bronen, R. A., Seibyl, J. P., Southwick, S. M., et al. (1995). MRI-based measurement of hippocampal volume in patients with combat-related posttraumatic stress disorder. *American Journal of Psychiatry, 152,* 973–981.

Bremner, J. D., Vythilingam, M., Vermetten, E., Nazeer, A., Adil, J., Khan, S., et al. (2002). Reduced volume of orbitofrontal cortex in major depression. *Biological Psychiatry, 51*(4), 273–279. doi: 10.1016/S0006-3223(01)01336-1

Breslow, R. A., & Smothers, B. A. (2005). Drinking pattern and body mass index in never smokers: National Health Survey, 1997–2001. *American Journal of Epidemiology, 161*(4), 368–376. doi: 10.1093/aje/kwi061

Brewer, J. A., Worhunsky, P. D., Gray, J. R., Tang, Y.-Y., Weber, J., & Kober, H. (2011). Meditation experience is associated with differences in default mode network activity and connectivity. *Proceedings of the National Academy of Sciences, 108*(50), 20254–20259. doi: 10.1073/pnas.1112029108

Brewer, M. B., & Gardner, W. (1996). Who is this "we"? Levels of collective identity and self representations. *Journal of Personality and Social Psychology, 71*(1), 83–93. doi: 10.1037/0022-3514.71.1.83

Brewer, N., Keast, A., & Rishworth, A. (2002). The confidence–accuracy relationship in eyewitness identification: The effects of reflection and disconfirmation on correlation and calibration. *Journal of Experimental Psychology: Applied, 8,* 46–58. doi: 10.1037/1076-898X.8.1.44

Brewin, C. R., Andrews, B., & Valentine, J. D. (2000). Meta-analysis of risk factors for posttraumatic stress disorder in trauma-exposed adults. *Journal of Consulting and Clinical Psychology, 68,* 748–766. doi: 10.1037/0022-006X.68.5.748

Brooks, L. (1990). Concept formation and particularizing learning. In P. Hanson (Ed.), *Information, language and cognition* (pp. 141–167). Vancouver, BC: University of British Columbia Press.

Brooks, L., Norman, G., & Allen, S. (1991). Role of specific similarity in a medical diagnostic task. *Journal of Experimental Psychology: General, 120,* 278–287. doi: 10.1037/0096-3445.120.3.278

Brosnan, S. F. (2010). Behavioral development: Timing is everything. *Current Biology, 20*(3), R98–R100. doi: 10.1016/j.cub.2009.12.009

Brosnan, S. F., & De Waal, F. B. (2003). Monkeys reject unequal pay. *Nature, 425,* 297–299. doi: 10.1038/nature01963

Brown, G. W., & Harris, T. O. (1989). Depression. In G. W. Brown & T. O. Harris (Eds.), *Life events and illness* (pp. 49–93). New York, NY: Guilford Press.

Brown, J. D., & Mankowski, T. A. (1993). Self-esteem, mood, and self-evaluation: Changes in mood and the way you see you. *Journal of Personality and Social Psychology, 64*(3), 421–430. doi: 10.1037/0022-3514.64.3.421

Brown, J. D., & Smart, S. A. (1991). The self and social conduct: Linking self-representations to prosocial behavior. *Journal of Personality and Social Psychology, 60*(3), 368–375. doi: 10.1037/0022-3514.60.3.368

Brown, P., & Elliot, R. (1965). Control of aggression in a nursery school class. *Journal of Experimental Child Psychology, 2,* 103–109. doi: 10.1016/0022-0965(65)90035-4

Brown, R. W., & McNeill, D. (1966). The "tip of the tongue" phenomenon. *Journal of Verbal Learning and Verbal Behavior, 5,* 325–337. doi: 10.1016/S0022-5371(66)80040-3

Brown, T. A., & Cash, T. F. (1990). The phenomenon of nonclinical panic: Parameters of panic, fear, and avoidance. *Journal of Anxiety Disorders, 4,* 15–29. doi: 10.1016/0887-6185(90)90021-Z

Bruck, M., & Ceci, S. J. (2009). Reliability of child witnesses' reports. In J. L. Skeem, S. O. Lilienfeld, & K. S. Douglas (Eds.), *Psychological science in the courtroom: Consensus and controversy* (pp. 149–171). New York, NY: Guilford Press.

Bruine de Bruin, W., Parker, A. M., & Fischhoff, B. (2007). Individual differences in adult decision-making competence. *Journal of Personality and Social Psychology, 92,* 938–956. doi: 10.1037/0022-3514.92.5.938

Brune, M. (2006). The evolutionary psychology of obsessive-compulsive disorder: The role of cognitive metarepresentation. *Perspectives in Biology and Medicine, 49*(3), 317–329. doi: 10.1353/pbm.2006.0037

Brunelli, M., Castellucci, V., & Kandel, E. R. (1976). Synaptic facilitation and behavioral sensitization in *Aplysia*: Possible role of serotonin and cyclic AMP. *Science, 194*(4270), 1178–1181. doi: 10.1126/science.186870

Bryant, F. B., & Veroff, J. (2007). *Savoring: A new model of positive experience.* Mahwah, NJ: Erlbaum.

Bryant, G. A., & Haselton, M. G. (2009). Vocal cues of ovulation in human females. *Biology Letters, 5*(1), 12–15. doi: 10.1098/rsbl.2008.0507

Bryden, M. P. (1982). *Laterality: Functional asymmetry in the intact brain*. New York, NY: Academic Press.

Bulik, C. M., Thornton, L., Root, T. L., Pisetsky, E. M., Lichtenstein, P., & Pedersen, N. L. (2010). Understanding the relation between anorexia nervosa and bulimia nervosa in a Swedish national twin sample. *Biological Psychiatry, 67*(1), 71–77. doi: 10.1016/j.biopsych.2009.08.010

Burch, M. R., & Bailey, J. S. (1999). *How dogs learn*. Hoboken, NJ: Howell Book House.

Burger, J. M. (2009). Replicating Milgram: Would people still obey today? *American Psychologist, 64*(1), 1–11. doi: 10.1037/a0010932

Burger, J. M., Messian, N., Patel, S., del Prado, A., & Anderson, C. (2004). What a coincidence! The effects of incidental similarity on compliance. *Personality and Social Psychology Bulletin, 30*, 35–43. doi: 10.1177/0146167203258838

Burke, S. C., Cremeens, J., Vail-Smith, K., & Woolsey, C. (2010). Drunkorexia: Calorie restriction prior to alcohol consumption among college freshmen. *Journal of Alcohol and Drug Education, 54*(2), 17–34.

Burton, L. A., Henninger, D., Hafetz, J., & Cofer, J. (2009). Aggression, gender-typical childhood play, and a prenatal hormonal index. *Social Behavior and Personality, 37*(1), 105–115. doi: http://dx.doi.org/10.2224/sbp.2009.37.1.105

Buscemi, N., Vandermeer, B., Friesen, C., Bialy, L., Tubman, M., Ospina, M., et al. (2007). The efficacy and safety of drug treatments for chronic insomnia in adults: A meta-analysis of RCTs. *Journal of General Internal Medicine, 22*(9), 1335–1350. doi: 10.1007/s11606-007-0251-z

Bushdid, C., Magnasco, M. O., Vosshall, L. B., & Keller, A. (2014). Humans can discriminate more than 1 trillion olfactory stimuli. *Science, 343*(6177), 1370–1372. doi: 10.1126/science.1249168

Bushman, B. J. (2002). Does venting anger feed or extinguish the flame? Catharsis, rumination, distraction, anger, and aggressive responding. *Personality and Social Psychology Bulletin, 28*, 724–731. doi: 10.1177/0146167202289002

Bushnell, I. W. R. (2001). Mother's face recognition in newborn infants: Learning and memory. *Infant and Child Development, 10*, 67–74. doi: 10.1002/icd.248

Buss, A. H., & Perry, M. (1992). The aggression questionnaire. *Journal of Personality and Social Psychology, 63*(3), 452–459. doi: 10.1037/0022-3514.63.3.452

Buss, D. M. (1985). Human mate selection. *American Scientist, 73*, 47–51.

Buss, D. M. (1989). Sex differences in human mate preferences: Evolutionary hypotheses tested in 37 cultures. *Behavioral and Brain Sciences, 12*, 1–49. doi: http://dx.doi.org/10.1017/S0140525X00023992

Buss, D. M. (1996). Evolutionary biology and personality psychology: Toward a concep-tion of human nature and individual dif-ferences. In G.-H. Jennings (Ed.), *Passages beyond the gate: A Jungian approach to understanding the nature of American psy-chology at the dawn of the new millennium* (pp. 108–125). Needham Heights, MA: Simon and Schuster Custom Publishing.

Buss, D. M. (1999). Human nature and indi-vidual differences: The evolution of human personality. In L. A. Pervin & O. P. John (Eds.), *Handbook of personality: Theory and research* (2nd ed., pp. 31–56). New York, NY: Guilford Press.

Buss, D. M., Larsen, R. J., & Westen, D. (1992). Sex differences in jealousy: Evolution, physiology, and psychology. *Psychological Science, 3*, 251–255. doi: 10.1111/j.1467-9280.1992.tb00038.x

Buss, D. M., & Schmitt, D. P. (1993). Sexual strategies theory: An evolutionary perspec-tive on human mating. *Psychological Review, 100*, 204–232. doi: 10.1037/0033-295X.100.2.204

Bustillo, J. R., Lauriello, J., Horan, W. P., & Keith, S. J. (2001). The psychosocial treat-ment of schizophrenia: An update. *American Journal of Psychiatry, 158*(2), 163–175. doi: 10.1176/appi.ajp.158.2.163

Byer, C. O., & Shainberg, L. W. (1995). *Living well: Health in your hands* (2nd ed.). New York, NY: HarperCollins.

Byrne, D. (1961). Interpersonal attraction and attitude similarity. *Journal of Abnormal and Social Psychology, 62*, 713–715. doi: 10.1037/h0044721

Cacioppo, J. T., & Berntson, G. G. (2001). The affect system and racial prejudice. In J. Bargh & D. K. Apsley (Eds.), *Unraveling the complexities of social life: A festschrift in honor of Robert B. Zajonc* (pp. 95–110). Washington, DC: American Psychological Association.

Cacioppo, J. T., & Berntson, G. G. (2011). The brain, homeostasis, and health: Balancing demands of the internal and external milieu. In H. S. Friedman (Ed.), *The Oxford handbook of health psychology* (pp. 73–91). New York, NY: Oxford University Press.

Cacioppo, J. T., Berntson, G. G., Adolphs, R., Carter, C. S., Davidson, R. J., McClintock, M. K., et al. (2002). *Foundations in social neuroscience*. Cambridge, MA: MIT Press.

Cacioppo, J. T., Berntson, G. G., & Klein, D. J. (1992). What is an emotion? The role of somatovisceral afference, with special emphasis on somatovisceral "illusions." In M. S. Clark (Ed.), *Emotion and social behavior: Review of personality and social psychology*(Vol. 14, pp. 63–98). Thousand Oaks, CA: Sage.

Cacioppo, J. T., Berntson, G. G., Larsen, J. T., Poehlmann, K. M., & Ito, T. A. (2000). The psychophysiology of emotion. In M. Lewis & J. M. Haviland-Jones (Eds.), *Handbook of emotions* (Vol. 2, pp. 173–191). New York, NY: Guilford Press.

Cacioppo, J. T., Berntson, G. G., Norris, C. J., & Gollan, J. K. (2011). The evaluative space model. In P. Van Lange, A. Kruglanski, & E. T. Higgins (Eds.), *Handbook of theories of social psychology* (Vol. 1, pp. 50–72). Thousand Oaks, CA: Sage.

Cacioppo, J. T., Berntson, G. G., Sheridan, J. F., & McClintock, M. K. (2000). Multilevel integrative analyses of human behavior: Social neuroscience and the complement-ing nature of social and biological approaches. *Psychological Bulletin, 126*(6), 829–843. doi: 10.1037/0033-2909.126.6.829

Cacioppo, J. T., Cacioppo, S., & Boomsma, D. (2014). Evolutionary mechanisms for lone-liness. *Cognition and Emotion, 28*, 3–21. doi: 10.1080/02699931.2013.837379

Cacioppo, J. T., Cacioppo, S., Capitanio, J. P., & Cole, W. W. (2015). The neuroendocri-nology of social isolation. *Annual Review of Psychology, 66*.

Cacioppo, J. T., Cacioppo, S., Gonzaga, G. C., Ogburn, E. L., & VanderWeele, T. J. (2013). Marital satisfaction and break-ups differ across on-line and off-line meeting venues. *Proceedings of the National Academy of Sciences, 110*(25), 10135–10140. doi: 10.1073/pnas.1222447110

Cacioppo, J. T., & Decety, J. (2011a). An intro-duction to social neuroscience. In J. Decety & J. T. Cacioppo (Eds.), *The Oxford hand-book of social neuroscience* (pp. 3–8). New York, NY: Oxford University Press.

Cacioppo, J. T., & Decety, J. (2011b). Social neuroscience: Challenges and opportuni-ties in the study of complex behavior. *Annals of the New York Academy of Sciences, 1224*(1), 162–173. doi: 10.1111/j.1749-6632.2010.05858.x

Cacioppo, J. T., & Gardner, W. L. (1999). Emotion. *Annual Review of Psychology, 50*, 191–214. doi: 10.1146/annurev.psych.50.1.191

Cacioppo, J. T., & Hawkley, L. C. (2005). People thinking about people: The vicious cycle of being a social outcast in one's own mind. In K. D. Williams, J. P. Forgas, & W. von Hippel (Eds.), *The social outcast: Ostracism, social exclusion, rejection, and bullying* (pp. 91–108). New York, NY: Psychology Press.

Cacioppo, J. T., & Hawkley, L. C. (2009). Perceived social isolation and cognition. *Trends in Cognitive Sciences, 13*, 447–454. doi: 10.1016/j.tics.2009.06.005

Cacioppo, J. T., Hawkley, L. C., Berntson, G. G., Ernst, J. M., Gibbs, A. C., Stickgold, R., et al. (2002). Do lonely days invade the nights? Potential social modulation of sleep efficiency. *Psychological Science, 13*, 384–387. doi: 10.1111/1467-9280.00469

Cacioppo, J. T., Hawkley, L. C., Kalil, A., Hughes, M. E., Waite, L., & Thisted, R. A. (2008). Happiness and the invisible threads of social connection: The Chicago Health, Aging, and Social Relations Study. In M. Eid & R. Larsen (Eds.), *The science of* well-being (pp. 195–219). New York, NY: Guilford Press.

Cacioppo, J. T., Hawkley, L. C., & Thisted, R. A. (2010). Perceived social isolation makes me sad: 5-year cross-lagged analyses of loneliness and depressive symptomatology in the Chicago Health, Aging, and Social Relations Study. *Psychology and Aging, 25*(2), 453–463. doi: 10.1037/a0017216

Cacioppo, J. T., Hughes, M. E., Waite, L. J., Hawkley, L. C., & Thisted, R. A. (2006). Loneliness as a specific risk factor for depressive symptoms: Cross-sectional and longitudinal analyses. *Psychology and Aging, 21*, 140–151. doi: 10.1037/0882-7974.21.1.140

Cacioppo, J. T., Marshall-Goodell, B. S., Tassinary, L. G., & Petty, R. E. (1992). Rudimentary determinants of attitudes: Classical conditioning is more effective when prior knowledge about the attitude stimulus is low than high. *Journal of Experimental Social Psychology, 28*, 207–233. doi: 10.1016/0022-1031(92)90053-M

Cacioppo, J. T., Norris, C. J., Decety, J., Monteleone, G., & Nusbaum, H. (2009). In the eye of the beholder: Individual differences in perceived social isolation predict regional brain activation to social stimuli. *Journal of Cognitive Neuroscience, 21*(1), 83–92. doi: 10.1162/jocn.2009.21007

Cacioppo, J. T., & Patrick, W. (2008). *Loneliness: Human nature and the need for social connection.* New York, NY: Norton.

Cacioppo, J. T., & Petty, R. E. (1981). Electromyograms as measures of extent and affectivity of information processing. *American Psychologist, 36*, 441–456. doi: 10.1037/0003-066X.36.5.441

Cacioppo, J. T., & Petty, R. E. (1984). The elaboration likelihood model of persuasion. *Advances in Consumer Research, 11*, 673–675. doi: 10.1007/978-1-4612-4964-1_1

Cacioppo, J. T., Petty, R. E., Feinstein, J. A., & Jarvis, W. B. G. (1996). Dispositional differences in cognitive motivation: The life and times of individuals varying in need for cognition. *Psychological Bulletin, 119*(2), 197–253. doi: 10.1037/0033-2909.119.2.197

Cacioppo, J. T., Petty, R. E., & Kao, C. F. (1984). The efficient assessment of need for cognition. *Journal of Personality Assessment, 48*, 306–307. doi: 10.1207/s15327752jpa4803_13

Cacioppo, J. T., Semin, G. R., & Berntson, G. G. (2004). Realism, instrumentalism, and scientific symbiosis: Psychological theory as a search for truth and the discovery of solutions *American Psychologist, 59*(4), 214–223. doi: 10.1037/0003-066X.59.4.214

Cacioppo, S., Bianchi-Demicheli, F., Frum, C., Pfaus, J. G., & Lewis, J. W. (2012). The common neural bases between sexual desire and love: A multilevel kernel density fMRI analysis. *Journal of Sexual Medicine, 9*(4), 1048–1054. doi: 10.1111/j.1743-6109.2012.02651.x

Cacioppo, S., Couto, B., Bolmont, M., Sedeno, L., Frum, C., Lewis, J. W., et al. (2013). Selective decision-making deficit in love following damage to the anterior insula. *Current Trends in Neurology, 7*, 15–19.

Cadoret, R. J., & Cain, C. (1981). Environmental and genetic factors in predicting adolescent antisocial behavior in adoptees. *Psychiatric Journal of the University of Ottawa, 6*, 220–225.

Caggiano, V., Rizzolatti, G., Pomper, J. K., Thier, P., Giese, M. A., & Casile, A. (2011). View-based encoding of actions in mirror neurons of area f5 in macaque premotor cortex. *Current Biology, 21*(2), 144–148. doi: 10.1016/j.cub.2010.12.022

Cain, W. S., & Gent, J. F. (1991). Olfactory sensitivity: Reliability, generality, and association with aging. *Journal of Experimental Psychology: Human Perception and Performance, 17*, 382–391. doi: 10.1037/0096-1523.17.2.382

Calcagni, E., & Elenkov, I. (2006). Stress system activity, innate and T helper cytokines, and susceptibility to immune-related diseases. *Annals of the New York Academy of Sciences, 1069*, 62–76. doi: 10.1196/annals.1351.006

Caldwell, D. F., & Caldwell, M. C. (1976). Cetaceans. In T. A. Sebeok (Ed.), *How animals communicate* (pp. 794–808). Bloomington, IN: Indiana University.

Calvin, W. H. (2004). *A brief history of the mind: From apes to intellect and beyond.* Oxford, United Kingdom: Oxford University Press.

Camelot Group. (2004). Living the dream: Jackpot winners reveal their millionaire lifestyles. Retrieved from http://www.camelotgroup.co.uk/Winnerfacts.pdf

Campbell, F. W., Maffei, L., & Piccolino, M. (1973). The contrast sensitivity of the cat. *Journal of Physiology, 229*(3), 719–731.

Canary, D. J., Stafford, L., Hause, K. S., & Wallace, L. A. (1993). An inductive analysis of relational maintenance strategies: Comparisons among lovers, relatives, friends, and others. *Communication Research Reports, 10*(1), 5–14. doi: 10.1080/08824099309359913

Canli, T. (2009). Neuroimaging of personality. In P. J. Corr & G. Matthews (Eds.), *The Cambridge handbook of personality psychology* (pp. 305–322). New York, NY: Cambridge University Press.

Canli, T., Qiu, M., Omura, K., Congdon, E., Haas, B. W., Amin, Z., et al. (2006). Neural correlates of epigenesis. *Proceedings of the National Academy of Sciences, 103*(43), 16033–16038. doi: 10.1073/pnas.0601674103

Cannon, M., Kendell, R., Susser, E., & Jones, P. (2003). Prenatal and perinatal risk factors for schizophrenia. In R. M. Murray, P. B. Jones, E. Susser, J. van Os, & M. Cannon (Eds.), *The epidemiology of schizophrenia* (pp. 74–99). Cambridge, United Kingdom: Cambridge University Press.

Cannon, W. (1927). The James–Lange theory of emotions: A critical examination and an alternative theory. *American Journal of Psychology, 39*, 106–124. doi: 10.2307/1415404

Cannon, W. (1929). *Bodily changes in pain, hunger, fear and rage* (2nd ed.). New York, NY: Harper and Row.

Cannon, W. (1932). *The wisdom of the body.* New York, NY: Norton.

Cannon, W., & Washburn, A. L. (1912). An explanation of hunger. *American Journal of Physiology, 29*, 441–454.

Cantalupo, C., & Hopkins, W. D. (2001). Asymmetric Broca's area in great apes. *Nature, 414*, 505. doi: 10.1038/35107134

Capela, J. P., Fernandes, E., Remião, F., Bastos, M. L., Meisel, A., & Carvalho, F. (2007). Ecstasy induces apoptosis via 5-HT(2A)-receptor stimulation in cortical neurons. *Neurotoxicology, 28*(4), 868–875. doi: 10.1016/j.neuro.2007.04.005

Capshew, J. H. (1993). Engineering behavior: World War II, Project Pigeon, and the conditioning of B. F. Skinner. *Technology and Culture, 34*, 835–857.

Carew, T. J., & Kandel, E. R. (1973). Acquisition and retention of long-term habituation in *Aplysia:* Correlation of behavioral and cellular processes. *Science, 182*(4117), 1158–1160. doi: 10.1126/science.182.4117.1158

Carlsmith, J. M., & Anderson, C. A. (1979). Ambient temperature and the occurrence of collective violence: A new analysis. *Journal of Personality and Social Psychology, 37*(3), 337–344. doi: 10.1037/0022-3514.37.3.337

Carpenter, W. T., Jr., Conley, R. R., Buchanan, R. W., Breier, A., & Tamminga, C. A. (1995). Patient response and resource management: Another view of clozapine treatment of schizophrenia. *American Journal of Psychiatry, 152*, 827–832.

Carskadon, M. A., Wolfson, A. R., Acebo, C., Tzischinsky, O., & Seifer, R. (1998). Adolescent sleep patterns, circadian timing, and sleepiness at a transition to early school days. *Sleep, 21*, 871–881.

Carstensen, L. L., Fung, H. H., & Charles, S. T. (2003). Socioemotional selectivity theory and the regulation of emotion in the second half of life. *Motivation and Emotion, 27*(2), 103–123. doi: 10.1023/a:1024569803230

Carstensen, L. L., Isaacowitz, D. M., & Charles, S. T. (1999). Taking time seriously: A theory of socioemotional selectivity. *American Psychologist, 54*(3), 165–181. doi: 10.1037/0003-066x.54.3.165

Carstensen, L. L., Turan, B., Scheibe, S., Ram, N., Ersner-Hershfield, H., Samanez-Larkin, G. R., et al. (2011). Emotional experience improves with age: Evidence based on over 10 years of experience sampling. *Psychology and Aging, 26*(1), 21–33. doi: 10.1037/a0021285

Cartwright, R. D. (1978). *A primer on sleep and dreaming.* Reading, MA: Addison-Wesley.

Carver, C. S., & Scheier, M. F. (2000). Origins and functions of positive and negative affect: A control-process view. In E. T. Higgins & A. W. Kruglanski (Eds.), *Motivational science: Social and personality perspectives* (pp. 256–272). New York, NY: Psychology Press.

Casanova, M. F., Switala, A. E., Trippe, J., & Fitzgerald, M. (2007). Comparative mini-columnar morphometry of three distinguished scientists. *Autism, 11*(6), 557–569. doi: 10.1177/1362361307083261

Caspers, S., Zilles, K., Laird, A. R., & Eickhoff, S. B. (2010). ALE meta-analysis of action observation and imitation in the human brain. *NeuroImage, 50,* 1148–1167. doi: 10.1016/j.neuroimage.2009.12.112

Caspi, A., Sugden, K., Moffitt, T. E., Taylor, A., Craig, I. W., Harrington, H., et al. (2003). Influence of life stress on depression: Moderation by a polymorphism in the 5-HTT gene. *Science, 301*(5631), 386–389. doi: 10.1126/science.1083968

Caspi, A., Williams, B., Kim-Cohen, J., Craig, I. W., Milne, B. J., Poulton, R., et al. (2007). Moderation of breastfeeding effects on the IQ by genetic variation in fatty acid metabolism. *Proceedings of the National Academy of Sciences, 104*(47), 18860–18865. doi: 10.1073/pnas.0704292104

Cassidy, J. (1988). Child–mother attachment and the self in six-year-olds. *Child Development, 59*(1), 121–134. doi: 10.2307/1130394

Cassidy, T., & Lynn, R. (1989). A multifactorial approach to achievement motivation: The development of a comprehensive measure. *Journal of Occupational Psychology, 162,* 301–312.

Caterina, M. J., Leffler, A., Malmberg, A. B., Martin, W. J., Trafton, J., Petersen-Zeitz, K. R., et al. (2000). Impaired nociception and pain sensation in mice lacking the capsaicin receptor. *Science, 220,* 306–313. doi: 10.1126/science.288.5464.306

Caterina, M. J., Schumacher, M. A., Tominaga, M., Rosen, T. A., Levine, J. D., & Julius, D. (1997). The capsaicin receptor: A heat-activated ion channel in the pain pathway. *Nature, 389,* 816–824. doi: 10.1038/39807

Cattell, R. B. (1969). *Description and measurement of personality.* Yonkers, NY: World Book. (Original work published 1946)

Cattell, R. B. (1971). *Abilities: Their structure, growth, and action.* Boston, MA: Houghton Mifflin.

Celesia, G. G. (2013). Conscious awareness in patients in vegetative states: Myth or reality? *Current Neurology and Neuroscience Reports, 13*(11), 1–9. doi: 10.1007/s11910-013-0395-7

Centers for Disease Control and Prevention. (2003). State-based prevalence data of ADHD medication treatment. Retrieved from http://www.cdc.gov/ncbddd/adhd/medicated.html

Centers for Disease Control and Prevention. (2004). Years of potential life lost report, average for United States 2001–2005. Retrieved from https://apps.nccd.cdc.gov/ardi/Report.aspx?T=YPLL&P=f214cf69-cad7-496f-ace2-2a09b9d6a126&R=804296a0-ac47-41d3-a939-9df26a176186&M=E2769A53-0BFC-453F-9FD7-63C5AA6CE5D7&L=40071693-2c38-4b92-87aa-21fc57dbc1ab

Centers for Disease Control and Prevention. (2007). Healthy aging: Preserving function and improving quality of life among older Americans. Retrieved from http://www.cdc.gov/nccdphp/publications/aag/aging.htm

Centers for Disease Control and Prevention. (2008). Update: Measles—United States, January–July 2008. *MMWR Surveillance Summaries, 57*(33), 893–896.

Centers for Disease Control and Prevention. (2009a). National suicide statistics at a glance: Suicide rates among persons ages 10 years and older, by race/ethnicity, United States, 2002–2006. Retrieved from http://www.cdc.gov/violenceprevention/suicide/statistics/rates01.html

Centers for Disease Control and Prevention. (2009b). NCHS data brief. Retrieved from http://www.cdc.gov/nchs/data/databriefs/db26.htm

Centers for Disease Control and Prevention. (2010a). Pyramid: Adverse Childhood Experiences (ACE) Study. Retrieved from http://www.cdc.gov/ace/pyramid.htm

Centers for Disease Control and Prevention. (2010b). What do we know about tobacco use and pregnancy? Retrieved from http://www.cdc.gov/reproductivehealth/tobaccoUsePregnancy/index.htm

Centers for Disease Control and Prevention (CDC). (2011a). Antidepressant use in persons aged 12 and over: United States, 2005–2008. Retrieved from http://www.cdc.gov/nchs/data/databriefs/db76.htm

Centers for Disease Control and Prevention. (2011b). Vital signs: Current cigarette smoking among adults aged $18 years—United States, 2005–2010. *Morbidity and Mortality Weekly Report.* Retrieved from http://www.cdc.gov/mmwr/pdf/wk/mm60e0906.pdf

Centers for Disease Control and Prevention. (2012a). Alcohol use and binge drinking among women of childbearing age: United States, 2006–2010. *Morbidity and Mortality Weekly Report, 61*(28), 534–538.

Centers for Disease Control and Prevention. (2012b). Summary health statistics for U.S. adults: National Health Interview Survey, 2011. Retrieved from http://www.cdc.gov/nchs/data/series/sr_10/sr10_256.pdf

Centers for Disease Control and Prevention. (2012c). Vital signs: Binge drinking prevalence, frequency, and intensity among adults—United States, 2010 Retrieved from http://www.cdc.gov/mmwr/preview/mmwrhtml/mm6101a4.htm?s_cid=mm6101a4_w

Centers for Disease Control and Prevention. (2013). Vital signs: Current cigarette smoking among adults aged 18 years with mental illness: United States, 2009–2011. *Morbidity and Mortality Weekly Report, 62,* 1–7. Retrieved from http://www.cdc.gov/media/dpk/2013/docs/dpk-vs-adult-smoking-mental-illness-hyde_MMWR.pdf

Centers for Disease Control and Prevention. (2014a). Alcohol-attributable deaths and years of potential life lost: 11 states, 2006–2010. *Morbidity and Mortality Weekly Report, 63*(10), 213–216.

Centers for Disease Control and Prevention. (2014b). National suicide statistics at a glance: Suicide rates among persons ages 10 years and older, by race/ethnicity, United States, 2005–2009. Retrieved from http://www.cdc.gov/violenceprevention/suicide/statistics/rates01.html

Centers for Disease Control and Prevention. (2014c). Adult cigarette smoking in the United States: Current estimates. Retrieved from http://www.cdc.gov/tobacco/data_statistics/fact_sheets/adult_data/cig_smoking/index.htm

Cerella, J., & Hale, S. (1994). The rise and fall in information-processing rates over the life span. *Acta Psychologica, 86,* 109–197. doi: 10.1016/0001-6918(94)90002-7

Chagnon, N. A. (1988). Life histories, blood revenge, and warfare in a tribal population. *Science, 239,* 985–992. doi: 10.1126/science.239.4843.985

Champagne, F., Francis, D. D., Mar, A., & Meaney, M. J. (2003). Variations in maternal care in the rat as a mediating influence for the effects of environment on the development of individual differences in stress reactivity. *Physiology and Behavior, 79,* 359–371. doi: 10.1016/S0031-9384(03)00149-5

Chao, L. L., Yaffe, K., Samuelson, K., & Neylan, T. C. (2014). Hippocampal volume is inversely related to PTSD duration. *Psychiatry Research: Neuroimaging, 222*(3), 119–123. doi: 10.1016/j.pscychresns.2014.03.005

Chaplin, J. P., & Krawiec, T. S. (1979). *Systems and theories of psychology.* New York, NY: Holt, Rinehart, and Winston.

Chapman, B., Fiscella, K., Duberstein, P., Kawachi, I., & Muennig, P. (2014). Measurement confounding affects the extent to which verbal IQ explains social gradients in mortality. *Journal of Epidemiology and Community Health.* doi: 10.1136/jech-2013-203741

Chapman, R. S. (1995). Language development in children and adolescents with Down syndrome. In P. Fletcher & B. MacWhinney (Eds.), *The handbook of child language* (pp. 641–663). Oxford, United Kingdom: Blackwell.

Chapman, S., & MacKenzie, R. (2010). The global research neglect of unassisted smoking cessation: Causes and consequences.

PLoS Medicine, 7(2), e1000216. doi: 10.1371/journal.pmed.1000216

Charmaraman, L., & Grossman, J. M. (2010). Importance of race and ethnicity: An exploration of Asian, Black, Latino, and multiracial adolescent identity. *Cultural Diversity and Ethnic Minority Psychology, 16*(2), 144–151. doi: 10.1037/a0018668

Chase, W. G., & Simon, H. A. (1973). Perception in chess. *Cognitive Psychology, 4,* 55–81. doi: 10.1016/0010-0285(73)90004-2

Chatrian, G. (1990). Coma and other states of altered responsiveness and brain death. In D. D. Daly & T. A. Pedley (Eds.), *Current Practice of Clinical Electroencephalography* (pp. 442–443). New York, NY: Raven Press.

Chaudhari, N., Landlin, A. M., & Roper, S. D. (2000). A metabotropic glutamate receptor variant functions as a taste receptor. *Nature Neuroscience, 3,* 113–119. doi: 10.1038/72053

Chaudhri, N., Sahuque, L. L., & Janak, P. H. (2008). Context-induced relapse of conditioned behavioral responding to ethanol cues in rats. *Biological Psychiatry, 64*(3), 203–210. doi: 10.1016/j.biopsych.2008.03.007

Chein, J., Albert, D., O'Brien, L., Uckert, K., & Steinberg, L. (2011). Peers increase adolescent risk taking by enhancing activity in the brain's reward circuitry. *Developmental Science, 14*(2), F1–F10. doi: 10.1111/j.1467-7687.2010.01035.x

Chemtob, C. M., Nomura, Y., Rajendran, K., Yehuda, R., Schwartz, D., & Abramovitz, R. (2010). Impact of maternal posttraumatic stress disorder and depression following exposure to the September 11 attacks on preschool children's behavior. *Child Development, 81*(4), 1129–1141. doi: 10.1111/j.1467-8624.2010.01458.x

Chen, C.-H., Wu, W.-X., & Chen, C.-Y. (2013). Ant-inspired collective problem-solving systems. *Journal of Vibration and Control, 19*(16), 2481–2490. doi: 10.1177/1077546312456231

Chen, S., Boucher, H. C., & Tapias, M. P. (2006). The relational self revealed: Integrative conceptualization and implications for interpersonal life. *Psychological Bulletin, 132*(2), 151–179. doi: 10.1037/0033-2909.132.2.151

Cherkas, L., Hochberg, F., MacGregor, A. J., Snieder, H., & Spector, T. D. (2000). Happy families: A twin study of humour. *Twin Research, 3,* 17–22. doi: http://dx.doi.org/10.1375/twin.3.1.17

Chertkow, H., Whitehead, V., Phillips, N., Wolfson, C., Atherton, J., & Bergman, H. (2010). Multilingualism (but not always bilingualism) delays the onset of Alzheimer disease: Evidence from a bilingual community. *Alzheimer Disease and Associated Disorders, 24*(2), 118–125. doi: 110.1097/WAD.1090b1013e3181ca1221

Chiao, J. Y., & Blizinsky, K. D. (2010). Culture–gene coevolution of individualism–collectivism and the serotonin transporter gene. *Proceedings of the Royal Society of London, Series B: Biological Sciences, 277*(1681), 529–537. doi: 10.1098/rspb.2009.1650

Chicago Social Brain Network. (2011). *Invisible forces and unseen powers: Gravity, gods, and minds.* Saddle River, NJ: Pearson.

Child, I. L. (1973). *Humanistic psychology and the research tradition: Their several virtues.* Oxford, United Kingdom: Wiley.

Cho, K., Ennaceur, A., Cole, J. C., & Suh, C. K. (2000). Chronic jet lag produces cognitive deficits. *Journal of Neuroscience, 20,* RC66.

Choi, I., Nisbett, R. E., & Norenzayan, A. (1999). Causal attribution across cultures: Variation and universality. *Psychological Bulletin, 125*(1), 47–63. doi: 10.1037/0033-2909.125.1.47

Chomsky, N. (1957). *Syntactic structures.* The Hague, Netherlands: Mouton.

Chrea, C., Valentin, D., Sulmont-Rosse, C., Mai, H. L., Nguyen, D. H., & Abdi, H. (2004). Culture and odor categorization: Agreement between cultures depends upon the odors. *Food Quality and Preference, 15,* 669–679. doi: 10.1016/j.foodqual.2003.10.005

Christakis, N. A., & Fowler, J. H. (2007). The spread of obesity in a large social network over 32 years. *New England Journal of Medicine, 357*(4), 370–379. doi: 10.1056/NEJMsa066082

Christakis, N. A., & Fowler, J. H. (2014). Friendship and natural selection. *Proceedings of the National Academy of Sciences, 111*(Suppl. 3), 10796–10801. doi: 10.1073/pnas.1400825111

Chua, A. (2011). *Battle hymn of the tiger mother.* New York, NY: Penguin Press.

Chua, H. F., Boland, J. E., & Nisbett, R. E. (2005). Cultural variation in eye movements during scene perception. *Proceedings of the National Academy of Sciences, 102,* 12629–12633. doi: 10.1073/pnas.0506162102

Chua, H. F., Ho, S. S., Jasinska, A. J., Polk, T. A., Welsh, R. C., Liberzon, I., et al. (2011). Self-related neural response to tailored smoking-cessation messages predicts quitting. *Nature Neuroscience, 14*(4), 426–427. doi: 10.1038/nn.2761

Cialdini, R. B. (2001). *Influence: Science and practice* (4th ed.). Boston, MA: Allyn & Bacon.

Cialdini, R. B., Borden, R. J., Thorne, A., Walker, M. R., Freeman, S., & Sloan, L. R. (1976). Basking in reflected glory: Three (football) field studies. *Journal of Personality and Social Psychology, 34*(3), 366–375. doi: 10.1037/0022-3514.34.3.366

Cialdini, R. B., Cacioppo, J., Bassett, R., & Miller, J. (1978). Low-ball procedure for producing compliance: Commitment then cost. *Journal of Personality and Social Psychology, 36,* 463–476. doi: 10.1037/0022-3514.36.5.463

Cialdini, R. B., & Goldstein, N. J. (2004). Social influence: Compliance and conformity. *Annual Review of Psychology, 55,* 591–621. doi: 10.1146/annurev.psych.55.090902.142015

Cialdini, R. B., Kenrick, D. T., & Baumann, D. J. (1981). Effects of mood on prosocial behavior in children and adults. In N. Eisenberg (Ed.), *The development of prosocial behavior* (pp. 339–359). New York, NY: Academic Press.

Cialdini, R. B., Vincent, J., Lewis, S., Catalan, J., Wheeler, D., & Darby, B. L. (1975). Reciprocal concessions procedure for inducing compliance: The door-in-the-face technique. *Journal of Personality and Social Psychology, 31,* 206–215. doi: 10.1037/h0076284

Cicero, T. J., Ellis, M. S., & Surratt, H. L. (2012). Effect of abuse-deterrent formulation of OxyContin. *New England Journal of Medicine, 367*(2), 187–189. doi: 10.1056/NEJMc1204141

Cipolotti, L., Husain, M., Crinion, J., Bird, C. M., Khan, S. S., Losseff, N., et al. (2008). The role of the thalamus in amnesia: A tractography, high-resolution MRI and neuropsychological study. *Neuropsychologia, 46*(11), 2745–2758. doi: 10.1016/j.neuropsychologia.2008.05.009

Clarke, A., & Butler, P. E. (2009). The psychological management of facial transplantation. *Expert Review of Neurotherapeutics, 9*(7), 1087–1100. doi: 10.1586/ern.09.42

Clegg, J., & Sheard, C. (2002). Challenging behaviour and insecure attachment. *Journal of Intellectual Disability Research, 46,* 503–506. doi: Challenging behaviour and insecure attachment.

Coan, J. A., Schaefer, H. S., & Davidson, R. J. (2006). Lending a hand: Social regulation of the neural response to threat. *Psychological Science, 17*(12), 1032–1039. doi: 10.1111/j.1467-9280.2006.01832.x

Coffey, S., Dansky, B. S., Carrigan, M. H., & Brady, K. T. (2000). Acute and protracted cocaine abstinence in an outpatient population: A prospective study of mood, sleep and withdrawal symptoms. *Drug and Alcohol Dependence, 59,* 277–286. doi: 10.1016/S0376-8716(99)00126-X

Cohen, E., Chazan, S., Lerner, M., & Maimon, E. (2010). Posttraumatic play in young children exposed to terrorism: An empirical study. *Infant Mental Health Journal, 31*(2), 159–181. doi: 10.1002/imhj.20250

Cohen, S., Alper, C. M., Doyle, W. J., Adler, N., Treanor, J. J., & Turner, R. B. (2008). Objective and subjective socioeconomic status and susceptibility to the common cold. *Health Psychology, 27*(2), 268. doi: doi: 10.1037/0278-6133.27.2.268

Cohen, S., & Herbert, T. B. (1996). Health psychology: Psychological factors and physical disease from the perspective of human psychoneuroimmunology. *Annual Review of Psychology, 47,* 113–142. doi: 10.1146/annurev.psych.47.1.113

Cohen, S., Tyrrell, D. A., & Smith, A. P. (1991). Psychological stress and susceptibility to the common cold. *New England Journal of Medicine, 325*(9), 606–612. doi: 10.1056/NEJM199108293250903

Cohn, D., & Taylor, P. (2010). Baby boomers approach age 65—glumly. Retrieved from http://pewresearch.org/pubs/1834/baby-boomers-old-age-downbeat-pessimism

Cohn, M. A., Fredrickson, B. L., Brown, S. L., Mikels, J. A., & Conway, A. M. (2009). Happiness unpacked: Positive emotions increase life satisfaction by building resilience. *Emotion, 9*(3), 361–368. doi: 10.1037/a0015952

Cole, F. S., Alleyne, C., Barks, J. D. E., Boyle, R. J., Carroll, J. L., Dokken, D., et al. (2011). NIH Consensus Development Conference Statement: Inhaled nitric-oxide therapy for premature infants. *Pediatrics, 127*(2), 363–369. doi: 10.1542/peds.2010-3507

Cole, J. (1955). Paw preference in cats related to hand preference in animals and man. *Journal of Comparative and Physiological Psychology, 48*, 137–140. doi: 10.1037/h0040380

Cole, M. (1999). Culture in development. In M. H. Bornstein & M. E. Lamb (Eds.), *Developmental psychology: An advanced textbook* (4th ed., pp. 73–123). Hillsdale, NJ: Erlbaum.

Cole, S. W., Conti, G., Arevalo, J. M. G., Ruggiero, A. M., Heckman, J. J., & Suomi, S. J. (2012). Transcriptional modulation of the developing immune system by early life social adversity. *Proceedings of the National Academy of Sciences, 109*(50), 20578–20583. doi: 10.1073/pnas.1218253109

Cole, S. W., Hawkley, L. C., Arevalo, J. M. G., & Cacioppo, J. T. (2011). Transcript origin analysis identifies antigen presenting cells as primary targets of socially regulated leukocyte gene expression. *Proceedings of the National Academy of Sciences, 108*, 3080–3085. doi: 10.1073/pnas.1014218108

Coleman, R. M. (1986). *Wide awake at 3:00 a.m. by choice or by chance?* New York, NY: W. H. Freeman.

College Board, The. (2009). 2009 college-bound seniors: Total group profile report. Retrieved from http://professionals.collegeboard.com/profdownload/cbs-2009-national-TOTAL-GROUP.pdf

Collins, A. M., & Loftus, E. (1975). A spreading activation theory of semantic processing. *Psychological Review, 82*, 407–428. doi: 10.1037/0033-295X.82.6.407

Colwell, K., Hiscock-Anisman, C., Memon, A., Rachel, A., & Colwell, L. (2007). Vividness and spontaneity of statement detail characteristics as predictors of witness credibility. *American Journal of Forensic Psychology, 25*(1), 1–25.

Comings, D. E., & Blum, K. (2000). Reward deficiency syndrome: Genetic aspects of behavioral disorders. *Progress in Brain Research, 126*, 325–341. doi: 10.1016/S0079-6123(00)26022-6

Committee on Public Education. (2001). Children, adolescents, and television. *Pediatrics, 107*(2), 423–426. doi: 10.1542/peds.107.2.423

Connelly, K., & Martlew, M. (1999). *Psychologically speaking: A book of quotations.* Oxford, United Kingdom: BPS Books.

Conners, C. K., Epstein, J. N., March, J. S., Angold, A., Wells, K. C., Klaric, J., et al. (2001). Multimodal treatment of ADHD in the MTA: An alternative outcome analysis. *Journal of the American Academy of Child and Adolescent Psychiatry, 40*, 159–167. doi: 10.1097/00004583-200102000-00010

Connidis, I. A. (1992). Life transitions and the adult sibling tie: A qualitative study. *Journal of Marriage and the Family, 54*(4), 972–982. doi: 10.2307/353176

Connolly, T., & Zeelenberg, M. (2002). Regret in decision making. *Current Directions in Psychological Science, 11*, 212–216. doi: 10.1111/1467-8721.00203

Consumerreports.com. (2009). Risky business. Retrieved from http://www.consumerreports.org/cro/magazine-archive/march-2009/money/risk-taking/overview/risk-taking-ov.htm

Cooper, J. (2011). Cognitive dissonance theory. In A. W. Kruglanski, E. T. Higgins, & P. A. M. V. Lange (Eds.), *Handbook of theories of social psychology* (Vol. 1, pp. 377–397). Thousand Oaks, CA: Sage.

Cooper, S. J., & Dourish, C. T. (1990). Multiple cholecystokinin (CCK) receptors and CCK–monoamine interactions are instrumental in the control of feeding. *Physiology and Behavior, 48*, 849–857. doi: 10.1016/0031-9384(90)90239-Z

Corballis, M. C. (2004). The origins of modernity: Was autonomous speech the critical factor? *Psychological Review, 111*, 543–552. doi: 10.1037/0033-295X.111.2.543

Corballis, M. C. (2009). The evolution of language. *Annals of the New York Academy of Sciences, 1156*, 19–43. doi: 10.1111/j.1749-6632.2009.04423.x

Corbett, M. (1991). *American public opinion.* White Plains, NY: Longman.

Coren, S. (1993). The Lateral Preference Inventory for measurement of handedness, footedness, eyedness, and earedness: Norms for young adults. *Bulletin of the Psychonomic Society, 31*(1), 1–3. doi: 10.3758/BF03334122

Coren, S. (1996a). *Sleep thieves.* New York, NY: Free Press.

Coren, S. (1996b). Daylight savings time and traffic accidents. *New England Journal of Medicine, 334*, 924-925. doi: 10.1056/NEJM199604043341416

Corkin, S. (2002). What's new with the amnesic patient H.M.? *Nature Reviews Neuroscience, 3*, 153–160. doi: 10.1038/nrn726

Cornford, F. M. (1957). *From religion to philosophy: A study in the origins of Western speculation.* New York, NY: Harper Torchbooks.

Correll, C. U., & Schenk, E. M. (2008). Tardive dyskinesia and new antipsychotics. *Current Opinion in Psychiatry, 21*(2), 151–156. doi: 110.1097/YCO.1090b1013e3282f53132

Corsi, P. (Ed.). (1991). *The Enchanted Loom.* New York: Oxford University Press.

Cosmides, L., & Tooby, J. (1997). Evolutionary psychology: A primer. Retrieved from http://www.psych.ucsb.edu/research/cep/primer.html

Costa, P. T., & McCrae, R. R. (2011). NEO Personality Inventory–Revised (NEO PI-R). Retrieved from http://www4.parinc.com/Products/Product.aspx?ProductID=NEO-PI-R

Courchesne, E. (1997). Brainstem, cerebellar and limbic neuroanatomical abnormalities in autism. *Current Opinion in Neurobiology, 7*, 269–278. doi: 10.1016/S0959-4388(97)80016-5

Cowan, N. (2000). The magical number 4 in short-term memory: A reconsideration of mental storage capacity. *Behavioral and Brain Sciences, 24*, 87–185. doi: http://dx.doi.org/10.1017/S0140525X01003922

Cowen, P. J. (2010). Not fade away: The HPA axis and depression. *Psychological Medicine, 40*(01), 1–4. doi: 10.1017/S0033291709005558

Cox, M. J., Owen, M. T., Henderson, V. K., & Margand, N. A. (1992). Prediction of infant–father and infant–mother attachment. *Developmental Psychology, 28*(3), 474–483. doi: 10.1037/0012-1649.28.3.474

Craddock, N., & Sklar, P. (2013). Genetics of bipolar disorder. *Lancet, 381*(9878), 1654–1662. doi: 10.1136/jmg.36.8.585

Craig, A., & Tran, Y. (2005). The epidemiology of stuttering: The need for reliable estimates of prevalence and anxiety levels over the lifespan. *Advances in Speech–Language Pathology, 7*(1), 41–46. doi: 10.1080/14417040500055060

Craig, I. W. (2007). The importance of stress and genetic variation in human aggression. *Bioessays, 29*(3), 227–236. doi: 10.1002/bies.20538

Craik, F. I. M., & Lockhart, R. S. (1972). Levels of processing: A framework for memory research. *Journal of Verbal Learning and Verbal Behavior, 11*, 671–684. doi: 10.1016/S0022-5371(72)80001-X

Craik, F. I. M., & Tulving, E. (1975). Depth of processing and the retention of words in episodic memory. *Journal of Experimental Psychology: General, 104*(3), 268–294. doi: 10.1037/0096-3445.104.3.268

Crick, F., & Koch, C. (2003). A framework for consciousness. *Nature Neuroscience, 6*, 119–126. doi: 10.1038/nn0203-119

Cross-Disorder Group of the Psychiatric Genomics Consortium. (2013). Genetic relationship between five psychiatric disorders estimated from genome-wide SNPs. *Nature Genetics, 45*(9), 984–994. doi: 10.1038/ng.2711

Csikszentmihalyi, M. (1990). *Flow: The psychology of optimal experience*. New York, NY: Harper and Row.

Csikszentmihalyi, M. (1996). *Creativity: Flow and the psychology of discovery and invention*. New York, NY: HarperCollins.

Cumming, G. (2012). *Understanding the new statistics: Effect sizes, confidence intervals, and meta-analysis*. New York, NY: Routledge.

Cuperman, R., & Ickes, W. (2009). Big Five predictors of behavior and perceptions in initial dyadic interactions: Personality similarity helps extraverts and introverts, but hurts "disagreeables." *Journal of Personality and Social Psychology, 97*(4), 667–684. doi: 10.1037/a0015741

Curtis, R. G., Windsor, T. D., & Soubelet, A. (2014). The relationship between Big-5 personality traits and cognitive ability in older adults: A review. *Aging, Neuropsychology, and Cognition* (ahead-of-print), 1–30. doi: 10.1080/13825585.2014.888392

Custance, D. M., Whiten, A., & Bard, K. A. (1995). Can young chimpanzees *(Pan troglodytes)* imitate arbitrary actions? Hayes & Hayes (1952) revisited. *Behaviour, 132*, 837–859. doi: 10.1163/156853995X00036

Cyders, M. A., & Coskunpinar, A. (2011). Measurement of constructs using self-report and behavioral lab tasks: Is there overlap in nomothetic span and construct representation for impulsivity? *Clinical Psychology Review, 31*(6), 965–982. doi: 10.1016/j.cpr.2011.06.001

Dabbs, J. M., Jr., & Janis, I. L. (1965). Why does eating while reading facilitate opinion change? An experimental inquiry. *Journal of Experimental Social Psychology, 1*, 133–144. doi: 10.1016/0022-1031(65)90041-7

Dabbs, J. M., Jr., Frady, R. L., Carr, T. S., & Besch, N. F. (1987). Saliva testosterone and criminal violence in young adult prison inmates. *Psychosomatic Medicine, 49*, 174–182.

Dabbs, J. M., Jr., & Hargrove, M. F. (1997). Age, testosterone, and behavior among female prison inmates. *Psychosomatic Medicine, 59*, 477–480.

Dabbs, J. M., Jr., & Morris, R. (1990). Testosterone, social class, and antisocial behavior in a sample of 4,462 men. *Psychological Science, 1*, 209–211. doi: 10.1111/j.1467-9280.1990.tb00200.x

Dahl, R. E., Holttum, J., & Trubnick, L. (1994). A clinical picture of child and adolescent narcolepsy. *Journal of the American Academy of Child and Adolescent Psychiatry, 33*, 834–841. doi: 10.1097/00004583-199407000-00009

Dallenbach, K. M. (1951). A puzzle-picture with a new principle of concealment. *American Journal of Psychology, 64*(3), 431–433. doi: 10.2307/1419008

Daly, R. (2006). Psychiatrists proactive in scope-of-practice battles. *Psychiatric News, 41*(5), 17–34.

Damasio, A. R. (1994). *Descartes' error: Emotion, reason, and the human brain.* New York, NY: Putnam.

Damasio, A. R., & Anderson, S. W. (1993). The frontal lobes. In K. M. Heilman & E. Valenstein (Eds.), *Clinical neuropsychology* (pp. 409–460). New York, NY: Oxford University Press.

Damasio, A. R., Bellugi, U., Damasio, H., Poizner, H., & Gilder, J. V. (1986). Sign language aphasia during left-hemisphere Amytal injection. *Nature, 322*, 363–365. doi: 10.1038/322363a0

Damasio, A. R., Grabowski, T. J., Bechara, A., Damasio, H., Ponto, L. L., Parvizi, J., & Hichwa, R. D. (2000). Subcortical and cortical brain activity during the feeling of self-generated emotions. *Nature Neuroscience, 3*, 1049–1056. doi: 10.1038/79871

Damasio, A. R., Tranel, D., & Damasio, H. (1991). Somatic markers and the guidance of behavior: Theory and preliminary testing. In H. S. Levin, H. M. Eisenberg, & A. L. Benton (Eds.), *Frontal lobe function and dysfunction* (pp. 217–229). New York, NY: Oxford University Press.

Damasio, H., Grabowski, T., Frank, R., Galaburda, A. M., & Damasio, A. R. (1994). The return of Phineas Gage: Clues about the brain from the skull of a famous patient. *Science, 264*, 1102–1105. doi: 10.1126/science.8178168

Dani, J. A., & Harris, R. A. (2005). Nicotine addiction and comorbidity with alcohol abuse and mental illness. *Nature Neuroscience, 8*(11), 1465–1470. doi: 10.1038/nn1580

Dannar, P. R. (2013). Millennials: What they offer our organizations and how leaders can make sure they deliver. *Journal of Values-Based Leadership, 6*(1), 3.

Danziger, K., & Ballantyne, P. F. (1997). Psychological experiments. In W. G. Bringmann, H. E. Luck, R. Miller, & C. E. Early (Eds.), *Pictorial history of psychology* (pp. 233–239). New York, NY: Oxford University Press.

Dapretto, M., Davies, M. S., Pfeifer, J. H., Scott, A. A., Sigman, M., Bookheimer, S. Y., et al. (2006). Understanding emotions in others: Mirror neuron dysfunction in children with autism spectrum disorders. *Nature Neuroscience, 9*(1), 28–30. doi: 10.1038/nn1611

Dark, J., Forger, N. G., Stern, J. S., & Zucker, I. (1984). Recovery of lipid mass after removal of adipose tissue in ground squirrels. *American Journal of Physiology, 249*(Pt. 2), R73–R78.

Darwin, C. (1859). *On the origin of species by means of natural selection, or the preservation of favoured races in the struggle for life.* London, United Kingdom: John Murray.

Darwin, C. (1871). *The descent of man and selection in relation to sex.* London, United Kingdom: John Murray.

Darwin, C. (1872). *The expression of emotions in man and animals.* London, United Kingdom: Murray.

Dauvilliers, Y., Montplaisir, J., Cochen, V., Desautels, A., Einen, M., Lin, L., et al. (2010). Post-H1N1 narcolepsy–cataplexy. *Sleep, 33*(11), 1428.

Davidson, R. J., & Irwin, W. (1999). The functional neuroanatomy of emotion and affective style. *Trends in Cognitive Sciences, 3*(1), 11–21. doi: 10.1016/S1364-6613(98)01265-0

Davidson, R. J., Putnam, K. M., & Larson, C. L. (2000). Dysfunction in the neural circuitry of emotion regulation—A possible prelude to violence. *Science, 289*, 591–594. doi: 10.1126/science.289.5479.591

Davis, C. G., & Nolen-Hoeksema, S. (2009). Making sense of loss, perceiving benefits, and posttraumatic growth. In S. J. Lopez & C. R. Snyder (Eds.), *Oxford handbook of positive psychology* (2nd ed., pp. 641–649). New York, NY: Oxford University Press.

Davis, J. A., Smith, T. W., & Marsden, P. V. (2006). General Social Survey (GSS). Retrieved from http://www.norc.uchicago.edu/projects/gensoc.asp

Davis, J. L. (2004). Researchers identify alcoholism gene: Alcohol addiction, high anxiety linked to same gene. Retrieved from http://www.webmd.com/content/article/87/99592.htm

Davis, J. L., & Rusbult, C. E. (2001). Attitude alignment in close relationships. *Journal of Personality and Social Psychology, 81*, 65–84. doi: 10.1037/0022-3514.81.1.65

Davis, M. (2007). An introduction to sine-wave speech. Retrieved from http://www.mrc-cbu.cam.ac.uk/people/matt.davis/sine-wave-speech/

Dawkins, R. (1976). *The selfish gene.* Oxford, United Kingdom: Oxford University Press.

de Gelder, B., Snyder, J., Greve, D., Gerard, G., & Hadjikhani, N. (2004). Fear fosters flight: A mechanism for fear contagion when perceiving emotion expressed by a whole body. *Proceedings of the National Academy of Sciences, 101*, 16701–16706. doi: 10.1073/pnas.0407042101

de Lecea, L., Kilduff, T. S., Peyron, C., Gao, X. B., Foye, P. E., Danielson, P. E., et al. (1998). The hypocretins: Hypothalamus-specific peptides with neuroexcitatory activity. *Proceedings of the National Academy of Sciences, 95*(1), 322–327. doi: 10.1073/pnas.95.1.322

De May, J., & Gladstone, B. (2009). The witnesses that didn't: Transcript. Retrieved from http://www.onthemedia.org/2009/mar/27/the-witnesses-that-didnt/transcript/

De Peri, L., Crescini, A., Deste, G., Fusar-Poli, P., Sacchetti, E., & Vita, A. (2012). Brain structural abnormalities at the onset of schizophrenia and bipolar disorder: A meta-analysis of controlled magnetic resonance imaging studies. *Current Pharmaceutical Design, 18*(4), 486–494. doi: 10.2174/138161212799316253

De Valois, R. L., & De Valois, K. K. (1980). Spatial vision. *Annual Review of Psychology, 31*, 309–341. doi: 10.1146/annurev.ps.31.020180.001521

de Vries, A. P., Kassam-Adams, N., Cnaan, A., Sherman-Slate, E., Gallagher, P. R., & Winston, F. K. (1999). Looking beyond the physical injury: Posttraumatic stress disorder in children and parents after pediatric traffic injury. *Pediatrics, 104*, 1293–1299. doi: 10.1542/peds.104.6.1293

Dear Abby. (January 14, 2006). Man ready to scrap marriage after wife wrecks his car. Retrieved from http://www.uexpress.com/dearabby/?uc_full_date=20060114

Deary, I. J., Penke, L., & Johnson, W. (2010). The neuroscience of human intelligence differences. *Nature Reviews Neuroscience, 11*, 201–211. doi: 10.1038/nrn2793

Deary, I. J., Strand, S., Smith, P., & Fernandes, C. (2007). Intelligence and educational achievement. *Intelligence, 35*(1), 13–21. doi: 10.1016/j.intell.2006.02.001

DeCasper, A. J., & Fifer, W. P. (1980). Of human bonding: Newborns prefer their mothers' voices. *Science, 208*, 1174–1176. doi: 10.1126/science.7375928

DeCasper, A. J., & Spence, M. J. (1986). Prenatal maternal speech influences newborns' perception of speech sounds. *Infant Behavior and Development, 9*, 133–150. doi: 10.1016/0163-6383(86)90025-1

DeCharms, R. (1968). *Personal causation.* New York, NY: Academic Press.

Deci, E. L., & Ryan, R. M. (2000). The "what" and "why" of goal pursuits: Human needs and the self-determination of behavior. *Psychological Inquiry, 11*, 227–268. doi: 10.1207/S15327965PLI1104_01

Deese, J. (1959). Influence of inter-item associative strength upon immediate free recall. *Psychological Reports, 5*, 305–312. doi: 10.2466/PR0.5.3.305-312

Della Rosa, P., Videsott, G., Borsa, V., Canini, M., Weekes, B. S., Franceschini, R., et al. (2013). A neural interactive location for multilingual talent. *Cortex, 49*(2), 605–608. doi: 10.1016/j.cortex.2012.12.001

Dement, W. (1960). The effect of dream deprivation. *Science, 131*, 1705–1707. doi: 10.1126/science.131.3415.1705

Dement, W., & Kleitman, N. (1957). The relation of eye movements during sleep to dream activity: An objective method for the study of dreaming. *Journal of Experimental Psychology, 53*, 339–346. doi: 10.1037/h0048189

Demitrack, M. A. (2007). Therapeutic neuromodulation: Clinical and research implications of a new therapeutic platform. *Psychiatric Annals, 37*(3), 165–174.

DeNeve, K. M., & Cooper, H. (1998). The happy personality: A meta-analysis of 137 personality traits and subjective well-being. *Psychological Bulletin, 124*(2), 197–229. doi: 10.1037/0033-2909.124.2.197

Dennett, D. C. (1991). *Consciousness explained.* Boston, MA: Little, Brown, & Co.

Dennis, W. (1966). Age and creative productivity. *Journal of Gerontology, 21*, 1–8.

Department of Health and Human Services, U.S. Public Health Service. (2007). Mental health: Culture, race, and ethnicity. Retrieved from http://www.surgeongeneral.gov/library/mentalhealth/cre/execsummary-1.html

Derksen, D. J. (2013). The Affordable Care Act: Unprecedented opportunities for family physicians and public health. *Annals of Family Medicine, 11*(5), 400–402. doi: 10.1370/afm.1569

Derntl, B., Windischberger, C., Robinson, S., Kryspin-Exner, I., Gur, R. C., Moser, E., et al. (2009). Amygdala activity to fear and anger in healthy young males is associated with testosterone. *Psychoneuroendocrinology, 34*(5), 687–693. doi: 10.1016/j.psyneuen.2008.11.007

Derogatis, L. R., & Coons, H. L. (1993). Self-report measures of stress. In L. Goldberger & S. Breznitz (Eds.), *Handbook of stress: Theoretical and clinical aspects* (2nd ed., pp. 200–233). New York, NY: Free Press.

Deschamps, J. C., & Doise, W. (1978). Crossed category membership in intergroup relations. In H. Tajfe (Ed.), *Differentiation between social groups* (pp. 141–158). London, United Kingdom: Academic Press.

Deutschman, A. Is your boss a psychopath? Retrieved from http://www.fastcompany.com/53247/your-boss-psychopath

DeYoung, C. G., Hirsh, J. B., Shane, M. S., Papademetris, X., Rajeevan, N., & Gray, J. R. (2010). Testing predictions from personality neuroscience. *Psychological Science, 21*(6), 820–828. doi: 10.1177/0956797610370159

Dew, J., & Wilcox, W. B. (2011). If momma ain't happy: Explaining declines in marital satisfaction among new mothers. *Journal of Marriage and Family, 73*(1), 1–12. doi: 10.1111/j.1741-3737.2010.00782.x

Di Pellegrino, G., Fadiga, L., Fogassi, L., Gallese, V., & Rizzolatti, G. (1992). Understanding motor events: A neurophysiological study. *Experimental Brain Research, 91*, 176–180. doi: 10.1007/BF00230027

Diamond, A., & Goldman-Rakic, P. S. (1989). Comparison of human infants and rhesus monkeys on Piaget's AB task: Evidence for dependence on dorsolateral prefrontal cortex. *Experimental Brain Research, 74*, 24–40. doi: 10.1007/BF00248277

Diamond, L. M. (2004). Emerging perspectives on distinctions between romantic love and sexual desire. *Current Directions in Psychological Science, 13*(3), 116–119. doi: 10.1111/j.0963-7214.2004.00287.x

Dias, B. G., & Ressler, K. J. (2013). Parental olfactory experience influences behavior and neural structure in subsequent generations. *Nature Neuroscience, 17*(1), 89–96. doi: 10.1038/nn.3594

Dickens, W. T., & Flynn, J. R. (2001). Heritability estimates versus large environmental effects: The IQ paradox resolved. *Psychological Review, 108*, 346–369. doi: 10.1037/0033-295X.108.2.346

Dickens, W. T., & Flynn, J. R. (2006). Black Americans reduce the racial IQ gap: Evidence from standardization samples. *Psychological Science, 17*, 913–920. doi: 10.1111/j.1467-9280.2006.01802.x

Diekelmann, S., & Born, J. (2010). The memory function of sleep. *Nature Reviews Neuroscience, 11*(2), 114–126. doi: 10.1038/nrn2762

Diener, E., Horwitz, J., & Emmons, R. A. (1985). Happiness of the very wealthy. *Social Indicators, 16*, 263–274. doi: 10.1007/BF00415126

Diener, E., Ng, W., Harter, J., & Arora, R. (2010). Wealth and happiness across the world: Material prosperity predicts life evaluation, whereas psychosocial prosperity predicts positive feeling. *Journal of Personality and Social Psychology, 99*(1), 52–61. doi: 10.1037/a0018066

Diener, E., & Seligman, M. E. P. (2004). Beyond money: Toward an economy of well-being. *Psychological Science in the Public Interest, 5*, 1–31. doi: 10.1111/j.0963-7214.2004.00501001.x

Diener, E., Suh, E. M., Lucas, R. E., & Smith, H. L. (1999). Subjective well-being: Three decades of progress. *Psychological Bulletin, 125*(2), 276–302. doi: 10.1037/0033-2909.125.2.276

Dierks, T., Linden, D. E., Jandl, M., Formisano, E., Goebel, R., Lanfermann, H., et al. (1999). Activation of Heschl's gyrus during auditory hallucinations. *Neuron, 22*, 615–621. doi: 10.1016/S0896-6273(00)80715-1

DiGrande, L., Perrin, M. A., Thorpe, L. E., Thalji, L., Murphy, J., Wu, D., et al. (2008). Posttraumatic stress symptoms, PTSD, and risk factors among lower Manhattan residents 2–3 years after the September 11, 2001, terrorist attacks. *Journal of Traumatic Stress, 21*(3), 264–273. doi: 10.1002/jts.20345

DiLalla, L. F., Kagan, J., & Reznick, J. S. (1994). Genetic etiology of behavioral inhibition among 2-year-old children. *Infant Behavior and Development, 17*, 405–412. doi: 10.1016/0163-6383(94)90032-9

Dion, K., Berscheid, E., & Walster, E. (1972). What is beautiful is good. *Journal of Personality and Social Psychology, 24*(3), 285–290. doi: 10.1037/h0033731

Dixon, L., Medoff, D. R., Wohlheiter, K., DiClemente, C., Goldberg, R., Kreyenbuhl, J., et al. (2007). Correlates of severity of smoking among persons with severe mental illness. *American Journal on Addictions, 16*(2), 101–110. doi: 10.1080/10550490601184415

Dolinoy, D. C., Huang, D., & Jirtle, R. L. (2007). Maternal nutrient supplementation counteracts bisphenol A–induced DNA hypomethylation in early development. *Proceedings of the National Academy of*

Sciences, 104, 13056–13061. doi: 10.1073/pnas.0703739104

Doll, R., Peto, R., Boreham, J., & Sutherland, I. (2004). Mortality in relation to smoking: 50 years' observations on male British doctors. *British Medical Journal, 328*(7455), 1519. doi: 10.1136/bmj.38142.554479.AE

Domanski, C. W. (2013). Mysterious "Monsieur Leborgne": The mystery of the famous patient in the history of neuropsychology is explained. *Journal of the History of the Neurosciences: Basic and Clinical Perspectives, 22*(1), 47–52. doi: 10.1080/0964704X.2012.667528

Domingue, B. W., Fletcher, J., Conley, D., & Boardman, J. D. (2014). Genetic and educational assortative mating among U.S. adults. *Proceedings of the National Academy of Sciences.* doi: 10.1073/pnas/1321426111

Donnay, G. F., Rankin, S. K., Lopez-Gonzalez, M., Jiradejvong, P., & Limb, C. J. (2014). Neural substrates of interactive musical improvisation: An fMRI study of "trading fours" in jazz. *PLoS One, 9*(2), e88665. doi: 10.1371/journal.pone.0088665

Dopfel, R. P., Schulmeister, K., & Schernhammer, E. S. (2007). Nutritional and lifestyle correlates of the cancer-protective hormone melatonin. *Cancer Detection and Prevention, 31*(2), 140–148. doi: 10.1016/j.cdp.2007.02.001

Dorries, K. M. (1992). Sex differences in olfaction in mammals. In M. J. Serby & K. L. Chobor (Eds.), *Science of olfaction* (pp. 355–376). New York, NY: Springer-Verlag.

Dovidio, J. F., & Gaertner, S. L. (2005). Color blind or just plain blind? The pernicious nature of contemporary racism. *NonProfit Quarterly.* Retrieved from http://www.nonprofitquarterly.org/index.php?option=com_content&view=frontpage&Itemid=1

Dresler, M., Eibl, L., Fischer, C. F., Wehrle, R., Spoormaker, V. I., Steiger, A., et al. (2013). Volitional components of consciousness vary across wakefulness, dreaming and lucid dreaming. *Frontiers in Psychology, 4*, 1–7. doi: 10.3389/fpsyg.2013.00987

Dronkers, N. F., Pinker, S., & Damasio, A. (2000). Language and the aphasias. In E. R. Kandel, J. H. Schwartz, & T. M. Jessell (Eds.), *Principles of neural science* (Vol. 4, pp. 1169–1185). New York, NY: McGraw-Hill.

Druckman, D. E., & Bjork, R. A. (Eds.). (1991). *In the mind's eye: Enhancing human performance.* Washington, DC: National Academy Press.

Druett, J. (2007). *Island of the lost: Shipwrecked at the edge of the world.* Chapel Hill, NC: Algonquin.

Dubernard, J.-M., Owen, E. R., Lanzetta, M., & Hakim, N. (2001). What is happening with hand transplants? *Lancet, 357*, 1711–1712. doi: 10.1016/S0140-6736(00)04846-7

Ducros, A. and Pasquet, P. (1978). Evolution de l'âge d'apparition des premières règles (ménarche) en France [Evolution of the age of first menstrual period (menarche) in France]. *Biométrie Humaine, 13*, 35–43.

Dudai, Y. (2004). The neurobiology of consolidations, or, How stable is the engram? *Annual Review of Psychology, 55*, 51–86. doi: 10.1146/annurev.psych.55.090902.142050

Dulaney, S., & Fiske, A. P. (1994). Cultural rituals and obsessive-compulsive disorder: Is there a common psychological mechanism? *Ethos, 22*(3), 243–283. doi: 10.1525/eth.1994.22.3.02a00010

Dunbar, R. I. M., & Shultz, S. (2007). Evolution in the social brain. *Science, 317*(5843), 1344–1347. doi: 10.1126/science.1145463

Dutton, D. G., & Aron, A. P. (1974). Some evidence for heightened sexual attraction under conditions of high anxiety. *Journal of Personality and Social Psychology, 30*, 510–517. doi: 10.1037/h0037031

Dweck, C. S. (2000). *Self-theories: Their role in motivation, personality, and development.* Hove, United Kingdom: Psychology Press.

Dyson-Hudson, N., & Dyson-Hudson, R. (1999). The social organization of resource exploitation in South Turkana. In M. A. Little & P. W. Leslie (Eds.), *Turkana herders of the dry savanna: Ecology and biobehavioural response of nomads to an uncertain environment.* Oxford, United Kingdom: Oxford University Press.

Dyson-Hudson, R., & Dyson-Hudson, N. (1995). *South Turkana homicide: A proximate view.* Paper presented at the Human Behavior and Evolution Conference, Santa Barbara, CA. Retrieved from http://www.hbes.com/HBES/abst95.htm#South_Turkana

Eberhardt, J. L., Davies, P. G., Purdie-Vaughns, V. J., & Johnson, S. L. (2006). Looking deathworthy: Perceived stereotypicality of Black defendants predicts capital-sentencing outcomes. *Psychological Science, 17*, 383–386. doi: 10.1111/j.1467-9280.2006.01716.x

Egeland, J. A., & Hostetter, A. M. (1983). Amish study: I. Affective disorders among the Amish. *American Journal of Psychiatry, 140*, 56–61.

Eglinton, E., & Annett, M. (1994). Handedness and dyslexia: A meta-analysis. *Perceptual Motor Skills, 79*, 1611–1616. doi: 10.2466/pms.1994.79.3f.1611

Ehlers, C. L. (2007). Variations in ADH and ALDH in Southwest California Indians. *Alcohol Research and Health, 30*(1), 14–17.

Eichel, S. K. D. (2002). Credentialing: It may not be the cat's meow. Retrieved from http://www.dreichel.com/Articles/Dr_Zoe.htm

Eichele, T., Debener, S., Calhoun, V. D., Specht, K., Engel, A. K., Hugdahl, K., et al. (2008). Prediction of human errors by maladaptive changes in event-related brain networks. *Proceedings of the National Academy of Sciences, 105*(16), 6173–6178. doi: 10.1073/pnas.0708965105

Einstein, A. (1945). A testimonial from Professor Einstein (Appendix II). In J. Hadamard (Ed.), *An essay on the psychology of invention in the mathematical field* (pp. 142–143). Princeton, NJ: Princeton University Press.

Ekman, P. (1996). Why don't we catch liars? *Social Research, 63*, 801–817.

Ekman, P., Davidson, R. J., & Friesen, W. V. (1990). The Duchenne smile: Emotional expression and brain physiology II. *Journal of Personality and Social Psychology, 58*(2), 342–353. doi: 10.1037/0022-3514.58.2.342

Ekman, P., Friesen, W. V., & Ellsworth, P. (1972). *Emotion in the human face: Guidelines for research and an integration of findings.* London, United Kingdom: Pergamon Press.

Elbert, T., Pantev, C., Weinbruch, C., Rockstroh, B., & Taub, E. (1995). Increased cortical representation of the fingers of the left hand in string players. *Science, 270*, 305–307. doi: 10.1126/science.270.5234.305

Elkind, D. (1967). Egocentrism in adolescence. *Child Development, 38*, 1025–1034. doi: 10.2307/1127100

Elkind, D., & Bowen, R. (1979). Imaginary audience behavior in children and adolescents. *Developmental Psychology, 15*, 38–44. doi: 10.1037/0012-1649.15.1.38

Eller, A., Abrams, D., Viki, G. T., & Imara, D. A. (2007). When my friend's friend is a police officer: Extended contact, cross-categorisation, and public–police relations of black and white people. *South African Journal of Psychology, 37*(4), 783–802.

Elliot, A. J. (1999). Approach and avoidance motivation and achievement goals. *Educational Psychologist, 34*(3), 169–189. doi: 10.1207/s15326985ep3403_3

Elliot, A. J., & Murayama, K. (2008). On the measurement of achievement goals: Critique, illustration, and application. *Journal of Educational Psychology, 100*(3), 613. doi: 10.1037/0022-0663.100.3.613

Ellis, A. (1975). *A new guide to rational living.* Upper Saddle River, NJ: Prentice Hall.

Ellis, H. C., & Hunt, R. R. (1983). *Fundamentals of human memory and cognition.* Dubuque, IA: William C. Brown.

Ellis Weismer, S., Lord, C., & Esler, A. (2010). Early language patterns of toddlers on the autism spectrum compared to toddlers with developmental delay. *Journal of Autism and Developmental Disorders, 40*(10), 1259–1273. doi: 10.1007/s10803-010-0983-1

Ellsworth, P. C. (1991). Some implications of cognitive appraisal theories of emotion. In K. T. Strongman (Ed.), *International Review of Studies on Emotion* (Vol. 1, pp.143–160). Chichester, United Kingdom: Wiley.

Ellsworth, P. C. (1994). William James and emotion: Is a century of fame worth a century of misunderstanding? *Psychological Review, 101*(2), 222–229. doi: 10.1037/0033-295X.101.2.222

Elman, C. (2011). The midlife years: Human capital and job mobility. In J. L. Angel, J. R. A. Settersten, & R. Settersten (Eds.), *Handbook of sociology of aging* (pp. 245–261). New York, NY: Springer.

Emery, N. J., Capitanio, J. P., Mason, W. A., Machado, C. J., Mendoza, S. P., & Amaral, D. G. (2001). The effects of bilateral lesions of the amygdala on dyadic social interactions in rhesus monkeys *(Macaca mulatta). Behavioral Neuroscience, 115*, 515–544. doi: 10.1037/0735-7044.115.3.515

Emlen, S. T., & Oring, L. W. (1977). Ecology, sexual selection, and the evolution of mating systems. *Science, 197*, 215–223. doi: 10.1126/science.327542

Emmons, R. A., Barrett, J. L., & Schnitker, S. A. (2008). Personality and the capacity for religious and spiritual experience. In O. P. John, R. W. Robins, & L. A. Pervin (Eds.), *Handbook of personality psychology: Theory and research* (3rd ed., pp. 634–653). New York, NY: Guilford Press.

Enard, W., Gehre, S., Hammerschmidt, K., Hölter, S. M., Blass, T., Somel, M., et al. (2009). A humanized version of *FOXP-2* affects cortico-basal ganglia circuits in mice. *Cell, 137*(5), 961–971. doi: 10.1016/j.cell.2009.03.041

Eng, M. Y., Luczak, S. E., & Wall, T. L. (2007). *ALDH2, ADH1B,* and *ADH1C* genotypes in Asians: A literature review. *Alcohol Research and Health, 30*(1), 22–27.

Engel, S. M., & Daniels, J. L. (2011). On the complex relationship between genes and environment in the etiology of autism. *Epidemiology, 22*(4), 486–488. doi: 10.1097/EDE.0b013e31821daf1c

Enoch, M. A. (2006). Genetic and environmental influences on the development of alcoholism. *Annals of the New York Academy of Sciences, 1094*(1), 193–201. doi: 10.1196/annals.1376.019

Entertainment Software Rating Board. (2014). ESRB rating process. Retrieved from http://www.esrb.org/ratings/ratings_process.jsp

Eppig, C., Fincher, C. L., & Thornhill, R. (2010). Parasite prevalence and the worldwide distribution of cognitive ability. *Proceedings of the Royal Society of London, Series B: Biological Sciences, 277*(1701), 3801–3808. doi: 10.1098/rspb.2010.0973

Erikson, E. H. (1963). *Childhood and society.* New York, NY: Norton.

Erikson, E. H. (1968). *Identity: Youth and crisis.* Oxford, United Kingdom: Norton.

Erol, R. Y., & Orth, U. (2011). Self-esteem development from age 14 to 30 years: A longitudinal study. *Journal of Personality and Social Psychology, 101*(3), 607–619. doi: 10.1037/a0024299

Eskelinen, M. H., & Kivipelto, M. (2010). Caffeine as a protective factor in dementia and Alzheimer's disease. *Journal of Alzheimer's Disease, 20*(Suppl. 1), 167–174. doi: 10.3233/JAD-1010-1404

Eslinger, P. J., & Damasio, A. R. (1985). Severe disturbance of higher cognition after bilateral frontal lobe ablation: Patient EVR. *Neurology, 35*, 1731–1741. doi: 10.1212/WNL.35.12.1731

Evans, P. D., Anderson, J. R., Vallender, E. J., Gilbert, S. L., Malcom, C. M., Dorus, S., et al. (2004). Adaptive evolution of ASPM, a major determinant of cerebral cortical size in humans. *Human Molecular Genetics, 13*, 489–494. doi: 10.1093/hmg/ddh055

Evans, P. D., Gilbert, S. L., Mekel-Bobrov, N., Vallender, E. J., Anderson, J. R., Vaez-Azizi, L. M., et al. (2005). Microcephalin, a gene regulating brain size, continues to evolve adaptively in humans. *Science, 309*, 1717–1720. doi: 10.1126/science.1113722

Eysenck, H. J. (1967). *The biological basis of personality.* Springfield, IL: Charles C. Thomas.

Fan, Y.-T., Decety, J., Yang, C.-Y., Liu, J.-L., & Cheng, Y. (2010). Unbroken mirror neurons in autism spectrum disorders. *Journal of Child Psychology and Psychiatry, 51*(9), 981–988. doi: 10.1111/j.1469-7610.2010.02269.x

Faraone, S. V., & Mick, E. (2010). Molecular genetics of attention deficit hyperactivity disorder. *Psychiatric Clinics of North America, 33*(1), 159. doi: 10.1016/j.biopsych.2004.11.024

Fechner, G. T. (1871). *Zür experimentalen aesthetik* [On experimental aesthetics]. Leipzig, Germany: S. Hirzel.

Federman, J. (Ed.). (1998). *National Television Violence Study: Executive summary.* Santa Barbara, CA: Center for Communication and Social Policy, University of California.

Fehr, E., & Rockenbach, B. (2004). Human altruism: Economic, neural, and evolutionary perspectives. *Current Opinion in Neurobiology, 14*, 784–790. doi: 10.1016/j.conb.2004.10.007

Feinberg, I. (1978). Efference copy and corollary discharge: Implications for thinking and its disorders. *Schizophrenia Bulletin, 4*, 636–640.

Feinstein, J. S., Adolphs, R., Damasio, A., & Tranel, D. (2011). The human amygdala and the induction and experience of fear. *Current Biology, 21*(1), 34–38. doi: 10.1016/j.cub.2010.11.042

Fejfar, M. C., & Hoyle, R. H. (2000). Effect of private self-awareness on negative affect and self-referent attribution: A quantitative review. *Personality and Social Psychology Review, 4*(2), 132–142. doi: 10.1207/S15327957PSPR0402_02

Feldman, M. B., & Meyer, I. H. (2007). Eating disorders in diverse lesbian, gay, and bisexual populations. *International Journal of Eating Disorders, 40*(3), 218–226. doi: 10.1002/eat.20360

Fenton, N., & Neil, M. (2012). *Risk assessment and decision analysis with Bayesian networks.* London, United Kingdom: CRC Press.

Fergusson, D. M., Boden, J. M., Horwood, L. J., Miller, A. L., & Kennedy, M. A. (2011). MAOA, abuse exposure and antisocial behaviour: 30-year longitudinal study. *British Journal of Psychiatry, 198*(6), 457–463. doi: 10.1192/bjp.bp.110.086991

Fergusson, D. M., Horwood, L. J., & Ridder, E. M. (2005). Tests of causal linkages between cannabis use and psychotic symptoms. *Addiction Research and Theory, 100*(3), 354–366. doi: 10.1111/j.1360-0443.2005.01001.x

Ferrari, P. F., Paukner, A., Ionica, C., & Suomi, S. J. (2009). Reciprocal face-to-face communication between rhesus macaque mothers and their newborn infants. *Current Biology, 19*(20), 1768–1772. doi: 10.1016/j.cub.2009.08.055

Ferrari, P. F., Visalberghi, E., Paukner, A., Fogassi, L., Ruggiero, A., et al. (2006). Neonatal imitation in rhesus macaques. *PLoS Biology, 4*(9), e302. doi: 10.1371/journal.pbio.0040302.

Ferri, C. P., Prince, M., Brayne, C., Brodaty, H., Fratiglioni, L., Ganguli, M., et al. (2005). Global prevalence of dementia: A Delphi consensus study. *Lancet, 366*(9503), 2112–2117. doi: 10.1016/S0140-6736(05)67889-0

Festinger, L. (1950). Informal social communication. *Psychological Review, 57*, 271–282. doi: 10.1037/h0056932

Festinger, L. (1954). A theory of social comparison processes. *Human Relations, 7*, 117–140. doi: 10.1177/001872675400700202

Festinger, L. (1957). *A theory of cognitive dissonance.* Stanford, CA: Stanford University Press.

Feusner, J. D., Neziroglu, F., Wilhelm, S., Mancusi, L., & Bohon, C. (2010). What causes BDD: Research findings and a proposed model *Psychiatric Annals, 40*(7), 349–355.

Fidler, D. J., Most, D. E., Booth-LaForce, C., & Kelly, J. F. (2008). Emerging social strengths in young children with Down syndrome. *Infants and Young Children, 21*(3), 207–220. doi: 10.1097/01.IYC.0000324550.39446.1f

Fiorito, G., & Scotto, P. (1992). Observational learning in *Octopus vulgaris. Science, 256*, 545–547. doi: 10.1126/science.256.5056.545

Fischhoff, B., de Bruin, W. B., Parker, A. M., Millstein, S. G., & Halpern-Felsher, B. L. (2010). Adolescents' perceived risk of dying. *Journal of Adolescent Health, 46*(3), 265–269. doi: 10.1016/j.jadohealth.2009.06.026

Fisher, P. A., Van Ryzin, M. J., & Gunnar, M. R. (2011). Mitigating HPA axis dysregulation associated with placement changes in foster care. *Psychoneuroendocrinology, 36*(4), 531–539. doi: 10.1016/j.psyneuen.2010.08.007

Fisher, R. P., & Geiselman, R. E. (2010). The cognitive interview method of conducting police interviews: Eliciting extensive information and promoting therapeutic jurisprudence. *International Journal of Law and Psychiatry, 33*(5–6), 321–328. doi: 10.1016/j.ijlp.2010.09.004

Fiske, S. T. (1998). Stereotyping, prejudice, and discrimination. In D. T. Gilbert, S. T. Fiske, & G. Lindzey (Eds.), *The handbook of social psychology* (4th ed., Vol. 2, pp. 357–411). New York, NY: McGraw-Hill.

Fiske, S. T., Cuddy, A. J. C., Glick, P., & Xu, J. (2002). A model of (often mixed) stereotype content: Competence and warmth respectively follow from perceived status and competition. *Journal of Personality and Social Psychology, 82*(6), 878–902. doi: 10.1037/0022-3514.82.6.878

Flegal, K. M., Carroll, M. D., Ogden, C. L., & Curtin, L. R. (2010). Prevalence and trends in obesity among U.S. adults, 1999–2008. *JAMA: Journal of the American Medical Association, 303*(3), 235–241. doi: 10.1001/jama.2009.2014

Fleischman, J. (2002). *Phineas Gage: A gruesome but true story about brain science.* Boston, MA: Houghton Mifflin.

Fletcher, H., & Munson, W. A. (1933). Loudness: Its definition, measurement, and calculation. *Journal of the Acoustical Society of America, 5*, 82–108. doi: 10.1002/j.1538-7305.1933.tb00403.x

Flexser, A. J., & Tulving, E. (1978). Retrieval independence in recall and recognition. *Psychological Review, 85*, 153–171. doi: 10.1037/0033-295X.85.3.153

Flom, R., & Bahrick, L. E. (2007). The development of infant discrimination of affect in multimodal and unimodal stimulation: The role of intersensory redundancy. *Developmental Psychology, 43*(1), 238–252. doi: 10.1037/0012-1649.43.1.238

Flynn, J. R. (1984). The mean IQ of Americans: Massive gains 1932 to 1978. *Psychological Bulletin, 91*(1), 29–51. doi: 10.1037/0033-2909.95.1.29

Flynn, J. R. (1999). Searching for justice: The discovery of IQ gains over time. *American Psychologist, 54*, 5–20. doi: 10.1037/0003-066X.54.1.5

Fodor, E. M. (1995). Subclinical manifestations of psychosis-proneness, ego strength, and creativity. *Personality and Individual Differences, 18*(5), 635–642. doi: 10.1016/0191-8869(94)00196-y

Fogassi, L., Ferrari, P. F., Gesierich, B., Rozzi, S., Chersi, F., & Rizzolatti, G. (2005). Parietal lobe: From action organization to intention understanding. *Science, 308*(5722), 662–667. doi: 10.1126/science.1106138

Ford, E. S., Bergmann, M. M., Kroger, J., Schienkiewitz, A., Weikert, C., & Boeing, H. (2009). Healthy living is the best revenge: Findings from the European Prospective Investigation into Cancer and Nutrition–Potsdam study. *Archives of Internal Medicine, 169*(15), 1355–1362. doi: 10.1001/archinternmed.2009.237

Forer, B. R. (1949). The fallacy of personal validation: A classroom demonstration of gullibility. *Journal of Abnormal and Social Psychology, 44*(1), 118–123. doi: 10.1037/h0059240

Forsyth, D. R., & Kerr, N. A. (1999). *Are adaptive illusions adaptive?* Boston, MA: American Psychological Association.

Forsyth, D. R., & Schlenker, B. R. (1977). Attributing the causes of group performance: Effects of performance quality, task importance, and future testing. *Journal of Personality, 45*(2), 220–236. doi: 10.1111/j.1467-6494.1977.tb00148.x

Foulkes, D. (1999). *Children's dreaming and the development of consciousness.* Cambridge, MA: Harvard University Press.

Fournier, J. C., DeRubeis, R. J., Hollon, S. D., Dimidjian, S., Amsterdam, J. D., Shelton, R. C., et al. (2010). Antidepressant drug effects and depression severity. *JAMA: Journal of the American Medical Association, 303*(1), 47–53. doi: 10.1001/jama.2009.1943

Foutz, A. S., Mitler, M. N., Cavalli-Sforza, G. L., & Dement, W. C. (1978). Genetic factors in canine narcolepsy. *Sleep, 1*, 413–421.

Fox, K. C., Nijeboer, S., Solomonova, E., Domhoff, G. W., & Christoff, K. (2013). Dreaming as mind wandering: Evidence from functional neuroimaging and first-person content reports. *Frontiers in Human Neuroscience, 7*, 412. doi: 10.3389/fnhum.2013.00412

Fox, M. C., & Mitchum, A. L. (2013). A knowledge-based theory of rising scores on "culture-free" tests. *Journal of Experimental Psychology: General, 142*(3), 979. doi: 10.1037/a0030155

Fox, P. W., Hershberger, S. L., & Bouchard, T. J., Jr. (1996). Genetic and environmental contributions to the acquisition of a motor skill. *Nature, 384*(6607), 356–358. doi: 10.1038/384356a0

Frances, A. (2010, March 1). It's not too late to save "normal": Psychiatry's latest DSM goes too far in creating new mental disorders. *Los Angeles Times.* Retrieved from http://articles.latimes.com/2010/mar/01/opinion/la-oe-frances1-2010mar01

Franco, Z. E., Blau, K., & Zimbardo, P. G. (2011). Heroism: A conceptual analysis and differentiation between heroic action and altruism. *Review of General Psychology, 15*(2), 99-113. doi: 10.1037/a0022672

Frank, M. G., & Ekman, P. (1993). Not all smiles are created equal: The differences between enjoyment and nonenjoyment smiles. *Humor: International Journal of Humor Research, 6*(1), 9–26. doi: 10.1515/humr.1993.6.1.9

Franken, D. (2002). *Personal strengths, positive psychology, optimum psycho-social lifeskills.* Holland, MI: Wellness Publications.

Frankl, V. E. (1959). *Man's search for meaning.* Boston, MA: Beacon Press.

Franks, N. R. (1989). Army ants: A collective intelligence. *American Scientist, 77*, 138–145.

Frazier, T. W., Thompson, L., Youngstrom, E. A., Law, P., Hardan, A. Y., Eng, C., et al. (2014). A twin study of heritable and shared environmental contributions to autism. *Journal of Autism and Developmental Disorders, 44*(8), 2013-2025. doi: 10.1007/s10803-014-2081-2

Freberg, K. J. (2011). *Intention to comply with food safety messages in a crisis as a function of message source and message reliability* (Doctoral dissertation). Retrieved from http://trace.tennessee.edu/utk_graddiss/970/

Frederick, J. Z., Dimitri, A. C., & Andrew, N. M. (2007). Associations between media viewing and language development in children under age 2 years. *Journal of Pediatrics, 151*(4), 364–368. doi: 10.1016/j.jpeds.2007.04.071

Fredrikson, M., Annas, P., Fischer, H., & Wik, G. (1996). Gender and age differences in the prevalence of specific fears and phobias. *Behaviour Research and Therapy, 34*(1), 33–39. doi: 10.1016/0005-7967(95)00048-3

Freedman, D. G. (1964). Smiling in blind infants and the issue of innate vs. acquired. *Journal of Child Psychology and Psychiatry, 47*, 171–184. doi: 10.1111/j.1469-7610.1964.tb02139.x

Freedman, D. G. (1974). *Human infancy: An evolutionary perspective.* Hillsdale, NJ: Erlbaum.

Freud, S. (1938). *The basic writings of Sigmund Freud.* New York, NY: Modern Library.

Freud, S. (1953). Interpretation of dreams. In J. Strachey (Ed.), *The standard edition of the complete psychological works of Sigmund Freud* (Vols. 4 and 5). London, United Kingdom: Hogarth Press. (Original work published 1900)

Freud, S. (1976). Analysis of a phobia of a five year old boy. In *The Pelican Freud library* (Vol. 8, Case Histories 1, pp. 169–306). Harmondsworth, United Kingdom: Penguin Books. (Original work published 1909)

Friederici, A. D. (2011). The brain basis of language processing: From structure to function. *Physiological Reviews, 91*(4), 1357–1392. doi: 10.1152/physrev.00006.2011

Friedman, J. M., & Halaas, J. L. (1998). Leptin and the regulation of body weight in mammals. *Nature, 395*(6704), 673–770. doi: 10.1038/27376

Friedman, M., & Rosenman, R. H. (1974). *Type A behavior and your heart.* New York, NY: Knopf.

Frisch, R. E. (1983). Fatness, menarche, and fertility. In S. Golub (Ed.), *Menarche: The transition from girl to woman* (pp. 5–20). Lexington, MA: Lexington Books.

Frischholz, E. J., Lipman, L. S., Braun, B. G., & Sachs, R. G. (1992). Psychopathology, hypnotizability, and dissociation. *American Journal of Psychiatry, 149*(11), 1521–1525.

Frith, U., & Frith, U. (1996). A biological marker for dyslexia. *Nature, 382,* 19–20. doi: 10.1038/382019a0

Frost, P. (2006). European hair and eye color: A case of frequency-dependent sexual selection? *Evolution and Human Behavior, 27,* 85–103. doi: 10.1016/j.evolhumbehav.2005.07.002

Fulkerson, J. A., Story, M., Mellin, A., Leffert, N., Neumark-Sztainer, D., & French, S. A. (2006). Family dinner meal frequency and adolescent development: Relationships with developmental assets and high-risk behaviors. *Journal of Adolescent Health, 39*(3), 337–345. doi: 10.1016/j.jadohealth.2005.12.026

Funder, D. C. (2009). Persons, behaviors and situations: An agenda for personality psychology in the postwar era. *Journal of Research in Personality, 43*(2), 120–126. doi: 10.1016/j.jrp.2008.12.041

Gailliot, M. T., & Baumeister, R. F. (2007). The physiology of willpower: Linking blood glucose to self-control. *Personality and Social Psychology Review, 11*(4), 303–327. doi: 10.1177/1088868307303030

Gailliot, M. T., Baumeister, R. F., DeWall, C. N., Maner, J. K., Plant, E. A., Tice, D. M., et al. (2007). Self-control relies on glucose as a limited energy source: Willpower is more than a metaphor. *Journal of Personality and Social Psychology, 92*(2), 325. doi: 10.1037/0022-3514.92.2.325

Galea, S., Ahern, J., Resnick, H., Kilpatrick, D., Bucuvalas, M., Gold, J., et al. (2002). Psychological sequelae of the September 11 terrorist attacks in New York City. *New England Journal of Medicine, 346*(13), 982–987. doi: 10.1056/NEJMsa013404

Gallese, V., Rochat, M. J., & Berchio, C. (2013). The mirror mechanism and its potential role in autism spectrum disorder. *Developmental Medicine & Child Neurology, 55*(1), 15–22. doi: 10.1111/j.1469-8749.2012.04398.x

Gallup, A. C., & Eldakar, O. T. (2012). The thermoregulatory theory of yawning: What we know from over 5 years of research. *Frontiers in Neuroscience, 6,* 1–13. doi: 10.3389/fnins.2012.00188

Gallup, G. G. (1970). Chimpanzees: Self-recognition. *Science, 167,* 86–87. doi: 10.1126/science.167.3914.86

Gallup, G. G., & Suarez, S. D. (1986). Self-awareness and the emergence of mind in humans and other primates. In J. Suls & A. Greenwald (Eds.), *Psychological perspectives on the self* (Vol. 3, pp. 3–26). Hillsdale, NJ: Erlbaum.

Galovski, T., & Lyons, J. A. (2004). Psychological sequelae of combat violence: A review of the impact of PTSD on the veteran's family and possible interventions. *Aggression and Violent Behavior, 9*(5), 477–501. doi: 10.1016/s1359-1789(03)00045-4

Galton, F. (1869). *Hereditary genius.* London, United Kingdom: Macmillan.

Galvan, A., Hare, T., Voss, H., Glover, G., & Casey, B. J. (2007). Risk-taking and the adolescent brain: Who is at risk? *Developmental Science, 10*(2), F8–F14. doi: 10.1111/j.1467-7687.2006.00579.x

Galyer, K. T., Conaglen, H. M., Hare, A., & Conaglen, J. V. (1999). The effect of gynecological surgery on sexual desire. *Journal of Sex and Marital Therapy, 25,* 81–88. doi: 10.1080/00926239908403981

Gantt, W. H. (1928). Ivan P. Pavlov: A biographical sketch. In I. P. Pavlov (Ed.), *Lectures on conditioned reflexes* (W. H. Gantt, Trans.) (pp. 11–34). New York, NY: International Universities Press.

Garb, H. N., Wood, J. M., Lilienfeld, S. O., & Nezworski, M. T. (2005). Roots of the Rorschach controversy. *Clinical Psychology Review, 25,* 97–118. doi: 10.1016/j.cpr.2004.09.002

Garcia, J., & Koelling, K. W. (1966). Relation of cue to consequence in avoidance learning. *Psychonomic Science, 4,* 123–124. doi: 10.3758/BF03342209

Gardner, H. (1976). *The shattered mind: The person after brain damage.* New York, NY: Knopf.

Gardner, H. (1983). *Frames of mind: The theory of multiple intelligences.* New York, NY: Basic Books.

Gardner, H. (1999). *Intelligence reframed: Multiple intelligences for the 21st century.* New York, NY: Basic Books.

Gardner, R. A., & Gardner, B. I. (1969). Teaching sign language to a chimpanzee. *Science, 165,* 664–672. doi: 10.1126/science.165.3894.664

Gardner, W., Gabriel, S., & Lee, A. Y. (1999). "I" value freedom, but "we" value relationships: Self-construal priming mirrors cultural differences in judgment. *Psychological Science, 10*(4), 321–326. doi: 10.1111/1467-9280.00162

Garmezy, N. (1991). Resilience and vulnerability to adverse developmental outcomes associated with poverty. *American Behavioral Scientist, 34*(4), 416–430. doi: 10.1177/0002764291034004003

Garrity, A., Pearlson, G., McKiernan, K., Lloyd, D., Kiehl, K., & Calhoun, V. (2007). Aberrant "default mode" functional connectivity in schizophrenia. *American Journal of Psychiatry, 164*(3), 450–457. doi: 10.1176/appi.ajp.164.3.450

Gawronski, B. (2004). Theory-based bias correction in dispositional inference: The fundamental attribution error is dead, long live the correspondence bias. *European Review of Social Psychology, 15,* 183–217. doi: 10.1080/10463280440000026

Gayán, J., Willcutt, E. G., Fisher, S. E., Francks, C., Cardon, L. R., Olson, R. K., et al. (2005). Bivariate linkage scan for reading disability and attention-deficit/hyperactivity disorder localizes pleiotropic loci. *Journal of Child Psychology and Psychiatry, 46,* 1045–1057. doi: 10.1111/j.1469-7610.2005.01447.x

Gazzaniga, M. S. (1967). The split brain in man. *Scientific American, 217,* 24–29. doi: 10.1038/scientificamerican0867-24

Gazzaniga, M. S. (2011). *Who's in charge? Free will and the science of the brain.* New York, NY: Ecco.

Gazzola, V., Aziz-Zadeh, L., & Keysers, C. (2006). Empathy and the somatotopic auditory mirror system in humans. *Current Biology, 16,* 1824–1829. doi: 10.1016/j.cub.2006.07.072

Geda, Y. E., Roberts, R. O., Knopman, D. S., Christianson, T. J. H., Pankratz, V. S., Ivnik, R. J., et al. (2010). Physical exercise, aging, and mild cognitive impairment: A population-based study. *Archives of Neurology, 67*(1), 80–86. doi: 10.1001/archneurol.2009.297

Geiser, S., & Studley, R. (2001). *UC and the SAT: Predictive validity and differential impact of the SAT I and SAT II at the University of California.* Retrieved from http://www.ucop.edu/sas/research/researchandplanning/pdf/sat_study.pdf

Genzel, L., Kroes, M. C., Dresler, M., & Battaglia, F. P. (2014). Light sleep versus slow wave sleep in memory consolidation: a question of global versus local processes? *Trends in Neurosciences, 37*(1), 10–19. doi: 10.1016/j.tins.2013.10.002

Gettler, L. T., McDade, T. W., Feranil, A. B., & Kuzawa, C. W. (2011). Longitudinal evidence that fatherhood decreases testosterone in human males. *Proceedings of the National Academy of Sciences, 108*(39), 16194–16199. doi: 10.1073/pnas.1105403108

Geuze, E., van Berckel, B. N., Lammertsma, A. A., Boellaard, R., de Kloet, C. S., Vermetten, E., et al. (2008). Reduced GABA$_A$ benzodiazepine receptor binding in veterans with post-traumatic stress disorder. *Molecular Psychiatry, 13*(1), 74–83. doi: 10.1038/sj.mp.4002054

Giancola, P. R. (2013). *Alcohol and aggression: Theories and mechanisms.* Chichester, United Kingdom: Wiley–Blackwell.

Gibbons, T., Pence, B., Bhattacharya, T., Mach, H., Ossyra, J., McCusker, R., et al. (2014). Diet, exercise, neurogenesis and cognition. *FASEB Journal, 28*(Suppl. 1), 1025.4.

Gibson, M. A. (2008). Does investment in the sexes differ when fathers are absent? Sex-biased infant survival and child growth in rural Ethiopia. *Human Nature, 19*(3), 263–276. doi: 10.1007/s12110-008-9044-2

Giesbrecht, T., Lynn, S. J., Lilienfeld, S. O., & Merckelbach, H. (2010). Cognitive processes, trauma, and dissociation— Misconceptions and misrepresentations: Reply to Bremner (2010). *Psychological Bulletin, 136*(1), 7–11. doi: 10.1037/a0018068

Gigerenzer, G. (2008). Why heuristics work. *Perspectives on Psychological Science, 3*(1), 20–29. doi: 10.1111/j.1745-6916.2008.00058.x

Gilbert, D. T., & Jones, E. E. (1986). Perceiver-induced constraint: Interpretations of self-generated reality. *Journal of Personality and Social Psychology, 50*, 269–280. doi: 10.1037/0022-3514.50.2.269

Gilbert, D. T., & Malone, P. S. (1995). The correspondence bias. *Psychological Bulletin, 117*(1), 21–38. doi: 10.1037/0033-2909.117.1.21

Gildersleeve, K., DeBruine, L., Haselton, M. G., Frederick, D. A., Penton-Voak, I. S., Jones, B. C., et al. (2013). Shifts in women's mate preferences across the ovulatory cycle: A critique of Harris (2011) and Harris (2012). *Sex Roles, 69*, 516–524. doi: 10.1007/s11199-013-0273-4

Gilger, J. W., Hanebuth, E., Smith, S. D., & Pennington, B. F. (1996). Differential risk for developmental reading disorders in the offspring of compensated versus noncompensated parents. *Reading and Writing, 8*(5), 407–417. doi: 10.1007/BF00404002

Gillihan, S. J., & Farah, M. J. (2005). Is self special? A critical review of evidence from experimental psychology and cognitive neuroscience. *Psychological Bulletin, 131*(1), 76–97. doi: 10.1037/0033-2909.131.1.76

Gillin, J. C., & Borbély, A. A. (1985). Sleep: A neurobiological window on affective disorders. *Trends in Neurosciences, 8*, 537–542. doi: 10.1016/0166-2236(85)90191-2

Gilovich, T., Medvec, V. H., & Savitsky, K. (2000). The spotlight effect in social judgment: An egocentric bias in estimates of the salience of one's own actions and appearance. *Journal of Personality and Social Psychology, 78*(2), 211–222. doi: 10.1037/0022-3514.78.2.211

Glanzer, M., & Cunitz, A. R. (1966). Two storage mechanisms in free recall. *Journal of Verbal Learning and Verbal Behavior, 5*, 351–360. doi: 10.1016/S0022-5371(66)80044-0

Gleeson, M. (2007). Immune function in sport and exercise. *Journal of Applied Physiology, 103*(2), 693–699. doi: 10.1152/japplphysiol.00008.2007

Gleick, J. (1992). *Genius: The life and science of Richard Feynman.* New York, NY: Pantheon.

Glynn, S. M. (1990). Token economy approaches for psychiatric patients: Progress and pitfalls over 25 years. *Behavior Modification, 14*, 383–407. doi: 10.1177/01454455900144002

Godden, D. R., & Baddeley, A. D. (1975). Context-dependent memory in two natural environments: On land and under water. *British Journal of Psychology, 66*, 325–331. doi: 10.1111/j.2044-8295.1975.tb01468.x

Goetz, C. G., Leurgans, S., Pappert, E. J., Raman, R., & Stemer, A. B. (2001). Prospective longitudinal assessment of hallucinations in Parkinson's disease. *Neurology, 57*, 2078–2082. doi: 10.1212/WNL.57.11.2078

Goff, D. C., & Evins, A. E. (1998). Negative symptoms in schizophrenia: Neurobiological models and treatment response. *Harvard Review of Psychiatry, 6*(2), 59–77. doi: 10.3109/10673229809000313

Goldscheider, F. K., & Waite, L. J.. (1991). *New families, no families? The transformation of the American home.* Berkeley, CA: University of California Press.

Goldsmith, T. H., & Zimmerman, W. F. (2001). *Biology, evolution, and human nature.* New York, NY: John Wiley.

Goldstein, A. P., Glick, B., & Gibbs, J. C. (1998). *Aggression replacement training: A comprehensive intervention for aggressive youth.* Champaign, IL: Research Press.

Goldstein, D. G., & Gigerenzer, G. (2002). Models of ecological rationality: The recognition heuristic. *Psychological Review, 109*, 75–90. doi: 10.1037/0033-295X.109.1.75

Goldstein, E. B. (2010). *Sensation and perception* (8th ed.). Belmont, CA: Cengage.

Goleman, D. (2006). *Social intelligence.* New York, NY: Random House.

Gollan, J. K., McCloskey, M., Hoxha, D., & Coccaro, E. F. (2010). How do depressed and healthy adults interpret nuanced facial expressions? *Journal of Abnormal Psychology, 119*(4), 804–810. doi: 10.1037/a0020234

Gonzalez-Maeso, J., Ang, R. L., Yuen, T., Chan, P., Weisstaub, N. V., Lopez-Gimenez, J. F., et al. (2008). Identification of a serotonin/glutamate receptor complex implicated in psychosis. *Nature, 452*(7183), 93–97. doi: 10.1038/nature06612

González-Maeso, J., Weisstaub, N. V., Zhou, M., Chan, P., Ivic, L., Ang, R., et al. (2007). Hallucinogens recruit specific cortical 5-HT(2A) receptor–mediated signaling pathways to affect behavior. *Neuron, 53*(3), 439–452. doi: 10.1016/j.neuron.2007.01.008

Goodall, J. (1971). *In the shadow of man.* Boston, MA: Houghton Mifflin.

Goodfriend, W., & Agnew, C. R. (2008). Sunken costs and desired plans: Examining different types of investments in close relationships. *Personality and Social Psychology Bulletin, 34*(12), 1639–1652. doi: 10.1177/0146167208323743

Gopnik, A., Capps, L., & Meltzoff, A. N. (2000). Early theories of mind: What the theory can tell us about autism. In S. Baron-Cohen, H. Tager-Flusberg, & D. J. Cohen (Eds.), *Understanding other minds: Perspectives from developmental cognitive neuroscience* (2nd ed., pp. 50–72). New York, NY: Oxford University Press.

Gordon, K. C., Baucom, D. H., & Snyder, D. K. (2004). An integrative intervention for promoting recovery from extramarital affairs. *Journal of Marital and Family Therapy, 30*, 213–231. doi: 10.1111/j.1752-0606.2004.tb01235.x

Gordon, N. (2002). Stuttering: Incidence and causes. *Developmental Medicine and Child Neurology, 44*(4), 278–281. doi: 10.1111/j.1469-8749.2002.tb00806.x

Goschke, T. (2014). Dysfunctions of decision-making and cognitive control as transdiagnostic mechanisms of mental disorders: Advances, gaps, and needs in current research. *International Journal of Methods in Psychiatric Research, 23*(S1), 41–57. doi: 10.1002/mpr.1410

Gosling, S. D., Mollaghan, D. M., & Van Lange, P. A. M. (2006). Animal research in social psychology: A bridge to functional genomics and other unique research opportunities. In P. A. M. Van Lange (Ed.), *Bridging social psychology: Benefits of transdisciplinary approaches* (pp. 123–128). Mahwah, NJ: Erlbaum.

Gosseries, O., Thibaut, A., Boly, M., Rosanova, M., Massimini, M., & Laureys, S. (2014). *Annales Françaises d'Anesthésie et de Réanimation, 33*(2), 65-71. doi: http://dx.doi.org/10.1016/j.annfar.2013.11.002

Gottesman, C. (2002). The neurochemistry of waking and sleeping mental activity: The disinhibition–dopamine hypothesis. *Psychiatry and Clinical Neurosciences, 56*, 345–354. doi: 10.1046/j.1440-1819.2002.01022.x

Gottesman, I. I. (1991). *Schizophrenia genesis.* New York, NY: W. H. Freeman.

Gottman, J. (2011). Gottman's relationship tips 101. Retrieved from http://www.gottman.com/49804/Self-Help-and-Tips.html

Gottman, J., Swanson, C., & Swanson, K. (2002). A general systems theory of marriage: Nonlinear difference equation modeling of marital interaction. *Personality and Social Psychology Review, 6*(4), 326–340. doi: 10.1207/s15327957pspr0604_07

Gouldner, A. (1960). The norm of reciprocity: A preliminary analysis. *American Sociological Review, 25*, 161–178. doi: 10.2307/2092623

Gouras, P. (1968). Identification of cone mechanisms in monkey ganglion cells. *Journal of Physiology, 199*(3), 533.

Goyal, M., Singh, S., Sibinga, E. S., Gould, N. F., Rowland-Seymour, A., Sharma, R., et al. (2014). Meditation programs for psychological stress and well-being: A systematic review and meta-analysis. *JAMA Internal Medicine, 174*(3), 357–368. doi: 10.1001/jamainternmed.2013.13018

Gräff, J., Joseph, N. F., Horn, M. E., Samiei, A., Meng, J., Seo, J., et al. (2014). Epigenetic priming of memory updating during reconsolidation to attenuate remote fear memories. *Cell, 156*(1), 261–276. doi: 10.1016/j.cell.2013.12.020

Grandin, T. (2010). *Thinking in pictures.* New York, NY: Vintage Books.

Granrud, C. E., Haake, J. J., & Yonas, A. (1985). Infants' sensitivity to familiar size: The effect of memory on spatial perception. *Perception and Psychophysics, 37*, 459–466. doi: 10.3758/BF03202878

Grant, A. M. (2003). The impact of life coaching on goal attainment, metacognition and mental health. *Social Behavior and Personality, 31*, 253–264. doi: http://dx.doi.org/10.2224/sbp.2003.31.3.253

Gray, J. A. (1970). The psychophysiological basis of introversion–extraversion. *Behaviour Research and Therapy, 8*(3), 249–266. doi: 10.1016/0005-7967(70)90069-0

Gray, J. A. (1987). Perspectives on anxiety and impulsivity: A commentary. *Journal of Research in Personality, 21*(4), 493–509. doi: 10.1016/0092-6566(87)90036-5

Gray, J. A., & McNaughton, N. (2003). *The neuropsychology of anxiety: An enquiry into the function of the septo-hippocampal system.* Oxford, United Kingdom: Oxford University Press.

Gray, J. R., & Thompson, P. M. (2004). Neurobiology of intelligence: Science and ethics. *Nature Reviews Neuroscience, 5*, 471–482. doi: 10.1038/nrn1405

Gray, P. B., Singh, A. B., Woodhouse, L. J., Storer, T. W., Casaburi, R., Dzekov, J., et al. (2005). Dose-dependent effects of testosterone on sexual function, mood, and visuospatial cognition in older men. *Journal of Clinical Endocrinology and Metabolism, 90*(7), 3838–3846. doi: http://dx.doi.org/10.1210/jc.2005-0247

Greenberg, J., Pyszczynski, T., & Solomon, S. (1986). The causes and consequences of a need for self-esteem: A terror management theory. In R. F. Baumeister (Ed.), *Public self and private self* (pp. 189–212). New York, NY: Springer-Verlag.

Greenspoon, J., & Ranyard, R. (1957). Stimulus conditions and retroactive inhibition. *Journal of Experimental Psychology, 53*, 55–59. doi: 10.1037/h0042803

Greenwald, A. G. (1980). The totalitarian ego: Fabrication and revision of personal history. *American Psychologist, 35*(7), 603–618. doi: 10.1037/0003-066X.35.7.603

Greenwald, A. G., & Farnham, S. D. (2000). Using the Implicit Association Test to measure self-esteem and self-concept. *Journal of Personality and Social Psychology, 79*, 1022–1038. doi: 10.1037/0022-3514.79.6.1022

Gregorian, R. S., Golden, K. A., Bahce, A., Goodman, C., Kwong, W. J., & Khan, Z. M. (2002). Antidepressant-induced sexual dysfunction. *Annals of Pharmacotherapy, 36*, 1577–1589. doi: 10.1345/aph.1A195

Gregory, R. L. (2005). The Medawar lecture 2001—Knowledge for vision: Vision for knowledge. *Proceedings of the Royal Society of London, Series B: Biological Sciences, 360*, 1231–1251. doi: 10.1098/rstb.2005.1662

Grether, J. K., Anderson, M. C., Croen, L. A., Smith, D., & Windham, G. C. (2009). Risk of autism and increasing maternal and paternal age in a large North American population. *American Journal of Epidemiology, 170*(9), 1118–1126. doi: 10.1093/aje/kwp247

Grieve, R., Indian, M., Witteveen, K., Anne Tolan, G., & Marrington, J. (2013). Face-to-face or Facebook: Can social connectedness be derived online? *Computers in Human Behavior, 29*(3), 604–609. doi: 10.1016/j.chb.2012.11.017

Grimm, S., Beck, J., Schuepbach, D., Hell, D., Boesiger, P., Bermpohl, F., et al. (2008). Imbalance between left and right dorsolateral prefrontal cortex in major depression is linked to negative emotional judgment: An fMRI study in severe major depressive disorder. *Biological Psychiatry, 63*(4), 369–376. doi: 10.1016/j.biopsych.2007.05.033

Grisham, J. R., Anderson, T. M., & Sachdev, P. S. (2008). Genetic and environmental influences on obsessive-compulsive disorder. *European Archives of Psychiatry and Clinical Neuroscience, 258*(2), 107–116. doi: 10.1007/s00406-007-0789-0

Grossman, M. (2007). *Unprotected.* New York, NY: Sentinel.

Grosso, G., Pajak, A., Marventano, S., Castellano, S., Galvano, F., Bucolo, C., et al. (2014). Role of omega-3 fatty acids in the treatment of depressive disorders: A comprehensive meta-analysis of randomized clinical trials. *PLoS One, 9*(5), e96905. doi: 10.1371/journal.pone.0096905

Groth-Marnat, G. (2009). *Handbook of psychological assessment* (5th ed.). New York, NY: Wiley.

Guignard, J.-H., & Lubart, T. (2006). Is it reasonable to be creative? In J. C. Kaufman & J. Baer (Eds.), *Creativity and reason in cognitive development* (pp. 269–281). New York, NY: Cambridge University Press.

Gunter, B. (1994). The question of media violence. In J. Bryant & D. Zillmann (Eds.), *Media effects: Advances in theory and research* (pp. 163–211). Hillsdale, NJ: Erlbaum.

Gustavson, C. R., Kelly, D. J., Sweeney, M., & Garcia, J. (1976). Prey–lithium aversions. I: Coyotes and wolves. *Behavioral Biology, 17*(1), 61–72. doi: 10.1016/S0091-6773(76)90272-8

Gutwinski, S., Löscher, A., Mahler, L., Kalbitzer, J., Heinz, A., & Bermpohl, F. (2011). Understanding left-handedness. *Deutsches Ärzteblatt International, 108*(50), 849–853. doi: 10.3238/arztebl.2011.0849

Guynn, M. J., McDaniel, M. A., Strosser, G. L., Ramirez, J. M., Castleberry, E. H., & Arnett, K. H. (2014). Relational and item-specific influences on generate–recognize processes in recall. *Memory & Cognition, 42*(2), 198-211. doi: 10.3758/s13421-013-0341-6

Guzman-Marin, R., Suntsova, N., Stewart, D. R., Gong, H., Szymusiak, R., & McGinty, D. (2003). Sleep deprivation reduces proliferation of cells in the dentate gyrus of the hippocampus in rats. *Journal of Physiology, 549*, 563–571. doi: 10.1113/jphysiol.2003.041665

Haber, R. N., & Haber, R. B. (1964). Eidetic imagery: I. Frequency. *Perceptual and Motor Skills, 19*, 131–138. doi: 10.2466/pms.1964.19.1.131

Haber, S. N., & Barchas, P. R. (1983). The regulatory effect of social rank on behavior after amphetamine administration. In P. R. Barchas (Ed.), *Social hierarchies: Essays toward a sociophysiological perspective* (pp. 119–132). Westport, CT: Greenwood Press.

Haemer, M. A., Huang, T. T., & Daniels, S. R. (2009). The effect of neurohormonal factors, epigenetic factors, and gut microbiota on risk of obesity. *Preventing Chronic Disease, 6*(3), A96.

Haerer, A. F. (1992). *DeJong's the neurologic examination* (5th ed.). Philadelphia, PA: J. B. Lippincott.

Haier, R. J. (2009). What does a smart brain look like? *Scientific American Mind, (20)*, 26–33. doi: 10.1038/scientificamerican-mind1109-26

Haier, R. J., Jung, R. E., Yeo, R. A., Head, K., & Alkire, M. T. (2005). The neuroanatomy of general intelligence: Sex matters. *NeuroImage, 25*, 320–327. doi: 10.1016/j.neuroimage.2004.11.019

Haier, R. J., Siegel, B. V., Jr., MacLachlan, A., Soderling, E., Lottenberg, S. & Buchsbaum, M. S. (1992). Regional glucose metabolic changes after learning a complex visuospatial/motor task: A positron emission tomographic study. *Brain Research, 570*, 134–143. doi: 10.1016/0006-8993(92)90573-R

Halaas, J. L., Gajiwala, K. S., Maffei, M., Cohen, S. L., Chait, B. T., Rabinowitz, D., et al. (1995). Weight-reducing effects of the plasma protein encoded by the obese gene. *Science, 269*, 543–546. doi: 10.1126/science.7624777

Hall, C. (1954). *A primer in Freudian psychology*, New York, NY: Meridian.

Hall, W. D. (2006). How have the SSRI antidepressants affected suicide risk? *Lancet, 367*(9527), 1959–1962. doi: 10.1016/s0140-6736(06)68860-0

Halmi, K. A., Casper, R. C., Eckert, E. D., Goldberg, S. C., & Davis, J. M. (1979). Unique features associated with age of onset of anorexia nervosa. *Psychiatry Research, 1*(2), 209–215. doi: 10.1016/0165-1781(79)90063-5

Halpern, D. F., Benbow, C. P., Geary, D. C., Gur, R. C., Hyde, J. S., & Gernsbacher, M. A. (2007). The science of sex differences in science and mathematics. *Psychological Science in the Public Interest, 8*(1), 1–51. doi: 10.1111/j.1529-1006.2007.00032.x

Halpern, J. H., & Pope, H. G., Jr. (2003). Hallucinogen persisting perception disorder: What do we know after 50 years? *Drug and Alcohol Dependence, 69*(2), 109–119. doi: 10.1016/S0376-8716(02)00306-X

Halverson, M. S., & Bolnick, D. A. (2008). An ancient DNA test of a founder effect in Native American ABO blood group frequencies. *American Journal of Physical*

Anthropology, 137(3), 342–347. doi: 10.1002/ajpa.20887

Hamamura, T. (2012). Are cultures becoming individualistic? A cross-temporal comparison of individualism–collectivism in the United States and Japan. *Personality and Social Psychology Review, 16*(1), 3–24. doi: 10.1177/1088868311411587

Hamel, M., Shaffer, T. W., & Erdberg, P. (2000). A study of nonpatient preadolescent Rorschach protocols. *Journal of Personality Assessment, 75*(2), 280–294. doi: 10.1207/s15327752jpa7502_8

Hamermesh, D. S., & Parker, A. M. (2005). Beauty in the classroom: Professors' pulchritude and putative pedagogical productivity. *Economics of Education Review, 24*(4), 369-376. doi: 10.1016/j.econedurev.2004.07.013 Hamilton, A. F. D. C. (2013). Reflecting on the mirror neuron system in autism: A systematic review of current theories. *Developmental Cognitive Neuroscience, 3*, 91–105. doi: 10.1016/j.dcn.2012.09.008

Hamilton, W. D. (1964). The genetical evolution of social behaviour: I . *Journal of Theoretical Biology, 7*(1), 1–16. doi: 10.1016/0022-5193(64)90038-4

Hamlyn, J., Duhig, M., McGrath, J., & Scott, J. (2013). Modifiable risk factors for schizophrenia and autism: Shared risk factors impacting on brain development. *Neurobiology of Disease, 53*(0), 3–9. doi: 10.1016/j.nbd.2012.10.023

Hampson, E. (1990). Estrogen-related variations in human spatial and articulatory-motor skills. *Psychoneuroendocrinology, 15*(2), 97–111. doi: 10.1016/0306-4530(90)90018-5

Hampson, E., & Kimura, D. (1988). Reciprocal effects of hormonal fluctuations on human motor and perceptual–spatial skills. *Behavioral Neuroscience, 102*(3), 456–459. doi: 10.1037/0735-7044.102.3.456

Hänecke, K., Tiedemann, S., Nachreiner, F., & Grzech-Sukalo, H. (1998). Accident risk as a function of hour at work and time of day as determined from accident data and exposure models for the German working population. *Scandinavian Journal of Work, Environment & Health, 24*, 43–48.

Haney, C., Banks, C., & Zimbardo, P. (1973). Interpersonal dynamics in a simulated prison. *International Journal of Criminology and Penology, 1*, 69–97.

Hansen, J., Winzeler, S., & Topolinski, S. (2010). When the death makes you smoke: A terror management perspective on the effectiveness of cigarette on-pack warnings. *Journal of Experimental Social Psychology, 46*(1), 226–228. doi: 10.1016/j.jesp.2009.09.007

Hansford, B. C., & Hattie, J. A. (1982). The relationship between self and achievement/performance measures. *Review of Educational Research, 52*, 123–142. doi: 10.3102/00346543052001123

Hare, R. D. (2002). *The predators among us.* Paper presented at the Canadian Police Association Annual General Meeting, St. John's, Newfoundland and Labrador.

Hare, R. D. (2006). Psychopathy: A clinical and forensic overview. *Psychiatric Clinics of North America, 29*(3), 709–724. doi: 10.1016/j.psc.2006.04.007

Harley, H. E., Xitco, M. J., Jr., Roitblat, H. L., & Herman, L. M. (1998, June). *Imitation of human models by bottlenose dolphins.* Paper presented at the Napoli Social Learning Conference, Naples, Italy.

Harlow, H. (1958). The nature of love. *American Psychologist, 13*, 573–685. doi: 10.1037/h0047884

Harlow, H. F., & Harlow, M. K. (1973). Social deprivation in monkeys. In W. T. Greenough (Ed.), *The nature and nurture of behavior: Readings from* Scientific American (pp. 108–116). San Francisco, CA: Freeman.

Harper, F. K., Schmidt, J. E., Beacham, A. O., Salsman, J. M., Averill, A. J., Graves, K. D., et al. (2006). The role of social cognitive processing theory and optimism in positive psychosocial and physical behavior change after cancer diagnosis and treatment. *Psycho-Oncology, 16*, 79–91. doi: 10.1002/pon.1068

Harper, K., Sperry, S., & Thompson, J. K. (2008). Viewership of pro-eating disorder websites: Association with body image and eating disturbances. *International Journal of Eating Disorders, 41*(1), 92–95. doi: 10.1002/eat.20408

Harrington, R. A., Lee, L.-C., Crum, R. M., Zimmerman, A. W., & Hertz-Picciotto, I. (2014). Prenatal SSRI use and offspring with autism spectrum disorder or developmental delay. *Pediatrics, 133*(5), e1241–e1248. doi: 10.1542/peds.2013-3406

Hart, A. J., Whalen, P. J., Shin, L. M., McInerney, S. C., Fischer, H., & Rauch, S. L. (2000). Differential response in the human amygdala to racial outgroup vs ingroup face stimuli. *NeuroReport, 11*, 2351–2355. doi: 10.1097/00001756-200008030-00004

Hart, B., & Pate, W. E. (2011, May). *Salaries, student debt, and employment opportunities in psychology.* Paper presented at the Midwestern Psychological Association Convention, Chicago, IL.

Hart, W., & Albarracin, D. (2009). The effects of chronic achievement motivation and achievement primes on the activation of achievement and fun goals. *Journal of Personality and Social Psychology, 97*(6), 1129–1141. doi: 10.1037/a0017146

Harvey, A., Watkins, E., Mansell, W., & Shafran, R. (2004). *Cognitive behavioural processes across psychological disorders.* New York, NY: Oxford University Press.

Haselton, M. G., Bryant, G. A., Wilke, A., Frederick, D. A., Galperin, A., Frankenhuis, W. E., et al. (2009). Adaptive rationality: An evolutionary perspective on cognitive bias. *Social Cognition, 27*(5), 733–763. doi: 10.1521/soco.2009.27.5.733

Haselton, M. G., Mortezaie, M., Pillsworth, E. G., Bleske-Rechek, A., & Frederick, D. A. (2006). Ovulatory shifts in human female ornamentation: Near ovulation, women dress to impress. *Hormones and Behavior, 51*, 40–45. doi: 10.1016/j.yhbeh.2006.07.007

Hathaway, S. R., & McKinley, J. C. (1940). A multiphasic personality schedule (Minnesota): I. Construction of the schedule. *Journal of Psychology, 10*, 249–254. doi: 10.1080/00223980.1940.9917000

Hathaway, S. R., & McKinley, J. C. (1943). *The Minnesota Multiphasic Personality Inventory manual.* New York, NY: Psychological Corporation.

Haug, T. T., Blomhoff, S., Hellstrom, K., Holme, I., Humble, M., Madsbu, H. P., et al. (2003). Exposure therapy and sertraline in social phobia: 1-year follow-up of a randomised controlled trial. *British Journal of Psychiatry, 182*, 312–318. doi: 10.1192/bjp.02.229

Hawkley, L. C., & Cacioppo, J. T. (2010). Loneliness matters: A theoretical and empirical review of consequences and mechanisms. *Annals of Behavioral Medicine, 40*(2), 218–227. doi: 10.1007/s12160-010-9210-8

Hawkley, L. C., Masi, C. M., Berry, J. D., & Cacioppo, J. T. (2006). Loneliness is a unique predictor of age-related differences in systolic blood pressure. *Psychology and Aging, 21*, 152–164. doi: 10.1037/0882-7974.21.1.152

Hawkley, L. C., Thisted, R. A., & Cacioppo, J. T. (2009). Loneliness predicts reduced physical activity: Cross-sectional and longitudinal analyses. *Health Psychology, 28*(3), 354–363. doi: 10.1037/a0014400

Hayak, Y., Walker, J. R., Li, C., Wong, W. H., Davis, L., Buxbaum, J. D., et al. (2001). Genome-wide expression analysis reveals disregulation of myelination-related genes in chronic schizophrenia. *Proceedings of the National Academy of Sciences, 48*, 4746–4751. doi: 10.1073/pnas.081071198

Haycock, P. C. (2009). Fetal alcohol spectrum disorders: The epigenetic perspective. *Biology of Reproduction, 81*(4), 607–617. doi: 10.1095/biolreprod.108.074690

Hecht, D. (2010). Depression and the hyperactive right hemisphere. *Neuroscience Research, 68*(2), 77–87. doi: 10.1016/j.neures.2010.06.013

Hecht, S., Shlaer, S., & Pirenne, M. H. (1942). Energy, quanta, and vision. *Journal of General Physiology, 25*, 819–840. doi: 10.1085/jgp.25.6.819

Heider, F. (1958). *The psychology of interpersonal relations.* New York, NY: Wiley.

Heinz, A. J., Beck, A., Meyer-Lindenberg, A., Sterzer, P., & Heinz, A. (2011). Cognitive and neurobiological mechanisms of alcohol-related aggression. *Nature Reviews Neuroscience, 12*(7), 400–413. doi: 10.1038/nrn3042

Held, B. S. (2004). The negative side of positive psychology. *Journal of Humanistic Psychology, 44*(1), 9–46. doi: 10.1177/0022167803259645

Helfinstein, S. M., Schonberg, T., Congdon, E., Karlsgodt, K. H., Mumford, J. A., Sabb, F. W., et al. (2014). Predicting risky choices from brain activity patterns. *Proceedings of the National Academy of Sciences, 111*(7), 2470–2475. doi: 10.1073/pnas.1321728111

Helliwell, J. F. (2003). How's life? Combining individual and national variables to explain subjective well-being. *Economic Modeling, 20*, 331–360. doi: 10.1016/S0264-9993(02)00057-3

Helpern, J. A., Adisetiyo, V., Falangola, M. F., Hu, C., Di Martino, A., Williams, K., et al. (2011). Preliminary evidence of altered gray and white matter microstructural development in the frontal lobe of adolescents with attention-deficit hyperactivity disorder: A diffusional kurtosis imaging study. *Journal of Magnetic Resonance Imaging, 33*(1), 17–23. doi: 10.1002/jmri.22397

Henkel, L. A., & Mather, M. (2007). Memory attributions for choices: How beliefs shape our memories. *Journal of Memory and Language, 57*(2), 163–176. doi: 10.1016/j.jml.2006.08.012

Hennenlotter, A., Schroeder, U., Erhard, P., Haslinger, B., Stahl, R., Weindl, A., et al. (2004). Neural correlates associated with impaired disgust processing in presymptomatic Huntington's disease. *Brain, 127*(6), 1446–1453. doi: 10.1093/brain/awh165

Henquet, C., Di Forti, M., Morrison, P., Kuepper, R., & Murray, R. M. (2008). Gene–environment interplay between cannabis and psychosis. *Schizophrenia Bulletin, 34*(6), 1111–1121. doi: 10.1093/schbul/sbn108

Herbst, N., Voderholzer, U., Thiel, N., Schaub, R., Knaevelsrud, C., Stracke, S., et al. (2014). No talking, just writing! Efficacy of an internet-based cognitive behavioral therapy with exposure and response prevention in obsessive compulsive disorder. *Psychotherapy and Psychosomatics, 83*(3), 165–175. doi: 10.1159/000357570

Herdt, G. H. (1987). *The Sambia: Ritual and gender in New Guinea.* New York, NY: Holt, Rinehart, and Winston.

Hergenhahn, B., & Henley, T. (2013). *An introduction to the history of psychology* (7th ed.). Belmont, CA: Cengage.

Herndon, J. G. (2010). The grandmother effect: Implications for studies on aging and cognition. *Gerontology, 56*(1), 73–79. doi: 10.1159/000236045

Herpertz, S. C., Werth, U., Lukas, G., Qunaibi, M., Schuerkens, A., Kunert, H. J., et al. (2001). Emotion in criminal offenders with psychopathy and borderline personality disorder. *Archives of General Psychiatry, 58*, 737–745. doi: 10.1001/archpsyc.58.8.737

Herrnstein, R. J. (1979). Acquisition, generalization, and discrimination reversal of a natural concept. *Journal of Experimental Psychology: Animal Behavior Processes, 5*, 116–129. doi: 10.1037/0097-7403.5.2.116

Herrnstein, R. J., & Boring, E. G. (1965). *A source book in the history of psychology.* Cambridge, MA: Harvard University Press.

Herrnstein, R. J., & de Villiers, P. A. (1980). Fish as a natural category for people and pigeons. In G. H. Bower (Ed.), *The psychology of learning and motivation* (Vol. 14, pp. 59–95). New York, NY: Academic Press.

Herrnstein, R. J., & Heyman, G. M. (1979). Is matching compatible with reinforcement maximization on concurrent variable interval variable ratio? *Journal of the Experimental Analysis of Behavior, 31*, 209–223. doi: 10.1901/jeab.1979.31-209

Herxheimer, A., & Waterhouse, J. (2003). The prevention and treatment of jet lag: It's been ignored, but much can be done. *British Medical Journal, 326*(7384), 296–297. doi: http://dx.doi.org/10.1136/bmj.326.7384.296

Herz, R. (2003). The effect of verbal context on olfactory perception. *Journal of Experimental Psychology: General, 132*, 595–606. doi: 10.1037/0096-3445.132.4.595

Hicks, T. V., Leitenberg, H., Barlow, D. H., Gorman, J. M., Shear, M. K., & Woods, S. W. (2005). Physical, mental, and social catastrophic cognitions as prognostic factors in cognitive-behavioral and pharmacological treatments for panic disorder. *Journal of Consulting and Clinical Psychology, 73*(3), 506–514. doi: 10.1037/0022-006x.73.3.506

Hill, M. N. (2014). Clearing the smoke: What do we know about adolescent cannabis use and schizophrenia? *Journal of Psychiatry & Neuroscience, 39*(2), 75–77. doi: 10.1503/jpn.140028

Himelboim, I., McCreery, S., & Smith, M. (2013). Birds of a feather tweet together: Integrating network and content analyses to examine cross-ideology exposure on Twitter. *Journal of Computer-Mediated Communication, 18*(2), 40–60. doi: 10.1111/jcc4.12001

Hinney, A., & Volckmar, A.-L. (2013). Genetics of eating disorders. *Current Psychiatry Reports, 15*(12), 1–9.

Hinton, D. E., & Good, B. (Eds.). (2009). *Culture and panic disorder.* Stanford, CA: Stanford University Press.

Hirshkowitz, M., & Moore, C. A. (1996). Sleep-related erectile activity. *Neurological Clinics, 14*, 721–737.

Ho, B.-C., Wassink, T. H., Ziebell, S., & Andreasen, N. C. (2011). Cannabinoid receptor 1 gene polymorphisms and marijuana misuse interactions on white matter and cognitive deficits in schizophrenia. *Schizophrenia Research, 128*(1–3), 66–75. doi: 10.1016/j.schres.2011.02.021

Ho, M. Y., & Fung, H. H. (2011). A dynamic process model of forgiveness: A cross-cultural perspective. *Review of General Psychology, 15*(1), 77–84. doi: 10.1037/a0022605

Hobson, J. M., & McCarley, R. W. (1977). The brain as a dream state generator: An activation–synthesis hypothesis of the dream process. *American Journal of Psychiatry, 134*, 1335–1348.

Hodgkin, A. L., & Huxley, A. F. (1952). A quantitative description of membrane current and its application to conduction and excitation in nerve. *Journal of Physiology, 117*, 500–544.

Hoebel, B. G., & Teitelbaum, P. (1966). Weight regulation in normal and hypothalamic hyperphagic rats. *Journal of Comparative and Physiological Psychology, 61*, 189–193. doi: 10.1037/h0023126

Hoeft, F., McCandliss, B. D., Black, J. M., Gantman, A., Zakerani, N., Hulme, C., et al. (2011). Neural systems predicting long-term outcome in dyslexia. *Proceedings of the National Academy of Sciences, 108*(1), 361–366. doi: 10.1073/pnas.1008950108

Hofling, C. K., Brotzman, E., Dalrymple, S., Graves, N., & Pierce, C. M. (1966). An experimental study in nurse–physician relationships. *Journal of Nervous and Mental Disease, 143*, 171–180.

Hofstede, G. (1980). *Culture's consequences.* Beverly Hills, CA: Sage.

Hofstede, G. (1984). The cultural relativity of the quality of life concept. *Academy of Management Review, 9*(3), 389–398. doi: 10.5465/AMR.1984.4279653

Hogan, C. L., Mata, J., & Carstensen, L. L. (2013). Exercise holds immediate benefits for affect and cognition in younger and older adults. *Psychology and Aging, 28*(2), 587. doi: 10.1037/a0032634

Holder, M. K. (1999). *Influences and constraints on manual asymmetry in wild African primates: Reassessing implications for the evolution of human handedness and brain lateralization* (Unpublished doctoral dissertation). Rutgers University, Piscataway, NJ.

Hollander, E., Liebowitz, M. R., Gorman, J. M., Cohen, B., Fyer, A., & Klein, D. F. (1989). Cortisol and sodium lactate-induced panic. *Archives of General Psychiatry, 46*(2), 135–140. doi: 10.1001/archpsyc.1989.01810020037007

Hollon, S. D., Thase, M. E., & Markowitz, J. C. (2002). Treatment and prevention of depression. *Psychological Science in the Public Interest, 3*(2), 39–77. doi: 10.1111/1529-1006.00008

Holmes, T. H., & Rahe, R. H. (1967). The social readjustment rating scale. *Journal of Psychosomatic Research, 11*, 213–218. doi: 10.1016/0022-3999(67)90010-4

Holt, L. H., Lotto, A. J., & Kluender, K. R. (1998). Incorporating principles of general learning in theories of language acquisition. In M. Gruber, C. D. Higgins, K. S. Olson, & T. Wysocki (Eds.), *Chicago*

Linguistic Society (Vol. 34, pp. 253–268). Chicago, IL: Chicago Linguistic Society.

Hölzel, B. K., Lazar, S. W., Gard, T., Schuman-Olivier, Z., Vago, D. R., & Ott, U. (2011). How does mindfulness meditation work? Proposing mechanisms of action from a conceptual and neural perspective. *Perspectives on Psychological Science, 6*(6), 537–559. doi: 10.1177/1745691611419671

Holzgrabe, U., Kapkova, P., Alptuzun, V., Scheiber, J., & Kugelmann, E. (2007). Targeting acetylcholinesterase to treat neurodegeneration. *Expert Opinion on Therapeutic Targets, 11*(2), 161–179. doi: 10.1517/14728222.11.2.161

Hopper, K., Harrison, G., Janca, A., & Sartorius, N. (2007). *Recovery from schizophrenia: An international perspective; A report from the WHO Collaborative Project, the international study of schizophrenia.* New York, NY: Oxford University Press.

Horn, J. L., & Hofer, S. M. (1992). Major abilities and development in the adult period. In R. J. Sternberg & C. A. Berg (Eds.), *Intellectual development* (pp. 44–99). Cambridge, United Kingdom: Cambridge University Press.

Horne, J. (1988). *Why we sleep: The functions of sleep in humans and other mammals.* New York, NY: Oxford University Press.

Horney, K. (1950). *The collected works of Karen Horney.* New York, NY: Norton.

Horney, K. (1967). *Feminine psychology.* New York, NY: Norton. (Original work published 1923–1937)

Hornsveld, R. H., Nijman, H. L., Hollin, C. R., & Kraaimaat, F. W. (2008). Aggression control therapy for violent forensic psychiatric patients: Method and clinical practice. *International Journal of Offender Therapy and Comparative Criminology, 52*(2), 222–233. doi: 10.1177/0306624X07303876

Horwitz, A. V., White, H. R., & Howell-White, S. (1997). Becoming married and mental health: A longitudinal study of a cohort of young adults. *Journal of Marriage and the Family, 58,* 895–907. doi: 10.2307/353978

Hostinar, C. E., Sullivan, R. M., & Gunnar, M. R. (2013). Psychobiological mechanisms underlying the social buffering of the hypothalamic–pituitary–adrenocortical axis: A review of animal models and human studies across development. *Psychological Bulletin, 140*(1), 256–282. doi: 10.1037/a0032671

Hourcade, J. P., Williams, S. R., Miller, E. A., Huebner, K. E., & Liang, L. J. (2013). Evaluation of tablet apps to encourage social interaction in children with autism spectrum disorders. *Proceedings of the SIGCHI Conference on Human Factors in Computing Systems,* 3197-3206. doi: 10.1145/2470654.2466438

House, J. S., Landis, K. R., & Umberson, D. (1988). Social relationships and health. *Science, 241,* 540–545. doi: 10.1126/science.3399889

Houston, S. M., Herting, M. M., & Sowell, E. R. (2013). The neurobiology of childhood structural brain development: Conception through adulthood. *Current Topics in Behavioral Neurosciences, 16,* 3–17. doi: 10.1007/7854_2013_265

Hoza, B., Waschbusch, D. A., Pelham, W. E., Molina, B. S. G., & Milich, R. (2000). Attention-deficit/hyperactivity disordered and control boys' responses to social success and failure. *Child Development, 71,* 432–447. doi: 10.1111/1467-8624.00155

Hrdy, S. B. (2005). Comes the child before the man: How cooperative breeding and prolonged postweaning dependence shaped human potential. In B. S. Hewlett & S. E. Lamb (Eds.), *Hunter–gatherer childhoods: Evolutionary, developmental and cultural perspectives* (pp. 65–91). New Brunswick, NJ: Transaction Publishers.

Hsu, L. K. G., Chesler, B. E., & Santhouse, R. (1990). Bulimia nervosa in eleven sets of twins: A clinical report. *International Journal of Eating Disorders, 9,* 275–282. doi: 10.1002/1098-108X(199005)9: 3<275::AID-EAT2260090305>3.0.CO;2-R

Hubel, D. H., & Livingstone, M. S. (1987). Segregation of form, color, and stereopsis in primate area 18. *Journal of Neuroscience, 7,* 3378–3415.

Hubel, D. H., & Wiesel, T. N. (1959). Receptive fields of single neurons in the cat's striate cortex. *Journal of Physiology, 148,* 574–591.

Hudson, J., Hiripi, E., Pope, H., & Kessler, R. (2007). The prevalence and correlates of eating disorders in the national comorbidity survey replication. *Biological Psychiatry, 61*(3), 348–358. doi: 10.1016/j.biopsych.2006.03.040

Hudspeth, A. (1983). The hair cells of the inner ear. *Scientific American, 248,* 54–64.

Hull, C. L. (1943). *Principles of behavior: An introduction to behavior theory.* Oxford, United Kingdom: Appleton-Century.

Humanoid Robotics Group (n.d.). Cog. Retrieved from http://www.ai.mit.edu/projects/humanoid-robotics-group/cog/overview.html

Hunt, H. T. (1989). *The multiplicity of dreams.* New Haven, CT: Yale University Press.

Hunt, J., & Eisenberg, D. (2010). Mental health problems and help-seeking behavior among college students. *Journal of Adolescent Health, 46*(1), 3–10. doi: 10.1016/j.jadohealth.2009.08.008

Hunt, M. (2007). Borderline personality disorder across the lifespan. *Journal of Women Aging, 19,* 173–191. doi: 10.1300/J074v19n01_11

Hupka, R. B., Lenton, A. P., & Hutchison, K. A. (1999). Universal development of emotion categories in natural language. *Journal of Personality and Social Psychology, 77,* 247–278. doi: 10.1037/0022-3514.77.2.247

Huston, A. C., Anderson, D. R., Wright, J. C., Linebarger, D. L., & Schmitt, K. L. (2001). *Sesame Street* viewers as adolescents: The recontact study. In S. M. Fisch & R. T. Truglio (Eds.), *"G" is for growing: Thirty years of research on children and Sesame Street.* Mahwah, NJ: Erlbaum.

Hyde, J. S. (1984). Children's understanding of sexist language. *Developmental Psychology, 20,* 697–706. doi: 10.1037/0012-1649.20.4.697

Hystad, S. W., Eid, J., Laberg, J. C., Johnsen, B. H., & Bartone, P. T. (2009). Academic stress and health: Exploring the moderating role of personality hardiness. *Scandinavian Journal of Educational Research, 53*(5), 421–429. doi: 10.1080/00313830903180349

Iacoboni, M., & Dapretto, M. (2006). The mirror neuron system and the consequences of its dysfunction. *Nature Reviews Neuroscience, 7*(12), 942–951. doi: 10.1038/nrn2024

Iacoboni, M., & Mazziotta, J. C. (2007). Mirror neuron system: Basic findings and clinical applications. *Annals of Neurology, 62*(3), 213–218. doi: 10.1002/ana.21198

Inoue, M., Koyanagi, T., Nakahara, H., Hara, K., Hori, E., & Nakano, H. (1986). Functional development of human eye movement in utero assessed quantitatively with real-time ultrasound. *American Journal of Obstetrics and Gynecology, 155,* 170–174. doi: 10.1016/0002-9378(86)90105-5

Insel, T. R. (2007). Post-traumatic stress disorder research at the National Institute of Mental Health. Retrieved from http://www.hhs.gov/asl/testify/2007/05/t20070524a.html

Institute of Medicine. (1994). *Growing up tobacco free: Preventing nicotine addiction in children and youths.* Washington, DC: National Academy Press.

International Coach Federation. (n.d.). Coaching FAQs. Retrieved from http://www.coachfederation.org/need/landing.cfm?ItemNumber=978&navItemNumber=567

International Society for the Study of Dissociation. (2005). Guidelines for treating dissociative identity disorder in adults. *Journal of Trauma and Dissociation, 6*(4), 69–149.

Inui, A., Asakawa, A., Bowers, C. Y., Mantovani, G., Laviano, A., Meguid, M. M., et al. (2004). Ghrelin, appetite, and gastric motility: The emerging role of the stomach as an endocrine organ. *FASEB Journal, 18*(3), 439–456. doi: 10.1096/fj.03-0641rev

Ioannou, C. C., Guttal, V., & Couzin, I. D. (2012). Predatory fish select for coordinated collective motion in virtual prey. *Science, 337*(6099), 1212–1215. doi: 10.1126/science.1218919

Ito, T. A., & Urland, G. R. (2003). The influence of processing objectives on the perception of faces: An ERP study of race and gender perception. *Cognitive, Affective, and Behavioral Neuroscience, 5,* 21–36. doi: 10.3758/CABN.5.1.21

Ittleson, W. H. (1952). *The Ames demonstrations in perception.* Princeton, NJ: Princeton University Press.

Iveson, C. (2002). Solution-focused brief therapy. *Advances in Psychiatric Treatment, 8,* 149–156. doi: 10.1192/apt.8.2.149

Jabbi, M., Swart, M., & Keysers, C. (2007). Empathy for positive and negative emotions in the gustatory cortex. *NeuroImage, 34*(4), 1744–1753. doi: 10.1016/j.neuroimage.2006.10.032

Jackson, B., Kubzansky, L. D., Cohen, S., Jacobs, D. R., Jr., & Wright, R. J. (2007). Does harboring hostility hurt? Associations between hostility and pulmonary function in the Coronary Artery Risk Development in (Young) Adults (CARDIA) study. *Health Psychology, 26*(3), 333–340. doi: 10.1037/0278-6133.26.3.333

Jackson, J. H. (1884). The Croonian lectures of evolution and dissolution of the nervous system: Lecture 1. *British Medical Journal, 1,* 591–593. doi: http://dx.doi.org/10.1136/bmj.1.1213.591

Jakupcak, M., Tull, M. T., McDermott, M. J., Kaysen, D., Hunt, S., & Simpson, T. (2010). PTSD symptom clusters in relationship to alcohol misuse among Iraq and Afghanistan war veterans seeking post-deployment VA health care. *Addictive Behaviors, 35*(9), 840–843. doi: 10.1016/j.addbeh.2010.03.023

Jambunathan, S., Burts, D. C., & Pierce, S. (2000). Comparisons of parenting attitudes among five ethnic groups in the United States. *Journal of Comparative Family Studies, 31,* 395–406.

James, D., & Drakich, J. (1993). Understanding gender differences in amount of talk: A critical review of research. In D. Tannen (Ed.), *Gender and conversational interaction* (pp. 281–312). New York, NY: Oxford University Press.

James, W. (1884). What is an emotion? *Mind, 9,* 188–205. doi: 10.1093/mind/os-IX.34.188

James, W. (1887). What is an instinct? *Scribner's Magazine, 1,* 355–365.

James, W. (1890). *Principles of psychology.* New York, NY: Henry Holt.

James, W. (1905). *The varieties of religious experience: A study in human nature.* New York, NY: Longmans, Green.

James, W. H. (2006). Two hypotheses on the causes of male homosexuality and paedophilia. *Journal of Biosocial Science, 38*(6), 745–761. doi: 10.1017/S0021932005027173

Jamison, K. R. (1993). *Touched with fire: Manic–depressive illness and the artistic temperament.* New York, NY: Free Press.

Jamison, K. R. (1995). Manic–depressive illness and creativity. *Scientific American, 272,* 62–67.

Jäncke, L., & Kaufmann, N. (1994). Facial EMG responses to odors in solitude and with an audience. *Chemical Senses, 19,* 99–111. doi: 10.1093/chemse/19.2.99

Jang, K. L., Livesley, W. J., & Vernon, P. A. (1996). Heritability of the Big Five personality dimensions and their facets: A twin study. *Journal of Personality, 64*(3), 577–591.

Janik, V. M., Sayigh, L. S., & Wells, R. S. (2006). Signature whistle shape conveys identity information to bottlenose dolphins. *Proceedings of the National Academy of Sciences, 103,* 8293–8297. doi: 10.1073/pnas.0509918103

Janis, I. (1972). *Victims of groupthink: A psychological study of foreign-policy decisions and fiascoes.* Oxford, United Kingdom: Houghton Mifflin.

Jansen, K. L. R. (1996). Using ketamine to induce the near-death experience: Mechanism of action and therapeutic potential. In C. Ratsch & J. R. Baker (Eds.), *Yearbook for ethnomedicine and the study of consciousness (jahrbuch für ethnomedizin und bewubtseinsforschung)* (pp. 55–81). Berlin, Germany: VWB Verlag.

Janszky, I., & Ljung, R. (2008). Shifts to and from daylight saving time and incidence of myocardial infarction. *New England Journal of Medicine, 359*(18), 1966–1968. doi: 10.1056/NEJMc0807104

Janusonis, S. (2008). Origin of the blood hyperserotonemia of autism. *Theoretical Biology and Medical Modelling, 5,* 10. doi: 10.1186/1742-4682-5-10

Jaques, E. (1965). Death and the midlife crisis. *International Journal of Psychoanalysis, 46,* 502–514.

Jelenchick, L. A., Eickhoff, J. C., & Moreno, M. A. (2013). "Facebook depression?" Social networking site use and depression in older adolescents. *Journal of Adolescent Health, 52*(1), 128–130. doi: 10.1016/j.jadohealth.2012.05.008

Jensen, R., & Burgess, H. (1997). Mythmaking: How introductory psychology texts present B. F. Skinner's analysis of cognition. *Psychological Record, 47*(2), 221–232.

Jepson, T., Ernst, M. E., & Kelly, M. W. (1999). Perspectives on the management of seasonal affective disorder. *Journal of the American Pharmaceutical Association, 39*(6), 822–829.

Jerabeck, J. M., & Ferguson, C. J. (2013). The influence of solitary and cooperative violent video game play on aggressive and prosocial behavior. *Computers in Human Behavior, 29*(6), 2573–2578. doi: 10.1016/j.chb.2013.06.034

Job, V., Dweck, C. S., & Walton, G. M. (2010). Ego depletion—Is it all in your head? Implicit theories about willpower affect self-regulation. *Psychological Science, 21*(11), 1686–1693. doi: 10.1177/0956797610384745

Job, V., Walton, G. M., Bernecker, K., & Dweck, C. S. (2013). Beliefs about willpower determine the impact of glucose on self-control. *Proceedings of the National Academy of Sciences, 110*(37), 14837–14842. doi: 10.1073/pnas.1313475110

Jodee. (2014). Prothinspo. Retrieved from http://www.worldsbestdietingtips.com/

Joel, S., Gordon, A. M., Impett, E. A., MacDonald, G., & Keltner, D. (2013). The things you do for me: Perceptions of a romantic partner's investments promote gratitude and commitment. *Personality and Social Psychology Bulletin, 39*(10), 1333–1345. doi: 10.1177/0146167213497801

Jo*ls, M. (2006). Corticosteroid effects in the brain: U-shape it. *Trends in Pharmacological Sciences, 27*(5), 244–250. doi: 10.1016/j.tips.2006.03.007

Johns, M. W. (1991). A new method for measuring daytime sleepiness: The Epworth sleepiness scale. *Sleep, 14*(6), 540–545.

Johnson, J. A. (2009). Wrong and right questions about persons and situations. *Journal of Research in Personality, 43*(2), 251–252. doi: 10.1016/j.jrp.2008.12.022

Johnson, M. K., Hashtroudi, S., & Lindsay, D. S. (1993). Source monitoring. *Psychological Bulletin, 114,* 3–28. doi: 10.1037/0033-2909.114.1.3

Johnson, P. L., Truitt, W., Fitz, S. D., Minick, P. E., Dietrich, A., Sanghani, S., et al. (2010). A key role for orexin in panic anxiety. *Nature Medicine, 16*(1), 111–115. doi: 10.1038/nm.2075

Johnson, S. P., & Aslin, R. N. (1995). Perception of object unity in 2-month-old infants. *Developmental Psychology, 31,* 739–745. doi: 10.1037/0012-1649.31.5.739

Johnson, W. G., Tsoh, J. Y., & Vanrado, P. J. (1996). Eating disorders: Efficacy of pharmacological and psychological interventions. *Clinical Psychology Review, 16,* 457–478. doi: 10.1016/0272-7358(96)00030-X

Johnston, L. D., O'Malley, P. M., Bachman, J. G., & Schulenberg, J. E. (2011). *Monitoring the future: National survey results on drug use, 1975–2010* (Vol. 1). Ann Arbor, MI: Institute for Social Research, University of Michigan.

Jones, E. E., & Nisbett, R. E. (1972). The actor and the observer: Divergent perceptions of the causes of the behavior. In E. E. Jones, D. E. Kanouse, H. H. Kelley, R. E. Nisbett, S. Valins, & B. Weiner (Eds.), *Attribution: Perceiving the causes of behavior* (pp. 79–94). Morristown, NJ: General Learning Press.

Jones, E. E., Rhodewalt, F., Berglas, S., & Skelton, J. A. (1981). Effects of strategic self-presentation on subsequent self-esteem. *Journal of Personality and Social Psychology, 41,* 407–421. doi: 10.1037/0022-3514.41.3.407

Jones, I. H., & Barraclough, B. M. (1978). Auto-mutilation in animals and its relevance to self-injury in man. *Acta Psychiatrica Scandinavica, 58*(1), 40–47. doi: 10.1111/j.1600-0447.1978.tb06918.x

Jones, M. C. (1924). The elimination of children's fears. *Journal of Experimental Psychology, 7,* 382–390. doi: 10.1037/h0072283

Jornada, L. K., Valvassori, S. S., Steckert, A. V., Moretti, M., Mina, F., Ferreira, C. L., et al.

(2011). Lithium and valproate modulate antioxidant enzymes and prevent ouabain-induced oxidative damage in an animal model of mania. *Journal of Psychiatric Research, 45*(2), 162–168. doi: 10.1016/j.jpsychires.2010.05.011

Joyner, K., & Kao, G. (2005). Interracial relationships and the transition to adulthood. *American Sociological Review, 70,* 563–581. doi: 10.1177/000312240507000402

Judge, T. A., Livingston, B. A., & Hurst, C. (2012). Do nice guys—and gals—really finish last? The joint effects of sex and agreeableness on income. *Journal of Personality and Social Psychology, 102*(2), 390–407. doi: 10.1037/a0026021

Jung, C. G. (1928). *Contributions to analytical psychology.* New York, NY: Harcourt Brace Jovanovich.

Juster, R.-P., McEwen, B. S., & Lupien, S. J. (2010). Allostatic load biomarkers of chronic stress and impact on health and cognition. *Neuroscience and Biobehavioral Reviews, 35*(1), 2–16. doi: 10.1016/j.neubiorev.2009.10.002

Juvonen, J. (2005). Myths and facts about bullying in schools. *Behavioral Health Management, 25,* 36–40.

Kagan, J. (1997). Temperament and the reactions to unfamiliarity. *Child Development, 68,* 139–143. doi: 10.2307/1131931

Kagan, J., Kearsley, R. B., & Zelazo, P. R. (1978). *Infancy: Its place in human development.* Cambridge, MA: Harvard University Press.

Kagohara, D. M., van der Meer, L., Ramdoss, S., O'Reilly, M. F., Lancioni, G. E., Davis, T. N., et al. (2013). Using iPods and iPads in teaching programs for individuals with developmental disabilities: A systematic review. *Research in Developmental Disabilities, 34*(1), 147–156. doi: 10.1016/j.ridd.2012.07.027

Kahn, D. (2013). Brain basis of self: Self-organization and lessons from dreaming. *Frontiers in Psychology, 4,* 408. doi: 10.3389/fpsyg.2013.00408

Kail, R., & Bisanz, J. (1992). The information-processing perspective on cognitive development in childhood and adolescence. In R. J. Sternberg & C. A. Berg (Eds.), *Intellectual development* (pp. 229–260). New York, NY: Cambridge University Press.

Kail, R., & Cavanaugh, J. C. (2010). *Human development: A life-span view,* 5th ed. Belmont, CA: Wadsworth/Cengage Learning.

Kalinowsky, L. B. (1986). History of convulsive therapy. *Annals of the New York Academy of Sciences, 462*(1), 1–4. doi: 10.1111/j.1749-6632.1986.tb51233.x

Kalisch, R., & Gerlicher, A. M. V. (2014). Making a mountain out of a molehill: On the role of the rostral dorsal anterior cingulate and dorsomedial prefrontal cortex in conscious threat appraisal, catastrophizing, and worrying. *Neuroscience & Biobehavioral Reviews, 42,* 1–8. doi: 10.1016/j.neubiorev.2014.02.002

Kamin, L. J. (1968). "Attention-like" processes in classical conditioning. In M. R. Jones (Ed.), *Miami symposium on the prediction of behavior: Aversive stimulation* (pp. 9–31). Miami, FL: University of Miami Press.

Kamin, L. J. (1969). Predictability, surprise, attention, and conditioning. In B. A. Campbell & R. M. Church (Eds.), *Punishment and aversive behavior* (pp. 279–296). New York, NY: Appleton-Century-Crofts.

Kandel, D. B. (1978). Similarity in real-life adolescent friendship pairs. *Journal of Personality and Social Psychology, 36,* 306–312. doi: 10.1037/0022-3514.36.3.306

Kandel, E. R., & Wurtz, R. H. (2000). Constructing the visual image. In E. R. Kandel, J. H. Schwartz, & T. M. Jessell (Eds.), *Principles of neural science* (4th ed., pp. 492–506). New York, NY: McGraw-Hill.

Kane, J. M., & Freeman, H. L. (1994). Towards more effective antipsychotic treatment. *British Journal of Psychiatry 165*(Suppl. 25), 22–31.

Kang, C., Riazuddin, S., Mundorff, J., Krasnewich, D., Friedman, P., Mullikin, J. C., et al. (2010). Mutations in the lysosomal enzyme–targeting pathway and persistent stuttering. *New England Journal of Medicine, 362*(8), 677–685. doi: 10.1056/NEJMoa0902630

Kaniasty, K., & Norris, F. H. (2008). Longitudinal linkages between perceived social support and posttraumatic stress symptoms: Sequential roles of social causation and social selection. *Journal of Traumatic Stress, 21,* 274–281. doi: 10.1002/jts.20334

Kanner, A. D., Coyne, J. C., Schaefer, C., & Lazarus, R. S. (1981). Comparison of two modes of stress measurement: Daily hassles and uplifts versus major life events. *Journal of Behavioral Medicine, 4,* 1–39. doi: 10.1007/BF00844845

Kant, I. (1978). *Anthropology from a pragmatic point of view* (V. L. Dodwell, Trans.). Carbondale, IL: Southern Illinois University Press. (Original work published 1798)

Kaplan, H., & Dove, H. (1987). Infant development among the Ache of Eastern Paraguay. *Developmental Psychology, 23,* 190–198. doi: 10.1037/0012-1649.23.2.190

Kaplan, R. M., & Kronick, R. G. (2006). Marital status and longevity in the United States population. *Journal of Epidemiology and Community Health, 60*(9), 760–765. doi: 10.1136/jech.2005.037606

Kaplan, R. M., & Saccuzzo, D. P. (2001). *Psychological testing: Principles, applications, and issues* (5th ed.). Belmont, CA: Wadsworth/Thomson Learning.

Karau, S. J., & Williams, K. D. (1993). Social loafing: A meta-analytic review and theoretical integration. *Journal of Personality and Social Psychology, 65,* 681–706. doi: 10.1037/0022-3514.65.4.681

Karraker, A., DeLamater, J., & Schwartz, C. R. (2011). Sexual frequency decline from midlife to later life. *Journals of Gerontology: Series B. Psychological Sciences and Social Sciences, 66B*(4), 502–512. doi: 10.1093/geronb/gbr058

Kasai, K., Yamasue, H., Gilbertson, M. W., Shenton, M. E., Rauch, S. L., & Pitman, R. K. (2008). Evidence for acquired pregenual anterior cingulate gray matter loss from a twin study of combat-related posttraumatic stress disorder. *Biological Psychiatry, 63*(6), 550–556. doi: 10.1016/j.biopsych.2007.06.022

Kass, A. E., Kolko, R. P., & Wilfley, D. E. (2013). Psychological treatments for eating disorders. *Current Opinion in Psychiatry, 26*(6), 549–555. doi: 510.1097/YCO.1090b1013e328365a328330e

Katzenberg, D., Young, T., Finn, L., Lin, L., & Mignot, E. (1998). A CLOCK polymorphism associated with human diurnal preference. *Sleep, 21,* 569–576.

Katzmarzyk, P. T., Church, T. S., Craig, C. L., & Bouchard, C. (2009). Sitting time and mortality from all causes, cardiovascular disease, and cancer. *Medicine and Science in Sports and Exercise, 41*(5), 998–1005. doi: 10.1249/MSS.0b013e3181930355

Kavé, G., Eyal, N., Shorek, A., & Cohen-Mansfield, J. (2008). Multilingualism and cognitive state in the oldest old. *Psychology and Aging, 23*(1), 70–78. doi: 10.1037/0882-7974.23.1.70

Kawashima, R., Okita, K., Yamazaki, R., Tajima, N., Yoshida, H., Taira, M., et al. (2005). Reading aloud and arithmetic calculation improve frontal function of people with dementia. *Journals of Gerontology: Series A. Biological Sciences and Medical Sciences, 60*(3), 380–384. doi: 10.1093/gerona/60.3.380

Kazek, B., Jamroz, E., Kajor, M., Grzybowska-Chlebowczyk, U., Ciupińska-Kajor, M., & Woś, H. (2013). The content of serotonin cells in duodenal biopsies of autistic patients. *Pediatria Polska, 88*(3), 230–235. doi: 10.1016/j.pepo.2013.03.005

Kearney, C. A., Albano, A. M., Eisen, A. R., Allan, W. D., & Barlow, D. H. (1997). The phenomenology of panic disorder in youngsters: An empirical study of a clinical sample. *Journal of Anxiety Disorders, 11,* 49–62. doi: 10.1016/S0887-6185(96)00034-5

Kearney, C. A., & Trull, T. J. (2012). *Abnormal psychology and life: A dimensional approach.* Belmont, CA: Wadsworth/Cengage Learning.

Kearns, D. N., Weiss, S. J., Schindler, C. W., & Panlilio, L. V. (2005). Conditioned inhibition of cocaine seeking in rats. *Journal of Experimental Psychology: Animal Behavior Processes, 31,* 247–253. doi: 10.1037/0097-7403.31.2.247

Keenan, J. P., Nelson, A., O'Connor, M., & Pascual-Leone, A. (2001). Self-recognition and the right hemisphere. *Nature*, *409*(6818), 305. doi: 10.1038/35053167

Keith, S. J., Regier, D. A., & Rae, D. S. (1991). Schizophrenic disorders. In L. N. Robins & D. A. Regier (Eds.), *Psychiatric disorders in America* (pp. 33–52). New York, NY: Free Press.

Keller, P. S., Blincoe, S., Gilbert, L. R., Dewall, C. N., Haak, E. A., & Widiger, T. (2014). Narcissism in romantic relationships: A dyadic perspective. *Journal of Social and Clinical Psychology*, *33*(1), 25–50. doi: 10.1521/jscp.2014.33.1.25

Kellogg, W. N., & Kellogg, L. A. (1933). *The ape and the child*. New York, NY: McGraw-Hill.

Kelly, T. L., Neri, D. F., Grill, J. T., Ryman, D., Hunt, P. D., Dijk, D. J., et al. (1999). Nonentrained circadian rhythms of melatonin in submariners scheduled to an 18-hour day. *Journal of Biological Rhythms*, *14*, 190–196. doi: 10.1177/074873099129000597

Keltner, D., & Ekman, P. (2000). Facial expression of emotion. In M. Lewis & J. Haviland-Jones (Eds.), *Handbook of emotions* (2nd ed., pp. 236–250). New York, NY: Guilford Press.

Kendall-Tackett, K., & Hale, T. W. (2010). The use of antidepressants in pregnant and breastfeeding women: A review of recent studies. *Journal of Human Lactation*, *26*(2), 187–195. doi: 10.1177/0890334409342071

Kendler, K. S., Walters, E. E., Neale, M. C., Kessler, R. C., Heath, A. C., & Eaves, L. J. (1995). The structure of the genetic and environmental risk factors for six major psychiatric disorders in women: Phobia, generalized anxiety disorder, panic disorder, bulimia, major depression, and alcoholism. *Archives of General Psychiatry*, *52*(5), 374–383. doi: 10.1001/archpsyc.1995.03950170048007

Kendzerska, T., Gershon, A. S., Hawker, G., Leung, R. S., & Tomlinson, G. (2014). Obstructive sleep apnea and risk of cardiovascular events and all-cause mortality: A decade-long historical cohort study. *PLoS Medicine*, *11*(2), e1001599. doi: 10.1371/journal.pmed.1001599

Kennedy, D. P., Gläscher, J., Tyszka, J. M., & Adolphs, R. (2009). Personal space regulation by the human amygdala. *Nature Neuroscience*, *12*, 1226–1227. doi: 10.1038/nn.2381

Kennedy, G. C. (1953). The role of depot fat in the hypothalamic control of food intake in the rat. *Proceedings of the Royal Society of London, Series B: Biological Sciences*, *140*, 578–592. doi: 10.1098/rspb.1953.0009

Kennis, M., Rademaker, A. R., & Geuze, E. (2013). Neural correlates of personality: An integrative review. *Neuroscience & Biobehavioral Reviews*, *37*(1), 73–95. doi: 10.1016/j.neubiorev.2012.10.012

Kenrick, D. T., Griskevicius, V., Neuberg, S. L., & Schaller, M. (2010). Renovating the pyramid of needs: Contemporary extensions

built upon ancient foundations. *Perspectives on Psychological Science*, *5*(3), 292–314. doi: 10.1177/1745691610369469

Kessler, R. C., Angermeyer, M., Anthony, J. C., De Graaf, R., Demyttenaere, K., Gasquet, I., et al. (2007). Lifetime prevalence and age-of-onset distributions of mental disorders in the World Health Organization's World Mental Health Survey Initiative. *World Psychiatry*, *6*(3), 168–176.

Kessler, R. C., Berglund, P., Demler, O., Jin, R., Koretz, D., Merikangas, K. R., et al. (2003). The epidemiology of major depressive disorder: Results from the National Comorbidity Survey Replication (NCS-R). *JAMA: Journal of the American Medical Association*, *289*(23), 3095–3105. doi: 10.1001/jama.289.23.3095

Kessler, R. C., Chiu, W. T., Demler, O., & Walters, E. E. (2005). Prevalence, severity, and comorbidity of twelve-month DSM-IV disorders in the National Comorbidity Survey Replication (NCS-R). *Archives of General Psychiatry*, *62*, 617–627. doi: 10.1001/archpsyc.62.6.617

Kessler, R. C., Sonnega, A., Bromet, E., Hughes, M., & Nelson, C. B. (1995). Posttraumatic stress disorder in the National Comorbidity Survey. *Archives of General Psychiatry*, *52*, 1048–1060. doi: 10.1001/archpsyc.1995.03950240066012

Kety, S. S., Rosenthal, D., Wender, P. H., & Schulsinger, F. (1968). The types and prevalence of mental illness in the biological and adoptive families of adopted schizophrenics. In D. Rosenthal & S. S. Kety (Eds.), *The transmission of schizophrenia* (pp. 345–362). Oxford, United Kingdom: Pergamon Press.

Keys, A., Brozek, J., Henschel, A., Mickelsen, O., & Taylor, H. L. (1950). *The biology of human starvation*. Minneapolis, MN: University of Minnesota Press.

Keysers, C., & Gazzola, V. (2010). Social neuroscience: Mirror neurons recorded in humans. *Current Biology*, *20*(8), R353–R354. doi: 10.1016/j.cub.2010.03.013

Khaw, K.-T., Wareham, N., Bingham, S., Welch, A., Luben, R., & Day, N. (2008). Combined impact of health behaviours and mortality in men and women: The EPIC–Norfolk prospective population study. *PLoS Medicine*, *5*(1), e12. doi: 10.1371/journal.pmed.0050012

Khoury, B., Lecomte, T., Fortin, G., Masse, M., Therien, P., Bouchard, V., et al. (2013). Mindfulness-based therapy: A comprehensive meta-analysis. *Clinical Psychology Review*, *33*(6), 763–771. doi: 10.1016/j.cpr.2013.05.005

Kiang, L., Witkow, M. R., Baldelomar, O. A., & Fuligni, A. J. (2010). Change in ethnic identity across the high school years among adolescents with Latin American, Asian, and European backgrounds. *Journal of Youth and Adolescence*, *39*(6), 683–693. doi: 10.1007/s10964-009-9429-5

Kiehl, K. A., Smith, A. M., Hare, R. D., Mendrek, A., Forster, B. B., Brink, J., et al. (2001). Limbic abnormalities in affective processing by criminal psychopaths as revealed by functional magnetic resonance imaging. *Biological Psychiatry*, *50*(9), 677–684. doi: 10.1016/S0006-3223(01)01222-7

Kihlstrom, J. F. (1997). Hypnosis, memory, and amnesia. *Philosophical Transactions of the Royal Society B: Biological Sciences*, *352*(1362), 1727–1732. doi: 10.1098/rstb.1997.0155.

Kihlstrom, J. F., & Barnhardt, T. M. (1993). The self-regulation of memory, for better and for worse, with and without hypnosis. In D. M. Wegner & J. W. Pennebaker (Eds.), *Handbook of mental control* (pp. 88–125). Englewood Cliffs, NJ: Prentice-Hall.

Kihlstrom, J. F., & Eich, E. (1994). Altering states of consciousness. In D. Druckman & R. A. Bjork (Eds.), *Learning, remembering, and believing: Enhancing performance* (pp. 207–248). Washington, DC: National Academy Press.

Kikkert, M. A., Ribbers, G. M., & Koudstaal, P. J. (2006). Alien hand syndrome in stroke: A report of 2 cases and review of the literature. *Archives of Physical Medicine and Rehabilitation*, *87*(5), 728–732. doi: 10.1016/j.apmr.2006.02.002

Kilham, W., & Mann, L. (1974). Level of destructive obedience as a function of transmitter and executant roles in the Milgram obedience paradigm. *Journal of Personality and Social Psychology*, *29*, 696–702. doi: doi: 10.1037/h0036636

Kim, H., & Markus, H. R. (1999). Deviance or uniqueness, harmony or conformity? A cultural analysis. *Journal of Personality and Social Psychology*, *77*, 785–800. doi: 10.1037/0022-3514.77.4.785

Kim, K. H., Relkin, N. R., Lee, K. M., & Hirsch, J. (1998). Distinct cortical areas associated with native and second languages. *Nature*, *388*, 171–174. doi: 10.1038/40623

King, P. M., & Kitchener, K. S. (2002). The reflective judgment model: Twenty years of research on epistemic cognition. In B. K. Hofer & P. R. Pintrich (Eds.), *Personal epistemology: The psychology of beliefs about knowledge and knowing* (pp. 37–61). Mahwah, NJ: Erlbaum.

King-Casas, B., Sharp, C., Lomax-Bream, L., Lohrenz, T., Fonagy, P., & Montague, P. R. (2008). The rupture and repair of cooperation in borderline personality disorder. *Science*, *321*(5890), 806–810. doi: 10.1126/science.1156902

Kirk, K. M., Bailey, J. M., & Martin, N. G. (2000). Etiology of male sexual orientation in an Australian twin sample. *Psychology, Evolution and Gender*, *2*(3), 301–311. doi: http://dx.doi.org/10.1080/14616660010024418

Kitayama, S., Chua, H. F., Tompson, S., & Han, S. (2013). Neural mechanisms of dissonance: An fMRI investigation of choice justification. *NeuroImage, 69*(0), 206–212. doi: 10.1016/j.neuroimage .2012.11.034

Klauke, B., Deckert, J., Reif, A., Pauli, P., & Domschke, K. (2010). Life events in panic disorder: An update on "candidate stressors." *Depression and Anxiety, 27*(8), 716–730. doi: 10.1002/da.20667

Klein, R. A., Ratliff, K. A., Vianello, M., Adams, R. B., Jr., Bahník, S., Bernstein, M. J., et al. (2014). Data from investigating variation in replicability: A "many labs" replication project. *Journal of Open Psychology Data, 2*(1), e4. doi: http:// dx.doi.org/10.5334/jopd.ad

Klein, S. B., Cosmides, L., & Tooby, J. (2002). Decisions and the evolution of memory: Multiple systems, multiple functions. *Psychological Review, 109*, 306–329. doi: 10.1037/0033-295X.109.2.306

Kleinmuntz, B., & Szucko, J. J. (1984). A field study of the fallibility of polygraph lie detection. *Nature, 308*, 449–450. doi: 10.1038/308449a0

Klima, E. S., & Bellugi, U. (1979). *The signs of language.* Cambridge, MA: Harvard University Press.

Kline, P. (2013). *Fact and fantasy in Freudian theory (RLE: Freud).* London, United Kingdom: Routledge.

Kling, K. C., Hyde, J. S., Showers, C. J., & Buswell, B. N. (1999). Gender differences in self-esteem: A meta-analysis. *Psychological Bulletin, 125*, 470–500. doi: 10.1037/ 0033-2909.125.4.470

Klonsky, E. D. (2007). The functions of deliberate self-injury: A review of the evidence. *Clinical Psychological Review, 27*, 226–239. doi: 10.1016/j.cpr.2006.08.002

Klonsky, E. D., & Muehlenkamp, J. J. (2007). Self-injury: A research review for the practitioner. *Journal of Clinical Psychology, 63*(11), 1045–1056. doi: 10.1002/jclp.20412

Klüver, H., & Bucy, P. (1939). Preliminary analysis of functions of the temporal lobe in monkeys. *Archives of Neurology and Psychiatry, 42*, 979–1000. doi: 10.1001/ archneurpsyc.1939.02270240017001

Knickmeyer, R., Baron-Cohen, S., Raggatt, P., & Taylor, K. (2005). Foetal testosterone, social relationships, and restricted interests in children. *Journal of Child Psychology and Psychiatry, and Allied Disciplines, 46*(2), 198–210. Doi: 10.1111/j.1469-7610 .2004.00349.x

Knight, D. C., Nguyen, H. T., & Bandettini, P. A. (2003). Expression of conditional fear with and without awareness. *Proceedings of the National Academy of Sciences, 100*(25), 15280–15283. doi: 10.1073/ pnas.2535780100

Knowlton, B. J., Squire, L. R., Paulsen, J. S., Swerdlow, N. R., Swenson, M., & Butters, N. (1996). Dissociations within nondeclarative memory in Huntington's disease. *Neuropsychology, 10*(4), 538–548. doi: 10.1037/0894-4105.10.4.538

Knyazev, G. G., Slobodskoj-Plusnin, J. Y., Bocharov, A. V., & Pylkova, L. V. (2011). The default mode network and EEG alpha oscillations: An independent component analysis. *Brain Research, 1402*, 67–79. doi: 10.1016/j.brainres.2011.05.052

Kochanek, K. D., Xu, J., Murphy, S. L., Miniño, A. M., & Kung, H.-C. (2011, March 16). Deaths: Preliminary data from 2009. *National Vital Statistics Reports, 59*(4), 5. Retrieved from http://www.cdc. gov/nchs/data/nvsr/nvsr59/nvsr59_04.pdf

Koeda, T., Seki, A., Uchiyama, H., & Sadato, N. (2011). Dyslexia: Advances in clinical and imaging studies. *Brain and Development, 33*(3), 268–275. doi: 10.1016/ j.braindev.2010.11.006

Koelega, H. S., & Koster, E. P. (1974). Some experiments on sex differences in odor perception. *Annals of the New York Academy of Sciences, 237*, 234–246. doi: 10.1111/j.1749-6632.1974.tb49859.x

Koenigsberg, H. W., Teicher, M. H., Mitropoulou, V., Navalta, C., New, A. S., Trestman, R., et al. (2004). 24-h monitoring of plasma norepinephrine, MHPG, cortisol, growth hormone and prolactin in depression. *Journal of Psychiatric Research, 38*(5), 503–511. doi: 10.1016/j.jpsychires .2004.03.006

Koffka, K. (1935). *Principles of Gestalt psychology.* London, United Kingdom: Lund Humphries.

Kohlberg, L. (1969). Stage and sequence: The cognitive-developmental approach to socialization. In D. A. Goslin (Ed.), *Handbook of socialization theory and research* (p. 379). Chicago, IL: Rand McNally.

Kohlberg, L. (1981). *The philosophy of moral development: Essays on moral development* (Vol. 1). San Francisco, CA: Harper and Row.

Kohlberg, L. (1984). *Essays on moral development: The psychology of moral development* (Vol. 2). San Francisco, CA: Harper & Row.

Kohler, C. G., Turner, T. H., Bilker, W. B., Brensinger, C. M., Siegel, S. J., Kanes, S. J., et al. (2003). Facial emotion recognition in schizophrenia: Intensity effects and error pattern. *American Journal of Psychiatry, 160*, 1768–1774. doi: 10.1176/appi. ajp.106.10.1768

Kokis, J. V., Macpherson, R., Toplak, M. E., West, R. F., & Stanovich, K. E. (2002). Heuristic and analytic processing: Age trends and associations with cognitive ability and cognitive styles. *Journal of Experimental Child Psychology, 83*(1), 26–52. doi: 10.1016/S0022-0965(02) 00121-2

Komarraju, M., Karau, S. J., & Schmeck, R. R. (2009). Role of the Big Five personality traits in predicting college students' academic motivation and achievement. *Learning and Individual Differences, 19*(1), 47–52. doi: 10.1016/j.lindif.2008.07.001

Konopka, G., Bomar, J. M., Winden, K., Coppola, G., Jonsson, Z. O., Gao, F., et al. (2009). Human-specific transcriptional regulation of CNS development genes by *FOXP2. Nature, 462*, 213–217. doi: 10.1038/ nature08549

Kopell, B. H., Machado, A. G., & Rezai, A. R. (2005). Not your father's lobotomy: Psychiatric surgery revisited. In Congress of Neurological Surgeons (2011). *Clinical neurosurgery* (Vol. 52; pp. 315–330). Retrieved from http://book2.neurosurgeon .org/?defaultarticle=&defaultnode=2671& layout=22&pagefunction=Load%20 Layout

Kopelman, M. D. (2002). Disorders of memory. *Brain, 125*(10), 2152–2190. doi: 10.1093/brain/awf229

Kosonogov, V. (2012). Why the mirror neurons cannot support action understanding. *Neurophysiology, 44*(6), 499–502. doi: 10.1007/s11062-012-9327-4

Kosslyn, S. M. (1978). Measuring the visual angle of the mind's eye. *Cognitive Psychology, 10*, 356–389. doi: 10.1016/ 0010-0285(78)90004-X

Kosslyn, S. M. (1980). *Image and mind.* Cambridge, MA: Harvard University Press.

Kosslyn, S. M. (1994). *Elements of graph design.* New York, NY: Freeman.

Kotov, R., Gamez, W., Schmidt, F., & Watson, D. (2010). Linking "big" personality traits to anxiety, depressive, and substance use disorders: A meta-analysis. *Psychological Bulletin, 136*(5), 768–821. doi: 10.1037/ a0020327

Krain, A. L., & Castellanos, F. X. (2006). Brain development and ADHD. *Clinical Psychology Review, 26*(4), 433–444. doi: 10.1016/j.cpr.2006.01.005

Kramer, B. J. (1993). Expanding the conceptualization of caregiver coping: The importance of relationship-focused coping strategies. *Family Relations, 42*(4), 383–391. doi: 10.2307/585338

Kravitz, D. A., & Martin, B. (1986). Ringelmann rediscovered: The original article. *Journal of Personality and Social Psychology, 50*, 936–941. doi: 10.1037/ 0022-3514.50.5.936

Krebs, H., Hogan, N., Hening, W., Adamovich, S., & Poizner, H. (2001). Procedural motor learning in Parkinson's disease. *Experimental Brain Research, 141*, 425–437. doi: 10.1007/s002210100871

Krijn, M., Emmelkamp, P. M. G., Ólafsson, R. P., Bouwman, M., van Gerwen, L. J., Spinhoven, P., et al. (2007). Fear of flying treatment methods: Virtual reality exposure vs. cognitive behavioral therapy. *Aviation, Space, and Environmental Medicine, 78*(2), 121–128.

Kross, E., Verduyn, P., Demiralp, E., Park, J., Lee, D. S., Lin, N., et al. (2013). Facebook use predicts declines in subjective well-being in young adults. *PLoS One, 8*(8), e69841. doi: 10.1371/journal.pone.0069841

Krous, H. (2014). Sudden infant death syndrome (SIDS), sudden unexpected death in infancy (SUDI), and sudden unexplained death in childhood (SUDC). In K. A. Collins & R. W. Byard (Eds.), *Forensic pathology of infancy and childhood* (pp. 193–206). New York, NY: Springer.

Krueger, R. F., South, S., Johnson, W., & Iacono, W. (2008). The heritability of personality is not always 50%: Gene–environment interactions and correlations between personality and parenting. *Journal of Personality, 76*(6), 1485–1522. doi: 10.1111/j.1467-6494.2008.00529.x

Kruger, J., & Dunning, D. (1999). Unskilled and unaware of it: How difficulties in recognizing one's own incompetence lead to inflated self-assessments. *Journal of Personality and Social Psychology, 77*, 1121–1134. doi: 10.1037/0022-3514.77.6.1121

Kuhl, B. A., Dudukovic, N. M., Kahn, I., & Wagner, A. D. (2007). Decreased demands on cognitive control reveal the neural processing benefits of forgetting. *Nature Neuroscience, 10*, 908–914. doi: 10.1038/nn1918

Kuhl, P. K. (2007). Is speech learning "gated" by the social brain? *Developmental Science, 10*(1), 110–120. doi: 10.1111/j.1467-7687.2007.00572.x

Kuhl, P. K. (2010). Brain mechanisms in early language acquisition. *Neuron, 67*(5), 713–727. doi: 10.1016/j.neuron.2010.08.038

Kuhn, D. (2008). Formal operations from a twenty-first century perspective. *Human Development, 51*(1), 48–55. doi: 10.1159/000113155

Kulik, J. A., Mahler, H. I. M., & Moore, P. J. (1996). Social comparison and affiliation under threat: Effects of recovery from major surgery. *Journal of Personality and Social Psychology, 71*, 967–979. doi: 10.1037/0022-3514.71.5.967

Kuo, L. E., Czarnecka, M., Kitlinska, J. B., Tilan, J. U., Kvetňanský, R., & Zukowska, Z. (2009). Chronic stress, combined with a high-fat/high-sugar diet, shifts sympathetic signaling toward neuropeptide Y and leads to obesity and the metabolic syndrome. In R. Kvetňanský, G. Aguilera, D. Goldstein, D. Jezova, O. Krizanova, E. L. Sabban, & K. Pacak (Eds.), *Stress, neurotransmitters, and hormones: Neuroendocrine and genetic mechanisms* (pp. 232–237). New York, NY: Wiley–Blackwell.

Kurihara, T., Kato, M., Sakamoto, S., Reverger, R., & Kitamura, T. (2000). Public attitudes towards the mentally ill: A cross-cultural study between Bali and Tokyo. *Psychiatry and Clinical Neurosciences, 54*, 547–552. doi: 10.1046/j.1440-1819.2000.00751.x

Kurina, L. M., Knutson, K. L., Hawkley, L. C., Cacioppo, J. T., Lauderdale, D. S., & Ober, C. (2011). Loneliness is associated with sleep fragmentation in a communal society. *Sleep, 34*(11), 1519–1526. doi: 10.5665/sleep.1390

Kurland, J. A. (1977). Kin selection in the Japanese monkey. *Contributions to Primatology, 12*, 1–145. doi: 10.1525/aa.1980.82.1.02a00600

Kurtz, R. G., Rozin, P., & Teitelbaum, P. (1972). Ventromedial hypothalamic hyperphagia in the hypophysectomized weanling rat. *Journal of Comparative and Physiological Psychology, 80*(1), 19–25. doi: 10.1037/h0032820

Kurzban, R., & Houser, D. (2005). Experiments investigating cooperative types in humans: A complement to evolutionary theory and simulations. *Proceedings of the National Academy of Sciences, 102*, 1803–1807. doi: 10.1073/pnas.0408759102

Kuster, J. M. (2005). Folk myths about stuttering. Retrieved from http://www.mnsu.edu/comdis/kuster/Infostuttering/folkmyths.html

Ladd, G. W., Buhs, E. S., & Seid, M. (2000). Children's initial sentiments about kindergarten: Is school liking an antecedent of early classroom participation and achievement? *Merrill–Palmer Quarterly: Journal of Developmental Psychology, 46*(2), 255–279.

Lagerspetz, K. M. J., & Lagerspetz, K. Y. H. (1983). Genes and aggression. In E. C. Simmel, M. E. Hahn, & J. K. Walters (Eds.), *Aggressive behavior: Genetic and neural approaches* (pp. 89–102). Hillsdale, NJ: Erlbaum.

Lahey, B. B. (1995). *Psychology: An introduction* (5th ed.). Dubuque, IA: WCB Brown & Benchmark.

Lai, C. S., Fisher, S. E., Hurst, J. A., Vargha-Khadem, F., & Monaco, A. P. (2001). A forkhead-domain gene is mutated in a severe speech and language disorder. *Nature, 413*, 519–523. doi: 10.1038/35097076

Lakin, J. L., Chartrand, T. L., & Arkin, R. M. (2008). I am too just like you: Nonconscious mimicry as an automatic behavioral response to social exclusion. *Psychological Science, 19*(8), 816–822. doi: 10.1111/j.1467-9280.2008.02162.x

Lane, A., Young, R., Baker, A., & Angley, M. (2010). Sensory processing subtypes in autism: Association with adaptive behavior. *Journal of Autism and Developmental Disorders, 40*(1), 112–122. doi: 10.1007/s10803-009-0840-2

Lane, R. E. (2001). Self-reliance and empathy: The enemies of poverty—and of the poor. *Political Psychology, 22*(3), 473–492. doi: 10.1111/0162-895X.00250

Lange, C. G. (1912). The mechanisms of the emotions. In B. Rand (Ed.), *The classical psychologists* (pp. 672–284). Boston, MA: Houghton Mifflin. (Original work published 1885)

Langenecker, S. A., Weisenbach, S. L., Giordani, B., Briceño, E. M., Guidotti Breting, L. M., Schallmo, M.-P., et al. (2012). Impact of chronic hypercortisolemia on affective processing. *Neuropharmacology. 62*(1), 217–225. doi: 10.1016/j.neuropharm.2011.07.006

Langley, J. (1921). *The autonomic nervous system.* Cambridge, United Kingdom: Heffer & Sons.

Langlois, J. H., Roggman, L. A., & Rieser-Danner, L. A. (1990). Infants' differential social responses to attractive and unattractive faces. *Developmental Psychology, 26*(1), 153–159. doi: 10.1037/0012-1649.26.1.153

Largo, R. H., Molinari, L., von Siebenthal, K., & Wolfensberger, U. (1996). Does a profound change in toilet-training affect development of bowel and bladder control? *Developmental Medicine and Child Neurology, 38*, 1106–1116. doi: 10.1111/j.1469-8749.1996.tb15074.x

Larrick, R. P., Nisbett, R. E., & Morgan, J. N. (1993). Who uses the cost–benefit rules of choice? Implications for the normative status of microeconomic theory. *Organization Behavior and Human Decision Processes, 56*, 331–347. doi: 10.1006/obhd.1993.1058

Larson, C. M., Pillsworth, E. G., & Haselton, M. G. (2012). Ovulatory shifts in women's attractions to primary partners and other men: Further evidence of the importance of primary partner sexual attractiveness. *PLoS One, 7*(9), e44456. doi: 10.1371/journal.pone.0044456

Lassek, W. D., & Gaulin, S. J. C. (2009). Costs and benefits of fat-free muscle mass in men: Relationship to mating success, dietary requirements, and native immunity. *Evolution and Human Behavior, 30*(5), 322–328. doi: 10.1016/j.evolhumbehav.2009.04.002

Latané, B., & Darley, J. M. (1968). Group inhibition of bystander intervention in emergencies. *Journal of Personality and Social Psychology, 10*, 215–221. doi: 10.1037/h0026570

Latané, B., Williams, K., & Harkins, S. (1979). Many hands make light the work: The causes and consequences of social loafing. *Journal of Personality and Social Psychology, 37*, 822–832. doi: 10.1037/0022-3514.37.6.822

Lau, J., & Chan, J. (2009). About critical thinking. Retrieved from http://philosophy.hku.hk/think/critical/improve.php

Laumann, E. O., Paik, A., Glasser, D. B., Kang, J.-H., Wang, T., Levinson, B., et al. (2006). A cross-national study of subjective sexual well-being among older women and men: Findings from the Global Study of Sexual Attitudes and Behaviors. *Archives of Sexual Behavior, 35*(2), 145–161. doi: 10.1007/s10508-005-9005-3

Law, M., & Tang, J. (1995). An analysis of the effectiveness of interventions intended to help people stop smoking. *Archives of Internal Medicine, 155*(18), 1933–1941. doi: 10.1001/archinte.1995.00430180025004

Lawrence, E., Rothman, A. D., Cobb, R. J., Rothman, M. T., & Bradbury, T. N. (2008). Marital satisfaction across the transition to parenthood. *Journal of Family Psychology, 22*(1), 41–50. doi: 10.1037/0893-3200.22.1.41

Lazar, S. W., Bush, G., Gollub, R. L., Fricchinoe, G. L., Khalsa, G., & Benson, H. (2000). Functional brain mapping of the relaxation response and meditation. *NeuroReport, 11,* 1581–1585. doi: 10.1097/00001756-200005150-00041

Lazar, S. W., Kerr, C., Wasserman, R. H., Gray, J. R., Greve, D., Treadway, M. T., et al. (2005). Meditation experience is associated with increased cortical thickness. *Neuro-Report, 16,* 1893–1897. doi: 10.1097/01.wnr.0000186598.66243.19

Lazarus, A. A. (2005). Multimodal therapy. In J. C. Norcross & M. R. Goldfried (Eds.), *Handbook of psychotherapy integration* (pp. 105–120). New York, NY: Oxford University Press.

Lazarus, R. S. (1966). *Psychological stress and the coping process.* New York, NY: McGraw-Hill.

Le, N., Loll, F., & Pinkwart, N. (2013). Operationalizing the continuum between well-defined and ill-defined problems for educational technology. *IEEE Transactions on Learning Technologies, 6*(3), 258–270. doi: http://doi.ieeecomputersociety.org/10.1109/TLT.2013.16

Le, Q. A., Doctor, J. N., Zoellner, L. A., & Feeny, N. C. (2014). Cost-effectiveness of prolonged exposure therapy versus pharmacotherapy and treatment choice in post-traumatic stress disorder (the optimizing PTSD treatment trial): A doubly randomized preference trial. *Journal of Clinical Psychiatry, 75*(3), 222–230. doi: 10.4088/JCP.13m08719

Le Lionnais, F. (1960). *The Orion book of time.* New York, NY: Orion.

Lea, M., & Spears, R. (1991). Computer-mediated communication, de-individuation and group decision-making. *International Journal of Man–Machine Studies, 34,* 283–301. doi: 10.1016/0020-7373(91)90045-9

Leaper, C., & Ayres, M. M. (2007). A meta-analytic review of gender variations in adults' language use: Talkativeness, affiliative speech, and assertive speech. *Personality and Social Psychology Review, 11*(4), 328–363. doi: 10.1177/1088868307302221

Leary, M. R. (2004). *The curse of the self: Self-awareness, egotism, and the quality of human life.* New York, NY: Oxford University Press.

Leary, M. R., & Downs, D. L. (1995). Interpersonal functions of the self-esteem motive: The self-esteem system as a sociometer. In M. H. Kernis (Ed.), *Efficacy, agency, and self-esteem* (pp. 123–144). New York, NY: Plenum.

Leary, M. R., Tambor, E. S., Terdal, S. K., & Downs, D. L. (1995). Self-esteem as an interpersonal monitor: The sociometer hypothesis. *Journal of Personality and Social Psychology, 68,* 518–530. doi: 10.1037/0022-3514.68.3.518

LeBlanc, S. A. (2003). *Constant battles: The myth of the peaceful, noble savage.* New York, NY: St. Martin's Press.

LeDoux, J. E. (2000). Emotion circuits in the brain. *Annual Review of Neuroscience, 23,* 155–184. doi: 10.1146/annurev.neuro.23.1.155

LeDoux, J. E. (2014). Coming to terms with fear. *Proceedings of the National Academy of Sciences, 111*(8), 2871–2878. doi: 10.1073/pnas.1400335111

LeDoux, J. E., Cicchetti, P., Xagoraris, A., & Romanski, L. M. (1990). The lateral amygdaloid nucleus: Sensory interface of the amygdala in fear conditioning. *Journal of Neuroscience, 10,* 1062–1069.

Lee, G. P., Meador, K. J., Loring, D. W., Allison, J. D., Brown, W. S., Paul, L. K., et al. (2004). Neural substrates of emotion as revealed by functional magnetic resonance imaging. *Cognitive and Behavioral Neurology, 17*(1), 9–17. doi: 10.1097/00146965-200403000-00002

Lee, H., Park, S.-A., Lee, Y.-A., & Cameron, G. T. (2010). Assessment of motion media on believability and credibility: An exploratory study. *Public Relations Review, 36,* 310–312. doi: 10.1016/j.pubrev.2010.04.003

Lee, H. S. (2010). Change in the singular racial concept of American society. *International Area Review, 13*(3), 51–72. doi: 10.1177/223386591001300303

Lee, J.-Y., Bachrach, D. G., & Lewis, K. (2014). Social network ties, transactive memory, and performance in groups. *Organization Science, 25*(3), 951–967. doi: 10.1287/orsc.2013.0884

Lee, M. R., Okazaki, S., & Yoo, H. C. (2006). Frequency and intensity of social anxiety in Asian Americans and European Americans. *Cultural Diversity and Ethnic Minority Psychology, 12*(2), 291–305. doi: 10.1037/1099-9809.12.2.291

Leichsenring, F. (2005). Are psychodynamic and psychoanalytic therapies effective? A review of empirical data. *International Journal of Psychoanalysis, 86,* 841–868. doi: 10.1516/RFEE-LKPN-B7TF-KPDU

Leichsenring, F., & Rabung, S. (2008). Effectiveness of long-term psychodynamic psychotherapy: A meta-analysis. *JAMA: Journal of the American Medical Association, 300*(13), 1551–1565. doi: 10.1001/jama.300.13.1551

Leichtman, M. (1995). Behavioral observations. In J. N. Butcher (Ed.), *Clinical personality assessment: Practical approaches* (pp. 251–266). New York, NY: Oxford University Press.

LePine, J. A., & Van Dyne, L. (1998). Predicting voice behavior in work groups. *Journal of Applied Psychology, 83,* 853–868. doi: 10.1037/0021-9010.83.6.853

Lerner, M. J., & Miller, D. T. (1978). Just world research and the attribution process: Looking back and ahead. *Psychological Bulletin, 85,* 1030–1051. doi: 10.1037/0033-2909.85.5.1030

Leroi, A. M. (2006). The future of neo-eugenics. *EMBO Reports, 7*(12), 1184–1187. doi: 10.1038/sj.embor.7400860

Leung, A. K.-Y., Kim, Y.-H., Zhang, Z.-X., Tam, K.-P., & Chiu, C.-Y. (2011). Cultural construction of success and epistemic motives moderate American–Chinese differences in reward allocation biases. *Journal of Cross-Cultural Psychology, 43*(1), 46–52. doi: 10.1177/0022022111405660

LeVay, S. (1991). A difference in hypothalamic structure between heterosexual and homosexual men. *Science, 253,* 1034–1037. doi: 10.1126/science.1887219

Levenson, R. W., Ekman, P., & Friesen, W. V. (1990). Voluntary facial action generates emotion-specific autonomic nervous system activity. *Psychophysiology, 27,* 363–384. doi: 10.1111/j.1469-8986.1990.tb02330.x

Leventhal, H., & Watts, J. C. (1966). Sources of resistance to fear-arousing communications on smoking and lung cancer. *Journal of Personality, 34,* 155–175. doi: 10.1111/j.1467-6494.1966.tb01706.x

Levine, M., Taylor, P. J., & Best, R. (2011). Third parties, violence, and conflict resolution. *Psychological Science, 22*(3), 406–412. doi: 10.1177/0956797611398495

Levinson, D., Darrow, C. M., Klein, E. B., Levinson, M. H., & McKee, B. (1974). The psychosocial development of men in early adulthood and the mid-life transition. In D. Ricks, A. Thomas, and M. Roff (Eds.), *Life history research in psychopathology* (Vol. 3, pp. 250–271). Minneapolis, MN: University of Minnesota Press.

Lewis, M., & Brooks-Gunn, J. (1979). *Social cognition and the acquisition of self.* New York, NY: Plenum Press.

Li, H., Bu, Q., Chen, B., Shao, X., Hu, Z., Deng, P., et al. (2014). Mechanisms of metabonomic for a gateway drug: Nicotine priming enhances behavioral response to cocaine with modification in energy metabolism and neurotransmitter level. *PLoS One, 9*(1), e87040. doi: 10.1371/journal.pone.0087040

Li, S.-C., Lindenberger, U., Hommel, B., Aschersleben, G., Prinz, W., & Baltes, P. B. (2004). Transformations in the couplings among intellectual abilities and constituent cognitive processes across the lifespan. *Psychological Science, 15*(3), 155–163. doi: 10.1111/j.0956-7976.2004.01503003.x

Libon, D. J., McMillan, C., Avants, B., Boller, A., Morgan, B., Burkholder, L., et al. (2012). Deficits in concept formation in amyotrophic lateral sclerosis. *Neuropsychology, 26*(4), 422. doi: 10.1037/a0028668

Lichtenberg, J. D., Lachmann, F. M., & Fosshage, J. L. (2013). *The clinical exchange: Techniques derived from self and motivational systems* (Vol. 16). London, United Kingdom: Routledge.

Lichtenstein, E., Harris, D. E., Birchler, G. R., Wahl, J. M., & Schmahl, D. P. (1973).

Comparison of rapid smoking, warm, smoky air, and attention placebo in the modification of smoking behavior. *Journal of Consulting and Clinical Psychology, 40,* 92–98. doi: 10.1037/h0034039

Lieberman, J. D., Solomon, S., Greenberg, J., & McGregor, H. A. (1999). A hot new way to measure aggression: Hot sauce allocation. *Aggressive Behavior, 25*(5), 331–348. doi: 10.1002/(SICI)1098–2337(1999)25: 5<331:AID-AB2>3.0.CO;2-1

Light, K. C., Grewen, K. M., & Amico, J. A. (2005). More frequent partner hugs and higher oxytocin levels are linked to lower blood pressure and heart rate in premeno-pausal women. *Biological Psychology, 69*(1), 5–21. doi: 10.1016/j.biopsycho.2004 .11.002

Liguori, A., Hughes, J. R., & Grass, J. A. (1997). Absorption and subjective effects of caffeine from coffee, cola and capsules. *Pharmacology Biochemistry and Behavior, 58*(3), 721–726. doi: 10.1016/s0091-3057(97)00003-8

Likert, R. (1932). A technique for the measurement of attitudes. *Archives of Psychology, 140,* 44–53.

Lilly, I. C. (1967). *The mind of the dolphin.* New York, NY: Doubleday.

Linehan, M. M., Armstrong, H. E., Suarez, A., Allmon, D., & Heard, H. L. (1991). Cognitive-behavioral treatment of chronically parasuicidal borderline patients. *Archives of General Psychiatry, 48*(12), 1060–1064. doi: 10.1001/archpsyc.1991 .01810360024003

Lisman, S. A. (1974). Alcoholic "blackout": State dependent learning? *Archives of General Psychiatry, 30,* 46–53. doi: 10.1001/ archpsyc.1974.01760070030005

Little, A. C., Jones, B. C., DeBruine, L. M., & Feinberg, D. R. (2008). Symmetry and sexual dimorphism in human faces: Interrelated preferences suggest both signal quality. *Behavioral Ecology, 19*(4), 902–908. doi: 10.1093/beheco/arn049

Liversedge, T., & Hirsch, N. (2010). Coma. *Anaesthesia & Intensive Care Medicine, 11*(9), 337–339. doi: 10.1016/j.mpaic.2010 .05.008

Livingstone, M. S., & Hubel, D. H. (1984). Anatomy and physiology of a color system in the primate visual cortex. *Journal of Neuroscience, 4,* 309–356.

Livshits, G., Kato, B. S., Wilson, S. G., & Spector, T. D. (2007). Linkage of genes to total lean body mass in normal women. *Journal of Clinical Endocrinology and Metabolism, 92*(8), 3171–3176. doi: http:// dx.doi.org/10.1210/jc.2007-0418

Lloyd-Richardson, E., Perrine, N., Dierker, L., & Kelley, M. L. (2007). Characteristics and functions of non-suicidal self-injury in a community sample of adolescents. *Psychological Medicine, 37,* 1183–1192. doi: http://dx.doi.org/10.1017/ S003329170700027X http://dx.doi. org/10.1017/S003329170700027X

Loe, I. M., & Feldman, H. M. (2007). Academic and educational outcomes of children with ADHD: Literature review and proposal for future research. *Ambulatory Pediatrics, 7*(Suppl. 1), 82–90. doi: 10.1093/jpepsy/jsl054

Loehlin, J. C., McCrae, R. R., Costa, P. T., & John, O. P. (1998). Heritabilities of common and measure-specific components of the Big Five personality factors. *Journal of Research in Personality, 32,* 431–453. doi: 10.1006/jrpe.1998.2225

Loftus, E. F. (1979). *Eyewitness testimony.* Cambridge, MA: Harvard University Press.

Loftus, E. F. (1997). Creating false memories. *Scientific American, 277*(3), 70–75.

Loftus, E. F. (2003). Our changeable memories: Legal and practical implications. *Nature Reviews Neuroscience, 4,* 231–234. doi: 10.1038/nrn1054

Loftus, E. F., & Palmer, J. C. (1974). Reconstruction of automobile destruction: An example of the interaction between language and memory. *Journal of Verbal Learning and Verbal Behavior, 13,* 585–589. doi: 10.1016/S0022-5371(74)80011-3

Luo, Y., Hawkley, L. C., Waite, L. J., & Cacioppo, J. T. (2012). Loneliness, health, and mortality in old age: A national longitudinal study. *Social Science & Medicine, 74*(6), 907–914. doi: 10.1016/j.socscimed .2011.11.028

Luo, Y., & Waite, L. J. (2014). Loneliness and mortality among older adults in China. *Journals of Gerontology: Series B. Psychological Sciences and Social Sciences, 69*(4), 633–645. doi: 10.1093/geronb/ gbu007

Lovaas, O. I. (1996). The UCLA young autism model of service delivery. In C. Maurice, G. Green, & S. C. Luce (Eds.), *Behavioral intervention for young children with autism: A manual for parents and professionals* (pp. 241–248). Austin, TX: Pro-Ed.

Lovaas, O. I., Freitag, G., Kinder, M. I., Rubenstein, B. D., Schaeffer, B., & Simmons, J. Q. (1966). Establishment of social reinforcers in two schizophrenic children on the basis of food. *Journal of Experimental Child Psychology, 4*(2), 109–125. doi: 10.1016/0022-0965(66)90011-7

Lowry, R. (Ed.). (1973). *A. H. Maslow: An intellectual portrait.* Monterey, CA: Brooks/ Cole.

Lubow, R. E., Ingberg-Sachs, Y., Salstein-Orda, N., & Gewirtz, J. C. (1992). Latent inhibition in low and high "psychotic-prone" normal subjects. *Personality and Individual Differences, 15,* 563–572. doi: 10.1016/ 0191-8869(92)90197-W

Lubow, R. E., & Moore, A. U. (1959). Latent inhibition: The effect of nonreinforced exposure to the conditioned stimulus. *Journal of Comparative and Physiological Psychology, 52,* 415–419.

Ludeke, S., Johnson, W., & Bouchard, T. J., Jr. (2013). "Obedience to traditional authority": A heritable factor underlying authoritarianism, conservatism and religiousness. *Personality and Individual Differences, 55*(4), 375–380. doi: 10.1016/j.paid.2013 .03.018

Lund, R., Christensen, U., Nilsson, C. J., Kriegbaum, M., & Hulvej Rod, N. (2014). Stressful social relations and mortality: A prospective cohort study. *Journal of Epidemiology and Community Health, 68:* 720–727. doi: 10.1136/jech-2013-203675

Luo, S., & Zhang, G. (2009). What leads to romantic attraction: Similarity, reciprocity, security, or beauty? Evidence from a speed-dating study. *Journal of Personality, 77*(4), 933–964. doi: 10.1111/j.1467-6494.2009.00570.x

Luo, S., Zhang, G., Watson, D., & Snider, A. G. (2010). Using cross-sectional couple data to disentangle the causality between positive partner perceptions and marital satisfaction. *Journal of Research in Personality, 44*(5), 665–668. doi: 10.1016/j.jrp.2010.08.006

Luo, Y., Hawkley, L. C., Waite, L. J., & Cacioppo, J. T. (2012). Loneliness, health, and mortality in old age: A national longitudinal study. *Social Science and Medicine, 74,* 907–914. doi: 10.1016/j.socscimed.2011 .11.028

Luo, Y., & Waite, L. J. (2014). Loneliness and mortality among older adults in China. *Journals of Gerontology: Series B. Psychological Sciences and Social Sciences* [Epub ahead of print]. doi: 10.1093/ geronb/gbu007

Luyckx, K., Tildesley, E. A., Soenens, B., Andrews, J. A., Hampson, S. E., Peterson, M., et al. (2011). Parenting and trajectories of children's maladaptive behaviors: A 12-year prospective community study. *Journal of Clinical Child and Adolescent Psychology, 40*(3), 468–478. doi: 10.1080/15374416.2011.563470

Lykken, D. T. (1982). Fearlessness: Its carefree charm and deadly risks. *Psychology Today, 16,* 20–28.

Lykken, D. T., & Tellegen, A. (1996). Happiness is a stochastic phenomenon. *Psychological Science, 7,* 186–189. doi: 10.1111/j.1467-9280.1996.tb00355.x

Lynn, M., & Simons, T. (2000). Predictors of male and female servers' average tip earnings. *Journal of Applied Social Psychology, 30,* 241–252. doi: 10.1111/j.1559-1816.2000.tb02314.x

Lyoo, I. K., Dager, S. R., Kim, J. E., Yoon, S. J., Friedman, S. D., Dunner, D. L., et al. (2010). Lithium-induced gray matter volume increase as a neural correlate of treatment response in bipolar disorder: A longitudinal brain imaging study. *Neuropsychopharmacology, 35*(8), 1743–1750. doi: 10.1038/npp.2010.41

Maccoby, E. E., & Martin, J. A. (1983). Socialization in the context of the family: Parent–child interaction. In P. Mussen & E. M. Hetherington (Eds.), *Handbook of child psychology* (Vol. 4, pp. 1–101). New York, NY: Wiley.

Maccoby, M. (2003). *The productive narcissist: The promise and perils of visionary leadership*. New York, NY: Broadway Books.

MacDonald, A., & Burrell, S. (2009). Infrequently performed studies in nuclear medicine: Part 2. *Journal of Nuclear Medicine Technology, 37*(1), 1–13. doi: 10.2967/jnm5.108.057851

Macleod, J., Davey Smith, G., Heslop, P., Metcalfe, C., Carroll, D., & Hart, C. (2002). Psychological stress and cardiovascular disease: Empirical demonstration of bias in a prospective observational study of Scottish men. *British Medical Journal, 324*, 1247. doi: http://dx.doi.org/10.1136/bmj.324.7348.1247

Maddi, S. (2013). *Hardiness: Turning stressful circumstances into resilient growth*. New York, NY: Springer.

Maggard, M. A., Shugarman, L. R., Suttorp, M., Maglione, M., Sugerman, H. J., Livingston, E. H., et al. (2005). Meta-analysis: Surgical treatment of obesity. *Annals of Internal Medicine, 142*(7), 547–559. doi: 10.7326/0003-4819-142-7-200504050-00013

Maher, B. (2001). Music, the brain, and Williams syndrome. *The Scientist, 15*, 20.

Maher, B. (2008). Poll results: Look who's doping. *Nature, 452*, 674–675. doi: 10.1038/452674a

Mahon, B. Z., & Caramazza, A. (2009). Concepts and categories: A cognitive neuropsychological perspective. *Annual Review of Psychology, 60*(1), 27–51. doi: 10.1146/annurev.psych.60.110707.163532

Mahon, B. Z., & Caramazza, A. (2011). What drives the organization of object knowledge in the brain? *Trends in Cognitive Sciences, 15*(3), 97–103. doi: 10.1016/j.tics.2011.01.004

Main, M., & Solomon, J. (1986). Discovery of an insecure–disorganized/disoriented attachment pattern. In T. B. Brazelton & M. W. Yogman (Eds.), *Affective development in infancy* (pp. 95–124). Westport, CT: Ablex.

Malle, B. F. (2006). The actor–observer asymmetry in attribution: A (surprising) meta-analysis. *Psychological Bulletin, 132*(6), 895–919. doi: 10.1037/0033-2909.132.6.895

Malone, E. (2006). Endangered languages. Retrieved from http://www.nsf.gov/news/special_reports/linguistics/endangered.jsp

Malt, B. C., & Smith, E. E. (1984). Correlated properties in natural categories. *Journal of Verbal Learning and Verbal Behavior, 23*, 250–269. doi: 10.1016/S0022-5371(84)90170-1

Månsson, H. (2000). Childhood stuttering: Incidence and development. *Journal of Fluency Disorders, 25*(1), 47–57. doi: 10.1016/s0094-730x(99)00023-6

Mantell, D. M. (1971). The potential for violence in Germany. *Journal of Social Issues, 27*, 101–112. doi: 10.1111/j.1540-4560.1971.tb00680.x

Mäntylä, T., & Nilsson, L.-G. (1988). Cue distinctiveness and forgetting: Effectiveness of self-generated retrieval cues in delayed recall. *Journal of Experimental Psychology: Learning, Memory, and Cognition, 14*(3), 502–509. doi: 10.1037/0278-7393.14.3.502

Marks, G. A., Shaffery, J. P., Oksenberg, A., Speciale, S. G., & Roffwarg, H. P. (1995). A functional role for REM sleep in brain maturation. *Behavioural Brain Research, 69*, 1–11. doi: 10.1016/0166-4328(95)00018-O

Markus, H. (1977). Self-schemata and processing information about the self. *Journal of Personality and Social Psychology, 35*(2), 63–78. doi: 10.1037/0022-3514.35.2.63

Markus, H. R., & Kitayama, S. (1991). Culture and the self: Implications for cognition, emotion, and motivation. *Psychological Review, 98*, 223–253. doi: 10.1037/0033-295X.98.2.224

Marmot, M. G., Rose, G., Shipley, M., & Hamilton, P. (1978). Employment grade and coronary heart disease in British civil servants. *Journal of Epidemiology and Community Health, 32*(4), 244–249. doi: 10.1136/jech.32.4.244

Marmot, M. G., Shipley, M. J., & Rose, G. (1984). Inequalities in death: Specific explanations of a general pattern? *Lancet, 323*(8384), 1003–1006. doi: 10.1016/S0140-6736(84)92337-7

Marner, L., Nyengaard, J. R., Tang, Y., & Pakkenberg, B. (2003). Marked loss of myelinated nerve fibers in the human brain with age. *Journal of Comparative Neurology, 462*(2), 144–152. doi: 10.1002/cne.10714

Marrast, L. M., Zallman, L., Woolhandler, S., Bor, D. H., & McCormick, D. (2013). Minority physicians' role in the care of underserved patients: Diversifying the physician workforce may be key in addressing health disparities. *JAMA Internal Medicine, 174*(2), 289–291. doi: 10.1001/jamainternmed.2013.12756

Marsh, A. A., & Blair, R. J. R. (2008). Deficits in facial affect recognition among antisocial populations: A meta-analysis. *Neuroscience and Biobehavioral Reviews, 32*(3), 454–465. doi: 10.1016/j.neubiorev.2007.08.003

Marshall, G. D., & Zimbardo, P. G. (1979). Affective consequences of inadequately explained physiological arousal. *Journal of Personality and Social Psychology, 37*(6), 970–988. doi: 10.1037/0022-3514.37.6.970

MarsVenus.com. (2007). Retrieved from http://www.marsvenus.com/

Martin, A., Wiggs, C. L., Ungerleider, L. G., & Haxby, J. V. (1996). Neural correlates of category-specific knowledge. *Nature, 379*, 649–652. doi: 10.1038/379649a0

Martin, P. (2008). Moderating effects of dispositional resilience on associations between hassles and psychological distress. *Journal of Applied Developmental Psychology, 30*(1), 53–60. doi: 10.1016/j.appdev.2008.10.005

Maslow, A. H. (1943). A theory of human motivation. *Psychological Review, 50*, 370–396. doi: 10.1037/h0054346

Maslow, A. H. (1950). *Self-actualizing people: A study of psychological health*. New York, NY: Grune and Stratton.

Mason, M. F., Norton, M. I., Van Horn, J. D., Wegner, D. M., Graftin, S. T., & Macrae, C. N. (2007). Wandering minds: The default network and stimulus-independent thought. *Science, 315*(5810), 393–395. doi: 10.1126/science.1131295

Mason, W. A., Capitanio, J. P., Machado, C. J., Mendoza, S. P., & Amaral, D. G. (2006). Amygdalectomy and responsiveness to novelty in rhesus monkeys (*Macaca mulatta*): Generality and individual consistency of effects. *Emotion, 6*(1), 73–81. doi: 10.1037/1528-3542.6.1.73

Masten, A. S., Hubbard, J. J., Gest, S. D., Tellegen, A., Garmezy, N., & Ramirez, M. (1999). Competence in the context of adversity: Pathways to resilience and maladaptation from childhood to late adolescence. *Development and Psychopathology, 11*(1), 143–169. doi: 10.1017/s0954579499001996

Masuda, T., & Nisbett, R. E. (2001). Attending holistically versus analytically: Comparing the context sensitivity of Japanese and Americans. *Journal of Personality and Social Psychology, 81*(5), 922–934. doi: 10.1037/0022-3514.81.5.922

Mathews, T. J., & Hamilton, B. E. (2009). Delayed childbearing: More women are having their first child later in life. Retrieved from http://www.cdc.gov/nchs/data/databriefs/db21.htm

Matsumoto, D., Consolacion, T., Yamada, H., Suzuki, R., Franklin, B. Paul, S., Ray, R., & Uchida, H. (2002). American–Japanese cultural differences in judgments of emotional expressions of different intensities. *Cognition and Emotion, 16*, 721–747. doi: 10.1080/02699930143000608

Matsumoto, D., & Hwang, H. S. (2011). Cooperation and competition in intercultural interactions. *International Journal of Intercultural Relations, 35*(5), 677–685. doi: 10.1016/j.ijintrel.2011.02.017

Matsumoto, D., Yoo, S. H., Nakagawa, S., et al. (2008). Culture, emotion regulation, and adjustment. *Journal of Personality and Social Psychology, 94*(6), 925–937. doi: 10.1037/0022-3514.94.6.925

Matthews, C. E., Chen, K. Y., Freedson, P. S., Buchowski, M. S., Beech, B. M., Pate, R. R., et al. (2008). Amount of time spent in sedentary behaviors in the United States, 2003–2004. *American Journal of Epidemiology, 167*(7), 875–881. doi: 10.1093/aje/kwm390

Maurer, D., & Maurer, C. (1988). *The world of the newborn*. New York, NY: Basic Books.

Mauro, J. (1992). Bright lights, big mystery. Retrieved from http://www.psychologytoday.com/articles/pto-19920701 2000030.html

Maxfield, M. C. (1990). *Effects of rhythmic drumming on EEG and subjective experiences* (Unpublished doctoral dissertation). Institute of Transpersonal Psychology, Menlo Park, CA.

Mayberg, H. S., Lozano, A. M., Voon, V., McNeely, H. E., Seminowicz, D., Hamani, C., et al. (2005). Deep brain stimulation for treatment-resistant depression. *Neuron, 45,* 651–660. doi: 10.1016/j.neuron.2005.02.014

Mayer, J. (1955). Regulation of energy intake and the body weight: The glucostatic theory and the lipostatic hypothesis. *Annals of the New York Academy of Sciences, 63,* 15–43. doi: 10.1111/j.1749-6632.1955.tb36543.x

Mayer, J. D., & Salovey, P. (1993). The intelligence of emotional intelligence. *Intelligence, 17,* 433–442. doi: 10.1016/0160-2896(93)90010-3

Mayer, J. D., & Salovey, P. (1997). What is emotional intelligence? In P. Salovey & D. Sluyter (Eds.), *Emotional development and emotional intelligence: Educational implications* (pp. 3–31). New York, NY: Basic Books.

Mazur, A., & Booth, A. (1998). Testosterone and dominance in men. *Behavioral and Brain Sciences, 21,* 353–363. doi: 10.1017/S0140525X98001228

Mazur, A., & Michalek, J. (1998). Marriage, divorce and male testosterone. *Social Forces, 77,* 315–331. doi: 10.1093/sf/77.1.315

Mazur, A., & Mueller, E. (1996). Facial dominance. In A. Somit & S. Peterson (Eds.), *Research in biopolitics* (Vol. 4, pp. 99–111). London, United Kingdom: JAI Press.

Mazure, C. M. (1998). Life stressors as risk factors in depression. *Clinical Psychology: Science and Practice, 5,* 291–313. doi: 10.1111/j.1468-2850.1998.tb00151.x

McArthur, L. Z., & Berry, D. S. (1987). Cross-cultural agreement in perceptions of babyfaced adults. *Journal of Cross-Cultural Psychology, 18*(2), 165–192. doi: 10.1177/0022002187018002003

McCall, M. (1997). The effects of physical attractiveness on gaining access to alcohol: When social policy meets social decision making. *Addiction, 92,* 597–600. doi: 10.1111/j.1360-0443.1997.tb02916.x

McCall, R. B. (1979). *Infants.* Cambridge, MA: Harvard University Press.

McCann, D., Barrett, A., Cooper, A., Crumpler, D., Dalen, L., Grimshaw, K., et al. (2007). Food additives and hyperactive behaviour in 3-year-old and 8/9-year-old children in the community: A randomised, double-blinded, placebo-controlled trial. *Lancet, 370*(9598), 1560–1567. doi: 10.1016/s0140-6736(07)61306-3

McCarley, R. W. (2007). Neurobiology of REM and NREM sleep. *Sleep Medicine, 8*(4), 302. doi: 10.1016/j.sleep.2007.03.005

McClelland, D. C. (1985). *Human motivation.* Glenview, IL: Scott, Foresman.

McClung, C. A. (2007). Circadian genes, rhythms and the biology of mood disorders. *Pharmacology and Therapeutics, 114*(2), 222–232. doi: 10.1016/j.pharmthera.2007.02.003

McComb, K., Baker, L., & Moss, C. (2006). African elephants show high levels of interest in the skulls and ivory of their own species. *Biology Letters, 2*(1), 26–28. doi: 10.1098/rsbl.2005.0400

McConnell, R.A., and Clark, T.K. (1991). National Academy of Sciences' opinion on parapsychology. *Journal of the American Society for Psychical Research, 85,* 333–365.

McCrae, R. R., & Costa, P. T. (1985). Updating Norman's "adequacy taxonomy": Intelligence and personality dimensions in natural language and in questionnaires. *Journal of Personality and Social Psychology, 49,* 710–721. doi: 10.1037/0022-3514.49.3.710

McCrae, R. R., & Costa, P. T. (1987). Validation of the five-factor model of personality across instruments and observers. *Journal of Personality and Social Psychology, 52,* 81–90. doi: 10.1037/0022-3514.52.1.81

McCrae, R. R., & Costa, P. T., Jr. (1997). Personality trait structure as a human universal. *American Psychologist, 52*(5), 509–516. doi: 10.1037/0003-066x.52.5.509

McCrae, R. R., Kurtz, J. E., Yamagata, S., & Terracciano, A. (2011). Internal consistency, retest reliability, and their implications for personality scale validity. *Personality and Social Psychology Review, 15*(1), 28–50. doi: 10.1177/1088868310366253

McDaniel, M. A. (2000). Big-brained people are smarter: A meta-analysis of the relationship between in vivo brain volume and intelligence. *Intelligence, 33,* 337–346. doi: 10.1016/j.intell.2004.11.005

McEwen, B. S. (2001). Invited review: Estrogens effects on the brain: Multiple sites and molecular mechanisms. *Journal of Applied Physiology, 91*(6), 2785–2801.

McEwen, B. S., & Gianaros, P. J. (2011). Stress- and allostasis-induced brain plasticity. *Annual Review of Medicine, 62*(1), 431–445. doi: 10.1146/annurev-med-052209-100430

McGaw, S., Shaw, T., & Beckley, K. (2007). Prevalence of psychopathology across a service population of parents with intellectual disabilities and their children. *Journal of Policy and Practice in Intellectual Disabilities, 4,* 11–22. doi: 10.1111/j.1741-1130.2006.00093.x

McGee, A. M., & Skinner, M. (1987). Facial asymmetry and the attribution of personality traits. *British Journal of Social Psychology, 26*(2), 181. doi: 10.1111/j.2044-8309.1987.tb00778.x

McGraw, A. P., Mellers, B. A., & Tetlock, P. E. (2005). Expectations and emotions of Olympic athletes. *Journal of Experimental Social Psychology, 41*(4), 438–446. doi: 10.1016/j.jesp.2004.09.001

McGuffin, P., Reveley, A., & Holland, A. (1982). Identical triplets: Non-identical psychosis? *British Journal of Psychiatry, 140,* 1–6. doi: 10.1192/bjp.140.1.1

McGuffin, P., Riley, B., & Plomin, R. (2001). Toward behavioral genomics. *Science, 291*(5507), 1232–1249. doi: 10.1126/science.1057264

McGurk, H., & MacDonald, J. (1976). Hearing lips and seeing voices. *Nature, 264,* 746–748. doi: 10.1038/264746a0

McKay, D. (2011). Methods and mechanisms in the efficacy of psychodynamic psychotherapy. *American Psychologist, 66*(2), 147–148. doi: 10.1037/a0021195

McKay, K. E., Halperin, J. M., Schwartz, S. T., & Sharma, V. (1994). Developmental analysis of three aspects of information processing: Sustained attention, selective attention, and response organization. *Developmental Neuropsychology, 10*(2), 121–132. doi: 10.1080/87565649409540572

McKelley, R. A., & Rochlen, A. B. (2007). The practice of coaching: Exploring alternatives to therapy for counseling-resistant men. *Psychology of Men and Masculinity, 8*(1), 53–65. doi: 10.1037/1524-9220.8.1.53

McKetin, R., McLaren, J., Lubman, D. I., & Hides, L. (2006). The prevalence of psychotic symptoms among methamphetamine users. *Addiction, 101*(10), 1473–1478. doi: 10.1111/j.1360-0443.2006.01496.x

McLean, D. E., & Link, B. G. (1994). Unraveling complexity: Strategies to refine concepts, measures, and research designs in the study of life events and mental health. In W. R. Avison & I. H. Gotlib (Eds.), *Stress and mental health: Contemporary issues and prospects for the future* (pp. 15–42). New York, NY: Plenum Press.

McNulty, J. K., Neff, L. A., & Karney, B. R. (2008). Beyond initial attraction: Physical attractiveness in newlywed marriage. *Journal of Family Psychology, 22*(1), 135–143. doi: 10.1037/0893-3200.22.1.135

McQueeny, T., Schweinsburg, B. C., Schweinsburg, A. D., Jacobus, J., Bava, S., Frank, L. R., et al. (2009). Altered white matter integrity in adolescent binge drinkers. *Alcoholism: Clinical and Experimental Research, 33*(7), 1278–1285. doi: 10.1111/j.1530-0277.2009.00953.x

Meaney, M. J. (2010). Epigenetics and the biological definition of gene ´ environment interactions. *Child Development, 81*(1), 41–79. doi: 10.1111/j.1467-8624.2009.01381.x

Mecca, A. M., Smelser, N. J., & Vasconcellos, J. (Eds.). (1989). *The social importance of self-esteem.* Berkeley, CA: University of California Press.

Medda, P., Perugi, G., Zanello, S., Ciuffa, M., & Cassano, G. B. (2009). Response to ECT in bipolar I, bipolar II and unipolar depression. *Journal of Affective Disorders, 118*(1–3), 55–59. doi: 10.1016/j.jad.2009.01.014

Meddis, R., Pearson, A., & Langford, G. (1973). An extreme case of healthy insomnia. *Electroencephalography and Clinical Neurophysiology, 35*, 213–214. Doi: 10.1016/0013-4694(73)90180-6

Mednick, S. A., & Kandel, E. (1988). Genetic and perinatal factors in violence. In T. E. Moffitt & S. A. Mednick (Eds.), *Biological contributions to crime causation* (pp. 40–54). Boston, MA: Martinus Nijhoff.

Medvec, V. H., Madey, S. F., & Gilovich, T. (1995). When less is more: Counterfactual thinking and satisfaction among Olympic medalists. *Journal of Personality and Social Psychology, 69*(4), 603–610. doi: 10.1037/0022-3514.69.4.603

Meeus, W. H. J., & Raaijmakers, Q. A. W. (1995). Obedience in modern society: The Utrecht studies. *Journal of Social Issues, 51*, 155–175. doi: 10.1111/j.1540-4560.1995.tb01339.x

Mehl, M. R., Vazire, S., Ramírez-Esparza, N., Slatcher, R. B., & Pennebaker, J. W. (2007). Are women really more talkative than men? *Science, 317*(5834), 82. doi: 10.1126/science.1139940

Meltzer, H. Y., Bobo, W. V., Lee, M. A., Cola, P., & Jayathilake, K. (2010). A randomized trial comparing clozapine and typical neuroleptic drugs in non–treatment-resistant schizophrenia. *Psychiatry Research, 177*(3), 286–293. doi: 10.1016/j.psychres.2010.02.018

Meltzoff, A. N., Kuhl, P. K., Movellan, J., & Sejnowski, T. J. (2009). Foundations for a new science of learning. *Science, 325*(5938), 284–288. doi: 10.1126/science.1175626

Melzack, R., & Wall, P. D. (1965). Pain mechanisms: A new theory. *Science, 150*, 971–979. doi: 10.1126/science.150.3699.971

Melzack, R., & Wall, P. D. (1983). *The challenge of pain.* New York, NY: Basic Books.

Mendel, G. (1865). Experiments in plant hybridization (W. Bateson & R. Blumberg, Trans.). Retrieved from http://www.esp.org/foundations/genetics/classical/gm-65-f.pdf

Mennella, J. A., & Beauchamp, G. K. (1996). The human infant's response to vanilla flavors in mother's milk and formula. *Infant Behavior and Development, 19*, 13–19. doi: 10.1016/S0163-6383(96)90040-5

Mennella, J. A., Jagnow, C. P., & Beauchamp, G. K. (2001). Prenatal and postnatal flavor learning by human infants. *Pediatrics, 107*, E88. doi: 10.1542/peds.107.6.e88

Menzel, E. W. (1978). Cognitive mapping in chimpanzees. In S. H. Hulse, H. Fowler, & W. K. Honig (Eds.), *Cognitive processes in animal behavior* (pp. 375–422). Hillsdale, NJ: Erlbaum.

Menzies, L., Chamberlain, S. R., Laird, A. R., Thelen, S. M., Sahakian, B. J., & Bullmore, E. T. (2008). Integrating evidence from neuroimaging and neuropsychological studies of obsessive-compulsive disorder: The orbitofronto-striatal model revisited. *Neuroscience and Biobehavioral Reviews, 32*(3), 525–549. doi: 10.1016/j.neubiorev.2007.09.005

Merritt, L. L., Martin, B. R., Walters, C., Lichtman, A. H., & Damaj, M. I. (2008). The endogenous cannabinoid system modulates nicotine reward and dependence. *Journal of Pharmacology and Experimental Therapeutics, 326*(2), 483–492. doi: 10.1124/jpet.108.138321

Mery, F., & Kawecki, T. J. (2005). A cost of long-term memory in *Drosophila. Science, 308*, 1148. doi: 10.1126/science.1111331

Merzenich, M. M., & Jenkins, W. M. (1993). Reorganization of cortical representations of the hand following alterations of skin inputs induced by nerve injury, skin island transfers, and experience. *Journal of Hand Therapy, 6*, 89–104. doi: 10.1016/S0894-1130(12)80290-0

Merzenich, M. M., Jenkins, W. M., Johnston, P., Schreiner, C., Miller, S. L., & Tallal, P. (1996). Temporal processing deficits of language-learning impaired children ameliorated by training. *Science, 271*, 77–81. doi: 10.1126/science.271.5245.77

Meyer, D. E., & Schvanevelt, R. W. (1971). Facilitation in recognizing pairs of words: Evidence of a dependence between retrieval operations. *Journal of Experimental Psychology, 90*, 227–234. doi: 10.1037/h0031564

Meyer-Bahlburg, H. F., Dolezal, C., Baker, S. W., & New, M. I. (2008). Sexual orientation in women with classical or non-classical congenital adrenal hyperplasia as a function of degree of prenatal androgen excess. *Archives of Sexual Behavior, 37*(1), 85–99. doi: 10.1007/s10508-007-9265-1

Meyer-Lindenberg, A., Domes, G., Kirsch, P., & Heinrichs, M. (2011). Oxytocin and vasopressin in the human brain: Social neuropeptides for translational medicine. *Nature Reviews Neuroscience, 12*(9), 524–538. doi: 10.1038/nrn3044

Michalski, D., Kohout, J., Wicherski, M., & Hart, B. (2011). 2009 doctorate employment survey. Retrieved from http://www.apa.org/workforce/publications/09-doc-empl/index.aspx

Micheau, J., & Marighetto, A. (2011). Acetylcholine and memory: A long, complex and chaotic but still living relationship. *Behavioural Brain Research, 221*(2), 424–429. doi: 10.1016/j.bbr.2010.11.052

Middleton, H., & Moncrieff, J. (2011). They won't do any harm and might do some good: Time to think again on the use of antidepressants? *British Journal of General Practice, 61*(582), 47–49. doi: 10.3399/bjgp11X548983

Mieda, M., Williams, S. C, Richardson, J. A., Tanaka, K., & Yanagisawa, M. (2006). The dorsomedial hypothalamic nucleus as a putative food-entrainable circadian pacemaker. *Proceedings of the National Academy of Sciences, 103*(32), 12150–12155. doi: 10.1073/pnas.0604189103

Milani, R. V., & Lavie, C. J. (2009). Reducing psychosocial stress: A novel mechanism of improving survival from exercise training. *American Journal of Medicine, 122*(10), 931–938. doi: 10.1016/j.amjmed.2009.03.028

Milevsky, A., Schlechter, M., Netter, S., & Keehn, D. (2007). Maternal and paternal parenting styles in adolescents: Associations with self-esteem, depression and life-satisfaction. *Journal of Child and Family Studies, 16*(1), 39–47. doi: 10.1007/s10826-006-9066-5

Milgram, S. (1963). Behavioral study of obedience. *Journal of Abnormal and Social Psychology, 67*, 371–378. doi: 10.1037/h0040525

Milgram, S. (1974). *Obedience to authority.* New York, NY: Harper & Row.

Milich, R., & Pelham, W. E. (1986). Effects of sugar ingestion on the classroom and playground behavior of attention deficit disordered boys. *Journal of Consulting and Clinical Psychology, 54*, 714–718. doi: 10.1037/0022-006X.54.5.714

Milinski, M., Semmann, D., & Jrambeck, H.-J. (2002). Reputation helps solve the "tragedy of the commons." *Nature, 415*, 424–426. doi: 10.1038/415424a

Miller, B. L., Seeley, W. W., Mychack, P., Rosen, H. J., Mena, I., & Boone, K. (2001). Neuroanatomy of the self: Evidence from patients with frontotemporal dementia. *Neurology, 57*(5), 817–821. doi: 10.1212/WNL.57.5.817

Miller, D. T., & Ross, M. (1975). Self-serving biases in the attribution of causality: Fact or fiction? *Psychological Bulletin, 82*, 213–225. doi: 10.1037/h0076486

Miller, G. A. (1956). The magical number seven, plus or minus two: Some limits on our capacity for processing information. *Psychological Review, 63*(2), 81–97. doi: 10.1037/h0043158

Miller, G. A., & Gildea, P. M. (1987). How children learn words. *Scientific American, 257*, 94–99.

Miller, J. G., & Bersoff, D. M. (1992). Culture and moral judgment: How are conflicts between justice and interpersonal responsibilities resolved? *Journal of Personality and Social Psychology, 62*(4), 541–554. doi: 10.1037/0022-3514.62.4.541

Miller, K. D., Choi, S., & Pentland, B. T. (2014). The role of transactive memory in the formation of organizational routines. *Strategic Organization, 12*(2), 109–133. doi: 10.1177/1476127014521609

Miller, N. E. (1944). Experimental studies in conflict. In J. M. Hunt (Ed.), *Personality and the behavior disorders* (pp. 431–465). New York, NY: Ronald Press.

Miller, R. (2007). Theory of the normal waking EEG: From single neurones to waveforms in the alpha, beta and gamma frequency ranges. *International Journal of Psychophysiology, 64*(1), 18–23. doi: 10.1016/j.ijpsycho.2006.07.009

Million, M., Angelakis, E., Maraninchi, M., Henry, M., Giorgi, R., Valero, R., et al. (2013). Correlation between body mass index and gut concentrations of *Lactobacillus reuteri, Bifidobacterium animalis, Methanobrevibacter smithii* and *Escherichia coli. International Journal of Obesity, 37*(11), 1460–1466. doi: 10.1038/ijo.2013.20

Millward, C., Ferriter, M., Calver, S., & Connell-Jones, G. (2008). Gluten- and casein-free diets for autistic spectrum disorder. *Cochrane Database of Systematic Reviews, 2*, CD003498. doi: 10.1002/14651858.CD003498.pub3

Milner, B. (1966). Amnesia following operation on the temporal lobe. In C. W. M. Whitty & O. L. Zangwill (Eds.), *Amnesia* (pp. 109–133). London, United Kingdom: Butterworth.

Milner, B. (1974). Hemispheric specialization: Scope and limitations. In F. O. Schmitt & F. G. Worden (Eds.), *The neurosciences: Third study program.* Cambridge, MA: MIT Press.

Milner, B. (2005). The medial temporal-lobe amnesic syndrome. *Psychiatric Clinics of North America, 28*, 599–611. doi: 10.1016/j.psc.2005.06.002

Mindess, A. (2006). *Reading between the signs* (2nd ed.). Boston, MA: Intercultural Press.

MindSign Neuromarketing. (2010). MindSign services: Neuropolitics. Retrieved from http://mindsignonline.com/services_pennsylvania.html

Mineka, S., & Cook, M. (1988). Social learning and the acquisition of snake fear in monkeys. In T. R. Zentall & B. G. Galef (Eds.), *Social learning: Psychological and biological perspectives* (pp. 51–73). Hillsdale, NJ: Erlbaum.

Mineka, S., Sutton, J., Craske, M. G., Hermans, D., & Vansteenwegen, D. (2006). Contemporary learning theory perspectives on the etiology of fears and phobias. In M. G. Craske, D. Hermans, & D. Vansteenwegen (Eds.), *Fear and learning: From basic processes to clinical implications* (pp. 75–97). Washington, DC: American Psychological Association.

Mirnics, K., Middleton, F. A., Marquez, A., Lewis, D. A., & Levitt, P. (2000). Molecular characterization of schizophrenia viewed by microarray analysis of gene expression in prefrontal cortex. *Neuron, 28*, 53. doi: 10.1016/S0896-6273(00)00085-4

Mischel, W. (1968). *Personality and assessment.* New York, NY: Wiley.

Mischel, W. (2004). Toward an integrative science of the person. *Annual Review of Psychology, 55*, 1–22. doi: 10.1146/annurev.psych.55.042902.130709

Mischel, W., Ebbesen, E. B., & Raskoff Zeiss, A. (1972). Cognitive and attentional mechanisms in delay of gratification. *Journal of*

Personality and Social Psychology, 21(2), 204–218. doi: 10.1037/h0032198

Mischel, W., & Shoda, Y. (1995). A cognitive–affective system theory of personality: Reconceptualizing situations, dispositions, dynamics, and invariance in personality structure. *Psychological Review, 102*(2), 246–268. doi: 10.1037/0033-295X.102.2.246

Mithoefer, M. C., Wagner, M. T., Mithoefer, A. T., Jerome, L., & Doblin, R. (2011). The safety and efficacy of ±3,4-methylenedioxymethamphetamine–assisted psychotherapy in subjects with chronic, treatment-resistant posttraumatic stress disorder: The first randomized controlled pilot study. *Journal of Psychopharmacology, 25*(4), 439–452. doi: 10.1177/0269881110378371

Mitchell, B. A., & Lovegreen, L. D. (2009). The empty nest syndrome in midlife families. *Journal of Family Issues, 30*(12), 1651–1670. doi: 10.1177/0192513x09339020

Mobbs, D., Lau, H. C., Jones, O. D., & Frith, C. D. (2007). Law, responsibility, and the brain. *PLoS Biology, 5*(4), 693–700. doi: 10.1371/journal.pbio.0050103

Mobbs, D., Petrovic, P., Marchant, J. L., Hassabis, D., Weiskopf, N., Seymour, B., et al. (2007). When fear is near: Threat imminence elicits prefrontal-periaqueductal gray shifts in humans. *Science, 317*, 1079–1083. doi: 10.1126/science.1144298

Mofenson, L. M. (2010). Protecting the next generation—Eliminating perinatal HIV-1 infection. *New England Journal of Medicine, 362*(24), 2316–2318. doi: 10.1056/NEJMe1004406

Moffitt, T. E., Caspi, A., Taylor, A., Kokaua, J., Milne, B. J., Polanczyk, G., et al. (2010). How common are common mental disorders? Evidence that lifetime prevalence rates are doubled by prospective *versus* retrospective ascertainment. *Psychological Medicine, 40*, 899–909. doi: 10.1017/S0033291709991036

Moldofsky, H., & Scarisbrick, P. (1976). Induction of neurasthenic musculoskeletal pain syndrome by selective sleep stage deprivation. *Psychosomatic Medicine, 38*, 35–44.

Molina, E., Cervilla, J., Rivera, M., Torres, F., Bellón, J. Á., Moreno, B., et al. (2011). Polymorphic variation at the serotonin 1-A receptor gene is associated with comorbid depression and generalized anxiety. *Psychiatric Genetics, 21*(4), 195–201. doi: 110.1097/YPG.1090b1013e3283457a3283448

Monk, C. S., Telzer, E. H., Mogg, K., Bradley, B. P., Mai, X., Louro, H. M. C., et al. (2008). Amygdala and ventrolateral prefrontal cortex activation to masked angry faces in children and adolescents with generalized anxiety disorder. *Archives of General Psychiatry, 65*(5), 568–576. doi: 10.1001/archpsyc.65.5.568

Monson, C. M., Taft, C. T., & Fredman, S. J. (2009). Military-related PTSD and inti-

mate relationships: From description to theory-driven research and intervention development. *Clinical Psychology Review, 29*(8), 707–714. doi: 10.1016/j.cpr.2009.09.002

Monti, M. M., Vanhaudenhuyse, A., Coleman, M. R., Boly, M., Pickard, J. D., Tshibanda, L., et al. (2010). Willful modulation of brain activity in disorders of consciousness. *New England Journal of Medicine, 362*(7), 579–589. doi: 10.1056/NEJMoa0905370

Montpetit, M. A., Bergeman, C. S., Deboeck, P. R., Tiberio, S. S., & Boker, S. M. (2010). Resilience-as-process: Negative affect, stress, and coupled dynamical systems. *Psychology and Aging, 25*(3), 631–640. doi: 10.1037/a0019268

Moon, C., Cooper, R. P., & Fifer, W. P. (1993). Two-day-olds prefer their native language. *Infant Behavior and Development, 16*, 495–500. doi: 10.1016/0163-6383(93)80007-U

Moore, B. R. (1992). Avian movement imitation and a new form of mimicry: Tracing the evolution of a complex form of learning. *Behaviour, 122*, 231–263. doi: 10.1163/156853992X00525

Moore, D. J., Mowen, J. C., & Reardon, R. (1994). Multiple sources in advertising appeals: When product endorsers are paid by the advertising sponsor. *Journal of the Academy of Marketing Science, 22*(3), 234–243. doi: 10.1177/0092070394223004

Moore, F. R., Cornwell, R. E., Law Smith, M. J., Al Dujaili, E. A. S., Sharp, M., & Perrett, D. I. (2011). Evidence for the stress-linked immunocompetence handicap hypothesis in human male faces. *Proceedings of the Royal Society of London, Series B: Biological Sciences, 278*(1706), 774–780. doi: 10.1098/rspb.2010.1678

Moors, A., Ellsworth, P. C., Scherer, K. R., & Frijda, N. H. (2013). Appraisal theories of emotion: State of the art and future development. *Emotion Review, 5*(2), 119–124. doi: 10.1177/1754073912468165

Morin, C. M., Culbert, J. P., & Schwartz, S. M. (1994). Nonpharmacological interventions for insomnia: A meta-analysis of treatment efficacy. *American Journal of Psychiatry, 151*(8), 1172–1180.

Morris, J. K., Wald, N. J., Mutton, D. E., & Alberman, E. (2003). Comparison of models of maternal age-specific risk for Down syndrome live births. *Prenatal Diagnosis, 23*, 252–258. doi: 10.1002/pd.568

Morris, M. W., & Peng, K. (1994). Culture and cause: American and Chinese attributions for social and physical events. *Journal of Personality and Social Psychology, 67*, 949–971. doi: 10.1037/0022-3514.67.6.949

Morse, S., & Gergen, K. J. (1970). Social comparison, self-consistency, and the concept of self. *Journal of Personality and Social Psychology, 16*, 148–156. doi: 10.1037/h0029862

Moscovici, S., Lage, S., & Naffrechoux, M. (1969). Influence of a consistent minority on the responses of a majority in a color perception task. *Sociometry, 32,* 365–380. doi: 10.2307/2786541

Moscovici, S., & Zavalloni, M. (1969). The group as a polarizer of attitudes. *Journal of Personality and Social Psychology, 12,* 125–135. doi: 10.1037/h0027568

Moskalenko, Y. E., Weinstein, G. B., Kravchenko, T. I., Mozhaev, S. V., Semernya, V. N., Feilding, A., et al. (2008). The effect of craniotomy on the intracranial hemodynamics and cerebrospinal fluid dynamics in humans. *Human Physiology, 34*(3), 299–305. doi: 10.1134/S0362119708030055

Mössner, R., Schuhmacher, A., Schulze-Rauschenbach, S., Kühn, K.-U., Rujescu, D., Rietschel, M., et al. (2008). Further evidence for a functional role of the glutamate receptor gene *GRM3* in schizophrenia. *European Neuropsychopharmacology, 18*(10), 768–772. doi: 10.1016/j.euroneuro.2008.05.007

Mota-Rolim, S. A., & Araujo, J. F. (2013). Neurobiology and clinical implications of lucid dreaming. *Medical Hypotheses, 81*(5), 751–756. doi: 10.1016/j.mehy.2013.04.049

Muehlenbein, M. P., & Bribiescas, R. G. (2005). Testosterone-mediated immune functions and male life histories. *American Journal of Human Biology, 17*(5), 527–558. doi: 10.1002/ajhb.20419

Mukamel, R., Ekstrom, A. D., Kaplan, J., Iacoboni, M., & Fried, I. (2010). Single-neuron responses in humans during execution and observation of actions. *Current Biology 20,* 750–756. doi: 10.1016/j.cub.2010.02.045

Mundorf, N., Weaver, J., & Zillmann, D. (1989). Effects of gender roles and self perceptions on affective reactions to horror films. *Sex Roles, 20*(11), 655–673. doi: 10.1007/bf00288078

Mundy, P., Block, J., Delgado, C., Pomares, Y., Van Hecke, A. V., & Parlade, M. V. (2007). Individual differences and the development of joint attention in infancy. *Child Development, 78*(3), 938–954. doi: 10.1111/j.1467-8624.2007.01042.x

Munker, H. (1970). *Farbige gitter, abbildung auf der netzhaut und übertragungstheoretische beschreibung der farbwahrnehmung* [Chromatic grids, projection to the retina, and translation theory-based description of the color perception]. Munich, Germany: Habilitationsschrift.

Muraven, M., & Baumeister, R. F. (2000). Self-regulation and depletion of limited resources: Does self-control resemble a muscle? *Psychological Bulletin, 126,* 247–259. doi: 10.1037/0033-2909.126.2.247

Murdoch, B. B., Jr. (1962). The serial position effect in free recall. *Journal of Experimental Psychology, 64,* 482–488. doi: 10.1037/h0045106

Murphy, B. L., Stoll, A. L., Harris, P. Q., Ravichandran, C., Babb, S. M., Carlezon, W. A., Jr., et al. (2012). Omega-3 fatty acid treatment, with or without cytidine, fails to show therapeutic properties in bipolar disorder: A double-blind, randomized add-on clinical trial. *Journal of Clinical Psychopharmacology, 32*(5), 699–703. doi: 10.1097/JCP.0b013e318266854c

Murphy, J. M., Gilligan, C., & Puka, B. (1994). *Moral development in late adolescence and adulthood: A critique and reconstruction of Kohlberg's theory.* New York, NY: Garland.

Murphy, K. D., Rose, M. W., Chinkes, D. L., Meyer, W. J., III, Herndon, D. N., Hawkins, H. K., et al. (2007). The effects of gamma-hydroxybutyrate on hypermetabolism and wound healing in a rat model of large thermal injury. *Journal of Trauma, 63*(5), 1099–1107. doi: 10.1097.TA.0b013e318157d9d0

Murray, H. A. (1938). *Explorations in personality.* New York, NY: Oxford University Press.

Murray, S. L., Holmes, J. G., Gellavia, G., Griffin, D. W., & Dolderman, D. (2002). Kindred spirits? The benefits of egocentrism in close relationships. *Journal of Personality and Social Psychology, 82,* 563–581. doi: 10.1037/0022-3514.82.4.563

Murphy, S. L., Xu, J., & Kochanek, K. D. (2013). Deaths: Final data for 2010. *National Vital Statistics Reports, 61*(4), 1–118.

Myers, D. G. (1993). *The pursuit of happiness.* New York, NY: Avon.

Nair, H. P., & Young, L. J. (2006). Vasopressin and pair-bond formation: Genes to brain to behavior. *Physiology, 21,* 146–152. doi: 10.1152/physiol.00049.2005

Nair, K. S. (1995). Muscle protein turnover: Methodological issues and the effect of aging. *Journals of Gerontology: Series A. Biological Sciences and Medical Sciences, 50,* 107–112. doi: 10.1093/gerona/50A.Special_Issue.1

Nardi, B., Marini, A., Turchi, C., Arimatea, E., Tagliabracci, A., & Bellantuono, C. (2013). Role of 5-HTTLPR polymorphism in the development of the inward/outward personality organization: A genetic association study. *PLoS One, 8*(12), e82192. doi: 10.1371/journal.pone.0082192

Narumi, J., Miyazawa, S., Miyata, H., Suzuki, A., Kohsaka, S., & Kosugi, H. (1999). Analysis of human error in nursing care. *Accident: Analysis and Prevention, 31,* 625–629. doi: 10.1016/S0001-4575(99)00021-4

Nasrallah, H. A., Hopkins, T., & Pixley, S. K. (2010). Differential effects of antipsychotic and antidepressant drugs on neurogenic regions in rats. *Brain Research, 1354,* 23–29. doi: 10.1016/j.brainres.2010.07.075

National Center on Addiction and Substance Abuse at Columbia University. (2007). The importance of family dinners IV. New York, NY: Author.

National Institute on Alcohol Abuse and Alcoholism (2014). Alcohol facts and statistics. Retrieved from http://www.niaaa.nih.gov/alcohol-health/overview-alcohol-consumption/alcohol-facts-and-statistics

National Institute of Child Health and Human Development. (2003). SIDS: Back to sleep public education campaign. Retrieved from http://www.nichd.nih.gov/sids/

National Institutes of Health. (2009). What causes ADHD? Retrieved from http://www.nimh.nih.gov/health/publications/attention-deficit-hyperactivity-disorder/what-causes-adhd.shtml

National Sleep Foundation. (2008). 2008 Sleep in America poll. Retrieved from http://www.sleepfoundation.org/sites/default/files/2008%20POLL%20SOF.PDF

National Sleep Foundation. (2009). Restless legs syndrome (RLS) and sleep. Retrieved from http://www.sleepfoundation.org/article/sleep-related-problems/restless-legs-syndrome-rls-and-sleep

Navara, K. J., & Nelson, R. J. (2007). The dark side of light at night: Physiological, epidemiological, and ecological consequences. *Journal of Pineal Research, 43,* 215–224. doi: 10.1111/j.1600-079X.2007.00473.x

Neal, D. T., & Chartrand, T. L. (2011). Embodied emotion perception: Amplifying and dampening facial feedback modulates emotion perception accuracy. *Social Psychological and Personality Science, 2*(6), 673–678. doi: 10.1177/1948550611406138

Nedeltcheva, A. V., Kilkus, J. M., Imperial, J., Schoeller, D. A., & Penev, P. D. (2010). Insufficient sleep undermines dietary efforts to reduce adiposity. *Annals of Internal Medicine, 153,* 435–441. doi: 10.7326/0003-4819-153-7-201010050-00006

Nee, D. E., Brown, J. W., Askren, M. K., Berman, M. G., Demiralp, E., Krawitz, A., et al. (2013). A meta-analysis of executive components of working memory. *Cerebral Cortex, 23*(2), 264–282. doi: 10.1093/cercor/bhs007

Needham, B. L., Adler, N., Gregorich, S., Rehkopf, D., Lin, J., Blackburn, E. H., et al. (2013). Socioeconomic status, health behavior, and leukocyte telomere length in the National Health and Nutrition Examination Survey, 1999–2002. *Social Science & Medicine, 85,* 1–8. doi: 10.1016/j.socscimed.2013.02.023

Negovsky, V. A., & Gurvitch, A. M. (2004). Post-resuscitation disease—A new nosological entity: Its reality and significance. *Resuscitation, 30,* 23–27. doi: 10.1016/0300-9572(95)00861-M

Neigh, G. N., Gillespie, C. F., & Nemeroff, C. B. (2009). The neurobiological toll of child abuse and neglect. *Trauma, Violence, and Abuse, 10*(4), 389–410. doi: 10.1177/1524838009339758

Neisser, U. (1967). *Cognitive psychology.* Upper Saddle River, NJ: Prentice-Hall.

Neisser, U., Boodoo, G., Bouchard, T. J., Boykin, A. W., Brody, N., Ceci, S. J., et al. (1996). Intelligence: Knowns and unknowns. *American Psychologist, 51*(2), 77–101. doi: 10.1037/0003-066X.51.2.77

Nelson, S. K., Kushlev, K., Dunn, E. W., & Lyubomirsky, S. (2014). Parents are slightly happier than nonparents, but causality still cannot be inferred: A reply to Bhargava, Kassam, and Loewenstein (2014). *Psychological Science, 25*(1), 303–304. doi: 10.1177/0956797613508561

Nelson, S. K., Kushlev, K., English, T., Dunn, E. W., & Lyubomirsky, S. (2013). In defense of parenthood: Children are associated with more joy than misery. *Psychological Science, 24*(1), 3–10. doi: 10.1177/0956797612447798

Neuner, F., Schauer, E., Catani, C., Ruf, M., & Elbert, T. (2006). Post-tsunami stress: A study of posttraumatic stress disorder in children living in three severely affected regions in Sri Lanka. *Journal of Traumatic Stress, 19*, 339–347. doi: 10.1002/jts.20121

Neville, H. J., Bavelier, D., Corina, D., Rauschecker, J., Karni, A., Lalwani, A., et al. (1998). Cerebral organization for language in deaf and hearing subjects: Biological constraints and effects of experience. *Proceedings of the National Academy of Sciences, 95*, 922–929.

Newcombe, T. M. (1929). *Consistency of certain extrovert–introvert behavior patterns in 51 problem boys.* New York, NY: Columbia University Teachers College Press.

Newell, A., & Simon, H. (1972). *Human problem solving.* Englewood Cliffs, NJ: Prentice Hall.

Newman, T. K., Syagailo, Y. V., Barr, C. S., Wendland, J. R., Champoux, M., Graessle, M., et al. (2005). Monoamine oxidase A gene promoter variation and rearing experience influences aggressive behavior in rhesus monkeys. *Biological Psychiatry, 57*(2), 167–172. doi: 10.1016/j.biopsych.2004.10.012

Nielsen, M., & Tomaselli, K. (2010). Over-imitation in Kalahari Bushman children and the origins of human cultural cognition. *Psychological Science, 21*, 729–736. doi: 10.1177/0956797610368808

Nielsen, T. A., Zadra, A., Simard, V., Saucier, S., Kuiken, D., & Smith, C. (2003). Typical dreams of Canadian university students. *Dreaming, 13*, 211–235. doi: 10.1023/B:DREM.0000003144.40929.0b

Nisbett, R. E., Aronson, J., Blair, C., Dickens, W., Flynn, J., Halpern, D. F., et al. (2012). Intelligence: New findings and theoretical developments. *American Psychologist, 67*(2), 130. doi: 10.1037/a0026699

Noaghiul, S., & Hibbeln, J. R. (2003). Cross-national comparisons of seafood consumption and rates of bipolar disorders. *American Journal of Psychiatry, 160*(12), 2222–2227. doi: 10.1176/appi.ajp.160.12.2222

Noël, X., Brevers, D., & Bechara, A. (2013). A neurocognitive approach to understanding the neurobiology of addiction. *Current Opinion in Neurobiology, 23*(4), 632–638. doi: 10.1016/j.conb.2013.01.018

Noelle-Neumann, E. (1984). *The spiral of silence: Public opinion—Our social skin.* Chicago, IL: University of Chicago Press.

Nolen-Hoeksema, S. (1991). Responses to depression and their effects on the duration of depressive episodes. *Journal of Abnormal Psychology, 100*, 569–582. doi: 10.1037/0021-843X.100.4.569

Nolen-Hoeksema, S. (2003). *Women who think too much: How to break free of overthinking and reclaim your life.* New York, NY: Henry Holt.

Nolen-Hoeksema, S., & Girgus, J. S. (1994). The emergence of gender differences in depression during adolescence. *Psychological Bulletin, 115*, 424–443. doi: 10.1037/0033-2909.115.3.424

Norcross, J. C., & Castle, P. H. (2002). Appreciating the Psy.D.: The facts. *Eye on Psi Chi, 7*, 22–26.

Nordenbæk, C., Jørgensen, M., Kyvik, K. O., & Bilenberg, N. (2014). A Danish population-based twin study on autism spectrum disorders. *European Child & Adolescent Psychiatry, 23*(1), 35–43. doi: 10.1007/s00787-013-0419-5

Norman, W. T. (1963). Toward an adequate taxonomy of personality attributes: Replicated factor structure in peer nomination personality ratings. *Journal of Abnormal and Social Psychology, 66*, 574–583. doi: 10.1037/h0040291

Northoff, G., Heinzel, A., de Greck, M., Bermpohl, F., Dobrowolny, H., & Panksepp, J. (2006). Self-referential processing in our brain: A meta-analysis of imaging studies on the self. *NeuroImage, 31*(1), 440–457. doi: 10.1016/j.neuroimage.2005.12.002

Nosek, B. A. (2007). Understanding the individual implicitly and explicitly. *International Journal of Psychology, 42*(3), 184–188. doi: 10.1080/00207590601068159

Nowak, M. A. (2006). Five rules for the evolution of cooperation. *Science, 314*, 1560–1563. doi: 10.1126/science.1133755

O'Brien, T. B., & DeLongis, A. (1996). The interactional context of problem-, emotion-, and relationship-focused coping: The role of the Big Five personality factors. *Journal of Personality, 64*(4), 775–813. doi: 10.1111/j.1467-6494.1996.tb00944.x

O'Keefe, J., & Nadel, L. (1978). *The hippocampus as a cognitive map.* Oxford, United Kingdom: Oxford University Press.

O'Malley, P., Lewis, M., Donehower, C., & Stone, D. (2014). Effectiveness of using iPads to increase academic task completion by students with autism. *Universal Journal of Educational Research, 2*(1), 90–97. doi: 10.13189/ujer.2014.020111

O'Neil, P. M., Smith, S. R., Weissman, N. J., Fidler, M. C., Sanchez, M., Zhang, J., et al. (2012). Randomized placebo-controlled clinical trial of lorcaserin for weight loss in type 2 diabetes mellitus: The BLOOM-DM study. *Obesity, 20*(7), 1426–1436. doi: 10.1038/oby.2012.66

O'Reardon, J. P., Solvason, H. B., Janicak, P. G., Sampson, S., Isenberg, K. E., Nahas, Z., et al. (2007). Efficacy and safety of transcranial magnetic stimulation in the acute treatment of major depression: A multisite randomized controlled trial. *Biological Psychiatry, 62*(11), 1208–1216. doi: 10.1016/j.biopsych.2007.01.018

O'Rourke, N., & Cappeliez, P. (2005). Marital satisfaction and self-deception: Reconstruction of relationship histories among older adults. *Social Behavior and Personality, 33*(3), 273–282. doi: 10.2224/sbp.2005.33.3.273

Odegard, T. N., Cooper, C. M., Lampinen, J. M., Reyna, V. F., & Brainerd, C. J. (2009). Children's eyewitness memory for multiple real-life events. *Child Development, 80*(6), 1877–1890. doi: 10.1111/j.1467-8624.2009.01373.x

Ogden, C. L., & Carroll, M. D. (2010, June). Prevalence of overweight, obesity, and extreme obesity among adults: United States, trends 1960–1962 through 2007–2008. *NCHS Health E-Stats.* Atlanta, GA: Centers for Disease Control and Prevention. Retrieved from http://www.cdc.gov/NCHS/data/hestat/obesity_adult_07_08/obesity_adult_07_08.pdf

Ogden, C. L., Carroll, M. D., Kit, B. K., & Flegal, K. M. (2014). Prevalence of childhood and adult obesity in the United States, 2011–2012. *JAMA: Journal of the American Medical Association, 311*(8), 806–814. doi: 10.1001/jama.2014.732

Olatunji, B. O., Davis, M. L., Powers, M. B., & Smits, J. A. (2013). Cognitive-behavioral therapy for obsessive-compulsive disorder: A meta-analysis of treatment outcome and moderators. *Journal of Psychiatric Research, 47*(1), 33–41. doi: 10.1016/j.jpsychires.2012.08.020

Olfson, M., & Marcus, S. C. (2009). National patterns in antidepressant medication treatment. *Archives of General Psychiatry, 66*(8), 848–856. doi: 10.1001/archgenpsychiatry.2009.81

Olsho, L. W., Koch, E. G., Halpin, C. F., & Carter, E. A. (1987). An observer-based psychoacoustic procedure for use with young infants. *Developmental Psychology, 23*, 627–640. doi: 10.1037/0012-1649.23.5.627

Olson, C. K. (2010). Children's motivations for video game play in the context of normal development. *Review of General Psychology, 14*(2), 180–187. doi: 10.1037/a0018984

Opris, I., & Casanova, M. F. (2014). Prefrontal cortical minicolumn: From executive control to disrupted cognitive processing. *Brain, 137*(7), 1863–1875. doi: 10.1093/brain/awt359

Orne, M. T., & Evans, F. J. (1965). Social control in the psychological experiment: Antisocial behavior and hypnosis. *Journal of Personality and Social Psychology, 1*, 189–200. doi: 10.1037/h0021933

Organisation for Economic Co-operation and Development. (2013). PISA 2012 results: Ready to learn: Students' engagement, drive, and self-beliefs. Retrieved from http://www.oecd.org/pisa/keyfindings/pisa-2012-results-volume-iii.htm

Osinsky, R., Reuter, M., Küpper, Y., Schmitz, A., Kozyra, E., Alexander, N., et al. (2008). Variation in the serotonin transporter gene modulates selective attention to threat. *Emotion, 8*(4), 584–588. doi: 10.1037/a0012826

Ostfeld, B. M., Esposito, L., Perl, H., & Hegyi, T. (2010). Concurrent risks in sudden infant death syndrome. *Pediatrics, 125*(3), 447–453. doi: 10.1542/peds.2009-0038

Oswald, F. L., Mitchell, G., Blanton, H., Jaccard, J., & Tetlock, P. E. (2013). Predicting ethnic and racial discrimination: A meta-analysis of IAT criterion studies. *Journal of Personality and Social Psychology, 105*(2), 171–192. doi: 10.1037/a0032734

Otsuka, Y. (2014). Face recognition in infants: A review of behavioral and near-infrared spectroscopic studies. *Japanese Psychological Research, 56*(1), 76–90. doi: 10.1111/jpr.12024

Owen, A. M., Hampshire, A., Grahn, J. A., Stenton, R., Dajani, S., Burns, A. S., et al. (2010). Putting brain training to the test. *Nature, 465*(7299), 775–778. doi: 10.1038/nature09042

Owen, M. J., Craddock, N., & Jablensky, A. (2007). The genetic deconstruction of psychosis. *Schizophrenia Bulletin, 33*(4), 905–911. doi: 10.1093/schbul/sbm053

Paluck, E. L., & Green, D. P. (2009). Prejudice reduction: What works? A review and assessment of research and practice. *Annual Review of Psychology, 60*, 339–367. doi: 10.1146/annurev.psych.60.110707.163607

Papp, L. A., Klein, D. F., Martinez, J., Schneier, F., Cole, R., Liebowitz, M. R., et al. (1993). Diagnostic and substance specificity of carbon dioxide–induced panic. *American Journal of Psychiatry, 150*, 250–257.

Paradiso, S., Ostedgaard, K., Vaidya, J., Ponto, L. B., & Robinson, R. (2013). Emotional blunting following left basal ganglia stroke: The role of depression and fronto-limbic functional alterations. *Psychiatry Research: Neuroimaging, 211*(2), 148–159. doi: 10.1016/j.pscychresns.2012.05.008

Pardo, C. A., & Eberhart, C. G. (2007). The neurobiology of autism. *Brain Pathology, 17*(4), 434–447. doi: 10.1111/j.1750-3639.2007.00102.x

Pargament, K. I., & Krumrei, E. J. (2009). Clinical assessment of clients' spirituality. In J. D. Aten & M. M. Leach (Eds.), *Spirituality and the therapeutic process: A comprehensive resource from intake to termination* (pp. 93–120). Washington, DC: American Psychological Association.

Parker, A. M., & Fischhoff, B. (2005). Decision-making competence: External validation through an individual-differences approach. *Journal of Behavioral Decision Making, 18*, 1–27. doi: 10.1002/bdm.481

Parrilla, L. (2006). O'Malley killer begins his sentence. *The Tribune,* San Luis Obispo, CA, p. B2.

Parrott, A. C. (2007). The psychotherapeutic potential of MDMA (3,4-methylenedioxymethamphetamine): An evidence-based review. *Psychopharmacology, 191*(2), 181–198. doi: 10.1007/s00213-007-0703-5

Parton, A., Malhotra, P., & Husain, M. (2004). Hemispatial neglect. *Journal of Neurology, Neurosurgery & Psychiatry, 75*(1), 13–21.

Pascual-Leone, A., & Torres, F. (1993). Plasticity of sensorimotor cortex representation of the reading finger in Braille readers. *Brain, 116*, 39–52. doi: 10.1093/brain/116.1.39

Paterson, D. S., Trachtenberg, F. L., Thompson, E. G., Belliveau, R. A., Beggs, A. H., Darnall, R., et al. (2006). Multiple serotonergic brainstem abnormalities in sudden infant death syndrome. *JAMA: Journal of the American Medical Association, 296*(17), 2124–2132. doi: 10.1001/jama.296.17.2124

Patterson, F. (1978, October). Conversations with a gorilla. *National Geographic,* 438–465.

Patterson, F. (1984). Self-recognition by gorilla *(Gorilla gorilla). Gorilla, 7*, 2–3.

Patterson, F. G. P., & Cohn, R. G. (1994). Self-recognition and self-awareness in lowland gorillas. In S. T. Parker, R. W. Mitchell, & M. L. Boccia (Eds.), *Self-awareness in animals and humans: Developmental perspectives* (pp. 273–290). New York, NY: Cambridge University Press.

Patterson, G. R., Chamberlain, P., & Reid, J. B. (1982). A comparative evaluation of parent training procedures. *Behavior Therapy, 13*, 638–650. doi: 10.1016/S0005-7894(82)80021-X

Patterson, K. D., & Pyle, G. F. (1991). The geography and mortality of the 1918 influenza pandemic. *Bulletin of the History of Medicine, 65*(1), 4–21.

Paul, A. M. (2010). *The cult of personality testing: How personality tests are leading us to miseducate our children, mismanage our companies, and misunderstand ourselves.* New York, NY: Simon and Schuster.

Paulhus, D. I. (1998). Interpersonal and intrapsychic adaptiveness of trait self-enhancement: A mixed blessing? *Journal of Personality and Social Psychology, 74*, 1197–1208. doi: 10.1037/0022-3514.74.5.1197

Pavlov, I. P. (1906). The scientific investigation of the psychical faculties or processes in the higher animals. *Science, 24*(620), 613–619. doi: 10.1126/science.24.620.613

Pavlov, I. P. (1927). *Conditioned reflexes.* Oxford, United Kingdom: Oxford University Press.

Pearce, J. M. S. (2005). A note on aphasia in bilingual patients: Pitres' and Ribot's laws. *European Neurology, 54*, 127–131. doi: 10.1159/000089083

Pearce, M. T., Ruiz, M. H., Kapasi, S., Wiggins, G., & Bhattacharya, J. (2010). Unsupervised statistical learning underpins computational, behavioural, and neural manifestations of musical expectation. *NeuroImage, 50*, 302–313. doi: 10.1016/j.neuroimage.2009.12.019

Pearson Assessments. (2005). MMPI-2. Retrieved from http://www.pearsonassessments.com/tests/mmpi_2.htm

Pegna, A. J., Khateb, A., Lazeyras, F., & Seghier, M. L. (2005). Discriminating emotional faces without primary visual cortices involves the right amygdala. *Nature Neuroscience, 8*(1), 24–25. doi: 10.1038/nn1364

Pelham, W. E., & Fabiano, G. A. (2008). Evidence-based psychosocial treatments for attention-deficit/hyperactivity disorder. *Journal of Clinical Child and Adolescent Psychology, 37*(1), 184–214. doi: 10.1080/15374410701818681

Pelios, L. V., MacDuff, G. S., & Axelrod, S. (2003). The effects of a treatment package in establishing independent academic work skills in children with autism. *Education and Treatment of Children, 26*, 1–21.

Peltokorpi, V. (2008). Transactive memory systems. *Review of General Psychology, 12*(4), 378–394. doi: 10.1037/1089-2680.12.4.378

Pepperberg, I. M. (2014). Interspecies communication with grey parrots: A tool for examining cognitive processing. In G. Witzany (Ed.), *Biocommunication of Animals* (pp. 213–232). Dordrecht, Netherlands: Springer. doi: 10.1007/978-94-007-7414-8_12

Perani, D., Paulesu, E., Galles, N. S., Dupoux, E., Dehaene, S., Bettinardi, V., et al. (1998). The bilingual brain: Proficiency and age of acquisition of the second language. *Brain, 121*, 1841–1852. doi: 10.1093/brain/121.10.1841

Perfect, T. J., & Askew, C. (1994). Print adverts: Not remembered but memorable. *Applied Cognitive Psychology, 8*(7), 693–703. doi: 10.1002/acp.2350080707

Perkins, T., Stokes, M., McGillivray, J., & Bittar, R. (2010). Mirror neuron dysfunction in autism spectrum disorders. *Journal of Clinical Neuroscience, 17*(10), 1239–1243. doi: 10.1016/j.jocn.2010.01.026

Perry, W. I. (1970). *Forms of intellectual and ethical development in the college years.* New York, NY: Holt, Rinehart, and Winston.

Peterson, C. (2006). *A primer in positive psychology.* New York, NY: Oxford University Press.

Peterson, C., & Seligman, M. E. P. (2004). *Character strengths and virtues: A handbook and classification.* Washington, DC: APA Press and Oxford University Press.

Peterson, C., Semmel, A., von Baeyer, C., Abramson, L. Y., Metalsky, G. I., &

Seligman, M. E. P. (1982). The attributional style questionnaire. *Cognitive Therapy and Research, 6*(3), 287–300.

Peterson, C., & Whalen, N. (2001). Five years later: Children's memory for medical emergencies. *Applied Cognitive Psychology, 15*(7), S7–S24. doi: 10.1002/acp.832

Peterson, C. C. (1996). The ticking of the social clock: Adults' beliefs about the timing of transition events. *International Journal of Aging and Human Development, 42*(3), 189–203. doi: 10.2190/mmdd-f9yp-npn8-720m

Peterson, L. R., & Peterson, M. J. (1959). Short-term retention of individual verbal items. *Journal of Experimental Psychology, 58*, 193–198. doi: 10.1037/h0049234

Petrides, M., Cadoret, G., & Mackey, S. (2005). Orofacial somatomotor responses in the macaque monkey homologue of Broca's area. *Nature, 435*(7046), 1235–1238. doi: 10.1038/nature03628

Petty, R. E., & Cacioppo, J. T. (1981). *Attitudes and persuasion: Classic and contemporary approaches.* Dubuque, IA: Wm. C. Brown.

Petty, R. E., & Cacioppo, J. T. (1986a). *Communication and persuasion: Central and peripheral routes to attitude change.* New York, NY: Springer-Verlag.

Petty, R. E., & Cacioppo, J. T. (1986b). The elaboration likelihood model of persuasion. *Advances in Experimental Social Psychology, 19*, 123–205. doi: 10.1016/S0065-2601(08)60214-2

Petty, R. E., Cacioppo, J. T., & Kasmer, J. (1988). The role of affect in the elaboration likelihood model of persuasion. In L. Donohew, H. Sypher, & E. T. Higgins (Eds.), *Communication, social cognition, and affect* (pp. 117–146). Hillsdale, NJ: Erlbaum.

Peverly, S. T., Brobst, K. E., & Morris, K. S. (2002). The contribution of reading comprehension ability and meta-cognitive control to the development of studying in adolescence. *Journal of Research in Reading, 25*(2), 203. doi: 10.1111/1467-9817.00169

Pew Research Center. (2010). The decline of marriage and rise of new families. Retrieved from http://www.pewsocial-trends.org/2010/11/18/the-decline-of-marriage-and-rise-of-new-families/

Phan, K. L., Wager, T., Taylor, S. F., & Liberzon, I. (2002). Functional neuroanatomy of emotion: A meta-analysis of emotion activation studies in PET and fMRI. *NeuroImage, 16*, 331–348. doi: 10.1006/nimg.2002.1087

Phelps, E. A., O'Connor, K. J., Cunningham, W. A., Funayama, E. S., Gatenby, J. C., Gore, J. C., et al. (2000). Performance on indirect measures of race evaluation predicts amygdala activation. *Journal of Cognitive Neuroscience, 12*, 729–738. doi: 10.1162/089892900562552

PhysOrg.com. (2006, July 28). First ever world map of happiness produced. Retrieved from http://www.physorg.com/news73321785.html

Piacentini, J., & Graae, F. (1997). Childhood OCD. In E. Hollander & D. Stei (Eds.), *Obsessive-compulsive disorders: Diagnosis, etiology, treatment* (pp. 23–46). New York, NY: Dekker.

Pietrzak, R. H., Goldstein, R. B., Southwick, S. M., & Grant, B. F. (2011). Prevalence and Axis I comorbidity of full and partial posttraumatic stress disorder in the United States: Results from Wave 2 of the National Epidemiologic Survey on Alcohol and Related Conditions. *Journal of Anxiety Disorders, 25*(3), 456–465. doi: 10.1016/j.janxdis.2010.11.010

Pilgrim, J. L., Gerostamoulos, D., & Drummer, O. H. (2011). Deaths involving MDMA and the concomitant use of pharmaceutical drugs. *Journal of Analytical Toxicology, 35*(4), 219–226. doi: 10.1093/anatox/35.4.219

Pinker, S. (1994). *The language instinct: The new science of language and mind.* London, United Kingdom: Penguin.

Piper, A., & Merskey, H. (2004). The persistence of folly: A critical examination of dissociative identity disorder. Part I. The excesses of an improbable concept. *Canadian Journal of Psychiatry, 49*(9), 592–600.

Pittenger, D. J. (1993). Measuring the MBTI . . . and coming up short. *Journal of Career Planning and Employment, 54*(1), 48–52.

Pitts, F. N., & McClure, J. N. (1967). Lactate metabolism in anxiety neurosis. *New England Journal of Medicine, 277*, 1329–1336. doi: 10.1056/NEJM196712212772502

Plomin, R., & Spinath, F. M. (2004). Intelligence: Genetics, genes, and genomics. *Journal of Personality and Social Psychology, 86*, 112–129. doi: 10.1037/0022-3514.86.1.112

Plotnik, J. M., de Waal, F. B. M., & Reiss, D. (2006). Self-recognition in an Asian elephant. *Proceedings of the National Academy of Sciences, 103*(45), 17053–17057. doi: 10.1073/pnas.0608062103

Plous, S. (1993). *The psychology of judgment and decision making.* New York, NY: McGraw-Hill.

Pol, H. E. H., Schnack, H. G., Posthuma, D., Mandl, R. C. W., Baaré, W. F., van Oel, C., et al. (2006). Genetic contributions to human brain morphology and intelligence. *Journal of Neuroscience, 26*(40), 10235–10242. doi: 10.1523/jneurosci.1312-06.2006

Pol, H. E. H., van Baal, G. C. M., Schnack, H. G., Brans, R. G., van der Schot, A. C., Brouwer, R. M., et al. (2012). Overlapping and segregating structural brain abnormalities in twins with schizophrenia or bipolar disorder. *Archives of General Psychiatry, 69*(4), 349–359. doi: 10.1001/archgenpsychiatry.2011.1615

Polya, G. (1957). *How to solve it.* Garden City, NY: Doubleday.

Pomarol-Clotet, E., Salvador, R., Sarro, S., Gomar, J., Vila, F., Martinez, A., et al. (2008). Failure to deactivate in the prefrontal cortex in schizophrenia: Dysfunction of the default mode network? *Psychological Medicine, 38*(8), 1185–1194. doi: http://dx.doi.org/10.1017/S0033291708003565

Pope, H. G., Jr., Katz, D. L., & Hudson, J. I. (1993). Anorexia nervosa and "reverse anorexia" among 108 male bodybuilders. *Comprehensive Psychiatry, 34*, 406–409. doi: 10.1016/0010-440X(93)90066-D

Pope, H. G., Jr., Kouri, E. M., & Hudson, J. I. (2000). Effects of supraphysiologic doses of testosterone on mood and aggression in normal men: A randomized controlled trial. *Archives of General Psychiatry, 57*(2), 133–140. doi: 10.1001/archpsyc.57.2.133

Porter, R. H., Makin, J. W., Davis, L. B., & Christensen, K. M. (1991). An assessment of the salient olfactory environment of formula-fed infants. *Physiology and Behavior, 50*, 907–911. doi: 10.1016/0031-9384(91)90413-I

Posey, D. J., Stigler, K. A., Erickson, C. A., & McDougle, C. J. (2008). Antipsychotics in the treatment of autism. *Journal of Clinical Investigation, 118*(1), 6–14. doi: 10.1172/JCI32483

Posner, M. I., & Keele, S. W. (1970). Retention of abstract ideas. *Journal of Experimental Psychology, 83*, 304–308. doi: 10.1037/h0028558

Poundstone, W. (1992). *Prisoner's dilemma.* New York, NY: Doubleday.

Povinelli, D. J. (1993). Reconstructing the evolution of mind. *American Psychologist, 48*, 493–509. doi: 10.1037/0003-066X.48.5.493

Prasad, S., & Steer, C. (2008). Switching from neurostimulant therapy to atomoxetine in children and adolescents with attention-deficit hyperactivity disorder: Clinical approaches and review of current available evidence. *Paediatric Drugs, 10*(1), 39–47. doi: 10.2165/00148581-200810010-00005

Pratt, L. A., & Brody, D. J. (2008, September). *Depression in the United States household population, 2005–2006* (NCHS Data Brief 7). Washington, DC: U.S. Department of Health and Human Services. Retrieved from http://www.cdc.gov/nchs/data/databriefs/db07.pdf

Premack, D. (1965). Reinforcement theory. In D. Levine (Ed.), *Nebraska Symposium on Motivation* (Vol. 13, pp. 3–41). Lincoln: University of Nebraska Press.

Premack, D. G., & Woodruff, G. (1978). Does the chimpanzee have a theory of mind? *Behavioral and Brain Sciences, 1*, 515–526.

Price, E. E., Lambeth, S. P., Schapiro, S. J., & Whiten, A. (2009). A potent effect of observational learning on chimpanzee tool construction. *Proceedings of the Royal Society of London, Series B: Biological Sciences.* doi: 10.1098/rspb.2009.0640

Priebe, S. (2006). The provision of psychotherapy: An international comparison. Retrieved from http://cep.lse.ac.uk/

textonly/research/mentalhealth/ StefanPriebe_provision-of-incapacity- benefit.pdf

Prinzie, P., Stams, G. J. J. M., Deković, M., Reijntjes, A. H. A., & Belsky, J. (2009). The relations between parents' Big Five personality factors and parenting: A meta-analytic review. *Journal of Personality and Social Psychology, 97*(2), 351–362. doi: 10.1037/a0015823

Provine, R. R. (1986). Yawning as a stereotyped action pattern and releasing stimulus. *Ethology, 72*, 109–122. doi: 10.1111/ j.1439-0310.1986.tb00611.x

Psychological Clinical Science Accreditation System. (2011). PCSAS mission. Retrieved from http://pcsas.org/mission-function. php

Psychological Clinical Science Accreditation System. (2014). PCSAS accredited programs. Retrieved from http://www.pcsas .org/accredited-programs.php

Public Broadcasting Service. (1998). DNA "fingerprinting." Retrieved from http:// www.pbs.org/wgbh/aso/resources/guide/ outcomesindex.html#DNA

Public Broadcasting Service. (2005). The story of ¼ smallpox—and other deadly Eurasian germs. Retrieved from http://www.pbs.org/ gunsgermssteel/variables/smallpox.html

Pyszczynski, T., Greenberg, J., & Solomon, S. (1991). A terror management analysis of self-awareness and anxiety: The hierarchy of terror. In R. Schwarzer & R. A. Wicklund (Eds.), *Anxiety and self-focused attention* (pp. 67–85). Amsterdam, Netherlands: Harwood Academic Publishers.

Qiu, D.-L., & Knopfel, T. (2007). An NMDA receptor/nitric oxide cascade in presynaptic parallel fiber–Purkinje neuron long-term potentiation. *Journal of Neuroscience, 27*(13), 3408–3415. doi: 10.1523/jneurosci .4831-06.2007

Quian Quiroga, R., Reddy, L., Kreiman, G., Koch, C., & Fried, I. (2005). Invariant visual representation by single neurons in the human brain. *Nature, 435*, 1102–1107. doi: 10.1038/nature03687

Quiroz, J. A., Machado-Vieira, R., Zarate, J. C. A., & Manji, H. K. (2010). Novel insights into lithium's mechanism of action: Neurotrophic and neuroprotective effects. *Neuropsychobiology, 62*(1), 50–60. doi: 10.1159/000314310

Raichle, M. E. (2010). The brain's dark energy. *Scientific American, 302,* 44–49. doi: 10.1038/scientificamerican0310-44

Raichle, M. E., & Snyder, A. Z. (2011). Intrinsic brain activity and consciousness. In S. Laureys & G. Tononi (Eds.), *The neurology of consciousness: Cognitive neuroscience and neuropathology* (pp. 81–88). New York, NY: Elsevier.

Raine, A., Lencz, T., Bihrle, S., LaCasse, L., & Colletti, P. (2000). Reduced prefrontal gray matter volume and reduced autonomic activity in antisocial personality disorder. *Archives of General Psychiatry, 57*, 119–127. doi: 10.1001/archpsyc.57.2.119

Raine, A., Stoddard, J., Bihrle, S., & Buchsbaum, M. (1998). Prefrontal glucose deficits in murderers lacking psychosocial deprivation. *Neuropsychiatry, Neuropsychology, and Behavioral Neurology, 11*(1), 1–7.

Rakic, P. (2000). Molecular and cellular mechanisms of neuronal migration: Relevance to cortical epilepsies. *Advances in Neurology, 84*, 1–14.

Raleigh, M. J., McGuire, M. T., Brammer, G. L., Pollack, D. B., & Yuwiler, A. (1991). Serotonergic mechanisms promote dominance acquisition in adult male vervet monkeys. *Brain Research, 559*(2), 181–190. doi: 10.1016/0006-8993(91)90001-C

Ramachandran, V. S. (1998). Consciousness and body image: Lessons from phantom limbs, Capgras syndrome and pain asymbolia. *Philosophical Transactions of the Royal Society of London, B: Biological Sciences, 353*, 1851–1859. doi: 10.1098/ rstb.1998.0337

Ramachandran, V. S. (2006). Mirror neurons and imitation learning as the driving force behind "the great leap forward" in human evolution. Retrieved from http://www. edge.org/3rd_culture/ramachandran/ ramachandran_p1.html

Ramachandran, V. S., & Rogers-Ramachandran, D. (2000). Phantom limbs and neural plasticity. *Archives of Neurology, 57*, 317–320. doi: 10.1001/archneur.57 .3.317

Rammstedt, B., & John, O. P. (2007). Measuring personality in one minute or less: A 10-item short version of the Big Five Inventory in English and German. *Journal of Research in Personality, 41*(1), 203–212. doi: 10.1016/j.jrp.2006.02.001

Rapkin, A. J., Mikacich, J. A., Moatakef-Imani, B., & Rasgon, N. (2002). The clinical nature and formal diagnosis of premenstrual, postpartum, and perimenopausal affective disorders. *Current Psychiatry Reports, 4*, 419–428. doi: 10.1007/s11920-002-0069-7

Rapoport, J. (1989). *The boy who couldn't stop washing: The experience and treatment of obsessive-compulsive disorder.* New York, NY: Dutton.

Rapoport, J. L., Giedd, J. N., Blumenthal, J., Hamburger, S., Jeffries, N., Fernandez, T., et al. (1999). Progressive cortical change during adolescence in childhood-onset schizophrenia: A longitudinal magnetic resonance imaging study. *Archives of General Psychiatry, 56*, 649–654. doi: 10.1001/archpsyc.56.7.649

Rasch, B., & Born, J. (2013). About sleep's role in memory. *Physiological Reviews, 93*(2), 681–766. doi: 10.1152/physrev.00032.2012

Rasmussen, T., & Milner, B. (1977). The role of early left-brain injury in determining lateralization of cerebral speech functions. *Annals of the New York Academy of Sciences, 299*, 355–369. doi: 10.1111/j.1749-6632.1977.tb41921.x

Rawlins, W. K. (2004). Friendships in later life. In J. F. Nussbaum & J. Coupland (Eds.), *Handbook of communication and aging research* (2nd ed., pp. 273–299). Mahwah, NJ: Erlbaum.

Raz, A., Kirsch, I., Pollard, J., & Nitkin-Kaner, Y. (2006). Suggestion reduces the Stroop effect. *Psychological Science, 17*(2), 91–95. doi: 10.1111/j.1467-9280.2006.01669.x

Reese, H. E., McNally, R. J., & Wilhelm, S. (2010). Facial asymmetry detection in patients with body dysmorphic disorder. *Behaviour Research and Therapy, 48*(9), 936–940. doi: 10.1016/j.brat.2010.05.021

Regan, C. (2000). *Intoxicating minds.* London, United Kingdom: Weidenfeld and Nicolson.

Reichenberg, A., Gross, R., Kolevzon, A., & Susser, E. S. (2011). Parental and perinatal risk factors for autism. In E. Hollander, A. Kolevzon, & J. T. Coyle (Eds.), *Textbook of autism spectrum disorders* (pp. 239–246). Arlington, VA: American Psychiatric Publishing.

Reicher, S., & Haslam, S. A. (2006). Rethinking the psychology of tyranny: The BBC prison study. *British Journal of Social Psychology, 45*, 1–40. doi: 10.1348/014466605X48998

Reinisch, J. M., Ziemba-Davis, M., & Sanders, S. A. (1991). Hormonal contributions to sexually dimorphic behavioral development in humans. *Psychoneuroendocrinology, 16*, 213–278. doi: 10.1016/ 0306-4530(91)90080-D

Reips, U.-D., & Orth, D. (2006). An Internet-based test of the Stock Choice Recognition Heuristic as an investment tool: More successful than experts, market and trust. Retrieved from http://www.psychologie. unizh.ch/sowi/reips/poster/ ReipsOrthJDM2005poster.pdf

Reisenzein, R. (1983). The Schachter theory of emotion: Two decades later. *Psychological Bulletin, 94*, 239–264. doi: 10.1037/0033-2909.94.2.239

Remez, R. E. (1998). Sine-wave speech. *Scholarpedia, 3*, 2394.

Remez, R. E., Rubin, P. E., Pisoni, D. B., & Carell, T. D. (1981). Speech perception without traditional speech cues. *Science, 212*, 947–950. doi: 10.1126/science.7233191

Rendell, L., Boyd, R., Cownden, D., Enquist, M., Eriksson, K., Feldman, M. W., et al. (2010). Why copy others? Insights from the social learning strategies tournament. *Science, 328*, 208–213. doi: 10.1126/ science.1184719

Renzulli, J. S., & Delcourt, M. A. (1986). The legacy and logic of research on the identification of gifted persons. *Gifted Child Quarterly, 30*, 20–23. doi: 10.1177/001698628603000104

Rescorla, R. A. (1966). Predictability and number of pairings in Pavlovian fear conditioning. *Psychonomic Science, 4*(11), 383–384. doi: 10.3758/BF03342350

Rescorla, R. A. (1968). Probability of shock in the presence and absence of CS in fear conditioning. *Journal of Comparative and Physiological Psychology, 66*, 1–5. doi: 10.1037/h0025984

Rescorla, R. A. (2004). Spontaneous recovery. *Learning & Memory, 11*, 501–509. doi: 10.1101/lm.77504

Rescorla, R. A., & Wagner, A. R. (1972). A theory of Pavlovian conditioning: Variations in the effectiveness of reinforcement and nonreinforcement. In A. H. Black & W. F. Prokasy (Eds.), *Classical conditioning, Vol. II: Current theory and research* (pp. 64–99). New York, NY: Appleton-Century-Crofts.

Restak, R. (1988). *Mind*. New York, NY: Bantam Dell.

Reyna, V. F. (2008). A theory of medical decision making and health: Fuzzy trace theory. *Medical Decision Making, 28*(6), 850–865. doi: 10.1177/0272989x08327066

Reyna, V. F., Estrada, S. M., DeMarinis, J. A., Myers, R. M., Stanisz, J. M., & Mills, B. A. (2011). Neurobiological and memory models of risky decision making in adolescents versus young adults. *Journal of Experimental Psychology: Learning, Memory, and Cognition, 37*(5), 1125–1142. doi: 10.1037/a0023943

Reyna, V. F., & Farley, F. (2006). Risk and rationality in adolescent decision making: Implications for theory, practice, and public policy. *Psychological Science in the Public Interest, 7*(1), 1–44. doi: 10.1111/j.1529-1006.2006.00026.x

Rhodes, N., & Wood, W. (1992). Self-esteem and intelligence affect influenceability: The mediating role of message reception. *Psychological Bulletin, 111*, 156–171. doi: 10.1037/0033-2909.111.1.156

Rhodewalt, F., Sandonmatsu, D. M., Tschanz, B., Feick, D. L., & Waller, A. (1995). Self-handicapping and interpersonal trade-offs: The effects of claimed self-handicaps on observers' performance evaluations and feedback. *Personality and Social Psychology Bulletin, 21*, 1042–1050. doi: 10.1177/01461672952110005

Ridley, M. (2003). *Nature via nurture*. New York, NY: HarperCollins.

Rijnbeek, B., de Visser, S. J., Franson, K. L., Cohen, A. F., & van Gerven, J. M. A. (2003). REM sleep effects as a biomarker for the effects of antidepressants in healthy volunteers. *Journal of Psychopharmacology, 17*(2), 196–203. doi: 10.1177/0269881103017002008

Rilling, J. K., & Sanfey, A. G. (2011). The neuroscience of social decision-making. *Annual Review of Psychology, 62*, 23–48. doi: 10.1146/annurev.psych.121208.131647

Rips, L. (1975). Inductive judgments about natural categories. *Journal of Verbal Learning and Verbal Behavior, 14*, 665–681. doi: 10.1016/S0022-5371(75)80055-7

Rips, L., & Collins, A. (1993). Categories and resemblance. *Journal of Experimental Psychology: General, 122*, 468–489. doi: 10.1037/0096-3445.122.4.468

Riskind, J. H., Moore, R., & Bowley, L. (1995). The looming of spiders: The fearful perceptual distortion of movement and menace. *Behaviour Research and Therapy, 33*(2), 171–178. doi: 10.1016/0005-7967(94)e0023-c

Rivers, W. H. R. (1905). Observations on the senses of the Todas. *British Journal of Psychology, 1*, 321–396. doi: 10.1111/j.2044-8295.1905.tb00164.x

Rivkin, M. J., Davis, P. E., Lemaster, J. L., Cabral, H. J., Warfield, S. K., Mulkern, R. V., et al. (2008). Volumetric MRI study of brain in children with intrauterine exposure to cocaine, alcohol, tobacco, and marijuana. *Pediatrics, 121*(4), 741–750. doi: 10.1542/peds.2007-1399

Rivkin, M. J., Flax, J., Mozell, R., Osathanondh, R., Volpe, J. J., & Villa-Komaroff, L. (1995). Oligodendroglial development in human fetal cerebrum. *Annals of Neurology, 38*(1), 92–101. doi: 10.1002/ana.410380116

Rizvi, S. L., et al. (2011). A pilot study of the DBT coach: An interactive mobile phone application for individuals with borderline personality disorder & substance use disorder. *Behavior Therapy, 42*, 589–600. doi: 10.1016/j.beth.2011.01.003

Rizzolatti, G., Fadiga, L., Gallese, V., & Fogassi, L. (1996). Premotor cortex and the recognition of motor actions. *Cognitive Brain Research, 3*(2), 131–141. doi: 10.1016/0926-6410(95)00038-0

Robberson, M. R., & Rogers, R. W. (1988). Beyond fear appeals: Negative and positive persuasive appeals to health and self-esteem. *Journal of Applied Social Psychology, 18*, 277–287. 10.1111/j.1559-1816.1988.tb00017.x

Robins, L. N., & Regier, D. A. (Eds.). (1991). *Psychiatric disorders in America: The Epidemiologic Catchment Area Study*. New York, NY: Free Press.

Rodin, J. (1986). Aging and health: Effects of the sense of control. *Science, 233*, 1271–1276. doi: 10.1126/science.3749877

Roediger, H. L., III, & Butler, A. C. (2011). The critical role of retrieval practice in long-term retention. *Trends in Cognitive Sciences, 15*(1), 20–27. doi: 10.1016/j.tics.2010.09.003

Roenneberg, T., Kuehnle, T., Pramstaller, P. P., Ricken, J., Havel, M., Guth, A., et al. (2005). A marker for the end of adolescence. *Current Biology, 14*, R1038–R1039. doi: 10.1016/j.cub.2004.11.039

Roesch, S. C., & Amirkhan, J. H. (1997). Boundary conditions for self-serving attributions: Another look at the sports pages. *Journal of Applied Social Psychology, 27*, 245–261. doi: 10.1111/j.1559-1816.1997.tb00631.x

Roese, N. J., & Summerville, A. (2005). What we regret most . . . and why. *Personality and Social Psychology Bulletin, 31*(9), 1273–1285. doi: 10.1177/0146167205274693

Roffwarg, H. P., Muzic, J. N., & Dement, W. C. (1966). Ontogenetic development of the human sleep–dream cycle. *Science, 152*, 604–619. doi: 10.1126/science.152.3722.604

Rogers, C. R. (1942). *Counseling and psychotherapy: New concepts in practice*. Boston, MA: Houghton Mifflin.

Rogers, C. R. (1951). *Client-centered therapy: Its current practice, implications and theory*. London, United Kingdom: Constable.

Rogers, C. R. (1980). *A way of being*. Boston, MA: Houghton Mifflin.

Rogers, L. J. (2000). Evolution of hemispheric specialization: Advantages and disadvantages. *Brain and Language, 73*(2), 236–253. doi: 10.1006/brln.2000.2305

Rogers, T. B., Kuiper, N. A., & Kirker, W. S. (1977). Self-reference and the encoding of personal information. *Journal of Personality and Social Psychology, 35*(9), 677–688. doi: 10.1037/0022-3514.35.9.677

Rokeach, M. (1968). The role of values in public opinion research. *Public Opinion Quarterly, 32*(4), 547–559. doi: 10.1086/267645

Rolls, E. T. (2000). The orbitofrontal cortex and reward. *Cerebral Cortex, 10*(3), 284–294. doi: 10.1093/cercor/10.3.284

Ronald, A., & Hoekstra, R. A. (2011). Autism spectrum disorders and autistic traits: A decade of new twin studies. *American Journal of Medical Genetics Part B: Neuropsychiatric Genetics, 156*(3), 255–274. doi: 10.1002/ajmg.b.31159

Roney, J. R., Hanson, K. N., Durante, K. M., & Maestripieri, D. (2006). Reading men's faces: Women's mate attractiveness judgments track men's testosterone and interest in infants. *Proceedings of the Royal Society of London, Series B: Biological Sciences, 273*, 2169–2175. doi: 10.1098/rspb.2006.3569

Roozendaal, B., McEwen, B. S., & Chattarji, S. (2009). Stress, memory and the amygdala. *Nature Reviews Neuroscience, 10*(6), 423–433. doi: 10.1038/nrn2651

Rorschach, H. (1921). Psychodiagnostik: Methodik und ergebnisse eines wahrnehmungsdiagnostischen experiments (deutenlassen von zufallsformen) [Psychodiagnostics: Methodology and results of diagnostic perceptual experiments (suggest leave of random shapes)]. *Arbeiten zur angewandten psychiatrie* (Vol. 2). Bern, Switzerland\: Bircher.

Rosales, F., Reznick, J. S., & Zeisel, S. (2009). Understanding the role of nutrition in the brain and behavioral development of toddlers and preschool children: Identifying and addressing methodological barriers. *Nutritional Neuroscience, 12*(5), 190–202. doi: 10.1179/147683009x423454

Rosch, E. (1973). Natural categories. *Cognitive Psychology, 4*, 328–350. doi: 10.1016/0010-0285(73)90017-0

Rosch, E. (1983). Prototype classification and logical classification: The two systems. In E. Scholnick (Ed.), *New trends in cognitive representation: Challenges to Piaget's theory* (pp. 73–86). Hillsdale, NJ: Erlbaum.

Rose, D., Fleischmann, P., Wykes, T., Leese, M., & Bindman, J. (2003). Patients' perspectives on electroconvulsive therapy: Systematic review. *British Medical Journal, 326*(7403), 1363. doi: 10.1136/bmj.326.7403.1363

Rose, J. (2011). Diverse perspectives on the Groupthink theory: A literary review. *Emerging Leadership Journeys, 4*(1), 37–57.

Rose, J. E., Behm, F. M., Murugesan, T., & McClernon, F. J. (2010). Silver acetate interactions with nicotine and non-nicotine smoke components. *Experimental and Clinical Psychopharmacology, 18*(6), 462–469. doi: 10.1037/a0021966

Roselli, C. E., Larkin, K., Resko, J. A., Stellflug, J. N., & Stormshak, F. (2004). The volume of a sexually dimorphic nucleus in the ovine medial preoptic area/anterior hypothalamus varies with sexual partner preference. *Endocrinology, 145*, 478–483. doi: http://dx.doi.org/10.1210/en.2003-1098

Rosenberg, J., & Tunney, R. J. (2008). Human vocabulary use as display. *Evolutionary Psychology, 6*, 538–549.

Rosenberg, M., Schooler, C., & Schoenbach, C. (1989). Self-esteem and adolescent problems: Modeling reciprocal effects. *American Sociological Review, 54*, 1004–1018. doi: 10.2307/2095720

Rosenberg, R., Mandell, D., Farmer, J., Law, J., Marvin, A., & Law, P. (2010). Psychotropic medication use among children with autism spectrum disorders enrolled in a national registry, 2007–2008. *Journal of Autism and Developmental Disorders, 40*(3), 342–351. doi: 10.1007/s10803-009-0878-1

Rosenberg, S. D., Rosenberg, H. J., & Farrell, M. P. (1999). The midlife crisis revisited. In S. L. Willis & J. D. Reid (Eds.), *Life in the middle* (pp. 47–73). San Diego, CA: Academic Press.

Rosenstein, D., & Oster, H. (1988). Differential facial responses to four basic tastes in newborns. *Child Development, 59*, 1555–1568. doi: 10.2307/1130670

Ross, D. C., Fischhoff, J., & Davenport, B. (2002). Treatment of ADHD when tolerance to methylphenidate develops. *Psychiatric Services, 53*(1), 102–102. doi: 10.1176/appi.ps.53.1.102

Ross, G. W., & Petrovitch, H. (2001). Current evidence for neuroprotective effects of nicotine and caffeine against Parkinson's disease. *Drugs and Aging, 18*(11), 797–806. doi: 10.2165/00002512-200118110-00001

Rotge, J.-Y., Langbour, N., Jaafari, N., Guehl, D., Bioulac, B., Aouizerate, B., et al. (2010). Anatomical alterations and symptom-related functional activity in obsessive-compulsive disorder are correlated in the lateral orbitofrontal cortex. *Biological Psychiatry, 67*(7), e37–e38. doi: 10.1016/j.biopsych.2009.10.007

Roth, A., & Fonagy, P. (1996). *What works for whom? A critical review of psychotherapy research.* London, United Kingdom: Guilford Press.

Roth, G., & Dicke, U. (2005). Evolution of the brain and intelligence. *Trends in Cognitive Sciences, 9*(5), 250–257. doi: 10.1016/j.tics.2005.03.005

Rothbart, M. K. (2007). Temperament, development, and personality. *Current Directions in Psychological Science, 16*(4), 207–212. doi: 10.1111/j.1467-8721.2007.00505.x

Rothbart, M. K. (2011). *Becoming who we are: Temperament and personality in development.* New York, NY: Guilford Press.

Rothbart, M. K., Ahadi, S. A., & Evans, D. E. (2000). Temperament and personality: Origins and outcomes. *Journal of Personality and Social Psychology, 78*(1), 122–135. doi: 10.1037/0022-3514.78.1.122

Rothbart, M. K., & Derryberry, D. (1981). Development of individual differences in temperament. In M. E. Lamb & A. L. Brown (Eds.), *Advances in developmental psychology* (Vol. 1, pp. 37–86). Hillsdale, NJ: Erlbaum.

Rothbart, M. K., Sheese, B. E., Rueda, M. R., & Posner, M. I. (2011). Developing mechanisms of self-regulation in early life. *Emotion Review, 3*(2), 207–213. doi: 10.1177/1754073910387943

Rothbaum, B. O., Rizzo, A. S., & Difede, J. (2010). Virtual reality exposure therapy for combat-related posttraumatic stress disorder. *Annals of the New York Academy of Sciences, 1208*(1), 126–132. doi: 10.1111/j.1749-6632.2010.05691.x

Rotter, J. B. (1966). Generalized expectancies for internal versus external control of reinforcement. *Psychological Monographs, 80*, 1–27. doi: 10.1037/h0092976

Rovee-Collier, C. (1997). Dissociations in infant memory: Rethinking the development of implicit and explicit memory. *Psychological Review, 104*, 467–498. doi: 10.1037/0033-295X.104.3.467

Rowland, L. W. (1939). Will hypnotized persons try to harm themselves or others? *Journal of Abnormal and Social Psychology, 34*, 114–117. doi: 10.1037/h0055818

Rucker, D., Padwal, R., Li, S. K., Curioni, C., & Lau, D. C. (2007). Long-term pharmacotherapy for obesity and overweight: Updated meta-analysis. *British Medical Journal, 335*(7631), 1194–1199. doi: http://dx.doi.org/10.1136/bmj.39385.413113.25

Rule, N. O., Ambady, N., Adams, R. B., Jr., Ozono, H., Nakashima, S., Yoshikawa, S., et al. (2010). Polling the face: Prediction and consensus across cultures. *Journal of Personality and Social Psychology, 98*(1), 1–15. doi: 10.1037/a0017673

Rule, N. O., Rosen, K. S., Slepian, M. L., & Ambady, N. (2011). Mating interest improves women's accuracy in judging male sexual orientation. *Psychological Science, 22*(7), 881–886. doi: 10.1177/0956797611412394

Ruscio, A., Stein, D., Chiu, W., & Kessler, R. (2010). The epidemiology of obsessive-compulsive disorder in the National Comorbidity Survey Replication. *Molecular Psychiatry, 15*(1), 53–63. doi: 10.1038/mp.2008.94

Rush, B. (1812). *Medical inquiries and observations upon the diseases of the mind.* Philadelphia, PA: Kimber & Richardson.

Rushton, D. H., Dover, R., Sainsbury, A. W., Norris, M. J., Gilkes, J. J., & Ramsey, I. D. (2001). Why should women have lower reference limits for haemoglobin and ferritin concentrations than men? *British Medical Journal, 322*, 1355–1357. doi: http://dx.doi.org/10.1136/bmj.322.7298.1355

Rushton, J. P., Fulker, D. W., Neale, M. C., Nias, D. K. B., & Eysenck, H. J. (1986). Altruism and aggression: The heritability of individual differences. *Journal of Personality and Social Psychology, 50*, 1192–1198. doi: 10.1037/0022-3514.50.6.1192

Russell, D., & Cutrona, C. (2010). *Stressful effects of where you live: Studying the influence of neighborhood context over time.* Paper presented at the World Conference on Stress and Anxiety Research, Galway, Ireland.

Russell, D., Peplau, L. A., & Cutrona, C. E. (1980). The revised UCLA Loneliness Scale: Concurrent and discriminant validity evidence. *Journal of Personality and Social Psychology, 39*(3), 472–480. doi: 10.1037/0022-3514.39.3.472

Russell, J. A. (1980). A circumplex model of affect. *Journal of Personality and Social Psychology, 39*, 1161–1178. doi: 10.1037/h0077714

Russo, R., & Mammarella, N. (2002). Spacing effects in recognition memory: When meaning matters. *European Journal of Cognitive Psychology, 14*, 49–59. doi: 10.1080/09541440042000133

Rust, J. (1999). Discriminant validity of the "Big Five" personality traits in employment settings. *Social Behavior and Personality, 27*(1), 99–108. doi: http://dx.doi.org/10.2224/sbp.1999.27.1.99

Ruwaard, J., Lange, A., Schrieken, B., & Emmelkamp, P. M. G. (2011). Efficacy and effectiveness of online cognitive behavioral treatment: A decade of Interapy research. *Studies in Health Technology and Informatics, 167*, 9–14. doi: 10.3233/978-1-60750-766-6-9

Rypma, B., Berger, J. S., Prabhakaran, V., Martin Bly, B., Kimberg, D. Y., Biswal, B. B., et al. (2006). Neural correlates of cognitive efficiency. *NeuroImage, 33*(3), 969–979. doi: 10.1016/j.neuroimage.2006.05.065

Rypma, B., & Prabhakaran, V. (2009). When less is more and when more is more: The mediating roles of capacity and speed in brain–behavior efficiency. *Intelligence, 37*(2), 207–222. doi: 10.1016/j.intell.2008 .12.004

Sabatini, R. M. E. (1997). The history of lobotomy. Retrieved from http://www .cerebromente.org.br/n02/historia/ lobotomy.htm

Sacco, K. A., Termine, A., & Seyal, A. (2005). Effects of cigarette smoking on spatial working memory and attentional deficits in schizophrenia: Involvement of nicotinic receptor mechanisms. *Archives of General Psychiatry, 62*(6), 649–659. doi: 10.1001/ archpsyc.62.6.649

Sackett, G. P. (1966). Monkeys reared in isolation with pictures as visual input: Evidence for an innate releasing mechanism. *Science, 154*, 1468–1473. doi: 10.1126/science.154.3755.1468

Sackheim, H. A., Prudic, J., Fuller, R., Keilp, J., Lavori, P. W., & Olfson, M. (2007). The cognitive effects of electroconvulsive therapy in community settings. *Neuropsychopharmacology, 32*, 244–254. doi: 10.1038/sj.npp.1301180

Sajatovic, M., Valenstein, M., Blow, F., Ganoczy, D., & Ignacio, R. (2007). Treatment adherence with lithium and anticonvulsant medications among patients with bipolar disorder. *Psychiatric Services, 58*(6), 855–863. doi: 10.1176/appi .ps.58.6.855

Sakai, Y., Shaw, C. A., Dawson, B. C., Dugas, D. V., Al-Mohtaseb, Z., Hill, D. E., et al. (2011). Protein interactome reveals converging molecular pathways among autism disorders. *Science Translational Medicine, 3*(86), 86ra49. doi: 10.1126/scitranslmed.3002166

Sakurai, T., Amemiya, A., Ishii, M., Matsuzaki, I., Chemelli, R. M., Tanaka, H., et al. (1998). Orexins and orexin receptors: A family of hypothalamic neuropeptides and G protein–coupled receptors that regulate feeding behavior. *Cell, 92*(5), 573–585. doi: 10.1016/S0092-8674(00)80949-6

Salazar, M., & Frincke, J. (2005, April). *Yesterday, today, and tomorrow. Careers in psychology: 2005. What students need to know.* Paper presented at the Annual Convention of the Western Psychological Association, Portland, OR.

Salmon, S. (2004). The PEACE curriculum: Expanded aggression replacement training. In A. P. Goldstein, R. Nensén, B. Daleflod, & M. Kalt (Eds.), *New perspectives on aggression replacement training* (pp. 171–188). Chichester, United Kingdom: Wiley.

Sanfey, A. G., Rilling, J. K., Aronson, J. A., Nystrom, L. E., & Cohen, J. D. (2003). The neural basis of economic decision-making in the Ultimatum Game. *Science, 300*, 1755–1758. doi: 10.1126/science.1082976

Santosa, C. M., Strong, C. M., Nowakowska, C., Wang, P. W., Rennicke, C. M., & Ketter, T. A. (2007). Enhanced creativity in bipolar disorder patients: A controlled study. *Journal of Affective Disorders, 100*(1–3), 31–39. doi: 10.1016/j.jad.2006.10.013

Sapolsky, R. M. (2001). *A primate's memoir.* New York, NY: Scribner.

Sapolsky, R. M., Krey, L. C., & McEwen, B. S. (1985). Prolonged glucocorticoid exposure reduces hippocampal neuron number: Implications for aging. *Journal of Neuroscience, 5*, 1222–1227.

Savage-Rumbaugh, S., Shanker, S. G., & Taylor, T. J. (1998). *Apes, language, and the human mind.* New York, NY: Oxford University Press.

Savine, R., & Sönksen, P. (2000). Growth hormone—Hormone replacement for the somatopause? *Hormone Research, 53*(Suppl. 3), 37–41. doi: 10.1159/ 000023531

Savin-Williams, R. C. (2006). Who's gay? Does it matter? *Current Directions in Psychological Science, 15*(1), 40–44. doi: 10.1111/j.0963-7214.2006.00403.x

Saxena, S. (2003). Neuroimaging and the pathophysiology of obsessive compulsive disorder (OCD). In C. H. Y. Fu, C. Senior, T. Russell, D. Weinberger, & R. Murray (Eds.), *Neuroimaging in psychiatry* (pp. 191–224). London, United Kingdom: Martin Dunitz.

Saxena, S., Brody, A. L., Maidment, K. M., Smith, E. C., Zohrabi, N., Katz, E., et al. (2004). Cerebral glucose metabolism in obsessive-compulsive hoarding. *American Journal of Psychiatry, 161*, 1038–1048. doi: 10.1176/appi.ajp.161.6.1038

Schachter, S. (1951). Deviation, rejection, and communication. *Journal of Abnormal Psychology, 46*, 190–207. doi: 10.1037/ h0062326

Schachter, S. (1959). *The psychology of affiliation: Experimental studies of the sources of gregariousness.* Stanford, CA: Stanford University Press.

Schachter, S., & Singer, J. (1962). Cognitive, social and physiological determinants of emotional state. *Psychological Review, 69*, 379–399. doi: 10.1037/h0046234

Schaffer, C. E., Davidson, R. J., & Saron, C. (1983). Frontal and parietal electroencephalogram asymmetry in depressed and non-depressed subjects. *Biological Psychiatry, 18*, 753–762.

Schaie, K. W. (1996). *Intellectual development in adulthood: The Seattle Longitudinal Study.* Cambridge, United Kingdom: Cambridge University Press.

Schechter, R., & Grether, J. K. (2008). Continuing increases in autism reported to California's developmental services system: Mercury in retrograde. *Archives of General Psychiatry, 65*(1), 19–24. doi: 10.1001/ archgenpsychiatry.2007.1

Schenck, C. H., Bundlie, S. R., Ettinger, M. G., & Mahowald, M. W. (1986). Chronic behavioral disorders of human REM sleep: A new category of parasomnia. *Sleep, 9*, 293–308.

Schimmelmann, B. G., Friedel, S., Nguyen, T. T., Sauer, S., Vogel, C. I. G., Konrad, K., et al. (2009). Exploring the genetic link

between RLS and ADHD. *Journal of Psychiatric Research, 43*(10), 941–945. doi: 10.1016/j.jpsychires.2009.01.003

Schjedlderup-Ebbe, T. (1922). Beiträge zur sozialpsychologie des haushuhns [Contributions to the social psychology of the house chicken]. *Zeitschrift für Psychologie, 88*, 225–252.

Schlaug, G., Forgeard, M., Zhu, L., Norton, A., Norton, A., & Winner, E. (2009). Training-induced neuroplasticity in young children. *Annals of the New York Academy of Sciences, 1169*, 205–208. doi: 10.1111/ j.1749-6632.2009.04842.x

Schlaug, G., Jäncke, L., Huang, Y., & Steinmetz, H. (1995). In vivo evidence of structural brain asymmetry in musicians. *Science, 267*, 699–701. doi: 10.1126/ science.7839149

Schnakers, C., Vanhaudenhuyse, A., Giacino, J., Ventura, M., Boly, M., Majerus, S., et al. (2009). Diagnostic accuracy of the vegetative and minimally conscious state: Clinical consensus versus standardized neurobehavioral assessment. *BMC Neurology, 9*(1), 35. doi: 10.1186/1471-2377-9-35

Schneider, F., Gur, R. C., Koch, K., Backes, V., Amunts, K., Shah, N. J., et al. (2006). Impairment in the specificity of emotion processing in schizophrenia. *American Journal of Psychiatry, 163*, 442–447. doi: 10.1176/appi.ajp.163.3.442

Schober, M. F., & Carstensen, L. L. (2010). Does being together for years help comprehension? In E. Morsella (Ed.), *Expressing oneself/expressing one's self: Communication, cognition, language, and identity* (pp. 107–124). Hove, United Kingdom: Psychology Press/Taylor & Francis.

Schön, D., Gordon, R., Campagne, A., Magne, C., Astésano, C., Anton, J.-L., et al. (2010). Similar cerebral networks in language, music and song perception. *NeuroImage.* doi: 10.1016/j.neuroimage.2010.02.023

Schroeder, S. (2008). Stranded in the periphery—The increasing marginalization of smokers. *New England Journal of Medicine, 358*(21), 2284–2286. doi: 10.1056/ NEJMe0802708

Schroeder, V., & Kelley, M. (2009). Associations between family environment, parenting practices, and executive functioning of children with and without ADHD. *Journal of Child and Family Studies, 18*(2), 227–235. doi: 10.1007/ s10826-008-9223-0

Schumann, C. M., Bauman, M. D., Machado, C. J., & Amaral, D. G. (2006). The social brain, amygdala, and autism. In S. O. Moldin & J. L. R. Rubenstein (Eds.), *Understanding autism: From basic neuroscience to treatment* (pp. 227–253). Boca Raton, FL: Taylor & Francis.

Schurz, G. (1985). Experimentelle überprüfung des zusammenhangs zwischen persönlichkeitsmerkmalen und der bereitschaft zum destruktiven gehorsam gegenüber autoritäten [Experimental examination of the relationship between personality characteristics and the readiness to destructive obedience to authorities]. *Zeitschrift für Experimentelle und Angewandte Psychologie, 32,* 160–177.

Schuster, M. A., Stein, L. H., Jaycox, R. L., Marshall, G. N., Elliott, M. N., Zhou, J., et al. (2002). After 9/11: Stress and coping across America. Retrieved from http://www.rand.org/pubs/testimonies/2005/CT198.pdf

Schwartz, B. (1984). *Psychology of learning and behavior* (2nd ed.). New York, NY: Norton.

Schwartz, B., Ward, A., Monterosso, J., Lyubomirsky, S., White, K., & Lehman, D. R. (2002). Maximizing versus satisficing: Happiness is a matter of choice. *Journal of Personality and Social Psychology, 83*(5), 1178–1197. doi: 10.1037/0022-3514.83.5.1178

Schwartz, C. E., Snidman, N., & Kagan, J. (1999). Adolescent social anxiety as an outcome of inhibited temperament in childhood. *Journal of the American Academy of Child and Adolescent Psychiatry, 38*(8), 1008–1015. doi: 10.1097/00004583-199908000-00017

Schwarz, M., & Susswein, A. J. (1992). Presence of conspecifics facilitates learning that food is inedible in *Aplysia fasciata. Behavioral Neuroscience, 106*(2), 250–261. doi: 10.1037/0735-7044.106.2.250

Scott, V., & Gijsbers, K. (1981). Pain perception in competitive swimmers. *British Medical Journal, 283,* 91–93. doi: http://dx.doi.org/10.1136/bmj.283.6284.91

Scully, J. A., Tosi, H., & Banning, K. (2000). Life event checklists: Revisiting the Social Readjustment Rating Scale after 30 years. *Educational and Psychological Measurement, 60,* 864–876. doi: 10.1177/00131640021970952

Segall, H. H., Campbell, D. T., & Herskovits, M. J. (1966). *The influence of culture on visual perception.* Indianapolis, IN: Bobbs-Merrill.

Segerstrom, S. C., & Miller, G. E. (2004). Psychological stress and the human immune system: A meta-analytic study of 30 years of inquiry. *Psychological Bulletin, 130,* 601–630. doi: 10.1037/0033-2909.130.4.601

Sekiguchi, A., & Kawashima, R. (2007). Cognitive rehabilitation—The learning therapy for the senile dementia. *Brain Nerve, 59*(4), 357–365.

Seksel, K., & Lindeman, M. J. (2001). Use of clomipramine in treatment of obsessive-compulsive disorder, separation anxiety and noise phobia in dogs: A preliminary, clinical study. *Australian Veterinary Journal, 79,* 252–256. doi: 10.1111/j.1751-0813.2001.tb11976.x

Seligman, M. E. P. (1971). Phobias and preparedness. *Behavior Therapy, 2*(3), 307–320. doi: 10.1016/s0005-7894(71)80064-3

Seligman, M. E. P. (1987, February). *Predicting depression, poor health, and presidential elections.* Paper presented at the Science and Public Policy Seminar sponsored by the Federation of Behavioral, Psychological and Cognitive Sciences, Washington, DC.

Seligman, M. E. P. (1990). *Learned optimism.* New York, NY: Simon and Schuster.

Seligman, M. E. P. (2002). *Authentic happiness: Using the new positive psychology to realize your potential for lasting fulfillment.* New York, NY: Simon and Schuster.

Seligman, M. E. P., Abramson, L. Y., & Semmel, A. (1979). Depressive attributional style. *Journal of Abnormal Psychology, 88,* 242–247. doi: 10.1037/0021-843X.88.3.242

Seligman, M. E. P., & Csikszentmihalyi, M. (2000). Positive psychology: An introduction. *American Psychologist, 55*(1), 5–14. doi: 10.1037/0003-066x.55.1.5

Selye, H. (1946). The general adaptation syndrome and the diseases of adaptation. *Journal of Clinical Endocrinology, 6,* 177–231. doi: http://dx.doi.org/10.1210/jcem-6-2-117

Selye, H. (1975). Confusion and controversy in the stress field. *Journal of Human Stress, 1*(2), 37–44. doi: 10.1080/0097840X.1975.9940406

Senju, A., Maeda, M., Kikuchi, Y., Hasegawa, T., Tojo, Y., & Osanai, H. (2007). Absence of contagious yawning in children with autism spectrum disorder. *Biology Letters, 3*(6), 706–708. doi: 10.1098/rsbl.2007.0337

Senju, A., Southgate, V., White, S., & Frith, U. (2009). Mindblind eyes: An absence of spontaneous theory of mind in Asperger syndrome. *Science, 325*(5942), 883–885. doi: 10.1126/science.1176170

Sereno, M. I., & Tootell, R. B. H. (2005). From monkeys to humans: What do we now know about brain homologies? *Current Opinion in Neurobiology, 15,* 135–144. doi: 10.1016/j.conb.2005.03.014

Setchell, J. M., & Wickings, E. J. (2005). Dominance, status signals and coloration in male mandrills (*Mandrillus sphinx*). *Ethology, 111,* 25–50. doi: 10.1111/j.1439-0310.2004.01054.x

Sethi, S. (2013). Treating youth depression and anxiety: A randomised controlled trial examining the efficacy of computerised versus face-to-face cognitive behaviour therapy. *Australian Psychologist, 48*(4), 249–257. doi: 10.1111/ap.12006

Shallice, T., & Warrington, E. K. (1970). Independent functioning of verbal memory stores: A neuropsychological study. *Quarterly Journal of Experimental Psychology, 22,* 261–273. doi: 10.1080/00335557043000203

Shaw, P., Cirelli, C., Greenspan, R. J., & Giulio Tononi, G. (2000). Correlates of sleep and waking in *Drosophila melanogaster. Science, 287,* 1834–1837. doi: 10.1126/science.287.5459.1834

Shaw, P., Eckstrand, K., Sharp, W., Blumenthal, J., Lerch, J. P., Greenstein, D., et al. (2007). Attention-deficit/hyperactivity disorder is characterized by a delay in cortical maturation. *Proceedings of the National Academy of Sciences, 104*(49), 19649–19654. doi: 10.1073/pnas.0707741104

Shaw, P., Greenstein, D., Lerch, J., Clasen, L., Lenroot, R., Gogtay, N., et al. (2006). Intellectual ability and cortical development in children and adolescents. *Nature, 440*(7084), 676–679. doi: 10.1038/nature04513

Shaw, P., Malek, M., Watson, B., Greenstein, D., de Rossi, P., & Sharp, W. (2013). Trajectories of cerebral cortical development in childhood and adolescence and adult attention-deficit/hyperactivity disorder. *Biological Psychiatry, 74*(8), 599–606. doi: 10.1016/j.biopsych.2013.04.007

Shaywitz, S. (1996). Dyslexia. *Scientific American, 275,* 98–105.

Shaywitz, S. E., Morris, R., & Shaywitz, B. A. (2008). The education of dyslexic children from childhood to young adulthood. *Annual Review of Psychology, 59,* 451–475. doi: 10.1146/annurev.psych.59.103006.093633

Shaywitz, S., Shaywitz, B. A., Pugh, K. R., Fulbright, R. K., Constable, R. T., Mencl, W. E., et al. (1998). Functional disruption in the organization of the brain for reading in dyslexia. *Proceedings of the National Academy of Sciences, 95,* 2636–2641.

Shedler, J. (2010). The efficacy of psychodynamic psychotherapy. *American Psychologist, 65*(2), 98–109. doi: 10.1037/a0018378

Shelton, J. F., Tancredi, D. J., & Hertz-Picciotto, I. (2010). Independent and dependent contributions of advanced maternal and paternal ages to autism risk. *Autism Research, 3*(1), 30–39. doi: 10.1002/aur.116

Shepard, R. N. (1990). *Mind sights: Original visual illusions, ambiguities, and other anomalies with a commentary on the play of mind in perception and art.* New York, NY: W. H. Freeman.

Sher, L. (2006). Alcohol consumption and suicide. *QJM: Monthly Journal of the Association of Physicians, 99*(1), 57–61. doi: 10.1093/qjmed/hci146

Sheridan, S. M., & Burt, J. D. (2009). Family-centered positive psychology. In S. J. Lopez & C. R. Snyder (Eds.), *Oxford handbook of positive psychology* (2nd ed., pp. 551–559). New York, NY: Oxford University Press.

Sherif, M., Harvey, L. J., White, B. J., Hood, W. R., & Sherif, C. (1961). *The Robbers Cave experiment: Intergroup conflict and cooperation.* Norman, OK: University of Oklahoma Institute of Intergroup Relations.

Sherman, D. K., & Kim, H. S. (2005). Is there an "I" in "team"? The role of the self in group-serving judgments. *Journal of*

Personality and Social Psychology, 88(1), 108–120. doi: 10.1037/0022-3514.88.1.108

Shi, J., Potash, J., Knowles, J., Weissman, M., Coryell, W., Scheftner, W., et al. (2011). Genome-wide association study of recurrent early-onset major depressive disorder. *Molecular Psychiatry, 16*(2), 193–201. doi: 10.1038/mp.2009.124

Shields, M. (2004). Stress, health, and the benefit of social support. *Health Reports (Statistics Canada, Catalogue 82-003), 15*, 9–38.

Shifren, J. L., Braunstein, G. D., Simon, J. A., Casson, P. R., Buster, J. E., Redmond, G. P., et al. (2000). Transdermal testosterone treatment in women with impaired sexual function after oophorectomy. *New England Journal of Medicine, 343*, 682–688. doi: 10.1056/NEJM200009073431002

Shih, M., & Sanchez, D. T. (2009). When race becomes even more complex: Toward understanding the landscape of multiracial identity and experiences. *Journal of Social Issues, 65*(1), 1–11. doi: 10.1111/j.1540-4560.2008.01584.x

Shin, S. H., Edwards, E. M., & Heeren, T. (2009). Child abuse and neglect: Relations to adolescent binge drinking in the National Longitudinal Study of Adolescent Health (AddHealth) Study. *Addiction and Behavior, 34*(3), 277–280. doi: 10.1016/j.addbeh.2008.10.023

Shin, S. H., Edwards, E., Heeren, T., & Amodeo, M. (2009). Relationship between multiple forms of maltreatment by a parent or guardian and adolescent alcohol use. *American Journal on Addictions, 18*(3), 226–234. doi: 10.1080/10550490902786959

Shiota, M. N., & Levenson, R. W. (2007). Birds of a feather don't always fly farthest: Similarity in Big Five personality predicts more negative marital satisfaction trajectories in long-term marriages. *Psychology and Aging, 22*(4), 666–675. doi: 10.1037/0882-7974.22.4.666

Ship, J. A., & Weiffenbach, J. M. (1993). Age, gender, medical treatment, and medication effects on smell identification. *Journals of Gerontology: Series A. Biological Sciences and Medical Sciences, 48*, M26–M32. doi: 10.1093/geronj/48.1.M26

Shu, L. L., Gino, F., & Bazerman, M. H. (2011). Dishonest deed, clear conscience: When cheating leads to moral disengagement and motivated forgetting. *Personality and Social Psychology Bulletin, 37*(3), 330–349. doi: 10.1177/0146167211398138

Shute, N. (2000). A maddening disconnect: Unraveling the mysteries of autism. Retrieved from http://www.usnews.com:80/usnews/issue/000605/autism.htm

Sia, C.-L., Tan, B. C. Y., & Wei, K.-K. (2002). Group polarization and computer-mediated communication: Effects of communication cues, social presence, and anonymity. *Information Systems Research, 13*(1), 70–90. doi: 10.1287/isre.13.1.70.92

Siegel, J. M. (2001). The REM sleep–memory consolidation hypothesis. *Science, 294*, 1058–1063. doi: 10.1126/science.1063049

Siegel, J. Z., & Crockett, M. J. (2013). How serotonin shapes moral judgment and behavior. *Annals of the New York Academy of Sciences, 1299*(1), 42–51. doi: 10.1111/nyas.12229

Siegfried, J. (2010). Airlines may charge fat people higher fares. Retrieved from http://www.examiner.com/airlines-airport-in-national/airlines-may-charge-fat-people-higher-fares

Siegle, G., Sagratti, S., & Crawford, C. (1999). *Effects of rumination and initial severity on response to cognitive therapy for depression.* Paper presented at the Meeting of the Association for the Advancement of Behavior Therapy, Toronto, ON.

Siever, L. J. (2008). Neurobiology of aggression and violence. *American Journal of Psychiatry, 165*(4), 429–442. doi: 10.1176/appi.ajp.2008.07111774

Silvia, P. J. (2005). Deflecting reactance: The role of similarity in increasing compliance and reducing resistance. *Basic and Applied Social Psychology, 27*, 277–284. doi: 10.1207/s15324834basp2703_9

Simon, H. A. (1957). *Models of man, social and rational: Mathematical essays on rational human behavior.* New York, NY: Wiley.

Simons, D. J., & Chabris, C. F. (1999). Gorillas in our midst: Sustained inattentional blindness for dynamic events. *Perception, 28*(9), 1059–1074. doi: 10.1068/p2952

Simons, L. G., & Conger, R. D. (2007). Linking mother–father differences in parenting to a typology of family parenting styles and adolescent outcomes. *Journal of Family Issues, 28*(2), 212–241. doi: 10.1177/0192513X06294593

Simons-Morton, B. G., Bingham, C. R., Falk, E. B., Li, K., Pradhan, A. K., Ouimet, M. C., et al. (2014). Experimental effects of injunctive norms on simulated risky driving among teenage males. *Health Psychology 33*(7), 616–627. doi: 10.1037/a0034837

Simpson, D. (2005). Phrenology and the neurosciences: Contributions of F. J. Gall and J. G. Spurzheim. *ANZ Journal of Surgery, 75*(6), 475. doi: 10.1111/j.1445-2197.2005.03426.x

Singer, M. I., Miller, D. B., Guo, S., Slovak, K., & Frierson, T. (1998). *The mental health consequences of children's exposure to violence.* Cleveland, OH: Cuyahoga County Community Mental Health Research Institute, Mandel School of Applied Social Sciences, Case Western Reserve University.

Singer, T., Kiebel, S. J., Winston, J. S., Dolan, R. J., & Frith, C. D. (2004). Brain responses to the acquired moral status of faces. *Neuron, 41*(4), 653–662. doi: 10.1016/S0896-6273(04)00014-5

Sinha, Y., Silove, N., & Williams, K. (2006). Chelation therapy and autism. *British Medical Journal, 333*(7571), 756. doi: http://dx.doi.org/10.1136/bmj.333.7571.756

Skene, D. J., Lockley, S. W., & Arendt, J. (1999). Use of melatonin in the treatment of phase shift and sleep disorders. *Advances in Experimental Medicine and Biology, 467*, 79–84. doi: 10.1007/978-1-4615-4709-9_10

Skerry, P. (2000). *Counting on the census? Race, group identity, and the evasion of politics.* Washington, DC: The Brookings Institution.

Skinner, B. F. (1953a). *Science and human behavior.* New York, NY: Macmillan.

Skinner, B. F. (1953b). Some contributions of an experimental analysis of behavior to psychology as a whole. *American Psychologist, 8*, 69–78. doi: 10.1037/h0054118

Skinner, B. F. (1960). Pigeons in a pelican. *American Psychologist, 15*, 28–37. doi: 10.1037/h0045345

Skinner, B. F. (1970). *Verbal behavior.* New York, NY: Appleton-Century-Crofts.

Skinner, B. F. (1971). *Beyond freedom and dignity.* New York, NY: Knopf.

Skodol, A. E., & Bender, D. S. (2003). Why are women diagnosed borderline more than men? *Psychiatric Quarterly, 74*(4), 349–360. doi: 10.1023/A:1026087410516

Skuse, D. H. (2000). Behavioural phenotypes: What do they teach us? *Archives of Disease in Childhood, 82*(3), 222–225. doi: 10.1136/adc.82.3.222

Slob, A. K., Bax, C. M., Hop, W. C., Rowland, D. L., & van der Werff ten Bosch, J. J. (1996). Sexual arousability and the menstrual cycle. *Psychoneuroendocrinology, 21*, 545–558. doi: 10.1016/0306-4530(95)00058-5

Slobodchikoff, C. N., Perla, B. S., & Verdoli, J. L. (2009). *Communication and community in an animal society.* Cambridge, MA: Harvard University Press.

Slotema, C. W., Blom, J. D., Hoek, H. W., & Sommer, I. E. (2010). Should we expand the toolbox of psychiatric treatment methods to include Repetitive Transcranial Magnetic Stimulation (rTMS)? A meta-analysis of the efficacy of rTMS in psychiatric disorders. *Journal of Clinical Psychiatry, 71*(7), 873–884. doi: 10.4088/JCP.08m04872gre

Slovic, P., Finucane, M., Peters, E., & MacGregor, D. G. (2002). The affect heuristic. In T. Gilovich, D. Griffin, & D. Kahneman (Eds.), *Heuristics and biases* (pp. 397–420). New York, NY: Cambridge University Press.

Smith, E. E., & Grossman, M. (2008). Multiple systems of category learning. *Neuroscience and Biobehavioral Reviews, 32*(2), 249–264. doi: 10.1016/j.neubiorev.2007.07.009

Smith, E. E., Shoben, E. J., & Rips, L. J. (1974). Structure and process in semantic memory: A feature model for semantic decisions. *Psychological Review, 81*, 214–241. doi: 10.1037/h0036351

Smith, T., & Lovaas, I. (1998). Intensive early behavioral intervention with autism: The UCLA Young Autism Project. *Infants and Young Children, 10,* 67–78. doi: 10.1007/s10803-008-0596-0

Sneed, D. (2006). Teen murder suspect's judgment could be impaired, says doctor. *The Tribune,* San Luis Obispo, CA, p. B1.

Sneed, J. R., Whitbourne, S. K., & Culang, M. E. (2006). Trust, identity, and ego integrity: Modeling Erikson's core stages over 34 years. *Journal of Adult Development, 13*(3–4), 148–157. doi: 10.1007/s10804-007-9026-3

Snyder, C. R. (1994). *The psychology of hope: You can get there from here.* New York, NY: Free Press.

Snyder, C. R., Berg, C., Woodward, J. T., Gum, A., Rand, K. L., Wrobleski, K. K., et al. (2005). Hope against the cold: Individual differences in trait hope and acute pain tolerance on the cold pressor task. *Journal of Personality, 73*(2), 287–312. doi: 10.1111/j.1467-6494.2005.00318.x

Snyder, C. R., Harris, C., Anderson, J. R., Holeran, S. A., Irving, L. M., Sigmon, S. T., et al. (1991). The will and the ways: Development and validation of an individual-differences measure of hope. *Journal of Personality and Social Psychology, 60,* 570–585. doi: 10.1037/0022-3514.60.4.570

Snyder, C. R., Rand, K. L., & Sigmon, D. R. (2002). Hope theory: A member of the positive psychology family. In C. R. Snyder & S. J. Lopez (Eds.), *Handbook of positive psychology* (pp. 257–276). New York, NY: Oxford University Press.

Society for Neuroscience. (2014). History of SfN. Retrieved from http://www.sfn.org/About/What-We-Do/History-of-SfN

Society of Psychological Hypnosis, Division 30 of the American Psychological Association. (n.d.). The official Division 30 definition and description of hypnosis. Retrieved from http://psychologicalhypnosis.com/info/the-official-division-30-definition-and-description-of-hypnosis/

Soon, C. S., Brass, M., Heinze, H.-J., & Haynes, J.-D. (2008). Unconscious determinants of free decisions in the human brain. *Nature Neuroscience, 11*(5), 543–545. doi: 10.1038/nn.2112

Soons, J. P. M., Liefbroer, A. C., & Kalmijn, M. (2009). The long-term consequences of relationship formation for subjective well-being. *Journal of Marriage and Family, 71*(5), 1254–1270. doi: 10.1111/j.1741-3737.2009.00667.x

Soria, V., Martinez-Amoros, E., Escaramis, G., Valero, J., Perez-Egea, R., Garcia, C., et al. (2010). Differential association of circadian genes with mood disorders: *CRY1* and *NPAS2* are associated with unipolar major depression and *CLOCK* and *VIP* with bipolar disorder. *Neuropsychopharmacology, 35*(6), 1279–1289. doi: 10.1038/npp.2009.230

Sorkhabi, N. (2005). Applicability of Baumrind's parent typology to collective cultures: Analysis of cultural explanations of parent socialization effects. *International Journal of Behavioral Development, 29*(6), 552–563. doi: 10.1177/01650250500172640

Soto-Faraco, S., Kingstone, A., & Spence, C. (2006). Integrating motion information across sensory modalities: The role of top-down factors. In S. Martinez-Conde, S. L. Macknik, L. M. Martinez, J. M. Alonso, & P. U. Tse (Eds.), *Progress in brain research* (Vol. 155, Part 2, pp. 273–286). New York, NY: Elsevier.

Sowell, E. R., Mattson, S. N., Kan, E., Thompson, P. M., Riley, E. P., & Toga, A. W. (2008). Abnormal cortical thickness and brain-behavior correlation patterns in individuals with heavy prenatal alcohol exposure. *Cerebral Cortex, 18*(1), 136–144. doi: 10.1093/cercor/bhm039

Sowislo, J. F., & Orth, U. (2013). Does low self-esteem predict depression and anxiety? A meta-analysis of longitudinal studies. *Psychological Bulletin, 139*(1), 213. doi: 10.1037/a0028931

Spearman, C. E. (1904). "General intelligence" objectively determined and measured. *American Journal of Psychology, 5,* 201–293. doi: 10.2307/1412107

Speer, A. M., Wassermann, E. M., Benson, B. E., Herscovitch, P., & Post, R. M. (2014). Antidepressant efficacy of high and low frequency rTMS at 110% of motor threshold versus sham stimulation over left prefrontal cortex. *Brain Stimulation, 7*(1), 36–41. doi: 10.1016/j.brs.2013.07.004

Spence, S. A., Brooks, D. J., Hirsch, S. R., Liddle, P. F. Meehan, J., & Grasby, P. M. (1997). A PET study of voluntary movement in schizophrenic patients experiencing passivity phenomena (delusions of alien control). *Brain, 120,* 1997–2011. doi: 10.1093/brain/120.11.1997

Sperling, G. (1960). The information available in brief visual presentations. *Psychological Monographs, 74* (11), 1–29. doi: 10.1037/h0093759

Sperry, R. W. (1982). Some effects of disconnecting the cerebral hemispheres. *Science, 217,* 1223–1226. doi: 10.1007/BF01115112

Spiegel, K., Tasali, E., Penev, P., & Van Cauter, E. (2004). Brief communication: Sleep curtailment in healthy young men is associated with decreased leptin levels, elevated ghrelin levels, and increased hunger and appetite. *Annals of Internal Medicine, 141*(11), 846–850. doi: 10.7326/0003-4819-141-11-200412070-00008

Spieker, L. E., Hürlimann, D., Ruschitzka, F., Corti, R., Enseleit, F., Shaw, S., et al. (2002). Mental stress induces prolonged endothelial dysfunction via endothelin-A receptors. *Circulation, 105*(24), 2817–2820. doi: 10.1161/01.cir.0000021598.15895.34

Spieler, D., Kaffe, M., Knauf, F., Bessa, J., Tena, J. J., Giesert, F., et al. (2014). Restless legs syndrome–associated intronic common variant in *Meis1* alters enhancer function in the developing telencephalon. *Genome Research, 24*(4), 592–603. doi: 10.1101/gr.166751.113

Spira, J. L., Pyne, J. M., Wiederhold, B., Wiederhold, M., Graap, K., & Rizzo, A. (2006). Virtual reality and other experiential therapies for combat-related posttraumatic stress disorder. *Primary Psychiatry, 13*(3), 58–64.

Sprengnether, M. (1990). The spectral mother: Freud, feminism and psychoanalysis. Ithaca, NY: Cornell University Press.

Springer, S. P., & Deutsch, G. (1998). *Left brain, right brain* (5th ed.). New York, NY: Freeman.

Squire, L. R. (1987). *Memory and the brain.* New York, NY: Oxford University Press.

Sroufe, L. A., Carlson, E. A., & Levy, A. K. (2003). Implications of attachment theory for developmental psychopathology. In M. E. Hertzig & E. A. Farber (Eds.), *Annual progress in child psychiatry and child development: 2000–2001* (pp. 43–61). New York, NY: Brunner-Routledge.

Stader, S. R., & Hokanson, J. E. (1998). Psychosocial antecedents of depressive symptoms: An evaluation using daily experiences methodology. *Journal of Abnormal Psychology, 107*(1), 17–26. doi: 10.1037/0021-843x.107.1.17

Stagnitti, M. N. (2008). Antidepressants prescribed by medical doctors in office based and outpatient settings by specialty for the U.S. civilian noninstitutionalized population, 2002 and 2005. Retrieved from http://www.meps.ahrq.gov/mepsweb/data_files/publications/st206/stat206.pdf

Stahl, L. A., Begg, D. P., Weisinger, R. S., & Sinclair, A. J. (2008). The role of omega-3 fatty acids in mood disorders. *Current Opinion in Investigational Drugs, 9*(1), 57–64.

Stanley, S. A., Connan, F., Small, C. J., Murphy, K. G., Todd, J. F., Ghatei, M., et al. (2003). Elevated circulating levels of cocaine- and amphetamine-regulated transcript (CART) in anorexia nervosa. *Endocrine Abstracts, 5,* OC30.

Steblay, N. M., Dysart, J., Fulero, S., & Lindsay, R. C. L. (2001). Eyewitness accuracy rates in sequential and simultaneous lineup presentations: A meta-analytic comparison. *Law and Human Behavior, 25,* 459–474. doi: 10.1023/A:1012888715007

Steele, C. M. (1997). A threat in the air: How stereotypes shape intellectual identity and performance. *American Psychologist, 52,* 613–629. doi: 10.1037/0003-066X.52.6.613

Steele, C. M., & Aronson, J. (1995). Stereotype threat and the intellectual test performance of African Americans. *Journal of Personality and Social Psychology, 69,* 797–811. doi: 10.1037/0022-3514.69.5.797

Stefanucci, J. K., & Proffitt, D. R. (2009). The roles of altitude and fear in the perception of height. *Journal of Experimental Psychology: Human Perception and Performance, 35*(2), 424–438. doi: 10.1037/a0013894

Steiger, B. (2000). *American Indian medicine dream book*. Atglen, PA: Whitford Press.

Stein-Behrens, B., Mattson, M. P., Chang, I., Yeh, M., & Sapolsky, R. (1994). Stress exacerbates neuron loss and cytoskeletal pathology in the hippocampus. *Journal of Neuroscience, 14*, 5373–5380.

Steinberg, L., & Levine, A. (1997). *You and your adolescent: A parent's guide for ages 10 to 20*. New York, NY: Harper Perennial.

Steinhausen, H.-C., Willms, J., & Spohr, H.-L. (1993). Long-term psychopathological and cognitive outcome of children with fetal alcohol syndrome. *Journal of the American Academy of Child and Adolescent Psychiatry, 32*, 990–994. doi: 10.1097/00004583-199309000-00016

Stephan, W. S., & Stephan, C. W. (2000). An integrated threat theory of prejudice. In S. Oskamp (Ed.), *Reducing prejudice and discrimination* (pp. 23–46). New York: Psychology Press.

Sternberg, R. J. (1985). *Beyond IQ: A triarchic theory of human intelligence*. New York, NY: Cambridge University Press.

Sternberg, R. J. (2004). A triangular theory of love. In H. T. Reis & C. D. Rusbult (Eds.), *Close relationships: Key readings* (pp. 213–227). Philadelphia, PA: Taylor & Francis.

Sternberg, S. (1966). High speed scanning in human memory. *Science, 153*, 652–654. doi: 10.1126/science.153.3736.652

Sternberg, S. (1967). Retrieval of contextual information from memory. *Psychonomic Science, 8*, 55–56.

Sternberg, S. (1969). Memory scanning: Mental processes revealed by reaction-time experiments. *American Scientist, 57*, 421–457.

Stevens, S. S. (1960). Psychophysics of sensory function. *American Scientist, 48*, 226–252.

Stewart, S. T., Cutler, D. M., & Rosen, A. B. (2009). Forecasting the effects of obesity and smoking on U.S. life expectancy. *New England Journal of Medicine, 361*(23), 2252–2260. doi: 10.1056/NEJMsa0900459

Stewart, W. K., & Fleming, L. W. (1973). Features of a successful therapeutic fast of 382 days' duration. *Postgraduate Medical Journal, 49*, 203–209. doi: 10.1136/pgmj.49.569.203

Steyn, P., Wallstrom, A., & Pitt, L. (2010). Consumer-generated content and source effects in financial services advertising: An experimental study. *Journal of Financial Services Marketing, 15*(1), 49–61. doi: 10.1057/fsm.2010.3

Stickgold, R., James, L., & Hobson, J. A. (2000). Visual discrimination learning requires sleep after training. *Nature Neuroscience, 3*, 1237–1238. doi: 10.1038/81756

Stickgold, R., & Walker, M. P. (2007). Sleep-dependent memory consolidation and reconsolidation. *Sleep Medicine, 8*(4), 331–343. doi: 10.1016/j.sleep.2007.03.011

Stokes, P. E. (1995). The potential role of excessive cortisol induced by HPA hyperfunction in the pathogenesis of depression. *European Neuropsychopharmacology, 5*(Suppl. 1), 77–82. doi: 10.1016/0924-977x(95)00039-r

Stoller, R. J., & Herdt, G. H. (1985). Theories of origins of male homosexuality: A cross-cultural look. *Archives of General Psychiatry, 42*, 399–404. doi: 10.1001/archpsyc.1985.01790270089010

Stomp, W., ten Duis, H.-J., & Nijsten, M. W. (2011). The impact of the lunar cycle on the incidence of trauma. *Trauma, 13*(2), 121–124. doi: 10.1177/1460408610384655

Stone, J., Perry, Z. W., & Darley, J. M. (1997). "White men can't jump": Evidence for the perceptual confirmation of racial stereotypes following a basketball game. *Basic and Applied Social Psychology, 19*(3), 291–306. doi: 10.1207/15324839751036977

Stoodley, C. (2014). Distinct regions of the cerebellum show grey matter decreases in autism, ADHD and developmental dyslexia. *Frontiers in Systems Neuroscience, 8*, 92. doi: 10.3389/fnsys.2014.00092

Strait, D. L., Kraus, N., Parbery-Clark, A., & Ashley, R. (2010). Musical experience shapes top-down auditory mechanisms: Evidence from masking and auditory attention performance. *Hearing Research, 261*(1–2), 22–29. doi: 10.1016/j.heares.2009.12.021

Strasburger, V. C. (2007). First do no harm: Why have parents and pediatricians missed the boat on children and media? *Journal of Pediatrics, 151*(4), 334–336. doi: 10.1016/j.jpeds.2007.05.040

Straus, S., Richardson, W. S., Glasziou, P., & Haynes, R. B. (2011). *Evidence-based medicine: How to practice and teach E.B.M.* (4th ed.). Edinburgh, Scotland: Churchill Livingstone.

Strauss, G. P., Harrow, M., Grossman, L. S., & Rosen, C. (2010). Periods of recovery in deficit syndrome schizophrenia: A 20-year multi–follow-up longitudinal study. *Schizophrenia Bulletin, 36*(4), 788–799. doi: 10.1093/schbul/sbn167

Streissguth, A. P., Aase, J. M., Clarren, S. K., Randels, S. P., LaDue, R. A., & Smith, D. F. (1991). Fetal alcohol syndrome in adolescents and adults. *JAMA: Journal of the American Medical Association, 264*, 1961–1967. doi: 10.1001/jama.1991.03460150065025

Strickland, B. R. (1992). Women and depression. *Current Directions in Psychological Science, 1*, 132–135. doi: 10.1111/1467-8721.ep10769766

Stroebe, W. (2010). The graying of academia: Will it reduce scientific productivity? *American Psychologist, 65*(7), 660–673. doi: 10.1037/a0021086

Ströhle, A. (2009). Physical activity, exercise, depression and anxiety disorders. *Journal of Neural Transmission, 116*(6), 777–784. doi: 10.1007/s00702-008-0092-x

Stroop, J. R. (1935). Studies of interference in serial verbal reactions. *Journal of Experimental Psychology, 18*, 643–662. doi: 10.1037/h0054651

Stuss, D. T. (2011). Functions of the frontal lobes: Relation to executive functions. *Journal of the International Neuropsychological Society, 17*(5), 759–765. doi: http://dx.doi.org/10.1017/S1355617711000695

Sugden, K., Arseneault, L., Harrington, H., Moffitt, T. E., Williams, B., & Caspi, A. (2010). Serotonin transporter gene moderates the development of emotional problems among children following bullying victimization. *Journal of the American Academy of Child and Adolescent Psychiatry, 49*(8), 830–840. doi: 10.1016/j.jaac.2010.01.024

Sung, H.-Y., Prochaska, J. J., Ong, M. K., Shi, Y., & Max, W. (2011). Cigarette smoking and serious psychological distress: A population-based study of California adults. *Nicotine and Tobacco Research*. doi: 10.1093/ntr/ntr148

Sunsay, C., & Rebec, G. V. (2008). Real-time dopamine efflux in the nucleus accumbens core during Pavlovian conditioning. *Behavioral Neuroscience, 122*(2), 358–367. doi: 10.1037/0735-7044.122.2.358

Suomi, S. J. (2006). Risk, resilience, and gene environment interactions in rhesus monkeys. *Annals of the New York Academy of Sciences, 1094*(1), 52–62. doi: 10.1196/annals.1376.006

Super, C. M. (1976). Environmental effects on motor development: The case of "African infant precocity." *Developmental Medicine and Child Neurology, 18*, 561–567. doi: 10.1111/j.1469-8749.1976.tb04202.x

Susswein, A. J., Schwarz, M., & Feldman, E. (1986). Learned changes of feeding behavior in *Aplysia* in response to edible and inedible foods. *Journal of Neuroscience, 6*, 1513–1527.

Sutton, R. M., & Douglas, K. M. (2005). Justice for all, or just me? More evidence of the importance of the self–other distinction in just world beliefs. *Personality and Individual Differences, 39*(3), 637–645. doi: 10.1016/j.paid.2005.02.010

Svoboda, E., McKinnon, M. C., & Levine, B. (2006). The functional neuroanatomy of autobiographical memory: A meta-analysis. *Neuropsychologia, 44*(12), 2189–2208. doi: 10.1016/j.neuropsychologia.2006.05.023

Swaminathan, R., Burrows, G., & McMurray, J. (1982). Energy cost of sodium pump activity in man: An in vivo study of metabolic rate in human subjects given digoxin. *IRCS Medical Science, 10*, 949.

Swap, W. C. (1977). Interpersonal attraction and repeated exposure to rewarders and punishers. *Personality and Social Psychology Bulletin, 3*(2), 248–251. doi: 10.1177/014616727700300219

Swedo, S. E., Leonard, H. L., Mittleman, B. B., Allen, A. J., Rapoport, J. L., Dow, S. P., et al. (1997). Identification of children with pediatric autoimmune neuropsychiatric disorders associated with streptococcal infections by a marker associated with rheumatic fever. *American Journal of Psychiatry, 154,* 110–112.

Syvalahti, E. K. G. (1994). I. The theory of schizophrenia: Biological factors in schizophrenia. *British Journal of Psychiatry, 164,* 9–14.

Szeszko, P. R., MacMillan, S., McMeniman, M., Chen, S., Baribault, K., Lim, K. O., et al. (2004). Brain structural abnormalities in psychotropic drug-naïve pediatric patients with obsessive-compulsive disorder. *American Journal of Psychiatry, 161*(6), 1049–1056. doi: 10.1176/appi. ajp.161.6.1049

Szymanski, L., & King, B. H. (1999). Practice parameters for the assessment and treatment of children, adolescents, and adults with mental retardation and comorbid mental disorders. *Journal of the American Academy of Child and Adolescent Psychiatry, 38*(Suppl. 12), 5S–31S. doi: 10.1016/S0890-8567(99)80002-1

Taheri, S., & Mignot, E. (2002). The genetics of sleep disorders. *Lancet Neurology, 1*(4), 242–250. doi: 10.1016/S1474-4422(02)00103-5

Talhelm, T., Zhang, X., Oishi, S., Shimin, C., Duan, D., Lan, X., & Kitayama, S. (2014). Large-scale psychological differences within China explained by rice versus wheat agriculture. *Science, 344*(6184), 603–608. doi: 10.1126/science.1246850

Tallal, P., Ross, R., & Curtiss, S. (1989). Familial aggregation in specific language impairment. *Journal of Speech and Hearing Disorders, 54,* 167–171. doi: 10.1044/ jshd.5402.167

Tang, Y.-Y., & Posner, M. I. (2009). Attention training and attention state training. *Trends in Cognitive Sciences, 13*(5), 223–227. doi: 10.1016/j.tics.2009.01.009

Tarumi, S., Ichimiya, A., Yamada, S., Umesue, M., & Kuroki, T. (2004). Taijin Kyofusho in university students: Patterns of fear and predispositions to the offensive variant. *Transcultural Psychiatry, 41*(4), 533–546. doi: 10.1177/1363461504047933

Tassi, P., & Muzet, A. (2001). Defining the states of consciousness. *Neuroscience & Biobehavioral Reviews, 25*(2), 175–191. doi: 10.1016/S0149-7634(01)00006-9

Taylor, D. A., & Altman, I. (1987). Communication in interpersonal relationships: Social penetration processes. In M. E. Roloff & G. R. Miller (Eds.), *Interpersonal processes: New directions in communication research* (pp. 257–277). Thousand Oaks, CA: Sage.

Taylor, L., Faraone, S. V., & Tsuang, M. T. (2002). Family, twin, and adoption studies of bipolar disease. *Current Psychiatry Reports, 4*(2), 130–133. doi: 10.1007/ s11920-002-0046-1

Taylor, R. (1990). Interpretation of the correlation coefficient: A basic review. *Journal of Diagnostic Medical Sonography, 6*(1), 35–39. doi: 10.1177/875647939000600106

Taylor, S. E. (2002). *The tending instinct: How nurturing is essential to who we are and how we live.* New York, NY: Henry Holt.

Taylor, S. E. (2006). Tend and befriend: Biobehavioral bases of affiliation under stress. *Current Directions in Psychological Science, 15*(6), 273–277. doi: 10.1111/j.1467-8721.2006.00451.x

Taylor, S. E., & Brown, J. D. (1988). Illusion and well-being: A social psychological perspective on mental health. *Psychological Bulletin, 103,* 193–210. doi: 10.1037/0033-2909.103.2.193

Taylor, S. E., & Master, S. L. (2010). Social response to stress: The tend-and-befriend model. In R. J. Contrada & A. Baum (Eds.), *The handbook of stress science: Biology, psychology, and health* (pp. 101–109). New York, NY: Springer.

Teasdale, J. D., Segal, Z. V., Williams, J. M. G., Ridgeway, V. A., Soulsby, J. M., & Lau, M. A. (2000). Prevention of relapse/recurrence in major depression by mindfulness-based cognitive therapy. *Journal of Consulting and Clinical Psychology, 68*(4), 615. doi: 10.1037/0022-006X.68.4.615

Terman, L. (1916). *The measurement of intelligence.* Boston, MA: Houghton Mifflin.

Terman, L. (1925). *Genetic studies of genius: Vol. 1. Mental and physical traits of a thousand gifted children.* Stanford, CA: Stanford University Press.

Terman, L. M., & Oden, M. H. (1959). *Genetic studies of genius: Vol. 5. The gifted group at mid-life.* Stanford, CA: Stanford University Press.

Terrace, H. S. (1979, November). How Nim Chimpsky changed my mind. *Psychology Today,* 65–76.

Terry, D. J. (1994). Determinants of coping: The role of stable and situational factors. *Journal of Personality and Social Psychology, 66*(5), 895–910. doi: 10.1037/ 0022-3514.66.5.895

Testa, M., Quigley, B. M., & Eiden, R. D. (2003). The effects of prenatal alcohol exposure on infant mental development: A meta-analytical review. *Alcohol and Alcoholism, 38*(4), 295–304. doi: 10.1093/ alcalc/agg087

Tetlock, P. E., Self, W. T., & Singh, R. (2010). The punitiveness paradox: When is external pressure exculpatory—and when a signal just to spread blame? *Journal of Experimental Social Psychology, 46*(2), 388–395. doi: 10.1016/j.jesp.2009.11.013

Thacher, P. V. (2008). University students and "the all nighter": Correlates and patterns of students' engagement in a single night of total sleep deprivation. *Behavioral Sleep Medicine, 6*(1), 16–31. doi: 10.1080/15402000701796114

Thannickal, T. C., Moore, R. Y., Nienhuis, R., Ramanathan, L., Gulyani, S., Aldrich, M., et al. (2000). Reduced number of hypocretin neurons in human narcolepsy. *Neuron, 27,* 469–474. doi: 10.1016/S0896-6273(00)00058-1

Theeboom, T., Beersma, B., & van Vianen, A. E. M. (2014). Does coaching work? A meta-analysis on the effects of coaching on individual level outcomes in an organizational context. *Journal of Positive Psychology, 9*(1), 1–18. doi: 10.1080/17439760.2013.837499

Thera*Scribe* [Computer software]. New York, NY: Wiley. Retrieved from http://www .wiley.com/legacy/therascribe/default.htm

Thierry, B. (1994). Emergence of social organizations in non-human primates. *Revue Internationale de Systémique, 8,* 65–77.

Thomas, A., & Chess, S. (1977). *Temperament and development.* New York, NY: Brunner/ Mazel.

Thomas, A., & Chess, S. (1989). Temperament and personality. In G. A. Kohnstamm, J. E. Bates, & M. K. Rothbart (Eds.), *Temperament in childhood* (pp. 249–261). New York, NY: Wiley.

Thomas, J. L., Wilk, J. E., Riviere, L. A., McGurk, D., Castro, C. A., & Hoge, C. W. (2010). Prevalence of mental health problems and functional impairment among active component and National Guard soldiers 3 and 12 months following combat in Iraq. *Archives of General Psychiatry, 67*(6), 614–623. doi: 10.1001/archgenpsychiatry.2010.54

Thomas, L. A., De Bellis, M. D., Graham, R., & LaBar, K. S. (2007). Development of emotional facial recognition in late childhood and adolescence. *Developmental Science, 10*(5), 547–558. doi: 10.1111/j.1467-7687.2007.00614.x

Thompson, M. A., Callaghan, P. D., Hunt, G. E., Cornish, J. L., & McGregor, I. S. (2007). A role for oxytocin and 5-HT(1A) receptors in the prosocial effects of 3,4-methyl-enedioxymethamphetamine ("Ecstasy"). *Neuroscience, 146*(2), 509–514. doi: 10.1016/j.neuroscience.2007.02.032

Thompson, P. M., Giedd, J. N., Woods, R. P., MacDonald, D., Evans, A. C., & Toga, A. W. (2000). Growth patterns in the developing brain detected by using continuum mechanical tensor maps. *Nature, 404,* 190–193. doi: 10.1038/35004593

Thompson, P. M., Vidal, C., Giedd, J. N., Gochman, P., Blumenthal, J., Nicolson, R., et al. (2001). Mapping adolescent brain change reveals dynamic wave of accelerated gray matter loss in very early-onset schizophrenia. *Proceedings of the National Academy of Sciences, 98*(20), 11650–11655. doi: 10.1073/pnas.201243998

Thorndike, E. L. (1913). *Educational psychology: Briefer course.* New York, NY: Teachers College.

Thornhill, R., & Gangestad, S. W. (1994). Human fluctuating asymmetry and sexual behavior. *Psychological Science, 5*(5), 297–302. doi: 10.1111/j.1467-9280.1994. tb00629.x

Thornton, L. M., Andersen, B. L., Crespin, T. R., & Carson, W. E. (2007). Individual trajectories in stress covary with immunity during recovery from cancer diagnosis and treatments. *Brain, Behavior, and Immunity, 21*(2), 185–194. doi: 10.1016/j.bbi.2006.06.007

Thorpe, W. H. (1963). *Learning and instinct in animals* (2nd ed.). Cambridge, MA: Harvard University Press.

Thyer, B. A. (2004). What is evidence-based practice? *Brief Treatment and Crisis Intervention, 4*(2), 167–176. doi: 10.1093/brief-treatment/mhh013

Tien, A. Y. (1991). Distribution of hallucinations in the population. *Social Psychiatry and Psychiatric Epidemiology, 26*(6), 287–292. doi: 10.1007/bf00789221

Tinbergen, N. (1951). *The study of instinct.* New York, NY: Oxford University Press.

Titone, D., Levy, D. L., & Holzman, P. S. (2000). Contextual insensitivity in schizophrenic language processing: Evidence from lexical ambiguity. *Journal of Abnormal Psychology, 109*(4), 761–767. doi: 10.1037/0021-843X.109.4.761

Tolman, E. C. (1948). Cognitive maps in rats and men. *Psychological Review, 55*(4), 189–208. doi: 10.1037/h0061626

Tolman, E. C. (1959). Principles of purposive behavior. In S. Koch (Ed.), *Psychology: A study of a science* (Vol. 2, pp. 92–157). New York, NY: McGraw-Hill.

Tolman, E. C., Richie, B. F., & Kalish, D. (1946). Studies in spatial learning: II. Place learning vs. response learning. *Journal of Experimental Psychology, 36*(3), 221–229. doi: 10.1037/h0060262

Travis, F. T. (2001). Autonomic and EEG patterns distinguish transcending from other experiences during Transcendental Meditation practice. *International Journal of Psychophysiology, 42*(1), 1–9. doi: 10.1016/S0167-8760(01)pp143-X

Treffert, D. A., & Wallace, G. L. (2004). Islands of genius. *Scientific American, 286,* 76–85.

Tribe, M. A. (n.d.). *Mexican wolf recovery program. Reporting period: January 1–December 31, 2010* (Progress Report 13). Retrieved from http://www.fws.gov/southwest/es/mexicanwolf/pdf/2010_progress_report_final.pdf

Trimble, J. E., Stevenson, M. R., & Worell, J. P. (2003). *Toward an inclusive psychology: Infusing the introductory psychology textbook with diversity content.* Washington, DC: American Psychological Association.

Triplett, N. (1898). The dynamogenic factors in pacemaking and competition. *American Journal of Psychology, 9,* 507–533. doi: 10.2307/1412188

Trivers, R. L. (1971). The evolution of reciprocal altruism. *Quarterly Review of Biology, 46*(1), 35–57. doi: 10.2307/2822435

Trivers, R., & Burt, A. (1999). Kinship and genomic imprinting. *Results and Problems in Cell Differentiation, 25,* 1–21. doi: 10.1007/978-3-540-69111-2_1

Trockel, M. T., Barnes, M. D., & Egget, D. L. (2000). Health-related variables and academic performance among first-year college students: Implications for sleep and other behaviors. *Journal of American College Health, 49*(3), 125–131. doi: 10.1080/07448480009596294

Troll, L., Neugarten, B. L., & Kraines, R. J. (1969). Similarities in values and other personality characteristics in college students and their parents. *Merrill–Palmer Quarterly, 15,* 323–336.

Trout, D. L. (1980). The role of social isolation in suicide. *Suicide and Life-Threatening Behavior, 10*(1), 10–23. doi: 10.1111/j.1943-278X.1980.tb00693.x

Trzesniewski, K. H., Donnellan, M. B., & Robins, R. W. (2003). Stability of self-esteem across the life span. *Journal of Personality and Social Psychology, 84*(1), 205–220. doi: 10.1037/0022-3514.84.1.205

Tsang, J.-A., Carpenter, T. P., Roberts, J. A., Frisch, M. B., & Carlisle, R. D. (2014). Why are materialists less happy? The role of gratitude and need satisfaction in the relationship between materialism and life satisfaction. *Personality and Individual Differences, 64,* 62–66. doi: 10.1016/j.paid.2014.02.009

Tulving, E. (1972). Episodic and semantic memory. In E. Tulving & W. Donaldson (Eds.), *Organization and memory* (pp. 381–403). New York, NY: Academic Press.

Tulving, E. (1983). *Elements of episodic memory.* Oxford, United Kingdom: Clarendon Press/Oxford University Press.

Tulving, E. (1985). How many memory systems are there? *American Psychologist, 40*(4), 385–398. doi: 10.1037/0003-066X.40.4.385

Tulving, E. (1989). Memory: Performance, knowledge, and experience. *European Journal of Cognitive Psychology, 1*(1), 3–26. doi: 10.1080/09541448908403069

Tulving, E. (1995). Organization of memory. In M. S. Gazzaniga (Ed.), *The cognitive neurosciences* (pp. 839–853). Cambridge, MA: MIT Press.

Tulving, E., & Psotka, J. (1971). Retroactive inhibition in free recall: Inaccessibility of information available in the memory store. *Journal of Experimental Psychology, 87*(1), 1–8. doi: 10.1037/h0030185

Tulving, E., & Thomson, D. M. (1973). Encoding specificity and retrieval processes in episodic memory. *Psychological Review, 80*(5), 352–373. doi: 10.1037/h0020071

Turati, C., Simion, F., Milani, I., & Umiltà, C. (2002). Newborns' preference for faces: What is crucial? *Developmental Psychology, 38*(6), 875–882. doi: 10.1037/0012-1649.38.6.875

Turnbull, H. W. (Ed.). (1959). *The correspondence of Isaac Newton* (Vol. 1). Cambridge, United Kingdom: Cambridge University Press.

Turkheimer, E., Haley, A., Waldron, M., D'Onofrio, B., & Gottesman, I. I. (2003). Socioeconomic status modifies heritability of IQ in young children. *Psychological Science, 14*(6), 623–628. doi: 10.1046/j.0956-7976.2003.psci_1475.x

Tversky, A., & Kahneman, D. (1981). The framing of decisions and the psychology of choice. *Science, 211,* 453–458. doi: 10.1126/science.7455683

Tversky, A., & Kahneman, D. (1987). Rational choice and the framing of decisions. In R. M. Hogarth & M. W. Reder (Eds.), *Rational choice: The contrast between economics and psychology* (pp. 67–94). Chicago, IL: University of Chicago Press.

Twenge, J. M. (2013). The evidence for Generation Me and against Generation We. *Emerging Adulthood, 1*(1), 11–16. doi: 10.1177/2167696812466548

Twenge, J. M., Baumeister, R. F., Tice, D. M., & Stucke, T. S. (2001). If you can't join them, beat them: Effects of social exclusion on aggressive behavior. *Journal of Personality and Social Psychology, 81,* 1058–1069. doi: 10.1037/0022-3514.81.6.1058

Twenge, J. M., Campbell, W. K., & Foster, C. A. (2003). Parenthood and marital satisfaction: A meta-analytic review. *Journal of Marriage and Family, 65*(3), 574–583. doi: 10.1111/j.1741-3737.2003.00574.x

Twenge, J. M., & Crocker, J. (2002). Race and self-esteem: Meta-analyses comparing Whites, Blacks, Hispanics, Asians, and American Indians and comment on Gray-Little and Hafdahl (2000). *Psychological Bulletin, 128*(3), 371–408. doi: 10.1037/0033-2909.128.3.371

U.S. Department of Education Office of Educational Research and Improvement. (1993). *National excellence: A case for developing America's talent.* Washington, DC: U.S. Government Printing Office.

U.S. Department of Justice. (2006). Crime in the United States. Retrieved from http://www.fbi.gov/ucr/cius2006/index.html

U.S. Department of Veterans Affairs. (2014). How common is PTSD? Retrieved from http://www.ptsd.va.gov/public/PTSD-overview/basics/how-common-is-ptsd.asp

U.S. Food and Drug Administration. (2002). What can I expect before, during, and after liposuction? Retrieved from http://www.fda.gov/cdrh/liposuction/expect.html

U.S. Food and Drug Administration. (2010). FDA approves new formulation for OxyContin. Retrieved from http://www.fda.gov/NewsEvents/Newsroom/PressAnnouncements/ucm207480.htm

U.S. National Center for Education Statistics. (2012). Digest of education statistics. Retrieved from http://nces.ed.gov/programs/digest/d12/tables/dt12_313.asp

Ullmann, L. P., & Krasner, L. (1965). *Case studies in behavior modification.* New York, NY: Holt, Rinehart, and Winston.

Underwood, B. J. (1957). Interference and forgetting. *Psychological Review, 64,* 49–60. doi: 10.1037/h0044616

United Nations. (2007). World population prospects: The 2006 revision. Retrieved from http://www.un.org/esa/population/publications/wpp2006/WPP2006_Highlights_rev.pdf

United Nations. (2009, June). World population prospects: The 2008 revision. Retrieved from http://data.un.org/Data.aspx?d=PopDiv&f=variableID%3A54

United Nations Office on Drugs and Crime. (2001). The seventh United Nations survey on crime trends and the operations of criminal justice systems (1998–2000). Retrieved from http://www.unodc.org/unodc/crime_cicp_survey_seventh.html

United Nations Office on Drugs and Crime. (2014). Global study on homicide. Retrieved from https://www.unodc.org/gsh/en/data.html

Üstün, T. B., Ayuso-Mateos, J. L., Chatterji, S., Mathers, C., & Murray, C. J. L. (2004). Global burden of depressive disorders in the year 2000. *British Journal of Psychiatry, 184*(5), 386–392. doi: 10.1192/bjp.184.5.386

Vaillant, G. E. (2003). A 60-year follow-up of alcoholic men. *Addiction, 98*(8), 1043–1051. doi: 10.1046/j.1360-0443.2003.00422.x

Vaillant, G. E., & Koury, S. H. (1993). Late midlife development. In G. H. Pollock & S. I. Greenspan (Eds.), *The course of life: Vol. 6. Late adulthood* (Rev. and exp. ed., pp. 1–22). Madison, CT: International Universities Press.

Vaitl, D., Gruzelier, J., Jamieson, G. A., Lehmann, D., Ott, U., Sammer, G., et al. (2013). Psychobiology of altered states of consciousness. *Psychology of Consciousness: Theory, Research, and Practice, 1*(Supplement 1), 2–47. doi: 10.1037/2326-5523.1.S.2

Valenstein, E. S. (1986). *Great and desperate cures.* New York, NY: Basic Books.

van Anders, S. M., Hamilton, L. D., & Watson, N. V. (2007). Multiple partners are associated with higher testosterone in North American men and women. *Hormones and Behavior, 51*(3), 454–459. doi: 10.1016/j.yhbeh.2007.01.002

van Anders, S. M., & Watson, N. V. (2006). Relationship status and testosterone in North American heterosexual and non-heterosexual men and women: Cross-sectional and longitudinal data. *Psychoneuroendocrinology, 31*(6), 715–723. doi: 10.1016/j.psyneuen.2006.01.008

Van Cauter, E., Leproult, R., & Plat, L. (2000). Age-related changes in slow wave sleep and REM sleep and relationship with growth hormone and cortisol levels in healthy men. *JAMA: Journal of the American Medical Association, 284*(7), 861–868. doi: 10.1001/jama.284.7.861

Van Haren, N. E., Cahn, W., Hulshoff Pol, H. E., & Kahn, R. S. (2012). Confounders of excessive brain volume loss in schizophrenia. *Neuroscience & Biobehavioral Reviews, 37*(10), 2418–2423. doi: 10.1016/j.neubiorev.2012.09.006

van Hell, J. G., & Tokowicz, N. (2010). Event-related brain potentials and second language learning: Syntactic processing in late L2 learners at different L2 proficiency levels. *Second Language Research, 26*(1), 43–74. doi: 10.1177/0267658309337637

Van Horn, J. D., Irimia, A., Torgerson, C. M., Chambers, M. C., Kikinis, R., & Toga, A. W. (2012). Mapping connectivity damage in the case of Phineas Gage. *PLoS One, 7*(5), e37454. doi: 10.1371/journal.pone.0037454

Van Knippenberg, D., & Wilke, H. (1992). Prototypicality of arguments and conformity to ingroup norms. *European Journal of Social Psychology, 22*(2), 141–155. doi: 10.1002/ejsp.2420220204

van Londen, L., Goekoop, J. G., van Kempen, G. M. J., Frankhuijzen-Sierevogel, A. C., Wiegant, V. M., van der Velde, E. A., et al. (1997). Plasma levels of arginine vasopressin elevated in patients with major depression. *Neuropsychopharmacology, 17*(4), 284–292. doi: 10.1016/S0893-133X(97)00054-7

van Rijn, S., Stockmann, L., Borghgraef, M., Bruining, H., van Ravenswaaij-Arts, C., Govaerts, L., et al. (2014). The social behavioral phenotype in boys and girls with an extra X chromosome (Klinefelter syndrome and trisomy X): A comparison with autism spectrum disorder. *Journal of Autism and Developmental Disorders, 44*(2), 310–320. doi: 10.1007/s10803-013-1860-5

van Veen, V., Krug, M. K., Schooler, J. W., & Carter, C. S. (2009). Neural activity predicts attitude change in cognitive dissonance. *Nature Neuroscience, 12*(11), 1469–1474. doi: 10.1038/nn.2413

Vargas, J. H., & Kemmelmeier, M. (2013). Ethnicity and contemporary American culture a meta-analytic investigation of horizontal–vertical individualism–collectivism. *Journal of Cross-Cultural Psychology, 44*(2), 195–222. doi: 10.1177/0022022112443733

Vaughn, B. E., & Bost, K. K. (1999). Attachment and temperament: Redundant, independent, or interacting influences on interpersonal adaptation and personality development? In J. Cassidy & P. R. Shaver (Eds.), *Handbook of attachment: Theory, research, and clinical applications* (pp. 198–225). New York, NY: Guilford Press.

Verdejo-Garcia, A., Clark, L., & Dunn, B. D. (2012). The role of interoception in addiction: A critical review. *Neuroscience and Biobehavioral Reviews, 36*(8), 1857–1869. doi: 10.1016/j.neubiorev.2012.05.007

Vermetten, E., Schmahl, C., Southwick, S. M., & Bremner, J. D. (2007). Positron tomographic emission study of olfactory induced emotional recall in veterans with and without combat-related posttraumatic stress disorder. *Psychopharmacology Bulletin, 40*(1), 8–30.

Vescio, T. K., Judd, C. M., & Kwan, V. S. Y. (2004). The crossed-categorization hypothesis: Evidence of reductions in the strength of categorization, but not intergroup bias. *Journal of Experimental Social Psychology, 40*(4), 478–496. doi: 10.1016/j.jesp.2003.09.005

Vestergaard-Poulsen, P., van Beek, M., Skewes, J., Bjarkam, C. R., Stubberup, M., Bertelsen, J., et al. (2009). Long-term meditation is associated with increased gray matter density in the brain stem. *NeuroReport, 20*(2), 170–174. doi: 10.1097/WNR.0b013e328320012a

Virués-Ortega, J. (2010). Applied behavior analytic intervention for autism in early childhood: Meta-analysis, meta-regression and dose-response meta-analysis of multiple outcomes. *Clinical Psychology Review, 30*(4), 387–399. doi: 10.1016/j.cpr.2010.01.008

Visser, B. A., Ashton, M. C., & Vernon, P. A. (2006). Beyond *g:* Putting multiple intelligences theory to the test. *Intelligence, 34*(5), 487–502. doi: 10.1016/j.intell.2006.02.004

Visser, S. N., Danielson, M. L., Bitsko, R. H., Holbrook, J. R., Kogan, M. D., Ghandour, R. M., et al. (2014). Trends in the parent-report of health care provider–diagnosed and medicated attention-deficit/hyperactivity disorder: United States, 2003–2011. *Journal of the American Academy of Child & Adolescent Psychiatry, 53*(1), 34–46. doi: 10.1016/j.jaac.2013.09.001

Vohs, K. D., & Heatherton, T. F. (2000). Self-regulatory failure: A resource-depletion approach. *Psychological Science, 11*(3), 249–254. doi: 10.1111/1467-9280.00250

Voineagu, I., Wang, X., Johnston, P., Lowe, J. K., Tian, Y., Horvath, S., et al. (2011). Transcriptomic analysis of autistic brain reveals convergent molecular pathology. *Nature, 474*(7351), 380–384. doi: 10.1038/nature10110.

Volkow, N. D., Wang, G.-J., Fowler, J. S., & Ding, Y.-S. (2005). Imaging the effects of methylphenidate on brain dopamine: New model on its therapeutic actions for attention-deficit/hyperactivity disorder. *Biological Psychiatry, 57*(11), 1410–1415. doi: 10.1016/j.biopsych.2004.11.006

Volkow, N. D., Wang, G.-J., Kollins, S. H., Wigal, T. L., Newcorn, J. H., Telang, F., et al. (2009). Evaluating dopamine reward pathway in ADHD: Clinical implications. *JAMA: Journal of the American Medical Association, 302*(10), 1084–1091. doi: 10.1001/jama.2009.1308

Vollebregt, M. A., van Dongen-Boomsma, M., Slaats-Willemse, D., & Buitelaar, J. K. (2014). What future research should bring to help resolving the debate about the efficacy of EEG-neurofeedback in children with ADHD. *Frontiers in Human Neuroscience, 8,* 321. doi: 10.3389/fnhum.2014.00321

vom Saal, F. S., VandeVoort, C. A., Taylor, J. A., Welshons, W. V., Toutain, P.-L., & Hunt, P. A. (2014). Bisphenol A (BPA) pharmacokinetics with daily oral bolus or continuous exposure via Silastic capsules in pregnant rhesus monkeys: Relevance for human exposures. *Reproductive Toxicology, 45*, 105–116. doi: 10.1016/j.reprotox.2014 .01.007

von Brücke, E. W. (1881). *Vorlesungen über physiologie* [Introductory lectures in physiology] (3rd ed.). Vienna, Austria: W. Braumüller.

Vuilleumier, P., Armony, J. L., Driver, J., & Dolan, R. J. (2001). Effects of attention and emotion on face processing in the human brain: An event-related fMRI study. *Neuron, 30*(3), 829–841. doi: 10.1016/ S0896-6273(01)00328-2

Vygotsky, L. S. (1962). *Thought and language.* Cambridge, MA: MIT Press. (Original work published 1934)

Wadee, A. A., Kuschke, R. H., Kometz, S., & Berk, M. (2001). Personality factors, stress and immunity. *Stress and Health: Journal of the International Society for the Investigation of Stress, 17*(1), 25–40. doi: 10.1002/1532-2998(200101)17:1<25::AID-SMI873>3.0.CO;2-N

Wagner, D. R. (1996). Disorders of the circadian sleep–wake cycle. *Neurological Clinics, 14*(3), 651–670. doi: 10.1016/S0733-8619(05)70278-4

Wainer, H., & Steinberg, L. S. (1992). Sex differences in performance on the mathematics section of the Scholastic Aptitude Test: A bidirectional validity study. *Harvard Educational Review, 62*(3), 323–336.

Waite, L. J., & Gallagher, M. (2001). *The case for marriage: Why married people are happier, healthier, and better off financially.* New York, NY: Random House.

Waite, L. J., Luo, Y., & Lewin, A. C. (2009). Marital happiness and marital stability: Consequences for psychological wellbeing. *Social Science Research, 38*(1), 201–212. doi: 10.1016/j.ssresearch.2008.07.001

Waldinger, R. J., & Schulz, M. S. (2010). What's love got to do with it? Social functioning, perceived health, and daily happiness in married octogenarians. *Psychology and Aging, 25*(2), 422–431. doi: 10.1037/ a0019087

Walker, A., & Shipman, P. (1996). *The wisdom of the bones: In search of human origins.* New York, NY: Knopf.

Wallston, K. (2005). The validity of the Multidimensional Health Locus of Control Scales. *Journal of Health Psychology, 10*(5), 623–631. doi: 10.1177/1359105305055304

Walster, E., Aronson, V., & Abrahams, D. (1966). Importance of physical attractiveness in dating behavior. *Journal of Personality and Social Psychology, 4*(5), 508–516. doi: doi: 10.1037/h0021188

Walters, S. (1994). Algorithms and archetypes: Evolutionary psychology and Carl Jung's theory of the collective unconscious. *Journal of Social and Evolutionary Systems, 17*(3), 287–306. doi: 10.1016/1061-7361(94) 90013-2

Walton, G. M., & Cohen, G. L. (2011). A brief social-belonging intervention improves academic and health outcomes of minority students. *Science, 331*(6023), 1447–1451. doi: 10.1126/science.1198364

Wan, C.-S., & Chiou, W.-B. (2010). Inducing attitude change toward online gaming among adolescent players based on dissonance theory: The role of threats and justification of effort. *Computers and Education, 54*(1), 162–168. doi: 10.1016/j. compedu.2009.07.016

Wang, J., Horlick, M., Thornton, J. C., Levine, L. S., Heymsfield, S. B., & Pearson, R. S., Jr. (1999). Correlations between skeletal muscle mass and bone mass in children 6–18 years: Influences of sex, ethnicity, and pubertal status. *Growth, Development, and Aging, 63*, 99–109.

Wang, Q. (2008). Emotion knowledge and autobiographical memory across the preschool years: A cross-cultural longitudinal investigation. *Cognition, 108*(1), 117–135. doi: 10.1016/j.cognition.2008.02.002

Wang, X. T., Kruger, D. J., & Wilke, A. (2009). Life history variables and risk-taking propensity. *Evolution and Human Behavior, 30*(2), 77–84. doi: 10.1016/j.evolhumbe-hav.2008.09.006

Wansink, B. (2006). *Mindless eating: Why we eat more than we think.* New York, NY: Bantam.

Wansink, B., & Sobal, J. (2007). Mindless eating. The 200 daily food decisions we overlook. *Environment and Behaviour, 39*, 106–123. doi: 10.1177/0013916506295573

Ward, D. (2006). *Stuttering and cluttering: Frameworks for understanding treatment.* New York, NY: Psychology Press.

Ward, B. W., Dahlhamer, J. M., Galinsky, A. M., & Joestl, S. S. (2014). Sexual orientation and health among U.S. adults: National Health Interview Survey, 2013. Retrieved from www.cdc.gov/nchs/data/ nhsr/nhsr077.pdf

Wasserman, R. C., Kelleher, K. J., Bocian, A., Baker, A., Childs, G. E., Indacochea, F., et al. (1999). Identification of attentional and hyperactivity problems in primary care: A report from pediatric research in office settings and the ambulatory sentinel practice network. *Pediatrics, 103*(3), E38. doi: 10.1542/peds.103.3.e38

Watkins, C. E., Campbell, V. L., & Nieberding, R. (1995). Contemporary practice of psychological assessment by clinical psychologists. *Professional Psychology: Research and Practice, 26*(1), 54–60. doi: 10.1037/0735-7028.26.1.54

Watkins, E., & Brown, R. G. (2002). Rumination and executive function in depression: An experimental study. *Journal of Neurology, Neurosurgery, and Psychiatry, 72*, 400–402. doi: 10.1136/jnnp.72.3.400

Watson, J. B. (1925). *Behaviorism.* Chicago, IL: University of Chicago Press.

Weber, W., & Newmark, S. (2007). Complementary and alternative medical therapies for attention deficit/hyperactivity disorder and autism. *Pediatric Clinics of North America, 54*(6), 983–1006. doi: 10.1016/j.pcl.2007.09.006

Wedekind, C., & Füri, S. (1997). Body odour preferences in men and women: Do they aim for specific MHC combinations or simply heterozygosity? *Proceedings of the Royal Society of London, Series B: Biological Sciences, 264*(1387), 1471–1479. doi: 10.1098/rspb.1997.0204

Wegner, D. M. (1986). Transactive memory: A contemporary analysis of the group mind. In B. Mullen & G. R. Goethals (Eds.), *Theories of group behavior* (pp. 185–208). New York, NY: Springer-Verlag.

Wegner, D. M. (1994). Ironic processes of mental control. *Psychological Review, 101*(1), 34–52. doi: 10.1037/0033-295X.101.1.34

Wegner, D. M., Erber, R., & Raymond, P. (1991). Transactive memory in close relationships. *Journal of Personality and Social Psychology, 61*(6), 923–929. doi: 10.1037/0022-3514.61.6.923

Wegner, D. M., Giuliano, T., & Hertel, P. (1985). Cognitive interdependence in close relationships. In W. J. Ickes (Ed.), *Compatible and incompatible relationships* (pp. 253–276). New York, NY: Springer-Verlag.

Weinberger, N. M. (2006). Food for thought: Honeybee foraging, memory, and acetylcholine. *Science Signaling: The Signal Transduction Knowledge Environment, 336,* pe23. doi: 10.1126/stke.3362006pe23

Weingartner, H., Miller, H., & Murphy, D. L. (1977). Mood-state–dependent retrieval of verbal associations. *Journal of Abnormal Psychology, 86*(3), 276–284. doi: 10.1037/ 0021-843X.86.3.276

Weinstock, M. (2005). The potential influence of maternal stress hormones on development and mental health of the offspring. *Brain, Behavior, and Immunity, 19*(4), 296–308. doi: 10.1016/j.bbi.2004.09.006

Weisberg, P., & Waldrop, P. B. (1972). Fixed-interval work habits of Congress. *Journal of Applied Behavior Analysis, 5*(1), 93–97. doi: 10.1901/jaba.1972.5-93

Weissman, M. M., Warner, V., Wickramaratne, P., Moreau, D., & Olfson, M. (1997). Offspring of depressed parents: 10 years later. *Archives of General Psychiatry, 54*(10), 932–940. doi: 10.1001/archpsyc.1997 .01830220054009

Welling, L. L. M., Jones, B. C., DeBruine, L. M., Conway, C. A., Law Smith, M. J., Little, A. C., et al. (2007). Raised salivary testosterone in women is associated with increased attraction to masculine faces. *Hormones and Behavior, 52*(2), 156–161. doi: 10.1016/j.yhbeh.2007.01.010

Wells, A. (2006). Metacognitive therapy for worry and generalised anxiety disorder. In G. C. L. Davey & A. Wells (Eds.), *Worry and its psychological disorders: Theory, assessment and treatment* (pp. 259–272). Hoboken, NJ: Wiley.

Wells, G. L., & Bradfield, A. L. (1998). "Good, you identified the suspect": Feedback to eyewitnesses distorts their reports of the witnessing experience. *Journal of Applied Psychology, 83*(3), 360–376. doi: 10.1037/0021-9010.83.3.360

Wells, G. L., Memon, A., & Penrod, S. D. (2006). Eyewitness evidence: Improving its probative value. *Psychological Science in the Public Interest, 7*(2), 45–75. doi: 10.1111/j.1529-1006.2006.00027.x

Wernicke, C. (1874). *Der aphasische symptom-enkomplex* [The aphasic symptom complex]. Breslau, Poland: Cohn & Weigart.

Wessely, S., & Kerwin, R. (2004). Suicide risk and the SSRIs. *JAMA: Journal of the American Medical Association, 292*(3), 379–381. doi: 10.1001/jama.292.3.379

Westbrook, D., & Kirk, J. (2005). The clinical effectiveness of cognitive behaviour therapy: Outcome for a large sample of adults treated in routine practice. *Behaviour Research and Therapy, 43*(10), 1243–1261. doi: 10.1016/j.brat.2004.09.006

Whisman, M. A., Dixon, A. E., & Johnson, B. (1997). Therapists' perspectives of couples' problems and treatment issues in the practice of couples therapy. *Journal of Family Psychology, 11*(3), 361–366. doi: 10.1037/0893-3200.11.3.361

White, A., & Hingson, R. (2014). The burden of alcohol use. *Alcohol Research, 35*(2), 201–218.

White, G. L. (1980). Physical attractiveness and courtship progress. *Journal of Personality and Social Psychology, 39*, 660–668. doi: 10.1037/0022-3514.39.4.660

White, S. A. (2013). *FoxP2 and vocalization*. In C. Lefebvre, B. Comrie, & H. Cohen (Eds.), *New Perspectives on the Origins of Language* (Vol. 144, pp. 211–236). Amsterdam, the Netherlands: John Benjamins Publishing Company.

Whorf, B. L. (1956). Science and linguistics. In J. B. Carroll (Ed.), *Language, thought, and reality: Selected writings of Benjamin Lee Whorf* (pp. 207–219). Cambridge, MA: MIT Press.

Widmeyer, W. N., & Loy, J. W. (1988). When you're hot, you're hot: Warm–cold effects in first impressions of persons and teaching effectiveness. *Journal of Educational Psychology, 80*(1), 118–121. doi: 10.1037/0022-0663.80.1.118

Widom, C. (1978). A methodology for studying non-institutionalized psychopaths. In R. D. Hare & D. Schalling (Eds.), *Psychopathic behaviour: Approaches to research* (pp. 71–84). Chichester, United Kingdom: Wiley.

Wilbanks, C. A. (2014). Alternative methods of predator control. Retrieved from http://agrilife.org/texnatwildlife/coyotes/table-of-contents/alternative-methods-of-predator-control/

Wilcox, H. C., Arria, A. M., Caldeira, K. M., Vincent, K. B., Pinchevsky, G. M., & O'Grady, K. E. (2010). Prevalence and predictors of persistent suicide ideation, plans, and attempts during college. *Journal of Affective Disorders, 127*(1–3), 287–294. doi: 10.1016/j.jad.2010.04.017

Wilensky, A. E., Schafe, G. E., Kristensen, M. P., & LeDoux, J. E. (2006). Rethinking the fear circuit: The central nucleus of the amygdala is required for the acquisition, consolidation, and expression of Pavlovian fear conditioning. *Journal of Neuroscience, 26*(48), 12387–12396. doi: 10.1523/JNEUROSCI.4316-06.2006

Wilke, A., Hutchinson, J. M. C., Todd, P. M., & Kruger, D. J. (2006). Is risk taking used as a cue in mate choice? *Evolutionary Psychology, 4*, 367–393.

Wilkinson, G. S. (1984). Reciprocal food sharing in the vampire bat. *Nature, 308*(5955), 181–184. doi: 10.1038/308181a0

Wilkinson, G. S. (1990). Food sharing in vampire bats. *Scientific American, 62*, 76–82.

Williams, H., Conway, M. A., & Cohen, G. (2008). Autobiographical memory. In G. Cohen & M. A. Conway (Eds.), *Memory in the real world* (pp. 21–90). New York, NY: Psychology Press.

Williams, J. H. G. (2008). Self–other relations in social development and autism: Multiple roles for mirror neurons and other brain bases. *Autism Research, 1*(2), 73–90. doi: 10.1002/aur.15

Williams, K. D. (2007). Ostracism. *Annual Review of Psychology, 58*, 425–452. doi: 10.1146/annurev.psych.58.110405.085641

Williams, L. M., Liddell, B. J., Kemp, A. H., Bryant, R. A., Meares, R. A., Peduto, A. S., et al. (2006). Amygdala–prefrontal dissociation of subliminal and supraliminal fear. *Human Brain Mapping, 27*(8), 652–661. doi: 10.1002/hbm.20208

Williamson, A. M., & Feyer, A.-M. (2000). Moderate sleep deprivation produces impairments in cognitive and motor performance equivalent to legally prescribed levels of alcohol intoxication. *Occupational and Environmental Medicine, 57*, 649–655. doi: doi:10.1136/oem.57.10.649

Williamson, R. A., Jaswal, V. K., & Meltzoff, A. N. (2010). Learning the rules: Observation and imitation of a sorting strategy by 36-month-old children. *Developmental Psychology, 46*(1), 57–65. doi: 10.1037/a0017473

Wilson, A. E., & Ross, M. (2000). The frequency of temporal and social comparisons in people's personal appraisals. *Journal of Personality and Social Psychology, 78*, 928–942. doi: 10.1037/0022-3514.78.5.928

Wilson, E. O. (1975). *Sociobiology: The new synthesis*. Cambridge, MA: Belknap Press.

Wilson, G. D., Cousins, J. M., & Fink, B. (2006). The CQ as a predictor of speed-date outcomes. *Sexual and Relationship Therapy, 21*(2), 163–169. doi: 10.1080/14681990600554215

Wilson, J. L., Peebles, R., Hardy, K. K., & Litt, I. F. (2006). Surfing for thinness: A pilot study of pro-eating disorder web site usage in adolescents with eating disorders. *Pediatrics, 118*(6), e1635–e1643. doi: 10.1542/peds.2006-1133

Wilton, P. (2002). A rule of thumb. *Canadian Medical Association Journal, 167*(12), 1367.

Wimmer, H., & Perner, J. (1983). Beliefs about beliefs: Representation and constraining function of wrong beliefs in young children's understanding of deception. *Cognition, 13*(1), 103–128. doi: 10.1016/0010-0277(83)90004-5

Witt, D. M., Carter, C. S., Lederhendler, I. I., & Kirkpatrick, B. (1997). Regulatory mechanisms of oxytocin-mediated socio-sexual behavior. *The integrative neurobiology of affiliation* (pp. 287–301). New York, NY: New York Academy of Sciences.

Witt, W. P., Cheng, E. R., Wisk, L. E., Litzelman, K., Chatterjee, D., Mandell, K., et al. (2014). Preterm birth in the United States: The impact of stressful life events prior to conception and maternal age. *American Journal of Public Health, 104*(S1), S73–S80. doi: 10.2105/AJPH.2013.301688

Wittchen, H.-U., & Hoyer, J. (2001). Generalized anxiety disorder: Nature and course. *Journal of Clinical Psychiatry, 62*(Suppl. 11), 15–19.

Wittgenstein, L. (1953). *Philosophical investigations* (G. E. M. Anscombe, Trans.). Oxford, United Kingdom: Blackwell.

Wobber, V., Wrangham, R., & Hare, B. (2010). Bonobos exhibit delayed development of social behavior and cognition relative to chimpanzees. *Current Biology, 20*(3), 226–230. doi: 10.1016/j.cub.2009.11.070

Wolpe, J. (1958). *Psychotherapy by reciprocal inhibition*. Palo Alto, CA: Stanford University Press.

Wolraich, M. L., Wilson, D. B., & White, J. W. (1996). The effect of sugar on behavior or cognition in children: A meta-analysis. *JAMA: Journal of the American Medical Association, 274*(20), 1617–1621. doi: 10.1001/jama.1995.03530200053037

Wood, J. M., Lilienfeld, S. O., Nezworski, M. T., Garb, H. N., Allen, K. H., & Wildermuth, J. L. (2010). Validity of Rorschach Inkblot scores for discriminating psychopaths from nonpsychopaths in forensic populations: A meta-analysis. *Psychological Assessment, 22*(2), 336–349. doi: 10.1037/a0018998

Wood, J. M., Nezworski, M. T., & Lilienfeld, S. O. (2003). *What's wrong with the Rorschach? Science confronts the controversial inkblot test*. San Francisco, CA: Jossey-Bass.

Woolley, A. W., Chabris, C. F., Pentland, A., Hashmi, N., & Malone, T. W. (2010). Evidence for a collective intelligence factor in the performance of human groups. *Science, 330*(6004), 686–688. doi: 10.1126/science.1193147

World Health Organization. (2003). WHO definition of health. Retrieved from http://www.who.int/about/definition/en/print.html

World Health Organization. (2006). Obesity and overweight. Retrieved from http://www.who.int/mediacentre/factsheets/fs311/en/index.html

World Health Organization. (2008). *WHO report on the global tobacco epidemic, 2008: The MPOWER package.* Geneva, Switzerland: World Health Organization.

World Health Organization. (2011a). Alcohol (Fact Sheet). Retrieved from http://www.who.int/mediacentre/factsheets/fs349/en/index.html

World Health Organization. (2011b). The International Classification of Diseases 11th Revision is due by 2015. Retrieved from http://www.who.int/classifications/icd/revision/en/index.html

Wright, G. A., Baker, D. D., Palmer, M. J., Stabler, D., Mustard, J. A., Power, E. F., et al. (2013). Caffeine in floral nectar enhances a pollinator's memory of reward. *Science, 339*(6124), 1202–1204. doi: 10.1126/science.1228806

Wrzesniewski, A., McCauley, C., Rozin, P., & Schwartz, B. (1997). Jobs, careers, and callings: People's relations to their work. *Journal of Research in Personality, 31*(1), 21–33. doi: 10.1006/jrpe.1997.2162

Wu, P.-L., & Chiou, W.-B. (2008). Postformal thinking and creativity among late adolescents: A post-Piagetian approach. *Adolescence, 43*(170), 237–251.

Wurtman, R. J. (2005). Genes, stress, and depression. *Metabolism, 54*(5, Suppl. 1), 16–19. doi: 10.1016/j.metabol.2005.01.007

Yalom, I. D. (1995). *The theory and practice of group psychotherapy* (4th ed.). New York, NY: Basic Books.

Yassa, M. A., & Stark, C. E. L. (2011). Pattern separation in the hippocampus. *Trends in Neurosciences, 34*(10), 515–525. doi: 10.1016/j.tins.2011.06.006

Yee, J. R., Frijling, J., Saber, M., Sterlinski, A., Tovar, S., Barlas, L., et al. (2010). *Oxytocin alters the behavioral, cardiovascular, and hormonal responses to a mild daily stressor.* Paper presented at the Society for Neuroscience, San Diego, CA.

Yee, N. (2006). The demographics, motivations and derived experiences of users of massively multiuser online graphical environments. *Presence: Teleoperators and Virtual Environments, 15*(3), 309–329.

Yehuda, R., Engel, S. M., Brand, S. R., Seckl, J., Marcus, S. M., & Berkowitz, G. S. (2005). Transgenerational effects of posttraumatic stress disorder in babies of mothers exposed to the World Trade Center attacks during pregnancy. *Journal of Clinical Endocrinology and Metabolism, 90*(7), 4115–4118. doi: http://dx.doi.org/10.1210/jc.2005-0550

Yerkes, R. M., & Dodson, J. D. (1908). The relation of strength of stimulus to rapidity of habit formation. *Journal of Comparative and Physiological Psychology, 18*, 459–482. doi: 10.1002/cne.920180503

Yotsutsuji, T., Saitoh, O., Suzuki, M., Hagino, H., Mori, K., Takahashi, T., et al. (2003). Quantification of lateral ventricular subdivisions in schizophrenia by high-resolution three-dimensional magnetic resonance imaging. *Psychiatry Research, 122*(1), 1–12. doi: 10.1016/S0925-4927(02)00105-1

Young, F. (2011). The Pearson correlation coefficient. Retrieved from http://forrest.psych.unc.edu/research/vista-frames/help/lecturenotes/lecture11/pearson.html

Young, P. C. (1952). Antisocial uses of hypnosis. In L. M. LeCron (Ed.), *Experimental hypnosis* (pp. 376–409). New York, NY: Macmillan.

Young, S. G., & Claypool, H. M. (2010). Mere exposure has differential effects on attention allocation to threatening and neutral stimuli. *Journal of Experimental Social Psychology, 46*(2), 424–427. doi: 10.1016/j.jesp.2009.10.015

Yu, Y. W., Chen, T. J., Wang, Y. C., Liou, Y. J., Hong, C. J., & Tsai, S. J. (2003). Association analysis for neuronal nitric oxide synthase gene polymorphism with major depression and fluoxetine response. *Neuropsychobiology, 47*, 137–140. doi: 10.1159/000070582

Yurgelun-Todd, D. (2007). Emotional and cognitive changes during adolescence. *Current Opinion in Neurobiology, 17*(2), 251–257. doi: 10.1016/j.conb.2007.03.009

Zadra, A. L., & Pihl, R. O. (1997). Lucid dreaming as a treatment for recurrent nightmares. *Psychotherapy and Psychosomatics, 66*, 50–55. doi: 10.1159/000289106

Zager, A., Andersen, M. L., Ruiz, F. S., Antunes, I. B., & Tufik, S. (2007). Effects of acute and chronic sleep loss on immune modulation of rats. *American Journal of Physiology. Regulatory, Integrative and Comparative Physiology, 293*(1), R504–R509. doi: 10.1152/ajpregu.00105.2007

Zajonc, R. B. (1965). Social facilitation. *Science, 149*(3681), 269–274.

Zajonc, R. B. (1968). Attitudinal effects of mere exposure. *Journal of Personality and Social Psychology Monograph Supplement, 9*(2), 1–27. doi: doi: 10.1037/h0025848

Zelazo, P. R. (1998). McGraw and the development of unaided walking. *Developmental Review, 18*(4), 449–471. doi: 10.1006/drev.1997.0460.

Zerjal, T., Xue, Y., Bertorelle, G., Wells, S., Bao, W., Suling, Z., et al. (2003). The genetic legacy of the Mongols. *American Journal of Human Genetics, 72*(3), 717–721. doi: 10.1086/367774

Zhang, T. Y., Chrétien, P., Meaney, M. J., & Gratton, A. (2005). Influence of naturally occurring variations in maternal care on prepulse inhibition of acoustic startle and the medial prefrontal cortical dopamine response to stress in adult rats. *Journal of Neuroscience, 25*(6), 1493–1502. doi: 10.1523/JNEUROSCI.3293-04.2005

Zhang, Y., Proenca, R., Maffei, M., Barone, M., Leopold, L., & Friedman, J. M. (1994). Positional cloning of the mouse obese gene and its human homologue. *Nature, 372*, 425–432. doi: 10.1038/372425a0

Zigler, E. (1967). Familial mental retardation: A continuing dilemma. *Science, 155*(3760), 292–298. doi: 10.1126/science.155.3760.292

Zigler, E., & Hodapp, R. (1986). *Understanding mental retardation.* New York, NY: Cambridge University Press.

Zimbardo, P. G. (1969). The human choice: Individuation, reason, and order vs. deindividuation, impulse and chaos. In W. J. Arnold & D. Levine (Eds.), *Nebraska symposium on motivation* (pp. 237–307). Lincoln, NE: University of Nebraska Press.

Zimmer, C. (2009). On the origin of tomorrow. *Science, 326*(5958), 1334–1336. doi: 10.1126/science.326.5958.1334

Zimmerman, F. J., Gilkerson, J., Richards, J. A., Christakis, D. A., Xu, D., Gray, S., et al. (2009). Teaching by listening: The importance of adult–child conversations to language development. *Pediatrics, 124*(1), 342–349. doi: 10.1542/peds.2008-2267

Zubin, J., & Spring, B. (1977). Vulnerability: A new view of schizophrenia. *Journal of Abnormal Psychology, 86*(2), 103–126. doi: 10.1037/0021-843X.86.2.103

Zuscho, H. (1982). Posttraumatic anosmia. *Archives of Otolaryngology—Head and Neck Surgery, 108*(2), 90–92. doi: 10.1001/archotol.1982.00790500026006

Name Index

Jones, B. C., 521
Jones, E. E., 473, 493, 495
Jones, I. H., 295, 476
Jones, M. C., 288
Jones, O. D., 123
Jones, P., 408
Jornada, L. K., 605
Joyner, K., 521
Jrambeck, H.-J., 526
Judd, C. M., 511
Judge, T. A., 457
Jung, C. G., 389, 453
Juster, R.-P., 633, 639
Juvonen, J., 476, 477, 478

Kagan, J., 261, 263, 424, 561
Kagohara, D. M., 600
Kahn, A. S., 247
Kahn, D., 203, 471, 480
Kahn, I., 345
Kahn, R. S., 551
Kahneman, D., 370
Kail, R., 419
Kaiser, J., 325
Kalinowsky, L. B., 596
Kalisch, R., 260
Kalish, D., 303
Kalmijn, M., 654
Kamin, L. J., 286
Kandel, D. B., 521
Kandel, E. R., 155, 286, 348, 572
Kane, J. M., 550, 604
Kang, C., 35
Kang, J.-H., 245
Kaniasty, K., 575
Kanner, A. D., 624
Kant, I., 184
Kao, C. F., 517
Kao, G., 521
Kapasi, S., 178
Kapkova, P., 349
Kaplan, H., 414
Kaplan, J., 311
Kaplan, R. M., 385, 654
Karau, S. J., 457, 517
Karney, B. R., 522
Karraker, A., 440
Kasai, K., 568
Kasmer, J., 517
Kass, A. E., 243
Kassam-Adams, N., 623
Kato, B. S., 239
Kato, M., 537
Katusic, S. K., 541
Katz, D. L., 241
Katzenberg, D., 202
Katzmarzyk, P. T., 640, 647, 648
Kaufmann, N., 262
Kave, G., 382
Kawachi, I., 385
Kawashima, R., 442
Kawecki, T. J., 319
Kaye, P. D., 379
Kazek, B., 130
Kearney, C. A., 537, 563
Kearns, D. N., 284
Kearsley, R. B., 261, 424
Keast, A., 344
Keehn, D., 425
Keele, S. W., 361
Keenan, J. P., 480, 481
Keene, R. G., 438
Keith, S. J., 550, 605
Kelder, A., 629
Keller, A., 188
Keller, P. S., 437

Kelley, M., 546
Kelley, M. L., 294
Kellogg, L. A., 379
Kellogg, W. N., 379
Kelly, D. J., 291
Kelly, J. F., 387
Kelly, M. W., 201
Kelly, T. L., 199
Keltner, D., 261, 662
Kemmelmeier, M., 484
Kendall-Tackett, K., 406
Kendall, R., 408
Kendler, K. S., 564
Kendzerska, T., 211
Kennedy, D. P., 118
Kennedy, G. C., 236
Kennedy, M. A., 528
Kennis, M., 464
Kenrick, D. T., 252, 253, 527, 654
Kenwood, C., 503
Kern, R. P., 51
Kerr, N. A., 478
Kerwin, R., 608
Kessen, W., 168
Kessler, R. C., 241, 443, 538, 547,
   552, 561, 563, 564, 565, 568, 623
Kety, S. S., 548
Keys, A., 252
Keysers, C., 311, 312
Khateb, A., 625
Khatri, P., 609
Khaw, K.-T., 435
Khoury, B., 609
Kiang, L., 433
Kiebel, S. J., 526
Kiehl, K., 571, 572
Kihlstrom, J. F., 224
Kikkert, M. A., 121
Kilham, W., 514
Kilkus, J. M., 632
Kim, H., 484
Kim, H. S., 496
Kim, J. E., 606
Kim, K. H., 383
Kim, Y.-H., 498
Kimura, D., 414, 492
King, B. H., 392
King, P. M., 435
King-Casas, B., 574
Kingstone, A., 177
Kirk, J., 595
Kirk, K. M., 247
Kirker, W. S., 352, 752
Kirkpatrick, B., 247
Kirsch, I., 224
Kirsch, P., 133
Kit, B. K., 239, 644
Kitamura, T., 537
Kitayama, S., 483, 497, 501
Kitchener, K. S., 435
Kittok, R., 216
Kivipelto, M., 219
Klann, N., 615, 616
Klauke, B., 564
Klavans, R., 5
Klein, D. J., 270
Klein, E. B., 439
Klein, R. A., 41
Klein, S. B., 319
Kleinmuntz, B., 265
Kleitman, N., 209
Klentz, B., 473
Klima, E. S., 383
Kline, P., 452
Kling, K. C., 475
Klonsky, E. D., 294

Kluender, K. R., 377
Kluver, H., 258
Knickmeyer, R., 410
Knight, D. C., 625
Knopfel, T., 349
Knowlton, B. J., 334
Koch, C., 162, 198
Koch, E. G., 178
Kochanek, K. D., 441
Koeda, T., 323
Koelega, H. S., 188
Koenigsberg, H. W., 632
Koffka, K., 12, 163
Kohlberg, L., 431
Kohler, C. G., 264
Köhler, W., 12
Kohout, J., 29
Kokis, J. V., 431
Kolevzon, A., 45
Kolko, R. P., 243
Komarraju, M., 457
Kometz, S., 629
Konopka, G., 82
Kopell, B. H., 597
Kopelman, M. D., 570
Koretz, D., 443
Kosonogov, V., 311
Kosslyn, S. M., 359
Koster, E. P., 188
Kotov, R., 457
Koudstaal, P. J., 121
Kouri, E. M., 106
Koury, S. H., 443
Kraaimaat, F. W., 614
Krain, A. L., 546
Kraines, R. J., 435
Kramer, B. J., 637
Kraus, N., 178
Kravitz, D. A., 517
Krawiec, T. S., 14
Krebs, H., 334
Kreiman, G., 162
Krey, L. C., 568
Kriegbaum, M., 631
Krijn, M., 612
Kristensen, M.P., 625
Kroes, M. C., 352
Kroger, J., 642
Kronick, R. G., 654
Kross, E., 40, 41
Krous, H., 211
Krueger, J.I., 476
Krueger, R. F., 463
Krug, M. K., 501
Kruger, D. J., 85, 98
Kruger, J., 476
Krumrei, E. J., 659
Kubzansky, L. D., 631
Kuepper, R., 219
Kugelmann, E., 349
Kuhl, B. A., 304, 345, 380
Kuhl, P. K., 304, 308, 380
Kuhn, D., 430
Kuiper, N. A., 352, 472
Kulik, J. A., 250
KunertKung, H.-C., 531
Kuo, L. E., 632
Kurihara, T., 537
Kurina, L. M., 208
Kurland, J. A., 527
Kuroki, T., 563
Kurtz, J. E., 466
Kurtz, R. G., 238
Kurzban, R., 525, 526
Kuschke, R. H., 629
Kushlev, K., 654

Kuster, J. M., 35
Kuzawa, C. W., 245
Kwan, V. S. Y., 511
Kyvik, K. O., 83

LaBar, K. S., 430
Laberg, J. C., 638
Lachmann, F. M., 590
Ladd, G. W., 661
Lage, S., 516
Lagerspetz, K. M. J., 528
Lahey, B. B., 294
Lai, C. S., 380
Laird, A. R., 311
Lakin, J. L., 226
Lalumière, M. L., 23
Lambeth, S. P., 311
Lammertsma, A. A., 568
Lampinen, J.M., 341
Lan, X., 497
Landis, K. R., 249, 490
Landlin, A. M., 186
Lane, A., 542, 543
Lane, A. M., 479
Lane, R. E., 460
Lange, A., 588
Lange, C. G., 266
Langenecker, S. A., 627
Langford, G., 210
Langley, J., 130
Langlois, J. H., 521
Lanzetta, M., 136
Largo, R. H., 414
Larkin, K., 248
Larkina, M., 419
Larrick, R. P., 371
Larsen, J. T., 257
Larsen, R. J., 523
Larson, C. L., 529, 572
Larson, C. M., 101
Lassek, W. D., 90
Latane, B., 517, 527
Lau, D. C., 241
Lau, H. C., 123
Lau, J., 38
Laumann, E. O., 245
Lauriello, J., 605
Lavie, C. J., 635, 636
LavoriLaw, J., 306, 601
Law, M., 307
Law, P., 306, 601
Lawrence, E., 438
Lazar, S. W., 224
Lazarus, A. A., 595
Lazarus, R. S., 622, 624, 635
Lazeyras, F., 625
Le Lionnais, F., 376
Le, N., 364
Le, Q. A., 376
Leaper, C., 38
Leary, M. R., 249, 476, 490
LeBlanc, S. A., 530
Lederhendler, I. I., 247
LeDoux, J. E., 258, 625
Lee, A. Y., 482
Lee, G. P., 125
Lee, H., 504
Lee, H. S., 521
Lee, K. M., 383
Lee, L.-C., 354, 406
Lee, M. A., 605
Lee, M. R., 562
Lee, Y.-A., 504
Leese, M., 596
Leichsenring, F., 590, 591
Leichtman, M., 465

Subject Index/Glossary

Development, 400–444. *See also individual headings*
adolescence, 428–435
childhood, 411–427
interpersonal relationships from perspective of, 444
late adulthood, 441–444
midlife, 438–441
newborn, 408–410
prenatal, 403–408, 404*f*
young adulthood, 435–437, 437*f*
Developmental psychology, 24. The psychological perspective that examines the normal changes in behavior that occur across the lifespan.
Developmental themes, 400–403
continuity *vs.* discontinuity, 402, 403*f*
nature *vs.* nurture, 400–402
universal *vs.* ecological development, 402–403
Dextroamphetamine, 603
DHA omega-3, 408
Diabetes, Type I and Type II, 236
Diagnostic and Statistical Manual of Mental Disorders (DSM), **537.** A system for classification of psychological disorders published by the American Psychiatric Association.
Diathesis-stress model, 560. A model that suggests that the experience of stress interacts with an individual's biological predisposition to produce a psychological disorder.
Diazepam (Valium), 611
Difference threshold, 152. The smallest detectable difference between two stimuli.
Discontinuity, continuity *vs.,* 402, 403*f*
Discrimination, 284. A learned ability to distinguish between stimuli.
Discrimination, 505. Unfair behavior based on stereotyping and prejudice.
Disorganized attachment, 424
Display rule, 262. A cultural norm that specifies when, where, and how a person should express an emotion, 262–264
Dispositional attribution, 493. A judgment assigning the cause of a person's behavior to personal qualities or characteristics.
Dissociative disorder, 569. A disorder characterized by disruptions in a person's identity, memory, or consciousness, 569–570
Dissociative identity disorders (DID), 570, 613
Distributed practice over time, 350–351
DNA. *See* Deoxyribonucleic acid (DNA)
Doctor of Philosophy (PhD) degree, 584, 585, 585*f*

Doctor of Psychology (PsyD) degree, 584, 585*f*
Dominant, 74. A feature of an allele that determines a phenotype in either the homozygous or heterozygous condition.
Door-in-the-face, 513. A persuasive technique in which compliance with a target request is preceded by a large, unreasonable request, 513, 513*f*
Dopamine, 142*t*, 143
addictive drugs, 222
ADHD and, 143, 546
hallucinogens and, 219
schizophrenia and, 143
Double-blind procedure, 54. A research design that controls for placebo effects in which neither the participant nor the experimenter observing the participant knows whether the participant was given an active substance or treatment or a placebo
Down syndrome, 381, 393, 393*f*
Dreaming, 209. A mental state that usually occurs during sleep that features visual imagery, 209–210
activation–synthesis theory of, 209
brain circuit activity and, 209
EEG and, 209
lucid, 210
sexual content and, 209
themes, 6*f*
Drive, 233. A state of tension and arousal triggered by cues important for survival.
Drive reduction, 233. The state of relief and reward produced by removing the tension and arousal of the drive state.
Dyslexia, 381–382

Eating. *See* Hunger; Obesity
Eating disorders, 241–243
anorexia nervosa, 241
binge-eating disorder, 242
bulimia nervosa, 241
homosexuals and, 241
hormones and, 243
pro-ana websites and, 243
Echoic memories, 321
Ecological development *vs.* universal development, 403–403, 425
Ectoderm, 403
Ego, 450. The component of Sigmund Freud's personality theory that is the self that others see, 450, 451*f*, 451, 452*f*
Egocentrism, 417. Limitations on the ability to understand the point of view of other people.
Elaboration Likelihood Model (ELM), 501. A model that predicts responses to persuasive messages by dis-

tinguishing between the central and peripheral routes to persuasion.
Electrical stimulation, 110*t*
Electroconvulsive therapy (ECT), 596. A biological treatment in which seizures are induced in an anesthetized patient; it is used primarily in the treatment of mood disorders that have not responded to medication or other treatments
Electroencephalogram (EEG), 110*t*
brain death and, 214, 215*f*
coma and, 213, 214*f*
dreaming and, 209
K-complexes and sleep spindles and, 203
meditation and, 224
during sleep, 203–204, 204*f*
waking and, 202–203, 203*f*
Embryo, 403. The term used to describe a developing organism between the zygote and fetus stages, or between 3 and 8 weeks following conception in humans.
Embryonic stage of development, 403, 404*f*
Emotion, 232. A combination of arousal, physical sensations, and subjective feelings that occurs spontaneously in response to environmental stimuli, 232–272
arousal produced by, 255–256, 256*f*
arts and, 256
biology of, 257–260–
amygdala, 257–259, 258*f*
autonomic activity and, 257, 260, 268
eye contact and detecting emotion, 258
fight–flight response and, 257, 268
hypothalamus and, 257
insula, 257–258, 259*f*
brain damage and, study of, 257
communication and, 256, 257*f*
continuous vs. discrete views of, 255, 255*f*
expressing, 260–264
biological influences on, 262–263
Botox and, 268–269, 269*f*
cultural influences on, 262–263
display rules and, 262–263, 263*f*
environmental influences on, 262
facial expressions and, 260–261
individual differences in, 263–264
infants and, developmental course shown by, 261, 262*f*
nonhuman primate species and, developmental course shown by, 261

"primary colors" of, 261
words for different emotional states and, 262
interpersonal relationships from perspective of, 272
interpreting, 264
cultural influences on, 264
individual differences in, 264
smiles, fake and genuine, 264
vs. motivation, 232–233
predicting, 257
theories of, 266–271, 266*f*
Cannon–Bard, 267–268
contemporary approaches, 270–271
James–Lange, 266–267
Schachter–Singer two-factor theory, 269–270
somatoviscereal afference model of emotion, 270–271
Yerkes–Dodson law and, 256
Emotional problems, bullying and, 76–77, 77*f*
Emotion-focused coping, 637. A response to stress that targets the negative emotions arising from the situation.
Empiricism, 7
"Empty nest" period, 440, 440*f*
Encoding, 318. The process of acquiring information and transferring it into memory.
Encoding specificity, 338. A process in which memories incorporate unique combinations of information when encoded.
Endocrine system (ES), 130. A system responsible for the release of hormones into the bloodstream, 130–133
glands of, 130–133, 132*f*
adrenal glands, 133
islets of Langerhans, 133
ovaries, 133
pineal gland, 132
pituitary gland, 132–133
testes, 133
thyroid gland, 133
hormones released by, 132–133
Endoderm, 403
Endogenous cannabinoids, 219
Endorphins, 142*t*, 143, 182, 223
Enteric nervous system, 130, 131*f*. Part of the autonomic nervous system consisting of neurons lining the gastrointestinal tract.
functions of, 130
Entity theory, 388
Epigenetics, 77. The study of the reversible development of traits by factors that affect how genes perform, 77–78, 81*f*
gene expression and, 78–79, 81*f*
of stress, 628
Epinephrine (adrenalin), 142*t*, 269, 626
Episodic memory, 329. A memory for personal experience.
Epworth Sleepiness Scale, 204

Ethical research. *See* Research ethics

Ethics of personality assessment, 469

Ethnic identity in adolescence, 433, 434*f*

Evidence-based practice (EBP), 583, 583*f*

Evoked potential, 110*t*

Evolution, 87. Descent with modification from a common ancestor, 87–102
behavior and, evolutionary influences on, 103
of human brain, 90–91, 91*f*
interpersonal relationships and, evolutionary perspective of, 102

Evolutionary mechanisms, 87–90
adaptation, 89–90
effects of, 88
fitness, 88
genetic drift, 88, 89*f*
migration, 87
mutation, 87
natural selection, 87–89

Evolutionary psychology, 23, 94, The psychological perspective that investigates how physical structure and behavior have been shaped by their contributions to survival and reproduction. *See also* Social behavior

Excellence motivation, 251

Exclusion, 491*f*

Exemplar, 361. A specific, "best case" member of a category used to represent the category, 361–362

Exercise, 635–636, 636*f*

Exhaustion, 622. The third and last stage of the general adaptation syndrome, characterized by depletion of physical and psychological resources.

Experiment, 48. A research method that tests hypotheses and allows researchers to make conclusions about causality, 48–53
artificiality in, 52
designing, 48, 49*f*
hypotheses tested using, 39–42
limitations of, 51
meta-analysis and, 52–53, 53*f*
multiple perspectives and, 53
operationalization and, 52
unethical, correlations and, 47, 48*f*
on video game use and aggression, 52, 52*f*, 53

Experimental group, 49. A group of participants that is exposed to the independent variable.

Explicit memory, 328. A conscious memory; also known as a declarative memory.

Extinction, 283. The reduction of a learned response. In classical conditioning, extinction occurs when the un-

conditioned stimulus no longer follows the conditioned stimulus. In operant conditioning, extinction occurs when the consequence no longer follows the learned behavior.

Extrasensory perception (ESP), 62

Extrinsic reward, 234. A reward from an outside source, 234

Extroversion, 456. One of the Big Five traits, also known as surgency, characterized by warmth, gregariousness, assertiveness, activity, excitement seeking, and positive emotion; opposite of introversion.

Eye contact, detecting emotion by, 258, 258*f*

Eyewitnesses, reliability of, 344

Facial expressions
emotions expressed by, 260–261
infants and, 256
of persons with depression, 556, 557*f*

Facial recognition
brain damage and, 213
of self, 480, 481*f*

Family therapy, 588. A type of therapy in which family members participate individually and in combination with other family members.

Fear, 625, 625*f*

Fetal alcohol syndrome (FAS), 407. A condition resulting from alcohol consumption by the mother during pregnancy that produces physical abnormalities and cognitive and behavioral problems in her child, 407–408, 407*f*

Fetal development, 403–405, 404*f*

Fetus, 403. The term used to describe a developing organism between the embryo stage and birth, or between 8 and approximately 40 weeks following conception in humans.

Fight–flight freeze system (FFFS), 464

Fight–flight response, 257, 268

First impressions, accuracy of, 491–492, 492*f*

Fitness, 88. The ability of one genotype to reproduce more successfully relative to other genotypes.

Fixed interval (FI) schedule, 299. A schedule of reinforcement in which the first response following a specified interval will be reinforced.

Fixed ratio (FR) schedule, 298. A schedule of reinforcement in which reinforcement occurs following a set number of behaviors.

Flashbulb memory, 341. An especially vivid and detailed memory of an emotional event, 341–342

Flow, 657. A state characterized by complete absorption in a current activity, such as work, problem solving, or creativity.

Flow chart, problem solving, 365*f*

Fluid intelligence, 385. The ability to think logically without the need to use learned knowledge, 385, 386*f*

Flynn effect, 391

Focal area of brain, seizures and, 216

Folic acid, 408

Food additives, hyperactivity and, 53–54, 54*f*

Food preferences before birth, 404

Foot-in-the-door, 513. A persuasive technique in which compliance with a small request is followed by compliance with a larger request that might otherwise have been rejected.

Forgetting, 345. A decrease in the ability to recall a previously formed memory, 345–347
decay and, 345–346
interference and, 346, 346*f*
motivated, 347

Formal operational stage, 417. Jean Piaget's stage of development beginning at age 12 and extending through adulthood and characterized by mature reasoning capabilities.

"4F" behaviors, 116

Fovea, 156. An area of the retina that is specialized for highly detailed vision.

FOXP-2 gene, 82, 82*f*, 376, 381, 381*f*

Framing effects, 370, 370*f*

Free association, 590. The psychoanalytic technique of encouraging a patient to say whatever comes to mind without attempting to censor the content.

Frequency, recognizing objects and, 163, 164*f*

Frontal lobe, 118. The most forward of the four lobes of the cerebral cortex; location of primary motor cortex and areas responsible for some of the most complex cognitive processes, 119, 120–121
ADHD and, 545
cognitive functions of, 120–121
importance of, Phineas Gage accident and, 121–122
orbitofrontal cortex and, 121–122, 122*f*
prefrontal cortex and, 121

Frontal lobotomy, 121

Fugu, 139

Functional fixedness. 365. A possible barrier to successful

problem solving in which a concept is considered only in its most typical form, 365, 366*f*

Functionalism, 13. An approach to psychology that saw behavior as purposeful and contributing to survival, 13–14, 15
James and, 12–14

Functional magnetic resonance imaging (fMRI), 108, 110*t*
lie detection and, 265, 265*f*
meditation and, 224
prosopagnosia and, 213
vegetative state and, 215*f*

Fundamental attribution error, 494. A failure to consider situational variables while making an attribution, leading to an overestimation of dispositional contributions when observing the behavior of others.

Fusiform Face Area (FFA), 213

GABA, 142*t*
seizures and, 216

Gamma rays, 150*f*, 155

Gamma wave, 203. A high frequency waveform recorded by electroencephalogram that accompanies the processing of sensory input.

Gantt chart in problem solving, 371*f*

Gate theory, 182. The theory that suggests that input from touch fibers competes with input from pain receptors, possibly preventing pain messages from reaching the brain, 182, 183*f*

Gays. *See* Homosexuality

Gender, self-esteem and, 475, 475*f*

Gene, 73. Small segment of DNA located in a particular place on a chromosome.
alleles for, 74
for behavior, 82
blond, 88, 89*f*
environmental influences on, 71–72, 72*f*
FOXP-2, 82, 82*f*, 376, 381, 381*f*
hemophilia and, 77, 80*f*
serotonin transporter, 76, 76*f*, 449*f*
shared with other species, 82*f*

Gene expression, 73. The process in which genetic instructions are converted into a feature of a living cell.

General adaptation syndrome (GAS), 621. Hans Selye's three-stage model for an organism's response to stressors, 621–622, 621*f*, 624

General intelligence (g), 385. A measure of an individual's overall intelligence as opposed to specific abilities.

Hunger, 235–243
cues for, 235–236
eating disorders, 241–243
fat stores and, 236–237
feeding and, stimulation of, 237
glucose and, 236
insulin levels and, 236
leptin levels and, 237–238
satiety and, 237–238, 238*f*
sensation of, 235–237
vegan food pyramid and, 235
Hunter–gatherer societies, 98
Huntington's disease, 83, 334
Hydrocephalus, 111
Hyperactivity and food additives, 53–54, 54*f*
Hyperbaric oxygen therapy, 602
Hyperpolarization, 138, 139*f*, 141
Hyperthymesia, 330
Hypnosis, 223. An altered state of consciousness characterized by relaxation and increased suggestibility, 223–224
Stroop Test and, 224, 224*f*
Hypnotherapist, 585
Hypothalamic-pituitary-adrenal (HPA) axis, 626. A circuit that responds to perceived stressors by initiating the release of cortisol into the bloodstream, 626–627, 626*f*
Hypothalamus, 116. A subcortical structure that participates in the regulation of thirst, temperature, hunger, sexual behavior, and aggression.
emotion and, regulation of, 257
endocrine system and, 132
"4F" behaviors and, 116
hunger and, 237*f*
lateral, feeding initiated by, 237
narcolepsy and, 211
panic disorder and, 563
pituitary gland and, 132
sexual orientation and, 248, 248*f*
ventromedial, satiety sensed by, 237, 238*f*, 239*f*
Hypothesis, 39. A proposed explanation for a situation, usually taking the form "if A happens then B will be the result.", 39–40
evaluating, 39–40
experiments used to test, 42–45

Iconic memory, 321
Id, 450. The component of Sigmund Freud's personality theory containing primitive drives present at birth, 450–451, 451*f*, 452*f*
Identity, 432. A consistent, unified sense of self.
If-then relationships, 461
Illusion
moon illusion, 166
Müller–Lyer illusion, 166, 167*f*
Munker illusion, 147, 148*f*
Ponzo illusion, 166, 168*f*
Turning the Tables illusion, 170, 171*f*
Imitation, 309. Copying behavior that is unlikely to occur

naturally and spontaneously, 309, 310–311
Immune system, 629. The body system that defends against infection and cancer, 629–630, 629*f*
Implicit Association Test (IAT), 508*f*
Implicit memory, 328. *See also* Nondeclarative memory
Imprinting, 278
INAH, 248, 248*f*
Incentive, 234. A reward that pulls an organism's behavior in a particular direction.
effectiveness of, 234, 234*f*
Incremental theory, 388
Independent variable, 48. An experimental variable controlled and manipulated by the experimenter; the "if A happens" part of a hypothesis.
Individual differences, 25. An approach to psychology that investigates variations in behavior from one person to the next.
Big Five theory and, 456–457, 456*f*
in cooperation and competition, 525
in expressing emotion, 263
in interpreting emotions, 264
social-cognitive learning theory and, 460–461
in susceptibility to hypnosis, 224
Individualism, 483, 483*f*, 484*f*
Indulgent parenting style, 426, 427f
Infants. *See also* Childhood development
audition and, 178
circadian rhythm and, 201
expressing emotions and, developmental course shown by, 261, 262*f*
facial expressions of, emotions and, 256
gustation and, 189
language and, 380
touch and, 181
vision and, 168–169
Inferences, schemas and, 336–337
Inferential statistics, 61. Statistical methods that allow experimenters to extend conclusions from samples to larger populations, 61–63, 64*f*
Information processing, 318. A continuum including attention, sensation, perception, learning, memory, and cognition, 318–319, 419
Informed consent, 65. Permission obtained from a research participant after risks and benefits of an experimental procedure have been thoroughly explained.
Infrared rays, 150*f*, 155
Infrasound, 173

In-group cooperation, reduction of bias through, 510, 510*f*
Inheritance
of traits, 87
Inhibition, 283. A feature of classical conditioning in which a conditioned stimulus actually predicts the nonoccurrence of an unconditioned stimulus.
Insecure attachment, 424. A pattern of infant–caregiver bonding that can take several forms but is generally characterized as less desirable for the child's outcomes than secure attachment, 424–425
Insight therapy, 590. A therapy that improves symptoms of psychological disorder by building the people's understanding of their situation.
Insomnia, 210. A sleep disorder characterized by an inability to either initiate or maintain normal sleep.
Instinct, 277. An inborn pattern of behavior elicited by environmental stimuli; also known as a fixed action pattern.
Instinctive drift, 304
Institutional animal care and use committees (IACUCs), 64
Institutional review boards (IRBs), 64
Instrumental conditioning, 293
Insula, 257. Regions of cortex located at the junction of the frontal and temporal lobes, 257–258, 258*f*
Insulin, 133
Intellectual disability, 392. A condition diagnosed in individuals with IQ scores below 70 and poor adaptive behaviors; historically known as mental retardation, 392–393, 393*f*
Intelligence, 384. The ability to understand complex ideas, adapt effectively to the environment, learn from experience, engage in reasoning, and overcome obstacles, 384–391. *See also* Intelligence quotient (IQ)
abilities and, general and specific, 385–387
assessing, 384–385
biological influences on, 389–391
brain structure and, 389, 389*f*
genetics, 390–391, 392*f*
cognitive perspective of interpersonal relationships and, 396
collective, 390–391, 391*f*
crystallized, 385, 386*f*
emotional, 387
extremes of, 392–395
fluid, 385, 386*f*
general, 385

giftedness, 394–395
impact on education, 388
social, 387
theories, 388
Intelligence quotient (IQ), 384. A measure of individual intelligence relative to a statistically normal curve, 384–385, 385*f*. *See also* Intelligence
brain structure and, 389, 389*f*
Flynn effect and, 391
giftedness and genius, 394–395
heritability of, 390
infectious disease and, 392*f*
intellectual disability and, 390–391, 392–394, 393*f*
phenylketonuria and, 390
twins and, 390
Interactome, 535
Interference, 346. Competition between newer and older information in memory.
forgetting and, 346, 346*f*
International Affective Picture System, 62
International Statistical Classification of Diseases and Related Health Problems, (ICD-10), 539
Interneuron, 112
Interpersonal relationships
biological perspective of, 30, 144
clinical perspective of, 575
cognitive perspective of, 396
consciousness perspective of, 226–227
developmental perspective of, 444
emotional perspective of, 272
evolutionary perspective of, 102
health psychology and, 661
learning perspective of, 313
memory perspective of, 354
personality perspective of, 484–485, 485*f*
psychological perspective of, 30
research methods perspective of, 67
sensation and perception perspective of, 189
social perspective of, 532
treatment perspective of, 615–616, 616*f*
Interpersonal self, 481. The self we are in the presence of other people, 610–611
Interpretation of Dreams, The (Freud), 209
Interstitial nucleus of the anterior hypothalamus (INAH), 248
Intrinsic reward, 234. A reward that arises internally.
Introspection, 5. Personal observation of your own thoughts, feelings, and behavior.
Introversion, 456. A dimension of one of the Big Five traits characterized by coolness, reserve, passivity, inactivity, caution, and negative emotion; opposite of surgency or extroversion.

IQ. *See* **Intelligence quotient (IQ),** 384. A measure of individual intelligence relative to a statistically normal curve.

Iris, 155. The brightly colored circular muscle surrounding the pupil of the eye, 155, 156*f*

Islets of Langerhans, 132, 132*f*, 133

Jamais vu, 216

James–Lange theory, 266. A theory of emotion that proposes that physical sensations lead to subjective feelings, 266–267, 266*f*
catharsis and, 266
subjective feelings changed by physical sensations and, 266–267

Jet lag, 132

Just-world belief, 497. The assumption that good things happen to good people and bad things happen to bad people.

Juvenile delinquency and self-esteem, 478

Kanzi, 379
Kavadis, 183
K-complexes, 203
Ketamine, 216
Knee-jerk reflex, 112, 115*f*
Knowledge, philosophical debate about source of, 7

Language, 375. A system for communicating thoughts and feelings using arbitrary signals, 478–488
biological psychology of, 377–379
building blocks of, 377
disorders, 377–378
Broca's aphasia, 378
Wernicke's aphasia, 378
FOXP-2 gene and, 376, 381, 381*f*
infants and, 380
learning, 380–381
morphemes and, 377
nonhuman animals and, language ability of, 378–379
origins of, 376
phonemes and, 377*f*, 377
processing, variations in, 381–383
American Sign Language (ASL) and, 383
dyslexia and, 381–382
multilingualism and, 382–383, 383*f*

Late adulthood, 441–444
cognitive development in, 442–443
entertainment in, aging brain and, 442–443
physical changes in, 441–442
social and emotional aspects of, 443–444
depression and, 443, 443*f*
relationships and, 443–444

Latent inhibition, 285. The slower learning that occurs when a conditioned stimulus is already familiar compared to when the conditioned stimulus is unfamiliar.

Latent learning, 302. Learning that occurs in the absence of reinforcement.

Lateral hypothalamus (LH), 237
Lateralization, 124–126
cognitive processes showing evidence of, 125
defined, 124
function of, 124–126
of language correlated with handedness, 126–127, 126*t*
lateral preference inventory and, 127*t*
right/left brain myths, 125
right/left brain processing of movement and sensation, 124–125
split-brain operation and, 124*f*, 125

Law of Effect, Thorndike's, 17–18, 19*f*
Leadership, psychopaths and, 572–573

Learned helplessness, 555. A state in which experiencing random or uncontrolled consequences leads to feelings of helplessness and possibly depression.

Learning, 277. A relatively permanent change in behavior or the capacity for behavior due to experience, 276–314
aggression and, 530
associative, 279–294
classical conditioning, 279, 281–290
operant conditioning, 279, 293–294
instincts and, animals' use of, 276–378
interpersonal relationships from perspective of, 313
nonassociative, 279
observational, 280, 308–313
reflexes and, animals' use of, 276–278

Lens, 155. The clear structure behind the pupil that bends light toward the retina, 188, 189*f*

Leptin, 237. A hormone secreted by fat cells that helps the body maintain an appropriate level of stored fat, 237–238

Lesbians. *See* Homosexuality
Lesions, 110*t*
Levels of awareness, Freud's, 452*f*

Levels of processing theory, 325. The depth (shallow to deep) of processing applied to information that predicts its ease of retrieval, 325–326, 326*f*

Lexical decision task, 331, 332*f*

Librium (chlordiazepoxide), 611
Lie detection, 265, 265*f*
Life coach, 586
"Light at the end of the tunnel" experience, 214
Light spectrum, 155, 173
Limbic system, 116. *See also* Subcortical structures
Linear perspective, 165, 167*f*
Lithium, 605, 606*f*
Lobes, 120–122, 120*f*
frontal, 120–122
occipital, 122
parietal, 122–123
temporal, 122

Locus of control, 460. A cognitive expectancy featured in social–cognitive learning theories of personality about the source of individual outcomes; an external locus of control sees outcomes as resulting from luck or chance, while an internal locus of control sees outcomes as the result of individual effort.

Loneliness, sleep and, 208–209

Longitudinal study, 55. An experimental design for assessing age-related changes in which data are obtained from the same individuals at intervals over a long period.

Long-term memory (LTM), 325. The final stage of the Atkinson–Shiffrin model that is the location of permanent memories, 325–337
levels of processing in, 325–326, 326*f*
moving information into, 325–326
organization in, 335–337
connectionist theories and, 335–336
inferences using schemas and, 336–337
spreading activation model and, 335, 335*f*
retrieval from, 337–341
types of, 328–331 (*See also* Declarative memory; Nondeclarative memory)
vs. working memory, 327–328, 327*f*

Long-term potentiation (LTP), 348. The enhancement of communication between two neurons resulting from their synchronous activation, 348, 349*f*
Loudness, perception of, 176, 177*t*, 177*f*
Love, brain imaging of, 67, 67*f*
LSD (lysergic acid diethylamide), 219

Lucid dreaming, 210. A conscious awareness of dreaming accompanied by the ability to control the content of the dream.

Lymphocyte, 629. White blood cells that are products of the immune system.
Lysergic acid diethylamide (LSD), 219

Magnetoencephalography (MEG), 110*t*

Major depressive disorder, 553. A disorder characterized by lengthy periods of depressed mood, loss of pleasure in normal activities, disturbances in sleep and appetite, difficulty concentrating, feelings of hopelessness, and possible thoughts of suicide, 553–560, 554*f*. *See also* Depression
causes of, 554–560
integration of perspectives on, 560
mindfulness-based cognitive therapy for, 609
prevalence of, 553–554, 554*f*
treatment for, 607–609, 608*f*, 609*f*

Major depressive disorder with seasonal pattern, 201. A mood disorder in which depression occurs regularly at the same time each year, usually during the winter months; formerly known as seasonal affective disorder (SAD).

Major histocompatibility complex (MHC), 102

Mania, 552. A period of unrealistically elevated mood.

Marijuana (cannabis), 219
Marriage, happiness and, 653–655, 654*f*
Massively multiplayer online role-playing games (MMORPGs), 301
Master of Divinity (MDiv) degree, 585
Matching hypothesis, 522
Maximizer *vs.* satisficer, 396
MDMA (Ecstasy), 222

Mean, 58. The numerical average of a set of scores, 58, 59*f*. *See also* Data

Measure, 46. A method for describing a variable's quantity.

Median, 59. The halfway mark in a set of data, with half of the scores above and half below, 59, 59*f*. *See also* Data

Medications. *See also* Antidepressant medication; Psychoactive drug antipsychotic, 582, 596, 600, 601*f*
for autism, 600–602, 601*f*
biological therapies and, 596
over-the-counter, 219
for schizophrenia, 603–605, 604*f*

Meditation, 224. A voluntary alteration of consciousness characterized by positive

Panic attack, 563. The experience of intense fear and autonomic arousal in the absence of real threat.

Panic disorder, 563. A disorder characterized by repeated panic attacks and fear of future attacks, 563–564
biological explanations of, 563
cognitive explanations of, 563
integrating perspectives on, 564
social explanations of, 563–564

Papillae, 186. Small bumps on the tongue that contain taste buds.

Paradoxical sleep, 204

Parapsychology, 62

Parasympathetic nervous system, 130. The part of the autonomic nervous system associated with rest, repair, and energy storage, 130–131
antagonistic effects on organs served by, 130, 131f
function of, 130
low fat stores and leptin levels and, 237

Parenting inventory, 439t

Parenting styles, 425–427, 426t, 427f
categories of, 425–426, 426t, 427f
authoritarian, 426–427
authoritative, 425–427
indulgent, 426
uninvolved, 426
child outcomes and, 427f
cultural influences on, 424

Parietal lobe, 118. The lobe of the cerebral cortex that lies at the top of the head between the frontal and occipital lobes; location of primary somatosensory cortex, 122–123, 123f
vestibular system and, 181

Parkinson's disease, 116, 143

Partial reinforcement, 298. The reinforcement of a desired behavior on some occasions but not others.

Partial reinforcement effect in extinction, 300. The more rapid extinction observed following continuous reinforcement compared to that following partial reinforcement, 300–301

Partner infidelity, 523, 523f
couples therapy for treating, 615–616, 616f

Patriarchal systems, 98

Pavlovian conditioning, 16, 281

Peer review, 40. The process of having other experts examine research prior to its publication.

Perception, 149. The process of interpreting sensory information, 148–154
auditory, 173–179
bottom-up processing and, 151
gustatory, 184–189
interpersonal relationships and, 189

measuring
absolute threshold and, 152f, 152
difference threshold and, 152
psychophysics and, 152, 152f
olfactory, 184–189
sensation and, 149
sensory adaptation and, 151
signal detection and, 153
somatosensory, 180–183
top-down processing and, 151
visual, 159–161

Periaqueductal gray, 114, 182

Peripheral nervous system (PNS), 109, 111. The nerves exiting the central nervous system that carry sensory and motor information to and from the rest of the body.
autonomic nervous system and, 130
somatic nervous system and, 129, 129f

Personality, 25, 449. An individual's characteristic way of thinking, feeling, and behaving, 449–485
assessment of (See Personality assessment)
biological bases of, 461–465
brain function, 463–464
brain structure, 463–464
evolution of, 464–465
genetics, 462–463, 462f, 463f
temperament, 461–462
classic behavioral approaches to, 453
description of, 449–450
humanists approach to, 454–455, 455f
interpersonal relationships from perspective of, 484–485, 485f
psychodynamic theories on, 450–453
rudimentary theory of, 9
self and, 471–484
situations affecting, 460–461
social–cognitive learning theories of, 460–461
trait theories of, 455–457

Personality assessment, 465–469
ethics of, 469
personality inventories, 466, 467f
projective tests, 467

Personality disorder, 570. A disorder characterized by impairments in identity, in personality traits, and in the establishment of empathy or intimacy, 541–546, 570–575
ADHD, 544–546, 546f
antisocial personality disorder, 571–573
autism spectrum disorder, 541–544, 542–543f
borderline personality disorder, 573–575, 574f
childhood, 541–546
psychopaths and, 571, 572
treatment for, 614

Personality inventory, 466. An objective test, often using

numbered scales or multiple choice, used to assess personality, 466, 467f

Person-centered therapy, 591. A humanistic therapy approach developed by Carl Rogers to help clients achieve congruence.

Persuasion, 501. A change in attitudes in response to information provided by another person, 501–504, 504f
age and intelligence of audience, 503
Elaboration Likelihood Model and, 501–502
medium used to communicate, 503
routes to, 502–504
central, 502
peripheral, 502–503
social media and, 503–504, 504f
user-generated messages and, 504f

Phantom limb, 181

Phenotype, 73. Observable characteristics.

Phenylketonuria (PKU), 390

Phenytoin (Dilantin), 407t

Philosophers, ancient
Aristotle, 7, 9
Descartes, 7
Freud, 14–15
Locke, 8
vs. psychologist, 6–7

Philosophy, 6. The discipline that systematically examines basic concepts, including the source of knowledge. See also Philosophers, ancient
brain and, 8–9
empiricism and, 8
knowledge, philosophical debate about source of, 7
microscope and, 8f, 9
nerve signaling and, speed of, 9
personality and, rudimentary theory of, 9

Phoneme, 377. A speech sound, 377f, 377

Phrenology, 107

Physical attractiveness, 522, 522f

Pineal gland, 132, 132f

Pinna, 174, 175f, 176

Pitch perception, 175f, 176

Pituitary gland, 132–133, 132f

Pituitary hormones, 132–133
adrenal glands activated by, 133
growth hormone, 133
oxytocin, 133
sex hormones, 133
thyroid gland activated by, 133
vasopressin, 133

Placebo, 54. An inactive substance or treatment that cannot be distinguished from a real, active substance or treatment.
effects on pain, 182

Plan in problem solving
carrying out, 371
making, 365–371
solutions in, 366–371

affect heuristic and, 369
algorithms and, 366–367
availability heuristic and, 367, 368f
deciding on, 369–371
generating, 366–368
recognition heuristic and, 368, 369f
representativeness heuristic and, 367

Pons, 113. A part of the brainstem located between the medulla and midbrain.

Ponzo illusion, 166, 168f

Population, 44. The entire group from which a sample is taken.

Positive emotions, 652–657. See also Happiness

Positive institutions, 660–661

Positive psychology, 651. An approach to psychology that emphasizes normal behavior and human strengths, 651–661
future and, 661–661
positive emotions and, 652–657
positive institutions and, 660–661
positive traits and, 657–660

Positive punishment, 297. A consequence that eliminates or reduces the frequency of a behavior by applying an aversive stimulus.

Positive reinforcement, 293, 294, 295

Positive traits, 657–660

Positron emission tomography (PET), 108, 110t

Postconventional morality, 431. Lawrence Kohlberg's stage at which moral choices are made according to personal standards and reason.

Posterior cingulate cortex (PCC), 117

Posttraumatic stress disorder (PTSD), 567. A disorder caused by the experience of trauma, which leads to flashbacks, dreams, hypervigilance, and avoidance of stimuli associated with the traumatic event, 567–569
biological explanations for, 568, 568f
cultural explanations for, 569
learning explanations for, 569
MDMA for, 222
norepinephrine activity and, 143
olfaction and, 188
social explanations for, 569
stress and, 620–623, 623f
symptoms, 567
treatment for, 612
veterans with, 575

Power of one, 516

Preconventional morality, 431. Lawrence Kohlberg's stage at which moral choices are made according to expectations of reward or punishment.

Science, *continued*
critical thinking in, 38–39
hypothesis in, 39–40
objectivity in, 36–37
theories in, 39
Sea slug, 275, 286
Secondary reinforcers, 296
Secondary sex characteristics, 429. Physical changes occurring at puberty associated with sexual maturity.
Secure attachment, 424. A pattern of infant–caregiver bonding in which children explore confidently and return to the parent or caregiver for reassurance, 424–425
Seizure, 216. An abnormal level of brain activation with a sudden onset.
GABA and, 216
generalized, 216, 216*f*
partial, 216, 216*f*
Selection in Relation to Sex (Darwin), 94
Selective serotonin reuptake inhibitors (SSRIs), 607–608, 608*f*
Self, 471. Patterns of thought, feelings, and actions we perceive in our own minds.
brain and, 480, 481*f*
culture and, modifying effects of, 482, 483*f*
definition of, 471
personality and, 471–484
self-awareness, 472–473, 473*f*
self-concept, 471–472, 472*f*
self-esteem, 473–477
self-regulation, 479–480, 479*f*
social, 481–484
Self-actualization, 253. A state of having fulfilled your potential, 15
Self-awareness, 194, 472. The special understanding of the self as distinct from other stimuli, 472–473, 473*f*
self-knowledge and, sources of, 473
Self-concept, 471. A person's description of their own characteristics, 471–472, 472*f*
Self-consciousness, 472, 473*f*
Self-control, 479, 479*f*
Self-efficacy, 460–461
Self-enhancement to protect self-esteem, use of, 475–476
Self-esteem, 473. A judgment of the value of the self, 473–480
academic performance and, 478
advantages of, 476
gender, race, culture and, 475, 475*f*
juvenile delinquency and, 478
self-enhancement to protect, use of, 475–476
social rejection and, signal for, 476, 477*f*
sources of, 474–475
Self-knowledge, sources of, 473
Self-regulation, 479–480, 479*f*

Self-schema, 471. A cognitive organization that helps us think about the self and process self-relevant information.
Self-serving bias, 496. Attributing success to dispositional factors while attributing failure to situational factors.
Semantic memory, 329. A general knowledge memory.
vs. episodic memory, 329
Sensation, 148. The process of detecting environmental stimuli or stimuli arising from the body. *See also* Perception
interpersonal relationships and, 189
microwaves and ultraviolet waves and, 149, 150*f*
transduction and, 150
Senses of newborn, 409–410, 410*f*, 411*f*
Sensitization, 279. An increased reaction to many stimuli following exposure to one strong stimulus, 279–280
Sensorimotor stage, 416. Jean Piaget's stage of development beginning at birth and ending at the age of 2 years and characterized by active exploration of the environment.
Sensory adaptation. 151. The tendency to pay less attention to a nonchanging source of stimulation.
Sensory homunculus, 181
Sensory memory, 320. The first stage of the Atkinson–Shiffrin model that holds large amounts of incoming data for very brief amounts of time, 320–325
short-term memory and, 321–323
Sperling's demonstration of duration of, 322*f*
working memory, 324–325, 324*f*
Sensory neuron, 112
Sensory sensitivity in autism spectrum disorder, 542, 543*f*
Separation anxiety, 424
Serial position effect, 327*f*
Serotonin, 142*t*, 143
hallucinogens and, 219
MDMA and, 222
REM and, 209
sudden infant death syndrome and, 211
Serotonin transporter gene, 76, 76*f*, 449*f*
Set point, 233. A value that is defended to maintain homeostasis.
Sex and adolescence, 429
Sex hormones, 133
Sexual motivation, 243–248
cross-cultural studies on, 245, 245*f*
evolutionary psychology perspective of, 243

hormones and, 244–247
menopause and, 244
ovulation and menstrual cycle and, 244–245, 244*f*
oxytocin, 246–247, 246*f*
stability of relationships and, 245–246, 246*f*
testosterone and, 244–246
vasopressin and, 246, 246*f*
preferences in mate characteristics, 244*f*
sexual orientation and, 247–248
Sexual orientation, 247. A stable pattern of attraction to members of a particular sex, 247–248
birth order and, 247
brain structures and, 248, 248*f*
cross cultural surveys on mate preferences, 243, 244*f*
genetics and, 247
hormones and, 247
sexual motivation and, 244, 247–248
Sexual selection, 96. The development of traits that help an individual compete for mates, 96–98
parental investment and, 96–97
traits influenced by, 97–98
Shift maladaptation syndrome, 200, 201*f*
Short-term memory (STM), 321. The second stage of the Atkinson–Shiffrin model that holds a small amount of information for a limited time, 321–323
chunking and, 323
rehearsal and, 322
retrieval from, 337
Signal detection, 153. The analysis of sensory and decision-making processes in the detection of faint, uncertain stimuli, 153
outcomes in, 153, 154*t*
perception and, 153
two-step process of, 153
Similarity, Gestalt principle of, 164, 165*f*
Simplicity, Gestalt principle of, 164
Sine wave speech, 179, 179*f*
Single cell recording, 110*t*
Sitting, death and, 647, 648*f*
Situational attribution, 493. A judgment assigning the cause of a person's behavior to the environment, 493, 516–519
deindividuation, 517
group polarization, 517–518, 518*f*
groupthink, 518–519
social facilitation, 516–517
social loafing, 517
Skin conductance response (SCR), 110*t*
Skinner boxes, 19
Sleep, 199. A normal state of consciousness characterized by reduced awareness of external stimuli, 203–207
benefits of, 205–207

circadian rhythms and, 199–202
health and, 631–632, 632*f*
loneliness and, 208–209
memory and, 352
regulation, serotonin and, 143
stages of (*See* Non-rapid eye movement (N-REM) sleep; Rapid eye movement (REM) sleep)
Sleep apnea, 211. A sleep disorder in which the person stops breathing while asleep.
Sleep disorders, 210
cataplexy, 210–211
insomnia, 210
narcolepsy, 210–211
nightmares, 210
restless legs syndrome and, 212
sleep apnea, 211
sleep terrors, 210
sudden infant death syndrome and, 211
Sleep spindles, 203
Sleep terror, 210. A sleep disorder occurring in non–rapid eye movement sleep in which the sleeper wakes suddenly in great distress, but without experiencing the imagery of a nightmare.
Smell. *See* Olfaction
Social anxiety disorder, 562. A disorder, previously known as social phobia, characterized by an unrealistic fear of being scrutinized and criticized by others.
treatment for, 610*f*, 615–616, 616*f*
Social behavior
altruism and, 96
cooperation and, 96
culture and, 98–99
origins of, 94–98
reciprocal altruism and, 96
sexual selection and, 97–98
social interactions and, outcomes of, 95*t*
Social–cognitive learning theory, 460. A theory of personality that features cognition and learning, especially from the social environment, as important sources of individual differences in personality, 460–461
if–then relationships and, 461
locus of control and, 460
reciprocal determinism and, 460–461
self-efficacy and, 460–461
Social facilitation, 304, 516. A situation in which the presence of other people changes performance, 516–517
Socialization, 490, 491*f*. *See also* Social relationships
Social learning, 280
Social loafing, 517. Reduced motivation and effort shown by individuals working in a group.

Social media, persuasion of, 503–504, 504f

Social norms, 511. Usually unwritten or unspoken rules for behavior in social settings, 511–516
  compliance, 512–514, 513f
  conformity, 511–512, 512f
  obedience, 514–515, 515f
  power of one, 516

Social psychology, 24. The psychological perspective that examines the effects of the social environment on the behavior of individuals.
  aggression and, 528–531
  attitudes and, 499–501
  attributions of behaviors and, 493–498
  cooperation and competition and, 524–528
  first impressions and, 491–492, 492f
  interpersonal relationships from perspective of, 532
  persuasion and, 501–503
  prejudice and, 505–511
  situational influences on behavior and, 516–519
  socialization and, 490, 491f
  social norms and, 511–516
  social relationships and, 520–523

Social rejection, 476, 477f

Social relationships, 520–523
  attraction and liking, 520–522, 520f
  building, 522, 522f
  ending, 522–523, 523f
  maintaining, 522

Social self, 481–484
  cultural influences on, 483–484
  interpersonal self, 481–483

Sociocultural influences
  on audition, 179, 179f
  on chemical senses, 188–189
  on somatosenses, 183
  on vision, 171

Somatic nervous system, 129. The part of the peripheral nervous system that brings sensory information to the central nervous system and transmits commands to the muscles, 129, 129f

Somatic symptom disorder, 570. A disorder characterized by physical symptoms that do not have an underlying medical cause.
  therapy for, 613–614

Somatosensation, 180. The body senses, including body position, touch, skin temperature, and pain, 180–183. *See also* Pain; Touch
  biology of, 180–183
  body position, 180–181
  pain, 182–183
  touch, 181–182
  sociocultural influences on, 183
  somatosensory stimuli and, 180

Somatovisceral Afference Model of Emotion (SAME), 270. A model of emotion in which a range of physical sensations from precise to general requires varying degrees of cognitive processing prior to subjective feelings, 270–271, 271f

Sound, localization of, 176–177, 178f

Sound features, 173f

Sound waves, 173, 173f, 174, 175f, 176, 179f

Source amnesia, 334

Specific phobia, 561. Fears of objects other than those associated with agoraphobia or social anxiety disorder, 561–562, 562f
  treatments for, 594f, 610, 610f

Sperling's demonstration of duration of memory, 322f

Spinal cord, 109. A long cylinder of neural tissue extending from the medulla of the brain down to the middle of the back; part of the central nervous system.
  spinal nerves, 112, 113f, 129
  spinal reflexes, 112, 115f

Spinning, 226

Split-brain operation, 124f, 125

Spontaneous recovery, 283. During extinction training, the reappearance of conditioned responses after periods of rest.

Spot light effect, 562

Spreading activation model, 335. A connectionist theory proposing that people organize general knowledge based on their individual experiences, 335–336, 335f

Squid, 137

Standard deviation, 60. A measure of how tightly clustered a group of scores is around their mean.

Stanford–Binet Intelligence Scales, 384

Statistical abnormality, 537, 538f

Statistical significance, 62. A standard for deciding whether an observed result is due to chance.

Stepping reflex, 409t

Stereotype, 505. A simplified set of traits associated with membership in a group or category, 509f

Stereotype threat, 507, 509f

Sternberg's triangular model of love, 522, 522f

Stimulant, 219. Any drug that increases the activity of the nervous system.

Storage, 319. The retention of information.

Stranger anxiety, 424

Stream of consciousness, 13

Stress, 620. An unpleasant emotional state that results from the perception of danger or threat, 620–638. *See also* Posttraumatic stress disorder (PTSD)

  biological correlates of, 624–627
    amygdala, 625–626, 625f
    epigenetics, 628
    gender differences, 627
    hippocampus, 627–628
    hypothalamic-pituitary-adrenal axis, 626–627, 626f
    socioeconomic status and, 628
    sympathetic adrenal-medullary system, 626–627, 626f
  coping with
    effectively, 635–638
    resilience and, 638–, 638f
    types of, 637–638
  depression and, 703
  described, 620
  general adaptation syndrome and, 621–622, 621f, 624
  health effects of, 629–634
  health and (*See under* Health)
  managing, 635–636, 636f
  pain and, 182–183
  PTSD and, 620–623, 623f
  response to, 620–622, 621f, 627
  schizophrenia and, 551f
  sources of, 622–624, 623f

Stressor, 620. A stimulus that serves as a source of stress.

Stroop Test, 224, 224f

Structuralism, 12. An approach in which the mind is broken into the smallest elements of mental experience.

Structuralists, 12
  Titchener, 12
  Wundt, 10–12

Stuttering, 35–36

Subcortical structures, 116–118, 117f
  amygdala, 117–118, 118f
  basal ganglia, 116
  cingulate cortex, 117
  hippocampus, 116–117
  hypothalamus, 116
  limbic system, 116
  nucleus accumbens, 118
  thalamus, 116

Sucking reflex, 409t

Sudden infant death syndrome (SIDS), 211. A sleep disorder in which an otherwise healthy infant dies while asleep.

Suicide, 558–559, 558f

Summation, 142

Superego, 450. The component of Sigmund Freud's personality theory that internalizes society's rules for right and wrong, or the conscience, 450–451, 451f

Supertasters, 186, 187

Survey, 44. A descriptive method in which participants are asked the same questions, 44–45, 46f, 50–51
  critical thinking used to evaluate, 40–41, 41f
  samples used in, 44
  self-report used in, 44
  on video game use and aggression, 45, 46–47f, 46, 49–50

Sympathetic adrenal-medullary (SAM) system, 626. A circuit that responds to perceived stressors by initiating the release of epinephrine and norepinephrine into the bloodstream, 626–627, 626f

Sympathetic nervous system, 130. The division of the autonomic nervous system that coordinates arousal, 130
  antagonistic effects on organs served by, 130, 131f
  function of, 130

Synapse, 140. A point of communication between two neurons.

Synaptic vesicles, 134, 135f, 140, 141f

Systematic desensitization, 289. A type of counterconditioning in which people relax while being exposed to stimuli that elicit fear.

Tardive dyskinesia, 605. A movement syndrome that results from the use of medications used to treat symptoms of schizophrenia.

Taste. *See* Gustation

Taste bud, 186. A structure found in papillae that contains taste receptor cells.

Taste receptors, 186, 187f

Temperament, 461. A child's pattern of mood, activity, or emotional responsiveness linked to later personality, 421–422, 422f, 461–462

Temporal lobe, 118. The lobe of the cerebral cortex that curves around the side of each hemisphere; location of primary auditory cortex.

Tend and befriend, 627. An alternative to fight or flight as a response to stressors; possibly more characteristic of females.

Teratogen, 406. A chemical agent that can harm the zygote, embryo, or fetus, 406–407, 406f, 407t

Testes, 132, 132f, 133

Testosterone, 244. A male hormone, 244–246
  aggression and, 529, 529f

Tests, memory improved by, 351

Tetanus (lockjaw), 141, 142f

Tetrahydrocannabinol (THC), 219

Thalamus, 116. A subcortical structure involved with the processing of sensory information, states of arousal, and learning and memory.
  auditory pathways and, 175
  consciousness and, 197–198, 197f
  olfactory pathways and, 184, 185f, 186
  pain pathways and, 182

Thalamus, *continued*
somatosensory pathways and, 181
unconsciousness associated with brain death and, 197
visual pathways and, 157–159, 158*f*, 160
Thale cress, 82, 82*f*
Theory, 39. A set of facts and relationships between facts that can explain and predict related phenomena. *See also individual headings*
Big Five, 456–457, 456*f*
Cannon–Bard, 266*f*, 267–268
cognitive development, Piaget's, 416–418, 416*t*
concept, 362
intelligence, 388
James–Lange, 266–267, 266*f*
opponent process, 160
psychodynamic, 450–453
Schachter–Singer two-factor, 266*f*, 269–270
scientific, 39
social-cognitive learning, 460–461
trichromatic, 159–160
utility, 369–370
Theory of mind (TOM), 420. The understanding that others have thoughts that are different from one's own, 420–421, 420*f*
Therapy
anxiety disorders and, 610–611
biological, 596–599
childhood disorders and, 600–603
dissociative identity disorders and, 613
integration of, 614
interpersonal relationships from the treatment perspective for, 615–616
personality disorders and, 614
psychologists providing, 580–589, 585*f*
psychotherapies, 590–595
schizophrenia and, 603–605, 604*f*
somatic symptom disorders and, 613–614
TheraScribe, 588
Theta wave, 203. A waveform recorded by electroencephalogram that is characteristic of lighter stages of non-rapid eye movement sleep, 203, 204*f*
Third variable, 46. A variable that is responsible for a correlation observed between two other variables of interest.
Thoughts, 358–364
as concepts, 359–364
as images, 358–359, 359*f*
Thyroid gland, 132, 132*f*, 133
Time, assessing effects of, 54–55
cross-sectional study, 54–55
longitudinal study, 55
mixed longitudinal study, 55
Tobacco use
health psychology and, 641–644, 642–643*f*

during pregnancy, 406, 408
Token economy, 305. An application of operant conditioning in which tokens that can be exchanged for other reinforcers are used to increase the frequency of desirable behaviors.
Tolerance, 217. The need to administer greater quantities of a drug to achieve the same subjective effect.
Tolman's Maze, 303, 303*f*
Tongue, 186–187
Tonic–clonic seizures, 216
Top-down processing, 151. A perceptual process in which memory and other cognitive processes are required for interpreting incoming sensory information.
Touch, 181–182. *See also* Somatosensation
infants and, 181
representation of, in primary sensory cortex, 181
sensory homunculus and, 181
touch pathways and, 181
touch receptors and, 181, 181*f*
Trait, 455. A stable personality characteristic.
Trait Hope Scale, 658–659
Trait theories of personality, 455–457, 455*f*
Big Five theory, 456–457, 456*f*
early, 456
Transactive memory, 354
Transcranial magnetic stimulation (TMS), 110*t*, 193
Transduction, 150. The translation of incoming sensory information into neural signals.
Transference, 591. A psychoanalytic technique in which the therapist uses the responses of the patient to the therapist to understand the patient's approach to authority figures in general.
Traumatic memories, erasing, 342
Trepanation drilled holes, 7, 9
Triangular model of love, Sternberg's, 522, 522*f*
Trichromatic theory, 159. A theory of color vision based on the existence of different types of cones for the detection of short, medium, and long wavelengths, 159–161
color deficiency and, 159, 160*f*
color vision and, 159–160, 159*f*, 161
cones in retina and, 159–160, 159*f*
vs. opponent process theory, 160
Trisomy 21. *See* Down syndrome
Trust
borderline personality disorder and, 574*f*
Turning the Tables illusion, 170, 171*f*
Tuskegee syphilis experiment, 65

Twins
DNA and, 71–72
homosexuality in, 247
IQ and, 390
Tympanic membrane, 174, 175*f*
Type A personality, 630. A competitive, workaholic, and in some cases hostile personality type.
Type B personality, 630. A mellow, "laid-back" personality type.
Type I diabetes, 236
Type II diabetes, 236

UCLA-R Loneliness Scale, 208
Ultrasound, 173, 174f
Ultraviolet waves, 149, 150f, 155, 169
Umami, 184
Unconditioned response (UCR), 282. A response to an unconditioned stimulus that requires no previous experience, 281*f*, 282
overcoming fear and, 288
Unconditioned stimulus (UCS), 282. A stimulus that elicits a response without any prior experience, 281*f*, 282
acquisition and, 282, 283*f*
addiction and, 289–290
element of surprise and, 286
extinction and, 283, 284*f*
higher order conditioning and, 285
overcoming fear and, 288
Rescorla–Wagner Model and, 286, 287*f*
taste aversion and, 286–287, 287*t*
Unconscious mind, 453. The part of mental activity that cannot be voluntarily retrieved.
Uninvolved parenting style, 426
Universal development *vs.* ecological development, 402–403
User-generated messages, 504*f*
Utility theory, 369–370

Vaccinations for autism spectrum disorder, 544, 545*f*
Validity, 57. A quality of a measure that leads to valid conclusions (i.e., the measure measures the concept it was designed to measure), 57
Valium (diazepam), 611
Variable, 45. A factor that has a range of values, 45–46
confounding variable, 49
in correlation, measuring, 45–46, 47*f*
dependent variable, 48
independent variable, 48
third variable, 46
Variable interval (VI) schedule, 299. A schedule of reinforcement in which the first response following a varying period of time is reinforced, 299–300
Variable ratio (VR) schedule, 98. A schedule of reinforcement in which reinforce-

ment occurs following some variable number of behaviors, 298–299
Varicella (chicken pox), 407*t*
Vasopressin, 133, 246, 246*f*
Vegan food pyramid, 235
Vegetative state (PVS), 213. An abnormal state following brain injury featuring wakefulness without consciousness.
characteristics of patients in, 213–214
comma and, 213
communicating with patients in, 214–215
fMRI and, 215*f*
Ventricles, 110, 112*f*
Ventromedial hypothalamus (VMH), 237, 238*f*, 239*f*
Vestibular system, 180. The system in the inner ear that provides information about body position and movement of the head, 180–181
Video game use and aggression
experiment on, 52, 52*f*, 52
questionnaire, 51
survey on, 45, 46–47*f*, 46, 49–50
Virtual reality for treating anxiety,612
Viruses, pregnant women exposed to, 408
Visible light, 155
Vision, 155. The sense that allows us to process reflected light, 155–171
astigmatism and, 169, 169*f*
biology of, 155–161, 156*f*
blind spots, 156, 156*f*
cornea, 155
fovea, 156
iris, 155
lens, 155
pupil, 155
retina, 155, 157*f*
rods and cones, 156, 157*f*
thalamus, 158, 158*f*, 160
color vision and, 159–160
depth and, recognizing, 164–168
differences in, developmental and individual, 168–169
farsightedness and, 169
infants and, 169
nearsightedness and, 169
objects and, recognizing, 162–168
older adults and, 169
perception and cognition, 159–161
sociocultural influences on, 171
visual pathways, 157–159
visual stimulus and, 155, 155*f*
Vision quests, 226
Visual codes, 321
Visual pathways, 157–159
optic nerve, 157
optic tracts, 158
primary visual cortex, 120*f*, 122

Waking, 199. A normal state of consciousness characterized by alertness and awareness of external stimuli, 203–204

beta, alpha and gamma waves, 203

circadian rhythms and, 199–202

daydreaming, or mind wandering and, 203

EEG during, 202–203, 203*f*

Epworth Sleepiness Scale and, 204

Waorani, 98

Wealth and happiness, 655–656, 655*f*

Web design, color vision and, 161, 161*f*

Wechsler Adult Intelligence Scale (WAIS), 384

Weight loss and obesity, 240–241

Wernicke's aphasia, 378

Wernicke's area, 378, 378*f*

White matter, 134

Williams syndrome, 381

Withdrawal, 217. Physical responses to the removal of some habitually administered drugs.

Women preferences for male features, 100

Working memory, 324. An extension of the concept of short-term memory that includes the active manipulation of multiple types of information simultaneously, 324–325, 324*f*

vs. long-term memory, 327–328, 328*f*

Xanax (alprazolam), 611

X chromosome, 75–77

X-rays, 150*f*, 155

Yanomamö, 98

Yawning, contagious, 277

Y chromosome, 75–77

Yerkes–Dodson law, 256. A description of the relationships among task complexity, arousal, and performance.

Young adulthood, 435–437

cognitive development in, 435–436

physical development in, 435

relationships in, 436–437

commitment to, 437

intimacy *vs.* isolation and, 436, 437*f*

marital satisfaction and, 437, 439*f*

Zeitgebers, 199–200

Zoe D. Katze, 223, 585–586

Zone of proximal development, Vygotsky's, 419*f*

Zygote, 403. The term used to describe a developing organism immediately following conception until the embryo stage, or the first 2 weeks following conception in humans, 403–404

20

Neuropsychology

Our eyes, working with our brains, allow most of us to see the world in three-dimensional depth and in full color, but some people have a condition that leaves them unaware of half of that world. Even though their eyes work properly, when these people look at a nice round pizza, they see only half a pizza. They are not suffering *from a mental illness of the kind we describe in the chapter on psychological disorders, but they most definitely have a problem in their brains. Understanding what the problem is, exactly where it is, and how it affects a person's behavior and mental processes takes us into the realm of* neuropsychology, *which is the focus of this chapter.*

Something was wrong with Max. He put away his car keys, his wallet, and a pair of dress shoes in their usual places, but when he tried looking for them later, he had no idea where they were. "You're just getting forgetful," his wife teased. But at breakfast one day, he used a piece of bacon to stir his coffee. Then, mistaking a candle on the table for a glass of juice, he tried to drink it, and he used a pancake as a napkin, wiping his mouth with it before placing it carefully on his lap. He seemed puzzled by these mistakes. His wife took him to a doctor. Suppose you were that doctor. How could you determine what was wrong with Max? You would have many possibilities to consider. Maybe he is choosing to do silly things just to annoy his wife. But if he is not acting oddly on purpose, just where does the problem lie? Perhaps something is amiss in his brain. The problem might reside somewhere in his memory systems, but it might also be in the realm of attention or some other psychological function. Of course, the problem might be something less specific. Perhaps he has just been working too hard or is having a reaction to a medication or some sort of dietary deficiency. He might be experiencing depression, or maybe an unrecognized infection is affecting his ability to remember and concentrate. In this chapter, we explore *neuropsychology,* a subfield in which specially trained psychologists study patients such as Max in an effort to pinpoint the nature and cause of a wide variety of puzzling behavioral and psychological problems. We will describe how this subfield developed, what it has revealed about the relationship between brain functions and psychological functions, and how neuropsychologists study patients on a case-by-case basis. We will also describe some of the most interesting examples of what can go wrong in the brain and how these problems can affect people's thoughts, actions, and abilities.

Foundations of Neuropyschology

Neuropsychology is the subfield of psychology whose goal is to explore and understand the relationships among brain processes, human behavior, and psychological functioning. *Neuropsychologists* are interested in how brain systems, and disruptions of those systems, affect a wide range of human abilities, including cognitive functioning (such as language, memory, attention, mathematical, and visual-spatial skills), motor functioning (such as walking or threading a needle), emotional functioning (such as the ability to express emotions and understand other people's emotional expressions), and social functioning (such as daily interactions with others). They are interested, too, in how dysfunctions in the brain relate to changes in personality and to the appearance of psychological disorders such as depression.

The field of neuropsychology rests on two main assumptions. The first is that many complicated mental tasks, such as memory or decision making, involve numerous subtasks that can be tested and studied separately (Lezak, Loring, & Howieson, 2004).

neuropsychology The subfield of psychology whose goal is to explore and understand the relationships among brain processes, human behavior, and psychological functioning.

805

For example, as described in earlier chapters, the ability to form a new memory usually requires a person to be awake, to pay attention, to receive sensations, to perceive those sensations, to form mental representations of that information, to be motivated to remember the information, and to have the language or other verbal skills necessary to express the information when it is retrieved from memory. If any of these subtasks fails, a person's memory would appear to fail in any number of everyday situations. With this assumption about subtasks in mind, neuropsychologists must not only figure out what complicated mental tasks a person can and cannot do but also identify the failure of one or more subtasks that may be at the root of the problem.

The second main assumption of neuropsychology is that different psychological processes are controlled by different brain regions or by different combinations of brain regions (Fodor, 1983; Heilman & Valenstein, 2003). Neuropsychologists use this assumption to draw conclusions about each patient they examine. After deciding what psychological processes are impaired, they work backward to infer what brain region or combinations of regions may not be working properly. This "working backward" approach is valuable, because many kinds of brain damage or disease are too subtle to be identified by physical examination or by various brain-scanning procedures (Nadeau & Crosson, 1995).

Using these two main assumptions, some neuropsychologists conduct research on how the human brain controls and organizes separate parts of complicated mental activities. These scientists, known as *experimental neuropsychologists,* most often study people with brain damage, but they sometimes do research on people with normal brains too. Their aim is to add to our knowledge of brain functioning among people in general. **Clinical neuropsychologists** use this knowledge to try to understand the problems that appear in particular individuals such as Max. They look for the best way to examine each person so as to determine the likelihood of brain damage or dysfunction, what psychological processes are impaired, exactly how they are impaired, and which are still operating properly (Heilman & Valenstein, 2003; Lezak, Loring, & Howieson, 2004; Scott, 2006). Most clinical neuropsychologists are to be found in hospitals and other health care settings, where they work with physicians to test people with brain damage.

For example, Max's physician decided to have him tested by a clinical neuropsychologist, who showed Max a long series of simple drawings of common objects and asked him to name each one. Experimental neuropsychological research on large numbers of people provided *norms* that told her what kind of performance she could expect on this test from people of Max's age and educational background. She could then compare his performance to these norms. As you might expect, Max's responses were not normal. For example, looking at the drawing of a pencil, he said he saw "a long, narrow protrusion of some kind." He called a paper clip "an object curling into itself." For eyeglasses, he said, "That's two circular devices suspended together." Clearly he was not naming things well—but why? Could his vision be bad? No, because he could correctly read words even when they were in small print. He could also produce reasonably accurate copies of the drawings, even though he could not always name the objects in them. This meant that he had sensed and perceived the drawings' shapes, angles, and spatial relationships. Did Max have a general problem with memory, as his wife had suggested? To test that idea, the neuropsychologist read him lists of words and later asked him to recall them. He did about as well on this memory test as most people of his age and level of education, so his memory seemed normal. The neuropsychologist next considered whether Max was no longer able to understand the concepts represented in the drawings. But this possibility was ruled out when he correctly defined the words *pencil, paper clip,* and *eyeglasses.* So he knew what these objects were, and when examples of them were placed into his hands while he was blindfolded, he could name them instantly. So Max could recognize these objects through his sense of touch but not through his sense of vision.

Why? The neuropsychologist concluded that Max still had normal function in brain areas that process basic visual sensations but that something was wrong in the brain regions that normally convert those sensations into recognizable visual

clinical neuropsychologists
Neuropsychologists who use tests and other methods to try to understand neuropsychological problems and intact functions in individual patients.

perceptions. Research on the brain told the neuropsychologist that this problem, called a *visual agnosia* (pronounced "ag-NOH-zhuh"), can occur when parts of the temporal lobes on both sides of the brain are not working properly (Bauer & Demery, 2003; Spalletta et al., 2007). Max's physician used that information to focus his medical care on those brain regions.

Max's case illustrates several important aspects of what neuropsychologists have learned about how the brain operates. Let's review some of what they have discovered and how these discoveries occurred.

A Brief History of Neuropsychology

Max's case shows **localization of function**, the idea that specific psychological functions can be affected by damage to specific brain areas. This concept probably seems obvious to you, especially if you have read about the brain in the chapters on biological aspects of psychology, sensation, and consciousness. But this "commonsense" notion was once a matter of considerable debate (Tyler & Malessa, 2000). In fact, for centuries, philosophers and scientists had been speculating about the role of different brain areas in different psychological functions (Eling, 2008; Kaitaro, 2001).

Early in the 1800s, for example, the dominant view was that the brain worked more or less as a single organ, such that no particular part was any more important than any other part in the control of mental life. An anatomist named Franz Gall disagreed with this view, arguing instead that particular brain areas controlled particular aspects of cognitive functioning (Zola-Morgan, 1995). Gall's claim turned out to be correct, and his legacy would be more widely honored except for the fact that Gall also mistakenly believed that brain areas, like muscles, get bigger as people use them. He believed, too, that each brain area is associated with certain behavior patterns or personality traits, such as honesty or love or aggressiveness. Finally, Gall assumed that as brain areas grew larger, there would be corresponding bumps in the skull just above them. After creating a map showing which brain areas were supposedly controlling which traits, he thought he could assess a person's psychological makeup by measuring the bumps on the skull. Gall's approach, which was known as *phrenology,* was a hit with the public because it appeared to offer a simple way measure personality (Benjamin & Baker, 2004). But assessing personality by feeling people's skulls was a far-fetched and easily refuted notion that led Gall's scientific colleagues to dismiss virtually everything he said about the brain's role in psychology. In fact, the ridicule heaped on phrenology tended to taint all theories about localization of function.

In 1861, though, everything changed. It was then that a famous and widely respected French surgeon, Paul Broca, examined a hospitalized patient whose leg had a serious deep-tissue infection called gangrene. (In this era before antibiotics, gangrene often required amputation.) It so happened that many years earlier, this patient had had a **stroke**—the official medical term is **cerebrovascular accident**, or CVA—a condition in which one of the blood vessels to the brain is blocked, causing permanent damage to the brain. The stroke left him unable to say anything but the word *tan,* which became the staff's nickname for him. Despite his speech difficulties, Tan could apparently understand spoken language because he easily followed verbal commands. Before anything could be done about Tan's gangrene, he died, and Broca ordered an autopsy. It showed a small **lesion**, or area of damage, in the left frontal lobe of Tan's brain (see Figure 20.1). Broca wondered if this lesion was related to Tan's speech problems, and if so, how such a small lesion could cause such a major and specific problem. Not long afterward, Broca requested an autopsy on another patient who had had language problems similar to Tan's and discovered a brain lesion in the same place as Tan's.

If lesions in this particular spot were somehow linked to these patients' speech disorders, the previously dismissed idea of localization of function might actually be correct. Indeed, a particular brain area could be involved in controlling a particular function such as speech (Broca, 1861, 1865). This is precisely what Broca proposed

localization of function The idea that specific psychological functions can be affected by damage to specific brain areas.

cerebrovascular accident (stroke) A loss of blood supply to some part of the brain, resulting in disruption of some aspect of behavior or mental processes.

lesion An area of damaged tissue in the brain.

FIGURE 20.1
Tan's Brain

When Tan died, Paul Broca discovered severe damage in the left frontal lobe of the cerebral cortex, just in front of the primary motor cortex. This site, now known as *Broca's area*, is involved in the ability to produce normal speech.

From Corsi, P., ed. The Enchanted Loom. New York: Oxford University Press, 1991. Musée Dupuytren, Paris. Photo courtesy of Dr. Jean-Louis Signoret

when he shared his observations in a lecture to the Anthropological Society of Paris. And because, unlike Gall, Broca held such high status in the scientific community, his support of localization of function made it a respectable idea. In fact, it created an upsurge of scholarly interest in localization of brain function that is still seen today. The resulting explosion of brain research that occurred in the past century and a half has not only confirmed localization but established that localization is more complex than anyone in Broca's time would ever have guessed.

Modules and Networks

More recent approaches to localization of function have introduced the idea that the brain is organized into discrete regions called **modules**, each of which adds its own unique kind of analysis of the information it receives (Fodor, 1983; Uttal, 2003). According to this *modularity* view, each module, located in a unique brain area, acts somewhat like a circuit board in a computer. That is, a module does not itself "control" any particular function, but it adds a needed piece to complete a larger puzzle that allows speech or some other function to occur. The analysis performed by a particular module can be used in many kinds of brain functions. And each brain function—whether it is detecting the edges of an object or making a decision about something—is accomplished through the support of a different team, or *network,* of modules (Mesulam, 1990). It is as if the brain were the head of a company with a vast array of employees, each with a specific skill, which can be organized and reorganized from one moment to the next into many different work teams to perform many different tasks.

Speaking and understanding language, for example, involves a network of modules in several brain areas (Ross, 2010). This means that damage to any part of the network will affect a person's language ability in some way, but the exact effect will depend on which part of the network is damaged. In Tan's case, for example, the lesion in his left frontal lobe disrupted his ability to speak but left him with the ability to understand what was said to him.

The brain regions underlying language are a particularly good example of a network that uses several modules. One of the interesting consequences of a system that is organized in this way is the potential for a *disconnection syndrome.* Such syndromes occur when various modules in a network, though themselves intact, are prevented from interacting (Geschwind, 1968). A classic example is *alexia without agraphia,* which literally means inability to read while still being able to write (Imtiaz, Nirodi, & Khaleeli, 2001; Sheldon, Malcolm, & Barton, 2008). The brain damage shown in Figure 20.2 could produce this kind of disconnection syndrome. Here, there is damage to the left occipital lobe, causing loss of vision, but only for what is on the right side of the visual field. The patient can still see the left side of the visual field. However, there is also damage to part of the corpus callosum, which connects the left and right hemispheres of the brain. This particular part of the corpus callosum normally allows

modules Regions of the brain that perform their own unique kind of analysis of the information they receive.

Left   Right

FIGURE 20.2
Alexia Without Agraphia
This is a classic example of a disconnection syndrome. Brain damage (in darker blue) has occurred in the left occipital lobe and part of the corpus callosum. As a result, no visual information can enter the left hemisphere. The left hemisphere brain regions that create writing are intact, so these patients can write. But because feedback from the visual system cannot get back to the language processing systems of the left hemisphere, the patients cannot read what they have written.

visual information from the left side of the world to cross from the right hemisphere into the left hemisphere, but now this pathway is blocked. Because the language-producing regions of the left hemisphere are intact, the person can still talk and write normally but can see only what lies in the left visual field. That information goes to the right hemisphere, but because it cannot cross from there into the left hemisphere, where most language functions reside, people with this kind of disconnection syndrome cannot read what they write. In effect, the visual processing of the words is disconnected from the brain regions that are needed to understand the meaning of the words.

Lesion Analysis

Much as Broca did so long ago, experimental neuropsychologists today still study localization of function by looking at the results of brain damage. This aspect of their work is sometimes called *lesion analysis* (Aharonov et al., 2003). To get an idea of how lesion analysis works, suppose that a man with normal mathematical ability has a stroke that damages his left parietal lobe (see Figure 3.15 in the chapter on biological aspects of psychology for the location of this area). Afterward, like other people with similar brain damage, he can no longer perform mathematical calculations. Do these observations confirm that the ability to do math is localized in the left parietal lobe in human brains? Possibly, but not necessarily. Critical thinking by experimental neuropsychologists leads them to consider other possibilities too.

For example, we have already seen that complex psychological functions often require the cooperation of many modules in different brain areas. So although mathematical ability may well be impaired by damage to the left parietal lobe, it may also be affected by damage to other regions in the "mathematics" network. Experimental neuropsychologists explore this possibility by studying the changes in math ability seen in large numbers of people with damage to many different regions of the brain. If they find that math ability is affected by left parietal lobe damage but nowhere else, they would be more confident in asserting that mathematical ability is localized in that area. If they find that damage in other areas also affects math ability, they would realize that this ability is not as localized as it might at first seem.

But lesion analysis must also address the question of just what function it is that has been damaged. For example, doing a mathematical calculation might require you to use several kinds of abilities, such as recognizing numbers and symbols, remembering the rules of addition or multiplication, keeping several numbers in your head as you do calculations, and being able to read or hear the math problem and report your answer. So if a brain lesion makes it hard for you to talk, you would not be able to answer the question "How much is 2 plus 2?" But this may not mean that there is anything wrong with your mathematical ability.

To help figure out exactly what problems a brain-damaged patient actually has, experimental neuropsychologists look at a complex mental task, such as reading or doing math, and—in light of research from sensation, perception, and cognitive psychology—try to identify all the abilities that a person's brain must combine to succeed at that task. They then try to determine which of these abilities are actually separate, or *dissociated,* perhaps because they are based in different brain modules in particular brain regions. One way to establish a dissociation between abilities is to study which components of a mental task are affected by which kinds of brain damage. An important example of dissociated abilities is described in the chapter on biological aspects of psychology. Damage to a particular area in the left frontal lobe disrupts a person's ability to speak fluently but leaves the person able to understand most of what others say. Damage to a different area in the left temporal lobe does the opposite, leaving the person able to speak easily but unable to understand what others are saying. We will discuss these conditions again later in this chapter. ("In Review: Foundations of Neuropsychology" summarizes milestones in the history of neuropsychology.)

IN REVIEW   Foundations of Neuropsychology

Principle	Main Figure or Era	Key Ideas
Localization of function	Franz Gall, early 1800s Paul Broca, mid-1800s	The idea that a specific psychological function could depend on a specific brain area
Modularity	Late 1900s	A revision of localization in which each brain area performs different, unique computations, which contribute to various psychological functions
Networks	Late 1900s	A perspective suggesting that different complex psychological functions rely on unique combinations of brain modules
Lesion analysis	1800s to the present	An approach to experimental neuropsychology in which psychological functions are linked to particular brain areas by studying patients with damage to those areas and comparing these people with people who have damage elsewhere or no damage

1. A person who studies individual patients to determine what kind of brain damage each one happens to have is called a _____.
2. The case of "Tan" helped establish the principle of _____.
3. In alexia without agraphia, the brain areas that control reading and writing are intact but cannot interact. This condition is called a _____.

Neuropsychological Assessment

So far we have discussed how the brain is organized and how neuropsychologists go about studying ways in which its functioning is related to behavior and behavior problems. Let's now consider how they decide when a person has such problems. Consider memory, for example. Everyone forgets things sometimes, even such familiar things as your best friend's phone number, the name of your roommate's brother, or where you left your car keys. But how much forgetfulness is normal and how much does it take to be labeled as excessive or problematic?

LINKAGES   What psychological tests are used in diagnosing neuropsychological disorders? (a link to Cognitive Abilities, p. 376)

To answer this question, neuropsychologists typically conduct a **neuropsychological assessment** by giving patients a large number of tests designed to measure a wide range of mental functions, such as general intelligence, memory, reading, motor coordination, naming pictures, and finding targets in a visual display. Some neuropsychologists prefer to use an individualized set of assessments uniquely tailored to each patient. In this way, they hope to measure the specific problems that a particular patient is most likely to have. In other cases, patients are given a standardized test battery, which includes a predetermined set of tests that are designed to complement one another and comprehensively address all aspects of psychological functioning. Many such test batteries have been carefully prepared and validated. Among the best-known examples are the Halstead-Reitan Battery, the Wechsler Adult Intelligence Scale, and the Luria-Nebraska Neuropsychology Battery. Standardized batteries offer the advantage of giving each patient the same tests in the same way, but they don't allow the neuropsychologist to tailor testing to focus on a patient's particular problems or unique situation. Accordingly, most clinical neuropsychologists start with a standard test battery and then administer additional tests that are particularly relevant to each case.

By giving a variety of tests, the clinical neuropsychologist can get a glimpse into many different aspects of a person's psychological functioning and also measure each area separately. Analyzing the overall pattern of results may help pinpoint where the difficulties in the brain may lie. But the results of neuropsychological testing, like the results of personality testing, intelligence testing, and academic testing, must be interpreted with caution. Many factors, such as age, education, and cultural background, can affect a person's performance on neuropsychological tests. With this in mind, each patient's performance on these tests must be compared with established averages, or norms. These norms are based on the test performance of thousands of people who are of the patient's own age, educational level, and cultural background but who have no known brain damage. Norms also give clinical neuropsychologists an idea of how often normal people's scores vary from the average and by how much. Having this information helps establish whether a score that looks deviant at first glance is actually

neuropsychological assessment Testing a patient's intelligence, memory, reading, motor coordination, and other cognitive and sensory functions in an effort to locate problems in the brain responsible for neuropsychological symptoms.

as unusual as it seems. Norms can also reveal when what seems like a minor deviation from the average is actually quite unusual and indicative of a potential problem.

Training for Neuropsychology

A large part of a clinical neuropsychologist's training is focused on learning about many different kinds of neuropsychological tests, how to administer and score them, and how to combine and interpret their results so as to reach the most accurate conclusions about patients' problems and the likely source of those problems (Boake, Yeates, & Donders, 2002). Neuropsychologists typically train in graduate school, earning a Ph.D. degree in clinical psychology with a special focus on neuropsychology and the many topics related to it. Before they can get a license to practice on their own, however, they must complete an internship. The internship usually includes a year or more of neuropsychological practice performed under the close supervision and mentoring of a licensed clinical neuropsychologist, typically in a university hospital setting. Once licensed, clinical neuropsychologists tend to be hired by health facilities where there is a need for testing patients for possible brain damage. Many neuropsychologists are employed directly by a hospital; others join specialty clinics where they work closely with physicians who focus on the diagnosis and treatment of brain disorders. Some may work in highly specialized facilities that offer programs focusing only on patients who have had a cerebrovascular accident or brain trauma. Experimental neuropsychologists are usually employed by universities, where they teach students, conduct their own research, and participate in testing patients as time permits.

Mechanisms of Brain Dysfunction

We have been talking a lot about brain damage, and perhaps you are wondering how brains get hurt.

Cerebrovascular Accidents

As you may have guessed by now, cerebrovascular accidents (strokes) are a common source of brain damage. The brain receives all the oxygen, sugar (glucose), and other nutrients it needs from the rich supply of blood flowing through it (see Figure 20.3). But brain cells cannot store much of this energy, so they must have a supply of fresh blood at all times (Acker & Acker, 2004). If a vessel bringing blood into some part of the brain becomes blocked, the brain tissue in that part of the brain will die, and whatever function that part of the brain usually did will be disrupted or destroyed (Caplan, 2004, 2005). When someone's behavior or mental processes are affected by brain damage from a loss of blood supply, the person is said to have had a cerebrovascular accident. Even very tiny CVAs can cause disabling symptoms if they take place in vital brain areas, but strokes in less vital areas may cause few, if any, symptoms.

Strokes can be quite dangerous. In fact, they are the third-leading cause of death in the United States (Heron et al., 2009). They tend to occur as people get older, but young adults and even children can have them. Unlike heart attacks, in which blood flow to the heart muscle is disrupted, a stroke usually involves little or no pain because there are no pain receptors in brain tissue. So a stroke victim may not immediately realize that anything is wrong. The resulting delay in seeking medical attention can be costly, because treatments that can help reduce the effects of a stroke must be administered as soon as possible after the stroke occurs (Hjelmblink, Holström, & Kjeldmand, 2010).

Like explosions that break windows a block away, strokes affect not only the area in which brain tissue has died but also the surrounding area. Fortunately, if cells in the area around a stroke have not actually died, they may start working again (Liebeskind, 2010). As a result, some people recover all or part of their lost functions. The amount of recovery depends on many factors, including the quality and speed of medical

FIGURE 20.3
The Brain's Blood Supply

TRY THIS Blood reaches the brain either through the carotid arteries on either side of the neck or through vertebral arteries entering through the base of the skull. Once in the brain, these arteries branch into the anterior cerebral artery, the middle cerebral artery, and the posterior cerebral artery. Each artery provides blood to specific brain areas. Consequently, a blockage in a particular blood vessel damages a specific, predictable part of the brain. Review the chapter on biological aspects of psychology to remind yourself of the functions associated with each area of the cerebral cortex. Then make a list of the functions that would most likely be affected by blockage in each of the arteries shown in this figure.

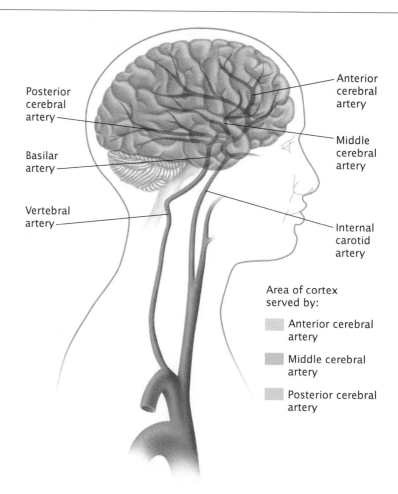

Posterior cerebral artery

Basilar artery

Vertebral artery

Anterior cerebral artery

Middle cerebral artery

Internal carotid artery

Area of cortex served by:

Anterior cerebral artery

Middle cerebral artery

Posterior cerebral artery

treatment, how large the stroke is and where it is located, the health of the remaining blood vessels and brain tissue, the quantity of salvageable tissue, the degree to which the remaining nervous system can reorganize along its original lines, and the kinds of rehabilitation programs undertaken after the stroke (Cramer, 2008; Frizzell, 2005; Heiss & Teasel, 2006; Kelley & Borazanci, 2009). To help the brain heal itself, some scientists are experimenting with chemicals that stimulate existing cells to grow; others are inserting stem cells into the brain to replace damaged tissue. As described in the chapter on biological aspects of psychology, though, restoring functions lost to a stroke takes more than just restoring the cell population in damaged brain areas. The new cells must also somehow be influenced to reestablish the right connections with other brain cells (Kalluri & Dempsey, 2008; Liu et al., 2009).

Traumatic Brain Injury

Another major cause of brain damage is **traumatic brain injury**, also known simply as **trauma** (Okonkwo, 2003). Trauma creates an impact on the brain, as when a person's head is struck by a baseball bat or a bullet or when during an accident the head moves suddenly or is thrown violently against some object. Traumatic events such as these can cause damage because the brain is not firmly attached to the skull. Instead, it floats within it, suspended in a bath of **cerebrospinal fluid**. So when the head is struck or violently accelerates or decelerates, the soft globe of brain bounces back and forth inside the skull, bumping up against bone and causing nerve fibers in many areas to stretch and tear.

The amount of brain damage resulting from trauma depends greatly on the amount of force involved in such situations. Further, unlike in strokes, where only the area in and around a disrupted blood supply is likely to be affected, the damage and disruption caused by trauma may be widespread. So whereas stroke patients may show very specific kinds of

traumatic brain injury (trauma) An impact on the brain caused by a blow or a sudden, violent movement of the head.

cerebrospinal fluid A clear liquid that surrounds and buffers the brain against vibration.

neuropsychological deficits, sometimes with striking dissociations between functions that are lost and those that are preserved, people with head injuries may display deficits that are far more diffuse, harder to specify, and involve many aspects of functioning (Wade, 2004), including cognitive and psychiatric problems (Malojcic et al., 2008; Schwarzbold et al., 2008). This may explain why we know much more about the neuropsychological symptom patterns that follow strokes than we do about those following brain traumas.

Neurodegenerative Diseases

Unlike the sudden symptoms that result from brain damage caused by stroke and trauma, other brain problems develop gradually. These more slowly developing symptoms often appear because **neurodegenerative diseases** are causing *neurodegeneration,* the gradual process of damage to brain cells (Mayeux, 2003). Three of the most prominent examples of neurodegenerative diseases are Alzheimer's disease, Parkinson's disease, and Huntington's disease. Each type of neurodegenerative disease affects a particular kind of brain cell or cells in a particular part of the brain, causing them to be the first to stop working properly (Cummings, 2003) and leaving the victim without the mental or physical functions those cells had once supported. The pattern of symptoms resulting from each neurodegenerative disease is different enough that neuropsychological assessment of a patient can lead to a diagnosis of which disease is affecting that patient (Brun, 2007; Miller, 2007).

Some kinds of neurodegeneration appear to be caused by infections, nutritional deficiencies, or genetic abnormalities, but despite intense research, we are still not sure about the specific causes of most such diseases. ("In Review: Mechanisms of Brain Dysfunction" summarizes the major causes of brain injury and dysfunction.)

IN REVIEW Mechanisms of Brain Dysfunction			
Brain Problem	**Onset**	**Underlying Process**	**Symptoms**
Cerebrovascular accidents (stroke)	Sudden	Blood flow is blocked in some part of the brain.	Specific to the area of the brain that is destroyed
Traumatic brain injury (trauma)	Sudden	Brain moves back and forth inside the skull.	Often nonspecific, diffuse
Neurodegenerative disease (neurodegeneration)	Gradual	A subset of neuron cell types becomes diseased and stops working properly.	Specific to the types of brain cells affected

1. The brain floats in a bath of _____ inside the skull.
2. The brain needs a constant flow of fresh _____ at all times.
3. Cerebrovascular accidents rank as the number _____ cause of death in the United States.

neurodegenerative diseases Conditions in the brain that result in a gradual loss of nerve cells and of the cognitive or other functions in which those cells are normally involved.

syndrome A pattern of symptoms associated with a specific disorder.

amnestic disorders Neuropsychological disorders that involve memory loss.

Neuropsychological Disorders

Let's now take a closer look at the **syndromes**, or patterns of symptoms, that clinical neuropsychologists typically see in patients who have suffered stroke, trauma, or neurodegenerative disease. These syndromes are referred to as *neuropsychological disorders* and include amnestic disorders, consciousness disturbances, perceptual disturbances, disorders of language and communication, disorders of movement, and disorders involving dementia.

LINKAGES What disorders are caused by damage to brain areas involved in memory? (a link to Memory, p. 272)

Amnestic Disorders

Amnestic disorders involve memory loss (often referred to as *amnesia*). Specific concerns about memory problems often bring people to clinical neuropsychologists for evaluation. These people are concerned partly because they rely heavily on memory, and any threat to its integrity can be extremely upsetting. But patients also tend to highlight memory problems because we all have a tendency to interpret almost any psychological deficit as being related to memory (Lezak, Loring, & Howieson, 2004). As in Max's case, for example, people who begin having trouble naming objects may say they are "forgetting" words, even though the problem could actually be one of language or visual recognition. Many older individuals, too, seek neuropsychological assessment because of worry that even minor forgetfulness might be an early sign of Alzheimer's disease. We discuss Alzheimer's in the section on dementia, but memory loss can occur in other neuropsychological syndromes too (Lucas, 2005).

For example, the ability to create new long-term memories can be impaired by damage in the brain's medial temporal lobes ("medial" means toward the middle of the brain), especially in the hippocampus (Ando et al., 2008; de Haan et al., 2006; Rosenbaum et al., 2008). Consider the famous case of H.M. (Scoville & Milner, 1957; Squire, 2009). In 1953, this 27-year-old man's epilepsy was so severe that he underwent brain surgery in an effort to stop his seizures. The surgery removed parts of both his left and right temporal lobes, including parts of the hippocampus on both sides. This radical treatment ended his seizures, but it left H.M. with a dense amnestic syndrome that persisted until his death at the age of 82 in 2008 (Mackay, 2006; Squire, 2009; see Figure 20.4). Although he was able to recall most details of his life from before the

FIGURE 20.4

H.M.'s Brain Surgery

H.M. underwent surgery that removed the hippocampus, amygdala, and part of the association cortex from both temporal lobes. As shown in these MRI scans comparing an intact brain with H.M.'s brain after surgery, H.M. had some hippocampus (H) but no entorhinal cortex (EC). In this image, (V) refers to the lateral ventricle, (f) refers to the fornix, (PH) refers to the parahippocampal cortex, and (Cer) refers to the cerebellum.

Coronal sections of typical person's brain

Coronal sections of H. M.'s brain

Courtesy Dr. Suzanne Corkin, Massachusetts Institute of Technology. Copyright © 1997 Society for Neuroscience. J. Neurosci., May 15, 1997, 17(10):3964-3979

FIGURE 20.5

Memory Without Awareness

People with amnesia due to medial temporal lobe damage may still learn from the experiences that they otherwise cannot recall. These stimuli show degraded versions of a drawing. Using stimuli similar to these, participants with amnesia first saw a very degraded version, then one less so, then another clearer one, and so on until they could name the item. Patients with amnesia were able to name items earlier if they had seen them before, even when they could not recall having seen them.

anterograde amnesia A loss of memory for events that occur after a brain injury.

Korsakoff's psychosis (Korsakoff's syndrome) An amnestic condition in people whose thiamine (vitamin B1) level is depleted by inadequate nutrition or alcoholism.

confabulation A characteristic of some neuropsychological disorders in which patients report false memories.

surgery, he had difficulty forming new memories. In other words, as discussed in the memory chapter, he had **anterograde amnesia**. When he met someone new, he was unable to recall the meeting, so the person seemed to be a stranger no matter how many times they met again. Similarly, new words he heard over the years—such as *computer, videotape, cell phone,* and *Jacuzzi*—never made it into his vocabulary. He wasn't even able to remember that time was passing, so he had few clues that he was getting older; to a great extent, he was mentally stuck in the 1950s.

Many of H.M.'s other mental capacities remained largely intact, however, providing a striking example of the dissociation that can occur between abilities lost and those retained after brain damage. His language function remained good; he recognized objects; he thought and reasoned; he remained intelligent, pleasant, and sociable; and he carried on very normal-sounding conversations. But even he was quite aware of his memory problem. He put it as follows: "Right now, I'm wondering, have I done or said something amiss? You see, at this moment everything looks clear to me, but what happened just before? That's what worries me. It's like waking from a dream. I just don't remember" (Milner, 1970, p. 37).

H.M. was carefully studied for years, and the lessons learned from him have prompted research on memory loss in other people after medial temporal lobe damage. When other people have amnesia caused by damage to the hippocampus, just like H.M., they also have difficulty remembering the new experiences or events of their lives. But also like H.M., it turns out that these individuals can still learn new skills and habits as a result of their new experiences. When they do a task over and over, they get better at it, meaning that they do form some kind of a memory. Nonetheless, they have no awareness of this learning and do not recall the experiences that led to it (see Figure 20.5).

Anterograde amnesia and other amnestic syndromes can be caused by events other than surgery in the hippocampus and medial temporal lobe. For example, certain brain infections, such as herpes encephalitis (Ando et al., 2008; Baringer, 2008), tend to damage these same parts of the brain and create an amnestic syndrome similar to that of H.M. Cerebrovascular accidents, too, can sometimes damage these regions, though they are usually on just one side of the brain, so the amnestic syndrome may not be as noticeable. Finally, as described later, these regions, and the memory functions they normally perform, can also be impaired by Alzheimer's disease (Wolk et al., 2010).

The hippocampus is not the only structure involved in memory. For example, as described in the chapter on biological aspects of psychology, the thalamus processes information from all the senses except smell and sends it on to the cerebral cortex for further processing. But the medial dorsal (middle and top) region of the thalamus is also part of the brain's *limbic system*, an interconnected set of structures that includes the hippocampus (see Figure 20.6). The medial dorsal thalamus is seldom damaged by trauma or stroke, but it is often damaged when people have **Korsakoff's psychosis**, also known as **Korsakoff's syndrome** (Butters, 1981), a condition in people whose thiamine (vitamin B1) is depleted by inadequate nutrition or alcoholism. Running low on thiamine is dangerous because this vitamin is needed to process glucose (sugar) for energy. Nerve cells of the medial dorsal thalamus are especially dependent on this function of thiamine (Marti, Singleton, & Hiller-Sturmhofel, 2003), so if thiamine deficiency is severe, nerve cells there are more likely to die than in other brain regions (Kumar, 2010; Vemuganti et al., 2006). The result is anterograde amnesia with an additional unusual feature: **confabulation**, or the creation of false memories, both spontaneously and in response to questions (Borsutzky et al., 2008; Butters, 1981). These individuals believe that they have had experiences that they have not actually had, and they "recall" them as if they were real. Research with other confabulating patients suggests that this condition may also occur following damage to the inferior medial prefrontal system (Turner et al., 2008). Other amnestic syndromes do not usually produce confabulation, so when clinical neuropsychologists test patients with severe anterograde amnesia and find confabulation too, they often suspect medial dorsal thalamic amnesia or inferior medial prefrontal amnesia.

FIGURE 20.6
The Limbic System
A number of closely connected structures form the limbic system, which controls many aspects of motivation and emotion.

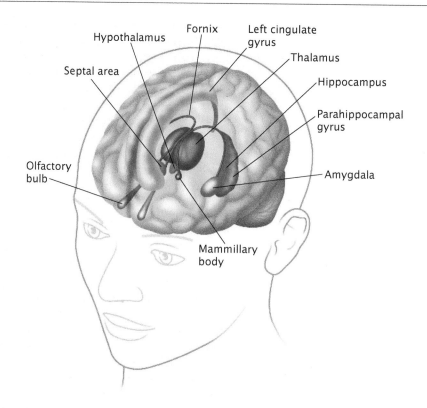

Consciousness Disturbances

Sometimes problems in the brain can create **consciousness disturbances**, which impair people's ability to be fully aware of the world around them (Bernat, 2009). One such problem occurs when there is disruption or damage to the **reticular formation**, also known as the *reticular activating system,* or *RAS.* The RAS is a long, tubelike structure that begins in the base of the brain and extends upward, eventually splitting into two halves that reach into both sides of the thalamus. As its name implies, the RAS normally serves to increase and decrease arousal in the rest of the brain and is partly responsible for our daily cycles of wakefulness and sleep (Izac & Eeg, 2006). If the RAS is severely damaged, the result can be an unconscious state known as a *coma.* People with lesser amounts of RAS damage may enter a *persistent vegetative state (PVS)* (Bekinschtein et al., 2005). Unlike patients in comas, people in a PVS may open their eyes and appear to wake up during the day and close their eyes and appear to sleep at night. They may also show a wider array of automatic movements than coma patients. For example, when food is put the mouth of someone in a PVS, chewing movements may occur, and sounds and touches may sometimes trigger facial expressions. But though EEG and fMRI scans show activity in some areas of these individuals' brains—including activity in speech-processing areas in response to familiar voices (Brenner, 2005; Eickhoff et al., 2008; Laureys, 2004; Magee, 2007; Schiff et al., 2005)—most patients remain unaware of their environment. The chances for recovery are often poor following significant damage to the RAS.

Even if the RAS is working properly to stimulate the rest of the brain, consciousness can be impaired if there are widespread disruptions in the functioning of both sides of the cerebral cortex, where other aspects of awareness are controlled (Stevens & Bhardwaj, 2006). Impairment of both sides of the cortex is most commonly caused by drugs such as alcohol or sleeping pills, but other causes include fever, seizures, chemical imbalances in the blood, hormonal disorders, and infections that have spread to the blood (Plum & Posner, 2000).

Other disturbances of consciousness have more complex and changing effects. People with **delirium**, for example, experience alternating periods of abnormally

consciousness disturbances Neuropsychological disorders in which there are impairments in the ability to be aware of the world.

reticular formation A collection of cells and fibers in the hindbrain and midbrain that are involved in arousal and attention.

delirium Periods of abnormally impaired or abnormally elevated levels of consciousness.

impaired consciousness and abnormally elevated levels of consciousness (Kahn et al., 2009; Torpy, 2008). The impairments in consciousness appear in many mental functions, usually including poor attention, poor memory, and disorientation. Elevated consciousness may appear as hallucinations (hearing sounds or seeing things that are not really there) or as episodes of mental agitation for no apparent reason. Indeed, a key feature of delirium is the rising and falling of consciousness (Plum & Posner, 2000). These patients may appear sleepy and "out of it" one minute and then far too attentive the next, as shown by reactions to every little sight and sound. Common causes of delirium include fever, poisons, infections that have reached the bloodstream, and the side effects of medication. Delirium can sometimes signal a medical emergency, but most of the time its psychological effects are not permanent. Delirium usually disappears when the underlying medical cause is corrected (Skrobik, 2009).

Neuropsychological testing of people in delirium is difficult (Milisen et al., 2006). Their attention and awareness can vary, sometimes dramatically, over the course of testing. In general, performance on almost any test is very poor, probably because patients with delirium cannot pay attention long enough or well enough to cooperate with the testing process. Indeed, their typical pattern of performance on neuropsychological tests is that there is no pattern—everything may look impaired.

Still other consciousness disturbances involve problems not in people's level of consciousness but in the nature or content of their consciousness. For example, a person may have a stroke that causes total paralysis of one side of the body, but the person may have no awareness that there is anything wrong. This condition is called *anosognosia* (pronounced "an-oh-sug-NOH-zhuh"), which means an absence of knowledge of disease (Langer, 2009). In such cases, it appears that brain damage causes not only an impairment in functioning but also an impairment in the ability to know about that impairment. This makes sense because the brain is the organ that we use to figure out when something is wrong. So if you have pain in your arm, sensory neurons tell the brain about it. But if the brain itself is hurt, it has nowhere to send its message.

People can have anosognosia with respect to a variety of problems, from paralysis to blindness to amputation of a limb (McGlynn & Schacter, 1989). It is also often seen in association with Alzheimer's disease (Pia & Conway, 2008). Anosognosia is more likely after damage to the right side of the brain (Nathanson, Bergman, & Gordon, 1952; Spalletta et al., 2007). Anosognosia is relatively common, occurring, for example, in more than 25 percent of all cerebrovascular accident cases (Starkstein et al., 1992). An unfortunate result is that these patients may not be motivated to get the prompt medical attention needed to limit the amount of damage that a stroke can cause. Anosognosia usually fades over time, but it may persist. When it does persist, it impairs patients' cooperation with rehabilitative treatments. They don't recognize that something is wrong, so they don't understand why treatment is necessary. There may be ways to improve awareness of neurological deficits, though. In one case, a man was unaware of the sudden and bizarre involuntary movements he had been making for several years. He could not see these movements, even when looking at himself in a mirror, but when watched himself on videotape, he instantly saw the problem (Shenker et al., 2004).

THINKING CRITICALLY

Can Someone Be Partially Paralyzed and Not Know It?

In anosognosia, a person denies any neurological deficit because there is no understanding that a problem exists. This phenomenon was first described long ago in relation to strokes that caused *hemiparesis,* a weakness or partial paralysis that affects just one side of the body (Babinski, 1914). Skeptics have argued that people with hemiparesis are still fully capable of knowing that they are partially paralyzed but that this knowledge would be so upsetting that they simply cannot admit it, even to themselves. According to this argument, anosognosia is not based on true unawareness but on the operation of an unconscious mental process similar to the ego defense mechanism that Freud called *denial* (see the chapter on personality).

What am I being asked to believe or accept?

Arguing against these skeptics are those who say that anosognosia occurs because the brain damage that causes hemiparesis also damages the parts of the brain that would allow the person to know that something is wrong. As a result, patients who seem unaware of hemiparesis or other problems are, in fact, truly unaware of them (Heilman, Barrett, & Adair, 1998; McGlynn & Schacter, 1989).

What evidence is available to support the assertion?

Those who believe that anosognosia is genuine unawareness point out that if it were the result of an ego defense mechanism, patients would deny any and all potentially upsetting deficits. Yet evidence from neurological examinations shows that some hemiparesis patients, for example, are aware that an arm is weak but not that a leg is weak (Berti, Ladavas, & Corti, 1996; Bisiach et al., 1986). Others are aware that they have a speech disturbance but not weakness in a limb (Bisiach et al., 1986; Breier et al., 1995).

Another problem with the ego defense mechanism argument is that anosognosia occurs much more often after right hemisphere brain damage, which causes left-side hemiparesis, than it does when left hemisphere brain damage causes right-side hemiparesis. It would seem that weakness on either side should be about equally upsetting and equally likely to cause anosognosia. In fact, because most people are right-handed, weakness on the right side might be even more upsetting and therefore *more* likely to result in psychologically motivated denial.

Additional evidence against the ego defense mechanism hypothesis comes from research showing that anosognosia can occur even when there is no threat of permanent paralysis. In a procedure pioneered by June Wada (Strauss & Wada, 1983), patients being evaluated for possible brain surgery had an anesthetic injected into one side of their brain at a time (Adair et al., 1995; Gilmore et al., 1992). This *Wada test* temporarily "turns off" either the left hemisphere or the right hemisphere without causing permanent brain damage. When the right hemisphere was "turned off" in this way, participants became paralyzed on the left side of their bodies. When they were asked about their experience, they recalled most details correctly, but most of them showed anosognosia—that is, they said that they did not notice any weakness or paralysis. When the left hemisphere was anesthetized, though, patients not only became weak on the right side but also later reported awareness of the paralysis. These data are hard to explain as being due to ego defense mechanisms because once participants had recovered from their left-side paralysis, why would they be motivated to deny that it had occurred?

Are there alternative ways of interpreting the evidence?

One problem with the Wada test is that it is difficult to compare the experiences that patients have during left- versus right-hemisphere anesthesia. The problem is that because speech areas are on the left side, people are usually unable to speak when their left hemisphere is "turned off." This doesn't happen on the right side, so the only way to do a direct comparison of the experience of left- versus right-hemisphere inactivation is to ask the patient questions after the anesthetic has worn off. If it were possible to talk to people during the left-hemisphere inactivation, perhaps they would show anosognosia because at that particular moment, there could be enough distress to motivate denial.

This interpretation is supported by research from decades ago with patients who had suffered a stroke causing hemiparesis (Weinstein & Kahn, 1955). When these patients' families were interviewed, it turned out that those patients who, before their stroke, had tended to cope with stress through denial were the ones most likely to deny their hemiparesis. Patients who did not show anosognosia were described by their families as less likely to have previously used denial as a coping strategy. These data suggest that denial of hemiparesis could be an exaggeration of a person's typical stress-coping tendencies.

What additional evidence would help evaluate the alternatives?

The results of this and other family report studies might be affected by *retrospective bias*. That is, once they know that their relative is denying hemiparesis, family members might be more likely to recall similar episodes of denial in the relative's past and to forget about episodes in which the patient had coped with stress in other ways. Similarly, if a relative isn't denying the symptoms caused by a stroke, perhaps family members will be less likely to recall incidents in which the patient did use denial in stressful situations.

One way around the problem of retrospective bias would be to do a *prospective* study in which a large group of individuals is identified, their typical stress-coping tendencies are assessed, and then they are contacted on a regular basis for many years. The ego defense mechanism hypothesis would be supported in such a study if the people in the group who were most likely to use denial as a coping mechanism are also the ones most likely to display anosognosia following a stroke.

What conclusions are most reasonable?

It is probably true that some individuals who suffer neurological deficits may use denial or other psychological defense mechanisms to avoid facing their distressing problems, but given the neurological evidence we have reviewed, it seems reasonable to conclude that most cases of anosognosia reflect a true lack of awareness of neurological deficit.

Perceptual Disturbances

As described in the chapter on perception, the brain must organize, recognize, and interpret the information we receive from our eyes, ears, and other senses if we are to make sense of the world. These vital perceptual functions depend on the normal operation of specific regions of the brain. For example, visual information from the eyes goes to the thalamus and then to particular areas in the occipital lobe of the cerebral cortex, where the information is analyzed further. From there, visual information is sent along two pathways. Along each of these pathways are a series of connected cortical regions that perform specialized analyses that allow us to experience different aspects of visual perception (Ungerleider & Mishkin, 1982; see Figure 20.7). The pathway leading toward the ventrolateral temporal lobe (on the sides of the head— "ventral" means toward the bottom part of the brain, and "lateral" means toward the outside of the brain) has been called the "what" system because the cortical regions

FIGURE 20.7

"What" Versus "Where" Visual Pathways

Research suggests that visual information reaching the primary visual cortex is sent along two separate but parallel systems. The "where" system focuses on an object's location in space and how it is moving. The "what" system determines the identity of the object.

along this pathway help us decide what we are seeing—a dog or a car, for example. The pathway leading toward the parietal lobe (near the top of the head) has been called the "where" system because it processes information about the location of objects and where those objects are in relation to one another. This system helps us understand, for example, that the dog is sitting in the car. Damage to our perceptual systems can result in **perceptual disturbances**.

For example, damage to the "what" pathway causes a condition called *visual agnosia* (Bauer & Demery, 2003). As in the case of Max, individuals with visual agnosia can see objects in the world, describe them, and even draw them, but they cannot identify them on the basis of their appearance (Rubens & Benson, 1971). So a visual agnosia patient can correctly define the word *apple* and, based on how it feels, correctly state that the neurologist has placed an apple in the person's hand. In other words, these patients still know what apples and other objects are, but they have lost the ability to link visual images of these objects to the part of the brain where that knowledge is stored.

Visual agnosia may leave some patients unable to name anything they see. For others, the problem occurs only when they try to name certain categories of objects (Bauer & Demery, 2003). For example, some people appear to have visual agnosia only for manufactured objects, such cars, books, or drinking glasses, but can still correctly identify on sight a tree, a dog, or any other living thing (Riddoch et al., 2008). In other cases, only manufactured objects can be named on sight (Riddoch et al., 2008; Thomas & Forde, 2006). These case observations suggest that information about natural versus manufactured objects must be processed in different ways by different brain areas. Visual agnosias can be even more specific. For example, there appears to be a brain system that is specialized for visual recognition of faces (Farah, 1996). When this aspect of the "what" system is damaged, the result is *prosopagnosia* (pronounced "proh-suh-pag-NOH-zhuh"), a condition in which a person can no longer recognize faces, even very familiar ones, including the patient's own face in a photograph or mirror (Barton et al., 2004; Bentin et al., 2007; Stephan & Caine, 2009). The facial recognition system appears to depend on temporal lobe structures; most people who develop prosopagnosia have damage to these areas on both sides of the brain (Ettlin et al., 1992), but sometimes a lesion on the right side alone is enough to produce a facial recognition syndrome (Barton et al., 2002).

In a different kind of face-related perceptual disturbance, people can still recognize faces, but they believe that a parent, a spouse, or some other familiar person has been replaced by an "imposter." This false belief, known as *Capgras syndrome* or *Capgras delusion* (pronounced "KAHP-grah") in recognition of the French psychiatrist who first reported it (Capgras & Reboul-Lachaux, 1923), tends to occur after temporal lobe damage. The damage appears to create a disconnection between brain areas that recognize faces from those that allow us to have a sense of familiarity (Ramachandran, 1998). Capgras delusions are usually permanent, though there is at least one case in which the condition was cured by antiseizure medication (Shenker, 2010).

What happens after damage to the "where" system? As you might expect, this kind of damage creates problems in the visual perception of objects in space and how they are related to one another. A particularly interesting example is called *simultanagnosia* (pronounced "sih-MUL-tun-ag-NOH-zhuh") (Wolpert, 1924), a condition in which a person can see parts of a visual scene but has difficulty perceiving the whole scene. In a sense, a person with simultanagnosia can see the "trees" but cannot see the "forest." So if simultanagnosia patients were to look at the pattern shown in Figure 20.8, they could see all the "Ts" but not the larger letter "H" formed by the smaller letters.

One patient described her perceptions as follows (Shenker, 2005):

Examiner: What do you see?

Patient: I see T, T, T, T, . . . Do I keep going?

FIGURE 20.8
A "Global-Local" Stimulus

TRY THIS People with simultanagnosia have difficulty seeing an H in this stimulus but see the Ts easily. Try showing this pattern to several friends. Unless any of them have a similar neuropsychological disorder, you should be able to confirm that they will report seeing both the little Ts and the larger letter H.

perceptual disturbances
Neuropsychological disorders in which there are impairments in the ability to organize, recognize, interpret, and make sense of incoming sensory information.

Examiner: Anything else?

Patient: T, T, T, T, . . . lots of Ts.

Examiner: Are there any other letters?

Patient: No.

Examiner: Is there an H?

Patient: No, just Ts.

Examiner: Is there a big letter?

Patient: No, I don't see one.

Examiner: Is there a big letter H?

Patient: No.

Examiner: Do the little letters together form the shape of a big letter H?

Patient: I don't see how.

Examiner: (*outlines the H with finger*) Do you see how this is a big H?

Patient: I don't see an H.

Simultanagnosia has been associated with damage or dysfunction on both sides of the brain, in the upper part of the parietal lobes (Coslett & Lie, 2008a, 2008b). Damage to the "where" system in a different region of the parietal lobes can cause *hemineglect* (Heilman, Valenstein, & Watson, 2000). This condition often occurs after a cerebrovascular accident and involves difficulty in seeing, responding to, or acting on information coming from either the right or, more often, the left side of the world (Heilman, Watson, & Valenstein, 2003). The side of space that is neglected is usually opposite the side where the parietal lobe lesion is located. A person with hemineglect will ignore food on one side of a dinner plate, fail to put makeup on one side of the face, and pay no attention to voices coming from one side of the room. As shown in Figure 20.9, when asked to draw a picture of, say, a flower or a clock, only half a drawing will be completed—the half on the side of space to which the person is still paying attention.

A fascinating aspect of hemineglect is that it is cannot be explained as being due to a lack of sensation from one side or the other. For patients with left hemineglect, it is as if the concept of "leftness" is lost, and so the left side of things is simply ignored (Bisiach, Capitani, & Tansini, 1979). This ignoring process is easy to demonstrate in some patients. The neuropsychologist simply holds up one hand on each side of the patient's visual field and then asks the patient to say when any fingers are wiggling. In many cases of hemineglect, patients may be able to correctly report when fingers are wiggling on the right *or* on the left, as long as the wiggling is only on one side at a time. When there is wiggling on both sides, though, these patients may report seeing it only on the side to which they pay attention. These cases demonstrate that some hemineglect patients are capable of seeing both sides of space; they don't have a pure sensory problem. They are simply more likely to pay attention to one side of the world and to ignore the other. The tendency to do so can be reduced, though. In one study, patients showed increased awareness of the normally neglected side of space while listening to music that put them in a more positive emotional state (Soto et al., 2009).

Some patients with hemineglect also have sensory problems. They may be blind in their left visual field, for example. It may seem surprising, but neuropsychologists can show that even in these patients, the tendency to ignore one side of space cannot be explained by their sensory loss. For example, patients with left hemineglect may not respond to the sound of a voice coming from the left. Is it because of a problem in their left ear? No, because the sound was heard by their right ear too. Also, left hemineglect patients may ignore the left side of an object even if the entire object appears in their right visual field.

FIGURE 20.9

Examples of Hemineglect on a Drawing Test

When shown an object and asked to draw it, patients with hemineglect leave out details from one side of the object.

Studying Hemineglect

Showing that hemineglect is not explained by sensory problems alone can be tricky. After all, in many cases of hemineglect, the brain damage that caused it also caused a loss of sensation from the same side. Also, most tests for hemineglect rely on giving a person some kind of sensory information to respond to. How can one show that hemineglect is not due to a sensory problem if you can only test for it by having people respond to the sensations they receive?

What was the researcher's question?

Edoardo Bisiach (Bisiach, Luzzatti, & Perani, 1979) reasoned that if hemineglect was truly a problem with understanding that a particular side of space exists, then this problem should persist even for a scene that is not viewed directly but is instead put together using only one's imagination.

How did the researcher answer the question?

Bisiach tested patients who had right hemisphere lesions and left-sided hemineglect. He created randomly shaped stimuli that looked a bit like clouds. The stimuli were passed behind a vertical slit so that as the image moved across, patients could see only a small "slice" of it at a time (see Figure 20.10). In other words, the only way to see the whole stimulus was to imagine all the "slices" assembled in the mind's eye. Patients were shown two of these passing images at a time, one passing by the top part of the slit and the other passing by the bottom part of the slit. On some trials, the two stimuli were identical; on other trials, only their left sides were different; and on still others, only their right sides were different. The patients' task was to decide if the two stimuli were the same or different.

What did the researcher find?

Patients with left-sided hemineglect were able to determine when the stimuli were different if the right sides were different. But these patients could not detect differences between the stimuli if the left sides were different.

What do the results mean?

Because of the slit, the patients could not see the left and right sides of the images at the same time. This means that their failure to notice differences on only the left side did not reflect an inability to see the left side of space. Instead, these results suggest that hemineglect occurs when patients ignore stimulation that is on a particular side of space, even when they are assembling that stimulation through memory and imagination.

FIGURE 20.10
Studying Hemineglect

Here are examples of the random cloudlike shapes used by Bisiach, Luzzatti, and Perani (1979) to explore whether hemineglect is a sensory problem. Hemineglect patients could see only vertical "slices" of these shapes as the patterns passed behind a narrow vertical slit. So to see these shapes as whole patterns and to decide whether pairs of patterns were the same or different, the patients had to build an image of each pattern in their minds.

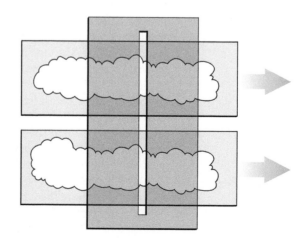

What do we still need to know?

Different kinds of hemineglect are produced by damage in different parts of the brain (Watson & Heilman, 1979). So it is not clear if Bisiach's patients, who had damage in their parietal lobes, are representative of all hemineglect patients. Notice, too, that the stimuli in Bisiach's study were all visual. Would the same results appear in research using imagined touches or sounds, for example? These are questions to be answered by further research on the fascinating topic of hemineglect.

LINKAGES

LINKAGES How does damage to language areas of the brain affect language abilities? (a link to Biological Aspects of Psychology, p. 90)

Language Disorders and the Brain

When people suffer disruptions in the functioning of brain regions that normally support their ability to speak, read, write, and understand language, specific aspects of these language skills will fail, resulting in corresponding disorders in the person's language abilities. The precise nature of these **language disorders**, also called **aphasias** (pronounced "uh-FAY-zhuhz"), can be identified using detailed neuropsychological testing. In this section, we discuss several subtypes of aphasias (Caplan, 2003a), each of which is associated with damage or dysfunction in a particular area of the brain's language centers.

Most aphasias occur as a result of damage to the left side of the brain, often from stroke or trauma but sometimes from a neurodegenerative disease process called *frontotemporal degeneration (FTD)* (Boxer & Miller, 2005; Rabinovici & Miller, 2010). FTD gradually kills nerve cells in the front section of the brain's temporal or frontal lobes, often on one side more than on the other (Neary, Snowden, & Mann, 1993; Yamamoto et al., 2009; see Figure 20.11). The result is similar to a stroke in the sense that FTD tends to affect a fairly specific brain area, but unlike the sudden symptoms of a stroke, FTD symptoms develop gradually over a period of years. If FTD is focused on the brain's language-related regions, the result is a condition called *primary progressive aphasia* (Grossman & Ash, 2004; Rogalski & Edmonds, 2008). Let's consider where these language-related brain regions are, what they normally do, and what else can happen when their functioning is disrupted.

As described in the chapter on biological aspects of psychology, the brain has several language areas. These interconnected regions work together as a network, and all of them must work properly in order for us to use and understand language. For example, it appears that *Broca's area* is vital to our ability to translate thoughts into words or writing that will be clear and meaningful to others. People who suffer damage to Broca's area (see Figure 20.12) display **Broca's aphasia**, which is manifested mainly in the loss of language fluency (Keller et al., 2009). That is, people with Broca's aphasia are no longer able to express themselves smoothly and easily (Kertesz, 1993). Instead, they speak in a halting, sputtering manner, with great effort and often with much frustration. There may be other symptoms as well, including a change in the kinds of words that individuals produce (Benson & Geschwind, 1971). Most of the words that patients with Broca's aphasia can still speak or write are those that refer to concrete objects, such as *book* or *pillow* or *water*, rather than those that refer to abstract ideas such as *justice* or *literature* or *weather*. These patients also tend to use mainly concrete nouns and verbs, leaving out the more abstract articles, adjectives, and adverbs they once spoke or wrote. This change in word usage results in a "telegraphic" speaking style that recalls a bygone era when people sending telegrams had to pay for each word in a message. A Broca's aphasia patient who once would have said, "Please give me the spoon," might now say simply, "Give spoon." Sometimes Broca's aphasic patients make mistakes when naming objects. Such naming errors are called *paraphasias*, and in Broca's aphasia, they tend to be *phonemic paraphasias*, or errors in the way a word should sound. So a person with Broca's aphasia might look at a pen and call it a "peb." Finally, people with Broca's aphasia may have some subtle problems in understanding grammar or other aspects of language (Cannizzaro, 2009; Caplan, 2003a, 2003b). In one such problem, called *agrammatism*, they may not understand that the sentences *The boy hit the girl* and *The girl was hit by the boy* express the same meaning

© Zephyr/Photo Researchers, Inc.

FIGURE 20.11
Frontotemporal Degeneration
In frontotemporal degeneration, a relatively limited part of the brain can become extremely shrunken, as shown here.

language disorders (aphasias)
Neuropsychological disorders in which there are disruptions in the ability to speak, read, write, and understand language.

Broca's aphasia A language disorder in which there is a loss of fluent speech.

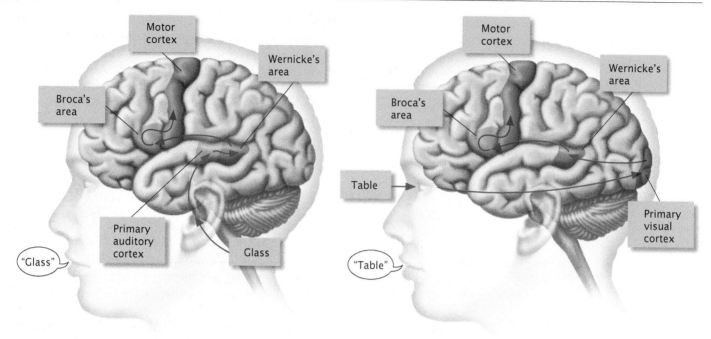

Repeating a Spoken Word

(A)

Reading a Word Out Loud

(B)

FIGURE 20.12

The Wernicke-Geschwind Model of Aphasia

The Wernicke-Geschwind model of aphasia accounts for many, but not all, of the findings associated with the major aphasias. The pathways shown in part A transmit information when a participant is instructed to repeat a spoken word. The image shown in part B traces the flow of information when the person is asked to read a written word out loud.

Wernicke's aphasia A language disorder in which there is a loss of ability to understand written or spoken language and to produce sensible speech.

People with aphasia caused by damage to *Wernicke's area* (see Figure 20.12) have a different pattern of problems (Goodglass & Kaplan, 1982). This area is involved in the ability to extract the meaning of language-related sensory information, so if its functioning is disrupted, people have difficulty understanding what they read or what others say (Kertesz, 1993). In fact, because everything everyone says sounds like nonsense to a person with **Wernicke's aphasia**, the world must seem like a suddenly strange and even unfriendly place where everyone *else* has a problem. Further, although people with Wernicke's aphasia still speak fluently and effortlessly, what they say is far from normal. Most notably, they make *semantic paraphasias,* that is, naming errors in which they use words that have the wrong meaning. So when trying to name a pen, they may call it a "book." In contrast to Broca's aphasia, people with Wernicke's aphasia tend to use lots of adverbs, adjectives, and articles but relatively few nouns and verbs. So the speech of a patient with Wernicke's aphasia may be incomprehensible. For example, when attempting to describe a picture of a woman and her children in the kitchen, a Wernicke's aphasia patient may say, "Over here is the top of the rest for the other rapid sheesh of many red sitters." This kind of output, combined with naming errors, can make the speech of a person with Wernicke's aphasia sound so disorganized that it may be mistaken for the "word salad" produced by some people with severe schizophrenia (Sambunaris & Hyde, 1994; see the chapter on psychological disorders). Yet because they do not recognize all the mistakes they are making or appreciate the oddness of their speech, people with Wernicke's aphasia are often puzzled and upset when others do not seem to understand them or respond as expected.

Damage in the brain's left hemisphere is associated with most language disorders, but communication problems can also occur after right-hemisphere damage. In general, people with right-hemisphere damage can still speak words well and can understand the words that they hear and see fairly well. However, they no longer use tone of voice properly when they speak, or they may no longer use other people's tone of voice to help them understand what those people mean (Ross & Monnot, 2008). This problem, called *aprosodia* (pronounced "ap-ruh-SOH-dee-uh"), can take several forms (Ross, 1981, 2006). For example, damage to the right frontal lobe can cause *expressive aprosodia,* in which people speak in such a dull monotone that it may be necessary for them to say something like "I am angry" in order to convey their emotional tone.

However, these patients may still be able to correctly understand and use cues from other people's tone of voice. By contrast, people with damage to the right temporal and parietal regions may have a *receptive aprosodia,* which means that they can use tone of voice correctly when they speak but have difficulty understanding the meaning of other people's tone of voice. So if someone were to sarcastically say, "Well, that was really smart," meaning just the opposite, a person with receptive aprosodia may miss the sarcasm, pay attention only to the words themselves, and say, "Thanks!"

Movement Disorders

The brain's motor pathways are "wired" to our muscles in ways that allow us to move our limbs and body, but the knowledge of how to move in order to effectively accomplish our goals is not built in to that system. Using silverware, pedaling a bicycle, sucking on a straw, or swinging a hammer are just a few examples of the many coordinated movements that each of us learn from experience. A network of special brain systems control such learned motor skills by instructing the brain's motor control centers to make the movements needed for each action sequence (Krakauer & Shadmehr, 2007; see Figure 20.13). These brain areas tell the motor system what combinations of movements to make for a specific kind of task. If a part of this special network is damaged, the result is a form of **apraxia** (pronounced "uh-PRAK-see-uh"), or **movement disorder**, in which learned motor skills are disrupted (McClain & Foundas, 2004).

There are two main types of apraxia (Heilman & Gonzalez-Rothi, 2003; Pearce, 2009). In *ideational apraxia,* the individual movements needed to perform a task are correctly executed but in the wrong order. So although a person with ideational apraxia can still open a tube of toothpaste, wet her toothbrush, squeeze paste onto the brush, insert the brush in her mouth, and do a good job of brushing, she might begin to brush before putting toothpaste on her brush, or she might squeeze the toothpaste tube first and then unscrew the cap.

A more common problem is *ideomotor apraxia,* which involves difficulties not in the sequence of skilled movements but in performing them (Wheaton & Hallett, 2007). So a person with ideomotor apraxia will try to execute each step in toothbrushing in

movement disorder (apraxia)
Neuropsychological disorders in which there are impairments in the ability to perform or coordinate previously normal motor skills.

FIGURE 20.13
The Initiation of Voluntary Movement
A network of brain regions is involved in initiating voluntary movements.

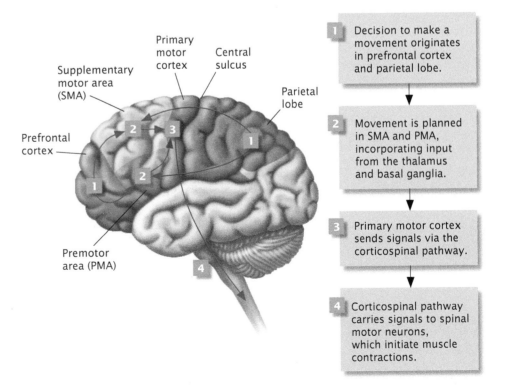

1. Decision to make a movement originates in prefrontal cortex and parietal lobe.

2. Movement is planned in SMA and PMA, incorporating input from the thalamus and basal ganglia.

3. Primary motor cortex sends signals via the corticospinal pathway.

4. Corticospinal pathway carries signals to spinal motor neurons, which initiate muscle contractions.

FIGURE 20.14

An Example of Apraxic Motor Behavior

When imitating the movements involved in using a common object, individuals with apraxia may mistakenly use an arm or a leg to represent that object. So instead of showing how they would move in order to use a tool, they act as if their limb is the tool itself.

Correct imitation   **Apraxic behavior**

its proper order but may have difficulty in positioning her hand to hold the brush and may be unable to time the sequence of arm and hand motions required to actually brush her teeth. In one kind of ideomotor apraxia, the person may use a finger or other body part as if it were a tool, perhaps brushing with the finger or using it to try to turn a screw. In such cases, the person cannot seem to figure out how to use the brush or screwdriver or other tool they once used with skillful ease (see Figure 20.14).

Dementia

We have already seen that in cases of delirium, people show reduced or heightened levels of consciousness, and many psychological abilities may fail at once. But these deficits are usually reversible, such that when the toxin or other cause of delirium disappears, the deficits do too. In conditions known as *dementia*, however, there is usually no waxing and waning of consciousness; wakefulness and alertness remain mostly normal, but many other mental functions are impaired (Knopman & Selnes, 2003; Manning, 2004). Specifically, in **dementia**, memory declines from its previous level, and there is also impairment in some other area of psychological functioning such as perceptual ability, language, or learned motor skills. In addition, to be diagnosed as dementia, the impairments must be significant enough to cause problems in the person's ability to function at work, in social situations, or in everyday tasks such as driving, cooking, or balancing a checkbook. In most cases, but not all, dementia is gradual, progressive, and irreversible. It has been estimated that about 34.4 million people worldwide have dementia (Wimo, Winblad, & Jönsson, 2010).

A condition known as *mild cognitive impairment (MCI)* may precede the appearance of some kinds of dementia (Dubois, 2004; Petersen & Morris, 2005). In *amnestic MCI*, for example, a person begins to have memory problems that are reflected in well-below-average scores on neuropsychological tests. There are no other deficits, though, and the person may have adapted well enough to the memory loss that there is no significant disruption in daily functioning. People with amnestic MCI may get worse, however, and about 2 to 10 percent of them each year progress to the point that they are considered to have dementia (Mitchell & Shiri-Feshki, 2009). Identifying people when they are still in this relatively early stage of memory loss is important partly because medication is available that might stabilize memory and delay the development of full-fledged dementia (Petersen et al., 2005; Tabert et al., 2006).

Dementia is often caused by a progressive neurodegenerative disease, and the most common of these, accounting for 60 to 80 percent of all cases, is Alzheimer's disease

dementia Neuropsychological disorders in which there are significant and disruptive impairments in memory, as well as in perceptual ability, language, or learned motor skills.

FIGURE 20.15
Brain Atrophy in Alzheimer's Disease

Alzheimer's disease causes some brain cells to stop working and eventually die, while other brain cells may be unaffected. Where brain cells die off, the cortex shrinks, leaving gaping spaces.

(Alzheimer's Association, 2009; Fratiglioni & Qiu, 2009). About 5.3 million people have Alzheimer's disease in the United States alone, where its economic costs are set at more than $148 billion a year and where its costs in personal suffering are incalculable (Alzheimer's Association, 2009). The percentage of people with Alzheimer's disease doubles after about every five years after the age of 60. As a result, about 13 percent of people over age 65 have this disease, and the chances of developing Alzheimer's disease increase dramatically after age 75 and again after 85 (Alzheimer's Association, 2009). With more people than ever living longer and longer lives, current estimates suggest that by the year 2050, Alzheimer's disease will affect as many as 16 million people in the United States (Alzheimer's Association, 2009).

Alzheimer's disease was first described in 1907 by the German neurologist Alois Alzheimer (Devi & Quitschke, 1999). He told of a 46-year-old woman identified as "Auguste D.," who had developed what Alzheimer described as an "early onset senility" (see Figure 20.15). When she died a few years later, he examined her brain and found two types of microscopic abnormalities. The first appeared as *neurofibrillary tangles*, which are dead and dying nerve cells that have become twisted and misshapen. The second abnormality was clumps of protein deposits, called *amyloid plaque*, lying around the outside of the dead and dying nerve cells. To this day, the ultimate diagnosis of Alzheimer's disease depends on the appearance of these tangles and plaque deposits (Graeber & Mehraein, 1999; Wengenack et al., 2008).

Today we know that the brain areas where neurofibrillary tangles are most numerous in Alzheimer patients are precisely the areas that fail to work properly and cause most of these patients' symptoms. As for amyloid plaque, scientists believe that it plays a key role in causing at least some forms of Alzheimer's disease. We all develop some of this plaque as we get older, but although it is toxic to nerve cells, it usually causes no more harm than other signs of aging, such as hair loss or wrinkles. However, in Alzheimer's disease patients, amyloid plaque is much more abundant than normal, and according to some researchers, this excessive amount of plaque causes the brain damage that results in Alzheimer's symptoms (Hardy, 2006; Swerdlow & Khan, 2009).

Studying the brains of deceased Alzheimer's patients has shown that the disease mainly damages neurons that use the neurotransmitter *acetylcholine* (Perry, 1980), especially those in the parietal and medial temporal lobes on both sides of the brain (Cummings, 2004; Knopman & Selnes, 2003). Because the parietal lobes are important for locating objects in space, Alzheimer's disease patients have difficulty drawing some kinds of shapes and may easily get lost as they drive or walk around. Many Alzheimer's patients are endangered every day by wandering away from home or from the care facility in which they live (Rolland et al., 2007). Because the left parietal lobe contains brain areas important for language, patients with Alzheimer's disease may also develop *anomia*, a condition in which it becomes hard to name objects even if they know what the objects are. The left parietal lobe usually also contains brain areas that are important in performing learned motor skills such as using a hammer or a spoon, so Alzheimer's patients commonly develop apraxia. And because the medial temporal lobes contain the hippocampus, these patients experience impairment in the ability to form new memories. Old memories, the ones already formed and stored elsewhere, usually remain accessible until the disease has progressed to its later stages. So as in the case of H.M., Alzheimer's disease patients may remember details from their early adulthood but not a conversation from yesterday. Finally, because the temporal lobes are also important for the ability to interpret visual sensations, patients with Alzheimer's disease sometimes develop visual agnosia and so may not recognize the objects they see.

In another kind of dementia, called **vascular dementia**, memory loss and other psychological deficits are caused by restrictions in the supply of blood to the brain (Kirschner, 2009; Topakian & Aichner, 2008). We have already mentioned that when a blood vessel in the brain is blocked, the brain cells die in the tissue that normally receives oxygen and nutrients from that blood vessel. Sometimes this loss of blood supply occurs in very tiny blood vessels, resulting in the death of only a tiny amount of

vascular dementia A form of dementia caused by multiple restrictions of the brain's blood supply.

brain tissue. Such injuries may not cause symptoms when they first occur, especially if vital areas are not affected, but if many small injuries occur repeatedly, more and more brain tissue is lost (Hallam et al., 2008), and the cumulative effect can be an impairment of memory and other psychological functions (Fisher, 1989).

Vascular dementia accounts for about 17 percent of the dementia seen in people over the age of 70, making it second only to Alzheimer's disease as a common cause of dementia (Alzheimer's Association, 2009). The two conditions may occur in the same individual (Topakian & Aichner, 2008), but the symptoms of vascular dementia often differ from those of Alzheimer's disease (Knopman, 2006). Vascular dementia patients show memory loss, including the forgetting of recent events, but in contrast to Alzheimer's disease, the hippocampus is usually relatively well preserved. So vascular dementia patients should still be able to form new memories. Why, then, do these people have difficulty remembering new material? In some cases, the answer may be that they have more of a problem in retrieving recent memories than in forming them. This subtle difference highlights the importance of careful neuropsychological assessment. Differences between vascular dementia and other impairments have also been found on behavioral tests (Milan et al., 2008), as well as in the appearance of deficits such as aphasia, apraxia, and dyslexia in vascular dementia patients (Topakian & Aichner, 2008).

A proper testing protocol can help establish the likely cause of a dementia. This information is useful because new medications are becoming available that can stop or slow the progression of certain dementias (Caccamo, Fisher, & LaFerla, 2009; Cummings, 2004). It is important for physicians to know exactly what form of dementia they are dealing with in each case so that they can prescribe the correct medication and help families plan for the future problems that dementia is likely to bring (Leifer, 2009). Drugs such as dimebolin (Dimebon), galantamine (Reminyl), and rivastigmine (Exelon) have been shown to be somewhat effective at slowing the progress of Alzheimer's disease and are well tolerated by patients (Burns et al., 2009; Doody et al., 2008; Small & Dubois, 2007). Certain antidepressant medications may have similar benefits (Hashioka et al., 2009), and antipsychotic drugs such as risperidone have shown potential for treating some of the behavioral and psychological symptoms of Alzheimer's disease (Oshima, 2008).

Choosing the right drug at the right time can help patients enjoy a better quality of life for a longer time and can delay for years the need for nursing home care (Geldmacher et al., 2003). Accordingly, it would be ideal if Alzheimer's disease and other dementias could be diagnosed even before their symptoms appear. Scientists are working to develop such early diagnostic tests based on molecular and brain imaging (Drzezga, 2008; Hallam et al., 2008; Nordberg, 2008; Wengenack et al., 2008), analysis of EEG brain waves (Gasser et al., 2008), refined neuropsychological assessment batteries (De Santi et al., 2008), and observation of various behavioral changes (Caputo et al., 2008). One study found, for example, that patients who displayed three or more subtle neurological abnormalities, such as difficulty with balance, were more likely than others to show cognitive decline over the next eight years (Inzitari et al., 2008). Another found that the inability to smell certain types of odors may be an early sign of Alzheimer's disease or dementia related to frontotemporal degeneration (FTD), and a third found that losing the ability to appreciate sarcasm may signal the presence of FTD (Kipps et al., 2009; McLaughlin & Westervelt, 2008).

Giving the right prescription at the right time is of little use, though, if, as often happens in cases of dementia, the patients forget—or are unable or unwilling—to take their medication on the proper schedule. To address this compliance problem, pharmaceutical companies have begun to offer some of their dementia medications in transdermal patches. When applied to the skin these patches automatically provide the correct daily drug dose (Small & Dubois, 2007).

Progress in the development of new medications and early diagnostic tests leads many researchers to hope that instead of just stopping or slowing the progress of dementia, it may someday be possible to reverse its course, allowing some patients to once again enjoy more normal cognitive functioning (Lacor, 2007). And as discussed in the human development chapter, the appearance of dementia may be delayed or prevented in those who spend their lives engaged in stimulating mental activity, interactions with friends, and healthy eating and exercise (Fratiglioni & Qiu, 2009). ("In Review: Major Neuropsychological Disorders" summarizes the various dysfunctions discussed here.)

IN REVIEW　　Major Neuropsychological Disorders

Syndrome	Type of Difficulty	Areas of Brain Malfunction
Apraxia	Making learned skilled movements even if not weak or confused	Usually left cerebral hemisphere parietal or frontal lobes
Visual agnosia	Attaching meaning to visual sensations	Temporal lobes, often bilateral
Anosognosia	Becoming aware of the loss of neurological function	Usually right cerebral hemisphere
Hemineglect	Paying attention to one side of space	Usually right parietal lobe
Aphasia	Using language as a communication system	Usually left cerebral hemisphere
Aprosodia	Using tone of voice as a communication tool	Usually right cerebral hemisphere
Dementia	Memory and at least one other psychological ability that are severe enough to impair functioning	Variable, depending on the cause of the dementia

1. A patient who has become forgetful but has no problems in other areas of cognitive function may be said to have _____.

2. A dementia patient whose hippocampus is relatively intact and can still form new memories probably has _____ dementia.

3. A patient with thiamine deficiency who is forgetful but makes up memories and believes they are real probably has _____.

LINKAGES

As noted in the introductory chapter, all of psychology's subfields are related to one another. Our discussion of language disorders illustrates just one way in which the topic of this chapter, neuropsychology, is linked to the subfield of biological psychology, which is described in the chapter on biological aspects of

CHAPTER 20
Neuropsychology

psychology. The Linkages diagram shows ties to two other subfields, and there are many more ties throughout the book. Looking for linkages among subfields will help you see how they all fit together and help you better appreciate the big picture that is psychology.

— LINKAGES —

How does damage to language areas of the brain affect language abilities?
(ans. on p. 823)

CHAPTER 3
Biological Aspects
of Psychology

What disorders are caused by damage to brain areas involved in memory?
(ans. on p. 826)

CHAPTER 7
Memory

What psychological tests are used in diagnosing neuropsychological disorders?
(ans. on p. 810)

CHAPTER 10
Cognitive Abilities

SUMMARY

Neuropsychology is the subfield of psychology whose goal is to explore and understand the relationships among brain processes, human behavior, and psychological functioning.

Foundations of Neuropsychology

There are two main assumptions in neuropsychology. The first is that complicated mental tasks such as memory involve many subtasks that can be studied separately. The second is that different psychological processes are controlled by different brain regions or different combinations of brain regions. Experimental neuropsychologists use these assumptions as they conduct research on how the brain controls and organizes human mental activity. *Clinical neuropsychologists* use the results of neuropsychological research to try to understand the nature and location of brain disorders seen in individual patients.

A Brief History of Neuropsychology

Neuropsychology's early history focused on debates over *localization of function,* the idea that specific psychological functions are governed by specific parts of the brain. Early evidence for this notion was dismissed by serious scientists, but by the 1860s, localization of function began to be accepted, and it now forms the basis for much of what we know about neuropsychological functioning.

Modules and Networks

Recent theories of localization center on the idea that the brain is organized into *modules,* each of which performs its own unique analysis of information and works together with varying combinations of other modules throughout the brain to perform all aspects of behavior and mental processes.

Lesion Analysis

Experimental neuropsychologists today use *lesion* analysis to try to understand the complexities of localization of function; they look at how damage (lesions)

in particular places in the brain relate to the appearance of particular problems.

Neuropsychological Assessment

Clinical neuropsychologists use a wide variety of *neuropsychological assessment* methods to help determine the nature of a patient's neuropsychological problems and even to suggest where in the brain the problem may lie. These tests may consist of a standardized group of instruments, such as the Halstead-Reitan Battery, or they may be an individualized combination of tests chosen by the neuropsychologist with a particular patient in mind. In most cases, a standard battery is followed by some additional individualized tests.

Training for Neuropsychology

To develop their skills, clinical neuropsychologists typically earn a Ph.D. in clinical psychology with a focus on neuropsychology and then complete a postdoctoral internship.

Mechanisms of Brain Dysfunction

Brain dysfunctions can be caused by a number of conditions.

Cerebrovascular Accidents

One of the main causes of brain damage and dysfunction is a *cerebrovascular accident* (*stroke*), which occurs when the blood supply to a part of the brain is blocked, causing the death of brain cells in that region and the loss of that brain region's ability to exercise its normal control over some aspect of behavior or mental processing. Strokes can be disabling and sometimes deadly.

Traumatic Brain Injury

Damage and dysfunction can also result from *traumatic brain injury* (*trauma*), a sudden impact on the brain caused by a blow to the head, sudden and violent head movements, or other events that literally shake the brain inside the skull. The amount of damage and dysfunction following such events depends mainly on the amount of force involved and the

degree to which the impact is cushioned by the action of the *cerebrospinal fluid.*

Neurodegenerative Diseases

Neurodegeneration is the gradual process of damage to brain cells caused by *neurodegenerative diseases* such as Alzheimer's, Parkinson's, and Huntington's or by infections, nutritional deficiencies, or genetic abnormalities.

Neuropsychological Disorders

The *syndromes,* or patterns of symptoms, associated with stroke, trauma, and neurodegenerative diseases appear as several kinds of neuropsychological disorders.

Amnestic Disorders

The hallmark of *amnestic disorders* is some significant disruption or loss of memory, as seen in conditions such as *anterograde amnesia,* in which new memories do not form, and *Korsakoff's psychosis* (*Korsakoff's syndrome*), in which memory distortions and *confabulations* are caused by a lack of thiamine.

Consciousness Disturbances

In *consciousness disturbances,* a person's normal awareness of the world is impaired. These conditions can range from loss of consciousness, as in coma or persistent vegetative state (which may result from damage to the *reticular formation*), to *delirium,* in which the patient alternates between reduced and elevated degrees of consciousness. In cases of anosognosia, a person may be paralyzed on one side of the body but have no awareness of the problem.

Perceptual Disturbances

People who experience *perceptual disturbances* may become unable to understand what objects, or certain categories of objects, are by looking at them (visual agnosia), may be unable to recognize faces (prosopagnosia), or have difficulty assembling the specific parts of a visual scene into a coherent whole (simultanagnosia). Patients with a perceptual disorder called hemineglect ignore one half of the world.

Language Disorders and the Brain

Language disorders usually result from damage to language areas on the left side of the brain and take the form of *aphasias,* in which the ability to speak or understand language is disrupted. The many forms of aphasia include *Broca's aphasia,* in which people can no longer speak fluently, and *Wernicke's aphasia,* which makes it difficult for people to understand what they read or hear, and although they can speak fluently, their speech makes little or no sense. Damage in the right side of the brain can result in aprosodia, the loss of ability to use tone of voice to express one's meaning or to understand the meaning of other people's speech.

Movement Disorders

Movement disorders, also known as *apraxias,* involve the inability to perform various motor skills or the inability to perform those skills in the correct order.

Dementia

Patients with *dementia* suffer gradually more significant and, usually, irreversible, loss of many mental functions, including impairment of memory, perception, language, and motor skills. It is usually caused by progressive neurodegenerative disorders such as Alzheimer's disease, though in *vascular dementia,* the cause is restrictions of the brain's blood supply. A condition known as mild cognitive impairment may precede the appearance of some forms of dementia.

LINKAGES TO FURTHER LEARNING

Now that you have finished reading this chapter, how about exploring some of the topics and information that you found most interesting? Here are some places to start.

Books

Oliver Sacks, *The Man Who Mistook His Wife for a Hat* (Simon & Schuster, 1985). Beautifully written and easily read stories describing real patients with specific neuropsychological syndromes such as aphasia, agnosia, and amnesia.

Kenneth M. Heilman, *Matter of Mind* (Oxford University Press, 2002). A readable review of some of the scientific basis for clinical neuropsychology, with stories illustrating syndromes and good discussions of lesion analysis and modularity.

Aleksandr R. Luria, *Mind of a Mnemonist: A Little Book About a Vast Memory* (Basic Books, 1968). Detailed case study written by a storied neuropsychologist that describes a man whose memory was so effective that he could not forget anything he learned.

Thomas Debaggio, *Losing My Mind: An Intimate Look at Life with Alzheimer's* (Simon & Schuster, 2003). A professional writer's autobiographical account of what it is like to have Alzheimer's disease.

Konrad Maurer and Ulrike Maurer, *Alzheimer: The Life of a Physician and the Career of a Disease* (Columbia University Press, 2003). A fascinating account of the German neurologist and his careful study of the first Alzheimer's disease patient.

Jenni A. Ogden, *Fractured Minds: A Case-Study Approach to Clinical Neuropsychology* (Oxford University Press, 2004). Vivid accounts of patients with a wide variety of neuropsychological syndromes.

On the Internet

 Access an integrated eBook and chapter-specific learning tools including flashcards, quizzes, videos, and more. Go to CengageBrain.com.

Want to maximize the value of your online study time? Take this easy-to-use study system's diagnostic pre-test, and it will create a personalized study plan for you. By helping you identify the topics that you need to understand better and then directing you to valuable online resources, it can speed up your chapter review. CengageNOW even provides a post-test so you can confirm that you are ready for an exam. Go to CengageBrain.com.

TALKING POINTS

Here are a few talking points to help you summarize this chapter for family and friends without giving a lecture.

1. Neuropsychologists try to understand how normal and abnormal brain functioning affects our behavior and mental processes.

2. Clinical neuropsychologists test patients with neuropsychological disorders to figure out which psychological functions have been disrupted and which brain areas might be causing the problems.

3. Most neuropsychologists have a Ph.D. in clinical psychology, and all have additional specialized training.

4. Neuropsychology is based on the assumption that particular psychological functions are controlled by particular areas of the brain.

5. Neuropsychological disorders are disruptions in behavior or mental processes caused by strokes, head trauma, or disease.

6. Certain kinds of brain damage not only cause paralysis or other disruptions in functioning but also leave the person unaware of the problem.

7. It is important to diagnose Alzheimer's disease early, while medication might still be effective in slowing the cognitive deterioration (dementia) caused by this disease.